Symbol	Definition
$F(K,N,T)$	The aggregate production function, depending on labor (N) and capital (K) inputs and technology T. Capital and technology are sometimes held constant.
$f(K/N)$	The intensive production function where average labor productivity depends upon the capital labor ratio (and technology when technological change is considered).
G	Government purchases of goods and services
G^D	Government purchase of goods produced domestically
G^F	Government purchases of goods produced overseas
GNP	Gross national product
h	The coefficient of the interest rate in the demand for money equation
$H(Y^P/Y)$	The coefficient of the output ratio in the output-inflation trade-off equation
i	The short-term nominal rate of interest
$i_{domestic}$	The domestic short-term nominal rate of interest. This is generally the same as i; the subscript ''domestic'' is used when international comparisons of rates are being made.
$i_{foreign}$	The foreign short-term nominal rate of interest
$i(1), i(2), i(3)$	The one-year, two-year, and three-year nominal rates of interest
i (long term)	The long-term nominal rate of interest
$i_{foreign}$ (long term)	The foreign long-term nominal rate of interest
I	Investment purchases by businesses (gross private domestic investment)
I_0	The autonomous part of investment demand
I_1	The marginal propensity to invest (MPI) from an investment function
I^D	Purchases of domestically produced investment goods
I^F	Purchases of investment goods produced overseas
I_P	Planned investment (the P subscript is dropped after Chapter 2)
I_R	Replacement investment
I_U	Unplanned investment (the U subscript is dropped after Chapter 2)
IM	Imports of goods and services
IM_0	The autonomous part of import demand

(continued inside back cover)

Macroeconomics,

FINANCIAL MARKETS, AND THE INTERNATIONAL SECTOR

Macroeconomics,

FINANCIAL MARKETS, AND THE INTERNATIONAL SECTOR

Martin Neil Baily
Professor of Economics and Public Policy
The University of Maryland and
The Brookings Institution

Philip Friedman
Provost, Vice President for Academic Affairs and Professor of Economics
Bentley College

Homewood, IL 60430
Boston, MA 02116

Senior sponsoring editor: *Gary L. Nelson*
Developmental editor: *Elizabeth Murry*
Project editor: *Gladys True*
Production manager: *Ann Cassady*
Cover designer: *Michael Warrell*
Cover illustrator: *David Shannon*
Interior designer: *Maureen McCutcheon*
Artist: *Carlisle Communications*
Compositor: *Arcata Graphics/Kingsport*
Typeface: *10/12 Palatino*
Printer: *R. R. Donnelley & Sons Company*

Library of Congress Cataloging-in-Publication Data

Baily, Martin Neil.
    Macroeconomics, financial markets, and the international sector /
Martin Neil Baily, Philip Friedman.
      p.   cm.
    Includes index.
    ISBN 0-256-03339-0
    1. Macroeconomics. 2. International finance. 3. International
trade. I. Friedman, Philip, 1945– . II. Title.
HB172.5.B339   1991
339—dc20   90–21840

Printed in the United States of America
1 2 3 4 5 6 7 8 9 0 DOC 8 7 6 5 4 3 2 1

To Vickie Baily and Sue Friedman with love for the partnership we have with them; and to the friendship we have together.

■ PREFACE

This is an exciting but challenging time to teach macroeconomics. Macroeconomic issues are being debated widely and the newspapers are full of stories about the exchange rate, recession fears, concerns about rising inflation, and interest rates. As a result of this wide interest in the economy, students are crowding into macro courses and they have high expectations of finding out how the economy works. They are often disappointed, because the models that they learn often seem too abstract, or unrelated to the events they read about, or in conflict with one other.

Over the years, we have taught macro to economics majors, MBA students, undergraduate business majors, master's students in public policy, and liberal arts and science majors with a general interest in economic policy. We have used a variety of different texts and added supplemental readings, particularly on financial markets. Despite the diverse backgrounds of the students in these courses and their differing political perspectives, we have found that they all wanted nearly the same thing. Students want a course that is not just a preparation for later courses, but one that will help them understand what is going on in the economic world around them.

Part of the difficulty that faculty face in macro courses is that within the economics profession there is disagreement about the basic approach to the subject, making it hard to give a coherent perspective to students. It is important to provide a fair and rigorous discussion of macroeconomic controversy so that economics majors or graduate students are prepared for advanced courses. At the same time, it is perhaps more important to satisfy the need of all students for a course that is relevant and interesting and that fits with what they observe about ongoing economic events and actual business behavior.

One way to teach macro is to present a standard Keynesian *IS-LM* model even though it is clearly unrealistic in its depiction of a single rate of interest linking the real and monetary sectors of the economy. Moreover, this model is also flawed because it is unable to tackle many modern policy issues or reflect the importance of expectations.

Modern neo-Keynesian analysis has helped with one problem of the standard Keynesian model by giving insights into why prices and wages are not fully flexible. But it does not really provide a version of the Keynesian model that solves the limitations of *IS-LM* analysis.

Another way to teach macro is to develop the monetarist model, or the more recent developments of classical thinking; the equilibrium business-cycle model or the real business-cycle model. These models have also yielded important insights into the working of the macroeconomy, but students are justifiably skeptical of models in which unemployment is voluntary, and in which markets are always clear and the economy returns quickly to full employment. Moreover, these models ignore many important issues, including the potential discrepancy between saving and investment at full employment and the role of the financial sector.

Finally, most macro models used in the standard texts pay too little attention to the international sector.

AN ALTERNATIVE APPROACH TO TEACHING MACROECONOMICS

We provide an alternative treatment of macroeconomics that is easy to understand despite the fact that it covers some new and challenging material. We believe that we have developed a coherent framework for understanding the macroeconomy that still does justice to the divergence of approaches within the profession. We have stressed the importance of expectations, financial markets, and the international sector. We have covered the microeconomic foundations of macroeconomic behavior, but not to the point where students will be trying to learn material that is more appropriate for doctoral courses in economics.

In our judgment, the business cycle and macroeconomic policy should be analyzed within an aggregate supply and demand framework in which there is some stickiness of wages and prices. Short-run fluctuations in output are driven primarily by changes in aggregate demand. Supply should not be neglected, of course; supply shocks are considered and we recognize that income in the long run is determined primarily by aggregate supply.

We begin with the standard *IS-LM* framework, but in the actual economy the financial sector is a critical element, since short-term nominal rates and long-term real rates do not necessarily move in tandem, we introduce major changes in this framework, developing what we have called the *IS-ALM* model. The *IS-ALM* model allows us to incorporate different rates of interest into the analysis and to show how these different rates are related by expectations. We describe a model where the financial sector provides the link that explicitly connects shifts in monetary conditions to changes in real investment demand.

We guide students step-by-step through the cash management decision that shows that it is the short-term nominal rate of interest that is determined in the money market and that is affected by monetary policy. We discuss the term structure of interest rates and the importance of real rates of interest and we show how business investment decisions are influenced by the long-term real rate of interest. We define the interest-rate gap as the difference between the long-term real rate that affects investment and the short-term nominal rate from the money market. We show how expectations about inflation and future Federal Reserve policy can alter this gap.

The interest-rate gap then allows us to analyze several current policy issues, including the problems with nominal interest rate targeting in an inflationary environment, the need for policy credibility, and the impact of expected monetary policy on the effectiveness of fiscal policy.

Obviously it is a big step for students to think about a model with expectations and more than one rate of interest. But we have successfully taught the material in this text to students with quite different backgrounds and interests. Many students have trouble understanding the standard *IS-LM* model, but we have found that the difficulty is not that the material is too technical; rather it is that students cannot relate what they are learning to what they read or hear about outside the classroom. Business majors and public-policy majors study financial markets with short-term and long-term interest rates and inflation and they want to know how these fit with the model that is being presented in class. Many of you have seen the confusion that students suffer when they read in the newspaper that higher expected money growth can lead to higher long-term rates of interest.

This text develops its ideas using only simple algebra (and not much of that), plus figures, and a series of numerical worked examples that we urge you to go over in class. They are designed to present the new material in a way that makes it accessible to as many students as possible.

THE IMPORTANCE OF THE INTERNATIONAL SECTOR

Extensive coverage of the international sector is essential in a modern macro course. We bring our first discussion of trade into Chapter 2 and show how demand is affected by net exports and vice versa. The main issue in the analysis of fiscal policy today is the relation between the budget deficit and the trade deficit (the new crowding out) and this is covered in Chapter 4. Then in two extensive separate chapters (11 and 12) we develop a discussion of the exchange rate and the impact of monetary and fiscal policy in an open economy. The fact that we have stressed the importance of interest rates and expectations in earlier chapters then yields an important payoff. The analysis of international interest-rate differentials and the expected rate of change of the exchange rate follows naturally from the earlier work.

FLEXIBILITY GAINED FROM SEPARATE SEGMENTS ON KEY TOPICS

This book is designed for students who have had at least one previous course in macroeconomics at the introductory level. The entire text can be presented easily in a two-course sequence. And by moving rapidly, the entire text can also be covered in a one-semester course if the students have had more exposure to economics than the typical introductory sequence of micro and macroeconomics. For well-prepared students, much of Chapters 1–5 can be covered quickly. And although we do not suggest it, some of the material on fiscal policy multipliers (in Chapter 4) and on controlling the money supply (in Chapter 5) can be omitted with only a small loss of continuity. Even so, for most curricula there is more material in the text than can be effectively covered in one semester or quarter.

A one-semester course using this book can be taught in several different ways by combining and/or omitting various chapters, and we expect that this is typically the way the book will be used. The particular combinations of chapters covered will depend upon the interests and preparation of students, the program of study in which the course is being offered, and the preferences of the instructor.

The core analysis of the book is presented in the first nine chapters and then following Chapter 9, there are a series of self-contained segments on key topics that give the instructor considerable flexibility in designing a course to meet differing needs and interests. The first of these segments is on supply-shock inflation. Chapter 9, the last one in the core, introduces the output-inflation trade-off and Chapter 10 then looks at supply shocks; notably at the impact of oil price increases.

The second segment consists of the two chapters on the international sector; this is followed by the third segment, consisting of two chapters on economic fluctuations (Chapters 13 and 14). The idea that the economy can generate endogenous fluctuations and, in particular, that investment demand depends upon changes in income is introduced early in the text, but only briefly. The two-chapter segment on economic fluctuations develops this idea much further and introduces the concepts of economic dynamics. We step carefully in presenting this material, however, because we have found that analysis using difference equations is difficult for students to follow. We use numerical examples and keep the analysis simple. In Chapter 14 we develop the idea of fluctuations that are generated within the financial sector and we assess the threat to stability posed by increased indebtedness.

In Chapters 15 and 16 we look at alternative viewpoints and recent developments in macroeconomics. We develop the ideas of the monetarist model, the equilibrium business-cycle model, and the real business-cycle model. We also discuss the neo-Keynesian efforts to explain sticky wages and prices in models of rational behavior. Although these chapters are the first time in the text that the monetarist and equilibrium viewpoints have been developed as alternative frameworks, the ideas of monetarist and rational expectations economists were introduced within our core analysis, particularly into the analysis of expectations and policy effectiveness.

The final two chapters deal with long-run growth and the recent productivity decline, with policy prescriptions following analysis.

The overall structure of the book is as follows.

Core Sections (Chapters 1–9)

Prologue and Introduction

Aggregate supply and demand

Income and expenditure

Money and *IS-LM*

Monetary and fiscal policy

Financial markets, rates of interest, and *IS-ALM*

Expectations about policy and inflation

Causes of inflation, the trade-off

Self-Contained Segments

Supply shocks and the policy dilemmas they create (Chapter 10)

The international sector; goods and capital flows (Chapters 11–12)

Economic fluctuations (Chapters 13–14)

Alternative approaches to macroeconomics (Chapters 15–16)

Long-run growth and the slowdown (Chapters 17–18)

THE APPROACH TO PEDAGOGY

The explanations in the text rely heavily on descriptions of simple, but relevant, economic scenarios. The micro basis of macroeconomics is imbedded in these descriptions. We try to make the writing accessible and direct, and references to the behavior of individuals in the economy are not confused with references to economic models. For example, we might say that a change in the behavior of consumers can be represented by a shift in the consumption function, rather than saying that consumers shifted up the consumption function. Students do not need a knowledge of calculus as a prerequisite, although some material allows students who know calculus to use that knowledge.

There are several specific learning features.

- Boxes that offer business, policy, or heuristic explanations are a feature of each chapter.
- Many chapters have numerical Worked Examples and there are discussion questions and problems at the end of every chapter.
- Key terms are given definitions that are set out in the margins where they first occur and then are collected in a list at the end of each chapter.
- Part openers are used to introduce major sections and offer an overview of an area of study.
- Summaries are provided at the end of each chapter.
- Key statements are highlighted to aid understanding.

SUPPLEMENTARY MATERIALS

This text is being prepared with a comprehensive package of supplementary materials, including a study guide, a test bank, an instructor's manual, and a computer disk that allows students to work through additional problems and exercises.

WHY WE WROTE THE BOOK IN THE WAY WE DID

Abstraction in economic modeling and in teaching is an art. Too little, and the complexity overwhelms insight; too much, and the abstraction tells no useful stories about reality. The standard *IS-LM* model was simple and attractive but woefully incomplete as a way of analyzing aggregate demand shifts. Alternative models have failed to capture a viable and complete picture of how the macroeconomy operates, although they have added insights. We have tried to bring the best aspects of the new economics to bear on the old framework in order to give a workable and exciting hybrid.

The benefits we derive from extending the old model are significant in terms of relevance to current economic issues. Students are given a richer description of the economy that is still tractable; in fact, we have found the richer model easier to teach, not harder. There is less to explain away. We know that there are several excellent books in the market, but we hope you will find that this one offers some real advantages. And please let us know your reactions to it and your suggestions for improvements.

ACKNOWLEDGMENTS

We have many debts to those who have helped us in the task of writing this book. We both learned macro as fellow graduate students at MIT and have been learning since then from many students and colleagues. Colleagues at The Brookings Institution, the University of Maryland, the University of North Carolina at Greensboro, and at Bentley College have provided help and support. Members of the review panel have worked hard and given invaluable advice and criticism at each round of revision and development. The following are among the helpful reviewers on this project.

Francis W. Ahking
University of Connecticut

Shaghil Ahmed
Pennsylvania State University

Christine Amsler
Michigan State University

Robert B. Archibald
College of William and Mary

Philip F. Bartholomew
University of Michigan—Dearborn

Alan S. Blinder
Princeton University

Scott Bloom
North Dakota State University

Barry Bosworth
The Brookings Institution

James H. Breece
University of Maine

Margaret Chapman
Illinois Wesleyan University

Rafael del Villar
Texas A&M University

Gary Dymski
University of Southern California

Charles Engel
University of Virginia

S. Nuri Erbas
University of Houston

Roger T. Kaufman
Smith College

Michael Klein
Clark University

John Laitner
University of Michigan

Kathleen Langley
Boston University

William J. Leonard
St. Joseph's University

Doug McMillin
Louisiana State University

Joe Peek
Boston College

Greg Pett
Baldwin-Wallace College

Richard Schiming
Mankato State University

Stephen L. Shapiro
University of Florida

William E. Spellman
Coe College

David E. Spencer
Brigham Young University

And special thanks should be given to Alan Blinder and Barry Bosworth who read the whole manuscript prior to the last round of revisions and made important suggestions for improvement. Thanks also to Martin Feldstein, who first asked us to tackle this book.

This book has taken long enough to write that we have outlasted changes of editorial staff at Irwin and even changes of corporate ownership. We owe much to the willingness of Irwin to let us take the time to write the book we wanted to write. Particular thanks go to Gary Nelson, who has been with the project over most of its gestation and has given much help and encouragement; to Kristen Rabe, who provided extensive and helpful editorial development work with early drafts; to Elizabeth Murry, who has provided invaluable editorial and organizational help as the manuscript has been completed; to Gladys True and Bruce Sylvester, who have copyedited the manuscript with more than the usual care and attention; and to Ray Canterbery of Florida State, who has reviewed the final manuscript and written some supplementary material for boxes. David Ring of SUNY—Oneonta has done an excellent job on short notice in preparing the study guide and test bank. Steve Fagin has collected data, plotted figures, and checked galleys for us with great skill. Jane Taylor and Sarah Hufham provided excellent typing assistance.

The final but greatest debt must go to our families. Vickie Baily and Sue Friedman have given us the kind of support and encouragement that is essential to the monumental task of writing a textbook. Spending time with them and our children (Nick, Katy, Chris, and Lizzie Baily, and Ethan,

Damon, and Sharon Friedman) gave us joy at times when work seemed never-ending. Without them there would be no book. Our children have been understanding of our commitment, and the prospect of seven college tuitions has provided a spur to our efforts.

Writing a jointly authored book requires much give-and-take and willingness to compromise. Fortunately, for us that has been easy. Working together has been a pleasure.

Martin Neil Baily
Philip Friedman

■CONTENTS

Macroeconomics,

FINANCIAL MARKETS, AND THE INTERNATIONAL SECTOR

PART I

Introduction

We introduce the study of macroeconomics in the following sections. The Prologue sets forth the issues that are the focus of macroeconomics, both the traditional concerns of economic performance and policy (how well the economy is doing and what policies can and should be pursued to assure that it does well) and the more recent issues concerning the workings of the economy in a world where financial markets have a significant impact on performance, where goods and services are traded in global markets, and where there has been a declining trend in the level of economic performance among industrialized nations. The prologue also sets out the way in which economic thought has developed, and concludes with a discussion of conceptual approaches and models that are used throughout the book.

Before we go on to describe how the economy works, we devote Chapter 1 to describing just what we measure when we refer to economic performance. Several aspects of overall or aggregate performance are discussed, followed by a description of the measurement of aggregate output—gross national product (GNP). We also describe the major features of national income accounting, which is the structure used to measure GNP and evaluate aggregate economic performance.

PROLOGUE
Issues and Ideas

TRADITIONAL CONCERNS AND CHANGING ISSUES

Newspapers are filled with reports about the economy: "Recession feared: Unemployment expected to rise as sales fall," "GNP is flat in the third quarter," "The dollar falls on all currency markets," "Congressional Budget Office predicts record deficit," "Banks raise the prime rate," "Consumer Price Index is up 5 percent," "Trade deficit widens," "Inflation fears cause a tightening of monetary policy: Interest rates rise." All of us are confronted with a confusing daily flow of huge quantities of economic information. We need a systematic way of sorting out this information so that we can make sense of it all.

We will be studying the determination of output, investment, foreign trade, inflation, and other major elements of the economy. We will try to see which of these elements are important and how they are interrelated.

To understand the interrelations, we use macroeconomic models of the economy. We start with simple models that focus on the basic relationships and then build up to more complicated models in order to get a deeper understanding of how the economy works. We need to understand the causes of both the long-term growth trends in the output of the economy and the short-term fluctuations that make up what is called the business cycle. *This is the core issue of macroeconomics: the determination of income and output, including their long-term growth and their short-term fluctuations.*

The Traditional Concerns of Macroeconomics

There have been frequent fluctuations in the U.S. economy and those of the other major industrial countries over the past century. When the levels of income and output in the economy fall, this reduces employment and may leave millions of workers without jobs. Business profits decline during periods of recession or depression and factories are underutilized. During the Great Depression of the 1930s, there was a massive collapse of income and output that left 25 percent of the work force unemployed in the worst year, 1933. There were also many business and bank failures at that time. Since World War II, there has been no recession that has rivaled the Great Depression in severity, but there have been serious recessions, including one in the early 1980s when unemployment peaked at 10 percent of the work force. We want to know why recessions occur and whether they can be reduced in severity.

When output and income fluctuate, there can also be problems associated with too much demand. When workers are in short supply and production capacity is stretched, prices can start to rise and the economy will experience accelerating inflation. *Another core issue of macroeconomics is the trade-off between output and inflation.* We will be looking at the nature and extent of that trade-off. How much acceleration of inflation will accompany a given increase in the level of output? How does the answer differ between the short run and the long run?

Inflation has been a serious problem in the U.S. economy since the mid-60s, particularly in 1974 and again in 1979 and 1980 when the cost of living rose by over 10 percent each year. The problems with inflation have arisen in part because of high levels of demand, but also because of inflationary supply shocks that hit the economy, particularly the price increases that were engineered by the oil-exporting nations. We will be looking at how the excessive pressure of demand interacted with inflationary shocks to supply and created a chronic problem with inflation in the 1970s and early 1980s.

Macroeconomic policy

For good or ill, the government exercises a major influence over the course of the economy. When the federal government changes tax rates, this affects the purchasing power of people in the private sector. When the Federal Reserve, the nation's central bank, decides to vary the supply of money in the economy, this affects interest rates and hence the decisions people make to borrow and to invest.

There are two distinct viewpoints that are held about the appropriate role for macroeconomic policymaking. One view is that the private sector of the economy is itself prone to fluctuations in output, caused by changes in the level of demand for goods and services. Recessions, in this view, occur when people are not buying the amount that businesses are willing to sell. Government policy can then be used to change the level of aggregate demand in the economy and pull it out of recession. Similarly, when there is the threat of inflation brought on by an excessive level of demand, government policy can be used to restrain demand in the economy.

The second viewpoint argues that the economy is basically stable when provided with a stable environment. The appropriate policy strategy for government is to intervene in the private sector as little as possible. The Federal Reserve should maintain a stable and predictable path for the amount of money in the economy. The attempt to improve the economy by using active policy measures has in practice been a source of instability. According to this view, government policy has been a major cause of fluctuations.

We will be looking at the effects of macroeconomic policies throughout this book. In our judgment, policies can help to pull the economy out of recessions and restrain booms. And they should be used in this way on occasion. But policy in practice has often been used badly and has frequently made the economy worse. There are significant problems involved in using any macroeconomic policy; serious dangers are inherent in certain policy strategies that have been followed in practice. We will be discussing both positive and negative effects of macroeconomic policies.

New Issues for Macroeconomics

Analyzing the short-term fluctuations of the economy has been the main emphasis of macroeconomics and will be the subject of much of this book. But there are other issues that have come to the fore in recent years, including financial markets and expectations, the trade deficit and the budget deficit, and the slowdown in productivity growth.

Financial markets and expectations

The study of financial markets and financial institutions has always been important, particularly when something has gone wrong in the financial sector. We know that the banking crisis and the stock-market crash both contributed to the collapse of the economy in the Great Depression. Today, the savings and loan industry is in crisis, although it has created more of a problem for taxpayers (who must foot the bill) than for the general level of economic activity.

In recent years it has been realized that financial markets and institutions play a crucial role in the working of the economy even when there is no specific crisis, a role that in the past has been given too little weight in the analysis of income and output. To understand how a modern economy works we must look at how financial markets work and how the spectrum of different interest rates is determined.

Households buying houses or corporations financing new office buildings will borrow long-term at a rate set in the mortgage market or long-term bond market. These markets are known collectively as the financial capital market. Moreover, when the companies and households decide whether or not to buy, they will take into account the effect of inflation on the value of the assets that they are thinking of buying. This means, effectively, that their decisions are affected by an interest rate that is adjusted for the impact of inflation.

Houses, office buildings, and factories are physical assets (also called tangible assets) and they lie at one end of the spectrum of different assets that exist in the economy. At the other end of the spectrum are short-term financial assets, such as Treasury bills (T bills). T bills are bonds issued by the U.S. Treasury that are redeemed after a few months and whose interest rate is set in the money market. Banks and corporate cash managers trade in the money market. They buy and sell T bills, weighing off the interest they can earn against their need for cash to run their businesses.

The Federal Reserve also trades in the money market. Monetary-policy changes will affect the interest rate on T bills and other short-term financial assets. Since 1970, monetary policy has become the main instrument for controlling income and inflation in our economy. *To see how monetary policy works we must see how changes in the money market, occurring at one end of the spectrum of different assets and interest rates, affect purchases of houses and office buildings at the other end.*

Figuring out how interest rates are determined in financial markets is a major part of the analysis of this book. In particular, we will see how expectations about the future course of economic policy will change interest rates today. *We will find that the effectiveness of government policy, both in changing output and in curbing inflation, depends upon how much credibility the policymakers have built up.* When people believe that the Federal Reserve is serious about raising interest rates and reducing inflation, then it becomes easier for these goals to be accomplished.

The international sector and the twin deficits

It used to be that macroeconomics could be applied to the U.S. economy with very little regard for the international sector. Exports and imports were a small fraction of output in the United States and the gap between exports and imports was small. Interest rates here at home were determined without much regard to interest rates abroad. The exchange rate of the dollar was fixed in relation to gold until 1971 and, even after that, fluctuations in the value of the dollar were fairly moderate. This situation has changed dramatically.

During the 1980s, there was a huge increase in the U.S. deficit in foreign trade. Imports exceeded exports by about $160 billion in 1987, led by a wave of goods from Japan and other Asian countries. Since then the trade deficit has come down, but it remains large, and the accumulation of past deficits means that foreign residents now hold enormous quantities of U.S. assets, including government and private bonds, U.S. real estate, and U.S. companies.

There is a counterpart to the large trade deficit, namely an equally large deficit in the federal budget. The problem of the twin deficits has become a vital one for policymakers. The budget deficit rose in the mid-1980s as a result of cuts in federal income taxes, and has been coming down gradually since then, helped by a surplus in the social security fund. This parallels pretty closely the rise and fall of the trade deficit, and the relationship is more than coincidence. Most of us used to think that the main effect of a cut in taxes was an increase in the level of income here at home, with some offsetting reduction in the level of capital spending (investment). But we have discovered something that a few wise people already knew, namely that the main effect of a cut in taxes is to open a gap between exports and imports.

The different economies of the world have become more closely linked. When the U.S. government decided to go on a borrowing spree in the 1980s, it found many foreigners ready and willing to lend to it—at the right interest rate. This inflow of foreign capital drove up the value of the U.S. dollar and made it very difficult for U.S. companies to sell overseas. Foreign goods became comparatively cheap and imports came flooding in.

Once the budget deficit started to come down, a fall began in the high U.S. interest rates that had lured the foreign capital here. The flow of capital slowed and the dollar started to fall also. The value of the dollar has taken a roller-coaster ride since the early 1980s.

In this book we will see how the determination of income and output is affected by the foreign sector. We will trace the impact of changes in U.S. income on the trade balance and we will see how imports and exports affect the level of U.S. income and output. We will show how the deficit in the federal budget led to a foreign-trade deficit and changed forever our view of fiscal policy. In two chapters devoted to the foreign sector specifically, we will examine the working of the foreign-exchange market and the way in which interest rates here and overseas affect the dollar. We will see how the internationalization of financial markets means that U.S. interest rates are influenced by world economic events. We will show how macroeconomic policymaking changes once markets are opened to international competition.

The large swings in the exchange rate between the dollar and other currencies in recent years have raised concern about the influence of speculators on the economy. People who know, or think they know, that the dollar is going to rise or fall will see a golden opportunity to move funds across national borders for a profit. The expectations that people have about the future value of the dollar can have a big influence on its value today. When we study international financial markets we will see how expectations about future currency values and future interest rates influence the economy.

The slowdown in productivity growth

The determination of the long-term rate of growth of the productive capacity of the economy has been part of macroeconomics for many years, but has taken on new importance because of the decline in the rate of productivity growth in the United States and other countries. In the short run, economic well-being is greatly affected by whether there is a boom or a slump and whether or not inflation is under control. But over the long run, living standards depend primarily on how much output can be produced—on supply. Since the late 1960s there has been a much slower rate of growth of U.S. productivity and this has led to slowly growing or even stagnating living standards for many families.

We will examine the traditional theory of long-term growth and we will also investigate the likely causes of the recent slowdown in productivity growth. The decline in growth has repercussions for the position of the United States in the international community. Many observers link the persistent trade deficit with the productivity problem. The value of the dollar has come down since 1985, but the trade deficit has been very slow indeed to decline. Does this indicate a fundamental loss of competitiveness for the U.S. economy? We will conclude our discussion of long-term growth and competitiveness by suggesting some policies that might help improve the productivity of the work force and encourage technological change.

The Importance of Macroeconomics to Decision Making

Understanding both the traditional concepts and the new issues of macroeconomics is important for its own sake. We want to understand how the world around us works. But this understanding also has practical value in two ways: for government policymaking and for decision making by individuals and businesses.

An understanding of how the economy works is essential for policymaking. Whatever one's philosophy, knowledge of the overall state of economic conditions is an absolute necessity before we can begin to understand, predict, or assess the impact of government policy. Some of the central questions of macroeconomic policy are:

1. Should the government try to prevent or mitigate the business cycle and protect the economy from recurring bouts of high unemployment and recession?

2. What policies will maintain reasonable price stability, and is there a trade-off between full employment and low inflation?

3. What policies allow the economy to benefit from trade and foreign investment?

4. What policies best promote long-term growth and increased productivity?

Besides its importance for policymaking, the second way in which knowledge of macroeconomics has practical value is that it contributes to better individual economic decisions and better business decisions. In this book we describe how economic conditions affect the outcome of those decisions. One reason students take economics courses is because they believe they will help them later in a variety of careers, as they certainly will. The relationships between individual or microeconomic decisions and the macroeconomy work both ways. Not only does the state of the economy affect individual decisions, but the combination of all the individual and business microeconomic decisions affects the state of the overall economy.

Macroeconomic conditions help us explain why it may be hard for McDonald's to find minimum-wage workers in New England, why the cost of living in our own city has risen, why the interest rate on a business bank loan or a new mortgage has changed, or why domestic auto sales are weak one year and strong the next.

The ability to understand and even predict general economic activity is important when making individual economic decisions. Businesses deciding on expansion plans need to estimate what the supply of potential workers is likely to be. A business needs to know whether a recession is likely when deciding if new investment in machinery is warranted.

People deciding whether or not to buy a house or a new car have to assess their chances of being laid off because of a recession. Households considering refinancing a mortgage should assess how interest rates are likely to change in order to decide whether they are picking a good time for the refinancing. Sometimes it is important to know that interest rates or stock-exchange movements are unpredictable. Many of the variables that are studied in macroeconomics are important for making both business and personal economic decisions.

When we get down to brass tacks and start building models and analyzing how income and interest rates are determined, we will find that we have to spend quite a lot of time learning concepts and working with models that are rather unrealistic. The steps we take are necessary ones, but it will be easy to lose sight of where all this is heading. As the semester goes on, it may be hard to remember what all those exciting issues of macroeconomics were. In order to help you keep the big picture in mind, we conclude this prologue with a survey of how macroeconomic ideas have developed.

EXPLAINING THE WAY THE ECONOMY WORKS: THE DEVELOPMENT OF MACROECONOMIC IDEAS

Adam Smith was the founder of modern economics. In *The Wealth of Nations* (1776) he considered the important macroeconomic issue of how aggregate supply and productivity grow over time. He argued that firms achieve increases in productivity by increased specialization (the "division of labor"). Each worker gets a narrow task to perform and becomes very good at it.

Smith and subsequent writers in the classical economics tradition, such as David Ricardo (1772–1823), also considered aggregate demand and emphasized the importance of gold and the money supply in the determination of the price level. But the emphasis of the classical tradition was on the theory of distribution, that is, how the income and output of the economy are divided up among wage income paid to workers, rental income paid to landowners, and profits paid to capitalists.

Although his ideas were not accepted by all classical writers, one of the most important contributors to classical thought on the macroeconomy was the French economist J. B. Say, who argued in 1803 that supply always creates enough demand to match the available supply. Say's Law argues that there will always be an adequate level of aggregate demand. In the economy as a whole, the argument goes, production generates exactly the right amount of income to allow people to pay for the sale of all of the goods that have been produced.

There is an important element of truth in Say's Law. Say originated the idea of the circular flow of income. The value of everything produced is received as income by those who produced it. Workers, capitalists, and land-owners split up the revenues associated with the sale of the goods and services produced. And then as this income is spent, it flows back to be paid out again as income. However, there is no guarantee that everything that is produced is sold. The experience of prolonged unemployment in the 1870s and, most importantly, the catastrophe of the Great Depression of the 1930s gave unmistakable evidence that Say's Law does not guarantee that aggregate demand is always large enough to insure production at potential output and full employment.

The neoclassical school developed in the 19th century and continues to be a central part of economics today. This school studied consumer choice, the behavior of firms, relative prices, and other issues that we now describe as microeconomics. The focus of neoclassical economics was on the workings of quickly clearing competitive markets. All economists agree that market forces work; they disagree over the speed with which prices adjust so that supply and demand are equal. In the long run there is no disagreement that market forces determine equilibrium, which is why neoclassical analysis is used today in macroeconomics to analyze long-term growth. In Chapter 17 we will develop the neoclassical growth model introduced by Robert Solow in 1956.

The neoclassical economists of the 1920s and 1930s saw first-hand the large fluctuations in the economy that were taking place and many of them explained these fluctuations in neoclassical terms. In particular, they argued that persistent unemployment was caused by an excessively high level of wages. Workers were pricing themselves out of jobs—an idea that remains important in the thinking of some macroeconomists today.

This idea has some truth to it. Almost all models of the business cycle suggest reasons why the excess supply of labor that occurs when there is high unemployment does not immediately lead to a sharp fall in wages. But most economists today, including ourselves, believe that variations in wages do not provide a tenable explanation of cyclical unemployment. There is very little evidence that recessions or depressions are periods when wages are unusually high. Wages are about the same when unemployment is high as they are when unemployment is low, so it is hard to say that when workers are laid off in recessions they are pricing themselves out of jobs.

John Maynard Keynes and Aggregate Demand in the Great Depression

Modern macroeconomics owes much to the revolution in thinking generated by the publication of the *General Theory of Employment, Interest and Money* by the British economist John Maynard Keynes in 1936.

The British economy suffered high unemployment after World War I and did not get back to full employment until the start of World War II, almost 20 years later. The economies of the industrialized world suffered their most severe business-cycle trough in the Great Depression of the 1930s. Keynes's theory was influenced by this experience and he argued that free-enterprise economies can become stuck in a recession or depression with no market mechanism strong enough to cure the problem. He argued that this can come about because aggregate demand can remain very low for a long enough period of time so that unemployment becomes a persistent problem. He said that economies lack sufficient self-correcting mechanisms to stimulate aggregate demand and restore full employment. He argued, further, that an economy's central bank trying to expand output and employment by increasing the amount of money in the economy might not be effective. It might be necessary, he argued, to increase demand by bypassing the marketplace and increasing the amount of direct government spending in the economy. Keynes's ideas gained support among some American economists, such as Seymour Harris of Harvard, Paul Samuelson of the Massachusetts Institute of Technology, and James Tobin of Yale. They and the British economist John Hicks helped to sort out Keynes's ideas and develop them. Those ideas have remained controversial, however, particularly among political conservatives, who judge that Keynesian thinking rationalizes government intervention in free markets.

The high point for Keynesian views in the United States was the 1960s. Articulate advocates for these views such as Walter Heller, who became the chairman of the Council of Economic Advisors under President John F. Kennedy, could point to the unprecedented success of the economy in the years following the development of Keynesian ideas. Unemployment was low, recessions were mild, and inflation was moderate. Economists even talked about fine-tuning macroeconomic policies to maintain full employment without inflation and judged that the big debate about macroeconomic policy was over. President Nixon, in the first Republican administration after the Democratic presidents Kennedy and Johnson, declared, "I am a Keynesian." Yet simultaneous with the ascendancy of Keynesian policies, the makings of a counterrevolution against Keynesian theory were already brewing.

Milton Friedman and Monetarism

Milton Friedman of the University of Chicago had never accepted the Keynesian framework. In 1963, with Anna Schwartz, he published the landmark volume, *A Monetary History of the United States,* which argued that the money supply is the primary engine determining fluctuations in aggregate demand.[1]

---

[1] Milton Friedman and Anna J. Schwartz, *A Monetary History of the United States* (Princeton, N.J.: Princeton University Press, 1963).

As an advocate of monetarism, Friedman attacked the Keynesian idea that monetary policy is a weak or ineffective instrument. On the contrary, he said, monetary policy caused or contributed to almost all of the recessions he studied and was the prime cause of the Great Depression. Further, Friedman argued that the Great Depression of the 1930s did not demonstrate the failure of the free-enterprise system and the need for government to stabilize the economy. Rather, it demonstrated the failure of government economic policies, especially monetary policy as conducted by the Federal Reserve Board (the U.S. central bank). Where Keynes argued that a central bank is incapable of helping an economy get out of a depression, Friedman argued that the Federal Reserve was responsible for getting the U.S. economy into a depression.

Milton Friedman's prescription for macroeconomic policy is to avoid fine-tuning and to set a stable rate of growth of the supply of money. This will allow the natural stability of the economy to emerge, he says. The rate of growh of the money supply should be chosen to allow for the growth of GNP, without being large enough to accommodate inflation.

Stagflation and the Rise of New Macroeconomic Theories

In the 1970s the problem of stagflation appeared, in which high unemployment and high inflation occur together. Following the problems of inflation in the late 1960s, this stagflation gave force to Milton Friedman's critique of Keynesian thinking; he blamed those economic problems on Keynesian policies.

The stagflation in the 1970s also cast doubt on the soundness of economic forecasts that were based on the Keynesian notion that changes in aggregate demand are the source of changes in short-run economic performance. If aggregate-demand fluctuations bring about either higher price levels with higher levels of output and employment or lower price levels with more unemployment, then how could inflation accelerate along with rising unemployment as it did in the 1970s?

Supply shocks

One response to the questions posed by stagflation was to focus on supply-side issues. The price level could rise and output fall if aggregate supply contracted over time (perhaps due to a reduction in oil supplies) rather than expanding as it usually does due to productivity improvements. Moreover, if the contraction in aggregate supply happened quickly, short-run fluctuations in output could no longer be assumed to be solely caused by fluctuations in aggregate demand. Inflationary supply shocks were analyzed within the same general framework as the Keynesian models, except that they pointed to the need to recognize shifts in aggregate supply along with shifts in aggregate demand.

Rational expectations and neoclassical markets

A more profound reaction to the problems associated with aggregate-demand models was the development of a fundamentally different theoretical approach to understanding how the economy works. The economic models based mostly on aggregate-demand fluctuations appeared to be inconsistent both with the reality of stagflation and with assumptions of rational economic behavior. These inconsistencies stimulated a new set of theories about economic fluctuations and government policies. Robert Lucas of the University of Chicago and Thomas Sargent of the University of Minnesota developed models embodying what is called rational expectations. Their models assert that people make everyday economic decisions based upon predictions about future economic behavior, including government policies that are rationally arrived at—and they make them fast. Like Milton Friedman, they argue that recessions are the result of misguided policy gyrations, but they say that policies designed to increase or decrease aggregate demand (monetary and fiscal policies) affect real output and employment *only to the extent that they surprise people.* For the most part, rational-expectations theorists also adopt the assumption that markets are neoclassical, that is, that prices and wages will adjust quickly in order to ensure equilibrium between supply and demand. To these theorists, policies that lead to anticipated changes in aggregate demand cannot work because people discount the price effects of such policy interventions. They argue that if people anticipate that the government is going to spend more money, these same people expect prices to rise, so they do not work any more when their wages rise—they know the wage increase is not real. Since people do not work more when the government spends more, the government's spending policy works only to raise prices, not to increase real output.

Recent Developments in Macroeconomic Ideas

The business cycle occurs with real reductions in output and employment, not just nominal changes in prices. Keynesian models assume that output and employment fall in a recession because of fluctuations in aggregate demand that affect output more than they affect the price level. This is the Keynesian assumption that prices and wages are sticky, so that they do not adjust quickly when supply and demand fluctuate. And a key criticism of Keynesian analysis made by monetarists and especially the rational-expectations economists was that slowly adjusting (sticky) prices were inconsistent with rational behavior.

In the face of this controversy over what causes output and employment to fluctuate, recent research in macroeconomics has taken two very different directions: neo-Keynesian and real–business-cycle theories.

Neo-Keynesian theory

One group, called neo-Keynesians, has been looking for the microeconomic foundations of Keynesian economics. Neo-Keynesians have been developing models in which they say there are good and rational reasons why firms or individuals might adjust prices or wages slowly. Some of the reasons they cite for price stickiness and wage stickiness are found in the inner workings of firms and organizations and in the relationships among firms, neither of which are observable in the marketplace. Neo-Keynesians may never be completely successful in convincing the economists who assume ultrarational behavior that they can explain price stickiness, but their efforts should be applauded. The search has proven useful along the way. It has given us a clearer picture of why price- and wage-stickiness occur by stressing the special character of both the employer–employee relationship and the company–customer relationship. Neo-Keynesians have also looked at how the organization of industry—with the absence of perfect competition in actual markets, with networks of firms that buy from and sell to each other as part of long-term relationships—may contribute to rational reasons for the overall stickiness of prices.

A variant on the neo-Keynesian theory is called post-Keynesian theory. The post-Keynesians retain the notion of price and wage stickiness developed by the neo-Keynesians. They use the idea of a price markup—"marking up" unit production costs by some amount—as one contributor to sticky prices. The group's main departure from neo-Keynesian economists is its focus upon income distribution and the effect it has upon the investment share of national income. In this view, the government needs an incomes policy to influence wages and profits in order to keep inflation in check without raising unemployment. In particular, using a tax incentive to encourage wage and price restraint was a popular idea during the 1980 presidential election, but has not received much attention since then.

Real–business-cycle theory

The other direction that recent research has taken—real–business-cycle theory—is very different from the research that has developed neo-Keynesian ideas. It attributes business-cycle changes in output and employment to changes in technology and to shocks in productive capacity rather than to changes in aggregate demand. This theory developed as economists who accepted the assumptions of rational expectations and neoclassical markets were not satisfied with the explanations of the business cycle in terms of surprises or shocks to aggregate demand. The new theory attempts to reconcile rational-expectations and neoclassical markets with the existence of real fluctuations in the economy. It adopts the neoclassical argument that wages and prices are not sticky and combines that with the rational-expectations argument that anticipated changes in aggregate demand cannot cause changes in output. These theorists argue that the existence of fluctuations in such real economic variables as output and employment is evidence of real business cycles. Recessions, they argue, are periods when production technology has deteriorated and so people decide not to work as much.

In our judgment, this theory does not provide a reasonable view of the business cycle, but the work of these economists has proven valuable. Major developments in technology, such as the automobile or the computer, are large enough to have macroeconomic effects. And the real–business-cycle theorists have shown that the impact of these changes in technology on output are surprisingly long-lasting.

A Modern Framework

The framework for describing the economy that we are using in this book owes much to Keynes and to the subsequent development of his ideas by Keynesians and neo-Keynesians. The reason for starting with a Keynesian framework is that in our judgment it provides the best basic structure available to describe the way our actual economy works. We start with the Keynesian framework and then we extend it to incorporate modern developments.

In our framework, shifts in aggregate demand, in the face of sticky prices and wages, are the major sources of short-term fluctuations in output. The economy experiences business-cycle recessions in which actual output is below potential output and there is excess unemployment because of inadequate aggregate demand. A recession is a time when the economy is operating inefficiently: there are people who want to work but do not have jobs; there are companies that would like to hire more workers and produce more output, but they do not because they could not sell the resulting output. And there are consumers who would be willing to spend more, but do not because their incomes are depressed as a result of the recession and the unemployment. Somehow the actions of these groups of people are not coordinated by the working of the economy in a way that maintains full employment.

There are two ways in which the activities and decisions of different groups in the economy may not be coordinated. The first of these involves saving and investment. In a primitive economy there is a direct link between the amount people save and the amount they invest for future production. A farmer produces wheat and consumes part of it. The remainder is saved and *automatically* the saving is invested in the form of seed for next year's wheat production. There is no coordination problem between saving and investment because the person doing the saving is also doing the investing. A modern economy is different, however. The decisions by families to consume part of their incomes and save the remainder, and the decisions by businesses to invest in new machines and factories are not coordinated. When businesses decide they want to cut back on their purchases of new machinery and factories, households may also decide to cut back on their consumption. Instead of a fall in investment being matched by a rise in consumption, the opposite happens and the result is a recession.

The second coordination problem arises with the adjustment of prices and wages. If workers find that there are not enough jobs, or if companies find that they cannot sell all of the output that they are producing, then the theory of competitive markets says that prices and wages should fall. An excess supply of workers looking for jobs should lead to a decline in wages. In practice, wages and prices adjust only very slowly to an excess of supply over demand. In fact there have been many situations in recent years where there has been persistent inflation even though the economy was in a recession. In such cases a coordinated reduction in wage and price increases would cut inflation and improve the economic situation for everyone, but each individual firm or each group of workers continues to push prices and wages up because every other firm or group of workers is doing the same thing. While it may be in the collective interest of the economy to reduce inflation without having a recession, there are no good coordination mechanisms that would achieve this.

Since we contend that these two coordination failures are an essential part of business-cycle fluctuations, we use a framework of analysis that incorporates them, rather than the monetarist, rational-expectations, or real–business-cycle models that do not. However, we do make use of important aspects of these models. Keynes was wrong in minimizing the effect of monetary policy and Milton Friedman was correct in stressing its power. Friedman was also correct in pointing to the dangers of inflation and even stagflation inherent in some policy prescriptions derived from earlier Keynesian models. Lucas and Sargent were correct in arguing that the economy is influenced not only by current policies, but also by people's expectations of policy in the future. In Chapters 15 and 16 we shall specifically address the monetarist and rational-expectations approaches to macroeconomics. But we shall be using their ideas much earlier than this. In our description of the macroeconomy, we recognize the important role that is played by expectations, especially expectations about the rate of inflation and the actions of economic policymakers.

We hope to offer readers a tool that will increase their understanding of the modern economy. We have attempted to synthesize the major contributions that have led to the development of modern macroeconomics. We have also attempted to incorporate ideas from the social-policy and business communities that do not always fit conventional economic modeling.

Any framework for understanding the macroeconomy has to be built up one step at a time. We shall start with a Keynesian model and expand the framework from there. Then we introduce financial markets, monetary and fiscal policies, expectations, inflation, the foreign sector, long-term growth, and productivity. However, the first step we have to take is a close look at just what it is that we measure when we measure macroeconomic performance.

CHAPTER 1

Measuring Economic Performance

KEY CONCEPTS FOR MACROECONOMICS

How do we assess the performance of the economy at the aggregate level? We have come to expect that an economy that is operating well will generate high and rising incomes, that most of the people who want jobs will have them, that there will be reasonable stability of prices, and that our economic relations with other countries will be in reasonable balance. We look now at how these ideas can be translated into specific measurable concepts. Then we use these concepts to see how the U.S. economy is doing.

Total income and production are the most important indicators of aggregate economic conditions, because they measure our society's ability to command economic resources. How much is available to spend on the consumption goods we enjoy? How much government spending can be made? How much shall we invest to maintain or increase production in the future? Are we borrowing from the rest of the world because we can't produce all that we spend, or are we lending and investing overseas because we are not spending all that we produce?

Gross National Product (GNP) The total amount of goods and services produced in the economy in a given period. **Nominal GNP** in a given period is measured using the prices that prevail in the same year. **Real GNP** in a given year values the output in that year in the prices that prevailed in a *base year*. Base years are changed periodically; the year used now is 1982.

The Gross National Product

The total amount of goods and services produced in the economy in a given year is called the **Gross National Product** or **GNP.** GNP is a gross measure of output, meaning that it does not include an adjustment for replacing capital that was used up in the productive process. GNP is also, for reasons we shall see shortly, a measure of aggregate income.

Nominal GNP measures the total amount of goods and services produced in a given year in terms of the dollars of the same year. However, a better way to measure the level of production in the economy is to use **real GNP,**

which calculates the value of output using the prices that prevailed in a base year. (Currently the base year is 1982.) Real GNP takes the nominal values of GNP year by year and removes the effect of inflation. We can compare values of real GNP in different years and see the change in the rate at which the economy is producing autos, loaves of bread, restaurant meals, nights in hotels, and other goods and services in our factories, offices, and businesses.

To assess economic performance over time we look at the *rate of growth of real GNP*. How well is the economy doing this year relative to last year or over a period of several years? Real GNP in 1989 was $4,144 billion (in 1982 dollars) compared to $4,024 billion in 1988, and so the rate of growth of real GNP from 1988 to 1989 was 3.0 percent [(4,144 − 4,024)/4,024 = 0.030 = 3.0 percent].

real GNP per person (or per capita)
Real GNP divided by the population.

To see how well the economy is providing resources for its citizens we look at **real GNP per person** (also called **real GNP per capita**). This takes real GNP and divides it by the number of people living in the United States. In 1989 it was estimated that the U.S. population was 248.8 million people, so that real GNP per person was about $16,700 in 1989. This figure compares to a real GNP per person of about $7,600 in 1948 and about $10,700 in 1965 (all figures in 1982 dollars). It places the United States very high in the international distribution of income. Real GNP per person in the United States is 20–25 percent higher than in France, West Germany, and Japan, and about 35 percent higher than in the United Kingdom.[1]

We show in Figure 1.1 how real and nominal GNP have changed between 1955 and 1989. Figure 1.1A looks at the levels of real and nominal GNP and it shows the tremendous growth that has taken place in the output of the economy. There has been a pronounced upward trend in real GNP but an even greater upward trend in nominal GNP. Prices have increased substantially over this period.

business cycle
A recurring fluctuation of aggregate output in the economy. Each cycle consists of a **peak** (the highest level of output and employment reached before a sustained decline in output), a **recession** or **contraction** (where output is falling for at least two quarters), a **trough** (the low point for output), and a **recovery** or **expansion** (where output is rising).

Figure 1.1B, showing the year-to-year percent rates of growth of real GNP over the same time period, reveals that growth has been far from smooth around this long-term trend. There are years of strong increase in real GNP and years of very small increase or even decline. These year-to-year fluctuations in growth make up the business cycle.

Business Cycles

A **business cycle** is a recurring fluctuation of real GNP. Each cycle consists of a **peak** (the highest level of output and employment reached before a sustained decline in output), a **recession** or **contraction** (where output is falling for at least two quarters), a **trough** (the low point for output), and a **recovery** or **expansion** (where output is rising).

---

[1] The source for these international comparisons is the Organization for Economic Cooperation and Development (OECD) in their publications *OECD Statistics, Paris, 1989,* and *OECD Main Economic Indicators, 1989,* both published in Paris, 1989.

FIGURE 1.1A   Real and Nominal Gross National Product, 1955–1989

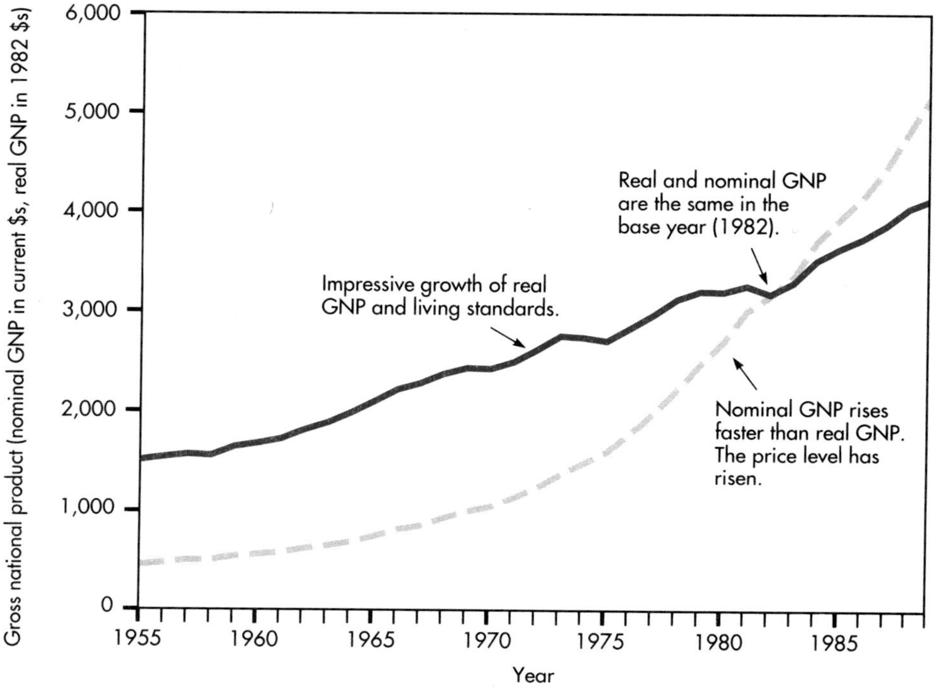

Source: U.S. Department of Commerce, Bureau of Economic Analysis.

Output fluctuates in business cycles, with production sometimes falling below the economy's capacity to produce and employment falling below full employment. And production sometimes goes above the level that can be produced with normal levels of utilization of the economy's resources. There has been no great regularity to business-cycle fluctuations in the U.S. economy. Some cycles have lasted only a couple of years and some have lasted many years. Since World War II, business expansions have been much longer than contractions, with the current expansion that started in 1982 continuing as of mid-1990.[2]

Business cycles consist of fluctuations in real GNP around a benchmark level that reflects the long-term–growth trend in the productive capacity of

---

[2] Robert J. Gordon, ed., *The American Business Cycle: Continuity and Change* (Chicago: University of Chicago Press, 1986).

FIGURE 1.1B   The Growth Rate of Real GNP, 1955–1989

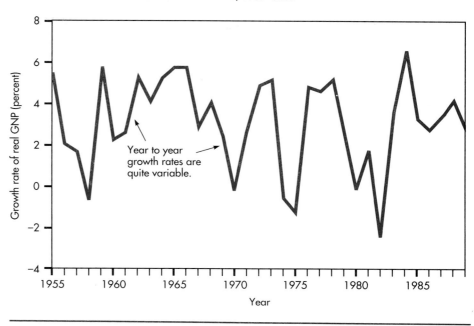

Source: U.S. Department of Commerce, Bureau of Economic Analysis.

the economy. The level of GNP that is used as a benchmark is called potential output. In our study of business-cycle fluctuations, we will be asking why real GNP is sometimes below potential output and sometimes above it. How is potential output defined?

Potential Output

potential output or potential GNP
The level of output (usually *real GNP*) that is produced when the capital and labor resources of the economy are fully utilized but not overutilized. Benchmark levels of unemployment and capital utilization have to be set to determine potential output.

Potential output or **potential GNP** is defined as the level of output that can be produced in a given year when the available capital and labor resources of the economy are fully utilized but not at so high a rate that it cannot be sustained. Potential output is not maximum output, since the maximum possible output we could produce if everyone worked 24 hours a day, seven days a week, and ran all our machinery at full throttle with no time taken for maintenance and no provisions for replacement is not a very meaningful number. We certainly could not sustain that level of effort for any length of time. Rather, potential output measures the *sustainable* productive capacity of the economy, once the benchmark for the level of utilization is set. And since potential output is not the maximum possible level of output, there

■ Nominal GNP, Real GNP, and the Price Level

The **price level** is an index number that reflects the prices of all the goods and services produced and sold in a particular year. Changes in the price level from year to year are measured as an average of the price changes in all the goods and services produced and sold. The bigger the amount spent on the product, the more important on average is its price increase.[3] If the economy produced only two goods, food and clothing, and if we spent three quarters of our incomes on food and one quarter on clothing, and if food prices rose by 10 percent in a year and clothing prices rose by 2 percent, then the price level would have risen by 8 percent [(0.75 × 10%) + (0.25 × 2%)].

Nominal GNP is the measure we get when we simply add up the dollar values of aggregate demand. The price level is related to nominal GNP and real GNP in the following way:

Nominal GNP = Real GNP × The price level

or alternatively

Real GNP = Nominal GNP / The price level.

Real GNP grew from $2.09 trillion in 1965 to $4.14 trillion in 1989. The value in 1965 dollars of all the goods and services produced in the economy in 1965 was $705 billion, that is, nominal GNP was $705 billion. In standard data sources the price level is expressed as an index number, 33.8 in 1965 or 126.3 in 1989, which relates the price level in any given year to the price level in a particular period or base year. The base year now being used is 1982. Real GNP is reported as "1989 GNP in 1982 dollars" or "1965 GNP in 1982 dollars." The price level in 1982 is set equal to 100 and then the price level in 1965 is the ratio of the price index in 1965 to the price index in 1982. So, the price level in 1965 was 0.338 of the price level in 1982 and 1965's real GNP in 1982 dollars is then $705 billion ÷ 0.338, which equals $2.09 trillion.

Similarly, the nominal GNP in 1989 was $5.23 trillion. The price level in 1989 was 1.263 (126.3 ÷ 100), so that 1989's real GNP in 1982 dollars is then $5.23 trillion ÷ 1.263, which equals $4.14 trillion.

Nominal GNP in 1989 was much greater than nominal GNP in 1965, but much of the increase in nominal GNP was the result of an increase in the level of prices. Real GNP increased between 1965 and 1989 but by roughly two times (4.10 ÷ 2.09) rather than the more than seven times (5.22 ÷ 0.705) indicated by comparing nominal values.

---

price level
A price index set equal to unity (or 100) in the *base year*. Changes in the price level over time reflect the average change of all prices. The *implicit price deflator for GNP* is one measure of the price level, equal to the ratio of *nominal GNP* to *real GNP*.

will be years when output exceeds potential output (that is, when capital and labor are utilized more intensively than the benchmark levels).

Potential output must be estimated and this is usually done using information on unemployment (a measure of the degree of utilization of the labor force) and business reports of how close firms are to full capacity (a measure of capital utilization). To measure potential output from this information, there has to be some benchmark for the level of utilization that corresponds to potential output. When Arthur Okun first introduced the concept in the early 1960s, he said that output was equal to potential output when there was 4 percent unemployment.[4] That benchmark has been adjusted—today

---

[3] The average used is a **weighted average.** See the discussion of price indexes and inflation on pp. 28–29.

[4] Arthur M. Okun, "Potential GNP: Its Measurement and Significance," in *Proceedings of the Business and Economic Statistics Section of the American Statistical Association,* 1962, pp. 98–104.

potential output corresponds to somewhere between 5 and 6 percent unemployment.

Comparing Output with Potential Output

Over the course of the business cycle, actual output can be either higher or lower than capacity. If actual output is less than capacity, the standard of living that is achieved is worse than it could have been—the economy is suffering unemployment of labor and underutilization of capital. That gap between what was produced and the potential to produce reflects a painful waste of opportunities for improving the economic lives of our citizens. Real GNP can also be greater than potential output for a time with very low unemployment and factories running overtime or extra shifts. The problem in this case is that inflation will accelerate.

The output ratio

output ratio
The ratio of actual output to *potential output,* usually given in percent terms.

A measure of economic performance that compares actual output to potential output is the **output ratio.** We can use potential output to measure short-run economic performance in terms of the output ratio or the output gap. The first of these is a key indicator of the state of the economy and is defined as the ratio of output to potential output:

$$\text{Output ratio} = \text{Output} \div \text{Potential output}.$$

Since real GNP is our main measure of output, the output ratio is usually defined as the ratio of real GNP to potential real GNP, and the ratio is multiplied by 100 to express it as an index number. Figure 1.2 shows the output ratio for the U.S. economy over the period 1955–88. It shows that there have been persistent business-cycle fluctuations, such as 1975–77 and 1982–84 when the economy operated well below potential output (that is, when the output ratio was well below 100 percent). And there was a long period in the 1960s when output was well above potential output (when the ratio was above 100 percent).

output gap
The difference between actual output and *potential output.* Can also be expressed as the percent difference between the two.

The **output gap** is just another way of expressing the same idea as that embodied in the output ratio. The output gap is defined either as the difference between output and potential output or the percent deviation of output from potential output:

$$\text{Output gap (in base-year dollars)} = \text{Output} - \text{Potential output}$$
$$\text{Output gap (in percent)} = \text{Percentage difference between output and potential output.}$$

For example, if the output ratio is 90 percent, the output gap is *minus* 10 percent and GNP is 10 percent below potential GNP. This would correspond to a dollar output gap of about $400 billion in today's economy (using 1982 dollars). The output gap indicates the percent change in GNP that would have had to occur in order to restore the economy to its benchmark level of utilization.

FIGURE 1.2   Ratio of Actual GNP to Potential GNP, 1955–1989

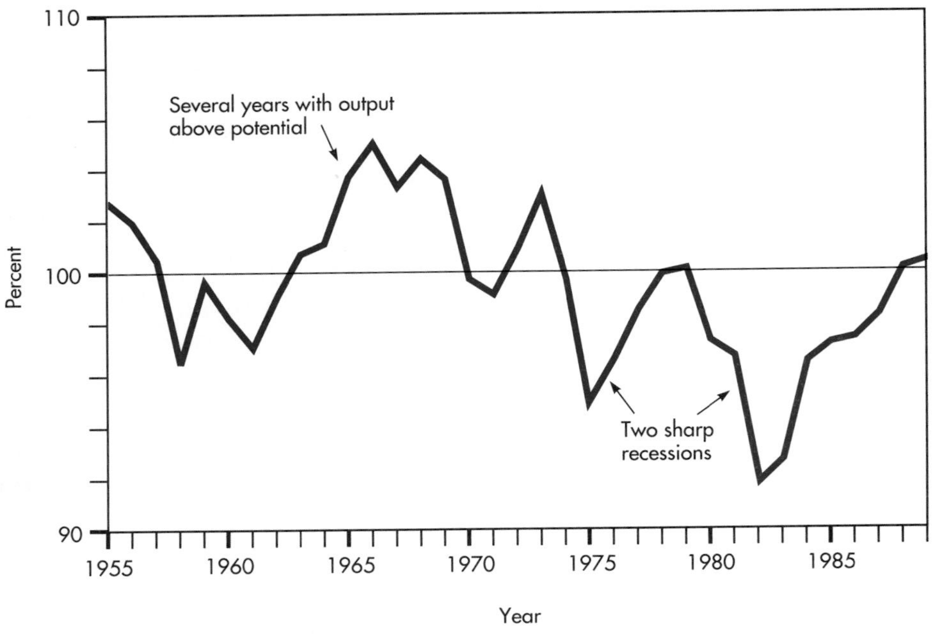

Source: U.S. Department of Commerce, Bureau of Economic Analysis. Potential GNP estimated by the authors.

Much of this book will be concerned with understanding why the output ratio differs from 100 percent and what, if anything, should be done to control those fluctuations. In discussions of income determination and fluctuations in the short run, we will often ignore the growth over time in potential output itself. In the long run, as a result of increases in the amount of labor and physical capital, plus investments in human skills and capabilities, technology, and knowledge, potential output grows over time. We return to look at long-run changes in potential output when we explore the issues of long-run growth and productivity.

The degree to which an economy operates at potential also affects the work force. Since the prospects for employment are so critical to the well-being of our population, macroeconomists pay special attention to whether or not the economy generates jobs for the people who want them.

Unemployment

The basic purpose of the economic system is to produce the goods and services that people demand. And this is why we have said that output and income are the most important measures of economic performance. But

FIGURE 1.3   The Unemployment Rate, 1929–1989

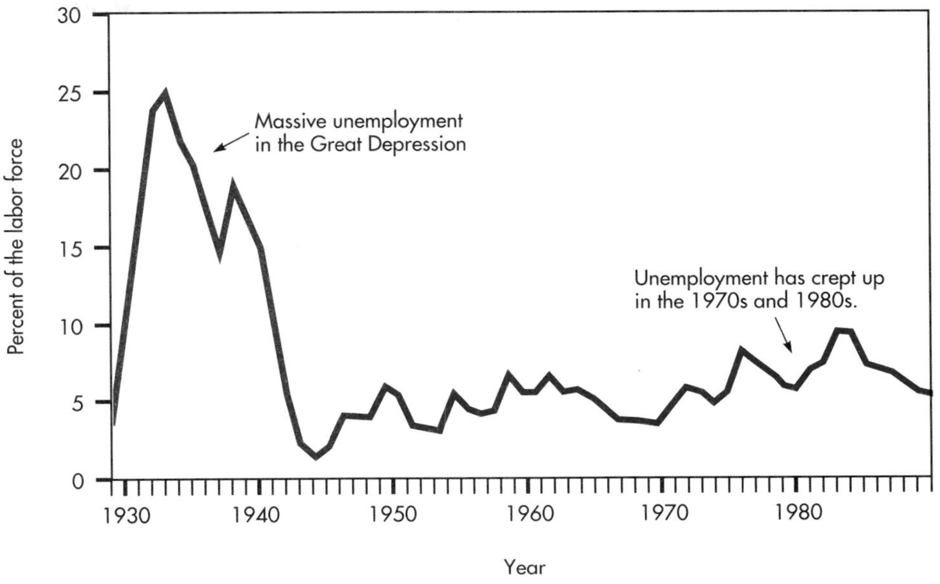

Source: U.S. Department of Commerce, Bureau of Economic Analysis: *Historical Statistics of the United States* (Washington, D.C.: U.S. Government Printing Office, 1971); and *Economic Report of the President, 1990* (Washington, D.C.: U.S. Government Printing Office, 1990).

a vital element in any successful economy is its ability to employ all or almost all of the individuals seeking employment.

Every month surveyors from the Census Bureau, a federal government agency, interview a sample of U.S. residents about their employment status. They ask someone in each family surveyed to say whether the family members have jobs, are actively looking for jobs, are on temporary layoff from a job, do not want to take paid employment, or are sick or unable to work. The number of people in the economy who either have jobs (are employed) or are unemployed is the total **labor force.** The unemployed are those people over 16 years old who are able to work and looking for work who do not have a job, or who are on layoff. The **unemployment rate** is then the percentage of the labor force that is unemployed and this provides a measure of the slack in the labor market, the economy's unused labor resources.

Figure 1.3 shows the unemployment rate for the U.S. economy from 1929 to 1989. The Great Depression in the 1930s is the period of the worst sustained unemployment in U.S. history. The unemployment rate averaged 19 percent over the 10 years 1931–40. Although the situation improved after 1933, the economy did not reach low unemployment rates until 1942. Very low unemployment rates were sustained throughout World War II and the

labor force
The total number of people in the economy who are either employed or unemployed.

unemployment rate
The percentage of the *labor force* that is unemployed. The unemployed are those looking for work or on layoff.

rate stayed low after the war until 1974. There have been two deep recessions since 1974 and a generally higher average rate of unemployment, but by 1989 the recovery had brought the rate close to 5 percent.

Some unemployment is inevitable in the normal operation of the economy, but in a recession unemployment exceeds this normal or natural level. There is no question that the public considers excessive unemployment a problem. Productive employment is vital to people's immediate well-being (both economic and psychological) and it is the source of experience and skill building that enhances our future well-being.

Full employment

Even when the economy is producing a level of output equal to potential output, there is a substantial amount of unemployment. Imagine a factory in the Midwest whose workers have been laid off and are looking for work, while there are jobs without qualified applicants in an insurance company on the West Coast. Even when the labor market is operating normally, workers can be separated from jobs by location and training. They will have to search for the right job; they may have to relocate; and they may have to wait for a new job to open up or wait for their old job to reopen.

Since some level of unemployment is normal, **full employment** in the economy is a misleading term. It doesn't mean that everyone is employed. Full employment is often used to describe the economy when it is operating with output equal to potential output and the unemployment rate is equal to the **natural rate of unemployment.** During the late 1980s potential output was reached when the natural rate of unemployment stood between 5 and 6 percent.

full employment
The level of employment that occurs when the economy is operating at *potential output.* The benchmark for potential output and for full employment are determined together.

natural rate of unemployment
The level of unemployment that occurs when output equals potential output.

productivity
The amount of output produced per unit of input. Often measured by **average labor productivity**—output per hour of work. Output per worker is often used as an alternative measure.

Productivity

Growing output benefits the economy in that more jobs are available. Rapid growth of output leads to reductions in unemployment. But there is an additional advantage when output increases more than the number of hours of work used to produce the output. When this occurs, **productivity** is increasing.

Although there are several different measures of productivity, the simplest useful measure is output per hour of work. This is called **average labor productivity** or often just productivity. Productivity is a measure of the efficiency of the economy—how much output is produced with a given amount of labor used. Figure 1.4 shows average labor productivity for the U.S. economy from 1948 to 1988. Productivity growth has been most impressive over this period, but growth has slowed since the early 1970s.

The Rate of Inflation

Inflation is an increase in the overall level of prices. Throughout the history of world economies there have been periods of time during which inflation was a serious problem. In modern times the price level has risen continuously

FIGURE 1.4   Business Productivity: Growth Rate per Year, 1948–1988

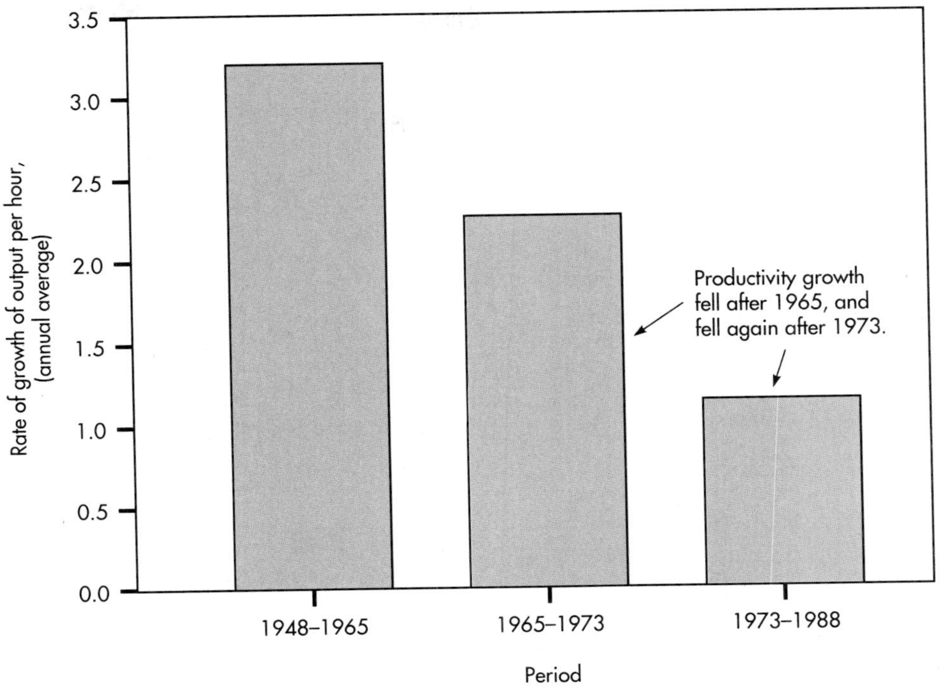

Source: U.S. Department of Labor, Bureau of Labor Statistics.

inflation
The rate of increase of the price level. A decrease in the price level—*deflation*—is measured as the negative of the rate of inflation. Inflation for consumer prices is measured as the rate of increase of the *consumer price index.*

in the United States since the mid-1950s, but the problem of high rates of inflation emerged in the United States and in most other economies in the mid-1960s. The rate of inflation is defined as the proportional or percent increase in the price level from one year to the next.

Rate of inflation = [Price level (given year) − Price level (prior year)]
÷ Price level (prior year).

Rate of inflation (in percent) = Percent rate of growth of the price level.

In the U.S. economy, there have been periods when the price level has fallen. This happened in the 1930s, for example. A falling price level is called *deflation* and the rate of deflation is simply the negative of the rate of inflation.

Although the price level has sometimes fallen, this has not been the normal case for the U.S. economy since the 1950s. As we noted earlier, the price level in 1989 was more than three times as high as it was in 1955. From 1965 to 1989, the rate of inflation has ranged mostly between 3 and 6

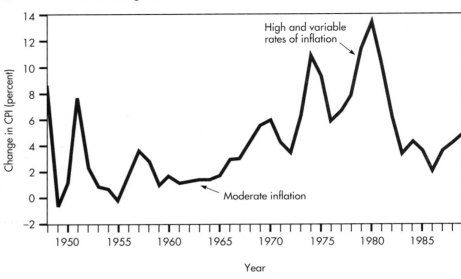

FIGURE 1.5   Percent Change in the Consumer Price Index, 1948–1989

Source: U.S. Department of Labor, Bureau of Labor Statistics.

percent with short bursts of higher inflation. Inflation has averaged nearly 5 percent a year over this period. Despite efforts to reduce inflation, it was still running at about 5 percent in 1990.

The price level as we are using it here is an index number that is based on all of the goods and services that are part of GNP. This price index is known as the **implicit price deflator for GNP.** It provides a measure of overall inflation, but it can give a misleading picture if there are changes over time in the kinds of goods produced in the economy.

An alternative price index, one whose changes capture inflation as it affects consumers, is the consumer price index.

implicit price deflator for GNP
The *price level* for all GNP. The deflator is computed as the ratio of *nominal GNP* to *real GNP*.

The consumer price index

consumer price index (CPI)
The index tracks the prices of the purchases made by typical households in a given year relative to the prices for the same collection of goods and services in a *base year*.

The **consumer price index** (CPI) is constructed by looking at changes in the prices of the things that typical households buy. Figure 1.5 shows the rate of inflation (annual percent change in the CPI) measured by this important price index. The CPI tracks the average annual rate of increase in the prices consumers pay for a representative group or "basket" of purchases.

There are thousands of different items purchased by consumers, but the U.S. Department of Labor's Bureau of Labor Statistics, the federal government agency that prepares the CPI, looks at a sample of these and then forms a **weighted average** of their rates of increase. Each price in the survey

weighted average
Used for calculating an overall measure when not all items are equally important. Instead of calculating an average by adding all the elements and dividing by the number of items, in a weighted average each item is counted (weighted) for relatively more or less in arriving at the average. The weight of an item reflects the relative importance or impact of that item in the aggregate measure.

is given a relative importance in the average, depending upon how large a fraction of the consumer dollar is spent on this type of good or service.

People dislike inflation intensely, but economists, who are used to evaluating economic conditions in real terms, after inflation adjustment, would argue that the intensity of dislike for inflation may be excessive and may stem partly from misunderstanding. If wage increases are followed by an increase in prices, this is seen as undoing well-deserved gains, even if the inflation itself was a major reason for the higher wages.

This is not to say economists cannot see real reasons to dislike inflation. There is a cost of inflation that is the added uncertainty in the economy that results from not knowing the real value of future revenues and returns. Increased uncertainty discourages investment and makes it hard for people to plan for retirement. A related reason why inflation is costly to the economy is that an unexpected burst of inflation surprises people and ends up changing the effective terms of contracts that have been agreed to. If you sell goods or services, or if you offer labor or rent capital, you expect to be compensated. Unexpected inflation can lower the real value of amounts received under the terms of a contract because the money received for goods and services rendered buys less when prices rise.

THE PERFORMANCE OF THE INTERNATIONAL SECTOR

imports
Domestic purchases of foreign goods and services.

exports
Purchases of domestically produced goods and services by foreigners.

trade balance
The difference between exports and imports of goods.

Increasingly, our economic concerns involve the U.S. performance in relation to other countries. Supply and demand do not stop at national borders. The goods and services available to U.S. consumers include **imports** from abroad, while the demand for our goods and services includes our **exports** (sales to the rest of the world). In addition, financial assets move across international borders at electronic speed. Interest rates and the availability of credit are no longer domestically determined.

In 1986 the United States imported $282 billion worth of manufactured goods, which was equal to 34 percent of the value of manufactured production here at home. The corresponding figure for 1966 was only 7 percent. Figure 1.6 shows how imports and exports have been rising as a percentage of GNP. Moreover, the **trade balance** (the gap between exports and imports) has also changed, going from a mild surplus to a large deficit.

Because of its increasing importance, we will look at the international sector by including imports, exports, exchange rates, and international movements of financial capital in our analysis. U.S. living standards depend upon our ability to produce products and services that compete effectively in world markets. By selling overseas, we earn the income to pay for those imported goods that cannot be produced domestically, except at higher costs than they can be produced abroad.

The value of the dollar also provides an indicator of our international economic performance. The value of the dollar, in common with all the major currencies, has fluctuated widely since the 1970s. However, these fluctu-

FIGURE 1.6   Exports and Imports as Percentages of GNP, 1948–1989

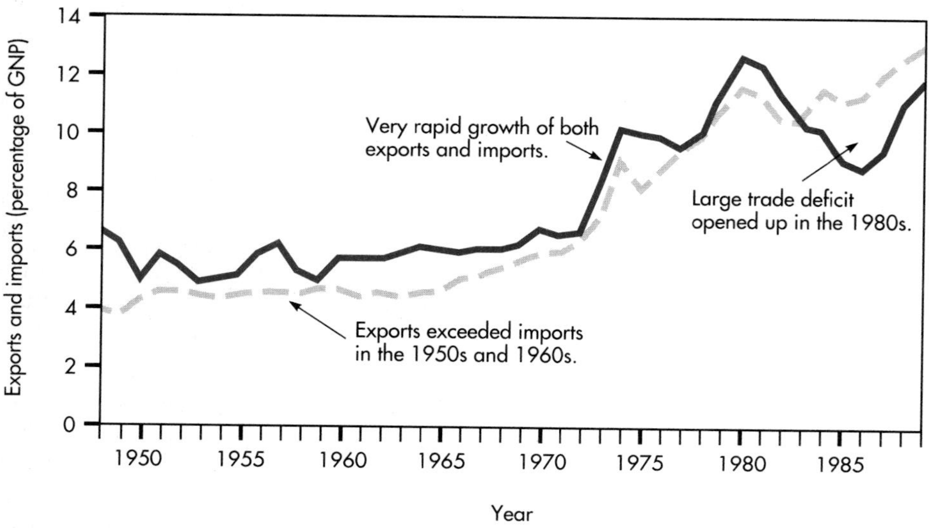

Source: U.S. Department of Commerce, Bureau of Economic Analysis.

ations have come around a declining trend of the dollar in relation to the German mark and the Japanese yen. In 1970 exchange rates were 3.6 marks per dollar and 360 yen per dollar. As of mid-1990 rates are 1.7 marks per dollar and 160 yen per dollar.

THE MACROECONOMIC SCORECARD: HOW ARE WE DOING?

We can assess macroeconomic performance in historical terms: How are we doing relative to our own past performance? And we can assess performance relative to other countries. The grades are mixed on both counts. We start with the long view and compare the postwar period from 1948 to the present, relative to economic performance over the period before World War II.[5]

- The post–World War II period, 1948–1989, is one of greatly increased stability in real GNP compared to earlier periods. *The business cycle has been reduced in severity.* In particular there has been no depression comparable to the Great Depression of the 1930s.

---

[5] Historical data can be found in U.S. Department of Commerce, *Historical Statistics of the United States.*

- The trend rate of growth of real GNP and the trend rate of productivity growth have been as high or higher than in earlier periods. *Living standards for most Americans have increased enormously since 1948.*

- The level of unemployment has been as low or lower since 1948 on average than it was in prior periods. There has also been a tremendous growth in the labor force and the fraction of the population that is employed. *The U.S. economy has created jobs for most of the people who have wanted them, especially compared to the disastrous experience of the 1930s.* (Certain groups in the economy have not shared fully in this general success, however, particularly minorities.)

- The average rate of inflation has been higher since 1948. In earlier periods prices would rise substantially but they would also fall. *The persistence of inflation is a phenomenon of the postwar economy.*

- Even though inflation was much lower prior to World War II, there was considerable instability in prices at that time. As the price level rose and fell, this generated a rather variable rate of inflation. *The variability of inflation has been somewhat lower since World War II.*

- *There has been a tremendous expansion of world trade since 1948,* with large increases in the volumes of both U.S. exports and imports.

Taken as a whole, therefore, there are several reasons to give a good grade to macroeconomic performance over the period 1948–1989. Real incomes, employment, and trade have all shown tremendous growth and reasonable stability. Inflation has been a recurrent problem, however.

If we break down the postwar period and compare performance in the 1970s and 1980s with the two decades prior to that, the picture does not look so good.

- The rate of inflation (measured by the consumer price index) averaged only 2 percent a year from 1948 to 1969. In the next 20 years inflation averaged over 6 percent a year.

- There were large fluctuations in real GNP in the 1970s and 1980s.

- The unemployment rate averaged 4.7 percent from 1948 to 1969. From 1970 to 1989, unemployment averaged 6.7 percent, a full two percentage points higher.

- The rate of increase of productivity has been much slower since the late 1960s than it was earlier. The rate of growth of real GNP has also slowed, but by less than productivity because there has been a large increase in employment, as the baby-boom generation entered the work force and the fraction of women in paid employment increased.

- The United States ran a surplus in its foreign trade and payments in most years from 1948 to 1983 (as measured in terms of current dollars). There has been a large foreign deficit since then. The deficit in foreign

THE INTERNATIONAL SCOREBOARD   Comparative Productivity Growth Rates

A serious misconception is being circulated about U.S. productivity. The following newspaper account is typical:

> Factory productivity in the United States lags still more behind other nations. Output per hour gained only 2 percent among U.S. manufacturers in 1989, exceeding only Sweden's 1.6 percent rise among 11 industrial countries, the Bureau of Labor Statistics said. Nine other nations topped the United States, led by gains of 6.4 percent in Norway, 5.8 percent in Japan, and 5.1 percent in the United Kingdom. U.S. productivity increases had tied for fifth among 12 nations from 1979 through 1987, but the U.S. rise in 1988 fell to 10th among the 12.*

Such statements err in treating the *rate of growth* in productivity as if it were the *level* of productivity. In absolute terms, factory productivity in the United States remains far above that of other industrialized nations. Nobody does it better, or nearly as well.

Even so, the U.S. trade balance has been upset by the *relative* improvement in manufacturing productivity growth in Europe and Japan, leading U.S. policymakers to bemoan the "great productivity slowdown" in this country. Thus, some economists have been probing the sources of productivity growth in hopes of speeding it up again.

Perhaps they are using their time unwisely. According to the *convergence hypothesis*, the overwhelming superiority of the American economy in the early years after World War II came of extraordinary circumstances and could not be sustained indefinitely.

In the late 1940s, the American market was eight times the size of the next largest market, allowing U.S. industry to benefit from large-scale production. Also, war refugees coming to America were among Europe's most skilled and intelligent workers. The U.S. populace was unmatched in higher educational attainment. America was richer than other countries, so the first mass market for just about everything, especially the automobile and television, began in the United States.

trade has been paralleled by a large deficit in the budget of the federal government.

The bad news is that performance has deteriorated in recent years. The macroeconomy is still doing well, but not as well as it did in the 1950s and 1960s. How does this performance look compared to that of other countries?[6]

- In recent years, inflation has been higher in Europe than in the United States. Japan has had very little inflation.

- Unemployment has been much higher on average in Europe than in the United States in recent years. It has stayed persistently high, rather than showing a cyclical pattern as U.S. unemployment has done. Japan has had very little unemployment.

- The level of productivity and the level of real GNP per person remain substantially higher in the United States than in Europe and Japan. The growth rates of productivity have been higher overseas than here,

---

[6] See sources cited in footnote 1.

This American lead in productivity growth had to wane as other nations rebuilt industrial bases over wartime ruins. Thus, the relative size of the American market has declined. Today it is not quite twice as large as the Japanese market and it will soon be outstripped by a unified European market that will provide Europeans with a per capita income close to that of the United States.

Many other elements besides internal market size affect productivity growth. For one thing, because of revolutionary improvements in telecommunication, computer technology, and transportation, as well as less trade restrictions, the world is in many ways a "global village." The Japanese can produce and sell six times as many video recorders as they themselves can buy.

Another reason affecting productivity is that a mature "post-industrial" economy like America's shifts labor and capital from one sector to another, replacing some high-productivity factory workers with low-productivity service industry workers. Americans willingly pay for such personal services as massages and hairstyling. Europe and Japan have yet to achieve such a full service sector in their respective economies.

Finally, the high productivity rates in Europe and Asia should prove to be as unsustainable in the long run as the U.S. rate of old—another consequence of convergence. When U.S. productivity slowed down in 1973–79 (negatively, by some measures) and again in 1979–86, the same thing happened to the productivity pace in every other advanced industrial nation, including Japan. As world nations become more globally alike and interdependent, they tend to experience the same economic ups and downs at about the same time.

Does convergence mean that the Third World countries are due for their own dynamic growth periods? Not necessarily. It is possible to accept the idea of convergence without extending it to the entire world. The least-developed countries, such as those in eastern Africa or in Central America, actually may be losing ground because they lack the basic minimal educational levels and industrial base required to take off.

but it does not look as if our productivity lead will be eliminated any time soon. Real GNP and employment have grown slowly in Europe.

- Japan and Germany are running large trade surpluses, in contrast to our large trade deficit.

Even though U.S. economic performance has deteriorated, it compares reasonably well with the other main industrial countries' economies. In fact, given all the gloom and doom that one hears about the economy, the relative U.S. performance looks surprisingly good. One reason for the gloom and doom is that people are always comparing the United States to Japan, particularly in terms of the two countries' performances in international trade. Japan's economy has done outstandingly well by a variety of measures and Japanese exports have taken some of our industries by storm. Keep in mind, however, that Japan's success has been somewhat selective. Many of its industries perform poorly. And Japan's success has come as part of a process of catch-up, so that living standards in Japan are still well below those in the United States.

We have looked at some of the key concepts that are used to measure macroeconomic performance and we have found a mixed picture in terms of assessing the U.S. economy. We turn now to a more detailed look at how the key performance measure, GNP, is computed and then broken down into components in the *National Income and Product Accounts*.

MEASURING OUTPUT: GROSS NATIONAL PRODUCT AND NATIONAL INCOME ACCOUNTING

intermediate goods and services
Goods and services sold to other firms to be used up in production or resold, as opposed to those sold for final use.

GNP is the total value of goods and services produced. It is measured by using the value of goods and services sold to final users plus the amount businesses add to their inventories. Since **intermediate goods and services** (goods and services sold from one firm to another as part of the process of production) will take on value when they are sold to final users, they are not counted in total GNP. An example of an intermediate good is the wheat sold to a miller. Its value, the value of the flour sold to the commercial bakery, and the value of the bread sold to the grocer are not counted separately in GNP because they are included in the value of the final product—the bread sold to consumers by the grocer. If a loaf of bread sells for $1.00, the value of a loaf of bread in GNP is $1.00. If we were to add intermediate sales, we would arrive at a value in excess of $1.00 because we would be *double counting*—counting some values several times, such as the value of the wheat.

Value Added

value added
The net contribution to the final value of a product made at each stage of production. Calculated by subtracting the cost of intermediate goods and services purchased from the value of sales plus additions to inventory.

GNP can be computed correctly by adding the value of production at each intermediate stage. GNP is the total of **value added** at each stage of production including the value added at the retail level. By this method we would add (1) the value of the wheat produced by the farmer (the value added by the farmer) plus (2) the value of the flour minus the cost of the wheat (the value added by the miller) plus (3) the value of the bread to the grocer minus the cost of the flour (the value added by the baker) plus (4) the value of the bread to the consumer minus the cost of the bread to the grocer (the value added at retail). The comparison of sales prices with value added is illustrated in the following table. The final results are the same, whether we use sales price to final consumer or the sum of value added.

	Sales price	Value added
Farmer's wheat sold to miller	$ .30	$ .30
Miller's flour sold to baker	.55	.25
Baker's bread sold to grocer	.90	.35
Grocer's bread sold to consumer	1.00	.10
Total	$2.75	$1.00

Using value added, we are simply adding up the share of the final value that was generated at each stage of production. The contribution to GNP is

$1.00 either way. The sum of the sales prices of all the intermediate goods (farmer's wheat, miller's flour, baker's bread), $2.75, has no economic meaning. It is not the contribution to GNP because it includes double counting of the intermediate goods.

In the United States, GNP is estimated directly from surveys of final sales and inventory changes. The European countries rely heavily on value-added taxes for revenue and they use the resulting tax returns of businesses to compute value added at each stage of production and add these to calculate GNP. In principle the two methods are equivalent, though in practice discrepancies may result from reporting errors.

Transfer of Assets

The value of purchases and sales of assets that are only transferred from one owner to another and not produced in a given year are also excluded from GNP. GNP is designed to measure production in a given year. When ownership of an asset is transferred from one person to another, nothing is added to production. Rather, goods produced in a previous year were counted in that year's GNP. If we did not exclude the sale of previously produced assets from GNP, we would be guilty of another form of double counting, that is, double counting over time rather than double counting via stages of production. For example, this year's sales of old houses or used cars do not count in this year's GNP because they were counted in GNP in the year they were produced. However, the value added by realtors or used-car dealers is added to this year's GNP.

Nonmarket Production

Some production is not traded in the market and so does not have a market price, but it is nevertheless part of GNP. If someone rents an apartment, the rental payment is counted in GNP as the value of the service she receives in being allowed to live in the apartment. If the building is converted to condominiums and the tenant buys the apartment, the measure of GNP stays the same because an allowance is made for imputing the rental value of the apartment that she still occupies. She is assumed to be renting the apartment from herself. A value for the imputed rent of owner-occupied houses and condominiums is estimated by the U.S. Department of Commerce and added to GNP.

Many nonmarket sources of goods and services are provided in our society, such as services produced inside the family structure and benefits offered to employees "in kind." These are not counted in GNP. Whether or not a nonmarket activity should be imputed into GNP is a judgment call based upon the size of the nonmarket activity, its variation from year to year, and the availability of market comparisons. The largest source of nonmarket contributions to GNP is the government. Government itself produces services as a result of such activities as the military, the FBI, and people who administer such programs as social security. These services are given a value in GNP equal to the amount of wages paid to government employees. This procedure may undervalue or overvalue the contribution of government to production because there is no test of market value applied to government output.

GNP Errors: The Underground Economy and Quality Change

Aside from difficulties in deciding what activities are to be included in GNP, there are problems in GNP measurement because some of the necessary data are missing or inaccurate.

The underground economy

Some production is market production but is missed by the usual methods of data collection because the people involved in it do not want the government to know about it. Some carpenters and babysitters want to be paid in cash because they are not going to pay tax on the income. And some businesses and professionals overstate their expenses and hence understate the value of their production.

Some economic activity is illegal in itself. Dealing in drugs, for example, is an activity that reportedly generates billions of dollars in revenues to the dealers. The people engaged in these activities do not report their activities for obvious reasons.

Some economists have suggested that the underground economy is very large and has become much larger in recent years. They argue that GNP is being understated by increasing amounts. This could be true, but there is not much evidence to support the idea. First, the illegal activities, such as drug dealing, are not ones that we want to include in GNP anyway. Trade in dangerous drugs is considered, as a matter of social judgment, to be a transfer among individuals, not a productive economic activity. Second, when the U.S. Department of Commerce computes its GNP figures, it already includes an amount that is an estimate of the underreporting of income and the over statement of expenses for tax reasons.[7]

No one doubts that the underground economy exists. The questions are whether it is much larger than the Department of Commerce thinks it is, which would lead to an understatement of the level of GNP, and whether it has grown more rapidly than the regular economy, which would lead to an understatement of the growth of GNP. The fall in income-tax rates in the 1980s has meant that the payoff to tax cheating has declined quite a bit, so the latter alternative seems unlikely.

Quality change

Real GNP gives the value of production in a given year using the prices that prevailed in the base year, currently 1982. But there are many items being produced in 1990 that were not produced at all in 1982 and many

---

[7] Carol S. Carson, "The Underground Economy: An Introduction," *Survey of Current Business* (May 1984, continued in the July 1984 issue).

more that have changed in quality. New models of computers, autos, and machine tools come out every year and have to be given a price based upon what they would have cost in 1982 if they had been produced then. For some goods, the estimates of the hypothetical 1982 prices are made in a very sophisticated way. For example, new-model computers are assigned a 1982 price that depends upon their speed, size of memory, and other characteristics. For some goods, however, price indexes are used that ignore changes in quality.

In general, the difficulties in taking account of quality change mean that the growth of real GNP is being understated. Living standards have actually grown more than the growth in real GNP would indicate. There is no clear indication, however, that this problem has become much worse over time or that it is very different for the United States than for any other country.

What GNP Tells Us

Our concern with measuring GNP helps us understand what GNP is and what it isn't. GNP is an overall measure of yearly economic performance. We are making a judgment that improved economic performance is positively related to the improved overall well-being of our society. Our focus on GNP and economic performance assumes that economic well-being is important, but we certainly do not place economic well-being above noneconomic values in our society.

When Robert F. Kennedy was running for president in 1968, he talked about the measure of a nation:

> The Gross National Product does not allow for the health of our children, the quality of their education or the joy of their play. It does not include the beauty of our poetry, or the strength of our marriages, the intelligence of our public debate or the integrity of our public officials. It measures neither our wit nor our courage, neither our wisdom nor our devotion to our country. It measures everything, in short, except that which makes life worthwhile, and it can tell us everything about America except why we are proud that we are Americans.

GNP fails to capture some very important elements of social well-being, such as the distribution of income or economic and political freedom of choice. What GNP does give us is a key measure of how well we are doing economically.

Production, Expenditure, and Income

Any given firm or household may produce more or less than it spends and it may spend more or less than its income. But *in the total economy, production, expenditure, and income are all equal.* This is the sense in which Say's Law is correct. Total production (the value of all of the goods and services produced in the economy in a year) equals the value of all expenditures made on goods and services; it also equals the value of all income payments received by those who produced the goods and services:

Production = Expenditure = Income.

The economywide equality of production, expenditure, and income is the basis for the accounting system we use to measure and evaluate aggregate economic performance.

The accounting system used by a company helps, among other things, to keep track of the value of goods it produced, the amounts received when they are sold, and the disbursements of income payments, such as wage payments. The **National Income and Product Accounts** do this for the whole economy, and the accounts balance as a result of the equality between production, expenditure, and income.

The total amount of expenditure that is made in the economy consists of **consumption** expenditures *(C)*, **investment** expenditures *(I)*, **government purchases of goods and services** *(G)*, and net foreign purchases (exports minus imports) called **net exports** *(X − IM)*. In the National Income and Product Accounts everything that has been produced in a given period is assigned to one of these four categories, so that the total value of production, *Y*, equals the total value of expenditure:

$$GNP = Y = C + I + G + X - IM. \tag{1.1}$$

Figure 1.7 gives the components of GNP in 1964 and 1989, showing that consumption is the largest component.

Consumption

Consumption includes all the items that households buy, including food, clothing, and such durable goods as autos and furniture. Sometimes it is hard to separate consumption from investment or intermediate goods. For example, construction materials are intermediate goods if used by the construction industry. They are consumption goods if households buy them for do-it-yourself projects around the home.

Investment

Investment in the National Income and Product Accounts is called gross private domestic investment and is made up of business expenditures on structures (factories, offices) and equipment plus expenditures on new residential structures (rental property, condominiums, and single-family houses). Notice in particular that investment is used here in a way that is different from the way it is used in the financial press. Investment does *not* mean the purchase of stocks, bonds, or other financial assets. It does mean the purchase of real assets such as machines and houses.

Investment also includes an important balancing item: change in inventories, known as **inventory accumulation.** The inclusion of inventory accumulation insures that production and expenditure are equal. Goods produced

---

National Income and Product Accounts
The accounting system used to organize and define aggregate economic measures. These accounts form the basis for macroeconomic analysis of output, income, and expenditure.

consumption
The total value of goods and services purchased by households.

investment
Gross private domestic investment is the total of new plant and equipment (machines and factories), nonresidential structures (offices, shopping centers), residential structures (houses and apartments), and *inventory accumulation* purchased in a given period.

government purchases of goods and services
The amount that local, state, and federal governments spend on goods and services. Includes such things as school supplies and missiles. Also includes salaries paid to government employees. Transfer payments are excluded.

net exports
Exports minus *imports*. Exports of goods and services minus imports of goods and services.

inventory accumulation
The change in business inventory in a given period. Goods produced but not yet sold are included in inventory. It is part of *investment* and is valued in GNP at the same market prices as comparable items that have been sold.

FIGURE 1.7   Components of U.S. Gross National Product, 1964 and 1989

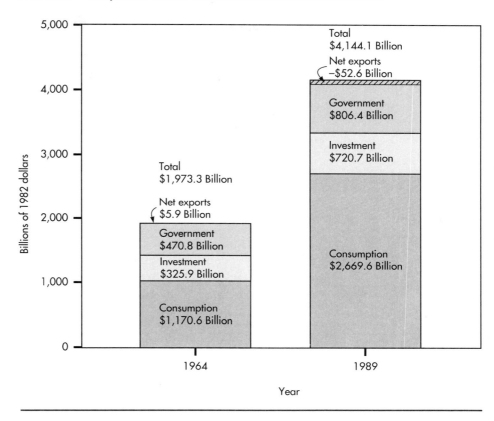

and not sold to an outside customer are kept by the producer as part of inventory.

When firms produce more than they sell, the unsold goods are added to inventories. Those inventories are included in investment and valued in GNP at the same market prices as comparable items that have been sold. If 100 pairs of shoes are produced and sold at $40 a pair, then $4,000 is added to GNP. If only 90 of the 100 pairs are sold, $4,000 is still added to GNP, this year.[8]

Government purchases
Government purchases of goods and services include purchases made by the federal government and by state and local governments. They include

---

[8] What if the 10 pairs of shoes that were unsold at the end of the year can only be sold during the next year, at a lower price? The lower price will be reflected in the value of shoe sales next year.

such things as military aircraft, computers, school supplies, and also the wages and salaries paid out to government employees. Certain transfer payments, such as social security retirement payments, are not included.

Net exports

Purchases of U.S.-made goods by foreign residents add to the total of U.S. expenditures. For instance, when a foreign government or foreign-based corporation buys a U.S.-made Cray supercomputer instead of a supercomputer produced in Japan, expenditures on goods and services in the United States rise. Therefore, exports, X, are an addition to total expenditures and are added to total expenditures.

On the import side, we see that imports, IM, are subtracted from total expenditures. Why is this? When an American consumer buys a Japanese-built Toyota instead of a U.S.-built Chevy, we can no longer count total consumption expenditures as the consumption portion of aggregate expenditures. Household expenditures on consumption goods, C, consist of expenditures on consumption goods produced here, C^D, plus consumption of foreign-made goods, C^F. Thus $C = C^D + C^F$. And the same is true for investment and government expenditures. Then the value of total expenditures that is equated to GNP is equal to expenditures on domestically produced goods plus exports:

$$\text{Total expenditures} = \text{GNP} = Y = C^D + I^D + G^D + X. \tag{1.2}$$

To calculate the expenditures on domestically produced consumption, investment, and government goods, we subtract the purchases of foreign goods from the totals:

$$\begin{aligned} C^D &= C - C^F \\ I^D &= I - I^F \\ G^D &= G - G^F. \end{aligned} \tag{1.3}$$

Then total imports are equal to the sum of all of the foreign purchases that are part of consumption, investment, and government purchases:

$$IM = C^F + I^F + G^F. \tag{1.4}$$

Substituting 1.3 into 1.4 we eliminate the need to account separately for the domestic and foreign components of consumption, investment, and government expenditures:

$$\text{GNP} = Y = C - C^F + I - I^F + G^D - G^F + X$$
$$\text{or}$$
$$\text{GNP} = Y = C + I + G + [X - (C^F + I^F + G^F)] \tag{1.5}$$
$$\text{or}$$
$$\text{GNP} = Y = C + I + G + (X - IM).$$

We subtracted imports in Equation 1.1 because total expenditures on consumption, investment, and government overstated the amount of U.S. national production by an amount equal to imports.

GNP, GDP, and Final Sales

There are two aggregate economic measures that are very close in value to total GNP but are not quite the same. They are useful for certain purposes and are often reported in the press along with GNP, so it is a good idea to know what they are.

Exports and imports in the national income accounts include the trade in oil, autos, and such, but they also include incomes on foreign-held assets, called *factor incomes*. When a U.S. multinational has a subsidiary overseas that earns a profit, this income is considered part of total U.S. GNP. The company that is resident here is considered to have exported a service to its foreign subsidiary. Similarly, foreign residents earn returns on assets that they hold in the United States, and these are part of imports and are subtracted from GNP.

It is often useful to know how much is actually being produced by factories and offices in the United States (for example, when studying the productivity of U.S. industries), so that net factor income is then taken out of GNP and the result is called **gross domestic product** (GDP). GDP is a measure of the outputs produced by factors of production residing in the United States.

gross domestic product (GDP)
GNP minus net factor income from overseas. GDP is a measure of the output produced by factors of production residing in the United States.

$$\text{GDP} = \text{GNP} - \text{Net exports of factor income.} \tag{1.6}$$

The calculation for 1989 (using 1982 dollars) is:

Gross national product	=	$4,144.1 billion
Less exports of factor income	=	106.2
Plus imports of factor income	=	77.5
Equals gross domestic product	=	$4,115.3.

The U.S. economy has traditionally earned more factor income overseas than it pays out. This situation may not continue, but net exports of factor income were positive in 1989. (There is a small rounding error in the figures given above.)

In predicting whether or not the economy is headed into a recession, it is useful to know whether U.S. residents are increasing their total buying. A figure that gives an indication of buying patterns is called **final sales.** To get to final sales from GNP, first the net factor incomes are excluded (just as for GDP); then the final-sales figure adds imports back into the total. Final sales includes the amount consumers are spending, regardless of whether it is on U.S.-made goods or foreign goods. Since we are looking for the buying power of U.S. residents, however, export sales are excluded, so these are subtracted from GNP. The last adjustment made is that changes in inventories are excluded. The amount of production that is placed in inventory is not considered part of the sales to final users. The computation for final sales in 1989 is shown next:

final sales
GNP minus exports plus imports minus change in business inventory.

Gross national product = $4,144.1 billion
Less net exports of factor income = 28.7
Equals gross domestic product = $4,115.3
Less other exports = 483.0
Plus other imports = 564.3
Less change in business inventory = 21.9
Equals final sales to domestic
purchasers = $4,174.8.

These figures indicate that sales to domestic purchasers were larger than GNP or GDP. In 1989, consumers, business investors, and the government were demanding more than the economy was producing here at home. The difference was made up by net foreign purchases.

Production and income

Total expenditure represents the amount paid for all the goods and services produced. The revenue from all these sales is then divided among those who produced the output. Labor income is paid to workers, while profit, interest, and rental income are paid to the owners of capital, land, and natural resources. The value of the production and the value of the expenditures equal the value of income received. Again, inventory accumulation plays an important balancing role. If a firm produces a good and it is not sold to a customer but is added to inventories, then the firm is considered to have received income from the sale of the good to itself. The income paid to itself automatically finances the inventory accumulation. If a firm is supplying a service, then when the service is not sold, it is not produced either. For example, telephone companies only "produce" as many phone calls as people actually make.

GNP and National Income

Production equals income, but in the National Income and Product Accounts there is a difference between GNP and national income. First we'll summarize the distinctions and then we'll discuss the reasons for them:

GNP − Capital consumption allowance = Net national product (NNP)

NNP − (Indirect business taxes + Business transfers + Business payments to government enterprise) = National income (NI)

NI = Employee compensation + Proprietors' income + Rental income of persons + Corporate profits + Net interest.

national income
The sum total of all income received by those who contributed to production. This includes the compensation of employees, proprietors' income, rental income, profit, and net interest.

National income (NI) is the sum total of all income received by those who contributed to production, within the country. It is defined as compensation of employees, proprietors' income, rental income, corporate profits, and net interest. The main sources of difference between GNP and NI are *depreciation* and *indirect taxes*.

The factories, office buildings, and machinery (capital goods) purchased by businesses during a year are part of production and are included in GNP.

capital stock
The collection of all capital goods (machines, factories, offices, etc.) still in use. Includes those purchased in previous years with adjustment for depreciation.

But GNP does not take account of the fact that capital goods depreciate over time. The **capital stock** consists of all the capital goods (machines, factories, offices) still in use, including those purchased in previous years. The extent to which the capital stock wears out is called depreciation. The name GNP indicates that it is a measure of output that is *gross* of depreciation rather than *net* of depreciation.

GNP is a good measure of total production, but it can be misleading as a measure of income in a given year. A business makes profit and other forms of business income, but uses up part of its capital stock. It subtracts from profit an allowance for the reduction of its existing capital. Business income net of depreciation is included in national income. In national income accounting, depreciation is called a **capital consumption allowance** measuring the capital consumed or used up in the production process. We do not have very good information on depreciation because the accounting rules for depreciation that businesses actually use are not connected to the true wearing out of the capital. They are creatures of our tax laws. Nevertheless, the U.S. Department of Commerce does estimate as best it can a measure of depreciation. GNP less depreciation is called **net national product** (NNP).

capital consumption allowance
The allowance reflects *depreciation* (the extent to which the capital stock wears out in a given period).

net national product (NNP)
The value of total production after the *capital consumption allowance (depreciation)* is deducted from GNP.

The next step in calculating national income is to subtract indirect taxes. Earlier, we argued that the production and sale of a good or service produce revenue and the revenue is paid to workers, managers, and owners as wage and profit income. When you pay $100 for something at the store, not all of that $100 is kept by the retailer, wholesaler, or manufacturer as wage or profit income. Some of it goes to government in what are called indirect taxes. These include state sales taxes and business property taxes, and there are also various state and federal excise taxes and duties. Thus, the value of production includes these indirect taxes, but the income resulting from the sale of the output does not include them. Indirect taxes are included in GNP but not in national income.

There are other small differences between measured GNP and national income. These are business transfer payments, net payments to government enterprises, and statistical discrepancies. Business transfers are the largest of these and include gifts that corporations make to individuals, universities, public television, and so on. These payments are included in GNP but not in national income.

The individual components that are subtracted from GNP to get national income are not computed in real- or constant-dollar terms. They do not correspond to particular goods and services with 1982 prices. The relation between GNP and national income for 1989 in current dollars is:

GNP (current dollars)	= $5,233.2
Less capital consumption allowances	= 552.2
Equals net national product	= 4,681.0
Less indirect taxes, etc.	= 416.0
Equals national income	= 4,265.0

Subtracting capital consumption allowances reduces GNP by 10.5 percent; indirect taxes and the other items are about another 8 percent.

Data revisions

The figures for real GNP that were given earlier in this chapter were based upon the revised estimates that were available to us as we wrote this book. The current-dollar figures just given are based upon preliminary estimates, because the revisions for national income were not yet available. It is important to keep in mind that a process of change and revision goes on in economic data all the time. And periodically, whole new series are introduced as there are changes in the base years used for price indexes. By the time you read this book, there will have been revisions made to many of the numbers that you will see here.

Government agencies can only provide numbers that are as good as the sources available to them. It takes time before tax returns are filed or company reports are made. It takes time before surveys and censuses can be completed and processed. We look now at one important economic area where there is only very sketchy information available, total national wealth.

Income and wealth

Individuals and businesses can make estimates of their wealth. Indeed, corporations are required to maintain balance sheets that give their assets and liabilities. The total of the assets of all the individuals and businesses in the economy does not add up to total national wealth, however, because the assets of one person may be the liabilities of another. One person may own some corporate bonds and another may own some stock in the same corporation. The bond is a liability of the company. The same company may own a factory in Europe as part of its assets. To calculate national wealth we must include only those assets that are not offset by liabilities.

national wealth
All tangible assets plus net foreign-asset holdings.

National wealth includes all the tangible assets in the economy and net foreign assets. Tangible assets are such things as houses, farmland, oil reserves, factories, shopping centers, and office buildings. National wealth excludes or nets out the borrowing and lending transactions among U.S. residents, such as corporate or U.S. government bonds, which are owed by one group of U.S. residents to another. However, the U.S. assets held by foreign residents, including government and private bonds, are considered a subtraction from national wealth. The assets U.S. residents hold overseas, including factories and foreign bonds, are included in national wealth.

The Federal Reserve Board estimated that our national wealth was $14.6 trillion in current dollars in 1988, about three times the size of GNP in the same year. This figure included a negative item of $533 billion, the estimate of the amount by which U.S. assets held by foreign residents exceeded the amount held by U.S. residents overseas. As you may have heard in the news, allegedly the United States has become the largest debtor nation in the world.

It is certainly true that our net–foreign-asset position has turned sharply for the worse in recent years. The Federal Reserve Board shows a positive foreign-asset position as recently as 1983; since then we have been borrowing heavily. However, the reported size of our current indebtedness is not a reliable figure. Many of our assets overseas were acquired in the 1950s and 1960s when U.S. multinational companies were setting up or expanding operations in other countries. The current value of these foreign operations, most of them very profitable, is being understated in the Federal Reserve's figure. The income earned by U.S. residents on their foreign assets in 1988 exceeded the income earned by foreigners on U.S. assets. We saw this same situation for 1989 when we looked at the adjustment of GNP to GDP.

This concludes our look at national income accounting. In the next chapter we will go from the framework established by the National Income and Product Accounts to a model in which income and output are determined when aggregate demand equals aggregate supply. At that next stage in the development of our framework, changes in aggregate demand will account for different equilibrium levels of income and output.

SUMMARY

- There are some key macroeconomic concepts that are used to assess the performance of the economy. Real GNP and real GNP per person are indicators of the overall level of economic activity and are important for living standards.

- Nominal GNP is equal to the price level times real GNP. There has been a strong upward trend in real GNP and the price level has risen substantially in the past 40 years.

- There have been fluctuations in the growth rate of real GNP, reflecting the recurrent changes in output that make up the business cycle. The phases of the cycle are the peak, recession, trough, and recovery.

- Cyclical variations in output occur around potential output, the benchmark level of output at full utilization of resources. The output ratio and the output gap look at output in relation to potential output.

- Generating an adequate level of employment growth is an important part of economic performance. Unemployment was very high in the Great Depression and has been much lower since, although there have been serious recessions since 1970.

- Productivity growth occurs when output grows faster than the inputs into production. Productivity growth has slowed in recent years.

- Inflation has been a persistent problem, especially since the mid-1960s.

- The international sector has become much more important to the U.S. economy in recent years. The United States is running a large trade deficit and the value of the dollar against the German mark and Japanese yen has fallen over time.

- The United States has performed well in many ways in the period since World War II compared to prior periods. There has been nothing comparable to the disastrous Great Depression.

- U.S. economic performance has deteriorated starting in the 1970s due to greater fluctuations in output, higher unemployment, higher inflation, slower productivity growth, and a large foreign-trade deficit.
- The National Income and Product Accounts have developed procedures for measuring income, expenditures, production, and the relationships among them. Aggregate production, GNP, excludes intermediate goods and the transfer of assets. It imputes values for nonmarket production, notably for government production and owner-occupied housing.
- The underground economy is hard or impossible to measure. The same is true of the effect of changes in the quality of goods and services. GNP excludes many aspects of life that are important to welfare.
- Production equals expenditure equals income. All goods produced are allocated to consumption, investment, government purchases, and net exports. All goods produced, even those not sold, generate income equal in value to the value of production.
- Gross domestic product (GDP) measures the amount actually produced in U.S. factories and offices, excluding net foreign income from GNP. Final sales indicates how much U.S. residents are spending.
- Depreciation is subtracted from GNP to get net national product (NNP). Then indirect taxes and some other transfers are subtracted to give national income. National income is the amount paid out in wages, profits, and interest to those who have contributed to national production.

KEY TERMS

average labor productivity

business cycle

capital consumption allowance

capital stock

consumer price index (CPI)

consumption

contraction

depreciation

expansion

exports

final sales

full employment

government purchases of goods and services

gross domestic product (GDP)

gross national product (GNP)

implicit price deflator for GNP

imports

inflation

intermediate goods and services

investment

labor force

National Income and Product Accounts

natural rate of unemployment

net exports

nominal GNP

output gap

output ratio

potential output or GNP

price level

productivity

real GNP

real GNP per person (per capita)

trade balance

unemployment rate

value added

weighted average

DISCUSSION QUESTIONS AND PROBLEMS

1. A large company is bargaining with its union over a three-year wage contract. What macroeconomic conditions should the parties take into account, and why?

2. Review the performance of the U.S. aggregate economy. Rank income, productivity, employment, and price-stability as goals for national policy.

3. Review the role of inventory accumulation as a balancing item in the National Income and Product Accounts.

4. In the short run, policies that reduce unemployment may worsen inflation. Do you think it likely that tolerating a high rate of inflation would allow us to maintain low unemployment in the long run?

5. Which of the following contribute to GNP? Indicate whether all or part of the transaction is a contribution.

   Someone sells 50 shares of stock to someone else.

   A couple hires a housekeeper to look after their children.

   IBM imports components, assembles them, and sells the computers to business customers.

6. Consider the following figures for the components of GNP in 1988 in billions of current dollars.

Personal consumption expenditures	3,235.1
Gross private domestic investment	750.3
Net exports of goods and services	−73.7
Government purchases of goods and services	968.9
Exports of factor income	94.7
Imports of factor income	66.6
Change in business inventory	27.9

   Use these numbers to calculate GNP, GDP, and final sales. The implicit price deflator for GNP in 1988 was 121.3. Calculate real GNP in 1988.

7. The *fixed-weight* GNP price index differs from the implicit price deflator. Year-to-year changes in the fixed-weight index reflect a weighted average of the price increases of all the goods and services in GNP, with the weights equal to the shares of the goods in 1982 GNP. These weights, therefore, do not change from year to year. When will the fixed weight index and the implicit deflator give different estimates of inflation? Which gives the better measure of inflation? Is it still true that nominal output equals price times real output with a fixed-weight index?

8. Use the following data on prices.

Year	GNP price deflator (1982 = 100)
1985	110.9
1986	113.9
1987	117.7
1988	121.3

   Calculate the rates of inflation for 1986, 1987, and 1988.

PART II

The Determination of Income and Expenditure

GNP and national income are measures of the state of the economy. We move from describing the state of the economy to explaining how it came about. We want to know the current level of income and why the current level is what it is. In the next two chapters, we describe a simple model of the economy where the sum of expenditures on goods and services adds up to aggregate demand and aggregate demand determines the level of income and output. This model gives us a good picture of the economy using only a few categories of expenditure—household consumption, business investment, and imports and exports—even though total expenditure is actually a result of millions of decisions made by millions of buyers and sellers.

The expenditure decisions of households and businesses in any given year add up to total expenditure in our simple model economy, and hence determine aggregate demand and income. But when we ask what determines how much these groups spend, we find that income is the most important factor influencing the expenditure decisions. Expenditure decisions determine income and income determines expenditure decisions. The model shows us how income and expenditure are determined together.

Expenditures are also affected by interest rates and by decisions made in financial markets. At a higher rate of interest, the same level of income will result in lower expenditures, which will ultimately lower income. In order to determine income, we also have to determine the rate of interest. This complication leads us to look at money and its role in aggregate demand. The model that combines money with expenditure decisions is called the *IS-LM* framework.

The model used in these next two chapters omits some important elements of the actual economy, notably, inflation and the role of government. Yet this simple model captures a basic idea: In any year, different expenditure decisions made by different people combine to make up aggregate demand and there is no guarantee that the sum of these decisions leads to a level of GNP that fully utilizes the economy's resources. There are periods when the economy falls into recession—we want to know why and under what circumstances a recession is likely to occur.

CHAPTER 2

Aggregate Supply and Demand and Income Determination

INTRODUCTION

In this chapter we shall set up a model of a very simple economy and then show how aggregate demand and supply interact to determine income and output within it and how changes in aggregate demand bring about short-run changes in income and output. This introductory model economy has no government sector, so there are no taxes and no government expenditures.

This simple model demonstrates the interaction between income and output in the economy. The level of aggregate demand in the model economy determines the level of production, but production generates income, which then feeds back into demand. The model shows how equilibrium is determined, given this interdependence among income, demand, and production.

Up to this point we have excluded the foreign sector, but we then extend the model to take a first look at the effect of imports and exports. We find that foreign trade can affect the levels of production and employment. A large trade deficit, as has existed in the United States for several years, reduces a nation's output and income.

We then develop the model by allowing for the impact of changing interest rates on investment. Conditions in the money market influence demand and production. There is a link between the money market and the level of production and employment.

In the prologue, we said that recessions can result from the failure to coordinate saving and investment decisions. We conclude the chapter by using the simple model to examine this idea.

AGGREGATE SUPPLY AND DEMAND AND PRICE STICKINESS

aggregate demand
The amount that households, businesses, and the government decide to purchase, plus net foreign demand.

The level of output in the economy is determined by the interaction of aggregate supply and aggregate demand. In an economy with government and foreign sectors, **aggregate demand** is the amount that households, businesses, and the government decide to purchase, plus net foreign demand. In the simple economy we are studying now, the government and foreign sectors are excluded, so aggregate demand includes only household demand and business investment demand.

aggregate supply
The amount of goods and services businesses offer for sale.

Aggregate supply is the amount of goods and services businesses offer for sale. It depends upon the productive capacity of the factories and offices in the economy and the prices businesses expect to receive. We are taking the productive capacity of the economy—the technology and the amount of capital—as given, giving us an aggregate-supply schedule that relates the output produced in the economy to the price level.

The Aggregate-Supply Schedule

Figure 2.1 depicts an upward-sloping aggregate-supply schedule indicating that firms are willing to supply higher levels of output at higher prices. It shows that an increase in aggregate supply (from Y_A to Y_B) will be associated with an increase in the price level (from P_A to P_B). However the figure says that for most levels of output, excluding the extremely high levels on the right-hand side of the aggregate-supply schedule, *large changes in the level of output bring about small changes in the price level.*

Supply elasticity

If a large percent rise in output generates a small percent increase in prices, then aggregate supply is described as elastic and it would be fairly well represented by a schedule such as that in Figure 2.1. The **supply elasticity** over the range shown in the figure (Y_A to Y_B) is defined as follows:

$$\text{elasticity of aggregate supply from } A \text{ to } B = \frac{\text{percent change from } Y_A \text{ to } Y_B}{\text{percent change from } P_A \text{ to } P_B} \tag{2.1}$$

In the U.S. economy, estimates indicate that in the short run, over a broad range of output levels, the aggregate-supply schedule is quite elastic, with elasticity measuring about five. As is marked in Figure 2.1, a change in output equal to about 5 percent of GNP will lead to a change in the price level of only about 1 percent *in the same year.*[1] That elasticity of about five

---

[1] The slope of the aggregate-supply curve can be inferred from inflation studies such as George L. Perry, "Inflation in Theory and Practice," *Brookings Papers on Economic Activity* 1 (1980), pp. 207–41; and Robert J. Gordon, "Inflation, Exchange Rates and the Natural Rate of Unemployment," in *Workers Jobs and Inflation*, Martin Neil Baily, ed. (Washington, D.C.: Brookings Institution, 1982).

FIGURE 2.1   The Aggregate-Supply Schedule

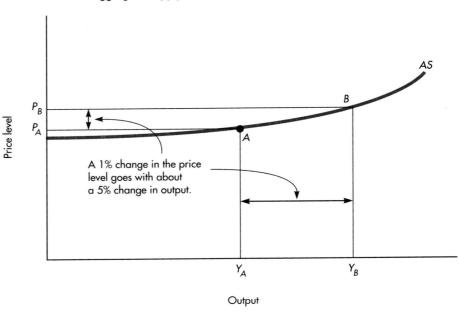

A 1% change in the price
level goes with about
a 5% change in output.

The aggregate-supply schedule is rather flat. A large change in output induces only a small
change in the price level in the same year.

---

corresponds to a fairly flat supply curve. An increase or decrease of real
GNP by 5 percentage points—equal to about $200 billion and about 2 million
workers unemployed—is a dramatic change in economic conditions. A one-
percentage-point change in the price level is much less significant. Moreover,
when GNP changes by 5 percent, there are much bigger changes in the
outputs of such cyclically sensitive parts of the economy as auto, appliance,
and machine-tool production. And yet the changes in the prices of these
goods may be even less than the change in the overall price level.

   In general, when there is a change in supply or demand in any market,
the response to the change will involve adjustments of both price and quantity.
Why is it that in the overall economy, the response of prices to changes is
fairly small compared to the larger changes in output? An important part
of the answer lies with timing. Prices adjust to changes in supply and demand,
but they adjust slowly—prices are sticky.

Price Stickiness
There are some perfectly competitive markets in the economy where prices
for standard commodities such as wheat or soybeans vary according to shifts

in supply and demand. And prices in these markets are quite volatile. But the price level in a modern economy is determined largely by companies that set their prices based upon what they see as their best long-run competitive strategy. There are several reasons why the prices the companies choose are not very responsive to short-run variations in demand.[2]

- In many markets there are a few firms that control a large fraction of sales. When the demand for the product falls, these large firms do not cut their prices because they do not want to trigger a price war with their competitors.

- Even when there are many firms in an industry, the products produced by each firm are a little different. A price cut in response to a fall in demand will not result in a large increase in sales because most customers are loyal to their usual suppliers. The gain from adjusting price to each firm is at most very small.

- Changing prices can be costly. New catalogs and price lists have to be prepared.

- Wages are also sticky, so that a major part of a firm's cost per unit is unchanged. Wages are sticky because (a) workers do not like the uncertainty of variable wages, (b) they regard wage cuts as unfair, and (c) firms are concerned that cutting wages in a recession will lower morale and reduce work effort as well as lead the best workers to quit.

- Many wages are set by wage contracts that insure wages will be sticky. These may be union contracts lasting several years or informal arrangements between workers and employers that rely upon the reputations of the employers that wages will not be varied when there are short-run fluctuations in the economy.

- Most goods are produced in several stages of production, usually in several industries. In order to lower the final sales price of a good by much when demand falls, there would have to be a coordinated reduction of prices at each stage of production—and that is very hard to achieve.

---

[2] Research that has looked at the stickiness of wages and prices and the implications includes George A. Akerlof and Janet L. Yellen, "A Near Rational Model of the Business Cycle, with Wage and Price Inertia," *Quarterly Journal of Economics* 100, Supplement, pp. 823–38; Costas Azariadis, "Implicit Contracts and Underemployment Equilibria," *Journal of Political Economy* 83 (1975), pp. 1183–202; Martin Neil Baily, "Wages and Employment under Uncertain Demand," *Review of Economic Studies* 41 (1974), pp. 37–50; Robert J. Barro, "A Theory of Monopolistic Price Adjustment," *Review of Economic Studies* 39 (1972), pp. 17–26; N. Gregory Mankiw, "Small Menu Costs and Large Business Cycles: A Macroeconomic Model of Monopoly," *Quarterly Journal of Economics*, 1985, pp. 529–37; Arthur M. Okun, *Prices and Quantities: A Macroeconomic Analysis* (Washington, D.C.: Brookings Institution, 1981); Lawrence Summers, *Understanding Unemployment* (Cambridge, Mass.: MIT Press, 1988); Alan S. Blinder, "A Shred of Evidence on Wage Stickiness," NBER Working Paper, 1989; Assar Lindbeck and Dennis Snower, "Efficiency Wages versus Insiders and Outsiders," in *Oxford Economic Papers* (Oxford, England: Clarendon Press, 1987).

In today's economy, one cannot expect the prices of complex products sold by large firms, such as aircraft or banking services, to have prices that vary as quickly and easily as do the prices of agricultural products. The forces of supply and demand assert themselves over time in all markets, but these market forces work slowly. In the short run, prices are sticky and the aggregate-supply schedule is very flat in showing how the price level varies over a given year in response to changes in aggregate output in that year.

Aggregate Demand and Output Changes in the Short Run

The aggregate-demand schedule represents the way in which the demand from the business and household sectors varies with changes in the price level. In Figure 2.2, an aggregate-demand schedule, AD, is shown intersecting with an aggregate-supply schedule, AS, at a level of output Y_A and price level P_0.

The aggregate-demand schedule is shown as downward-sloping in Figure 2.2 and the reason for this is that when the price level is lower and the amount of money in the economy is fixed, then interest rates will fall and this will encourage spending. This is not the usual intuitive way one thinks about downward-sloping demand schedules. In microeconomic models a demand schedule slopes downward because people will shift from buying one good to buying another when their *relative* prices change. But in macroeconomics, at the aggregate level, a general change in the price level that involves no change in people's real incomes will not change aggregate spending by any similar mechanism. We will look at the relation between the price level and aggregate demand in a later chapter.

Changes in the economy other than changes in the price level can lead to shifts in the aggregate-demand schedule. We show the effect of leftward and rightward shifts in the aggregate-demand schedule in Figure 2.2. For example, a decline in income would lead to a shift such as that from AD to AD'. And an increase in income will lead to a shift such as the one from AD to AD''.

As we study the short-run fluctuations of output in these early chapters we will concentrate on the impact of shifts in the aggregate-demand schedule, particularly those resulting from changes in income, rather than on the movements along the aggregate-demand schedule associated with changes in the price level. This is an oversimplification, but is not too serious a problem, provided we focus on recessions or situations where there are slack resources in the economy. Figure 2.2 illustrates the error we are making by neglecting the effects of changes in the price level on aggregate demand.

If aggregate demand falls to AD', output will fall to Y_C and the price level will fall to P_1. By neglecting the effect of the price-level change, we would erroneously conclude that output falls to Y_B rather than Y_C. Since

FIGURE 2.2   Shifts in Aggregate Demand

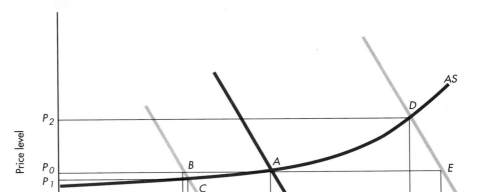

By neglecting the effect of changes in the price level on aggregate demand, we make an error. To the left of *A*, the error is small.

the aggregate-supply schedule is elastic but not perfectly flat, there is an error $(Y_B < Y_C)$, but not a terribly serious one. Most of the change in output $(Y_A - Y_C)$ was caused by the shift in aggregate demand. $(Y_A - Y_B$ is approximately equal to $Y_A - Y_C$.) We are ignoring the small movement along the demand schedule (point *B* to point *C*) after it shifted, so we are overstating slightly the effect of the demand shift.

Notice, however, that we have shown in Figure 2.2 that the aggregate-supply schedule slopes up more steeply at levels of output higher than Y_A. If aggregate demand were to shift all the way out to *AD''*, then output would increase to Y_D and the price level to P_2. If we were then to ignore the price-level change, we would be making a serious error by predicting that output was Y_E, a level that is higher than the actual output, Y_D. Even in the short run, neglecting the price-level change would not be appropriate for studying the impact of a large increase in aggregate demand on an economy with very low unemployment that was operating at almost full capacity. Ignoring

■ The Vertical Aggregate Supply Schedule: A Very Different Perspective

The nature of the aggregate supply schedule is a matter of great controversy and disagreement in macroeconomics and some economists argue that the schedule is not flat at all; it is actually very steep, or even vertical. A vertical supply schedule means that when aggregate demand increases, this will cause prices and wages to rise rather than real output and employment. This is illustrated below.

The Effect of an Increase in Aggregate Demand with a Vertical Aggregate Supply Schedule

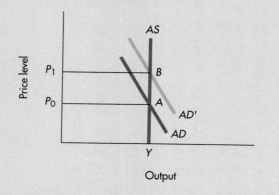

With a vertical aggregate supply schedule, the shift in the aggregate demand schedule from *AD* to *AD'* will increase the price level from P_0 to P_1 with no change in the level of income.

The idea of a vertical aggregate supply schedule

is based upon models of the economy in which markets are competitive and all wages and prices adjust quickly in order to eliminate any imbalance between supply and demand. With perfect markets, an increase in aggregate demand will increase individual prices and wages without changing relative prices or the real wage (the wage in relation to the price level). This means that no firm has an incentive to produce more and no worker has an incentive to work more, so that output remains unchanged.

The real issue here in assessing the slope of the aggregate supply schedule is timing. Most economists, including ourselves, agree that the aggregate supply schedule is vertical in the long run. Prices and wages adjust to ensure equilibrium in the long run. But when we observe business-cycle fluctuations in the economy, we see imperfect markets with sticky wages and prices. We also see that changes in aggregate demand fall mainly on output in the short run. This is why we assume a rather flat aggregate supply schedule for the analysis of short-run income changes.

The different assumptions about the slope of the supply schedule have important implications for the role of policy. We are developing a framework in which economic policy can affect aggregate demand and hence income and output. If there is a vertical aggregate supply schedule, these aggregate demand policies will have no effect on output. In Chapters 15 and 16 we present the alternative view of the economy where prices adjust very quickly, and where policies that change aggregate demand are to be avoided.

the price-level effects would result in a serious overstatement of the resulting increase in output.

The analysis of the next few chapters is geared to the study of the short-run changes in an economy where there are slack resources, an economy where increases or decreases in aggregate demand primarily affect output and have only a minor effect on the price level.

AGGREGATE SUPPLY AND DEMAND AND QUANTITY ADJUSTMENT

In Chapter 1, we said that GNP is equal to the sum of consumption expenditure, investment expenditure, government expenditure, and net exports. In the economy we are studying now, there is no government and no foreign trade, so that GNP *(Y)* is equal to the sum of consumption *(C)* and investment *(I)*:

$$Y \equiv C + I. \tag{2.2}$$

identity
An equation that is true by definition for all values of the variables in the equation.

Equation 2.2 describes a simple accounting relationship, an identity. An **identity** is an equation that is true by definition for all values of the variables in the equation. (The three-line equality sign indicates that the relation is an identity.) Identities turn up frequently. For example, the total number of people in a group of families is identically equal to the average family size times the number of families. This holds true because of the way in which an average is defined.

Equation 2.2 is an identity because *Y* is defined as total output and then each good or service that is part of total output is defined either as part of consumption or as part of investment. In particular, total investment includes the buildings and machines that businesses order from other businesses, but investment as measured in the national income accounts also includes any goods that are produced but not sold. Unsold goods become part of inventory accumulation and are included in total investment in the accounts. This means that the fact that Equation 2.2 is always satisfied does not tell us very much at all about how GNP is determined. In particular, it does not tell us whether or not aggregate demand is less than, equal to, or greater than aggregate supply. Only if the unsold goods held in inventory were intended to be part of inventory will the economy be in equilibrium.

The economy is in equilibrium when producers do not wish to change the level of output they are producing. In this model, the economy is assumed to be in equilibrium only if there are no unintended changes in inventories.

In addition, we will assume that the way in which the economy adjusts when it is not in equilibrium also depends upon what is happening to inventories. We will assume that businesses decide to increase or decrease their level of production depending upon whether inventories are piling up or are being depleted. If businesses in general are producing more than the amount they are selling plus the amount they planned to add to or subtract from inventories, they will reduce production. If businesses are producing less than the amount they are selling plus the amount that they planned to add to inventory, then they will expand production.

Planned and Unplanned Expenditures

The level of investment that is planned by businesses (I_p) includes only their expected or intended change in inventory. However, firms can wind up with larger or smaller inventories than they wanted as they react to custom-

FIGURE 2.3A   Excess Supply and Inventories Pile Up

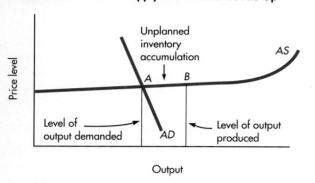

FIGURE 2.3B   Excess Demand and Inventories Are Depleted

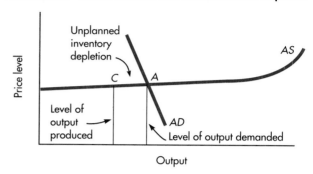

ers' orders. This unanticipated or unplanned change in inventory is part of businesses' expenditure on investment, regardless of the fact that it was unplanned or unwanted. Total investment *(I)* is the sum of the planned and unplanned *(I_U)* components:

$$I = I_P + I_U. \tag{2.3}$$

Unplanned investment *(I_U)* will be positive if inventories are piling up, or negative if they are being run down.[3] This lets us give the condition for equilibrium in the goods market in terms of investment. *There is goods-market equilibrium when there is no unplanned investment* ($I_U = 0$) *so that planned investment and actual or realized investment are equal* ($I = I_P$).

The Quantity of Goods Supplied Adjusts to Equal Aggregate Demand

Figure 2.3 illustrates how the response of businesses to changes in unplanned inventory works within the aggregate–supply-and-demand framework. In Figure 2.3A, we show the case where businesses produced more goods than they could sell. The level of production is at *B*, but the level of aggregate demand is at *A*. In this case, businesses produced too much and unsold inventories piled up (point *B* minus point *A*), making I_U positive. Firms move to stop the accumulation of unwanted inventories by reducing production. The quantity of output produced moves to the left, from *B* toward *A*.

The opposite case is shown in Figure 2,3B. In this case, there was an unplanned depletion of inventory (point *A* to point *C*), and I_U was negative. Firms respond to this by increasing their production. The quantity of output produced moves to the right, from *C* toward *A*. As shown in Figure 2.4,

---

[3] Typically businesses will have some planned changes in inventory, so that, strictly speaking, I_U refers to the gap between actual inventory adjustments and planned inventory adjustments.

FIGURE 2.4 Quantity Adjustments to Aggregate Demand

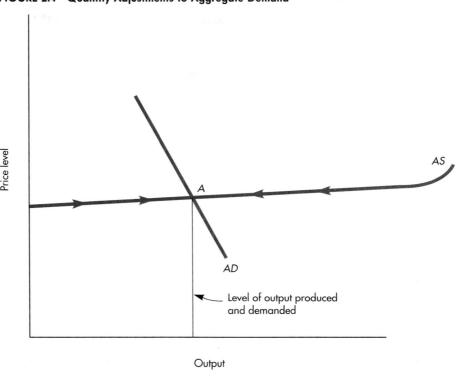

The quantity produced adjusts until *AD* equals *AS* at point *A*. The economy is in equilibrium at point *A*.

whether unintended inventory changes are too high or too low, the reaction of firms (reducing or increasing production) brings about an adjustment of the quantity of goods supplied to equal aggregate demand (movement toward point *A*).

Studies of businesses have found that in practice they respond quickly to any piling up or running down of inventories. If sales are less than expected and inventories start to pile up, businesses cut back on production and start laying off workers within a month or two. If inventories are being depleted, companies start to use overtime and then increase hiring in order to expand production. The idea that there are quick quantity (output and employment) adjustments in the economy in response to gaps between supply and demand is one that matches well with observed business behavior.[4]

[4] The behavior of inventories is shown in Alan S. Blinder and Douglas Holtz-Eakin, "Inventory Fluctuations in the United States since 1929," in *The American Business Cycle: Continuity and Change*, Robert J. Gordon, ed. (Chicago: University of Chicago Press for National Bureau of Economies Research, 1986), pp. 183–236.

■ Do Inventory Adjustments Take Place in the Service Sector?

We have talked about how businesses adjust their production in response to a piling up or running down of inventories. And we described equilibrium as "goods-market equilibrium." But we know that the majority of employment in our economy is now in services. Aren't we ignoring the service sector?

Yes, we have shortchanged the service sector in this discussion. One reason is that cyclical fluctuations in the economy are very heavily concentrated in the goods-producing sector of the economy. In a recession, it is construction, autos, machine tools, and other similar industries that take the biggest declines in output and employment. In fact, the service sector often continues to increase employment right through a recession. Still, some specific service industries do decline in recessions, so let's look at how they adjust.

Service industries can almost never hold inventories. There is no way to hold an inventory of haircuts when there are too many barbers for the number of customers. In the electricity-generation service industry, it is possible to store electricity rather than run a power plant, but the storage is so expensive that it is rarely done. In general, there are no inventories of service outputs.

Excess supply in a service industry will show up as excess capacity. There will be too many barbers for the number of customers; too many lawyers and not enough clients (don't we wish); too much generating capacity for the demand for electricity. The response of service firms to this excess capacity will be similar to the response of goods producers to unplanned additions to inventory. Service firms will slowly lay off workers and reduce capacity.

Excess demand in a service firm will mean that customers may be turned away or will have to wait some time before being able to buy the service. In this situation, service firms will respond just like goods producers with inventories running down. They will increase hiring and expand production.

The adjustment of supply to variations in demand in service industries is similar to the adjustment in goods industries, even though there are no inventories of services. Unplanned excess capacity or unplanned shortages of capacity are similar to unplanned inventory changes. When we talk about goods-market equilibrium, you should think of this as equilibrium in the sector that produces goods and services.

The National Income Identity and the Equilibrium Condition

We said earlier that the definitions used in the National Income and Product Accounts ensure that output equals the sum of consumption and investment and that this is an identity that always holds. What is not always true is the equality of intended production with aggregate demand. The national income identity can describe both equilibrium and disequilibrium conditions by substituting planned and unplanned investment for total investment:

$$Y \equiv C + I_P + I_U. \tag{2.4}$$

Since unplanned investment refers to unplanned changes in inventories, equilibrium between the quantity of goods produced and aggregate demand takes place when unplanned inventories are zero. The national income identity becomes an equilibrium condition when $I_U = 0$:

$$Y = \text{Aggregate production or aggregate supply } (AS)$$
$$C + I_P = \text{Aggregate demand } (AD) \tag{2.5}$$

When

$$\text{Aggregate supply } = \text{ Aggregate demand,}$$
$$Y_e = C + I_P.$$

The economy is in goods-market equilibrium when output equals consumption plus planned investment. Equation 2.5 does not always hold, but when it does hold, it reflects an equilibrium of supply and demand in the goods market.[5] The left-hand side of the equation is aggregate output, that is, aggregate supply. The right-hand side of the equation is consumption demand plus investment demand. Investment demand includes all the purchases of factories and equipment that businesses wanted to make and excludes the unintended changes in inventories.

Having specified the condition for goods-market equilibrium, the task now is to determine how this equilibrium comes about: At what level of output, Y, will there be equality between supply and demand? Since we have argued that production will adjust to meet aggregate demand, we will answer this question by seeing how the components of aggregate demand are determined. We begin with consumption demand.

Consumption demand and the consumption function

Demand originating in the household sector is called consumption demand. We describe the relationship between consumption and those economic variables that determine the decision to consume by a **consumption function.** Although several variables are important, for now we will discuss only the simplest and most important part of that relationship: the fact that consumption depends upon income. In general, households spend more on consumption goods when they have higher incomes. As a result, the sum of consumption by all households increases as aggregate income increases. Households buy more when income rises. We describe the relation between income and consumption by using a simple straight-line consumption function where C is consumption demand:

$$C = C_0 + C_1 Y. \tag{2.6}$$

Earlier we used the term Y to denote output, but as we saw in Chapter 1, output and income are equal, so that Y also denotes income. In this straight-

consumption function
The relationship between consumption and those economic variables that determine the decision to consume.

---

[5] Notice that in this equilibrium condition, the regular equal sign has replaced the identity sign and we have written Y_e instead of Y to emphasize that this is the level of income where there is goods-market equilibrium.

line consumption function, C_0 is a positive constant and C_1 is the slope of the line.[6]

average propensity to consume (APC)
The fraction of income that households spend on consumption, expressed as a ratio C/Y.

The average propensity to consume.   The consumption function given in Equation 2.6 indicates that a smaller portion of income is devoted to consumption at higher levels of income. We can see this by looking at the fraction of income that households spend on consumption, the ratio C/Y, called the **average propensity to consume** (APC). In our consumption function, the APC is given as:

$$\text{APC} = \frac{C}{Y} = \frac{C_0 + C_1 Y}{Y} = \frac{C_0}{Y} + C_1 \qquad (2.7)$$

C_0 is positive and called the *autonomous* part of consumption, the portion of consumption expenditure not affected by income. Then since C_1 is constant and C/Y declines as Y increases, the APC must decline as income increases.

In an economic recovery, as income rises, consumption rises, but consumption as a proportion of income falls—the APC declines. In a recession, as income falls, consumption falls, but consumption as a proportion of income rises—the APC rises. For example, as shown in Figure 2.5, during the recession and recovery of 1981–83, there was a rise in the APC with the fall in income from 1981 to 1982 plus a fall in the APC with a rise in income during the recovery from 1983 to 1984. Consumption made up just over 62 percent of GNP in 1981, but as the economy went into the deep recession, this rose to almost 66 percent of GNP. As the economy began to grow out of the recession, the APC started to come down again.

The consumption relation that we have described where the APC varies with income is the one that is probably most applicable to the analysis of short-run fluctuations in the economy. However, when we look at the long-run growth of the economy, we find that consumption has been a fairly constant fraction of income. (C_0 is very close to zero when we look at long-run data.) The reason for the difference is that short-run fluctuations in income are temporary changes and families react differently to temporary income changes than they do to the long-run growth in income, which is seen as permanent. In Chapter 13 we explore the effect of temporary and permanent income changes on consumption.

---

[6] In general, terms such as C_0 and C_1 are called the *parameters* or *coefficients* of a function. When the values of consumption and income change, the relationship between income and consumption will not change as long as the coefficients of the consumption function are constant.

In empirical studies of the actual economy, the coefficients of equations are estimated using *econometric analysis*. Econometrics combines statistics with economic theory to subject data to statistical tests. For example, the shape of the consumption function and, thus, the interpretation of saving behavior associated with income would change if the coefficients were different. Whether the value of C_0 was zero or positive and whether the value of C_1 was constant or changed with income can be ascertained by using data on consumption and income, calculating the values of the coefficients, and finding out whether there is a high or low statistical probability that the coefficients that are estimated are estimates of "true" values that conform to the prior notions of their size or sign.

FIGURE 2.5   The Average Propensity to Consume: Consumption as a Proportion of GNP in Recession and Recovery, Third Quarter 1981 to First Quarter 1984

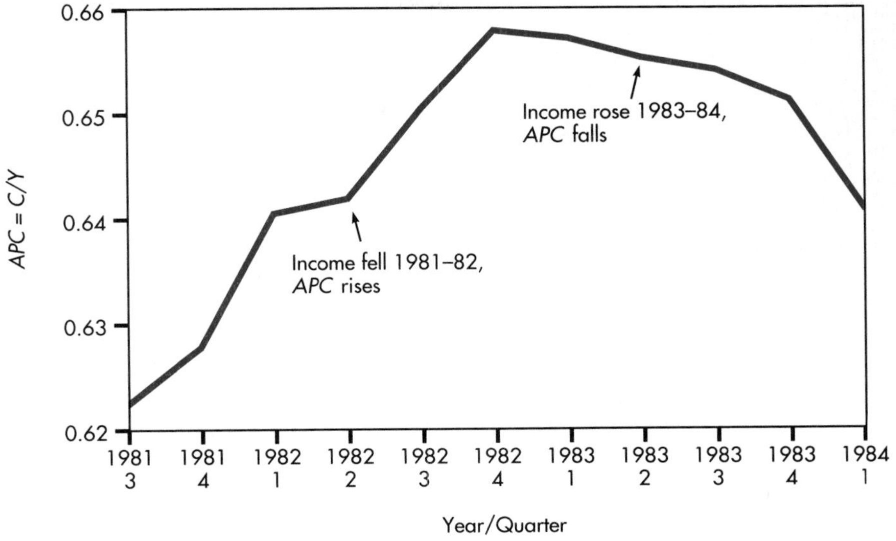

Income rose 1983–84, APC falls

Income fell 1981–82, APC rises

The APC rises as income falls (1981–82) and falls as income rises (1983–84).

Source: U.S. Department of Commerce, Bureau of Economic Analysis.

The marginal propensity to consume.   Part of any increase in income is allocated to consumption and part is allocated to saving. The consumption function describes the relationship between increases in income and the resulting increases in consumption. If income rose by $1 million and consumers increased their consumption expenditures by $750,000 then the value of C_1, which is the slope of the consumption line, would be 0.75. The slope indicates the amount of increased consumption (ΔC) that results from an amount of increased income (ΔY). This fraction ($\Delta C / \Delta Y$) is called the **marginal propensity to consume** (MPC). Equation 2.8 shows the coefficient C_1 in our consumption function is equal to the MPC:

$$\Delta C = C_1 \Delta Y$$

$$\text{MPC} = \frac{\Delta C}{\Delta Y} = C_1.$$

2.8

marginal propensity to consume (MPC)
The amount of increased consumption (ΔC) that results from an amount of increased income (ΔY) expressed as ($\Delta C / \Delta Y$).

For any marginal increase in income (ΔY), the MPC indicates the propensity among consumers to increase (ΔC) consumption expenditures. Since changes in consumption bring about changes in aggregate demand, this means that the MPC is important to our understanding of the determination of aggregate demand.

Figure 2.6 shows the linear consumption function that we have described. Three different levels of income are shown (Y_D, Y_A, and Y_B) along with three corresponding levels of consumption (C_D, C_A, and C_B). Starting at income level Y_A (point A along the consumption function), an increase in income to Y_B (line segment AC) results in an increase in consumption, C_A to C_B (line segment BC). The slope of the consumption line (Equation 2.9, $BC \div AC$) is equal to the MPC:

$$BC = \Delta C$$
$$AC = \Delta Y$$

$$\text{MPC} = \frac{BC}{AC} = \frac{\Delta C}{\Delta Y} \tag{2.9}$$

Different values of the MPC would be depicted by differing slopes of the consumption line. A steeper-sloped consumption line would reflect a larger increase in consumption for any increase in income—the line segment BC would be larger in relation to AC than illustrated here, thus there would be a higher MPC.

The way in which the average propensity to consume (APC) varies with income is also shown in Figure 2.6. At income level Y_D and consumption level C_D, the APC is the ratio of consumption to income:

APC at point $D = C_D \div Y_D$.

The value of the APC at D is the same as the slope of the line OD. At the higher levels of income and consumption, at points A (Y_A and C_A) and B (Y_B and C_B), the APC is still the ratio of consumption to income:

APC at $A = C_A \div Y_A$,
APC at $B = C_B \div Y_B$.

Apart from consumption, the other source of demand in our economy is investment, so we turn now to analyze the investment function.

Investment demand and the investment function

Demand for final goods originating from the business sector, *investment demand*, was introduced in Chapter 1. We describe the relationship between investment and those economic variables that determine the decision to invest by an **investment function.** Investment demand follows consumption as the main source of aggregate demand coming from the private sector of the economy. In addition to being important to aggregate demand, investment is also important because of the role it plays in maintaining and increasing the productive capacity of the economy.

The main components of investment are business structures (new office

investment function
The relationship between investment demand and those economic variables that determine the decision by firms to purchase capital goods.

FIGURE 2.6   The Consumption Function, the MPC, and the APC

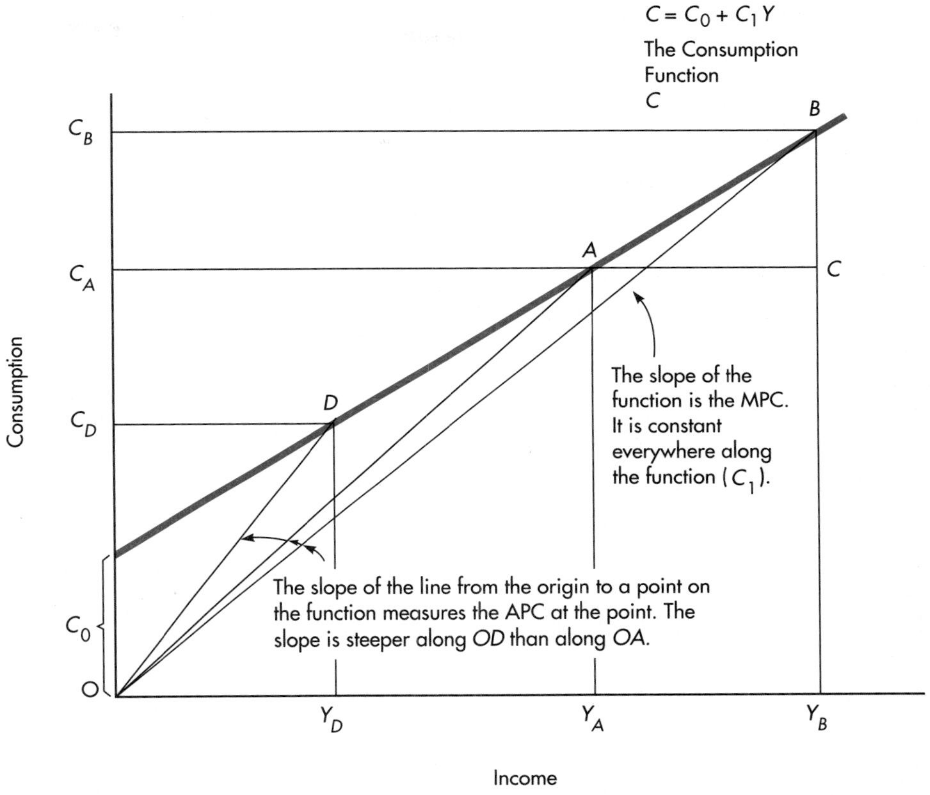

$$C = C_0 + C_1 Y$$

The Consumption Function

The slope of the function is the MPC. It is constant everywhere along the function (C_1).

The slope of the line from the origin to a point on the function measures the APC at the point. The slope is steeper along *OD* than along *OA*.

Consumption (vertical axis)

Income (horizontal axis)

buildings and factories), business equipment (machine tools, computers, and office furniture), and residential structures (new apartment buildings and single-family houses). The decisions to purchase these investment or capital goods are made primarily by the people that manage businesses in the economy. When households decide to buy houses or condominiums, rather than renting, they are making business-investment decisions also. Household demand for residential structures is included in investment demand.

planned investment
The amount businesses want to spend on capital goods including the amount they want to add to their inventories. Planned investment differs from actual investment by the amount of unplanned changes in inventory accumulation.

Planned investment.   **Planned investment** is the amount businesses would like to spend on capital goods plus the amount they want to add to their inventories. The reason businesses decide to buy capital goods is that they foresee profits accruing to them from using these capital goods. A firm will add capacity if it sees the potential for increased production and sales, or if it can lower the costs of producing to meet its current level of sales. A real estate company will build an office building or an apartment block based upon the anticipated rents that it will receive.

We will identify two variables that affect the level of investment demand: the level of income or output in the economy, Y and the interest rate in the economy, denoted by r. We specify an investment-demand function incorporating these two variables:

$$I_P = I_0 + I_1 Y - I_2 r. \tag{2.10}$$

The most important influence on investment demand has been found to be the level of income and output in the economy. If income is depressed and the economy is in a recession, then businesses do not expect to be able to use new equipment and factories profitably. Instead they anticipate slow sales, unused production capacity, and reduced profitability from any additions to their equipment or factories. A high level of income means that firms will anticipate strong demand from consumers and from other businesses, so that adding capacity makes sense.

marginal propensity to invest (MPI)
The amount of increased investment (ΔI_p) that results from an amount of increased income (ΔY) expressed as $(\Delta I_P/\Delta Y)$.

The responsiveness of investment demand to income (I_1) is called the **marginal propensity to invest** (MPI). Figure 2.7 shows the investment function. When income rises $(Y_A$ to $Y_B)$, the level of investment expenditures rises by the MPI times the increase in income (investment demand rises from I_A to I_B). The function is shown for some particular value (r_1) of the interest rate, so the intercept $(I_0 - I_2 r_1)$ is the level of investment expenditure that is not related to the level of income.

Investment demand and the interest rate. The interest rate affects the decision to invest directly when businesses borrow to buy capital goods. If the bank charges interest on money it is lending, or if a company must issue a corporate bond to finance the investment, then the interest will be a cost to the company that must be subtracted from the profits earned by the investment. Even if investment is financed by a company out of its retained earnings, the interest rate is still important. The company could pay out the earnings as dividends and allow shareholders to earn interest by buying bonds with the money. Or the company could use the earnings to repay past debts that it has incurred and thereby reduce its interest burden.

Household investment in new houses is very sensitive to the interest rate, because most new houses are financed by mortgages. The most visible impact of interest rates on investment in the U.S. economy occurs in the housing sector. High interest rates have played an important role in initiating recessions. There were sharp declines in residential construction that began with high mortgage interest rates in the 1974–75 recession and again in the 1982 recession.

The responsiveness of investment to the interest rate is reflected in the interest parameter in the investment function (I_2) in Equation 2.10. The negative sign of the interest parameter indicates that the higher the interest rate, the lower is investment demand.

FIGURE 2.7   The Investment Function

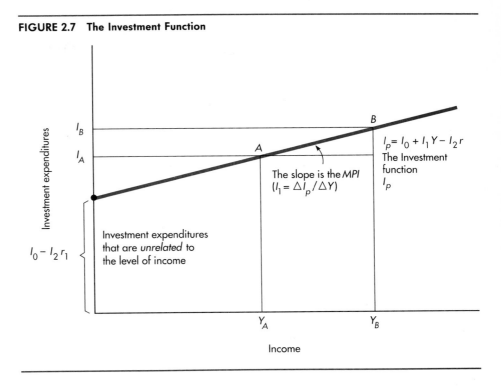

Figure 2.8 shows how the investment function moves up or down depending upon changes in the interest rate. At a given level of income (Y_A), the higher the interest rate, the lower is investment demand. As shown, investment demand is lower at point D than at point A.

With a given rate of interest, investment demand rises with income. When income increases from Y_A to Y_B, investment demand rises from I_A to I_B as shown in Figure 2.8 (point A to point B when $r = r_1$). If at point B the rate of interest rose (r_1 to r_2), then investment expenditures would drop from I_B to I_C (point B to point C when there is no change in income).

In the actual economy, income and the interest rate both change and their changes are often interrelated. In fact, a rise in income often accompanies a rise in the interest rate. We are describing here the *separate* effects on investment demand, first of income changes and then of interest-rate changes. In any practical case we would look at the *combined* effect of changes in both income and the interest rate.

Variability of investment.   We have pointed to income and the interest rate as two important influences on the level of investment demand. But in practice there are many factors influencing investment demand, making it a part of

FIGURE 2.8   Investment Demand Varies with Both Income and the Rate of Interest

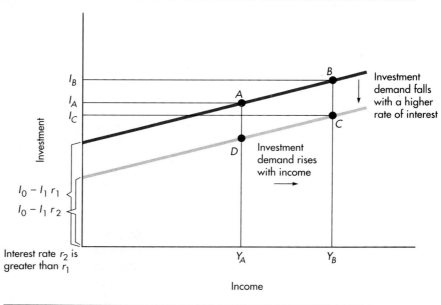

demand that is very variable and hard to predict. *The variability of investment demand is a major source of instability in aggregate demand.*

One view of investment demand is that it depends upon not only the level of production in the current period but also the level of production in the previous period. The **accelerator model** of investment says that investment demand depends upon the change in income and production. When income rises, businesses will need more machines than they needed in the previous period. Investment will be high. When income falls, businesses will have more than enough machines and will not buy new ones. We look at the accelerator model in Chapter 13, where we see how the accelerator model predicts large swings in investment demand.

Changes in technology or major changes in raw-materials prices can also affect investment. The increases in oil prices lead to increased investment in some industries and declines in others. The development of the computer has led to increases in business-equipment investment. In our model, when we consider what happens as a result of a change in these other determinants of investment demand, we describe those effects as shifts in investment demand. A shift in investment demand is illustrated as a change in the intercept term (I_0) of the investment function. Technology and business confidence are the kinds of things that result in shifts in I_0. These will shift the

accelerator model
The accelerator model of investment says that investor demand depends upon the change in income

investment function up or down in the same manner (but for different reasons) as the changes in the interest rate shown in Figure 2.8.

GOODS-MARKET EQUILIBRIUM

The condition that insures goods-market equilibrium in this simple economy was given in Equation 2.5, which we restate here:

$$Y_e = C + I_P.$$

In this expression, Y_e denotes the equilibrium level of income and output. Since we have developed functions that show how consumption demand and planned-investment demand are determined, we can substitute these into the equilibrium condition to give

$$Y_e = C_0 + C_1 Y_e + I_0 + I_1 Y_e - I_2 r. \tag{2.11}$$

If we know the values of the parameters in the consumption and investment functions and the rate of interest, we can solve Equation 2.11 for the level of income where there is no unplanned investment, that is, where aggregate supply equals aggregate demand. We will have used our knowledge of the components of aggregate demand to determine equilibrium income. We select income terms (Y terms) on the left-hand side of Equation 2.11 and factor them out to give

$$Y_e(1 - C_1 - I_1) = C_0 + I_0 - I_2 r.$$

Dividing both sides by $(1 - C_1 - I_1)$ gives

$$Y_e = (C_0 + I_0 - I_2 r) \div (1 - C_1 - I_1).$$

Rearranging terms and adding parentheses, we get an expression that describes equilibrium in the goods market:

$$Y_e = \frac{1}{1 - (C_1 + I_1)} \times (C_0 + I_0 - I_2 r). \tag{2.12}$$

Determining Aggregate Demand

Equation 2.12 determines the level of aggregate demand where the value of income equals the value of output with no unintended increases or decreases in inventories. This is the expression of equilibrium of aggregate demand and supply that we have been working toward. At this level of income, businesses will not increase or decrease supply. Thus, this level of aggregate demand equal to aggregate supply represents goods-market equilibrium for the economy.

For the time being we are going to study the determination of equilibrium income with the rate of interest taken as given. For example, we could suppose that the interest rate was fixed by monetary policy. This is a useful simplifying assumption that we later will change to see how the interest rate affects goods-market equilibrium. We write r as $\bar{r}$ to denote that we are fixing the interest rate.

In this equilibrium solution, C_0, I_0, and $I_2\bar{r}$ represent the *autonomous* parts of expenditure. These components of expenditure include the intercept terms in the consumption and investment schedules plus the part of investment demand that varies with the interest rate, $I_2\bar{r}$. This last term is included at this stage of our analysis in what we have called "autonomous" expenditure because here we are assuming a fixed interest rate.

Equilibrium income is proportional to total autonomous expenditure. The factor of proportionality is given a special name: the **multiplier.**

multiplier
In the simple income determination model the level of equilibrium income is proportional to autonomous expenditure. The factor of proportionality is called the multiplier, so that, for example, if the multiplier were three, then equilibrium income would be three times autonomous expenditure.

Equilibrium income = Multiplier × Autonomous expenditure

$$Y_e = \frac{1}{1 - (C_1 + I_1)} \times (C_0 + I_0 - I_2\bar{r})$$

In this simple model of the economy the multiplier is equal to $1 \div [1 - (C_1 + I_1)]$ and it depends upon the marginal propensities to spend in the model: the marginal propensity to consume (MPC) and the marginal propensity to invest (MPI). As we develop the simple model of the economy later, the exact expression for the multiplier will change. But the concept will continue to be important. *Equilibrium in the goods market occurs where the levels of income and output are equal to aggregate demand—the autonomous parts of expenditure (the ones that do not vary with income) times the multiplier.*

WORKED EXAMPLE 2.1   Determining Aggregate Demand and Goods-Market Equilibrium: Autonomous Expenditure and the Multiplier

In the first several chapters of this book, we will use a numerical example to illustrate the ideas being presented. As far as possible, we will carry over the numbers at each successive stage. We start by showing how to solve for goods-market equilibrium and the multiplier.

Question: In a simple economy the consumption function is given as follows:

$C = 600 + 0.7Y$.

Income (Y) and consumption (C) are in billions of dollars. The investment function is

$I_P = 250 + 0.1Y - 10\bar{r}$.

In this expression the interest rate is expressed as an annual percentage.

(*a*) If the interest rate is 5 percent, what is the value of autonomous expenditure in this economy?

(*b*) What is the value of the multiplier in this economy?

(c) Solve for the level of income that gives goods-market equilibrium. What are the levels of consumption and investment at this level of income?

(d) If the MPC were to increase to 0.75, what would be the new multiplier and the new level of equilibrium income?

Answer: Always go to the condition that output equals aggregate demand. In our simple model, there is only consumption and investment demand, so we get

$$Y_e = \underset{\text{(consumption)}}{600 + 0.7Y_e} + \underset{\text{(investment)}}{250 + 0.1Y_e - 10\bar{r}}.$$

If you try to solve the problem by remembering the expressions for the multiplier or autonomous expenditure, you will get into trouble in later questions because both of these will be different in later problems. Since the interest rate is 5 percent, we get

$$Y_e = 600 + 0.7Y_e + 250 + 0.1Y_e - (10 \times 5).$$

Now collect all the terms with Y_e in them on the left-hand side and all the other terms on the right-hand side:

$$Y_e[1 - (0.7 + 0.1)] = 600 + 250 - 50$$
$$Y_e(0.2) = 800.$$

Now divide both sides by the bracketed term:

$$Y_e = \frac{1}{0.2} \times 800.$$

We can now start answering the questions. Part (a) asks for autonomous expenditure. The answer is 800. It is the sum of all the terms that do not contain Y_e. Part (b) asks for the multiplier, which we already just about worked out when we collected the terms with Y_e in them. The multiplier in this model is $(1 \div 0.2) = 5$. The answer to part (b) is 5.

The question then asks for the level of equilibrium income. We have also done most of this too.

$$Y_e = \frac{1}{0.2} \times 800$$
$$= 4,000.$$

The first part of the answer to part (c) is $4 trillion. The level of consumption and planned investment are found by substituting back into the consumption and investment functions.

$$C = 600 + (0.7 \times 4,000) = 3,400$$
$$I_P = 250 + (0.1 \times 4,000) - 50 = 600.$$

The rest of the answer to part (c) is that consumption is $3.4 trillion and investment is $600 billion.

Part (d) of the question asks about the effect of increasing the MPC. This means there is a new consumption function:

$$C = 600 + 0.75Y_e.$$

Substituting this function rather than the original one gives

$$Y_e = 600 + 0.75Y_e + 250 + 0.1Y_e - (10 \times 5).$$

We are assuming the interest rate stays at 5 percent. Collecting terms in the same way as before gives

$$Y_e[1 - (0.75 + 0.1)] = 600 + 250 - 50$$
$$Y_e(0.15) = 800$$
$$Y_e = 1 \div 0.15 \times 800$$
$$= 5,333.$$

The new multiplier is $(1 \div 0.15) = 6.67$, and the new equilibrium level of income is $5.33 trillion.

The question illustrates how sensitive the multiplier and the level of equilibrium income are to small changes in the MPC. A change in the MPI would have also been important. The multiplier is related to the *sum* of the marginal propensities because small marginal propensities generate small increases in aggregate demand when income rises, while large marginal propensities generate large increases in aggregate demand for the same size increase in income.

When economists use statistical means to estimate the size of the multiplier, the values are below those used in these examples, ranging from 1.5 to 3.5, depending upon a variety of assumptions about how to do the estimation. This is because our model economy has, so far, ignored important factors that reduce the multiplier, namely, taxes and foreign trade.

The determination of equilibrium income is shown in Figure 2.9. The dark blue line $[(C + I_P)_0]$ through point E is the aggregate-demand line. It shows the investment function added to (sitting on top of) the consumption function. Consumption and planned investment are added vertically to give total expenditures $(C + I_P)$. In the figure, the points all along the 45-degree line are where the vertical and hortizontal distances are equal. The point where the aggregate-demand line intersects with the 45-degree line (point E) is the point where the vertical distance (aggregate demand) equals the horizontal distance (output or aggregate supply).

Adjustment to Equilibrium

If the economy is not at a point of equilibrium income, aggregate supply and demand will adjust so that the economy reaches equilibrium. Suppose aggregate production or supply exceeds the total of consumption demand and planned-investment demand $(Y_A > Y_e)$, at point A in Figure 2.9; point A' along the aggregate demand line is below point A along the 45-degree line). This would mean that inventories are piling up and that there is unintended inventory accumulation. Producers respond to this by cutting back production (a drop in aggregate supply) and *this means a fall in income, because*

FIGURE 2.9   The Determination of Goods-Market Equilibrium

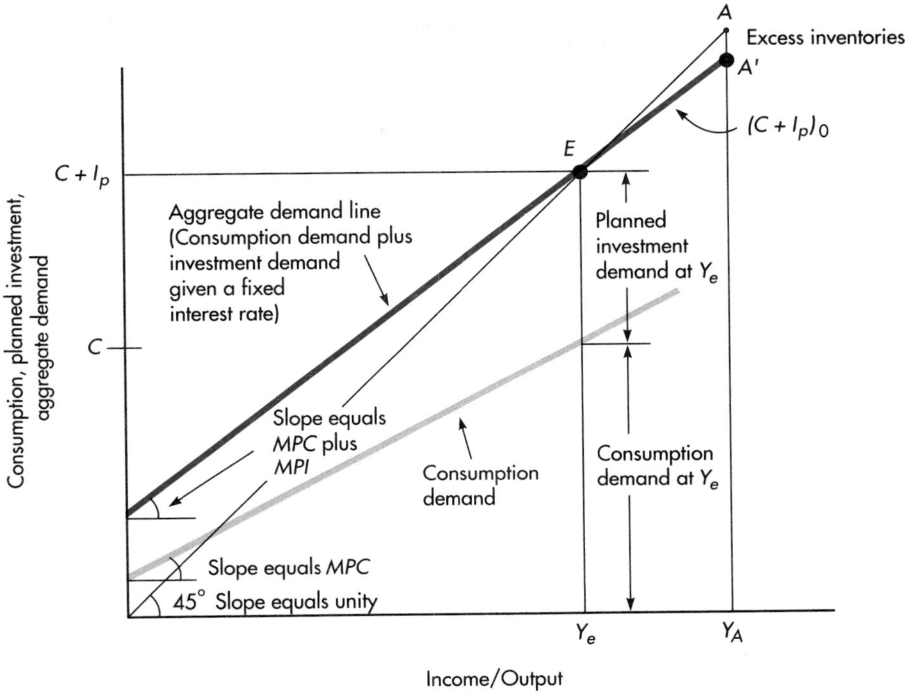

The aggregate demand line crosses the 45-degree line at point *E*.

income is generated by production. The fall in income shows up most obviously in layoffs of workers and a decline in the wage income that they earn. When income falls this causes a fall in consumption demand and in planned-investment demand (a drop in aggregate demand), because both depend upon income. So if the economy starts from a point where supply exceeds planned demand (point *A*), then as firms cut production to close the gap, they end up causing a further reduction in demand, meaning that the gap may not be closed until there are further reductions in income (point *A* to point *E*).[7]

---

[7] We have neglected one aspect of the adjustment process. When excess inventories pile up, not only will firms cut production to match demand, they will go beyond this to work off the excess inventories. In practice this can give rise to overshooting of equilibrium, a phenomenon known as an inventory cycle. Despite this effect, the fundamental condition that insures convergence to equilibrium is shown by Equation 2.13.

In this model of the economy adjustments of income and production to equilibrium are akin to a dog chasing its own tail. Producers cut production to match demand and end up pushing down demand. This property of the economy reflects the fact that we are studying macroeconomics, not microeconomics. If a single firm cuts production because its sales are weak, the effect on total income in the economy is trivial and so the effect on the demand for its product is trivial. If all firms together cut production, then total income falls and so does demand. Even though we are using a very simple model, this idea of production adjustment gives us an important insight into why real economies go into recessions. If inventories start piling up, then businesses cut back and demand falls, causing further declines in production and hence demand.

The same story can be told in reverse for expansions. If inventories are running down, firms expand production, hire workers, generate more income, and create more demand. The economy goes into a boom.

Even though the adjustment to equilibrium income does involve a series of reactions, the process does come to an end, and the economy does move to a new equilibrium. *The economy will move into equilibrium provided the marginal propensities to spend are not too large.* If the sum of the marginal propensity to consume (C_1) and the marginal propensity to invest (I_1) is less than unity, then the simple-model economy we have just described will adjust to an equilibrium level of output. This condition on the propensities to spend is shown in Equation 2.13 where the sum of the MPC and MPI is less than one:

$$C_1 + I_1 < 1. \tag{2.13}$$

If the sum of the marginal propensities to spend equals or exceeds unity, then the multiplier is either infinite or negative, neither of which describe an adjustment process that resembles the workings of any actual economy.

Having shown how equilibrium in the goods market is determined in this simple economy, and having looked at how the economy adjusts to equilibrium, we can now ask how the economy is affected by shifts in the consumption function or the investment function. How does the equilibrium level of income and output change when the consumption or investment schedule shifts?

Changes in Equilibrium Income and the Multiplier

The relationships between income and the interest rate and the demand for consumption and investment expenditures can change. Households may become more optimistic about future income; firms may find that they would rather invest more even at the current income and interest rate. We capture these changes in demand by allowing for a shift in the consumption and/or investment functions.[8] This increase or decrease in the autonomous part of consumption, C_0, or of investment, I_0, initially increases aggregate demand, which eventually leads to a change in equilibrium income that is a multiple of the initial change in expenditures. Small shifts in the consumption- or investment-demand schedules will lead to much larger changes in income and output. The reason is that when businesses or customers step up their expenditures, demand rises, and then producers respond by increasing output. The boost in output then raises employment and income. And the increase in income then induces a further increase in demand. There is a similar chain-reaction process working to reduce equilibrium output when the demand schedules shift down.

The description we have just given of how a small shift in the demand schedules will result in a larger increase in equilibrium income is similar to the description we gave earlier of the adjustment of the economy to a given equilibrium. This similarity is because both stem from the same basic idea: Aggregate demand and aggregate supply are not independent. An initial increase in demand stimulates an increase in supply that in turn induces further increases in income and so on.

The effect of shifts in the demand schedules on equilibrium income can be analyzed algebraically using the term $1 \div [1 - (C_1 + I_1)]$ in Equation 2.12—the multiplier. The multiplier gives the factor of proportionality between equilibrium income and autonomous expenditure and it also indicates that a *change* in autonomous expenditure results in a *change* in income.

The multiplier and a change in investment demand

Suppose that there is increased optimism among businesses about future sales. One source of optimism in the real economy could be a falling value of the dollar, which makes U.S. products more attractive to foreign buyers. Such a change in business confidence would be translated into the expectation of higher profitability from capital investment. At any level of income and interest rate there would be a higher level of expenditure on investment goods. The change in planned investment would be represented by an increase in autonomous investment ($\Delta I_0 > 0$).

In Figure 2.10 we show the increase in autonomous investment as an increase in aggregate demand [the line $(C + I_P)_0$ shifts up to the line $(C + I_P)_1$]. The new aggregate-demand line is parallel to the old aggregate-demand line,

---

[8] Changes in the demand for consumption and/or investment expenditures can also be due to increases or decreases in the marginal propensities to spend (MPC and MPI). These changes would be shown as twists or changes of slope in the straight-line consumption and investment functions used in graphical analysis of an adjustment to equilibrium. We ignore this type of change for now. However, we do use just such a change in Chapter 4 when we look at how changes in income tax rates change equilibrium income.

FIGURE 2.10   Graphical Analysis of the Multiplier: An Autonomous Increase in Investment Demand

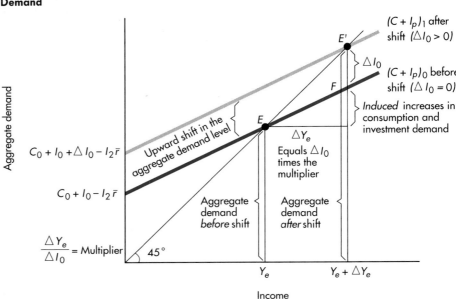

and the vertical rise of the line is equal to the increase in autonomous investment expenditure (ΔI_0). As the new, higher aggregate-demand line (ΔI_0) slides along the 45-degree line, equilibrium income is shown to increase by the change in autonomous investment times the multiplier.

Returning to the algebraic description of the model, the new level of planned investment is

$$I_P = I_0 + \Delta I_0 + I_1 Y - I_1 \bar{r}.$$

This new planned level of expenditure on investment goods starts an increase in aggregate demand that eventually results in an increase in equilibrium income that is a multiple of the initial increase in demand.

We show this to be the case by working through the changes in the equilibrium condition that reflect the change in investment demand. Before the increase in autonomous investment demand, the equilibrium condition was

$$Y_e = (C_0 + I_0 - I_1 \bar{r}) \div (1 - C_1 - I_1)$$

or

$$Y_e \times (1 - C_1 - I_1) = (C_0 + I_0 - I_1 \bar{r}).$$

After the increase in autonomous investment expenditure the equilibrium condition becomes

$$(Y_e + \Delta Y_e) \times (1 - C - I_1) = (C_0 + I_0 + \Delta I_0 - I_1 \bar{r}).$$

Subtracting the first of these two from the second gives

$$\Delta Y_e \times (1 - C_1 - I_1) = \Delta I_0.$$

Dividing by $(1 - C_1 - I_1)$ gives the expression that describes the change in equilibrium income:

$$\Delta Y_e = \frac{1}{1 - (C + I_1)} \times \Delta I_0. \tag{2.14}$$

The change in equilibrium income and output is equal to the multiplier times the change in the autonomous portion of planned investment.

The multiplier formula shows that the final increase in equilibrium income is larger than the initial increase in autonomous expenditure. This is illustrated in Figure 2.10 where equilibrium income rises (point E to point E') by the aggregate-demand line $(C + I_p)_1$ intersecting with the 45-degree line. A vertical shift in the aggregate-demand line by the amount of the initial increase in autonomous investment expenditure (ΔI_0) causes a larger horizontal shift $(Y_e$ to $Y_e + \Delta Y_e)$ in the point of intersection.

Using a numerical example, if planned investment increases by $1 billion and the sum of the MPC and MPI is 0.75, then output increases by $4 billion dollars. How did each dollar of increased investment expenditure result in $4 of increased output and income?

A given amount of increased expenditure triggers a chain reaction. The added expenditure initially raises output and income directly in those firms that supply the increased product. The rise in income then triggers an increase in consumption and investment for those who work for those suppliers. These new expenditures then trigger another round of increased income and increased consumption and expenditure and so on. Total demand is the sum of consumption and investment demands. In this example, an investment-demand increase of $1 billion adds $1 billion directly to aggregate demand and stimulates an extra $3 billion of subsequent production. The $3 billion of subsequent production comes about in the adjustment process leading to the new equilibrium level of income.

The $1 billion increase of income resulting from a $1 billion increase in investment demand is the initial or first-round effect. The second-round effect of the rise in investment expenditure includes two elements that then follow from the increase in income. Consumers spend a fraction (C_1) of that extra billion dollars of income. And then the same rise of income of $1 billion also triggers a change in planned investment over and above the initial change in autonomous planned investment. Investment expenditure increases when firms spend a fraction (I_1) of the extra billion dollars of income. The second-round effect is therefore the total of the marginal propensities $(C_1 + I_1)$. If

$(C_1 + I_1)$ equals 0.75, then the second-round effect on income and expenditure is \$750 million.

The \$750 million of production and expenditure from the second round also generates extra income. Consumers and firms spend a fraction $(C_1 + I_1)$ of the fraction $(C_1 + I_1)$ of the initial increase in income and expenditure. In our example, the third round of expenditure and income is 0.75 of \$750 million, which is \$562.5 million. In general, the third-round effect is $(C_1 + I_1) \times (C_1 + I_1)$ or $(C_1 + I_1)^2$.

This process goes on indefinitely for additional rounds. So the initial increase in demand of \$1 billion leads to a much larger final effect on output and income because of the chain reaction it induces.

Those of you familiar with the algebra of series will realize that the final change in income and output that results from the initial investment stimulus can be described by the relation

$$\Delta Y_e = \Delta I_0 \times [1 + (C_1 + I_1) + (C_1 + I_1)^2 + (C_1 + I_1)^3 + \ldots]. \qquad (2.15)$$

Each term in parentheses represents a successive round of the chain reaction—unity on the first round, $(C_1 + I_1)$ on the second round, $(C_1 + I)^2$ on the third round, $(C_1 + I)^3$ on the fourth round, and so on. The sum of this series is just equal to $1 \div [1 - (C_1 + I_1)]$, the multiplier. Looking at the sum of an infinite series gives us exactly the same answer as we found before.

We said earlier that the economy will converge to a new equilibrium level of income provided the sum of the marginal propensities to consume and to invest are less than unity. Equation 2.15 gives additional understanding of this condition. As long as the sum of the marginal propensities to spend are below unity, each successive term in the series in Equation 2.15 gets smaller and smaller and the total converges to the expression for the multiplier.

The multiplier and a change in consumption demand

Although we have looked at the multiplier effect in terms of a change in investment demand, the same analysis applies to a change in autonomous consumption. If consumers become more optimistic and decide that a recession any time soon is unlikely, they will spend more now and save less. Or perhaps the consumption of automobiles increases with no offsetting reduction in other purchases because gasoline prices have fallen, financing arrangements are improved, or new car models are more attractive. Regardless, if consumption shifts up, sales revenues go up, automakers and other producers will respond with higher production, and the chain reaction works itself out in the same manner as described for investment demand. An upward shift in the consumption function will raise demand. The extra demand stimulates production and then income, causing a further increase in consumer demand and planned investment:

$$\Delta Y_e = \frac{1}{1 - (C + I_1)} \times \Delta C_0.$$

■ **The Multiplier at Work**

Multiplier analysis is used to evaluate and describe how economic repercussions work in an economy. Consider how the multiplier sequence would be used to describe the effect of a change in demand on a specific industry, its work force, and the surrounding community.

The Detroit-area economy is dominated by the automobile industry, an industry that is large and important enough to have a widespread impact. If auto manufacturers expect a very good year, they may increase production and raise their targets for capital-goods purchases. Auto production and employment will both be higher than usual. The increased levels of production and employment in the industry raise income and production in the Detroit area directly. Workers at the factories then have more than the usual amount of money to spend at the stores and restaurants in the Detroit area. So the higher-than-usual demand for autos thus spills over into extra demand and better business for other companies in Detroit. And, of course, there are successive rounds of spillover. The stores and restaurants hire more workers and those workers in turn spend money. The impact of a very good year in autos will move beyond Detroit, and eventually beyond Michigan, as auto suppliers and their communities are affected. Ultimately, the impact of increased activity in the automobile industry is felt throughout the nation.

Unfortunately, the process also works in reverse. When the auto industry is depressed, output and income fall, first in the factory, next in Detroit, then ultimately throughout the economy. The effects of changes in demand are felt most strongly in the immediate area of the change. Then as the impact widens in area, it lessens in degree, much like the ripples in a pond after someone has tossed in a pebble.

As shown in Figure 2.10, an increase in any part of autonomous expenditure of the same size as the increase in autonomous expenditure on investment goods (substitute ΔC_0 for ΔI_0 in the figure) would have the exact same effect on the vertical movement of the $(C + I_P)$ line, causing an equal increase in income. In general, for either consumption-demand shifts or investment-demand shifts, *the change in income or output is equal to the change in autonomous expenditure (ΔC_0, ΔI_0, or the sum of the two) times the multiplier.*

WORKED EXAMPLE 2.2   The Effect of Changes in Autonomous Expenditure

Consider the same simple economy that we used in the first example. We will look at the case where the MPC is 0.7. The consumption and investment schedules and equilibrium income in that case were

$$C = 600 + 0.7Y$$
$$I_P = 250 + 0.1Y - (10 \times 5)$$
$$Y_e = 4,000.$$

We are assuming that the interest rate remains at 5 percent throughout.

Question: (a) What is the effect on equilibrium income of a decrease in autonomous consumption (C_0) from \$600 to \$550?

(b) What is the effect on equilibrium income of an increase in autonomous investment (I_0) from \$250 to \$300?

Answer: We will do this problem two ways. The long way is to solve for the new equilibrium income.

$$Y = 550 + 0.7Y + 250 + 0.1Y - (10 \times 5)$$
$$Y[1 - (0.7 + 0.1)] = 750$$

$$Y_e = \frac{1}{0.2} \times 750$$

$$= 3{,}750.$$

The answer to part *(a)* is that equilibrium income falls to \$3.75 trillion. Now we do the problem the quick way.

$$\Delta Y_e = \text{multiplier} \times \Delta C_0$$
$$= 5\,(-50) = -250.$$

So the level of income goes from \$4,000 to \$3,750, the same answer we got doing it the long way.

Finding the effect of an increase of \$50 in the autonomous part of investment is similar to finding the effect of the increase in autonomous consumption. We could solve for the new equilibrium level of income, or we can use the multiplier. We will do it the long way first.

$$Y = 600 + 0.7Y + 300 + 0.1Y - (10 \times 5)$$
$$Y[1 - (0.7 + 0.1)] = 850$$

$$Y_e = \frac{1}{0.2} \times 850$$

$$= 4{,}250.$$

The new equilibrium income is \$4.25 trillion. Using the multiplier gives

$$\Delta Y_e = \text{multiplier} \times \Delta I_0$$
$$= 5 \times 50 = 250.$$

Equilibrium income rises by \$250 billion—the same answer as before.

This problem illustrates how modest fluctuations in investment demand or consumption demand can turn into major fluctuations in the economy. The model we are using is very simple; in reality multipliers are smaller than the value of 5 used in this example. But the idea remains important. In his analysis of the Great Depression, Keynes believed that a decline in business investment had dragged the whole economy down.

THE FOREIGN SECTOR: A FIRST LOOK

The impact of foreign trade on the economy has become so important that we want to introduce the foreign sector at this point. We will ask how the foreign sector affects the multiplier and how shifts in autonomous expenditure have an impact on the balance of imports and exports. Looking at these issues now is a digression, but it is a useful digression. The ideas we look at now will remain important in our subsequent work. For a while, we will have to remove the foreign sector from our analysis again in order to avoid excessive complexity.

When consumers and firms can buy from overseas, part of consumption demand and planned-investment demand consists of foreign purchases. Thus, when the economy imports goods and services *(IM)*, this is a subtraction from the total demand for domestically produced goods and services. On the other hand, when foreigners purchase goods and services from U.S. producers, these exports *(X)* are an addition to the demand for domestically produced goods. With a foreign sector, therefore, the condition for equilibrium income becomes:

$$Y_e = C + I_P + X - IM. \tag{2.16}$$

We have already looked at what determines consumption and investment demand so now we simply consider the factors that determine exports and imports. There are three main factors. The first is that the volume of imports depends upon the level of domestic income. The more income that people have to spend, the more they spend on imports. The second factor is that the volume of exports depends upon the level of income overseas. If Europe has a recession, U.S. exports decline. And third, both imports and exports depend upon the prices of imports and exports. This last factor is reflected in the value of the dollar—the U.S. exchange rate relative to other countries' currencies. In this first look at trade we cannot take account of all three of these. Instead we will only focus here on the *effect of domestic income on the demand for imported goods and services.*

Import Demand, Income, and the Trade Balance

In this discussion, the relationship between imports and income is simply described by a linear function much like the consumption and investment functions. Equation 2.17 shows the import function:

$$IM = IM_0 + IM_1Y. \tag{2.17}$$

marginal propensity to import (MPM)
The amount of increased imports (ΔIM) that results from an amount of increased income (ΔY) expressed as ($\Delta IM/\Delta Y$).

balance of trade
The difference between exports and imports.

In Equation 2.17, IM_0 represents the autonomous part of imports. IM_1 is the **marginal propensity to import,** which is positive and shows how imports increase as domestic income increases. Figure 2.11 illustrates the import function. The higher is income ($Y_A > Y_B$), the higher are imports ($IM_A > IM_B$). Since the exchange rate and foreign income are taken as fixed, the demand in other countries for U.S. goods and services (export demand) is predetermined. In this first look at trade, the level of exports doesn't change so that exports ($X = \overline{X}$) are shown as a horizontal line in Figure 2.11.

Also shown in the figure is the **balance of trade,** the difference between exports and imports. Whenever the import line is above the horizontal export line (as when point *A* is above *A'*), there is a deficit—imports exceed exports.

FIGURE 2.11   The Import Function and the Trade Balance

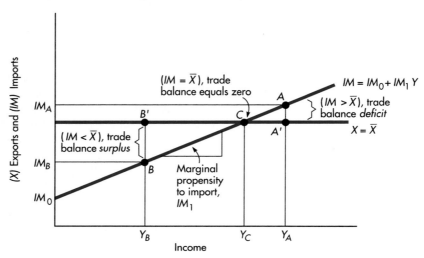

Exports can be larger or smaller than imports at different levels of income.

When the import line is below the export line (as when point B is below B'), there is a surplus. The trade balance is zero $(\overline{X} = IM)$ when the import function crosses the export line (point C). The level of income (Y_C) at which the trade balance is zero is not necessarily an equilibrium level of income, nor is it a preferred target for equilibrium. Equilibrium can, and does, come about at levels of income that generate trade deficits or trade surpluses and we would not argue that policy should be directed at changing the trade balance. We note, however, that one sure way to change the trade balance is to change the equilibrium level of income. A trade deficit can be converted into a trade surplus if the economy slides into a recession (point A to point B as income goes from Y_A to Y_B).

Goods-Market Equilibrium with Foreign Trade

We find the equilibrium level of income, accounting for foreign trade, by substituting the consumption, investment, export, and import functions into the expression for equilibrium income (2.16):

Equilibrium
Income = Consumption + Investment + Exports − Imports
$$Y_e = (C_0 + C_1 Y_e) + (I_0 + I_1 Y_e - I_2 \bar{r}) + (\overline{X}) - (IM_0 + IM_1 Y_e).$$

Collecting terms and solving for equilibrium income gives the equilibrium condition with a foreign sector:

$$Y_e = \frac{1}{1 - (C_1 + I_1) + IM_1} \times (C_0 + I_0 - I_2\bar{r} + \overline{X} - IM_0). \tag{2.18}$$

Equilibrium has been affected; *the multiplier is smaller as a result of the marginal propensity to import.* To give an example, in our model, if IM_1 were 0.1 and the sum of the marginal propensities to consume and invest were 0.8 ($C_1 + I_1 = 0.8$), then the denominator of the multiplier expression would be 0.3 and the multiplier would be 3.3. In a closed economy, with no imports, the denominator of the multiplier expression is 0.2 (1 − 0.8) and the multiplier itself is 5. The presence of imports has reduced the size of the multiplier. Because some of any increase in income is spent on imports, a change in autonomous expenditure has a smaller effect on income with foreign trade than without it.

This effect for the U.S. economy is important. The successive rounds of expansion, following an increase in investment or consumption, have a smaller effect because *part of each increase in income "leaks" overseas in the form of demand for imports,* rather than adding to domestic demand.

The effect of trade on the multiplier is only one part of the effect of trade on income. Autonomous expenditure has also changed. Exports $(\overline{X})$ increase autonomous expenditures, while the autonomous portion of imports (IM_0) is a subtraction from such expenditure. In general, total exports will be larger than the purely autonomous part of imports. *Autonomous expenditure is increased as a result of the foreign sector.* The demand for domestic goods coming from overseas can benefit demand.

As a result of the foreign sector, the multiplier is smaller but autonomous expenditure is larger. What is the overall effect of the foreign sector on equilibrium income? The answer can go either way. One way to think about the overall effect is as follows. Consider an economy with no foreign trade where the economy was in equilibrium. Then suppose that the country opened its borders and allowed imports and exports. If it were to turn out that export demand were just equal to import demand, then the presence of the foreign sector would have had no net effect on demand and, hence, on equilibrium income. In other words, if the trade balance is zero (as in Equation 2.19),

$$X = IM = IM_0 + IM_1Y_e, \tag{2.19}$$

then the foreign sector is neither boosting nor decreasing equilibrium income. Exports are adding to demand the same amount that imports are subtracting.

International trade among market economies is not constrained to be balanced. The condition of balanced trade expressed in Equation 2.19 does not always hold in practice; exports may be greater or less than imports. Net foreign demand may raise or lower equilibrium income. In 1980 the United States had a surplus of exports over imports, so foreign trade was boosting U.S. demand and income. In 1987 there was a huge deficit, so that the foreign sector was reducing U.S. demand.

Changes in equilibrium income and the trade balance

Suppose the economy starts out with exports and imports in balance. ($Y_e = Y_C$ in Figure 2.11.) Then suppose there is an increase in autonomous investment. The impact on equilibrium income follows from the new expression for the multiplier. From Equation 2.18,

$$\Delta Y_e = \frac{1}{1 - (C_1 + I_1) + IM_1} \times \Delta I_0.$$

The change in equilibrium income is the new multiplier times the change in I_0. When equilibrium income changes, imports also change:

$$\Delta IM = IM_1 \times \Delta Y_e. \tag{2.20}$$

Since exports are fixed, there is now a deficit on the foreign account (point A to point A' in Figure 2.11) as imports exceed exports. *Starting from trade balance, an increase in income will result in a trade deficit.* And, of course, the same idea holds in reverse. *A fall in income will induce a trade surplus or reduce a preexisting deficit.*

The impact of income on trade is important in practice. One reason for the large U.S. trade deficit in the mid-1980s was that the U.S. economy experienced strong income growth after 1982 and this pulled in imports.

WORKED EXAMPLE 2.3   The Foreign Sector and Aggregate Demand

We are going to take the same economy that was used in the earlier worked examples and add in the import and export functions. We get the following relations:

$$C = 600 + 0.7Y$$
$$I_p = 250 + 0.1Y - (10 \times 5)$$
$$IM = 50 + 0.1Y$$
$$\overline{X} = 450.$$

Question: (a) What are the multiplier and equilibrium income in this economy?

(b) Is there a trade surplus or deficit in equilibrium?

(c) How do your answers change if exports increase to 510?

(d) How do your answers change if exports go back to 450, but the marginal propensity to import increases to 0.2?

Answer: Use the condition that output equals aggregate demand, where demand includes exports and subtracts imports. We are assuming that the rate of interest remains at 5 percent throughout.

$$Y_e = 600 + 0.7Y_e \quad + 250 + 0.1Y_e - (10 \times 5) + 450 - (50 + 0.1Y_e).$$
$$\text{consumption} \quad \text{investment} \qquad \text{exports} \qquad \text{imports}$$

Now collect all the terms involving Y_e on the left-hand side and all the autonomous terms on the right-hand side:

$$Y_e \times [1 - (0.7 + 0.1 - 0.1)] = 600 + 250 - 50 + 450 - 50$$
$$Y_e \times (0.3) = 1{,}200$$
$$Y_e = (1 \div 0.3) \times 1{,}200$$
$$= 4{,}000.$$

We have found that the equilibrium level of income is $4 trillion and the multiplier is $1 \div 0.3 = 3.3$. So we have the answer to part *(a)*. To find the surplus or deficit, we substitute the equilibrium level of income into the import function:

$$IM = 50 + (0.1 \times 4{,}000) = 450.$$

Then the trade balance is equal to exports minus imports:

$$\text{Trade balance} = X - IM$$
$$= 450 - 450 = 0.$$

The answer to part *(b)* is that there is no deficit or surplus, so trade is balanced. Actually, we knew it would come out this way because the level of equilibrium income, at $4 trillion, is the same as it was with no foreign trade.

To get the answer to part *(c)* we can use the long way and solve again for equilibrium income or we can use the multiplier. The multiplier is unaffected by the increase in exports, which are part of autonomous expenditure. This time we will just use the short way:

$$\Delta Y_e = \text{multiplier} \times \Delta \overline{X}$$
$$= (1 \div 0.3) \times 60$$
$$= 200.$$

So equilibrium income increases from $4 trillion to $4.2.

The trade balance is affected both by the increase in exports and by the increase in imports caused by the increase in income:

$$\text{Trade balance} = 510 - [50 + (0.1 \times 4{,}200)]$$
$$= 510 - (50 + 420)$$
$$= 510 - 470$$
$$= 40.$$

This completes the answer to part *(c)*. The trade balance did turn positive and equilibrium income increased as a result of the increase in exports. But the improvement in the trade balance was not dollar for dollar with the increase in exports. As income rose, this sucked more imports into the economy.

The increase in the marginal propensity to import will change the multiplier but not autonomous expenditure. The safest way to answer part *(d)* is just to solve again for equilibrium income. We will do the problem this way, but you can probably see how to get the answer quicker by adjusting the size of the multiplier.

$$Y_e = 600 + 0.7Y_e + 250 + 0.1Y_e - (10 \times 5) + 450 - (50 + 0.2Y_e)$$
$$Y_e \times [1 - (0.7 + 0.1 - 0.2)] = 600 + 250 - 50 + 450 - 50$$
$$Y_e \times (0.4) = 1,200$$
$$Y_e = (1 \div 0.4) \times 1,200$$
$$= 3,000.$$

The multiplier has fallen from 3.3 to 2.5 = $1 \div 0.4$. This is a huge change and has dropped the level of equilibrium income to $3 trillion. Clearly, a rise in the marginal propensity to import of this magnitude is a very major change. One lesson from this example is that countries that import a lot (small countries particularly) will lose a much larger fraction of any increase in income to imports than countries that do not trade much. When the marginal propensity to import is high, the multiplier is small. To solve for the trade balance, we substitute in the level of income:

$$\text{Trade balance} = 450 - [50 + (0.2 \times 3,000)]$$
$$= 450 - 650 = -200.$$

The trade balance has fallen into a $200 billion deficit. This completes the answer to part *(d)*. This example illustrates that a large increase in the MPI will have a devastating effect on the economy, although remember that the increase in import propensity in the example was not matched by an offsetting rise in exports. A rise in exports and imports together need not lower demand or income.

The fact that we have ignored the effect of exchange-rate movements is obviously a limitation on the analysis so far. The overvalued dollar after 1982 was important to the growing U.S. deficit. But the effect of income on imports is large and shows up quickly. In the past, most countries fixed their exchange rates, at least for a period, so that income changes were then the key factor causing changes in the trade balance. Even today, many European countries try to maintain their exchange rates at fixed or fairly fixed levels relative to the German mark. With this constraint, they are afraid of policies that encourage an increase in equilibrium income because of concern about the resulting deficit in trade.

This concludes our first look at the foreign sector. We have seen how exports add to the total demand for goods produced in the United States and that when Americans buy foreign goods rather than U.S.-made goods this is a subtraction from U.S. demand. The net effect of the foreign sector on demand depends upon whether we are running a surplus or a deficit on our foreign account.

We have also seen how changes in income here in the United States affect whether we run a trade deficit or a surplus. Strong growth in income tends to increase our imports, as Americans buy more foreign goods as well as more domestic goods.

THE FOREIGN SECTOR WHEN EXCHANGE RATES WERE FIXED

During 1946–1971, the domestic U.S. economy closely resembled the model we have just discussed in the previous section, "The Foreign Sector: A First Look." This model is characterized by fixed exchange rates, set during this time period by the Bretton Woods agreement. Developed by the Allies toward the end of World War II, the Bretton Woods system fixed exchange rates among international currencies. Under this system, the U.S. dollar was the reserve currency and dollars could be freely converted to gold by foreign central banks. The price of the dollar was effectively fixed because it was tied to the value of gold at $35 an ounce.

Today we sometimes regard this era nostalgically, at least from an economic perspective. During most of the two decades following World War II, the price level was stable, interest rates were low, and the international value of the dollar was tied to the official price of gold. Yet during the 1950s, the U.S. international payments deficit rose from an annual average rate of $1.5 billion to $3.7 billion. From our vantage point in the 1990s, after witnessing $100 billion annual foreign payments deficits, this figure does not seem alarming, yet it concerned U.S. policymakers. Under the Bretton Woods system, a U.S. trade deficit could seriously affect the value of the dollar. The Eisenhower administration began to worry because foreign banks were demanding gold for their official dollar holdings, portending a forced-dollar devaluation through a rise in the price of gold. In the days of fixed exchange rates, maintaining gold reserves was an important U.S. economic goal, as gold reserves directly related to the price of the dollar.

Under the Bretton Woods system, gold would continue to be transferred to foreign banks unless the balance of payments deficit was cured. This cure could be achieved by tightening money, lowering U.S. purchases abroad, and raising U.S. interest rates. By simultaneously attracting foreign investors into dollar-denominated assets and lowering U.S. demand for foreign goods, the balance of payments deficit would stabilize and the drain on U.S. gold reserves would stop.

The Eisenhower administration pursued these policies and as a result President Kennedy inherited an economic recession when he took office in 1961. Yet despite his campaign promise to "get the country moving again," Kennedy feared foreign investors would start to distrust the dollar if the federal budget ran a deficit, so his fiscal policy was only mildly expansionary and the Federal Reserve kept interest rates from falling. Only the 1961 Berlin crisis, which brought more foreign investment to the "safe haven" of the United States and an increase in defense spending, boosted aggregate demand enough to lift the economy out of the recession.

The international considerations that were important to the United States in the 1950s and 1960s are still important today, despite abandonment of the Bretton Woods system in the early 1970s. In the summer of 1990 the U.S. economy was sluggish, yet the Federal Reserve was maintaining higher-than-warranted interest rates for fear foreign investors would run from dollar-denominated assets. Toward the end of the summer the Mideast conflict put further downward pressure on the dollar. The Fed was dually concerned with avoiding a domestic recession (further threatened by rising oil prices) and stemming the dollar's fall on the international market. While conditions governing the dollar's exchange rate are different today than they were under a fixed exchange rate system, the domestic versus international policy dilemma still exists.

GOODS-MARKET EQUILIBRIUM, INTEREST RATES, INVESTMENT, AND SAVING

We have looked at how equilibrium income is determined by aggregate supply and demand in the goods market. Equilibrium income was determined *assuming a fixed interest rate*. That was a useful simplification and gave us insights into the real economy, about how changes in production feed back into changes in demand. However, interest rates do change and those changes affect the level of equilibrium income. The interest rate is determined in part by financial markets and in part by the supply and demand for real goods and services. The interest rate is the link between the money and financial markets and the goods market. We have to see how the interest rate affects goods-market equilibrium and vice versa.

We will end this chapter by simply asking what happens when the rate of interest changes. The next chapter will take up the question of what brings about a change in the rate of interest. It turns out that we already have done most of the work to answer the first question, but we will have to go back to a closed economy without foreign trade. The reason for this is ease of exposition. We could carry forward what we have done so far, but the analysis gets cluttered and algebraic. We can show some important attributes of an economy where the interest rate changes without explicit reference to the foreign sector.

We will also make another change in order to simplify the exposition. *From now on in the algebraic discussion we will refer only to points of goods-market equilibrium. Total investment* (I) *and planned investment* (I_P) *will always be the same and we will refer only to investment* (I). *Unless specifically noted, income* (Y) *will be equilibrium income* ($Y = Y_e$). When we talk about changing Y, from now on, we are talking about changes in the level of income for which the goods market is in equilibrium.

Interest Rates and Aggregate Demand

The interest rate affects aggregate demand through investment demand. An increase in the interest rate leads to a fall in investment demand, and a decrease in the interest rate leads to a rise in investment. Figure 2.12 shows how equilibrium income is determined at two rates of interest, r_1 and r_2, where r_2 is lower than r_1. At interest rate r_1, equilibrium income is at Y_1. At the lower rate of interest, r_2, the investment-demand function shifts up, the aggregate-demand line moves up ($[C + I]_1$ to $[C + I]_2$), and the equilibrium point shifts out (E_1 to E_2). The result of the drop in the interest rate is much the same as the result of an increase in autonomous expenditure; it causes investment demand to rise at the same initial level of income. The multiplier effects of that initial increase in investment expenditure drive up equilibrium income (Y_1 to Y_2).

Algebraically the upward shift in the investment function is given as follows:

FIGURE 2.12 The Effect of a Fall in the Rate of Interest on Goods-Market Equilibrium

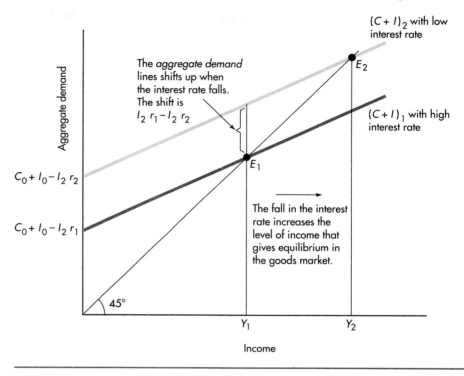

Investment demand at $r_1 = I_0 + I_1Y - I_2r_1$
Investment demand at $r_2 = I_0 + I_1Y - I_2r_2$
Shift in investment demand $= I_2r_1 - I_2r_2$.

The effect of this shift in the investment-demand function on equilibrium income then follows from the multiplier analysis:

$$\Delta Y = \frac{1}{1 - (C_1 + I_1)} \times (I_2r_1 - I_2r_2)$$

$$= Y_2 - Y_1. \tag{2.21}$$

A decline in the rate of interest is like a shift in the autonomous component of investment. It produces a multiplied response, an increase in income.

Suppose that the economy has been in a recession for a while, and then the rate of interest falls (perhaps because of a policy change by the

Federal Reserve Board). This fall in the rate of interest increases the demand for investment goods, particularly new houses and other construction.[9] This increase in investment demand has an initial, or first-round, effect on income and output. Then the initial rise in income generates second-round effects on both consumption demand and investment as the multiplier process works its way through the economy. The final result of the fall in the interest rate is an increase in equilibrium income.

The process also works in reverse. If the rate of interest rises, this can induce a drop in housing starts and other investment demand, leading to a multiplied decline in income and output. Changes in the rate of interest have proven to be a powerful influence on aggregate demand in the U.S. economy.

Equilibrium Income and the Interest Rate: The *IS* Schedule

We have just found that the equilibrium level of income is different at a low rate of interest than at a high rate of interest. Another way of saying this is that *the goods market is in equilibrium with many different combinations of income and the interest rate.* In our example, the combination of a high interest rate and a low level of income (r_1, Y_1) gives goods-market equilibrium. But the combination of a low rate of interest and a high level of income (r_2, Y_2) also gives goods-market equilibrium. And of course there are many other combinations of interest rate and income in between that will give goods-market equilibrium.

The combinations of interest rate and income that generate equilibrium in the goods market make up what is known as the IS *schedule.* The *IS* schedule is shown in Figure 2.13. The pairs of values of the interest rate and income (r_1 and Y_1 at point E_1, and r_2 and Y_2 at point E_2) used in Figure 2.12 are identified along the *IS* schedule (points E_1 and E_2) in Figure 2.13. The *IS* schedule is downward-sloping because high interest rates discourage investment and therefore reduce equilibrium income.

The slope of the *IS* schedule is important because it shows how much equilibrium income will change with a change in the interest rate. If a lower interest rate stimulates a large increase in aggregate demand, then the *IS* schedule will be flat. If a lower interest rate stimulates only a small increase in aggregate demand, then the *IS* schedule will be steep. In later chapters we look at the conditions that lead to large or small interest-rate effects.

---

[9] When general business conditions are healthy, changes in the interest rate are more likely to affect investment demand than when general business conditions are suffering from recession or expectations of recession. A lower interest rate will be a weak incentive to invest when business prospects are poor.

FIGURE 2.13 The IS Schedule

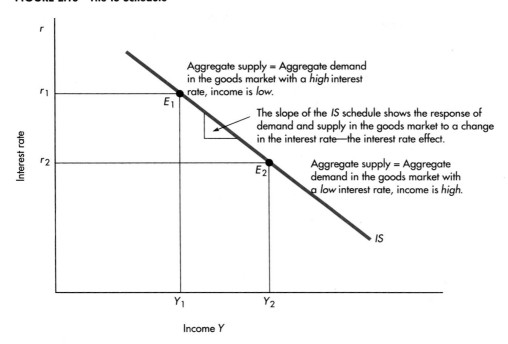

The *IS* schedule shows the combinations of income and interest rate that are consistent with goods-market equilibrium.

WORKED EXAMPLE 2.4 Finding the *IS* Schedule

The *IS* schedule is derived from the same relation as the one we have been using to solve for equilibrium income. We find the *IS* schedule by equating output and aggregate demand. The difference is that we are now considering the interest rate as a variable rather than as a fixed number. This means that *instead of solving for* Y, *we will solve for the equation that shows how* r *varies with* Y. We will use the same investment and consumption functions that we used in the earlier examples:

$$C = 600 + 0.7Y$$
$$I = 250 + 0.1Y - 10r.$$

We have excluded exports and imports, but we will now let the interest rate vary rather than being fixed at 5 percent.

Question: (a) With the relations just shown, what is the *IS* schedule?

(b) What is the slope of this schedule?

(c) What are the levels of income along the *IS* schedule corresponding to interest rates of 5, 3, and 7 percent?

Answer: Output equals aggregate demand gives the following:

$$Y = 600 + 0.7Y + 250 + 0.1Y - 10r.$$

Now collect the terms with *r* in them on the left-hand side. And on the right-hand side collect two terms: one with the autonomous components of expenditure and the other with the terms involving *Y*. Notice that since the interest rate varies, it is treated separately. The interest-rate term is no longer included in autonomous expenditure:

$$10r = 850 + [(0.7 + 0.1) - 1]Y.$$

Now divide by 10, the coefficient on the interest-rate term, and simplify the coefficient on *Y*:

$$r = 85 - 0.02Y.$$

We have now answered part *(a)*. The preceding equation is the *IS* schedule. It is a linear—straight-line—relation and the slope is the coefficient on *Y*. The answer to part *(b)* is that the slope of the *IS* schedule is −0.02. This slope means that if we compare two points that are both in goods-market equilibrium, and the rates of interest differ by one percentage point, then the levels of income will differ by −50, as shown by the fact that $-0.02 \times (-50) = 1$.

Another way to get this answer is as follows. We have an investment function in which each percentage-point change in the interest rate changes investment demand by −10. A change of 1 percentage point in the rate of interest is like a change in autonomous investment of −10. Then, since the multiplier is 5 in this model, this induces a change of −50 in income. The slope of the *IS* schedule is then the ratio of the change in the interest rate ($\Delta r = 1$) to the change in income ($\Delta Y = -50$). So the slope ($\Delta r \div \Delta Y$) is given by $1 \div (-50) = -0.02$.

We know from the earlier examples that when the interest rate is 5 percent, then the equilibrium level of income is 4,000. So the first answer to part *(b)* is $4 trillion. If we had not already worked out that answer, we could have found it directly from the *IS* schedule.

$$5 = 85 - 0.02Y(\text{given } r = 5).$$

Divide through by 0.02 to get

$$250 = 4,250 - Y(\text{given } r = 5)$$

$$Y(\text{given } r = 5) = 4,000.$$

An interest rate of 3 percent is 2 percentage points below the 5 percent level, so the increase in income is −2 times the −50 for each percentage-point change in the interest rate $(-2)(-50) = 100$. The new equilibrium level of income is 4,100 or $4.1 trillion.

A rate of interest of 7 percent is 2 percentage points above the 5 percent value we used earlier, so income decreases by 100 [2 (−50) = −100]. The new equilibrium level of income is 3,900 or $3.9 trillion.

We could have obtained these answers directly from the *IS* schedule, so we can also check these answers now by seeing if they hold in the *IS* schedule.

$$3 = 85 - (0.02 \times 4,100)$$

$$7 = 85 - (0.02 \times 3,900).$$

Both answers check out. This completes part *(c)* of the question.

It would be a useful exercise to draw the *IS* schedule that we have found in this example. Do not draw all values of income down to zero. Have income run from 3,000 up to 4,500. With a vertical axis set at 3,000, the *IS* schedule will hit this axis at a rate of interest of 25 percent. The schedule is a straight line that then hits the horizontal axis at 4,250. As we have said, it has a slope of −0.02.

Investment and saving

The *IS* schedule gives points of goods-market equilibrium. These are also points where saving equals investment. Households receive income in the form of wages, interest, and dividends from companies. Part of this income is used for consumption and the remainder is saved. **Saving** is defined as income less consumption:

saving
Saving is the part of income that is not used for consumption.

$$S \equiv Y - C.$$

The condition for equilibrium in the goods market is that income equals aggregate demand. Using the definition of saving allows this condition to be expressed as follows:

$$Y = C + I, \text{ which implies } Y - C = I = S.$$

The condition for goods-market equilibrium is that saving (S) *equals planned investment* (I), and this tells us something important.

Production generates income in the household sector. Income is used partly for consumption, while some of it is set aside as saving. The part set aside for saving does not contribute directly to demand, so saving reduces aggregate demand. On the other hand, there is demand generated by businesses making investment. When the subtraction from demand (saving) equals the addition to demand (investment), then there is goods-market equilibrium. The amount of investment is influenced by the rate of interest, so *the* IS *schedule shows the points of goods-market equilibrium, where the interest rate encourages just the amount of investment by businesses that equals the saving being made by households.*

In this discussion, saving represents income that does not become part of aggregate demand. This suggests that when saving is relatively large, then consumption and hence aggregate demand will be relatively small. Indeed, if an economy is in a recession where demand is too low, saving is too high. If, for example, consumers suddenly decreased spending at all levels of income (a drop in C_0), there could be too much saving given the level of investment businesses plan to make. Then income would fall, lowering both saving and investment until the two are equal.[10] However, it would be wrong to think of saving as a detriment to the economy. By the act of saving, households refrain from consuming all of the goods and services produced. If business can gain access to those resources, perhaps by borrowing funds from savers, then business can make investments in capital goods that increase potential output. An economy's capability for growth is affected by its capacity for saving. If saving and investment can rise together, this will provide more capital resources for the long-run growth of the economy.

Increased saving can help the economy by freeing resources or it can hurt the economy by creating a shortage of demand. Which of the two cases applies depends upon whether or not there is *coordination* between saving and investment. If higher saving is accompanied by higher investment the economy is helped. If higher saving leads to a recession, the economy is hurt.

Saving–investment coordination

The idea that a failure of coordination between saving decisions and investment decisions could lead to recession is the major conclusion to be drawn from the work of John Maynard Keynes. Keynes argued that saving could exceed planned-investment demand (which is the same as saying that consumption demand plus investment demand is less than output). In this situation, the result is excess supply of goods and services in the economy along with falling production and income. The equality of saving and investment is then restored, but only by a reduction of income as the economy goes into a recession.

Prior to Keynes, economists had not considered that coordinating saving and investment decisions was a problem. The rate of interest was seen as the mechanism that brought the two into equality, without there being any fluctuations in income. And many economists still hold this view today. The insight of Keynes has not been universally accepted by any means.

An important reason for this continued skepticism is that Keynes's own discussion of the determination of the interest rate and its impact on the economy was not valid or at least was not applicable to contemporary economic situations. Providing a better understanding of the determination of interest rates and the role of financial markets in influencing the goods market has been a major effort of modern macroeconomics and will be a major task of this book. *The* IS *schedule is a key element in this since it incorporates both the Keynesian idea that income and output adjust to bring saving and investment into*

---

[10] Starting from a position of $S > I$, equilibrium will be reached as long as saving falls by more than investment as income declines. Investment declines by ($I_1 \times \Delta Y$). Saving declines by $(1 - C_1)\Delta Y$. As long as ($C_1 + I_1$) is less than unity, saving declines by more than investment as income falls.

equality, and the classical/neoclassical idea that the rate of interest adjusts to do this. The next step is to start the analysis of the money market and the way interest rates are determined.

SUMMARY

- Aggregate supply and aggregate demand determine equilibrium income. In the short run the aggregate-supply schedule is fairly flat. Businesses are willing to supply the market demand at a given price. When production plans do not match demand, businesses will increase or decrease their inventories.

- Using the concepts of the National Income and Product Accounts ensures equality between aggregate output and expenditure, but this is only an identity. It is true by definition, and the key definition that makes it true is that changes in inventory (positive or negative) are automatically counted as additions to or subtractions from investment.

- Goods-market equilibrium requires a more restrictive condition, namely that aggregate supply equals aggregate demand with no unplanned investment. This point of equilibrium is important because if the economy is not in equilibrium, it will move toward it. Businesses will expand or contract their production depending upon whether inventories are piling up or running down.

- The consumption function relates consumption demand to the level of income using a simple straight-line function. The average propensity to consume, APC, is the average share of income devoted to consumption. The marginal propensity to consume, MPC, is the share of each additional dollar devoted to consumption.

- Planned investment demand is the amount businesses wish to add to their stock of capital goods and any planned increase in inventories. Investment demand depends positively on income and negatively on the rate of interest. The marginal propensity to invest is the change in investment demand resulting from a change in income.

- Equilibrium income can be determined with a given rate of interest. It is the level of income that equates supply and planned demand, using the consumption and investment functions to determine demand. Equilibrium income is equal to the multiplier times autonomous expenditure, and this same relation holds for changes in income. When there is a shift in autonomous expenditure, the resulting change in equilibrium income is equal to the multiplier times the change in the autonomous portion of expenditure.

- The foreign sector also affects aggregate demand. Exports are an addition to demand, while imports are a subtraction. A new expression for equilibrium income can be derived in which the multiplier is lower because of the marginal propensity to import, while autonomous expenditure is higher. The overall effect of the foreign sector depends upon whether exports exceed imports (raising income) or imports exceed exports (lowering income).

- Domestic income affects the foreign sector. If the economy expands, imports will increase but exports will not, so the effect may be a trade deficit.

■ We go back to an economy without foreign trade to consider the effect of a change in the rate of interest. A shift in the rate of interest changes investment demand and this brings about a multiplied change in equilibrium income. There is a particular level of income that goes with each rate of interest. The *IS* schedule traces out the combinations of income and the rate of interest such that supply equals planned demand and the goods market is in equilibrium.

■ Higher saving reduces aggregate demand but releases resources that can be used by firms for investment purchases. If firms buy capital goods with the resources released by saving, then saving will have increased the economy's ability to raise income by raising future potential output. An increase in saving that is coordinated with an increase in investment will maintain demand and help the long-run growth of the economy. If saving and investment are not coordinated, then the result will be income fluctuations and recessions.

KEY TERMS

accelerator model	investment function
aggregate demand	marginal propensity to consume (MPC)
aggregate supply	marginal propensity to import (MPM)
average propensity to consume	marginal propensity to invest (MPI)
balance of trade	multiplier
consumption function	planned investment
identity	saving
inventory investment	supply elasticity

DISCUSSION QUESTIONS AND PROBLEMS

1. Does price stickiness mean that there is no inflation?
2. Why might an employer refrain from dropping wages when demand drops for the company's product?
3. How does aggregate supply adjust to meet aggregate demand?
4. If the consumption function is represented by a straight line, how can the share of income spent on consumption goods decline as income rises?
5. Draw the investment function assuming a fixed rate of interest. How does it shift if the rate of interest increases or decreases?

6. Aggregate demand equals aggregate supply. In the simple model of the economy in this chapter, consumption and planned investment are the two components of aggregate demand. How can their sum exceed or fall short of aggregate supply?

7. Show graphically how equilibrium income is determined from the sum of consumption demand and investment demand. Show how a shift in autonomous expenditure leads to a multiplied shift in equilibrium income.

8. Discuss changes in economic behavior that would increase or decrease the multiplier. What effect would such changes have on equilibrium income?

9. How does the foreign sector affect equilibrium income? How would the trade balance be affected by a recession?

10. If saving is greater than investment at a given rate of interest, what happens to equilibrium income?

11. If autonomous spending increases by $50 billion and the multiplier is 3, what is the increase in equilibrium income? Assume that the interest rate is constant.

12. Canada has its exports equal to its imports. The U.S. economy goes into a recession. What happens to the Canadian foreign balance (balance of trade)?

13. The United States has its exports equal to its imports. There is a fall in autonomous expenditure in the U.S. economy. What happens to the U.S. foreign balance (balance of trade)?

14. Consider a closed economy (no foreign sector) without a government sector that is described by the following equations:

$$C = 700 + 0.6 \times Y \qquad \text{(Consumption)}$$
$$I_p = 300 + 0.2 \times Y - 40 \times r \qquad \text{(Investment)}$$

Assume that the interest rate is fixed at 5 percent by monetary policy.

   a. Calculate the magnitude of autonomous spending.
   b. Calculate the multiplier and the level of income that gives goods market equilibrium.
   c. What is the level of saving in equilibrium?
   d. If, for some reason, output was at the level 5,500, what would the level of unplanned inventory accumulation be?
   e. If the level of autonomous investment, (I_0), were to rise to 400, what would the effect be on equilibrium income?

15. Using the consumption and investment functions from question 6, find the *IS* schedule.

16. Consider an open economy (with foreign trade), but without a government sector described by the following equations:

$$C = 300 + 0.7 \times Y \qquad \text{(Consumption)}$$
$$I_p = 110 + 0.1 \times Y - 30 \times r \qquad \text{(Investment)}$$
$$IM = 10 + 0.2 \times Y \qquad \text{(Imports)}$$
$$\overline{X} = 250 \qquad \text{(Exports)}$$

Assume that the interest rate is fixed at 5 percent by monetary policy.

    a Calculate the multiplier in this open economy and the equilibrium level of income.

    b. Calculate the balance of trade, $(\overline{X} - IM)$.

    c. Assume that there is a reduction in export demand of 30, i.e., $\Delta \overline{X} = -30$. By how much does equilibrium income change? By how much does the trade balance worsen?

    d. If there were no foreign trade in this economy, what would the value of the multiplier be?

■ APPENDIX 2A
Algebraic Analysis of the IS *Schedule*

We use the linear relationships for the consumption and investment functions that were described in the text:

$$C = C_0 + C_1 Y.$$

$$I = I_0 + I_1 Y - I_2 r.$$

We then write the condition that output equals the sum of consumption and investment demand:

$$Y = C_0 + C_1 Y + I_0 + I_1 Y - I_2 r.$$

Collecting terms gives

$$r = \frac{[C_0 + I_0]}{I_2} - \frac{[1 - (C_1 + I_1)]Y}{I_2}.$$

This equation is then the *IS* schedule. The constant term depends upon autonomous expenditure and the interest-sensitivity of investment (the coefficient I_2). Changes in autonomous expenditure cause the schedule to shift without changing slope, with increases in autonomous expenditure causing the schedule to shift to the right. Changes in I_2 cause both shifts and rotations of the schedule, since this term also appears in the slope term (the coefficient on Y).

    To interpret the slope of the *IS* schedule, $\Delta r / \Delta Y$, recall the definition of the multiplier:

Multiplier $= 1 \div [1 - (C_1 + I_1)]$.

It follows that the slope of the *IS* schedule, the interest-rate effect on equilibrium income, is the following:

Slope of $IS = -1 \div$ (Multiplier $\times$ Interest-sensitivity of investment).

The minus sign indicates that the *IS* schedule slopes downward. It is flatter, the larger is the interest-sensitivity of investment. A given change in the interest rate, Δr, will cause a larger change in income, ΔY, the bigger is the induced change in investment (the larger is I_2) and the bigger is the effect on income of the induced change in investment (the larger is the multiplier).

CHAPTER 3

The Monetary Economy, Aggregate Demand, and Equilibrium Income

INTRODUCTION

Money is obviously important in our economy. Without money we would be forced either to provide for ourselves without buying and selling in the market, or to spend time and energy in bartering for goods and services. Money facilitates exchange. In this chapter, we will look at how money supports the workings of individual markets in our economy and then turn our attention to the roles of money and the interest rate in the overall economy.

We saw in Chapter 2 that goods-market equilibrium, where aggregate supply equals aggregate demand, can occur at high or low levels of income, depending upon the interest rate (shown in Chapter 2 as points along the *IS* schedule). Interest rates are set in financial markets, where many different kinds of financial assets are traded, such as Treasury bills and long-term corporate bonds. These assets differ in how easily they can be resold and in how risky they are. For our first look at how the interest rate is determined, we will focus here on the **money market** and the determinants of money supply and money demand. The money market is where people increase or decrease the amount of money they hold by selling or buying short-term bonds that carry very little risk of default, such as Treasury bills. Among the largest participants in this market are corporate financial officers who buy and sell short-term bonds in order to strike a balance between the interest their companies can earn on Treasury bills against the company's need to hold money to pay its bills.

As we study the money market, we will find that the level of output in the real economy also influences what happens in the money market. Because of the two-way interaction between income and the interest rate, we need

money market
The money market is where people increase or decrease the amount of money they hold by selling or buying short-term bonds that carry very little risk of default, such as Treasury bills.

to combine the analysis of equilibrium in the money market (called *LM* analysis) with the analysis of equilibrium in the goods market (*IS* analysis).

Interest rates rise and fall on Wall Street, while jobs and production increase and decrease in factories and offices around the country. How do the two parts of the economy affect each other? In this chapter we will use *IS-LM* analysis to provide an important part of the answer.

A MONETARY ECONOMY

money
Money is an asset that can be used to make transactions; that is, money is used to buy things and is accepted by people selling things.

We know that **money** plays a large part in determining overall economic activity, but what is money? Is it the paper and coins in your pocket? Is it your credit cards or your bank balance? Is a savings account money? If so, what about a savings bond, common stock, a pension account, or an insurance policy? How about gold or silver or platinum? If we are going to find out how money, more of it or less of it, affects the aggregate economy, we have to start by knowing what it is.

Money is an asset that can be used to make transactions; that is, money is used to buy things and is accepted by people selling things. Formally, there are three different concepts of money, called *M*1, *M*2, and *M*3. We will give these alternative definitions of money a little later, but in order to get a handle on the concept of money, we will look first at the role of money in our economy—what money does for us and for the market economy.

Barter, Markets, and Money

barter
Direct trading for goods and services without using money.

Without money or markets, goods and services would have to be exchanged through direct trading via **barter.** For example, the currency of the Soviet Union, the ruble, cannot be converted directly into dollars. So when the Pepsi-Cola company set up an agreement to sell Pepsi in the Soviet Union, it arranged to accept vodka in exchange—a barter arrangement. Similarly, if we did not have money here in the United States, there would still be goods and services exchanged among Americans. The reasons for exchanging goods and services exist with or without money—exchange is conducted for mutual advantage.

There are costs to using barter rather than using money, particularly the costs in time spent searching out advantageous trades. People who make shoes and need food and clothing would have to find people with food who want shoes and people with clothing who want shoes. Barter requires a matching of people and needs, which can be very difficult to achieve. There is a serious coordination problem for the organization of production and consumption when barter is the main form of exchange. This microeconomic coordination problem was solved by two social economic inventions: organized markets and money. Markets reduced the costs of searching for particular goods and services and smoothed out extreme price differences for the same goods. With money, it is easier for producers to specialize, thereby increasing productive efficiency. They can concentrate on one activity and then exchange their production for money and use the money to buy the things that they need.

In a modern society economic activities are specialized. Workers and the owners of capital goods combine their efforts in production. The production of output generates income for employees and owners of capital. Money is not necessary for paying wages and profits, but it is very convenient. In a shoe factory, workers and the owners of capital could be paid with shoes, while in an umbrella factory they could be paid with umbrellas. They then would have to barter shoes or umbrellas for the rest of their needs. With money, people can sell their labor to a producer, receive money in exchange, and then buy the things that they need.

Transactions and the Medium of Exchange

In modern economies workers are willing to accept money in exchange for their labor, while firms accept money in exchange for the products they produce and offer for sale. Everyone believes he or she can offer money and get goods and services in return. As long as businesses accept money for products, workers will accept money for labor. Money has value because of its ability to execute exchange, not because the money has any value as a product itself.

transaction
A single act of exchange of goods or services between a buyer and a seller.

Those who earn income receive a flow of payments in money; each receipt adds to the amount of money they have on hand. They also use the money to buy things, and this depletes their holdings of money. At any particular time, *people and companies hold inventories or stocks of money*. The major reason why households, firms, and institutions hold stocks of money is to accomplish **transactions**. A transaction occurs whenever one person offers money in exchange for a good, a service, or an asset and another person accepts the money. There is a transaction when we buy food at the grocery store, and there is a transaction when your employer pays you at the end of the week or the month for the labor you have supplied. An important part of the role of money in the economy is that it serves as a **medium of exchange.**

medium of exchange
An asset that is used for transactions purposes.

> *Money is a medium of exchange.* It is an asset that is used for transactions purposes, and consists of currency and coin and any bank account or other financial asset that allows for the writing of checks.

demand deposits
Bank deposits that can be withdrawn upon on demand.

Bank accounts that allow for check writing are considered to be part of the money supply. These bank accounts are called **demand deposits** because the funds in the account can be withdrawn upon demand. Most checks are written on demand deposits.

Unit of account

It might be possible to work out a market trading system without money if everyone who received income did so in kind (shoe-factory workers, manag-

■ **Money Loses Value When There Is a Loss of Public Trust
   in the Monetary System**

Money has no intrinsic value; it has value in exchange. If you don't believe this, try eating a $20 bill for dinner, instead of exchanging the $20 for a steak and a salad. The ability of money to execute exchange is based on the trust that the goods and services people will demand and pay for with money will be produced and available when people take their money to the market. The trust implicit in a monetary system is based upon the maintenance of a socially understood relationship governing the way in which money is created and distributed in the economy. That trust is enhanced by laws that make money legal tender, good for paying taxes and bills, and free from counterfeiting. It is also enhanced by the government keeping its commitment to maintain the scarcity of money (i.e., not creating it at such a rate that the value of goods purchased with money drops precipitously, causing a breakdown of trust). If you worked 160 hours last month earning $10 per hour (after taxes), you have a good notion of how much of what goods and services you can buy for $1,600. You would

pay for food, shelter, clothing, and entertainment and you might be able to save a little. But how would you react if by the end of the month, because of a sudden increase in the amount of money, your take home pay only bought 70 percent or 50 percent or 30 percent of what you thought it would buy? When $1,600 ran out before a month had passed, you would feel cheated. If government fails to safeguard its money, there is a breakdown of trust; and if the trust is completely broken, money is no longer used in the economy. The result is economic crisis and a return to barter, because there is no money that people will accept.

In the period between the two World Wars there were *hyperinflations* in Europe that led to major economic dislocations and breakdowns of the monetary systems. In more recent years there have been very high rates of inflation in several countries. Israel, Brazil, and Argentina all had rates of inflation around 10–15 percent *per month* for periods in the 1980s.

ers, and suppliers would receive shoes, umbrella factories would pay in umbrellas, and so on) and then they traded goods and services without carrying around an inventory of them. The trades would have to be recorded in an information bank and all the exchanges could be reconciled and cleared at the end of the day. People's holdings of shoes, umbrellas, and any other good or claim to service would then be recalculated. Even if supercomputers were capable of this daily relisting and clearing of what everybody owned, it would be a cumbersome project. To know where you stood at the end of the day you would have to study the listed inventory of possessions and claims in detail. For accounting purposes, *it is much easier to convert all your assets into a common value or common units using the prices of all of the goods and claims on goods and services. Prices are stated in units of a commonly valued asset. Money serves this accounting function.*

> *Money is a unit of account.* It serves as the way in which we keep account of who has a claim on what resources. As a unit of account money also allows for a common way of using prices to value wealth.

Money's role as a unit of account doesn't determine the amount of money people want to hold. Either we have a monetary system or we don't. Once we have one, money serves as a unit of account. There is a seemingly paradoxical nature to the unit-of-account benefits provided by money. If an individual holds more or less money, there is no change in the unit-of-account benefits provided by money, but for the entire economy, the value of money as a unit of account disappears if money is not scarce. Like chips in a poker game, they can only be meaningfully used to keep score if their quantity is limited. We will take a closer look at the unit-of-account aspect of money when we describe the supply of money.

The medium-of-exchange and unit-of-account services provided by money are unique to money, but money also provides a value that is not unique. Money is one among many vehicles for holding wealth. The amount of money you have is part of your total wealth, along with other types of financial and real assets.

Financial Assets and Money

financial asset
A contract that gives the holder a claim on the issuer of the asset. The terms of the contract vary widely from a fixed future payment (as in the case of certain bonds) to a claim that is conditional upon future events (as in the case with certain types of corporate stocks).

stocks
There are two separate definitions to be used in context. (1) Stocks are the plural of stock—a fixed quantity, as in the stock of money, meaning the fixed quantity of money. (2) Stocks refer to corporate equities, a particular type of asset. These are the common or preferred stocks, which are the ownership shares of corporations.

wealth
The total value of all assets.

A family that sits down to add up its economic assets would include the value of tangible assets, such as a house or a car, plus the value of **financial assets,** such as **stocks** (ownership shares or claims on business and/or real assets), **bonds** (financial assets that pay a fixed dollar return to their owners over a given period of time), and **money**—including bank accounts and cash. The sum of a family's economic assets is its **wealth** and wealth is accumulated by saving over time. Household spending and saving patterns describe how much of their wealth people hold in various forms such as stocks, bonds, real estate, and money.

> *Money is a financial asset.* Financial assets are claims on the issues of the asset. People save, in part, by owning financial assets in order to store values for the future. Money is one kind of financial asset. Money, other financial assets, and tangible assets (also called physical assets or real assets) are part of our total wealth.

Businesses also add up their assets. These may include tangible assets such as factories and inventory and financial assets, including money. Businesses are owned by shareholders, and the value of their shares becomes part of the wealth of the people who own them. Businesses, like households, also make independent decisions about how much money to hold along with a variety of other corporate assets.

The fact that money is one of many financial assets complicates the analysis of the monetary economy. The answer to the question *what is money?* is no longer obvious. There are ways of making purchases without an asset (e.g., credit cards). And there are assets that are very close to money (for example, short-term bonds) that cannot be used directly to buy goods and services. When we want to know how much money is being held, do we include

■ The Messy Problem of Defining Money: If We Can Shop with Credit Cards, Why Aren't Credit Cards Money?

Even were we to limit our definition of money to those assets that were held for medium-of-exchange or transactions purposes, there would be problems with any single definition of money because some assets are used for transactions purposes more than others and because there are mechanisms, such as *credit cards* for accomplishing, though not settling, transactions without using assets. This problem with the definition of money has become even harder in recent years because the deregulation of banks and other institutions has led to the creation of new types of accounts. The most often used definitions of money are described next, and credit cards do not appear in any of them.

A purely transaction-based definition of money is *M*1. This includes *currency* plus accounts on which checks can be written (that is demand deposits) and *travelers checks*.

An almost purely transactions-based definition of money that includes some easily transferable savings accounts is *M*2. This consists of everything in *M*1, plus *overnight repurchase agreements* (RPs), U.S. dollar accounts held in Europe (that is, *Eurodollars*) accounts held in *money-market mutual funds*, and *savings deposits*, including small *time deposits*.

A definition that gets even further away from pure transactions purposes is *M*3. This includes everything in *M*2 plus large time deposits and other accounts that are used less frequently for transactions purposes.

Based on the notion that money is the amount people can readily use for transactions, one might include unspent lines of credit on credit-card accounts (they are used all the time to make purchases) and exclude time deposits (which are bank accounts that if used to make purchases quickly must pay a penalty). In practice, the definitions of *M*1, *M*2, and *M*3 include items that are all *assets*, meaning individuals see them as part of their total wealth. Credit-card accounts allow people to borrow very easily, but then the bank that issues the card must hold money in order to pay the merchant that accepted the card. And the cardholder must then repay the bank. Credit cards certainly affect how much money people want to hold, but credit cards are excluded from the definition of money because they are not assets.

Time deposits are on the borderline. They are assets and can be used for transactions with only a little difficulty. They are included in one definition and excluded from another.

bond
A financial claim on an issuer with a specified interest payment and redemption value. The actual return on a bond is a combination of interest payments and any gain or loss in the value of the bond at the time it is sold.

assets, such as savings accounts? Are these assets also money even though they are different from checking accounts and cash?

There is no completely satisfactory way to define money, in practice. There are three main definitions of money that are used regularly, *M*1, *M*2, and *M*3. (See the preceding box.) And there are even additional ones favored by some economists. *We will concentrate on the idea that money is an asset that is used to make transactions.* And when we look at figures on money to assess monetary policy or judge whether there have been changes in the demand for money, we will look at both the *M*1 and the *M*2 definitions of money. *M*1 includes currency and bank accounts with checking privileges. It corresponds mostly directly to the idea of money held for transactions purposes. *M*2 includes everything in *M*1 plus small savings accounts and money-market accounts. Many of these accounts now have check-writing privileges also, so that *M*2 can also be considered as mostly money.

*M*3 and the even broader money concepts are useful for some purposes, but do not really fit with the concept of money we are using here. They contain assets that are more like bonds. They can be converted into money, but are not actually money themselves.

THE MARKET FOR MONEY

In macroeconomics we do not generally choose to study supply and demand in the market for any specific good or service. We do not look at supply and demand in the auto market or the insurance market. We do study consumption, investment, government expenditures, and net exports, but these are categories of goods and services. We make an exception in the case of money, because it is different from other goods and services and it plays an especially large part in determining interest rates, inflation, equilibrium income, and overall economic activity.

The Demand for Money

It might seem strange to talk about the demand for money since we all want more money rather than less, but it is important to remember that money as we discuss it here is different from income or wealth. When people say they want more money rather than less, what they generally mean is that they want more income or more wealth. They want to be richer or wealthier.

In macroeconomics, the demand for money has a narrower meaning: it is *the portion of our wealth we want to hold in the form of money.* The demand for money describes what motivates people to allocate their stock of wealth into a nonmonetary portion and a monetary portion. Big corporations may have billions of dollars of assets and they allocate a few millions to money in the form of checking account deposits (demand deposits) and cash. Poor families may have some furniture, a car, some debts, and a hundred dollars in cash. When we study the demand for money, the decisions of the big companies are going to be quantitatively more important than the decisions of the poor family. But in both cases, the demand for money is a decision to allocate part of wealth to be held in the form of money.

Transactions and the demand for money

Money is used to make transactions. If people, firms, and institutions are going to purchase more goods and services over a period of time, they will need more money. *When the number of transactions rises in the economy, the demand for money will rise.*

There are many things that will influence the number of transactions in the economy. For example, in a modern economy most goods are manufactured in several stages of production. Raw materials are turned into components and components are assembled into cars or computers. Money is used

to facilitate the transactions at each stage of production, as component manufacturers buy raw materials and assemblers buy components. The number
of transactions increases as the complexity of the economy increases.

However, changes in the way in which production is organized take
place slowly. Institutions change gradually and the structure of markets
changes slowly. In looking at the demand for money in a given year, the
most important determinant of the volume of transactions is the level of
income. The more income people have, the larger is the volume of transactions
they will want to make. A higher stock of money will be demanded in order
to undertake a higher value of transactions, so *the demand for money will
increase along with increases in income.*

We show in Equation 3.1 a simplified demand-for-money relation in
which the amount of money demanded (M_d) depends only on income:

$$M_d = k \times Y. \tag{3.1}$$

In this specification, money demand is proportional to the amount of income.
The constant of proportionality, k, does not have to be unity, since money
passes from person to person or firm to firm and is not used up in each
exchange of money for goods and services. Over a period of time, one dollar
can buy more than one dollar's worth of goods and services. In the 1980s,
the stock of money in the U.S. economy was about one sixth the size of
U.S. GNP using the $M1$ definition of money and about two thirds the size
of GNP using the $M2$ definition.

Another way of looking at the demand for money is to note that

$$\frac{1}{k} = \frac{Y}{M_d}. \tag{3.2}$$

The ratio of income to the amount of money demanded tells us how many
times a dollar is spent and respent in the economy in a one-year time period.
If the ratio of income to money demand is high, then dollars turn over
rapidly in the economy. If the ratio of income to dollars is low, then dollars
turn over slowly. Because of this relationship between the ratio of income
to money and the rapidity with which money changes hands, we call the
ratio of income to money the **velocity of money.** The velocity of money is
defined as the ratio of income to the stock of money:

velocity of money
The ratio of income to money,
usually described by the term
V. Velocity measures the number of times a dollar turns over
in a year.

$$V \equiv \frac{Y}{M}. \tag{3.3}$$

In this simple case where money demand is equal to k times income, comparing
Equation 3.2 with Equation 3.3 shows that 1 divided by k will equal the
velocity of money. We said that $M1$ is about a sixth of GNP in the U.S.
economy. This means that the velocity of $M1$ is about 6, the velocity of $M2$
is about 1½.

Figure 3.1 illustrates the relation between the demand for holding an

---

FIGURE 3.1   The Transactions Demand for Money and the Level of Income

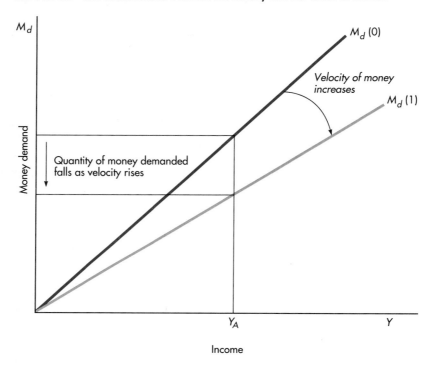

An increase in the velocity of money reduces the quantity of money demanded at a given level of income.

---

amount of money and the level of income shown in Equation 3.1. Since the slope of the money-demand function is equal to the ratio of money demand to income *(k)*, the *steeper* the schedule, the *lower* is the income velocity of money. In Figure 3.1, the *less steeply* sloped demand-for-money schedule $[M_d(1)]$ reflects a situation where the velocity of money is higher than on the more steeply sloped demand-for-money schedule $[M_d(0)]$.

A low velocity of money, as seen along $M_d(0)$ where money demand is a large fraction of income, indicates that individuals and firms are letting funds stay in their bank accounts for a period of time and not actively working to remove those funds quickly. A high velocity of money, as seen along $M_d(1)$ where money demand is a smaller fraction of income, indicates that individuals and firms are actively working to remove those funds quickly. People and firms will remove funds from their bank accounts to buy goods and services and they will also remove funds to buy financial assets.

Financial-asset holding and the demand for money

At any given time a household, individual, or organization has certain assets and **liabilities.** The net value of their assets is their wealth.[1] The household or organization's list of all its assets and liabilities is its **portfolio.** Since savers have a choice of vehicles for storing value—real and financial assets and their different types—they have to decide on the proportions of various types of assets in their portfolio. When people or firms decide how to allocate assets in a portfolio, they are making a **portfolio choice.** The decision about how much money to hold represents a part of the overall portfolio choice. For some people the choice may be whether to draw down the amount in a checking account in order to pay off a credit-card bill this month or, alternatively, to pay off only a minimum amount and maintain a higher checking-account balance. For some firms, the choice will be whether to move money out of checking accounts and into brokerage accounts so they can buy a variety of assets such as stocks and bonds.

In deciding how much money to hold as part of their portfolios, individuals and corporations will weigh the benefit of holding money against the cost of holding money. The benefit of holding assets in the form of money is the certainty that the asset can be quickly and readily used to purchase goods and services. The cost of holding money as an asset comes from the fact that money either earns no interest or has a very low interest rate.

Other assets yield a higher return than money and this gives them an advantage over money. The disadvantage of holding these assets is that they cannot be used directly for transactions and when they are sold or converted into money, this involves costs. There are costs, in the form of brokerage fees or even the time and trouble involved, when converting non-money assets to money. A corporate financial officer who buys and sells bonds too frequently will incur large brokerage fees that wipe out any interest earned.[2]

We will assume that firm managers choose between two alternatives: holding money or holding bonds. At any given interest rate on bonds, a

liability
Any claim that requires future payment.

portfolio
A listing of the set of assets and liabilities held by a household or organization.

portfolio choice
The decision about the proportions of different assets and liabilities held in a portfolio.

---

[1] The total net value of wealth includes the value of assets such as a house and stocks and bonds minus the value of liabilities, such as a mortgage or other debts.

[2] The cost of holding money is the difference between the interest that could have been earned on bonds or other alternative nonmoney financial assets and the interest that can be earned on money. The interest rate that can be earned on money varies from zero for holders of cash and owners of commercial demand deposits to competitively set rates on money-market accounts. When all money is taken into account, the interest rate earned on money is considerably lower than that which is earned on any other financial asset. Moreover, when interest rates rise in the economy, the spread between the rates earned on money and on other financial assets increases. In order to understand why there are changes in the relationships among different interest rates, we need to describe the different demands that exist for various types of financial assets. Until we do so in Chapter 6, where we introduce the financial sector and financial markets, we will continue to refer to a single rate of interest. In Chapter 6 we also look more closely at the cost of not holding money (the brokerage-type costs associated with converting assets from a nonmoney form into money and vice versa).

balance is struck between the benefits of holding bonds and earning their interest and the benefits of holding money. When interest rates rise, the balance is upset because bonds appear relatively more attractive than money. Money balances decline and bond holdings increase. This continues until a new balance is struck.

Taking funds out of checking accounts and purchasing financial assets when interest rates rise is an activity that makes more sense for corporations or individuals with large amounts of wealth than for the typical household. Yet even those with small balances sometimes make extra trips to the bank or automatic teller machine (ATM) to switch funds out of checking accounts to money-market accounts in order to take advantage of the interest rate. Even so, when funds are moved back and forth between money and bonds, most of the action is taking place through large financial institutions and corporations.

Corporations have so much to gain by increasing or decreasing their checking-account balances in response to the interest rate that they actively manage their accounts. In many firms there is a corporate financial operation with the sole responsibility of handling the funds that are moved into and out of checking accounts. This management of money balances is called **cash management.** When the interest rate changes, the amount of gain that can accrue to cash management is large enough to change the proportion of money that firms want to hold relative to the level of income. Financial institutions and corporations hold 70–75 percent of all demand deposits.

cash management
Moving funds between check-able accounts and financial assets in order to finance transactions while minimizing the cost of holding money.

Firms hold an inventory of money in order to make transactions, but the size of that inventory of money is affected by the rate of interest in the economy. Relative to the money-demand relation we gave in Equation 3.1, *the amount of money held for transactions purposes is reduced because individuals and companies hold smaller checking-account balances in order to earn interest on bonds.*

In Equation 3.4, we give a demand-for-money equation showing the effect of changes in the interest rate and changes in income:

$$M_d = kY - hr. \tag{3.4}$$

With a zero interest rate, the demand for money would be proportional to the level of income. Each percentage-point increase in the interest rate reduces money demand by an amount h. In this demand-for-money equation, *at a given level of income, the demand for money is lower the higher the rate of interest.*

Figure 3.2 illustrates a demand-for-money schedule that responds to changes in income and the interest rate like the one shown in Equation 3.4. In the figure, $[M_d(r, Y_0)]$ is drawn so that at a given income level (Y_0), money demand is a downward sloping function of the interest rate.

Just as in the description of the transaction demand for money, a rise in the level of income will increase the demand for transactions and the

FIGURE 3.2 The Demand for Money Balances as a Function of the Interest Rate

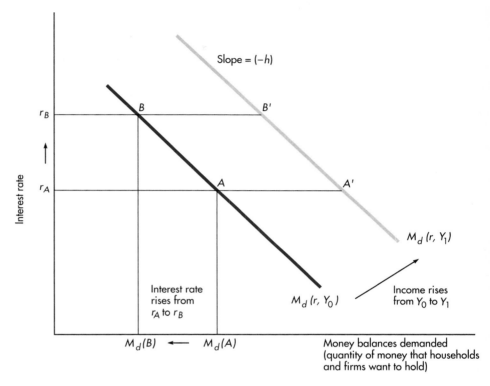

When income is constant, money demand is a negative function of interest.

demand for money. A rise in the level of income will increase the demand for money at all interest rates. This is shown as an outward shift of the demand schedule [$M_d(r,Y_0)$ to $M_d(r,Y_1)$]. At any rate of interest, such as r_A or r_B, the quantity of money demanded is now higher than it was at a lower level of income (point A to A' and point B to B').

At any given level of income, when the interest rate that can be earned on other financial assets increases, less money is held. When the rate of interest rises from r_A to r_B, the quantity of money demanded drops [e.g., $M_d(A)$ to $M_d(B)$ along $M_d(r,Y_0)$] as checking-account balances are drawn down in order to buy bonds. This is shown by the negative slope ($-h$) along the demand schedule (point A to point B).

WORKED EXAMPLE 3.1   How the Velocity of Money Is Affected by the Rate of Interest

The income velocity of money is a measure of how often money turns over or, conversely, how long money balances are held between payment periods. One way of looking at how the rate of interest affects the demand for money is through changes in velocity.

Question: Consider the following demand-for-money schedule, where income is in billions of dollars and the interest rate is calculated as a percentage.

$$M_d = 0.4Y - 80r.$$

(a) What is the demand for money when income is $4 trillion ($4,000 billion) and the interest rate is 5 percent? What is the velocity of money?

(b) With the level of income taken as given, how would your answer change if the interest rate were 1 percent? If it were 10 percent? Explain.

(c) When interest rates change in the economy, income often changes also. Suppose income is $3.8 trillion ($3,800 billion) when the interest rate is 10 percent. What is the velocity of money now?

Answer: If we substitute the values for income and the rate of interest we get the following:

$$M_d = (0.4 \times 4,000) - (80 \times 5) = 1,200.$$

The demand for money is $1.2 trillion. The velocity is the ratio of income to money:

$$\text{velocity} = V = \frac{4,000}{1,200} = 3.33.$$

If the interest rate drops to 1 percent, then we can see that the demand for money rises to $1.52 trillion:

$$M_d = (0.4 \times 4,000) - (80 \times 1) = 1,520.$$

If the rate of interest rises to 10 percent, the demand for money falls to $800 million:

$$M_d = (0.4 \times 4,000) - (80 \times 10) = 800.$$

The velocity of money is 2.63 in the case where the interest rate is 1 percent (4,000 ÷ 1,520) and 5.0 in the case where the interest rate is 10 percent (4,000 ÷ 800). The velocity of money falls as the interest rate falls because corporations and individuals have less incentive to reduce their money holdings. The velocity rises as the interest rate rises, as corporations reduce their checking-account balances in order to take advantage of the interest opportunity.

If the level of income were to rise at the interest rate of 10 percent, the demand for money would drop again:

$$M_d = (0.4 \times 3,800) - (80 \times 10) = 720.$$

The demand for money is $720 million and the velocity is now 5.28 (3,800 ÷ 720). The velocity of money increases as income falls in this model. This is the result of the particular form of the money-demand equation that we used, and it might not always be the case.

We have seen how a change in the rate of interest affects the demand for holding a stock of money, but in order to see how the demand for money interacts with the supply of money to determine the interest rate, we need to see how the supply of money is determined.

The Supply of Money

Money is a financial asset designed to accomplish transactions and to serve as a unit of account. Money can only provide these functions if money is scarce, that is, if the supply of money is fixed or grows at a limited rate. In most modern economies, the money supply is controlled by the banking system and the government's monetary authority—the central bank. We will assume now that the money supply is fixed by the policy actions of the U.S. central bank, the Federal Reserve or Fed. The money supply does not vary with income or the interest rate unless the Fed chooses to change it—that is, the money supply is fixed exogenously.[3] Such a money supply is described by the vertical lines in Figure 3.3.

The amount of money in the economy changes only when the Fed takes action to make it change. In Figure 3.3, a change in the money supply is shown as a shift in a fixed quantity. An increase is depicted by an outward shift $[M_s(0)$ to $M_s(1)]$ and a decrease by an inward shift $[M_s(1)$ to $M_s(0)]$.

Money-Market Equilibrium

Once the Fed has set the money supply, holders of money can make individual decisions about how much money to hold, but *the total amount of money will not change.* Equilibrium in the money market means that money demand is equal to a fixed money supply:

$$M_s = M_d$$
$$= kY - hr. \tag{3.5}$$

---

[3] A more careful analysis of the money supply awaits in Chapters 5 and 16. There it is shown that the money supply is created by the central bank and the banking system. The rate of interest can affect the decisions of bankers, and as such the money supply is often reported as being a slightly positively sloped function of the interest rate. We are assuming here that the Fed can undo any increase or decrease in interest-induced changes in the money supply. That is a strong assumption because the Fed lacks perfect information as well as perfect control. Therefore, the vertical money-supply schedule reflects the dominant role of the Fed in affecting the supply of money.

FIGURE 3.3   The Supply of Money

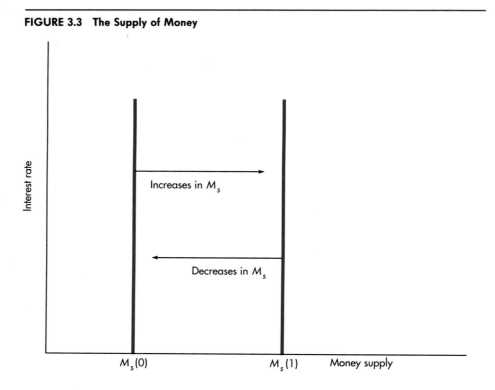

Money supply is set by the Fed through monetary policy. It is exogenously determined.

Since the supply of money is fixed, if the demand for money is higher or lower than the supply of money, then the adjustment has to take place in money demand. If there is less or more money demanded than available, the actions of money holders in trying to acquire or get rid of money will bring about a change in the quantity of money demanded so as to have money holders satisfied with holding the amount of money available. In the money market, the interest rate adjusts to bring money demand into equilibrium with money supply.

Figure 3.4 depicts a particular demand for money, $M_d(r, Y_0)$, at the level of income (Y_0). The figure shows that the supply of money and the demand for money are equal at the interest rate, r_0 (point A).

In Figure 3.4, when the interest rate is r_1 (lower than r_0), the amount of money demanded along $M_d(r, Y_0)$ exceeds the amount of money supplied (point B to point B'), at the level of income (Y_0). We have an excess demand

FIGURE 3.4   Money-Market Equilibrium

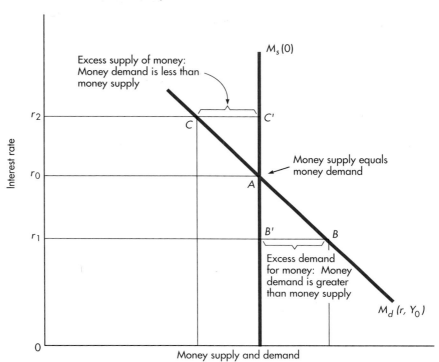

Money supply is fixed and money demand is for a given level of income (Y_0).

for money because the interest rate is too low. When the amount of money demanded exceeds the amount of money available, everyone wants more money than is available. The cash managers of corporations try to readjust their portfolios to increase the amount of money they have and reduce the amount of bonds. They can do this by selling bonds or by buying fewer bonds.[4] But since there is no more money available, the only affect of this attempted readjustment is that the interest rate on bonds will rise.

If the level of income remains unchanged, the resulting rise in the interest rate *reduces* the excess demand for money. Money is like tickets for a popular concert. No matter how much excess demand exists for a particular show,

[4] The interest rate will change as asset holders manage their cash balances by selling financial assets to get money. When there are more sellers than buyers, the price of financial assets falls. When the price of financial assets falls, the interest rate rises.

THE EURODOLLAR: AN INTERNATIONAL DIMENSION OF THE U.S. MONEY SUPPLY

Economists tend to simplify things by saying that the American money supply, as exogenously determined by the Federal Reserve, is dispensed by U.S. banks. This simplification takes some liberties with the definition of the U.S. money supply as well as with its location. Increasingly the U.S. dollar has become an international medium of exchange; many dollar-denominated time deposits are held in foreign branches of U.S. banks and in American branches of foreign banks under federal jurisdiction.

Now consider the complication to U.S. monetary policy posed by Eurodollars. These are still U.S. dollars but ones which are in time deposits in banks legally resident outside of the United States. Maturities on these time deposits vary. Some are overnight funds, virtually defying the definition of a "time" deposit. Other Eurodollar funds rest in certificates of deposit (CDs) with maturities of three months or more. These funds are very similar to CDs found in your local bank, except their size is usually at least one million dollars an increment. Eurodollar deposits are created by wire or cable transfers of an underlying balance held in a U.S. correspondent bank—a bank which by agreement conducts home-country business for an otherwise nonaffiliated foreign bank.

Eurodollar deposits have many useful purposes. These deposits are convenient interest-bearing funds for holding excess corporate liquidity, and they also function as a major source of short-term bank loans for working capital. These short-term loans help finance imports and exports, facilitating international trade.

The exact size of the Eurocurrency market is uncertain, but present estimates put it at $5 trillion (more than twice its size in 1982). About 60 percent of this market is comprised of Eurodollars. Much of the Eurodollar's appeal comes from the higher interest rates paid for foreign held dollar-denominated demand deposits, as compared to interest rates paid within the United States and on lower interest rates charged on loans. This narrow interest spread is possible because deposits are made in large, unsecured amounts and the borrowers tend to be large corporations or governments whose credit-worthiness and loan size qualify them for low interest rates.

There is another important reason why interest on Eurodollar deposits is so high. Unlike domestic U.S. banks, Eurodollar banks do not have to comply with U.S. reserve requirements or policy strictures. In effect, the Eurodollar market is not regulated. Federal Reserve policies cannot really affect these "offshore" banks, yet foreign bankers who deal in Eurodollars are nonetheless cognizant of Federal Reserve activity.

Given the greater rewards and risks in the Eurodollar market, some turbulence can result. When it comes to the conduct of U.S. monetary policy, the existence of a global Eurodollar market can be confusing. The Federal Reserve can directly create or destroy only *domestic* bank deposits. Meanwhile massive amounts of Eurodollars can flow in and out of U.S. banks in the time it takes to execute a computer command. The dollar is truly an international currency; therefore, we have difficulty sometimes even defining *the* money supply, much less controlling the part of it that lies beyond our immediate influence.

that demand cannot create extra seats on the night of the concert. Ticket prices are bid up by those who want to attend until demand is brought into line with the fixed supply and those who sell their tickets are willing to exchange tickets for money.

In the economy, if the total amount of money held does not change, the supply of money is fixed like the supply of concert tickets. If there is an excess demand for money, then the interest rate will rise and reduce the demand for money until people and firms are satisfied with holding the unchanged amount of money balances. In the figure, there is excess money demand when the interest rate is r_1. When the interest rate rises (r_1 goes back to r_0), the amount of money demanded declines. This process continues as long as the demand for money exceeds the supply. At point A, there is no longer any excess demand for money. Money demand equals money supply and there is a particular combination of interest rate (r_0) and income (Y_0) associated with money-market equilibrium.

WORKED EXAMPLE 3.2 Money-Market Equilibrium

Suppose that the money-demand relation is the following.

$$M_d = (0.4 \times Y) - (80 \times r)$$

What is the rate of interest when the money market is in equilibrium? As before, we assume that income is $4 trillion ($4,000 billion). Suppose that the supply of money is $1.2 trillion ($1,200 billion). What is the rate of interest?

$$M_s = 1,200 = M_d = (0.4 \times 4,000) - (80 \times r)$$
$$80 \times r = 1,600 - 1,200 = 400$$
$$r = 5.$$

The solution is that the interest rate is 5 percent.

Suppose, however, that the interest rate were lower than 5 percent at the same level of income. If the interest rate were 3 percent, the quantity of money demanded would be

$$M_d = (0.4 \times 4,000) - (80 \times 3) = 1,360.$$

There would then be an excess demand for money of $160 billion:

$$M_d = 1,360 > M_s = 1,200.$$

The $160 billion excess demand disappears when the interest rate rises by enough (from 3 to 5 percent) to drive the demand for money back into equilibrium with a fixed money supply of $1.2 trillion.

Income and interest rates in money markets: The *LM* schedule
We have looked at equilibrium in the money market when the level of income remained unchanged. Now we are ready to see how changes in income bring about changes in the money market.

Starting with money demand equal to money supply, if income were to change, the value of transactions would go up or down and so would the size of money balances demanded by asset holders. However, the supply of money is unchanged and, therefore, the increase or decrease in income

FIGURE 3.5   Changes in Equilibrium Income and Money-Market Equilibrium: The *LM* Schedule

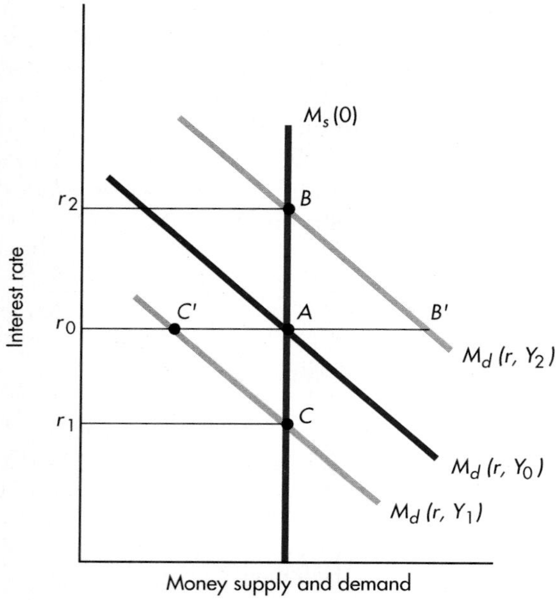

Money supply equals money demand at different levels of income and different interest rates.

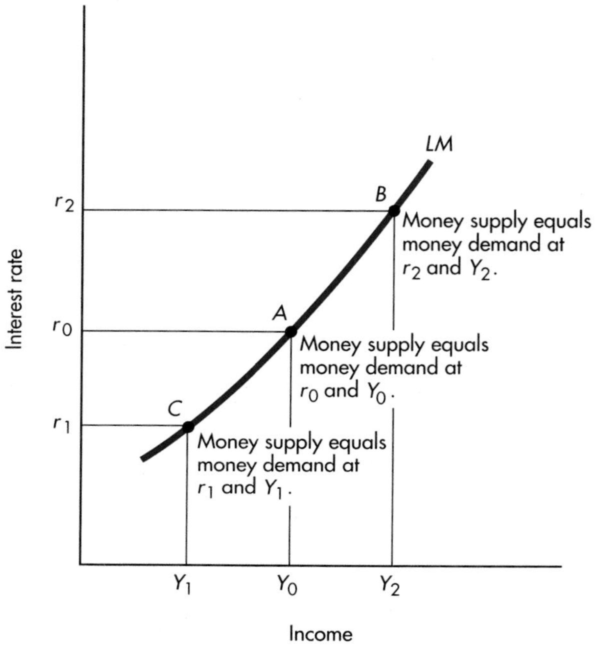

The money market is in equilibrium at all points along the *LM* schedule.

creates either excess supply of money or excess demand for money. When there is equilibrium in the money market, money demand is brought into line with the fixed money supply and *there is a higher or lower interest rate associated with money-market equilibrium at a higher or lower level of income.*

In the diagram on the left-hand side of Figure 3.5, the money market is initially in equilibrium at point A, with income at Y_0 and the interest rate at r_0. An increase in income (Y_0 to Y_2) raises the quantity of money demanded (point A to point B'). Now there is excess demand for money. By the same process as was described before, the excess demand for money brings about an increase in the interest rate. The interest rate continues to rise (r_0 to r_2) until the demand for money is once again equal to the supply of money (point B on the left-hand side of Figure 3.5).

When income went up, money demand went up, but there wasn't any more money. Asset holders held the same amount of money after income rose as before. *However, there was a change in the money-market equilibrium that* resulted from a higher income; namely, there was an increase in the desire to hold money because there were more transactions, and there was a decrease in the desire to hold money because the interest rate had gone up.

If the level of income fell, the analysis would run in reverse. At a lower level of income, the demand for money declines because transactions demand declines.[5] In the diagram, the lower demand for money $(M_d(r,Y_1))$, which is illustrated by an inward shift of money demand, comes into equilibrium with money supply at a lower rate of interest (point A to point C).

There are now three levels of income $(Y_0, Y_1,$ and $Y_2)$ associated with three different interest rates $(r_0, r_1,$ and $r_2)$. In all cases, the demand for money equals the supply of money. The diagram on the right-hand side of Figure 3.5 shows the pairs of equilibrium income and interest rate (points A, B, and C) along a line called the **LM schedule.** *The LM schedule gives all the combinations of income and interest rates where different levels of money demand equal a fixed money supply. The money market is thus in equilibrium everywhere along the* LM *schedule.*

LM schedule
Gives all the combinations of income and interest rates where money demand equals money supply.

WORKED EXAMPLE 3.3   Income and Money-Market Equilibrium: The *LM* Schedule

We continue with the worked example used in 3.2 but we let income go up from $4 trillion (Y_0) to $4.3 trillion (Y_2). We assume at the outset the interest rate is 5 percent. Money demand is now given as follows:

$$M_d = (0.4 \times 4{,}300) - (80 \times 5)$$
$$= 1{,}720 - 400 = 1{,}320.$$

Since the supply of money is only $1.2 trillion (1,200), there is excess demand for money, $M_d > M_s$. This means that the interest rate must rise. When the interest rate has risen to 6.5 percent, the money market is in equilibrium again.

$$M_d = (0.4 \times 4{,}300) - (80 \times 6.5)$$
$$= 1{,}720 - 520 = 1{,}200.$$

We have now found two points on the *LM* schedule:

1. $Y = \$4$ trillion, $M_d = M_s = 1{,}200$, $r = 5$ percent
2. $Y = \$4.3$ trillion, $M_d = M_s = 1{,}200$, $r = 6.5$ percent.

If income falls from $4 trillion to $3.8 trillion, this drop in income of $200 billion causes the quantity of money demanded to fall by $80 billion (0.4×200). With a rate of interest of 5 percent, there is an excess supply of money of $80 billion. As

---

[5] This is always a troublesome concept. How can firms and households want less money when income is falling? The way out of this puzzle is to remember that the demand for money is a demand for a portfolio or proportion of assets held in the form of money. Households and firms certainly want more *income,* but when income is falling, they want to hold a smaller portion of their wealth in the form of money. Because income is falling, cash managers need to hold smaller money balances and they buy bonds to increase earnings. Of course, every cash manager does the same thing so interest rates fall.

cash managers try to buy bonds, the interest rate falls until it drops from 5 percent to 4 percent. At the new lower interest rate, the amount of money demanded once more equals the amount supplied. This gives us a third point on the *LM* schedule:

3. $Y = \$3.8$ trillion, $M_d = M_s = 1{,}200$, $r = 4$ percent.

The *LM* schedule is upward-sloping because the higher the level of income, the greater has to be the interest rate that will bring money demand back down into equilibrium with a fixed money supply. In general, starting with equilibrium in the money market (any given point on the *LM* schedule), an increase in income is associated with a higher level of money demand. Since the money supply is set by the Fed, money demand is unsatisfied at higher income. The excess demand for money brought about by the increase in income generates an increase in the rate of interest. The quantity of money demanded remains the same all along the *LM* schedule as the higher interest rate cancels the increase in demand due to higher incomes.

GOODS MARKETS AND MONEY MARKETS TOGETHER: THE *IS-LM* FRAMEWORK

We are now ready to answer the question left open at the end of Chapter 2. If the *IS* schedule represents goods-market equilibrium at different rates of interest, what interest rate actually prevails and where is equilibrium? The answer comes from combining goods-market equilibrium *(IS)* with money-market equilibrium *(LM)*. We will look at how the two markets interact to jointly determine income and the interest rate. We will also use the *IS-LM* framework to describe how changes in economic conditions drive the economy from one equilibrium to another.

Equilibrium Income and the Interest Rate

We can see how the goods-market and money-market equilibriums are jointly determined by combining the information contained in the *IS* and *LM* schedules. In Figure 3.6, *IS* and *LM* are shown together. The point of intersection of the *IS* and *LM* schedules (point *A*, with interest rate r_A and income Y_A) is the one combination of interest rate and income common to both schedules. This point is a very important one for the economy—it is the equilibrium point where both the goods market and the money market are in equilibrium.

In the figure we can see that a level of income higher than equilibrium $(Y_B > Y_A)$ would require a higher-than-equilibrium rate of interest $(r_B > r_A)$ along the *LM* schedule (point *B*). But at the same time, this higher level of income would require a lower-than-equilibrium rate of interest $(r_{B'} < r_A)$ along the *IS* schedule (point *B'*). This inconsistency is because Y_B is a level of income that is in excess of equilibrium—one that cannot be maintained. At the equilibrium level of income (Y_A) the rate of interest (r_A) is consistent

FIGURE 3.6   Equilibrium in the Goods Market *(IS)* and Money Market *(LM)*

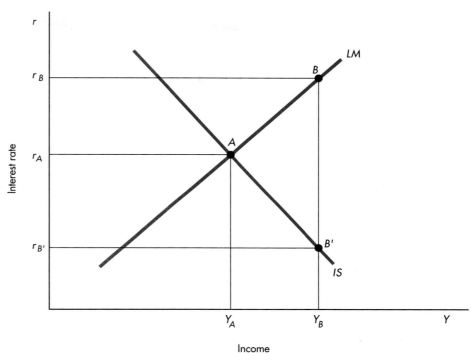

Income

Both goods and money markets are in equilibrium at point A. If income were Y_B then the interest rate consistent with money-market equilibrium (point B) is higher than the interest rate consistent with goods-market equilibrium (point B').

with equilibrium income in both the money market *(LM)* and the goods market *(IS)*.

WORKED EXAMPLE 3.4   Solving for Equilibrium with *IS* and *LM*

Combining consumption and investment demands into aggregate demand equal to income gives an *IS* schedule as shown in Chapter 2:

$$Y = C + I$$
$$C = 600 + 0.7Y$$
$$I = 250 + 0.1Y - 10r.$$

The *IS* schedule is:

$$r = 85 - 0.02Y.$$

The money-market relations in the previous worked examples were as follows:

$$M_s = M_d$$
$$M_d = 0.4Y - 80r$$
$$M_s = 1,200$$
$$1,200 = 0.4Y - 80r.$$

If we put the interest-rate term on the left-hand side and divide by 80, this gives the equation for the *LM* schedule:

$$r = 0.005Y - 15.$$

The point of intersection of *IS* and *LM* is found by solving for the level of income for which the interest rate is the same along both schedules:

$$85 - 0.02Y = 0.005Y - 15.$$

Collecting terms gives

$$0.025Y = 100$$
$$Y = 4,000.$$

We have found that both the goods market and the money market are in equilibrium at an income of $4 trillion. The equilibrium rate of interest can be found from substituting into either the *IS* or the *LM* schedule. (Do both as it gives a good check.) Either way, we find that the rate of interest is 5 percent.

If income were higher, the *LM* schedule would require a higher interest rate; then equilibrium in the goods market would require a lower rate of interest than 5 percent. Investment would need more of a stimulus to sustain a higher level of income. The *IS* schedule would require a lower interest rate at a higher level of income. But if income were higher, equilibrium in the money market would require a higher rate of interest. The higher income would increase the demand for money. Since the supply of money is fixed, the interest rate would rise. Hence the goods market and money market could not both be in equilibrium. The same holds true for any other combination of interest rate and income level.

The *IS* schedule gets its name from the simple condition that at all levels of equilibrium income, planned investment equals saving. The reason why *LM* is called *LM* is less clear. One explanation is that *M* stands for money supply and *L* for money demand—sometimes called liquidity preference. The *LM* schedule then shows when money supply and demand are equal.

The Tendency toward Equilibrium

The equilibrium point has economic meaning beyond being a lucky accident. When the economy is not at the equilibrium point, markets work so as to bring about changes in income and interest rates, which move the economy toward the equilibrium point. Since the conditions of supply and demand in some or all markets often change, the economy is not always in equilibrium.

FIGURE 3.7 Adjustment toward Equilibrium Following Money-Market Shift

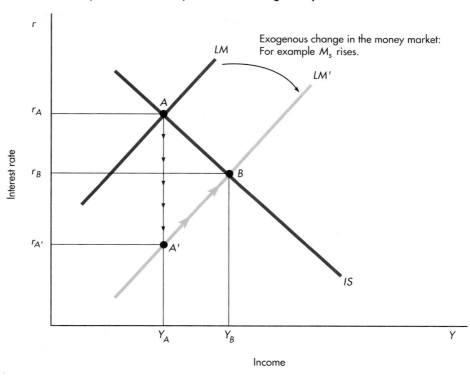

It may be moving from one equilibrium state to another. Further, markets do not adjust to change instantaneously or at the same rate of adjustment.

We illustrate how the economy adjusts to market forces in Figure 3.7. Initially the economy is in equilibrium at point A. The level of income Y_A and interest rate r_A result in both goods-market equilibrium (on the IS schedule) and money-market equilibrium (on the LM schedule).

To see how the economy adjusts, we suppose that there is a change in money-market conditions—for example, an increase in the supply of money. Following such a shift, there is an excess supply of money balances and money-market equilibrium will now take place only if the demand for money increases. In order to increase money demand, either the rate of interest falls or the level of income rises, or both. This implies in the figure that there has been an outward shift of the LM schedule (LM to LM'). Everywhere along the new LM schedule *(LM')*, money demand equals money supply at lower interest rates and/or higher incomes. At point A, the supply of goods and services equals the demand for goods and services, but the supply of money exceeds the demand for money. The goods market is in equilibrium but the money market is not—the economy is not in equilibrium. Households and firms are holding more money than they would like to hold given the level of the interest rate and income.

Are interest rates too high or is income too low at point A in Figure 3.7? In general the answer is both. The reactions to changes in market conditions occur simultaneously, with adjustments in one market feeding into and causing subsequent adjustments in other markets. However, some adjustments take place faster than others, and it will simplify our interpretation of the tendency toward equilibrium if we describe reactions as taking place in a particular sequence.[6] We can say that the first reaction in the economy will be that the interest rate will change. The money market adjusts to equilibrium rather quickly and the interest rate falls. The interest rate adjusts before income adjusts because it takes a lot less time for cash managers, reacting to excesses or insufficiencies of cash balances, to buy or sell bonds than it takes for production managers, reacting to excesses or insufficiencies of inventories, to decrease or increase production. Working with the overly simple assumption that money markets completely adjust before goods markets start to adjust, the fall of the interest rate continues (point A to point A' in Figure 3.7) until the money market is in equilibrium. (Point A' is on the new LM schedule, LM'.) With the interest rate $(r_{A'})$ this low, the goods market is not in equilibrium. (Point A' is not on the IS schedule.)

The adjustment of income to equilibrium is prompted by the reduction of the interest rate. When the interest rate fell, firms increased their expenditures on capital goods. Unplanned reductions in inventories begin to stimulate economywide increases in production. As production rises, so does income. The adjustment of income to equilibrium can be seen in Figure 3.7 as a movement of income, toward equilibrium income (point A' to point B).

Let's review where we are. First, cash managers wanted to hold less money than the available money supply—the interest rate was too high. The interest rate dropped and that stimulated capital-investment spending by firms. The rise in investment spending had a multiplier effect, so income began to rise. But as income rose (point A' to point B), cash managers wanted to hold more money to meet increased transactions needs. As the goods market adjusted to equilibrium with increases in production and income, the money market adjusted to the rising demand for money and the interest rate (which first fell) then rose part of the way back (from r_A to r_B).

Let us illustrate the adjustment to equilibrium with another example.

---

[6] These adjustment mechanisms have been a bit oversimplified. While there are certainly market forces driving the economy toward the equilibrium point, in practice there may be overshooting of the level of income as well as overshooting of the interest rate. Income in the economy often ends up moving back and forth around the equilibrium point. The adjustments around equilibrium will be discussed later in Chapter 13 when we look at economic fluctuations.

FIGURE 3.8 Adjustment toward Equilibrium Following Goods-Market Shift

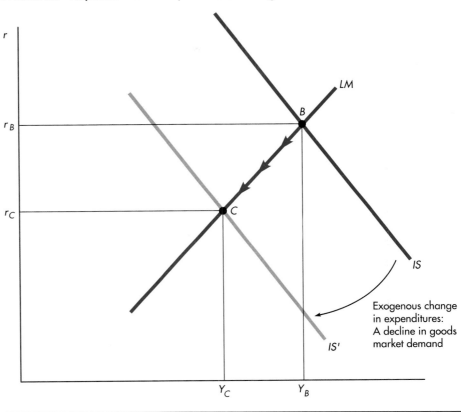

In Figure 3.8 the economy is described as being initially in equilibrium at point *B*. Then suppose that there is an exogenous reduction in the demand for goods and services—one not initiated by either a drop in income or a rise in the interest rate. Perhaps fears of a future economic downturn cause consumers and investors simply to decide to spend less out of current income. Aggregate demand then falls below aggregate supply. The multiplier process amplifies the initial decline in income. Excess inventories are piling up and firms are cutting back production. Output falls. This fall in income affects the money market, because the volume of transactions and hence the demand for money both decline. The lowering of income creates an excess supply of money that is quickly brought into equilibrium at a lower rate of interest. Through the multiplier, income continues to fall. Since the money market can adjust more quickly than the goods market, the money market remains in equilibrium with a smaller transaction demand for money being balanced by an increase in money demand brought on by lowered interest rates. The path to adjustment is along the *LM* schedule from point *B* to point *C*.

In contrast with the shift in the money market in Figure 3.7, where the interest rate first fell and then rose, here in Figure 3.8, where there was a shift in the goods market, the interest rate fell in conjunction with the fall in income.

Multiplier and interest-rate effects

When aggregate demand changes, the economy adjusts from one equilibrium to another and changes take place in both money markets and goods markets, thereby affecting both income and the interest rate. This is a different description of the impact of changes in aggregate demand from that set out in the multiplier process. In the description of the multiplier process, the rate of interest was taken as given.

multiplier effect
The change in income that would occur following a shift in the *IS* schedule if there were no change in the rate of interest.

It is useful to think of the effect on equilibrium income of the adjustment from one equilibrium to another following a shift in the *IS* schedule as being comprised of (1) a **multiplier effect,** where changes in income result from shifts in money markets and goods markets with no change in the interest rate and (2) an **interest-rate effect,** following a shift in conditions in the goods market. The interest rate effect is the change in income resulting from the change in the rate of interest.

interest rate effect
Following a shift in conditions in the goods market, the interest rate effect is the change in income resulting from the change in the rate of interest.

We illustrate the multiplier and interest-rate effects in Figure 3.9. An increase in aggregate demand has occurred due to an exogenous increase in demand in the goods market. The impact of this increase in demand on equilibrium in the goods market is shown as an outward shift in the *IS* schedule (*IS* to *IS'*). If the rate of interest had not changed, then income would rise by the initial exogenous increase in expenditures times the multiplier, which is the full amount of the shift in the *IS* schedule—from point *A* to point *A'*. This shift (Y_A to $Y_{A'}$) is the multiplier effect. In addition, in the absence of any other exogenous change, the increase in income will drive up the demand for money, resulting in a higher rate of interest (r_A to r_B). The higher rate of interest reduces the level of expenditure on investment goods below what it would be with no rise in the interest rate. Equilibrium takes place in the goods market at a lower level of income and production because of the higher interest rate. This reduction in income ($Y_{A'}$ to Y_B from point *A'* to point *B'*) is the interest-rate effect.

This concludes our introduction to the money market and to *IS-LM* analysis. We began our description of the economy in Chapter 2 by saying that, in the short run, changes in aggregate demand account for changes in the level of income. This idea still holds, but the analysis in this chapter has become more complex. We have to look to interest rates and money markets as well as goods markets in order to describe the state of aggregate demand. The determination of the interest rate was found in the money market, but the money market was also affected by the level of income.

FIGURE 3.9   The Multiplier and Interest-Rate Effects

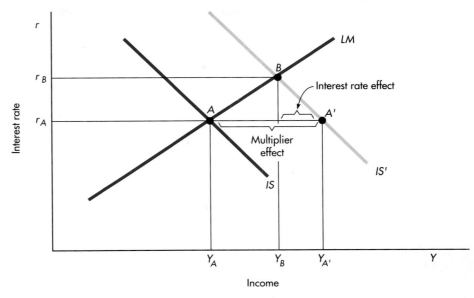

Adjustment to equilibrium takes place through the interaction of the multiplier with changes in the interest rate. The change in income at the initial rate of interest with no change in the interest rate is the multiplier effect. The reaction of income to changes in the interest rates is the interest-rate effect.

In the next two chapters, we will use the *IS-LM* model to see how the government can stimulate or retard aggregate demand, thus affecting the level of income and interest rates. When the government changes its level of expenditures or taxation, aggregate demand will change and we will see the effect of that policy change in a movement of the *IS* schedule. When the Fed changes the amount of money supplied to the economy, equilibrium will change in the money market and we will see the effect of that policy change in a movement of the *LM* schedule.

SUMMARY

- The demand for money is derived from the services provided by money. Money facilitates *transactions* and avoids the need for barter.
- Money serves as *a medium of exchange.* Since transactions increase with income, the demand for money increases along with increases in income.

- Money serves as a *store of value*. When the interest rate that can be earned on other financial assets goes up, the demand for holding money goes down. The demand for money will decrease along with increases in the interest rate.

- Since money is a financial asset, families have to decide on the proportions of assets in their portfolios. When people or firms decide how to allocate assets in a portfolio, they are making a *portfolio choice*. The decision about how much money to hold represents a part of the overall portfolio choice.

- Money consists of currency, coin, and any bank account or other financial asset that allows for the writing of checks. There is no ideal definition of money in practice. The M1 and M2 definitions of money are both useful. There are also extended definitions of money.

- The money supply is controlled by the banking system and the Federal Reserve. We take the money supply as fixed exogenously by the Fed. If the amount of money demanded exceeds the amount of money available, there will be an overall excess demand for money balances. The interest rate will rise until cash managers want to hold the amount of money that is available.

- The combinations of income and interest rates where money demand equals money supply are described along the *LM schedule*. Because higher levels of income increase the demand for money, higher levels of income are associated with higher levels of the interest rate. The *LM* schedule slopes up to the right.

- The point of intersection of the *IS* and *LM* schedules is the one combination of interest rate and income common to both schedules. This is the point where both the goods market and the money market are in equilibrium.

- If there is a shift in either the *IS* or the *LM* schedule, there will be an adjustment process. The money market adjusts more quickly than the goods market. We discuss the case where the money market is always in equilibrium and the goods market responds over time to changes in the interest rate. Investment demand changes and this has a multiplied effect on income.

- The change in income that results from an exogenous shift in expenditure (a shift in the *IS* schedule) can be described as consisting of *a multiplier effect* (the change in income that would occur if there were no change in the interest rate) and an *interest-rate effect* (the change in income due to the change in the interest rate).

KEY TERMS

barter	liability
bond	*LM* schedule
cash management	medium of exchange
currency	money
demand deposits	money market
financial asset	multiplier effect
interest-rate effect	portfolio

portfolio choice   velocity of money

stocks   wealth

transaction

DISCUSSION QUESTIONS AND PROBLEMS

1. Along the *IS* schedule, when interest rates decline, equilibrium income rises. Why is this? Describe a circumstance when lower interest rates would not necessarily result in higher income?

2. If the introduction of credit cards reduces the amount of money that people hold in order to make a given volume of transactions, how would this affect the *LM* schedule? How would it change the level of income in the economy?

3. Cash managers economize on money balances as the interest rate rises. Is there a limit on this process or could the velocity of money rise indefinitely?

4. When the demand for money exceeds the supply, what restores money-market equilibrium in the short run (before there is any change in income)? What happens to the interest rate as income changes?

5. Along the *IS* schedule, higher incomes are associated with lower interest rates, while along the *LM* schedule, higher incomes are associated with higher interest rates. If income increases, do interest rates rise or fall?

6. Describe the path of income and interest rates as the economy adjusts from one equilibrium to another following a shift in the *IS* schedule. Separate the change in income into the multiplier effect and the interest-rate effect.

7. Consider the following money-demand relation.

   $$M_d = 0.6Y - 120r \qquad \text{(Money Demand)}$$

   a. What is the demand for money when income is $4 trillion ($Y = 4,000$) and the interest rate is 5 percent ($r = 5$)?

   b. What is the velocity of money?

   c. What is the velocity of money when the interest rate is 10 percent? 2 percent?

   d. Does the velocity of money rise or fall when income increases with a constant rate of interest?

   e. Suppose that the supply of money is $2.196 trillion ($M_s = 2,196$) and income is $4 trillion ($Y = 4,000$). What is the rate of interest in money-market equilibrium?

   f. Suppose that the supply of money is $1.44 trillion ($M_s = 1,440$) and income is $4 trillion ($Y = 4,000$). What is the rate of interest?

8. Consider now an *IS-LM* model. The money supply is fixed and the interest rate is determined in the model. The economy is now described by the following equations:

$C = 950 + 0.65Y$	(Consumption)
$I = 350 + 0.1Y - 20r$	(Investment)
$M_d = 0.6Y - 120r$	(Money Demand)
$M_s = 2,196$	(Money Supply)

a. What is the equation that describes the *IS* schedule?
b. What is the slope of this *IS* schedule? What does the slope of the *IS* schedule show?
c. What is the equation that describes the *LM* schedule (Hint: 2,196 = 12 × 183)?
d. The equilibrium level of income is 4,760 and the equilibrium interest rate is 5.5 percent. Show how these values are obtained.

■ APPENDIX 3A
Algebraic Treatment of IS and LM

We derived the *IS* schedule in the appendix to Chapter 2. Recall what we found. We used linear relationships for the consumption and investment functions:

$$C = C_0 + C_1 Y$$
$$I = I_0 + I_1 Y - I_2 r.$$

We then solved for goods-market equilibrium:

$$r = \frac{C_0 + I_0}{I_2} - \left[\frac{1 - (C_1 + I_1)}{I_2}\right] Y.$$

This equation is the *IS* schedule. We now have schedules for money demand and supply:

$$M_d = kY - hr;$$
M_s is fixed by the Fed.

Setting money demand equal to money supply leads to the *LM* schedule:

$$M_s = M_d = kY - hr.$$

Solving for *r* gives

$$r = \left(\frac{k}{h}\right) Y - \frac{M_s}{h}.$$

This relation is the *LM* schedule. The equilibrium level of income in the economy is then found by setting the interest rates to be equal. This gives the point of intersection of *IS* and *LM*:

$$\frac{C_0 + I_0}{I_2} - \left[\frac{1 - (C_1 + I_1)}{I_2}\right] Y = \left(\frac{k}{h}\right) Y - \frac{M_s}{h}.$$

This can be solved for the equilibrium value of *Y*, which can then be substituted back into the *LM* or the *IS* schedules to find the equilibrium value of *r*. To try and present the algebraic expressions more simply, we define two terms that we just call *A* and *B*:

$$A = \frac{C_0 + I_0}{I_2} + \frac{M_s}{h}$$

$$B = \frac{1 - (C_1 + I_1)}{I_2} + \frac{k}{h}.$$

Then equilibrium income is just equal to $A \div B$. And substituting the resulting value for income back into the LM schedule is the simplest way to get the equilibrium interest rate, r.

We can look at the expressions for A and B and see how changes in economic behavior represented by changes in the terms in A and B, will raise and lower equilibrium income. Increases in autonomous expenditures, $(C_0 + I_0)$, will certainly raise income. So will increases in the money supply.

Increases in the multiplier, $1 \div [1 - (C_1 + I_1)]$, will lower B and hence will also raise equilibrium income. Increases in k mean that there is more demand for money for transactions, with any given level of income. With a given supply of money, this will push up interest rates and hence lower equilibrium income.

Changes in the interest-responsiveness parameters, I_2 and h, have ambiguous effects. They affect both A and B. Changes in these parameters will change the slopes of both the IS and the LM schedules and have offsetting overall effects. If either h or I_2 goes to zero, the analysis will have to be redone.

■ **APPENDIX 3B**
Disequilibrium, Excess Supply, and Excess Demand

In this chapter, we looked at how the economy would adjust when it started away from equilibrium. We argued that whenever the economy is in disequilibrium it will move toward equilibrium. But we used a very simplified assumption, namely that the money market moves immediately into equilibrium. Now we will look at the adjustment process a bit more generally.

Any equilibrium point is surrounded by areas of disequilibrium where goods and money markets are both in either excess supply or excess demand. In the money market, excess supply leads to lower interest rates, which increase money demand. Excess money demand, on the other hand, leads to higher interest rates, which reduce money demand. In the goods market, excess supply leads to a decrease in production, which then has a feedback effect of reducing demand, but eventually equilibrium is reached at a lower level of income. Finally, in the goods market, excess demand leads to a production increase, which via the multiplier leads to yet higher demand and production, until equilibrium is reached at a higher level of income. In Figure 3B.1 and the accompanying Table 3B.1, the four sectors of *IS-LM* disequilibrium are separately indicated by roman numerals I–IV.

Table 3B.1 shows conditions of excess supply and demand and the initial tendency toward changes in the interest rate and income in each sector. For example, in sector I (point A, at Y_A, in the figure), there is an excess supply of both money and goods.

FIGURE 3B.1   Adjustment to Equilibrium

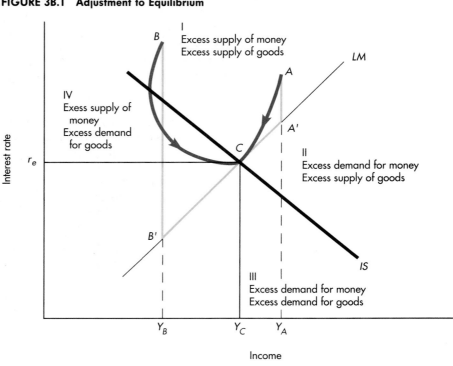

TABLE 3B.1   Disequilibrium and Adjustment in the *IS-LM* Framework

| Sector | Money market | Initial tendency for change | | Goods market |
		Interest rates	Income	
I	Excess supply of money	Down	Down	Excess supply of goods
II	Excess demand for money	Up	Down	Excess supply of goods
III	Excess demand for money	Up	Up	Excess demand for goods
IV	Excess supply of money	Down	Up	Excess demand for goods

The tendency in the money market is to drive down interest rates (point A to A') and the tendency in the goods market is to lower income (Y_A down to Y_C, point A' to point C). As we said earlier, the drop in the interest rate will occur more quickly than the fall in income, but both will be occurring together. This is shown by the curve between point A and point C in the figure.

The adjustment to equilibrium may also take the economy out of one sector and into another sector, where the subsequent tendency toward equilibrium of income and the interest rate will be different from the initial tendency. In Figure 3B.1, when the economy is out of equilibrium as described by point B (Y_B) in sector I, the initial tendency is for a falling interest rate with falling income, the same as at point A, as a result of excess supply in both money market and goods market. However, the rapid adjustment of the money market takes the economy through sector IV to money-market equilibrium at point B'. In the figure at point B', the interest rate is below equilibrium and there is an excess demand for goods and services. In contrast with the case at point A, income rises (Y_B up to Y_E). The rise in income triggers an increased demand for money balances and the interest rate reverses direction (point B' to point C) as the goods market comes into equilibrium along the LM schedule. As in the case that started with point A, the separation of effects is an exaggeration. The initial downward tendency of both income and interest rate followed by a rise in both is shown by the curve between points B and C in the figure.

PART III

The Role of Government in Determining Equilibrium through Monetary and Fiscal Policies

The model of the economy we have described in Part II included only private sector decision makers. Consumers and firms, seeking their own best economic interests, made separate decisions concerning the amount of income they would spend on a variety of goods and services. When the sum of these separate expenditures equaled the amount of goods and services produced and supplied in the economy, the economy had reached an equilibrium level of income.

The government also makes separate expenditure decisions. It purchases a significant fraction of total goods and services. Its expenditure decisions are motivated differently than those of households or businesses, which means we have to include government expenditures separately in aggregate demand. In order to pay for its expenditures, the government collects taxes and borrows from the private sector. The government also has to decide how much tax revenue to raise and how much to borrow.

As well as taxation and expenditure decisions, the government also has control over the amount of money in the economy. Decisions that the government makes about the supply of money have a major impact on the level of demand coming from the private sector.

Fiscal policies describe the means by which government acquires revenue and the amount and type of expenditures it undertakes. Monetary policies describe the government's control of the money supply and the banking system, mostly done through the purchases and sale of financial assets by the central bank. An understanding of how both fiscal and monetary policies affect the economy is essential to an understanding of economic performance. These policies can help offset recessions, but they can also do serious harm to the economy. We will argue in Chapter 4 that the federal budget deficit has been the main cause of the serious U.S. trade deficit.

CHAPTER 4

The Government and Aggregate Demand
Fiscal Policy, Budgets, and the Interest Rate

INTRODUCTION

government purchases of goods and services
The goods and services that the government buys from the private sector plus the salaries of government employees.

The size of **government purchases of goods and services** (including purchases by state, local, and federal agencies) measures the direct impact of the government on aggregate demand. In 1989 total government purchases were 19.5 percent of GNP. Of this total, about 42 percent represented federal purchases and the remaining 58 percent were state and local purchases. Government purchases include the salaries of government employees; this part is counted as government production—the government buys this production from itself. The remaining portion of government purchases (over 80 percent) consists of goods and services that the government buys from the private sector, everything from office-building rentals to missiles, school supplies, and computers.

Government purchases of goods and services were 2.6 percent of GNP in 1929 but rose to over 40 percent of GNP during World War II (totaling 57 percent of GNP in 1944 during the height of the war). Military expenditures fell at the end of the war, so that in 1947 government demand was only 17 percent of GNP. The Cold War and the growth of various federal programs pushed the percentage up again, so that by 1955 government demand was 24 percent of GNP. This percentage has varied since then but fell during the 1980s, down to 19.5 percent of GNP by 1989.

government expenditures or outlays
The government's purchases of goods and services plus transfer payments and interest on government debts.

Total **government expenditures or outlays** exceed government purchases of goods and services because the federal, state, and local governments all allocate transfer payments to be paid to people and institutions. Transfer

136

payments include such things as social-security retirement and disability payments, unemployment insurance, agricultural subsidies, and interest on the government's debts. In 1989, total federal-government expenditures were about three times the size of federal purchases of goods and services. Transfer payments (including interest on the national debt) make up the largest part of federal spending. However, transfer payments are a relatively small portion of state and local expenditures, which exceed the purchases of goods and services by only about 11 percent. States and localities devote their budgets primarily to providing goods and services. During the 1980s, total government expenditures remained a fairly constant share of GNP. Total state, local, and federal outlays were equal to just over 36 percent of GNP in 1989.

The government finances its expenditures by raising revenues, including direct taxes (such as federal and state income taxes) and indirect taxes (such as property taxes and sales taxes). In the 1980s there was an increase in the budget deficit (the gap between government receipts and government expenditures or outlays), which grew from 1.3 percent of GNP in 1980 to 3.4 percent of GNP in 1986. The deficit has fallen since then, to 1.9 percent of GNP in 1989. These deficits have been incurred by the federal government (a $207 billion deficit in 1986 in current dollars), with small surpluses by state and local governments partially offsetting the federal deficit. The large federal deficit has been financed by issuing federal-government bonds (Treasury bills and bonds).

The role of government in the economy is sufficiently large and different from the private sector's role so as to require our treating the government as a separate element of the economy. In this chapter we focus primarily on the fiscal policies of government. Fiscal policies describe the means by which government gets revenue and distributes transfer payments, and the amount and kinds of goods and services that the government purchases in the economy. We want to see how the government's fiscal decisions about the total amount of expenditures and taxation affect aggregate demand.

The *IS-LM* framework that we developed in Chapters 2 and 3 included only private-sector decision makers. Consumers and firms pursued their own best economic interests. They made separate decisions concerning the amount of income they would spend on a variety of goods and services and the amount of money they would hold at any level of income and interest rate. These separate expenditure and financial decisions generated an equilibrium level of income and interest rate.

In this chapter we add the expenditure decisions and taxation policies of government to our description of the determination of income and the interest rate. We include government purchases as part of aggregate demand and we see how taxes and transfer payments affect the income people have to spend.

This treatment of the role of the government ignores some aspects of government economic actions. For example, regulatory policies and standards alter economic behavior by requiring the compliance of firms and individuals.

The most important part of government policy that we are either going to ignore or going to treat in a very simple way in this chapter is monetary policy. Through the actions of their monetary authorities (the Fed in the United States), governments affect the supply of money in the economy. In this chapter we look at money-market conditions only to the extent that they alter the effectiveness of **fiscal policy.** But before we look at how fiscal policy affects aggregate demand, we should look at what goods and services the government is buying and why.

fiscal policy
Government actions concerning tax revenues, transfers, and the amount of government purchases.

WHAT IS THE GOVERNMENT BUYING AND WHY?

State and local governments provide the basic public services such as schools, roads, and public libraries. They also provide some public-welfare programs. Figure 4.1 shows how the state and local expenditure pie was divided in Fiscal Years 1965–66 and 1986–87. Over the intervening two decades, expenditures on education first rose and then fell, trends that have reflected the increased student population during the baby-boom years and the fall in the number of students in recent years. Public welfare has risen in relative importance over the period.

The composition of federal expenditures is shown in more detail for the 1980s in Table 4.1. We can see that during the 1980s, the federal government's expenditures on defense and interest on past debt had the most growth in their share of total expenditures, while education, energy, natural resources, agriculture, income security, transportation, VA benefits, and other expenditures had reductions in their shares. Defense expenditures rose as a result of the Reagan administration's commitment to strengthen the military. Military spending may fall in the 1990s with the reduction in cold war tensions. The rise in the share of expenditure going to pay interest came about because of the large budget deficits.

The composition of government expenditures is a tangible representation of how our democracy regards the relative importance of competing needs and programs. The rise and fall of the shares of different parts of the budget represent the rise and fall of the priorities attached to activities being funded. Sometimes our political process works well, bringing about changes in expenditures that mirror changes in social priorities. Sometimes expenditure decisions reflect a politician's wish to be reelected and/or the pressures applied by special interests. When expenditure decisions can avoid inappropriate political pressures, there are three main rationales for government expenditures: the provision of public goods, support for the needy, and the provision of merit goods.

Public Goods, Income Distribution, and Merit Goods

There are certain goods called **public goods** that have a special claim to be provided by the government. Public goods are consumed in common and have two key properties: *nonexcludability* and *nonrivalry*. Not all public goods

FIGURE 4.1   State and Local Government Expenditures by Function, 1966 and 1987

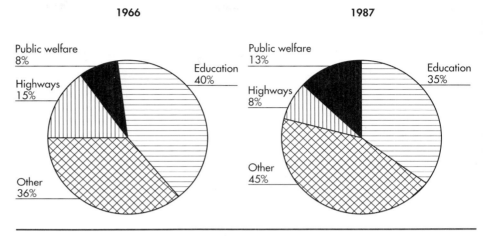

Note: "Other" includes expenditures for libraries, hospitals, health, employment security administration, veterans services, air transportation, water transport and terminals, parking facilities, transit subsidies, police protection, fire protection, correction, protective inspection and regulation, sewerage, natural resources, parks and recreation, housing and community development, sanitation other than sewerage, financial administration, judicial and legal services, general public buildings, other governmental administration, interest on general debt, and general expenditures, not elsewhere classified.
Source: National Income and Product Accounts.

public goods
Goods and services that to some extent have the properties of nonrivalry and nonexcludability.

have both of these properties to the same extent, but one clear example of a public good is national defense. Individuals within the same country cannot be excluded from the benefits of the defense being provided for the country as a whole. And the amount of defense provided to one citizen does not subtract from the defense provided to other citizens. Other public goods include public-health expenditures and scientific research.

Free markets work best for private, individually consumed goods and services. They do not work well for public goods, particularly because of the problem of nonexcludability. If people benefit from their consumption of national defense irrespective of the amount they buy individually, it is unlikely that they will voluntarily pay for military services. If national defense were privately supplied and if only a very few were willing to contribute to its purchase, then too little would be supplied. Through the public provision of national defense we all contribute to its provision at a level that is determined socially.

Another major purpose for government expenditures is to provide income support for those in a society who are judged to be needy and deserving of public consideration: the elderly, the disabled, and others unable to support themselves. Leaving aside the intense debate over exactly which groups belong in this category and what the level of support should be, these social

TABLE 4.1   Federal Government Expenditures, Fiscal Years 1980, 1984, 1988
(billions of current-year dollars)

	1980		1984		1988	
	Bil$	%	Bil$	%	Bil$	%
Defense	134	23%	227	27%	290	27%
Health and Medicare	55	9	88	10	123	12
Education and training	32	5	28	3	32	3
Energy, natural resources, and agriculture	33	6	33	4	34	3
Transportation	21	4	24	3	27	3
Income security	87	15	113	13	129	12
Social security	119	20	178	21	219	21
VA benefits	21	4	26	3	29	3
Net interest	53	9	111	13	152	14
Other expenditures[a]	57	10	56	7	66	6
Total outlay of funds	591	100%	852	100%	1,064	100%

Note: Categories include both purchases of goods and services and transfer payments. The federal fiscal year starts in October, so that, for example, Fiscal Year 1989 runs from October 1, 1988, to September 30, 1989. Undistributed offsetting receipts are omitted.

Dollar values shown are current dollars with no inflation adjustment.

[a] Includes international affairs, science, space, technology, commerce and housing credit, regional development, and governmental administrative costs.

Source: *Historical Tables Budget of the U.S. Government,* U.S. Department of Commerce.

transfers are an important part of the mission of government, and these programs have become a large part of the federal budget.

Some public expenditures are for goods that are neither public goods nor for the needy, but they are still considered to have merit—these are *merit goods*. For instance, a small part of government expenditure helps support public libraries and art galleries. A major part of government spending goes for education, which is justified partly as a help to children who lack their own resources, partly because education is a public investment in future productivity, and partly because of what is seen as the intrinsic merit of education.

The process of deciding which goods have special merit and which do not is prone to abuse and partisanship. Unfortunately, not all goods and services purchased by government are really public goods, transfers to the needy, or merit goods. In some cases public funds are used to serve narrow private interests. Most of us oppose pork-barrel projects that benefit special interests, although we often disagree on what these are. Citizens are also

■ The Dilemma of Choosing among Competing Public Goods: Hospitals and Health Services

The Veterans Administration is considering building a new hospital and locating it in a small town in the Midwest. The citizens of the town are understandably happy. The chamber of commerce of the town is excited about the prospect when contemplating the economic effects of the construction and the salaries paid to physicians and staff. There are three other communities in the state who are less than pleased because they were bypassed. The local American Legion is supportive. While the state and local Vietnam veterans organizations support VA hospitals, they want the VA to set up a counseling service and outreach program, statewide. If forced to choose, the Vietnam vets prefer a delay on the hospital and immediate progress on the outreach program. The existing local hospitals, both private and public, are convinced that the additional beds provided by the VA would produce excess capacity in the region and lead to cost inefficiencies. A collection of Congresspeople from the East and West are dubious about the VA's plans, since they see little benefit from the location decision and they have important public-health projects pending in their communities.

A recent study from a health-research agency indicates that trauma centers are more effective in prolonging longevity than full-service hospitals and another study shows that in spite of a huge 11 percent of the federal budget being spent on health care in the United States, public health services are inadequate. Finally, the Veterans Administration is justifiably concerned with the increasingly difficult health problems of an aging group of veterans at the same time that VA critics argue that there is enough waste in the VA bureaucracy to pay for all the health-care needs of veterans for the next two decades. Should the hospital be built and, if so, how big should it be, what services should it provide, and how much money should be spent?

Perhaps surprisingly, macroeconomics does not attempt to answer questions such as this, because the decision, *on average*, does not affect the overall performance of the economy! Of course it makes a difference whether or not the government is effective and efficient in its choices, and as citizens we should not be complacent about the inadequacies of government expenditure programs, but as economists, we have to expect that from one year to the next, the proportion of waste and error associated with any level of government expenditure is constant.

prone to put aside their objections to special-interest projects when the project in question benefits them or their neighbors. Many people argue that government expenditures are too large, but the issue of exactly which government expenditures should be made is fraught with conflict and self-interest.

We cannot, unfortunately, model the conflicts and self-interests that go into the determination of government spending decisions, and so we are forced to make a simplifying assumption about how government purchases of goods and services are determined as we study their aggregate-demand effects. We will assume that *government purchases of goods and services*, G, *are part of autonomous expenditure.* We assume that the size of G is fixed by policy.

Government can generate a good deal of conflict when it raises taxes to pay for its outlays just as it can stir up controversy through its spending decisions. We turn next to look at taxes and transfer payments.

TAXES, TRANSFERS, AND THE TAX FUNCTION

The government takes away part of the income of individuals and corporations in the form of taxes and it contributes to the income of individuals and organizations in the form of transfer payments. By the amount of tax that households and institutions pay, the government affects private spending decisions and hence affects aggregate demand.

Gross and Net Tax Revenues

Taxes are levied to pay for government expenditures. Tax revenues are overwhelmingly the largest source (over 90 percent) of the funds used by the government to pay for its spending. Yet, because the federal government can spend in excess of, or less than, the amount collected from tax revenues, we will assume that *taxes are determined separately from expenditures.* The government can and often does run budget deficits and it has at times run surpluses.

The federal income tax, levied on households and corporations, generates the largest share of total tax revenue. Payroll taxes (such as the taxes used to support social security or unemployment compensation), sales taxes, state and local income taxes, and property taxes account for most of the rest of tax revenue. The total of all tax revenue collected by all forms of government is **gross tax revenue** (T_g). Table 4.2 shows the major categories of federal tax receipts. As in Table 4.1, the figures are current dollar values and the years are fiscal years.

gross tax revenue
The total of all tax revenue collected by all forms of government.

In recent times the major change in the sources of tax revenues has been a decline in income taxes and a rise in payroll taxes. In the late 1970s and continuing through the 1980s, federal taxation of individual and corporate incomes fell as percentages of total federal tax revenue. During the same period, contributions for social security increased. Tax reform in 1986 lowered individual income taxes and raised the share of revenue coming from the corporate income tax. Because many corporate deductions were eliminated, corporate taxes rose even though the tax rate on corporate income fell from 46 percent to 34 percent. By 1988, the share of tax paid out of individual income had continued to decline, but the share from corporate income tax had risen again, although not back to its 1980 share.

Transfer payments

transfer payments
Income payments made by the government to households and institutions. Interest payments on the debt are included in transfers.

The government pays out money to the private sector in the form of **transfer payments** (T_p). The decision to allocate these transfer payments is made as part of the budgetary process, and the payments are part of total government expenditures. However, *transfer payments affect aggregate demand differently than government purchases of goods and services. Transfers are an addition to the income of the recipient rather than a direct part of aggregate demand.* In public discussions surrounding a government budget, there is usually a commingling of transfers and purchases of goods and services. In the newspaper you might find trans-

TABLE 4.2   Federal Government's Gross Tax Revenues, Fiscal Years 1980, 1984, 1988
(billions of current-year dollars)

	1980		1984		1988	
	Bil$	%	Bil$	%	Bil$	%
Individual income tax	244	47%	298	45%	401	44%
Corporate income tax	65	13	57	9	95	10
Social insurance taxes and contributions	158	31	239	36	334	37
Excise tax	24	5	37	6	35	4
Other[a]	26	5	34	5	44	5
Gross tax revenue *(Tg)*	517	100%	666	100%	909	100%

[a] Includes estate tax, gift tax, customs, and miscellaneous receipts.
Source: *Historical Tables Budget of the U.S. Government,* U.S. Department of Commerce.

fers and government purchases mixed together in a discussion of whether we can afford high levels of both defense spending (purchases) and social-security payments (transfers). In the analysis of aggregate demand, income, and output, we cannot mix these two together. How a transfer is spent and on what it is spent are determined by the recipient of the transfer and not by the government. We will treat transfer payments as an offset to gross tax revenues. They are negative taxes since, in total, the net amount we all pay to the government is equal to our tax payments minus the transfers that the government gives back to us.

Taxes and Income

net tax revenue
The total or gross tax revenue collected by the government minus transfer payments (including interest on the debt).

The government takes away income in the form of gross tax revenue (T_g) and adds to income the amount paid out as transfer payments (T_p). **Net tax revenue** (T) is the difference between these two, gross tax receipts minus transfers $(T = T_g - T_p)$. Increases or decreases in net tax revenues have an impact on private expenditure decisions. However, the size of net tax revenues is related to the level of income.

Both components of net tax revenue (gross tax revenue, T_g, and transfer payments, T_p) have predictable relationships to the level of national income. During good economic conditions when national income is relatively high, there are more people employed, wages per employee are higher, and business profits are higher. Since income taxes and payroll taxes are collected as percentages of wages, salaries, and profits, *when income is high, gross tax revenues are high.* For transfer payments, when income and employment are high, unemployment is low, so that unemployment-insurance payments are low. When employment opportunities are good, people decide to delay retirement, so that social-security retirement payments are reduced. In addition, a smaller portion of the population applies for welfare, so welfare payments are lower. *When income is high, transfer payments are low.* The relationships between gross tax revenues and income and between transfer payments and income work together, so that *net tax revenues rise when income rises and fall when income falls.*

The tax function

Equation 4.1 describes the relationship between net tax revenues and income via a *tax function*. The tax function is analogous to the consumption and investment functions we have already described:

$$T = T_0 + T_1Y. \tag{4.1}$$

This tax function is an economic description of how net tax revenues vary with income. Some taxes (for example, property taxes) do not vary with income. The tax function reflects this in its first term (T_0), the autonomous part of tax revenue, which is unconnected to income. Most taxes, such as income and payroll taxes, do vary with income and so do transfers. This is reflected in the second term (T_1Y). The constant slope (T_1) is also called the **marginal propensity to tax** or MPT and it says that marginal tax receipts rise as a constant fraction of income (Y). Every additional dollar of income generates a fraction of a dollar (T_1) of additional tax revenue.

marginal propensity to tax
The change in net tax revenue resulting from a change in income.

The U.S. federal tax code is written with tax brackets that increase with income. The size and number of brackets have changed over time. There have been as few as 3 brackets and as many as 12 brackets with taxes that ranged from 10 percent to 94 percent of taxable income. In spite of this changing structure, studies of actual taxes paid indicate that taxes rise proportionally with income. It is estimated that in 1988, except for the very poorest families, most households paid between 22 and 25 percent of their income in federal, state, and local taxes.[1] A tax function with a constant MPT, such as the one we use, is an adequate approximation of the actual tax structure in the U.S. economy.

Disposable income

The amount of income available for people to spend and save is the amount left over after transfers are added to income and gross tax receipts are subtracted from income. This net level of income is called **disposable income** (Y_d):

disposable income
Income plus transfers minus gross tax receipts.

$$Y_d = Y - T_g + T_p = Y - T. \tag{4.2}$$

---

[1] Joseph A. Pechman, "The Future of the Income Tax," *American Economic Review* 80, no. 1 (March 1990), pp. 1–20; and Pechman, *Who Paid the Taxes, 1966–84?* (Washington, D.C.: Brookings Institution, 1985).

Disposable income (Y_d) is just total income (Y) less net tax payments (T).[2] When taxes are collected, *consumption expenditures are determined by the level of disposable income, not by the level of total income.* Because aggregate demand is affected directly by government expenditures and indirectly by net taxes through changes in consumption expenditures, we need to rework our description of goods-market equilibrium to account for the roles of government expenditures and net taxes.

GOODS-MARKET EQUILIBRIUM WITH TAXES AND GOVERNMENT SPENDING

We can now incorporate taxes and government spending into the *IS-LM* framework. We start by reworking the *IS* schedule. Including government purchases *(G)* in aggregate demand changes the condition for goods-market equilibrium. Aggregate demand now includes consumption demand, investment demand, and government demand—which is equal to government purchases of goods and services and fixed by policy. The condition for goods-market equilibrium is

$$Y = C + I + G. \tag{4.3}$$

Government adds to demand through its purchases of goods and services, but it also reduces private consumption demand through its taxation. Since disposable income is the portion of income consumers are free to either spend or save (that is, dispose of), the consumption function has to be changed so that *consumption depends on disposable income:*

$$C = C_0 + C_1 Y_d \quad \text{or} \quad C = C_0 + C_1(Y - T). \tag{4.4}$$

We will assume that the inclusion of government does not change investment demand or its relation to income and the interest rate, so that the investment function remains as described in Chapter 2, rewritten here as

$$I = I_0 + I_1 Y - I_2 r. \tag{4.5}$$

We now replace the terms for consumption and investment expenditure *(C* and *I* in Equation 4.3) with the expressions for consumption demand (Equation 4.4) and investment demand (Equation 4.5). We add the autonomous level of government demand *(G)* to aggregate demand and the result is a new equilibrium condition. We show the substitutions that lead to the equilibrium condition in steps. First,

$$Y = C_0 + C_1 Y_d + I_0 + I_1 Y - I_2 r + G.$$

---

[2] In the National Income and Product Accounts disposable income excludes the profit income that businesses retain. We do not follow this procedure; instead we assign all profit income to the owners of the businesses because the income belongs to the owners and they take it into account when deciding how much to consume and how much to save.

Then, since disposable income is equal to total income minus net tax revenue,

$$Y = C_0 + C_1(Y - T) + I_0 + I_1Y - I_2r + G.$$

The one remaining substitution replaces net tax revenues (T) with the tax function, so that the result of these substitutions of functions for expenditures and revenues is the condition for goods-market equilibrium:

$$Y = C_0 + C_1[Y - (T_0 + T_1Y)] + I_0 + I_1Y - I_2r + G. \tag{4.6}$$

Equation 4.6 can be rearranged to give an *IS* schedule, the combinations of income and the interest rate for which there is goods-market equilibrium. The steps involved in doing this are given in the appendix to this chapter. The resulting *IS* schedule is

$$r = \frac{(C_0 + I_0 + G - C_1T_0)}{I_2} - \frac{\{1 - [C_1(1 - T_1) + I_1]\}Y}{I_2}. \tag{4.7}$$

This is a complex expression that is not easy to interpret and you should not try to memorize it. The appendix looks at this algebraic expression and shows how fiscal-policy variables (government spending and taxes) have affected both the position and the slope of the *IS* schedule. As an alternative to the algebra, we give here a numerical example (Worked Example 4.1) to show the effect of introducing government. The example shows that the *IS* schedule has become steeper because part of any increase in income that is stimulated by a fall in the interest rate and an increase in investment will go to the government in the form of higher taxes. The *IS* schedule will also move to the right as a result of introducing government purchases, which add to aggregate demand.[3]

WORKED EXAMPLE 4.1   Finding the *IS* Schedule with Taxes and Government Purchases of Goods and Services

We use the same investment function that appeared in earlier worked examples, but *we have changed the consumption function.*[4] Consumption now depends upon disposable income and we have set autonomous consumption at $80 billion, much lower than in the earlier worked examples.

$C = 80 + 0.7Y_d$
$I = 250 + 0.1Y - 10r.$

There is a tax function as follows:

$T = 300 + 0.2Y.$

---

[3] Autonomous taxes (T_0) shift the *IS* to the left, but they are smaller than government purchases and have a smaller effect on demand, so that the effect of adding G predominates.

[4] The numbers used in these examples for marginal propensities and multipliers are illustrative only. Actual estimates vary over a considerable range and in many cases are smaller or larger than those used here.

We assume that there is $1,290 billion of government purchases of goods and services:

$G = 1,290$.

The condition for goods-market equilibrium is then

$Y = C + I + G$
$\quad = 80 + 0.7Y_d + 250 + 0.1Y - 10r + 1,290$
$\quad = 80 + 0.7[Y - (300 + 0.2Y)] + 250 + 0.1Y - 10r + 1,290$.

Collecting terms gives

$Y = (80 - 210 + 250 + 1,290) + (0.56Y + 0.1Y) - 10r$.

Putting the interest-rate term on the left-hand side and the income terms on the right-hand side and dividing by 10 gives

$r = 141 - 0.034 \times Y$.

This is the new *IS* schedule. What happens if the interest rate is 5 percent?

$0.034Y = 141 - 5 = 136$

$Y = 4,000$.

We have used numbers that give the same level of income at the same rate of interest as the worked examples in Chapter 3. Notice, however, that the *IS* schedule is not the same. The constant term is higher (it was 85 in Worked Example 3.4 and now it is 141) and the coefficient on income is higher. (It was 0.02 in Worked Example 3.4 and now it is 0.034.) The new *IS* schedule is shifted to the right and is steeper than before. Why has this happened?

There is no rule that says that the *IS* schedule is automatically shifted to the right when the government sector is added. This result depended on the particular values we chose for taxes and spending. If we had set government purchases and taxes differently, we could have come up with a different result. Even though there is no rule, however, it is likely that the government sector will add to aggregate demand. It is no surprise that the *IS* schedule is shifted to the right. Recall that we lowered the level of autonomous expenditure in the consumption function compared to the earlier worked examples. This had the effect of lowering demand and shifting the *IS* schedule to the left, an effect that was more than offset by government's net effect on demand. Government is having a substantial net positive impact on aggregate demand in our example, because government spending goes directly into aggregate demand while taxes reduce income, which then reduces demand less than dollar for dollar.

The *IS* schedule including a tax function is steeper than the *IS* schedule without a tax function because the schedule reflects the smaller multiplier effect caused by marginal taxes. The multiplier represents successive rounds of expenditure, income gain, and subsequent expenditure. With marginal taxes, some fraction of each dollar increase in income is lost to taxes. The multiplier is smaller because each round of expenditure is smaller, subsequent income gains are smaller, and so are subsequent rounds of expenditures and so on.

In Chapter 2 we developed the idea of the multiplier by fixing the interest rate and we are going to do the same thing here. In practice, an unchanged interest rate in the face of a fiscal change would require the cooperation of the monetary authorities. The Fed would have to adjust monetary policy to maintain a constant interest rate and it is not clear that the Fed would do this or even could do it. At this point, however, we are not concerned with how monetary policy is made. We are taking a step-by-step approach to understand the effects of fiscal policy. We can then take what we learn from this exercise and apply it in the case where the interest rate varies.

Equilibrium with an Unchanged Interest Rate

With a given interest rate, equilibrium income can be determined from the goods-market–equilibrium condition—if the interest rate is known, then a particular point on the *IS* schedule is known, determining equilibrium income. By solving Equation 4.6 for the value of Y that just satisfies goods-market demands, we find equilibrium income. The solution involves collecting Y terms to the left-hand side and factoring out Y:

$$Y[1 - C_1(1 - T_1) - I_1] = C_0 - I_0 - I_2 r + G - C_1 T_0.$$

Dividing both sides by $[1 - C_1(1 - T_1) - I_1]$ results in the following expression for goods-market–equilibrium income with a given interest rate $(\bar{r})$:

$$Y = \frac{1}{1 - C_1(1 - T_1) - I_1} \times (C_0 + I_0 - I_2\bar{r} + G - C_1 T_0). \qquad (4.8)$$

$$\begin{array}{c} \text{Equilibrium} \\ \text{income} \end{array} = \begin{array}{c} \text{Autonomous-} \\ \text{expenditure} \\ \text{multiplier} \end{array} \times \begin{array}{c} \text{Autonomous} \\ \text{expenditure} \end{array}$$

Rewriting the autonomous-expenditure multiplier using marginal propensities gives

$$\text{Autonomous-expenditure multiplier} = \frac{1}{1 - \text{MPC}(1 - \text{MPT}) - \text{MPI}}.$$

autonomous-expenditure multiplier
The effect of an increase in autonomous expenditure on equilibrium income when these are taxes.

Equilibrium income in the goods market with a given interest rate is equal to the **autonomous-expenditure multiplier** times *autonomous expenditure* and this has the same form as the solution for goods-market equilibrium that we had in Chapter 2 before we introduced government expenditures and taxation. However, when we introduced the multiplier in Chapter 2 we talked simply about "the multiplier." Now we are putting a specific label on this multiplier because there will be different multipliers depending upon which fiscal policy is being changed.

Looking at the autonomous-expenditure term, remember that since we are holding the interest rate constant and focusing only on the multiplier effect, we have included as part of autonomous expenditures the portion of investment demand that is affected by the interest rate.

The terms that are new in the expression for autonomous expenditure (compared to Chapter 2) are government spending and the autonomous part of taxes $(G - C_1 T_0)$. In general, total government purchases, G, will be much larger than the purely autonomous part of tax receipts. So this new term has raised the total size of autonomous expenditures.

Taxes respond to income, so that the marginal propensity to tax appears in the multiplier. The autonomous-expenditure multiplier depends upon the marginal propensity to tax $(T_1$ or MPT$)$ as well as the marginal propensity to consume $(C_1$ or MPC$)$ and the marginal propensity to invest $(I_1$ or MPI$)$. Higher taxes reduce the level of disposable income left over from any increase in income. This effect is reflected in the multiplier since the marginal propensity to tax *increases* the denominator of the expression for the multiplier and *decreases* the size of the multiplier.

Both autonomous expenditure and the multiplier have been changed by the introduction of the government sector. Autonomous expenditures have been increased, while the multiplier has been decreased. The government sector has had offsetting effects on goods-market equilibrium, raising aggregate demand through government purchases and lowering demand through net taxation.

The autonomous-expenditure multiplier and government spending

The autonomous-expenditure multiplier shows how aggregate demand will change when there is a change in autonomous expenditure—be it a change in the autonomous parts of consumption, investment, and/or government purchases. The multiplied effect of a change in autonomous expenditure when there is a government collecting taxes is different from one with no taxation. If taxes are a function of the level of income, as they are in most modern economies, then there are **tax leakages** that reduce the multiplier. A boost in any autonomous expenditure will cause income to rise, but the rise in income drives up tax receipts which in turn leads to smaller increases in expenditure in the subsequent rounds of the multiplier. We refer to tax payments as leakages because they drain off resources each time demand is recycled through the economy. The heavier the leakage, the smaller the ultimate impact of any initial change. The effect of a change in autonomous expenditure on income is shown in Equation 4.9:

tax leakages
The increased net tax revenue associated with an increase in income. Because tax leakages reduce the increase in spending that follows an increase in income, they reduce the multiplier.

$$\Delta Y = \frac{1}{1 - \text{MPC}(1 - \text{MPT}) - \text{MPI}} \times \Delta(C_0 + I_0 - I_2 \bar{r} + G - C_1 T_0).$$

| Change in income | = Autonomous-expenditure multiplier | × Change in autonomous expenditures | (4.9) |

Since an increase in the marginal propensity to tax (the tax rate, T_1) reduces the multiplier, *the higher the tax rate, the lower the multiplier effect* on equilibrium income.

**WORKED EXAMPLE 4.2   The Autonomous-Expenditure Multiplier
with Tax Leakages**

Question: Consider an economy where the marginal propensity to consume is
0.7 and the marginal propensity to invest is 0.1.

(a) What is the autonomous-expenditure multiplier when the marginal propensity
to tax is zero?
(b) How does this answer change if the marginal propensity to tax is 0.2?
(c) What will be the increases in income resulting from an increase of $1 billion
in autonomous expenditure in the two cases?

Answer: The autonomous-expenditure multiplier is given in Equation 4.9. Substituting in the values given in part (a) of the question leads to

$$\text{Multiplier} = \frac{1}{1 - 0.7(1 - 0) - 0.1} = 5.$$

Repeating this procedure for part (b) of the question gives

$$\text{Multiplier} = \frac{1}{1 - 0.7(1 - 0.2) - 0.1} = 2.94.$$

Equation 4.9 can also be used to answer part (c) of the question:

Change in income when MPT is zero = 5 × 1 = $5 billion
Change in income when MPT is 0.2 = 2.94 × 1 = $2.94 billion.

A given increase in autonomous expenditure will result in a smaller increase in income
($5 billion versus $2.94 billion) in case (b) than in case (a). This is because in case (b)
tax payments rise along with the rise in income.

We saw in Chapter 2 that the multiplier can be looked at as a sequence
of increases in income that stimulate further increases in demand. The same
is true here. For simplicity we ignore changes in investment demand; then
each dollar of increase in autonomous expenditure has, first, a direct effect
that increases demand by $1. This raises income by $1 in the model with
no taxes. However, with taxes, disposable income goes up only by (1 −
MPT). Of this increase in disposable income, a fraction (MPC) is spent, so
demand goes up by [MPC × (1 − MPT)]. On the next round of the process,
the increase in demand is [MPC × (1 − MPT)] times the previous round's
increase income. After the process has worked its way through the economy,
the final increase in demand is the sum of all the terms:

$$[\text{MPC} \times (1 - \text{MPT})] + [\text{MPC} \times (1 - \text{MPT})]^2 + [\text{MPC} \times (1 - \text{MPT})]^3 +$$
. . . $[\text{MPC} \times (1 - \text{MPT})]^n$. . .

This series would sum up to the autonomous-expenditure multiplier if we
had also taken account of investment changes.

Changes in government purchases.   There is an important implication of what we have found. *Since government purchases of goods and services are part of autonomous expenditure, a change in government purchases will change equilibrium income.* When the government increases its demand for aircraft or computers, this adds directly to total demand in the economy and there are then further increases in income as the multiplier works through the economy. When the government cuts back on its purchases, this will reduce demand in the economy and could trigger a recession.

In Worked Example 4.2 we found that a $1 billion increase in autonomous expenditure would lead to a $2.94 billion increase in income, assuming the marginal propensities that were given in the example, including a marginal propensity to tax of 0.2. This example applies directly to the case of a $1 billion increase in government purchases of goods and services, which would raise income by $2.94 billion. *An increase or decrease in government purchases will have a multiplied effect on income.* And, in practice, this gain in income may come partly from output and partly from prices.

A change in the level of government purchases in the economy will have the intended or unintended effect of changing income. In practice, the biggest changes in government purchases occur when there is a war. If the economy was at full employment before the war starts, then the wartime increase in government purchases will raise income above capacity and may well lead to inflation. Inflations have often accompanied wars. Alternatively, if the economy was in a recession when the war started, then the increase in income may be helpful economically. This was the case with World War II, when large increases in defense spending pulled the U.S. economy out of the high unemployment of the Great Depression.

Changes in income may be the unintended side effects of changes in government purchases that are made because of national defense or for other reasons, but there is also the possibility that *increases or decreases in government purchases may be used deliberately to affect income.* Policymakers may decide that they want to increase or decrease the level of income or employment in the economy and they can use government purchases as a way of achieving this.

The model we have used in this section, in which the government increases its demand and thus increases income and employment in the economy, was the one used by John Maynard Keynes to argue that government spending should be used to bring the British economy out of its long depression of the 1920s and 1930s.[5]

There have been cases more recent than the Great Depression where government purchases have been changed with the intention that this would

---

[5] Keynes argued that there would be little or no change in the rate of interest following the increase in government spending because the economy has excess money during depression periods—the so-called *liquidity trap*. Most analysts have disagreed with this view, however, and have not found evidence to support the idea of a liquidity trap.

change income. For example, President Kennedy increased defense spending in the 1960s partly in order to alleviate recession. But these cases are not very common. Government programs normally have to be justified based upon their merits and usually have a long time horizon. Kennedy increased defense spending mostly because he believed there was a need for more missiles. The fact that this would then help overcome the recession was a bonus. When fiscal policy is used to change income and there is no clear basis for changing government spending for other reasons, it is generally taxes and transfers that are changed.

The lump-sum–tax multiplier

Some taxes such as taxes on property, business, or trade licenses are collected from individuals and institutions regardless of their level of income. In some economies there is a minimum tax liability that each citizen or family must pay. The 1990 poll taxes initiated in the United Kingdom by the Thatcher government are of this type. Public unrest over the Thatcher poll tax was a reaction to the regressive nature of the tax. The poor, by paying the same dollar amount as the rich, end up paying taxes that are a much higher percentage of their income than is the case with the rich. These taxes are fixed by tax policy in dollar amount—they have to be paid as a lump sum.

lump-sum taxes
Taxes fixed by tax policy in dollar amount and collected from individuals and institutions regardless of their level of income.

Lump-sum taxes, such as property taxes, are included in the term T_0 in our analysis, so they are a negative portion of autonomous expenditure $(-C_1 T_0)$. If a family has to pay a certain dollar amount of lump-sum tax, T_0, then family income falls by T_0 dollars. The effect on expenditures of a fall in income is described by the marginal propensity to consume, C_1, and so, for every dollar of lump-sum tax, expenditure is reduced by C_1 dollars. This is why the term $(-C_1 \Delta T_0)$ shows up in the lump-sum–tax multiplier:

Change in income for a change in lump-sum taxes

$$\Delta Y = \frac{1}{[1 - C_1(1 - T_1) - I_1]} \times [(-C_1 \Delta T_0)]$$

$$= \frac{-C_1}{[1 - C_1(1 - T_1) - I_1]} \times \Delta T_0 \qquad (4.10)$$

$$= \frac{-\text{MPC}}{1 - \text{MPC}(1 - \text{MPT}) - \text{MPI}} \times \Delta T_0.$$

Change in = Lump-sum–tax × Change in
income   multiplier   lump-sum
                              taxes

lump-sum–tax multiplier
The effect of a change in lump-sum taxes on equilibrium income.

The **lump-sum–tax multiplier** has the opposite sign to the autonomous-expenditure multiplier and it is multiplied by the marginal propensity to consume (MPC). *So an increase in lump-sum taxes reduces income with the magnitude of the effect being smaller than the one for a change in expenditure.*

Worked Example 4.3   The Lump-Sum–Tax Multiplier

Question: What is the change in equilibrium income resulting from an increase of $1 billion in property taxes?

Answer: The effect of the $1 billion increase in property taxes can be obtained from Equation 4.10:

$$\Delta Y = \frac{-0.7}{[1 - 0.7(1 - 0.2) - 0.1]} \times 1$$
$$= \frac{-0.7}{0.34 \times 100} = -(0.7 \times 2.94) \times 1$$
$$= -2.06.$$

If property taxes increase by $1 billion, this reduces disposable income immediately by $1 billion. Households will reduce consumption expenditures by a fraction of the drop in disposable income. (The fall in consumer spending equals $-MPC \times \Delta T_0 = -0.7 \times 1 = -0.7$.) This fall in consumption then has a multiplier effect on income as there are successive rounds of reduction in demand. The final result is that income falls by $2.06 billion ($-0.7 \times 2.94 = 2.06$).

The tax-rate multiplier

In practice, governments often alter taxes through a change in the tax rate (T_1, or MPT). Tax-rate changes have an important characteristic—*the impact of any tax-rate change depends both upon the amount of change in the rate and upon the level of income that the economy starts out with before the change in the tax rate.* A given increase in the tax rate will bring about a larger increase in the amount of taxes paid and a larger reduction in the equilibrium level of income at higher levels of income than at lower levels of income. This may seem puzzling, but notice that a change in tax rates affects the economy by changing the amount of tax dollars paid to the government out of different levels of income. If income in the economy is $4 trillion and the tax rate rises by 5 percentage points, disposable income falls initially by $200 billion. This is followed by a multiplier reaction that includes the increased tax leakage. However, if income were initially $5 trillion, the same rise in tax rate would result in a $250 billion fall in disposable income, followed by a multiplier reaction. The reduction in equilibrium income will be larger in the latter case where income was originally higher. The *tax-rate multiplier* gives the effect on income of a change in the tax rate, ΔT_1:

Effect on income of a change in the tax rate
$$\Delta Y = \frac{-C_1 Y}{1 - C_1(1 - T_1) - I_1} \times \Delta T_1$$

$$\text{Change in income} = \text{Tax rate multiplier} \times \text{Change in tax rate}$$

$$\Delta Y = \frac{-C_1 Y}{1 - C_1(1 - T_1) - I_1} \times \Delta T_1$$

$$= \frac{-\text{MPC} \times Y}{[1 - \text{MPC}(1 - \text{MPT}) - \text{MPI}]} \times \Delta \text{MPT}.$$

Notice that the tax-rate multiplier is just the lump-sum–tax multiplier times the level of income. The higher the level of income, the greater is the tax-rate multiplier. Deriving this expression for the change in goods-market–equilibrium requires the use of calculus. The following worked example demonstrates numerically how the level of income affects the tax-rate–multiplier effect.

WORKED EXAMPLE 4.4   The Tax-Rate–Multiplier Effect

We start with an economy before a change in the tax rate:

Income = $4 trillion ($4,000 billion)
MPC   = 0.7, MPI = 0.1, MPT = 0.20

Then the tax rate is changed. MPT is reduced by 5 percentage points, to 0.15, so that the change in the tax rate is −0.05.

$$\Delta Y = \frac{-C_1 Y}{1 - C_1(1 - T_1) - I_1} \times \Delta T_1$$

$$= \frac{(-0.7 \times 4,000)}{1 - 0.7(1 - 0.2) - 0.1} \times (-0.05)$$

$$= -2.06 \times 4,000 \times (-0.05)$$

$$= +412.$$

In this example, with a constant rate of interest and with income initially at $4 trillion, a decline in the marginal tax rate from 20 percent to 15 percent of income would result in an increase of income of $412 billion.

If the initial level of income were lower, say $3,000 billion, then the change in income from the tax cut would also be lower. It would be derived in exactly the same way as the calculation just shown, except that 3,000 would appear instead of 4,000. The resulting increase in income would then be $309 billion.

In the worked example, the reduction in the tax rate by 5 percentage points represents a major change in the tax code that would have a large effect on income—increasing income by over 10 percent. Tax-rate changes as large as these can be powerful devices for changing equilibrium income.

Monetary policy and money-market conditions often operate independently of fiscal-policy changes. There is no guarantee that the monetary authorities can or will coordinate policies so that a change in taxation or government expenditure occurs with a constant rate of interest. The changes in income that we computed holding the rate of interest constant were too large. We now use the *IS-LM* framework in which the interest rate adjusts along the *LM* schedule as goods-market equilibrium changes. The impact of a change in tax policy is the combined result of the multiplier effect and the interest-rate effect.

FISCAL POLICY AND MONEY-MARKET CONDITIONS

As we allow for changes in the interest rate, we will find that the time we have spent studying multiplier effects has not been wasted. Changes in fiscal policy will be represented by shifts in the *IS* schedule and the size of the horizontal shifts in the *IS* following a tax change or a change in government purchases of goods and services will be equal to the changes in income that we have just computed with a constant rate of interest (a similar result to the one we saw in Chapter 2). That is to be expected. The horizontal shifts in the *IS* schedule reflect the multiplier effect. With no change in the interest rate, the change in income is equal to the multiplier effect with no offsetting interest-rate effect.

Fiscal Policy and Interest-Rate Effects

In Figure 4.2 we use shifts in the *IS* schedule to represent the effects of increases in government purchases and in lump-sum taxes of the same amount. The former shifts the *IS* schedule to the right (to *IS'*) and the latter shifts the *IS* to the left (to *IS"*). The leftward shift due to the tax change is shown as smaller than the rightward shift due to the increase in government purchases. This is because of the difference in the multipliers for the two changes.

Consider first the effect of the increase in government purchases of goods and services. In Figure 4.2, the shift from *A* to *B* describes the full multiplier effect of the increase in government spending. With no change in the interest rate, income would rise from Y_A to Y_B. However, with a fixed *LM* schedule, there is an interest-rate increase (r_A to r_C) that then leads to a partially offsetting decline in income (the interest-rate effect). The final increase in income (Y_A to Y_C) is less than the increase that is given by the multiplier effect alone.

The shift from *A* to *D* describes the full multiplier effect of the increase in lump-sum taxes. With a fixed *LM* schedule, there is a fall in the interest rate (r_A to r_E) that then leads to a partially offsetting increase in income (the interest-rate effect). The final decrease in income (Y_A to Y_E) is less than the decrease that is given by the multiplier effect alone.

We have found, therefore, that *the effectiveness of fiscal policy in bringing about changes in income is reduced by the movements of the interest rate that occur with an unchanged monetary policy.* If the fiscal-policy changes are being used appropriately in order to increase income when it is too low, or to decrease

FIGURE 4.2   The Effects of an Increase in Government Purchases or an Increase in Lump-Sum Taxes

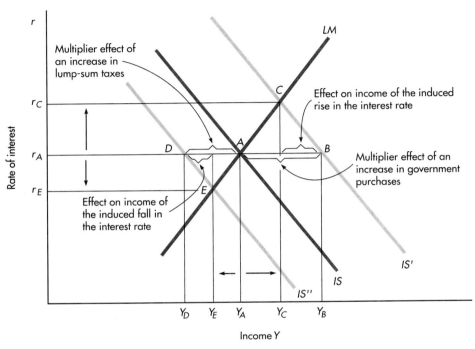

An increase in government purchases raises income $(Y_A$ to $Y_C)$ and the interest rate $(r_A$ to $r_C)$. An increase in lump-sum taxes lowers income $(Y_A$ to $Y_E)$ and the interest rate $(r_A$ to $r_C)$.

it when it is too high, then this is bad news. The policy is not as effective in bringing about an economic improvement. If the fiscal-policy change is made for other reasons (to fight a war, for example), then the mitigating effects of interest-rate changes may be helpful in preventing an overheated economy. The rise in the interest rate will reduce private spending and allow for the increase in public spending.

Figure 4.3 shows the case of changes in the tax rate (the MPT). The effects of both increases and decreases in the tax rate are shown and this case is a bit more complicated. A change in the tax rate will change the slope of the *IS* schedule, with increases in the tax rate making the schedule steeper (from *IS* to *IS'*, so that income falls from Y_A to Y_B and the interest rate falls from r_A to r_B), and decreases in the tax rate making the schedule flatter (from *IS* to *IS"*, so that income rises from Y_A to Y_C and the rate of interest rises from r_A to r_C).

FIGURE 4.3   The Effects of an Increase or a Decrease in the Tax Rate (the MPT)

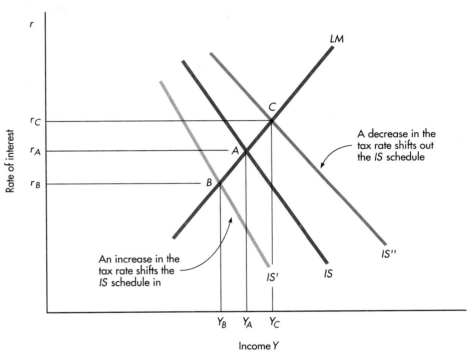

An increase in the tax rate makes the *IS* schedule steeper, while income and the interest rate fall. A decrease in the tax rate makes the *IS* schedule flatter, while income and the interest rate rise.

The simplest way to understand why the *IS* schedule changes its slope as it shifts in this case is to look back at Worked Example 4.1. We saw there that introducing taxes that depend upon income had the effect of making the *IS* schedule steeper. An increase in the tax rate (an increase in MPT) will strengthen this effect. Decreases in the tax rate will make the *IS* schedule more like the case with no taxes, so the *IS* is flatter. Another way to understand the result is to recall that the tax-rate multiplier changes with income. The multiplier and hence the horizontal shift of the *IS* schedule is greater at low rates of interest/high levels of income than at high rates of interest/low levels of income.

We have found that when the money supply remains constant (the *LM* schedule is fixed), the effectiveness of fiscal policy in altering income is reduced. Now we are going to show that the extent to which this occurs depends upon money-market conditions and the nature of money demand in particular. *The way money demand responds to changes in income and the interest rate has an important impact on the effectiveness of fiscal policy.*

Money demand and fiscal-policy effectiveness

The way in which the demand for money responds to income and the interest rate depends mostly on the way in which businesses adjust their money holdings. If the cash managers that administer business checking accounts increase their demand for money a lot when income rises, and if these cash managers are unwilling to reduce their demand for money by much when the rate of interest rises, then an expansionary fiscal policy will have little effect on income. Let's see how this happens.

Figure 4.4 depicts an economy that is initially in equilibrium at point *A*. There is then either a cut in taxes or an increase in government purchases. The effect of this is depicted as a rightward shift of the *IS* schedule (from *IS* to *IS'*). Suppose that money-market conditions in this economy can be represented by a schedule such as the one shown as *LM* in the figure. In this case, the expansionary fiscal policy has increased income from Y_A to Y_B. As the fiscal policy increases demand in the goods market, this increases income and the rise in income boosts the demand for money as people make more transactions. Since the supply of money is fixed, there is no more money available and so the interest rate starts to rise. Money-market equilibrium is restored once cash managers and households are content to hold the fixed money supply, even though they are making more transactions. Provided the increase in money demand generated by the rise in transactions is not too great, and provided people are willing to change their money demand in response to a higher interest rate, the magnitude of the interest-rate rise (shown as the increase r_A to r_B in Figure 4.4) will not be very large.

Suppose now that conditions in the money market in this economy can be represented by a schedule like the one labeled *LM'* in the figure.[6] In this case, the fiscal expansion will still lead to an increase in income. But as income rises, either the transactions demand for money rises sharply or

---

[6] The demand-for-money relation we used in Chapter 3 was the following:

$$Md = kY - hr.$$

The case of a steeply sloped money-demand schedule is the same as the case of a small interest-rate effect on the demand for money balances (i.e., the value of the term *h* is small). *A small interest-rate term in the money-demand equation leads to a steep LM schedule and a large interest-rate effect in the money market.* When *h* is small, it takes a larger change in interest rates to bring about money-market equilibrium following a fiscal expansion than it does when *h* is large. The effectiveness of fiscal policy is dampened by a large interest-rate effect (small value of *h*) in money markets.

Estimates of the interest-rate effect in money markets come from estimates of the demand for money balances. See John P. Judd and J. L. Scadding, "The Search for a Stable Money Demand Function," *Journal of Economic Literature XX*, no. 3 (Sept. 1982).

FIGURE 4.4   The Effect of an Expansionary Fiscal Policy Depends upon the Responsiveness of Money Demand

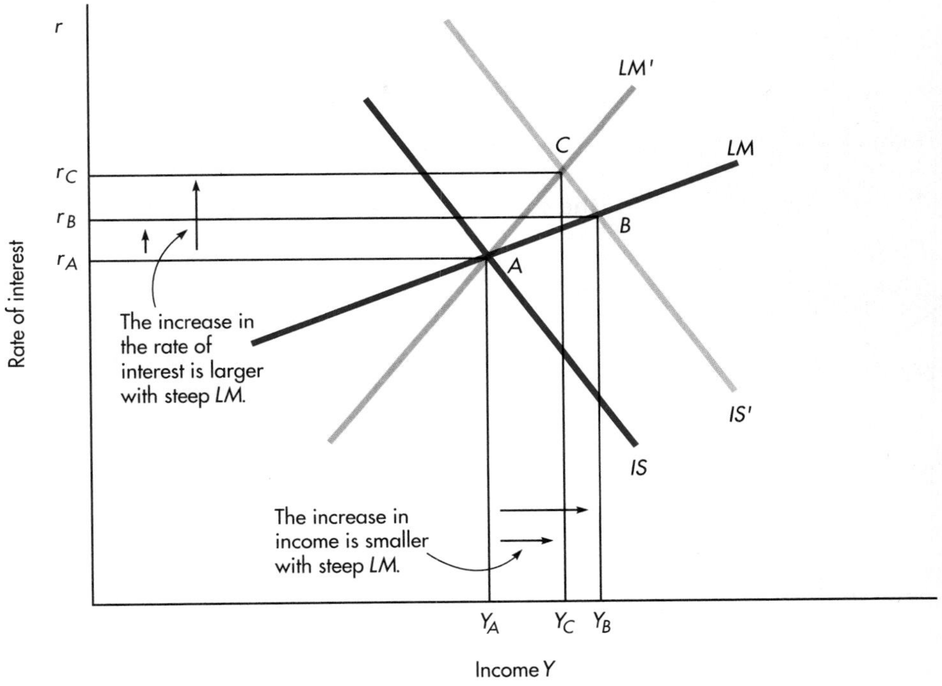

For a given shift in *IS,* the change in income will be smaller with a steep *LM* schedule.

cash managers are not willing to cut back on their money demand much when the interest rate starts to rise—or both are true. Then the only way to maintain money-market equilibrium in this economy is by a large increase in the interest rate (shown as the increase from r_A to r_C in Figure 4.4). *The large increase in the interest rate then has a large negative effect on investment demand. This reduces the effect of the fiscal expansion on income.* Income rises only from Y_A to Y_C in this case. The fiscal expansion has not been very effective in raising income.

Monetarist economists have criticized Keynes for his advocacy of fiscal policy as a way of pulling an economy out of recession. One reason for their opposition to fiscal policy is that monetarists do not think that money demand changes much when the interest rate changes. The *LM* schedule is then very steep and fiscal policy is ineffective.

Crowding out

An increase in government purchases increases aggregate demand, but it will also increase interest rates, as we have just seen. This is an important consideration if fiscal policy is being used deliberately in order to raise income. It is also an important consideration if government purchases are being increased for other reasons. An increase in government purchases will raise the rate of interest and this will have an adverse effect on investment, a phenomenon known as **crowding out.** Crowding out occurs when increases in government spending displace private spending, particularly private investment. Investment crowding out can also occur as a result of tax cuts. Tax cuts that increase disposable income and increase consumption will also cause the interest rate to rise and can have an adverse effect on investment.

crowding out

A reduction in investment resulting from an increase in government spending or a reduction in taxes.

The investment function (Equation 4.5) shows how investment demand depends upon income and the interest rate. If there is a fiscal policy change that results in changes in income and the interest rate, then there will be a change in investment demand as a result (Equation 4.11).

$$\Delta I = I_1 \Delta Y - I_2 \Delta r. \tag{4.11}$$

The change in investment demand, ΔI, depends upon the change in income, ΔY, the change in the rate of interest, Δr, and the responsiveness of investment demand to these changes (the magnitudes of I_1 and I_2). An increase in government spending or a cut in taxes will raise income and therefore raise investment demand. But an increase in government spending or a tax cut will also increase the rate of interest and this will lower investment demand. The extent to which crowding out is a problem depends upon which of these two effects is more important.

We can see that the problem of crowding out is closely related to our previous discussion of money-market conditions and the effectiveness of policy. If money demand is relatively unresponsive to changes in the interest rate (steep *LM* schedule), then this will mean that any increase in government spending or cut in taxes will raise income by relatively little and will raise the interest rate a lot. *Crowding out becomes a serious problem when the* LM *schedule is steep.*

However, the steepness of the *LM* schedule is not the only factor. The responsiveness of investment demand to income changes and interest-rate changes is also important to an assessment of crowding out. Generally, it is thought that if the economy is in a recession and there are slack resources, investment will be fairly responsive to increases in income and not very responsive to changes in the rate of interest. *The crowding-out effect of increased government spending is not very serious if there is slack capacity in the economy in the first place. On the other hand, if income in the economy is already above potential output so that capacity is being overused, then adding increased pressure of government demand is likely to crowd out private investment spending.*

How important has crowding out been in practice? We have learned an important lesson about this in the past few years as a result of the large tax cuts that began in 1981. We have found that crowding out is very important indeed but not quite in the way we had thought. The expansionary fiscal policy has led to substantially higher interest rates, so that the *LM* schedule is certainly steep enough to make crowding out a real concern (Δr was large.) On the other hand, the magnitude of the effect of the high interest rates on investment was not all that great. (I_2 was not very large.) Private domestic investment in the U.S. economy in the 1980s was undoubtedly lower than it would have been because of the very high interest rates, but it was not particularly low overall. An important reason is that the steady growth of income after 1982 helped to sustain reasonably strong investment. (The $I_1\Delta Y$ term was important over this period.) Crowding out of the kind we have just described did not turn out to be all that important in the 1980s.

The crowding out that did turn out to be important occurred in the foreign sector. The tax cuts of the 1980s led to a large deficit in foreign trade. The difference between imports and exports is called **net foreign investment**. *The tax cuts of the 1980s led to a crowding out of net foreign investment.* We will examine this idea later in this chapter after we have looked at the issue of the budget deficit. The crowding out of net foreign investment is closely linked to the large budget deficits of the 1980s.

net foreign investment
Purchases of foreign assets by U.S. residents minus purchases of U.S. assets by foreign residents. It equals net exports.

Up until now we have assumed that taxes and government spending are determined separately. We talked about the effect of increases in government spending without saying where the resources are coming from to pay for the extra spending. In practice the relation between total spending and total revenues is an important one for the government and may affect fiscal-policy decisions. We now turn to an analysis of the government budget and the problem of the deficit.

GOVERNMENT FINANCE AND THE BUDGET BALANCE

The government raises tax revenue to finance its expenditures. If tax revenues always equaled expenditures, the budget would always be in balance. But often, actual revenues either fall short of or overshoot actual expenditures. When tax revenues exceed government expenditures, the result is a *budget surplus*. When government expenditures exceed net tax revenues, the result is a *budget deficit*. A budget surplus or deficit is defined, equivalently, as either the difference between net tax revenue *(T)* and government purchases of goods and services *(G)* or else the difference between gross tax revenues (T_g) and total government expenditures [government purchases *(G)* plus transfers (T_p)]. We refer to the surplus or deficit as the **budget balance** *(B):*

budget balance
The difference between government receipts and government outlays. When receipts exceed outlays, the budget balance is a *budget surplus*. When receipts fall short of outlays, the budget balance is a *budget deficit*.

$$\begin{aligned} B &= T - G \\ &= T_g - T_p - G \\ &= T_g - (G + T_p). \end{aligned} \tag{4.12}$$

When the government balance *(B)* is positive, there is a surplus, but when *B* is negative, there is a deficit. Over the past several years in the United States, the cumulative effects of deficits have outweighed surpluses.

The Budget Deficit

Table 4.3 shows the combined receipts and expenditures of the federal, state, and local governments as they appear in the National Income and Product Accounts. These include government purchases, total tax receipts, and transfer payments. The table also notes the overall government balance, which was a deficit in each of the years shown. The figures are in current dollars, unadjusted for inflation. The table shows that government purchases, receipts, and transfers have all been rising, but that total receipts have not matched the sum of government expenditures and transfer payments. The result has been a deficit that widened until 1986. Since then the deficit has been coming down, mostly because of an increase in social-security tax revenues. The social-security tax rate has gone up and the ratio of workers to retirees has risen too as the baby-boom generation has entered the work force. By 1989, the deficit was down to $104.9 billion.

The overall government deficit is a result of the fact that the federal government has been making expenditures greatly in excess of its receipts for several years now. How does it manage to do this?

Borrowing from the central bank

One possible way in which the federal government can cover a deficit is that it can issue government bonds and have the Fed buy the bonds, thereby financing the deficit through an increase in the supply of money. Does this happen in practice?

In general, *the Fed does not automatically supply money to cover federal budget deficits.* And for good reason. This would lead to an increase in the supply of money that was uncontrolled by deliberate monetary policy, but instead was driven by the need to cover a fiscal shortfall. The result would likely be inflationary. The main way in which federal deficits in the United States are financed is by borrowing from the public. This is not true in some other countries, however.

Some European countries in the 1920s and 1930s and Latin American countries in the 1980s have made expenditures well in excess of their tax revenues and have been unable to borrow the difference. They have therefore forced their own central banks to print money to cover the shortfall of revenues. They have imposed an expansionary monetary policy on their economies in support of their fiscal policies and the result in all cases has been inflation. The underlying causes of the difficulties in these countries have been political and economic problems that preceded the excess government spending. Some governments have spent on the military in the hope of preventing or controlling political unrest. Many countries have provided large subsidies to private or public enterprises that were in danger of bankruptcy. This last difficulty has also become important in Eastern Europe in the 1990s. There are many enterprises in the Eastern Bloc that have huge deficits and are being kept afloat by government subsidies. The governments lack the tax revenue to

TABLE 4.3   Federal, State, and Local Government Receipts and Expenditures, Calendar Years 1980–1989 (billions of current-year dollars)

	1980	1984	1986	1989
Receipts	$855.1	$1,172.9	$1,347.4	$1,673.8
Less purchases of goods and services	530.3	735.9	872.2	1,036.7
Less transfer payments and net interest	359.3	542.0	619.3	742.0
Equals budget balance (deficit)	−34.5	−105.0	−144.1	−104.9

Note: Differences between the data in Table 4.3 and data in Tables 4.1 and 4.2 are because Table 4.3 uses calendar year figures rather than fiscal year figures.

pay these subsidies and are finding it difficult to borrow. They are increasing their money supplies in order to maintain expenditures, and the danger of accelerating inflation in these countries is very real.

Borrowing from the public

In the United States, federal-government borrowing is generally done through the Treasury, which sells Treasury bills and bonds to the general public. (Treasury bills are just short-term bonds). When the Treasury sells these bonds, the proceeds go to the government to close the gap between tax revenues and government expenditures. Some states and municipalities also borrow by using bonds and this borrowing is included in the total of government borrowing. State and local levels of government have not been net borrowers in recent years, mostly because they have been building up pension funds for their employees.

Once Treasury bonds have been sold, the federal government is obliged to pay the owners of the bonds an amount of *interest* every year and then to repay the loan or *principal* after a fixed amount of time. *There is a cost to the public from deficit financing.* By borrowing, the government has covered its deficit in the short run without increasing taxes, but since the interest on the debts must be paid, this means that a larger fraction of future tax revenues must be devoted to debt service and not to public services.

There is much controversy surrounding the federal budget deficit, how harmful it is, and whether concerns about the deficit should limit the use of fiscal policy to increase income in recessions. The key point about budget surpluses and deficits is that they are a form of government saving or dissaving. *The government's decision to save or dissave affects the total of national saving in the economy. A budget deficit is a subtraction from saving, and the effects of this can be either good or bad.*

The Effect of the Budget Balance on Saving

With no government sector, equilibrium income occurs where saving equals planned investment. A similar condition relates saving and investment when we include government in the model. In Chapter 2 we assumed that there was no government sector, so that saving was defined as income minus consumption. Now we need to define two different concepts of saving, private saving and national saving. **Private saving** *(S)* is equal to disposable income (Y_d) minus consumption:

private saving
The part of private income not consumed. It is computed as total income minus net taxes minus consumption. Private saving can be split into personal saving and business saving (retained earnings).

$$S = Y_d - C = Y - T - C.$$

The goods-market–equilibrium condition is given by

$$Y = \text{Aggregate demand} = C + I + G.$$

Subtracting consumption and government spending from income gives

$$Y - C - G = I.$$

Then subtracting and adding net taxes gives

$$(Y - T - C) + (T - G) = I$$

or

$$S + B = I.$$

national saving
The total of private saving plus the government's budget surplus (or minus the government's budget deficit). It can be given gross or net of depreciation.

Saving plus the budget balance equals investment. The sum of private saving and the budget balance is often called **national saving,** so that *goods-market equilibrium occurs when national saving equals investment.*

When the budget is balanced $(B = 0)$, government expenses are paid for by net tax revenues $(G = T)$. In this case, the relationship between private saving and planned investment is the same as if there were no government sector.

If the budget is in surplus $(B > 0)$, tax revenues exceed government expenditures $(G < T)$ and this is the same as having the government save a portion of its tax revenue. The income received by the government is not all spent when it runs a surplus. This represents extra national saving that can then be used for investment, if there is enough investment demand to make use of it. National saving is larger than private saving in this case.

Finally, the most common case for the U.S government is that it is running a deficit $(B < 0)$, spending more than it earns in revenues $(G > T)$. The resources of saving available for planned investment are lower than they would have been otherwise, because the resources devoted to meeting government expenditures exceeded the tax revenues collected to pay for them. Here, national saving is less than private saving.

The relationship between the budget balance, saving, and planned investment helps us to see both the pluses and minuses of using deficit spending to cure a recession.

Short-term and chronic deficits

When the economy is in a recession, there is inadequate aggregate demand and this can be seen as a problem of coordination between the level of planned investment and the level of national saving. When planned investment falls below the amount of private saving generated in the economy when income and output are equal to potential output, then there is a fall in income. The economy reaches a new equilibrium in which investment equals saving once again, but at a lower level of income and employment.

In this situation, a cut in taxes or an increase in government purchases that creates a budget deficit provides a subtraction from private saving. Total national saving is then less than private saving, and if the difference is enough to bring national saving back into alignment with investment at full-employment income, then the lack of coordination between investment and private saving will have been overcome.

The use of deficits to solve the coordination problem should be seen only as a short-term approach, however. The coordination problem should not be used as an excuse to run chronic large deficits, since these shift the economy toward more government spending or more consumption as sources of aggregate demand and crowd out investment. If the economy has fallen into a recession because of inadequate investment, then it is better to reverse this and increase investment than to rely on demand fueled by deficit spending in the long run.

Since deficits can be either good or bad, policymakers need to have a correct view of whether or not there is a deficit problem. And it turns out that this is quite difficult to obtain because *the deficit itself changes when the economy changes.* Let's see how this happens.

The Budget Deficit over the Business Cycle

We start the discussion of the effect of the economy on the deficit by looking at an economy that is about to go into a recession. Perhaps the recession begins with businesses becoming less optimistic about future sales and profits. Because of worsened expectations, firms target a lower level of planned investment. Production decreases, leading to further reductions in purchases of capital goods, and this reduction in investment is amplified throughout the economy through the multiplier process. If there are no offsetting positive changes in aggregate demand, the economy will go into a recession. Since income has fallen, tax revenues have fallen by an amount equal to the change in income times the marginal propensity to tax ($\Delta Y \times$ MPT). If the budget was balanced before the recession ($B = 0$), the fall in income will move the government budget into deficit ($B < 0$). *Even if there is no change in policy, a recession by itself will create or worsen a deficit because of the dependence of tax revenues and transfers on income.*

Faced with this new, lower equilibrium income, fiscal policymakers in

■ The Balanced-Budget Multiplier and the Saving-Investment Imbalance

We found in our earlier discussion that in the case of a fixed interest rate, a change in government purchases has a bigger effect on equilibrium income than a change in taxes of the same magnitude. The multiplier for government purchases is bigger than the one for tax changes. This result has been used to argue that expansionary fiscal policy can help pull the economy out of a recession without worsening the budget deficit. We see here how this idea works and look at the paradoxical result that the problem of an imbalance between saving and investment can, in principle, be alleviated even without government dissaving.

When the *balanced-budget multiplier* was first derived, it was assumed that investment demand was fixed.* The problems of a rising interest rate and the resulting crowding out of investment were both ignored. This limits the usefulness of the result, but it makes it easier to see the important consequences, so we will follow this approach here.

The condition for goods-market equilibrium with government purchases is

$$Y = C + I + G.$$

Then there is a change in government purchases (ΔG), a change in tax revenues (ΔT), and, by assumption, no change in investment $(\Delta I = 0)$.

The change in tax revenues comes about because of a change in tax rates $(\Delta T_0, \Delta T_1,$ or both) and also because income changes (hence $\Delta T = \Delta T_0 + \Delta T_1 \times \Delta Y)$. But the trick that makes the balanced-budget multiplier easy to compute in this model is that we do not need to know exactly how much each of these has contributed to the final increase in tax revenues. We know that the change in consumption will be equal to the MPC times the change in disposable income $(\Delta C = \text{MPC} \times \Delta Y_d)$. And then the change in disposable income equals the change in total income minus the change in tax revenues $(\Delta Y_d = \Delta Y - \Delta T)$. This means that we can write the following expression for the change in equilibrium income:

$$\Delta Y = \text{MPC}(\Delta Y - \Delta T) + \Delta G.$$

Then an expansionary fiscal policy that leaves the budget balance unchanged must have the property that the increase in tax revenue is equal to the increase in government purchases.

Balanced-budget fiscal-policy change implies $\Delta G = \Delta T$.

Substituting this into the expression for the change in income and collecting terms gives

$$\Delta Y = \text{MPC}(\Delta Y - \Delta G) + \Delta G$$
$$= \text{MPC}(\Delta Y - \Delta T) + \Delta T.$$

Hence

$$\Delta Y = \Delta G = \Delta T.$$

This is the famous result that a balanced-budget increase in taxes and government purchases of, say, $10 billion will increase equilibrium income by $10 billion also. *The balanced-budget multiplier is unity*, given the assumption we have made about investment being unchanged.

At first glance the balanced-budget–multiplier re-

* William A. Salant, "Taxes, Income Determination and the Balanced Budget Theorem," *Review of Economics and Statistics* 39 (May 1957).

the administration and Congress may find it difficult to decide on the appropriate policy changes. Should they cut government programs and raise taxes to cure the deficit, but worsen the recession? Or should they increase government programs and cut taxes to move the economy out of recession, but worsen the deficit?

sult seems very paradoxical. We have argued here that an expansionary fiscal policy helps pull the economy out of recession by alleviating the imbalance between private saving and private investment. But since the balanced-budget multiplier is unity, the increased income is equal to the increase in taxes $(\Delta Y = \Delta T = \Delta G)$, and hence *there is no change in disposable income and no change in either private or national saving ($\Delta S = 0$ and $\Delta B = 0$) as a result of the fiscal-policy change.* How can a balanced-budget change that involves no change in the deficit alleviate the problem of the imbalance between saving and investment?

If an economy is in a recession, saving equals investment, but at a level of income below potential. Any increase in income will increase saving and lead to an excess of saving over investment. This is certainly true in the case we are looking at here where investment demand is assumed fixed, and it is also true more generally. Thus the answer to the paradox is that a balanced-budget fiscal policy has engineered an increase in income without any increase in saving. So the equality between saving and investment is maintained even though income is higher.

Even though balanced-budget increases in taxes and expenditures do not involve any explicit dissaving, they will still reduce the fraction of total income that is saved. The government is spending all of its extra revenue $(\Delta T = \Delta G)$. It is a large "consumer" that is saving no part of its additional income. After the expansion, a smaller fraction of total income is being saved, because the share controlled by government has risen.

In terms of its effect on saving, therefore, a bal-anced-budget change has some of the same pluses and minuses as an expansionary fiscal policy that generates a deficit. And, of course, if we allowed for changes in interest rates and investment, the same potential for crowding out will also exist with balanced-budget changes.

At the present time, few, if any, economists advocate the use of balanced-budget fiscal policies as a way of deliberately smoothing income fluctuations. Such policies would involve large increases in taxes and government spending, leading to large stop-and-go spending programs and great uncertainty about tax rates. Moreover, the fact that such procedures would avoid changes in the deficit do not eliminate their impact on the fraction of total income that is saved.

Despite the fact that the balanced-budget multiplier is of limited relevance for antirecession policies, this does not mean that the basic result is unimportant. The balanced-budget multiplier carries an important lesson for the effects of increases in government purchases that occur for other reasons. When there are large increases as a result of war or a defense buildup, then these will be expansionary even if taxes are increased by enough to pay for the extra spending. This has been important in practice. When government purchases increased as a result of the Vietnam War spending, this did not lead to a budget deficit for several years. Nevertheless, the overall effect of the increased size of the government sector was expansionary—too expansionary, in fact—and there was an acceleration of inflation. To avoid the expansionary effects of increased government expenditures, tax revenues have to be raised by more than the increase in government purchases.

The basic problem here is that *the budget deficit is giving a false indication of the status of the budget during recessions.* When the economy goes into a recession, it looks as though there is a deficit problem when there is not. And the problem of giving false signals is not restricted to recessions. When the economy goes into a boom, it can look as though there is no deficit

cyclically adjusted budget
The budget surplus or deficit that would occur with current tax rates and expenditure programs if the level of output and income in the economy were equal to potential output.

problem when in fact there is one. A way to avoid this problem is to define a concept called the **cyclically adjusted budget.**

The cyclically adjusted budget

The idea of the cyclically adjusted budget is that the impacts of cyclical changes in income on the deficit are removed, and what remains provides a measure of the underlying or longer-term status of the deficit.[7] The cyclically adjusted budget (CAB) is defined as the budget surplus or deficit that would exist if the economy were at full employment, that is, if output were equal to potential output:

$$CAB = T_0 + T_1 Y^P - G$$

The level of net tax revenues that would occur if output were equal to potential is not known, of course; it has to be estimated.

structural deficit
If the cyclically adjusted budget is in deficit, then the economy has a structural deficit.

Once the CAB has been estimated, the actual deficit in any year can be divided into two parts. If the cyclically adjusted budget is in deficit, then it is said that the economy has a **structural deficit.** And the extent to which the actual deficit exceeds the structural deficit is then classified as the **cyclical deficit:**

cyclical deficit
The budget deficit minus the structural deficit.

Total deficit = Structural deficit + Cyclical deficit.

In any given year, the actual deficit will be greater in magnitude than the structural deficit if output is less than potential output and there will then also be a cyclical deficit. If output is greater than potential output, then there will be a cyclical surplus.

Figure 4.5 shows the total budget deficit and estimates of the structural and cyclical components. Evident in the figure are both the rising structural deficits in the 1980s and the substantial cyclical deficits in the early 1980s, particularly in 1982.

Cyclical deficits and the automatic stabilizers

The cyclical deficit is the amount by which the government budget is in deficit as a result of a level of output that is below potential output. In the view of many economists, including ourselves, policymakers should not worry too much about the cyclical deficits that are caused by recessions. Cyclical deficits are an indication that the economy has **automatic stabilizers** that are helping to offset recessions.

automatic stabilizers
Transfers and tax reductions that are activated when income falls, without the need for new authorizations or legislation from Congress.

Automatic stabilizers consist of any transfers and tax reductions that are activated in a recession without the need for new authorizations or legislation from Congress. Programs such as unemployment insurance help to sup-

---

[7] The task of evaluating the status of the deficit and fiscal policy is discussed in Olivier J. Blanchard, "Debts, Deficits and Finite Horizons," and Edward M. Gramlich, "Fiscal Indicators." Both are Working Papers of the OECD Department of Economics and Statistics, April 1990, nos. 79 and 80, respectively.

FIGURE 4.5   The Structural, Cyclical, and Total Deficits

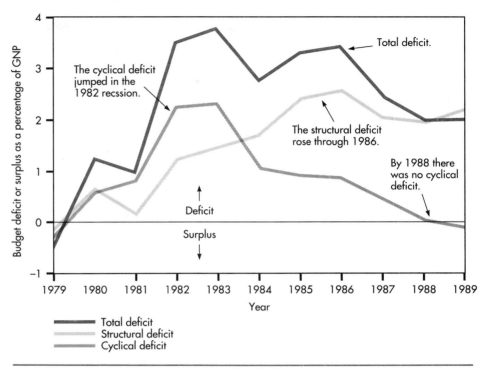

Source: Computed by the authors using data from the Bureau of Economic Analysis, U.S. Department of Commerce.

port workers who are laid off by providing them with income. Laid-off workers who receive unemployment benefits continue spending, thereby bolstering aggregate demand. As well as unemployment insurance, other transfer programs such as welfare and social security also help to sustain aggregate demand during a recession. By reducing the decline in equilibrium income and output, these transfer programs act as automatic stabilizers.

The fact that income and sales taxes also vary with the level of income and expenditure means that they too act as automatic stabilizers. The reduction in gross tax revenues during recessions helps sustain aggregate demand. The government is taking less income out of the economy. The combination of reduced taxes and increased transfers in recessions means that disposable income (Y_d) falls by less than income (Y).

The workings of the automatic stabilizers have already been incorporated into our analysis. When net tax revenues vary with income, this leads to a reduction in the multiplier. This means that the changes in equilibrium income and the shifts in the *IS* schedule that result from changes in autonomous

■ **An Argument Against Amending the U.S. Constitution to Require a Balanced Federal Budget**

Statement of

Alice M. Rivlin*

Senior Fellow

The Brookings Institution

before the

Subcommittee on Economic and Commercial Law

Committee on the Judiciary

U.S. House of Representatives

July 10, 1990

Mr. Chairman, I am happy to be back again before this Committee to explain why I believe that amending the Constitution to require balance in the federal budget would be unwise. I share with the proponents of H.J. Res. 268 a strong belief that the economy would be much healthier in the future if currently projected budget deficits were eliminated. I fervently hope that the budget negotiations now going on between the White House and the Congress will result in a firm plan to move the budget from deficit to surplus over the next several years through some combination of tax increases and spending cuts. I do not believe, however, that amending the Constitution would either help with current deficit problems or contribute to sounder economic policy in the long run. I would like to explain my reasons for these views.

First, balance in the federal budget is not always best for the economy. Currently projected deficits are damaging the economy, primarily because they are reducing national saving, raising interest rates, and discouraging investment at a time when we badly need the government to be leaning in exactly the opposite direction. Private saving rates are low and substantial investment is needed to improve productivity. If the government ran surpluses instead of deficits in the unified budget in the 1990s, it would add to the pool of saving, put downward pressure on interest rates, make investment more attractive to the private sector and to state and local governments, and lessen the dependence of the U.S. economy on inflows of foreign capital. That is why I think it is so important that the budget negotiations succeed.

The Constitution, however, is an expression of permanent policy and economic conditions are not permanent. Imagine that in the next century Americans begin saving at much higher rates, consumption lags, and unemployment drifts upward to persistently higher levels. Running a deficit in the federal budget might then seem far wiser than it does today.

Or, imagine that some major technological breakthrough in the 21st century necessitates massive public investment in a new form of transportation

* The views expressed in this statement are those of the author and do not necessarily reflect the views of other staff members, officers, or trustees of the Brookings Institution.

expenditures (such as fluctuations in investment demand) are smaller in an economy with taxes and transfers.

In the short run, allowing the automatic stabilizers to work and even supplementing them with active adjustments to tax rates can improve economic stability without major cost. *Short-run cyclical deficits are not a problem that should stop the use of fiscal policy when the economy needs an increase in aggregate demand.*

or communication, without which our economy cannot remain competitive. Borrowing to finance this needed public investment would certainly be appropriate. I see no reason why today's fiscal conditions should be invoked to put constitutional road blocks in the way of future Congresses taking actions to respond to fiscal conditions that may be very different from current ones.

Second, any procedural device that focuses attention exclusively on the short run will lead to short-sighted policies. Opponents of writing fiscal policy into the Constitution have pointed out for years that a balanced budget amendment would provide incentives to achieving balance in the upcoming budget year by means that could be detrimental to the economy or to the effectiveness of government in the longer run. Possibilities range from outright gimmicks, such as delaying payments or artificially accelerating revenues, to mandating costs on the private sector or states and localities, or forgoing needed maintenance in our defense establishment.

These arguments are no longer speculative. The experience with Gramm-Rudman-Hollings has dramatized the extraordinary ingenuity of budgeteers in both the executive branch and the Congress in finding ways to appear to meet short-run budget targets while making it more difficult to reduce deficits in the longer run. Congress and the President need to work together to formulate and implement long run budget policies. They should not enshrine short-sightedness in the Constitution.

Finally, implementation and enforcement of this amendment would introduce considerable uncertainty and inefficiency to government operations. Estimates of revenue are notoriously uncertain, since they are sensitive to unpredictable changes in the economy and in taxpayer behavior. Outlay estimates are similarly difficult to make, since they also depend on economic conditions and on changes in payment lags under government programs with long leadtimes. If the amendment were in effect, shifts in the economy, natural disasters, or international crises could easily cause frequent excesses of outlays over estimated revenues or actual receipts. At such moments, a minority of the Congress could exact a high price for joining the super majority that would be necessary to avoid disruption of essential government services.

In short, Mr. Chairman, I believe both the American economy and the American political system would be ill-served by adding the amendment to our Constitution. I hope that instead of passing the amendment, the Congress will devote its energies to turning current deficits into surpluses and demonstrating that those who believe the Constitution must be amended to save democratic government from itself are over-pessimistic. Thank you, Mr. Chairman.

Structural deficits

The concerns over the deficit that started in the middle 1980s and are continuing into the 1990s were generated by an ever-increasing deficit during the economy's longest post–World War II expansion. The long-term growth of government debt was more rapid than the growth of GNP. The economy was generating larger and larger structural deficits. This concern led to a movement to contain the deficit through formula, such as the Gramm-Rudman-Hollings deficit-reduction legislation, or through proposals for a constitutional amendment requiring a balanced budget.

The trouble with proposals to curb deficits with formulas such as the Gramm-Rudman-Hollings proposal is that these formulas may prevent the automatic stabilizers from working and discourage the use of tax-rate reductions to deal with severe recessions. But the reasons that these proposals are being made and supported are quite legitimate. The large structural deficits of the 1980s that seem to be continuing into the 1990s have done considerable damage to the economy and will continue to do damage. Large structural deficits crowd out investment; specifically they have crowded out net foreign investment. This has created serious difficulties for many of our industries in the 1980s and is eroding our national wealth because we are piling up huge foreign debts.

GOVERNMENT DEBT, SAVINGS, AND THE INTERNATIONAL SECTOR

In an open economy where there is foreign trade, aggregate supply and demand include the international sector and equilibrium is described by the expanded relation that we saw in Chapter 2:

$$Y = GNP = C + I + G + (X - IM).$$

Net exports $(X - IM)$ are part of GNP and part of aggregate demand. The relationship between saving, investment, and budget balances now has to be extended also. We rearrange the preceding terms by subtracting consumption and government purchases from both sides and by adding and subtracting net taxes:

$$(Y - C - T) + (T - G) = I + (X - IM)$$
$$\text{that is} \qquad S + (T - G) = I + (X - IM) \qquad\qquad (4.13)$$
$$S + B = I + (X - IM).$$

This means that

Private saving + Government saving = Domestic
investment + Net exports

that is,

National saving = Domestic investment + Net foreign investment.

If there is no government surplus or deficit $(B = 0)$ and net exports are zero $(X = IM)$, then Equation 4.13 shows that private saving equals domestic investment $(S = I)$ and we are back to the simple relation between saving and investment. But in an open economy, private saving does not always equal domestic investment. Instead, it is national saving that equals the total of domestic and net foreign investment. Let's take a look at the net–foreign-investment component.

U.S. foreign investment is the amount of foreign assets purchased by

U.S. residents. Foreign residents also purchase assets in the United States and the difference between the two is net foreign investment. This is equal to net exports because there must be a balance of foreign-exchange transactions. We will discuss this further in Chapter 12, but the basic idea is that when the U.S. economy is exporting more than it is importing, as was the case some years back, then there must be net foreign investment being made by U.S. residents overseas in order to provide enough dollars for the foreigners to pay for the excess of U.S. exports over U.S. imports. Similarly, when the U.S. economy is importing more than it is exporting, as has been true for the past several years, there must be a corresponding net investment by foreign residents in the United States (net foreign investment in the U.S. accounts is negative) in order to provide the foreign exchange for Americans to buy the excess of imports over exports.

In order to see how the budget deficit ended up crowding out net foreign investment, it is helpful to make one more manipulation of the condition given in 4.13. Subtracting investment from both sides gives the following:

$$(S - I) + B = X - IM. \tag{4.14}$$

The actual figures for the U.S. economy based on this condition are shown in Table 4.4. Notice that in the table we are using values in 1982 dollars for calendar years and not fiscal years. The figures will not correspond directly with values given in earlier tables. Any difference between figures does not affect the basic story, however. The government deficit tripled in size between 1980 and 1983.

Alternative Impacts of the Budget Deficits of the 1980s

In the early 1980s the U.S. government began to dissave on a large scale. There were several possible consequences of this that the economy might have followed. We can use Equation 4.14 and our *IS-LM* analysis to see what they are.

Helping to sustain income

The economy went into a moderate recession in 1980 and made a partial recovery in 1981. Then in 1982, the economy went into a deep recession initiated by inflation and monetary policy and exacerbated by a collapse of business confidence. Table 4.4 reveals that there was a substantial gap between private saving and domestic investment over the period 1980–83, a gap that sharply increased in 1982 after domestic investment fell by 13 percent between 1981 and 1982.

The budget deficits were both cyclical and structural, with the latter becoming more important after 1982. The tax cuts that came into effect in 1982 and 1983 were enacted because the administration argued that the burden of federal taxation was too great and was undermining incentives to work and invest. But as it happened, the timing of the tax cuts was excellent and

TABLE 4.4   Saving and Investment, the Government Budget Balance, and Net Foreign Investment, 1980–1987 (billions of 1982 dollars)

	Excess of saving over domestic investment $(S - I)^a$	Government budget balance (Negative values are deficits.) $B = (T - G)^b$	Net foreign investment (Negative values are deficits.) $(X - IM)^c$
1980	$42.1	−$40.3	$1.8
1981	40.3	−31.6	8.7
1982	117.8	−110.8	7.0
1983	81.2	−123.8	−42.6
1984	0.8	−97.5	−96.7
1985	17.2	−118.8	−101.6
1986	9.5	−126.6	−117.1
1987	−28.6	−93.8	−122.4

Note: These figures give the elements of the following equation:

$$(S - I) + B = X - IM.$$

The excess of private saving over investment plus the budget balance equals net foreign investment.
[a] Gross private saving minus gross private domestic investment; computed as a residual.
[b] Federal, state, and local government budgets combined; current-dollar values divided by the implicit deflator for GNP.
[c] The balance on the current account divided by the implicit deflator for GNP.
Source: *Economic Report of the President,* February 1990.

they became a well-timed expansionary fiscal-policy change. The main effect of the budget deficits in these years was to help sustain aggregate demand, boost income, and help overcome the gap between private saving and domestic investment. Income still fell, but the 1982 recession would have been much worse without the expansionary effects of the deficit in these years.

Prior to 1983, there was a small excess of exports over imports (positive net foreign investment) so that the foreign sector was helping to sustain demand and income also.

Both income and investment started to rise rapidly after 1982. In fact, by 1984 domestic investment was 47 percent higher than it had been in 1982. The expansionary fiscal policy combined with an easing of monetary policy had generated a recovery, and the cyclical deficit was being reduced. It was time for fiscal policy to become less expansionary and to reduce the structural deficit. In practice the total and structural deficits continued to grow, partly because the drive for tax reductions was so politically popular.

Impacts that did not happen

As the structural deficit grew in the mid-1980s, two impacts were predicted to follow. Private saving might have increased and domestic investment might have been reduced, and in fact neither of these happened. Let's look first at these "dogs that did not bark" because what we learn from what did not happen is just as interesting as what we learn from what did happen.[8]

Private saving might have increased (but did not).   Taxpayers are responsible for the government's debts. When the federal government began to borrow heavily, this meant that the interest payments that it would be making in the future to service its debts would have to be paid out of taxes that would be collected in the future. When taxpayers saw the federal deficit rise in the 1980s, they could have increased their own saving, setting aside additional resources, knowing that either their taxes or their children's taxes would have to be higher in the future. One possible outcome of the large federal-budget deficits, therefore, is that *private saving could have increased to offset the dissaving of the government sector.* Did this happen? No, it did not. Private saving actualy fell as a percentage of GNP in the 1980s.

Relatively few economists actually thought that private saving would rise to offset the fall in government saving, so that the fact that this option did not materialize was not a big surprise to most people. There is one school of thought that predicted it, however. Supporters of the Barro-Ricardo hypothesis argue that private-saving decisions will offset government-saving decisions. This hypothesis seems to have been clearly refuted by the experience of the 1980s.[9] Taxpayers did not base their saving decisions on long-run forecasts of future tax payments; they tend to focus on more personal and short-term factors.

Domestic investment might have fallen. (Arguably it fell some.)   The structural deficits of the 1980s were generated by tax cuts. This shift to an expansionary fiscal policy can be represented by a rightward shift of the *IS* schedule. Since monetary policy was not terribly expansionary, the result of the rightward shift of the *IS* schedule was to raise interest rates. Many economists argued that the growing deficits and the rising interest rates that they produced after 1983 would have a disastrous effect on domestic investment. In actual practice the increase in interest rates did have a negative effect on domestic investment, but this was largely offset by the positive impact on investment demand of the growth in income. We discussed this issue earlier when we talked about crowding out. The growth of total domestic investment was somewhat weak in 1985 and 1986, but the level of investment demand generally held up surprisingly well in the face of the high interest rates.

Saving was predicted to increase by some economists, but it did not. Investment was expected to collapse by many economists, but it did not.

---

[8] In a famous case Sherlock Holmes deduced that the theft of a racehorse must have been an inside job because the dog guarding the stable did not bark.

[9] Robert J. Barro, "Are Government Bonds Net Wealth?" *Journal of Political Economy* 82 (November/December 1974). For a discussion of this idea see also Douglas Bernheim, "Ricardian Equivalence: An Evaluation of Theory and Evidence," *NBER Macroeconomics Annual,* 1987.

The net result was that *by 1984 the imbalance between saving and investment had been eliminated*. (See Table 4.4.) And that only leaves one way for the budget deficit to be offset. Net foreign investment, which had already started to turn negative by 1983, became very large and negative in 1984 and beyond. Table 4.4 shows that net exports went from a positive $8.7 billion in 1981 to a negative $122.4 billion by 1987. *The structural deficits of the 1980s had the effect of crowding out net foreign investment.*

The Twin Deficits of the 1980s (and 1990s?)

As the economy recovered after 1982, income grew strongly, and the increasing level of income led to increased imports. This effect of income on imports was part of our analysis in Chapter 2, where we saw that net exports will tend to turn negative with increases in income here at home. *Part of the reason that the U.S. economy had negative net exports in the 1980s was the strong recovery of income.*

This was by no means the whole story, however. We have already noted that the growing structural budget deficits combined with monetary restraint led to very high rates of interest in the U.S. economy. And this meant that U.S. interest rates were very high compared to interest rates overseas. As a result, buying U.S. bonds became very attractive to foreign savers and they started to buy lots of them. There was of course no shortage of supply of U.S. bonds, because the federal government had a budget deficit and the Treasury had to issue huge numbers of bills and bonds to cover the shortfall of tax revenues compared to expenditures. *The United States started to finance its budget deficit by selling bonds to residents of foreign countries.* Saving made by foreigners was transferred to the U.S. economy in the form of negative net foreign investment from the perspective of the U.S. economy. Foreign saving was used to offset the U.S. federal-government deficit.

When residents of foreign countries buy U.S. bonds, they write checks in their local currencies and give them to banks or other financial institutions to arrange the purchase of the bonds. The bank or other institution must then go to the foreign-exchange market and change the local currency into dollars. In effect, foreign residents demand dollars when they decide to buy U.S. bonds and this increases the demand for dollars. When the demand for dollars increases, this will drive up the foreign-exchange value of the dollar. In 1980, it took 1.81 German marks to buy one dollar, but by 1985, it took 2.94 German marks to buy a dollar. The change in the value of the yen was less dramatic, but still important. In 1980 it took 227 Japanese yen to buy a dollar, but by 1985 it took 238 yen. *The increase in U.S. interest rates encouraged residents of foreign countries to buy U.S. assets and this led to an increase in the value of the U.S. dollar.*

When U.S. companies sell their products overseas, they must compete against local companies and against companies from third countries. An important element in determining who gets the sale, of course, is the price that will be charged. But the prices that a U.S. company will charge in, say, Germany or Australia depend upon the value of the dollar in international exchange. When the value of the dollar is high, U.S. goods sold overseas will become more expensive for foreigners to buy. And it may well become less profitable for U.S. companies to sell overseas. This means that *U.S. exports will fall when the value of the dollar increases.*

A similar argument goes for foreign companies that sell in the U.S. market. When the dollar rises in value, this makes foreign goods very cheap and Americans buy a lot of them. The U.S. market becomes a very profitable place for foreign companies to sell. *U.S. imports rise when the value of the dollar rises.* And since exports fall and imports rise when the dollar rises, it follows that *net exports will turn negative when the dollar increases.*

We have now traced out how the budget deficits of the 1980s led to the trade deficits of the same period.[10] The twin deficits together form one of the most serious economic problems of this period, one that is continuing into the 1990s. Many Americans believe that the trade problems of the U.S. economy are the result either of poor performance by U.S. firms or of protectionist policies overseas. But these views are not correct. It is certainly true that there are U.S. companies that perform poorly as well as companies that perform well. And it is certainly true that many foreign countries protect their own industries much more than the United States does. And these factors may be important in determining which industries run deficits and which industries run surpluses. But all of these things were true in 1980, when net exports were positive. They cannot be blamed for the overall trade deficits of the 1980s. The real cause of the trade deficits has been the structural budget deficits.

After 1985 the dollar started to fall again. The trade and budget deficits have also fallen, although both remain very large as of 1990. What does the future hold? The key question that we cannot resolve here is the extent to which the budget deficit will be reduced by agreements between the president and Congress to raise taxes or to cut expenditures. Eventually the budget deficit will be eliminated, but it will make a difference if we wait for this to happen gradually or act now to cut the twin deficits. The longer we wait, the larger will be the stock of bonds and other assets that will have been bought by residents of foreign countries. We will have to pay the interest on those obligations. Indeed, interest payments on the national debt are already a major budget expense.

Moreover, it is not certain that we can continue forever getting foreigners to finance our deficit even if we want to. At some point it will become harder and harder to attract foreign funds, and interest rates here in the United States will start to rise. It is quite possible that in the 1990s budget

---

[10] In Chapters 11 and 12 we look at the foreign sector in more detail and give a more complete explanation of the effect of the tax cuts on net exports.

deficits will crowd out domestic investment, even though this did not happen much in the 1980s.

Conclusions about Fiscal Policy

We have seen both the potential gains from using fiscal policies and the problems that can occur. An expansionary fiscal policy will increase demand in the goods market (shift the *IS* schedule to the right) and this will raise income. But the stimulation to aggregate demand from a purely fiscal expansion normally results in a rising interest rate and the crowding out of investment is a concern. How much of a concern depends upon the interest-rate effect, upon the nature of the money market, and upon how long the fiscal policy lasts.

The problems that result from using fiscal policy to increase income are not terribly serious if the policies smooth out short-run variations of income over the business cycle. Since it is hard to mobilize both the administration and Congress to take action on taxes or expenditures (it is impossible today given the debate over the structural deficit), the automatic stabilizers seem the ideal vehicle by which fiscal policy can improve the performance of the economy in the 1990s. There are good reasons to have in place programs such as unemployment insurance that support workers without jobs plus retirement and disability programs for those who cannot work. Maintaining or strengthening these income-support programs because they help the needy will have the beneficial side effect of improving the overall stability of the economy.

Running a large budget deficit over several years can create serious problems. Indeed, deficits have created serious problems in the 1980s that continue into the 1990s. Large structural deficits raise the rate of interest, and they distort the foreign-exchange market and the value of the dollar. Such policies will crowd out either foreign investment or domestic investment or both.

In our discussions of fiscal policy we found that money-market conditions made a difference. We did not talk much about monetary policy. At this point we need to take a systematic look at the role of monetary policy. This is the task of Chapter 5.

SUMMARY

- The government purchases goods and services, which adds to aggregate demand. Government expenditures include transfers and are much larger than purchases—transfer payments including interest on the debt and social security make up the majority of federal spending.
- Political pressures affect the spending decisions. Rationales for government spending include public goods, income support for the needy, and merit goods.

- The government raises tax revenues to finance its spending, but it often borrows to cover deficits.

- Net tax revenues, equal to gross tax revenues minus transfer payments, rise and fall with rising and falling income.

- Consumers make consumption and saving decisions with respect to disposable income (income minus net tax payments).

- Fiscal-policy changes include changes in the level of government purchases and changes in tax rates and transfers.

- With the government sector, equilibrium income is determined by equating aggregate demand $(C + I + G)$ to output (Y). Taxes (T) affect the consumption function.

- Increases in government purchases boost aggregate demand and raise equilibrium income through the multiplier effect. Taxes that depend upon income reduce the autonomous-expenditure multiplier because of the leakages of income into tax revenues. The reduction in the multiplier results in a steeper *IS* schedule.

- Tax cuts also raise aggregate demand. The multiplier is smaller for taxes than for government purchases.

- Increasing government purchases with a given money supply raises the interest rate. The interest-rate effect cuts into the expansion of aggregate demand.

- The interest-rate effect following a fiscal expansion can crowd out domestic investment.

- The government does not have to match expenditures with tax revenues. The difference between tax revenues and government expenditures is the government budget balance. When expenditures exceed revenues, the balance is in deficit. When revenues exceed expenditures, the balance is in surplus.

- Deficits can help cure recession; however, chronic deficits reduce the resources available for capital formation. Businesses may reduce investment in an economy with large chronic deficits. Large deficits erode the amount of national saving in the economy.

- The budget balance can be adjusted for cyclical changes in income. The deficit can be split into cyclical and structural components. In the 1980s, the U.S. federal government ran large structural deficits. These are continuing into the 1990s.

- Much of the impact of the large deficits of the 1980s has been higher rates of interest and negative net exports. Domestic investment has been maintained through negative net foreign investment. This situation may not continue.

KEY TERMS

automatic stabilizers

autonomous-expenditure multiplier

budget balance

crowding out

cyclical deficit

cyclically adjusted budget

disposable income

fiscal policy

government expenditures or outlays

government purchases of goods and services

gross tax revenue   net tax revenue

lump-sum taxes   private saving

lump-sum–tax multiplier   public goods

marginal propensity to tax   structural deficit

national saving   tax leakages

net foreign investment   transfer payments

DISCUSSION QUESTIONS AND PROBLEMS

1. What determines which goods and services are supplied by government and which are supplied by private markets?

2. If increasing government expenditures leads to higher levels of equilibrium income, are we always better off when government expenditures are increased?

3. The federal-government budget combines expenditures and transfer payments into a total government outlay. Why do we separate government purchases and transfer payments in our analysis?

4. Explain how an increase in government purchases brings about a shift in the *IS* schedule. How does the size of the shift depend upon the multiplier effect? How does the resulting increase in GNP depend upon the interest-rate effect?

5. Why is the multiplier different in an economy with government than in an economy without government?

6. Review the algebraic expressions for the following multipliers:
   Government purchases
   Lump-sum taxes
   Tax rates
   Balanced budget (optional).

7. What is crowding out? If crowding out occurs, how do the trade balance and availability of foreign capital affect the results of a fiscal-policy expansion?

8. How is the effectiveness of fiscal policy affected by money-market conditions?

9. How can the government spend more than it receives in tax revenues? Who supplies the missing funds?

10. Is running a deficit ever a reasonable policy tool?

11. What is wrong with long-run deficits? What happens to national saving?

12. If government purchases and taxes increase by the same amount, what is the effect on
    a. The budget balance?
    b. The equilibrium level of income?
    c. The share of GNP in the public and private sectors?
    d. Private saving, national saving, and the fraction of GNP that is saved?

13. The algebraic model of the economy is solved for equilibrium income by substituting functions for the terms in

$$Y = C + I + G.$$

Why are taxes not included in this equilibrium condition?

14. Distinguish between government expenditures and government purchases. What part of government expenditures is an addition to aggregate demand and what part is an addition to national income? Use the following list of federal government programs to calculate the value of expenditures and purchases:

	$ Billions
Defense	200
Veterans benefits	30
Farm subsidies	20
Transportation	30
Social security	150
Net interest payments	120

15. Calculate the values of the following: equilibrium income, the autonomous-expenditure multiplier, the lump-sum–tax multiplier and the *IS* schedule for an economy described by the following relationships:

$$C = 100 + 0.8Y_d$$
$$T = 300 + 0.2Y - 20r$$
$$T = 250 + 0.25Y$$
$$G = 1,200.$$

The interest rate is set by the monetary authority at: $r = 10$ percent. Compare the results you find with those shown in Worked Example 4.1. Which changes in the numerical values given in the above relationships compared to the values in Worked Example 4.1 contributed to increasing or decreasing equilibrium income and why?

■ APPENDIX 4A
IS-LM *with Taxes and Government Purchases*

In the text we derived the condition for goods-market equilibrium. We reprise some of this derivation now and then go on to obtain the *IS* schedule. Consumption depends upon disposable income:

$$C = C_0 + C_1Y_d$$
$$= C_0 + C_1(Y - T).$$

Investment demand or planned investment is still a function of income and the interest rate:

$$I = I_0 + I_1Y - I_2r.$$

We can insert into the goods-market–equilibrium condition, the expressions for consumption demand, investment demand, and the autonomous level of government demand:

$$Y = C + I + G$$
$$= C_0 + C_1 Y_d + I_0 + I_1 Y - I_2 r + G$$
$$= C_0 + C_1 (Y - T) + I_0 + I_1 Y - I_2 r + G$$
$$= C_0 + C_1 [Y - (T_0 + T_1 Y)] + I_0 + I_1 Y - I_2 r + G.$$

This was the equation we found in the text. To obtain the *IS* schedule, we put the interest-rate term on the left-hand side and then collect the income terms together and the autonomous terms together:

$$r = \frac{(C_0 + I_0 + G - C_1 T_0)}{I_2} - \frac{\{1 - [C_1(1 - T_1) + I_1]\}}{I_2} \times Y.$$

This expression is then the *IS* schedule. It may be useful to compare this schedule to the one that we obtained in Chapter 3 when there was no government sector:

$$r = \frac{(C_0 + I_0)}{I_2} - \frac{[1 - (C_1 + I_1)]}{I_2} \times Y.$$

What are the differences? Looking at the first expression in parentheses on the right-hand side in the first equation, we see that the term $(G - C_1 T_0)$ has been added. This reflects the net change in autonomous expenditure due to the addition of government. It will almost certainly be positive. The *IS* schedule has been shifted; it strikes the vertical axis at a higher interest rate.

Looking at that equation's second term in brackets on the right, we see that $(1 - T_1)$ has been inserted. This represents the effect of induced taxes on the multiplier. This term makes the expression in the bracket larger, which makes the slope of the *IS* schedule steeper.

Assume that we have the same money-market relationships that existed before the introduction of fiscal policy. The *LM* schedule is unchanged:

$$r = \frac{k}{h} Y - \frac{M_s}{h}.$$

The equilibrium level of income in the economy is then found by setting the interest rates equal. This gives the point of intersection of *IS* and *LM*:

$$\frac{(C_0 + I_0 + G - C_1 T_0)}{I_2} - \frac{\{1 - [C_1(1 - T_1) + I_1]\}}{I_2} \times Y = \frac{k}{h} Y - \frac{M_s}{h}.$$

Without plugging in specific values for the parameters, we cannot say whether this solution for income and the interest rate will occur at a higher level of income and a higher interest rate or at a lower level of income and a lower rate of interest than in the case with no government sector. Usually we expect the former case.

CHAPTER 5

Monetary Policy, the Federal Reserve, and the Money Supply

INTRODUCTION

In this chapter we describe and analyze the conduct of *monetary policy*, the policy decisions and actions that affect the banking system and the money supply. By its ability to change conditions in the money market, the Fed can bring about changes in aggregate demand. We use the *IS-LM* framework to describe the influence of the Fed's monetary-policy actions on the aggregate economy. Changing the supply of money will change the equilibrium interest rate (shift the *LM* schedule) and the level of income. At the end of Chapter 4, we looked at the effect of fiscal policy in an open economy, where there are trade and capital flows. At this point we are going back to a closed economy. A full treatment of monetary and fiscal policy in an open economy appears in Chapters 11 and 12.

Having seen the effects of changes in the supply of money, we look next at the determination of the money supply and how the Fed is able to adjust its size. We start this process by looking at banks and the monetary system that create and change the size of the stock of money. We describe how depository institutions contribute to the growth of the money supply through the transfer of funds among checkable deposit accounts. Then we look at how the Federal Reserve (Fed), the U.S. economy's central bank and monetary authority, controls the supply of money through the banking system. The supply of money is changed when the Federal Reserve changes the amount of reserves that banks can draw on to issue loans.

CHANGING THE MONEY SUPPLY: MONETARY POLICY

When we studied fiscal policy, we found that an expansionary fiscal policy did not lead to the full impact on income that would be predicted from an analysis of the multiplier effect alone. This happens because the increase in income raises the demand for money, which drives up the rate of interest, and the interest-rate effect then reduces aggregate demand. This was represented by an outward shift of the *IS* leading to a new equilibrium occurring at a higher interest rate along a given *LM* schedule.

Fiscal policy does not necessarily have to be restrained by a higher interest rate. When both monetary and fiscal policymakers decide that the level of income should be increased, they can use a *coordinated policy* of fiscal and monetary expansion. In such a case, the increase in income may reflect the full impact of the multiplier effect.

Coordinated Monetary and Fiscal Policies

A coordinated antirecession policy is illustrated in Figure 5.1. Prior to any policy actions, the economy is in equilibrium in a recession (point R), with the interest rate at r_0 and the level of income below potential output (Y_R). The government uses expansionary fiscal-policy tools (lowers taxes and/or raises government expenditures) to boost goods-market demand. The *IS* schedule shifts to *IS'*. At the same time the Fed increases the money supply—the effect of this being shown by a shift of the *LM* schedule to *LM'*. The result is an increase in income (from Y_R to Y_A) with a stable rate of interest.

Of course, coordinated policies can also be used to reduce demand. If the economy is in equilibrium at too high a level of income and is experiencing inflation that both the Fed and the fiscal authorites wish to curb, then a coordinated fiscal and monetary contraction will reduce the level of income while keeping the interest rate stable.

While there are great advantages to coordinated monetary and fiscal policies, in practice these policies are not always coordinated. In recent years, independent monetary policy has been a major force in the economy.

Independent Monetary Policy

Monetary and fiscal policies may not be coordinated because the Fed may decide that it disagrees with the fiscal-policy actions that are being made by the Congress and the administration. The Fed is often more concerned about inflation than is Congress because the Fed sees itself as the protector of the value of the currency. Elected officials may be more concerned about high unemployment, especially those in Congress who face reelection every two years.

FIGURE 5.1   Using Monetary and Fiscal Policies to Cure a Recession

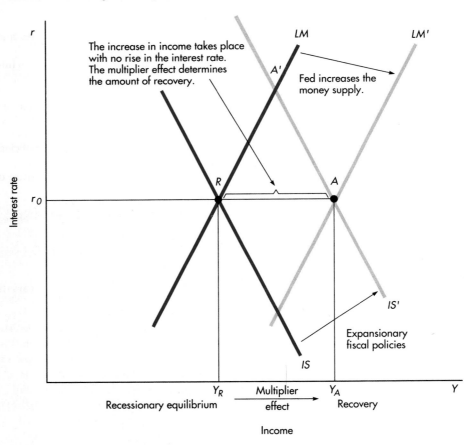

A coordinated change in both monetary and fiscal policies can change income while keeping the rate of interest stable. The increase in income takes place with no rise in the interest rate. The multiplier effect determines the amount of recovery.

Since 1978, particularly, the Fed has asserted considerable independence of action, supported by the leadership of two strong chairmen: Paul Volcker, who held office from 1978 until 1987, followed by Alan Greenspan, the current chairman as of 1990. In 1979, Paul Volcker announced that the Fed was committed to a stable target for the money supply, regardless of changes in the interest rate. The reason for the change in policy was a rapidly escalating inflation. Volcker was willing to see the economy go into the deep 1982 recession and to face strong criticisms from Congress.

■ Politics and Economic Policy

The outcome of American political elections is often decided by the health of the U.S. economy. Reagan's 1980 campaign challenge to voters' well-being was a direct appeal to their pocketbooks. It is generally agreed that Bush's 1988 presidential victory was favorably affected by U.S. economic performance that year. Despite the October 1987 stock market crash and a severe summer drought preceding the election, U.S. economic growth in 1988 was 3¼ percent and unemployment was at a 14-year low. At the same time the inflation rate remained steady at a 4 percent annual rate.

While American presidents usually bear the ultimate praise or blame for U.S. economic performance, the determination of U.S. economic policy is decided by many different players. The Federal Reserve is chiefly responsible for monetary policy which influences interest rates and monetary growth. The White House and Congress are jointly responsible for fiscal policy decisions, which determine the federal budget and spending priorities. The different considerations for controlling fiscal and monetary policies means that friction between the several decision-making bodies often emerges. This was illustrated by the Bush Administration's standoff with Congress over the 1991 federal budget in October 1990.

The differences in policy coordination are seen more clearly in the relationship between the executive branch and the Federal Reserve. By virtue of their office, U.S. presidents are the de facto leaders of their political parties and as such are interested in how their economic policies will affect election prospects. Thus, the White House usually places its highest priority on maintaining economic growth. The Federal Reserve, concerned most directly with monetary policy, places a higher premium on price stability than on economic growth. The Fed is generally more responsive to the international ramifications of its monetary policies, as these policies extend more directly beyond U.S. borders, as opposed to the more domestic nature of fiscal policy.

Since the 1988 presidential election, U.S. economic performance has worsened. By September 1990 the United States appeared closer to a recession than it had in recent years, because of both rising inflation and sluggish economic growth. While the White House would like to avert a recession, the Fed is more concerned with keeping inflation to a minimum. In recent years the Fed has placed a priority on keeping inflation in check and has sometimes resisted easing credit to make possible a fiscal expansion which would aid economic growth. The Federal Reserve's status as an independent decision-making government agency makes it more immune to political pressures than either the White House or Congress. It is most often because of this greater independence from political considerations that disagreements over the course of U.S. economic policy often occur between the Fed and the White House.

In the 1990s, the debate about the deficit and the appropriate levels of taxation and government spending means that active fiscal policy is unlikely to be employed to change the level of income, beyond the automatic stabilizers. In the absence of fiscal-policy direction, the Fed is left with the task of using monetary policy alone to influence the level of income and output. The administration may not always agree with the Fed's decisions, as the box above discusses.

On other occasions, the Fed may take independent actions with the full approval of the other branches of government. For example, during the

FIGURE 5.2   Changes in Income and the Interest Rate Resulting from Independent Monetary Policy

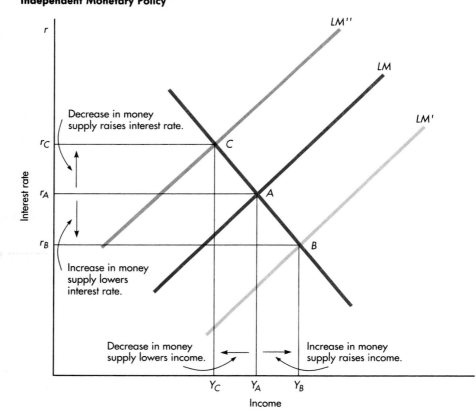

1980s there were several episodes of financial-market instability, such as the stock-market crash in 1987, which could have resulted in significant disruption and credit contraction. The Fed, under chairmen Volcker and Greenspan, acted to stabilize financial markets under crisis, continuing the role of the Fed as a provider of liquidity and stability in financial markets.[1]

We can see how an independent monetary policy works with the *IS-LM* framework as Figure 5.2 illustrates. The economy is depicted at an initial equilibrium (point *A*) with a level of income Y_A and an interest rate r_A. If the Fed then decides to increase the supply of money, this will initially

[1] Andrew F. Brimmer, "Central Banking and Systemic Risks in Capital Markets," *Journal of Economic Perspectives* 3 (Spring 1989), pp. 3–16.

result in an excess supply of money. As people then adjust their portfolios, the result is a fall in the rate of interest. The *LM* schedule shifts down or to the right, to *LM'*. The fall in the rate of interest stimulates investment, and over time the economy moves to point *B*, with a high level of income (Y_B) and a lower rate of interest (r_B).

The effect of a reduction in the supply of money is shown by the shift of the *LM* schedule from *LM* to *LM''*. There is an initial excess demand for money that leads to an increase in the rate of interest, and then a reduction in investment demand and a fall in income. The economy moves to point *C*, with income Y_C and interest rate r_C.

Even without a change in fiscal policy it is possible for monetary policy to affect the level of income and the interest rate. Independent monetary policy is an important instrument of control that can help the economy through sound policy actions or can hurt the economy through misguided actions.

WORKED EXAMPLE 5.1.   Monetary Policy: The Effect of Increasing the Supply of Money

In Worked Example 4.1 in Chapter 4 we found an *IS* schedule, given values for the components of demand in the goods market (the consumption function, the investment function, the tax function, and the level of government spending):

$$r = 141 - 0.034Y.$$

The money-market relations used in Worked Example 3.2 in Chapter 3 were as follows:

$$M_d = 0.4Y - 80r$$
$$M_s = 1,200.$$

The *LM* schedule then comes from setting money supply equal to money demand and rearranging terms:

$$r = 0.005Y - 15.$$

To find the level of income at the intersection of the *IS* and *LM* schedules, we set the interest rates equal:

$$141 - 0.034Y = 0.005Y - 15.$$

Solving this equation gives the equilibrium as $Y = 4,000$, that is, income is $4 trillion. Substituting back into either the *IS* or the *LM* equation gives the interest rate as 5 percent.

Question: Consider the economy just described. Suppose that the Fed now decides to expand the supply of money in order to increase income. If it increases M_s to 1,300, what happens to income?

Answer: The new *LM* schedule is given as follows:

$$M_d = 0.4Y - 80r$$
$$= 1,300 = M_s$$
$$r = 0.005Y - 16.25.$$

The new *IS-LM* equilibrium is then given by

$$141 - 0.034Y = 0.005Y - 16.25.$$

Solving this gives a value for Y of 4,032. The level of equilibrium income has increased by \$32 billion as a result of the monetary expansion. The rate of interest has dropped to 3.9 percent and this stimulated investment and raised income.

The interest-rate responsiveness of investment

An expansion of the money supply stimulates aggregate demand by driving down the rate of interest and encouraging investment expenditures (an outward shift of the *LM* schedule and a slide down the *IS* schedule). The increase in investment then leads to higher income and output. This means that *the effectiveness of monetary policy depends upon how much additional investment is induced by a given fall in the interest rate.* If the amount of induced investment demand is large, then monetary policy is an effective way of increasing income. If the amount of induced investment demand is small, then monetary policy is not an effective way of increasing income. With the slope of the *LM* schedule taken as given, *the effectiveness of monetary policy depends on the slope of the* IS *schedule.*

The case where investment expenditures do not respond by very much to a lowered interest rate is shown in the right-hand side (panel B) of Figure 5.3, where the *IS* schedule is steeply sloped. The shift in the *LM* schedule induces only a small increase in income. (The shift from Y_A to Y_B is small.)

The alternative case is illustrated in the left-hand portion (panel A) of Figure 5.3 where the *IS* schedule has a relatively flat slope. The expansion of the money supply is shown as a shift in the *LM* schedule, which raises income by more when investment is interest-rate–responsive (Y_A to Y_B in panel A) than when investment is not interest-rate–responsive (Y_A to Y_B in panel B).

While some kinds of capital investment do not change much when the interest rate changes (those kinds being the ones where the risks are high and the expectation of profits are more important than borrowing costs), there are others that are quite responsive (those long-term projects made by businesses in office buildings, shopping malls, and apartment buildings plus purchases of houses and cars by households).

The responsiveness of investment may also vary with general economic conditions. In an economic slump a reduction in the interest rate is not likely to stimulate much of an increase in expenditure on investment goods. Keynes argued that this was the case in the Great Depression[2] and that was a major reason why he claimed that monetary policy was ineffective during that period.

---

[2] J. R. Hicks, "Mr. Keynes and the Classics: A Suggested Interpretation," *Econometrica* 5 (April 1937), pp. 147–59.

FIGURE 5.3   The Effectiveness of Monetary Policy Depends on the Interest-Rate Effect in the Goods Market

A   A small drop in the interest rate generates a large increase in investment expenditures.

B   A large drop in the interest rate generates a small increase in investment expenditures.

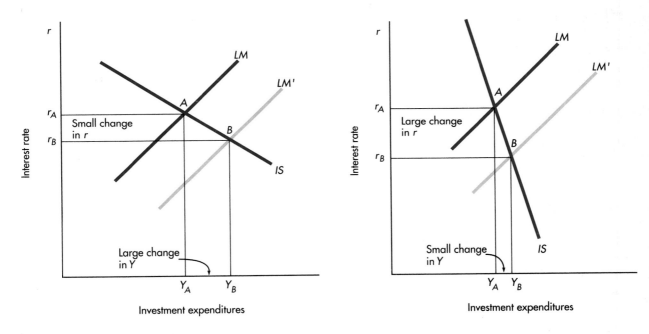

When the *IS* schedule is flat, monetary policy is an effective way of changing income. When the *IS* schedule is steep, monetary policy has a small effect on income.

Monetary policy was used aggressively in the 1980s. The reaction of investment demand to monetary-policy changes was strong. This period, during which monetary policy was the sole instrument of economic policy, revealed the power of changes in monetary policy to affect income. If we ever have another deep depression, Keynes's argument about the ineffectiveness of monetary policy may be important, but it is not relevant for the use of policy in normal economic conditions.

The interest-rate responsiveness of money demand
In Chapter 4 we found that the effectiveness of fiscal policy depends upon the responsiveness of money demand—the slope of the *LM* schedule. We will see now that the impact of a given monetary-policy change also depends

FIGURE 5.4   The Effectiveness of Monetary Policy Depends on the Interest Responsiveness of Money Demand (the slope of the *LM* schedule).

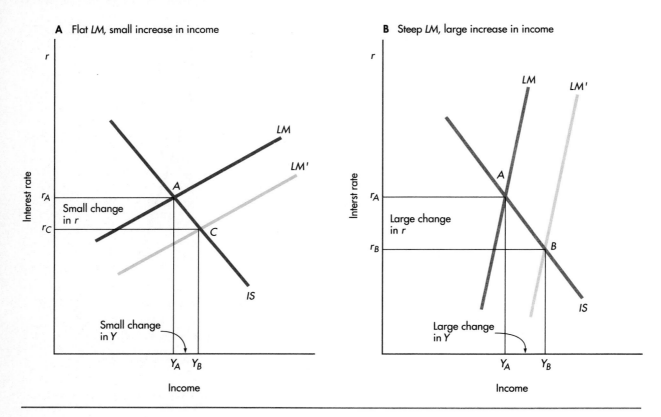

upon the responsiveness of money demand. The *LM* schedule gives points of money-market equilibrium and its slope depends upon the response of money demand to changes in both income and the interest rate. Here we will focus primarily on the responsiveness of money demand to the interest rate.

When money demand is not very responsive to changes in the interest rate, the *LM* schedule is steeply sloped as shown here in the right-hand panel of Figure 5.4. In this case, the response to a given increase in the money supply is a large fall in the rate of interest (r_A to r_B). The drop in interest rate stimulates investment and this then increases income. An increase in the supply of money leads first to an excess supply of money. As people try to reduce their money holdings, this increases the demand for bonds or bills and drives down the rate of interest. Since, in this case, money demand is not very responsive to changes in the interest rate, it takes a large reduction in the interest rate to restore money-market equilibrium. Equilibrium income rises from Y_A to Y_B, moving along *IS* from point *A* to point *B*.

If a drop in the interest rate results in a large increase in the demand for money, then the *LM* schedule will be relatively flat. This case is shown in the left-hand panel of Figure 5.4, where the drop in the interest rate, from r_A to r_C, is a smaller reduction than in the former case. In this case where the demand for money is quite responsive to changes in the rate of interest, the increase in the supply of money brings about a modest fall in the rate of interest. Hence, the stimulation to investment is also modest. Income rises, but the gain in income from Y_A to Y_C is smaller than the gain from Y_A to Y_B.

We saw in Chapter 4 that the effectiveness of fiscal policy depends upon the interest responsiveness of the demand for money (slope of the *LM* schedule). We have found now that the effectiveness of monetary policy in changing income also depends upon the extent to which people change their demand for money when the interest rate changes. To summarize the findings from this chapter and from Chapter 4:

- When people do not change their demand for money by much when the interest rate changes then the *LM* schedule is relatively steep, and monetary policy is relatively effective and fiscal policy is relatively ineffective in changing income.

- When the demand for money changes a lot when the interest rate changes then the *LM* schedule is relatively flat and monetary policy is relatively ineffective and fiscal policy is relatively effective in changing income.

WORKED EXAMPLE 5.2.   The Case of a Steeper *LM* Schedule

Take up the same model economy that was given in Worked Example 5.1. But suppose now that there is a different money-demand schedule, one for which the demand for money is less responsive to changes in the rate of interest. We assume also that the response to income is smaller. This new money-demand schedule is as follows:

$M_d = 0.36Y - 48r$.

Question: *a*. With this money-demand schedule and a money supply of 1,200, find the new *LM* schedule and show that it intersects the *IS* schedule at a level of income of 4,000 and an interest rate of 5 percent. How does the slope of this new *LM* schedule compare to the one in Worked Example 5.1?

b. What is the effect on income and the rate of interest of an increase in the money supply of $100 billion?

Answer: The new *LM* schedule is found by setting money supply equal to the new money demand:

$M_s = 1,200 = 0.36Y - 48r$

so that

$$r = 0.0075Y - 25.$$

To show that $Y = 4,000$ and $r = 5$ are points on the new *LM* schedule, these values can be substituted in:

$$5 = (0.0075 \times 4,000) - 25$$
$$= 5$$

so that we have shown that this *LM* schedule passes through the same point as the original one. (That is why we made the income coefficient smaller when we made up the example.) The new *LM* schedule still intersects the *IS* where income is $4 trillion and the interest rate is 5 percent.

The slope of this *LM* schedule is 0.0075 rather than 0.005. This is a 50 percent increase in the slope. This completes the answer to part *(a)* of the question.

What happens if the Fed increases the money supply by 100 with this money-demand relation that is less responsive to the interest rate? The new *LM* schedule is

$$M_s = 1,300 = 0.36Y - 48r$$

so that

$$r = 0.0075Y - 27.08.$$

We then set the *IS* and *LM* interest rates equal:

$$141 - 0.034Y = 0.0075Y - 27.08.$$

Solving this gives the result that $Y = 4,050$. Thus, *a given increase in the supply of money has had a larger impact on income with the steeper* LM *schedule.* (Income rose by $50 billion rather than the $32 billion in Worked Example 5.1.)

Substituting into either *IS* or *LM* gives the interest rate. For the *IS,*

$$141 - (0.034 \times 4,050) = 3.3.$$

The interest rate fell to 3.3 percent in contrast with a fall to only 3.9 percent in Worked Example 5.1. The greater decrease in the interest rate gives a greater stimulus to investment and a larger increase in income.

Starting in the 1970s, changes in the regulation of the banking system have affected the responsiveness of money demand. This has had an impact on the relative effectiveness of monetary and fiscal policy.

Bank deregulation and monetary policy

deregulation
Removal or relaxation of regulations governing the composition of bank assets and the payment of interest on deposit liabilities.

One of the effects of the **deregulation** of banks and other financial institutions is that in contrast to the rules in effect under regulation, banks are now allowed to pay interest on some parts of the money supply and on assets that are close substitutes for money. It is still the case that holding money involves some sacrifice of interest, but *for those who are holding money that* *pays interest, the cost of holding it is now equal to the spread or difference between the interest on bonds and the interest on money.*

When the interest rate on bonds increases, banks will compete directly or indirectly to attract deposits and the interest rate paid on money itself will rise. The differential or spread between the rate on money and the rate on other short-term bonds will increase in this situation, so that the interest cost of holding money will still rise as the interest rate on bonds rises. But overall, *when people can earn interest on money, the incentive to shift to bonds following a given increase in the interest rate on bonds is lessened. People will reduce their demand for money less in response to a given rise in the interest rate on bonds.*

One effect of bank deregulation, therefore, has been to increase the amount by which the interest rate has to change to bring money demand into equilibrium following a change in income. *Bank deregulation has steepened in the* LM *schedule, which has made monetary policy more effective and fiscal policy less effective.*

At this time we do not have any clear evidence as to how important a change this has been, but there is a sense among policymakers that fiscal policy is not as effective as was once thought, and changes in the money market as a result of deregulation have contributed to this thinking.

This conclusion provides a good lead in for us to start looking specifically at the banking system and how banks and the Fed create the supply of money.

THE BANKING SYSTEM: BANKS AND DEPOSITORY INSTITUTIONS

We have argued that money is distinguished from other financial assets by the fact that it is used for transactions purposes. The various definitions of money ($M1$, $M2$, and $M3$) were listed in Chapter 3. The money concepts that correspond most closely to money as a transaction medium are $M1$ and $M2$. The amounts of the different assets that make up these money concepts are shown for various years in Table 5.1.

These definitions of money consist of currency plus balances in accounts that offer checking privileges, or balances that can be moved very easily into checkable accounts. Checkable accounts are money because checks written on these accounts are accepted in exchange for goods and services. A check drawn on a checkable account can be converted into cash or transferred to another account on demand. Hence, checkable accounts are also called *demand deposits. We will use as our working definition of the money supply that it consists of currency held by the public plus demand deposits.*[3]

A demand deposit is a liability of a **commercial bank** or other financial institution such as a thrift institution or a money-market mutual fund. It is

commercial bank
A bank that is authorized to issue checking accounts to individuals and commercial customers.

___
[3] We are using the term *demand deposits* to cover a broad range of assets that have some checking privileges. There is also a narrowly defined concept of demand deposits that includes only commercial-bank checking accounts.

TABLE 5.1   The Composition of the Money Supply, 1976–1988 (billions $)

	1976	1980	1984	1988
Currency	81.6	116.7	158.5	214.9
Demand deposits at commercial banks	224.3	265.2	248.3	298.8
Travelers checks	2.8	4.2	5.2	6.9
Other checkable deposits, including S&Ls (thrifts)	2.7	30.5	145.5	283.7
Total M1	311.4	416.6	557.5	804.3
Overnight RPs[a] and eurodollars, money-market funds, savings, small time deposits	852.2	1214.8	1814.2	2272.8
Total M2	1163.6	1631.4	2371.7	3077.1

[a] An RP is a repurchase agreement.
Sources: Various editions of *Economic Report of the President* and the *Federal Reserve Bulletin.*

an asset of the customer who opened the account and deposited the funds. These private institutions, called depository institutions, together make up the banking system. The liabilities of these institutions are the demand deposits that are part of the money supply. Currency is supplied by the Fed, the only supplier of legal tender in the United States.

For many years the different institutions that made up the banking system were distinguished by the kinds of assets that they held and by the ways in which they were regulated. For example, regulations formulated in the 1930s directed thrift institutions, such as credit unions, mutual saving banks, and especially **savings-and-loan banks** (S&Ls) to specialize in holding residential-mortgage loans as their primary asset. At the time, S&Ls were savings banks where customers held savings accounts, but these thrift institutions could not issue checking accounts. Commercial banks were free to hold a wider variety of assets, including consumer and commercial loans, and they could issue checking accounts.

Both S&Ls and commercial banks faced restrictions on the interest they could pay depositors, but S&Ls were allowed to pay a slightly higher interest rate than commercial banks so that S&Ls could attract deposits that were then used for mortgages. This regulatory environment remained unchanged from the 1930s through the 1970s. During that period, due to the regulations that affected them, the commercial banks issued most of the demand deposits included in the money supply.

In the 1970s and 1980s, following a period of inflation and fluctuating interest rates, the government undertook a policy of deregulation. Many of the regulations governing the composition of bank assets and the payment

savings-and-loan banks
(S&Ls) Those banks where customers hold savings accounts. Prior to deregulation, they could not issue checking accounts. They were directed to specialize in residential-mortgage loans as their primary asset. Now they are similar to commercial banks.

■ The S&L Crisis

The rapid rise of nominal interest rates in the 1970s and the deregulation of the banking system that followed placed savings-and-loan institutions (thrifts) in serious jeopardy. The S&Ls operated within a regulated market to provide residential-mortgage lending. They did so by offering fixed-interest accounts that earned less than mortgages, and the spread between mortgage rates and savings-account rates provided the profit needed to run the S&Ls as commercial financial institutions. With the rapid run-up in nominal interest rates and the advent of alternative banking services, S&Ls saw themselves losing depositors. At that time, when depositors withdrew their funds from S&Ls, the thrifts couldn't sell off their mortgage holdings or successfully require homeowners to prepay their mortgages. The government "solved" the problem by allowing S&Ls to compete for deposits by offering competitively high interest rates on savings accounts. Unfortunately the solution was as bad as the original problem.

Many thrifts acted responsibly and they gradually found out how to compete with other financial institutions. Yet too many thrifts, having no experience in those markets and receiving signals from government regulators to fix the problem by earning higher returns, went on a lending binge. These institutions reallocated hundreds of billions of dollars, with a good deal of it invested in shaky ventures. The depositors who put money into the S&Ls were not concerned about the risk taking, because the federal government was providing insurance up to $100,000 on each savings account.

Bank deregulation also led to a relaxation of the government's oversight responsibility for assuring that thrifts followed sound banking practices. Fraud and corruption exacerbated some of the ill effects of unwise lending practices.

By the late 1980s, the *S&L crisis* exploded. Thrifts that together owed depositors hundreds of billions (deposits insured by the government) became insolvent, holding assets that were worth much less on the market than they were on the books of the S&Ls. The government was bound by the insurance it had provided and so it intervened by buying the thrifts or negotiating deals with healthy banks to buy the thrifts. All these transactions were subsidized with public funds. The Resolution Trust Corporation was formed to sell off the assets that the government acquired when the insolvent thrifts were dissolved. Since the assets were of a depreciated or even a nonexistent value, the government-created Resolution Trust Corporation faces years of borrowing funds and years of slowly liquidating the acquired assets. Estimates of the ultimate cost to taxpayers of bailing out the thrifts have been rising steadily—the official estimate as this is written is that as much as $300 billion of taxpayers money will be needed to deal with the S&L crisis.

---

of interest on deposit liabilities were relaxed. S&Ls were no longer charged with the primary task of supplying mortgage credit. Commercial banks had to share the franchise for issuing checkable accounts with thrifts and money-market mutual funds. Financial institutions were forced to alter their strategies for competing among each other, and the differences among kinds of banks were reduced or eliminated. Following deregulation, the services provided by a checkable account (payment by check, fund transfer, or automatic teller machines) were very similar among different types of financial institutions.

As a result of the deregulation of depository institutions, there was a dramatic change in the composition of the money supply with a rapid increase in checkable deposits held outside of commercial banks. By the end of the 1980s, the part of the money supply that consisted of checking-account deposits in commercial banks remained a large share of the narrowest definition of the money supply. (Thirty-seven percent of the total $M1$ and 51 percent of the noncurrency portion of $M1$ was held in commercial-bank demand-deposit accounts.) However, commercial-bank checking-account balances made up only 10 percent of the noncash portion of $M2$.

Because of the similarity of services among depository institutions, *we will analyze the monetary system using commercial banks as representative of all depository institutions.* By describing how commercial banks create demand deposits we will explain the process by which the banking system and the Fed create money.

Money Creation, Loans, and Reserves

Commercial banks are *financial intermediaries,* that is, they come between borrowers and lenders. They borrow from their depositors and use the funds to make business and personal loans. In the process they "create money" because their liabilities are demand deposits that can be used for transactions, while their assets consist of a portfolio of loans that are not money. They are not creating wealth, for a bank's assets and liabilities are balanced. But by spreading risks over large numbers of different loans, they have, in a sense, transformed their assets (a portfolio of loans with various risks and maturities) into money (the demand deposits that are the banks' liabilities). A key element in the money-creation process is the **fractional reserve system.**

reserves
A depository institution's reserve-account balances plus cash held in the bank (vault cash). Reserves held by depository institutions are available to meet withdrawal demands that exceed deposits.

Households and the cash managers of business firms deposit funds in bank checking accounts. These banks then want to lend out most of their funds to earn interest on them. After all, banks pay for the costs of their operations and earn a profit by charging fees for financial services and by receiving interest on the loans that they make. However, banks must hold **reserves** because their depositors may withdraw some of the funds that have been deposited. If your bank held no reserves of currency and you wanted to cash a check at the bank, the bank would not have any cash on hand. When you buy something and pay by check, the person you buy the item from will probably deposit the check in another bank and so your bank will have to pay out funds to the other bank. To do this, your bank must have funds in its **reserve account.**

reserve account
Banks and other depository institutions hold funds in accounts with the Federal Reserve. These are reserve accounts and are included in total bank reserves.

Under the fractional reserve system, banks need hold only a fraction of the funds that have been deposited in their accounts in the form of reserves, and they can then lend out the rest. A bank is in equilibrium when it has a desired level of reserves and it is servicing its depositors by giving them checking privileges and, perhaps, paying some interest on their deposits. In this situation, the bank is earning no interest on its reserves, but it is earning interest on its loans. Because the interest rate on loans is higher than the average interest rate on its deposits, it can make a profit.

fractional reserve system
The system under which banks need only hold a fraction of the funds deposited in the form of reserves.

TABLE 5.2   First Newtown Bank

Assets	Liabilities
+$10,000 cash	+$10,000 DD (restaurant)

During the 18th and 19th centuries, when gold circulated as money, reserves were held in the form of gold coins and bullion. In 1933, the U.S. government eliminated the use of gold coin as part of the currency. Gold is no longer an important part of reserves. Reserves are now held by banks in the form of U.S. currency (sometimes called *vault cash*) and special deposit accounts that banks have at the Fed (reserve accounts). These two parts of bank reserves are both liabilities of the Fed. Reserve accounts are like checking accounts that banks hold with the Fed; banks write checks to other banks using these accounts. Banks earn no interest on their reserve accounts in the United States. And notice that *bank reserves are not included in the money supply*. Cash held by the public is part of the money supply, but the cash and reserve accounts held by banks are not.

Deposits, reserves, and loans

To see how the banks and the fractional reserve system create money, we will use a numerical example. A bank, First Newtown Bank, opens for business in a town that didn't have a commercial bank. The bank attracts a commercial depositor, a local restaurateur. This restaurant accepts only cash payments. The first deposit the restaurateur makes in the new bank is $10,000 in cash. The $10,000 is deposited in a checking account, creating a demand deposit *(DD)*. The effect of the deposit on the bank's balance sheet is shown in Table 5.2.

At this point the amount of money supply has not changed. The cash has become part of the bank's reserves and, since bank reserves are not included in the money supply, $10,000 of cash has been subtracted from the supply of money. Offsetting this decrease in the money supply is the $10,000 demand deposit that represents an increase in the money supply. In other words, the money supply has not changed at this point because the restaurateur has simply exchanged $10,000 in currency for $10,000 in a checking account. This is only the beginning, however.

For simplicity we assume that First Newtown sends all of the $10,000 in currency to the Fed, where it is deposited in First Newtown's reserve account. The bank intends to leave only a portion of the $10,000 in the reserve account and lend out the rest to earn interest. The portion of the $10,000 that the bank can lend out depends upon the level of reserves the bank holds. For U.S. banks, this is basically determined by the Fed.

The reserve ratio

reserve ratio
The ratio of total reserves to demand deposits.

The size of the loan that the bank can offer is limited by the **reserve ratio** (*Rr*) and, subject to a minor qualification, *the reserve ratio is set by the Fed.* The reserve ratio is the fraction of demand deposits held as reserves:

$$Rr = \frac{\text{Reserves}}{\text{Demand deposits}}$$

$$Rr = \frac{R}{DD}. \tag{5.1}$$

If the Fed sets the ratio at 10 percent, then in our example First Newtown must hold at least $1,000 in reserves. Maintaining a $1,000 reserve means that First Newtown Bank can generate income by lending up to $9,000.

We assume a reserve ratio of 10 percent in our discussion here. The actual reserve requirements set by the Fed depend on the types of deposits (checkable and noncheckable), total size of all deposits, and the length of time the deposits are intended to be kept in a depository institution. If a large number of depositors decide to shift between checking accounts and savings accounts, the required reserve ratio changes to reflect the changing composition of deposits. This means that, in principle, the actual reserve ratio can and will change without any change in Fed policy. In practice the Fed adjusts its policy to make sure that when the public shifts among different kinds of accounts, the money supply is not altered unintentionally. In December 1989, required reserves were 10.3 percent of the deposits included in *M*1 and 2.0 percent of the deposits included in *M*2.

The ability of the Fed to control reserve requirements has increased in the past few years. Prior to the Depository Institutions Decontrol Act and the Monetary Control Act of 1981, only deposits in commercial banks that were members of the Federal Reserve System were subject to Fed reserve requirements. Following that act, all deposit-insuring financial institutions became subject to a range of minimum reserve requirements set by the Fed.

The banking system creates money

Returning to our example, the bank's credit manager finds that the local record store is interested in borrowing $9,000. When the loan is approved, a checking account with a $9,000 balance is issued to the record store. Table 5.3 is the balance sheet of First Newtown Bank after the loan approval but before the record store spends any loan proceeds.

The bank can make a loan, the borrower now has new money, and the restaurateur still has a deposit of $10,000. Now we see that once the First Newtown Bank has made its first loan, the banking system has created money.

TABLE 5.3   First Newtown Bank's New Balance Sheet

Assets	Liabilities
+$10,000 Reserves	+$10,000 DD (restaurant)
+$ 9,000 Loan (record store)	+$ 9,000 DD (record store)

The restaurateur owns a $10,000 demand deposit. She has the same amount of money she had before she deposited the cash in First Newtown Bank. There is also the record store's $9,000 demand deposit, which previously did not exist. The money supply increased by $9,000 when First Newtown Bank lent 90 percent of the restaurant owner's deposit to the record store.

The process of money creation does not stop with this first step. Of course the record store did not borrow $9,000 in order to keep it in the bank. The record store purchases $9,000 worth of compact discs from a record distributor. The record distributor is located out of town and banks with City National Bank. City National Bank sends the check to the Fed. The Fed takes $9,000 out of First Newtown Bank's reserve account and credits it to the reserve account of City National Bank.

City National Bank now has a lending opportunity similar to that which faced First Newtown Bank. City National Bank can lend 90 percent ($8,100) of its newly acquired $9,000 in cash reserves. City National Bank lends the money to an auto mechanic for tools, and the tool supplier banks with Second Country Bank in another city. The balance sheets of these three banks, as shown in Table 5.4, reflect the next stage of increases in the money supply.

In Table 5.4 the money supply has increased by another $8,100. This example started with a $10,000 deposit of cash in First Newtown Bank (the original +$10,000). There is now $27,100 of demand deposits in all three of these banks together. There was a $17,100 net increase in the supply of money as the banking system responded to the initial deposit. And the process is far from over.

The original cash deposit of $10,000 has not left the banking system; it has only been distributed among several banks. When these successive rounds of lending and interbank transfer of reserves is over, the original $10,000 will reside in the reserve accounts of many banks. But as long as no one takes cash out of the banks, the original deposit of $10,000 has added $10,000 to the reserves of the banking system. Table 5.5 is the consolidated balance sheet for the entire banking system, with the first three banks listed separately. By looking at the entire banking system, we see the banks' role in expanding the money supply.

TABLE 5.4   Three Banks' Balance Sheets

Assets	Liabilities
First Newtown Bank	
+$1,000 Reserves	+$10,000 DD (restaurant)
+$9,000 Loan (record store)	
City National Bank	
+$ 900 Reserves	+$ 9,000 DD (record distributor)
+$8,100 Loan (auto mechanic)	
Second Country Bank	
+$8,100 Reserves	+$ 8,100 DD (tool manufacturer)

TABLE 5.5   Consolidated Balance Sheet for the Banking System

Assets	Liabilities
First Newtown Bank	
+$ 1,000 Reserves	+$ 10,000 DD (restaurant)
+$ 9,000 Loan (record store)	
City National Bank	
+$ 900 Reserves	+$ 9,000 DD (record distributor)
+$ 8,100 Loan (auto mechanic)	
Second Country Bank	
+$ 810 Reserves	+$ 8,100 DD (tool manufacturer)
+$ 7,290 Loan	
Another Bank	
+$ 729 Reserves	+$ 7,290 DD (another borrower)
+$ 6,561 Loan	
.	.
.	.
Total-Banking-System Balance Sheet	
+$10,000 Reserves	+$100,000 Demand deposits[a]
+$90,000 Loans	

[a] The sum of $10,000 + $9,000 + $8,100 + $7,290 and so on is the same as $10,000 \times [1 + 0.9 + (0.9)^2 + (0.9)^3 \ldots + (0.9)^n \ldots]$. This equals $100,000. The same figure can also be found from the value of cash brought to the banking system as new reserves divided by the reserve ratio ($R/Rr = \$10,000/0.1 = \$100,000$).

The money supply and the amount of reserves

Prior to the original cash deposit, the money supply includes $10,000 in cash. After the deposit, the cash becomes part of bank reserves and is no longer part of the money supply, so this reduces the money supply by $10,000. However, $100,000 of demand deposits have been created. There is, therefore, a net increase of $90,000 in the money supply. The simple act (by the restaurateur in this example) of rearranging the form in which money is held—from cash to demand deposit—changes the money supply because the rearrangment adds reserves to the banking system. The $10,000 in cash deposited at First Newtown Bank becomes $10,000 in reserves. Eventually, this increase in reserves allows the banking system to expand the money supply by $90,000, balanced by an equal increase in loans.

Another way to see why the money supply rises by $90,000 in the example is as follows. Individuals and firms can choose to hold their money in the form of demand deposits *(DD)* or in the form of currency or cash *(Cp)*. The sum of these two is equal to the money supply:

$$\text{Money supply} = \text{Demand deposits} + \text{Cash held by the public}$$
$$M_s = DD + Cp. \tag{5.2}$$

The amount of demand deposits equals the amount of reserves divided by the reserve ratio. Substituting R/Rr for DD in the definition of the money supply yields

$$M_s = Cp + \frac{R}{Rr}. \tag{5.3}$$

The money supply depends on the cash held by the public *(Cp)*, the amount of reserves *(R)*, and the reserve ratio *(Rr)*. In our example, cash held by the public decreased by $10,000 and reserves increased by $10,000 when the restaurateur deposited her cash. The reduction in cash held by the public was balanced by an increase in demand deposits. The initial increase in demand deposits of $10,000 ultimately lead to an increase of $100,000 in demand deposits. The change in the money supply, shown in Equation 5.4, is the sum of the reduction of cash held by the public and the total increase in demand deposits:

$$\Delta M_s = \Delta Cp + \left[\Delta R \times \left(\frac{1}{Rr} \right) \right]$$
$$= -\$10,000 + \left(\$10,000 \times \frac{1}{0.1} \right) \tag{5.4}$$
$$= +\$90,000.$$

The banking system, by keeping reserves that are a fraction of their banks' demand-deposit liabilities and lending out the rest, is able to take any increase in reserves and increase the money supply by a multiple of the increase in reserves. A small increase in reserves can lead to a large increase in the money supply.

We have seen how the banking system creates money by using a simplified example. Now we take account of some complications and give a more general picture of how the money supply is determined in practice.

The Determinants of the Money Supply

monetary base
The sum of bank reserves and cash held by the public.

money multiplier
The money supply divided by the monetary base. The money-multiplier equation (5.11) shows how the money multiplier depends upon the currency ratio and the reserve ratio.

To see how the money supply is determined we need to understand two important concepts: the **monetary base** (the stock of funds that can be used by the banking system to expand the money supply) and the **money multiplier** (the degree to which the money supply is expanded out of the monetary base).[4] When we know what the monetary base and the money multiplier are, then we can measure the money supply. When we see how the Fed can control and change the monetary base and the money multiplier, we will see how the Fed controls the money supply.

The monetary base

The monetary base is defined as currency held by the public plus bank reserves. Bank reserves include both reserve accounts and currency held by the banks (vault cash):

$$MB = R + Cp. \tag{5.5}$$

The monetary base consists of all the outstanding "currency" that the Fed has issued in the past. Some part of this currency is now being used by the public. Part is in the banks. And part of it has been given back to the Fed to be deposited in the reserve accounts that banks hold with the Fed. In December 1989, the monetary base was $285.2 billion.

In practice, the Fed does not issue only currency. It can also issue checks that banks then deposit directly in their reserve accounts. A check for $1 million drawn on the Fed is essentially equivalent to $1 million in currency. A bank could cash the Fed's check and receive currency if it wanted to.

Part of the monetary base is currency held by the public. If it is increased, with demand deposits unchanged, there would be a direct increase in the money supply since this currency is counted as part of the money supply.

If instead bank reserves are increased, this does not change the money supply immediately, but the banking system can then initiate a sequence of lending and redepositing, which increases demand deposits and, hence, the money supply.

Although banks use the reserves in the monetary base to increase loans

---

[4] The way in which the money supply is determined is discussed in Federal Reserve Bank of Chicago, *Modern Money Mechanics* (Chicago, 1975).

and deposits, banks do not affect or control either the size or the composition of the monetary base. *The size of the monetary base has been set by the Fed's past actions. Changes in the monetary base are the result of Fed policy decisions.*

The money multiplier

The relationship between the size of money supply and the size of the monetary base is called the *money multiplier (MM)*:

$$M_s = MM \times MB. \tag{5.6}$$

The money supply equals the money multiplier times the monetary base. If policymakers and financial-market participants know the value of the money multiplier, they can forecast how much money will change when there is a change in the monetary base. Since the monetary base is changed by Fed policy, *the money multiplier determines how Fed actions are translated into money-supply changes.* The composition of the money multiplier can be found by using the definitions for the money supply and the monetary base.

We have that

$$MM = \frac{M_s}{MB},$$
$$M_s = DD + Cp, \text{ and}$$
$$MB = R + Cp$$

Putting these conditions together gives

$$\frac{M_s}{MB} = \frac{(DD + Cp)}{(R + Cp)}.$$

Then dividing through by *DD* and using the fact that reserves are equal to the reserve ratio times demand deposits *(Rr = R/DD, so that R = Rr × DD)* yields the following expression for the money multiplier:

$$MM = \frac{1 + \dfrac{Cp}{DD}}{Rr + \dfrac{Cp}{DD}} \tag{5.7}$$

currency ratio
The ratio of currency held by the public to demand deposits.

The currency ratio. We define the term *(CP/DD)* in the money-multiplier equation as the **currency ratio** *(Cr)*. It is the ratio of cash held by the public to demand deposits. The currency ratio reflects the decision by the public as to how they divide the total of their stock of money among the amount held as currency and the amount held as demand deposits. The currency-ratio decision is determined by households and businesses as they balance the advantages and disadvantages of using currency versus checks to buy goods and services. The currency ratio is a determinant of the money multiplier because a change in the public's cash holding changes the bank's reserves, which in turn changes the amount of demand deposits.

Using the currency ratio, we can rewrite the money multiplier in simpler form:

$$MM = \frac{(1 + Cr)}{(Rr + Cr)}.$$ (5.8)

We now have the result that *the money multiplier depends upon two key ratios: the reserve ratio* (Rr) *and the currency ratio* (Cr). In December 1989, the money multiplier was 2.8 for the $M1$ definition of money and 11.3 for the $M2$ definition.

We are now well on the way toward our goal of seeing how the money supply is determined and controlled by the Fed. But we have to deal with one more complication at this point.

excess reserves
The amount of bank reserves held over and above the minimum amount required. The **excess-reserve ratio** is the ratio of excess reserves to demand deposits.

Excess reserves.   We have been assuming that banks expand loans to the maximum amount allowable. If that's the case, the reserve ratio is determined by the minimum reserve ratio set by the Fed. In reality there may be times when banks reassess the risks of lending and conclude that they exceed the return to loans. In this situation, the actual reserve ratio is higher than the minimum or required reserve ratio. The reserves held over and above the minimum amount required are called **excess reserves.** Since the total reserves *(R)* held by the banking system are equal to the Fed-mandated minimum or **required reserves** *(RR)* plus any excess reserves *(EX)*, the reserve ratio needs to reflect both minimum reserves and excess reserves. The total reserve ratio is found by dividing the two parts of total reserves by demand deposits:

required reserves
The minimum level of reserves that must be held. The **required reserve ratio** is the ratio of required reserves to demand deposits.

$$\frac{R}{DD} = \frac{RR}{DD} + \frac{EX}{DD} \qquad \text{or}$$

$$Rr = RRr + EXr.$$ (5.9)

When excess reserves are held, the reserve ratio is comprised of the **required reserve ratio** *(RRr)* and the **excess-reserve ratio** *(EXr)*.

Banks attempt to keep their excess reserves to a minimum. During the 1970s excess reserves fluctuated around 1 percent of total reserves while during the 1980s the ratio rose close to 2 percent. The higher interest rates experienced in the earlier period may have contributed to the profitability of further squeezing down the level of excess reserves. On a day-to-day basis, fluctuations in deposits and withdrawals mean that often some banks do have more reserves than they need (positive excess reserves) and some banks have less (negative excess reserves). On a very short-term basis, often overnight, banks that need reserves will borrow from the banks whose reserves are too high. These short-term borrowing and lending transactions occur in what is called the **federal funds market.**

federal funds market
The market among banks for short-term borrowing and lending of bank reserves.

In our bank example, the First Newtown Bank was shown as having excess reserves as it responded to the initial cash deposit. In practice, this bank would have lent these excess reserves in the federal funds market. In normal economic situations, the positive and negative excess reserves of different individual banks are channeled into the federal funds market and offset each other. This means that the banking system as a whole has a very low net excess reserve ratio. In December 1989, required reserves were $59.068 billion while excess reserves were $0.923 billion.

On those rare occasions when the interest rate in the federal funds market is very low, or when banks are worried about a sudden wave of withdrawals by their depositors, banks in general may decide to hold back on maximizing loans and the banking system will generate higher net excess reserves.

The money-supply equation

We have said that the money supply is determined by the money multiplier and the monetary base. We can now set out a complete expression for the money supply. In Equation 5.10 we substitute the term *(RRr + EXr)* for the reserve ratio and generate a final version of the money multiplier *(MM)*:

$$MM = \frac{(1 + Cr)}{(RRr + EXr + Cr)}. \tag{5.10}$$

The size of the money supply equals the money multiplier times the monetary base, so that in Equation 5.11 we give the money-supply equation:

$$M_s = MM \times MB$$
$$= \left(\frac{1 + Cr}{RRr + EXr + Cr}\right) \times MB. \tag{5.11}$$

This expression for the money supply is complex and you should not try to memorize it. It is important to get a general sense of what factors are important in the determination of the money supply. (1) The monetary base is equal to currency plus bank reserves. The higher the monetary base, the higher is the money supply. (2) The currency ratio is equal to the public's holding of currency divided by the amount of deposits. The currency ratio appears in both the numerator and the denominator of the money-multiplier expression but, even so, when the ratio goes up, the money supply goes down. (3) The reserve ratio is equal to reserves divided by deposits. Reserves are almost entirely made up of required reserves. When the reserve ratio goes up, the money supply goes down.

Let's take a look at how the different elements in Equation 5.11 lead to a given overall money supply. We use the M1 definition of money for December 1989. The ratio of currency held by the public was 38.6 percent *(Cr = 0.386)*. The required reserve ratio was 10.3 percent *(RRr = 0.103)* and the excess reserve ratio was 0.16 percent *(EXr + 0.0016)*. This yields the money multiplier of 2.8 that we gave earlier [(1 + 0.386)/(0.103 + 0.0016 + 0.386) = 2.8]. The monetary base in December 1989 was $285.2 billion, so that the money supply ($M1$) was equal to \$797.6 (\$285.2 $\times$ 2.7966 = 797.6, where we have used an unrounded figure for the money multiplier).

Changes in the Money Supply and the Monetary Base

The money supply changes when any of these monetary factors changes. For example, if the currency ratio had been 0.3 in December 1989 with no other changes, then the money multiplier would have been 3.2 and the money supply ($M1$) would have been \$916.4 billion.

In the First Newtown Bank example given earlier, the money supply increased because of a decrease in the currency ratio when \$10,000 cash that had been held by the public was deposited in the bank. Notice however that the money multiplier in practice is smaller than it was in that example. In the example, none of the initial \$10,000 deposit ended up as additional cash held by the public. It all went into reserves and stayed there (as if Cr were zero). Also there were no excess reserves in the example ($EX_r = 0$). In the First Newtown example, therefore, the money multiplier for the \$10,000 increase was simply ($1/Rr = 10$), the inverse of the reserve ratio.

Changes in the money supply can also be induced by changes in the economic conditions that affect the money multiplier. For example, if banks see greater risks and decide to reduce their lending, the excess reserve ratio could rise, reducing the money multiplier and the money supply. The same might be said about banks' response to exceedingly low rates of interest. If rates were so low that in spite of good economic prospects banks still curtailed lending, there would be a change in the money supply induced by changes in the interest rate.

An increase in the monetary base will also increase the money supply. In the previous example, if the central bank had loaned \$10,000 to a depositor, then \$10,000 of new reserves would have been created. If the money multiplier is 2.8, \$10,000 of new reserves turns into a \$28,000 increase in the money supply.

In practice, changes in the currency ratio or the amount of excess reserves are not major factors in changing the money supply in normal times. Gradual changes in people's desire to hold currency can be adjusted for by offsetting Fed actions and excess reserves are usually very small. For the purposes of our analysis of cyclical fluctuations in the economy and monetary policy, we will assume that the currency ratio and the excess reserve ratio are constant. This means that the money multiplier is controlled by the Fed when it sets the required reserve ratio. Then *since the Fed also controls the monetary base, our analysis has shown how the Fed sets the overall money supply.*

Because of the large impact that monetary policy has on the economy, the chairman of the Fed's Board of Governors is often called the second most powerful public figure in our economy. We look now at how the Fed operates.

THE FEDERAL RESERVE SYSTEM

The manner in which monetary policy decisions are made is quite different from the way in which fiscal policy decisions are made. In the United States, fiscal policy is directed by the executive and legislative branches of government. Both the president and members of Congress are elected and thus strongly influenced by electoral and political concerns. The conduct of monetary policy is carried out by an independent Federal Reserve that is much less influenced by political concerns.

The Board of Governors of the Fed has seven members appointed to 14-year terms by the president and confirmed by the Senate. The board sets the overall policy goals for the Fed. The other primary decision-making group within the Fed is the Federal Open Market Committee (FOMC). The FOMC is composed of the seven members of the Board of Governors plus five members who are chosen in rotation from the 12 regional Federal Reserve banks. The FOMC determines what the Fed's monetary policy will be.

While there has rarely been unanimity of opinion about the direction of economic policy among members of the FOMC, in the past, the FOMC had been strongly influenced by the chairman of the Board of Governors. The Fed chairman is often, but not always, influenced by the economic-policy directions taken by the president. The Fed has a relation to economic policy not unlike the relationship of the Supreme Court to the body of U.S. law. The Fed's board members, as is the case with Supreme Court justices, are appointed by the president and they are not completely immune from political pressures, but they often make decisions that are not to the liking of the president.

The FOMC meets regularly every few weeks to consider the state of the economy and decide on the direction of its policy actions. It gives instructions to the staff of the Fed that have the effect of changing the money supply, either by changing the monetary base or by changing the money multiplier. The money multiplier can be changed if the Fed alters the required reserve ratio, but this is rarely done and we postpone the discussion of this approach. The main mechanism for monetary control is changing the monetary base through the control of reserves, using **open-market operations.** Open-market operations are the day-to-day purchases or sales of Treasury securities that are made by Fed staffers, mostly on the New York financial markets, following the directions given to them by the FOMC. We look at how this process works to change bank reserves.

open-market operations
The buying and selling of government securities, that is, Treasury bills and bonds. They are used to vary the size of bank reserves.

Open-Market Operations

The Federal Reserve system actually consists of 12 regional banks, which means that each regional bank has its own balance sheet of assets and liabilities. But in Table 5.6 we show a simplified balance sheet for the Federal

TABLE 5.6   A Simplified Balance Sheet of the Federal Reserve

Assets		Liabilities	
U.S. Treasury securities	80%	Fed reserve notes	76%
		Bank and depository reserve accounts *(RA)*	15
Other assets	20	Other liabilities	9

Reserve System as a whole, created by consolidating the balance sheets of the 12 regional Federal Reserve banks.

Since the Fed's assets consist primarily of U.S. government (Treasury) securities, it can buy and sell them in large quantities in the open market. Because the Fed acts through brokers, it participates in the market just like any other securities dealer. However, the Fed's motivation for buying and selling is quite different from that of the private purchaser. Private holders of Treasury securities want to earn interest on their investment, capture capital gains from changes in the prices of securities, or both. The Fed wants to control the money supply by changing the size of the monetary base.[5]

When the Fed buys securities (Treasury bonds or bills), its payment for those securities automatically increases the reserves of the banking system. *Open-market purchases of government securities increase reserves and hence the monetary base.* When the Fed sells securities, its payment for those securities automatically decrease the reserves of the banking system. *Open-market sales reduce the monetary base.* Increases or decreases in the monetary base then generate increases or decreases in the supply of loans and changes in the money supply.

Open-market purchases: increasing the monetary base

Table 5.7 illustrates how a Fed open-market purchase of securities raises the monetary base by showing the impact of an open-market purchase on three balance sheets: the Fed's, a private corporation's, and a commercial bank's.

In this example, the Fed purchases $1 million worth of government securities from a private corporation. The corporation sells these bonds to the Fed because the Fed offers a high enough price for the securities to induce the corporation to sell. The Fed pays for the securities by writing a check on itself. By making this transaction, the Fed has increased its own assets by $1 million (the bond) and increased its own liabilities by $1 million (the

---

[5] Jack M. Guttentag, "The Strategy of Open Market Operations," *Quarterly Journal of Economics* 80 (February 1960), pp. 1–30.

TABLE 5.7 Balance Sheets Describing a Fed Open-Market Purchase: An Increase in the Monetary Base

Assets	Liabilities
Federal Reserve	
+$1,000,000 Government bonds	+$1,000,000 Bank's reserve account
Corporation	
−$1,000,000 Government bonds	
+$1,000,000 Demand deposit	
Commercial bank	
+$1,000,000 Reserves	+$1,000,000 DD (corporation)
+$ 100,000 Required	
+$ 900,000 Excess reserves available for loans	

check issued by the Fed). The corporation deposits the Fed's check into its corporate checking account. This Fed check is different from a check drawn on another commercial bank. When a check is deposited in one bank, it is usually drawn against another bank and the monetary base does not change. In this case the Fed's check is returned to the Fed, which accepts the check and credits the bank's reserve account at the Fed. Thus the check issued by the Fed has become part of the reserves of the banking system and *the net effect of the Fed's open-market purchase is an increase in reserves and hence an increase in the monetary base.*

Because reserve-account balances and currency are liabilities of the Fed, the Fed can increase the monetary base by simultaneously increasing its own assets and liabilities.[6] The $1 million open-market purchase has led to an increase in the reserve accounts of the banking system. If the reserve ratio is set at 0.1 then following the open-market purchase and the deposit

---

[6] In the Fed balance sheet shown in Table 5.6, the Fed's liabilities were shown to be mostly Federal Reserve notes (cash, either Cp or Cb) and the reserve accounts (RA) of banks and other depository institutions. All reserves and all cash (the components of the monetary base) are the liabilities of the Fed. The monetary base will increase or decrease when the liabilities of the Fed increase or decrease and the Fed can change the size of its liabilities. This is done when the Fed simultaneously increases or decreases both its assets and its liabilities. There is no mystery here. Any financial entity can simultaneously raise or lower assets and liabilities. When a corporation borrows money, its liabilities rise by the size of the debt and its assets rise by the size of the money balance and/or real assets purchased with the proceeds of its borrowing. What is different here is that changes in the firm's level of assets and liabilities do not affect the money supply—the lender's money balance goes down and the borrower's money balance goes up. In contrast, changes in the Fed's level of assets and liabilities do in fact change the monetary base and ultimately change the money supply.

of the Fed's check with the bank, the bank's minimum or required reserves have increased by $100,000, while total reserves have increased by $1 million. There are $900,000 in excess reserves available for loans. When the bank lends those excess reserves, it creates a multiple increase in the amount of loans and money in the economy. The open-market purchase increases the monetary base and the increase of the monetary base leads to an increase of the money supply. If the money multiplier is 2.8 as it was approximately in 1989, then the $1 million open-market purchase results in a $2.8 million increase in the money supply.

Open-market sales: decreasing the monetary base

When the Fed wants to reduce the money supply, it sells Treasury securities. Private purchasers buy the securities by writing checks payable to the Fed. Instead of directly presenting those checks to the depository institution on which they were drawn, the Fed simply debits their reserve accounts. The reduction in reserves leaves banks with a shortage of required reserves. Banks react to the reserve shortage by building up reserves. Reserves are accumulated when banks reduce the amount of new loans issued relevant to the amount of loan repayments it receives. Businesses find it harder to have lines of credit renewed, let alone continue or expand borrowing. The economywide contraction of credit works in the opposite direction from the expansion of the money supply. The money supply is reduced. Tighter credit, along with an excess demand for money, drives up the interest rate and drives down the level of income.

The expansion or contraction of the money supply via open-market operations is both subtle and powerful. The Fed can vary its stance (that is, expand or contract on a daily basis) to a small or large degree, depending upon the size of its open-market purchases or sales. The power of open-market operations comes from the Fed's control over the monetary base. Each dollar increase or decrease in the monetary base results in a multiplied increase or decrease in the money supply via the money multiplier.

This analysis of the way in which the Fed changes reserves has omitted one important qualification. The Fed has a commitment to the banks that they can actually borrow reserves if they are suddenly caught short. We take a look now at the question of *borrowed reserves*.

Borrowed Reserves

The Fed allows banks to borrow reserves to meet its reserve requirements. In our earlier banking example, suppose that by acquiring deposits and making loans, First Newtown Bank has grown to $100,000 in deposits. The reserve ratio is set at 10 percent and the bank holds $10,000 in reserves and $90,000 in loans.

If the restaurateur now decides to remove her $10,000 from First Newtown Bank, the bank will not be able to meet the withdrawal without depleting

TABLE 5.8   The Role of Borrowed Reserves: First Newtown Bank

Assets	Liabilities
$10,000 Reserves	$100,000 Demand deposits
$90,000 Loans	
−$10,000 Cash to the restaurateur	−$ 10,000 Demand deposits
	$ 90,000 Net demand deposits
+$ 9,000 Borrowed reserves	+$ 9,000 owed to Fed

its reserves and having its reserve ratio fall below the required ratio. Since the bank cannot convert its loans to cash in the short run, it is faced with a problem. One solution is that the bank could go into the federal funds market and borrow reserves from another bank. But if many banks were trying to borrow reserves at the same time, there would not be enough excess reserves to solve the cash-withdrawal problem. The rate of interest on federal funds would rise dramatically but the amount of reserves available in the banking system would still be inadequate. The solution to the problem caused by cash withdrawal (inadequate reserves) is for banks to get help from the Fed. In our example, the bank borrows $9,000 from the Fed to meet the restaurateur's withdrawal and the bank maintains its required level of reserves. Table 5.8 illustrates the role of borrowed reserves.

The bank ends up with $90,000 in demand deposits, holding a 10 percent reserve position of $9,000. The bank did not have to reduce its loan portfolio to generate cash for the withdrawal. There is no contraction of credit available to businesses. The money supply did not contract because even as the rise in the currency ratio reduced the money multiplier, the increase in borrowed reserves increased the monetary base.

If borrowed reserves were freely available, this would undermine the Fed's control of reserves and hence its control of the money supply. This is why in practice, *the Fed is willing to lend reserves only on a temporary basis.* The Fed is called the *lender of last resort,* meaning that banks only borrow from the Fed when, in the short run, they have no alternative. Banks have to comply with minimum reserve requirements and those banks that have borrowed reserves must eventually reduce their loans and their demand deposits. The Fed's willingness to supply borrowed reserves enables banks to manage fluctuations in the withdrawal demands of their depositors without being forced to sell off their other assets too quickly and hence at a loss. It allows the banks to make a smooth transition when the Fed decides to change the money supply. In December 1989, borrowed reserves were $0.266 billion out of total reserves of almost $60 billion.

The discount rate

When banks borrow from the Fed, they must pay interest. The interest rate that the Fed charges on borrowed reserves is called the **discount rate.** In principle, therefore, the Fed could control the amount of borrowed reserves by varying the cost of borrowing. In practice, the discount rate in the United States is not primarily used as a *direct* way of affecting the amount of borrowing banks do.

discount rate
The interest rate that the Fed charges on borrowed reserves.

The Fed mostly uses the discount rate as a signal to financial markets about the direction of monetary policy. When the Fed raises the discount rate, it is signaling its intention to reduce the money supply. It is giving a warning to banks that they should start adjusting their loan activity accordingly. Banks read the discount-rate signal and they reduce their loan portfolios in anticipation of further Fed action. When the Fed lowers the discount rate, it is signaling its intention to increase the money supply.

Changing the Required Reserve Ratio

If the Fed decides to change the required reserve ratio, the result is an immediate change in the reserve position of the banks and other depository institutions. If the required reserve ratio is lowered, banks will have more reserves than they need to meet the new lower minimum requirements. Banks, finding themselves with unwanted excess reserves, will convert those reserves into loans or they will buy government or corporate bonds. Either way, bank credit has expanded economywide and the result is an increase in the money supply. The reduction in the required reserve ratio has left the amount of reserves unchanged, but the proportion of loans and money that can be supported by those reserves has increased—the money supply will increase because there has been an increase in the money multiplier.

Conversely, when the reserve ratio is raised, banks have insufficient reserves, which causes each bank to try to replace those reserves. Since there has been no increase in the monetary base, as the banks attempt to increase reserves, they do so by reducing the amount of loans and the money supply falls. Changes in the reserve ratio are rare. The Fed seldom changes the reserve ratio in such a dramatic fashion. On the rare occasions when the Fed has undertaken a significant change in the reserve ratio, the effect of such changes on the money supply has been substantial.

Some Important Issues Yet to Tackle

In this chapter we have looked at how the Fed can control and change the supply of money. We began by using the *IS-LM* framework to examine how monetary and fiscal policy interact and how monetary policy can be used independently. However, many of the most important contemporary issues concerning monetary and fiscal policy have not yet been dealt with. This

■ **The Fed's Seldom-Used Big Gun: Changing the Reserve Ratio**

The Fed changes the reserve ratio only when faced with the need for drastic policy action. When the reserve ratio is changed, the effect is powerful, because it can immediately change the behavior of all depository institutions. The last time there was a large change in the reserve ratio was as part of a Fed policy action in 1937, when the reserve ratio was increased by 33 percent. The resulting contraction of credit and the money supply helped to pro-long the Great Depression. Since the 1937 experience, the Fed has learned to avoid policy actions that bring about sudden and massive changes in the money supply. Circumstances do occasionally call for dramatic action, but, the use of the reserve ratio is not usually seen as an appropriate vehicle for significant changes in monetary policy. Most of the Fed's policy changes take place through its ability to change the monetary base.

chapter has used the standard *IS-LM* treatment of monetary and fiscal policy and the lessons from this analysis are important ones to learn. But in our judgment, this framework can also give misleading answers.

Part of the problem is that we have not yet tackled inflation. Another problem is that the *LM* schedule relates to the interest rate set in the market for short-term assets whereas the *IS* schedule describes equilibrium in goods markets that include long-term investments in physical assets such as houses or machinery. We have not distinguished between real and nominal interest rates nor have we differentiated between short-run and long-run interest rates. It is the role of financial markets to set the relationship between short-term and long-term rates of interest and to take account of the impact of inflation on these rates, so we next turn to an analysis of financial markets and investment decision making.

SUMMARY

- A coordinated policy of monetary and fiscal expansion may be able to raise income without increasing the rate of interest.
- With a given level of income, an increase in the supply of money creates an excess supply of money that in turn causes the interest rate to fall. Investment demand is stimulated and income increases.
- When money demand is not very responsive to the interest rate it requires a large change in the rate in order to restore money market equilibrium following a change in income.

- A steep *LM* schedule will occur if money demand is not very responsive to the interest rate. Financial-market deregulation has meant that part of the money supply pays interest and this has contributed to the steepening of the *LM* schedule.
- A given shift in the money supply will have a large effect on income when the *LM* schedule is steep and/or the *IS* schedule is flat.
- The supply of money is determined by the money multiplier and the monetary base. Increases in the monetary base result in a multiple increase in the money supply.
- The monetary base is comprised of reserves and cash held by the public.
- The monetary system, also called the banking system, consists of depository institutions that offer checkable deposit accounts. Most checkable account balances are held in banks.
- A bank's assets include reserves, which must be a minimum fraction of the amount of checkable deposit accounts in the bank. The remainder of the bank's assets are loans.
- The size of the increase in the money supply is determined by the money multiplier, which in turn is determined by the ratio of reserves to demand deposits (the reserve ratio) and the ratio of cash held by the public to demand deposits (the currency ratio).
- The Fed changes the money supply by changing the monetary base and/or the money multiplier.
- The Fed has partial control over the money multiplier by setting required reserves and direct control over the monetary base by managing open-market operations.
- Open-market operations are purchases and sales of government securities. The amounts are determined by the Federal Reserve's Open Market Committee (FOMC). These purchases are designed to affect the level of reserves in the banking system.
- When the Fed sells government securities, it takes reserves out of the banking system and thus reduces credit and reduces the money supply. When the Fed buys government securities, it adds reserves to the banking system, which allows banks to increase credit and thus increase the money supply.

KEY TERMS

commercial bank	money multiplier
currency ratio	open-market operations
deregulation	required reserve ratio
discount rate	required reserves
excess-reserve ratio	reserve account
excess reserves	reserve ratio
federal funds market	reserves
fractional reserve system	savings-and-loan banks
monetary base	

DISCUSSION QUESTIONS AND PROBLEMS

1. How is an increase in the money supply matched by a change in money demand?

2. What happens to the interest rate when the money supply increases? Initially? Subsequently?

3. Who controls the money multiplier?

4. Describe the role of banks in increasing the money supply.

5. What might contribute to an increase or decrease in the money multiplier?

6. When the Fed buys or sells securities, what happens to the monetary base?

7. Suppose the currency ratio is 0.2, the reserve ratio is 0.05, and the monetary base is $300 billion. What is the money supply? What happens to the money supply if the currency ratio falls to 0.15? What happens to the money supply if the reserve ratio rises to 0.06? What happens to the money supply if the Fed uses open-market operations to increase the monetary base by $10 billion?

8. What does the Fed have to know about economic conditions, bank behavior, and the public's preferences in order to know how large an increase in the monetary base is necessary in order to bring about a targeted increase in the money supply?

9. How does an open-market purchase by the Fed that increases both the assets and the liabilities of the Fed lead to an increase in the money supply?

10. Review the way in which the effectiveness of monetary policy changes with different slopes of the *IS* and *LM* schedules. Explain the differences in terms of the behavior of holders of money and firms deciding to purchase investment goods.

PART IV

The Macroeconomy and Financial Markets

In Part IV we recast the *IS-LM* framework in the light of the financial sector and changes in the rate of inflation. Up to this point we have been describing *IS* and *LM* as intersecting at equilibrium, but a more accurate description is that *IS* and *LM* represent equilibrium in separate markets. The financial sector connects changes in the money market to changes in the goods market and vice versa. The financial sector consists of financial markets where individuals, corporations, the government, and financial institutions trade financial assets and it provides the means by which borrowers get access to funds supplied by savers. This sector is important to the working of the economy because in most cases savers and borrowers are not the same economic agents, neither do they share common preferences. Savers want at least part of their assets in a form which offers little risk and gives them ready access to their funds. Borrowers using funds to buy capital goods are subject to considerable risk and cannot repay loans quickly or unexpectedly. Financial institutions help to serve the needs of both lenders and borrowers and they make a profit by taking advantage of the spread between short-term and long-term rates of interest. We will look at the role played by financial institutions and markets in our economy by concentrating on the determination of different rates of interest.

Distinguishing among different interest rates is important because interest rates vary enormously by type. The interest rate that equates money supply and demand and the interest rate that influences the demand for capital goods turn out to be different from one another. The interest rate determined in the money market is a short-term nominal rate of interest, while the interest rate that affects investment is a long-term real rate. Nominal rates of interest are the ones that are commonly posted by banks or quoted in the financial press. Real rates of interest have been adjusted for inflation. Until now we have ignored the impact of inflation and changes in the price level on equilibrium income. We will now introduce inflation into the analysis, starting by developing the relationship between real and nominal rates of interest.

CHAPTER 6

Financial Assets, Real Interest Rates, and the Yield Curve

INTRODUCTION

In the actual economy there are many different rates of interest earned by a variety of different financial assets, and interest rates also differ in terms of whether or not they are adjusted for inflation. The interest rate that affects the level of investment demand is not the same as the one determined by equilibrium between money supply and demand. Assuming a single interest rate of interest, as we did in the first part of this book, does not represent the workings of the economy in a realistic manner. An increase or decrease in one rate of interest does not necessarily mean that there will be an equal change in all other rates. In fact rates can and do move by very different amounts; they may even move in opposite directions.

In this and subsequent chapters we recognize the variety of interest rates and look at how they are related. Specifically we want to know how to connect changes in money-market interest rates with changes in the interest rates that affect investment demand.

So far, we have generally ignored the effect of inflation and changes in the price level on the money market and on investment demand. The real world is quite different. When price increases are sustained, the buying power of money and the value of financial assets are reduced. Smart borrowers and lenders will take into account the effects of inflation on the value of their debts and their financial assets.

In order to understand how money and financial markets affect jobs and production—the link between the real and the monetary sectors of the economy—we must consider both inflation and the variety of interest rates. We are going to separate the *IS* and the *LM* schedules and then see how they can be put back together again.

As we investigate different rates of interest we also look at some of the ways in which *expectations* affect the economy. If bond buyers expect interest rates to change tomorrow, that expectation will affect how much they are willing to pay for bonds today and hence it affects interest rates today.

Expectations about the nature of future macroeconomic policies are particularly important. On Wall Street, all the major financial houses attempt to predict the actions of the Fed, and those predictions influence trading in financial assets. Financial institutions know that expectations about future monetary policy have an impact on current interest rates.

We find that expectations also play an important role as we assess the impact of inflation. It is the amount of inflation that is expected in the future that affects the attractiveness of holding money and other financial assets.

The different assets being traded on financial markets in the economy and the interest rates that are determined in these markets can be lined up along a spectrum. At one end of the spectrum is money, an asset that earns no interest or a low rate, but is safe and can be used for transactions. Next come short-term bonds (such as Treasury bills), followed by longer-term bonds. Then come corporate shares (common stock traded on stock exchanges) and, finally, real assets such as machines and office buildings. The markets in the assets along this spectrum are interrelated. When the Fed uses open-market operations at one end of the spectrum, it ultimately affects investment spending at the other. *We want to know how changes in money markets work their way into changes in the demand for real investment goods.*

We will start our analysis in this chapter by looking at the way in which the financial officers of companies move funds between short-term bonds, on the one hand, and their companies' checking accounts, on the other. We introduce inflation into the picture and see how this affects, or does not affect, the money-demand decision. This analysis shows that the demand for money depends on the short-term nominal interest rate and hence that the *LM* schedule should be drawn against this interest rate. We then take the next step along the spectrum of assets by looking at the relation between short-term and long-term rates of interest—at the term structure and the yield curve. In Chapter 7 we will move further along the spectrum and relate investment demand to borrowing costs.

CASH MANAGEMENT

The **money market** is where corporations, financial institutions, and individuals buy and sell short-term financial assets as part of their **cash-management** activities.[1] Buyers and sellers use the money market to adjust their portfolios

---

[1] The economic theory of cash management was developed by William Baumol, "The Transactions Demand for Cash: An Inventory Theoretic Approach," *Quarterly Journal of Economics*, November 1952; and James Tobin, "The Interest Elasticity of Transactions Demand for Cash," *Review of Economics and Statistics*, August 1956.

cash management
The movement of funds into and out of money through the purchase and sale of money-market assets. The goal of cash management is to maximize interest earned after deducting financial-transactions costs (FTCs) while providing sufficient cash to cover ongoing expenses.

money market
Where corporations, financial institutions, and individuals buy and sell short-term financial assets. Buyers and sellers, including cash managers, use the money market to adjust their portfolios so that they contain the desired mix of money and short-term bonds.

so that they contain the mix of money and short-term bonds that best fits the needs of these individuals or organizations. The short-term assets that are traded in the money market include Treasury bills (Treasury bonds with less than one year's duration, often called T bills), federal agency securities, dealer loans and repurchase agreements (RPs), bank certificates of deposit (CDs), federal funds, commercial paper, bankers acceptances, financial futures, and Eurodollar deposits.[2] Money-market assets can be converted to money (sold) very quickly with only a small risk that they will not fetch the price at which they were purchased. But these money-market assets cannot be used directly to buy goods and services (make transactions). Individuals and corporations deciding how much money to hold as part of their portfolios will weigh the benefit of holding money against the cost of holding money.

The Costs and Benefits of Cash Management

To carry out transactions people have to have money, but money is only needed at the very last moment before making a purchase. People and companies that are intending to buy something can cash in bonds or other assets the day they need to use money to make the purchase. In the United States, banks are not allowed to pay interest on the checkable demand deposits of corporations, so that any amount held by a corporation in a demand deposit represents a pure loss of interest.[3] This loss of interest is the *opportunity cost* of holding money. The person or firm holding money is missing the opportunity to earn interest (or more interest) associated with holding a financial asset other than money.

To minimize the loss of interest, business financial managers often transfer funds into and out of demand deposits. Deciding upon the frequency of transfers, determining which financial assets to buy and sell, and executing those transfers is called *cash management*. (The word *cash* here is used as a generic term covering all forms of money and does not refer simply to currency.)

The extent to which people or companies are willing to make transfers back and forth, into and out of money, depends upon the gain they can secure in earned interest balanced against the cost and time and trouble of making all the financial transactions that are involved. The income generated

---

[2] The money market describes a collection of several markets for a variety of very short term, highly marketable financial securities. It is the market for *nonmoney short-term assets*, yet, this is the market where cash managers trade money for its nearest substitutes and it is commonly called the money market. We simplify the discussion by assuming that all of the trade-offs between money and nonmoney assets take place between money and money-market assets.

[3] The Federal Reserve regulates the use of checkable deposit accounts and the Fed restricts access to interest-earning checking accounts to individuals. Corporations do not have access to interest-bearing checking accounts. The Fed's rationale for this rule is that it improves the effectiveness of its control of the money supply.

by the extra interest that is earned through holding short-term financial assets must be enough to repay the brokerage fees and the time and effort incurred in the process of continually buying and selling those assets. The more money a company holds, the less it has to pay in brokerage fees and the less time and effort have to be expended on cash management. These savings are the benefits of holding money.

Households also engage in cash management. When a significant asset is liquidated (as with the sale of a house or automobile), the household's cash position is suddenly increased. If the purchase of the next house or car is not immediate, it makes sense for the household to purchase a short-term asset, earn interest, and then sell the financial asset when the time arrives to buy the house or car. Although it would not be unusual for a household to buy interest-earning assets after liquidating a large asset such as a house, household cash-management activities take place with much less frequency than do such activities by corporations and financial institutions. In particular, households are unlikely to change their demand for money by very much when interest rates change. The dollars saved through day-to-day cash management are usually quite low for households.

This is not true for corporations and financial institutions. The optimal cash-management strategy will change when the rate of interest changes. And the behavior of these groups is very important for overall money demand. A large fraction of the short-term financial assets in the economy are owned or controlled by entities that actively engage in cash management.

The Average Cash Balance

average cash balance
The average amount held in all forms of money over a period of time.

The focus of our analysis of cash management is the **average cash balance.** We use an extended example of corporate cash management to look at how the average cash balance is affected by the short-term nominal interest rate and the cost of financial transactions. Then, since the average cash balance held by households and companies is also equal to the demand for money, we will have shown how money demand depends on these same variables.

In our example, a company needs $100,000 each day to meet its ongoing and regular expenses. It starts each month with a $3 million initial deposit in its checking account derived from its sales revenues. It spends the funds a day at a time, until, at the end of the month, it has a zero bank balance.[4] The firm then starts the next month with another $3 million deposit that it draws down daily and so on. This firm's average cash balance is $1.5 million, which is simply the average of its daily balances. Since we have assumed a smooth drawdown of funds over time, this is equal to the average of the initial monthly balance of $3 million and the final monthly balance of zero.

---

[4] For the purposes of this example, the year consists of 12 months, each with 30 days.

FIGURE 6.1   Average Cash Balances

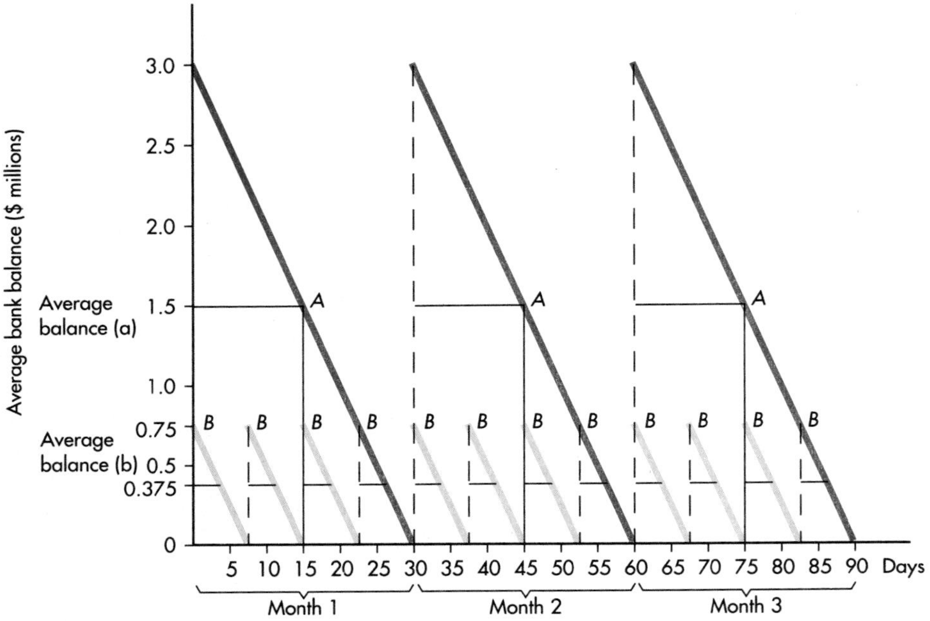

(a): $1,500,000 average balance. Initial balance is $3,000,000 every 30 days.
(b): $375,000 average balance. Initial balance is $750,000 every 7½ days.

The average balance (a) is shown in Figure 6.1 as the amount left in the checking account halfway through any month (days 15, 45, 75 . . .). Since the firm has the same average balance each month during the year, its average annual bank balance is also $1.5 million.

Suppose that this cash manager had been able to juggle the company's receipts and expenditures in such a way that she had maintained a zero average balance in the company's checking account, instead of the actual average cash balance of $1.5 million. In this case, she could have bought $1.5 million of any of a number of short-term financial assets in the money market. We will assume, for simplicity, that the cash manager compares the alternatives of holding T bills versus holding money. She ignores all the other money-market alternatives. We use T bills to represent all money-market assets.

If T bills earned interest equivalent to an annual rate of 10 percent, and the firm kept an average of $1.5 million invested in T bills for an entire year, the firm would earn $1.5 million × 0.1 = $150,000 per year in interest.

This $150,000 interest figure represents the opportunity cost of holding a $1.5 million balance in a checking account. By holding an average checking-account balance of $1.5 million, the company is forgoing interest of $150,000.

In practice it will never be possible or even desirable for the cash manager to keep a zero checking-account balance. Expenses for salaries, materials, and other factors are incurred on an ongoing basis and bills have to be paid. And of course, in actual practice, unlike in our example, receipts and expenses do not always occur smoothly and predictably. The cash manager must allow enough cash to cover uncertainty in the company's inflows and outflows of funds. (This is sometimes referred to as the precautionary demand for money.)

But one possible way of meeting ongoing expenses while still taking advantage of the opportunity to earn interest is to hold a smaller amount of money in a checking account and to use part of the monthly funds to buy T bills. Whenever the checking account runs down, the firm sells T bills and replenishes the checking account. This approach generates interest and hence reduces the forgone interest, but there is a downside. The firm incurs costs associated with buying and selling T bills.

financial-transactions costs (FTCs)
The explicit costs (brokerage fees) and implicit costs (cash-management expenses) of exchanging or buying and selling financial assets.

The costs of buying and selling financial assets are called **financial-transactions costs (FTCs).** Some FTCs are explicit, such as the brokerage cost of buying and selling T bills, commercial paper, and other bonds. Other financial-transaction costs are implicit, such as a portion of the salaries and expenses of a firm's accounting and financial offices.

Making the trade-off between the FTCs and the interest earned by T bills is the essence of cash management. Because FTCs are not zero, the average cash balances that people and companies hold will be somewhat larger than the absolute minimum necessary to meet the need for goods and services transactions.

WORKED EXAMPLE 6.1   The Effect of Trading T Bills Every Seven-and-a-Half Days.

Question: Instead of depositing $3 million in its checking account at the beginning of the month, the cash manager deposits only $750,000 and buys T bills with the rest. Because the firm still faces a $100,000 daily expenditure, its bank balance will have to be replenished four times a month (every 7½ days) instead of once per month. This replenishment will require four financial transactions per month (one at the beginning of the month, one after 7½ days, one after 15 days, and the final one after 22½ days). The result of this approach to cash management is that the firm will have an average bank balance of $375,000. This is shown as points *B* in Figure 6.1 where each quarter of the month has the same pattern of cash balances, starting out at $750,000 and declining evenly to zero. Show that this cash management strategy will increase the company's profit. What happens if the cash manager raises the frequency of financial transactions to five per month?

Answer: The firm will start out each month by buying $2.25 million worth of T bills—the portion of its monthly $3 million not initially placed in its checking account. Then the amount of T bills is reduced by $750,000 every time the checking account is replenished. By using the money market, the firm's opportunity cost of holding money declines from $150,000 per year ($1.5 million × 0.1) to $37,500 per year ($375,000 × 0.1).

The decline in the opportunity cost has occurred because the firm is earning $112,500 in interest per year on its average holding of T bills. This amount can be arrived at by observing that, since the average cash balance has declined from $1.5 million to $375,000, the average T-bill holding has increased from zero to $1.125 million ($1.5 million − $375,000). Then the average holding of $1.125 million earns $112,500 at 10 percent, assuming the same average holding is maintained for a year.

To get the same answer another way, note that the cash manager starts the month with $2.25 million in T bills. She holds this amount for a quarter of a month and then cashes in $750,000 worth of T bills, leaving $1.5 million. These are held for another quarter of a month until the next $750,000 is cashed in, leaving $750,000 still there. The T-bill balance drops to zero for the final quarter of the month. The average holding over the month is then (2.25 + 1.5 + 0.75 + 0.0) ÷ 4 = $1.125 million.

The firm engages in financial transactions four times each month. If each FTC has a cost of $750, and there are 4 per month or 48 per year, then the annual cost is $36,000 (48 × 750). The firm will generate a profit from cash management of $76,500 ($112,500 − $36,000).

If buying and selling T bills is such a good thing, why not go even further? If the cash manager increased the frequency of financial transactions to five times per month,[5] she could earn an additional $7,500 in annual interest. (The average cash balance would have fallen to $300,000 and the average T-bill holding would have risen by $75,000, to $1.2 million.) However, there would now be a total of 60 transactions per year and the additional 12 FTCs would cost $9,000 per year. The increase in the cost of transactions exceeds the extra interest earned and the company would be worse off. The cash manager maximizes the profitability of her operation by engaging in four monthly transactions, but not five.

Worked Example 6.1 shows how the optimal cash-management strategy and, hence, the company's demand for money depend upon the balance between the interest earnings and the size of the FTCs. We can then infer from this model that when the interest rate on T bills increases, this will increase the frequency of financial transactions and reduce the demand for money. At higher T-bill rates, firms are encouraged to hold lower average cash balances. In the appendix to this chapter we provide an algebraic treatment of the cash-management decision that shows these results more formally.

We have used this discussion of cash management to introduce the discussion of financial markets and to focus on the connection between the demand for money and the demand for short-term financial assets. We are now going

---

[5] We have considered here only alternative strategies involving an integral number of transactions each month. Strictly speaking, by allowing some months to have more transactions than others, the manager could do slightly better by averaging a little over four transactions a month.

■ **Real and Nominal GNP**

In our analysis of the *IS-LM* framework we have described the decisions firms and individuals make about consumption and investment. These are decisions about the quantities of goods purchased and how they vary with income. They are decisions about *real* consumption and investment and how they depend upon *real* income. Real income and real GNP measure the total value of income and output in the economy after adjusting for inflation. They are measured in the dollars of a given base year, 1982.

Expenditures and output denoted by the symbols *C, I, G,* and *Y* in our analysis referred to **real values** or inflation-adjusted values. Tax revenue, *T,* was also an inflation-adjusted or real value.

When we explicitly refer to a **nominal value** (for example, nominal income), we will precede the value with the symbol *P.* (For example, nominal income is shown as *PY.*) This particular use of symbols is consistent with the relationship drawn from aggregate supply-and-demand equilibrium:

P(the price level) × *Y* (real income)
= *PY* (the nominal or current dollar value of income).

Note however that we do not use this same notation for real and nominal money demand, as we will discuss shortly.

---

to introduce changes in the price level to see how real interest rates are determined and to show that the demand for money is a demand for real money balances. We will develop the relation between money demand and the interest rate further, but we need to introduce inflation so that we can see whether it is the real or the nominal rate of interest that affects money demand.

INFLATION, REAL MONEY DEMAND, AND REAL INTEREST RATES

nominal values
Values of such things as the money supply and income expressed in current-dollar terms. Interest rates and rates of return unadjusted for inflation.

real values
Values of such things as the money supply, income, and interest rates adjusted for inflation.

Inflation has become a pervasive phenomenon in our economy. The cost of living has risen in almost every year for over 40 years, increasing by over 600 percent between 1946 and 1989. In this and the next couple of chapters we will study the effects of inflation—what it does to money demand and interest rates. In Chapters 9 and 10 we tackle the causes of inflation. We start our analysis of the effects of inflation by seeing how it affects money demand.

The Nominal and Real Stocks of Money

The demand for money is affected by the price level because it is the dollar amount of transactions (not just the number of transactions) that generates a demand for money. In order to purchase a certain quantity of a good, the amount of money required is proportional to the price charged for that good.

A firm that buys three tons of steel wire at \$3,000 a ton requires \$9,000. If steel wire costs \$6,000 a ton, then \$18,000 is required, or twice as much. If the price level doubled, meaning that the average change in prices is twofold, then there would be a doubling of the demand for money balances needed to accomplish the same volume of transactions.

The current year's value of the money supply is the *nominal money stock.* At the end of 1959, the nominal money stock was \$140 billion for the *M*1 definition and \$298 billion for the *M*2 definition. By the end of 1989 these values had risen to \$798 billion for *M*1 and \$3,217 billion for *M*2. In nominal terms there was 5 to 10 times as much money in 1989 as there was in 1959, depending on which money concept we look at. However, the price level *(P)* in 1989 was 4.2 times higher than it was in 1959 so that the stock of money in terms of transactions (the purchases and sales that people wanted to make) had risen by much less.

The real stock of money is defined by the ratio of the nominal money stock to the price level:[6]

$$\text{Real money stock} = \frac{M_s}{P}.$$

Looking at the real stock of money involves an adjustment for the effects of inflation in a way that is just like the adjustment of income or GNP. Since the price level is equal to unity (or index 100) in the base year (1982), the real and nominal stocks of money are the same in that year. But since the price level has risen by a factor of over four over this time period, the growth of the real money stock is much less than the growth of the nominal money stock. For example, in 1959 the real money stock was \$461 billion in 1982 dollars, using the *M*1 definition, and this had risen to \$632 billion by 1989, a rate of increase of 1.0 percent per year. Over the same period, the real stock of *M*2 increased by 4.4 percent per year.

The nominal stock of money grew faster than the price level over this period, so that the real money stock increased. It is the growth rate of the real stock that we look at when we want to know how changes in the money market affect and are affected by income, expenditure, asset holding, and interest rates.

The Nominal and Real Rates of Interest

Along with nominal and real values for income, expenditures, and assets, there are nominal and real concepts of the interest rate. We will now use

---

[6] We have now defined Y and PY as real and nominal income, respectively, but we define M_s as the nominal stock of money and M_s/P as the real stock. In both cases the concepts are similarly defined: The real and nominal values are related to each other by dividing through by the price level. But obviously it is a bit confusing to have Y indicating real income while M_s/P indicates the real money stock. Nevertheless, this notation follows common practice in macroeconomics.

real and nominal rates of interest
The nominal rate of interest is the one reported by a bank or financial institution. It is denoted by the symbol i. The real rate of interest is adjusted for inflation and is denoted by the symbol, r.

the letter r as the symbol for the **real rate of interest** and the letter i as the symbol for the **nominal rate of interest.**

Adjusting interest rates for inflation is more complicated than adjusting other nominal concepts. When someone buys a bond costing $100 that promises to pay $105 at the end of one year, then the bond is said to carry a nominal interest rate of 5 percent ($i = 0.05 = 5$ percent). If there is inflation in the economy, so that the price level is expected to increase over the course of the year, then the $105 paid at the end of the year is not expected to buy 5 percent more goods and services. Depending upon how much increase there has been in the price level over the year, part, all, or more than all of the 5 percent return will have been eroded by inflation. Notice that *it is the change of the price level, or the rate of inflation—not the price level itself—that counts here in assessing the return.* And since the bond purchase will result in a return that will be paid in the future, and since the inflation that will occur cannot be known with certainty, *it is the expected rate of inflation that is relevant when people are deciding about buying or selling bonds.*

WORKED EXAMPLE 6.2   Computing the Real Rate of Interest

Question: Consider a situation where it is expected that there will be no inflation next year and a lender is considering lending $1 million for a year at 5 percent interest. In this case the lender expects to be able to buy goods and services with a real value of $1,050,000 at the end of the year. The real rate of interest in this case is 5 percent, the same as the nominal rate of interest (with no inflation, $r = i$). Line 1 of Table 6.1 shows the simple case where $1,000,000 is lent for one year at 5 percent and there is no inflation.

Suppose now that there were an inflation of 10 percent expected for the year. What will the real rate of interest be in this case, assuming no change in the nominal rate of interest? What will the nominal rate of interest have to be in order to yield a real rate of interest of 5 percent when there is 10 percent expected inflation?

Answer: With 10 percent inflation expected, lenders will expect to lose 10 percent of the value of their loans when they are repaid. If the nominal rate of interest remains at 5 percent (i is still $0.05 = 5$ percent), the lender receives $1,050,000 (the loan repayment plus interest) but because of the 10 percent inflation, the loan repayment plus interest is worth 10 percent less than the nominal amount of the repayment. After the effects of inflation, the real value of the loan repayment plus interest is only $954,545 ($1,050,000 \div 1.10$). In this case, the real rate of interest is -4.5 percent [$r = -4.5$ percent $= -0.045 = (954{,}545 - 1{,}000{,}000)/1{,}000{,}000$]. This is shown on line 2 of Table 6.1.

The lender loses purchasing value by making this loan. The real return to the lender is negative because even after lending money at interest, the lender's investment buys a smaller quantity of goods and services after one year than could have been bought at the beginning of the year.

Suppose the lender expects 10 percent inflation and he wants his investment to be able to purchase 5 percent more goods and services after being lent for one year. How high would the nominal rate of interest have to be to yield a real rate of

TABLE 6.1   Lending, Inflation, and Interest Rates

(a) Expected inflation rate this year	(b) Lent funds	(c) Nominal interest rate	(d) Funds repaid next year	(e) Real value next year	(f) Real rate of interest
1. 0	$1,000,000	5%	$1,000,000 × 1.05 = $1,050,000	$1,050,000	5%
2. 10%	$1,000,000	5%	$1,000,000 × 1.05 = $1,050,000	$1,050,000 ÷ 1.10 = $954,545	−4.5%
3. 10%	$1,000,000	15.5%	$1,000,000 × 1.15 = $1,155,000	$1,155,000 ÷ 1.10 = $1,050,000	5%

interest of 5 percent? The answer is that when there is 10 percent inflation, the nominal rate of interest has to be 15.5 percent ($i = 0.155 = 15.5$ percent) in order to yield a real rate of interest of 5 percent ($r = 0.05 = 5$ percent). This is shown on line 3 of Table 6.1, where the dollar amount of the loan repayment plus interest at an interest rate of 15.5 percent is $1,155,000. When this amount is reduced by the 10 percent expected rate of inflation, the value of the repayment plus interest is indeed $1,050,000 = $1,155,000 ÷ 1.1, so the real rate of interest is 5 percent.

In general, the real rate of interest, r, is defined in terms of the nominal rate of interest, i, and the expected rate of inflation, Exp$\Delta P/P$, as follows:

$$1 + r = \frac{(1 + i)}{(1 + \text{Exp}\Delta P/P)} \tag{6.1}$$

Equation 6.1 says that one plus the real rate of interest is equal to one plus the nominal rate of interest divided by one plus the expected rate of inflation. Note that the values of the interest rates and the rate of inflation are not expressed in percentages. This means, for example, that in the case where the nominal rate of interest was 15.5 percent and the expected rate of inflation was 10 percent, then the real rate of interest of 5 percent is calculated as follows: $0.05 = [(1 + 0.155) \div (1 + 0.10)] - 1$.

It is often useful to use an approximation for the real rate of interest. As shown in Equation 6.2, the real rate of interest is approximately equal to the nominal rate minus the rate of inflation:

$$r = i - \text{Exp}\Delta P/P \tag{6.2}$$

In this same example that we have just used, the approximation from Equation 6.2 generates a real rate of interest of 5.5 percent rather than 5 percent. (The simple form of the equation allows us to express the interest rate either as a pure number or as a percentage.) From Equation 6.2,

$r = 0.155 - 0.10 = 0.055$, or alternatively,
$$= 15.5\% - 10\%$$
$$= 5.5\%.$$

The accuracy of this approximation depends upon the size of the rates. At low rates of interest and inflation, such as we normally find in the U.S. economy, the simple formula works fairly well. At higher rates the approximation will produce a larger error.

The concept of the real rate of interest is an important one for economic decision making. As we will find in the next chapter, the real rate of interest is the rate that is most relevant for the decisions by businesses whether to purchase new investment goods.

But what about the money market? When there is inflation, will people hold more money or less money? There is no simple answer to that question, but we can begin to resolve the issue by returning to our corporate example and looking at the effect of an increase in the price level on the cash manager.

Real Average Cash Balances and Inflation

We are now going to go back to our worked example, with the following changes. We will assume that the cash manager expects that prices will rise in the future at 5 percent a year and it is now also the case that the nominal rate of interest is 15.5 percent. This means that the real rate of interest is still 10 percent, the same as in the first cash-management example. This means that for this new example, *we have changed both the nominal rate of interest and the expected rate of inflation, but we have kept the real rate of interest unchanged.* We will find that the increase in the nominal rate of interest has affected the demand for cash balances. The cash manager's situation has changed in two important respects. First, the increase in the nominal rate of interest changes the relative returns from holding money in a checking account compared with holding T bills. And second, the increase in the price level will increase the amount of money needed in order to make a given volume of transactions.

WORKED EXAMPLE 6.3   The Effect on Cash Management of Inflation and an Increase in the Nominal Rate of Interest

Recall the situation we described in Worked Example 6.1. The cash manager needed to provide her firm with the funds to cover $3 million in monthly expenditures. When T bills earned 10 percent ($i = 0.1$), her demand for an average money balance was $375,000 and she held an average T-bill account of $1,125,000. The total average balance of checking and money-market accounts together was $1.5 million, and she had arranged for her company to hold a quarter of it in the form of money. In that cash-management example, we assumed no changes in the price level, hence, no inflation.

Suppose that the expected rate of inflation is now 5 percent and the nominal rate of interest is now 15.5 percent. This means that the real rate of interest is still 5 percent, the same as in Worked Example 6.1.

$$\text{Exp } \Delta P/P = 0.05$$
$$i = 0.155$$
$$r = 0.1$$

Question: Show that it is profitable for the cash manager to make five financial transactions per month. What does this imply about the demand for money? How does money demand then change over time as the price level increases?

Answer: Suppose the manager increases the number of financial transactions she makes from 48 to 60 per year (i.e., from four to five times a month). An increase in the number of financial transactions was not profitable in the earlier example, but it will be now. The checking account is opened with $600,000 and drawn down to zero in five days, so that the average money balance is now $300,000 and the average T-bill balance is now $1,200,000 (one half of $3,000,000 − $600,000). The manager now holds only 20 percent of the company's monthly funds in the form of money. Cash-management costs are now $45,000 (60 FTCs at $750 each) and interest earnings are $186,000 (1,200,000 at 15.5 percent). Her net earnings are $141,000 ($186,000 − $45,000). She has gained substantially from the switch to more frequent transfers of funds. *The increase in the nominal rate of interest has induced a lower demand for money, even though the real rate of interest has stayed the same.*

The second effect of inflation is that as the inflation proceeds from year to year, the price level will increase and the cash manager will find that her company needs a large average checking-account balance to cover monthly expenses. Assuming that the firm's expenses rise in line with the general inflation, the cash manager will find that, a year from now, she needs to cover $3.15 million in monthly expenses, up 5 percent from the $3 million a month she is meeting at present. Obviously if the company expands or contracts its real activities, that will have an impact too, but for the sake of this example we are assuming that the real volume of goods-and-services transactions is constant.

A year from now, the manager finds that on average prices have gone up by 5 percent. The checking account is still replenished every five days, but now with $630,000, and it is still drawn down to zero at the end of five days. The average money balance is $315,000 and the average T-bill balance is $1,260,000. Cash-management costs are $47,250 (60 FTCs at $787.50 each), because we are assuming that the cost of each financial transaction also went up by the rate of inflation: those brokerage fees went up and so did costs in the cash-management department. Interest earnings are now $195,300 (1,260,000 at 15.5 percent). The company's net earnings from cash management have also inceased by 5 percent to $148,050 (195,300 − 47,250) compared with $141,000 a year before. The real value of cash-management activity is just the same as it was after the rise in expected inflation first occurred.

In Table 6.2 we summarize the effect of a simultaneous increase in both inflation and the nominal rate of interest. Column (a) shows the case we used in Worked Example 6.1, where there is no inflation and the nominal rate of interest is 10 percent. The average nominal money balance is $375,000 and this is the same as the real money demand since the price level does not change. Column (b) shows the first year in the case where there is 5 percent inflation expected and the nominal rate of

TABLE 6.2 Real Average Cash Balances, Inflation, and the Price Level

	(a) Years 1 and 2, no inflation	(b) Year 1 with inflation	(c) Year 2 with inflation
Nominal interest rate	10%	15.5%	15.5%
Real interest rate	10%	10%	10%
Expected inflation rate	0%	5%	5%
Current year's price level	1.00	1.00	1.05
Average nominal money demand	$375,000	$300,000	$315,000
Average real money demand	$375,000 ÷ 1.00 = $375,000	$300,000 ÷ 1.00 = $300,000	$315,000 ÷ 1.05 = $300,000

interest is 15.5 percent. Compared to column (a), the increase in the nominal rate of interest has reduced the average cash balance (money demand) from $375,000 to $300,000.

The price level is unity in year 1 because inflation is expected, but it has not yet changed prices. This means that the real money demand in year 1 is also $300,000. Both the real demand and nominal demand for money were lower in year 1 in case b than in case a, when no inflation was expected and the nominal rate of interest was low.

As the inflation proceeds, the increased nominal rate causes cash managers to economize on real money balances. But the demand for real cash balances does not undergo further change—it remains at $300,000 in both year 1 and year 2. However, each year of inflation increases the price level, so the nominal demand for money balances has to be adjusted accordingly. Cash managers need higher nominal balances in order to provide adequate funds to cover day-to-day expenditures. In year 2, shown in column c, the average nominal money balance of $315,000 is 5 percent higher than the nominal balance of $300,000 of a year earlier.

The Worked Example shows that *when inflation is matched by an increase in the nominal rate of interest, the firm's demand for nominal money balances first falls in reaction to the higher nominal interest rate and then rises over time with an increase in prices.* The firm's demand for real money balances also falls in reaction to the higher nominal interest rate. Then, as the dollar value of transactions increases with inflation, the dollar value of the money demanded to make these transactions keeps up over time. But as long as the inflation rate and the nominal interest rate stay constant, the demand for real balances does not change because of the ongoing changes in the price level.

INTERNATIONAL CASH MANAGEMENT AND THE DOLLAR AS A SAFE HAVEN

Cash management can have international ramifications. In international corporations cash managers have to decide how to distribute their cash and short-term bills among the different countries and currencies of the world. International cash managers want to earn the best return on their assets, but they are also concerned about risks. In particular, they do not want to buy assets with high probabilities of default.

Historically, the United States has been seen as a safe place to hold assets. When international tensions mount, cash managers around the world decided to buy U.S. T bills. The U.S. was a *safe haven* for funds, but this pattern seems to have been broken in 1990, following the Iraqi invasion of Kuwait.

Why did this happen? One initial response might be that the vulnerability of the U.S. economy to the fortunes of Middle Eastern oil supplies allowed investors to see weakness where there once was strength. But if this were so, how could the yen rise against the dollar? Japan is wholly dependent on other nations, including those in the Persian Gulf, for its oil supplies. In fact, oil counts for more than half of its national energy consumption. Yet its currency rose as strongly against the dollar as did that of Britain, a net oil exporter (albeit a marginal one). Germany is also a big oil importer, but the deutsche mark surged against the dollar. Oil dependence did not appear to figure consistently in the dollar's fall against major international currencies.

A more persuasive explanation is the rise in foreign interest rates, especially those in Germany and Britain, while U.S. interest rates held firm. In this climate, dollar-denominated assets such as T bills looked less attractive. A third possibility is that heightened expectations of a U.S. recession lowered the value of the dollar.

But these are short-term economic consider-ations, incapable in and of themselves of truly undermining the dollar's traditional position as a comparatively secure asset. Something else had to be going on. The dollar also plummeted against the Swiss franc, even though interest rates in Switzerland were much lower than those in other favored European countries—lower, even, than those in the United States. There is our clue. When investors turn to Swiss financial instruments, security concerns are usually the reason. When the issue is the relative riskiness of currencies, political risk sometimes overwhelms economic risk.

The dollar's decline as a safe haven for international investors may well be a reaction to the realignment of global alliances. Before investors came in from the Cold War they feared that any armed conflict or threat of one could escalate into a confrontation between the United States and the U.S.S.R. Europe was regarded at such times as a very unsafe place and hence as a very risky depository for investors. Thus, when a superpower conflict threatened, European as well as Arab and Japanese investors would move into dollar-backed securities such as U.S. bonds or stocks. The surging demand for dollars then sent the dollar's value soaring relative to the value of the mark, pound, yen, and other currencies.

With the warming of American and Soviet relations in the 1980s, the associated investment risk in European currencies also diminished. International investors now began to feel that their funds were safe there—safer, perhaps, than in the United States, where the dollar floated fitfully on a sea of economic troubles. Comparative political risk may not be the entire explanation for the dollar's decline as an international investment haven, but it cannot be dismissed as an important factor in this decline.

Looking at the effect of the interest rate on money demand, the demand for *real* money balances has gone down because the higher *nominal* interest rate has led to a decrease in money demand. This is a paradoxical and important result: *The demand for real money balances reacts to changes in the nominal rate of interest rather than to changes in the real rate of interest.*

One of the important lessons of macroeconomics is that most rational business and economic decisions are made based upon real values of variables: real income, real taxes, and real interest rates. And the same idea does hold for decisions about the demand for money as well. The reason that the demand for the real stock of money is affected by the nominal interest rate is because the cash manager is comparing the return from T bills and the return from money. The increase in the price level will erode the two assets' values to the same degree regardless of the proportion held of each. So an increase in inflation does not shift the trade-off between the two assets. A rise in the nominal rate of interest makes holding T bills relatively more profitable than holding money.

We asked at the beginning of this section how inflation would change the demand for money. And we have found that the answer to this question is complex. An increase in expected inflation will lower the demand for money if it is also associated with an increase in the nominal rate of interest. In our example, we assumed that the inflation was matched by an increase in the nominal rate of interest that kept the real rate of interest constant, so the combination of inflation and a higher nominal rate of interest did lead to the reduction in money demand. But it was the change in the nominal rate of interest that had the effect. In the actual economy, inflation usually does lead to changes in the nominal rate of interest, but the changes do not always end up leaving the real rate of interest constant.

As well as the link between inflation and the interest rate, we also found that as inflation proceeds over time, the demand for nominal money will rise in proportion to the rise in the price level. *The demand for money is a demand for a real stock of money.*

We now take the lessons from the analysis of cash management and apply them to the demand for money and equilibrium in the money market described along the *LM* schedule.

THE DEMAND FOR MONEY AND MONEY-MARKET EQUILIBRIUM REVISITED

Our analysis of corporate cash management shows that the real money stock that a firm would like to hold varies negatively with the nominal interest rate on short-term financial assets, i, and negatively with the cost of financial transactions, *FTC*. If we continue to assume that real income, Y, provides a proxy for the volume of transactions (purchases of goods and services), then

---

FIGURE 6.2   The Demand for Real Money Balances

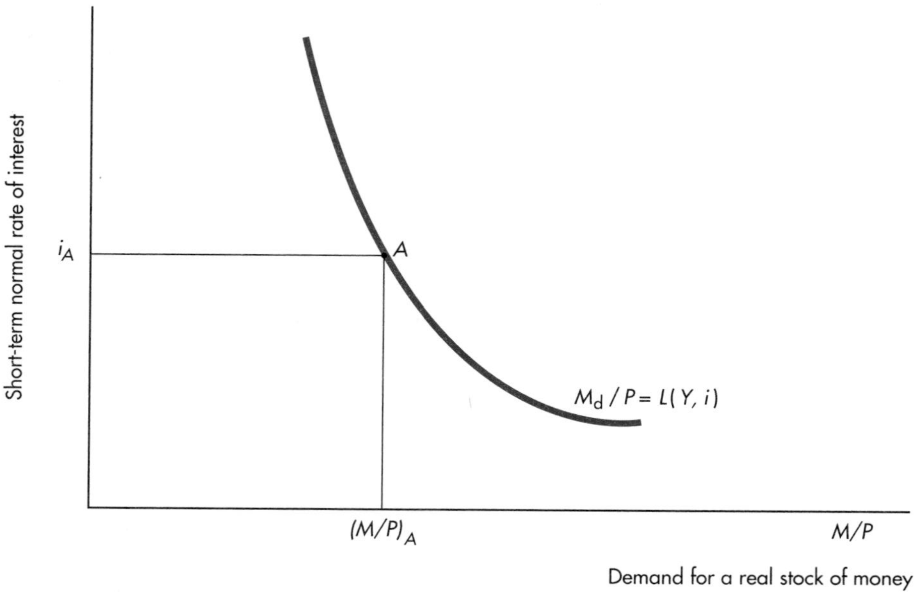

Demand for a real stock of money

Real money demand depends upon real income and the short-term nominal interest rate. At higher levels of interest, the schedule becomes steeper as cash managers reach the point where they can no longer easily economize on average cash balances.

---

demand varies positively with income and we have a new form for the money-demand function:

$$\frac{M_d}{P} = L(Y, i). \qquad (6.3)$$

In Equation 6.3 we have omitted an explicit term for financial-transactions costs (FTC). These costs change slowly and are not generally a major source of changes in money demand. The demand for money given in Equation 6.3 is shown in Figure 6.2. The schedule (M_d/P) shows how the demand for money varies with the short-term nominal interest rate. In the figure, we are holding constant income, the price level, and financial-transactions costs.

In contrast with the demand-for-money schedule introduced in Chapter 3, here we show the schedule as a curve that becomes steep at high interest rates. This is because there are limits to how much people and firms can economize on money. At very low interest rates the demand-for-money schedule becomes rather flat, because T bills provide little advantage over holding money.

The Real Supply of Money

In Chapter 5, we described the Fed's control over the monetary base, the money multiplier, and size of the money supply. The Fed has direct control over the nominal money supply (M_s). The real stock of money is the real money supply and we will assume that by adjusting the nominal money supply to match changes in the price level, the real money supply can also be taken as set by the Fed.

Many economists would challenge this assumption. Classical economists argued that if the nominal money supply, M_s, is increased, then the price level increases quickly until the real money supply (M_s/P) returns to its original level. They questioned whether the Fed can determine the real stock of money, and many monetarist economists today would concur with this classical assessment.

We believe that taking the real money supply as set by the Fed is a reasonable assumption for the analysis of short-run fluctuations in the economy. The rate of inflation is determined by many factors and does not change quickly in response to short-run changes in demand or in the nominal money supply. The Fed does not have any direct control over the price level, but at any point in time the Fed is aware of both the level and rate of change of the price level and the Fed can take monetary actions targeted at the real supply of money.

Assuming that the Fed sets the real money supply does not mean that we assume that the Fed always keeps the real money supply constant when the price level changes. For example, if the price level rose by 10 percent, the Fed could choose to keep the real money supply unaffected by making an accommodating rise in the nominal money supply of 10 percent. The Fed would then be choosing a constant real money supply. But alternatively, the Fed could leave the nominal money supply unchanged, in which case the Fed would be choosing a 10 percent decline in the real money supply.

While we disagree with the monetarist position on this issue in the short run, we do acknowledge that in the long run there is a connection between the money supply and the price level that means that the Fed does not ultimately determine the real money stock. The relation between the short run and the long run is discussed further in Chapters 9 and 15.

Money-Market Equilibrium and the Short-Term Interest Rate

Money-market equilibrium occurs when the demand for real-money balances equals the real stock of money:

$$\frac{M_s}{P} = \frac{M_d}{P}$$

$$\frac{M_s}{P} = L(Y, i).$$

(6.4)

This equilibrium condition in the money market is one of the most important in macroeconomics. Issues involving the efficacy of monetary and fiscal policy turn on the roles of income, prices, interest rates, and transactions costs in affecting money-market equilibrium. Alternative viewpoints about the way the economy behaves are reflected in different assumptions about how money-market equilibrium comes about.

In our analysis, money demand has to adjust to equal the given money supply through changes in the short-term nominal rate of interest. We illustrate the money-market equilibrium in Figure 6.3. The money market starts in equilibrium (point A) at an interest rate (i_A), which induces the quantity demanded of real money balances to be equal to the real supply of money, set by the Fed.

If income changes, the effect on the demand for money is shown as a shift of the schedule. Figure 6.3 shows such a shift $[(M_d/P)$ to $(M_d/P)']$. Along $(M_d/P)'$, the demand for money is smaller at any rate of interest (point A to point B). With a smaller money demand, there is an increased demand for T bills and this triggers a fall in the short-term interest rate which then increases money demand. This is shown in Figure 6.3 as a movement along the money-demand schedule (point B to point C). Money demand goes down (point A to B) because of lower income and up (point B to C) because of a lower interest rate. The net result is that cash managers' average checking-account balances are unchanged—first they fall, then they rise back up— but the short-term rate of interest has declined from i_A to i_C.

As we said, this shift could have resulted from a decrease in income or possibly a decrease in FTC. Either of these changes will lead cash managers to want to hold less money and more T bills. How will that change in T-bill demand lead to a change in the short-term interest rate?

T-bill prices and the short-term rate of interest

The rate of interest on a particular type of financial asset is determined through supply and demand in the market for this asset, while the effective rate of interest on an asset is directly linked to the price at which the asset is traded.

Consider the example of a financial asset consisting of an IOU that promises to pay $1,000 in one year. The IOU does not pay out anything until it is redeemed after one year. The borrower buys the IOU for less than $1,000 at the beginning of the year and then receives the $1,000 at the end of the year. The effective interest rate on the IOU depends upon the price paid for it, relative to $1,000. The higher the price paid for the IOU, the less is gained after one year and therefore the lower is the rate of interest earned.

FIGURE 6.3   **Equilibrium in the Market for Real Money Balances**

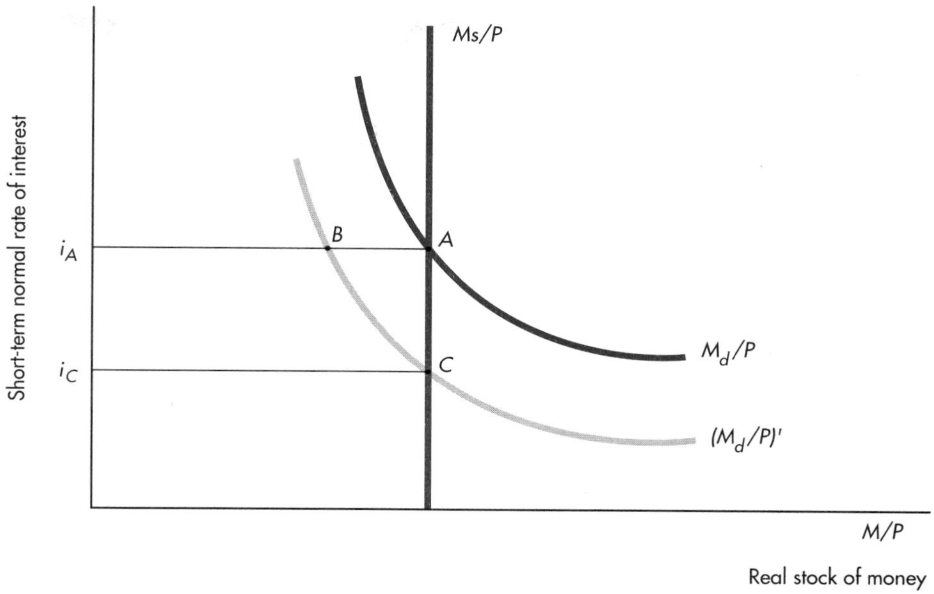

With a fixed real money supply (set by the Fed), a fall in real money demand, [M_d/P to $(M_d/P)'$], lowers the interest rate until money-market equilibrium is restored. The decline in money demand could have come from a decline in income.

Let's look at the effective interest rates on a $1,000 IOU payable in one year for different initial prices:

Initial price of the IOU	$600	$750	$900	$950	$990
Gain when the IOU is paid off	$400	$250	$100	$50	$ 10
Interest rate calculated by taking the gain as a percent of the price paid	66.7%	33.3%	11.1%	5.3%	1%

In this example, the interest rate was earned completely through the capital gain. A financial asset such as this is called a *zero coupon bond*. T bills are the most common example of such an asset.

Most other financial assets are not zero coupon bonds; they promise to pay a dollar amount each quarter or each year for a certain number of years. A bond then represents a claim on the interest as well as the repayment. For these assets also, there is an inverse relation between the interest rate on the bond and its price. A dollar amount of interest to be paid per year (for example, $100 per year) represents a higher return or interest rate when the bond is purchased for $500 than if the same bond paying $100 per year were purchased for $2,000. For all bonds—T bills, one-year bonds, 10-year bonds, perpetuities (bonds that are never redeemed) and so on—an inverse price/interest-rate relation exists.

WORKED EXAMPLE 6.4   When There Is a Change in Money Demand, How Does the Change in the Short-Term Interest Rate Come About?

Question: A three-month Treasury bill is an IOU issued by the U.S. Treasury. At the end of three months the U.S. Treasury promises to pay the owner of the T bill a fixed amount, say $10,000. When the bill is first issued, it will sell in the money market at a price below $10,000. For example, if the T bill sold for $9,765, the owner would gain $235 after three months. When expressed as an annual rate of interest, this gain is 10 percent. How is this interest rate calculated? What is the interest rate if the price of the T bill is $9,879?

Answer: First calculate the percent gain or return after three months.

Purchase price	*Redemption value*	*Gain*
$9,765	$10,000	$235

3-month gain = ($235 ÷ $9,765) × 100 = 2.41 percent

Then the annual interest rate is calculated by assuming that the proceeds from the redemption are reinvested every three months in T bills at the same interest rate. The result of doing this is calculated as follows:

Value of holding three-month T bills for four periods in succession with reinvestment

1st: $9,765 × 1.0241 = $10,000
2nd: $10,000 × 1.0241 = $10,241
3rd: $10,241 × 1.0241 = $10,488
4th: $10,488 × 1.0241 = $10,741

Annual gain

($10,741 − $9,765) ÷ ($9,765) × 100 = ($976 ÷ $9,765) × 100 = 10 percent

The interest rate on an annual percent basis in this example is just 10 percent. In general, the annual rate, i, is found by compounding the three-month rate (i_3) four times:

$$1 + i = (1 + i_3) \times (1 + i_3) \times (1 + i_3) \times (1 + i_3) = (1 + i_3)^4$$
$$i = (1 + i_3)^4 - 1.$$

Applying this formula in the example gives

$$0.1 = 1.0241^4 - 1.$$

Thus $i = 0.10$ or 10 percent. This completes the answer to the first part of the question.

The same method can be used to calculate the interest rate when the price of the T bill rises to $9,879. In this case, the three-month return is given by

$$(1 + i_3) = 10,000 ÷ 9,879 = 1.0122.$$

Then the annual interest rate is given by

$$0.05 = 1.0122^4 - 1.$$

Thus i in this case is 0.05 or 5 percent.

This worked example has confirmed, therefore, the inverse relation between the price of T bills and the annual percent rate of interest. The increase in price of the T bill from \$9,765 to \$9,879 meant that the interest rate fell from 10 percent to 5 percent.

We show in Figure 6.4 how equilibrium in the money market (panel A) is linked with equilibrium in the T-bill market (panel C). In panel B we show the relationship between T-bill prices and their interest rates, a schedule calculated using the method shown in Worked Example 6.1. Numerical values from that example are shown in the figure.

In Figure 6.4C we show the supply (S_T) and demand (D_T) for T bills in equilibrium at a price, $P_T[A]$. Moving to Figure 6.4B, we see that this price of T bills implies a particular interest rate, i_0, on T bills. Then in Figure 6.4A, we see that equilibrium in the money market also occurs at the same rate of interest, i_A. The T-bill market and the supply of and demand for money are two sides of the same money market where cash managers trade money for T bills. Money supply and demand are equal at an equilibrium interest rate that corresponds to the equilibrium price of T bills. The relationship between the prices of assets and interest rates connects these two parts of the financial market.

If the price of T bills were above its equilibrium price (for example, if the price of T bills were \$9,879), then there would be an excess supply of T bills (Figure 6.4C). Tracking this back to Figure 6.4A, we see that this price of T bills corresponds to a short-term nominal interest rate of 5 percent, and this represents a situation of excess demand for money. The alternative case is also shown in Figure 6.4, where the price of T bills is \$9,765, resulting in an excess demand for T bills and an excess supply of money.

The *LM* Schedule and the Short-Term Nominal Interest Rate

In Chapter 3, the *LM* schedule was drawn by showing how increases in income raised the demand for money. Because the supply of money was fixed, this resulted in a higher interest rate. We have used our analysis of cash management to deepen our understanding of that relationship and to modify money-market equilibrium to take account of inflation. These changes also imply a modification in the *LM* schedule. Through examples, we have found that the demand for real money balances depends upon three factors. First is the real volume of transactions and, hence, the level of real income. Second, it depends upon the nominal rate of interest on short-term assets—

FIGURE 6.4   Connecting Money Supply and Demand and the T-Bill Market

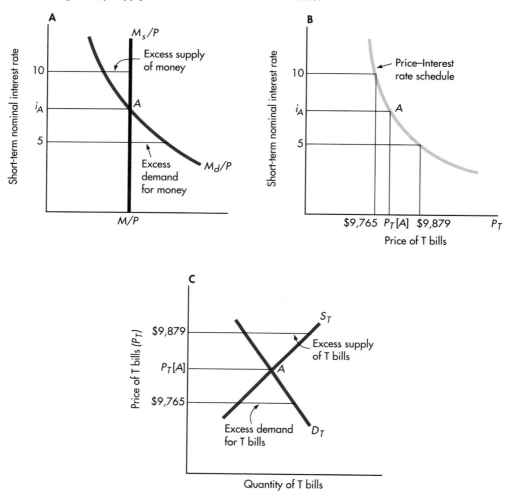

we use the rate on T bills. Cash managers will intensify their economizing of money balances at higher nominal rates of interest. Third, the demand for real money balances depends upon FTCs, the costs of moving back and forth between money and T bills. We argued that the Fed effectively controls the real supply of money and that equilibrium in the money market takes

FIGURE 6.5   The Money Market and the *LM* Schedule Revisited

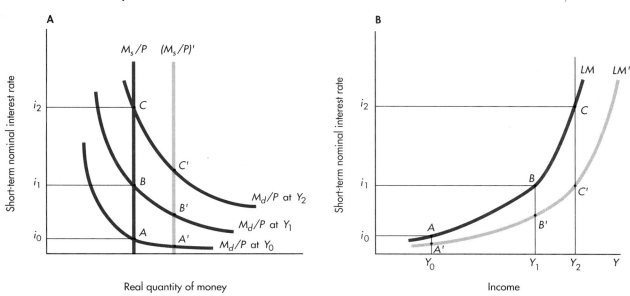

The impacts of changes in income and changes in the real supply of money upon money-market equilibrium are different at different interest rates. At higher interest rates and higher levels of income the interest-rate effects of a monetary expansion are stronger.

place as cash managers buy and sell T bills in order to maintain their optimal portfolio of money and bills. Purchases and sales of T bills raise and lower the price of T bills and this automatically results in changes in the short-term nominal rate of interest.

The *LM* schedule shows the points where the money market is in equilibrium. Based upon what we have learned in this chapter, we now have a modified *LM* schedule as shown in the right-hand panel of Figure 6.5. There are four differences between this *LM* schedule and the one used in previous chapters. First, the interest rate shown on the vertical axis is the short-term nominal rate. Second, as shown in the left-hand panel of the figure, the money-supply and money-demand schedules that combine to give the *LM* schedule are real money supply and the real money demand. Third, the *LM* schedule is shown as a curve. This shape incorporates the idea that at high rates of interest, cash managers have done about as much as they can to economize on their holdings of money. Fourth, changes in FTCs will shift the money-demand schedule and, hence, the *LM* schedule.

The left-hand panel of the figure shows three different demand schedules corresponding to three levels of income. Increases in income, from Y_0 to Y_1 to Y_2, mean that money-market equilibrium occurs at increasingly higher rates of interest. The short-term nominal rate of interest is higher at point B than at point A and higher still at point C. The preceding description of money-market equilibrium applies to the case of a fixed money supply. If the real money supply increases [from (M_s/P) to $(M_s/P)'$], then the rate of interest will be lower at each level of income—compare points A', B', and C' with points A, B, and C.

Monetary policy will be more or less effective depending upon whether interest rates or income change by more or less when there is a change in monetary policy. Our interest in the shape of the LM schedule is related to our understanding of monetary and fiscal policies. Monetary-policy changes bring about shifts in the real money supply that are reflected in shifts in the LM schedule. When the real money supply is increased, the reduction in the short-term nominal interest rate is lower at low levels of the interest rate and higher at high levels of the interest rate. At low levels of the interest rate the opportunity cost of holding money is low. Cash managers are holding, and continue to hold, a large portion of their funds in the form of money. There is a small excess supply of money brought about by the increase in the money supply. This small increase in the excess supply of money results in a relatively small increase in the demand for T bills. T-bill prices rise by a little and the short-term nominal rate of interest falls by a relatively small amount (point A to A' in Figure 6.5).

At high interest rates the opportunity cost of holding money is high. Cash managers are holding, and continue to hold, a small portion of their funds in the form of money. There is a large excess supply of money brought about by the increase in the money supply that results in a relatively large increase in the demand for T bills. T-bill prices rise by a lot and the short-term nominal rate of interest falls by a relatively large amount (point C to C' in Figure 6.5).

The impact of a change in monetary policy affects the money market differently at different interest rates and this is reflected in how the LM schedule is shifted. An increase in the real money supply reduces low interest rates a little and reduces high interest rates a lot (LM to LM' and points A, B, and C to points A', B', and C' in Figure 6.5B).

We have taken a careful look at how, under varying conditions, the LM schedule reflects changes in monetary equilibrium. The money market and the LM schedule are at one end of a spectrum of assets that runs from relatively riskless cash to quite risky real assets such as fixed business investment goods (capital goods). We are now going to move along the spectrum. The next stop is to look at the relation between the interest rate on T bills and the interest rates on longer-term Treasury bonds.

SHORT-TERM AND LONG-TERM INTEREST RATES

term structure of interest rates
The relationship among interest rates, depending upon the maturity of the assets.

Many companies and financial institutions and households hold longer-term Treasury securities in preference to holding T bills. These longer-term financial assets usually have higher rates of interest than T bills and therefore yield a higher return, but there are some offsetting disadvantages to longer-term assets. The long-term nominal interest rate is not usually equal to the short-term nominal interest rate and the two rates sometimes move differently. We want to ask now how the rate varies with the maturity of financial assets and how the gap between the long and short rates of interest varies with changing economic conditions. We are going to look at the **term structure of interest rates,** which describes the way in which interest rates vary depending upon the maturity of the assets on which the interest is being paid.

The first important link between the short-term and long-term interest rates is that long-term interest rates depend upon expectations about future short-term rates. Leaving aside differences in the riskiness of different assets, the interest rate on long-term bonds reflects an average of current and expected future interest rates on short-term bonds. Let's see how this works.

Expected Future Interest Rates

The short-term interest rate today is the rate on a bill issued today that matures a few months or a year from now. These bills are being issued all the time, and new ones will be issued a year from now. What will the rate of interest be on these short-term assets a year from now? That is an important question for an investor deciding whether or not to hold a long-term bond. An investor thinking of buying a three-year bond could instead buy a one-year bill now and then another one a year from now and a third two years from now. How do these alternatives compare?

If there is no risk, then the return from holding a three-year bond must be the same as the return from holding three one-year bonds. Were the return to a three-year bond different from the return to three one-year bonds, investors would buy whichever had a higher return and sell whichever had a lower return—raising the price and lowering the interest rate on the higher-returning bond and lowering the price and raising the interest rate on the lower-returning bond. Trading in financial markets would tend to equalize returns. Suppose that the interest rate on one-year bonds this year, $i(1)$, is 7.2 percent. This one-year rate is expected to be 7.0 percent next year and 6.8 percent the year after that. What is the rate of interest on a three-year investment, $i(3)$, that generates the same three-year return as these three one-year investments? One million dollars invested consecutively in three one-year bonds will earn a return as follows:

$$\$1,000,000 \times 1.072 \times 1.070 \times 1.068 = \$1,225,000.$$

The three-year interest rate, $i(3)$, that yields the same return as three consecutive one-year investments is then given by

$$\$1,000,000 \times [1 + i(3)]^3 = \$1,225,000.$$

The three-year rate, $i(3)$, is 7 percent. In general, the three-year interest rate, $i(3)$, and the current and expected future one-year rates, $i(1)$, are related as follows:

$$[1 + i(3) \text{ in year one}]^3 = [1 + i(1) \text{ in year one}] \times$$
$$[1 + i(1) \text{ expected in year two}] \times$$
$$[1 + i(1) \text{ expected in year three}].$$

This relation means that, ignoring risk differences, the long-term interest rate on a bond would be equal to the average of the expected short-term interest rates over the period until the bond matures.[7] And this result can be applied for two-year, four-year, and longer-term interest rates also.

If expectations about future one-year rates were to change, then the current three-year rate would change, without there being any change in the current one-year rate. In the preceding example, if the expectation of the one-year rate in the third year fell from 6.8 percent to 5.3 percent, the current three-year rate $[i(3)]$ would fall from 7 percent to 6.5 percent since

$$(1.072) \times (1.070) \times (1.053) = (1.065)^3.$$

The current short rate remains at 7.2 percent as the current longer rate falls. *A change in the expectation of a future short interest rate will change the relationship between current short rates and current long rates. It will change the term structure of interest rates.*

Interest-Rate Risk

We have looked at the relation between short-term and long-term nominal rates of interest without considering the difference in risk. In practice, there is more risk associated with buying a long-term bond than in buying a short-term bond. Interest rates in the future are not known with certainty. Expectations about interest rates may not be realized.

If a three-month T bill was purchased when the interest rate was 5 percent, we showed earlier that the T bill would sell for $9,879. If rates double to 10 percent, T-bill prices would fall to $9,765. A doubling of the interest rate on T bills results in only a little more than a 1 percent loss in the value of the three-month security. So in the case of T bills, the loss of value that

---

[7] Formally, this relation among rates is that the long rate is the geometric mean of the short rates. The geometric mean is an average taken by multiplying N elements and taking the Nth root of the product, in contrast with the arithmetic mean, which is taken by adding N elements and dividing the sum by N. For rates of interest that are not terribly large or do not change much over time, the simple average of the expected short rates is very close to the geometric mean.

occurred with a rather large change in the rate of interest was not very great. The same is not true of longer-term financial assets, however.

At the opposite end of the spectrum from T bills are infinitely long term government bonds called *consols* or *perpetuities*. These bonds are promises to pay a stated amount each year forever, but they are never redeemed. For perpetuities, there is a very simple relation between the interest rate and the price of the bond. Suppose a perpetuity promises to pay $100 per year forever. Then if its price is $2,000, the interest rate is 5 percent ($100 ÷ $2,000). If the price were $1,000, the interest rate on a consol would be 10 percent ($100 ÷ $1,000). The same change in the rate of interest that resulted in about a 1 percent change in the value of a T bill would have led to halving of the price of a perpetuity. In general, long-term bonds lose much more in value than do short-term bonds following a given change in the rate of interest.

Long-term bonds have much more variability in price than do short-term bonds. Buying a long-term bond exposes the lender to much greater risk as a result of interest-rate changes (**interest-rate risk**) than is the case when buying a short-term bond. The longer the bond's **term to maturity,** the greater is the change in price associated with a given change in the rate of interest. *Interest-rate risk is more substantial when the term to maturity is longer.*

Liquidity preference

The fact that short-term financial assets are less affected by interest-rate risk than are long-term assets means that regardless of changes in economic conditions, short-term financial assets can be quickly sold for very near their purchase price. This quick resale characteristic of short-term financial assets is called **liquidity.** A T bill is quite liquid because it is issued by the federal government, is for a short maturity, and is traded in a well-developed market. A second mortgage held on a residential dwelling is quite illiquid because it is an obligation on a particular household, is for a long maturity, and is not as easily sold as a T bill. The second mortgage is, however, more liquid than the house itself.

If different assets offer the same rate of return, most asset holders, most of the time, would prefer the asset with the most liquidity. This preference for low-risk assets is described as their **liquidity preference.** Because of the preference for liquidity, investors require a higher rate of return on assets that are less liquid. In order to compensate for the greater risk of long-term assets, these assets can be expected to carry a higher rate of interest. The preference for liquidity can be expressed as a **liquidity premium** added to long-term rates over and above the interest rate on short-term assets. The liquidity premium is the difference between long-term and short-term interest rates that holders of long-term assets demand in exchange for the loss of liquidity.

The liquidity premium is the reason why short-term rates are generally lower than long-term rates. But the spread between long and short rates

interest-rate risk
The risk borne by the owner of a financial asset that the price of the asset will change when market interest rates change.

term to maturity
The length of time between the current period and an obligation's date of required repayment of principal.

liquidity
The quick-resale characteristic of short-term financial assets. Assets that can be sold quickly for a value very close to the value that would be obtained by waiting are called liquid assets.

liquidity preference
The preference for liquidity, meaning that investors require a higher rate of return on assets that are less liquid than others. The preference for liquidity can be expressed as a **liquidity premium** (the difference between long-term and short-term interest rates that holders of long-term assets demand in exchange for the loss of liquidity).

■ The Tension between Risk and Return

People are often confused as to why different interest rates are charged on what might appear to be the same kind of bond. Why not always hold savings in the form which will yield the highest rate of interest? Part of the answer is related to risk.

Perhaps the simplest place to put savings is in a time deposit, where a principal lump sum is invested for a certain period at a fixed rate of interest. At the end of the period one gets back the principal plus the accrued interest earned on the sum. Old-style mortgages and promissory notes worked this way; certificates of deposit and certain types of bonds still do. It is a less liquid way to save money than stuffing it into an old shoe box, but it is generally a superior way to save because you benefit from the willingness of others to pay you for the use of your money, which has a *time value*.

Savings accounts are like time deposits, except that the term of investment is open-ended and the possibility of partial withdrawal without penalty exists. In such a circumstance, you have more flexibility as your preference for liquidity changes. Interest income also is earned on savings accounts. The possibility of earning interest while holding a relatively safe investment instrument is also the reason for holding conservative instruments such as government and high-grade corporate bonds, certain mutual funds and preferred stocks, and, traditionally at least, the common stocks of public utility companies.

At higher levels of risk are instruments in which the returns, including capital appreciation, depend on the resale value of the security or asset. This includes growth stocks as well as the various speculative instruments (options, warranties, futures, etc.) of the securities and commodities markets, and sometimes interest on real property.

When deciding on where to invest your savings,

Value Curves of Scotch Whisky at 6% and NOW Account at 5%.

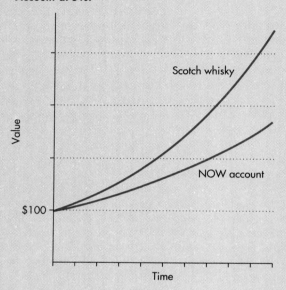

one of your key concerns is the comparison of projected yields and relative risks. As the accompanying figure shows, when we compare the yield on a Scotch whisky investment at 6 percent and on a NOW account at 5 percent, the differential, slight at first, gradually widens as the effect of compounding increases. Like the Scotch itself, the whisky investment improves with time.

Against this advantage in long-term returns must be weighed the Scotch whisky's lower safety factor as an investment. Compared to money in the bank, whisky is a riskier asset. Its greater potential return on investment may not justify its greater risk factor.

varies considerably and it is even possible for the relationship between short and long rates to be reversed with the short rate above the long rate. Clearly, in those cases, the short rate of interest is expected to change in the future. We need to combine our analysis of the relation between long rates and expected future short rates with what we have just said about liquidity.

Combining Expectations and the Liquidity Premium

There is a liquidity premium on long interest rates compared with short rates. To see how this can be combined with what we learned earlier about the relation between long and short rates, we go back to our earlier example. We assume now that there is a 2 percent premium on the long rate so that the long rate will be around 7 percent when the short rate is around 5 percent. See how this works in our example when the current and future one-year rates are 5.2 percent, 5.0 percent, and 4.8 percent and the 2 percent premium is expected to remain the same in future years.[8] Then the three-year rate $[i(3)]$ is given as

$$[1 + i(3)]^3 = (1.052 + 0.02) \times (1.050 + 0.02) \times (1.048 + 0.02)$$
$$= 1.223 = (1.07)^3.$$

Once again, the three-year rate is 7 percent.

Combining expectations and liquidity preference gives a more realistic description of the relationship among interest rates: *Long-term rates on Treasury bonds are generally higher than short-term rates (T-bill rates) because of liquidity preference, but changes in expectations about future short-term rates can augment, reduce, or even more than offset the liquidity premium.*

The general relation between the short-term rate of interest and the long-term rate of interest that these examples illustrate is that *the rate of interest on Treasury bonds equals the average of the current and expected future short rates (T-bill rates) plus a liquidity premium.* The average includes the short rates for those future years that are relevant for a particular long rate. The rate on a 10-year bond equals the average of expected short rates over the next 10 years plus a liquidity premium, and so on for bonds of different maturities.

The term structure and the yield curve

At a given point in time the rates of interest that prevail in the market can be observed. If these rates are arrayed by maturity, the relationships among rates is called the term structure of interest rates, that is, how rates vary by the term to maturity of bonds. There is an important branch of economics that studies the term structure, and many academic economists who have

---

[8] Someone wanting to make a three-year investment will pay more in FTCs with three one-year bonds than with one three-year bond. We are assuming that the liquidity premium includes an adjustment for differences in the transaction costs associated with the different bonds.

become expert in this area (referred to in the financial industry as the "rocket scientists") have taken positions in Wall Street firms in recent years. Because the relationships between a bond's interest rate and its maturity involve expectations, the shape of the term structure and changes in that shape can provide useful information about the likelihood of interest rates in the future.

The term structure is used, by those who understand it, as a forecasting tool and as a tool for creating profitable investment strategies. And there is plenty of opportunity to lose money also for those whose understanding is not as good as they thought it was because of the uncertainty associated with all markets.

We describe the term structure by plotting interest rates (yields) on different bonds against maturity. The bonds differ only in that they have different terms to maturity. The resulting figure is called the **yield curve.** Figure 6.6 shows four different yield curves using rates on U.S. Treasury securities of different maturities. The two schedules shown as *AA* (1985) and *AA* (1987) are **normal yield curves** where the short rate of interest is below the long rate. The reason that this is normal is that the liquidity premium rises with maturity and the yield curve flattens out with increases in maturity. Long-term bonds are riskier and require a higher interest rate, but the differences in liquidity among medium-term bonds (2–10 years) and long-term bonds (10–30 years) is not usually very large. Notice that the maturity along the horizontal axis is not drawn to scale.

If the short-term rate of interest is expected to remain constant into the future, then the rising yield curve simply reflects the rising liquidity premium, but this is not always the case.

yield curve
The array of interest rates on bonds by term to maturity. A **normal yield curve** has short-term rates lower than long-term rates. An **inverted yield curve** has short-term rates higher than long-term rates.

Expectations and the shape of the yield curve

If the short rate of interest is expected to change in the future, then the yield curve will reflect the impact of both the liquidity premium and the changes in expectations. *Holding the liquidity premium constant, an expectation that the short-term rate of interest will fall in the future will tend to reduce the current long-term rate of interest.* This was illustrated in the earlier example, where we found that when the current short rate was expected to fall in successive years, then the long rate fell. While in the example the liquidity premium was taken as zero, the same result comes through even with the liquidity premium added in. It is even possible for the short-term rate of interest to be higher than the long-term rate, when expectational effects overcome the liquidity premium.

When the short-term rate of interest is actually higher than the long rate, we call it an **inverted yield curve** because the normal relationship of higher long-term rates and lower short-term rates has been inverted. This is unusual, but not impossible. The yield curve was inverted for periods of time in 1973, 1974, 1979, 1980, 1981, and 1989. Inverted yield curves based

FIGURE 6.6   The Yield Curves on U.S. Government Securities (Treasury Bills, Notes, and Bonds), Selected Years, 1974–1987

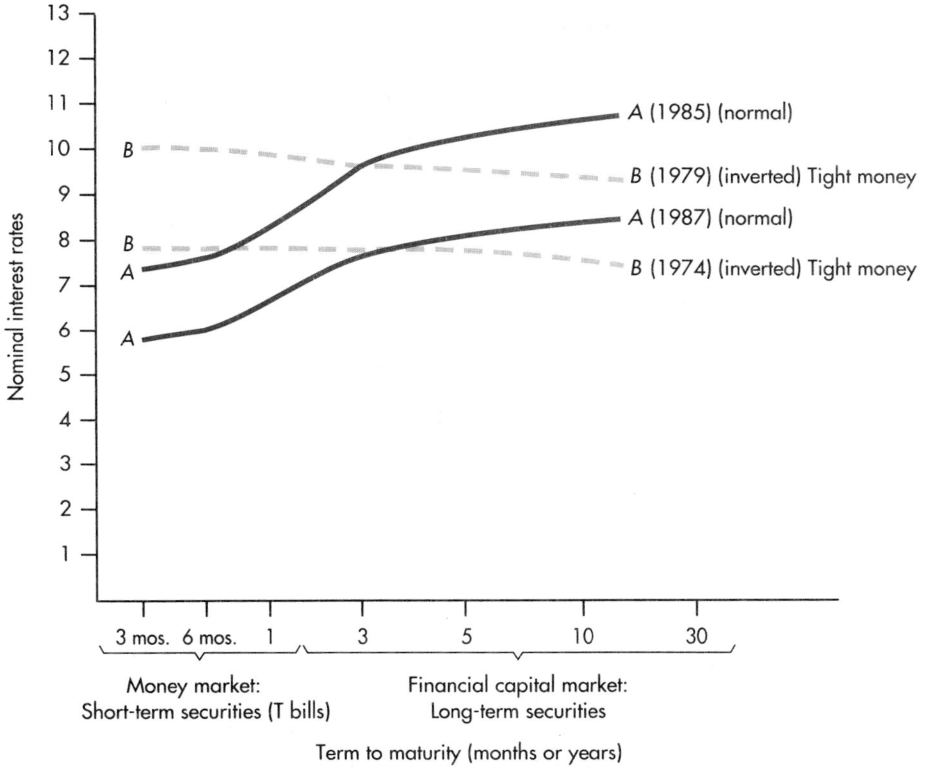

Source: *Economic Report of the President,* various issues (Washington, D.C.: U.S. Government Printing Office).

upon actual experience in the U.S. economy are shown in Figure 6.6 as *BB* (1974) and *BB* (1979).

Inverted yield curves generally arise when the economy is at a high level of income and the Fed is following a contractionary policy. The economy has a strong demand for money for transactions purposes and the Fed is cutting back the supply of money and this drives the rate of interest on T bills very high. Traders in financial markets expect, however, that these very high short-term rates will be lower in the future, so the long-term rate of interest, which incorporates the average of current and future short rates, is lower than the current short rate.

The observation of an inverted yield curve is generally taken to be a signal of an impending reduction of aggregate demand, perhaps even the start of a recession. This is because an inverted yield curve generally reflects the initial stages of a contractionary monetary policy, before long-term rates are affected. Investors recognize that while short rates are currently high, the contractionary effect of tighter monetary policy is going to reduce aggregate demand in the future. The result of the expected fall in income is a drop in the demand for borrowing, reducing rates along the entire yield curve.

A different change in the shape of the yield curve will occur if the economy is already in a recession and the Fed decides to battle the recession by expanding the money supply. Then the yield curve may become unusually steep; that is, short-term rates may drop relative to long-term rates. When the short-term rate of interest is expected to rise, then the yield curve becomes steeper. Here the long rate is much higher than the short rate because the long rate includes not only the liquidity premium but also the expected rate increase. This represents the initial stages of a monetary expansion. In a recession, the current rate on T bills falls very low, but the market expects aggregate demand to rise as the economy grows out of its recession. The expected growth in aggregate demand also leads to an expected increase in credit demand and income, both of which contribute to the expected rise in rates in the future.

Conclusions about the Money Market, the Yield Curve, and *IS-LM*

Interest rates change as a result of changes in income and as a result of policy moves by the Fed. In our analysis through Chapter 5 we considered only a single interest rate, so it made sense to talk about "the" interest rate rising or falling. If it were the case in practice that there was always a normal yield curve, then this simplification would be acceptable. If, for example, 1985 and 1987 are compared in Figure 6.6, one can simply talk about a general fall in the interest rate between those years.

But in fact the yield curve can twist or change shape. Is the interest rate higher in 1985 than in 1979 or is it lower? The answer is not clear because the long-term rate was higher in 1985, but the short rate was lower. This is why it is important to analyze the determinants of the term structure.

Monetary-policy shifts lead to changes in the short-term interest rate and these are transmitted down the yield curve and change the long rate. But expectations play an important role in determining how much the long rate changes. Is the rise in the short-term rate expected to persist or to be over very soon? Will the economy grow strongly or go into a recession affecting money demand and interest rates in the future? People's expectations about the economy have a big impact on how monetary policy affects the long-term rate of interest. And the long-term rate of interest is a key mechanism by which changes in interest rates affect expenditures and hence the goods market, the real economy.

We will go on in the next chapter to look at the relationship between the long-term interest rate and equilibrium in the goods market. We will reintroduce the distinction between real and nominal rates. Inflation expectations will be shown to play a significant role in the relation between the long-term nominal rate of interest and investment demand.

SUMMARY

- The different assets being traded on financial markets in the economy and the interest rates that are determined in these markets can be lined up along a spectrum from short term to long term.

- The interest rate that is determined by equilibrium in the money market along the *LM* schedule is different from the interest rate that affects investment demand along the *IS* schedule.

- Companies or wealthy individuals transfer funds into and out of demand deposits on frequent occasions. Deciding upon the frequency of transfers, determining which financial assets to buy and sell, and executing those transfers is called cash management. The average "cash" balance is equal to the demand for money.

- Cash managers adjust their portfolios of money and T bills. The real demand for money depends upon real income, the short-term nominal rate of interest, and the financial-transactions costs (FTC) of moving back and forth between money and T bills.

- The demand-for-money schedule becomes steeper at high rates of interest because there are limits to the extent to which cash managers are willing or able to reduce their money holdings.

- In an economy that experiences inflation, it is important to distinguish real values from nominal values. Consumption, investment, government purchases, net exports, and taxes should all be measured with real values, adjusted for inflation.

- The demand for money is a demand for a real stock of money. Nominal money demand rises in proportion to the price level. The demand for real money balances is affected by the short-term nominal rate of interest. Changes in the expected rate of inflation affect the real demand for money to the extent that they change the nominal interest rate.

- The real return to financial investment is measured by the real rate of interest. The real rate of interest on a bond is approximately equal to the nominal rate of interest minus the rate of inflation that is expected over the lifetime of the bond.

- At the long-term end of the spectrum of assets we find that bonds carry interest-rate risk. The prices of long-term bonds are much more variable than the prices of short-term bonds.

- Because of risks, long-term bonds carry a liquidity premium. Short-term rates are on average lower than long-term rates.

- When short-term rates are expected to rise in the future, this increases the current long-term rate of interest. When short-term rates are expected to fall, this decreases the long-term rate.

- The yield curve shows how the interest rates on different bonds vary with the maturities of these bonds. In practice the yield curve will reflect the effect of both the liquidity premium and the expected future pattern of rates.

- A normal yield curve slopes upward because the liquidity premium increases with maturity.

- During business-cycle peaks, the demand for money is high and the Fed is usually imposing monetary restraint to cool off the economy. The short-term rate of interest is very high but is expected to fall. This can create an inverted yield curve, where short-term rates are higher than long-term rates.

- In recessions, short-term rates are usually much lower than long-term rates and the yield curve is unusually steep.

KEY TERMS

average cash balance	nominal values
cash management	nominal rate of interest
financial-transactions cost	normal yield curve
interest-rate risk	real rate of interest
inverted yield curve	real values
liquidity	term structure of interest rates
liquidity preference	term to maturity
liquidity premium	yield curve
money market	

DISCUSSION QUESTIONS AND PROBLEMS

1. Why would a cash manager not insure that cash is always available for the firm by simply keeping a larger than necessary balance in the corporate checking account?

2. If deregulation of financial markets spurs competition among brokers that lowers financial-transactions costs, will this affect short-term interest rates? How?

3. When the price level rises and the dollar costs of wages and materials rise, what does this do to a cash manager's demand for money balances?

4. How can a change in nominal interest rates affect the demand for real money balances?

5. Is it likely that the effect on interest rates of an increase in the real supply of money will be different at higher or lower levels of income or higher or lower interest rates?

6. If investors have a preference for liquidity, how can short-term interest rates ever exceed long-term rates?

■ APPENDIX 6A
Money Demand as an Inventory Problem: The Square-Root Rule

The cash manager has to decide how many times to transfer funds between T bills and cash per month. If her monthly income is Y_m and she makes four transactions per month, then her company's average cash balance is $Y_m \div (4 \times 2)$. This is the result we found in the chapter, where the monthly income was $3 million and the average cash balance was $375,000 = $3,000,000 \div 8$. In general, if there are n transactions per month, then the average cash balance is $Y_m \div (n \times 2)$. The opportunity cost of a cash balance of this size over the course of a year is then $(i \times Y_m) \div (n \times 2)$, when the annual interest rate is i.

With n transactions per month, the cost of financial transactions is $12 \times n \times FTC$. This means that the company's total cost of cash management plus forgone interest is just the sum of these two terms:

Total cost of cash management = $[(i \times Y_m) \div (n \times 2)] + [12 \times n \times FTC]$.

The cash manager must minimize this cost. To find the value of n that does this requires calculus. The condition that determines the optimal frequency of transfers, n, for cost minimization is the following. Cost of cash management is minimized when

$$n = \sqrt{\frac{i \times Y_m}{2 \times 12 \times FTC}}.$$

Using the values in our example in the chapter, this expression gives an optimal number of transactions of 4.08 per month. We found that 4 per month was optimal because we were looking only at integers. The expression for the optimal number of transactions can then be used to find the average cash balance (average money demand), which we saw earlier was equal to $Y_m \div (n \times 2)$. Substituting in gives

$$\text{Average cash balance} = \sqrt{\frac{(12 \times Y_m) \times FTC}{2 \times i}}.$$

Since 12 times the monthly income is the annual income, this completes the result we are looking for. The average cash balance and, hence, money demand depend positively on income and on FTCs and negatively on the rate of interest. The dependence in all three cases involves the square root.

This model of money demand as a form of inventory holding is a very important one that shows the key determinants of money demand, but the detailed result should not be taken too literally. In the actual economy, money demand does not follow a square-root rule exactly. For many people the optimal cash-management strategy involves no monthly transactions into and out of bonds.

CHAPTER 7

The Demand for Investment Goods, Financial Intermediaries, and the Interest-Rate Gap

INTRODUCTION

The short-term nominal rate of interest is determined in the money market, but as we will see in this chapter, aggregate demand and the decision to purchase investment goods respond to the long-term real rate of interest. Since movements in the short-term nominal rate are not necessarily connected one for one with movements in the long-term real rate, we need to show how financial markets and financial intermediaries bridge the gap between changes in money-market conditions and changes in investment demand which affect the real economy.

The description of the way the gap is bridged was started in Chapter 6, where we moved along the yield curve from short-term assets traded in the money market toward the longer-term assets and saw how their nominal rates depend on the liquidity premium and on expected future short-term interest rates. Our strategy for working out the connections between money and goods markets continues in this chapter where we describe the spectrum of assets, tracing the relationship among the different rates of return that allows us to re-establish the link between the *LM* schedule at one end of the spectrum and the *IS* schedule at the other.

However, before we finish the task of showing how the financial sector fits in the gap between money and goods markets, we start this chapter by jumping from money markets and financial assets directly to the goods market. We show how investment demand is affected by the long-term real rate of interest; only after showing this do we turn to look at the importance of risk and liquidity in saving and investment decisions, and the important role played by financial intermediaries in mediating between the desire of savers for security (low risk) and easy access to their money (high liquidity), and the desire of borrowers to have stable long-term repayment schedules.

Financial intermediaries and the financial capital market provide a bridge between those who want to borrow so as to purchase capital goods and those who want to lend either by buying financial assets or by depositing funds in a financial institution. In addition to providing intermediation between lenders and borrowers, financial intermediaries play an independent role in influencing investment decisions.

We conclude the chapter by returning to the task of connecting money and goods markets by defining the gap that separates the money market and the goods market as the difference between the short-term nominal rate of interest and the long-term real rate of interest. This is *the interest-rate gap*—the gap that separates the *IS* and *LM* schedules. We examine how the short-term nominal rate may move either together with or differently from the long-term real rate, and how changes in money-market conditions may or may not affect change in aggregate demand and equilibrium income.

INVESTMENT DEMAND AND THE LONG-TERM REAL RATE OF INTEREST

Investment demand is that part of aggregate demand represented by expenditure on capital goods. When households or firms buy houses, autos, factories, and business equipment, they are making long-term investments in the productivity of these capital goods. In that sense, the household decision to purchase a house is similar to the business decision to buy an office building.[1] We describe the decisions to make investment expenditures as business decisions.

Business investment demand is the demand for capital goods and the planned accumulation of inventories. Firms invest in order to maintain or increase profits. Capital goods allow the firm to initiate or increase production. The firm that can produce more and sell the increased product at a price that covers costs will maintain or increase its profitability.

How much to invest in new equipment, factories, and inventories depends primarily upon the expectation of future sales. Higher sales are met by increasing production, which usually requires more capital goods. From the point of view of an individual firm, if capital goods were not purchased in the

---

[1] A careful distinction between durable goods purchased by consumers (mostly houses, autos, and appliances) and durable goods purchased by firms (factories, equipment, and inventories) is deferred to Chapter 13, where the impact of a change in income on the desired capital stocks of households and businesses is discussed. There we explore the separate roles of the variability in household investment demand and business investment demand in contributing to fluctuations in economic activity.

face of higher sales, the unit cost of increased production will rise, eroding profits.

At the aggregate level, when income is expected to rise in the economy, firms increase their level of planned investment because higher sales are expected. The role of income in our simple investment-demand function (described in Chapter 2),

$$I = I_0 + I_1 Y - I_2 r$$

was a rough approximation for the role played by expected income in determining investment demand. Income, including expectations of future income, is the most important determinant of investment demand, but it is not the only one. At this point we will focus on the interest cost of making the investment expenditure as a determinant of investment demand. *Changes in the interest cost of capital spending provide the main link between the money market and monetary policy on the one hand and investment demand and the goods market on the other.*

The decision to purchase capital goods is a portfolio decision. A firm is deciding among several alternatives as it allocates the company's wealth. It could pay out funds as dividends to its shareholders or issue new shares. It could buy financial assets (such as bonds), retire some of the bonds it has issued in the past, or issue new bonds. It could buy out another company or buy a division or factory from another company. And finally, it could decide to purchase new capital goods. In making the decision to adopt some of these options, or others, the company's managers will examine the relative risks and returns from the alternative choices.

Which capital good to purchase and which corporate project to undertake are critical managerial decisions. These decisions go beyond simple portfolio considerations—they are critical strategic decisions for individual firms. However, as we study the level of investment demand in the total economy, most of the factors that are important for individual firms will average out, and the interest cost of capital spending becomes an important determinant of aggregate investment.

Financing Investment

Households, small businesses, and large corporations all purchase capital goods. How do they pay for them? Corporations can finance capital purchases by borrowing from banks or other financial institutions and they can sell bonds. Alternatively, corporations can finance capital purchases by using retained earnings or by issuing new equity shares and selling them in stock markets such as the New York or American Stock Exchanges or through private placement using investment bankers. When a corporation borrows from a bank or sells a corporate bond, it promises to pay a specific rate of interest on the liability it has assumed. Either way, the interest rate it will pay on its liability is the long-term rate of interest.

■ The Purchase of Capital Goods, Corporate Strategy, and Interest Rates

When the economy is booming, firms scramble to buy capital goods. Corporate managers spend money on new plant and equipment so that they will have a cost-effective way to meet the current and future increases in product demand. The managers use a variety of criteria to decide which investment projects to select and how large the investment budget should be: internal rates of return, hurdle rates (minimum returns), payback periods, and even strategic budget allocations. These are all designed to approximate a comparison of the expected return to the capital expenditure with the cost of allocating financial resources to that expenditure. Saying that the decision to purchase capital goods is a portfolio decision does not mean that the decision is made regardless of the business fortunes that the firm faces at any point in time. A lower interest rate will not bring about an increase in capital-goods expenditures if firms expect a collapse in the demand for their products. A higher rate of interest will not slow down the demand for capital goods if firms expect consumers to go on a buying spree. Rather, the statement about capital-goods purchases being a portfolio decision means that, after business (demand) conditions are accounted for, firms will increase or decrease their level of capital investment as the cost of that investment decreases or increases.

When a corporation issues equity shares (stocks), it must offer the buyers of these shares the expectation of a future return (dividends and capital gains). The exact amount of the payments is unknown in advance, but nevertheless the owners expect to gain a return, and that requirement for a return represents the cost of equity finance to the firm. When a company retains profits in order to invest, it is implicitly signaling its shareholders the expectation that it will earn an adequate rate of return on the investment, a return that will eventually benefit the shareholders.

Corporations, therefore, calculate an effective cost of equity finance that is analogous to the long-term rate of interest that they pay on debt finance. Even though there are important differences between bond financing and equity financing,[2] there is a relationship between the cost of equity finance and the rate of interest on long-term financial assets. Increases in the long-term rate of interest will raise corporations' overall cost of financing investment.

When a family or individual buys a house, the purchase is typically financed with a mortgage. The mortgage interest rate is a long-term rate of interest. When long-term interest rates rise, this increases the cost of financing a new home and has a negative effect on the demand for housing. The effect of increases in interest rates on housing demand is even exacerbated

---

[2] The firm's cost of acquiring capital goods is called the *cost of capital*. This cost is calculated using the relationship between the cost of equity finance and the long-term real rate of interest. Considerations of financial risk, depreciation, and tax laws affect the results. In general terms the cost of capital is imputed from the cost of borrowing funds in financial markets for a period of time similar to the expected life of the capital good.

by the institutional rules of thumb that mortgage lenders use. A family has to qualify for a mortgage by showing that it has income of at least some fixed multiple of the size of the mortgage payment—the family income must be three to four times the mortgage payment. If the interest rate rises from 10 to 11 percent, this raises the annual interest cost of a $100,000 mortgage from $10,000 to $11,000, and it raises the income threshold for lending by a multiple of that amount, making it harder for families to qualify.

Small businesses often use loans to finance their operations. Small retailers finance inventory with loans. Many construction companies build condominiums or even single-family homes speculatively, without specific customers lined up. They rely on loans to pay for labor and materials before the first sales are made. Increases in interest rates therefore have a direct effect on these business investment decisions.

Opportunity-cost view of the interest rate

opportunity cost of funds
The rate of interest on financial assets that could have been earned had the funds that are used for other purposes been used instead to purchase a financial asset. That rate represents the *opportunity cost of investment.*

When we talk about the interest cost of investment, we are assuming that financing investment out of retained earnings or using existing wealth to buy a house is similar to borrowing or issuing new shares. The concept of the **opportunity cost of funds** helps to clarify this idea. If a firm buys capital goods with its own funds, the firm is usually committing those funds for the life of the capital investment and it gives up the opportunity to invest those funds in financial assets.[3] The firm has chosen to invest in itself over a long term. In this case, the long-term rate of interest on financial assets represents the opportunity cost of investment. The same idea applies when a family cashes in its IRAs or CDs and uses the proceeds toward partial payment for a house. That family could have continued to earn interest on savings while financing a larger portion of the house purchase with a mortgage. The forgone interest represents the opportunity cost of financing the house purchase.

Discounting and Present Discounted Values

We have seen that there is an interest-cost component to the cost of investment, whether the investment is financed directly by borrowing or by investing existing funds. The reason for the interest-cost component is that investment expenditures are made in the present and their benefits are earned in the future. Investment decisions always involve time.

In order to evaluate whether or not to undertake a given investment project, a firm must evaluate the stream of profits it expects to receive in future periods. It then compares this with the costs of the project. And in making this evaluation, the value of profits earned in the future has to be discounted. **Discounting** reduces the value of future cash receipts in order

---

[3] Sometimes capital goods are resold before the end of their lives. In general, however, a firm assesses its investments over a long time horizon.

discounting
Using an interest rate or discount rate to reduce the value of future cash receipts in order to find out how much those receipts would be worth compared to funds received in the present.

present discounted value
The total discounted value of a stream of future returns.

to find out how much those receipts would be worth compared to funds received in the present. Dollars that will be received in the future are not as valuable as dollars received now, and the trade-off between present dollars and future dollars depends upon the rate of interest. By means of the example in the following subsection ("Evaluating an Investment Project"), we show that *the long-term rate of interest is used to discount future profits*. This means that a higher long-term rate of interest will reduce the value of the future benefits earned by an investment project and will lead to less investment. The opposite is true for a lower long-term rate. We will also use this example to show how inflation changes investment decisions. We will find that the real rate of interest is the one that affects investment decisions.

When a stream of future returns (receipts to be received over several years) is discounted correctly and then added up, the total amount is called the **present discounted value** of the flow of returns. We look at the role of discounting and interest rates in investment demand by looking at how a business evaluates the costs and benefits of a particular investment project.[4]

Evaluating an investment project
In this example, a firm is considering whether or not to expand its retail-distribution facilities by opening a new location. The future profits from the new unit's sales will have to be compared with the cost of opening the facility. The conditions surrounding this investment-project example are described as follows:

- *Opening a new retail operation costs $1,500,000.*
  This covers the construction of the facility, buying equipment, putting in inventory, and other start-up costs.

- *The firm plans to operate the facility for four years.*
  It is corporate policy to sell off the facility as a franchise operation after the first four years.

- *The firm's managers expect that the facility will generate a profit of $350,000 a year in each of its first four years.*

- *It is estimated that at the end of four years, the firm can sell the facility to a franchisee for $500,000.*

One way to evaluate the project is to simply add up all the returns. A return of $350,000 in each of four years totals $1.4 million. Add the return from selling the franchise for $500,000 and the total inflow of funds is $1.9 million. On a dollar-to-dollar basis the firm would make a $400,000 profit, but dollar-to-dollar comparisons miss an essential aspect of asset valuation. The $1.5 million initial investment expenditure is incurred immediately, but the $1.9 million return flows in over a four-year period. When evaluating

---

[4] In the business literature this evaluation process is often referred to as discounted cash flow analysis, or net present value analysis.

any asset such as this investment project, it is important to figure out not only how large the returns are, but also when they are received.

A return that is paid out one, two, three, or more years in the future is not worth as much as a return paid today. Therefore, *future returns should not be compared to current expenditures on a dollar-to-dollar basis.* In order to compare future returns with the current cost of the investment project, the firm has to compare the value of returns spread out over four years to the value of an immediate return received today.

Present discounted values.   One way to understand discounting is to suppose that the firm goes to a bank and asks to borrow funds now that will be repaid with the $350,000 profit that will be available a year from now. How much could the firm borrow? Since the bank charges interest for the year's use of the money, the firm would receive less than $350,000 from the bank at the beginning of the year. The amount received from the bank now is the *present discounted value (PV)* of the profit and the amount to be repaid is the *future value (FV),* which is $350,000.

The amount that has to be repaid after one year *(FV)* equals the amount received *(PV)* plus the dollar value of interest charged by the bank on that amount *(PV ×* interest rate). At this point in the example, we are assuming that there is no inflation, so that there is no difference between the nominal and real rates of interest. To avoid problems later when we introduce inflation, we will simply use "discount rate" here (rather than substituting a particular interest rate *r* or *i*), and then later we will talk about which is the relevant interest rate to use as a discount rate. The relationship between present value and future values is

$$PV + (PV \times \text{discount rate}) = FV$$
$$PV\,(1 + \text{discount rate}) = FV \tag{7.1}$$
$$PV = \frac{FV}{(1 + \text{discount rate})}.$$

As long as it has the alternative of borrowing, *the firm will not be willing to pay more than the interest on next year's profit in order to have access to next year's profit today.*

If the bank charges an interest rate of 15 percent, the firm receives $304,350 today and has to repay the $350,000 loan next year. This is because the amount received ($304,350) plus the interest ($304,350 × 0.15 = $45,650) is just equal to $350,000. The present value of $350,000 to be paid a year from now is $304,350 at 15 percent interest:

$304,350 = $350,000 ÷ (1 + 0.15).

Suppose now that the firm borrows funds for two years, to be paid back with its second year's profit; the bank will give the firm $264,650. The bank knows that the amount received, $264,650, plus interest, $39,700, is just equal to $304,350 at the end of one year and $304,350 plus interest in the second year is suffcient to repay $350,000 at the end of the second year:

$264,650 \times (1.15) = \$304,350$ after the first year
$304,350 \times (1.15) = \$350,000$ after the second year so that
$264,650 \times (1.15)^2 = \$350,000$
$264,650 = \$350,000 \div (1.15)^2$.

The present discounted value of the second year's profit is lower than the present discounted value of the first year's profit because it is discounted twice. Returns that arrive in more distant years are discounted even more. *In general, the present discounted value (PV) of a given amount, n years in the future, is equal to the future value discounted by $1 \div (1 + \text{discount rate})^n$*. This relationship between present and future values and the discount rate is

$$PV = \frac{FV}{(1 + \text{discount rate})^n}. \tag{7.2}$$

The discount rate that is used in the calculation of present values reflects the opportunity cost of funds used for capital purchases.

Returning to the firm and its distribution facility, discounting can be used to evaluate the investment project regardless of how the firm finances the facility, whether through borrowing or via internally generated funds. Since this is a four-year project, an alternative use of these funds would be the purchase of a bond with a four-year term to maturity. Because most investment projects involve the purchase of capital goods that are expected to return value over a multiyear horizon, *the relevant discount rate used to evaluate investment projects is a long-term rate of interest.*[5]

In Table 7.1, the present-discounted-value calculation for the distribution facility indicates that the retail-distribution-facility project has a present discounted value of just under $1.3 million. Since the project requires an investment of $1.5 million, this evaluation would lead to rejecting the project with a 15 percent discount rate.

We used this example of an evaluation of an investment project in order to find out how interest rates affect investment demand. In this case, the interest rate was so high that a project that seemed viable on a cash-flow basis was rejected on a present-discounted-value basis.

What would the evaluation of the project look like if the long-term interest rate were lower? Table 7.2 shows the evaluation of the project when the long-term rate of interest is 5 percent instead of the previous 15 percent. With a lower long-term interest rate, the project has a present value in excess of $1.6 million, a figure that exceeds the initial investment cost of $1.5 million. At the lower interest rate, the evaluation of present discounted value leads to the acceptance of the project. *When the interest rate used to discount investment*

---

[5] Discounting uses the long-term rate over the life of the project (i.e., a 10-year rate for a 10-year project) rather than discounting the first year's return by the one-year rate and the second year's return by the two-year rate, and so on because a capital project of 10 years' length is not liquid in each year.

TABLE 7.1   Present Value of the Distribution Facility (long-term interest rate = 15 percent)

	Return estimates		Present values
Year 1	$350,000 ÷ 1.15	= $	304,350
Year 2	$350,000 ÷ (1.15)^2	= $	264,650
Year 3	$350,000 ÷ (1.15)^3	= $	230,130
Year 4	$350,000 ÷ (1.15)^4	= $	200,115
Sale of facility to franchisee:			
Year 4	$500,000 ÷ (1.15)^4	= $	285,875
Total present value			$1,285,120

TABLE 7.2   Present Value of the Distribution Facility (long-term interest rate = 5 percent)

	Return estimates		Present values
Year 1	$350,000 ÷ 1.05	= $	333,333
Year 2	$350,000 ÷ (1.05)^2	= $	317,460
Year 3	$350,000 ÷ (1.05)^3	= $	302,343
Year 4	$350,000 ÷ (1.05)^4	= $	287,946
Sale of facility to franchisee:			
Year 4	$500,000 ÷ (1.05)^4	= $	411,351
Total present value		=	$1,652,433

projects declines, there is an increase in the present discounted value of projects and an increase in the number of projects that are undertaken.

Investment demand, inflation, and the real rate of interest

Because investment projects extend many years into the future, the evaluation of an investment project should take into account the effect of inflation on the future stream of profits. In the distribution-facility example, suppose the firm's managers expect a particular rate of inflation over the life of the project. Taking inflation into account changes their estimate of future profits.

If the level of *real* activity remains constant (that is, if the distribution facility is distributing the same volume of goods each year), then inflation will increase the dollar values of both future revenues and future costs of goods sold and hence increase their difference—future profit. When both sales and costs rise at the same rate as the rate of inflation, profit will also increase at the same rate as inflation.

TABLE 7.3   Present Value of the Distribution Facility with Future Returns Showing a 6.5 Percent per Year Rate of Inflation and Discounted at a 15 Percent Long-Term Nominal Interest Rate

	New return estimate: interest			
	Original estimate	Effect of inflation	Discounting future values	Present discounted values
Year 1	$350,000 $\times$	(1.065)	$= \$372,750 \div 1.15$	$= \$ \ 324,130$
Year 2	$350,000 $\times$	$(1.065)^2$	$= \$396,979 \div (1.15)^2$	$= \$ \ 300,173$
Year 3	$350,000 $\times$	$(1.065)^3$	$= \$422,782 \div (1.15)^3$	$= \$ \ 277,986$
Year 4	$350,000 $\times$	$(1.065)^4$	$= \$450,263 \div (1.15)^4$	$= \$ \ 257,439$
Sale to franchisee:				
Year 4	$500,000 $\times$	$(1.065)^4$	$= \$643,233 \div (1.15)^4$	$= \$ \ 367,771$
Total estimated *PV*				$\$1,527,499$

Using a particular value for the expected rate of inflation, in this case 6.5 percent per year, we show in Table 7.3 how the present discounted value *(PV)* of the project is recalculated accounting for inflation. Notice that this calculation assumes that the rise in the resale value of the facility to the franchisee has also mirrored the expected rate of inflation.

The verdict is that even at a nominal interest rate of 15 percent, the facility looks like a good investment when adjusted for expected inflation. When inflation was ignored, the discount rate of 15 percent was high enough to make the project look undesirable. With inflation factored in, the project looks acceptable in spite of the 15 percent discount.

In Table 7.3, inflation is introduced by estimating its effect on the dollar returns from the project. The dollar or nominal values of the returns are then discounted using the nominal rate of interest. From the point of view of the individual firm, that is the right way to do the calculation. When we analyze investment demand in the overall economy, we cannot introduce a specific inflation adjustment into the expected returns of all the separate investment projects. Rather, *we account for the effects of inflation on the future stream of profits by using an inflation-adjusted discount rate, that is, we use the real rate of interest.*

Discounting the original estimate of real profit by the real rate of interest (the approach taken when analyzing the overall economy) generates the same present discounted value of an investment project as increasing future profits by the expected rate of inflation and discounting future profits by the nominal rate of interest (as was done in Table 7.3).

There is often confusion over this point—how can a real rate and a

TABLE 7.4   Present Value of the Distribution Facility Discounting with a Long-Term Real Rate of Interest of 7.98 Percent

	Original return	Discounting future values	Present discounted values
Year 1	$350,000	÷ (1.0798)	= $ 324,130
Year 2	$350,000	÷ (1.0798)^2	= $ 300,173
Year 3	$350,000	÷ (1.0798)^3	= $ 277,986
Year 4	$350,000	÷ (1.0798)^4	= $ 257,439
Sale to franchisee:			
Year 4	$500,000	÷ (1.0798)^4	= $ 367,771
Total estimated *PV*			= $1,527,499

nominal rate generate the same evaluation of an investment project? The answer is that the real rate already includes an inflation adjustment so the future stream of returns does not have to reflect inflation. In Table 7.3, future profits were increased by the inflation rate of 6.5 percent and discounted by the nominal long-term rate of interest of 15 percent. The real rate of interest in that example is calculated using the relationship between real and nominal rates shown in Chapter 6, Equation 6.1:

$$r = \{[1 + i(\text{long term})] \div (1 + \text{Exp}\Delta P/P)\} - 1$$
$$.0798 = (1.15 \div 1.065) - 1.$$

The long-term real rate of interest, r, in this example is equal to approximately 8 percent, calculated by adjusting the long-term nominal rate of interest, i(long term), for expected inflation. Using this value for the real rate to evaluate the distribution-facility project (shown in Table 7.4) results in the same estimate of the present value of the project that was obtained by calculating the nominal returns expected in future years (including the impact of inflation) and discounting these by the nominal interest rate (Table 7.3).

This example illustrates a general and important conclusion: *When the long-term real interest rate increases, the present discounted values of investment projects decline. When the present values of investment projects decline, fewer projects are viable.* Some of these projects will be scrapped or delayed, and the aggregate level of investment demand goes down. *The level of investment demand depends upon the long-term real rate of interest.* The relevant interest rate used in the simple investment-demand function

$$I = I_0 + I_1 Y - I_2 r \tag{7.3}$$

is the long-term real rate.

This relationship between the long-term real interest rate and the slope of investment demand is illustrated in Figure 7.1. Here, along the investment-demand line labeled AA, the level of income Y_A is taken as given. When the long-term real rate of interest rises from r_0 to r_1 along AA, the decrease in the demand for investment expenditures, from $I[A]_0$ to $I[A]_1$, depends upon the interest-rate slope of investment demand. The increase in the long-term real rate of interest generates a lower present discounted value of investment projects, a higher opportunity cost of funds, and a higher borrowing cost for funds used to purchase capital goods. All of these circumstances are summarized by the observation that the long-term real interest rate has risen, reducing the demand for investment goods at a given level of income.

While nominal interest rates and inflation do not necessarily move together, it helps us understand why it is the long-term real rate of interest that affects investment demand by considering the case where the nominal interest rate rises and the inflation rate rises *by just enough so that there is no change in the real rate of interest.* The rate of inflation has to rise by approximately the same amount as the rise in the nominal rate to keep the real rate constant. For instance, if the nominal rate of interest used in the preceding example rose from 15 percent to 26.5 percent and the rate of inflation increased from 6.5 percent to 17.15 percent, then the following relation holds.

$$r = \{[1 + i(\text{long term})] \div (1 + \text{Exp}\Delta P/P)\} - 1$$
$$.0798 = (1.265 \div 1.1715) - 1.$$

And the real rate is unchanged at 7.98 percent. Future returns are discounted more, which reduces present values, but future returns are expected to increase more because of inflation, which raises present discounted values. The result is that both present discounted values and investment demand are unchanged.

When a company or a family borrows from the bank and the contract is signed, that contract specifies the rate of interest that is being charged on the loan. That rate of interest is the nominal rate of interest. The real rate of interest is something that both borrowers and lenders calculate for themselves and it takes into account the fact that inflation will erode the value of the dollars that are used to make future interest payments and to repay the loan.

A lower real rate of interest encourages borrowing and discourages lending. The real rate of interest is lower when the rate of inflation is higher for any given nominal rate of interest. A family deciding to buy a house takes into account the fact that the dollar value of its income, the prices of all the things that it buys, and the value of its house can be expected to rise over time with inflation. The family is much more willing to take out a 10 percent mortgage when there is 5 or 6 percent inflation than when prices are stable.

FIGURE 7.1   Investment Demand and the Interest Rate

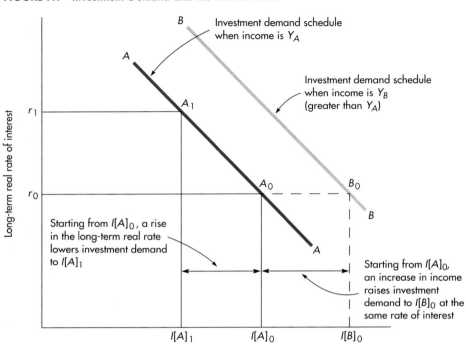

The investment-demand schedule shows how investment varies with the long-term real rate of interest. The schedule shifts when income changes.

On the other hand, those who are considering lending funds will be less likely to do so in the face of inflation. Consider a worker coming up to retirement age and saving for the future. He is going to be less willing to sell property and lend the proceeds at 10 percent, perhaps by buying a bond, when there is inflation than when there is price stability.

The preceding analysis concluded that the long-term real rate of interest drives investment demand, but there is an important qualification to that result. We have been assuming that inflation affects all prices to the same degree (the costs of the labor, capital, and materials that a firm incurs in production along with the prices of the goods and services that firm sells). That has often been the case during inflationary periods, but it is not always the case. For example, rising energy prices in 1973 and again in 1979 helped generate an increase in the rate of inflation. Nominal interest rates did not rise by as much as the price level, which actually drove real interest rates below zero for a while. With such a low level of real interest rates, investment demand might have been expected to increase, but in fact, investment demand did not surge. Companies did not think that the profits from their own investment projects would necessarily increase in line with inflation.

Long-Term Real Rates of Interest and the *IS* Schedule

Earlier in this text, the *IS* schedule described the different levels of equilibrium in the goods market that were associated with different interest rates, without specifying which interest rate was involved. A lower interest rate induced increases in investment demand, which, via a multiplier process, raised income. We have now found that it is decreases in the long-term real rate of interest that stimulate investment demand. The reduction in the long-term real rate of interest represents two effects on investment demand: (1) the reduction in opportunity cost, which through discounting raises the present discounted value of investment projects, making more of them attractive, and (2) a lower rate is a surrogate for an increase in the availability of funds that can be borrowed from financial intermediaries for the purpose of purchasing investment goods. We start the reworking of the *IS* schedule by looking at the opportunity-cost effect on investment demand and then go on to the issue of financial intermediaries and the availability of funds.

In Figure 7.1, when the long-term real rate of interest falls from r_1 to r_0, investment demand rises from $I[A]_1$ to $I[A]_0$ along AA, assuming no change in income. In the goods market, the increase in investment demand brings about an induced increase in income. Now at a higher level of income, the demand for investment goods is higher. The schedule labeled BB illustrates the higher level of investment demand and the new higher equilibrium level of income, Y_B, that result from a drop in the long-term real rate of interest. The points A_1 and B_0 in Figure 7.1 (which show that a lower real rate generates higher investment demand and a higher level of income) are also shown as two points of goods-market equilibrium along the *IS* schedule in Figure 7.2. At point B_0, the level of expenditure on capital goods is higher than at point A_0 because income is higher; capital expenditures at point B_0 are higher than at point A_1 because the real rate of interest is lower.

In this section we have used an extended example of evaluating an investment project in order to show that investment demand depends upon the long-term real rate of interest. One of the important considerations that we have not yet dealt with in this analysis is risk. Purchasing capital goods involves substantial risk. The way this risk is passed on to different groups of asset holders is a major determinant of the different rates of interest earned by the holders of these assets. Risk and liquidity are key factors separating the different types of assets along the spectrum from money to physical capital.

FIGURE 7.2   The *IS* Schedule with the Long-Term Real Rate of Interest

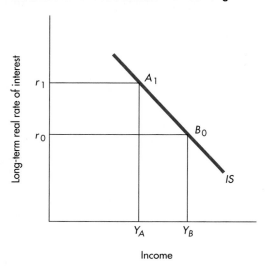

The *IS* schedule shows combinations of the long-term real rate of interest and income that give goods-market equilibrium.

THE SPECTRUM OF ASSETS, RISKS, AND LIQUIDITY

We have been examining the spectrum of assets from both ends: the money market at one end and investment demand at the other. It will help us at this point to review the spectrum itself, so Table 7.5 lists the different types of assets with examples of each type in parentheses.

We have split the different assets into three parts in Table 7.5. In the top part of the table are the financial assets that are backed by the government and are essentially free from the possibility of default. These assets are held by some savers on a long-term basis and by cash managers on a short-term basis for transactions purposes. In Chapter 6, we examined the relation among the assets in this first group, seeing how decisions are made to move between T bills and money (items 1 and 2) and we looked at the term structure and the yield curve that relate T-bill rates to rates on longer-term government bonds (items 2 and 3).

In the bottom part of the table are the real assets that are held by investors (including businesses) and the residential housing held by households. In this chapter, we have grouped items 7, 8, and 9 together as capital goods and then asked how the demand for new capital goods (investment) varies with the cost of financing.

TABLE 7.5   The Spectrum of Assets

---

1. Money (currency, demand deposits)
2. Short-term financial assets (T bills)
3. Safe long-term financial assets (Treasury bonds)

4. Long-term financial assets (corporate bonds, mortgages, bank loans)
5. Corporate stocks and shares
6. Shares of private or unincorporated businesses

7. Relatively safe real assets (houses)
8. Capital goods owned and operated by corporations or established businesses
9. Capital goods owned by small businesses or unincorporated businesses

---

The cost of financing investment depends upon the return that must be paid to holders of assets listed under items 4, 5, and 6. These are the assets that make up the middle part of the table and they are the ones held by the savers who have financed the purchases of the real assets.

As we look at the different assets in the spectrum, the risk and liquidity associated with each of them are crucial elements in the determination of their returns. Inevitably there is risk incurred and a loss of liquidity when anyone makes real investments. This creates a difficulty for savers who want to hold assets with low risk and high liquidity. We need to incorporate risk and liquidity into our analysis in order to see what separates the money market (with assets at the top of the spectrum) from the goods market (where investment demand reflects the demand for new capital goods).

Project Risk and Default Risk

Investment projects are evaluated and compared by estimating future returns and calculating present discounted values. Investment in capital goods is risky because anticipated future values may not be realized. The actual real returns to an investment project may be different from the present discounted value that was estimated at the time of the initial investment. The annual real profit from the distribution facility we used in the earlier example ($350,000) was estimated when the project was evaluated. It is not likely that actual profits will turn out to be exactly this value. There is *project risk* associated with the specific success or failure of investment projects.

Some of the project risk from investment falls directly on the managers that run the businesses that make the investments. And households that own residential housing and the proprietors of small businesses are carrying risk when they purchase real estate or other capital goods. But some of the risk is passed back to the savers that provided the financing. People that buy corporate stocks and shares bear a substantial amount of uncertainty. If a company makes poor investment decisions, its dividends will decline and the value of the stock will fall. The general performance of the economy will affect the stock averages. Holding a portfolio of stocks in 1929 turned out to be a bad idea; stocks did badly again in the 1970s. Stocks did well in the 1980s, but there was a sharp decline in the market in October 1987. Savers who buy stocks do take on substantial risks and, since people generally are averse to taking risks, the real return from stocks over the long term has had to be high in order to compensate people for this willingness to take risk. *There is a substantial risk premium built into stock prices and returns; managers have to take this into account when they use retained earnings or new equity issues to finance company investments.*

Savers who provide financing in the form of long-term bonds or direct loans also bear some of the underlying project risks. There is *default risk.* Default risk for bondholders arises because there is some probability that the issuers of an asset will fail to meet a promised payment. Default risk explains the differences in interest rates among different issuers of the same type of financial asset. For example, the interest rate that investors will require to purchase the corporate debt of large, well-established computer companies such as IBM or Digital Equipment Corporation is lower than the rate investors will require on the debt of a small, recently established computer company. The probabilities that the large established companies will fail to meet an interest payment on their corporate bonds are not zero, but they are much lower than the likelihood that a small, newly created computer company will be unable to meet its debt payments.

Default risks have been very important in the mortgage market in the 1980s and 1990s. Declines in local economies, combined with the fall in the real-estate market in some parts of the country (particularly in Texas) have forced or encouraged some businesses and families to stop paying on their mortgages, leaving the banks and S&Ls with properties worth less than the outstanding mortgage value.

Since people are mostly averse to taking risks with their funds, a premium usually has to be paid to bondholders so that they are willing to exchange dollars today for an uncertain repayment of dollars in the future. And as in the case of equity financing, *the risk premium in bond interest rates that arises from default risk is built into the decisions of those who invest in capital goods.*

One of the consequences of the fact that project risks are passed on to savers is that *if there is an economywide increase in the level of uncertainty associated with future returns, that will raise the cost of capital and lower the level of investment demand.* And of course, the opposite can occur where there is an increased optimism about the course of the economy and risk premiums fall. This reduces the cost of capital, and investment is encouraged.

Inflation Risk

The present value of the new retail-distribution facility described in the earlier example was uncertain because the real profits or returns from the project were uncertain. But in addition, the real rate of interest used to discount the returns to the project is not known with certainty ahead of time. Inflation may turn out to be different after the fact than the rate that was expected beforehand, and consequently the real interest rate is different from the one used to evaluate the project. There is *inflation risk* associated with the financing of investment.

In the example of the distribution facility, the decision to invest in the company's facility was based upon an expected rate of inflation of 6.5 percent over four years. At the time when the facility was initiated, the current long-term nominal rate of interest was 15 percent. The expected real rate of interest was almost 8 percent. What happens if the rate of inflation comes in at only 2 percent a year over the next four years? The real rate of interest will turn out to be almost 13 percent, not 8 percent. The estimate of future returns was based upon an estimate that profits would grow with inflation at 6.5 percent per year. If the returns only grew at 2 percent per year while the borrowing cost was locked in at the time the funds were borrowed and the facility was initiated, the facility would turn out to be a losing proposition. The fact that the real rate turned out to be much higher than expected would turn a viable investment into one that would not have been undertaken if the firm had accurately predicted the future rate of inflation.

Inflation also affects savers who buy financial assets. When these are purchased, the buyer knows that inflation will reduce the dollar value of the returns from the asset. However, if the inflation rate turns out to be higher than was expected, then the real return on that asset turns out to have been lower than was expected. If inflation turns out lower than expected, the real return turns out greater than expected.

In the face of inflation, the real rate of interest on assets is uncertain, while surprises in the inflation rate generate unexpected gains and losses among borrowers and lenders. Unexpectedly high inflation has the effect of reducing the real rate of interest paid by borrowers and received by lenders. This means that unexpected inflation redistributes from lenders to borrowers. Unexpectedly low inflation or deflation redistributes from borrowers to lenders. During the 1970s, unexpected increases in the rate of inflation meant that real rates of interest that were positive, based upon the amount of inflation expected when the loans were made, turned into negative real rates when inflation rates jumped. Conversely, during the early 1980s, unexpected declines in the rate of inflation meant that real rates of interest turned out to be higher than expected.

In principle it should be possible for borrowers and lenders to agree to interest or principal payments that are adjusted depending on the rate of inflation (indexed) and thereby reduce the risk to both sides. And in some countries this has occurred. There have been mortgages issued in South America indexed to inflation; there are British government bonds that are indexed to inflation also. In the United States, however, indexed bonds are not generally available. One possible reason is that any particular inflation may affect borrowers and lenders differently. For example, the inflation of the 1970s raised the cost of living dramatically but it did not increase the returns of businesses proportionally. Private businesses are therefore reluctant to issue bonds that are indexed to inflation.

Whatever the reason, in practice bonds are not adjusted for inflation in the U.S. economy, so that both purchasers and sellers of bonds know that if there is inflation over the period until the bond matures then this will affect the real value of interest and principal payments. The nominal interest rate that is determined in the market for the bonds has to reflect the expected rate of inflation. Moreover, there is considerable uncertainty about the extent of the inflation, uncertainty that increases with the duration of the bond. Long-term bonds will also carry a risk premium that compensates the purchasers of the bond for the inflation risk of those securities.

Liquidity

Real assets are generally very illiquid. It is very difficult to sell off machines or factories quickly without taking a substantial loss. At the bottom of the list of assets given in Table 7.5, the assets of small businesses are particularly risky (many small businesses go bankrupt) and are very illiquid. Selling off the inventory of a failed retail-distribution facility at a reasonable price is not easy.

Residential housing is seen by many families as being a safer investment than some stocks and bonds, but there is no question that a house is very illiquid. Realtors' fees are 6 percent or so of the selling price of a house and it can often take several months or more to sell a home, or at least sell it for its full market value.

Stocks and bonds are generally much more liquid than are real assets. Provided they are the liabilities of well-established companies, they can be sold quickly in organized markets, such as the New York exchanges. But these assets are less liquid than short-term bonds or T bills. Of course, the assets that are part of the money supply are the most liquid of all.

Liquidity is an attribute that is valued in the marketplace. We introduced the idea of a liquidity premium for long-term government bonds in Chapter 6, and this same premium affects other assets also. Assets that are illiquid will command a lower price or must offer a higher expected rate of return than more liquid assets. *There is a liquidity premium that is incorporated into the market rate of return to assets that are illiquid.* The premium is paid to savers/ lenders who are willing to give up liquidity, just as the risk premium is paid to savers who are willing to give up safety.

An important consequence of differences in liquidity among assets is that there can be changes in the market "price" of liquidity, that is, in liquidity premiums. If there are credit restrictions introduced or a credit crunch resulting from monetary policy, then there will be an increase in the value placed on liquidity by the market. This will raise the liquidity premium and hence raise the cost of capital, and this will reduce investment demand.

The Gap between Savers and Investors

Risk and liquidity do not always move together. Shares of General Motors are probably riskier than residential housing, but they are much more liquid. But despite the complications that arise when we look at a complex economy with many different types of assets, we can still make a broad generalization about them. Real assets generally involve long-term commitments, carry high risk, and have low liquidity. Company managers or people who own these real assets directly carry some of the risk and they have to adjust their actions because of the low liquidity. But these owners or managers of the real assets are not willing to accept all of the risk. They try to pass some of it back to the savers that put up the financing. This creates a problem for the economy, because when savers are deciding how to allocate their assets, they look for low risk and high liquidity. They prefer to hold safe financial assets rather than risky real assets. There is a gap between the preferences of savers and the fact that investors want to minimize their own risks.

People save and accumulate assets and they generally prefer to hold assets that are safe and can be liquidated easily. If two assets are expected to earn the same rate of return, then savers will usually choose the one that has lower risk and greater liquidity. When people make their portfolio decisions about how to allocate their assets, they will demand a higher rate of return to compensate for any loss of liquidity or increase in risk.

The reverse is true for borrowers. Companies borrowing in order to build new office buildings or shopping centers want to issue long-term bonds, because the payoff from their investments is long-term. And families buying houses want long-term mortgages so that they can pay off these loans in predictable installments over long periods of time.

The equilibrium in the market for alternative assets has to reflect the preferences of the savers and the borrowers. As we move down the spectrum of assets, the rate of return that the market requires rises with the increases in risk and decreases in liquidity. On the investment side, a prospective business project has to earn a higher expected return than the return on less risky financial assets.

financial intermediary
Any institution that borrows by issuing financial liabilities and that uses the proceeds to purchase assets, both real and financial.

The existence of differential rates of return earned on different assets presents a profit opportunity that is exploited by institutions called **financial intermediaries.** Many intermediaries specialize in issuing short-term liabilities (they borrow short) and holding loans and other long-term assets (they lend long). These institutions also provide an important service. They are the

nonbank intermediaries
Intermediaries that are prevented by regulations from issuing checking accounts and making loans.

intermediaries that help meet the needs of both borrowers and lenders. They channel saving into investment. Commercial banks are one kind of financial intermediary and they issue the most liquid asset of all, namely demand deposits. They lend in the form of business and personal loans. Other financial intermediaries (called **nonbank intermediaries** or sometimes, even less elegantly, nonbank banks) include insurance companies, pension funds, finance companies, and investment companies.

FINANCIAL INTERMEDIARIES: BRIDGING THE GAP

The different rates of interest that are paid on different kinds of assets in the economy have given rise to institutions whose very existence and profitability rely on the gaps among these rates. Financial intermediaries make money by helping to bridge the gap between money-market interest rates and the return to investments in real assets. Financial intermediaries operate in the *financial capital market*, where savers bring funds to lend and investors go to borrow. Financial intermediaries function as a go-between for these two groups, taking funds from savers and lending them out to borrowers.[6]

The mismatch between savers and investors would have serious implications for the level of saving and investment in the economy if there were no financial intermediaries. If the only source of funds that firms could borrow to finance the purchase of real investment goods were the funds made available directly by investors, then there would be a market equilibrium with a lower level of saving equal to a lower level of investment. Businesses that borrow to build factories and buy equipment would find it harder to borrow if they could only go directly to savers. The development of financial intermediation was part of the "solution" of the problem of the gap between savers and investors. Financial intermediaries do not eliminate the differences in rates of return, but by gathering and assessing information and by pooling risks, they reduce the differentials.

Financial intermediaries evaluate the creditworthiness of potential borrowers. For example, commercial banks, thrifts, and mortgage bankers employ professional staffs that evaluate and originate mortgage-loan applications and handle the monthly payments. Other financial intermediaries such as pension

---

[6] The economic analysis of financial intermediaries has been an area of great interest recently. See, for example, Bruce C. Greenwald and Joseph E. Stiglitz, "Financial Market Imperfections and Business Cycles," Working Paper no. 2494 (Cambridge, Mass.: National Bureau of Economic Research, January 1988); Ben S. Bernanke and Alan S. Blinder, "Credit, Money, and Aggregate Demand," Working Paper no. 2534 (Cambridge, Mass.: NBER, March 1988); Frederic S. Mishkin, "Understanding Real Interest Rates," Working Paper no. 2691 (Cambridge Mass.: NBER, August 1988); and Mark Gertler and R. Glen Hubbard, "Financial Factors in Business Fluctuations," Reprint no. 1251 (Cambridge, Mass.: NBER, August 1989). Textbooks of interest in this area are Frederic S. Mishkin, *The Economics of Money, Banking and Financial Markets*, 2nd ed. (Glenview, Ill.: Scott Foresman, 1989) and George G. Kaufman, *Money, the Financial System and the Economy*, 3rd ed. (Boston: Houghton Mifflin, 1981).

funds and insurance companies evaluate the riskiness of bonds issued by corporations. When financial intermediaries earn a higher interest rate than they pay out, part of this is a return to their activities of evaluating credit and servicing loans. By gathering information and monitoring the activities of borrowers, they reduce the risks associated with direct investment. The credit analysis and monitoring activities allow small businesses and individuals to borrow from a bank even though these borrowers could not successfully sell IOUs in the bond market.

Financial intermediaries also pool the risks involved in lending. Because they hold a large portfolio of assets including loans, the default risk and project risk associated with any particular loan are small in comparison to overall risk. Moreover, if the intermediaries' asset portfolios are diversified (that is, if the business activities of the borrowers are unrelated), then the risk of the entire portfolio of loans and assets can be lower than the risk associated with any single investment. Risk pooling and diversification enhance the attractiveness of intermediation to savers, which lowers the cost of capital for borrowers, thereby connecting the goods market (*IS* schedule) with the financial capital market. Further, the profit potential from intermediation compensates them for taking on the interest-rate risks of lending long-term and borrowing short-term, thereby connecting the financial capital market with the money market (*LM* schedule).

Financial intermediaries charge fees for the specific services they provide (such as investment advice or loan processing) and they make a profit by paying out a lower interest rate to lenders than the rate received from borrowers. Prior to the deregulation of financial institutions in the 1970s and 1980s, thrift banks or S&Ls were a classic example of this process. Individuals and families opened savings accounts with S&Ls that earned, say, 5 percent a year interest. People wanting mortgages borrowed from S&Ls and paid perhaps 8 percent a year interest. The difference between the rates of interest paid to depositors and charged to borrowers is the **interest-rate spread** earned by the S&Ls. The spread paid for the costs of running the institution, provided for losses when some borrowers defaulted, and generated a profit. The public was willing to deposit funds at a low rate because they received a safe asset, namely an insured savings account.

Though the interest-rate spread generated profits, it would appear that the S&Ls were in a risky position—they had short-term liabilities (deposits) and long-term assets subject to default (mortgages). S&Ls reduced this risk through risk pooling; they each had a large number of depositors and mortgage loans. S&Ls, like other financial intermediaries, made use of the benefits of pooling to allow individual depositors the flexibility of withdrawing funds when needed. As long as only a few deposits were withdrawn at once and the interest-rate spread was positive, the institution as a whole remained sound. The basic principle of financial intermediation is valid—although of course problems with intermediation can occur as we have seen with the S&Ls.

interest-rate spread
The difference between the rate of interest paid to depositors and the rate charged to borrowers.

■ Why Do Savers Stay Away from the Stock Market?

Surveys of family finances have found that a very large fraction of households have funds in savings accounts or similar types of assets and hold no stocks and shares at all.* This is a surprising result since over the past 100 years the real rate of return to stocks has been about 6 percentage points higher than the real return to savings accounts or similar safe financial assets. Even over periods of 10 years or so, having funds in the stock market has almost always yielded a higher return than having funds in savings accounts.

It is natural that people should be willing to accept a somewhat lower rate of return from safe assets than they get from the stock market, which is certainly riskier and less liquid. But the extent to which people seem averse to risk in this area is puzzling, particularly because even quite wealthy families often hold no stocks. They do not even hold mutual funds where the risks are reduced by holding small amounts of many different stocks.

People accept risk in other parts of their lives; in fact people often fail to buy insurance to cover quite common occurrences and they are often willing to gamble on unfavorable terms, such as on lotteries or horse races. What can explain the aversion to stocks?

First, one can ask if the underlying facts are correct. Is it not true that many people have pensions or insurance policies that are invested in the stock market? Most pension funds are "defined-benefit plans" in which the retirees will receive a pension linked to their salary or to the cost of living. The retiree's income is not affected directly by the performance of the stock market, unless the fund actually goes broke. Insurance-policy payouts are also affected very little by the performance of the stock market. So the existence of pension plans and insurance policies does not explain the paradox.

The most likely explanation for the fact that so many people hold no stocks is that they underestimate the advantage from holding stocks and overestimate the risk. The stock market got a bad name in the 1930s and was not helped by its short-run gyrations in the 1980s. Many people today still view the stock market as a place for gambling and not a place for retirement saving. Even for many economists, including ourselves, the fact that the stock market had performed so much better than safe financial assets over the long run was a surprise when it was first discussed in the recent literature.

The unwillingness of so many people to hold stocks has implications for the economy. The aversion to risk that so many savers show means that businesses that want to borrow funds in the capital market would face very high borrowing costs were it not for financial intermediaries that can reduce the risks to savers. Financial intermediaries are indeed playing a crucial role in our economy.

* The basic puzzle of the low rate of stock holding was posed by Rajnish Mehra and Edward C. Prescott in "The Equity Premium: A Puzzle," *Journal of Monetary Economics,* 15 (March 1985), pp. 145–61. This article spawned a lively literature with many different hypotheses to explain the puzzle.

Corporations as financial intermediaries

An industrial corporation is not usually thought of as a financial intermediary, but in some respects it is. At any given moment, a large corporation will have many different products being marketed. It will have a large research-

and-development (R&D) program that is looking for new products and processes in several areas. It will have a variety of investment projects underway that are located in different regions of the country and often around the world. Such a corporation has a professional management team. Some managers are responsible for marketing and distribution activities. Some managers are running the existing plants, trying to reduce cost or increase output. Some managers are assessing corporate investment strategy and others are managing R&D projects.

The company does not know which of its marketing strategies will work best or which of its products will pay off most profitably in the next year. It does not know which investment or R&D projects are likely to be the winners and which the losers, but it can expect that the winners and losers will balance out to some extent, hopefully with more of the former than the latter. The fact that there are many projects going on at once means that the company is pooling its risks. A large corporation is taking advantage of risk pooling just as a financial intermediary does.

The managers of the company are spending part of their time doing just what the loan officer in a financial intermediary is doing. They are evaluating the feasibility and likely profitability of a series of potential investment projects. They are paid to assess the extent of inflation risk and project risk.

The ownership of a company may be privately held by a small number of people, but often ownership of the large, publicly held firm is spread among thousands or even millions of people and institutions. Ownership is divided into shares, and shares can be bought or sold on the stock market. Those who own a company's shares do not typically manage it. The owners rely on the professional managers to evaluate investment opportunities, decide which are the best ones, and determine how much of the company's profit should be retained for future investment, how much the company should pay out in dividends, and how much borrowing the company should do. The managers determine a company's corporate strategy.

Just like financial intermediaries, corporations make money by paying out lower returns on their liabilities than the rates they receive on their assets. A typical factory or shopping mall has a required rate of return that is higher than the required rate of return on corporate shares. The difference in rates of return provides a surplus that pays the salaries, bonuses, and expenses of the corporate managers. It also pays the corporate income tax that the government levies.

The role of the corporation as a financial intermediary provides an important service to shareholders. Individual shareholders do not have the expertise that would allow them to assess the individual projects that the corporation undertakes. Moreover, when investors buy shares in an established company, they hold an asset that can readily be resold. Shares are much more liquid than the real assets that are owned by the corporation issuing the shares.

Consequences of Financial Intermediation

Financial intermediation is vitally important for connecting saving and investment through financial markets and the various rates of interest. The existence of banks and other financial intermediaries is also important because they can have a *direct* effect on investment by small businesses, on housing, and even on corporate investment. This effect is direct rather than the result of a change in the interest rates charged to borrowers by the intermediaries.

Credit rationing

credit rationing
When financial intermediaries reduce the quantity of credit and/or access to credit by rationing rather than only by raising the interest rate they charge on loans.

When the Fed contracts the money supply, banks are forced to reduce loans and then they ration credit, rather than simply raising the interest rate they charge on bank loans. **Credit rationing** may be occurring because intermediaries are faced with borrowers whose risks are changing in a changing economic environment and the intermediaries are not capable of quickly and accurately reevaluating those risks. Also, intermediaries have long-established relationships with their primary customers (borrowers), the intermediaries want to hold on to their customers, and they may choose to temporarily allocate a smaller quantity of credit rather than raise rates to market-clearing levels. This type of behavior in the financial market is the equivalent of sticky prices in the general economy. It does not last very long, as rates eventually rise, and it does not reflect behavior in the financial markets for traded assets. It is an aspect of market adjustment in the financial sector that results from intermediation. Companies that cannot get loans will cut back on inventory investment. Builders unable to get construction loans will cut back on housing starts. This often happens at the same time that higher interest rates in the financial capital market lead to higher mortgage rates, which push down housing demand.

Because there was regulation of interest rates in the 1950s and 1960s, interest rates in the financial capital market did not change by very much. In that environment, credit rationing was particularly important in connecting changes in money-market conditions and monetary policy with changes in the demand for real investment goods. When the Fed decided that the economy was overheating, it would cut the money supply and encourage banks to ration credit. The credit crunch resulted in a restriction of investment demand that cut aggregate demand with very little change in interest rates.

Financial-sector deregulation and the growth of nonbank financial intermediaries have led to an increased level of competition among lenders. This development rendered credit rationing somewhat less important than in earlier periods, but it is still a factor in restricting the growth of aggregate demand when the Fed chooses to follow a contractionary monetary policy. Moreover, credit rationing may occur because of a change in the degree of risk that managers of financial intermediaries believe they can bear. Credit rationing was reported during 1990 as intermediaries responded to the tightened requirements for loan reserves imposed by regulators as an aftermath of the S&L crisis.

Intermediation failure

The fact that financial institutions and even large corporations act as financial intermediaries helps to solve the problem of the gap between savers and investors, but financial intermediation creates some problems of its own. Intermediaries can fail, thereby creating a credit crisis. This has happened recently where S&Ls have failed as a result of deregulation, fraud, or inefficient management, as we saw in Chapter 5. And the same problems can also occur with corporations and the role that they play as intermediaries.

Managers of publicly owned corporations are hired by corporate boards of directors to be stewards of the interests of shareholders. Most often they carry out their responsibilities well. However, some managers and corporate boards of directors may fail to use corporate funds appropriately, they may pay themselves salaries that do not reflect their contribution to the firm's effectiveness, or they may provide themselves with excessive corporate perks or finance business expansions through takeovers (buying out another company) that have little real chance of paying off. In principle, takeovers are an aspect of intermediation. Corporate managers use financial resources under their control to gain ownership and control of the real capital being employed by the target firm (the company they seek to take over). This process is designed to police the behavior of corporate managers. Companies run by poor management teams will be the object of takeovers by companies with more effective management. In some cases, takeovers actually have worked out that way, but in practice this mechanism can also fail. Takeover bids are very expensive. And often the managers of the company doing the taking over are no more efficient than the managers of the takeover target.[7]

Intermediation failure in the aggregate economy.   The problems of intermediation that we have described may possibly be quite large, but with the exception of unusual periods such as the Great Depression of the 1930s, they do not generally play a big part in determining fluctuations in income and output. For macroeconomic analysis, the existence of financial intermediaries, including corporations, is important because these institutions separate saving and

---

[7] The problem of misallocation of resources that results when the personal interests of corporate managers are not aligned with shareholders' interests has been studied by financial economists. They have developed a model called *agency theory* to describe the economic consequences of the misalignment of interests between a principal (i.e., owner or stockholder) and an agent (i.e., manager). See Michael Jensen and W. W. Meckling, "Theory of the Firm: Managerial Behavior, Agency Costs and Ownership Structure," *Journal of Financial Economics* 3 (October 1976), pp. 305–60; Steve Shavell, "Risk Sharing and Incentives in the Principal and Agent Relationship," *The Bell Journal of Economics* 10 (Spring 1979), pp. 55–73; Sherwin Rosen, "Authority, Control, and the Distribution of Earnings," *The Bell Journal of Economics* 13 (Autumn 1982), pp. 311–23; and Alan J. Marcus, "Risk Sharing and the Theory of the Firm," *The Bell Journal of Economics* 13 (Autumn 1982), pp. 369–78.

The effect on economic fluctuations that stem from financial arrangements such as takeovers, LBOs, and junk bonds that allow for changes in the relationship between principal and agent are explored in Chapter 14.

investment decisions and can therefore exacerbate a failure of coordination between saving and investment.

We have commented before that a modern economy is very different from a simple primitive economy. In the primitive economy, saving is also investment. In a modern economy, the saving and investment decisions are made separately and they may or may not be coordinated. If saving were to increase because people are optimistic about the future returns from investing in factories, then the increase in saving will lead to an increase in stock-market values, and this will encourage corporate managers to invest more. In this case the saving and investment decisions are coordinated. But if people are saving more because they fear bad times, then they will increase their demand for safe, liquid assets. The interest rates on short-term assets will probably fall as the demand is increased for these assets. But that shift of asset demand will probably be accompanied by an increase in risk premiums and a drop in share prices. Consequently, long-term interest rates on bank loans or risky bonds may not fall; they may even rise.

Corporate managers and the loan officers of financial intermediaries have their own ideas about when it is a good time to invest and do not rely only on changes in interest rates or the stock market to indicate whether investment should increase or decrease. The competitive economic environment that these managers work in certainly compels them to respond to some degree to changes in financial markets, but managers' expectations about future sales and profitability are much more important than short-run fluctuations in interest rates. In particular, an increase in saving is a reduction in the demand for consumer goods. An increase in saving may lead to excess capacity in industries that are producing consumer goods, including durable goods. Even if long-term interest rates were to fall when saving increases, excess capacity may have a greater influence in reducing the demand for investment goods than the positive effect of the fall in rates.

Changes in interest rates are not a completely effective mechanism for coordinating saving and investment decisions. The miscoordination of saving and investment continues to generate recessions where output and employment drop in spite of financial markets that freely determine interest rates.

Conclusions on intermediation

Financial institutions help make money markets operate smoothly. They borrow funds from those who want to save, but who also want to hold assets with less risk and more liquidity than are available through direct investment. The connection between the financial capital market and the goods market arises, to a large degree, through the activities of bank and nonbank financial intermediaries. A modern economy could not operate without a financial sector, but we do pay a price for the development of financial markets and intermediation. Financial markets are prone to rapidly fluctuating interest rates, and the process of intermediation itself can exacerbate a breakdown of coordination between saving and investment, leading to recessions. In a primitive economy where saving and investment always occur together, there is no coordination problem, but the level of saving and investment is low and so is income.

The complexity of the modern economy's range of financial markets also exacts a price from those of us who try to understand the workings of economic policy. We have found that there is a split between the *IS* and *LM* schedules. Now we are going to attempt to put those schedules back together. To do this we will carry forward the conclusion that we drew from the analysis of investment demand and discounting. The demand for investment goods and hence equilibrium of supply and demand in the goods market shown along the *IS* schedule depends upon the long-term real rate of interest and the current level of income.

In one sense the *IS* schedule provides much too simple a view of what is involved in investment decisions. But the simplicity can be helpful for our purposes. The *IS* schedule is useful for studying the impact of policy. The links between the short-term nominal interest rate and long-term real rate do not ensure perfect coordination between saving and investment, but policy-induced changes in interest rates are still capable of having a powerful effect on the economy.

THE GAP BETWEEN SHORT-TERM NOMINAL AND LONG-TERM REAL RATES OF INTEREST

We need to capture in a simple way as much as we can of the analysis of the money market, inflation, the investment decision, risk, and the effect of intermediation. Inevitably we will have to leave many interesting elements out, but we can focus on the most important ones that will give us an understanding of how policy affects the economy.

1. We assume that equilibrium in the money market determines the short-term nominal rate of interest and we have assigned the letter *i* to this rate. The *LM* schedule gives the combinations of real income (*Y*) and the short-term nominal interest rate *(i)* for which there is money-market equilibrium.

2. There is a gap between the short-term nominal rate and the nominal interest rate on risky long-term financial assets. This latter rate is the nominal interest rate that is relevant for corporate borrowing to finance investment. Alternatively, we can think of this as the mortgage rate that households then pay when they finance home purchases. We have assigned the notation *i*(long term) to this interest rate.

3. This gap between the short and long nominal rates [the gap between *i* and *i*(long term)] reflects *expectations about future short rates, a liquidity premium, and a risk premium*. This gap does not remain constant, but will vary in response to economic conditions, including policy changes. Since we will be looking frequently at the effect of changes in the yield curve and the term structure, we will call the gap the **maturity premium** *(MP)*. The

maturity premium
The difference in interest rates that investors require in order for them to hold a longer-term, higher-risk asset rather than a shorter-term, lower-risk asset.

relationship between the short-term and long-term nominal rates of interest can then be expressed as

$$MP = i(\text{long term}) - i$$
$$i + MP = i(\text{long term}).$$
(7.4)

For example, with a short-term rate of 5 percent and a maturity premium of 5 percent, the long-term rate will be 10 percent. Usually the long-term rate will be well above the short-term rate. Certainly this will be the case with a normal yield curve.

4. The gap between real and nominal rates of interest is the inflation rate that is expected to prevail over the life of the asset. Equation 7.5 gives the simple approximation of the relation between the real and nominal rates described in Chapter 6:

$$r = i(\text{long term}) - \text{Exp}\Delta P/P.$$
(7.5)

Combining the relationships between real and nominal rates (Equation 7.4) and between long and short rates (Equation 7.5) and rearranging the terms then gives us an approximate expression for the gap between the long-term real rate of interest (r) and the short-term nominal rate of interest (i):

$$r = i + MP - \text{Exp}\Delta P/P.$$
(7.6)

The long-term real rate of interest is the short-term nominal rate plus the maturity premium minus the expected rate of inflation. For example, if the short-term nominal rate of interest were 5 percent, the maturity premium were 5 percent, and the expected rate of inflation were 4 percent, then the long-term real rate of interest would be 6 percent $(5 + 5 - 4 = 6)$.

The relationship among the different rates of interest is illustrated in Figure 7.3. The left-hand panel shows the maturity premium depicted as a straight line. It describes the gap between short-term and long-term nominal rates of interest and it is used in this form to represent one part of the connection between the *IS* and *LM* schedules. It shows a 5 percent short-term nominal interest rate (point *A*) and a normal yield curve *(AB)*, resulting in a maturity premium of 5 percent. The long-term nominal rate (point *B*) is then 10 percent, as shown in the center of the figure.

The right-hand panel of the diagram connects long-term nominal rates with long-term real rates of interest. It uses an *inflation line,* based on the approximate relationship between real and nominal rates, to show how different expected rates of inflation transform a given long-term nominal interest rate into a long-term real rate. The inflation line is one part of the connection between the *IS* and *LM* schedules. With a particular rate of inflation, any long-term nominal rate of interest (point *B*) marked along the middle vertical axis is converted into a long-term real rate that is 4 percent lower marked along the right-hand vertical axis (point *E*). Starting at point *B* with an expected inflation rate of 4 percent, sliding along the inflation line *(BC)* until the particular rate of inflation is found, takes us to point *D*. At point *D*, the real rate

FIGURE 7.3   Connecting the Short-Term Nominal Rate and the Long-Term Real Rate

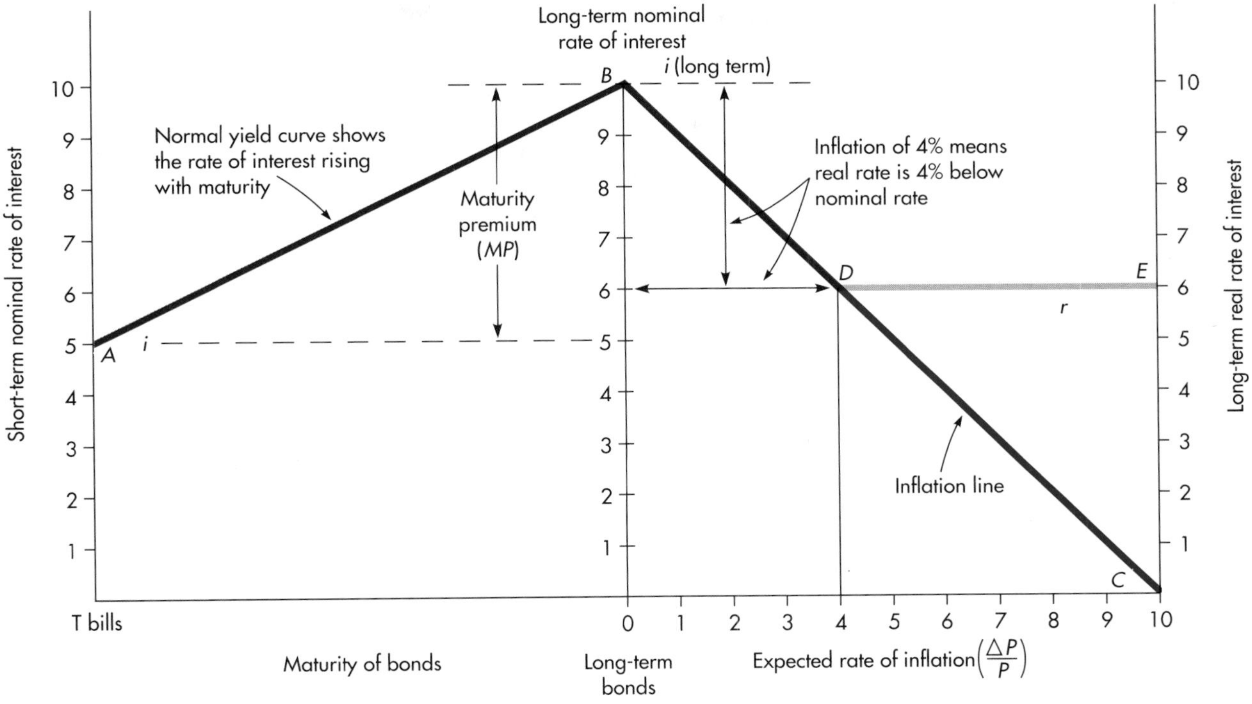

The figure shows the relation between the short-term nominal rate and the long-term real rate, based on the maturity premium and the rate of inflation.

is 6 percent, as shown at point E on the right-hand axis of the panel.

Suppose now that the short-term nominal rate of interest were to fall from 5 percent to 3 percent with no change in the maturity premium or the expected rate of inflation. This is shown in Figure 7.4 by the drop of the yield curve (AB to $A'B'$). The figure also shows how the long-term real rate of interest is affected. The long-term nominal rate also falls by 2 percentage points (B to B') and this moves the inflation line down by 2 percentage points (BC to $B'C'$). Notice that in this example we have assumed that the rate of inflation has remained the same at 4 percent. Therefore, the long-term real rate is found along the new inflation line (point D') and it is 4 percent rather than 6 percent (point E' rather than point E). In this simple case, the decline of 2 percentage points in the short-term nominal rate of interest has led to an equal decline of 2 percentage points in the long-term real rate of interest. The two rates have simply moved together.

FIGURE 7.4   A Uniform Drop in Interest Rates

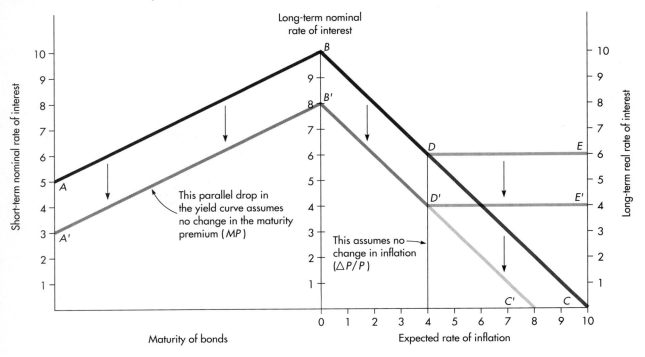

A fall in the short-term nominal rate by 2 percentage points leads to a fall in the long-term nominal rate by 2 points also, with no change in *MP* or Δ*P/P*.

The Interest-Rate Gap

If, in the actual economy, changes in interest rates were always of the simple kind we just described—with no change in the maturity premium or the expected rate of inflation—it would not be necessary, from a macroeconomic point of view, to distinguish among the different interest rates. In such an economy, information about changes in any rate of interest would be equivalent to information about changes in all rates of interest. However, financial markets in the actual economy are not connected in lockstep. Interest rates, the maturity premium, and the expected rate of inflation can move together or independently, and when they do, this leads to changes in the **interest-rate gap.**

The interest-rate gap is defined as the long-term real rate of interest minus the short-term nominal rate of interest. Given the relation between the two interest rates that we found in Equation 7.5, it also follows that *the*

interest-rate gap
The difference between the long-term real rate of interest and the short-term nominal rate. It is equal to the maturity premium minus the expected rate of inflation.

■ Supply and Demand in the Financial Capital Market

We saw earlier that changes in supply and demand in the T-bill market lead to changes in the price of T bills and hence to changes in the short-term nominal rate of interest. A similar relation holds for long-term bonds. Equilibrium of supply and demand in the financial capital market determines the long-term nominal rate of interest. When the rate of inflation is unchanged, shifts in the supply of and demand for financial capital that change the long-term nominal rate of interest are then carried over to changes in the long-term real rate of interest.

The financial capital market is comprised of a wide variety of financial assets and institutions, all of which operate to connect borrowers with lenders. But we can think about the concept of supply and demand in the bond market to represent the workings of the much larger financial capital market. The equality of supply and demand in the financial capital market means that borrowers and lenders have determined a price for bonds. Determining a price for bonds also determines a long-term nominal rate of interest.

Through changes in the amount of borrowing and lending that take place in financial capital markets, financial-market conditions affect the real economy. The amount of borrowing and lending is determined by wealth holders, savers, and investors and by the actions of financial institutions, especially financial intermediaries.

---

interest-rate gap is the maturity premium minus the expected rate of inflation. We show these relations in Equation 7.6a:

$$r = i + r_{gap}$$
$$r_{gap} = r - i = MP - \text{Exp}\Delta P/P. \qquad (7.6a)$$

The interest-rate gap is an important concept. It can be either positive or negative depending upon whether or not the maturity premium exceeds expected inflation. Since inflation has been high in the past 20 years, the interest-rate gap has often been negative in practice over this period. When we know what the interest-rate gap is or how it changes, we will know how to link the money market and the goods market. To understand more about the interest-rate gap, we look at a series of changes in inflation and interest rates, using illustrative examples to help us see when the interest-rate gap may widen or narrow, or turn positive or negative. This will equip us for Chapter 8 where these examples are applied to actual economic-policy changes.

A fall in the expected rate of inflation

Suppose that the rate of inflation expected to prevail over the life of a long-term bond declined, with no change in the maturity premium. For example, suppose the maturity premium remains constant at 5 percent and the expected rate of inflation falls from 4 percent to 2 percent. Then the interest-rate gap will rise to 3 percent.

With 4 percent inflation: $r_{gap} = MP - \text{Exp}\Delta P/P$
$$= 5\% - 4\% = 1\%.$$
With 2 percent inflation: $r_{gap} = MP - \text{Exp}\Delta P/P$
$$= 5\% - 2\% = 3\%. \tag{7.7}$$

We have found that, *holding the maturity premium constant, a fall in the expected rate of inflation leads to an increase in the interest-rate gap.*

A decline in the maturity premium

Suppose there is a decline in the maturity premium with no change in the expected rate of inflation. This could come about because financial investors believe that short-term nominal rates of interest will be lower than they had previously expected them to be. Or perhaps there is an expectation of improved economic conditions, so that the risk premium on corporate bonds declines. Suppose, for example, that the maturity premium fell from 5 to 3 percent as the yield curve became flatter (expected inflation stays the same). This case is shown in Equation 7.8.

With 5 percent maturity premium: $r_{gap} = MP - \text{Exp}\Delta P/P$
$$= 5\% - 4\% = 1\%.$$
With 3 percent maturity premium: $r_{gap} = MP - \text{Exp}\Delta P/P$
$$= 3\% - 4\% = -1\%. \tag{7.8}$$

We have found that, *holding expected inflation constant, a decline in the maturity premium leads to a fall in the interest-rate gap.* In this example the interest-rate gap is negative as the maturity premium is now less than expected inflation.

Maturity premium and inflation moving together

In our examples so far we have looked at the impact of changing only one variable at a time. But the actual economy rarely produces such simple effects. Indeed, the underlying shifts in the economy that lead to a change in one variable will usually change other variables also. Changes in expectations about inflation will usually be accompanied by changes in expectations about the risks of financial investment and future interest rates. One important example of this is where there is a change in the expected rate of inflation and a change in the maturity premium by the same amount in the same direction. This is illustrated by Equation 7.9.

With 5 percent maturity premium and 4 percent expected inflation,

$$r_{gap} = MP - \text{Exp}\Delta P/P$$
$$= 5\% - 4\% = 1\%. \tag{7.9}$$

With 3 percent maturity premium and 2 percent expected inflation,

$$r_{gap} = MP - \text{Exp}\Delta P/P$$
$$= 3\% - 2\% = 1\%.$$

Equal changes in both the maturity premium and the expected rate of inflation will leave the interest-rate gap unchanged.

The Interest-Rate Gap and Interest-Rate Changes

Changes in the expected rate of inflation or changes in the maturity premium can, and usually will, lead to changes in the interest-rate gap. When the short-term nominal rate of interest changes, there will often be a change in the interest-rate gap and therefore there will not usually be an equal change in the long-term real rate of interest. The impact of an initial increase in the short-term nominal rate of interest upon the long-term real rate of interest is reinforced if the maturity premium rises. It is offset if this premium falls. The impact of an initial increase in the short-term nominal rate of interest on the long-term real rate is reinforced by a decrease in expected inflation. It is offset if expected inflation rises. A summary of how various combinations of change in the maturity premium and the expected rate of inflation affect the relationship between the short-term nominal and the long-term real rate of interest is given in Table 7.6.

These alternatives are important because monetary policy works by changing the short-term nominal rate of interest. *In order for monetary policy to be effective, its impact on short-term nominal rates has to be transmitted via the financial capital market into a change in the long-term real rate of interest.* For example, suppose the Fed decides to follow a contractionary monetary policy and raises the short-term nominal rate of interest. What will happen to investment demand and, hence, income and output? It is certainly possible for the increase in the short-term nominal rate to go one for one into the long-term real rate of interest. But it is also possible for the change in the short-term nominal rate to be accompanied by a change in the long-term real rate that is greater or even much greater. The monetary contraction would have a supercharged effect. In other cases, the outcome of a change in the short rate is uncertain. It is even possible in principle, if unlikely in practice, for a monetary contraction to be followed by a stimulus to investment.

Different interest rates matter: fluctuations in the interest-rate gap

The long-term real rate of interest rate and the gap between this rate and the short-term nominal rate are vital concepts for macroeconomic theory and policy. But there is a serious difficulty involved in using them because they are not directly observable. The problem, of course, is that they involve the expected future rate of inflation and there is no ideal way of knowing what this is. Different participants in financial markets have different views of the likely course of inflation, while individual companies planning their own investment projects will have their own estimates of the likely increases in the prices of their own products over the lifetime of the investment projects. Indeed, as we saw when we did the example of a new distribution facility, business managers do not even have to compute the real rate of interest explicitly; they can estimate their future profits in dollars and then use the nominal rate of interest to discount them.

Economists have typically used two strategies in order to make estimates

TABLE 7.6   Possible Outcomes for the Long-Term Real Rate of Interest Following an Increase in the Short-Term Nominal Rate of Interest

	Maturity premium rises; expected inflation falls.	Interest-rate gap rises.	Increase in the long-term real rate exceeds the increase in the short-term nominal rate.
Short-term nominal rate increases.	Equal changes or no changes in maturity premium and expected inflation.	Interest-rate gap unchanged.	Increase in the long-term real rate matches the increase in the short-term nominal rate.
	Maturity premium falls; expected inflation rises.	Interest-rate gap falls.	Small increase or decrease in the long-term real rate.

of real rates of interest. One strategy is to assume that the expected future rate of inflation is an average of past rates of inflation. This approach uses what are called adaptive expectations. The second strategy is to assume that people are able to make rational forecasts of the future, so that the expected rate of inflation differs only randomly from the rate of inflation that actually occurs. This approach assumes what are called rational expectations.[8] Formal methods for coming up with estimates of expected inflation by either of these strategies can be very complex,[9] but we have used instead a simple combined approach in order to indicate the main movements in the long-term real rate of interest and the interest-rate gap during the 1970s and 1980s.[10]

In Figure 7.5, we show the interest rate on three-month T bills, representing the short-term nominal rate of interest. Then we show two alternative

---

[8] We discuss the way in which expectations are formed and the alternatives of adaptive expectations and rational expectations in Chapter 9.

[9] See for example Frederic S. Mishkin "Understanding Real Interest Rates," Working Paper No. 2691 (Cambridge, Mass.: National Bureau of Economic Research, August 1988).

[10] We looked at data covering the period from 1970 to 1987 and we computed an estimate of expected inflation using the average rate of increase of the price level over the period running from five years prior to the date shown through three years after this date, making a separate estimate for each quarter of each year. This meant, for instance, that the expected rate of inflation in the second quarter of 1981 was equal to the average rate of inflation over the period from the second quarter of 1976 to the second quarter of 1984 (the inflation rate was calculated using the fixed-weight GNP price index, not the implicit deflator for GNP). This method combines in a rough way the backward-looking view embodied in the adaptive expectations approach and the forward-looking view of the rational expectations approach. We have a greater weight to past values than to future values because the rate of inflation over this period was variable and hard to predict, so that even the best informed decision makers could not have forecast the actual path of inflation very far into the future. As a check, however, we tried a variety of combinations of time-periods with essentially similar results to the ones found here.

FIGURE 7.5 **The Short-Term Nominal Rate of Interest (the three-month T-bill rate) and Two Estimates of the Long-Term Real Rate of Interest**

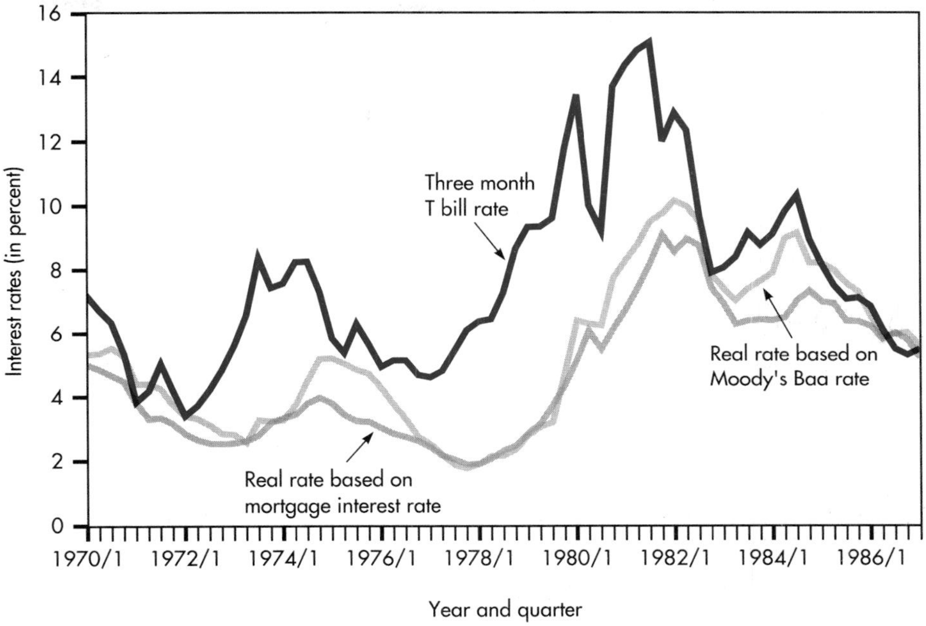

Source: Computed by the authors with data from the Federal Reserve Board and the U.S. Department of Commerce.

measures of the long-term real rate of interest, based upon the interest rate of mortgages on new homes and the interest rate on corporate bonds rated Baa by Moody's rating service. In both cases the long-term nominal rates of interest (on mortgages or bonds) were adjusted for inflation using our estimate of expected inflation.

The short-term nominal rate of interest over this period was high and very variable and there was a tendency for interest rates to be higher in the 1980s than in the 1970s. There were three peaks in the short-term rate, occurring in 1974–75, in 1980, and then in 1981–82. The long-term real rate of interest was less than the short-term nominal rate over almost the entire period, so that the interest-rate gap was generally negative. Expected inflation was substantial over this period and exceeded the maturity premium, at least for the mortgage interest rate and the Moody's Baa rate.

There were two significant peaks in the long-term real rates occurring in 1975 and then in 1982. Both of these coincided with severe recessions, and this is consistent with the view that tight money first raised short-term nominal interest rates and then long-term real rates and contributed to both recessions. This pattern is particularly marked in the case of the 1982 recession.

The peak in the real rate of interest in 1975 is not very pronounced. In the period 1973–75 there was an oil embargo, the first oil price increase, and the resignation of President Nixon. The uncertainties that these created contributed to a loss of business and consumer confidence and weakness in investment quite apart from the impact of monetary tightness and high interest rates. In terms of our economic modeling, the *IS* schedule was shifting down to the left at this time, lowering both income and interest rates.

Figure 7.6 shows one version of the interest-rate gap explicitly using the real rate of interest based on Moody's Baa rate minus the T-bill rate. It is notable that the gap is often large in magnitude and it varies considerably. And because of this variability, it follows that changes in the short-term nominal rate of interest are not simply translated one-for-one into changes in the long-term real rate. It is clear that trying to use a model of the economy with only a single rate of interest is a serious mistake. The most striking result from Figure 7.6 is that the interest-rate gap becomes large and negative when there is a sharp increase in the T-bill rate and it becomes small or even turns positive when the T-bill rate falls sharply. If there is a contraction in the real stock of money that drives up short-term nominal rates of interest, then long-term real rates do not immediately follow the increase in the short rate. Similarly, if the Fed expands the money supply and lowers short-term rates, then real rates do not necessarily fall right away.

Another important conclusion from both figures concerns the behavior of the long-term real rate and the interest-rate gap in the 1980s. Both real rates of interest fell from the peak in 1982, but they still stayed extremely high. And the interest-rate gap went almost to zero, becoming slightly positive in 1986. This period was one where there was a very expansionary fiscal policy with a large budget deficit. The recovery in the 1980s was being helped by the tax cuts (the *IS* schedule was shifted to the right), that raised income and kept real interest rates high.[11] There was also a sharp decline in expected inflation over this period that helped turn the interest-rate gap positive.

There are many different possible real rates that can be calculated so that the data shown in Figures 7.5 and 7.6 should only be taken as examples. In particular, the real rate used to discount business investment projects will probably be higher than the rates shown in Figure 7.5 because the risk premiums will be much higher. The interest-rate gap is positive for many business investment decisions.

Despite this, however, the simple calculations used in the figures have shown us that interest rates do not always move together and that we need to look at variations in the interest-rate gap and what causes them. In the next chapter we will use the interest-rate gap to link the *IS* and *LM* schedules and then use this to evaluate the effects of specific policy changes.

---

[11] This period was discussed in Chapter 4.

FIGURE 7.6   The Interest Rate Gap: The Difference between the Real Moody's Baa Bond Rate and the Three-Month T-Bill Rate

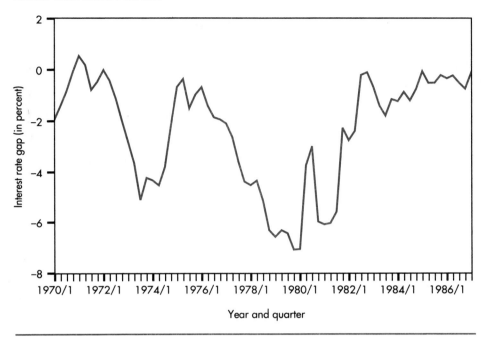

Year and quarter

Source: Computed by the authors as described in the text.

SUMMARY

- A company purchasing capital goods is making a long-term investment. The opportunity cost of using funds to purchase a capital good is the return on best alternative use of the funds. The long-term rate of interest is a proxy for the opportunity cost.

- A company wishing to issue debt to finance investment or a household wishing to obtain a mortgage to buy a house will want to repay the debt over the long term. The long-term rate of interest will affect the decision to make debt-financed investments.

- The present value of dollars to be received n years in the future is calculated by dividing the future value by $(1 + \text{discount rate})^n$. This is called discounting.

- The present value of an investment project is the sum of the discounted flow of returns from it, using the long-term rate of interest as a discount rate.

- An increase in the long-term rate of interest will reduce the present value of investment projects. The number of projects undertaken will be reduced or the size of some will be reduced and the demand for investment in the economy will fall.

- If returns from an investment project are given in dollars, they can be discounted using the nominal rate of interest. If the returns are given in real terms, after inflation adjustment, then they are discounted using the real rate of interest. The answer is the same.

- For a given level of income, real investment demand increases when the long-term real rate of interest falls, while real investment demand decreases when that rate rises.

- The *IS* schedule relates the level of income to the long-term real rate of interest.

- Savers prefer to hold assets that are safe and liquid. Investors/borrowers financing risky investment projects want to repay loans over long periods with stable repayment schedules.

- Asset-market equilibrium will involve substantial differences in rates of returns on assets with different risks and liquidity. These differences in returns provide a profit opportunity for financial intermediaries who can bridge the gap between savers and investors.

- Financial intermediation is vital to the working of a modern economy, but investment decisions are not always coordinated with saving decisions and can result in recession.

- The short-term nominal rate of interest is determined in the money market at one end of the spectrum of assets *(LM)*. The long-term real rate of interest affects investment and goods-market equilibrium *(IS)*. The difference between the two rates is the interest-rate gap.

- A single interest rate should only be used to describe equilibrium in the *IS-LM* framework if there is a lockstep relationship between the short-term nominal rate of interest and the long-term real rate of interest (that is, only if the interest-rate gap does not change). This is unlikely in practice.

- The interest-rate gap is the maturity premium minus the expected rate of inflation. A rise in the maturity premium and/or a fall in the expected rate of inflation will cause the interest-rate gap to increase.

- When the interest-rate gap changes, changes in the long-term real rate of interest will not be the same as the changes in the short-term nominal rate of interest.

KEY TERMS

credit rationing	maturity premium
discounting	nonbank intermediaries
financial intermediary	opportunity cost of funds
interest-rate gap	present discounted value
interest-rate spread	

DISCUSSION QUESTIONS AND PROBLEMS

1. Describe how a pension fund operates as a financial intermediary. Do the same for an insurance company and a real-estate holding company.

2. Savers who deposit funds in a financial intermediary receive a lower rate of interest than the rate paid by families or companies who borrow from the intermediary. Why don't the savers lend directly to the borrowers?

3. The following is a breakdown of gross fixed investment by type for 1987 (in billions of 1982 dollars):

Producer's durable equipment		$325.5
Information-processing equipment	139.4	
Industrial equipment	61.4	
Transportation equipment	59.1	
Other	65.6	
Nonresidential structures		125.5
Residential structures		189.4
Total private domestic fixed investment		640.4
Inventory investment		34.4
Total private domestic investment		674.8

When these investments were made, what time horizons do you think were used to evaluate their profitability?

4. Explain the different impacts of inflation on the returns from an investment project and the returns from a 30-year bond. Use your answer to explain why the real rate of interest affects investment demand.

5. If there is an increase in the supply of real money balances and a fall in the short-term nominal rate of interest, would investment demand rise? What might change so that investment was not affected?

6. Consider a firm's manager deciding whether to expand the firm's retail facilities by opening a new location. Suppose that opening this new facility costs $650,000. The firm plans to operate the facility for three years. The firm's manager expects that the facility will generate a profit of $200,000 a year in each of its first three years. The manager expects to sell the facility for $275,000 at the end of three years. Suppose that the long-term nominal rate of interest is 15 percent. Also suppose that the firm's manager expects there to be an inflation of 2 percent per year over the life of the project. Further, the manager expects that the sales, costs, and resale value of the facility will rise at the same rate as the rate of the inflation.

   a. What are the present discounted values of first year's, second year's, and third year's profit?

   b. What is the total present value of this project? Should the firm undertake the project?

   c. Now suppose that the rate of inflation turns out to be less than what the manager expected; it is 0 percent a year over the next three years. Would the project still have a present value greater than its cost? (Assume that the long-term nominal interest rate is still at 15 percent.)

CHAPTER 8

Macroeconomic Policy When Financial Markets Incorporate Expectations about Inflation and Economic Policy

INTRODUCTION

"Investment Falls, Interest Rates at 8 Percent"

"Investment Rises, Interest Rates at 8 Percent"

"White House and Congress Agree on Tax Hike—Fears of Recession Are Alleviated"

"Unemployment Rate Rises and Stock Market Rallies

When headlines such as these have appeared in newspapers, it is hard to make sense of them using the basic *IS-LM* description of the economy. How can an 8 percent rate of interest lead to both an increase and a decrease in investment? How can a tax hike (which is a contractionary fiscal policy that should raise the chances of a recession) make a recession seem less likely? If stock prices reflect anticipated corporate profits, why should stock prices rise when an increase in unemployment suggests declining business prospects and low profits?

One possible explanation for these seemingly contradictory headlines is that newspaper people and the experts they have interviewed simply do not understand the economy. And indeed there are often misleading reports written on the economy. Whenever the stock market changes, there are 20 "experts" to explain it, regardless of whether the market rose or fell. But misinformation is not the only explanation since in many cases such headlines are accurate, though incomplete, descriptions of economic reality. The actual economy is more complex than the economy described by a simple *IS-LM* model of aggregate demand. When macroeconomic commentators discuss and interpret the state of the economy, they are implicitly or explicitly using a model of the economy that includes much more than the simple *IS-LM* framework. In this chapter we will be describing the effects of macroeconomic policies using the model of the economy that we have developed in the previous two chapters—one that accounts for the influences that changes in expected inflation and changes in the maturity premium have on financial markets and on aggregate demand.

We will see how to connect equilibrium in the money market with equilibrium in the goods market, using the interest-rate gap, and we construct an *LM* schedule that is augmented to account for changes in inflation and the maturity premium. The augmented *LM* schedule, called *ALM*, is a schedule that describes the different levels of income and the long-term real rates of interest that obtain when the money market is in equilibrium, taking as given particular values of the maturity premium and expected inflation. When the maturity premium or the expected rate of inflation change, the augmented *LM* schedule will shift. The augmented LM schedule (the *ALM* schedule) together with the *IS* schedule form the *IS-ALM* framework for policy analysis. This framework will allow us reconcile the seemingly contradictory headlines and, more importantly, it will allow us to account for the effects of changes in expected inflation and financial-market conditions on the conduct of economic policy. In particular we will see the effect of changing expectations about monetary policy. What people think the Fed is going to do in the future will affect what happens in the economy today.

EXPECTATIONS IN GOODS MARKETS AND MONEY MARKETS

How can an 8 percent interest rate both raise and lower investment spending? If the interest rate being quoted is the long-term nominal rate, then if the expected rate of inflation dropped by 2 percentage points a year, say from 6 percent to 4 percent, the 8 percent nominal rate of interest implies a real rate of interest rising from 4 to 6 percent. A rise to a 6 percent real rate is steep and could cause investment to fall. At other times, a rise in the expected inflation rate from 4 to 6 percent a year would mean that the same 8 percent nominal rate of interest would imply a drop of 2 percent in the real rate of interest, which could be seen as a decline to a low real rate, so investment expenditures may increase.

How can a tax hike, which we would expect to lower aggregate demand, work to reduce recessionary fears? Suppose that it is known that the Fed is very concerned about the budget deficit. Unless there is some reduction in the deficit, the Fed is expected to pursue a tight monetary policy. This will lead to higher short-term nominal interest rates in the future. Investors' **expectations** about future Fed actions and future interest rates affect current long-term interest rates. *Concerns about the future course of Fed policy may actually be affecting today's long-term real rate of interest, depressing investment demand,*

expectations
A market participant's view of future circumstances (for example, inflationary expectations, interest-rate expectations, and economic-policy expectations).

and increasing the threat of recession. In such a case, when a tax hike is announced, the concerns about future tight money disappear and recession fears are calmed.

How can a rise in the unemployment rate, which usually is associated with a reduction in income and expenditure, stimulate stock prices, which are usually associated with a rise in income and expenditure? Any sign of a reduction in aggregate demand (such as a rise in unemployment) can, in the short run, generate expectations of lower inflation rates. A drop in the inflation rate reduces the probability of the Fed's pursuit of monetary contraction in the future. Just as in the tax-hike scenario, if concerns about a Fed contraction are reduced, this will lower long-term interest rates. Lower long-term rates on bonds will improve the stock market because financial managers will shift funds out of bonds and into stocks.

This discussion illustrates an important issue in current macroeconomic policy analysis: *People in financial markets form expectations about the Fed's policy actions, and these expectations affect their behavior.* In recent years financial markets have shown extreme sensitivity to changes in expectations about Fed policy positions. Financial managers and traders of financial assets know that the Fed's policy choices depend upon the behavior of the economy and that the behavior of the economy depends upon Fed policy. In order to understand what is happening to output and interest rates today, we have to look at the effects of this second-guessing by both policymakers and financial analysts.

In the previous chapter we saw that changes in the interest rate in the money market can be very different from the movements in the long-term real rate of interest that affects investment. The difference in the rates is reflected in changes in the interest-rate gap. In this chapter we will see how these disparate shifts accompany changes in economic policy. Expectations about the duration and extent of either a monetary-policy or fiscal-policy initiative will affect the term structure of interest rates. For example, short-term nominal rates of interest can rise or fall with little or no change in the long-term real rate. This disconnection of one type of interest rate from another means that monetary policy can cause money-market conditions to change (shift the *LM* schedule) but have little effect on the long-run real rate of interest. Hence the policy will have little effect on output. Alternatively, a fiscal-policy change (shifting the *IS* schedule) may also lead to a shift in the term structure that raises long-term interest rates and offsets the effect of the fiscal policy—again there is little effect on output. *The effectiveness of policy depends importantly on expectations.*

Since we have shown here and in the previous chapter how and why equilibrium in the goods and money markets (*IS* and *LM* schedules) can become disconnected because of the effect of changes in inflation and maturity premiums on financial markets, the task of this chapter is to put *IS* and *LM* back together again and then revisit the workings of economic policy. The first task is to see how the *LM* schedule is affected by inflation.

INFLATION AND THE *LM* SCHEDULE

The *LM* schedule is made up of combinations of the short-term nominal rate of interest and income for which the money market is in equilibrium. If there is inflation in the economy, this means that the price level is changing over time. But changes in the price level will change the real money supply for a given nominal money supply. If P changes, then M_s/P is affected, for a given M_s. In building our extended or augmented model, we need to take into account the impact of inflation on the real stock of money.

Inflation and the Real Supply of Money

Inflation erodes the size of the real stock of money for a given nominal money stock. Figure 8.1 shows the money market, where the demand for real money balances (M_d/P) is initially equal to the real supply of money (M_s/P) at point A. Since inflation raises the price level (P to P' to P'' to P'''), the real money supply declines, as shown in a series of shifts to the left of the schedule $(M_s/P', M_s/P'', M_s/P''')$.

The demand for real money balances does not change as the price level changes because the transactions demand for nominal money rises at the same rate as the increases in the price level (holding real income and the nominal rate of interest constant). Remember, a cash manager facing a 10 percent rise in prices will demand a 10 percent higher average cash balance to cover her firm's monthly purchases.

So if higher prices erode the real money supply and the demand for real money balances remains constant, then money-market equilibrium occurs at higher and higher short-term nominal rates of interest (points *B*, *C*, and *D*). *With a fixed nominal supply of money, an increase in the price level contracts the real money supply and shifts the* LM *schedule.* Figure 8.2 shows the shifts of the *LM* schedule (*LM'*, *LM''*, and *LM'''*) that accompany inflation when the nominal money supply is unchanged.

Current and expected rates of inflation

Earlier, when we looked at the way in which interest rates are adjusted for inflation, the inflation adjustment was for the *expected* future rate of inflation. Here, when we look at the role of inflation in changing the price level and the size of the real supply of money, we are looking at the *current* rate of inflation, and the two are not necessarily the same. When the rate of inflation has been constant for a long period of time, the current rate and the expected future rate of inflation are probably about the same. However, when the current rate changes from year to year, then people will not usually expect that the future rate of inflation is going to be the same as the actual rate of inflation this year.

For example, from 1978 until 1981 the current rate of inflation rose rapidly, but during that period the Fed engaged in a policy of tightening the growth

FIGURE 8.1   Inflation and the Real Money Supply

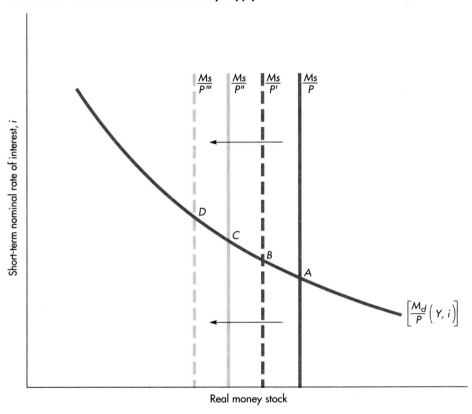

As the price level rises, a fixed nominal supply of money will lead to a declining real stock of money balances.

of the money supply with the publicly stated purpose of reducing the rate of inflation. Overall expectations were determined by the degree to which individuals either believed the Fed and expected a reduction in inflation or were skeptical and expected inflation to accelerate. What was clear during that period was that inflationary expectations were not simply equal to the current rate of inflation in any given year. Overall, the expected rate of inflation was probably less than the current rate because enough people expected that the upward burst of inflation would eventually be reversed—which in fact happened.

It is important, therefore, to keep the distinction clear between the expected future rate of inflation, $\text{Exp}\Delta P/P$, and the current or actual rate of inflation, $\text{Current}\Delta P/P$. The current rate of inflation is the rate at which the

FIGURE 8.2 Inflation and the *LM* Schedule with a Fixed Nominal Money Supply

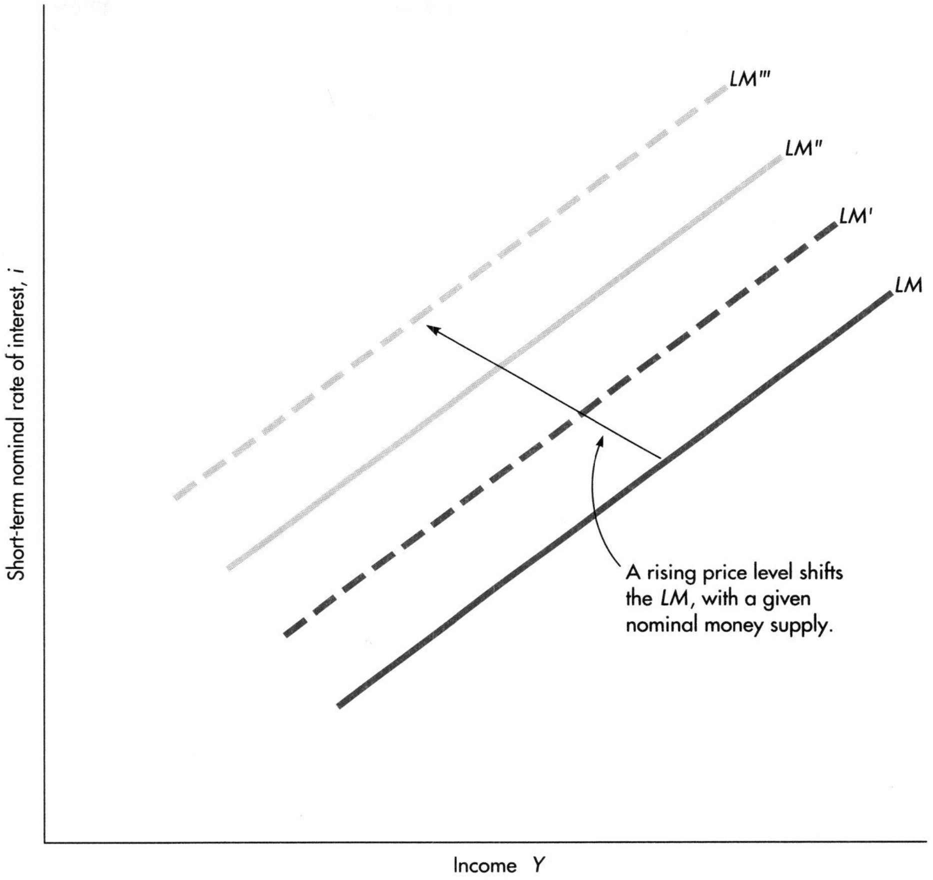

A rising price level shifts the *LM*, with a given nominal money supply.

As the price level rises and the real stock of money declines, the *LM* schedule shifts up or to the left.

price level is actually changing over time. The expected future rate of inflation is used in computing real interest rates.

Money Growth and the Real Money Supply

When the Fed uses open-market operations to change the money supply, it can decide to increase, decrease, or keep constant the real money supply, even when there is inflation occurring in the economy. The Fed can choose to take an anti-inflationary position by maintaining a rate of increase in the nominal money supply that is less than inflation. It can even hold the nominal money supply constant or reduce it. In all of these cases the real money supply will fall. Alternatively, the Fed can offset the effect of inflation on the real money supply by increasing the nominal supply of money in proportion to the rise in the price level. This policy would maintain a fixed real supply of money. The Fed can even increase the nominal money supply faster than inflation and thus increase the real money supply. These alternatives are as follows:

contractionary monetary policy
When the Fed sets the rate of growth of the money supply to be less than the rate of inflation.

A **contractionary monetary policy** occurs when $\Delta M_s/M_s < \text{Current}\Delta P/P$. (The real money supply is falling.)

An **inflation-accommodating monetary policy** occurs when $\Delta M_s/M_s = \text{Current}\Delta P/P$. (The real money supply is constant.)

An **expansionary monetary policy** occurs when $\Delta M_s/M_s > \text{Current}\Delta P/P$. (The real money supply is increasing.)

inflation-accommodating monetary policy
When the Fed increases the nominal supply of money at the same rate as the rate of inflation. This policy keeps the real money supply constant.

The *LM* schedule gives points of money-market equilibrium, and this means that if the Fed is following an inflation-accommodating policy, and there are no shifts in the money demand schedule, then the *LM* schedule will remain stationary. That makes the inflation-accommodating policy a useful benchmark. It means that the *LM* schedule will not be shifting because policy change has offset the effect of a rising price level.

expansionary monetary policy
When the Fed sets the rate of growth of the money supply to be faster than the rate of inflation.

If the Fed is choosing to increase the nominal supply of money more slowly than the actual rate of inflation, then this contractionary monetary policy will cause the *LM* schedule to shift upward and to the left. Alternatively, an expansionary policy will shift the *LM* schedule down to the right.

At different times the Fed has chosen each of the alternative policy options just described. For example, the Fed followed an expansionary policy in 1982–84 to combat the effects of the 1982 recession. A contractionary policy was pursued again in 1988–89 in order to restrain aggregate demand. Inflation had begun to accelerate in 1988–89, following a low level of inflation in 1987.

We are not saying which of the policy alternatives is more likely or more desirable. At this point, we are simply setting up the framework for policy analysis so that we can evaluate the appropriate policy actions. We summarize what we have found as follows:

A contractionary monetary policy reduces the real money supply and causes the *LM* schedule to shift up to the left.

An inflation-accommodating policy keeps the real money supply constant and causes the *LM* schedule to remain stationary.

An expansionary monetary policy increases the real money supply and causes the *LM* schedule to shift down to the right.

■ **Allowing for the Growth of Real Income**

In the actual economy, potential output grows over time with increases in the labor force and the stock of capital and with gradual improvements in technology. And we have not taken this increase in potential output and income into account when we defined the monetary-policy alternatives. We certainly could incorporate the economy's growth trend into the discussion. The reason we have not done this is that there are already several different variables changing and lots of issues to deal with when we talk about policy, so that adding complications is costly. The model becomes harder to understand.

When we apply the conclusions of our policy analysis to actual experience, however, it is helpful to keep in mind that potential output is growing. The Fed on average will aim for a rising real stock of money in order to meet the economy's increased need for transactions as the economy grows.

GOODS MARKETS AND MONEY MARKETS RECOMBINED: THE *IS-ALM* FRAMEWORK

Finding the equilibrium levels of income and interest rates in money markets and goods markets (putting *IS* and *LM* back together) means finding the conditions under which the money market, the goods market, and the financial markets that connect them are all in simultaneous equilibrium. At any level of income, the money market will be in equilibrium at some short-term nominal rate of interest. Expectations about the future course of the economy, expressed within the financial capital market, determine the size of the maturity premium and the expected rate of inflation. This gives the relation between the short rate and the long-term real rate of interest. If all markets are in equilibrium together, they will jointly determine equilibrium of aggregate demand.

Figure 8.3 depicts such an equilibrium, using the representations of the maturity premium and the expected inflation line shown in Chapter 7. In Figure 8.3 it is assumed that the economy is in full equilibrium with both the money market and the goods market in equilibrium. In the far-left panel of the figure, the money market is assumed to be in equilibrium at a level of income Y_A with a short-term nominal rate of interest of 5 percent ($i = 5$ percent). The center-left panel then assumes that there is an equilibrium maturity premium of 5 percentage points ($MP = 5$ percent), incorporating the term structure of interest rates and the premiums for risk and liquidity. The long-term nominal rate of interest is then 10 percent [i(long term) $= 10$ percent]. The center-right panel of Figure 8.3 then assumes that the expected rate of inflation in the economy is 4 percent ($\text{Exp}\Delta P/P = 4$). This is subtracted from the long-term nominal rate of interest, giving a 6 percent long-term real rate of interest ($r = 6$ percent). In the far-right panel it is assumed that the goods market is in equilibrium with a long-term real rate of interest of 6 percent and a level of income equal to Y_A.

FIGURE 8.3 The Money Market and the Goods Market Connected by the Financial Capital Market

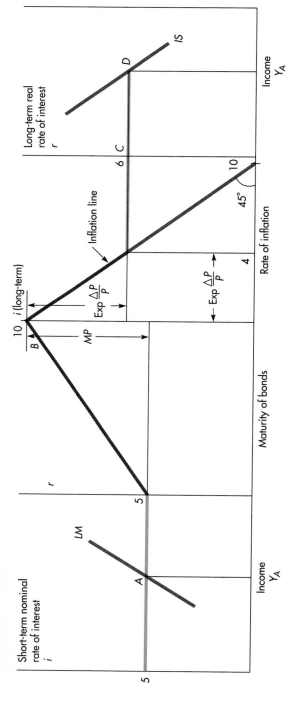

There is equilibrium in this model of the economy when the short-term nominal rate of interest along the *LM* schedule is at the same level of income (Y_A) at which the long-term real rate of interest along the *IS* schedule.

Figure 8.3 provides a visual depiction of the gap between the money market on the left and the goods market on the right and shows how the maturity premium and the expected rate of inflation bridge the gap between them. But we still have to see what conditions will hold in an actual equilibrium and how policy changes will affect that equilibrium.

The interest-rate gap, which incorporates both the maturity premium and the expected rate of inflation, allows us to bring the money market and the goods market together in a single diagram. We will develop the conditions that must hold in an *IS-ALM* equilibrium, and once we have determined equilibrium income in this *IS-ALM* framework, we can use the model in the same way we used *IS-LM* to describe how the economy reacts to autonomous shifts in expenditure or changes in policy.

The Interest-Rate Gap and the Augmented *LM* Schedule

To find the *IS-ALM* equilibrium we need the combinations of income and the long-term real rate for which all markets are in equilibrium. To do this, we adjust the *LM* schedule for the gap between the short-term nominal rate and the long-term real rate: the interest-rate gap. Recall how the different interest rates and the interest-rate gap are defined:

$$r = i + MP - \text{Exp}\Delta P/P$$
$$= i + r_{gap}. \tag{8.1}$$

The long-term real rate of interest, r, is equal to the short-term nominal rate plus the interest-rate gap.

The augmented *LM* schedule

augmented *LM* schedule
The *ALM* is an *LM* schedule that has been augmented by the interest-rate gap. With a particular maturity premium and inflationary expectations, the *ALM* describes the different levels of income and the long-term real rates of interest that obtain when the money market is in equilibrium.

The *LM* schedule is the collection of interest rates and income where the money market is in equilibrium. It is drawn with values of the short-term nominal rate of interest on the vertical axis. We now draw an **augmented LM schedule,** called *ALM,* which also depicts money-market equilibrium. However, the *ALM* describes the different values of the long-term real rate, r, that are consistent with that money-market equilibrium, the maturity premium, and the expected rate of inflation. Along the *ALM,* the long-term real rate, r, appears on the vertical axis. *The ALM is an LM schedule that has been shifted by the term structure and expected inflation, that is to say, it has been shifted by the interest-rate gap:*

$$ALM = LM + r_{gap}. \tag{8.2}$$

Figure 8.4 shows the two schedules. At a level of income Y_A, the short-term nominal interest rate that emerges from the money market is shown on the vertical axis as i_A while the long-term real rate is shown as r_A. The interest-rate gap is shown as positive and it separates the two rates.

FIGURE 8.4   The *ALM* Schedule and the *LM* Schedule

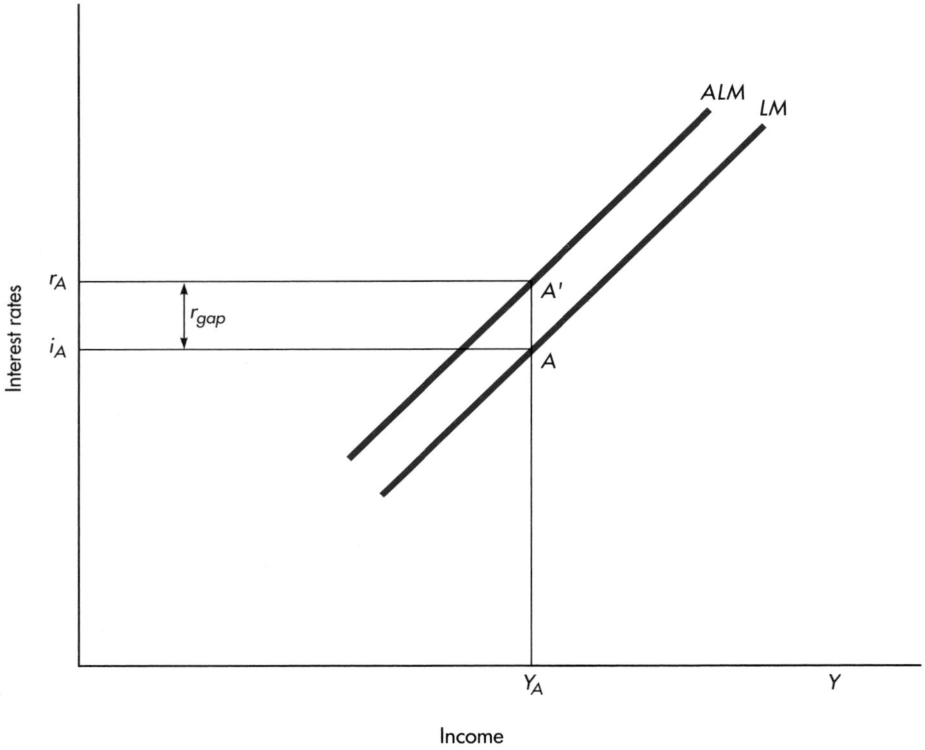

The *ALM* schedule is displaced by the interest-rate gap from the *LM* schedule.

WORKED EXAMPLE 8.1   Constructing the *ALM* Schedule

In Chapter 5, Worked Example 5.1, we used the following *LM* schedule:

$i = 0.005Y - 15$.

At the time, we did not label the interest rate in this way because we were not making a distinction among rates. Now we have to keep track. The *LM* schedule relates the short-term nominal rate and the level of income.

Assume that the maturity premium and the expected rate of inflation are as follows (in percentages):

$MP = 5$
$Exp\Delta P/P = 3$.

Question: With the preceding values for the *LM* schedule, the maturity premium, and the expected rate of inflation, calculate the interest-rate gap and derive the *ALM* schedule.

Answer: The interest-rate gap is computed as the maturity premium minus the expected rate of inflation:

$$r_{gap} = MP - \text{Exp}\Delta P/P$$
$$= 5 - 3 = 2.$$

The answer to the first part of the question is that the interest-rate gap is 2 percent. Then the answer to the second part of the question is found as follows:

$$ALM \quad r = i + r_{gap} = LM + r_{gap}$$
$$= 0.005Y - 15 + 2$$
$$= 0.005Y - 13.$$

This gives the answer to the second part of the question. The *ALM* schedule is displaced vertically upward by 2 percentage points relative to the *LM* schedule, an amount equal to the interest-rate gap.

If the interest-rate gap changes, with no change in money-market conditions, then the *ALM* schedule will shift up or down relative to the *LM* schedule. Remember that the long-term real rate of interest is the rate relevant for making real investment-expenditure decisions, such as housing purchases and corporate borrowing.[1]

The interest-rate gap reflects expected inflation and a maturity premium that includes a risk premium for lending funds to finance the purchase of real capital goods. Changes in any of these factors can and will change the interest-rate gap. *Whenever the interest-rate gap changes, the* ALM *schedule will shift relative to the* LM *schedule.*

Figure 8.5 illustrates the effect of change in r_{gap} with no change in other conditions in the money market (no shift in the *LM* schedule). The interest-rate gap is shown as becoming negative, reflecting a decline in the maturity premium and/or a rise in expected inflation. In the figure this is shown as

---

[1] The long-term real rate relevant for making decisions about investment expenditures is of course different for different projects or purchases depending upon the individual risk associated with each purchase. When we replaced the long-term nominal rate on Treasury bonds with the rate on mortgages and corporate bonds, we implicitly assumed that there is a stable connection among the spectrum of long-term rates on assets with various risks. One of the functions of financial capital markets is to determine a price of financial assets that reflects those risks. An increase or decrease in the long-term nominal rate on Treasury bonds will be reflected in financial markets by a change in all other rates on various long-term financial assets. Changes in business and financial market conditions will alter the connections between the rate on Treasury bonds and the interest rates on other long-term financial assets. Differences in assets' risks that are not related to term to maturity are the subject of a separate and well-developed branch of financial economics concerned with the pricing of capital assets.

FIGURE 8.5   A Change in the Interest-Rate Gap

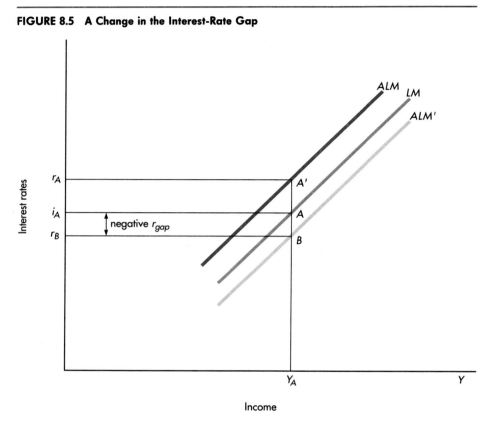

Income

If the interest-rate gap changes, the *ALM* schedule shifts. The shift from *ALM* to *ALM'* occurs with a negative interest-rate gap.

a shift of the *ALM* schedule from *ALM* to *ALM'*. The drop in r_{gap} was large enough so that for a given level of income, the long-term real rate fell (r_A to r_B) below the short-term nominal rate (i_A) and the *ALM'* schedule lies below the *LM* schedule.

The Conditions for Equilibrium

We can now draw a single diagram containing both the *IS* and *ALM* schedules. In Figure 8.6, the intersection of the two schedules gives the point *(A)* where both the goods market and the money market are in equilibrium. The long-term real rate of interest that prevails at the point of intersection is r_A and the level of income is Y_A. This point is one in which the goods market, the money market, and the financial capital market that connects them are all

FIGURE 8.6   The Economy Is in *IS-ALM* Equilibrium at Point A

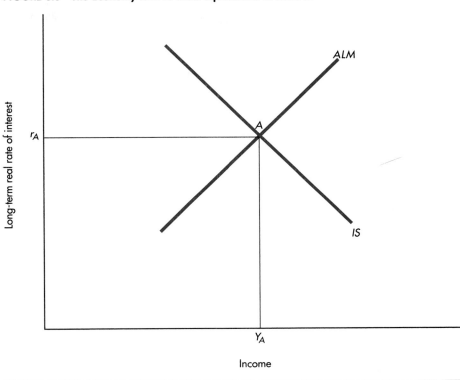

in equilibrium. The main conditions that must hold in aggregate-demand equilibrium are the following:

- The long-term real interest rate, r_A, and the level of income, Y_A, must be the values that occur at the intersection of *IS* and *ALM*. This just says in words what the figure shows.
- The interest-rate gap must reflect the economy's expectations about future interest rates and inflation.
- The money market must be in equilibrium with the real money supply equal to money demand at the equilibrium level of income, Y_A.
- To maintain consistency: The short-term nominal rate of interest that accompanies money-market equilibrium has to be the same as the short-term rate, i_A, implied by the equilibrium rate of interest, r_A, and the interest-rate gap ($r = i + r_{gap}$).

If these conditions are satisfied, then the intersection of *IS* and *ALM* (point A in Figure 8.6) does indeed represent a point of aggregate demand equilibrium.

WORKED EXAMPLE 8.2   Solving for Equilibrium in the *IS-ALM* Framework

The conditions for equilibrium in the money market in an economy can be described by the following *LM* schedule:

$i = 0.005Y - 15.$

Assume that the maturity premium and the expected rate of inflation are as follows (in percentages):

$MP = 5$
$Exp\Delta P/P = 3.$

The conditions for goods-market equilibrium can be described by the following *IS* schedule (used earlier in Chapter 5):

$r = 141 - 0.034Y.$

The interest rate in this equation is the long-term real rate.

Question: What are the values for the level of income and the long-term real, short-term nominal, and long-term nominal rates of interest when the economy is in equilibrium?

Answer: The first step is to construct the *ALM* schedule. This was done in Worked Example 8.1:

$r = 0.005Y - 13.$

The next step is to set the *ALM* and *IS* schedules equal, to find their point of intersection, and then to solve for *Y:*

$0.005Y - 13 = 141 - 0.034Y$ so that
$0.039Y = 154$
$Y = 3,949.$

The equilibrium level of income in this economy is $3.949 trillion, a value that is lower than the value of $4 trillion that we found in the worked example in Chapter 5. The difference is the result of the 2–percentage-point interest-rate gap. The interest rate used here to affect investment demand is 2 percentage points higher, resulting in a lower level of investment demand and a lower level of equilibrium income.

The interest rate *r* can be solved by substituting back into either the *IS* schedule or the *ALM* schedule:

$(0.005 \times 3,949) - 13 = 6.74 = 141 - (0.034 \times 3,949).$

In equilibrium in this example, the long-term real rate of interest is 6.74 percent. The short-term nominal rate of interest then differs from *r* by the interest-rate gap of 2 percentage points:

$r = i + r_{gap}$
$6.74 = i + 2$ so that
$i = 4.74.$

The equilibrium value of the short-term nominal rate of interest is 4.74 percent.

The long-term nominal rate of interest differs from the short-term nominal rate by the maturity premium:

$$MP = i(\text{long term}) - i$$
$$i(\text{long term}) = i + MP$$
$$= 4.74 + 5 = 9.74.$$

In equilibrium, the long-term nominal rate of interest is equal to 9.74 percent.

This example illustrates the importance of differences in interest rates. If we had tried to apply the *IS-LM* framework to the actual economy, which interest rate would we have used? The T-bill rate would be at only 4.74 percent. The long-term nominal interest rate on corporate bonds or mortgages is 9.74 percent. The rate relevant for investment decisions is 6.74 percent.

Expectations and equilibrium

One reason we have developed this extended model is that it is more realistic than the simple *IS-LM* framework that we used previously. Everyone knows that there are different interest rates, and it is confusing and unrealistic if we analyze the economy and ignore this. But that is not the only, nor even the main reason. Changes in the economy (including changes in financial-market conditions, expectations, and economic policies) will lead to variations in the interest-rate gap. The impact of policy changes on equilibrium income cannot be inferred simply by assuming that all rates of interest move together in lock-step fashion.

This analysis points to the role of expectations in determining the interest-rate gap and in influencing the equilibrium level of income. If there is a change in expectations about inflation, future interest rates, or economic policies, this will cause a shift in the *ALM* schedule and hence a shift in the equilibrium level of income.

Before we explore this, however, we have to acknowledge a limitation to what we have done. The *ALM* schedule is drawn with the interest-rate gap taken as determined autonomously. In other words, the schedule is drawn with the interest-rate gap as constant along the schedule. This is an oversimplification. When we study the effects of policy changes in the actual economy, there will be situations that we will have to represent as moves along the *ALM* schedule together with simultaneous changes in the interest-rate gap (shifts in the *ALM* schedule).

The interest-rate gap reflects expectations about future interest rates and future inflation so that by taking the interest-rate gap as determined autonomously, we have assumed these expectations are set autonomously. One reason for making this assumption is that there is considerable argument about how in fact expectations are determined. Research on this issue continues and there is no wholly satisfactory or generally accepted model of the way in which expectations are formed. An evaluation of the determinants of expected inflation, Fed policies, and future interest rates is something that is currently being done at the frontier of economics.

In the next section of this chapter we look at the "what if" question. What if the expected rate of inflation changes? Or what if the term structure changes? We will then turn to look at the economy's experience with the way in which economic policy actions or other economic events have brought about changes in expectations. Since the issue of how expectations are formed is unresolved, when we describe the role of expectations in this chapter, we will use ideas drawn from alternative views about how expectations are determined.

Changes in Expected Inflation

The study of macroeconomics is made difficult by the fact that in the actual economy many different things change at once. For example, it is hard to see the effect of a fiscal-policy change if monetary policy changes at the same time. Similarly, in the actual economy, changes in expected inflation are quite likely to go along with changes in the current rate of inflation or changes in the maturity premium. But in order to keep our analysis manageable, we are going to look at one thing at a time. We will consider what happens if there is a change in the expected rate of inflation but the maturity premium stays the same. We are also assuming that the Fed is following an inflation-accommodating policy, keeping the real money stock constant. In this case, the LM schedule does not shift, but the ALM schedule will shift because of changes in inflationary expectations.

With the maturity premium taken as given, a rise or fall in the expected rate of inflation will decrease or increase the interest-rate gap. Figure 8.7 illustrates this. An increase in the expected rate of inflation reduces the interest-rate gap by moving the ALM schedule down (from ALM to ALM') and cutting the real rate of interest (r_A to r_B). The reduction in real interest encourages investment and increases equilibrium income from Y_A to Y_B. Conversely, a decrease in expected inflation moves the ALM schedule up (from ALM to ALM'') and results in an increase in the real rate of interest (r_A to r_C) and a decrease in equilibrium income from Y_A to Y_C.

The results shown in Figure 8.7 reflect a direct link between people's expectations about inflation and current income. The intuition behind this effect is as follows: If people believe that inflation is going to accelerate, they decide that buying investment goods (such as houses, shopping centers, and factories) is better than holding financial assets such as money and bonds whose value is going to be eroded by inflation. Investment demand increases (those investment goods look like a better buy) and so does income.

In the case we just described, inflation was expected to increase while the Fed pursued an inflation-accommodating monetary policy, reflected in a fixed LM schedule. In the new equilibrium, the level of income is higher, so with a fixed LM schedule, the nominal rate of interest in the money market will be higher. And with a constant maturity premium, the long-term nominal rate of interest will also be higher. This is illustrated in Figure

FIGURE 8.7 Changes in Expected Inflation and the ALM

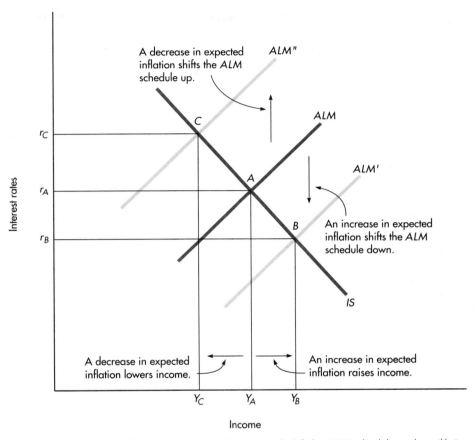

A change in the rate of inflation expected in the future will shift the *ALM* schedule and equilibrium income. An increase in inflation raises income, while a decrease in inflation lowers income. The maturity premium is assumed to remain constant.

8.8. The right-hand panel shows the shift in the *ALM* schedule from *ALM* to *ALM'* along the *IS* schedule that was also depicted in Figure 8.7. In the left-hand panel we see that the resulting rise in income leads to an increase in the demand for money, which drives up the short-term nominal rate from i_A to i_B. The T-bill rate increases as the equilibrium moves from *A'* to *B'* along the given *LM* schedule. In this case, *the result of an increase in expected inflation is an increase in equilibrium income accompanied by both increases and decreases in interest rates. Nominal rates of interest rise (short and long) while the long-term real rate falls.*

FIGURE 8.8   Expected Inflation and the Real Rate of Interest

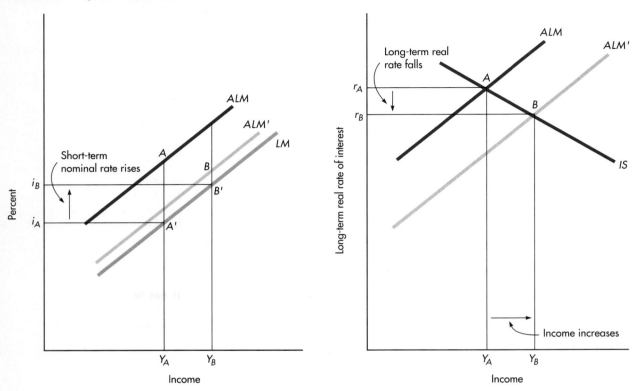

An increase in expected inflation leads to higher income, a lower long-term real interest rate, and a higher short-term nominal interest rate. Note: This result can change if the maturity premium changes.

In the new equilibrium, the long-term nominal rate of interest has increased, but by less than the rise in expected inflation. The interest rates on bonds have increased to compensate lenders in part for the increase in inflation they expect to occur over the life of the bonds they are holding.

WORKED EXAMPLE 8.3   The Effect of an Increase in Expected Inflation

Consider the economy that was described in Worked Example 8.2

Question: What happens to equilibrium income and interest rates if the expected rate of inflation rises from 3 percent to 6 percent, with the maturity premium and the current rate of inflation remaining constant?

Answer: The *LM* schedule remains the same:

$$i = 0.005Y - 15.$$

But the interest-rate gap has changed:

$$r_{gap} = MP - \text{Exp}\Delta P/P$$
$$= 5 - 6 = -1.$$

This gives a new *ALM* schedule:

$$r = 0.005Y - 16.$$

Equilibrium income is found by setting the *ALM* equal to the *IS*. This gives

$$0.005Y - 16 = 141 - 0.034Y$$
$$0.039Y = 157$$
$$Y = 4,026.$$

The equilibrium level of income in this economy is $4.026 trillion, an increase of $76 billion compared to the level of income in the case where the expected inflation was only 3 percent. The higher level of income comes about because the rise in inflationary expectations resulted in a drop in r_{gap} and in the long-term real rate. The drop in the long-term real rate then stimulated income.

The interest rate r can be solved by substituting back into either the *IS* schedule or the *ALM* schedule:[a]

$$0.005 \times 4,026 - 16 = 4.13 = 141 - 0.034 \times 4,026.$$

The long-term real rate of interest is 4.13 percent. It has been sharply reduced by the increase in expected inflation. The short-term nominal rate of interest then differs from the long-term real rate by the interest-rate gap, which is now equal to -1:

$$r = i + r_{gap}$$
$$4.13 = i - 1 \quad \text{so that}$$
$$i = 5.13.$$

The short-term nominal rate of interest in this economy is 5.13 percent. The long-term nominal rate of interest differs from the short-term nominal rate by the maturity premium:

$$i(\text{long term}) = i + MP$$
$$= 5.13 + 5 = 10.13.$$

The long-term nominal rate of interest is equal to 10.13 percent. This example, when contrasted with Worked Example 8.2, illustrates the fact that an increase in expected inflation, holding the maturity premium and the current rate of inflation constant, leads to a decrease in the real rate of interest, an increase in income and an increase in nominal interest rates.

[a] Due to rounding errors that have been carried along in these worked examples, these calculations generate slightly different values of r or Y depending upon whether the values are solved from *IS* or *ALM*. In the preceding exercise the real rate is 4.13 from *ALM* (left-hand solution) and 4.116 from *IS* (right-hand solution).

The effect of increases in expected inflation on aggregate demand was seen in the countries of Eastern Europe. Many of these countries announced plans to deregulate prices and it was then widely expected that prices would increase rapidly. Consumers rushed to the stores to buy whatever was available. Even items such as canned food or toilet paper became "capital goods" because they could be stored and used later. Unfortunately, the increases in aggregate demand were not translated into increases in real output and income in these countries. There were so many problems on the supply side of these economies that additional supply was not necessarily forthcoming.

Some economists believe that the impact that changes in inflation expectations have on income has been an important source of instability in the U.S. economy in earlier periods.[2] The drop in prices during the Great Depression of the 1930s probably generated the expectation that the rate of inflation had turned negative. This had an effect that was in the opposite direction from the one described in Figure 8.8. A change from a positive or zero expected rate of inflation to a negative rate results in an increase in the real rate of interest. This made the purchase of investment goods unattractive and thereby cut both investment demand and real income. The deflation that occurred at that time, it is argued, contributed to the drops in aggregate demand and income.

Expected inflation separates the real rate of interest from the nominal rate. The results we have found for a change in expected inflation are important, but they should be viewed with caution because we have assumed a constant maturity premium. We will see later that allowing for changes in the maturity premium could generate different conclusions about the movement of real and nominal interest rates.

Inflationary expectations and interest-rate targets for monetary policy

When the Fed follows a policy of targeting nominal interest rates, the Fed's open-market committee instructs its traders to make open-market purchases and sales (thereby expanding or contracting the money supply) depending upon whether the interest rate on T bills is above or below a target range. We will show that this interest-rate–targeting strategy looked like a sound policy when it was analyzed using the standard *IS-LM* framework. But the *IS-ALM* framework shows that the policy of nominal-interest-rate targeting can lead to serious problems. These problems became apparent in actual practice.

interest-rate targeting
A goal for monetary policy that uses changes in the money supply to keep a nominal rate of interest within a target range.

Analyzing interest-rate targeting with standard IS-LM.   A key rationale for the use of **interest-rate targeting** was that the Fed wanted to make sure that fluctuations in money markets did not lead to fluctuations in real income and employment. During the 1930s, instability in financial markets and in the banking system had contributed to the instability in the economy. Changes in the

---

[2] J. Bradford DeLong and Lawrence H. Summers, "The Changing Cyclical Variability of Economic Activity in the United States," in *The American Business Cycle*, ed. Robert J. Gordon (Chicago: 1986), pp. 679–734.

FIGURE 8.9   Analyzing Interest-Rate Targeting with Standard *IS-LM*

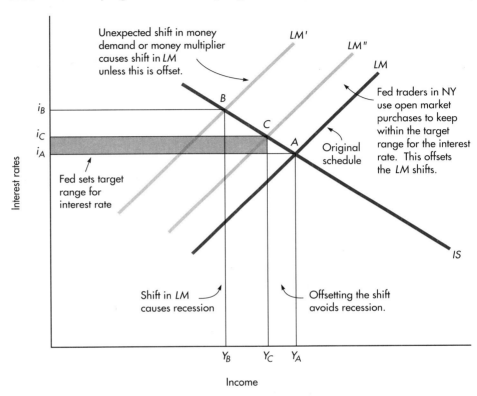

A conventional *IS-LM* model can make a case for interest-rate targeting. This approach will offset the effects of unexpected shifts in the *LM* schedule. The question is: Which interest rate is targeted?

public's demand for currency had been a particular problem during that period as people demanded cash, fearing bank failures. This reduced the money multiplier and hence the money supply. The Fed had learned the lesson of the Great Depression, and during the period following World War II until the late 1960s, the Fed used a policy of interest-rate targeting because it thought this would mean that unpredictable fluctuations in money demand or the demand for cash would automatically be dampened.

The argument used to support a policy of interest-rate targeting was derived from the standard *IS-LM* framework. Figure 8.9 illustrates the argument. It shows an economy in equilibrium (point *A*) at an interest rate i_A and a level of income Y_A. The Fed's interest-targeting policies were directed at nominal rates of interest, mostly short-term, though occasionally policy was employed that distinguished among short-term and long-term rates. Since during the period of time when interest-rate targeting was pursued, distinguishing among real, nominal, short-term, and long-term interest rates was not part of the general analysis, we can presume that the appropriate rate of interest to use in the *IS-LM* framework is a nominal rate of unspecified term.

The way interest-rate targeting is supposed to work is illustrated by examining the reactions to an unexpected increase in money demand or cash demand. The higher demand for money then generates a higher interest rate, which in turn generates a new equilibrium with a lower level of income. The increase in money demand is shown in the figure by a shift in the *LM* schedule, to *LM'* (point A to point B). The increase in money demand pushes up the interest rate (i_A to i_B) and a higher rate of interest drives down investment demand (along *IS*), resulting in a lower level of income (Y_A to Y_B). The unexpected shift in money demand has brought on a recession.

This discussion assumed no offsetting action by the Fed. Suppose now that the Fed uses a policy of interest-rate targeting. In order to fulfill its role of providing a buffer that insulates the real economy from the effects of unexpected financial-market changes, the Fed sets an interest-rate target range (i_A to i_C). When the interest rate rises outside the target range, as it did when money demand shifted (i_A to i_B), then the Fed's traders in New York are instructed to make open-market purchases. This insures that the Fed acts quickly to offset the tight money conditions that would have occurred when money demand increased. In the figure, the policy of interest-rate targeting is seen as an offsetting shift of the *LM* schedule, moving it back to *LM''* (point A to point C) where the economy is in equilibrium with only slightly higher interest rates and slightly lower income (Y_B to Y_C).

As described by the *IS-LM* framework, therefore, interest-rate targeting should greatly reduce the impact of the shift in money demand on income.

Monetarist criticism of interest-rate targeting and *IS-ALM* analysis.   Monetarists criticized the Fed's use of interest-rate targets. In particular, they argued that this approach led directly to the problems with inflation that afflicted the economy beginning in the late 1960s. The criticism goes directly to the problems we have discussed with the standard *IS-LM* framework. The Fed used the nominal rate of interest in setting its interest-rate target range. But when expected inflation increases, the gap between real and nominal rates of interest changes.

In the mid-1960s aggregate demand in the economy was very strong. Monetary and fiscal policymakers had acted deliberately to stimulate an economy that suffered two recessions from 1958 to 1962. Fiscal policy remained expansionary throughout the remainder of the 1960s because of transfer payments and government spending made to support both the Vietnam War and extended social programs. Figure 8.10 illustrates this situation, showing both the *LM* schedule and the *IS-ALM* framework. The strong growth of

FIGURE 8.10   Targeting Nominal Interest Rates Can Lead to Excessive Monetary Expansion and Inflation

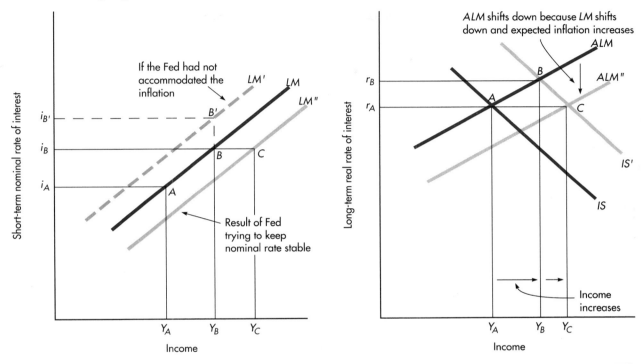

demand is shown as a shift from *IS* to *IS'*. This boosted income from Y_A to Y_B, and initially the increase in income raised both the nominal rate and real rate of interest (i_A to i_B along the *LM* schedule and r_A to r_B along the *ALM* schedule).

At point *B*, the economy was overheating as the high level of aggregate demand led to an increase in inflation. Monetarists argued that the Fed should have kept the growth of the nominal money supply below the rate of inflation. Had that policy been followed, the real money supply would have declined. We show the impact of this alternative policy as a shift in the *LM* schedule up and to the left (from *LM* to *LM'*, the dashed schedule in the left-hand panel of Figure 8.10). If this policy had been followed, the short-term nominal rate of interest would have increased by more than the increase that actually occurred. (The interest rate would have increased to $i_{B'}$ along *LM'*.)

This policy would have required the Fed to abandon its policy of keeping the rate of interest inside of a target range ($i_{B'}$ in Figure 8.10 is greater than i_C in Figure 8.9) so in practice, the Fed did not do this. Instead, the Fed followed an expansionary monetary policy, trying to keep nominal interest rates down.

As current inflation increased and the Fed seemed to be willing to accommodate this inflation, there was an increase in expected inflation also. The combination of the increase in the real money supply (*LM* to *LM″*) and the increase in expected inflation (which lowered the interest-rate gap) pushed the long-term real rate of interest down. This is shown in the figure by the shift from *ALM* to *ALM″*. The result was that the economy moved to point *C*, where the real rate of interest returned to r_A and this then triggered a further increase in income, from Y_B to Y_C. The short-term nominal rate of interest was held at i_B, rather than being driven back to i_A.

The Fed was expanding the nominal supply of money in an unsuccessful attempt to reduce *nominal* interest rates. The economy was overheating because the *real* rate of interest had remained low. As time went on, the situation got worse. The increases in income brought about by the continued expansion of the real supply of money kept the nominal rate of interest high and led to further increases in both actual and expected inflation. Monetarists argued that the Fed's efforts to keep nominal interest rates down in the face of rising inflation in the late 1960s led to a severely overheated economy and a legacy of inflation.

These criticisms have not gone unchallenged. There were other factors leading to the overheating of the economy—the Vietnam War and Great Society expenditures boosted aggregate demand (shifted the *IS* schedule out) and started the inflationary process. But there remains an important truth in what the monetarists said. The Fed was viewing the economy as if it were described by standard *IS-LM* analysis. The Fed did not fully appreciate the effect of inflation on real interest rates and tried, unjustifiably and unsuccessfully, to hold down nominal rates of interest. Partly this was to protect banks and savings and loans that had made long-term lending commitments at low nominal rates of interest. Their depositors were pulling money out of these institutions due to higher interest rates offered by other financial intermediaries. Partly the Fed failed to recognize the separate roles of expectations and real and nominal rates.

We have looked at the effect of changes in expected inflation using a simplifying assumption that the maturity premium is constant. We next use the *IS-ALM* framework to analyze the economic effects of changes in the maturity premium. We start out with a parallel simplifying assumption that the expected rate of inflation is constant.

The Financial Sector and Changes in the Maturity Premium

With expected inflation taken as given, an increase in the maturity premium will increase the interest-rate gap. This can occur if expected future interest rates or the risk premium rise. Since the two cases are somewhat different from each other, we will deal with them in sequence.

FIGURE 8.11   An Increase in the Maturity Premium

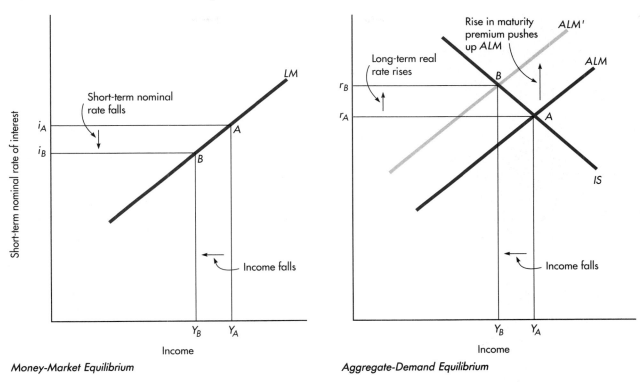

Money-Market Equilibrium   *Aggregate-Demand Equilibrium*

This leads to a fall in income, a rise in the long-term real rate, and a fall in the short-term nominal rate, with expected inflation assumed to be constant.

We look first at the effect of an increase in the maturity premium caused by an increase in expected future interest rates. In the right-hand panel of Figure 8.11 the *ALM* schedule is drawn initially for a normal yield curve, where expected future short interest rates are expected to be about the same as current rates and the risk premium is also normal. The rise in the maturity premium is reflected in an upward shift of the *ALM* schedule (*ALM* to *ALM'*) in the right-hand panel. The higher long-term real interest rate (r_A to r_B) then initiates a reduction in expenditures along *IS* and a fall in income (Y_A to Y_B).

In the left-hand panel of Figure 8.11 the *LM* schedule is shown and we see that the fall in income has reduced the demand for money and this has led to a fall in the short-term nominal rate of interest. The current interest rate on T bills has fallen as a result of the rise in expected future short-term interest rates.

In the earlier analysis, we found that an increase in expected inflation resulted in movements of different interest rates in opposite directions. The same thing has happened with a rise in the maturity premium, except that in this case the long-term rates of interest (both real and nominal) have risen, while the short-term nominal rate has fallen. A shift in expected inflation changes the gap between real and nominal rates. A change in the maturity premium changes the gap between short and long rates.

We have used our model to describe how changes in expectations affect different interest rates, but how are these changes in expectations reflected in the behavior of buyers and sellers of securities in the financial market? If there is a change in expectations, so that financial investors believe that interest rates will be higher in the future, they will sell long-term bonds and buy short-term bills. This allows them to hold their funds in short-term assets and wait for the expected rise in rates to materialize and then buy long-term assets at a later date. The initial movement out of long-term assets will drive down the price of these assets and raise the long-term nominal rate of interest. The increased demand for short-term assets, such as T bills, increases the price of these assets and decreases the short-term rate of interest. The change in expectations makes the yield curve steeper. The spread between long-term rates (mortgages and corporate bonds) and short rates (T bills) rises and the maturity premium increases.

WORKED EXAMPLE 8.4   The Effect of an Increase in the Maturity Premium

Consider the economy that was described in Worked Example 8.2.

Question: What happens to equilibrium income and interest rates if the maturity premium rises from 5 percent to 7 percent while the real money supply is held constant along with the expected rate of inflation?

Answer: The *LM* schedule remains the same:

$$i = 0.005Y - 15.$$

The rise in *i*(long, nominal) causes the interest-rate gap to change:

$$r_{gap} = MP - \text{Exp}\Delta P/P$$
$$= 7 - 3 = 4.$$

This gives a new *ALM* schedule:

$$r = 0.005Y - 11.$$

Equilibrium income is found by setting the *ALM* equal to the *IS*. This gives

$$0.005Y - 11 = 141 - 0.034Y \quad \text{so that}$$
$$0.039Y = 152$$
$$Y = 3,897.$$

The equilibrium level of income in this economy is \$3.897 trillion, a decrease compared to the case where the maturity premium was only 5 percent. The interest rate r can be solved by substituting back into either the *IS* schedule or the *ALM* schedule:

$$0.005 \times 3{,}897 - 11 = 8.49 = 141 - (0.034 \times 3{,}897).$$

The long-term real rate of interest is 8.49 percent. It has been sharply increased by the rise in the maturity premium. The short-term nominal rate of interest i then differs from r by the interest-rate gap, which is now equal to 4:

$$r = i + r_{gap}$$
$$8.49 = i + 4 \quad \text{so that}$$
$$i = 4.49.$$

The short-term nominal rate of interest in this economy is 4.49 percent. This rate has fallen with the rise in the maturity premium. The long-term nominal rate of interest differs from the short-term nominal rate by the maturity premium:

$$i(\text{long, nominal}) = i + MP$$
$$= 4.49 + 7 = 11.49.$$

The long-term nominal rate of interest is equal to 11.49 percent. The expectation of a future rise in rates (steepening of the yield curve) caused an increase in the maturity premium. This example illustrates the fact that the increase in the maturity premium (holding expected inflation and the current rate of inflation constant) leads to an increase in the long-term rates of interest, both real and nominal, a decrease in income, and a decrease in the short-term money-market interest rate.

An increase in the risk premium

Our focus on the maturity premium and interest rates underscores an important insight into the workings of the macroeconomy—circumstances in financial markets can influence real economic performance. One source of such influence can come about from a change in the perceived risks of undertaking investment. If risks are perceived to rise, then investors will require a higher risk premium in order to lend funds for capital projects. The higher rates will reduce aggregate demand and the result will be that an increase in the perception of riskiness may in fact contribute to bringing about a reduction in business activity.

When financial investors and businesses change their expectations of the project risks associated with new investments, this will affect both the goods market through investment demand (the *IS* schedule) and financial markets through the maturity premium (the *ALM* schedule). When corporate managers see an increased risk of failure for new factories or offices, they will reduce their demand for new investment goods even with a given cost of financing. When households become more concerned about their incomes and the return to holding real estate, they will scale back their demand for new housing even with a given mortgage rate.

FIGURE 8.12   An Increase in the Risk Premium

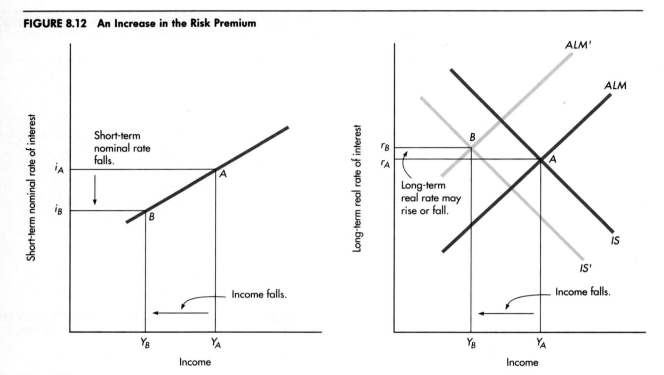

When investment becomes riskier, this leads to a change in both *ALM* and *IS*. Income and the short-term nominal rate of interest both fall. The long-term real rate may rise or fall.

On the financial side, when financial investors see companies having trouble meeting debt payments or see a rise in the default rate on mortgages, they will raise the risk premium they demand for holding bonds and mortgages. An increase in the risk premium will also lead to a decline in the stock market, bringing about an increase in the cost of equity financing.

Figure 8.12 illustrates the effect of the change in expectations. In the right-hand panel, the increase in the risk premium has raised the maturity premium and pushed the *ALM* schedule up to the left to *ALM'*. At the same time, the reduction in investment demand by businesses has shifted the *IS* schedule down to the left to *IS'*. As a result of both effects, the level of income has fallen in the economy. *A reduction in confidence can have a powerful effect in bringing on recessions.* It reduces the willingness of businesses to buy new capital goods and it reduces the willingness of savers to finance the purchases of these goods.

Since both the supply of funds to the financial capital market and the demand for funds have declined, one cannot say in general whether the

■ **Short-Term Nominal Interest Rates and Inflation: The Yield Curve Can Change Shape at Either End**

The link from the money markets through the financial sector to the goods market can work in the opposite direction. Changes in the long-term real rate of interest can bring about changes in the short-term nominal rate.

When we studied the conditions determining equilibrium in the money market, we did it by looking at a corporate cash manager adjusting her portfolio to earn as much interest as she could, while providing a large enough balance in a checking account to pay the company's bills. And she had to weigh off transactions costs against interest earnings forgone. This model of portfolio choice led to a specification for money demand in which money demand depends upon income (because this measures the volume of transactions) and the short-term nominal rate of interest (the rate that is relevant for choosing between money and short-term bonds such as T bills).

In practice, portfolio managers can also choose to shift assets from short-term T bills into long-term bonds, or vice versa. There is not a rigid separation between the two types of bonds and this means that changes in the long-term nominal rate of interest can affect money-market equilibrium. For example, an increase in the long-term nominal rate of interest could lead cash managers to shift funds out of T bills into long-term bonds in order to take advantage of the higher long-term rate. This, in turn, lowers the demand for T bills and the short-term rate begins to rise. An increase in the long-term nominal rate of interest therefore spills over into an increase in the short-term nominal rate of interest, even though there has been no change in the money supply or the level of income.

The spillover of long-term rates into short-term rates is important in understanding some issues. For example, the rate of interest on T bills was consistently higher in the 1980s than was true in the 1950s, and a major reason for this is that inflation is consistently higher than it used to be. Inflation affects the choice between long-term bonds, on the one hand, and real assets such as houses and office buildings, on the other, so inflation drives up the long-term nominal rate of interest. This, in turn, means that inflation will also increase short-term rates. We oversimplified the analysis of money-market equilibrium when we ignored this possibility.

long-term real and nominal rates of interest will rise or fall. There is no ambiguity about the response of short-term safe assets, however. The T-bill rate will fall as the decline in income reduces the transactions demand for money. This is shown in the left-hand panel of Figure 8.12.

The findings from this analysis can be seen in actual recessions. Between 1981 and 1982, the economy went into a steep recession and there was a drop in confidence and an increase in the risk premium. The interest rate on T bills fell by nearly 4 percentage points between these two years, while the interest rate on new mortgages increased slightly, as did the interest rate on corporate bonds rated Baa by Moody's Investors Service. The interest rate on the higher-rated Aaa bonds fell slightly between these two years. Between 1929 and 1933, there was a similar pattern as the economy fell into the Great Depression. The interest rate on short-term safe assets was low in 1933, falling to less than one half of one percent for T bills. The interest rate on Baa bonds rose to nearly 8 percent in 1933.

Besides reflecting the effects of changing expectations in financial markets, changes in the maturity premium are related to the effects of economic policies. We will look at these as we try to take into account the interactions among policy, inflation, and the maturity premium.

MACROECONOMIC POLICY, THE FINANCIAL SECTOR, AND POLICY EXPECTATIONS

We have shown how changes in expectations affect the workings of the economy through the financial sector. In forming expectations, those who trade assets in the financial sector will also form expectations about the future course of policy. Policy expectations themselves are likely to affect the course of economic events.

The Policy Regime and the Effectiveness of Monetary Policy

The people, firms, and institutions who actively participate in financial markets spend much of their time trying to forecast interest rates. These expectations about interest rates depend importantly on what those in financial markets think the Fed is going to do in the future. If participants in financial markets suddenly decide that the Fed is going to shift to a more contractionary or tight money policy in the future, this raises expected future interest rates. This increase in expected future rates then has an immediate impact in raising the long-term nominal rate of interest. *Expectations of future Fed policy have an impact on current long-term interest rates.*

The fact that expected future policy has an impact on interest rates today means that when we assess the effectiveness of policy, both monetary and fiscal, we have to ask how policy affects expectations. Suppose that a change in monetary policy is announced. The degree to which people believe that the policy will in fact happen and their expectations of how long it will be maintained can actually influence the current interest rate and hence the level of income.

We used the *IS-LM* framework to describe the impact of monetary and fiscal policies on the economy in Chapters 4 and 5. In that discussion, we found that the degree to which income responds to changes in interest rates (and hence the slopes of the *IS* and *LM* schedules) is important in assessing the effectiveness of policy. In our analysis of policy in this chapter, we will show how *expectations about the future course of monetary policy can be another important determinant of policy effectiveness.* The impact on the economy of a shift in monetary policy depends upon whether the policy change is the result of a short-run action or a longer-run policy strategy. A longer-run policy strategy is often called the **policy regime.** Let us see how the policy regime affects the outcome of a particular policy shift.

policy regime
The policymakers' actions over time indicate how the Fed is likely to react to economic events. People then form their expectations about future policy on the basis of this regime.

The ineffectiveness of a policy change that is expected to be temporary

It is widely believed that if the Fed tries to fine-tune the economy (make small adjustments in aggregate demand that keep income near some target level of income) by using short-term monetary contractions or expansions, then it will find that its efforts are not effective. Why is that?

Suppose the economy has been experiencing relative stability for some time—income, inflation, interest rates, and the rate of growth of the money supply have undergone only minor fluctuations. Now suppose that in this stable environment, the Fed wants to trim back aggregate demand. The Fed decreases its open-market purchases of T bills, thereby bringing about a reduction in the growth of the nominal money supply. Since there is no immediate change in the rate of inflation, the slowdown of the growth of the nominal money supply means that there has been a contraction of the real money supply.

With a stable economy, investors, cash managers, and many other members of the economy could easily believe that this action does not mean that the Fed has decided to pursue a sustained contractionary monetary policy. Rather, there could be an expectation that the monetary contraction is only temporary. There has been no perceived change in the policy regime.

The policy regime is like the climate. It indicates the way in which the Fed normally responds to economic situations. People form expectations about the climate on the basis of fairly long-run experience. An unusual turn in the weather, such as a hot day in winter, does not change people's view of the climate. Similarly, if people have learned that the Fed normally tries to maintain a full-employment economy, a shift to monetary contraction in an otherwise stable economy does not change their view of the policy regime. They will expect the Fed to reverse and change policy rather quickly.

Given that the policy is seen as temporary, what will happen to the economy? The monetary contraction will certainly affect the money market. There will be a rise in the short-term nominal interest rate. But the rise in this rate will not necessarily generate a corresponding increase in the long-term nominal and real rates of interest. Let's see why.

First, since the monetary-policy contraction is seen as temporary, higher short-term rates will not change expectations about future short-term nominal rates of interest in the economy. Bond holders will see the current rise in short-term rates as a spike and not a sustained increase. They will not attempt major adjustments in their portfolios and so the interest rate on long-term Treasury bonds will rise only a little.

Second, a monetary contraction that is seen as temporary is unlikely to have much effect on the risk premium. While risk premiums are hard to predict, it is unlikely that a policy change that is seen as temporary will bring on a major or prolonged recession or a financial crisis.

Third, a contractionary monetary policy may lead to some small reduction in the expected rate of inflation. But as we will see in Chapter 9, the expected rate of inflation changes only slowly in response to policy moves and it will change hardly at all in response to a temporary policy contraction. There will likely be little change in inflationary expectations as a result of this temporary policy shift.

Since neither long-term nominal rates nor expected inflation changes by very much, *the temporary monetary contraction does not have much effect on the long-term real rate of interest.* The *ALM* schedule moves very little as a result of a temporary monetary contraction. A small change in the long-term real rate of interest can still have some effect on investment demand. There will be some projects that are postponed as a result of even a small change in the long rate. But since the purchase of capital goods involves a long-term commitment and is financed with long-term borrowing, *the effect of a small change in the long-term real rate will itself be small.*

Temporary gyrations of the money supply will cause gyrations in short-term interest rates but will not lead to corresponding changes in the long-term real rate of interest and hence will not have much effect on income.

The effectiveness of a policy change that is expected to be sustained

The conclusion about the ineffectiveness of a temporary shift in monetary policy can be contrasted with the effectiveness of a monetary contraction that is believed to be sustained. Consider the case where the Fed has established a policy regime under which monetary contractions are not quickly reversed, even if a contraction results in recession. When there is a reduction in the real money supply, people will believe that the contraction is just the beginning of a sustained policy of tight money. As a result, the policy will be effective. One or more of the three conditions linking a rise in short-term nominal rates with a rise in long-term real rates will hold. Expected future short rates will likely rise along with the current short-term rate. In financial markets, all securities will trade at a lower price/higher interest rate because everyone expects higher interest rates to last. Thus, in this case, the rise in the current short-term rate of interest will be accompanied by an increase in expected future short rates with no tendency for the yield curve to flatten.

In terms of the risk premium, a policy of monetary contraction that is expected to be sustained will raise concerns about a recession and a possible financial crunch and will increase the probability of defaults—both for businesses and for household mortgages.

As a result of the stability of the yield curve and the increase in the risk premium, therefore, the maturity premium will not fall and may well rise in response to a sustained monetary contraction. The long-term nominal rate of interest will rise along with the short-term nominal rate.

In terms of expected inflation, a strategy of long-term monetary restraint will certainly reduce expected inflation somewhat. Some economists believe that expected inflation will fall quickly if the Fed follows a credible policy of sustained monetary contraction. We think this view is overly optimistic,

EXPECTATIONS ARE REVISED QUICKLY IN THE CAPITAL MARKET

An easing of monetary policy that is expected to be permanent will influence the long-term real interest rate. For example, on July 19, 1990, Federal Reserve Chairman Alan Greenspan testified before the Senate Banking Committee. He quietly suggested that the Fed had eased credit "slightly" the prior Friday because it had become concerned that the credit crunch was beginning to have very real effects on economic activity. This move did not constitute a fundamental shift in monetary policy, he quickly added, though he did feel that the economy was a bit closer to a recession than it had been earlier in the year. Greenspan was really saying that the fear of inflation had fallen a notch in the Fed's priorities. Yet on the very same day the Consumer Price Report was released, and it showed an uptick in inflation.

Long-term U.S. Treasury bond prices quickly fell nearly one point, or about $10 for every $1,000 of face value. Stock prices also tumbled in sympathy with bond prices. Of course, lower bond prices mean higher nominal interest rates. Bond sellers apparently reacted both to the unexpected news on increasing inflation and to Greenspan's lessening fears of higher prices. In particular, bond investors worried that Mr. Greenspan was responding to political pressure to ease interest rates instead of clinging to his goal of zero inflation growth. Bond prices fall even if bond buyers merely *expect* inflation.

Thus, expected inflation rose and the long-term real interest rate (adjusting the nominal interest rate by the heightened expectational inflation) moved lower. This probably is the opposite result of what Greenspan sought.

but at the least there would be some decline in expected inflation in this case.

It follows, therefore, that *in the face of a sustained monetary contraction, the increase in the long-term nominal rate of interest will probably result in an increase in the long-term real rate of interest.* The belief that the monetary policy will be sustained, contributes to the transmission of the Fed's policy action from the money market to the goods market. Table 8.1 summarizes the different effects of a policy-induced rise in short-term nominal rates that is perceived as temporary with one that is perceived to be sustained.

Figure 8.13 illustrates the comparison of policies that are perceived to be either temporary or prolonged. A monetary contraction that is expected to be long-term shifts the *ALM* schedule (*ALM* to *ALM''*) by more than the shift for a temporary policy (*ALM* to *ALM'*). The increase in the long-term real rate following a contraction that is expected to be sustained (r_A to r_B) reduces expenditures on interest-sensitive purchases and reduces income. The increase in the long-term rate (r_A to r_C) following a contraction that is expected to be temporary is small, if it occurs at all. A monetary contraction that is perceived to be temporary will bring about little reduction in income.

When it formulates its policies, the Fed needs to take account of expectations. If financial-market participants come to learn that changes in the direction of monetary policy will be reversed quickly, then they will regard any policy move as merely temporary. This will make the Fed's policies relatively

TABLE 8.1   The Links between a Rise in the Short-Term Nominal Rate of Interest and a Rise in the Long-Term Real Rate of Interest

	A monetary contraction that is expected to be temporary	A monetary contraction that is expected to be prolonged
Short-term nominal interest rate	Rises	Rises
Expected future short rates	No change	Rise
Maturity premium	Falls	Rises or stays the same
Expected inflation	Little Change	Falls
Long-term real interest rate	Little change	Rises

ineffective. But, if financial-market participants learn that when the Fed embarks on a change of direction for monetary policy, the Fed usually makes a commitment to sustain the change over a considerable period of time or until the Fed's objectives (e.g., reducing inflation or stimulating demand) have been realized, then financial markets will take Fed actions seriously and these actions will become more effective. The Fed must establish the credibility of its policies in order for those policies to be effective.

Fiscal Policy and the Fed's Expected Reaction

We have found that a temporary change in monetary policy can be relatively ineffective in changing income, and there is a similar point to be made about fiscal policy—a tax cut that is believed to be temporary is also relatively ineffective. The reason for this is that consumption decisions are based on a longer-term view of income (a concept called permanent income) rather than just on current income. A temporary tax cut will not change people's perceptions of their long-term or permanent income and hence will have only a small effect on consumption. We discuss the permanent-income hypothesis and its implications for fiscal policy in Chapter 13.

In this chapter, however, we want to discuss a different aspect of fiscal policy. The effectiveness of a fiscal-policy action, even one that is thought to be sustained, depends upon expectations about the Fed's monetary-policy response to the fiscal-policy action. For example, starting with the same stable economy we described previously, suppose Congress enacts a reduction in tax rates. This cut in taxes increases disposable income, consumption, and hence aggregate demand along the lines that we discussed in Chapter 4.

FIGURE 8.13   Monetary Policy and Policy Expectations

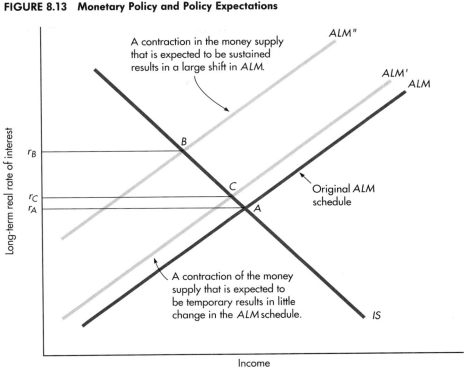

A contraction in the money supply that is expected to be sustained results in a large shift in *ALM*.

A contraction of the money supply that is expected to be temporary results in little change in the *ALM* schedule.

Original *ALM* schedule

The effect of monetary policy on the economy depends upon whether it is expected to be temporary or sustained.

In Figure 8.14 the effect of the cut in taxes is shown by a rightward movement of the *IS* schedule from *IS* to *IS'*. If there is no change in money-market conditions as a result of the fiscal policy, the *ALM* schedule will not change and the equilibrium will move from point *A* to point *B*. The fiscal policy will have increased income (from Y_A to Y_B) with the multiplier effect being partially offset by the rise in interest rates. The increase in the demand for money raises the short-term rate and, with no change in the interest-rate gap, this will translate into an equal increase in the long-term real rate. This description of the effect of an expansionary fiscal policy does not differ from the description given in Chapter 4.

In practice, however, the effect of a fiscal-policy change will depend on how the Fed responds. Consider first the case where the Fed is expected to try and keep nominal interest rates stable.

■ Short-Term Interest Rates and the Postponement Effect

We have argued that investment demand is affected by the long-term real rate of interest. But short-term rates can have an effect too because of the *postponement effect*. An increase in short-term rates that is believed to be temporary will result in only a small increase in long-term rates. But the increase in short rates may still have an impact on investment demand, if it also leads to the expectation that the small increase in long rates will soon be reversed.

Suppose that the mortgage rate rises, but families believe that this will soon be reversed. They may decide to wait six months or a year before buying a house, whereas if they had thought that the mortgage rate would stay high, then they would go ahead and buy anyway. There is no longer any advantage in waiting. A small, temporary change in the mortgage rate may have an effect on home purchases due to the postponement effect.

The postponement effect is important, but it does not change the conclusion about the importance of credibility to policy effectiveness. In order for Fed policy to be effective, it must be transmitted to long rates—and the mortgage rate is a long rate. The mortgage rate must increase before there can be an effect on housing demand. Moreover, once a contractionary policy has raised long rates and brought about a fall in investment and a fall in income, then both long and short rates of interest will fall again. A sustained and effective policy that raises the mortgage rate will in fact be followed by a decline in the mortgage rate after a year or two. The postponement effect on investment demand will be part of the economy's response to a sustained monetary policy and part of the reason it is effective. A sustained and effective contractionary monetary policy is not one that tries to raise interest rates forever.

In recent years the postponement effect has become less important. Some of the people wanting to buy houses who expect the mortgage rate to fall will go ahead and buy anyway, and then refinance the mortgage if their expectations turn out to be correct.

Even though it is less important than it used to be, the postponement effect still occurs, however, and it suggests that short-term interest rates will have some impact on investment demand even though the long-term rate is much the more important factor. We have oversimplified our discussion by ignoring the impact of short rates on investments.

Fiscal policy when the Fed stabilizes interest rates

We saw earlier that at one time the Fed was committed to maintaining stable nominal interest rates. When the Fed tries to do this, it will automatically follow an expansionary monetary policy when there is an expansionary fiscal policy. An expansionary fiscal policy tends to increase rates and then monetary policy tries to bring them down, so that it is then coordinated with the fiscal-policy change.

Once this policy regime of interest-rate stabilization was anticipated by financial markets, the result was that fiscal policy became very effective. People expected that the Fed would respond to an expansionary fiscal policy by loosening monetary policy. Then *the expectation that monetary policy was about to change was sufficient by itself to cause a simultaneous flattening of the yield curve.* The increase in the short-term nominal rate was thought to be temporary, keeping the long-term nominal rate of interest from rising very far. The policy expectation prevented the real rate of interest from rising by

FIGURE 8.14   Fiscal Expansion If People Expect Monetary Ease

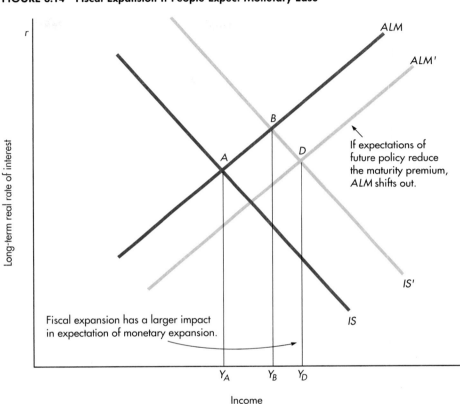

If people expect that the fiscal expansion will be accompanied by an easing of monetary policy in the future, then the impact of the fiscal expansion on income will increase.

very much, even before the monetary expansion kicked in. The flatter yield curve and smaller maturity premium pushes the *ALM* schedule down somewhat, as shown by the shift from *ALM* to *ALM'*. We find therefore that a given fiscal expansion leads to a larger increase in income than would be the case if long and short rates of interest moved together.

This case where the Fed is expected to reinforce the effect of tax changes is applicable to the 1950s or 1960s. It is not applicable to the economy of the 1980s and 90s however. The situation has become exactly the opposite.

Fiscal policy when the Fed maintains aggregate demand

The situation of the late 1980s created a very different view of the relation between the Fed and fiscal policy. The policy regime has changed for two reasons.

First, the Fed abandoned its attempts to maintain stable nominal rates of interest because of the problems that resulted from this policy strategy. The Fed still uses interest rates as a guide to its actions, but recognizes the importance of real interest rates as well as nominal rates.

Second, the Fed is very concerned about the adverse effects of the current large structural deficit and wishes to encourage deficit reduction. The national debate over fiscal policy in the 1990s focuses on proposals to raise taxes or cut expenditures to reduce the deficit. The Bush administration, having gained the White House on a pledge of no new taxes, was nevertheless searching for a budget compromise with the Congress during its first years in office. If enacted, these combinations of budget cuts and tax increases would be contractionary, but few people in financial markets expect that the Fed would respond to such policy moves with a monetary contraction or even monetary neutrality. Rather, if there are successful efforts to cut the deficit, the Fed is expected to allow and even encourage nominal interest rates to decline by easing monetary policy. The reduction in aggregate demand that stems from cutting the budget deficit would be offset by the stimulus to aggregate demand from lower real rates.

This case is the opposite from the previous one. The Fed is not expected to change monetary policy in the same direction as fiscal policy. If fiscal policy expands aggregate demand, the Fed will pull aggregate demand back down, and if fiscal policy drives aggregate demand down, the Fed will pull it back up. There is now the expectation that the Fed will attempt to maintain aggregate demand in the face of fiscal-policy actions.

Figure 8.15 illustrates the impact on fiscal policy of the expectations that the Fed will act to maintain aggregate demand in the face of a fiscal contraction designed to reduce the deficit. A contractionary fiscal policy shifts the *IS* schedule to the left, but at the same time it creates the expectation of lower interest rates in the future, since the Fed is expected to ease money. Expectations of future monetary policy are reflected in an outward shift of the *ALM* schedule because of a fall in the maturity premium.

The case shown in the figure is the one where the fiscal contraction does not lead to any cut in income at all as the *ALM* schedule shifts to *ALM'*. This case would probably require some increase in the real money supply to lower short rates, together with the expectation of continued low rates in the future to keep the maturity premium down.

This discussion helps explain why some economists' advice to Congress and the administration in recent years has been supportive of efforts to cut the budget deficit. Economists rarely recommend policies that would head the economy into recession and they were not making such recommendations in this case. Because of the expectations about a monetary-policy response, a contractionary fiscal policy would not necessarily bring on fears of a recession. Since many people worried that the Fed's concern about the deficit would lead the Fed to tighten monetary policy and therefore induce a recession, so deficit-reduction measures alleviate the fears of a recession. When

FIGURE 8.15   Effect of Deficit Cutting in the 1990s

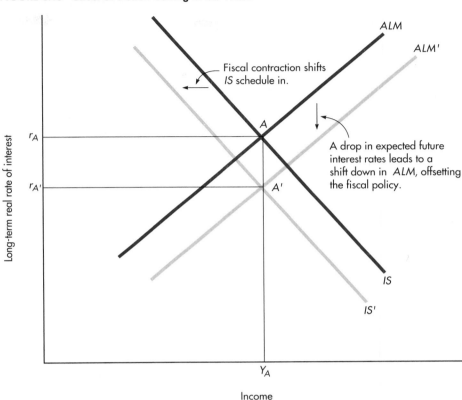

People are concerned about the federal budget deficit and Fed policy, given the deficit. Steps to cut the deficit are contractionary and shift *IS* to *IS'*. But expected future interest rates decline, so the maturity premium declines and *ALM* shifts to *ALM'*. The final outcome is uncertain, but income could remain constant.

actions are taken to reduce the deficit, this eases the Fed's concern and actually reduces the chances of a recession. (Opinion is somewhat divided on this issue; see the box by Peter Passell of *The New York Times*.)

Inflation-Sensitive Policy Expectations

Earlier in this chapter (Figure 8.8) we examined the effect of a change in the expected rate of inflation on real and nominal interest rates, but that analysis assumed a fixed maturity premium. Taking the maturity premium as given, an increase in expected inflation leads to a fall in the long-term *real* rate of interest and hence an increase in investment and income.

The Tax Rise Question

Economic Analysis

Congress may be prepared to buy the White House's rationale for putting a tax increase on the negotiating table now. But few independent analysts accept the Administration's peculiar argument that rising unemployment makes the case for a quick budget fix more compelling than it was a few months or a few years ago. Indeed, by conventional economic logic the timing seems perverse: an increase in taxes or a cut in spending would let air out of an economy that may already be sagging.

Still, most analysts believe that the potential long-term gains from a budget accord are well worth the modest risk of pushing the economy into a recession. "Whatever the reason the mood has shifted in Washington, I wouldn't say no," concludes Francis Bator at Harvard's Kennedy School of Management.

Lagging Government receipts combined with larger-than-anticipated costs of the savings and loan bailout, the White House contends, have pushed the 1990 deficit up by as much as $40 billion above official Administration estimates, and sent the projected 1991 deficit into the stratosphere.

The Last Straw

The resulting need to finance the Government with borrowed cash, the White House argued, was pushing up interest rates for private borrowers, raising business costs and threatening to choke off investment. Fresh evidence of economic weakness, an increase in unemployment, proved the last straw: An immediate dose of deficit reduction was needed to ward off a recession.

Congressional sources scoff at the idea that Richard G. Darman, the President's budget director, has only recently discovered that the 1990 deficit was far larger than the official Administration projection, or that the 1991 deficit could easily exceed the Gramm-Rudman deficit reduction targets by $100 billion. But the likely economic consequence, the notion that fiscal restraint would save the economy from a recession, drew guffaws from economists.

"I nearly blew a gasket when I heard it was time to cut the deficit because the economy was weak," said Prof. Robert Solow. A back-of-the-envelope calculation suggests why.

A big cut in Federal spending or an increase in taxes next year—the consensus speculation is in the neighborhood of $40 billion—would initially reduce demand for goods and services by roughly the same amount. And according to Henry Aaron of the Brookings Institution, the "multiplier effect" on total income would be 1.5 to 2 times as great, as reduced purchases by those directly affected would lead other individuals and businesses to pull in their horns. That might reduce total demand by nearly 2 percent, wiping out the 2 percent growth in G.N.P. forecast by many private economists.

Would Lower Interest Rates

One reason not to be unduly alarmed is that the impact of fiscal restraint would be partly offset by a "crowding in" of investment, as the reduced demand by consumers eased the demand for credit, lowering interest rates and making it cheaper for businesses to expand. Indeed, the White House seems to be suggesting that "crowding in" would more than offset the impact on consumer spending and actually save the economy from recession.

A recession need not happen even if fiscal restraint works as conventional wisdom suggests because policy makers would not sit by passively as factories were shuttered. "The Federal Reserve has made it abundantly clear that it would respond to a swing in the deficit by pushing down interest rates," Mr. Aaron said. Along with stimulating business investment, lower rates would tend to reduce the value of the dollar, since foreign investors would no longer be lured to buy dollar-denominated securities bearing high interest rates. A lower dollar, in turn, would help United States exporters, by making American products cheaper in overseas markets.

In any case, most economists seem prepared to take the risk of a downturn because they are so eager to curb the Treasury's voracious appetite for private savings and pare its dependence on foreign capital. "We passed up seven years of good times to cut the deficit," Mr. Solow points out. And he, like many economists, would settle for cutting it at a bad time.

Financial investors viewed the prospect of deficit reduction favorably also. Five days later, *The New York Times* reported that the stock market had hit new highs as a result of investor optimism over the attempts to reduce the deficit. Of course this optimism may soon evaporate. At this time, we have no way of knowing whether the efforts to reduce the deficit will be successful. There have been several unsuccessful attempts in the past.

Source: Peter Passell, *The New York Times*, May 10, 1990. Copyright © 1990 by The New York Times Company. Reprinted by permission.

In practice, however, the maturity premium cannot be taken as given when expected inflation changes. A rise in inflationary expectations will also trigger a change in expectations about future Fed policy and hence about future interest rates. When the Fed has a firm commitment to fighting inflation, then an increase in expected future inflation will also lead to the expectation of contractionary monetary policy and higher interest rates in the future. In the face of a rise in inflationary expectations coupled with an anti-inflationary Fed, the maturity premium may rise by enough so that the long-term real rate of interest will actually increase even though the rate of inflation falls. Once we take into account the Fed's response to inflation, an increase in expected inflation may actually cause a fall in income.

An increase in expected inflation with an anti-inflationary policy regime

In October 1979, the Fed, under its newly appointed chairman, Paul Volcker, announced that it was no longer going to use interest-rate targets but was going to set a stable path for the growth of the money supply. This specific commitment did not last long, because the economy fell into a very deep recession by 1982 with unemployment rising above 10 percent in September of that year. The Fed countered the deep recession by abandoning its commitment to a constant rate of growth of the money supply. But nevertheless, an important change in the policy regime had taken place.

The unemployment rate went over 7 percent in 1980 and remained above this level until mid-1986. The Fed signaled its willingness to combat inflation, even at the expense of high unemployment. It was willing to act to avoid economic collapse, but it was not willing to restore full employment until inflation was under control. With this new policy regime established in the 1980s, financial markets in the 1990s now react negatively to fears of rising inflation. When financial-market participants observe that the rate of inflation is rising, they revise their expectations of both inflation and monetary policy. They anticipate that the Fed will react to the higher inflation by tightening monetary policy so long-term interest rates rise as a result of the fears of higher inflation.

The case where an increase in expected inflation leads to the expectation of contractionary monetary policy is illustrated in Figure 8.16. The increase in expected inflation in itself lowers the long-run real rate. (The *ALM* schedule moves to *ALM'*.) But the increase in the maturity premium (*ALM'* to *ALM''*) reflects a rise in the long-run nominal rate, perhaps by enough to leave the real rate unchanged or even higher than it was initially. If so, the new level of income is a little lower (Y_A to Y_B) than before inflation expectations rose.

The increase in the maturity premium may be enough, or even more than enough, to keep up the long-term real rate of interest following an increase in expected inflation. Reading the signals from financial markets is not easy, but many participants in financial markets today believe that fears of inflation, especially fears of the Fed's reaction to inflation, could actually

FIGURE 8.16   Effect of Increase in Expected Inflation with Inflation-Fighting Fed

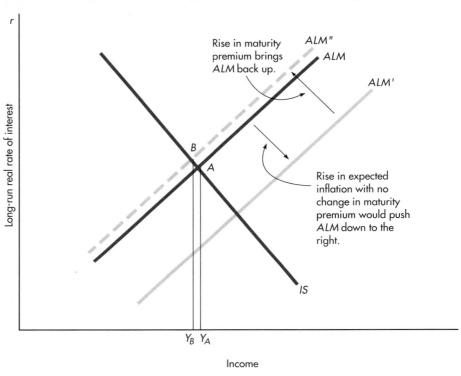

An increase in expected inflation in itself, shifts the *ALM* schedule to *ALM'*, just as in Figure 8.4. People expect the Fed to respond to higher inflation, which raises the maturity premium. The *ALM* schedule moves back and may even end up above the original *ALM* schedule.

raise interest rates enough to cause a recession or at least the threat of recession.

If fears of higher inflation can push up the long-term real rate of interest, so too unexpectedly low inflation reduces the maturity premium. The winding down of inflation in the mid-1980s helped keep down the real rate of interest, even though there were other forces keeping the real rate high at the time, notably the budget deficit.

In this chapter we have found that reconnecting *IS* and *LM* in the *IS-ALM* framework has meant looking at the interest-rate gap between the short-term interest rate that is determined in the money market and the long-term real rate that affects investment. Changes in the gap can reinforce or undo the relationships between a change in the money market and an impact in the goods market and vice versa. The interest-rate gap changes mostly as a result of changes in expectations about the future course of interest rates, risk, inflation, and economic policy. Expectations can change the equilibrium in the economy as well as influencing the effectiveness of policy.

Up to this point we have only alluded indirectly to the fact that we are assuming that inflation (current or expected) is determined autonomously. In practice, of course, inflation is brought about by changes in aggregate supply and demand and economic policy. In the next two chapters, where we describe the sources of inflation, we will see that expectations continue to play an important role in determining economic events.

SUMMARY

- When the price level changes, the real money supply and the *LM* schedule remain constant as long as the Fed increases or decreases the nominal supply of money in proportion to the change in the price level. This is an inflation-accommodating policy.

- Faster money growth is expansionary and the *LM* schedule shifts down to the right. Slower money growth is contractionary and the *LM* schedule shifts up to the left.

- In equilibrium, there is an interest-rate gap equal to the maturity premium minus the expected rate of inflation. This is equal to the long-term real rate of interest minus the short-term nominal rate of interest.

- Shifts in the interest-rate gap change the relationship between the money market and the goods market. For example, a given change in monetary policy has a direct effect on money markets. It has an equal effect on the real economy only when there is no change in the interest-rate gap.

- The augmented *LM* schedule, called *ALM*, is an *LM* schedule that has been shifted by the interest-rate gap.

- With a given maturity premium and inflationary expectations, the *ALM* describes the different levels of income and the long-term real rates of interest that obtain when the money market is in equilibrium.

- Money-market equilibrium is described along an *LM* schedule. For a given *LM* schedule, the *ALM* schedule will shift when the interest-rate gap changes.

- Holding the maturity premium constant, an increase in expected inflation will reduce the real rate of interest, stimulate investment demand, and increase the level of equilibrium income—the *ALM* schedule shifts down.

- Holding expected inflation constant, an increase in the maturity premium will raise the real rate of interest, dampen investment demand, and reduce the equilibrium level of income—the *ALM* schedule shifts up.

- In practice, both the maturity premium and the expected rate of inflation will change at the same time, not necessarily in the same direction.

- When the Fed undertakes a monetary contraction, there is a rise in short-term nominal rates—the *LM* schedule shifts up. If the monetary contraction is expected to be temporary, the effectiveness of monetary policy is weakened—aggregate demand and income are only slightly affected. There will be a reduction in the interest-rate gap as the maturity premium falls.

■ If the monetary contraction is expected to be sustained, the effectiveness of monetary policy is strengthened—aggregate demand and income are strongly affected. Long-term nominal interest rates will increase in line with the increase in short-term rates.

■ The effect of a fiscal policy on the economy depends in part upon the Fed's response to that policy.

■ If expected Fed policy is to target a constant nominal rate of interest, fiscal policy will be very effective in changing income.

■ If expected Fed policy is to maintain a stable level of aggregate demand, fiscal-policy changes will have little effect on income. Cutting the deficit will not induce a recession because in anticipation of the Fed response, the interest-rate gap falls.

■ Because of expectations about the Fed's reaction to inflation, an increase in inflationary expectations can drive up the interest-rate gap. The long-term real rate of interest may not fall and may even rise.

KEY TERMS

augmented *LM* schedule

contractionary monetary policy

expansionary monetary policy

expectations

inflation-accommodating monetary policy

interest-rate targeting

policy regime

DISCUSSION QUESTIONS AND PROBLEMS

1. Review the ways in which investment decisions and cash-management decisions are affected by expectations, inflation, and different interest rates. How do the different responses lead to a separation of the goods market and the money market?

2. What is the interest-rate gap? How does it connect money-market equilibrium along an *LM* schedule with financial-capital-market equilibrium along an *ALM* schedule?

3. If the interest-rate gap fell by 2 percentage points, could you determine the new equilibrium level of the long-term real rate of interest simply by assuming that the short-term nominal rate remained constant and subtracting 2 percentage points from the long-term real rate?

4. If the Fed unexpectedly increased the rate of growth of the money supply, what would be the most likely immediate effect on short-term nominal interest rates? What would happen to the interest-rate gap?

5. Are the effects of monetary-policy actions on the real economy different for policy changes that are expected to be temporary or permanent? Why?

6. Why did monetarists criticize the Fed for following a policy of targeting the nominal rate of interest? What did they suggest as an alternative? In this alternative, what would happen to expectations about monetary policy?

7. If financial and business investors believe that there has been an increase in the riskiness of investments, can that change in expectations affect equilibrium output? How? What happens to the maturity premium?

8. Show how the *ALM* shifts when there is a change in the short-term nominal rate of interest, the expected rate of inflation, or the maturity premium. Indicate which variables are changing and which are being held constant.

9. Consider an economy described by the following equations:

   IS $r = 70 - 0.0125Y$
   LM $i = 0.004Y - 12.5$

   Assume that the maturity premium, *MP*, is 6.3 percent and that the expected rate of inflation is 3 percent.

   $MP = 6.3$
   $Exp\Delta P/P = 3.$

   Further, assume that the Fed is following an accommodating monetary policy, so that the real stock of money remains constant at the given rate of current inflation.

   a. What is the interest-rate gap?
   b. What is the equation that describes the *ALM* schedule?
   c. What are the equilibrium levels of income and long-term real rate of interest?
   d. What is the long-term nominal rate of interest in equilibrium?
   e. What is the short-term nominal rate of interest in equilibrium?
   f. Now suppose that expected rate of inflation declines from 3 percent to 1 percent. Assume that the maturity premium and current rate of inflation are constant. What are the new equilibrium levels of income and long-term real rate of interest?
   g. What impact does a decline in the expected rate of inflation have on the difference between real and nominal rates of interest?
   h. Suppose that the expected rate of inflation goes back to its old level (i.e., to 3 percent), but the maturity premium rises from 6.3 percent to 9.5 percent. What are the new equilibrium levels of income and long-term real rate of interest? What impact does the increase in the maturity premium have on the short-term nominal interest rate?

10. Suppose the Fed reduces the real money supply and raises the short-term nominal rate of interest.
   a. What happens to the maturity premium and the expected rate of inflation if this policy action is expected to be temporary?
   b. What happens to the maturity premium and the expected rate of inflation if this policy action is expected to be sustained?
   c. Compare the impact on income in the two cases.

11. What happens to the maturity premium following an increase in expected inflation if the Fed is committed to an anti-inflationary policy regime?

REVIEW AND PREVIEW

SUMMARY OF WHAT WE HAVE COVERED SO FAR

The primary focus of the first part of the book has been on understanding how income is determined and how economic forces and policies affect income. We have looked at a model of the economy where changes in aggregate demand determine income. Aggregate demand is affected by decisions made in markets and by the government. We have concentrated on three interrelated markets; the market for goods and services, the market for money and short-term financial assets, and the financial capital market where longer-term financial assets are used to finance purchases of new capital goods.

In the market for goods and services (the goods market), aggregate demand for goods and services arises out of the separate sectors of demand: consumers, businesses, government, and foreign buyers. In general, an increase in demand in any sector generates an increase in income which feeds into a further increase in demand and so on, until a new equilibrium level of income is reached. Aggregate demand is also affected by interest rates, where a higher long-term real rate of interest reduces the demand for capital goods. The combinations of long-term real rate of interest and the levels of income generated by the separate demands of consumers, businesses, government and the foreign sector is called the *IS* schedule. Equilibrium income cannot be determined by the goods market alone since the equilibrium level of income depends upon the level of the long-term real rate of interest.

In the money market, the demand for money balances is driven by cash managers seeking to balance the transactions benefits of holding money against the opportunity cost of foregoing the higher short-term nominal returns that can be earned by holding money-market instruments—particularly T bills. There is then a two-way interaction between the goods market and the money market, as the level of income generated in the goods market affects the demand for money. And in addition, the short-term nominal rate of interest determined in the money market affects the long-term real rate that affects the goods market.

The connection between the money market and the goods market takes place in the financial capital market. Short-term nominal rates of interest are linked to long-term real rates by a maturity premium involving risk and expected future interest rates, and also by the expected rate of inflation. We summarize the difference between rates in the money and goods market by defining the interest-rate gap. At various levels of income, there are short-term nominal rates of interest that are associated with equilibrium in the money market. When those rates are adjusted by the interest-rate gap, the resulting combination of long-term real rates and income is called the *ALM* schedule, the combination of real rates and income where money markets and financial capital markets are in equilibrium, given inflationary expectations and the level of income.

Income is determined by aggregate demand and aggregate demand is set when money, financial capital, and goods markets all come into equilibrium—depicted as the intersection of *IS* and *ALM*. Policy can be used to affect aggregate demand and hence income. Fiscal policy works by changing taxes, transfers, and government expenditures. Monetary policy works through open market operations, bank reserves, and cash management reactions in the money market. Expectations about inflation, the future of interest rates, and future policy actions will all combine to influence the way in which monetary and fiscal policies impact upon income.

SUMMARY OF WHAT WE ARE COVERING IN THE REST OF THE BOOK

We have described how inflation affects decisions in the money and capital markets through the money supply and real rates of interest. Policy and income are influenced by the current and expected rates of inflation. But up until now we have not said what determines the rate of inflation and how it may be influenced by policy changes or other economic forces. Inflation arises as a result of actions taken by individuals, business, and government. In Chapters 9 and 10 we look at how inflation is generated and at the consequences of inflation for economic performance and policymaking. The discussion starts with aggregate demand as the source of inflation and that approach leads to the idea of a trade-off between output and inflation. The trade-off approach is followed by a look at how changes in aggregate supply can be the source of inflation.

We have already introduced the foreign sector into the description of aggregate demand. In the second part of the book we go much further by describing the roles that foreign exchange and international financial markets play in affecting domestic economic performance and policies. The international sector is revisited at the end of the book when we look at the recent experience of industrialized economies with productivity, long-term growth, and competitiveness.

Another issue that was not addressed in the first part of the book was the fact that income exhibits fluctuations, rising and falling over time, and tracing out a pattern that has been called a business cycle, where recession is followed by recovery. We offer several explanations of the variability of income: built-in variations in expenditures by households and business as well as international and financial sources of variability. We then look at stabilization policies—policies designed to curb or dampen the variability of income. Much of the controversy among economists turns on the issue of whether or not government policies can in fact contribute to reducing variability or whether policies exacerbate fluctuations. That controversy is examined when we look at a different view of the economy—one in which it is assumed that prices adjust quickly to changes in supply and demand, where demand is driven mostly by changes in the money supply, and where economic decision makers act upon the rational expectations they form about economic conditions.

Finally, we look at the determinants of the long-run trend of income. We look at the sources of growth in aggregate supply and how that growth allows for the growth of real income over time. We point to the serious issue of a decline in growth rates in advanced economies and the consequences of that decline for living standards as well as policies designed to deal with the decline.

PART V

Inflation

From year to year, some prices fall, but most rise. In most economies, the overall price level grows, albeit at an uneven rate. We need to know why this inflation occurs. We have already seen how inflation and the expectation of inflation affects decisions throughout the economy. Now we turn to the *causes* of inflation.

Prices in markets are set as a result of decisions taken by individuals, business, and government. Inflation is caused by shifts in supply and demand conditions in markets that then lead businesses to decide to raise prices and wages. If there are continuing increases in aggregate demand with a fixed aggregate supply, then prices will keep increasing. That basic approach to inflation is where we start—inflation generated by a continuing rise in aggregate demand. In the short run, before the economy can fully adjust to a jump in aggregate demand, there will be an increase in production that accompanies the rising price level. The aggregate demand approach coupled with less than immediate adjustment of inflationary expectations leads to the notion of a trade-off between output and inflation.

Aggregate supply also has a role to play in inflation. First a rise in the cost of goods and services can become built in to costs and prices so that aggregate supply will catch up with shifts in aggregate demand. And if increases in inflation are anticipated, upward shifts in aggregate supply can occur even with no increase in aggregate demand, so that inflation becomes a self-fulfilling prophecy. Further, there have been sudden contractions of the supply of specific commodities, such as oil, and ended up affecting the overall rate of inflation.

Finally, in all of the discussion of inflation, policy questions are critical. The reactions of policymakers to inflation was important in forming our picture of how the economy works. Now we go beyond policy reactions and investigate the role of policymakers in bringing about a particular rate of inflation.

CHAPTER 9

The Trade-Off between Output and Inflation

INTRODUCTION

Inflation is a rise in overall prices, an ongoing increase in the price level. In a dynamic economy, there are always changes in supply-and-demand conditions in individual markets that lead to increases in some prices and decreases in others and this does not necessarily result in any overall inflation. But when increases in prices outweigh reductions in prices and on average the economy experiences a rise in the overall price level, there is inflation.

Inflation is seen as a burden or a cost to the economy, especially when it surprises people. When you sell goods or services, when you offer your labor to an employer, or when you rent out capital assets to be used by others, you agree on an amount that you will be paid. An unexpected burst of inflation can lower the real value of wages received or other compensation because the funds received for work done or for goods provided buy less when prices rise.

People appear to dislike inflation intensely even when there is no element of surprise. In part, this may stem from a misunderstanding. People often believe that increases in their wages or salaries are the result of their own efforts. They do not always realize that part of the increase that they have received is attributable to general inflation. If wage increases are followed by increases in prices, wage earners may well see the inflation as undoing well-deserved gains, no matter that the inflation itself was a major reason for the higher wages. Even when there is no misunderstanding involved, however, there is still a cost of inflation—the added uncertainty in the economy that results from not knowing the real value of future revenues and returns.

In Chapters 6 through 8 we found that inflation has a real impact on the economy through the reaction of financial markets to both the actual rate of inflation and inflationary expectations. Here we look at the causes of inflation. Inflation is caused by economic conditions in the goods markets as well as financial markets.

The first place to look for a cause of inflation is aggregate demand. Higher demand in most of the markets in the economy brings about more output, but only at higher prices. Higher output raises production costs; higher demand means that producers can raise the prices that they charge while still being able to sell their output.

As well as increases in aggregate demand, there are other factors that can contribute to inflation. Inflation can be caused by inflation itself. Once inflation has been started, by demand or supply changes, it may generate its own momentum. The expectation of inflation may itself become a cause of inflation.

In addition, shocks to aggregate supply can cause inflation. An inflationary supply shock is a sudden and significant increase in the price level at which a given level of output is produced. The shock can be permanent, such as the long-run and possibly fundamental decline in productivity growth that started in the late 1960s. Or a shock can be temporary, such as the sudden OPEC-oil-price increases of the 1970s, increases that were largely reversed in the 1980s, although they may be returning in the 1990s with the renewed Mideast conflict. In any case, a supply shock will generate a boost to inflation. The surge in inflation can then generate enough momentum to cause continuing inflation.

In this chapter, we introduce changes in both aggregate supply and demand as sources of inflation, but we then go on to concentrate on the aggregate demand side, together with the formation of inflationary expectations. We look at the implications for monetary policy of demand-induced inflation. In the next chapter, we see how changes in aggregate supply conditions (supply shocks) can affect inflation and the implications of this for economic policy.

SHIFTS IN AGGREGATE SUPPLY AND DEMAND AND THE PRICE LEVEL

Looking at the simple model of aggregate supply and demand, we see how an increase in aggregate demand can raise the price level. In Figure 9.1, the rise in the price level is caused by the outward shift of aggregate demand along the rising portion of the aggregate supply schedule. In the figure, aggregate demand is increased twice, as shown by two successive shifts in the aggregate demand schedule. The first shift is from $AD(A)$ to $AD(P)$, and the second shift is from $AD(P)$ to $AD(B)$. The price level also rises in two steps along the aggregate supply (AS) schedule—first from P_A to P^P, followed by the increase from P^P to P_B.

The successive increases in aggregate demand (point A to point P followed by point P to point B) bring about increasingly larger increases in price, particularly as the level of income exceeds potential output (Y^P). The price level increases by more as income exceeds potential output because businesses

FIGURE 9.1   Aggregate Supply and Demand and the Price Level

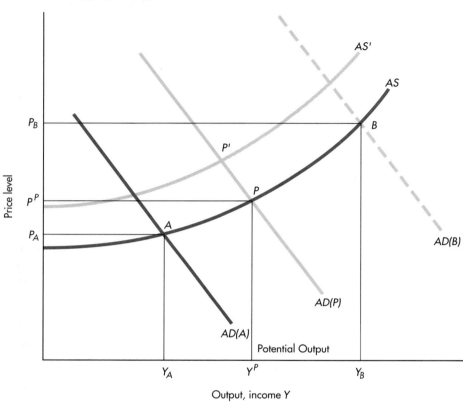

The price level changes in response to shifts in both supply and demand.

are near full capacity. Increases in production raise costs by more when firms are operating near full capacity than when there is excess productive capacity.

The figure also illustrates how a rise in the price level can be caused by a contraction in aggregate supply or a supply shock. The worsening of aggregate supply conditions *(AS to AS')* raises the price level with no change in aggregate demand conditions (point *P* to point *P'*).

The aggregate supply and demand model shown in Figure 9.1 provides a framework for illustrating the separate determinants of inflation. It suggests an important difference between inflation driven by increases in demand and inflation driven by reductions in supply. In the case of aggregate supply shifts, output falls as prices rise. In the case of aggregate demand shifts, there is an increase in output as prices rise. And this latter case suggests, in turn, the existence of an important trade-off. Increases in aggregate demand will induce higher levels of output, but at the cost of higher prices.

The simple model of Figure 9.1 is useful, but inflation is not about a one-time increase in the price level of the kind just described. Inflation refers to a continuing rise in prices over time and is measured by the rate of growth of prices. We want to understand why the rate of inflation increases or decreases and the consequences of these changes. That understanding comes from looking at the way in which higher demand leads to higher output and a higher rate of inflation—the output–inflation trade-off.

THE OUTPUT–INFLATION TRADE-OFF

output–inflation trade-off
The change in the rate of inflation associated with a change in the output ratio.

To understand the **output–inflation trade-off,** we start with the observation that the price level reflects the average of thousands of individual prices. In individual markets there is not always equilibrium between supply and demand; instead *prices adjust at a rate that depends upon the discrepancy between demand and supply.* In any given market there is a prevailing market price; if demand exceeds supply at this price, then the price will increase. If supply exceeds demand, then price falls. At a high level of aggregate demand, demand will be high in many individual markets. This will bring forth a high level of output, but it will also mean that there are also more markets for which demand exceeds supply and hence there will be more prices that are increasing than prices that are decreasing. There will be inflation.

The Trade-Off with Competitive Markets

The economy has many different markets and the balances between supply and demand can be rather different from one to another. The goods and services produced in each industry or market require different kinds of labor that in turn are supplied in multiple labor markets.[1] Their technologies are different and the factories or offices that make up their capital inputs are distinct. This means that there can be an excess of supply relative to demand in one market and, simultaneously, an excess of demand relative to supply in another. In Figure 9.2 we consider supply and demand conditions in two competitive markets in the economy. One of the markets is in excess supply and the other is in excess demand.

The two markets shown in the figure can reflect demand and supply conditions in different industries or geographic regions. Items produced in one market are not perfect substitutes for those produced in another market. Even though the firms and workers who are in the unfortunate position of

---

[1] Richard G. Lipsey, "The Relation between Unemployment and the Rate of Change of Money Wage Rates in the United Kingdom, 1862–1957: A Further Study," *Economica* 28 (February 1960).

FIGURE 9.2   Supply and Demand in Two Competitive Markets

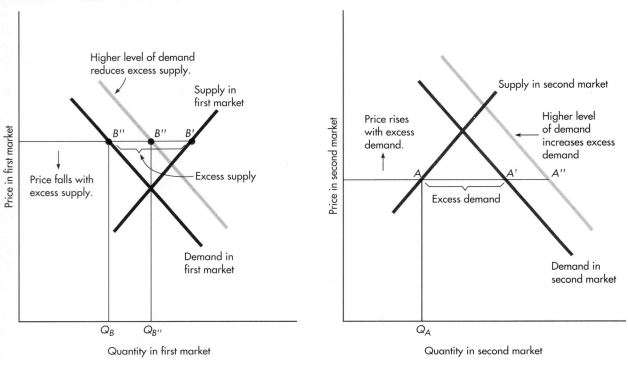

A higher level of demand leads to greater output but also to inflation.

being in excess supply are ready and willing to work more and produce more, these workers and factories cannot easily or quickly change production technologies and distribution systems so as to produce and sell the different products that are in excess demand. This division among markets is shown in the figure where the market shown in the right-hand panel indicates an excess demand for its products. Demand exceeds the supply at the going price (the distance AA') and there is a shortage of capacity and job vacancies. Output is equal to Q_A, constrained by the willingness of producers to sell at the going price. The market in the left-hand panel shows the opposite situation. There is an excess supply (the distance BB'); that is to say there is slack capacity and unemployed workers in this region or industry. Output is at Q_B, constrained by the willingness of consumers to buy at the going price.

The prices will adjust in these markets. The price of the product and the workers' wages will be increasing in the market with excess demand

and decreasing in the market with excess supply. When there is excess demand, prices and wages will increase as firms in these regions or industries bid against each other for the available pool of workers, and markups are increased. When there is excess supply, prices and wages will fall as workers compete for jobs and companies compete for customers. There will be no general inflation, however, as long as excess supply and excess demand balance each other out. Price increases in one market will offset decreases in the other. The economy is then in aggregate equilibrium. And individual prices are adjusting to equate supply and demand in both markets.

Consider now the case of a higher level of aggregate demand, so that the demand schedules in both of the markets are above or to the right of the original demand schedules (shown as the shifted demand schedules in both panels). In the market that had an excess supply (the left-hand panel) output will be higher as firms can sell more (at Q_B''). In addition, the extent of the excess supply will be reduced. (It is now BB'' rather than BB'.) In the market that has excess demand, there is no change in supply; rather, the excess demand will be greater in the market (the distance AA'').

Comparing the case with a higher level of demand to the previous case, we find that the higher level of demand has resulted in a higher level of output through its impact on the market that was suffering from excess supply. But as well as the impact of higher demand on output, there will also be an impact on prices. We assume that the price in the market with excess demand will rise faster following the increase in demand. The rate of price increase depends upon the size of the gap between supply and demand; it depends upon the amount of excess demand in the market. In similar fashion, we assume that the price in the market with excess supply will fall more slowly following the increase in demand. The extent of the excess supply has been reduced, and hence the rate of price decline is smaller.

Taking both markets together, therefore, we find that the increase in aggregate demand has changed the balance between price increases and decreases. Price is rising faster in the excess demand market and falling more slowly in the excess supply market, so that the average price, (the price level) is now increasing; there is inflation. The increase in demand has therefore shown us the trade-off between output and inflation. The higher level of aggregate demand has led to more output at the cost of inflation.

We have just considered the case of a higher level of aggregate demand, but we could just as easily have considered the case where aggregate demand was lower. A low level of aggregate demand will induce a low level of output as firms in the market with excess supply are able to sell less. And there will be deflation, as prices rise less rapidly in the market with excess demand and prices fall more rapidly in the market with excess supply.

This model of two markets can be extended to a model economy with many competitive markets. If this is done, the analysis (called general equilibrium analysis) becomes extremely complex and it is hard to be sure exactly how individual prices or the overall price level will behave. But the intuitive lesson from such a model with many markets is that *there is an equilibrium level of aggregate demand and output for which there is no inflation (the price level is stable). Higher levels of aggregate demand will lead to higher levels of output combined with inflation. Lower levels of aggregate demand will lead to lower levels of output combined with negative rates of inflation (deflation).*

The equilibrium level of output where there is price stability is important. This level of output corresponds to what we have been calling potential output. When output is equal to potential output, there is no inflationary pressure coming from excess demand in the economy as a whole. Once we take account of expected inflation, we will see that in the actual economy there can be (and usually is) inflation even when output is equal to or below potential output. But the idea of potential output as the point where the forces of excess supply in some markets balance out the forces of excess demand in others, remains an important one. When output is below potential output, there is net excess supply, and inflation will be decreasing. When output is above potential output, there is net excess demand, and inflation is increasing.

For any given level of output relative to potential output, the rate of inflation or deflation reflects the speed at which the markets in the economy adjust in response to the gaps between supply and demand. This speed of adjustment is something that economists do not agree on. One school of thought (the equilibrium–business-cycle theory discussed in Chapter 16) argues that the adjustment occurs very quickly indeed, so that excess supply and demand are eliminated almost immediately. An increase in aggregate demand that results from an increase in the nominal supply of money will lead to a rapid proportional rise in the price level. The equilibrium level of output will be restored quickly, and any trade-off between output and inflation is only a short-lived phenomenon.

However, if markets adjust slowly, as we believe they do, the situation is different. An increase in aggregate demand will induce a slow but persistent inflation and output will be above its equilibrium for some time. The mainstream view among economists is that the speed of adjustment is slow, so that prices are sticky in response to changes in demand.

The trade-off with sticky prices

Few markets are perfectly competitive with completely flexible prices. Instead, many markets are dominated by companies that sell products that are unique; they have customers with loyalty to their brand; and they use extensive advertising to persuade existing and potential customers of the advantages of their products. Large companies, and many small companies as well, set the prices they will charge for their products rather than simply taking a market price as given. And in many cases companies have established contractual arrangements with their suppliers and their customers. In addition, many companies maintain some slack capacity and they are almost always glad to sell more when demand increases.[2]

It is very hard to model realistically the way in which output and prices adjust in response to excess supply or demand. A firm that sets its price will try to anticipate what the response of its competitors will be and how its customers will then respond to what all the competing firms in the market have done. The two branches of economics that deal with the problem of how prices and wages are set are called *game theory* (named because choosing a pricing strategy is a bit like choosing a strategy in poker or chess) and *contract theory*. Unfortunately these theories have shown us a lot about the complexity of the problem and not enough about the likely solutions. There are, however, some ways in which the lessons from the model of competitive markets should be modified once we take into account the way prices adjust in practice.

First, in the competitive market model pictured in Figure 9.2, an increase in demand will not lead to any increase in output in markets where there is already excess demand. In the actual economy, increases in demand will increase output in most markets. Second, many wages and prices are set either by formal contracts or by implicit understandings between buyers and sellers. Wage contracts are particularly important. These contracts—explicit or implicit—make prices and wages slow to adjust to demand changes. And third, prices and wages are often stickier downward than upward. If firms cannot hire enough workers, they will increase wages, but they may not cut wages when there are layoffs.[3]

Relative to what might be expected from the model of competitive market adjustment, therefore, the output–inflation trade-off in the actual economy will be flatter, with inflation responding only a little to demand changes. And it will be flatter at low levels of output than at high levels. And since markets where there is excess supply will show little decline in prices due to **price stickiness,** while markets with excess demand will show increases in prices, it follows that there will have to be more markets with excess supply than there are markets with excess demand at the level of aggregate output where there is no inflationary pressure. This last point is important because it affects the way we think about potential output.

price stickiness
A characteristic of the economy wherein prices do not immediately and completely adjust to changes in supply and/or demand.

Potential output and the natural rate of unemployment

Potential output is a benchmark for the economy. It is the level of output that does not strain the available supply of labor or the productive capacity

---

[2] Robert E. Hall, "The Relation between Price and Marginal Cost in U.S. Industry," Working Paper no. 1786 (Cambridge, Mass.: National Bureau of Economic Research, January 1986).

[3] Price and wage stickiness and the role of contract theory and implicit contracts are discussed in Chapter 16.

of the economy and hence does not lead to inflationary pressure. But in order to restrain inflationary pressures in the economy, it is necessary to maintain excess supply in many markets. When output equals potential output, there are many underutilized factories and many workers without jobs.

natural rate of unemployment
The rate of unemployment associated with output equal to potential output, hence the unemployment rate that is consistent with a stable rate of inflation.

An economy that is producing at potential output generates a particular level of unemployment called the **natural rate of unemployment.** Potential output and the natural rate of unemployment are defined together, representing equivalent benchmarks for the economy. In the U.S. economy in the 1980s and thus far in the 1990s, the natural rate has been in the 5–6 percent range and for much of that period actual output has been in fact equal or near potential. When the unemployment rate is equal to the natural rate, the economy is said to be at *full employment,* but keep in mind that in 1990 when there was a 5–6 percent unemployment rate, there were about 6 million people looking for work. It is unfortunate that our economy cannot reduce unemployment further without creating inflationary pressure. There is hope that the natural rate of unemployment will fall in the 1990s as we see a decline in the fraction of the work force that is made up of high-unemployment groups such as teenagers.

We now summarize what we have found. The simple model of supply-and-demand adjustment suggests that the rate of inflation depends upon the extent to which there is more excess demand than excess supply. This leads to the idea of a trade-off in which fluctuations in demand lead to changes in output relative to potential output and changes in the rate of inflation. This same idea can also be applied to the analysis of markets that do not have perfect flexible prices, but stickiness suggests a relatively flat trade-off, especially at low levels of output. In addition, when prices are sticky, the concept of potential output changes. When the economy is at potential output, this does not mean that the economy is operating as efficiently as possible. Achieving a level of output above potential output leads to more jobs and more profits. The cost is higher inflation.

The Short-Run Output–Inflation Trade-Off

short-run output–inflation trade-off
The change in the rate of inflation associated with a change in the output ratio that takes place over a short period of time, before expectations of inflation are revised.

The **short-run output–inflation tradeoff** for the aggregate economy relates the output ratio to the current rate of inflation. The short-run trade-off is shown in Equation 9.1:

$$\text{Current } \Delta P/P = H(Y/Y^P). \tag{9.1}$$

The **output ratio** (Y/Y^P) was introduced in Chapter 1, but since that is a while back at this point, we reproduce the definition. It is the ratio of current output to potential output:

$$\text{Output ratio} = Y/Y_P = \text{Current GNP/Potential GNP.}$$

It is usually expressed as a percentage. When current output is 5 percent higher than potential output, the output ratio is equal to 105 percent. When

---

FIGURE 9.3   The Short-Run Output–Inflation Trade-Off

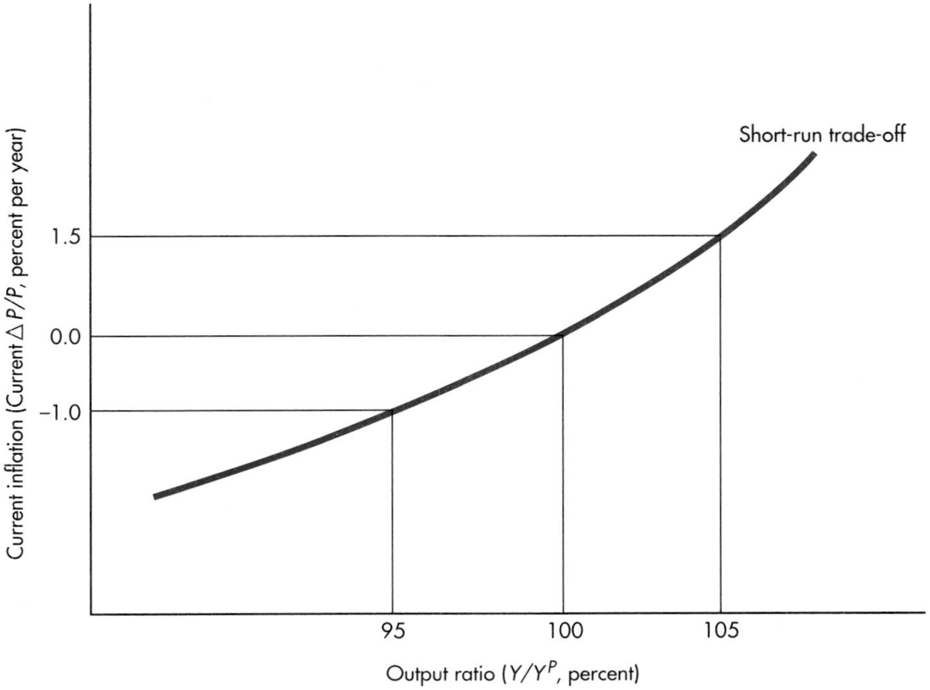

The trade-off is drawn assuming zero expected inflation.

---

output ratio
The ratio of actual output to potential output, measured in percentage of potential output.

current output is 5 percent lower than potential output, the output ratio equals 95 percent.

In Equation 9.1, the letter H indicates a functional relation, where higher values of the output ratio cause higher values of inflation. This captures the idea that when output is high relative to potential, there are many markets with excess demand, and prices are rising on average. Current inflation increases when the output ratio increases. The output–inflation trade-off given in Equation 9.1 is shown in Figure 9.3. The horizontal axis in the figure shows the output ratio, expressed as a percentage. The vertical axis shows the rate of price inflation. The figure shows a zero rate of inflation when the output ratio is 100 percent and positive and negative rates when the ratio is above or below this level. This happy situation would only occur in practice if there were a zero expected rate of inflation.

Since inflation rises with output, the output–inflation trade-off slopes up to right. The trade-off is also shown to be curved, getting steeper at higher levels of the output ratio. We discussed earlier how this property of the trade-off comes from the fact that excess supply may not reduce prices by much.

The Phillips curve and the output–inflation trade-off

The analysis of the trade-off between output and price inflation in the goods market began with the work of A. W. Phillips on the labor market. In 1958 he described a negative relationship between the rate of change in wages and the unemployment rate. This finding about the workings of labor markets is now called the *Phillips curve*.[4] It was based on observations of data for the British economy over many years. Lower rates of unemployment were associated with higher rates of increase in wages. Phillips' analysis of the British data indicated that the values of the trade-off between the two had remained very stable over time.

In Figure 9.4, we depict a Phillips curve. It shows wage increases varying with the unemployment rate in the economy. At point *A*, the unemployment rate is 6 percent and the rate of wage increase 1 percent. If unemployment falls to 4 percent, the rate of wage increase rises to 2 percent (point *B*).

The curve that Phillips found was used by U.S. policymakers in the 1960s in their theories of the output–inflation trade-off. This was done by linking the labor market to the goods market in two key steps. The first step was to show the relation between output and unemployment (**Okun's law**) and the second was to link the rate of wage increase to the rate of price inflation.

Okun's law
The relationship between output and unemployment. If output exceeds potential output, then the unemployment rate will be below the natural rate of unemployment.

Relating unemployment to output: Okun's law.   The link between output and unemployment is known as *Okun's law*, a relationship estimated by Arthur Okun in the early 1960s.[5] Calling this relationship a law is a rather old-fashioned terminology. Economists do not talk about laws much these days, but in this case the relation it expresses has withstood the test of time quite well and so the name has stuck. The "law" relates the unemployment rate at any point in time to the natural rate of unemployment and the output gap. In a modern version of Okun's law, each percentage-point rise in the output gap reduces the unemployment rate by about 0.4 of a percentage point. When the output gap is negative (current output is less than potential output), then the unemployment rate is above the natural rate. When the output gap rises to zero (current output equals potential output), then unemployment equals the natural rate. If the output gap were to go above zero (current

---

[4] A. W. Phillips, "The Relation between Unemployment and the Rate of Change of Money Wage Rates in the United Kingdom, 1861–1957," *Economica* 25 (November 1958). A precursor to the Phillips curve is attributed to Irving Fisher. In 1926 he wrote an article titled "A Statistical Relation between Unemployment and Price Changes" which was reprinted in *Journal of Political Economy*, March/April 1973, pp. 496–502.

[5] Arthur M. Okun, "Potential GNP: Its Measurement and Significance," reprinted in Okun's *The Political Economy of Prosperity* (Washington, D.C.: Brookings Institution, 1970), pp. 132–45.

FIGURE 9.4 The Phillips Curve

Phillips suggested that there is a stable relation between wage increases and unemployment.

output in excess of potential), the economy would be in a boom with unemployment dipping below the natural rate. Okun's law is shown as

$$\text{Unemployment rate} = \text{Natural rate of unemployment} \\ - 0.4 \, (\text{Output gap}). \tag{9.2}$$

While there is no consensus as to the size of the natural rate of unemployment in the U.S. economy, most estimates range between 5 and 6 percent. Since inflation was beginning to increase as of 1990 (at a time when the unemployment rate was between 5 and 6 percent), the 6 percent figure is probably the best current estimate. Recalling the definition of the output gap, this means that Okun's law can be given as

$$\text{Unemployment rate} = 6 - 0.4[(Y/Y^P) - 100]. \tag{9.3}$$

Some alternative values for output and the unemployment rate from Equation 9.3 are then as follows:

Unemployment rate	Output ratio
4 percent	105 percent of Y^P
6 percent	100 percent of Y^P
8 percent	95 percent of Y^P

Using Okun's law to relate unemployment to output was one of the two steps required to go from the relationship between unemployment and wage increases to the output–inflation trade-off. The second step is to relate increases in wages to price inflation.

Relating wage increases and productivity to inflation.   The connection between wages and inflation works through costs. When there is an industrywide increase in the cost of production, the rise in cost is reflected in an upward shift in the supply schedule of that product. To the degree that demand is not perfectly elastic, the rise in costs will result in a rise in price.

For the economy as a whole, wage costs are the largest fraction of total cost even though for many companies, the largest fraction of their own costs comes from the parts and materials that they buy from other companies. Recall that GNP is equal to the total value added at each stage of production. What is important to overall inflation is the fraction of value added that is labor cost. For the U.S. economy, that fraction is about 70 percent. And the remainder reflects the markup over labor costs that then becomes the return to capital.

productivity
A measure of output per unit of input.

Productivity growth allows prices to grow more slowly than wages. For instance, producers may face higher wages each year, but their labor costs will rise more slowly than wages if output per hour of work increases, that is, if productivity increases. As long as there is productivity growth in the economy, firms can pay for wage increases without raising prices. Since 1979, productivity has increased by about 1 percent a year.[6]

The Phillips curve and the trade-off.   The unemployment rate can be linked to the output ratio by recalling Okun's law. Lower output means higher unemployment. Wages are connected to prices because businesses would increase their prices by the amount of wage increases minus the increase in productivity. This means that higher rates of wage increase translate into higher rates of price inflation. Thus the Phillips curve, by connecting unemployment to inflation, was a precursor of the output–inflation trade-off.

The relation between the original Phillips curve and the output–inflation

---

[6] Productivity growth exceeded 3 percent per year from 1945 to 1973, but the rate of growth fell below 2 percent and stayed there after 1973. The growth of productivity is critically necessary in order for an economy to provide an improving real income over time. We will look at the determinants of productivity more closely in Chapters 17 and 18.

trade-off that was developed in the 1960s has had to be revised since then. First, even though labor costs are the largest component of cost for the economy as a whole, prices and labor costs do not always move together. When demand is strong, businesses do raise markups, so that price inflation will be greater than cost increases at high levels of the output ratio. When the output ratio is low, markups are compressed and price inflation is less than cost increases. The output–inflation trade-off reflects this tendency for markups to rise and fall with variations in demand.

Second, prices can move very differently from labor costs when there are shocks to the supply of nonlabor inputs. When world energy prices and agricultural prices rose sharply, this led to increases in the U.S. prices of these commodities, increases that were not linked to wage increases.

Shifts of the output–inflation trade-off

The concept of the output–inflation trade-off was introduced into U.S. policy-making discussion in the early 1960s.[7] Indeed, the behavior of the U.S. economy during much of the 1960s strongly supported the existence of the trade-off. As the output ratio increased, inflation gradually increased and there was almost a consensus among economists that policymakers could choose the combination of the output ratio and the level of inflation that was the best compromise and that they could use policy tools to reach that goal.

The consensus of support for the idea of a stable trade-off was short-lived however. Unfortunately for the well-being of the U.S. economy, the trade-off started to move around a good deal. During the 1970s there was both more inflation and more unemployment than had been the case earlier. A new description of economic discomfort entered the national vocabulary— the **misery index** (the sum of the unemployment and inflation rates), with the index rising to new heights in the 1970s. The experience of rising inflation and falling income that occurred in the 1970s was called **stagflation,** the combination of stagnating or falling income and high inflation.

The 1970s confirmed for many economists an idea that had been forming in the late 1960s—that the simple stable trade-off, as in Equation 9.1, was an incomplete description of the determination of inflation. The trade-off relation was shifting and the reasons had to be determined. Figure 9.5 shows how a shifting trade-off describes how the relationship between inflation and output changes over time.

For a particular short-run trade-off (SR–TO:1) the movement along the curve (point *A* to point *B*) shows the conventional pattern of rising inflation with rising output. The U.S. economy experienced such movements along the trade-off between 1963 and 1967. However, when the economy experiences increases of inflation with flat income, as occurred from 1967 to 1969, then

misery index
The sum of the unemployment rate and the rate of inflation. The misery index rises particularly during stagflation.

stagflation
A worsening of the output–inflation trade-off where the rate of inflation rises while there is a constant or reduced level of output.

---

[7] Paul A. Samuelson and Robert M. Solow, "Analytical Aspects of Anti-Inflation Policy," *American Economic Review* 50 (May 1960), pp. 177–94.

FIGURE 9.5   Shifts in the Short-Run Trade-off

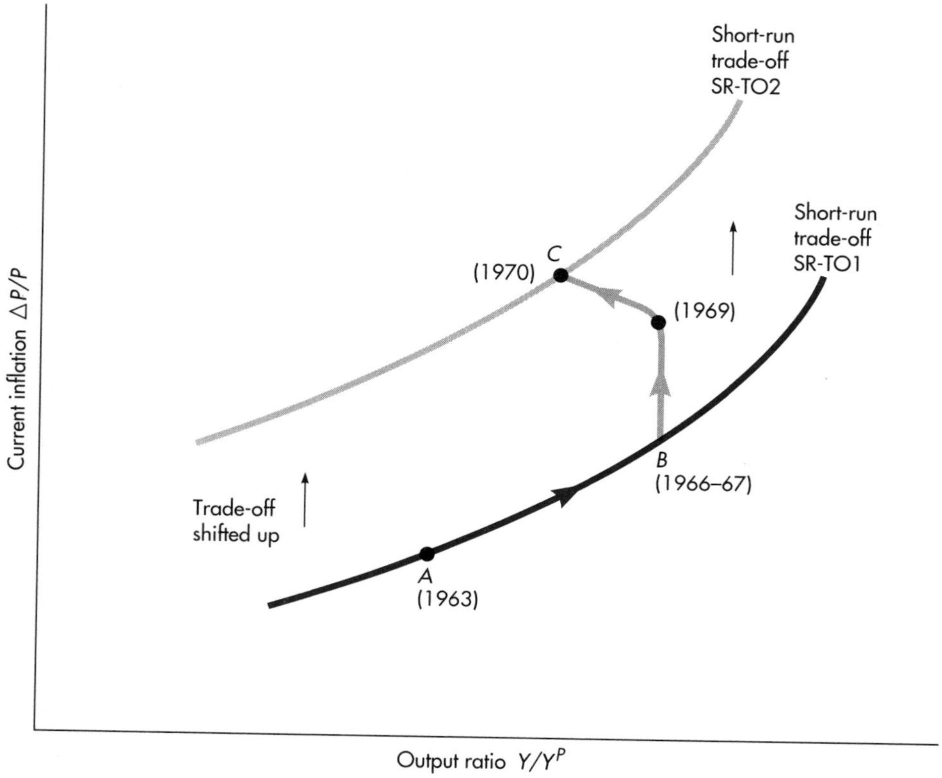

Movements along the short-run trade-off (such as A to B) involve modest increases in inflation. As the trade-off shifts, inflation can rise, even as output falls.

the trade-off is shifting up. This was even more apparent from 1969 to 1970, when inflation increased with a falling output ratio. We show in Figure 9.5 that the trade-off shifted from SR–TO:1 to SR–TO:2 (point B to point C).

The trade-off that we gave in Equation 9.1 was in fact a short-run trade-off. Over time, the trade-off itself may shift, so that inflation and output worsen together. There are two main explanations for such shifts: supply shocks and changes in inflationary expectations. Changes in inflationary expectations can explain the shifts because businesses set their prices based upon what managers think other prices are going to be in the future. This means that when there is an expectation of a higher rate of inflation, current inflation can accelerate even though the growth of input is slowing down or even when output is falling. In this chapter we look to inflationary expectations as an explanation of the shifts of the trade-off. Further discussion of how supply shocks shift the trade-off is postponed to the next chapter.

INFLATION, OUTPUT, AND EXPECTATIONS

The current rate of inflation depends upon what people think the rate of inflation will be as well as upon the current level of income or output in the economy. If the expected rate of inflation rises, the current rate of inflation will rise even if income is equal to 100 percent of potential. In fact, if inflationary expectations are rising rapidly, inflation may increase even when income is below potential. This is what is meant by saying that changes in expectations lead to shifts in the short-run trade-off.

For example, when labor unions bargain for wages increases, the size of the increases they demand depends upon how much inflation they expect over the course of the wage contract. The larger the expected rate of inflation, the greater the increase in revenues that will be expected by businesses, and so they will be willing to grant larger wage increases to union and nonunion workers alike. *As the expectation of inflation is built into actual wage contracts, this in turn raises costs and contributes to next year's actual inflation rate.* In addition, suppliers of materials have expectations about the amount of inflation that will occur over the duration of a contract to deliver goods over the coming year. The larger is the rate of inflation they expect, the higher is the price that they seek for deliveries. The rise in materials prices is then incorporated into the actual inflation in finished-goods prices.

The simple output–inflation trade-off shifts up or down depending upon whether expected inflation increases or decreases. An increase in inflationary expectations can raise the current rate of inflation even though there is no change in the output ratio. This formulation is shown in Equation 9.4:

$$\text{Current}\Delta P/P = H(Y/Y^P) + \text{Exp}\Delta P/P. \tag{9.4}$$

The current rate of inflation (Current$\Delta P/P$) is determined by the output ratio (Y/Y^P) and the expected rate of inflation (Exp$\Delta P/P$). As shown in Figure 9.6, increases in the expected rate of inflation lead to higher current rates of inflation for any given value of the output ratio. For example, at an output ratio of $(Y/Y^P)_A$ the rate of inflation will rise from the level at A to the level at A' and then to the level at A'', with successive increases in the expected rate of inflation. Similarly, if the output ratio is $(Y/Y^P)_B$, then inflation will be B, B', or B'', depending upon expected inflation. The short-run trade-off shifts up (first from SR–TO:1 to SR–TO:2 and then from SR–TO:2 to SR–TO:3) with each increase in the expected rate of inflation.

The trade-off between current output and current inflation is still a valid concept for the short run. If the expected rate of inflation can be taken as given in the short run, then the current rate of inflation depends upon the current output ratio; hence the short-run trade-off. But when people expect

Figure 9.6   Expected Inflation and the Trade-Off

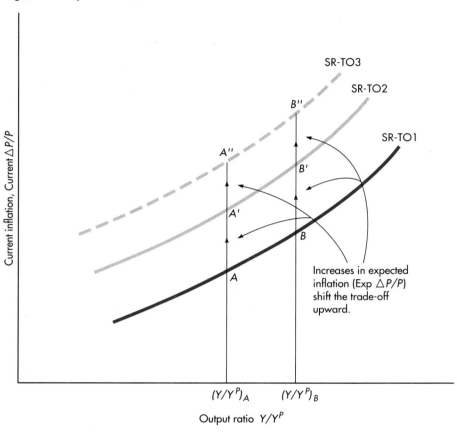

If expected inflation increases, the short-run trade-off shifts upward.

inflation to occur, there is no longer any guarantee that current inflation will be zero when the output ratio is 100 percent. U.S. inflation was in the range of 4 to 5 percent in early 1990 when output was equal to potential output.

WORKED EXAMPLE 9.1   Current Inflation Depends upon the Output Ratio and Expected Inflation

Consider the following relation for the determination of the current rate of inflation:

$$\text{Current}\Delta P/P = 0.2[(Y/Y^P) - 100] + \text{Exp}\Delta P/P.$$

Suppose the output ratio and the expected rate of inflation take on the following values over an 11-year period:

Year	Output ratio	Expected inflation
One	100	0.0
Two	104	0.0
Three	108	0.8
Four	108	2.4
Five	104	4.0
Six	100	4.8
Seven	96	4.8
Eight	92	4.0
Nine	92	2.4
Ten	96	0.8
Eleven	100	0.0

Question: (a) Evaluate the current rate of inflation for each of the 11 years.

(b) In what years did the economy experience output and inflation moving in opposite directions? Did it ever experience the opposite case?

(c) Comment on the relation between current and expected inflation in this economy. Are the values for expected inflation plausible?

Answer: The answer to part (a) is worked out as follows:

Year	Trade-off relation	Expected inflation	Current rate of inflation
One	0.2(100 − 100)	+ 0.0	= 0.0
Two	0.2(104 − 100)	+ 0.0	= 0.8
Three	0.2(108 − 100)	+ 0.8	= 2.4
Four	0.2(108 − 100)	+ 2.4	= 4.0
Five	0.2(104 − 100)	+ 4.0	= 4.8
Six	0.2(100 − 100)	+ 4.8	= 4.8
Seven	0.2(96 − 100)	+ 4.8	= 4.0
Eight	0.2(92 − 100)	+ 4.0	= 2.4
Nine	0.2(92 − 100)	+ 2.4	= 0.8
Ten	0.2(96 − 100)	+ 0.8	= 0.0
Eleven	0.2(100 − 100)	+ 0.0	= 0.0

The answer to part (b) is that output stayed the same from years three to four while inflation rose. Output actually fell from years four to five, while inflation rose. And output fell again from years five to six while inflation stayed the same. The years from three to six look pretty much like a perverse trade-off. The change from year four to year five certainly has output and inflation moving in opposite directions.

These were periods of stagflation, in that output stagnated or declined while inflation worsened.

The economy did experience the opposite case, where output grew but inflation declined or remained constant. This happened in years nine through eleven.

For part *(c)*, note that the numbers that are given for expected inflation in this example are actually the previous year's rate of inflation. In other words, the example used the following relation for expected inflation:

$\text{Exp}\Delta P/P$ = Actual inflation of the previous year.

Is this plausible? Expected inflation is probably not determined as mechanically as this. Expected inflation is based on the past experience of more than one previous year and may be based on other information too. In the text we discuss the ways in which expected inflation is determined.

The short-run trade-off still exists but it may provide a treacherous guide to policy over the longer run. If increases in inflation in the short run result in increases in expected inflation in the longer run, the rate of inflation may increase in future periods even if output drops back. The key question, therefore, is: What determines expected inflation?

Expectations Formed by the Past History of Inflation

If changes in inflationary expectations are an important reason why the U.S. economy suffered from stagflation, we need to know how expectations are formed and what causes them to change. Economists point to two primary determinants of inflationary expectations. The first is that expected inflation depends upon past inflation. People have **adaptive expectations,** where they revise their view of future inflation as a result of experience. The second is that expectations of inflation depend on a rational and future-oriented view of supply and demand conditions in the economy. In practice, both of these factors are important, but in our judgment the actual experience of past inflation is the more important.

adaptive expectations
Where the expected rate of inflation is revised each period as a result of the experience of actual inflation.

If inflation was high in the past, the expected rate of inflation will also be high. People expect an established inflation to continue. Most economists who argue for this view of the way expectations are determined believe that it is inflation experienced in the economy over an extended period that is important. Increases or decreases in inflation that are temporary have a small effect on the expected rate. For example, if the rate of inflation has been running at about 6 percent a year for some time and then it drops to 4 percent, the expected rate of inflation stays fairly close to 6 percent. If the current rate of inflation then stays down at 4 percent for several more periods, the expected rate gradually comes down also.

An important variation on this idea is that past inflation gets into expectations and hence into current inflation through a catch-up process. For example, if after a labor contract is negotiated inflation turns out to be higher than was expected, then workers will ask for larger wage increases to make up for the unexpected loss of buying power.

Past inflation and shifts in the trade-off

If inflationary expectations are formed from the prior history of the inflation rate, or if workers and firms try to catch up with past inflation, then the expected rate of inflation becomes a *built-in rate of inflation*. This means that a certain rate of inflation gets built into the economy and can only be removed by sustained changes in output. A built-in rate of inflation alters the implications of the output–inflation trade-off.

When we first developed the idea of a trade-off, the analysis suggested that inflation would cease as soon as output was below potential output. Once we take account of expected inflation, this is no longer the case. Inflation will be reduced by lowering output, but in the short run a level of output that is below potential output is not sufficient to overcome the effects of high expected inflation. For example, if inflation had been averaging 10 percent per year for 10 years, businesses and workers would use 10 percent as a benchmark rate of increase for contracts for the next year's products. Actual inflation in the eleventh year would be somewhat higher or lower than 10 percent, depending upon whether output was above or below potential output.

According to this view of inflation, the reason that the problem of stagflation appears is that when output is held above potential output for some time, the resulting acceleration of current inflation is then gradually incorporated into increases in expected inflation. Then higher expected inflation continues to drive up current rates of inflation, even after output growth stalls.

Short-run and intermediate-run trade-offs.   The intermediate run is a period of roughly two to eight years and is a crucial period for policymaking. What happens over this time horizon will determine the success or failure of a policy in the political arena. We can define an **intermediate-run trade-off** between output and inflation that is very important for this policymaking time horizon. First, take a fixed time period of two or more years. Then if the output ratio is increased to some point and held at the new higher level for the fixed period of time, the intermediate-run trade-off gives the increase in inflation over this period.

We illustrate the intermediate-run trade-off in Figure 9.7. The economy is initially represented (point A) with an output ratio of $(Y/Y^P)_A$ and current inflation of $(\text{Current}\Delta P/P)_A$. The output ratio is then increased to $(Y/Y^P)_B$ and held for a period of years at this higher level. Over the time period, the increase in current inflation leads to an increase in expected inflation and the short-run trade-off rises from SR–TO:1 to SR–TO:2. By the end of the intermediate-run time period, the current rate of inflation has reached

intermediate-run trade-off
The increase in inflation that occurs when the output ratio increases by a given amount for a given period of years.

FIGURE 9.7   The Intermediate-Run Trade-off

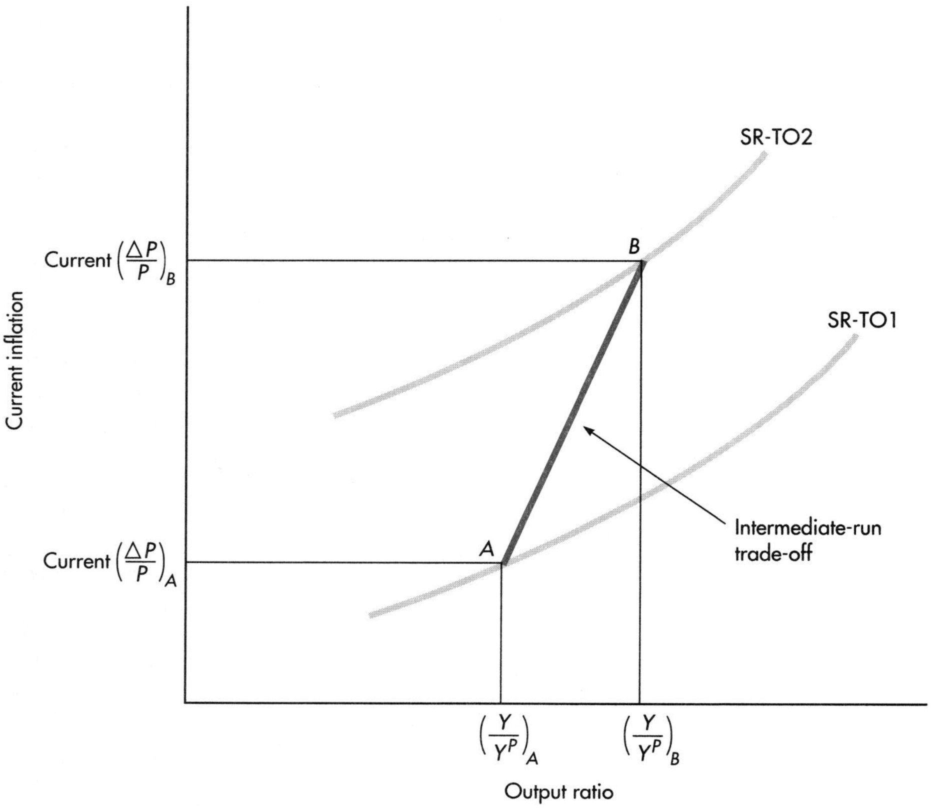

The intermediate-run trade-off is steeper than the short-run trade-off.

(Current$\Delta P/P)_B$ and the economy is at point B. The segment AB then gives the intermediate-run trade-off for the given increase in output and the given time period.

The intermediate-run trade-off will be steeper than the short-run trade-off. The economy faces very different options when policy choices are being made over a somewhat longer time horizon. An increase in output above potential results in a larger increase in the current rate of inflation in the intermediate run than it does in the short run because expectations catch up with experience.

The vertical long-run trade-off.   The preceding discussion understates the severity of the long-run inflation problem that results from holding output above

long-run trade-off
The change in the rate of inflation associated with a change in the output ratio that takes place over a period of time long enough for goods-market and labor-market expectations of inflation to completely catch up with the current rate of inflation.

potential output. Given enough time for the economy to adjust, there is a vertical **long-run trade-off,** meaning that as long as output remains above potential output (as long as Y/Y^P is greater than 100 percent), there will be inflationary pressure in the economy and the acceleration of inflation will continue. We defined potential output as the level of output produced by the economy at the point where the effect of excess supply in some markets balances off the effect of excess demand in others. At that point, there would be an adjustment of relative prices in the economy, but no net inflationary pressure from aggregate demand. But this means, of course, that whenever output is above potential, there is inflationary pressure, while whenever output is below potential, there is deflationary pressure.

This argument has important implications. It means that the very long-run trade-off is vertical, that is to say, *there is no trade-off between output and inflation in the very long run.* There is still a short-run trade-off in this case, but if output remains above potential output, the rate of inflation keeps on rising as shown in Figure 9.8. In the figure, the combinations of output and inflation that are sustainable in the long run lie on the same vertical line. In this case *only one level of output is consistent with a stable rate of inflation: where output is equal to potential output.* Any sustained increase in aggregate demand that raises output above potential output will generate increases in inflation that are modest in the short run. This is shown in the figure by the movement from point A to B along a short-run trade-off (SR–TO:1). A sustained increase in aggregate demand will result in continuing acceleration of inflation, with ever-increasing inflation in the very long run (points B' and C). *Potential output is the highest level of output that can be reached without generating rising inflation in the very long run.*

The process works in reverse for levels of output below potential output. If the economy starts at point D, and there is then a recession that reduces the output ratio, this will initially reduce inflation by only a small amount (point D to point D'). But at D', the current rate of inflation is below the expected rate of inflation and so the expected rate starts to decline. The short-run trade-off starts to shift down. In the long-run, with the same level of output, the economy moves from point D' to E to F.

WORKED EXAMPLE 9.2   The Trade-Off in the Short Run, the Intermediate Run, and the Long Run

Consider the following relation for the determination of the current rate of inflation:

$$\text{Current}\Delta P/P = 0.2[(Y/Y^P) - 100] + \text{Exp}\Delta P/P$$
$$\text{Exp}\Delta P/P = 0.5(\Delta P/P \text{ of previous year}) + 0.5(\Delta P/P \text{ of two years prior}).$$

Suppose that output in this economy has been equal to potential output and the rate of inflation has been 5 percent a year for several years. Then output increases to 105 percent of potential and stays there.

FIGURE 9.8   The Vertical Long-Run Trade-off

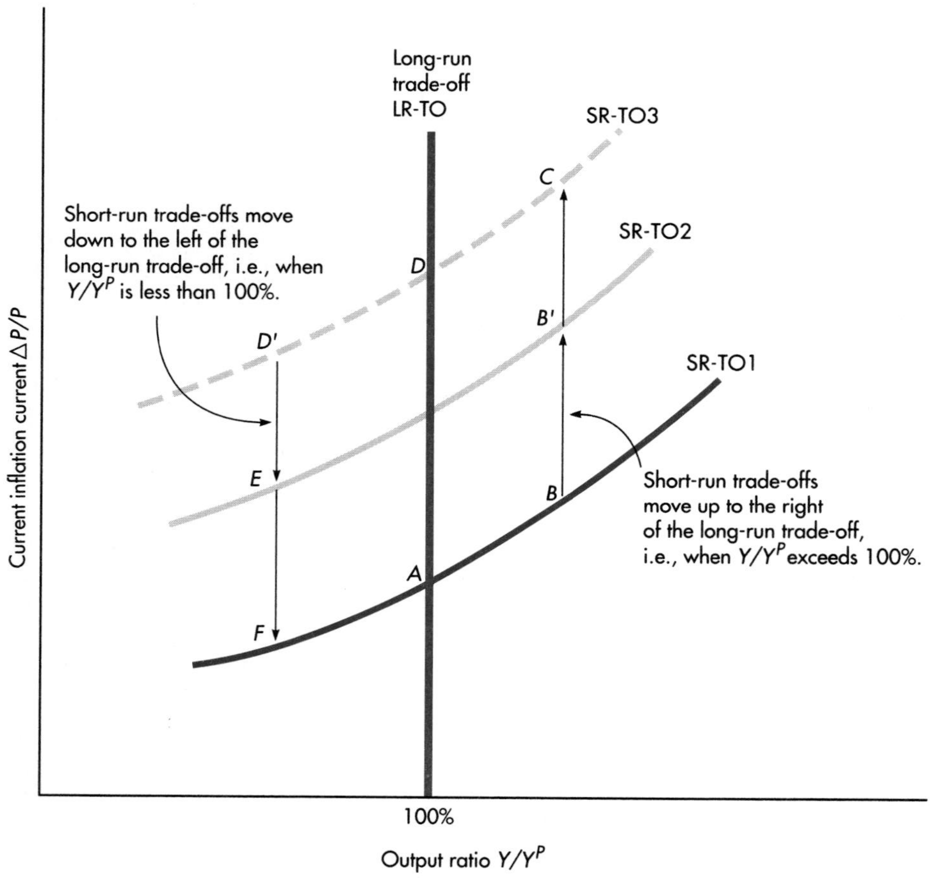

Current inflation current $\Delta P/P$

Long-run trade-off LR-TO

SR-TO3

SR-TO2

SR-TO1

Short-run trade-offs move down to the left of the long-run trade-off, i.e., when Y/Y^P is less than 100%.

Short-run trade-offs move up to the right of the long-run trade-off, i.e., when Y/Y^P exceeds 100%.

C

D

B'

D'

E

B

A

F

100%

Output ratio Y/Y^P

There is no trade-off in the very long run. When output remains above potential output, inflation accelerates.

Question: (a) How does inflation evolve in this economy?
(b) What is the slope of the short-run trade-off?
(c) What is the slope of the two-year trade-off?
(d) What is the slope of the eight-year trade-off?
(e) What is the slope of the long-run trade-off?

Answer: (a) The rates of inflation that evolve in this economy are shown as follows over eight years:

Year	Trade-off relation	Expected inflation	Current rate of inflation
One	0.2(105 − 100)	+ (0.5 × 5.00) + (0.5 × 5.00)	= 6.00
Two	0.2(105 − 100)	+ (0.5 × 6.00) + (0.5 × 5.00)	= 6.50
Three	0.2(105 − 100)	+ (0.5 × 6.50) + (0.5 × 6.00)	= 7.25
Four	0.2(105 − 100)	+ (0.5 × 7.25) + (0.5 × 6.50)	= 7.88
Five	0.2(105 − 100)	+ (0.5 × 7.88) + (0.5 × 7.25)	= 8.56
Six	0.2(105 − 100)	+ (0.5 × 8.56) + (0.5 × 7.88)	= 9.22
Seven	0.2(105 − 100)	+ (0.5 × 9.22) + (0.5 × 8.56)	= 9.89
Eight	0.2(105 − 100)	+ (0.5 × 9.89) + (0.5 × 9.22)	= 10.55

The rates of inflation have been rounded. The calculations were made without rounding, so there will be small discrepancies if you check through the figures. We see that inflation gets gradually larger over time with a sustained increase in output.

(b) The short-run trade-off gives the relation between output and inflation within the same year, taking the expected rate of inflation as given. The calculations just given indicate that the 5–percentage-point increase in output has raised inflation by 1 percentage point. The slope of the short-run trade-off is $1 \div 5 = 0.2$.

(c) The two-year trade-off looks at the effect after two years of a change in the level of output that is sustained over the two-year period. The preceding calculations indicate that inflation has risen by 1.5 percentage points after two years (6.5 − 5). Thus the slope of the two-year trade-off is $1.5 \div 5 = 0.3$. This is steeper than the short-run trade-off.

(d) The eight-year trade-off looks at the effect after eight years of a change in the level of output that is sustained over the eight-year period. The preceding calculations indicate that inflation has risen by 5.55 percentage points after eight years (10.55 − 5). Thus the slope of the eight-year trade-off is $5.55 \div 5 = 1.11$. We see that the slopes of the intermediate-run trade-offs are getting steeper as the time period increases.

(e) The long-run trade-off has a vertical slope. Inflation will continue to accelerate as long as output remains above potential output. Another way of understanding this is to see that the only way in which current inflation can equal expected inflation is if the output ratio equals 100.

The intuitive logic behind the idea of a vertical long-run trade-off was put forward by Edmund Phelps and Milton Friedman in the late 1960s.[8] Consider two economies that are the same in every way, except that in one the rate of inflation is 10 percent a year, and in the other it is 3 percent a year. The people in the high-inflation economy have all become thoroughly used to the 10 percent rate. Why would the high-inflation economy have higher output? Does that make sense? Phelps and Friedman say no. Workers

[8] Edmund S. Phelps, "Phillips Curves, Expectations of Inflation and Optimal Unemployment over Time," *Economica* 34 (August 1967), pp. 254–81; Milton Friedman, "The Role of Monetary Policy," *American Economic Review* 58 (March 1968), pp. 1–17.

will have the same inflation-adjusted wages in the two economies and will work as long and as hard in the 10-percent–inflation economy as they do in the 3-percent–inflation economy. Producers will add 10 percent per year to their prices and consumers, having earned 10 percent more per year in dollars, will be buying the same real value of goods and services as their counterparts in the 3-percent inflation economy. The real factors determining supply and demand will be the same in the two economies and so the level of output will be the same.[9]

The idea that the rate of inflation will keep getting larger if output is held above some critical point is plausible to most economists. In this sense, the Phelps-Friedman hypothesis of a vertical long-run Phillips curve has won broad acceptance.[10] As we discuss policies toward inflation, we will assume that there is a vertical trade-off in the long run—that is, no effective trade-off in the long run. However, this does not eliminate the need to look at the impact of aggregate demand policies on inflation and output in the short and intermediate runs. Policy is seldom pursued with an eye to the very long run, and conditions never remain unchanged between the time a policy action is initiated and the time its long-run consequence appears.

Expectations Formed by Rational Forecasts of Inflation

The alternative view of inflationary expectations argues that they are formed by people's forecasts of the behavior of the economy. Past inflation may be used as an important guide to the future course of inflation, so that, in practice, expectations may look as if they are based only on past inflation. But if there is some valid reason why inflation is likely to increase in the future, then expected inflation will increase also and will be different from past inflation. For example, if the Fed is expected to increase the rate of growth of the money supply, then people may expect this to increase aggregate demand and raise prices in the future. This will increase the expected rate of inflation and this forecast of future inflation can increase current inflation even before there is any change in current income.

In this view, stagflation can come about as follows: When the Fed attempts to fight inflation by reducing the growth rate of the money supply, people do not believe that the Fed will stick to its guns—they think that the monetary

---

[9] There is a complication that we are ignoring. With a high rate of inflation, the real return to money is large and negative. To the extent that money is substitutable for real assets, this will reduce the real money stock in the high-inflation economy.

[10] Many economists remain skeptical of the implications of the hypothesis when output is below potential output. If output were sustained at, say, 98 percent of potential, the hypothesis says that this should first cause inflation to decline. Then price decreases will commence; and finally prices will start declining faster and faster. The idea of accelerating deflation seems implausible. However, Milton Friedman does not accept the Phillips-curve framework in the form it has been presented in this chapter. He believes that an economy has a strong tendency to return to the natural rate of unemployment. The thought experiment of holding output at 98 percent of full-employment output is not one he would find valid.

contraction will be quickly reversed. Stagflation occurs because people expect aggregate demand to continue to expand and thus they expect the inflation rate to continue to climb even though current monetary policy is restrictive. Monetary policy previously had been expansionary for several years, so that when tighter monetary policy is introduced, people believe that the Fed will quickly give up its anti-inflationary policy and re-inflate the economy.

In principle this view makes sense. We have already seen in Chapter 8 that financial markets reflect people's expectations about monetary policy and that this can affect the economy. The problem with applying the rational-forecast model to the trade-off is that in practice it has not been found that the direct response of wages and prices to policy changes has been very large. Prices and wages are set in markets that are rather different from financial markets. Typical unions, businesses, employees, or customers do not adjust their wages and prices all that much in response to what they think the Fed will do.

Given this, we will continue to assume that the expected rate of inflation that affects the current rate of inflation in labor markets and goods markets is based on the past history of inflation. At the end of this chapter and in Chapter 16 we will look further into the rational-expectations view.

INFLATION, MONETARY POLICY, AND AGGREGATE EQUILIBRIUM

The *IS-ALM* framework is used to describe the role of aggregate demand in determining equilibrium. By combining aggregate demand (from *IS-ALM*) with aggregate supply (represented by the output–inflation trade-off), we now have a model of the macroeconomy where inflation is determined along with output and income. Inflation is determined within the economy along with other economic factors. Policy actions that change economic conditions also change the rate of inflation. In the remainder of this chapter we look at the nature of the full supply-and-demand equilibrium and at the linkage between policy actions and their impact on rates of inflation.

The Trade-Off and the *IS-ALM* Framework Combined

When the *IS-ALM* analysis of aggregate demand is combined with the trade-off analysis of aggregate supply, the resulting framework describes how aggregate supply and demand simultaneously determine the level of output, interest rates, and the current rate of inflation in the economy. The left-hand part of Figure 9.9 shows the *IS-ALM* diagram as we used it in Chapter 8, showing the combinations of output and long-run real rates of interest that are consistent with equilibrium. In this example, the economy is in *IS-ALM* equilibrium (point *A*) at a point where income and output are equal to potential output. This means that the *IS-ALM* equilibrium in this economy occurs where the output ratio is 100 percent. We use, as an example, a 6-percent real long-run rate of interest that corresponds to this level of income.

The fact that the economy is in long-run equilibrium also has implications for the maturity premium and hence for the short-run nominal rate of interest. In long-run equilibrium, with a given expected rate of inflation and no change in expected future interest rates, there should be a normally sloped yield curve, one that is neither inverted nor abnormally steep. We will assume a maturity premium of 5 percent, and since the expected rate of inflation is 4 percent, the interest-rate gap is 1 percent:

$$r_{gap} = MP - Exp\Delta P/P$$
$$= 5\% - 4\% = 1\%.$$

Since we are depicting an economy in full equilibrium, the demand for money must equal the supply of money at the short-run nominal interest rate that is consistent with this interest-rate gap:

$$i = r - r_{gap}$$
$$= 6\% - 1\% = 5\%.$$

The short-term nominal rate of interest is 5 percent. The money market must be in equilibrium with output equal to potential output and a 5 percent rate of interest on T bills.

In addition, if the economy is at a point of long-run equilibrium, the Fed must be accommodating the inflation, reflected in an *LM* schedule that remains stable. In this example, this means that the rate of growth of the money supply equals 4 percent per year and the real money supply remains constant.[11]

The short-run and long-run trade-offs are drawn on the right-hand side of Figure 9.9. The economy is shown to be in equilibrium (points *A* in both the left and right panels of the figure) with a rate of inflation of 4 percent. The rate of inflation is not changing because the current rate of inflation equals the expected rate of inflation. At this initial long-run equilibrium, the short-run curve (SR–TO) and the long-run vertical trade-off (LR–TO) intersect.

A 4 percent rate of inflation is expected in both financial markets and goods markets. With a maturity premium of 5 percent and a short-run nominal rate of interest of 5 percent, the long-run nominal rate

$$i(long, nominal) = i + MP$$
$$10\% = 5\% + 5\%$$

is 10 percent. This squares with a long-term real rate of interest of 6 percent and an expected rate of inflation of 4 percent. The model is in long-run equilibrium with expected inflation in both markets that is consistent with actual inflation.

---

[11] This discussion assumes a given constant level of potential output. If we allowed for gradual increases in potential output, then long-run equilibrium would require growing income and the real money supply would have to grow in order to accommodate the increase in the volume of transactions.

FIGURE 9.9   Output and Inflation Determined Together: Long-Run Equilibrium

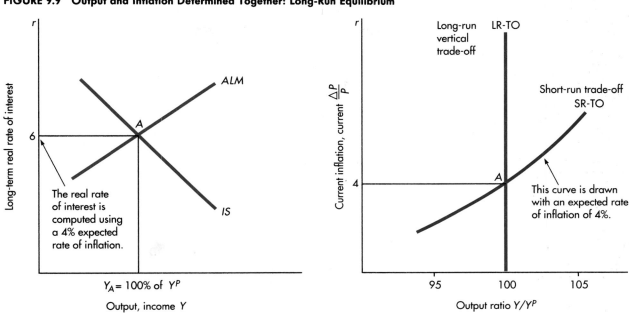

Bringing *IS-ALM* and the inflation trade-off together shows how output, inflation, and interest rates are determined. The case shown is one of long-run equilibrium.

We have now described an economy in full aggregate supply and demand equilibrium. The *IS-ALM* relations describe the demand equilibrium, with money-market and financial-market equilibrium in the background. The output–inflation trade-offs give aggregate supply equilibrium, with long-run equilibrium occurring where the trade-offs intersect.

In the equilibrium we have described, *there is only one level of output that lies on the long-run–trade-off schedule.* Output must equal potential output if the economy is to be in long-run equilibrium. By contrast, we chose the rate of inflation arbitrarily. *Provided the Fed is willing to accommodate the current rate of inflation, whatever it is, full equilibrium can occur at many different rates of inflation.* This contrast between output and inflation in the long run seems to correspond to what we see in long-run historical data for the U.S. economy. We find that output does tend to fluctuate around potential output, but that inflation has been rather different in different time periods.

Of course, the fact that many rates of inflation have occurred does indicate that the Fed has been willing to accommodate these different rates of inflation. If the Fed had behaved differently, we could turn the model around and say that the only rate of inflation consistent with long-run equilibrium is where inflation equals the rate of nominal-money-supply growth. But if the Fed had insisted on, say, zero inflation, then in our judgment, the economy would have spent long periods out of equilibrium with high unemployment.

Differing expectations in goods markets and financial markets

Connecting aggregate demand with aggregate supply through *IS-ALM* and the trade-off leaves unresolved an important question about expectations that was only mentioned in the beginning of this chapter. Is the expected rate of inflation in financial markets the same as the expected rate of inflation in the output-inflation trade-off? In the analysis of financial markets, the expected rate of inflation was used to derive the long-term real rate of interest. That expected rate of inflation is the one that financial investors expect to occur in the future years during which long-term bonds pay interest. This expected rate of inflation may not be the same as the expected rate of inflation that occurs in goods and labor markets that is used in the trade-off relation.

Expectations are likely to be the same in all markets in the long run in an economy with a stable entrenched inflation rate. Expectations are less likely to be the same in the short run as markets adapt at different rates to changes in aggregate supply and/or demand. In Figure 9.9, the trade-off diagram indicates that point *A*, where the rate of inflation is 4 percent, is a point of long-run as well as short-run equilibrium. This means that the current rate of inflation is the same as the expected rate of inflation, and the expected rate of inflation is 4 percent in all markets.

The fact that we used an example in which there is consistency of inflationary expectations in goods markets and financial markets assures us that the *IS-ALM* and the trade-off analyses can fit together consistently. It made sense to assure consistency when we were looking at a position of very long-run equilibrium. If the economy has an entrenched rate of inflation of 4 percent, then this rate will be incorporated both into decisions about wages and prices and into decisions about interest rates.

The presence or absence of consistency within models of the economy has become a major issue among macroeconomists in recent years. Rational-expectations economists have criticized what they see as inconsistencies in the way in which expectations are treated in traditional models of the economy. These criticisms are not always valid, however. During periods of adjustment in the economy, there is no compelling reason to believe that the expected rate of inflation used to set wages and prices is the same as the one that enters the real-interest-rate calculations made by participants in the financial capital market. The corporate managers making decisions about hiring workers and the people who are deciding whether to accept jobs are not influenced in the same way by the same information as those making decisions to buy or sell financial assets. The expected-inflation term in the trade-off relation reflects the inertia created by wage and price contracts, not just pure forward-looking expectations. Moreover, traders in bill and bond markets are generally much more concerned with guessing the Fed's next move than are workers and employers around the country who may not even know or care much about the latest wrinkle of monetary policy. As we look at short-run adjustments, we will not always expect the same consistency we would look for in a very long-run equilibrium.

The Trade-Off and Monetary Policy

When we first looked at monetary policy we made reference to a dilemma facing the Fed. If there is any trade-off between output and inflation, even if it is temporary, the Fed may have to choose between an expansionary monetary policy, which increases output and employment but leads to higher inflation, and contractionary policies, which reduce inflation at the expense of reductions in income and employment. This dilemma is posed even more starkly when there is no trade-off in the long run. Expansionary monetary policy that moves income above potential output not only generates a higher rate of inflation in the short run, it also sparks a longer-run acceleration of inflation. In the short and intermediate runs, the Fed's choice is about the trade-off between income and inflation. In the very long run, the Fed's choice is only about the level of inflation in the economy and not about the level of output.

Fighting inflation with monetary policy

Monetary policy is often employed to cut a rate of inflation considered to be too high by the Fed. This was the case in the early 1980s when the Fed acted to undo the legacy of inflation of the late 1960s and the 1970s and stop the acceleration of inflation that was taking place in the early 1980s. Table 9.1 shows inflation, the output ratio, and the growth rate of the real stock of money for the U.S. economy for the years 1979–84. There are two measures of inflation shown: the rate of growth of the Consumer Price Index (the CPI) and the GNP deflator. The CPI is an important indicator of how inflation is affecting consumers and it is used in wage contracts and to index various government programs. It shows the 1979–81 explosion of inflation. The CPI is rather volatile, reflecting the gyrations of food and energy prices over this period. Indeed, because of defects in the way it was computed at that time (defects since corrected), it exaggerated inflation over the period. The next column of Table 9.1 shows the growth rate of the GNP deflator as an alternative measure. It is less volatile, but it still reveals the seriousness of the inflation problem at the time.

According to the table, inflation fell to about 4 percent by 1984 and monetary contraction played a major role in this reduction in inflation. Since in the actual economy, potential output grows each year, the real money stock has to grow also to accommodate the increased demand for transactions. Over the years 1979–81, the real money stock fell rather than rising. This put tremendous pressure on financial markets. The output ratio, shown in

TABLE 9.1   Inflation, the Rate of Change of the Real Stock of Money, and the Output Ratio, 1979–1984

Year	Current inflation percent per year		Rate of change of real money stock		Output ratio
	CPI	GNP Deflator[a]	$\frac{M1}{P}$	$\frac{M2}{P}$	
1979	14.3	8.5	−1.2	−0.8	100.2
1980	17.8	9.3	−2.1	−0.2	97.5
1981	12.1	9.3	−2.9	0.2	96.9
1982	4.1	6.2	2.0	2.3	92.0
1983	2.3	4.1	5.5	7.7	92.9
1984	4.5	4.0	2.0	4.4	96.6

[a] The figures given are for the fixed-weight GNP price index. This adjusts the GNP deflator for changes in the composition of output.
Source: *Economic Report of the President 1990.*

the last column in the table, fell from about 100 percent in 1979 to 92 in 1982. Notice two important facts, however. First, the fall in the real money supply came about because the Fed refused to accommodate the inflation, even though the nominal money stocks rose in every year. And second, there is a lag between the reduction of the money supply and the decline of the economy. The rates of increase or decrease in the money stocks are December-to-December values. That means, for example, that the real stock of M1 was 2.9 percent lower in December 1981 than it had been in December 1980. The economy had started to go into a recession in 1981, and then unemployment peaked in 1982 at 10.7 percent of the labor force in the fourth quarter of that year.

In 1978–79 the Fed initiated a gradual approach to fighting inflation. The real supply of money fell and there were credit controls enacted for a while in 1980 to induce some rationing of credit. The economy went into a very short recession in 1980, but then monetary policy was eased a little and the credit controls were relaxed. The economy actually started to recover again in late 1980. Inflation had jumped sharply in 1979; it rose again in 1980 and remained very high in 1981. The Fed decided it was not going to accommodate this inflation and it was prepared to accept the consequences of the cumulative decline in the real money stock from 1979 to 1981.

Events in the actual economy over this period were complex, reflecting the effects of supply shocks, fiscal-policy changes, and changes in the international sector as well as the monetary-policy changes that are our focus now. In particular, energy and food prices were rising sharply and driving up inflation through 1980. Then these prices fell back again. We will abstract

FIGURE 9.10   Short-Run Effects of a Sharp Monetary Contraction

Left panel — vertical axis: Long-term real interest rate; horizontal axis: Output, income Y. Curves labeled ALM', ALM, IS. Annotation: "Sharp monetary contraction, shifts ALM." Points A' at 11, A at 4.5. Horizontal axis marks: $Y_{A'} = 92\%$ of Y^P, $Y_A = 99\%$ of Y^P.

Right panel — vertical axis: Current rate of inflation $\Delta P/P$ (with r); horizontal axis: Output ratio Y/Y^P. Curves labeled LR-TO, SR-TO:A, SR-TO:A'. Points A at 9.8, A' at 5.9. Annotations: "At first, there is only a small change in the short-run trade-off." and "Contraction induces recession." Horizontal axis marks: 92, 99 100.

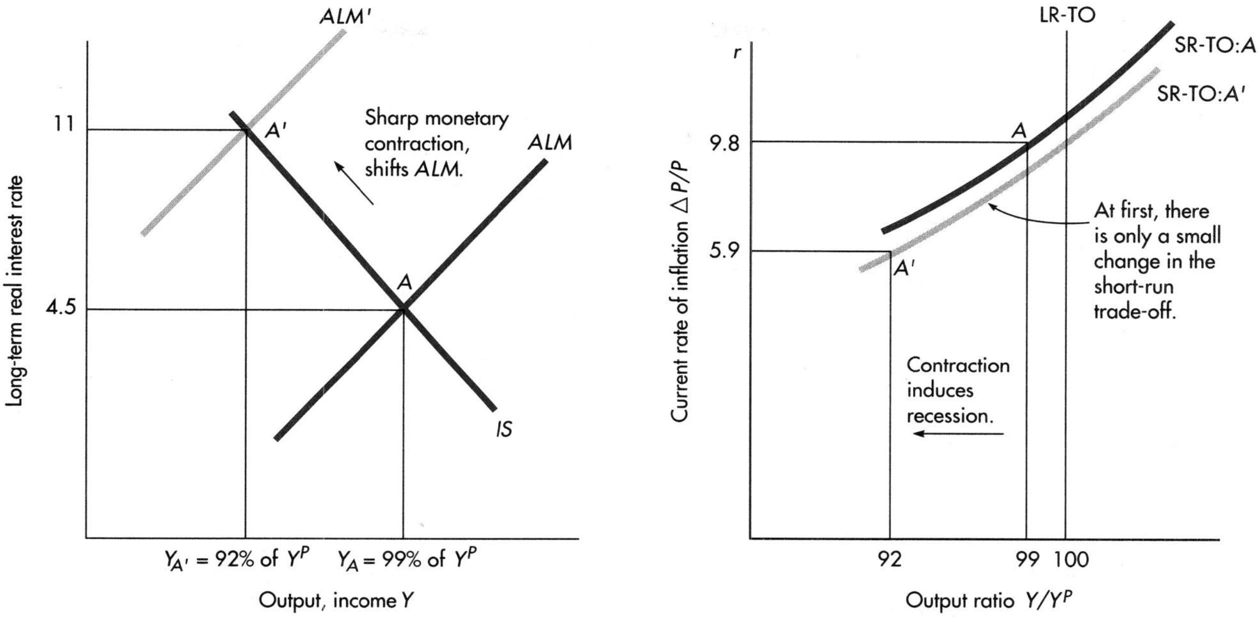

Inflation is reduced, but at the expense of very high unemployment.

from these supply shocks for the time being. In Figure 9.10 we look at a simplified analysis of the results of a monetary contraction.

Roughly in line with conditions that existed in the U.S. economy in 1979–80, the economy in its initial situation is shown in Figure 9.10 as having a very high expected rate of inflation (8 percent both for the trade-off and for financial markets), reflecting the fact that there had been high inflation in the past and that the Fed was not expected to act dramatically to reduce inflation. We will assume an initial output ratio of 99 percent, so that the current rate of inflation was slightly below expected inflation. (It is shown as 9.8 percent.) These initial conditions are reflected in points *A* in both panels of Figure 9.10.

We assume now that the Fed has a policy goal of reaching a new long-run equilibrium in which output is equal to potential output and the rate of inflation is going to be reduced from 9.8 percent to 4 percent. The policy goal used in this example is approximately in line with the actual economic policies that were followed. Since the Fed wants to take a major step toward reducing inflation quickly, it sets a rate of growth of the money supply well below the current rate of inflation—the rate of growth of the real money supply is negative.

The drop in the real money supply increased short-term rates and was accompanied by a decline of expected inflation in financial markets (we assume a fall from 8 percent to 6 percent). This raised the real rate of interest (we assume from 4.5 percent to 11 percent) and reduced output (point A to point A'). This is shown as a large shift in the ALM schedule *(ALM to ALM')* and a plunge of output to 92 percent of potential.

In the right-hand panel of Figure 9.10, the output ratio at point A was already slightly to the left of the long-run trade-off (LR–TO), the economy having moved a short distance along the short-run trade-off (SR–TO:A). In the following year, there is then a small downward shift of the short-run trade-off (SR–TO:A to SR–TO:A'), a shift that occurred because inflationary expectations in the goods and labor markets dropped by a modest amount (we assume from 8 percent to 7.5 percent; values not shown in the figure). The fall in expected inflation here is assumed to be less than the fall that occurs in financial markets. The reduction of current inflation to 5.9 percent then comes from the combination of the movement along the short-run trade-off and the downward shift of the trade-off (point A along SR–TO:A to point A' along SR–TO:A').

This was a quick and substantial reduction of inflation, but it was achieved with a very large drop in output. Unfortunately, because of the sluggish response of wages and prices and the inertia built into expected inflation, this very large reduction in output only drove down inflation part way toward the long-run target.

In financial markets, the impact of the reduction of the real supply of money pushed up short-term nominal rates by much more than the increase in the long-term nominal rate on Treasury bonds. The yield curve was flattened and credit conditions were tightened. The interest-rate gap does fall, but as bond traders decided that the Fed was serious about restraining money growth, the drop in inflationary expectations and the increase in the risk premium added to the mild rise in long-term nominal rates and caused a substantial rise in the long-term real rate. The ALM schedule shifted up from ALM to ALM'. Table 9.2 summarizes the effects of the monetary contraction under the columns headed point A and point A' (the columns headed Point B and Point C refer to Figure 9.11).

Over the next few years output grew faster than potential output (the output ratio was increasing), but the level of output remained below potential (the ratio remained below 100). The economy was operating to the left of the long-run trade-off line, so that expected inflation in the goods market and the short-run trade-off both fell. Current inflation was gradually reduced to the 4 percent range. Figure 9.11 depicts the adjustment. The Fed gradually eased monetary policy, allowing the economy to grow. This is shown by the down shifts of the ALM schedule, from ALM' to ALM" to ALM'". The short-run trade-off was also shifting down, from SR–TO:A' to SR–TO:B to

TABLE 9.2   Fighting Inflation with Monetary Policy

	Point A	Point A'	Point B	Point C
Output ratio:	99	92	94	100
Short-term nominal rate:	10%	14%	11%	5%
Long-term nominal rate:	12.5%	17%	13%	8%
Current inflation:	7.8%	5.9%	4.8%	4%
Expected inflation: (financial markets)	8%	6%	4%	4%
Long-term real rate:	4.5%	11%	9%	4%
Interest-rate gap:	−5.5%	−3%	−2.5%	−1%
Expected inflation: (trade-off/goods market)	8%	7.5%	6%	4%

SR–TO:C, so that inflation was falling even though output and the output ratio were rising. The economy is depicted in mid-adjustment at Point B and then at Point C, where it has reached a new long-run equilibrium, where the current rate of inflation and the expected rates of inflation in both financial markets and goods markets were 4 percent.

The Fed pursued a contractionary nonaccommodating policy and the economy suffered through a period of tight money, high real interest rates, and falling aggregate demand. This is the classic "credit-crunch" scenario of an economy entering a slowing or a recession because of financial-market constraints initiated by the Federal Reserve. This drove the economy into a deep recession and a prolonged period where output was below potential output. The Fed reduced inflation by engineering a severe recession and then re-expanded the real money supply in order to sustain a moderate recovery.

If, after 1979, the Fed had continued to pursue a gradualist strategy for reducing inflation by keeping output below potential output but not far below it, the time it would have taken to combat inflation would have been longer. On the other hand, the severe economic distress and bankruptcies of 1982 and 1983 might have been avoided. Although we have not talked here about instability, the choice between a short, sharp recession and a long, mild recession may be made in practice on the basis of concerns about unstable economic changes. Some members of the Board of Governors of the Fed considered the histories of extremely rapid inflations such as those in Europe in the 1920s and in Argentina, Brazil, and Israel in recent times, and they worried about a repetition of these in the United States in the 1980s. If the Fed believes that a high rate of inflation is not stable, then a sharp reduction in money growth is indicated. This concern about inflation rising out of control influ-

FIGURE 9.11   The Economy Returns to Full Employment with Moderate Inflation

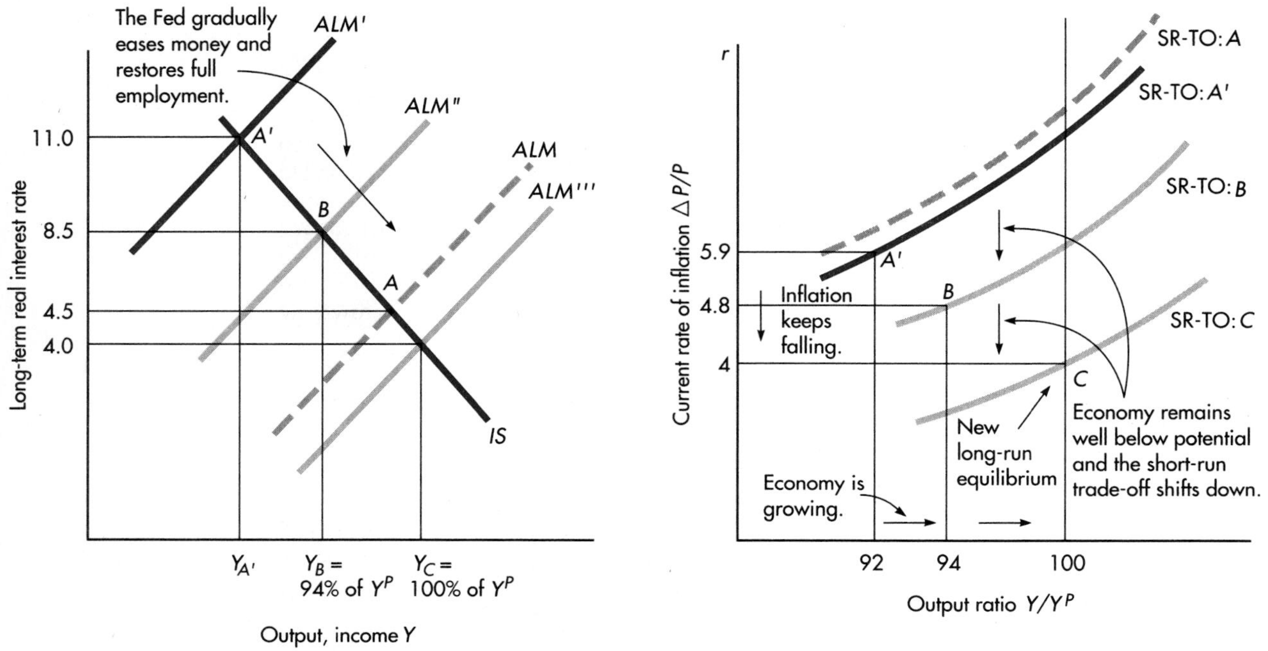

The Fed gradually eases money and restores full employment.

Left panel: Long-term real interest rate (vertical axis) versus Output, income Y (horizontal axis). Curves labeled ALM′, ALM″, ALM, ALM‴, IS. Interest rate values: 11.0, 8.5, 4.5, 4.0. Points A′, B, A. Horizontal axis marks $Y_{A'}$, $Y_B = $ 94% of Y^P, $Y_C = $ 100% of Y^P.

Right panel: Current rate of inflation $\Delta P/P$ (vertical axis) versus Output ratio Y/Y^P (horizontal axis). Curves labeled SR-TO:A, SR-TO:A′, SR-TO:B, SR-TO:C. Inflation values: 5.9, 4.8, 4. Points A′, B, C. Horizontal axis marks 92, 94, 100.

Labels: "Inflation keeps falling." "Economy is growing." "New long-run equilibrium" "Economy remains well below potential and the short-run trade-off shifts down."

enced the Fed to use a sharp reduction of money growth. Some economists, such as James Tobin of Yale University, worried that too sharp a recession could have led to a repeat of the Great Depression of the 1930s. In mid-1982 the Fed actually eased off on its policy of tight money because it too was worried about a depression. The Fed wanted a sharp recession, but not a major depression.

The sacrifice ratio.   Our example illustrated that there is a substantial cost to reducing inflation. The economy operates for some period of time at a lower level of output and with a higher level of unemployment than it would have had if the policy of contraction had not been followed. One measure of that cost is called the **sacrifice ratio,** which is calculated as the number of percentage points of lost GNP per year given up for each percentage-point reduction of inflation. Robert J. Gordon has estimated the sacrifice ratio for the U.S. economy as about six.[12] This means that it takes an output

sacrifice ratio
The loss in GNP, measured as a percentage, associated with a 1 percent reduction in the rate of inflation.

[12] Robert J. Gordon, "Inflation, Exchange Rates and Unemployment," in *Workers, Jobs, and Inflation,* Martin Neil Baily, ed. (Washington, D.C.: Brookings Institution, 1982).

■ Fiscal Policy and Inflation during the Recovery

We have oversimplified the discussion of the 1980s because we have ignored changes that shifted the *IS* schedule over this period, notably major fiscal-policy changes.

Tax cuts were enacted in 1981 and came into effect over the next three years, leading to a very expansionary fiscal policy and a chronic deficit. The fiscal expansion did help the economy to recover from the 1982 recession, but instead of eliminating the deficit as the economy approached full employment, the deficit has continued. This has led to an unbalanced recovery with higher long-term interest rates than those shown in Table 9.2, and a large trade deficit.

If monetary and fiscal policy had worked together in the 1980s to reduce inflation, rather than having a situation where the Fed had to use monetary policy to balance the very expansionary fiscal policy, then the same reduction of inflation could have been achieved without such high real rates of interest. The trade deficit would have been lower, and investment and long-term growth would have been fostered.

ratio of 99 for six years or a ratio of 94 for one year in order to bring about a long-run reduction of 1 percentage point in the inflation rate. In our example, the inflation rate started at 8 percent and ended up at 4 percent. This translates into 24 percent of lost GNP (4 percent of GNP for six years). This is quite a price. It is more than a third of consumption in a given year and this will be painful whether it comes about through a short, sharp recession or through a longer, but milder recession.

Inflationary expectations and credibility concerning the policy regime.   In this chapter we have assumed that the expected rate of inflation that determines the position of the trade-off is set by the past history of inflation—adaptive expections that adjust slowly to changes in the current rate. When this is the case, it is very difficult to reduce an entrenched inflation, as we saw in the preceding example. But what if expected inflation is really determined by a future-oriented perspective, so that past inflation is only relevant if it predicts future behavior. If this is the case, then perhaps policymakers could hasten the adaptation of the economy to a lower rate of inflation by acting explicitly to change expectations. If they could, inflation would drop quickly and the sacrifice ratio would be much smaller. The political and economic pain caused by the sharp reductions in output could be softened or even avoided.

In 1980, some policymakers in both the United States and Great Britain believed that inflation could be reduced more easily if there was a firm and credible policy of reduced money growth. Based on an implicit adoption of the views of rational-expectations economists, they thought that the slow adjustment of expected inflation came about because firms and workers did not believe that a policy of slow money growth would be sustained. If the Fed would only demonstrate its commitment to low inflation, then expected inflation would come down very quickly and inflation itself would just melt away without the cost of serious recession.

The hope of ending inflation without recession was not realized in either Great Britain or the United States. There are two contending conclusions that economists can draw from this episode. Either this is evidence that firms and workers do not set prices using expectations of inflation that are formed by rational forecasts of future inflation or else, in this case, policymakers were simply not able to demonstrate the necessary **credibility.** While both countries were able to reduce their inflation rates, both also experienced deep recessions in the process.

Tracing through the effects of economic policy has now become a richer exercise. We have looked at short-, intermediate-, and long-term effects, the impacts of inflation on output and output on inflation, short-term and long-term interest rates, real and nominal interest rates, and the workings of financial markets all together.

In the next chapter we go on to consider the other source of a worsening trade-off between output and inflation, namely the role played in inflation and inflationary expectations of supply shocks and/or shifts in aggregate supply.

credibility
The degree to which market participants believe that policymakers will maintain a policy direction (e.g., the believ-ability of the Fed's commitment to an anti-inflationary policy regime).

SUMMARY

- Inflation is a continuing rise in the overall level of prices.
- Inflation both affects economic decisions and is determined by economic conditions.
- Aggregate demand, expectations, and shocks to aggregate supply are the main determinants of inflation. This chapter has studied the first two of these.
- When output is equal to potential output, there is no inflationary pressure from aggregate demand. A high level of aggregate demand means that output is above potential output and the markets for which there is excess demand outweigh the number or importance of markets for which there is excess supply. This means that there are more prices adjusting upward than there are prices adjusting downward, and the result is an overall inflation. Variations in aggregate demand lead to an output–inflation trade-off.
- Stickiness of prices leads to a flat trade-off, especially at low levels of output. And there is widespread excess supply even when output equals potential output.
- The output–inflation trade-off started with the Phillips curve. Unemployment is related to the output ratio through Okun's law. Wages are the largest portion of costs while costs are related to prices. Productivity growth allows wages to grow faster than prices.
- The idea of a stable output–inflation trade-off became an important policy guideline in the 1960s, but the experience of the U.S. economy at the end of the 1960s and

throughout the 1970s showed that there is not a simple and stable trade-off between output and inflation. We characterize changes in the relationship between output and inflation as shifts of the short-run trade-off.

- The two major candidates for sources of shifts in the short-run trade-off are changes in the expected rate of inflation and changes in aggregate supply conditions.

- Expected inflation as it affects the trade-off is based on the past history of inflation and changes more slowly than in financial markets.

- When firms and workers expect the rate of inflation to increase, they build these expectations into their decisions about the prices they are setting in the present and hence into the current rate of inflation.

- In the goods and labor markets, as increases in inflation are incorporated into expected inflation, the intermediate-run increases in inflation associated with higher output are much greater. The slopes of the intermediate-run trade-off is relatively steep.

- In the very long run it is likely that no amount of increase in output above potential output can be sustained. Only higher prices will be generated, so there is no trade-off. That is to say, the long-run trade-off is vertical.

- With positive expected inflation, potential output is no longer the point where there is zero inflation. It is the point where inflation neither accelerates or decelerates. Output levels above or below potential will cause inflation to increase or decrease.

- When policymakers try to reduce inflation, a decrease in output will bring about only a small reduction in inflation in the short run, but a much larger reduction in the long run.

- In the very long run, policy to change demand cannot change the level of output or unemployment in the economy.

- The output–inflation trade-off, incorporating expectations, can be combined with the *IS-ALM* framework to provide a more complete picture of the economy in which output, inflation, and interest rates are all determined together.

- If the economy is in equilibrium, then the level of output determined within the *IS-ALM* (aggregate demand) framework must match the output and inflation relation embodied in the short-run, intermediate-run, and long-run trade-offs (aggregate supply).

- Since both the aggregate demand and the aggregate supply relationships involve expectations, it is important to determine whether or not expected inflation and expected interest rates are consistent with a given equilibrium point. If expected inflation changes, for example, then this will change the equilibrium of the economy.

- Monetary-policy changes will affect inflation directly through changes in aggregate demand and indirectly through changes in inflationary expectations.

- The existence of short-run and intermediate-run trade-offs presents a difficult policy choice: Inflation can be reduced, but the cost is a reduction in output. In the U.S. economy it takes about 6 percent-years of lost output to bring about a 1 percent reduction in inflation. A credible anti-inflation policy may be able to reduce this sacrifice ratio.

KEY TERMS

adaptive expectations

credibility

intermediate-run trade-off

long-run trade-off

misery index

natural rate of unemployment

Okun's law

output–inflation trade-off

output ratio

price stickiness

productivity

sacrifice ratio

short-run output–inflation trade-off

stagflation

DISCUSSION QUESTIONS AND PROBLEMS

1. A rise in the demand for some goods and services drives up their prices. Why isn't there a fall in the prices of goods and services whose demand has not increased, leaving the price level unaffected?

2. What are some of the economic conditions that can fuel an increase in aggregate demand that leads to inflation? Which conditions are likely to be sustainable over time and which are likely to be self-limiting?

3. How does the connection between wages, productivity, and inflation as well as Okun's law provide the link between the Phillips curve and the trade-off between inflation and the level of output?

4. Why would stagflation be measured by a misery index? Why is stagflation so economically painful?

5. Stagflation can be described as a worsening of the short-run output–inflation trade-off. Show how such a short-run trade-off shifts in the face of stagflation. What could account for the shift?

6. What are the two contrasting views of how inflationary expectations are formed? How is the notion of a trade-off affected either way?

7. Which trade-off is steepest: short-run, intermediate-run, or long-run? Why?

8. What does the trade-off mean for the use of economic policy actions to:
   a. stimulate the economy in a recession
      (1) in the short run
      (2) in the long run
   b. fight inflation
      (1) in the short run
      (2) in the long run
   c. target nominal interest rates
   d. target a stable rate of growth of the money supply

9. "If there is no trade-off between output and inflation in the long run, it does not matter whether or not monetary policy is used to fight inflation or accommodate inflation." Comment.

■ APPENDIX 9A
Short-Term Rates and Money-Growth Targeting during the Recovery

In 1979 the Fed publicly abandoned the practice of targeting nominal interest rates and said that it would attempt to maintain a stable rate of growth for the nominal money supply. This approach to monetary policy was the one supported by monetarists. This new approach did not last very long, however. As the economy plunged into recession in 1982, the Fed eased policy and the nominal money supply grew rapidly in the recovery of the 1980s. The monetarists then criticized the Fed for abandoning the policy of stable money growth so quickly. They forecast an increase in the rate of inflation as a result of the rapid rate of money growth, but this turned out to be incorrect. Inflation did not accelerate in the mid-1980s. This time the Fed was correct and the monetarists were wrong. What was going on?

The demand for money balances rose because expected inflation and nominal interest rates declined. We take a closer look at this result by analyzing how changes in inflation expectations affect financial markets. Figure 9A.1 shows the *LM* and *ALM* schedules together. At the outset (points *A*), current inflation is very high and expected inflation is even higher. The short-term nominal rate of interest is already high (10 percent), but the expected rate of inflation is so large that the interest-rate gap is large and negative (−5.5 percent). The *ALM* schedule lies below the *LM* and the economy is depicted at points marked *A* on both the *LM* and *ALM*.

The Fed then undertakes its change in policy and the monetary contraction is described as an upward and inward shift of the *LM* schedule to *LM'*, inducing a sharp spike in short-term interest rates (from 10 to 14 percent, point *A'* on the *LM* schedule). In the financial markets, the expected rate of inflation drops and long-term nominal rates of interest increase with the rise in short rates and because of growing concern about risk. The *ALM* schedule has shifted up to *ALM'* and the economy goes into the deep recession (point *A'* on the *ALM'* schedule).

Over time, both current and expected inflation fall, as the Fed is easing monetary policy with rapid monetary growth and pushing the *LM* schedule way down relative even to its initial position. (It ends up at *LM''*.) The *ALM* schedule has moved, (to *ALM''*) but not by as much because the interest-rate gap has come down. The rapid expansion of the money supply has not generated excessive growth of income and hence there is no acceleration of inflation. In the final equilibrium (points *C*) the short-term nominal rate is down to 5 percent and the long-term real rate is 4 percent.

The demand for the real stock of money is much higher after inflation and nominal interest rates have been brought down. (The T-bill rate has fallen from 14 percent at *A'* to 5 percent at *C*.) The Fed has had to adjust its policies to allow for this greater money demand by allowing a period of rapid growth in the nominal supply of money.

Once the new long-run equilibrium has been reached, the Fed can indeed do as the monetarists suggest and bring down the rate of growth of the nominal money supply. Inflation at the conclusion of this process is now 4 percent, so that an inflation-accommodating policy means that nominal money should grow at 4 percent. But sticking to a fixed money-growth target during the earlier period when inflation and money demand were rapidly changing would have been disastrous.

FIGURE 9A.1   Short-Term Nominal Rates and Long-Term Real Rates over the Contraction and Recovery

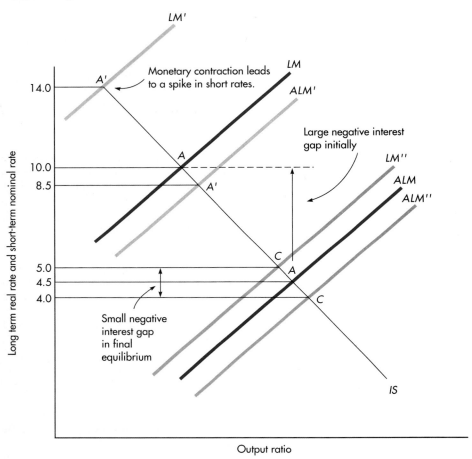

During recovery the *LM* schedule shifts from *LM'* to *LM''*. The growth of the money supply is rapid.

CHAPTER 10

Supply Shocks and Supply-Side Inflation

Inflation and unemployment were both higher in the U.S. economy in the 1970s than in any comparable period after World War II. The adverse experience of that decade changed people's views about what could be expected from the performance of the economy and it changed people's views about the success of economic policy. Living standards grew very slowly over the decade and even declined in some years. Consumers, workers, and business people all found this a difficult period. Economists were forced to reassess their views on the ability of the economy to maintain full employment and reasonable price stability. Old ideas of how the economy works had to be discarded or modified.

Besides economic effects, the bouts of very rapid inflation over this period and a worsened output–inflation trade-off had important social and political consequences. The defeat of President Gerald Ford by Jimmy Carter has been linked to the burst of inflation in 1974 followed by the recession in 1975 and 1976 that resulted from fighting the inflation. Four years later, it was President Carter's turn to face voters' anger over inflation, as he was defeated by Ronald Reagan, partly because of the burst of inflation of 1979–80 and the recession of 1980. The election of President Bush in 1988 was helped substantially by the fact that the Reagan–Bush administration was credited with curbing the inflationary legacy of the 1970s.

In Chater 9 we saw that inflation can be initiated by high levels of aggregate demand. Inflation may develop a momentum as people come to expect inflation. Once inflation is established, workers and firms change the conditions under which they are willing to supply output: They change their price-setting and wage-setting behavior. Expected inflation causes the aggregate supply schedule to keep rising over time; that is to say, it causes the output–

inflation trade-off to shift up. But in the analysis in Chapter 9, it was aggregate demand that initiated the process.

The acceleration of inflation that occurred in the 1970s was not initiated primarily by aggregate demand. Inflation was much worse in the 1970s than can be explained either directly by demand in that decade or by the legacy of excess demand from the 1960s. And there are other cases where changes in the rate of inflation have occurred that were not initiated by demand changes. Inflation declined more rapidly in the 1980s than can be accounted for purely by the recessions of 1980 and 1982—severe though they were. And the conflict with Iraq in 1990 appears to have resulted in another surge in inflation coming from oil price increases.

supply shock
A change in supply conditions, often associated with a large and rapid rise in the relative prices of commodities or raw materials.

There have been sharp rises and falls in inflation caused partly or wholly by abrupt shifts in aggregate supply that are not directly related to past inflation or demand. These shifts have come to be called **supply shocks.** In this chapter we explain the increases in inflation that took place in the 1970s and we look at how the reversal of those shocks helped the Fed to reduce inflation in the 1980s. When an inflation is initiated by a supply shock, the output–inflation trade-off worsens because higher costs drive up prices with no offsetting increases in output. Rather, the economy experiences both worsened unemployment and worsened inflation. Supply shocks are an important part of the explanation for stagflation.

When shocks occur, inflation rises and output falls, confronting policymakers with a dilemma that is similar to the dilemma created when expected inflation builds up. Either policies can be anti-inflationary, which will make the reduction in output even worse, or policies can focus on increasing output and employment, but at the cost of further fueling inflation. The fact that policymakers have to choose between two unpleasant options is why administrations of either party become unpopular when supply shocks hit.

SUPPLY SHOCKS AS A CAUSE OF INFLATION

adverse supply shock
A large and rapid increase in the relative prices of key commodities.

favorable supply shock
A large and rapid reduction in the relative prices of key commodities.

Supply shocks can take different forms and not all of them are alike. But the supply shocks that have been the most important in affecting U.S. inflation involve large changes in the relative prices of certain key commodities. When the supply conditions for a particular product change, so that its price relative to the price of other goods goes up enough to affect the overall price level, the economy is experiencing an **adverse supply shock.** A large reduction in the relative price of a key commodity will have the opposite effect and reduce the overall price level. This is a **favorable supply shock.**

A supply shock comes about when at least two circumstances exist in the economy. First, the national expenditure on the product suffering the supply shock is a large enough portion of GNP so that the increase in price measurably affects the price level. Second, in the case of an adverse supply shock, there has to be enough downward rigidity in wages and other prices so that the effect of the shock is not canceled by the fall in other prices. If these conditions are met, then there will be an increase in the price level in the economy for any given level of output, that is, there will be an upward shift in the aggregate supply schedule. Mostly when we refer to supply shocks we will be talking about adverse shocks.

The increases in the price of imported oil that were initiated by the Organization of Petroleum Exporting Countries (OPEC) in 1973 and again in 1978–79 provide the clearest examples of supply shocks. U.S. energy producers suddenly faced very different market conditions for their products. The world price of oil had jumped so U.S. energy producers were able to sell their own production at a much higher price, despite some price controls. This was true for U.S. oil producers and also for natural-gas and coal producers whose prices were linked to the price of oil. Since energy production is a significant part of GNP and non-energy prices did not fall, the increase in the price of energy led to a significant increase in the overall price level.

In Figure 10.1, the economy is represented at an initial equilibrium at point A, with a level of income Y_A and a price level of P_A. A supply shock is shown as an inward movement of aggregate supply (AS to AS'). With the aggregate demand curve unchanged, the economy will move to a new equilibrium (point A to point B) with a lower level of income (Y_A to Y_B) and a higher price level (P_A to P_B).

There is a limited amount that policymakers can do in the short run to change the conditions that lead to the supply shock. Using economic policy as a tool to increase the domestic supply of oil, for example, would mean encouraging additions to the nation's reserves or stimulating improvements in the technology for oil extraction. Such policies, even if successful, take a long time to work. Increasing energy efficiency requires investment in new equipment and other long-term strategies. *In the short run, policymakers have to decide whether to respond to the shock by changing aggregate demand.* They could increase aggregate demand to increase the level of output but with more inflation, or they could decrease aggregate demand to reduce inflation but also further reduce output.

Given that the supply shock has occurred and the economy now has lower output and a higher price level, policymakers face a dilemma. We illustrate the policy dilemma in Figure 10.1. Policymakers could reduce aggregate demand (AD to AD') and further reduce output (Y_B to Y_C) in order to bring the price level back down to its original level. Alternatively, they could stimulate aggregate demand (AD to AD'') in order to restore the original level of output and thereby further increase the price level (P_B to P_C). Both of these alternatives are unattractive.

In their effect on inflation, adverse supply shocks are similar to increases in expected inflation in that they shift the aggregate supply schedule and create serious dilemmas for policy. But in an important respect, adverse supply shocks are much worse. When OPEC raised the price of oil and domestic energy producers raised their prices, this had an adverse effect on the cost of living of the average American. We commented earlier that the

---

FIGURE 10.1   Output and the Price Level Following a Supply Shock

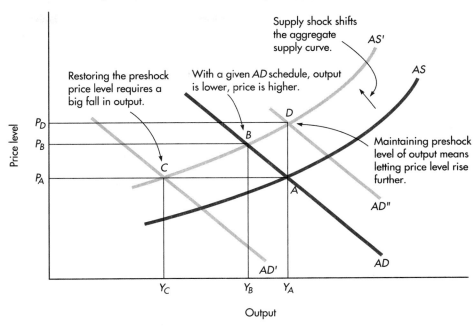

Supply shock shifts the aggregate supply curve.

Restoring the preshock price level requires a big fall in output.

With a given *AD* schedule, output is lower, price is higher.

Maintaining preshock level of output means letting price level rise further.

An adverse supply shock raises the price level and lowers output. Shifting aggregate demand can raise output at the expense of higher prices or reduce output to cut prices.

---

cost of a pure monetary inflation may not be terribly high. But there is no problem in identifying the costs of supply-shock inflation. After adjusting for inflation, workers' wages were only slightly higher in 1989 than they were in the late 1960s because of the various adverse changes in supply conditions that have occurred. Workers saw supply-shock inflation as reducing their real incomes and they were right. We look now at the sources of these supply shocks.

Adverse Supply Shocks in the 1970s

In the 1970s a series of dramatic supply shocks hit the economy that involved basic commodities such as energy, food, and other materials.[1] To some extent these relative price increases were subsequently reversed, but they caused serious economic difficulties along the way.

---

[1] The role of commodity prices in inflation in the 1970s is discussed in Barry Bosworth and Robert Z. Lawrence, *Commodity Prices and the New Inflation* (Washington, D.C.: Brookings Institution, 1982).

OPEC and energy prices

The Organization of Petroleum Exporting Countries was formed in 1960. In addition to the dominant Arab nations, OPEC has non-Arab countries as members, all of which face very different economic conditions and which subscribe to very different economic ideologies. Moreover, not all oil producers joined OPEC. At first OPEC had little influence on oil prices; it was an attempt by oil-exporting countries to get a somewhat better deal from the large oil companies that then dominated the world energy market. Given the diversity of its membership, it was not at all clear that OPEC could form a cartel that would successfully raise the price of oil higher than the competitive market price and keep oil prices stable at that higher level. Yet in fact, the OPEC cartel was successful in raising the price of oil by enforcing production quotas on its membership, and the price quadrupled in 1973 and rose again in 1979 and 1980.[2] (See the following box, "The Rise and Fall of Oil Prices.")

The increases in the price of imported oil in 1973 and 1978–80 had an impact on overall inflation in the United States because both the domestic supplies of oil and the domestic demand for oil were inelastic—neither demand nor supply in the United States could easily be changed in response to the changes in the price of oil. On the supply side, the flow of oil that can be drawn from a given base of reserves cannot easily be changed without impairing the longer-run productivity of the field. U.S. oil producers could not quickly respond to the price rise with quantities that were sufficiently high to undo the impact of a reduction in foreign supplies. Also, the supplies of alternative sources of energy, such as natural gas, could not be quickly increased by enough to matter. On the demand side, oil is a significant part of total raw-material use in the economy, and it was hard to reduce energy use quickly because energy efficiency is generally built into the existing stock of machines, furnaces, motor vehicles, and appliances. Improvements in energy efficiency came about slowly as these capital goods were replaced.

The two big jumps in the price of oil, in 1973 and 1979, were important inflationary shocks to the economies of oil-consuming countries, including the United States. In 1973 the United States used 17.3 million barrels of oil a day. Refined petroleum products rose in price by about $5.50 a barrel as a result of the OPEC actions, so that an oil "levy" of $35 billion was imposed on oil users—about 2½ percent of GNP. The second shock was much bigger. Oil rose in price by about $21 a barrel in 1979, imposing an oil levy of $144 billion on users—about 6½ percent of our GNP.[3] In addition, the price of

---

[2] Facts about energy prices and uses are given in Robert L. Loftness, *Energy Handbook*, 2nd ed. (New York: Van Nostrand, 1984), and in Congress of the United States, Office of Technology Assessment, *Energy Use and the U.S. Economy* (Washington, D.C.: U.S. Government Printing Office, June 1990).

[3] These figures are taken from Alan S. Blinder, "Anatomy of Double-Digit Inflation in the 1970s," in *Inflation Causes and Effects*, R. E. Hall, ed. (Chicago: 1982).

■ Oil Shocks, Wage and Price Controls, and Stagflation: The 1970s

What happens when the price of a raw material necessary in the production of a large share of output and consumption sharply rises? This is precisely what happened during the 1970s—not once but twice. In the first instance, it happened during a time of full employment.

The inflationary effect of the first oil price shock during this era was complicated by President Nixon's surprising introduction of price and wage controls in August 1971. The president reacted to what was then perceived as evidence that inflation was heating up. Based on prior U.S. experience, the 6 percent annual inflation rate *was* scary. The wage and price controls he imposed held prices down to the 3.9 to 4.3 percent range in 1971–72 and resulted in shortages.

From 1972 to 1974 the price of Saudi Arabian oil increased from $1.90 per barrel to $9.76 per barrel. This price rise was instigated by an Arab oil embargo and an increasing degree of market control among OPEC members. In the U.S. the price hike quickly filtered to gasoline pump prices, which jumped nearly 40 percent from September 1973 to May 1974. The second oil shock came during 1979 and was related to the war between Iran and Iraq. It resulted in an oil price increase from $12.70 to $28.67 per barrel during 1978–80.

The abrupt and steep price hikes destabilized the economies of most of the oil-importing industrial countries. In the case of the U.S., real GNP declined by 0.6 percent and 1.2 percent during 1974 and 1975, respectively, and by 0.4 percent during 1980. Unemployment rose in each period. This was the stagnation; the "flation" part of stagflation came from the jump in inflation from 5.7 percent in 1973 to 9.3 percent by 1975 and from 8.6 percent in 1979 to 9.4 percent in 1981. The term *stagflation* was coined to characterize what happened in the wake of the oil shocks.

Meanwhile, what had been happening to price and wage controls? President Nixon gradually removed the controls in 1973 and 1974, precisely at the time of the first major oil price shock. Workers were pushing for the higher wages denied by wage controls, and firms raised markups in an attempt to catch up with the profit losses they suffered during the price freeze. This "catching up" not only accelerated the inflation rate but also increased the expected rate of inflation.

At the same time nominal wages in the United States were *downwardly* rigid. Thus, the leftward shift in aggregate supply from the higher cost of production due to higher oil prices was not offset by falling wage costs. Instead, output and employment fell. Tight monetary policy by the Fed during 1973 and 1974 and a tight fiscal policy in 1973 reinforced the shock-induced decline in output. The "Great Recession" of 1974–75 was the result.

One possible explanation for the strong U.S. recovery between the two 1970s price shocks, relative to the European experience, was the decline in U.S. real wages. U.S. unions have fewer wage contracts with wages indexed to inflation than do European labor unions. For this reason, the Fed followed the same tactics after the 1979 oil shock with the same result—recession, hopefully to be followed by lower inflation and economic recovery. This time unemployment rose so rapidly that Fed policy was prematurely reversed before subduing inflation. Inflation accelerated again and the Fed held down the monetary brakes for a much longer time in 1981 and 1982. Then came the steepest and most prolonged recession since the Great Depression.

The economic drama of the 1970s and early 1980s is not due entirely to oil on troubled waters. The wage and price controls were poorly handled, and monetary policy itself was quite unstable.

competing fuels such as coal and natural gas also rose when the price of oil increased, adding to the levy on energy users.

Eventually, however, the cartel did unravel as new suppliers came into the market and some OPEC members exceeded their production quotas and sold oil at lower prices. The price of oil adjusted for inflation fell throughout the 1980s, providing a positive supply shock that helped the reduction of inflation in the 1980s. As well as oil prices, there were other supply shocks.

Agricultural shocks and food prices

The prices consumers paid for food rose by 15 percent in 1973 and by 14 percent in 1974. Food is an important component of the cost of living and hence has a large weight in the Consumer Price Index (CPI). These price increases (coming on top of rising gasoline prices and utility bills) cut living standards and left many households fearful about the future. Food is of course purchased on a frequent and regular basis, so that noticeable increases in food prices may be perceived by many as evidence of general inflation.

Food prices are set in world markets, where small differences in supply and demand generate large fluctuations in price. The variability of individual food prices is normal; the rapid rise in overall food prices was the shock. These agricultural price shocks were preceded by bad weather conditions. The Soviet Union made major grain purchases that reduced the supply of grain in the rest of the world and contributed to the run-up in grain prices. And since fertilizers are made from oil and gas, the energy crisis also had an impact on food production and prices.

Food prices are also affected by government actions. In the United States, until the early 1970s, farm policy included acreage restrictions and grain reserves in an attempt to stabilize prices. By 1973 the stabilization program had been abandoned and the grain reserve had been depleted, so that when the Soviets entered the market as a major grain purchaser, the effect on prices was dramatic. Food-price hikes coupled with oil-price hikes comprised a devastating series of price and supply shocks that impacted the entire economy.

Slowdown in the growth of labor productivity

Labor productivity describes the amount of output per unit of labor input.[4] If labor productivity grows, workers are producing more per hour than before, so they can be paid more per hour without necessarily raising prices. The growth in labor productivity allows for a gap between the rate of growth of wages and the rate of inflation.

A productivity increase means that it takes fewer hours of labor to produce a unit of output, so that *increases in productivity lower unit labor costs*. The wage rate is the amount an employer has to pay for each hour of work, so that *increases in wages raise unit labor costs*. As shown in Equation 10.1, the growth of unit labor cost *(ULC)* is equal to the difference between the rate of wage increase and the rate of growth of labor productivity:

---

[4] Labor input is often measured as hours worked. Output per unit of labor is a measure of total output per hour. This is often compared with wages measured as wages per hour. The hourly wage includes fringe benefits and payroll taxes prorated on an hourly basis. The hourly wage figure is often referred to as *hourly compensation*.

$$\text{Growth of } ULC = \text{Growth of wages}$$
$$- \text{Growth of labor productivity.} \tag{10.1}$$

Unit labor costs are constant when the growth of wages equals the growth of labor productivity; they increase when wages grow faster than labor productivity. This means that *a decrease in the rate of productivity growth will add to the rate of increase of unit labor costs, unless it is offset by a decline in the rate of growth of wages.*

Productivity growth slowed down in the late 1960s and then slowed sharply after 1973, so that in order to avoid an acceleration of unit labor costs, the rate of wage increase would have had to slow also. In practice, the rate of wage growth did not slow, at least not for several years, so that unit labor costs did accelerate. Then with costs rising for most firms in the economy, business managers were able to pass on the cost increases in higher prices. The acceleration of unit labor costs led to an acceleration of price inflation.

Supply Shocks and the Price Level

Supply shocks have a direct effect on the price level. When the prices paid for U.S. agricultural output and energy output rose sharply relative to other prices, this raised the overall U.S. price level, as measured by the GNP deflator. The increases in the relative prices of the agricultural and energy sectors are shown in Figures 10.2A and B. The 1971–85 period is shown in the figure, split into two parts. In Figure 10.2A we show the price indexes over the 1971–78 period for the output of the agricultural and the mining sectors of the U.S. economy, together with the price index for all of GNP except for these two sectors. These price indexes normally have 1982 as a base year, but we have divided the indexes by their 1971 values so that all three are set equal to 100 in 1971 instead of in 1982. This is done in order to show more clearly how prices evolved after 1971.

Figure 10.2A shows how the price of agricultural output rose very rapidly between 1972 and 1973. After that, agricultural prices fell back a little until there was a second milder price increase in 1978.

The price of the output of the mining sector in the United States primarily reflects the prices of crude oil, natural gas, and coal. The combined effect of the price increases in these energy-producing sectors was a massive jump in the price of mining output between 1973 and 1974. Following the OPEC price increase, the price of U.S. energy output would have occurred earlier than it did, except that price controls on energy products were in effect in that period.

The price of mining output continued to increase more rapidly than other prices even after 1974. The United States is gradually exhausting its most available sources of oil and gas, so that costs of drilling and extraction have risen. The supply schedule for the U.S. industry has been moving

FIGURE 10.2   The Price of Agricultural Output, the Price of Mining Output, and the Price of GNP Except for These Two Sectors

A.   Price indexes, 1971–1978, set equal to 100 in 1971.

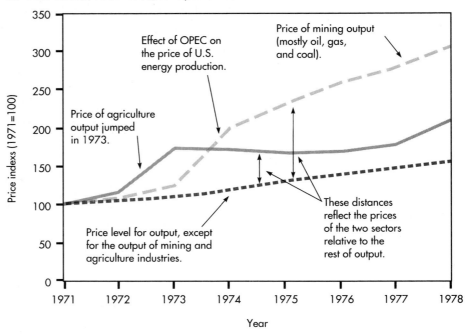

B.   Price indexes, 1978–1985, set equal to 100 in 1978.

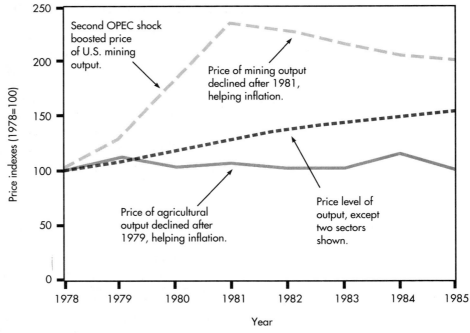

up. If foreign energy had remained cheap and available, this would have led to a fall in U.S. output. Since in fact foreign energy became more expensive and was at times limited in supply, this has kept U.S. energy output and prices high.

Figure 10.2B repeats the same exercise over the 1978–85 period. We have reset the price indexes again, this time to equal 100 in 1978. This figure shows that prices in the agricultural sector did not contribute to the increase in the overall 1979–81 price level. On the contrary, increases in agricultural productivity have lowered costs in the 1980s and have helped to keep the price level down.

The price of mining output rose faster than the price of other goods throughout the 1970s, and then there was another massive price boost between 1979 and 1981 that pushed up the overall price level. At that point, U.S. energy prices began to fall as a result of the breakdown of the OPEC cartel and the cumulative effects of increased efficiency by consumers and the increase of supply by non-OPEC energy sources. The relative price of mining output then fell after 1981.

The agricultural and mining sectors made up 4.7 percent of total GNP in 1972. The combined price index for these two sectors together went up by 64 percent between 1972 and 1974, so that in the absence of any offsetting declines in other prices, this price shock added about 3 percentage points directly to the overall price level ($0.047 \times 0.64 = 0.0299 = 3$ percent). In 1979, the mining sector was 2.9 percent of total GNP and the price index for this sector went up by 84 percent between 1979 and 1981. Leaving aside changes in other prices, this added 2.4 percent to the overall price level.

We have found therefore that large price changes in important sectors of the economy can have an impact on the overall price level. But if this had been the end of the story, the overall effect on inflation would not have been that bad. Adding 3 percent to the price level over a two-year period means adding about 1½ percent to the annual inflation rate for two years. Of course there were other adverse changes in supply conditions over this period (particularly the productivity-growth slowdown), so that the total effect of the supply shocks was larger than this. But even so, the direct effect of the supply shocks on the price level was not huge.

Unfortunately, however, this was not the end of the story. We have not yet examined the indirect effects of the supply shocks.

Supply Shocks, the Cost of Living, and Wages

The U.S. price level reflects the price of U.S. production. When OPEC raised the cost of oil, this affected the U.S. price level directly only as a result of the shift in the supply schedule of U.S. producers. But when the cost of energy and food rose sharply, this had a dramatic effect on the cost of living of U.S. consumers. U.S. consumers buy oil and agricultural products from both U.S. and foreign producers.

The indirect effect of the adverse supply shocks is that when the cost of living increased, this led to an acceleration in the rate of wage increase. And then, finally, the acceleration of wage growth led to general inflation. The impact of the supply shocks on the price level became a continuing inflation problem.

Changes in the U.S. cost of living

The way in which food and energy prices affected the U.S. cost of living is illustrated in Figure 10.3. The figure shows the rates of increase of three parts of the Consumer Price Index (CPI) averaged over various periods. Recall that the CPI is an index that changes over time as a weighted average of the rates of change of the various goods and services that are purchased by a representative consumer. Figure 10.3 uses a breakdown of the CPI into three parts: first, the price of food (16.3 percent of the total); second, the price of energy (7.4 percent of the total); and, third, everything else (76.3 percent). The price of food at the consumer level reflects prices at grocery stores and restaurants. The price of energy is computed by seeing how much consumers spend on energy through such items as their electricity and natural-gas bills and their gasoline purchases.

Over the 1965–71 period, food and energy prices rose more slowly than the prices of other goods and services in the CPI. This situation changed abruptly from 1971 to 1975 when both food-price and energy-price increases were much greater than other price increases. From 1975 to 1982 the situation was a little different again as food prices rose somewhat more slowly than other goods' and services' prices, but this time energy costs were jumping. After 1982, costs of both food and energy went up much less than the costs of other items, so that these sectors were holding down the overall increase in the cost of living in the 1980s, as they had in the 1960s.

The supply shocks that drove up food and energy prices had an important impact on the cost of living faced by U.S. consumers. One consequence of this was political. U.S. voters were angry at the erosion of their living standards and demanded change. Another important consequence is that workers demanded higher wage payments in an attempt (fruitless as it turned out) to offset the run-up in food and energy costs.

The cost of living and wage increases

Increases in the prices of imported and domestically produced food and energy were bound to have an adverse effect on the cost of living of the average consumer. The supply shocks represented a real cost to the average American. There were different ways in which the costs could have been paid, however. One possibility is that wages, salaries, and corporate profits could have been reduced in dollar terms following the supply shocks. In this case, the prices outside of mining and agriculture would have fallen following the supply shocks. The shocks would not have increased the price level as there would only have been changes in relative prices. A second

FIGURE 10.3 The Average Annual Rate of Growth of Food Prices, Energy Prices, and Prices of Other Items in the Consumer Price Index, 1965–1985

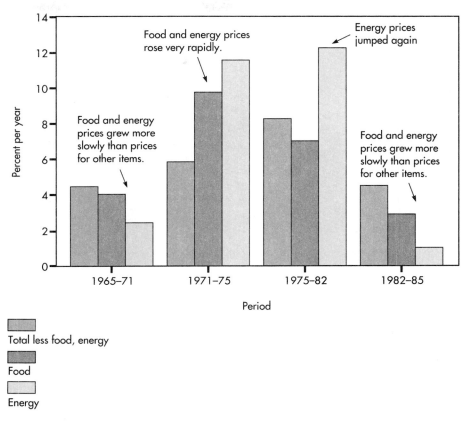

Total less food, energy

Food

Energy

Note: The figures for 1965–71 are the averages of the annual growth rates for each of the six years. Other periods' figures were calculated similarly.

possibility is that wages and other prices might have been unaffected by the supply shocks. They could have increased by the same amount that they would have increased without the shocks. In this case the effect of the shocks would have been to increase the price level and increase the cost of living, but there would have been no persistent effect on inflation. There would have been a short-term boost to inflation, of course, just in order to raise the price level, but the inflation would have stopped quickly.

Unfortunately, neither of these possibilities are what actually happened. Instead, the increases in the cost of living that were the result of the supply shocks then led to increases in money wages. Figure 10.4 illustrates what happened. From 1965 to 1971 the rate of increase in hourly compensation

FIGURE 10.4   Average Annual Rate of Growth of Hourly Compensation for Workers in the Business Sector, 1965–1985

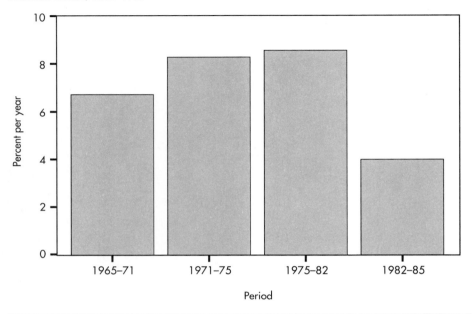

Hourly compensation includes employer payments for fringe benefits. The figure for 1965–71 is the average of the annual growth rates for each of the six years. Other periods' figures were calculated similarly.

(wages plus fringe benefits) was already high. Over this period, there had been a very strong demand for labor and very low unemployment. The expected rate of inflation had increased in the 1960s, as we saw in Chapter 9, and this increase in the expected rate of inflation had been built into wage increases. Then after 1971 the rate of increase of hourly compensation began to grow even more rapidly in response to the increases in the cost of living. This is a particularly striking fact for the 1975–82 period, when the rate of increase of hourly compensation accelerated even though the demand for labor was very weak and the rate of unemployment was much higher than it had been for 20 years or more previous to that.

The most straightforward explanation of the acceleration of wages is that the supply shocks created a problem of catch-up. Workers found their real wages had been reduced unexpectedly by the increase in energy and food prices, and they wanted to be compensated. For union workes with contracts that included cost-of-living adjustments, this compensation happened automatically. Then, employers were willing to grant similar wage increases to nonunion workers because it was equitable and because they expected every other firm to do the same.

■ Import Prices and Housing Costs in the CPI

The main supply shocks that affected the economy in the 1970s stemmed from the three causes that we have already talked about: food prices, energy prices, and the slowdown in productivity growth. But there were two additional factors that affected the CPI over this period: the value of the dollar and the way in which the cost of homeownership was measured.

Import prices. We have seen that the cost of living was affected by the increased cost of foreign oil as well as the increased cost of domestic energy. The effect of the prices of imported goods on the U.S. cost of living applies more generally than just to oil prices. The value of the dollar against foreign currencies fell after 1971. The fall in the dollar in the 1970s was a sudden event at the end of a long period of fixed exchange rates. The value of the U.S. dollar on foreign-exchange markets had been held artificially high for some time, so when the exchange rate was finally allowed to float, it fell dramatically. This fall in the value of the dollar meant that we had to pay more for the foreign goods that we bought. When we offered our own goods in the international marketplace, we got fewer foreign goods in return.

The sharp increase in the prices of oil and food that we discussed earlier came about partly because of the decrease in the dollar's exchange rate, so the falling dollar is part of the energy- and food-price explanation of the supply shock. But in addition to commodities' prices, other imported goods' prices also increased as the dollar fell. As the dollar fell, U.S. producers of products that competed with imports raised their markups because the pressure of competition from cheap imports was reduced. Increases in the prices of some products generated increases in the costs of other products, contributing to inflation.

The decline in the dollar in the 1970s has not been the only change in the value of the currency that has affected inflation. The decline in the dollar after 1985 also had a small but important adverse impact on inflation. And the rise of the dollar from 1980 to 1985 held down the U.S. cost of living and was a contributor to the decline of inflation over this period. In general, *major swings in the value of the dollar will have an effect on overall U.S. inflation.*

Homeownership and Measurement Error. The Consumer Price Index includes the cost of housing as one of the goods and services that consumers buy. About 20 percent of the total CPI reflects the cost of homeownership, picking up the fact that many families in the United States live in their own homes. For many years the U.S. Department of Labor's Bureau of Labor Statistics (BLS) used the monthly payment on new mortgages as an important part of homeownership costs. When mortgage interest rates rose in the 1970s, this then showed up in monthly payments and boosted the CPI. The particular procedures used by BLS resulted in an overstatement of true average homeownership costs.

For one thing, the majority of homeowners had mortgages with fixed interest rates and they were not affected by the rise in rates. The BLS was assuming all homeowners were facing higher mortgage payments. Second, the rise in inflation that accompanied the rise in nominal interest rates meant that the real rate of interest did not rise as much as the nominal rate. Mortgage holders benefited from the inflation because it reduced the real value of their indebtedness. Subsequently, the method of computing the CPI was changed and the procedure used now uses an estimate of what the rent would be on houses that people own themselves.

The result of the way in which homeownership costs were computed is that CPI inflation was exaggerated in the early 1970s. The CPI was not an accurate measure of inflation over this period. From 1971 to 1975 the price deflator for the goods purchased by consumers (consumption in the GNP accounts) rose about 1 percentage point a year slower than the CPI.

Even though it contained errors, the CPI was still widely used to adjust (or index) government programs and wage contracts. Many union contracts contain an indexing provision where wage increases are tied to CPI increases over the prior year. And Social Security benefits are also tied to the CPI. The measurement error ended up having real effects on people's incomes.

price–wage spiral
The ongoing process whereby increases in wages raise unit labor costs, contributing to a higher rate of inflation and still higher wages.

The supply shocks initiated a process that is sometimes called a **price–wage spiral.** Prices rose in some sectors of the economy and for imported goods, and this led to increases in the cost of living and then to increases in wages. The increases in wages then led to an increase in prices throughout the economy. We can explore how this price–wage spiral works using the identity between output and income.

The price–wage spiral

There is an identity that relates income and output and we have used this identity many times. This identity holds for real output and real income and also for nominal output and nominal income. We have used the former relation up until now, but to see the impact of a supply shock we now make use of the identity in nominal terms:

$$\text{Nominal value of output} = PY = \text{Nominal value of income}$$
$$= \text{Nominal wage income} + \text{Nominal value of payments to capital.} \quad (10.2)$$

Equation 10.2 simply states that the value of output is paid out either to workers or to the owners of the businesses for which they work. Of course in practice there are many small businesses where the owner and the worker are the same. And some of the capital here will include agricultural land and reserves of oil and gas. But these complications do not change the overall identity.

If we now take the identity in Equation 10.1 and divide through by real output (Y) we obtain the following:

$$\frac{PY}{Y} = P = \frac{\text{Wage income}}{Y} + \frac{\text{Capital income}}{Y} \quad (10.3)$$

Price level = Unit labor cost + Unit payments to capital.

Equation 10.3 tells us that the price level is equal to the amount paid to labor per unit of output produced and the amount paid to capital (including the amount paid to the owners of land and natural resources). This equation is actually a formalization of something that we saw in Chapter 9 when we looked at the relation between the Phillips curve and the output–inflation trade-off. We said there that increases in wages (a component of unit labor costs) will usually lead to increases in the price level. We have now broadened the analysis to include payments to capital.

The first component on the right-hand side of Equation 10.3 reflects the cost of wages for labor used to produce, distribute, and market the goods and services produced in the economy. The second reflects two elements. There are costs associated with the purchase, rent, or lease of the plant, equipment, and land, plus the carrying costs of inventory that are used in production and distribution. These capital costs are often viewed as a return to capital investment and are included in profits in company accounts. But on top of this, there may be an additional markup added to unit costs that reflects the generation of an economic profit, a return over and above the normal return to capital. If any particular firm is making less than a normal return on its capital, then its price is less than full cost and its "additional" markup is actually negative.

Equation 10.3 is an identity because the total payment to capital is defined as whatever is left over (positive or negative) after paying the labor costs.[5] When the average markup is positive for the economy as a whole, this means companies are earning returns greater than the normal return on capital. In a competitive economy, such excess profits will attract new firms and/or cause the expansion of existing ones. This increased competition drives down any excess return and eliminates the markup. When the markup is negative on average, this will encourage firms to shift their production into other lines or to close down plants. The reduction in capacity reduces supply and prices rise to restore the normal return on capital. Of course, at the time that a supply shock hits the economy, there will be substantial changes in "markups" in the affected industries. Farm incomes rose and the profits of energy producers increased significantly in 1973–74. But once the shock has passed, market adjustments will mean that prices in most industries will stay fairly close to the sum of labor and normal capital costs. This means that *when the price of labor rises, this cost increase is seen as a general increase in the cost of doing business and is passed along into final prices.*

Notice the importance of the productivity-growth slowdown at this point. When productivity growth slowed, this meant that any given increase in wages would lead to a higher rate of growth of unit labor costs and hence a higher rate of price increase. The only way to avoid an upward movement of inflation is to cut the rate of wage growth. In practice the opposite happened in the 1970s. *The slowdown in productivity growth that started in the 1970s coupled with an acceleration of wages translated into an even larger acceleration of price inflation.*

We have now given a descriptive analysis of how the supply shocks have resulted in a broader inflationary surge. The cost of living increased and this led to a push by workers to try to recoup some of the decline in their living standard. As workers demanded higher wages, firms were willing to grant the increases knowing that every other firm was doing the same. The general increase in wages took place despite a decline in the growth of

---

[5] We define the cost of capital as the price a firm would have to pay to lease or rent plant and equipment in order to produce its products. Even if the firm owns its own capital, the cost of capital figures into the cost of a product because the firm must pay for its capital out of revenues. The owners of a company own all the assets of the company, and so they usually own much of the capital used by the company in production. They receive as their return the residual income after labor costs, materials costs, and rental payments for capital not owned by the company have been paid. This residual return includes both an implicit payment for the capital owned by the company plus any markup beyond the cost of capital.

Sometimes the markup can be negative for a time for a company that is not able to earn the normal return on the capital that it owns—price is less than average unit cost. Sometimes the markup is large for a short period of time for a company producing a product for which there has been a short-run increase in demand—price is then greater than unit cost.

labor productivity and so it led to a general increase in prices. We will now return to the model of inflation and the trade-off that we introduced in Chapter 9 and see how the effect of the supply shocks can be incorporated into this analysis.

SUPPLY SHOCKS AND THE SHIFTING TRADE-OFF

An adverse supply shock initially pushes up the price level. This means that it has an effect that worsens the short-run output–inflation trade-off. It causes a temporary upward blip in the trade-off. Equation 10.4 gives a modified version of the short-run trade-off described in Chapter 9. Here, the current rate of inflation depends upon the output ratio $[H(Y/Y^P)]$, the expected rate of inflation $[Exp(\Delta P/P)]$, and the direct but temporary effect of the supply shock on inflation *(SS)*:

$$\text{Current inflation } \Delta P/P = H(Y/Y^P) + Exp(\Delta P/P) + SS. \qquad (10.4)$$

We can see what this specification implies by using an example of an increase in both agricultural prices and energy prices. Suppose that there is a 4-percentage-point increase in the price level as a result of these supply shocks and it happens over a single year. This means that the rate of inflation is increased by 4 percent for one year as a result of the direct effect of the changes in the relative prices of these commodities. This means that SS is equal to 4 in the year in which the supply shock strikes and is then zero thereafter. This example obviously is simplified relative to the actual supply shocks, but it captures the main idea.

Figure 10.5 illustrates the short-run impact of a supply shock assuming no changes in other prices or changes in expectations. Initially, the economy is experiencing stable inflation at full capacity (output ratio at 100 percent). This is shown as a point (point A) along a short-run trade-off (SR–TO:1). The economy then experiences a supply shock. The impact of the shock shifts the short-run trade-off upward (SR–TO:1 to SR–TO:2 by the amount SS). In general we would expect output to fall in the short run following the supply shock. The price level has been increased and unless the Fed takes specific action in response to this, the real stock of money will fall. If output falls (point C), then the economy faces the situation of stagflation, where both output and inflation are worse following the supply shock. However, the recession has mitigated the inflationary effects of the supply shocks $[(\Delta P/P)_C < (\Delta P/P)_B]$. The fall in the real stock of money following the supply shock does induce an offsetting fall in output that helps to reduce the impact of the shock on inflation.

If it is possible for the Fed to act very quickly to restore the real money supply so that it maintains the same level of output (output ratio remains at 100 percent), then the new level of inflation is shown along SR–TO:2 at point B. Current inflation has increased by the full amount of the supply-shock effect $[(\Delta P/P)_B = (\Delta P/P)_A + SS]$.

FIGURE 10.5   The Short-Run Effect of a Supply Shock on Inflation

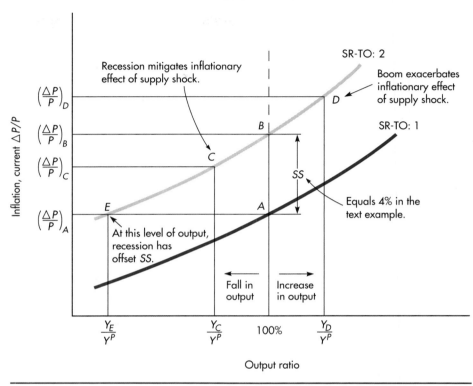

And finally it is possible, although unlikely, that the Fed is so anxious to avoid recession that it overshoots and increases the real stock of money. Then income will increase above potential (to point D) and the economy will experience an even greater increase in inflation than that caused by the direct effect of the supply shock [$(\Delta P/P)_D > (\Delta P/P)_B$]. The increase in output above potential generates an aggregate-demand–driven inflation that exacerbates the inflationary effects of the supply shock.

Figure 10.5 gives the alternative outcomes for the economy in the year that the supply shock actually hits. Policy can react by accommodating the resulting inflation surge, fighting it, or even exacerbating it. Once the initial shock has passed, however, the question then becomes: What next?

The Transition from Supply Shocks to Chronic Inflation

A supply shock will turn into a continuing inflation problem if expected inflation increases as a result of the shock. In the earlier part of this chapter we suggested that this is exactly what happened as a result of the price–

■ Potential Output and Supply Shocks

Some schools of thought represent potential output differently from the way we describe it. Some economists contend that supply shocks reduce potential output. Therefore, noninflationary full employment must be redefined as whatever rate of unemployment it takes to avoid any increase in inflation, no matter how high the unemployment.

In Figure 10.5 the supply shock is assumed not to alter potential output; rather, any reduction of output is a temporary drop below potential. Why? An oil price hike does not change the economy's capacity to produce goods and services by very much in the short run.

When there is a jump in the price of an essential raw material, the business firm passes along the extra cost of production to the final customer. For example, since chemical fertilizers are made from petroleum by-products, a successful naval blockade of the Persian Gulf will lead to higher fertilizer prices for American farmers. This, in turn, will lead to higher food prices. The fertilizer firm will use the same amount of crude petroleum as before, and the farmer will use almost the same amount of fertilizer. In the short run, businesses do not change their production recipes by much. Rather than change the mode of production, they raise prices and maintain production at former levels.

Over time, chemical firms and farmers can take steps to reduce their use of crude petroleum. Some of these kinds of changes contributed to the decline in American productivity growth during the 1970s and 1980s. If innovations lead to production processes in which petroleum is no longer an essential input, productivity would increase. Nonetheless, supply shocks are the hares, and changes in production processes are the tortoises.

Now we come to the alternative view. Suppose the economist defines potential output as the level of output just sufficient to keep the acceleration of inflation at zero. Then when the oil price shock comes, potential output will fall dramatically in the same year the supply shock hits. In Figure 10.5, the economy would have to operate at point E in order to avoid any acceleration of inflation. Compared to an unchanged level of potential output, the output ratio that precludes any increase in inflation would be at Y_E/Y^P. At this newly defined level of potential output, output would equal 100 percent of potential.

We do not agree with this alternative definition of potential output as a benchmark. The unemployment rate would be intolerably high at point E, perhaps as high as 14 percent for a large supply shock (like the one in the example where SS is 4 percent). Moreover, by this awkward definition, potential output would suddenly shoot way up the following year when the supply shock had run its course!

We prefer instead to define potential output as the level of output that will not lead to accelerating or decelerating inflation *in the absence of supply shocks*. We would prefer to estimate potential output from benchmark levels for unemployment and factory utilization plus the long-run trend of growth in the capacity of the economy.

wage spiral that was precipitated by a supply shock. In Figure 10.6, we illustrate the case in which the supply shock does lead to an increase in expected inflation, so that the short-run trade-off does not return to its original position even after the supply shock passes.

We assume, just as in Figure 10.5, that the supply shock has initially shifted the short-run trade-off from SR–TO:1 to SR–TO:2. We assume further

FIGURE 10.6 Inflation and the Trade-Off Once the Supply Shock Has Ended

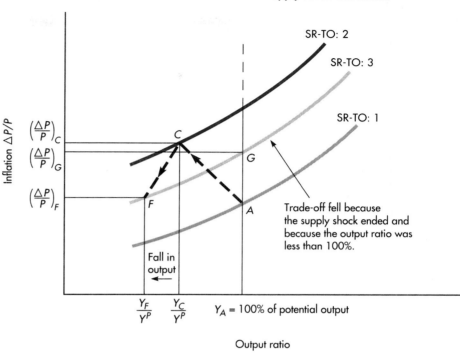

that the rise in the price level is not accommodated by the Fed, so that there is a reduction in the real stock of money and hence in the output ratio. The economy moves from point *A* to point *C*.

We consider now the period following the supply shock. The economy improves after the supply shock has passed, but it does not immediately return to its preshock equilibrium. In Figure 10.6, the new short-run trade-off is represented by SR–TO:3. The trade-off is better than it was when the shock first hit (SR–TO:3 lies below SR–TO:2), but worse than before the shock hit, because the shock has increased expected inflation (SR–TO:3 lies above SR–TO:1).

The particular combination of inflation and output experienced along the shifted short-run trade-off depends upon aggregate demand conditions following the shock. In the case shown in Figure 10.6, income continues to fall (Y_C to Y_F) in the year following the shock. This case means that the inflationary effects of the supply shock have been almost eliminated. The economy has experienced a fairly severe recession, but only a temporary surge in inflation.

Supply shocks and expected inflation

We have argued that the supply shocks of the 1970s increased the expected rate of inflation. This meant that the shocks resulted in a persistent inflation problem, not just a one-time increase in the price level, followed by a serious recession to offset the inflationary effect of the shock. And we would argue that the opposite situation happened in the 1980s, when the decline in energy and food prices helped to reduce expected inflation.

The idea that supply shocks will change expected inflation is controversial. Rational-expectations economists argue that changes in the relative prices of food and energy do not lead directly to changes in expected inflation. They say that if there was a legacy of higher expected inflation as a result of the relative price changes of the 1970s, then this must have been because of the way policymakers reacted to the shocks. If the Fed accommodates supply shocks, then people will make a rational judgment that inflation will be higher in the future. But if the Fed had not allowed money growth to increase, then there would have been no increase in expected inflation.

We disagree with the rational-expectations perspective on this. We argue that expected inflation, as it affects price and wage setting, is strongly affected by the actual experience of past inflation. And in the case of the supply shocks, there was also a push by both union and nonunion workers for catch-up wage increases. But the rational-expectations economists are certainly correct to stress the role of monetary policy in determining the course of inflation following a supply shock. *If a supply shock leads to persistent inflation, then it must be the case that monetary policy is accommodating the inflation.* Next we examine the role of policy.

SUPPLY-SHOCK INFLATION AND ECONOMIC POLICY

If there is no change in monetary policy and no increase in the nominal supply of money following a supply shock, then the increase in the price level will generate a lower real stock of money that will in turn reduce real income. Unless the Fed follows an inflation-accommodating monetary policy, there will be a fall in income following the supply shocks. Such a fall was described in Figure 10.6 (Y_A to Y_C to Y_E). In the *IS-ALM* framework we would describe this decline in the real money stock [(M_S/P) falls as P rises] as an inward shift of the *ALM* schedule.

If the Fed does respond to a supply shock, it has two very different policy alternatives. First, the Fed can accommodate the inflation by increasing the rate of growth of the money supply to match the new, higher rate of inflation. Inflation accommodation would maintain the level of the real money stock, thus allowing income and output to return quickly to their preshock levels. Alternatively, the Fed could refuse to accommodate the inflation by keeping the growth of the nominal supply of money below the rate of inflation. This would mean that income continues to fall after the supply shift and stays below potential until inflation has gone back to its preshock level.

In practice, over the 1971–87 period policymakers were continuously torn between the two goals of maintaining income and employment on the one hand, and reducing inflation on the other. At different times, the Fed embraced both inflation-accommodating and anti-inflationary policies. Indeed, policy oscillated as first inflation and then unemployment was thought to be the greater problem. Given the trade-off, it is not obvious that the Fed could have or should have tried to immediately eliminate any inflationary consequences of the supply shocks. Nevertheless, there was a higher inflation rate during the period than would have been experienced had an anti-inflationary policy been applied consistently. Prior to reviewing the rather confusing and inconsistent policies that were actually followed during this period, we will look at the two very different options that confronted policymakers: accepting the higher inflation in order to drive output toward potential output or bringing inflation back down to its preshock level and accepting the loss of income and the increase in unemployment. Combinations of these two policies made up the actual course of policy actions in response to the adverse supply shocks of the 1970s.

Targeting a Return toward Potential Output

When policymakers are more concerned with sustaining income and keeping down unemployment than with controlling inflation, their policy response following a supply shock will be to use economic policy actions that are targeted at income. The initial effect of the supply shock has been to initiate an inflationary spiral, reduce the real stock of money, and lower real income. Following this, expansionary fiscal or monetary policy or both could be used to bring output back toward potential output. Fiscal policy could be used to lower taxes and/or increase government expenditures, and monetary policy could expand the rate of growth of the money supply. The result of this policy of stimulating aggregate demand is to drive income up toward potential output, but with a higher long-run rate of inflation than existed before the combination of supply shock and the expansionary policy actions. In Figure 10.7 we return to the *IS-ALM* framework and the output–inflation trade-off to show the case where expansionary monetary policy is used after a supply shock to stimulate aggregate demand. The initial effect of the shock is shown as a movement from point *A* to point *C* in both panels of the figure. The right-hand panel shows the shift of the trade-off from SR–TO:1 to SR–TO:2, just as in Figure 10.6. The left-hand panel shows the shift in the *ALM* schedule that accompanies this change. The rise in the price level has reduced the real money supply *(ALM* to *ALM'),* but then the Fed accommodates the inflation so the real money supply grows again. (The *ALM* schedule moves back to its previous position and *ALM"* coincides with *ALM.*) The trade-off has moved down following the end of the supply shock (to SR–TO:3, the same as in Figure 10.6). The economy has returned to the level of employment

FIGURE 10.7   Inflation and a Quick Return to Full Employment Following a Supply Shock

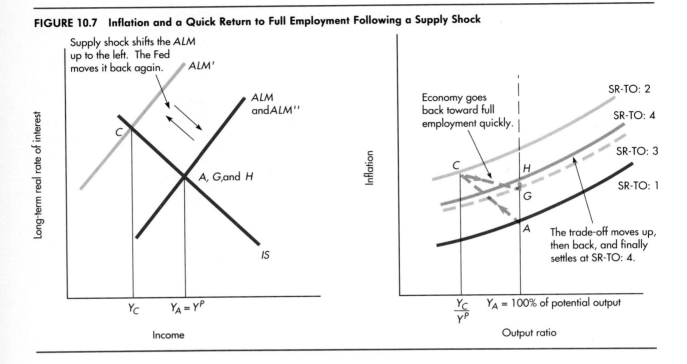

that existed before the supply shock, in this case to potential output (points *G* in both panels; points *A* and *G* coincide in the left panel).

In subsequent years, the Fed maintains the level of output by adjusting the nominal money supply. This avoids any additional cost in jobs and production, but there is a long-run boost to inflation. The new long-run equilibrium is shown at point *H* on SR–TO:4, where the economy has had to accept high chronic inflation. Point *H* coincides with points *A* and *H* in the left panel.

It is also the case that nominal interest rates are higher in the new long-run equilibrium. The real interest rate is the same as it was originally, but expected inflation is higher as expected inflation has been incorporated into pricing decisions in financial markets and goods markets.

In the example shown in Figure 10.7, the Fed has returned the economy quickly to potential output and has accepted a long-run legacy of higher inflation. The short-run trade-off is above its preshock position. The way in which the trade-off moves in this case is illustrated also in Worked Example 10.1, where expected inflation depends upon the actual rate of inflation over the prior two years.

We have seen that if the Fed decides to accommodate the supply-shock inflation, then there will be a higher rate of inflation indefinitely. The alternative strategy is to allow the increase in inflation to reduce the real stock of money and hence to bring on recession.

WORKED EXAMPLE 10.1 The Effect of a Supply Shock on Inflation with Inflation-Accommodating Monetary Policy (Output Returns Quickly to Potential Output)

Consider the following particular output–inflation trade-off when there is a supply shock, *SS:*

$$\text{Current } \Delta P/P = 0.2[(Y/Y^P) - 100] + \text{Exp } \Delta P/P + SS$$

coupled with the following relationship which determines inflationary expectations based upon past rates of inflation:

$$\text{Exp } \Delta P/P = 0.5(\Delta P/P \text{ of previous year}) + 0.5 \, (\Delta P/P \text{ of two years prior}).$$

Question: Suppose that output in this economy has been equal to potential output and the rate of inflation has been 5 percent a year for several years. Then there is a supply shock of 6 percent for one year. (*SS* equals 6 for one year and is then zero after that.) Output falls to 95 percent of potential in the year of the shock and is then restored to 100 percent in subsequent years. Show how inflation evolves in this economy.

Answer: The rates of inflation that evolve in this economy are shown as follows over the eight years starting with the initial shock. The rates of inflation have been rounded, but the calculations were made without rounding, resulting in small discrepancies.

Year	Short-run trade-off relation	+	Expected inflation	+	Supply shock	=	Current inflation
0	0.2(100 − 100)	+	[(0.5 × 5.00) + (0.5 × 5.00)]	+	0.00	=	5.00
	Supply shock starts.						
1	0.2(95 − 100)	+	[(0.5 × 5.00) + (0.5 × 5.00)]	+	6.00	=	10.00
	Supply shock ends.						
2	0.2(100 − 100)	+	[(0.5 × 10.00) + (0.5 × 5.00)]	+	0.00	=	7.50
3	0.2(100 − 100)	+	[(0.5 × 7.50) + (0.5 × 10.00)]	+	0.00	=	8.75
4	0.2(100 − 100)	+	[(0.5 × 8.75) + (0.5 × 7.50)]	+	0.00	=	8.12
5	0.2(100 − 100)	+	[(0.5 × 8.12) + (0.5 × 8.75)]	+	0.00	=	8.44
6	0.2(100 − 100)	+	[(0.5 × 8.44) + (0.5 × 8.12)]	+	0.00	=	8.28
7	0.2(100 − 100)	+	[(0.5 × 8.28) + (0.5 × 8.44)]	+	0.00	=	8.36
8	0.2(100 − 100)	+	[(0.5 × 8.36) + (0.5 × 8.28)]	+	0.00	=	8.32

The rather mechanical way that expected inflation is formed as a two-year average is giving an up-and-down movement to inflation. But despite this, the example provides an important lesson. It illustrates the way in which the shock feeds back into expected inflation.

With no sustained recession to offset the supply shock, there is a long-run boost to inflation. Inflation will settle indefinitely at rate that is about 3 percent higher than the rate it started at, as a result of the one-time supply shock (inflation started at 5 percent and ended at just over 8 percent). The shock gave an initial boost to inflation of 6 percent; that was partly offset by a one-year decline in output.

In this example, monetary policy is playing an important role in the background by accommodating the increase in inflation in order to restore the level of output.

Reducing Inflation to Preshock Levels

The strategy of allowing the real stock of money to decline following the supply shock and then living with the resulting deep recession describes Fed policy in the 1980s. We covered this approach to inflation fighting in Chapter 9 and so now we compare two alternative anti-inflation strategies: the sustained-recession approach and the cold-turkey policy. In both cases we use worked examples to illustrate. In Worked Example 10.2, we trace out the effect of a sustained moderate recession.

WORKED EXAMPLE 10.2   Anti-inflationary Policy: A Sustained Recession

We assume the same output–inflation trade-off and expectation formation with a supply shock that we have used previously.

Current $\Delta P/P = 0.2[(Y/Y^P) - 100] + \text{Exp } \Delta P/P + SS$

Exp $\Delta P/P = 0.5(\Delta P/P$ of previous year$) + 0.5(\Delta P/P$ of two years prior$)$.

Question: Suppose that output in this economy has been equal to potential output and the rate of inflation has been 5 percent a year for several years. Then there is a supply shock of 6 percent for one year. (SS equals 6 for one year and is then zero after that.) Output falls to 95 percent of potential in the year of the shock and is then held at this level until the increase in inflation has been eliminated. What rates of inflation are generated in this economy?

Answer: The rates of inflation that evolve in this economy are shown below. The rates have been rounded, but the calculations were made without rounding, resulting in small discrepancies.

The level of output for year 6 was calculated as the level needed to reduce inflation just to 5 percent. Expected inflation in year six was 5.72 percent $[(0.5 \times 5.56) + (0.5 \times 5.88)]$. This had to be reduced by 0.72 percent and this gave the figure of 96.4 percent for the output ratio $[0.2(96.4 - 100) = -0.72]$. A similar calculation is used to find the figure of 98.6 for year 7.

This example illustrates the substantial price that must be paid in order to restore the old level of inflation. Inflation jumped up to 10 percent in the year that the supply shock hit. This was reduced to 5 percent by holding output to 95 percent of potential during years two through five and at 96.4 percent of potential in year six, and at 98.6 percent of potential in year 7. This was a loss of 25 percent of GNP over the four years.

Year	Short-run trade-off relation	+	Expected inflation	+	Supply shock	=	Current inflation
0	0.2(100 − 100)	+	[(0.5 × 5.00) + (0.5 × 5.00)]	+	0.00	=	5.00
	Supply shock starts.						
1	0.2(95 − 100)	+	[(0.5 × 5.00) + (0.5 × 5.00)]	+	6.00	=	10.00
	Supply shock ends; recession is continued.						
2	0.2(95 − 100)	+	[(0.5 × 10.00) + (0.5 × 5.00)]	+	0.00	=	6.50
3	0.2(95 − 100)	+	[(0.5 × 6.50) + (0.5 × 10.00)]	+	0.00	=	7.25
4	0.2(95 − 100)	+	[(0.5 × 7.25) + (0.5 × 6.50)]	+	0.00	=	5.88
5	0.2(95 − 100)	+	[(0.5 × 5.88) + (0.5 × 7.25)]	+	0.00	=	5.56
	After inflation rate is restored to preshock level, monetary policy expands to allow for an increase in output.						
6	0.2(96.4 − 100)	+	[(0.5 × 5.56) + (0.5 × 5.88)]	+	0.00	=	5.00
7	0.2(98.6 − 100)	+	[(0.5 × 5.00) + (0.5 × 5.56)]	+	0.00	=	5.00
8	0.2(100 − 100)	+	[(0.5 × 5.00) + (0.5 × 5.00)]	+	0.00	=	5.00

This gives a sacrifice ratio of 5 since (25 ÷ 5) = 5, which is somewhat below the estimate of 6 that has been made for the sacrifice ratio for the actual economy.

Our discussion of policy responses to a supply shock indicates that neither of the two responses considered so far looks terribly appealing. This is just what one would expect, given that policy actions cannot immediately replace the loss of output that the economy suffered. There is either going to be an increase in inflation that could last indefinitely, or there is going to be a sustained recession. No wonder that in practice, policymakers oscillated between the two alternatives for several years. Adverse supply shocks are hard to deal with.

Another even more drastic approach has been suggested by rational-expectations economists, namely that the Fed should establish credibility in its anti-inflationary policies by taking a very hard line: Allow almost no increase in inflation at all, restore the economy to the preshock inflation rate very quickly, and reap the benefits of a faster drop in inflation as a result of a downward shift in inflationary expectations. This is a result of establishing policy credibility.[6]

Extreme anti-inflationary policies and policy credibility

If there is a belief that the Fed will choose to pursue a very hard anti-inflationary policy following a supply shock, then that policy could result in inflationary

---

[6] We explore the credibility issue in greater depth in Chapter 16. The credibility-policy suggestion does not require that there be strictly no initial increase in inflation, but rather that inflation is eliminated quickly and that the anti-inflationary policy is sustained.

expectations that were lower than those that would be calculated based upon past inflation. The improvement in expectations (a drop in Exp $\Delta P/P$ unrelated to past rates of inflation) should contribute to the effectiveness of anti-inflationary monetary policy.

We will use the following policy targets to reflect the Fed's attempt to convince financial and goods-market participants of the seriousness of its purpose:

1. Limit the effect of the supply shock in the current year to one half of the supply-shock impact.
2. Undertake whatever degree of monetary contraction is necessary in order to return and keep the current rate of inflation at the preshock level in all subsequent years.

Unfortunately, in order to maintain credibility by employing such a set of policies, the Fed may have to contract the money supply severely, perhaps bringing about a deep recession. Whether or not this credibility-building approach to inflation fighting—kicking inflation cold-turkey—is worthwhile depends upon just how much of a reduction in expected inflation is brought about by the establishment of anti-inflationary credibility.[7] If a cold-turkey policy works, then inflationary expectations will be reduced in each year by more than would have occurred in the absence of the credibility-building policy. The **credibility effect** is a reduction in inflationary expectations due to the belief that the Fed will be committed to restoring the preshock inflation rate as quickly as possible. *The greater the reduction in expected inflation due to credibility effects, the milder will be the recession necessary to restore inflation to its preshock level.*

credibility effect
The reduction in inflationary expectations that comes from being convinced that the Fed is in fact following a tough anti-inflationary policy.

WORKED EXAMPLE 10.3   Establishing Anti-Inflationary Credibility via a Cold-Turkey Approach to Dealing with a Supply Shock

The output–inflation trade-off with a supply shock is defined as

Current $\Delta P/P = 0.2[(Y/Y^P) - 100] + \text{Exp } \Delta P/P + SS.$

In this example, inflationary expectations are formed out of past inflation. However, to illustrate the potential benefits of credibility, we assume that the expected rate of inflation is reduced by 1 percentage point when there is a credible anti-inflationary policy in effect.

Exp $\Delta P/P = 0.5(\Delta P/P$ of previous year$) + 0.5(\Delta P/P$ of two years prior$)$
$- 1.0$ if the anti-inflation policy is credible.

Question: Suppose that output in this economy has been equal to potential output and the rate of inflation has been 5 percent a year for several years. Then there is a

---

[7] Our approach here exaggerates the differences between the sustained-recession case and the cold-turkey case by attributing no reduction in inflationary expectations to the Fed's anti-inflation stance in the sustained-recession case.

supply shock of 6 percent for one year. (*SS* equals 6 for one year and is then zero after that.) Monetary policy is used to keep the inflation rate from rising by more than 3 percent in spite of the supply shock. How large a reduction of output is needed and what subsequently happens to inflation in the economy?

Answer: The rates of inflation that evolve in this economy are shown as follows over the four years starting with the initial shock.

Year	Short-run trade-off relation	+	Expected inflation with credibility	+	Supply shock	=	Current inflation
0	$0.2(100 - 100)$	+	$[(0.5 \times 5.00) + (0.5 \times 5.00)]$	+	0.00	=	5.00
	Supply shock starts; monetary contraction keeps the current inflation rate from reflecting more than one half of the supply shock.						
1	$0.2(85 - 100)$	+	$[(0.5 \times 5.00) + (0.5 \times 5.00)]$	+	6.00	=	8.00
	Supply shock ends; the deep recession coupled with the relatively mild increase in the inflation rate makes the Fed's anti-inflationary policy credible.						
2	$0.2(97.5 - 100)$	+	$[(0.5 \times 8.00) + (0.5 \times 5.00) - 1.00]$	+	0.00	=	5.00
3	$0.2(97.5 - 100)$	+	$[(0.5 \times 5.00) + (0.5 \times 8.00) - 1.00]$	+	0.00	=	5.00
	Inflation has been restored to preshock levels and the economy has been restored to the preshock equilibrium.						
4	$0.2(100 - 100)$	+	$[(0.5 \times 5.00) + (0.5 \times 5.00)]$			=	5.00

Output is equal to 100 percent of potential and inflation is 5 percent in subsequent years. In contrast with the previous example where output was not allowed to fall below 95 percent of potential output, a serious enough contraction, in this case the initial contraction in output was down to 85 percent of potential. If this example described an actual event, a recession of that depth would exceed any that has been experienced in the United States since the 1930s.

The figures for output in years two and three were the levels needed to reduce inflation to 5 percent. In both years expected inflation would have been 6.5 percent $[(0.5 \times 8.00) + (0.5 \times 5.00)]$ if there were no credibility effect. In this example expected inflation in those years, including the credibility effect, was 5.5 percent. Inflation had to be reduced by 0.5 percent and this meant an output ratio of 97.5 percent $[0.2(97.5 - 100) = -0.5]$. Output would have had to be reduced by less if the credibility effect were stronger and it would have had to be reduced by more if the credibility effect were weaker. In practice, the impact of credibility is not known.

This example illustrates the depth of the recession that must be endured in order to reduce inflation so quickly. In this example, the loss of GNP totaled 20 percent over three years in this cold-turkey case versus 25 percent over six years in the sustained-recession case. The cold-turkey approach benefits from the credibility effect, but though the recession is shorter, it is nevertheless much deeper. While the total loss of GNP is somewhat less here than in the more gradual approach, there are significant dangers in using so drastic a cut in output. We have assumed here and in the discussions in the text that goods-market equilibrium (the *IS* schedule) will remain stable as the Fed hits the economy with a recession. In the real economy, investor or consumer confidence might be broken by a recession as deep as the one just described, leading to an unstable decline in output.

On the basis of the experience of the 1970s and 1980s, there is controversy among macroeconomists as to whether or not the credibility effects are significant enough to warrant the cold-turkey approach and whether or not expectations in all markets would respond to Fed policies. There is also a controversial debate over whether or not such credibility-building policies were actually pursued. Whatever the truth is about the potential benefits of a credible anti-inflation policy, policy was not credible in its fight against inflation in the 1970s. We look now at the 1970–79 period, a time when the Fed did not follow a clear strategy for policy.

Policy Vacillation, 1970–1979

The economy had its first experience with stagflation from 1968 to 1970 and the Fed reacted to this by encouraging output growth. It allowed very rapid growth in the nominal supply of money, enough to allow for strong growth in the real stock of money from 1970 to the end of 1972. Inflation was curbed temporarily in late 1971 and 1972 by the use of wage and price controls (see the box on page 408), but the controls were gradually being released in 1973 when the supply shocks hit. Inflation accelerated first as businesses were allowed to make price increases that they had wanted to make earlier, and then the supply shocks added to inflation. The inflation caused by the shocks did become a major concern of the Fed during 1973 and the growth of the nominal money supply actually slowed after 1973, even as inflation was still accelerating. This meant that the real money supply declined sharply in 1974–75, resulting in a sharp recession. Monetary policy was then eased in 1975–76 because of the concern about high unemployment and there was then a recovery of output growth in the economy lasting through 1979.

Over this period, therefore, the Fed did not follow a consistent policy. It encouraged growth until 1973. Then it became scared by the run-up in inflation and sent the economy into a tailspin in 1974–75. Then it became nervous about the recession and let growth pick up rapidly. By 1978, inflation was accelerating as a new set of supply shocks hit, especially the second oil-price increase of 1979. By the end of 1979, the economy was again experiencing double-digit inflation in the CPI and nearing it in the GNP deflator.

By 1979 the U.S. economy had been through a decade and a half of inflation that was higher than it had been before 1964. The increase in inflation was caused by the one-two punch of the excess aggregate demand of the late 1960s and the supply shocks of the 1970s. Following the second round of inflationary shocks in 1978–80, events initially followed much the same pattern as was experienced following the earlier shocks. There was a continuation of the earlier vacillation. The economy went into a recession in 1980, but the Fed again got cold feet and stimulated aggregate demand in the economy. A partial recovery started even before the end of 1980 and inflation remained high. By 1981, however, the Fed decided that enough was enough and we have described the consequences of this decision to tackle inflation.

One aspect of the success of the anti-inflation strategy of the 1980s that we did not discuss in Chapter 9, however, was the favorable effect of the decline in food and energy prices.

Favorable Supply Shocks, 1981–1988

Not all supply shocks are adverse and not all of the reduction in the rate of inflation in the 1980s can be traced to the recession and the change in monetary policy. Some of the reduction was due to the good fortune of positive shifts of supply. When there is a sudden reduction in the price of commodities or materials, the economy experiences a favorable supply shock. In terms of the output–inflation trade-off, SS becomes negative and the current rate of inflation is lower because of the direct effect of the shock. Of course, this boon to the economy in the form of a lower price level has exceptional effects just like (though in the opposite direction from) those that occur under stagflation.

Through much of 1980s, energy and food prices fell and this was an important source of the drop in the price level. There was a downward shift in the short-run trade-off. Food and energy prices fell in real terms by from 1 to 4 percent per year from 1981 to 1986 and oil prices collapsed in 1986, falling by more than 20 percent in real terms that year. Another positive supply shift in the United States was the upward movement in the foreign-exchange value of the dollar, a trend that continued along with falling energy and food prices until 1985. By putting downward pressure on the prices of imports sold in the United States, the revaluation of the dollar contributed to overall lower prices.

The positive supply shocks also contributed to a decline in inflationary expectations. As the built-in rate of inflation came down, the short-run trade-off slowly fell. From 1981 to 1988 the annual rate of inflation was low and the rate of real output growth was high.

Supply Shocks and the Output–Inflation Trade-Off: Conclusions

An adverse supply shock or series of shocks can initiate an increase in the rate of inflation. The supply shock worsens the output–inflation trade-off, but it is the reaction of policymakers and the formation of inflationary expectations that follow the supply shock(s) that determine the long-run course of inflation. Following a supply shock, there are a spectrum of choices to be made ranging from quickly regaining potential output—at the cost of suffering a persistently higher inflation rate—or, alternatively, quickly reducing the inflation rate to preshock levels—at the cost of suffering a very deep and potentially unstable recession.

The sharp burst of inflation in the 1970s coincided with sharp upward movements in certain key prices, particularly for food, energy, imports, and other raw materials. These price increases fed directly into higher costs of

IRAQI INVASION AND THE FED'S DILEMMA

The GNP growth rate had already slowed to a crawl by spring 1990, then in early August came the Iraqi invasion of Kuwait. The immediate economic effect was a surge in oil prices.

The oil price increase started with fears of diminished oil supplies, as Iraq seized Kuwait's oil fields and the West declared an embargo on oil purchases from either country. Fears of an oil shortage bid up prices on the spot market from $20 to $28 per barrel. Those increases, in turn, pushed up the prices of term contracts, which are often set on delivery and based partly on spot prices. Oil firms then hiked wholesale prices of already refined gas—based on the cost of *replacing* it. In a few days, average pump prices rose at least 16 cents in a reflection of wholesale price changes.

In some respects the United States was in a better position than it was in 1973, at the time of the first oil shock. Oil demand had been slipping as economic growth had slowed. After 1973 the United States reduced by about 40 percent the amount of oil and gas needed to produce a dollar of GNP. That is, there was energy conservation and some changes in production methods. By 1990 surplus oil supplies were available from countries such as Venezuela and Mexico. Moreover, the government has a 790-million-barrel Strategic Petroleum Reserve.

As this is written we do not know whether there will be a full-blown mideast war or a quick, peaceful end to the crisis, but even the increase in oil prices so far has faced the Fed with a dilemma, as the *Washington Post* reported in August 1990.

> Top Federal Reserve policy makers met yesterday to confront a dilemma: how to keep inflation under control and the U.S. economy out of recession with oil prices up more than $8 dollars a barrel in a month.
>
> The problem is not just that the Iraqi invasion of Kuwait sent oil prices soaring, but that it happened at a time when the economy had already lost its wind and inflation was stubbornly high. Higher oil prices only made the Fed's dilemma more acute.
>
> "The jump in oil is like a tax on the economy and a bubble on the inflation rate," said analyst Ray Stone of Stone & McCarthy, a financial markets research firm. "It's got to be a tough time at the Fed."
>
> In fact, it is no less of a tough time for the U.S. economy. While there is no sign of a serious nationwide slump, some parts of the country and some industries are headed downhill, unemployment has begun to rise and higher oil prices have begun to work their way through the economy. Consumers were already spending cautiously when the invasion occurred, and some forecasters fear the new uncertainty about economic prospects will cause them to zip up their pocketbooks.
>
> For a moment, put yourself in the shoes of Fed Chairman Alan Greenspan or one of the other key central bank officials who sat around the table in the Fed board room yesterday.
>
> Even if you favored easing monetary policy to give a boost to the economy—lowering short-term interest rates by adding cash to the banking system—you might have paused. If financial markets took the move the wrong way and bid up long-term interest rates because of a fear the Fed was abandoning its effort to bring inflation under control, then easing policy might backfire. After all, the level of long-term rates is usually more important to the economy than short-term rates, most economists believe.
>
> Suppose, on the other hand, that your principal concern is making sure that inflation does not get out of hand (several of the officials around the table yesterday have taken that position in the past on the grounds that the way to maximize long-term economic growth is to lower inflation). In that case, you did not want to pump money into the economy at a faster rate.
>
> Nevertheless, even an anti-inflation hawk might hesitate to stand by while the economy drops into a recession if only for fear of a political backlash against the Fed that could restrict its freedom to fight inflation in the future.

doing business, having a direct and immediate effect on the then current rate of inflation. They also had an indirect effect on inflationary expectations. When the energy and materials prices stopped increasing rapidly, inflation rates came back down, but the effect of cost increases on expectations left a legacy of inflation that was hard to deal with. If materials prices had quickly reversed direction—falling after having risen, rather than simply slowing their rate of increase—then a positive supply shock would have followed on the heels of a negative supply shock, effectively canceling out the direct effects and generating little or no increase in expectations. Unfortunately that is not the way the economy worked in the 1970s. It was not until the 1980s that there was a sustained fall in energy prices.

Up until the 1970s, most of the inflation we had experienced had been initiated by increases in aggregate demand and sustained by inflationary expectations. Increases in costs, including wage increases in excess of productivity growth, were the consequence of previous increases in demand. Generally speaking, autonomous increases in costs were not the initiating factor in inflation until the supply shocks of the 1970s.

There were no good ways to deal with the legacy of inflation, especially during those years when the trade-off worsened. American workers and consumers were reeling from the effects of the increases in their gasoline, home-heating, and grocery bills brought about by the food and energy shocks. As they demanded higher wages to pay those bills, they induced a continuing inflation, because the bills had to be paid by someone. Higher wages meant higher costs passed along as higher prices. Policymakers responded first by bringing on a recession and then by allowing growth, as people found those high bills even harder to pay out of unemployment checks. Finally, a period of high unemployment in the early 1980s and positive shocks throughout the period combined to reduce inflation and inflationary expectations. The renewal of conflict in the Mideast in 1990 may lead to a new adverse supply shock, facing the Fed with a familiar policy dilemma (see box, "The Iraqi Invasion and the Fed's Dilemma").

SUMMARY

- Inflation can be initiated by shifts in aggregate supply as well as by increases in aggregate demand.
- If there are large changes in the relative prices of important commodities and no offsetting changes in other prices, then these relative price changes will change the overall price level. The result is called a supply shock.
- In order for supply shocks to contribute to an increase in both the overall price level and the rate of inflation, the national expenditures on the products suffering the supply shocks have to be large portions of GNP and there has to be downward rigidity in other prices, particularly real wages.

- The relative prices of energy and agricultural products have changed sharply; the price of both groups of commodities rose in the early 1970s. Energy prices rose again in the late 1970s. Both relative prices have fallen subsequently. These changes were important supply shocks. A supply shock such as the OPEC price increase means that we have to pay more for foreign oil. There is no simple way to avoid the costs that this imposes.

- The productivity slowdown and changes in the value of the dollar were supply shocks of a somewhat different kind. The slowdown in the growth of labor productivity led to a rise in the unit labor costs. Since there was no offsetting reduction in the rate of growth of wages, this also contributed to inflation. The changes in the value of the dollar changed Americans' cost of living as foreign goods became more or less expensive.

- In a supply-shock inflation, the economy experiences an initial increase in the price level as the price of the output of U.S. producers in affected sectors increases. The cost of living increases because of both the increase in the price of domestic output and because of the rise in the prices of imported commodities. The increased cost of living then affects wages, and the acceleration of wage inflation leads to increased price inflation. There is a price–wage spiral.

- In terms of the output–inflation trade-off, an adverse supply shock results in an initial upward shift in the trade-off. The subsequent price–wage spiral then results in an increase in expected inflation.

- In the absence of any offsetting action by the Fed, a supply shock will raise the price level and reduce the real stock of money. This will reduce output. The Fed can choose to sustain the real money stock and avoid the contractionary effects of the shock.

- A supply shock confronts policymakers with a dilemma—once the shock has occurred, inflation rises. Aggregate demand policies can then be directed either at fighting the rise in inflation (thereby making the reduction in output worse) or policies can stimulate aggregate demand to return output and employment to their preshock levels (at the expense of making inflation worse).

- Once the impact of the supply shock has passed, inflation will fall and then subsequent increases or decreases in aggregate demand will determine whether there is a continuing or even a worsening legacy of inflation or whether income expands toward potential.

- When anti-inflationary policies are chosen, these involve reducing aggregate demand.

- If the Fed takes a completely tough line and seeks to bring inflation back to its original level right away, then it will create a major reduction in the real money supply and a very serious recession, though inflation will eventually start to decline and output will return to potential.

- The effectiveness of the anti-inflationary policy is enhanced to the degree that the Fed is able to establish its credibility as an inflation fighter, thereby reducing inflationary expectations.

- In practice, policymakers vacillated between the goal of fighting inflation and the goal of reducing unemployment. The result was that during the 1970s, the economy oscillated between very high inflation and very high unemployment. Then, in the 1980s, a determined course of inflation fighting was chosen.

■ Supply shocks can be positive. In the mid-1980s such positive supply shifts occurred because of a collapse of oil prices and a decline in the prices of imported goods.

■ Positive supply shocks, combined with an anti-inflationary monetary policy, drove down both inflation and inflationary expectations in the 1980s, but the rise in oil prices in 1990 threatens a new adverse supply shock.

KEY TERMS

adverse supply shock
credibility effect
favorable supply shock
price–wage spiral
supply shock

DISCUSSION QUESTIONS AND PROBLEMS

1. Contrast the explanation for stagflation that is based wholly on inflationary expectations with the explanation based upon supply shocks.

2. How is a supply shock different from the normal process by which relative prices change in the economy?

3. What are the choices that policymakers face when confronted with a supply shock? List some costs and benefits of alternative responses.

4. Use the following relationships,

    The output–inflation trade-off with a supply shock

    Current $\Delta P/P = 0.3[(Y/Y^P) - 100] + \text{Exp } \Delta P/P + SS$

    The formation of inflationary expectations

    Exp $\Delta P/P = 0.75(\Delta P/P$ of previous year$) + 0.25(\Delta P/P$ of two years prior$)$

    to trace out the reaction of the economy over several years to a supply shock of 4 percent for one year. Inflation has been stable at 3 percent per year prior to the shock. In the absence of an overt policy response, output falls to 98 percent of potential in the year of the shock.

    a. Assume that the output ratio returns to 100 percent the year after the shock has passed and stays at 100 percent. What has been the long-run effect of the supply shock on inflation?

    b. Assume that the output ratio stays at 98 percent until inflation is brought back to 3 percent a year or less. How long does this take?

PART VI

The International Sector

Modern national economies are not isolated from worldwide events. Rather than being *closed* economies, where economic activity is isolated within the country, modern economies are *open*, and so are influenced by global economic circumstances. In open economies, goods, services, and capital are traded in international markets where resources flow between nations. In the United States during the 1970s and 1980s, there was a growing appreciation of just how important international economic events were in shaping the domestic economy. Activity that took place outside the country affected individual households and businesses throughout the United States.

In the next two chapters we examine the open economy. We look at the value of the dollar, the balance of payments, the balance of trade and net exports, and relate them to aggregate income. We describe the workings of international financial markets where currencies and other financial assets are exchanged and where the exchange rates among currencies are determined.

We look at the way in which the world economy affects an open domestic economy by extending the *IS-ALM* analysis to include international markets. In an open economy, income, along with interest rates and other aggregate measures of economic conditions, are not wholly determined by domestic conditions. In analyzing the performance of an open economy it is necessary to understand the behavior of foreign consumers, investors, borrowers, and governments.

Domestic policymaking is more complicated in an open economy than in a closed economy, but this analysis of an open economy provides a better view of economic reality. We look at how the effectiveness of domestic monetary and fiscal policies is altered by the international sector. We also examine the effectiveness of international economic policies such as trade restrictions and exchange control which are designed to influence domestic performance by bringing about changes in international conditions.

CHAPTER 11

International Trade, Capital Movements, and the Exchange Rate

INTRODUCTION

Economic policymakers, business managers, and the general public are now well aware of the importance of the international economy. This awareness has developed relatively later in the United States than in the rest of the world. For much of U.S. history, especially during the period from 1945 until the 1970s, economic events overseas and across borders were of secondary importance to the United States. From the late 1940s through the late 1950s the Japanese and European societies were struggling with recovery from the devastation of World War II. During that period, the United States dominated the world's economy.

The U.S. economy remains by far the largest national economy in the world, but U.S. GNP has dropped from approximately 50 percent of world GNP in the 1950s to 30 percent in the 1980s. The Western European economy accounts also for about 30 percent share of world GNP, while the Japanese economy accounts for around another 10 percent. Many U.S. industries are now more concerned about foreign competition than about fluctuations in domestic demand. There has been a dramatic change in international economic relationships.

In this chapter and the next we will try to answer several questions about international economic relationships and the U.S. economy. What determines the exchange rate of the dollar for other currencies? Why does the value of the dollar fluctuate? Why did the U.S. economy change, going from a *net exporting nation* (one that sold more to the world than it bought from the world) to the reverse, a *net importing nation?* In order to pay for the excess of its imports over its exports, the United States has gone from being the leading creditor nation, lending more to other countries than any other nation, to being, by the late 1980s, the leading *debtor nation,* borrowing more money than any other. How did these changes in international economic relationships affect equilibrium income, economic performance, and economic policies?

International considerations add reality to our description of the economy. However, they also add significant complexity. In order to deal with this complexity, we focus on how international markets affect the domestic economy rather than attempting to describe the workings of the world economy as a whole. We approach the role of trade in the domestic economy in several steps. In this chapter, we look at what determines imports and exports at a given level of income. This simplicity allows us to focus on the exchange rate of the dollar as a primary factor determining the balance of our trade.

We then look at the international purchases and sales of assets. These depend on interest rates and expectations about the future value of the exchange rate. The flows of exports and imports and the flows of capital assets are the major determinants of the demand for and supply of foreign currency—often called foreign exchange—so that in the second part of this chapter we turn the analysis around and look at how the supply of and demand for foreign exchange determine the exchange rate. In the next chapter, we return to the *IS-ALM* framework in order to look at the role played by international trade in macroeconomic performance and macroeconomic policy.

INTERNATIONAL TRADE AND FOREIGN EXCHANGE

foreign exchange
Foreign currency that is purchased or sold in foreign-exchange markets.

The international exchange of goods and services sometimes happens through direct bilateral exchange. For example, in the 1930s, Hitler's finance minister convinced the government of Hungary to exchange Hungarian pork for German aspirin—without the use of money. The exchange was undertaken because neither country had free access to foreign markets and because Hitler was able to coerce an exchange of goods favorable to Germany. More recently, in the 1970s in some countries that still practiced exchange control industrial products were traded directly for oil during the period when there were oil shortages. However, most international trade is accomplished by an importer who first obtains foreign currency and then uses foreign currency to purchase foreign goods. Foreign currencies (i.e., **foreign exchange**) are traded or exchanged for one another in international financial markets or, more specifically, **foreign-exchange markets.** Foreign-exchange markets relieve international traders of the need to barter aspirin for pigs or transistors for oil. Trades of foreign exchange facilitate and accompany the trade of foreign goods and assets. But what happens in the foreign-exchange market also influences the amounts of goods and assets traded.

The decision to buy an imported good depends upon many factors, but in this discussion we are keeping income and tastes constant, so it is the *price* of a good being imported or exported that we will focus on as the factor that affects the decision to purchase it. In general, therefore, *the volume of exports from the United States will be higher when the prices paid by foreigners for U.S. products is lower.* The price that is relevant is the price that foreigners pay in their own currency. By a similar argument, *the volume of imports into the United States will be higher when the prices paid by U.S. purchasers are lower.* And the price that is relevant is the price that Americans pay in dollars.

For example, a decision by a foreign airline to buy Boeing aircraft is certainly affected by many different economic and political factors (reliability and energy consumption, for example), but if we take those other factors as given, it is the price of, say, Boeing's 757 relative to the European Airbus that is most important. Further, even if the airline chooses Boeing, the number of planes imported is likely to be smaller in the case of a high price for Boeing airplanes than the number of planes imported when the price of U.S.-produced aircraft is low.

Boeing will offer to sell its planes to the foreign airline at a particular price in dollars. But to the managers of the airline, the price of Boeing aircraft (that is, the price in marks, yen, lira, or whatever is the home currency of the purchaser) depends upon how many dollars can be bought with its currency as well as depending upon the price Boeing charges for its planes.

The Exchange Rate

exchange rate
The number of units of foreign currency that can be purchased for one unit of another currency (for example, the number or fraction of marks, yen, lira, pounds, or other currencies that can be purchased with one U.S. dollar).

The number of units of one currency that can be purchased with one unit of another currency is called the *foreign-currency exchange rate* or simply the **exchange rate.** When referring to exchange rates it is important to be clear about how the rate is expressed. One can look at the exchange rate between any two currencies in two possible ways. For example, one can look at the number of German marks exchanged for one British pound or, alternatively, the reciprocal of this number is the fraction of a pound that can be purchased with a single German mark. Foreign exchange rates are published daily in many newspapers; usually the exchange rates with the dollar are expressed both ways, such as number of marks per dollar, or fraction of a dollar per mark.

The general practice in the United States is to express *dollar* exchange rates as so many units of foreign currency that can be purchased with one dollar—2 German marks per dollar, 150 Japanese yen per dollar, and so on. This means that if the amount of foreign currency that the dollar can buy falls (that is, if the dollar becomes worth less in foreign-exchange markets), then the value of the dollar has fallen. *A fall in the value of the dollar is a decline in the exchange rate.* For example, if the dollar is exchanged for 130 yen rather than for 150 yen, then the exchange rate of the dollar has fallen against the yen.

This practice is not universally followed, however. For example, the exchange rate of the dollar with the British pound is often expressed in terms of the number of dollars per pound, say, $1.60 per pound. We will not use

THE EXCHANGE RATE: DOLLARS FOR YEN OR YEN FOR DOLLARS, WHICH WAY IS IT?

Readers be warned, international trade economists do it differently. One of the most confusing concepts in economics is the way in which the rate of exchange between two currencies should be expressed. As we indicate in the text, we choose to express the rate as the number of units of foreign currency that can be purchased with one dollar (for example, 130 yen to the dollar). This approach is commonly used in the media and it squares with the intuitive idea of *appreciation* or *devaluation* of the dollar. When the exchange as we have defined it goes up (e.g., from 130 yen to 150 yen), the dollar buys more foreign currency—the dollar has appreciated. When the exchange rate goes down (e.g., from 130 yen to 110 yen), the dollar buys less foreign currency—the dollar has depreciated.

Unfortunately, this approach is the inverse of the concept that international trade economists focus upon when they describe foreign-exchange markets. They define the exchange rate in terms of the price of foreign exchange, so that the yen to dollar exchange rate is the cost of purchasing one yen with dollars. If the exchange rate in our terms is equal to 130 yen to the dollar, the inverse would be $0.0077 (77/100ths of a dollar) per yen. If the dollar appreciates, from 130 yen to 150 yen to the dollar (dollar purchases more yen), then the exchange rate, expressed as the cost of yen, declines in dollar terms, in this example dropping from $0.0077 to $0.0067. The appreciating dollar means that yen purchased in foreign exchange markets are now cheaper to buy with dollars, exactly the concept that trade economists wish to show. But it also means that their definition of the dollar exchange rate falls when the dollar appreciates! This is very confusing and so we define the exchange rate as yen per dollar rather than dollars per yen. For those who go on to further studies in international economics, however, you will find that the trade economists' definition will usually appear in international economics texts and journals.

this alternative. We will stick to the convention of saying that U.S. exchange rates are expressed as units of foreign currency per dollar—the exchange rate with the pound in this example is then 0.625 British pounds per dollar (1 ÷ 1.6 = 0.625).

Changes in the Exchange Rate and the Flow of Trade

The exchange rates between the U.S. dollar and all other currencies are important in determining how much product from other countries is imported by U.S. buyers and how much U.S. product is exported to foreign buyers. For example, let's see how the exchange rate affects the choice of purchasing either a U.S.-made or German-made automobile. In the early 1980s the exchange rate between the U.S. dollar and the West German mark (deutsche mark or DM) was around two DM to the dollar. This means that during that time period, a German car that was sold to a U.S. dealer for DM60,000 by a German exporter cost $30,000 when purchased in the United States. At an exchange rate of two DM to the dollar, the U.S. import-car dealer had to pay $30,000 to purchase the DM60,000 needed to buy the German car. Of course the dealer must also pay for shipping and for a small tariff that is levied on imported cars. (A tariff is just an excise or sales tax imposed by the government on imported goods.) The final customer in the United States might pay $40,000 to cover all these costs, including the dealer's markup. The number of BMWs or Audis that Americans would then buy depends upon the comparison of these German cars at $40,000 with the alternatives facing car buyers in the United States.

In an earlier period, the dollar exchanged for four marks, so that German automobiles that cost DM60,000 were substantially cheaper for U.S. customers. At four marks to the dollar it takes only $15,000 for a car dealer to cover the same factory cost in DM. For this example, let's assume that shipping costs and dealer markups stayed the same in all periods (approximately $10,000). Then an American customer would pay around $25,000 for the German car. As the value of the dollar fell to three marks, it took $20,000 for a car dealer to cover the factory cost in DM, so that the American customer would pay around $30,000 for the German car. By 1989 the DM had risen to 1.80 DM to the dollar, and a DM60,000 automobile would have had a base price to U.S. dealers of $33,333 and a U.S. selling price of over $43,333 without any change in the price of the cars in marks. As summarized in the following tables, that sort of shift in exchange rates helped convert the BMW and Audi from upper-mid-priced cars to high-priced luxury cars in just a few years.

DM/$ exchange rate	Price of a German auto in the U.S.*
4.00	$25,000
3.00	$30,000
2.00	$40,000
1.80	$43,333

* Including approximately $10,000 in U.S.-based charges.

The same story runs in reverse for U.S. exports. U.S.-made aircraft or computers are expensive to foreign customers when the dollar is high and inexpensive when the dollar is low. It follows, therefore, that *an increase in the value of the dollar will encourage imports by making them cheaper, and it will discourage exports by making them more expensive.*

The trade-weighted exchange rate

The exchange rate of the U.S. dollar against the German mark affects U.S. trade with Germany, while the exchange rate of the U.S. dollar against the yen affects trade with Japan. In fact, these exchange rates also affect our exports to other countries where our companies compete for sales against Japanese and German firms. There are many different exchange rates, each of which has some effect on U.S. imports and exports, and they all change at different rates and in different directions. In order to characterize the average levels of all the different exchange rates, we need a summary measure of the exchange rates between the U.S. dollar and the currencies of our major trading partners.

From the U.S. point of view, we measure the value of the dollar relative to other currencies using an approach similar to the one used to measure the domestic price level and inflation. The domestic price level is computed as an index number that changes over time depending on the average change in all the different prices that go into the index. Similarly, the values of the many different foreign currencies are combined into a summary index number called the *nominal trade-weighted exchange rate,* sometimes simply the **nominal exchange rate index.** The nominal exchange rate index, denoted by the symbol *ex,* changes over time depending on the overall or average rates of exchange of many currencies for one particular currency. This index is set equal to 100 in a base year and it then changes over time depending on how the dollar moves, on average, relative to all the important foreign currencies. The computation uses a weighted average, where the weights are the relative importance of the countries in U.S. trade.

For example, if the United States traded with two countries (say, 40 percent of its trade with Germany and 60 percent with Japan) and the exchange rate of the dollar against the mark declined by 20 percent and the exchange rate of the dollar against the yen declined by 30 percent over some period since the base year, then the nominal exchange rate index would have declined by 26 percent $[0.4 \times (-20) + 0.6 \times (-30) = -26]$. The nominal exchange rate index would then be $(100 - 26) = 74$.

In practice, the United States trades with many countries so the index incorporates many currencies. As Figure 11.1 shows, the U.S. nominal exchange rate (dashed line) has gone through rising and falling periods since 1973. If the nominal exchange rate goes up, as it did from 1980 through 1985, then it takes more foreign currency to purchase dollars—dollars are more expensive to foreigners. If the nominal exchange rate goes down, as it did after 1985, dollars are less expensive to foreigners.

The inflation-adjusted real exchange rate

Changes in the nominal exchange rate index describe changes in the average exchange rate between dollars and foreign currencies, but it does not necessarily reflect changes in the relative prices of U.S. and foreign products. Because inflation rates are different across countries, the nominal exchange rate can go off track as an indicator of how the prices of foreign goods sold in the United States are changing relative to the prices of goods both produced and sold in the U.S.

Take an example where the rate of inflation is 10 percent per year in the United States and 3 percent in Germany. The buying power of the dollar in the United States is falling 7 percent faster than the buying power of the

nominal exchange rate index
An index of the values of the dollar where the contribution of any particular nominal exchange rate for any one foreign currency contributes to the value of the index based upon the share of total trade conducted with that country. The index is denoted by the symbol *ex.*

FIGURE 11.1   Nominal and Real Exchange Rate Indexes for the U.S. Dollar, 1973–1989

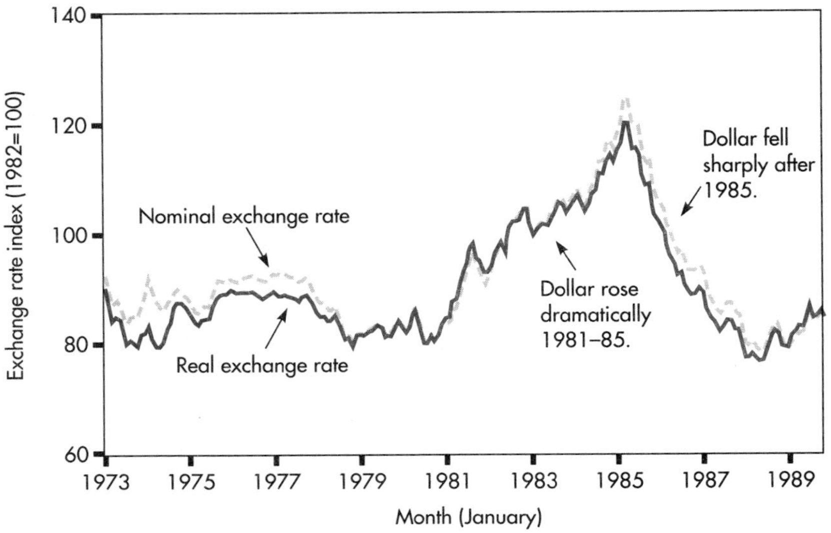

The U.S. exchange rate varies quite a bit from month to month and has shown sustained swings in value. The real and nominal exchange rates move together most of the time.

Source: *World Financial Markets,* various issues (New York: Morgan Guaranty Trust).

mark in Germany. If the exchange rate between the dollar and the German mark were to decline by 7 percent from one year to the next, then German buyers would be getting 7 percent more dollars for their marks, but the decline in the exchange rate would be exactly undone by the change in relative prices in the two countries. The number of Mercedes it took to trade for one Boeing 757 would be the same in the two years. (At least, this would be true on average for many goods.) This means that when a change in the exchange rate simply compensates for differences in inflation rates, the relative prices of U.S. imports (from Germany) and U.S. exports (to Germany) do not change.

Since it is changes in relative prices that lead to changes in the demands for imports and exports, we want to find out how changes in the exchange rate affect the relative prices of internationally traded goods and services in general. We need a measure of exchange rates that is adjusted for the effect of any difference in the rates of inflation between the United States and its trading partners. We make the inflation adjustment between any two currencies by computing an inflation-adjusted exchange rate called the **real exchange rate index** and denoted by the symbol *rex*. Changes in the real exchange

real exchange rate index
The nominal exchange rate index adjusted for changes in the relative price levels in the United States and its trading partners. Relative to the nominal index, it changes over time depending on whether inflation is more or less rapid in the United States than in other countries. The index is denoted by the symbol *rex*.

rate (calculated as an index) indicate a change in the buying power of the currency in one country compared to the buying power of the currency in another. The computation of the change in the real exchange rate index for the U.S. dollar in relation to the other world currencies is shown in Equation 11.1:

Percent change in the real exchange rate index = Percent change in the nominal exchange rate index + Difference between U.S. and foreign inflation rates (11.1)

$$\frac{\Delta rex}{rex} = \frac{\Delta ex}{ex} + \frac{\Delta P}{P} - \frac{\Delta P_f}{P_f}.$$

The real exchange rate rises or falls whenever there is a change in the nominal exchange rate that is higher or lower than the difference between inflation rates across countries. For example, if the nominal exchange rate of the dollar were to rise by 5 percent from one year to the next, and over the same period the U.S. inflation rate were 3 percent higher than the average in other countries, the real exchange rate between the United States and the rest of the world would rise by 8 percent. For foreign purchasers of U.S. products and assets, the cost of buying dollars has gone up by 5 percent and the relative cost of goods and services in the United States has gone up by 3 percent.

Equation 11.1 uses the rate of change of the nominal exchange rate index and the rates of inflation to calculate a rate of change of the real exchange rate index. If we want to compare the price levels of traded goods and services in one economy and in the rest of the world rather than rates of change (i.e., how expensive are U.S.-traded goods and services compared with those from the rest of the world), we can do so by computing the levels of the indexes. In Equation 11.2 we show that the real exchange rate (*rex*, shown here as an index), the U.S. price level *(P)*, and the world or foreign price level *(P_f)*, are related as follows:

$$rex = (P \times ex) \div P_f. \tag{11.2}$$

In the preceding example, the nominal exchange rate had fallen from 100 to 74. If the U.S. price level had risen by 30 percent (to 130 or 1.3) and the average foreign price level had risen by 20 percent (to 120 or 1.2) over the same period, then the real exchange rate would have fallen to 80.2 as determined from $(74 \times 130) \div 120 = 80.2$.

Figure 11.1 showed the real exchange rate of the dollar (solid line) along with the nominal exchange rate. We see that there is a difference between the two exchange rates, but that most of the variations in the nominal exchange rate are paralleled by changes in the real exchange rate. This is surprising since it might appear that differences in inflation rates between countries could account for a sizable portion of the changes in the nominal exchange rate. However, as is shown in the figure, *most of the change in nominal exchange*

FIGURE 11.2 **With Income Given, Exports and Imports Depend on the Exchange Rate**

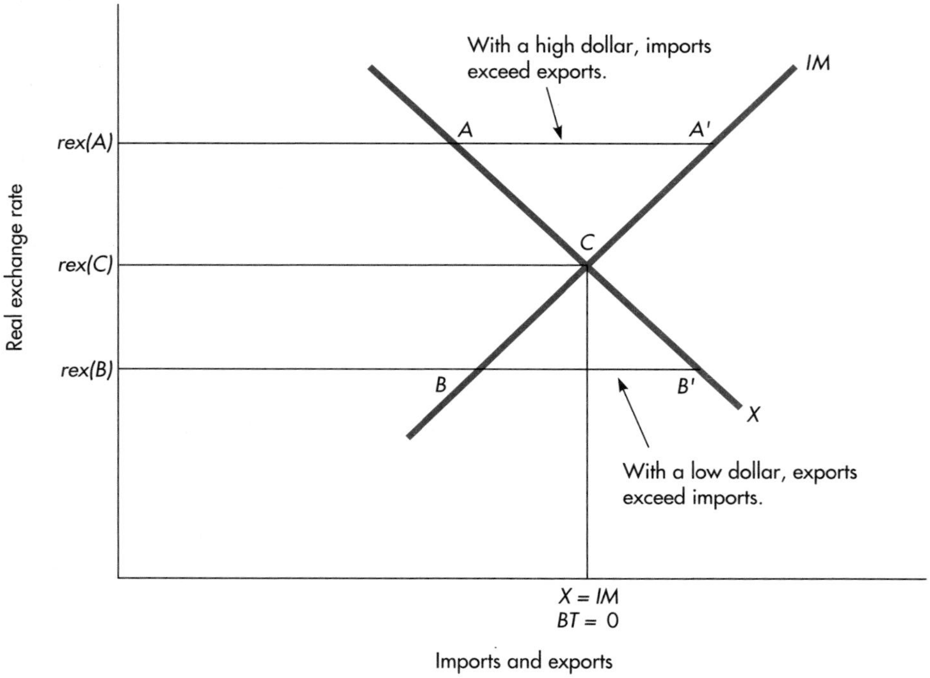

rates in industrial economies result from changes in the real exchange rate, rather than being principally driven by differences in inflation. We will return to discuss the implications of this important observation later.

The Trade Balance and the Exchange Rate

We first introduced exports and imports in Chapter 2, where we showed how trade is affected by equilibrium income and how, in turn, trade affects aggregate demand. In doing so, we ignored the effect of changes in the exchange rate on the balance of trade. Here we are doing the opposite—we are looking at how a change in the exchange rate affects the trade balance, holding income constant. Obviously, in practice, both income and the exchange rate are important in determining trade. Before we are through we will have to take account of both effects and the interaction between them. But for the time being we continue to take income as constant.

U.S. exports depend on how much foreigners have to pay for the goods and services that we offer for sale overseas, while U.S. imports depend on how much we have to pay for the things that foreigners offer for sale to U.S. customers. *Changes in a country's real exchange rate will, therefore, affect its balance of trade.*

In Figure 11.2 we illustrate the relationship between the real exchange rate and exports *(X)* and imports *(IM)*. From the U.S. point of view, a high real exchange rate [*rex(A)*] means that imported goods are relatively inexpensive and imports are high (point *A′*). At the same real exchange rate, U.S. exports are relatively costly and exports are low (point *A*). At this high real exchange rate [*rex(A)*], imports exceed exports and the balance of trade is negative (point *A* − point *A′*).

Conversely, at a low exchange rate [*rex(B)*] imports will be low (point *B*) and exports will be high (point *B′*). At this low real exchange rate the balance of trade is positive (point *B′* − point *B*). The figure shows that at some exchange rate [shown as *rex(C)* in Figure 11.2] exports equal imports and the balance of trade is zero (point *C*). But the fact that the trade balance can be zero does not imply that in fact the exchange rate will necessarily adjust so that a country's trade balance will be zero. For instance, the U.S. balance of trade was positive through much of the 1950s and was negative in the 1980s. At point *A* in the figure, the negative trade balance means only that U.S. purchasers are buying more products from the world than they are selling to the world. *This deficit in trade could be balanced by other items such as foreign purchases of U.S. assets. Thus, there is no guarantee that the trade balance (the international purchases and sale of goods and services) will be balanced over any particular period of time.*

What Figure 11.2 does imply is that a fall in the real exchange rate will lead to a reduction in a trade deficit or an increase in the surplus, and vice versa for a rise in the real exchange rate. Does this relation shown in the figure hold in actual practice?

Table 11.1 gives data for the real exchange rate and the balance of merchandise trade in the U.S. economy during the late 1970s and 1980s. There is some support for the relationship between high exchange rates and trade deficits. There is a tendency toward reductions in the deficit associated with periods of decline in the exchange rate, while during periods of a rising exchange rate there is a tendency toward increases in the trade deficit. For example, the exchange rate fell after 1977 and this was followed by a decline in the trade deficit in 1979 and 1980. This same pattern occurred again after 1985, as the deficit had begun to fall by 1988.

However, this pattern does not hold at all times and when the exchange rate falls, the balance of trade does not immediately improve. In fact, *when the exchange rate falls, there is a clear tendency for the trade deficit to get worse before it gets better.* This can be seen in 1978, 1986, and 1987. This same pattern also sometimes works in reverse, when the exchange rate rises. For example, the deficit fell in 1989 even though the exchange rate rose.

TABLE 11.1   The Real Exchange Rate Index and the Balance of Trade for the United States, 1977–1989

	Real exchange rate index (1982 = 100)	Balance of trade (billions of current dollars)
1977	83.3	−31.0
1978	75.4	−33.9
1979	74.5	−27.5
1980	75.9	−25.5
1981	90.2	−28.0
1982	100.0	−36.4
1983	105.0	−67.1
1984	115.0	−112.5
1985	118.2	−122.1
1986	92.6	−145.1
1987	81.2	−159.5
1988	78.9	−127.2
1989	84.4	−108.6

Source: *Economic Report of the President* (Washington, D.C.: U.S. Government Printing Office, February 1990).

Trade adjustment lags and the J-curve

The trade balance often worsens at first following a reduction in the exchange rate. The balance of trade traces out what is called a **J-curve.**[1] There are several reasons why the balance of trade may not always improve when the exchange rate falls. One reason is that both domestic and foreign income can and will change, but we are ignoring income changes at this point. But the most important reason is that it takes time for changes in the exchange rate to bring about shifts in the real flows of exports and imports, while changes in the exchange rate immediately change the dollar or nominal value of imports—even before there is any change in the real volume of imports.

The increase in exports and the decrease in imports that follow a reduction in the exchange rate take place with a considerable time delay or **trade adjustment lag.** To increase sales abroad, exporters must expand the number of dealers or retailers that carry their products; they must advertise and convince foreign customers of the availability and reliability of their products. On

J-curve
The pattern of the trade balance following a reduction in the exchange rate, where the trade balance first worsens and then improves above its initial level.

trade adjustment lag
In international trade, the time delay between a change in the exchange rate and changes in the volumes of imports and exports.

---

[1] The J-curve and the adjustment of trade flows are discussed in Rudiger Dornbusch and Paul Krugman, "Flexible Exchange Rates in the Short Run," *Brookings Papers on Economic Activity* 7, no. 3 (1976), pp. 558–66; Jeffrey D. Sachs, "The Current Account and Macroeconomic Adjustment in the 1970s," *Brookings Papers on Economic Activity* 12, no. 1 (1981), pp. 201–68; and Paul Krugman, "The J-Curve, the Fire Sale and the Hard Landing," *American Economic Review* 79, no. 2 (May 1989), pp. 31–35.

the import side, when the dollar falls, imports become more expensive. But people will have grown to like Japanese cars and stereo equipment, Danish furniture, and Italian wines and they keep buying these and other imports even as their prices rise in the United States. Suppliers of imports, having established a market share in the United States, lose that market position rather slowly. Foreign suppliers would rather suffer a reduction in markups than allow all of the change in the exchange rate to be reflected in higher prices of imports in U.S. markets. Of course, neither the preference for imports nor the reductions in profits for foreign suppliers can be maintained indefinitely if the real exchange rate keeps falling.

The trade balance and the J-curve

The value of the trade balance shown in Table 11.1 is in current dollars—the nominal value of the trade balance. This current dollar balance is important because it reflects the contribution of trade flows to the supply of and demand for foreign exchange. But we must now take account of the fact that this dollar trade balance can change when prices and the exchange rate change, whether or not the physical qualities of goods exported and imported change.

The dollar value of exports (PX) *equals the physical volume of exports* (X) *times the U.S. price level* (PX = P × X). This is the amount of dollars that are demanded by foreigners in order to buy U.S. goods. On the import side, *the dollar value of imports* (PIM) *equals the physical volume of imports* (IM) *times the foreign price level* (P_f) *divided by the exchange rate* (PIM = IM × P_f ÷ ex). This is the amount of dollars that U.S. importers will convert into foreign currencies in order to buy foreign goods. For example, if the U.S. imports 1 million Japanese autos at 2 million yen per auto and the dollar–yen exchange rate is 200 yen per dollar, then the U.S. import bill is $10 billion (1,000,000 × 2,000,000 ÷ 200 = $10 billion).

A decline in the exchange rate—a fall in *ex*—has the effect of making a given quantity of foreign goods more expensive for Americans to buy. This means that the current-dollar cost of imports will rise as a result of the fall in the exchange rate, even if the physical quantity of imports remains unchanged. Suppose that the value of the dollar drops to 150 yen with no change in the yen price of Japanese autos and suppose further that the number of autos imported does not change in the short run; then the U.S. import bill will increase to $13.3 billion or $13,300 per vehicle (1,000,000 × 2,000,000 ÷ 150 = $13,333 billion). *A constant physical volume of imports represents a higher dollar cost of imports when the value of the dollar declines (an increase in the value of the yen).*

In general, the demand for Japanese imports in the United States is not perfectly inelastic, meaning that the volume of Japanese goods purchased in the United States will decline as the prices of these goods increases. But in practice it is quite inelastic, especially in the short run. This means that the demand for imported products does not change very much when their prices change. Given this, the auto-import bill would rise even if Japanese auto manufacturers lowered their yen prices somewhat to remain competitive in U.S. markets and even if the Japanese automakers lost some sales because of the price rise. For instance, suppose there were a fall in the value of the dollar from 200 yen per dollar to 150 yen per dollar, imported car prices in yen dropped to 1.8 million yen per car, and sales volume fell by 5 percent to 950,000 vehicles. The import bill in current dollars would still rise (from $10 billion a year to $11.4 billion) because the *dollar price* of cars would go up by more than the reduction in volume of cars bought (the price rise is 20 percent, $10,000 to $12,000, compared to the 5 percent fall in quantity).

The effect on the current-dollar balance of trade of a drop in the exchange rate (a decline in the dollar) is therefore the outcome of the following effects:

1. The physical volume of U.S. exports will rise because they are now cheaper for foreigners to buy. U.S. exporters may also decide to raise the price in dollars of their foreign sales after a dollar decline, so the value of U.S. exports will rise more than the volume. This effect improves the trade balance.

2. The physical volume of U.S. imports declines because imports are more expensive. Foreign companies may also decide to trim their profit margins. Both of these effects improve the trade balance.

3. A given physical volume of imports requires more dollars to pay for the foreign currency needed to buy imports, even if import prices may have come down somewhat. Following a decline in the exchange rate, there is a decline in the terms at which our goods exchange for their goods, as measured by a fall in the price of exports relative to the price of imports. This effect is called a decline in the **terms of trade** and this decline worsens the current-dollar trade balance.

terms of trade
The value of imports received in exchange for exports, measured by comparing the prices of exports to the prices of imports.

In practice, for some time after the decline in the exchange rate the third factor dominates the first two. The current-dollar trade balance traces out a J-curve following a fall in the exchange rate. Figure 11.3 shows the J-curve, where the trade balance first falls (worsens) and then rises (improves) above the initial level.

Even though we are taking a simplified view of changes in trade flows, we can see the workings of the J-curve in the actual economy. For example, the dollar exchange rate started to fall in 1985, fell in 1986, and declined again in 1987. But the current-dollar trade balance continued to deteriorate until late in 1988. One consequence of the trade adjustment lags and the J-curve is that policymakers, and perhaps traders in international markets, can become confused about the fundamental relationships between exchange rates and trade flows. For example, a country running a trade deficit experiences a decline in its exchange rate. At first, this worsens the deficit; sophisticated policymakers and traders know why and are patient, waiting for the improvement in the balance of trade. However, some in the policy arena may lobby for protection of domestic producers in the form of import quotas

FIGURE 11.3   The J-Curve

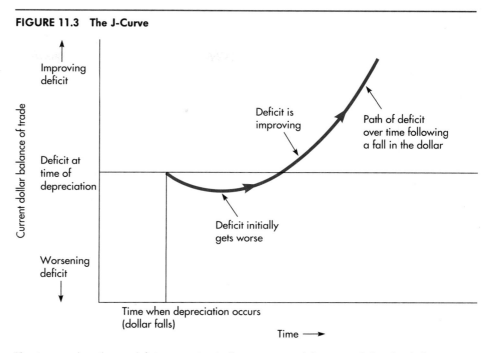

The J-curve describes a deficit worsening before improving following a fall in the dollar.

in part because the decline in the currency is not working to reduce the trade deficit.

Some international investors may lose confidence in the currency and speculate on further declines in the currency. Policymakers and decision makers need to understand adjustment lags and the J-curve in order to make sound decisions about international trade.

THE BALANCE OF PAYMENTS ON CURRENT ACCOUNT

The best measure of aggregate economic performance in a given year is the total income generated in that year. In an open economy (one that trades internationally), this is still the case, but in order to determine income we have to take account of the effect of the international sector. The effect on national income from the foreign sector includes traded goods and services, investment income, and other international transfers and receipts. The ways in which international transactions affect income are evaluated in the National Income and Product Accounts as part of the **balance of payments on current account.** We look at the components of the current account one part at a time.

balance of payments
The system of accounts describing international financial flows, including the **balance of payments on the current account** (the value of the trade balance plus the net balances of international items that affect income) and the **balance of payments on the capital account** (the net exchanges of foreign assets). The current-account balance is the negative of the capital-account balance.

balance of trade
The part of net exports consisting of the revenues from the sale of goods abroad (**merchandise exports**) and the expenditures on goods purchased from other countries (**merchandise imports**), including trade in services, such as insurance and transportation.

The Current Account

The main impact on income from the foreign sector consists of the revenues from the sale of goods abroad (**merchandise exports**) and the expenditures on goods purchased from other countries (**merchandise imports**). Total merchandise exports and imports also include trade in services, such as insurance and transportation. The value of merchandise exports less the value of merchandise imports is called the balance of merchandise trade or just the **balance of trade.**

The balance of trade

The United States had a net surplus in merchandise trade every year from 1946 to 1970. During that period the biggest U.S. exports were agricultural products, chemicals, and capital goods such as aircraft, communications equipment, and other machinery. There was a tremendous worldwide demand for U.S. capital goods in the 1950s and 1960s as other countries wanted access to U.S. technology and production methods. Traditionally the U.S. strength in exporting has been in high-tech products and this has remained the case into the 1990s, although the United States no longer has the dominant position it used to have.

The merchandise trade balance turned negative in 1971 and has been negative in almost every year since then. The deficit rose sharply in the 1980s, reaching a peak of almost $160 billion in 1987. It has been contracting since then, falling to $109 billion by 1989. The principal U.S. imports in the 1980s and 1990s have been oil, autos, machinery, agricultural products, semiconductors, other computer-related components, and consumer goods. These figures are all given in current dollars, that is, with no adjustment for inflation.

Income earned on foreign assets and transfers

Because U.S. residents earn income on their ownership of foreign assets just as foreign residents earn income on their ownership of U.S. assets, the balance of merchandise trade does not account for all of the foreign effects on domestic income. For example, U.S. residents may hold bonds issued by foreign governments or foreign companies. They may hold foreign real estate or the stocks of foreign companies. In addition, many U.S. companies have foreign subsidiaries. These foreign assets yield a flow of income to their American owners. Similarly, foreigners own U.S. assets, bonds, stocks, real estate, and so on. These U.S.-based assets generate a flow of income to their foreign owners.

The United States has a substantial inflow of investment income, derived largely from the earnings of the foreign subsidiaries of U.S. multinational corporations. This source of income has continued to grow in recent years. Yet, what has changed is the tremendous growth in the outflow of investment income in the 1980s, as foreigners have purchased large amounts of U.S. bonds, stocks, and real estate and have acquired ownership of some companies previously owned by U.S. residents. In 1981, the United States had a $34 billion net inflow of investment income. By 1988, this had fallen to a net inflow of $2 billion and the figure is expected to become a net outflow of income during the 1990s.

Income flows are also generated by fees and royalties. U.S. companies hold key patents in many areas of technology and they license foreign companies to use the technology. This generates a flow of fees and royalties to the United States. There is a smaller reverse flow of payments by U.S. companies to foreign licensors. Books, movies, television shows, and other entertainment and media products also generate international income flows. There is also a net outflow of income from the United States to foreign companies and governments from Americans' expenditures on foreign travel and transportation.

As well as the return on assets, payments known as *international transfer payments* are also made. Some of these payments stem from private financial transfers (i.e., gifts). There are many residents of one country who have ties to families in other countries. Monetary and in-kind gifts are sent in both directions, and the monetary transfers show up in the balance of payments. U.S. corporations and philanthropic institutions also make charitable contributions overseas. Other transfers result from the grants and aid that the U.S. government makes to foreign countries, most of it in the form of military assistance.

The Current-Account Deficit

When the net balances of all these different items that affect income are added to the trade balance, the resulting figure is called the balance of payments on the current account, or just the current account:

Current-account balance = Balance of trade +
Net investment income +
Net royalties +
Net transfers +
Net travel receipts.

The current-account balance is reported regularly, along with the trade account, and these figures give a good indication of whether the U.S. economy is generating a positive or negative flow of income in its foreign activities.

Table 11.2 shows the U.S. Department of Commerce's current-account and National Income Account figures for 1970, 1980, and 1988. In 1970, the balance of trade was in surplus as was the balance of payments. The nation exported $2.6 billion more to the rest of the world than it imported. The United States did transfer a little more than $6 billion net to the rest of the world, but it earned a little more than $6 billion on its foreign investment. In 1970, the balance of trade and the balance of payments were not seriously affecting income in the United States.

TABLE 11.2   The U.S. Current Account and Net Exports, 1970, 1980, and 1988
(billions of dollars)

	1970		1980		1988	
Balance of trade		$2.6		−$25.5		−$127.2
Exports	$42.5		$224.3		$319.3	
Imports	−39.9		−249.7		−446.5	
Net investment income		6.2		30.4		2.2
Receipts from abroad	$11.7		$72.5		$107.8	
Payments to abroad	−5.5		−42.1		−105.6	
Net travel, transfers, and other services (fees, royalties, etc.)		−6.5		−3.4		−1.5
Balance of payments on current account		2.3		1.5		−126.5

Source: *Economic Report of the President* (February 1990).

By 1980, the level of trade activity had increased and its composition had changed. The U.S. economy had switched from being a net exporter to being a net importer of merchandise. There was a deficit in merchandise trade (−$25.5 billion) and a net outflow resulting from travel and other transfers (−$3.4 billion). These deficits were offset by a substantial positive balance of investment income (+$30.4 billion), to give a positive current-account balance of $1.5 billion. By these measures, firms, households, and institutions in the United States purchased more from the world than they sold, but they more than paid for their excess purchases with income earned on foreign investments.

By 1988, foreign-investment income was no longer able to finance the rapidly rising level of net imports. The current account had swung into a substantial balance-of-payments deficit (−$126.5 billion). The main cause of the swing was the huge increase in the deficit on merchandise trade (−$127.2 billion). American consumers preferred and demanded imported goods to a greater degree than ever before in the 20th century. Net investment income also decreased (from $30.4 billion in 1980 to $2.2 billion in 1988) because foreigners had been investing heavily in U.S. assets between 1980 and 1988. The detailed current account is not available for 1989 as this is written, but the overall figures are available and they indicate that the situation had improved somewhat, with the current-account deficit down to −$108.6 billion. Regardless of that improvement, there had been a major change in the international economic relationship between the U.S. economy and the economies of the rest of the world.

When the current account is in surplus, as it was in the United States in 1980, the nation is generating more income from its export sales and its foreign investments than it is paying out for imports and as returns to foreign investors. In the aggregate, international economic activities contribute to raising national income in an economy that is running a surplus on its current account balance of payments. When the current account is in deficit (as it was in the United States in 1988 and 1989), the nation is generating less income from its export sales and its foreign investments than it is paying out for imports and as returns to foreign investors. Overall, in an economy with a balance-of-payments deficit, the impact of the foreign sector on income is negative. Of course, this does not mean that the economy that is running a balance-of-payments deficit would be better off without trade since consumers and firms benefited from their purchases of imported goods and services. Any artificial restrictions that might be placed on the import of foreign goods and services or the export of capital would raise the costs of acquiring comparable products and services along with increasing the cost of borrowing capital.

The current account and net exports

The items in the current account that add to U.S. income include the export of goods and services and income from foreign assets owned by U.S. residents. The total of these is included in what is called exports in the National Income and Product Accounts, with one important exception that we will discuss in a moment. Similarly, the import of goods and services plus income payments to foreigners on U.S. assets are included in imports in the National Income and Product Accounts, again with an important exception. This means that, in principle, the balance of payments on current account should equal the figure for net exports $(X - IM)$ in the National Income and Product Accounts. Indeed, we will talk about net exports in this book as if the two were equal.

The exceptions we are talking about and the reason that the published figure for net exports does not equal the current-account balance is that *international transfer payments are excluded from the figure for net exports in the National Income and Product Accounts.* The discrepancy has become very large in recent years—nearly $58 billion in 1989. The "transfer payment" that has grown substantially in recent years is the payment of interest on the federal government's debt to foreign residents. The federal government has been financing its deficit with foreign borrowing. One can argue about how to treat private foreign transfers in the national accounts, but there is no question that the interest payments to foreigners on the debt we have run up should be considered a subtraction from our national income. The official figure for net exports is misleading. When we talk about net exports here, we will use the figure from the balance on current account, not the official net export figure. (See the box on problems with net exports.)

International flows of goods and income involve foreign-exchange transactions and are determinants of supply and demand in the foreign-exchange market. But these flows are not the only contributors to the supply of and demand for dollars. We look now at the purchases and sales of assets: capital inflows and outflows.

■ Problems in Computing Net Exports in the National Income and Product Accounts

The reason that payments to foreigners on the national debt are excluded from the official figure is that all interest payments on the national debt have traditionally been considered transfers and hence excluded from GNP. And in the case of interest payments to U.S. residents, that is correct. The taxes that are paid by one U.S. resident are a subtraction from his or her income, but the interest received by the U.S. resident that owns the bond is an addition to his or her income. Therefore, there is no net addition to U.S. income resulting from interest payments on the debt that are made to U.S. residents. But this is not the case for payments of interest to foreign residents. The taxes that are paid by U.S. residents that are then paid out to foreign residents are indeed a subtraction from our national income. Other major industrial countries recognize this and we expect that the official U.S. procedures will change soon.

The problem of foreign transfers is not the only serious problem that afflicts the figure for net exports in the national accounts. The calculation of real or constant-dollar net exports is hard to do. The goods that we export and the goods that we import are very different, and so there is no good price deflator that covers both exports and imports. In the National Income and Product Accounts, separate export and import price deflators are used to compute the net export figure used in real GNP. These deflators are based upon the export and import prices that prevailed in 1982. When these price indexes are used for other years, the resulting real values for net exports can be very misleading. The table below illustrates the problem.

The real and nominal values are fairly close together when we are looking at the 1980s—years close to the base year of 1982. But changes in the *relative* prices of import goods and export goods that took place in earlier years are enough to make a surplus in net exports in current dollars look like a deficit in real dollars. Up and down movements in oil prices have made it particularly difficult to adjust imports for inflation.

During the 1950–70 period the United States was able to sell its advanced machinery and chemicals overseas for high prices and to buy raw materials for low prices. In later years, we experienced increases in the prices that we paid for raw materials— especially oil—and were forced to keep prices down in the increasingly competitive high-tech export market. When we apply 1982 prices to our trade flows of the 1950s and 1960s, it looks as if we were doing much worse than in fact was the case.

The United States suffered from what is called a decline in the terms of trade in the 1970s. Changes in the terms of trade, reflecting changes in relative prices, create particular problems for measuring net exports. But changing relative prices can also distort other components of GNP. The solution is to use what are called "chain indexes" rather than selecting a single base year.

Year	Net exports (billions of current dollars)	Net exports (billions of 1982 dollars)
1960	5.9	− 4.0
1970	8.5	−30.0
1977	1.9	−35.5
1982	26.3	26.3
1989	−50.9	−56.3

Source: *Economic Report of the President.*

INTERNATIONAL FINANCIAL ASSETS AND THE EXCHANGE RATE

Foreign currency is bought and sold in order to buy or sell foreign assets. U.S. companies and individuals buy foreign assets for much the same reasons as they hold domestic assets—they are balancing expected returns and anticipated risks. For example, some U.S. pension funds include foreign stocks and bonds in their portfolio of assets. U.S. multinational companies purchase factories and office buildings overseas. Pension-fund managers and multinational corporate treasurers may think that the returns to foreign assets are higher than the return to U.S. assets, or they may think that the overall risk of their portfolio of assets is reduced by diversifying and including foreign assets. Similarly, foreigners purchase U.S. assets, such as U.S. government securities, real estate in New York or Los Angeles, or factories in Ohio. All of these transactions involve foreign exchange. For example, a Japanese insurance company may decide to purchase an office building in Los Angeles. It deposits money into an account in a Japanese bank and the bank then arranges to exchange the amount in yen into a deposit in a dollar account in a U.S. bank. This money is then used to purchase the building. Because international investors require foreign exchange, international buyers and sellers of assets participate in foreign-exchange markets along with importers and exporters of goods and services.

In this section we examine the way in which international flows of capital are affected by interest rates and expectations about the future exchange rate. We will find that changes in interest rates and changes in expected future exchange rates will lead to inflows or outflows of capital.

Interest Rates and Expectations

Individuals and institutions that manage portfolios of assets look for the best combination of risk and return they can find. If the best opportunities are from buying financial assets in another country, then this is what they will do. Similarly, companies with profits to reinvest will weigh the returns from a new factory at home against buying out a foreign company or expanding one they already own.

When people or companies hold foreign assets, there is an extra source of possible gain or loss, over and above the rate of interest or rate of profit earned by the asset itself. When there are fluctuations in the exchange rate of the currencies involved, this means that the values of foreign assets also vary. Gains or losses in the domestic value of an asset can be reversed or increased by changes in currency values.

Consider specifically the return to holding a foreign financial asset such as a foreign government or commercial bond. The return on the bond will depend upon the interest earned on the asset and on the future value of the asset when these are converted back to domestic currency. Since the rate of conversion that will apply to the future payments of interest and

EXCHANGE-RATE RISK AND FOREIGN ASSETS

Consider a Japanese insurance company that bought a Los Angeles office building in 1985, expecting to take advantage of the real-estate boom in southern California. In 1985 the dollar/yen exchange rate was approximately 250 yen to the dollar. If the Japanese investors looked at their investment in 1988, they would find that each dollar's worth of investment would only purchase 125 yen in foreign-exchange markets. Even if the real-estate market in Los Angeles turned out to be a booming market, doubling the dollar value of the same building in three years, the building would only be worth the same in yen as it was when it was purchased. A 100 percent appreciation of the value of the asset for a domestic investor would have netted a 0 percent return to the foreign investor.

Even if the building was bought to be held for many years, rather than to be sold quickly, and no accounting recognition was made of the changes in the market value of the office building, the Japanese insurance company would still suffer from the immediate effect of the decline in the dollar because the flow of rental income from the property and the future value of leases would be much less in yen in 1988 than they were in 1985.

In foreign investments, as in the purchase of all assets, the expected return has to outweigh the risks in order for the asset to be traded at a given price.

principal is the future exchange rate, the decision to purchase a foreign asset is affected by both the interest rate earned on the asset and expectations about the future value of the exchange rate.

For example, an investor in Germany is considering buying a two-year bond. He could buy a German bond with an interest rate of 5 percent or a U.S. bond yielding 8 percent. Because of the 3 percent **foreign-interest-rate differential,** the U.S. bond looks attractive. Indeed, many German and Japanese investors and pension funds bought U.S. bonds in the 1980s precisely because of the differential return. But for the German thinking of purchasing the U.S. bonds, the higher return had to be balanced against the expected change in the exchange rate. If the dollar were to fall by 6 percent over two years (approximately 3 percent a year), then the German purchasing the U.S. bond earning 8 percent would get the same return in marks as another German investor would earn if he had purchased a 5 percent bond at home.

This example suggests that even though interest rates on similar assets may differ across economies, the expected rate of return on those assets can be equal. The condition under which expected returns are equalized is shown in Equation 11.3:

foreign-interest-rate differential The difference between the nominal rate of interest earned by the holder of a foreign bond and the nominal rate of interest earned by the holder of a domestic bond with the same maturity and risk.

Nominal foreign-interest-rate differential = Expected percent change in the nominal exchange rate

$$i_{\text{foreign}} - i_{\text{domestic}} = \text{Exp}(\Delta ex/ex). \qquad (11.3)$$

Across countries, the expected rate of return from holding bonds will be the same when the difference between the nominal rate of interest of a foreign bond ($i_{foreign}$) and the nominal rate of interest of a similar domestic bond ($i_{domestic}$) equals the expected change in the nominal exchange rate, Exp($\Delta ex/ex$).

In the example of the German investors, $i_{U.S.}$ is 8 percent, i_{German} is 5 percent, and the mark is expected to improve against the dollar by 3 percent per year, bringing the higher U.S. return back into line with the return available at home in Germany.

To German investors	
$i_{foreign} - i_{domestic}$	= Exp($\Delta ex/ex$)
U.S. 8% − German 5%	= +3% expected annual increase in the German mark relative to the dollar.

From the U.S. point of view, the dollar is expected to fall against the German mark (-3 percent per year) giving a 3 percent per year gain to U.S. holders of German currency. This expected gain from holding German marks converts the low 5 percent return on German bonds into an expected 8 percent return for U.S. investors, which is equal to what U.S. investors could earn at home.

To U.S. investors	
$i_{foreign} - i_{domestic}$	= Exp($\Delta ex/ex$)
German 5% − U.S. 8% =	− 3% expected annual decrease in the dollar relative to the German mark.

expected-return equalization
The expected returns from holding bonds in two different countries are the same when the foreign-interest-rate differential is equal to the expected rate of change of the exchange rate.

If Equation 11.3 holds for any particular pair of foreign and domestic bonds, we will say there is **expected-return equalization.** When the expected returns are equalized, financial investors will not see any rate-of-return advantage from moving funds from bonds in one country to bonds in the other.[2]

International Capital Mobility

What would guarantee expected-return equalization? Equality would exist among returns if capital were perfectly mobile—funds left one economy or currency and entered another in the face of the smallest differential in expected

---

[2] The condition for expected-return equalization can be expressed in real terms as well as nominal terms:

$$r_{foreign} - r_{domestic} = Exp(\Delta ex/ex) + \Delta P/P - \Delta P_f/P_f$$

or

$$r_{foreign} - r_{domestic} = Exp(\Delta rex/rex).$$

Clearly, interest rates across economies will not be equalized among assets of different risks and maturities in either real or nominal terms. This condition holds for similar bonds of the same term to maturity over the period of time until maturity.

capital mobility
The ability of investors to sell assets in one economy, purchase foreign exchange, and buy assets in another economy. If there is expected-return equalization, then there is **perfect capital mobility.**

returns. This narrowing of differentials could only occur if investors were free to move capital from one economy to another (by selling and buying international assets) with no government restrictions and no financial-transactions costs. This is called **capital mobility.**

If interest-rate equalization occurs in practice, then it is said that there is **perfect capital mobility** or, equivalently, that U.S. financial assets and foreign assets are *perfect substitutes.* The question is: Will the equalization condition be satisfied in practice? Is capital perfectly mobile in practice?[3]

In the 1970s and 1980s, the technology of wire transfers, satellite communications, and computers coupled with foreign-exchange markets has greatly reduced the transactions costs of buying and selling assets into and out of multiple currencies. In foreign-exchange markets, funds move in and out of the dollar, yen, mark, and pound on a daily basis. Small changes in interest differentials generate millions of dollars worth of foreign-exchange trades that take place around the world, 24 hours a day. These modern characteristics of international financial markets suggest that international capital has indeed become very mobile.

On the other hand, bonds and other long-term assets in different countries are not the same in terms of their riskiness, marketability, or terms and conditions for redemption at maturity. British, German, Japanese, and other foreign investors will usually find it easier and less risky to invest at home than overseas, and likewise for American investors.

So what is the answer concerning capital mobility? *The extent to which capital is mobile internationally depends upon the nature of the capital.* Multinational companies do not move their factories very often, certainly not in response to short-run considerations. Physical capital is not very mobile at all because factories in one country are not perfect substitutes for factories in another country. Pension funds and other large stock and long-term–bond holders do shift their assets overseas, but they assess risks and returns on a long-term basis and their decisions tend to have a lot of inertia in them. Stocks and long-term corporate bonds in different countries are closer substitutes than are factories, but they are not perfect substitutes for each other either.

By contrast, the risk of default on government securities is very low for any of the major industrial countries. The risks coming from the variability of future interest rates are also low for short-term bills. So *expected-return equalization comes very close to holding for short-term government bills,* such as the interest rate on U.S. Treasury bills compared to the interest rate on German or Japanese government short-term bills. *There is almost perfect capital mobility for short-term government bills and bonds.*

---

[3] International capital mobility is discussed in Martin S. Feldstein and Charles Horioka, "Domestic Saving and International Capital Flows," *Economic Journal,* June 1982; and Jeffrey Frankel and Donald Mathieson, "International Capital Mobility: What Do Saving–Investment Correlations Tell Us?" *IMF Staff Papers,* September 1987.

Changing interest rates and capital flows

The expected-return–equalization condition can also tell us how investors will behave when there is a change in the interest-rate differential. Suppose at the outset that expected returns are equalized between U.S. and German bonds, but that the interest rate then rises in the United States. At first, the interest rate in Germany remains unchanged and the expected rate of change of the dollar with respect to the German mark also remains the same as it was before U.S. rates rose. This means that the expected returns are no longer equalized. For example, suppose that the U.S. interest rate rose from 8 percent to 10 percent, with the German intererst rate remaining at 5 percent and the expected rate of change of the exchange rate remaining at a 3 percent rate of decline of the dollar. To both German and U.S. investors, the U.S. bonds now look more attractive:

To German investors	
$i_{foreign} - i_{domestic}$	$> \text{Exp}(\Delta ex/ex)$
U.S. 10% − German 5%	$> +3\%$

From the point of view of a German resident contemplating an investment in U.S. bonds, the interest differential exceeds the expected improvement in the value of the mark. The German investor will want to sell German bonds and buy dollars so as to buy U.S. bonds.

To U.S. investors	
$i_{foreign} - i_{domestic}$	$< \text{Exp}(\Delta ex/ex)$
German 5% − U.S. 10%	$< -3\%$

From the perspective of a U.S. investor contemplating investing in German bonds, the expected gains from holding a bond that pays off in marks (+3 percent per year since the dollar is expected to fall by 3 percent per year) is not enough to overcome the advantage offered by the higher U.S. interest rate. U.S. investors will want to sell their German bonds and buy U.S. bonds.

The increase in the U.S. interest rate, therefore, leads to an increase in the demand for U.S. financial assets. If the increase in the interest-rate differential is generalized so that U.S. rates rise on average relative to other countries, there will be an overall increase in the demand for U.S. bonds. Foreigners will exchange their currency for U.S. dollars and then they will increase their purchases of these bonds. U.S. residents will purchase fewer foreign bonds, resulting in a reduction in the demand for foreign currencies by U.S. residents. Thus, rising U.S. interest rates relative to foreign interest rates result in foreign capital flowing into U.S. financial markets and a reduction of the outflow of U.S. capital overseas. *A rise in U.S. interest rates leads to a net capital inflow.*

If the U.S. interest rate falls relative to foreign interest rates, capital will flow in the reverse direction. Holders of U.S. assets will sell them in order to buy foreign assets and there will be a reduction in the purchases of U.S. assets by foreigners. *A fall in the U.S. interest rate, with no corresponding changes in foreign interest rates or in the expectation of exchange-rate movements, leads to a net capital outflow.*[4] Financial investors respond to changes in the interest rate by selling one asset, trading the currency generated by the sale for another currency, and using the newly purchased currency to purchase another asset. In general, changes in interest-rate differentials cause international inflows and outflows of capital as investors seek the highest return.

The expected exchange rate and capital flows

We have seen that changes in interest rates can bring about changes in the inflows and outflows of capital and that these flows involve trading dollars and foreign currencies. But so far we have not said anything about the expected rate of increase or decrease in the exchange rate—the expected *future* value of the dollar relative to other currencies.

The fact that the exchange rate turns out to be different in six months or a year is no surprise to international investors. Their decisions to hold assets in different countries is based upon an expectation about how the value of the currencies will change relative to each other in the future. If their expectations change, international investors rework their decisions about which assets to hold.

Take the example where there is expected-return equalization between U.S. and German bills, with an expected 3 percent decline in the dollar against the mark, matched by a 3 percent interest differential. If there was then a change in economic conditions that affected the German economy rather more adversely than the U.S. economy (for example, increased political instability in eastern Europe), then expectations about the decline of the dollar relative to the mark would have to be revised. Suppose, for example, that expectations change so that the value of the dollar in terms of marks is expected to be only 1 percent lower next year instead of 3 percent lower. The comparison of U.S. and German bills would be

To U.S. investors
$i_{German} - i_{U.S.} < Exp(\Delta ex/ex)$
5%   − 8% < 1% expected decline in the dollar.

---

[4] Here we are ignoring the possibility that the increased demand for dollars used to buy U.S. bonds will affect the expected change in the exchange rate. The determination of the exchange rate in a supply-and-demand model, where changes in capital flows are included among the variables that affect those exchange rates, is described later in this chapter.

To the U.S. holder of the German notes, the interest differential (3 percent advantage in holding U.S. T bills) is now greater than the loss that is now expected as a result of the expected decline in the dollar (1 percent). American financial investors will sell their German notes, exchange the marks they receive for dollars, and buy U.S. T bills. There will be a capital inflow to the United States as American investors move their assets back to the United States and also as German investors decide to purchase U.S. financial assets instead of German assets.

For a given interest-rate differential, an increase in the expected future value of a currency will lead to an inflow of capital. A decrease in the expected future value of a currency will lead to an outflow of capital.

We have now examined how interest rates and expected future values of the exchange rate affect decisions to buy and sell foreign assets. We saw that there will be inflows of financial assets—especially short-term assets—when U.S. interest rates rise relative to foreign interest rates and when the expected future value of the U.S. dollar increases. There will be outflows of financial assets in the opposite cases.

We have seen in this and the preceding sections how trade flows and capital flows are affected by the exchange rate, by interest rates, and by the expected future exchange rate. *We are now going to refocus our discussion from one where the exchange rate affects trade and capital flows to one where capital flows, exports, and imports affect the exchange rate.* The supply of and demand for dollars in the foreign-exchange market are determined by trade and capital flows. Supply and demand then determine the exchange rate.

SUPPLY AND DEMAND IN THE FOREIGN-EXCHANGE MARKET

In foreign-exchange markets, currencies are traded at prices (exchange rates) that reflect supply and demand. The balance of trade and capital flows, both of which are affected by changes in the exchange rate, also contribute to determining the exchange rate.[5] The balances of trade and capital flows are also affected by fundamental economic factors such as income, interest rates, and expectations. We will pull these factors together into a model of the foreign-exchange market.

We analyze the foreign-exchange market in terms of the supply of dollars being brought into the market by those wishing to purchase foreign currencies

---

[5] Exchange rates are determined in foreign-exchange markets where the supplies of and demands for foreign exchange are affected by a myriad of market forces. This characteristic of exchange rates makes the forecasting of changes in exchange rates subject to a very large degree of error. As a result of the inability of economists to forecast exchange rates, a recent body of research has emerged that argues that exchange-rate movements are indistinguishable from random events. (See Richard Meese, "Currency Fluctuations in the Post–Bretton Woods Era," *Journal of Economic Perspectives,* Winter 1990.) In this view, exchange rates are determined by everything and therefore by no individual factor in particular. This is a nihilistic reaction to the complexity of the foreign-exchange market, but it does point to an important conclusion: Exchange rates reflect the impact of a host of international factors.

■ The Balance of Payments on Capital Account

We saw earlier that exports and imports of goods and services are recorded in the balance of payments on the current account. There is a similar account for asset flows called the *balance of payments on the capital account*, which is also called simply the *capital account*. The table below shows the capital account for the United States in 1970, 1980, and 1988. Comparing the balances on current account in Table 11.2 with the balances on capital account in the table below reveals that these balances add to zero. This is true in principle because the inflows of goods and services and income to the U.S. economy represented by a current-account deficit have to be paid for by an outflow of dollars. In order to pay for the excess inflows of foreign goods and services reflected in the current-account deficit, there have to be sales of assets to the world economies in excess of purchases of assets from the world economies. *The deficit in the current account is balanced by a surplus in the U.S. capital account.*

Look at the relationship between the capital account and the current account in the United States in 1988. The current-account balance was a deficit of $126.5 billion. The sum of net private foreign investment and net foreign-government investment of $126.5 billion is by definition equal to the amount by which the U.S. economy ran a current-account deficit with the rest of the world.

The U.S. Capital Account 1970, 1980, and 1988 (billions of dollars)

	1970	1980	1988
Private U.S. investment overseas	−$10.2	−$72.8	−$81.5
Private foreign investment in the United States*	−0.8	67.9	169.7
Net private foreign investment	−11.0	−4.9	88.2
Change in U.S. assets held by foreign governments	6.9	15.5	38.9
Change in foreign assets held by U.S. government	1.8	−12.1	−0.6
Net official foreign investment	8.7	3.4	38.3
Balance on capital account	−2.3	−1.5	126.5

* Includes statistical discrepancy.
Source: *Economic Report of the President* (Washington, D.C.: U.S. Government Printing Office, February 1990).

and the demand for dollars from those who are offering foreign currencies in exchange for dollars. Both the supply of and demand for dollars in the foreign-exchange market are derived from the demands for goods and assets that are involved in international transactions. From the U.S. vantage point, the supply of dollars is derived from the demand for foreign goods and foreign assets by U.S. residents. From the foreign vantage point, the demand for dollars is derived from the demand for U.S. goods and U.S. assets by foreign residents.

The capital account shows us that we paid for the deficit on the current account in 1988 through net sales of U.S. assets to private foreign residents and to foreign governments. Net private asset sales totaled $88.2 billion—private foreign investment in the U.S. exceeded private U.S. investment abroad by that amount. Since U.S. investment in the rest of the world did not change by much in the 1980s, this figure reflects the fact that private investors in the rest of the world greatly increased their purchases of U.S. assets ($67.9 billion in 1980 to $169.7 billion in 1988). The U.S. capital account shows that U.S. residents made substantial investments overseas, while foreigners likewise made substantial investments in the U.S. economy. The balance was a small net outflow of private capital in 1970 (−$11.0 billion) and a large net inflow in 1988 (+$88.2 billion).

Rising private U.S. investment overseas represents an increase in the holdings of foreign assets by U.S. residents. It is a positive item in our national wealth. In the capital account, however, this capital flow is shown with a negative sign because it represents the dollars supplied by U.S. investors in exchange for foreign currency used to purchase the foreign assets—an outflow of U.S. dollars to buy foreign capital (i.e., an outflow of U.S. capital).

The mix between long-term and short-term investments is different for foreigners investing in the United States than for private U.S. investment overseas. Traditionally, U.S. companies established products, brand names, and production technology within the United States and then engaged in *direct foreign investment*—setting up production facilities abroad to make and sell Ford cars, IBM computers, or Kellogg's corn flakes in overseas markets. Foreigners did relatively less direct foreign investment and purchased U.S. assets by buying short-term bonds in the United States. In the late 1980s, this pattern started to change as more foreign companies bought out U.S. companies or set up subsidiaries here.

The remainder of the capital-account balance—the remainder of the way in which the U.S. economy paid for its deficit—came from the large level of U.S. assets (net $38.3 billion in 1988, mostly financial securities and much of it Treasury bills and bonds) held by foreign governments. The governments of our trading partners financed our excess imports by purchasing U.S. financial securities.

Reflected in the entries under changes in foreign assets held by governments, the capital account shows that governments participate actively in current markets. Foreign-exchange intervention occurs as central banks conduct foreign-exchange open-market operations. They buy and sell foreign currencies in the exchange markets by increasing or decreasing their reserves of foreign-currency assets. In 1980, the Federal Reserve Board was increasing its holdings of foreign assets—by $12.1 billion—while foreign governments were increasing their holdings of dollar assets—by $15.5 billion. The interventions on both sides of the market came close to offsetting each other (+$3.4 billion). In 1988, foreign governments were taking larger dollar positions (+$38.9 billion) while the Fed took smaller foreign-exchange positions (−$0.6 billion) so that the net capital inflow accounted for by governments buying U.S. dollars added substantially (+$38.3 billion) to the supply of funds in the U.S. financial market.

Equilibrium in the Market for a Single Foreign Currency

Given that there are many different currencies, there are in practice many different foreign-exchange markets. For example, there is a market for the exchange of dollars for Japanese yen. This market is pictured in Figure 11.4. As we explained earlier, a rise in the dollar exchange rate (fall in the yen) makes U.S. exports more expensive to Japanese buyers. This increase in expense reduces the volume of U.S. exports to Japan and so the demand

FIGURE 11.4   Supply and Demand in the Dollar/Yen Exchange Market

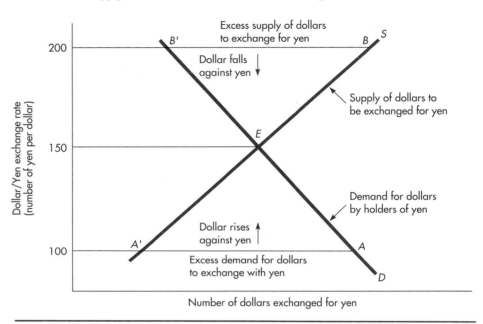

for dollars declines. Thus, the demand schedule for dollars from the Japanese is shown with a negative slope in the figure. At the same time, as the dollar exchange rate rises, imports from Japan become cheaper for U.S. consumers, and the volume of imports increases as does the supply of dollars from the United States to purchase yen in order to purchase imported goods. The supply of dollars to be exchanged for yen has a positive slope in the figure. The equilibrium, as in any market, is determined when supply and demand are equal, shown as the point of intersection of the schedules (point *E*). The equilibrium value is shown as 150 yen per dollar, about the value that prevailed in early 1990.

When the foreign-exchange market is not in equilibrium, the exchange rate will adjust to bring about an equilibrium. When the dollar exchange rate is low (for example, at 100 yen per dollar in the figure), there is an excess demand for dollars. The quantity of dollars demanded by the Japanese, point *A*, exceeds the quantity of dollars supplied, point *A'*. This excess demand for dollars causes a rise in the dollar exchange rate until it has reached the equilibrium value, thereby eliminating the excess demand.

When the price of the dollar is above the equilibrium value (for example, 200 yen per dollar as shown in the figure), there is an excess supply of dollars, which drives down the exchange rate toward its equilibrium value.

FIGURE 11.5   Supply and Demand, the Real Exchange Rate, and the Foreign-Exchange Market

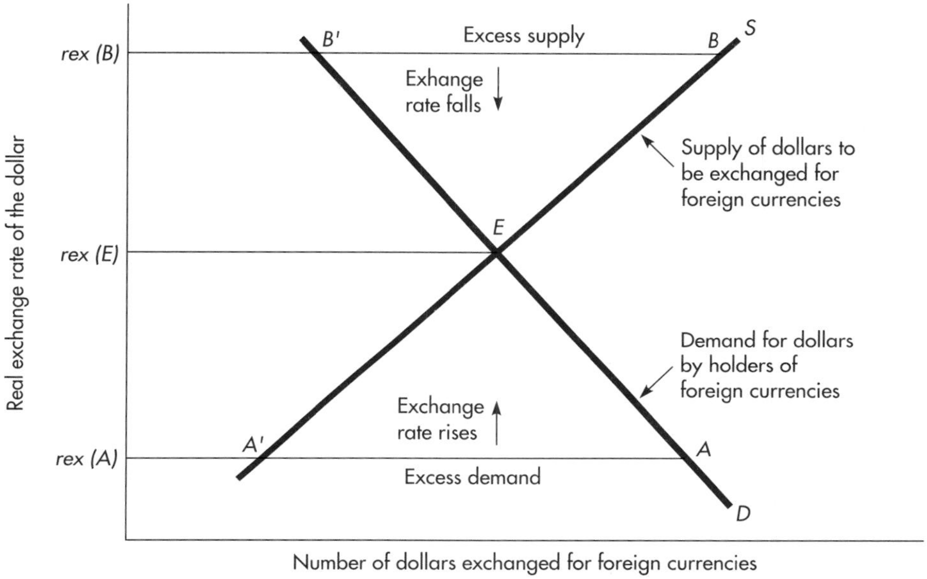

Equilibrium of the Real Exchange Rate

The exchange rates of the dollar against the currencies of America's major trading partners are determined in markets such as the one we have described for the dollar and the yen. In order to maintain a manageable view of the foreign-exchange market, we will assume a single foreign-exchange market, where the value of the real exchange rate is determined by the total demand for and supply of dollars to be exchanged into all foreign currencies. This foreign-currency–exchange market is depicted in Figure 11.5. We show the foreign-currency–exchange market as having the same characteristics as the single-currency market pictured in Figure 11.4. The supply of dollars rises with an increase in the real exchange rate because imports in general become less expensive to U.S. residents. The demand for dollars by foreigners falls with an increase in the real exchange rate because U.S. goods become more expensive to foreign residents. The equilibrium real exchange rate is determined at point *E*, where the schedules intersect. When there is excess supply of dollars or excess demand for dollars, then the exchange rate adjusts.

In this discussion we have ignored possible complications introduced by the slow adjustment of imports and exports to changes in the exchange rate—J-curve effects. In Chapter 12 we will look at possible anomalies in the foreign-currency market created by these lags and by currency speculation.

TABLE 11.3   Changes in the Exchange Rate: Shifting the Supply of and Demand for Dollars

---

Factors affecting the supply schedule of dollars in the foreign exchange market:

  Outward shifts in the supply of U.S. dollars are derived from:

    Increases in the demand for imports which are derived from:
      Increases in U.S. income

    Increases in the demand for foreign capital, real or financial, which are derived from:
      Increases in nominal foreign interest rates and/or
      Decreases in the expected future value of the dollar

Factors affecting the demand schedule for dollars in the foreign exchange market:

  Outward shifts in the demand for dollars are derived from:

    Increases in the demand for exports which are derived from:
      Increases in income in the rest of the world

    Increases in the demand for U.S. capital, real or financial, which are derived from:
      Increases in nominal U.S. interest rates and/or
      Increases in the expected future value of the dollar

Changes in the exchange rate

Glancing at the financial pages of the newspaper over a period of time will reveal that exchange rates change frequently. Figure 11.1 showed that there were large and sustained shifts in the real exchange rate of the dollar in the 1970s and 1980s. Movements in the exchange rate are caused by shifts of supply and demand in the foreign-exchange market.

The demand for dollars by the rest of the world depends on the worldwide demand for U.S. goods and/or U.S. assets. Increases in the demand for either U.S. goods or assets will generate an outward shift in the demand for dollars. The supply of dollars is derived from the demand for foreign goods and assets; increases in either will be reflected in an outward shift of the supply of dollars. We describe the working of the foreign-exchange market by looking at the major sources of shifts of supply and demand. As a guide to the discussion, the connections between the domestic and foreign demands for goods and assets and the supply and demand for foreign exchange are summarized in Table 11.3. In the table and in the discussion that follows, we are introducing changes in income into the analysis of the foreign-exchange market. Up until this point in this chapter, we have assumed constant income, both at home and abroad, but we are now changing that assumption.

The exchange rate and income

A rise in income in the United States generates an increase in the demand for imports. Since American customers want to purchase more foreign goods, they also increase their demand for foreign currencies. In the foreign-exchange

FIGURE 11.6 **Income and the Exchange Rate**

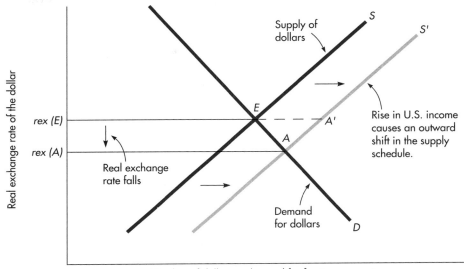

Number of dollars exchanged for foreign currencies

An increase in U.S. income leads to a fall in the real exchange rate.

market, more dollars are offered for sale in order to purchase more foreign exchange. The effect of a unilateral increase in U.S. income on the foreign-exchange market is shown in Figure 11.6 as an outward shift in the supply schedule *(S* to *S').* At the initial exchange rate, *rex(E),* the increase in U.S. income has increased the demand for imports and therefore increased (shifted) the supply of dollars being offered for foreign currencies. Since in this example there has been no change in the income of other countries, the demand for dollars has not shifted. There is an excess supply of dollars (point *A'* − point *E)* and the real exchange rate will fall.

The falling exchange rate makes imports more expensive, partially offsetting the increase in imports and hence partially offsetting the increased supply of dollars. And the fall in the exchange rate also increases the demand for U.S. exports and hence increases the demand for dollars by foreign buyers. The new equilibrium is established at point *A.*

The result of a rise in the level of U.S. income is a reduction in the real exchange rate of the U.S. dollar (ignoring other possible changes in the economy.) And the process works in the opposite direction also—*a fall in income in the United States will lead to a rise in the value of the dollar.*

FIGURE 11.7   The Impact of U.S. Interest Rates on the Exchange Rate

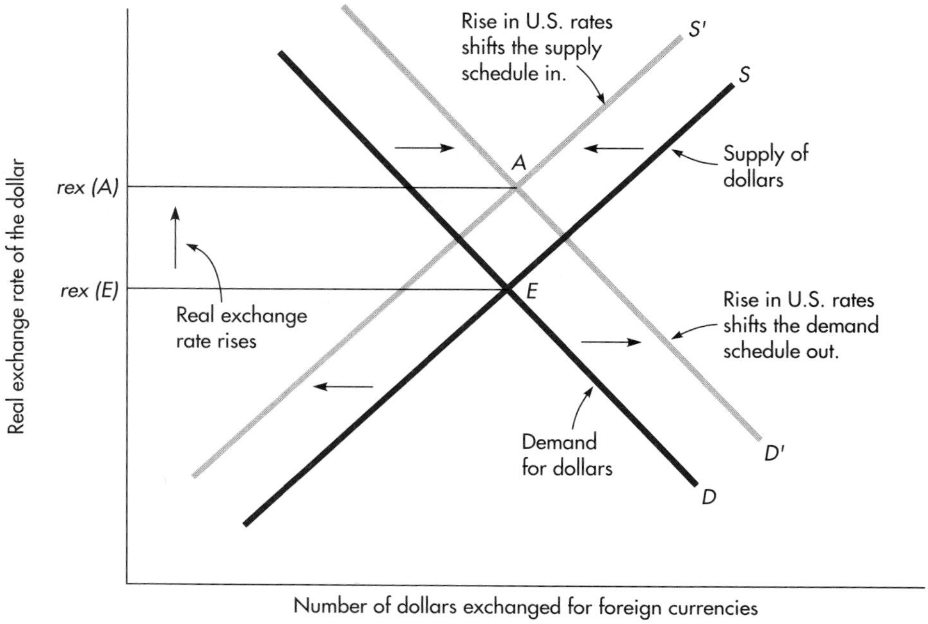

An increase in U.S. interest rates that raises the differential with foreign rates will increase the exchange rate.

The exchange rate and the interest differential

A change in the interest rate differential will also affect the exchange rate. For example, if the differential changes because there is an increase in rates of interest in the United States that is unmatched by interest-rate changes in the other major economies, foreign investors will sell assets denominated in foreign currencies, buy dollars, and then buy U.S. assets. In Figure 11.7 this is shown as an outward shift in the demand for dollars (*D* to *D'*). At the same time, American investors will reduce or eliminate their purchases of foreign assets and in so doing bring fewer dollars to the market seeking to exchange them for foreign currencies. This is shown as an inward shift in the supply of dollars (from *S* to *S'*). Both of these changes in behavior will raise the value of the dollar.

The impact of changes in interest rates on the dollar has been found to be very powerful, particularly in the mid-1980s when monetary policy drove up U.S. interest rates. High interest rates in the United States attracted foreign investors and their demand for the dollar kept the real exchange rate high.

FIGURE 11.8 An Increase in the Expected Future Value of the Dollar Will Increase the Current Value of the Dollar.

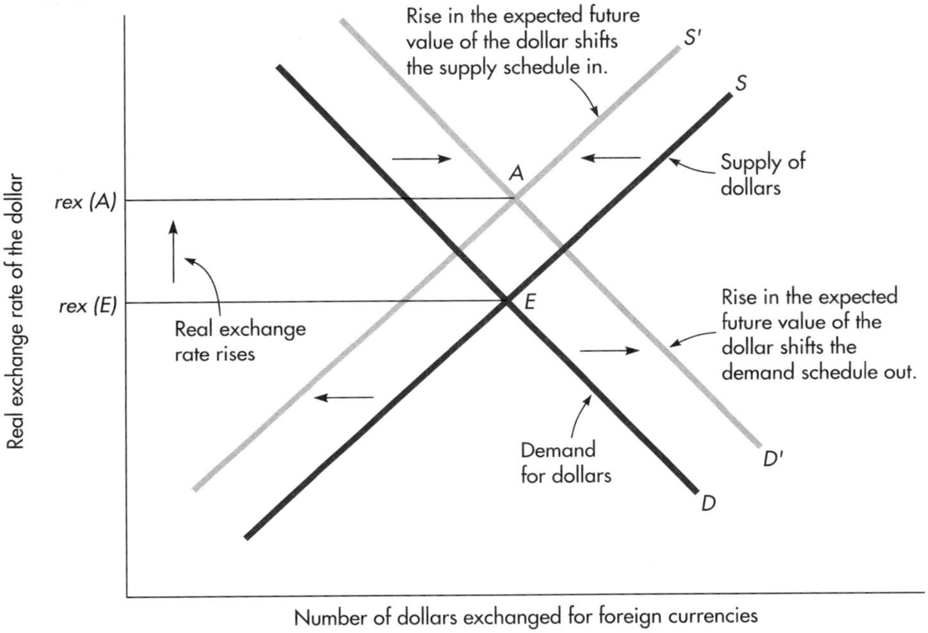

Expectations and the exchange rate

Changing economic circumstances lead to changed expectations about the future value of the dollar. There are many possible events that could change expectations. For example, predictions that U.S. manufacturers were losing their ability to develop new products might lead to the expectation of a reduced capacity to export and hence to the expectation of a lower future dollar-exchange rate. Or, a positive development, such as the discovery of a giant oil field in Alaska, might lead to the expectation of reduced oil imports and a higher expected value of the dollar.

For a given interest-rate differential, international financial markets are in equilibrium with a particular expected rate of appreciation or devaluation of each currency. (Recall the expected-return–equalization condition.) But if that expectation is altered, the interest-rate differential no longer makes up for expected changes in currency values and in practice, large movements of capital around the world are generated because of changes in expectations. Figure 11.8 shows the impact on the foreign-exchange market of an increase in the expected future value of the dollar. Either the rate of appreciation of the dollar has increased or the expected rate of decline has slowed down.

THE EXCHANGE RATE AND THE PURCHASING POWER OF THE DOLLAR: DO CAPITAL FLOWS AND INTEREST-RATE DIFFERENTIALS REALLY MATTER?

Some economists have used a simplified theory of purchasing power to predict whether or not there will be long-run changes in exchange rates and in what direction. The theory is simplified because it assumes that most of the changes in the supply of and demand for foreign exchange depend upon the supply of and demand for imports and exports. While this approach clearly excludes other factors that can affect exchange rates (such as assets flows, interest-rate differentials, and expectations), the proponents of this *purchasing-power–parity* approach argue that the relative prices of traded goods are important in determining trade flows, which in turn are the most important factors affecting the equilibrium value of the exchange rate.*

The purchasing-power–parity (PPP) theory of exchange-rate determination is based on the following argument. Take a representative sample of tradeable goods (autos, clothing, stereos, agricultural products, and so on) and see how much they cost in the United States. Then look at other countries and see how much the same basket of goods costs when dollars are exchanged at the prevailing exchange rates and the goods are purchased in the local currencies. If, as a result, you find that the same basket of goods can be purchased for less overseas, then the dollar is too high. If it takes more dollars to buy those goods overseas, the dollar is too low. The PPP theory, therefore, says that the exchange rate will adjust so that there is parity or equality between the purchasing power of the dollar in the United States and its effective purchasing power overseas.

The rationale for the PPP hypothesis is that if parity does not hold, then either U.S. importers will find they can buy more goods overseas and sell them at a profit at home, or U.S. exporters will increase their overseas sales. The supply of and demand for dollars will be out of balance and the exchange rate will change.

Any tourist can tell you that the PPP theory does not hold precisely. Prices are very different in different countries. Some of the reasons for this are easy enough to see. For example, most European countries have high value-added taxes and high taxes on gas and tobacco. Retail prices in Europe are often

* A discussion of the failure of the purchasing-power–parity theory is in Jacob Frankel, "The Collapse of Purchasing Power Parities during the 1970s," *European Economic Review* 16 (May 1981), pp. 145–66.

For concreteness, let us think about a case where the dollar is expected to rise in value over time, and then the expected rate of appreciation increases because of some favorable news about the U.S. economy. There is a capital inflow to the United States as a result of this favorable news. The effect of the capital inflow on the foreign-exchange market is shown in the figure as an outward shift of the demand schedule (from D to D') and an inward shift of the supply schedule (from S to S'). The result is that the value of the dollar will increase. *The current exchange rate will rise in anticipation of the future appreciation.*

For some given expectation about the future value of the dollar, an increase in today's value of the dollar has the effect of lowering the expected rate of increase of the dollar in the future. As the dollar rises, the market reaches a point where the rise in the current value of the dollar has a sufficient higher than the prices of the equivalent items in the U.S. In addition, not all goods and services are traded internationally. This is particularly true of services. A haircut costs a lot more in New York City than in most foreign countries. It costs more than a haircut in Alabama, for that matter. A service such as this is not subject to national or international competition. In addition, even with goods that are traded, many countries impose trade restrictions. Tariffs or quotas also allow price differences to persist.

The existence of taxes, nontraded goods, and trade restrictions explains why a very literal view of the PPP model fails to hold. But a somewhat weaker test of the theory should still hold. Because trade restrictions are changed only slowly, it should follow that the main year-to-year changes in exchange rates are simply those that compensate for differences in inflation rates. If the PPP theory is correct, the equilibrium *real* exchange rate should remain fairly stable over time. The values of the real exchange rate given in Figure 11.1 show that there is no indication that the nominal rate is simply adjusting for inflation differences. The PPP theory is contradicted by the evidence.

The failure of the PPP theory in itself is not of great consequence. But in this case, the failure is telling us something surprising about the behavior of the exchange rate. Exchange-rate movements since the mid-1970s have often resulted in large disparities in the prices of tradeable goods across countries, and these have resulted in large swings in trade balances. The U.S. dollar was low in the mid-1970s against the European currencies, allowing U.S. producers to undercut European producers and creating economic stress in these countries. The U.S. dollar became extremely high in 1984–85, leading to a huge U.S. trade deficit and substantial difficulties throughout U.S. manufacturing. The theory of comparative advantage says that trade will cause difficulties in some industries even when the exchange rate is correct. But exchange-rate swings in practice have created feast-or-famine conditions across the board at different times in all of the major industrial countries.

Why do exchange rates move in ways that violate the PPP theory and lead to large trade deficits and surpluses? The answer is that the factors that we know were excluded from the PPP theory have a major impact on the actual exchange rate. Capital flows are very large and respond to differences in interest rates. The response of the exchange rate to changes in the interest rate help explain why persistent swings in the exchange rate have taken place that violate purchasing power parity.

negative effect on the expected rate of appreciation of the dollar so that expected returns are once again equalized between U.S. assets and assets in other currencies.

Thus, for a given interest-rate differential, a change in the expected future value of the dollar will change the current value of the dollar until the expected rate of appreciation or depreciation has been restored and this has then restored the equality of expected returns to interest-bearing assets held in different currencies.

One example of a change in expectations that led to a change in the current exchange rate occurred in Britain when Margaret Thatcher took office as prime minister. Many investors felt increased confidence in British economic performance and the British pound rose to $2.40 in 1980–81. However, increases in exchange rates that are fueled solely by expectations can be very fragile. Disillusion set in with the reality of British economic performance, and the pound fell almost to $1.00 in 1985. The expectations were not being realized and investors became convinced that the British exchange rate was going to fall. These negative changes in expectations reversed the shifts in the supply of and demand for British currency, driving the exchange rate back down.

Interest rates, expectations, and market equilibrium

We have looked at the separate effects of changes in interest rates and changes in expectations about the exchange rate. In general, these things will be changing together. In particular, *a change in the interest-rate differential between the United States and other countries will lead to capital inflows or outflows, to a change in the current exchange rate, and to a change in the expected rate of appreciation or depreciation of the dollar.* For example, an increase in the U.S. rate of interest will cause a capital inflow to the United States that raises the current value of the dollar. As the current value of the dollar increases, people look at the likely future value of the dollar and decide that the expected rate of appreciation of the dollar has been reduced. There has been an increase in the dollar today, so there will be a smaller rate of capital gain in the future. *International-capital-market equilibrium will hold once again (expected returns will be equalized again) after the increase in the U.S. interest rate with a wider interest-rate differential between the United States and other countries and a smaller expected rate of increase in the dollar (or a larger expected rate of decrease).*

This process went on in the 1980s. The interest-rate differential between the United States and other countries widened, leading to capital inflows into the United States and a rising dollar. Gradually, the possibility of a dollar decline became greater, until in mid-1985 concern about the value of the dollar became strong enough to overcome the higher interest return to U.S. assets. The capital inflow began to slow and the dollar started to fall. The expectations of a fall in the dollar that had been building up were then realized and there was a continuing reduction in the real exchange rate of the dollar over the next three years.

In this chapter we have looked at how changes in prices and interest rates affect imports, exports, capital flows, and the exchange rate. We did this mostly within the context of a given level of income. In the next chapter we will extend our description of international economics to include macroeconomic policies and the determination of equilibrium income in open economies.

Because of capital flows, adjustment lags, and the J-curve effect, the trade balance can and does remain in surplus or deficit for extended periods. The direction and magnitude of the trade balance will have a continuing effect on the rate of growth of domestic income. Specifically we will see how trade affects aggregate demand and how interest rates in an open economy affect the conduct of monetary and fiscal policy. We will bring the international sector into the *IS-ALM* framework.

SUMMARY

- Consumers and businesses buy and sell internationally because trade is less costly than self-sufficiency.

- International trade is accomplished by an importer (in cooperation with an international bank) first obtaining foreign exchange and then using the foreign currency to purchase foreign goods. Foreign currencies are exchanged or traded for one another in *foreign-exchange markets*.

- The price of foreign currency is called the *exchange rate*. Exchange rates can be expressed in two ways. We use the convention that the exchange rate of the dollar for a foreign currency is equal to the number of units of the currency that can be exchanged for one dollar. A rise in the dollar exchange rate means the dollar buys more foreign currency and a fall in the exchange rate means the dollar buys less foreign currency.

- The values of many different foreign currencies are combined into a summary index number called the *nominal trade-weighted exchange rate* or the *nominal exchange rate (ex)*.

- When changes in the nominal exchange rate occur simply to reflect international differences in inflation, there is no change in the relative prices of goods and services traded between the countries.

- When changes in the nominal exchange rate are adjusted for the differences in rates of inflation, the resulting index is called the *real exchange rate (rex)*. Changes in the real exchange rate affect the amounts of goods and services that are imported and exported. Increases in the real exchange rate increase imports and reduce exports.

- The improvement in the trade balance that accompanies a reduction in the exchange rate takes place with a considerable time delay or *trade adjustment lag*. The real volumes of imports and exports are slow to adjust. When the value of the dollar declines, the dollar cost of imports rises, worsening the balance of trade. Following a fall in the exchange rate, the trade balance first usually falls and then rises above the initial level, tracing out a J-shaped curve over time.

- Foreign transactions are enumerated as part of the *balance of payments*.

- The value of merchandise exports less the value of merchandise imports is called the *balance of trade*.

- The balance of trade does not account for all of the foreign effects on domestic income because U.S. residents earn income on their ownership of foreign assets, while foreign residents earn income on their ownership of U.S. assets.

- When the net balances of items that affect income are added to the trade balance, the resulting figure is called the *balance of payments on the current account*.

- The current account includes the income generated by foreign-asset holdings and excludes the purchases and sales of the foreign assets themselves.

- When the current account is in surplus, international economic activities contribute to raising national income. When the current account is in deficit, the impact of the foreign sector on income is negative.

- In principle, the current-account balance should equal net exports. In practice, the official figure for net exports incorrectly excludes payments to foreigners on U.S. Treasury securities. We will use the current-account figure as our measure of net exports.

- Foreign currency is bought and sold because people and companies want to buy foreign assets as well as foreign goods and services.

- The decision to purchase a foreign asset is affected both by the interest rate earned on the asset and by expectations about the future value of the exchange rate.

- Short-term financial capital will move internationally, seeking the best return, until the interest rates earned on bonds of comparable quality in different countries differ by the amount of the expected rate of change in the exchange rate. There is then *expected-return equalization.*

- Changes in the interest differential and/or the expected rate of change in the exchange rate will trigger capital flows into or out of a currency and a country's financial market.

- Exchanges of foreign assets appear in the *balance of payments on the capital account.* The balances on current account and the balances on capital account sum to zero because the inflows of goods and services represented by a current-account deficit have to be paid for by a sale (outflow) of assets represented by a capital-account surplus.

- The exchange rate affects the flow of traded goods, services, and assets, yet the exchange rate is determined, in foreign-exchange markets, by those same flows.

- In foreign-exchange markets, foreign currencies are traded at prices (exchange rates) that reflect the supply of and demand for foreign exchange.

- The demand for foreign exchange (foreign currencies) is derived from the domestic demand for imports and for foreign capital.

- The supply of foreign exchange is derived from the foreign demand for exports and domestic capital.

- Movements in the exchange rate are caused by shifts in the supply of and demand for foreign exchange.

- Changes in income and interest rates as well as expectations about the future value of the exchange rate will cause shifts in the supply of and demand for foreign exchange and hence will cause changes in the current exchange rate.

KEY TERMS

balance of payments

balance of payments on the current account

balance of trade

capital mobility

exchange rate

expected-return equalization

foreign exchange

foreign-exchange markets

foreign-interest-rate differential

J-curve

merchandise exports

merchandise imports

nominal exchange rate index *(ex)*

perfect capital mobility

real exchange rate index *(rex)*

terms of trade

trade adjustment lag

DISCUSSION QUESTIONS AND PROBLEMS

1. How can a surplus in the balance of payments on the current account be reconciled with a deficit in the balance of trade for the same country in the same year?

2. What is the relationship between the current account and the capital account?

3. If there was a rise in the exchange rate between the U.S. dollar and the Japanese yen from 125 yen to 150 yen, would the yen become more or less expensive to holders of dollars?

    Assume that there have been no other changes except the exchange-rate shift just cited. Will Japanese products be more or less expensive for U.S. purchasers? Will U.S. exports be more or less expensive for Japanese customers?

4. Suppose that the value of imports to Canada are distributed as follows:

U.S.	60%
Japan	25%
Great Britain	15%

    and the exchange rates last year (the base year) for the Canadian dollar (C$) in terms of the currencies of its trading partners were

    1 C$ = 0.85 U.S.$
    1 C$ = 125 yen
    1 C$ = 0.5 U.K. pound

    and the exchange rates this year are

    1 C$ = 0.75 U.S.$
    1 C$ = 150 yen
    1 C$ = 0.65 U.K. pound.

    a. Did the Canadian-dollar trade-weighted exchange rate rise or fall? By what percent?

    b. What happened to the Canadian-dollar/U.S.-dollar exchange rate?

    c. What are you presuming about the allocation of Canadian imports among the three countries? Calculate the change in the Canadian-dollar trade-weighted index using different trading proportions from those previously indicated. Explain reasons why you expect the trading proportions to change in the direction you choose.

    d. If the rate of inflation in Canada was 6 percent per year while inflation was 5 percent per year in the United States, 1 percent per year in Japan, and 10 percent per year in Great Britain, calculate the percent change in the real exchange rate between the first and second years. Use constant trading proportions.

5. Explain how the balance of trade can worsen after a fall in the real exchange rate.

6. Suppose the short-term nominal rate of interest was 5 percent per year in Japan and 6 percent per year in Germany. Would investors necessarily prefer German securities to Japanese securities?
   a. If the treasurer of a multinational corporation were indifferent as to holding short-term German government notes in marks or short-term Japanese government notes in yen, what does that indifference imply about the exchange rate between yen and marks?
   b. How would the expected returns to financial investment be related across economies if capital were perfectly mobile between nations?

7. If there is an increase in the real rate of interest in the United States relative to the rest of the world, what is likely to be the effect on the demand for dollars in foreign-exchange markets?
   a. What would you expect to happen to the U.S. exchange rate?
   b. What other likely changes in markets could result in the exchange rate moving in the opposite direction from that which you indicated in (a)?

■ APPENDIX 11A
Calculating the Effect of a Change in the Exchange Rate on the Balance of Trade: The Marshall-Lerner Condition and the J-Curve

The condition that describes the responsiveness of exports and imports to changes in the exchange rate is called the Marshall-Lerner condition after the two economists who first investigated the question. We can see the effects of price and exchange-rate changes on the trade balance using the following expression for current-dollar net exports:

$$\text{Current-dollar net exports} = PX - (PIM \div ex) \tag{A11.1}$$
$$= P \times X - (P_f \times IM) \div ex.$$

In this expression, X represents the volume of U.S. exports measured in 1982 dollars. The U.S. price level, P, is assumed to be the same as the price of U.S. exports. P is measured as an index equal to unity in 1982. P_f represents an index of the prices of imports in foreign currency set equal to unity in 1982. IM represents the volume of U.S. imports, measured in units of inflation-adjusted foreign currency.

The real exchange rate *(rex)* adjusts for movements in the U.S. price level relative to the foreign price level:

$$rex = (ex \times P) \div P_f.$$

Substituting this into the preceding expression gives

$$\text{Current-dollar net exports} = P \times [X - (rex \times IM)]. \tag{A11.2}$$

In this expression for net exports, if the real exchange rate rises and volumes of exports and imports do not change (if neither X nor IM changes), then net exports will worsen.

In order for a reduction in the real exchange rate to result in an improvement in current-dollar net exports, the combined effects of the rise in exports and the fall in imports must be large enough to offset the direct effect of the rise in the real exchange rate. In other words, a change in the real exchange rate (Δrex) will lead to a change in terms in the square bracket in Equation A11.2, and this change must be positive following a decline in the real exchange rate if the current-dollar balance is to improve.

The Marshall-Lerner condition is satisfied if

$$\Delta[X - (rex \times IM)] > 0 \text{ for } \Delta rex < 0. \tag{A11.3}$$

Applying the change operator Δ inside the bracket then gives

$$\Delta[X - (rex \times IM)] = \{\Delta X - [(\Delta rex \times IM) + (rex \times \Delta IM)]\} > 0 \text{ for } \Delta rex < 0. \tag{A11.4}$$

This result is approximate as the term $(\Delta rex \times \Delta IM)$ is ignored. We now define E_x as the elasticity of exports with respect to changes in the exchange rate and E_{IM} as the elasticity of imports.

$$E_x = \frac{-\Delta X/X}{\Delta rex/rex} \text{ and } E_{IM} = \frac{\Delta IM/IM}{\Delta rex/rex}. \tag{A11.5}$$

The minus sign in the definition of the export elasticity indicates that exports decline when the exchange rate rises. If we divide Equation A11.4 by $(-\Delta rex \times IM)$ and substitute in the elasticities from Equation A11.5, we find the Marshall-Lerner condition for a decline in the exchange rate to increase net exports:

$$E_x \left(\frac{X}{rex \times IM} \right) + E_{IM} > 1.$$

An example will illustrate how the condition works. Suppose that initially exports are only 80 percent of imports, that is, $X \div (rex \times IM)$ equals 0.8 and that a 10 percent decline in the exchange rate will increase exports by 7 percent $(E_x = 0.7)$ and decrease imports by 5 percent $(E_{IM} = 0.5)$. Then the Marshall-Lerner condition is satisfied $[(0.7 \times 0.8) + 0.5 > 1]$, so that net exports will improve.

An approximate condition is often given if net exports are not too far from balance. If it is approximately true that $X = rex \times IM$, then the Marshall-Lerner condition becomes

$$E_x + E_{IM} > 1.$$

The sum of the elasticities must be greater than unity.

Based on the experience of the 1980s, the Marshall-Lerner condition is satisfied for the U.S. economy. Net exports declined when the dollar rose and improved when the dollar fell. Keep in mind, however, that income does not remain constant in practice and the adjustment process takes time because the short-run elasticities of exports and imports are small. The condition is not satisfied at first and then later it is satisfied. This worsening of the trade balance followed by an improvement in the trade balance has been described as the J-curve effect.

CHAPTER 12

Macroeconomic Policy in an International Economy

INTRODUCTION

Aggregate income, interest rates, exchange rates, and inflation are all affected by the international economy. In this chapter we continue the discussion of trade and capital movements and incorporate them into the analysis of income determination. In addition, we look at the impact of monetary and fiscal policies in an open economy. In the 1970s and 1980s, U.S. businesses learned the hard way that they must reckon with tough competition from overseas. And U.S. policymakers have learned that the choices they face are affected by the foreign sector. Monetary and fiscal policies can change the trade balance and the exchange rate, which, in turn, influence the effectiveness of these policies in changing interest rates, employment, output, and inflation.

Our analysis of macroeconomic policy is based upon the current set of international monetary arrangements, which include the current system of fluctuating exchange rates. This system has only been in place since 1971–1973, so we also take a look at how the international economy operated in an earlier period when governments controlled currency markets, so that exchange rates were more or less fixed. It is quite possible that in the future there could be a return to arrangements that involve greater government intervention in the foreign-exchange market.

We start by reviewing the results of the simple income and expenditure model (introduced in Chapter 2) where exports add to demand and imports subtract from demand, assuming no changes in the exchange rate. We then go on to describe the role of exchange-rate changes in determining equilibrium.

AGGREGATE DEMAND IN AN INTERNATIONAL ECONOMY

Aggregate demand in an open economy is just the total of purchases by U.S. residents (regardless of where the goods originated) plus net exports *(NX = X − IM)*:

$$Y = C + I + G + NX. \hspace{3cm} 12.1$$

To see how the foreign sector influences the level of income in the U.S. economy, we need to look at the determinants of net exports, just as we looked at the determinants of consumption and investment demand.

In the simple exposition offered in Chapter 2, we started out with an autonomously determined level of exports. On the import side, we assumed that a rise in domestic income raises overall expenditures causing both the domestic and foreign components of consumption and investment to increase. This meant that imports increased as a result of a rise in income. The fact that imports rise when domestic income rises means that, with exports and the exchange rate fixed, *net exports decline as the level of income rises*.

Net exports are part of aggregate demand in the domestic economy, so that a change in income will have a feedback effect on aggregate demand and income. The foreign sector, like consumption and investment, is influenced by income and also helps to determine income. When net exports are positive the foreign sector provides a net addition to aggregate demand. Negative net exports are a net subtraction from demand.

We saw in Chapter 2 that the multiplier is smaller in an open economy than in a closed one. In an open economy, the increase in imports that occurs as income rises means that any increase in aggregate demand will leak partly into increased imports. Goods that are purchased from overseas do not generate increases in production and employment here in the United States, so the wage and profit income resulting from the production of these goods is not U.S. income. Imports are leakages like taxes or saving in that they mitigate the multiplier effect of a given stimulus to income.

Goods-Market Equilibrium with a Foreign Sector

The *IS* schedule describes the combinations of the level of income and the long-term real interest rate that ensure goods-market equilibrium—where output equals aggregate demand. In an open economy, the *IS* schedule describes the same relationship as it does in a closed economy except that the foreign-trade multiplier is smaller than the multiplier in a closed economy. Therefore, taking the exchange rate as given, a reduction in the long-term real rate of interest may generate the same initial increase in investment expenditure as in a closed economy but, because of import leakages, the increase in income is smaller. This means that, *with a given exchange rate, goods-market equilibrium in an open economy will be described by an IS schedule that has a steeper slope than the IS schedule that describes the goods market in a closed economy.*

Recall that the slope of the *IS* schedule has implications for policy. For example, monetary policy works by changing interest rates, which induces a change in investment and income. The effectiveness of monetary policy depends upon the size of the interest-rate effect—the interest-rate responsiveness of expenditure changes as described by the slope of the *IS* schedule.

As well as affecting the economy's responsiveness to interest-rate changes, the foreign-trade sector can also affect the level of aggregate demand (shift the *IS* schedule). For example, if U.S. firms are successful in bringing to market innovations in products that appeal to foreign customers, those innovations would increase the foreign demand for U.S. goods. Assuming no change in the exchange rate, U.S. exports will increase. And this will raise the level of autonomous expenditure. Figure 12.1 shows the effect of this increase in autonomous expenditure as a shift of the *IS* schedule from *IS* to *IS'*. As a result of an increase in foreign demand for U.S. exports, aggregate demand has increased. If the money supply is unchanged following the changes in export demand, the increase in export demand would raise income and the interest rate. As shown in Figure 12.1, the economy would move from point *A* to point *B*.

The exchange rate and the *IS* schedule

In the actual economy, changes in international economic conditions are seldom restricted to changes in the foreign demand for U.S. exports. Interest rates and exchange rates are likely to change as income and trade flows change. We have seen, however, that the effect of changes in the exchange rate on imports and exports can be slow in coming. A change in the exchange rate that is short-lived (i.e., the rate goes up for only a few months and then returns to its previous level) is not likely to have a marked effect on the flow of trade. In order to study the effects of the foreign sector within the *IS-ALM* framework, we will use an *IS* schedule that is based upon a fixed value for the level of exports and a given import function. *Shifts in net exports that are related to sustained changes in the exchange rate are shown as causing shifts of the IS schedule.*

An increase in the exchange rate will eventually lead to an increase in imports and a decrease in exports. This means that *a sustained increase in the exchange rate will cause the IS schedule to shift back to the left.* Figure 12.2 illustrates such a shift, from *IS* to *IS'* as a result of a sustained increase in the value of the dollar. A reduction in the dollar has the opposite effect. After some lag, it will cause the *IS* schedule to shift to the right. This is shown as the shift from *IS* to *IS"*.

Money-Market Equilibrium with a Foreign Sector

In an economy where goods, services, and financial capital are traded internationally, financial markets are affected by international market conditions.

FIGURE 12.1   The Impact of Increasing Exports

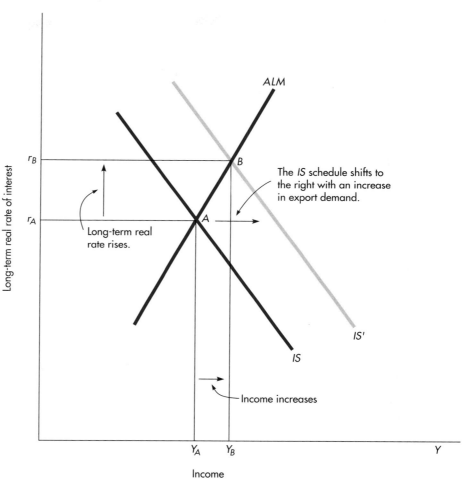

Rising export demand shifts the *IS* schedule to the right.

Interest rates here in the United States are affected by interest rates overseas, with the effect of the international sector occurring primarily through the demand for money and other financial assets.

In terms of the supply of money, the Fed can still exercise control, if it chooses to do so. The Fed and the U.S. banking system, which is controlled by the Fed, are the only agencies that can supply U.S. money (money that can be used to make transactions in the United States). Of course, foreigners can go into the foreign-exchange market and buy dollars, but only by finding

FIGURE 12.2   Goods-Market Equilibrium and Sustained Changes in the Exchange Rate

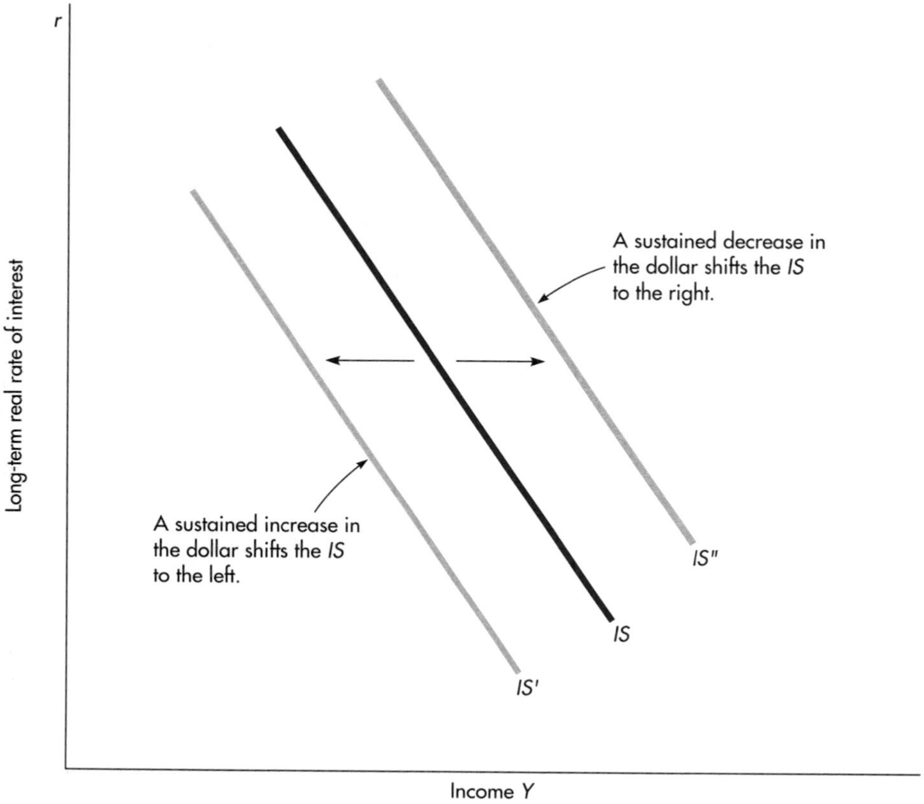

A sustained decrease in the dollar shifts the *IS* to the right.

A sustained increase in the dollar shifts the *IS* to the left.

IS"

IS

IS'

Long-term real rate of interest

Income *Y*

someone else willing to sell those dollars. The foreign-exchange market allows dollars to be traded at varying exchange rates but it cannot create dollars. Fundamentally, therefore, even in an open economy, the Fed can maintain its control over the U.S. money supply.

The Fed can choose to maintain its control over the supply of money in the U.S. economy, but it may end up giving up this control if it also tries to fix the exchange rate. As we will see later in this chapter, if the Fed decides to set the value of the dollar in foreign exchange markets, it will find this difficult or impossible to do if it is also trying to control the quantity of the U.S. money supply.

In the 1950s and 1960s the Fed did try to conduct a monetary policy that met the needs of the domestic economy and at the same time maintain a fixed exchange rate for the U.S. dollar in relation to gold. To the extent to which it succeeded, it did so by not using a very active monetary policy domestically and by relying on other countries to adjust their policies. The U.S. dollar was so dominant in world markets that the Fed could let other countries adjust their monetary policies or their exchange rates.

Over the 1971–1973 period, the Fed abandoned its commitment to maintain a fixed value of the dollar in relation to gold or other currencies. Since then, there has been a flexible–exchange-rate system, so that *we will assume now that the Fed sets the money supply and lets the exchange rate vary.* However, this does not mean that exchange rates are set in completely free markets. Foreign central banks have often intervened in the market, buying and selling dollars and affecting exchange rates, at least in the short run. Later in the chapter, we look at the case where the Fed intervenes in foreign-exchange markets.

U.S. and foreign interest rates

Even though the Fed can control the U.S. money supply, the ability of corporate cash managers to move money across international borders does affect money demand and the nature of money-market equilibrium. The cash manager balances liquidity (given a firm's need for cash for transactions) against the return on T bills or other interest-bearing assets. In an open economy, cash managers can substitute foreign-currency assets for T bills. Although holding foreign assets usually involves greater risks because of exchange-rate fluctuations, if the return earned on the foreign assets is large enough, it will induce some cash managers to increase their holding of foreign assets and decrease their holdings of T bills. For example, a fall in short-term U.S. interest rates not matched by a similar fall in short-term foreign rates will make bills or notes denominated in foreign exchange look more attractive.

This same argument works for the counterpart to the cash manager in a foreign firm. Japanese corporate treasurers may hold a portfolio including U.S.-government T bills. A fall in the U.S. short-term nominal interest rate causes the Japanese cash manager to shift out of these U.S. assets and seek alternatives, including yen-denominated assets.

Because cash managers here and overseas can shift their portfolios into or out of U.S. T bills, U.S. money demand and hence financial-market equilibrium in the United States (as shown by the position of the *LM* schedule) will shift if foreign interest rates change. For example, if the interest rate on short-term Japanese government bills rises, then some cash managers will decide to reduce their holdings of U.S. T bills and increase their holdings of Japanese short-term assets. In order to bring the U.S. money market back into equilibrium, the interest rate on U.S. T bills will rise too. This is shown as a shift from *LM* to *LM'* in Figure 12.3. At a given level of income, Y_A, the short-term nominal interest rate will rise in the United States when foreign short-term rates rise. *There is an international transmission of interest movements that results from the movements of short-term capital across national borders.* The effect on the money market of an increase in foreign interest rates is shown as an upward shift of the *LM* schedule.

FIGURE 12.3   Money-Market Equilibrium and Foreign Interest Rates

A rise in foreign interest rates pulls up the *LM* schedule.

LM'

LM

U.S. rate rises when foreign rates rise.

Short-term nominal rate of interest

Y_A

Income *Y*

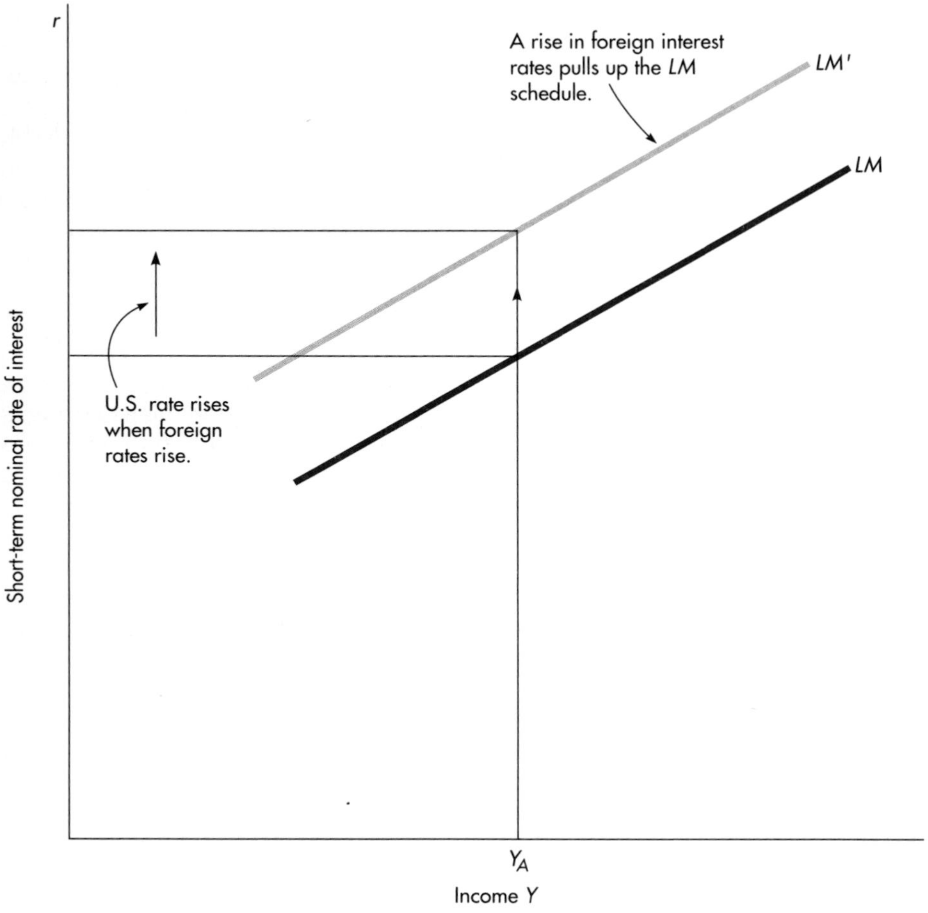

While corporate cash managers concentrate on short-term assets, pension funds, insurance companies, and mutual funds are making longer-term investments and are willing to hold long-term bonds in order to receive the higher yield that these bonds usually offer. The institutions making these long-term investments can also choose to hold foreign bonds rather than domestic bonds if the interest rates overseas are sufficiently attractive. This means that, presuming no change in inflationary expectations or the maturity premium (no change in r_{gap}), an increase in the long-term nominal interest rate overseas will encourage U.S. asset holders to sell U.S. long-term bonds, and this will lower the prices of these bonds and raise the long-term nominal

FIGURE 12.4   Capital-Market Equilibrium and Foreign Rates

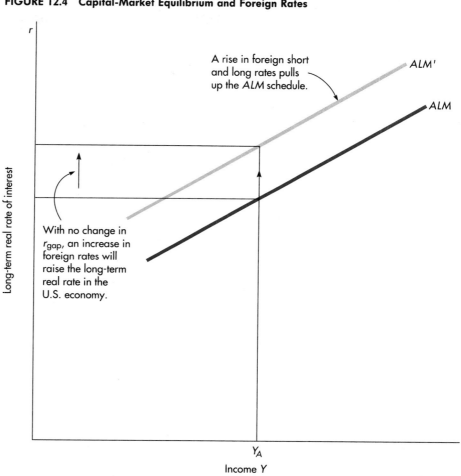

The effect of the rise in foreign rates on the *ALM* assumes no change in r_{gap}. If the rise in foreign rates is only in short-term rates or is seen as temporary, the effect on U.S. long-term real and nominal rates will be very small—r_{gap} will fall.

rate of interest in the United States. There is an international transmission of long-term interest rates as well as one for short-term interest rates. Figure 12.4 depicts the effect on the U.S. capital market of an increase in both short- and long-term interest rates overseas—the *ALM* schedule shifts up, from *ALM* to *ALM'*. Holding income and the expected future exchange rate constant, *when foreign interest rates rise, there is a corresponding rise in U.S. interest rates.*

We have just said that there is an international transmission of interest

THE DOLLAR THAT SOARED ONLY TO CRASH

During the early 1980s, because of its twin trade and budget deficits, the United States replaced Brazil as the world's largest debtor nation. The United States consumed much more than it could produce at home and paid for the difference by borrowing from abroad.

Of course not all debt is bad. Lots of businesses and countries start up or grow more prosperous by judiciously borrowing funds. Suppose the increase in U.S. borrowing from abroad had been used to upgrade plant and equipment for the American auto industry. These investments would have increased U.S. car manufacturers' ability to compete against foreign carmakers and could have brought in profits with which, among other things, the debt could have been retired.

Instead of being used for investment spending, much of the foreign borrowed funds merely helped fuel a consumer-led economic expansion. Ironically, lots of the profits went back overseas for goods that were made in Europe and Japan. The spending binge made everyone feel good, but it was largely wasteful from a long-term standpoint. It was as if college students had spent their tuition loans on vacations instead of education.

At the same time foreign demand for high-yield CDs, U.S. bonds, and stocks increased the international value of the dollar. Between 1980 and 1985 the U.S. dollar rose by a trade-weighted average of about 50 percent. However, economists concluded at the time that most of the rise was not related to the competitive position of American industry. If comparative costs of production alone had determined exchange rates, the dollar would have scarcely budged from its 1980 level. But foreign in-

vestors have traditionally viewed the United States as a safe haven; its high interest rates supported by massive deficit spending have attracted lots of foreign funds. For Americans, imports were cheap and they flowed into the United States.

At the same time Americans flocked abroad. College students traveling to Munich could stay the weekend in a Hofhaus for what formerly had been the price of a single night's stay. Their parents could fly to London rather than New York, buy a new wardrobe at Harrod's instead of Bloomingdale's, and still save money—or so they claimed. At the same time the prices of U.S. goods and services to foreigners were effectively marked up 40 percent. Many U.S. businesses could not survive such a price increase for their products. Indeed, many export- and import-competing U.S. industries were severely damaged by the soaring dollar.

Eventually the negative effects of the dollar's rise surfaced. The slowdown in U.S. exports due to the high-priced dollar—though it had helped to keep U.S. domestic prices in check during the expansion—led to widespread predictions of recession.

In 1986 the prospect of a recession prompted a new U.S. policy of intervention in the foreign exchange markets. The U.S. Treasury and the Federal Reserve, in cooperation with other foreign governments and central banks, began to sell dollars for other currencies in order to reduce the dollar's trade value.

The policy change, combined with a change in expectations among private investors, reversed the dollar's rise. By 1988, the dollar fell back to the level it had at the start of the decade.

rates, so that when foreign interest rates change, this leads to changes in U.S. rates (the *LM* and *ALM* schedules shift). But the spillover from foreign interest rates to U.S. interest rates should not be overemphasized—the shifts in the *LM* and *ALM* schedules are not very great. There are two main reasons for this. First, when foreign interest rates change, a large part of the impact on the U.S. economy is the result of changes in the dollar-exchange rate. A rise in short-term nominal rates of interest overseas will lead to a net capital outflow from the United States and a decline in the value of the dollar, as we saw in Chapter 11. *A change in the differential between the United States and foreign interest rates will change both the current value of the dollar and the expected rate of change of the dollar, as well as U.S. interest rates.* Expected return equalization will be achieved partly by a change in the short-term nominal rate here in the United States and partly by a change in the expected rate of appreciation or depreciation of the dollar (see Equation 11.3 in Chapter 11). The second reason that changes in foreign rates will have only a modest effect on U.S. rates applies to the case of long-term real rates of interest. Real assets in the United States are not close substitutes for real assets overseas, so that expected returns on these assets will not equalize. In particular, if the change that has taken place in foreign financial markets is primarily seen as a short-term change (one that changes only short-term rates), then there will be little change in the long-term real rate of interest in the United States (little change in the *ALM* schedule). Mostly, the impact will fall on the value of the dollar.

Equilibrium Income *(IS-ALM)* in an Open Economy

We describe the goods-market and financial-market influences on aggregate demand equilibrium using the *IS-ALM* framework. In Figure 12.5 the equilibrium level of income and the long-term real rate of interest are shown as the intersection of the *ALM* and *IS* schedules at point *A*. We now want to explore how the interest rate and the level of equilibrium income are affected by the fact that the economy is open.

Consider first the case of a closed economy. An increase in autonomous expenditure in this economy is shown by a shift of the *IS* schedule to the right. The amount of the shift in *IS* that would occur in a closed economy is shown in the figure by *IS'*. The closed economy would move to a point such as that depicted as point *B*. (The level of income is Y_B and the interest rate is r_B.)

By contrast, in an open economy, the multiplier is smaller and so the shift in the *IS* schedule is smaller. In Figure 12.5, the schedule *IS"* depicts the response of the open economy to an equivalent increase in autonomous expenditure. The economy will move to a point such as that depicted as point C_0. (The level of income is Y_C and the interest rate is r_C.) In Figure 12.5 the schedule *IS"* is drawn taking account of the change in imports that resulted from the increase in income. The import leakage is the reason why income at *C* is less than that at point *B*.

We have not yet taken account of changes in the exchange rate and their impact on net exports. A movement of the *IS* schedule to the right has two important effects on the exchange rate. The increase in income will (1) cause a decline in net exports and this will raise the supply of dollars into the foreign-exchange market and tend to lower the value of the dollar.

FIGURE 12.5   Impact of Rising Autonomous Expenditure

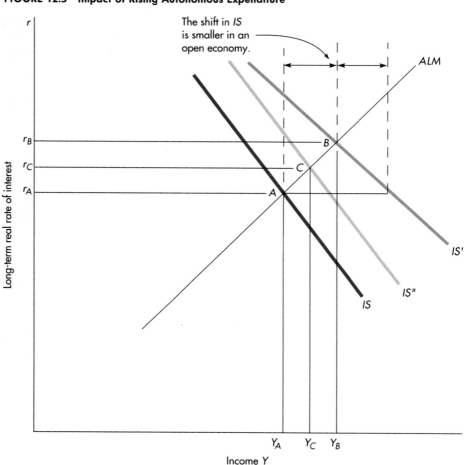

An increase in autonomous expenditure has a smaller effect in an open economy than in a closed economy.

And (2) it will cause U.S. interest rates to increase (as the *IS* schedule slides up the *ALM* schedule) and this will lead to a net inflow of capital (raising the demand for dollars in the foreign-exchange market) and tend to increase the value of the dollar. In general, these offsetting forces can come out either way. But there is one important case where we know that an increase in autonomous expenditure will lead to an increase in net exports and the value of the dollar. This is the case where there is an exogenous increase in export demand.

Increased export demand

An exogenous increase in export demand could have come about as a result of an increase in foreign income or a reduction in foreign-government restrictions (tariffs and trade barriers) on imports. Initially, an increase in export demand is like any other increase in autonomous expenditure—it will raise income and raise the interest rate. Imports will rise as the level of income rises, but except under very unusual circumstances, imports will not rise by as much as the initial increase in export demand. So an increase in export demand will raise net exports also. Since the increase in export demand has raised both interest rates and net exports, the result will certainly be an increase in the value of the dollar.

Over time, the increase in the value of the dollar will reduce exports and increase imports. This will reduce income and gradually eliminate the increase in net exports. An exogenous increase in export demand will gradually set off a self-correcting response (the rise in the dollar) that will tend to restore the original level of income and restore the original level of net exports. This adjustment process is shown in Figure 12.6. The economy is pictured initially at point A (the intersection of IS and ALM). There is then an increase in export demand and this pushes the IS schedule out to IS'. The economy is now at point B and the level of income and the rate of interest are both higher. (Y_B is higher than Y_A, and r_B is higher than r_A.) Over time, the increase in the exchange rate reduces net exports, and the IS schedule drifts back to the left. This is shown by the dashed lines in Figure 12.6. Eventually, the IS schedule will go back close to its original position. The exchange rate will remain higher in the long run, provided the factors that led to the initial increase in foreign demand for U.S. exports are sustained. *The long-run effect of a sustained increase in the demand for U.S. exports is that there will be little or no change in income or the interest rate in the United States. There will be an increase in the value of the dollar.*

A fall in foreign interest rates

We continue with our analysis of IS-ALM in an open economy by looking at the impact of a change in foreign interest rates on the U.S. economy. In our analysis of a closed economy we found that interest rates change in reaction to changes in the goods market or the U.S. money market. The effects of changing market conditions upon interest rates were described by shifts in the IS or the ALM schedules. In an open economy there can be changes in interest rates even in the absence of changes in domestic conditions. There is an international transmission of interest rates that has an effect on domestic income. For instance, a reduction in foreign interest rates will send capital into the U.S. financial market and drive down U.S. interest rates, thereby affecting domestic aggregate demand. In Figure 12.7 we show the effect of such a foreign–interest-rate decline through a downward shift in the ALM schedule, from ALM to ALM'. Income rises from Y_A to Y_B as the

FIGURE 12.6   The Effect of an Exogenous Increase in Export Demand

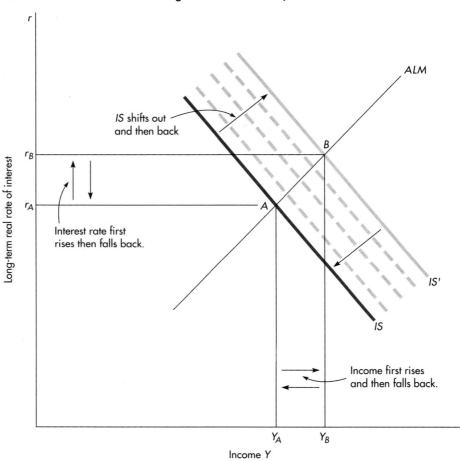

An increase in export demand is expansionary. But the dollar rises and reverses the initial impact.

fall in U.S. interest rates encourages domestic investment (the *ALM* slides along the given *IS* schedule).

This is not the end of the story, however. So far we have looked at the effect of a change in foreign interest rates on U.S. interest rates, while ignoring the impact on the U.S. exchange rate. When foreign interest rates decline, this will lead not only to some decline in U.S. interest rates, but it will also change the international interest differential and raise the value of the dollar. The drop in foreign interest rates (which makes foreign assets less attractive) generates a capital inflow that raises the exchange rate. If the drop in foreign

FIGURE 12.7   The Impact of a Fall in Foreign Interest Rates

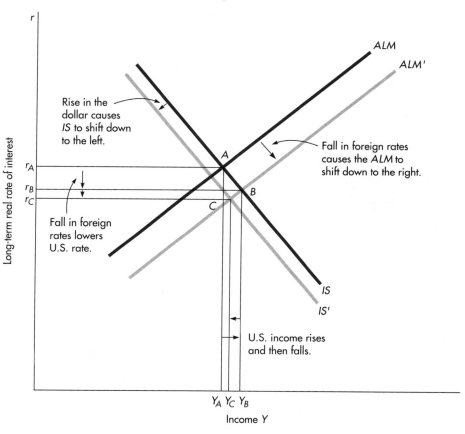

In this illustrative example, income is shown rising from Y_A to Y_B and then falling back part way, to end up at Y_C.

rates is sustained, the increase in the dollar will decrease our exports and increase our imports. This response in the goods market to a change in the exchange rate is shown as a leftward shift of the *IS* schedule (*IS* to *IS′*). Over the longer run, the initial positive impact on U.S. income of the reduction of foreign rates is offset by the subsequent negative impact on income of the rise in the dollar. As income first rises and then falls back, the U.S. interest rate will fall further (to r_C in the figure).

Given the size of the U.S. economy, the impact on U.S. income from foreign–interest-rate changes is likely to be fairly small. For smaller countries, however, the short-run impact of foreign–interest-rate changes may be larger.

In the 1980s, the large U.S. economy had very high interest rates, which thereby raised interest rates in international markets.

The European countries complained at that time that their interest rates were driven up by the high U.S. rates and that this was an obstacle to their efforts to reduce unemployment. This is the reverse of the case in Figure 12.7. From the European perspective, U.S. interest rates are the foreign rates and they rose rather than fell. This then had a spillover effect that raised European interest rates. Thus there is some basis for the European complaint. On the other hand, it is arguable whether the United States was really a major cause of slow growth in Europe. The rise in the U.S. dollar that went with the rise in U.S. interest rates led to a surge of U.S. imports, including imports from Europe. Over time, aggregate demand in the European goods market was increased (the European economy's *IS* schedule was shifted out) by the rise in U.S. interest rates.

DOMESTIC MACROECONOMIC POLICIES IN AN OPEN ECONOMY

The effects of domestic macroeconomic policy in an open economy are different from the effects in a closed economy—sometimes the foreign sector reinforces and sometimes the foreign sector works against policy actions.[1] Increases in aggregate demand that raise interest rates will cause capital inflows, changes in the exchange rate, and reductions in the balance of trade, all of which alter the effectiveness of policy actions.

Monetary Expansion and Capital Outflows

Expansionary monetary policy is designed to stimulate aggregate demand— first lowering the short-term nominal rate of interest and then lowering the long-term real rate of interest (assuming no offset from changes in maturity premiums or inflationary expectations in financial markets). The impact of a monetary-policy action on equilibrium is affected by the openness of the economy to international markets. First, the goods market is less interest-rate–responsive in an open economy than in a closed economy. (The *IS* schedule is steeper.) A given decline in the real interest rate induced by monetary policy has less of an effect on income in an open economy. Second, in an open economy, a reduction in the real rate of interest also reduces

---

[1] The basic framework for studying policy in an open economy is known as the Mundell-Fleming model. Robert Mundell, "Capital Mobility and Stabilization under Fixed and Flexible Exchange Rates," *Canadian Journal of Economics*, November 1963; and Marcus Fleming, "Domestic Financial Policies under Fixed and Floating Exchange Rates," *IMF Staff Papers*, November 1962. This framework has been extended by many authors since then. See, for example, Rudiger Dornbusch, *Open Economy Macroeconomics* (New York: Basic Books, 1980); John Campbell and Richard Clarida, "The Dollar and the Real Interest Rate," *Carnegie Rochester Conference Series* (Amsterdam: North Holland, 1987); Ralph Bryant et al., eds., *Empirical Macroeconomics for International Economies* (Washington D.C.: Brookings Institution, 1988); Paul de Grauwe, *International Money, Postwar Trends and Theories* (Oxford, England: Oxford University Press, 1989).

the real exchange rate. The fall in the real rate of interest changes the interest-rate differential between foreign and domestic financial assets. Financial managers will readjust their portfolios to hold more foreign assets and fewer domestic assets. This causes capital outflows, which reduce the real exchange rate. Initially, the lower real exchange rate will have little effect on the real volumes of exports and imports. Over time, however, net exports rise, adding to the increase in aggregate demand.

To summarize: Monetary policy has a different impact on income in a closed rather than in an open economy. One difference makes monetary policy less effective (steeper *IS* schedule). But the second difference is more important over time. A monetary policy action also changes the exchange rate. *In an open economy, in the intermediate run, monetary policy becomes a stronger instrument for controlling income, because it works not only as a result of changing investment demand but also through changing the exchange rate and hence net exports.* This conclusion about the strengthening of monetary policy is one of the most important results obtained from the analysis of macroeconomic policy in an open economy.

Short-run reactions to monetary expansion

A monetary expansion lowers the short-run nominal rate of interest and then lowers the long-run real rate. The expansion of the open economy initially occurs just as it did in a closed economy: The lower real interest rate stimulates capital expenditures that in turn generate a multiplier process of increased aggregate demand. However, because of changes in the exchange rate and the international interest-rate differential, the story of the short-term effects of a monetary expansion in an open economy is somewhat different from the story in a closed economy.

We look at this policy effect by starting with an economy producing at less than potential output. In Figure 12.8A, the *IS-ALM* intersection (point *A*) describes an economy in a recession *(Y_A)*. The Fed initiates a monetary expansion in order to stimulate aggregate demand and increase income. There is a drop in the short-term nominal interest rate, and once financial markets decide that the Fed is committed to expansion, then the long-term rate comes down. This is illustrated by an outward shift of the *ALM* schedule (*ALM* to *ALM'*). The fall in the rate of interest will increase investment demand and hence income. (The economy is shown moving from *A* to *B*.)

Even before the fall in the interest rate has led to a change in income, there are effects in the foreign-exchange market. The drop in U.S. short-term interest rates starts a capital outflow. As dollar-denominated assets are sold and foreign-denominated assets are purchased, this increases the supply of dollars and reduces the demand. In addition, the first effect of the fall in the exchange rate is to worsen the trade balance in current dollars—the J-curve. Imports are more expensive and this raises the supply of dollars in the foreign-exchange market. The combined effect of these shifts is that the supply schedule for dollars to the foreign-exchange market shifts out (*S*

FIGURE 12.8 **The Effect of a Monetary Expansion in the Short Run**

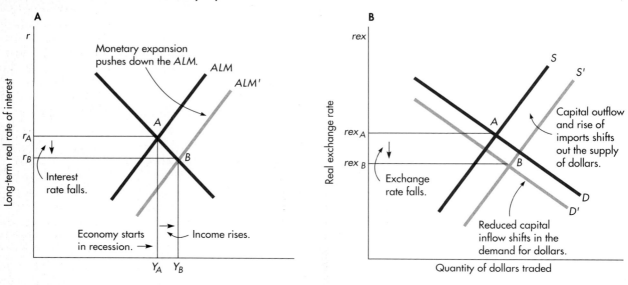

to S' in Figure 12.9B) and the demand schedule for dollars shifts in (D to D' in Figure 12.9B). As a result, the real exchange rate falls (point A to point B in Figure 12.8B).

Let's summarize what we can expect during the first year of an expansionist monetary policy in an open economy.

The short-term rate of interest declines. This results in a capital outflow and the value of the dollar declines.

The long-term nominal interest rate declines. The expected rate of inflation may rise. The long-term real rate of interest declines. (The ALM shifts down.)

Investment demand increases. This causes the level of income (a move along the IS) to rise. The increase in income leads to an increased demand for imports.

The dollar's fall increases the real volume of exports and reduces the real volume of imports.

However, real net exports will probably move into deficit (or a surplus will be reduced). The nominal value of net exports will turn negative as described by the J-curve.

There has been an increase in income and a decline in the real rate of interest, but there has also been a fall in the value of the dollar and a deterioration in the trade balance. Taking account of the foreign sector has suggested that the short-run effects of monetary expansion may lead to some undesirable consequences.

The Fed's dilemma in an open economy

We have argued that the Fed has often faced a policy dilemma: Expansionary monetary policy can stimulate aggregate demand but it may also increase inflation. At times, the Fed has also faced an additional constraint on any proposed expansionary policies. The Fed, cognizant of the fact that the United States is an open economy, has sometimes set for itself an additional policy goal: to manage the value of the dollar in foreign-exchange markets. If, in the opinion of the Fed, the dollar is falling too quickly, the Fed may engage in policy intended to "defend" the dollar.

When the economy is stuck at a level of income below potential and, in addition, the dollar is considered to be too low, the Fed faces several policy options. We look at two policy extremes. *First, the Fed could defend the dollar and ignore the below-potential income.* This would call for tight money policies. Interest rates would rise along with the value of the dollar, and inflation (though presumably low) would be reduced. The cost would be a worsening of the problem of low income and high unemployment. *Second, the Fed could stimulate aggregate demand (raising income and employment) and ignore the falling exchange rate.* This would require instituting a monetary expansion. The economy would suffer a net capital outflow and the real exchange rate would fall. In addition, there will be a short-term worsening of the current account and net exports as the dollar falls. This perverse movement of net exports will not last, but in the short run it is seen as an adverse result of the Fed's actions—they have driven down the dollar and made the current-dollar trade balance worse! The benefit of this policy, of course, is an increase in income.

It's easy to see why the Fed would be tempted to intervene in the foreign-exchange market, using its reserves of foreign exchange and trading currencies in the market to manage the dollar. And the same dilemma may also confront the central banks of other countries in the same situation. Many countries in recent years have intervened in currency markets in order to try and "defend" or "restrain" the values of their currencies without sacrificing their domestic income and employment. Later in the chapter we will look at the efficacy of such intervention.

Intermediate-run reactions to monetary expansion

While a monetary expansion appears to worsen trade balances in the short run, the effects of the monetary expansion over a longer period of time look better in several respects. The fall of the real exchange rate works to improve the balance of trade, further stimulating aggregate demand, and reinforcing the effectiveness of monetary policy. In Figure 12.9A, the effect on aggregate demand of an improved balance of trade is pictured as an

FIGURE 12.9   The Effect of a Monetary Expansion in the Intermediate Run

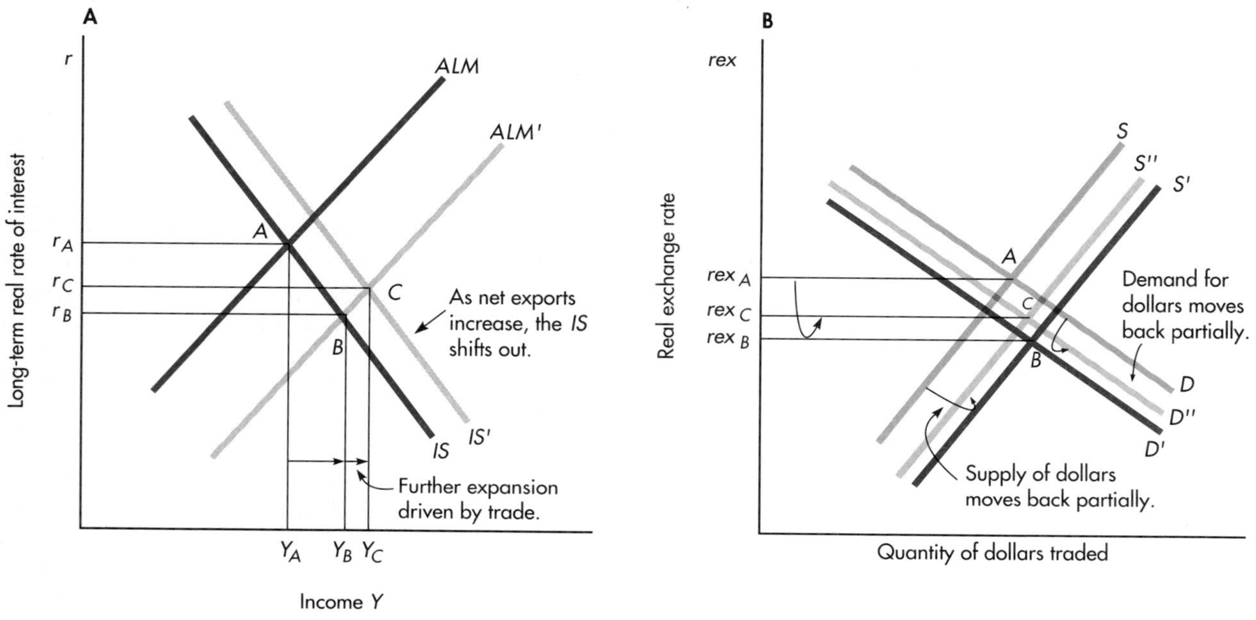

outward shift of the *IS* schedule (*IS* to *IS'*). The economy has moved to a higher level of income (Y_C is greater than Y_B) with some recovery of interest rates (r_C is greater than r_B but r_C is still lower than r_A) as the economy expanded.

In the foreign-exchange market, there has been some recovery of the value of the dollar. An increase in exports raises the demand for dollars, an effect that is reinforced by the impact on capital inflows of the rise in interest rates. Decreasing imports, even in current dollars, reduce the demand for dollars, while the rise in interest rates also reduces capital outflows. In Figure 12.9B, these changes are shown by the shifts from S' to S'' and D' to D''. The exchange rate goes to rex_C.

Inflation and the exchange rate

None of these intermediate-run effects of monetary policy will help the policy-makers get out of the dilemma posed by the output–inflation trade-off. In an open economy as well as in a closed economy, monetary expansion stimulates aggregate demand. We started by looking at an economy that was below potential, so in this case the expansionary policy will not lead to increased inflation. But if inflation was too high to start with, then the dilemma of wanting to reduce inflation as well as reduce unemployment is just as bad as it was in a closed economy—in fact it may even be worse. As we mentioned in Chapter 10, a decline in the dollar can create a small supply shock.

A fall in the exchange rate increases the rate of inflation. The impact of the exchange rate on inflation is both direct and indirect.[2] The direct impact is seen most clearly in the Consumer Price Index.[3] Consumers buy foreign-made goods and when these become more expensive, the cost of living increases. The indirect inflationary impact occurs in the ways that follow from the analysis of costs in Chapter 10; that is, costs coming from wages and markups may be increased by a fall in the dollar and hence increase inflation. First, an increase in consumer prices pushes wage inflation up, as consumer prices feed into the price–wage spiral. Second, U.S. companies that compete with imports may be able to expand their markups because imports are no longer as price-competitive.

If the dollar increases, this process works in reverse. *An increase in the dollar reduces domestic inflation.* The effects on inflation of both an increase and a decrease in the dollar were seen in recent years. From 1981 to 1985, the dollar rose, contributing to the rapid decline in inflation that occurred in those years. After 1985, the dollar declined again and this contributed to the mild increase in inflation that occurred after 1985.

Fiscal Expansion and Capital Flows

Expansionary fiscal policy works by increasing aggregate demand directly (shifting out the *IS* schedule). In a closed economy in which the Fed pursues a policy that maintains the *ALM* schedule in a fixed position, fiscal expansion raises the real rate of interest. In an open economy, fiscal policy has an even smaller impact on income than in a closed economy. The rise in the real rate of interest that results from the fiscal expansion causes capital inflows, which increase the real exchange rate, ultimately worsening the balance of trade and working against the expansionary policy. This is the second key aspect of macroeconomic policy in an open economy: *Fiscal policy is relatively ineffective in raising income without the support of monetary policy.* This does not mean that a fiscal expansion has no effects at all. It will generate a trade deficit.

In Figure 12.10A we show how a fiscal expansion (*IS* to *IS'*) has increased aggregate demand (point *A* to point *B*). Output is higher at *B*, even though for a given increase in government expenditures or reduction in taxes, the

---

[2] Robert J. Gordon, "Inflation, Flexible Exchange Rates and the Natural Rate of Unemployment," in *Workers Jobs and Inflation*, ed. Martin Neil Baily (Washington D.C.: Brookings Institution, 1982). A rise in the exchange rate may force a small reduction in export prices.

[3] The CPI is a better measure of the impact of trade on domestic prices than the GNP deflator since the price of imports does not enter directly into the GNP deflator. This is because imports are not explicitly part of GNP.

FIGURE 12.10 **The Effect of a Fiscal Expansion in the Short Run and the Intermediate Run**

A

Long-term real rate of interest

r

ALM

r_A

r_C

r_B

B

C

A

Fiscal expansion raises income in the short run; the effect weakens over time as a result of trade deficit.

Interest rate rises in the short run. It falls back partially in the intermediate run.

IS'

IS''

IS

Y_A Y_C Y_B

Income

B

rex

Real exchange rate

rex $_B$

rex $_C$

rex $_A$

S'
S''
S

B

A

D'
D''
D

The exchange rate rises in the short run and then partially falls back in the intermediate run.

Quantity of dollars traded

increase in output is smaller in an open economy than in a closed economy because of import leakages. The growth of output has increased imports and has had a negative impact on net exports.

In the foreign-exchange market, the increase in the demand for imports raises the supply of dollars, which lowers the real exchange rate. However, the increase in the real rate of interest brings capital flowing in and this tends to decrease the supply of dollars and also to increase the demand for dollars. There are therefore offsetting changes at work in the foreign-exchange market. The experience of the United States, shown particularly by the period 1983–1985, is that the overall effect of a fiscal expansion is to raise the exchange rate. Foreigners responded to higher U.S. interest rates by bringing in huge amounts of capital, more than enough to maintain the exchange rate. The shifts in supply and demand in the foreign-exchange market are shown in Figure 12.10B. (The supply of dollars shifts from S to S' and the demand for dollars shifts from D to D'.)

The initial effect of the fiscal expansion, therefore, is to increase income and bring about a rise in the real exchange rate as a result of capital inflows. Over time, however, the higher exchange rate works to reduce aggregate demand, undermining the effectiveness of fiscal policy.

Intermediate-run effects of a fiscal expansion

The intermediate-run effects of the foreign sector on fiscal policy are also shown in Figure 12.10. The rise in the exchange rate has led to an increase in imports and a decrease in exports and so the *IS* curve has shifted back (*IS'* to *IS"* in Figure 12.10A), generating a level of income and the real rate of interest that are both lower than they were after the short-run reaction to fiscal expansion. (Y_C is lower than Y_B and r_C is lower than r_B.)

In the foreign-exchange market, capital inflows are still occurring, but they have slowed down as interest rates have dropped back. More importantly, over time the deterioration of the trade balance is increasing the supply of dollars and reducing the demand for them. The end result is that the supply and demand schedules have moved back in the intermediate run, bringing the exchange rate partway back toward its initial starting point. (The supply of dollars shifts out from *S'* to *S"*, the demand for dollars shifts down from *D'* to *D"*, and the exchange rate moves to rex_C.)

Comparing Policy Tools in an International Environment

Now that we have added the foreign sector, we have a different perspective on the effectiveness of fiscal and monetary policies. International capital flows place a constraint on policymaking. Policy that generates a rise or fall in real interest rates while stimulating aggregate demand also generates inflows or outflows of capital and a rising or falling exchange rate. In an open economy, policymakers no longer have a captive financial sector.

The conclusion about monetary policy is that it is more effective in an open economy because the change in the real rate of interest brings about a response in capital movements that ultimately reinforces policy.

On the fiscal-policy side, we find an earlier conclusion is strengthened. *Fiscal policy will have little effect on the level of aggregate demand in the intermediate or long run.* This was a result that had already emerged from our discussion in Chapter 9 of the absence of trade-off in the long run. We found there that a fiscal expansion would raise the rate of inflation and this would lower the real money supply, offsetting the effect of the expansion, unless monetary policy was changed too. We have found in this chapter that there is another force that will weaken the impact of a fiscal policy on income. A fiscal expansion will lead to a rise in the exchange rate and a decline in net exports.

The final conclusion is not that fiscal policy should be abandoned as an instrument for affecting aggregate demand. *In the short run, fiscal policy can have a major impact on demand if it is used forcefully, but in the long run, there is little leverage that can be applied through fiscal policies.* Keep in mind also, that we are talking here about aggregate demand policies. Fiscal policy and the deficit will affect national saving and the long-term rate of growth of potential output in the economy.

Another way in which fiscal and monetary policies differ, once we look at the open economy, is in their effects on inflation. We noted earlier that a

THE IMPACT OF A FISCAL EXPANSION DEPENDS ON POLITICAL EXPECTATIONS

When President Mitterand of France took office in 1981, he decided to pursue expansionary policies. At the time, there was substantial uncertainty among French investors and among foreign investors about the future economic policies of the Mitterand government, especially about the possibility of nationalization of private assets. There was an outflow of capital caused by this uncertainty and the outflow was exacerbated by the expansionary policies as investors became concerned about the government's commitment to pay interest on its debts. The expansionary policies, therefore, were accompanied by an outflow of capital, not an inflow. The value of the French franc fell sharply.* Mitterand was forced to retrench on his expansionary program.

When the impact of policy changes depends upon people's expectations, there are few absolutes in policy analysis. The impact of a fiscal expansion raised the dollar in the United States partly because investors had confidence in the Reagan administration and its commitment to business. The same policy had a different effect, at least for a while, when investors distrusted the Mitterand administration.

* The expansionary policy was not a pure fiscal expansion. Monetary policy was also eased and this contributed to the fact that interest rates in France did not rise following a fiscal expansion in the way they did following the U.S. tax cuts.

monetary expansion would reduce the exchange rate and this would have a small impact in raising inflation as import costs rose. The opposite applies to fiscal policy, where a fiscal expansion drives up the exchange rate, and this will lower costs in the U.S. economy. These effects on inflation are over and above the standard effects of policy, where a change in policy changes the level of income and hence changes the output ratio.

Because of the direct effects of the exchange rate on costs, an expansion that is led by fiscal policy may be a little less inflationary than a policy led by monetary policy. And when a contractionary policy is called for, then a monetary contraction will raise the exchange rate and help to lower inflation, while a fiscal contraction will lower the exchange rate and increase inflation.

In the early 1980s, very expansionary fiscal policy, combined with a somewhat restrictive monetary policy, drove up the exchange rate. This helped the reduction of inflation in those years. Subsequently the dollar came back down again and inflation began to accelerate slightly. The favorable effects of the rising dollar in the early 1980s have been lost as a result of the falling dollar in the late 1980s.

These impacts of monetary and fiscal policy on inflation should not be overemphasized. First, the effect of exchange-rate changes on inflation is not very large to begin with. And second, the impact of the exchange rate on inflation will wear off over time. When the exchange rate rises, there are long-run forces that will bring it back down, so that the cost gains will be lost in the long run.

International Interest-Rate Equalization and Long-Run Equilibrium

International movements of capital in and out of economies tend to equalize expected returns on different assets. The condition for expected return equalization was given in Chapter 11 in Equation 11.3 and we reproduce that equation here:

Nominal foreign-interest-rate differential = Expected percent change in the nominal exchange rate

$$i_{\text{foreign}} - i_{\text{domestic}} = \text{Exp } (\Delta ex/ex).$$

Expected return equalization applies most directly to short-term government assets, such as T bills and their foreign equivalents. It says that *the only way in which the interest rates on U.S. and foreign short-term government assets can differ is if the exchange rate is expected to change.* Investors must be expecting a rise in the exchange rate any time the U.S. T-bill rate is above the rate on equivalent foreign assets. They must be expecting a declining exchange rate any time U.S. rates are above foreign rates.

We have been using this relation to describe the effects of monetary and fiscal policies. For example, we said that a monetary expansion would lower the T-bill rate in the United States and that this would lead to a capital outflow and lower the exchange rate. Equilibrium in the asset market would once again be restored (the preceding condition is satisfied again) with a lower value for the U.S. rate of interest (i_{domestic} is lower) and a higher expected rate of change of the exchange rate (Exp$\Delta ex/ex$ is higher).

In the short- and intermediate-run time periods it is perfectly possible for there to be expectations of either a rising or a falling exchange rate. However, in the long run, if economic conditions among countries are stable, then real exchange rates should be stable. With stable expectations about exchange rates, *equalization of expected returns will imply interest-rate equalization.* Since economic conditions among countries are unlikely to ever actually be stable (changes in technology, comparative advantage, and aggregate demand occur all the time) this case of long-run stability is not directly applicable for describing the year-to-year relationships among actual economies. Nevertheless, the notion of long-run stability is an important one for understanding the direction of international economic relationships in the long run.

We analyze international effects in the long run by looking at a world economy in which all markets are in long-run stable equilibrium; there are no transactions costs involved in moving assets overseas; and the risks of default on bonds are small (or are the same in different countries). What does this world of stability and perfect capital mobility look like? *In such a long-run stable world economy, the long-term real rate of interest in the U.S. economy is the same as the long-term real rate overseas.* Interest-rate equalization depends upon three conditions: an internationally stable relationship between short-term and long-term interest rates, stability in international inflation expectations, and stable exchange rates.

1. *International equalization of the maturity premium.* The long-term nominal rate of interest differs from the short-term nominal rate of interest because of risk and because short-term rates may change in the future. If the world economy had settled down into a long-run equilibrium in which interest rates did not change over time and where the risks of default can be ignored, then the gap between the short-term nominal and the long-term nominal rates of interest would be the same in the United States as in the rest of the world:

$$i_{\text{foreign}}(\text{long-term}) - i_{\text{foreign}} = i_{\text{domestic}}(\text{long-term}) - i_{\text{domestic}}. \quad (12.2)$$

If this condition is satisfied, then any tendency for capital movements to equalize short-term interest rates will also lead to equalization of long-term rates.

2. *Expected inflation differentials.* Even in long-run equilibrium, rates of inflation may differ between the United States and the rest of the world. These differences in rates of inflation could mean that nominal interest rates (both short and long) will not equalize. However, the relationship between the interest-rate differential and the expected rate of change in the exchange rate can be expressed in real terms as well as nominal terms:

$$\text{Nominal: } i_{\text{foreign}} - i_{\text{domestic}} = \text{Exp} \ (\Delta ex/ex)$$

$$\text{Real: } r_{\text{foreign}} - r_{\text{domestic}} = \text{Exp} \ (\Delta ex/ex) + \ \Delta P/P - \Delta P_f/P_f \quad (12.3)$$

or

$$r_{\text{foreign}} - r_{\text{domestic}} = \text{Exp}(\Delta rex/rex).$$

In real terms, the condition under which investors are indifferent between holding U.S. and foreign assets is that *the real–interest-rate differential is equal to the expected rate of change in the real exchange rate.*

3. *Long-run exchange-rate stability.* In a long-run stable world equilibrium, we would expect that the real exchange rate would remain constant. Suppose that were not the case, so that one exchange rate is constantly rising. The country's exports are becoming more and more expensive over time. Its imports are becoming steadily cheaper and cheaper relative to domestic production. Eventually, trade flows will force an adjustment and the exchange rate must stop rising. *Long-run stable equilibrium requires stable real exchange rates and this will mean that the real exchange rate is not expected to change* [Exp $(\Delta rex/rex) = 0$].

Under these three conditions, long-term real interest rates will be equalized in the long run across economies. Then combining the results for the maturity premium, the expected rate of inflation, and the stability of the exchange rate (combining Equations 12.2 and 12.3) gives the following conclusion:

$$r_{foreign} - r_{domestic} = 0$$

or   (12.4)

$$r_{foreign} = r_{domestic}.$$

Under conditions of a long-run stable equilibrium, there is full interest-rate equalization. One way of representing this condition is to presume that the worldwide foreign interest rate that is set in international capital markets $(r_{foreign})$ is determined outside of the capital market of any particular economy. In the United States, in the long run, this then fixes the long-run level of the U.S. interest rates as equal to the long-run level of internationally determined interest rates. Figure 12.11 illustrates this idea. The horizontal line at $r_{dom} = r_{for}$ shows this common level of the foreign and U.S. rates of interest, and the economy is shown initially at a point of long-run equilibrium, with the *IS* and *ALM* schedules intersecting at *A,* at the common world interest rate. How does the domestic economy adjust to fiscal- or monetary-policy changes when the interest rate is determined internationally?

A fiscal expansion with interest-rate equalization

Suppose now that there is a change in fiscal policy or, indeed, any change in the economy that increases the level of income associated with goods-market equilibrium. (In Figure 12.11, the *IS* schedule moves to the right to *IS.*) Short- and long-term rates of interest rise and generate capital inflows, just as we described earlier. (The economy moves to point B.) And these capital inflows will drive up the real exchange rate of the dollar. Over time, this rise in the dollar will lead to a negative shift in net exports and a fall in income. (The *IS* schedule shifts back.) However, we can see that in long-run equilibrium, because the domestic U.S. interest rate must come into line with the internationally determined interest rate, the exchange rate will adjust and goods-market equilibrium will keep changing until the economy has gone back to the initial equilibrium. Long-term interest-rate equalization is shown in Figure 12.11 by the dashed lines indicating that the *IS* schedule keeps moving back to the initial equilibrium position (point *B* to point *A*). If there is full long-run equalization of interest rates, then in the long run, fiscal policy will have no effect on income. (Of course the conditions that bring about interest-rate equalization are such that equalization is best regarded as a tendency rather than as a necessary conclusion.)

A monetary expansion with interest-rate equalization

Long-run interest-rate equalization can completely neutralize fiscal policy, but what of the effect on monetary policy? Consider, for example, a monetary expansion in a perfectly stable open economy. The first effect is a reduction in interest rates all along the yield curve. As shown in Figure 12.12, the long-run real rate of interest declines *(ALM* to *ALM').* The fall in rates then leads to increased investment and income (in the figure, the shift from point *A* to point *B*), but it also leads to capital outflows and a fall in the exchange

FIGURE 12.11   The Effect of a Fiscal Expansion in the Very Long Run

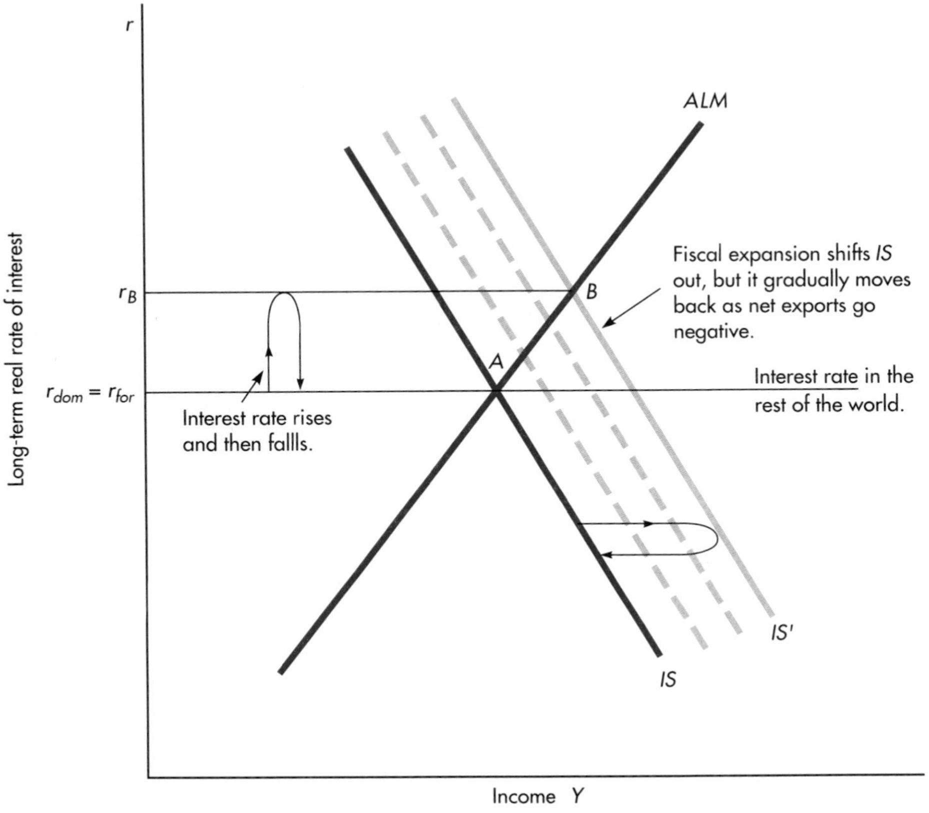

Income and the interest rate go back to their original levels.

rate. The fall in the exchange rate generates a positive shift in net exports that increases income (the *IS* schedule shifts to *IS'*). In the long run this process must go on until the new equilibrium is reached where the U.S. interest rate is once more at the world interest rate but there is a higher level of income. (The economy moves to point *C*.) *In the long run, monetary policy is very effective at raising income, but the increase in income comes about through a rise in net exports rather than an increase in the level of domestic investment.*

These findings about the effect of policy in an open economy in the long run are striking, but they must be taken cautiously. Just as we indicated in the fiscal-policy case, the conditions that have to be in force are long-run conditions of an economy that is not subject to change. In the actual economy, changes are taking place all the time so that we would be unlikely to see

FIGURE 12.12   **The Effect of a Monetary Expansion in the Very Long Run**

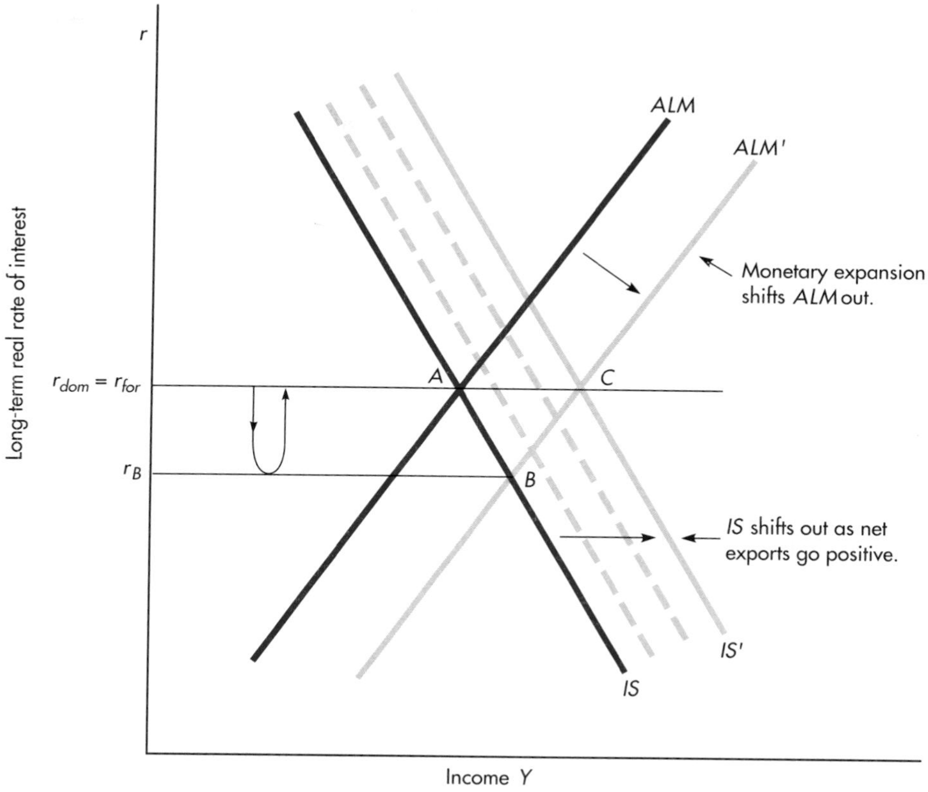

Income is higher but the interest rate has gone back to its original level.

these results hold exactly in practice. Having an understanding of long-run tendencies is helpful, however, even in evaluating short-run policy responses.

Conclusions on interest-rate equalization and policy in the long run

In situations where a policy change is sustained over a long time period and where interest-rate equalization is complete, a sustained fiscal stimulus is likely to generate a trade deficit rather than a sustained rise in income. Conversely, the effects of monetary expansion can be enhanced by a trade surplus. These long-run policy conclusions rest on the strong assumptions that were made in order to show equalization. In actuality, there is never a situation where the world economy has settled down into a long-run stable equilibrium. The amount of risk involved in investments in different countries will never be the same, and there are many other reasons why there will not be perfect capital mobility except for short-term government securities. The gap between the short-term nominal rate of interest and the long-term nominal rate will not be the same in different countries.[4]

INTERNATIONAL ECONOMIC POLICIES

Participation in the international economy offers policymakers another set of policy options: the ability to regulate international transactions. Countries can attempt to affect their economies by controlling the flow of capital and/ or traded goods and services across their borders. The control can be direct as in the cases of tariffs and trade restrictions and it can be indirect as in the case of intervention in foreign-currency markets. All of these policies operate under the principle that the market forces that determine international exchange can be manipulated to domestic advantage. In general, economists question this type of control from the point of view of economic efficiency. Nevertheless, the use of tools to restrict the workings of international markets are employed, to one degree or another, by policymakers in every economy. First we look at policies that use indirect control of trade. Then we go on to look at policies that work through central-bank operations in international financial markets.

Trade Policies

Increases in net exports will increase aggregate demand. This means that trade policies, including restrictions on imports can, in principle, be used to increase income and employment. We look now at this issue. Will policies that raise the trade balance as opposed to autonomous improvements in the trade balance raise real income or only nominal income? Is there any difference between the effect of autonomous increases in exports spawned by improved business practices and national economic policies directed at reducing imports? Does protectionism work? First, we will look at increases in exports that stem from improved competitiveness. Second, we will look at an artificial circumstance, where the trade balance improves because imports are restricted.

Competitiveness and increased exports
If exchange rates are allowed to adjust freely in response to market forces and trade is unrestricted, selling to the rest of the world requires firms in a country to design, produce, and market products or services that can compete

---

[4] *The New York Times* of March 6, 1990, in a story titled "Rate Moves: No Global Link," noted that 10-year nominal interest rates in Japan, West Germany, and the United States had moved in very different directions in the prior weeks. It cited several reasons why capital does not flow around the world to equalize rates and it quoted Paul Samuelson as follows: "Interest rates in one ocean bay are affected by rates in another ocean bay. But they don't mingle perfectly."

effectively in world markets. During the 1980s there was concern that many U.S. firms had lost their ability to compete effectively in international markets. But in the past few years, the manufacturing sector of the U.S. economy has increased its rate of productivity growth and worked more effectively than in the past to increase its competitiveness. Some of this improved competitiveness has come from investment by foreign companies in the United States. These foreign companies have brought technology and new management methods into the U.S. economy. Both the efforts of domestic companies and the investment by foreign companies have helped U.S. exports and reduced U.S. imports for any given exchange rate. Overall competitiveness has improved and this has had a beneficial effect on U.S. income.

The effect of an improvement in competitiveness on aggregate demand was shown in Figure 12.1. We saw there that the initial effect of the increase in exports is to raise aggregate demand and raise income. In the U.S. economy in the last few years, this has indeed been the case, where a falling trade deficit has helped to sustain the growth of aggregate demand. As we noted in the discussion of Figure 12.1, however, the longer-run effect of increases in competitiveness is to increase the value of the dollar relative to where it would be otherwise. The increase in the real exchange rate then gradually eliminates the aggregate demand effects of the increased demand for exports, by restraining exports and encouraging imports.

The gradual elimination of the aggregate demand effect of improved competitiveness does not mean that there are no long-run benefits. The increases in efficiency that have taken place in the manufacturing sector, partly in response to foreign competition and foreign investment, have improved overall productivity and efficiency; this translates into higher living standards for Americans. In addition, an increase in the real exchange rate means that we can buy foreign goods under more favorable terms, and that too is a plus for U.S. living standards.

Increasing competitiveness helps the trade balance and income in the short run and improves living standards in the long run. But some policymakers suggest benefits can also be gained from restricting trade.

Protectionism, tariffs, and decreased imports

The trade balance can be improved by protectionist policies such as restricting imports through the use of tariffs. Placing a tariff on imports raises the prices of imports and import substitutes. Imports decline as the balance of trade improves. The effect on the level of aggregate demand of the imposition of trade restrictions is similar to the effect of an increase in the demand for U.S. exports, although the specifics are different. Initially, the trade restrictions will reduce imports and have no effect on exports. The *IS* schedule shifts to the right initially as a result of the increase in net exports, and income and the interest rate rise. But the trade surplus and the higher interest rate then lead to an increase in the value of the dollar and there is a gradual reduction in exports and an increase in imports. Over time, the *IS* schedule shifts back to the left again. The effect of trade restrictions on aggregate demand is temporary, just as the effect of an increase in export demand was temporary.

In terms of the long-run effects on real income, however, trade restrictions and increased competitiveness are very different in their impact. Increasing competitiveness will expand trade, encouraging exports and then using the foreign exchange resources to buy more foreign goods. By contrast, the trade restrictions have reduced both imports and exports. Typically, trade restrictions are imposed because of the loss of jobs in industries that compete against imports. And the restrictions can succeed in doing this. But the unseen effect of the restrictions is to reduce exports also, which means fewer jobs in exporting industries. The efficiency of the economy in production is reduced as a result of the restrictions.

One cannot say unequivocally, however, that tariffs would reduce real income in the United States. The U.S. economy is very large and foreign companies that sell in the U.S. market face very competitive conditions. A tariff on imported goods might force foreign companies to cut the prices they will receive for their goods in the U.S. market. The price we pay as consumers would go up, but the tariff revenue would help pay our taxes. The United States can use its large size as a way of getting better terms in international trade, just as monopolists can make a profit by restricting output. Of course other countries will suffer as a result and they may then retaliate. Trade restrictions that are unilaterally placed on imports by one country often lead to *retaliation*, whereby the affected country places tariffs on imports from the initiating country. A trade war can ensue, resulting in lower trade for all countries.

Moreover, raising import restrictions eventually leads to import substitution that has a longer-run repercussion effect. When domestic buyers finally move away from the higher-priced imports, the income of other countries falls, causing them to demand fewer exports. As we indicated earlier, this repercussion effect has not been traced as the primary cause of recessions in the United States, but it has been seen as the basis for severe contraction in economies where trade is a much larger share of national income. During the 1930s in the midst of the Great Depression, most European countries attempted to improve their own trade balances and their domestic aggregate demand by passing legislation or enacting policies sharply restricting imports.[5] In Europe a downward spiral of the level of trade contributed to the deepening of the depression.

Since World War II the free-market economies of the world have used an international agreement called GATT (General Agreement on Tariffs and

---

[5] Philip Friedman, "The Welfare Costs of Bilateralism: German–Hungarian Trade, 1933–1938," *Explorations in Economic History* 13, no. 2 (January 1976), pp. 113–25; and "An Econometric Model of National Income, Commercial Policy and the Level of International Trade: The Open Economies of Europe, 1924–1938," *Journal of Economic History* 37, no. 1 (March 1978), pp. 148–80.

Trade) to prevent the wholesale escalation of tariffs and the economy-weakening effects of trade wars.

The large trade deficits of the 1980s have continued into the 1990s and have led to calls for restrictions on trade. But such restrictions would not work in the long run except to the extent that they help reduce the underlying cause of the deficit, namely the federal budget deficit.

The Twin Deficits, and the Decline of the Dollar after 1985

The macroeconomic policy that has had the biggest impact on the international sector of the U.S. economy in recent years has been the large federal budget deficit. We have argued in this chapter that a fiscal expansion has only a limited impact on aggregate demand in the long run because it is largely offset by a trade deficit. There is crowding out of net foreign investment (net exports) as the long-term real rate of interest increases. And there has been an ample demonstration of the validity of this argument in the 1980s.

In Chapter 4 we showed how the budget deficit reduces national saving and we repeat the basic identity here.

$$ \underset{\text{private saving}}{S} \quad + \quad \underset{\text{budget balance}}{G - T} \quad = \quad \underset{\text{investment}}{I} \quad + \quad \underset{\substack{\text{net exports} \\ \text{(net foreign investment)}}}{X - IM} $$

The budget balance turned sharply negative in the 1980s and since there was no offsetting increase in private saving, national saving was also sharply reduced (national saving $= S + G - T$). One possible consequence of this was that domestic investment, I, might have been curtailed, and to some extent this did indeed occur. But the main consequence of the fall in national saving was that net exports shifted into deficit (net foreign investment became negative).

What we did not do in Chapter 4 was to trace the effect of the expansionary fiscal policy on interest rates, capital inflows, the value of the dollar, and finally, the trade deficit. We can now fill in the missing parts of the story based upon the analysis of the effects of policy in this chapter.

An expansionary fiscal policy, such as the one that was instituted from 1981 to 1983, raises income and the interest rate. (The *IS* schedule shifts out to the right.) The increase in the interest rate then leads to a capital inflow, and the capital inflow then changes the supply of and demand for dollars and raises the exchange rate. The real exchange rate rose from about 80 in 1980 to around 120 in 1985 (see Figure 11.1) and this tremendous run-up in the dollar made the United States into a profit gold mine for foreign companies selling here and made it extremely difficult for U.S. companies to export. The government deficit was translated into a foreign deficit by changes in interest rates and capital flows.

The broad outlines of what happened in the first half of the 1980s can therefore be understood in terms of the interaction of trade flows and capital flows in response to shifts in the goods market and the money market (supply and demand in the foreign-exchange market and the *IS-ALM* framework). But the actual experience of the late 1980s also provides some important insights and some unresolved questions about the longer-term trade situation. The dollar fell sharply from 1985 until early 1989 and since then it has risen a little (through mid-1990). Why did the dollar fall and what will the future value of the dollar be?

The decline in the dollar after 1985

The budget deficit pushed up interest rates in the United States and led to an appreciation of the dollar from 1980 to 1985. But after 1985, the dollar came back down again. What explains this? We can better understand the drop in the dollar after 1985 by returning again to the expected return equalization condition: The interest-rate differential between the United States and the rest of the world is equal to the expected rate of change of the exchange rate. This condition helped us to understand that a fiscal expansion increases U.S. interest rates and the size of the differential. The resulting capital inflows then led to an increase in the value of the dollar. The new equilibrium is reached with U.S. interest rates above foreign interest rates, and with a high value for the dollar, *but with the dollar expected to fall in the future.* In other words, the fact that the dollar declined in the late 1980s was something that was built into expectations in the early 1980s when the dollar was rising— although the exact timing and magnitude of the swings in the dollar were not necessarily well-anticipated.[6]

exchange-rate overshooting
A persistent interest rate differential leads to a large swing in the exchange rate.

Exchange-rate overshooting.   The fact that the dollar rose as much as it did in the early 1980s and fell sharply after 1985 has been described as **exchange-rate overshooting.** The exchange-rate swings were much larger than many people expected. The capital inflows and outflows in response to changes in fiscal policy and the resulting changes in the international interest-rate differential were very large indeed. How large are the swings in the exchange rate that we should expect from a fiscal-policy change and how long will they last? We will try to give an answer to this question, but keep in mind that if we or anyone else could really predict exchange-rate movements precisely, we would not be writing textbooks. We would be sitting in the sun in the Bahamas enjoying the profits of our speculations in the foreign-exchange market.

   Suppose the interest rate on foreign short-term securities is, say, 5 percent and a fiscal-policy change (or indeed some other change in the U.S. economy) has pushed up the T-bill rate to 10 percent. Suppose that the U.S. exchange rate was 100 initially and investors judge that this is the long-run equilibrium value for the U.S. dollar. The key question now is how long U.S. interest

---

[6] One economist who predicted the sharp decline in the dollar was Stephen Marris. *Deficits and the Dollar: The World Economy at Risk* (Washington, D.C.: Institute for International Economics, 1985).

rates will remain above world rates. Suppose investors think that U.S. rates will remain at the high level of 10 percent for one year and then fall back to 5 percent. In order that investors be indifferent between holding T bills and foreign bills, the exchange rate must then be expected to fall by 5 percent over the next year. Since the long-run value of the dollar is 100, it follows that the exchange rate will rise to 105 when U.S. interest rates rise to 10 percent. That way the dollar can fall by 5 percent over the coming year and end up back in equilibrium.

Now let's think about the case where U.S. interest rates are expected to rise to 10 percent and stay there for two years. In order for investors to be indifferent between holding T bills and foreign short-term securities, the value of the dollar must be expected to fall by 5 percent a year for two years. And if the long-run equilibrium value of the dollar is still 100, this means that when U.S. rates rise to 10 percent and are expected to remain at this level for two years, then the exchange rate will rise by about 10 percent (to 110.3). That way the dollar can fall 5 percent a year for two years and still end up in equilibrium (back at 100). An interest differential of 5 percentage points for five years will cause an immediate jump in the exchange rate of 28 percent (5 percent compounded for five years).

If investors see policies instituted that they expect to lead to high U.S. rates of interest that persist over several years, then the exchange rate will rise dramatically. In other words, when short-term and long-term interest rates rise together, this will be accompanied by large changes in the exchange rate. In the early 1980s when fiscal expansion was instituted in the United States, it was not done as a short-run measure to stabilize the economy. It was done as part of the Reagan program of tax reduction. Investors reasoned, correctly, that the United States would have a budget deficit and high interest rates for several years. Consequently, there was a large rise in the value of the dollar. By 1985, however, the natural growth of tax revenues plus the measures taken to raise social-security taxes were forecast to gradually reduce the deficit and bring down interest rates. So after 1985 the dollar started to fall also.

Of course, in practice investors do not know how long policies will last or how long interest rates will stay high. Once investors decided that the interest-rate differential was not enough to sustain the very high value of the dollar, and once that view became widespread, the dollar started to fall quickly.

In the period since 1988 the dollar has gone back up again, probably as a result of a reassessment of the interest-rate situation.[7] In the United States, the growth of income and the continued federal budget deficit have meant that the interest-rate differential between U.S. interest rates and foreign interest rates that existed at the start of the 1980s persisted throughout the decade.

---

[7] As this book is being completed in mid-1990, the dollar has dropped again as a result of concerns about the economic consequences of the Iraqi invasion of Kuwait.

TABLE 12.1   Short-Term Nominal Interest Rates in the United States, Germany, and Japan, 1981–1989 (T Bills or their equivalent, annual average percentages)

	U.S.	Germany	Japan
1981	14.03	12.05	7.58
1982	10.61	8.81	6.84
1983	8.61	5.73	6.49
1984	9.52	5.96	6.32
1985	7.48	5.40	6.47
1986	5.98	4.58	4.96
1987	5.78	3.97	3.87
1988	6.67	4.28	3.96
1989	8.11	7.04	4.73

Source: *Federal Reserve Bulletins.*

(See Table 12.1.) *As long as U.S. interest rates are above world rates, the value of the dollar must remain above its long-run equilibrium level.*

We would argue therefore that large swings in the value of the dollar in the 1980s were in fact the predictable consequence of the domestic fiscal and monetary policies of the period. But it is also likely that the fluctuations in the dollar, including the large day-to-day fluctuations in currency values, are being driven, not by the fundamentals of real interest-rate differentials, but by short-term speculation. If the dollar starts rising, some traders buy expecting further increases and quick profits. Foreign-exchange speculation adds another element to understanding exchange-rate movements. Concerns about speculation have led to interventionist policies by central banks and even a call for a system of fixed exchange rates.

Fixed– and Flexible–Exchange-Rate Policies and Currency Speculation

Up to this point we have described the working of the foreign-exchange market as if it were a free market where the exchange rate was determined by the forces of supply and demand, unimpeded by government actions or regulations.

From before World War II until 1971, governments intervened heavily in determining foreign-exchange rates by committing to a system of **fixed exchange rates.** Exchange rates were fixed by arrangements among central banks around the world. The central banks pledged to maintain the value of their currencies against another key currency. From 1948 to 1971 the dollar was the key currency, which required the United States to pledge to maintain the value of the dollar against gold.

Fixed–exchange-rate systems are attractive to policymakers when they fear "excess" fluctuations in exchange rates. Fixed–exchange-rate systems tend to break down when the established fixed rates fail to reflect the underlying economic relationships among economies. Following a period in the late

fixed exchange rates
Prices of foreign currencies set in relationship to each other. This can occur either through all currencies having a fixed value in terms of an international monetary standard such as gold, or via an arrangement among worldwide central banks. Central banks agree that that they will intervene in foreign exchange markets to keep exchange rates from changing.

1960s and early 1970s of rising inflation and an escalating outflow of capital, President Nixon, over the period 1971–1973, uncoupled the U.S. dollar from the fixed–exchange-rate arrangements that were maintained among central banks.

The current **flexible–exchange-rate system** evolved at that time, but even though the new system allowed for fluctuations in exchange rates, it has not been the case that international financial markets were free from government intervention. Foreign central banks, and on occasion the U.S. Fed, still pursued exchange-rate policies. There is **central bank foreign exchange intervention.** Rather than trying to fix rates, they engaged in the buying and selling currencies in an attempt to influence the value of exchange rates.

In the 1990s, based on arguments that currency speculation is generating wild swings in exchange rates, policymakers are considering whether or not, after 20 years of flexible rates, they should return to a fixed-rate system. The case for or against switching to a fixed–exchange-rate system in order to avoid currency swings turns on the question of how currency speculation works, its benefits, and some of the problems it creates.[8]

Foreign-currency speculation

A financial investor who was convinced that the dollar was going to depreciate in the very near future would anticipate making a profit that was solely due to the change in the currency value. Any interest-rate differential would be small relative to the potential gain from guessing correctly the coming depreciation. With access to credit, an investor could speculate in currencies without having any assets herself.

Consider the case of a speculator who believes the dollar will fall against the yen in the next few months. She can borrow money in dollars and then exchange the dollars for yen and buy an interest-bearing asset in Japan, such as a short-term bond. Then she can wait until the dollar falls and bring the money back to the United States at a profit.

Suppose she borrows $1 million at a 10 percent rate of interest in New York, changes this into 200 million yen (at 200 yen to the dollar), and holds a Japanese government security paying a 3 percent rate of interest. If she waits one month and the dollar falls to 180 yen to the dollar, she can sell the yen (receiving approximately 200,500,000 yen, including the one month's interest), move the money back to New York, and receive approximately

flexible exchange rates
Exchange rates that can change values in response to changes in supply and demand for currencies in foreign exchange markets.

central bank foreign exchange intervention
The buying and selling of foreign exchange by central banks in order to affect the exchange rate.

---

[8] The basic case for flexible exchange rates was given by Milton Friedman, "The Case for Flexible Exchange Rates," *Essays in Positive Economics* (Chicago: University of Chicago Press, 1953). This same view was put forward more recently by Martin S. Feldstein, "Let the Market Decide," *The Economist* December 8, 1988. See the box on p. 512.

A long-time critic of speculation and a supporter of fixed exchange rates has been Charles Kindleberger, *Manias, Panics and Crashes* (New York: Basic Books, 1978). Recent empirical assessments of the effect of speculation are Jeffrey Frankel and Richard Meese, "Are Exchange Rates Excessively Variable," *NBER Macro Annual*, 1987; David M. Cutler, James Poterba, and Lawrence Summers, "Speculative Dynamics," Working Paper no. 3242 (Cambridge, Mass.: National Bureau of Economic Research, January 1990).

currency or foreign exchange speculation
Buying and selling foreign exchange and/or foreign exchange futures contracts for the purposes of profiting from changes in exchange rates.

$1,114,000. After paying the interest on the loan (about $8,000), the speculator has made a return of almost $106,000. But of course this return was made on a highly risky and speculative transaction. If the exchange rate had risen to 220 yen to the dollar over the course of the month, she would have been facing a loss of $96,600. Foreign currency is itself a foreign financial asset and investors who buy foreign currencies so that they can convert back to dollars at a profit are engaging in **currency speculation.**

Speculation can be beneficial for the economy. When shifts in supply and demand occur in currency markets, there can be temporary imbalances between supply and demand. Currency traders are willing to bridge the gap between supply and demand in the short run; they gather information, take risks, and do what is called "making the market" in foreign exchange. This means that they help maintain a smoothly functioning market where people can make the currency transactions they need in order to finance trade.

Because importers and exporters want to alleviate some of the risks of doing business in foreign currencies, speculation is a necessary consequence of international trade under a flexible–exchange-rate system.

Exchange risk and hedging.   All firms operate in the face of risk. Demand for their product can fall off, the cost of production can increase, and as a result profits are uncertain. Firms generally are willing to pay for insurance in order to reduce the risks associated with their foreign-exchange transactions. The profit of a U.S. firm that buys materials or components from abroad and/or sells products internationally is subject to *exchange risks*. Its foreign accounts receivable and accounts payable will change in value when the exchange rate shifts. Companies find themselves becoming speculators in foreign currencies even though they do not want to do this.

One of the benefits of having foreign-exchange speculators is that they provide firms with the ability to insure against exchange risk. If an importer has accounts payable (monies it owes for purchases that it expects to pay in near future) denominated in foreign currency, the importer can insure against or *hedge* the exchange risk by entering into a contract with a financial institution. The contract would obligate the financial institution to exchange a fixed amount of foreign currency for a fixed amount of dollars at a point in the future. The financial institution charges a fee for offering the contract.

foreign exchange forward contracts
A contract to buy or sell a quantity of foreign currency at a set future date, but at a price known today. A forward contract occurs between a bank and an individual or firm.

Such a **foreign exchange forward contract** provides insurance because the importer will know with certainty how much it will cost in dollars to obtain the foreign currency needed to pay his bills. The existence of futures contracts helps to facilitate international trade. Those who want to shed the risks associated with exchange rates can find speculators who, for a price, will enter foreign-exchange markets and accept exchange-rate risks.

Destabilizing speculation

A free market with a system of fluctuating exchange rates worries many policymakers because they fear that speculation may not always be beneficial.

They believe that speculation may drive exchange rates away from equilibrium. If speculation causes unnecessarily large swings in exchange rates,
the benefits of flexible exchange rates may be outweighed by risks. Speculation
can be destabilizing if changes in the exchange rate fuel further changes in
the same direction. We look at two possible sources of destabilizing speculation.

Self-fulfilling prophecy.   If a rumor can lead to a fall in the exchange rate and
the fall in the rate is taken as evidence that the rumor is correct, causing
the rate to continue to fall, we have the makings of a self-fulfilling prophecy.[9]
In earlier examples, we showed that investors would sell a currency if its
expected rate of depreciation worsened. The rumor of an impending depreciation changes the expected rate of depreciation, which in turn generates a
capital outflow from the country whose currency may decline. The exchange
rate then actually falls, confirming everyone's suspicion about the rumor so
even more capital leaves, and the situation continues.

Expectations are affected by the confidence that investors have in the
future value of a currency. If confidence in a currency decreases, investors
revise downward their estimates of future values. This creates still less confidence and a further fall. Conversely, a gain of confidence leads to a rise in
the currency and further self-fulling increases in the exchange rate. Speculation
that feeds on itself can create a *"bubble"* (in which the exchange rate for a
currency shoots up in a speculative frenzy) or a *panic* (when sales generate
falling exchange rates that drive sales further down).

Not everyone believes that self-fulfilling prophecies exist or are important.
Their key argument is that such speculation loses money, because it involves
selling currencies when they are too low and buying them when they are
too high. People who lose money by speculating will stop doing it, leaving
the market to those who buy when a currency is too low and sell when it
is too high—this will make the rate more stable. A similar argument is made
by economists that endorse the assumption of rational expectations. They
apply this assumption to the currency market and argue that if exchange-
rate speculation simply feeds on itself, then this implies that speculators
are ignoring information about the fundamentals that determine the exchange
rate. Why would such information be ignored, they say.[10]

The J-curve and the demand for foreign exchange.   Speculation may be destabilizing in the short run, because the quantities demanded of imports and exports
do not change immediately following changes in the exchange rate. The J-
curve described the implication of the lags that exist in trade. A fall in the
exchange rate between the dollar and the yen lowers the price of U.S. exports

---

[9] Self-fulfilling behavior in international markets is discussed by Maurice Obstfeld, "Rational
and Self-Fulfilling Balance of Payments Crises," *American Economic Review* 76 (March 1986).

[10] There is a lively discussion among economists as to whether speculative bubbles can be
consistent with rational expectations. See Maurice Obstfeld, footnote 9.

SETTING THE PRICE OF GOLD, THE BRETTON WOODS SYSTEM, AND FIXED EXCHANGE RATES

Prior to World War II, President Franklin D. Roosevelt fixed the dollar by setting the price of gold at $35 an ounce. The principal reason that the president instituted the fixed–exchange-rate system (actually reinstated the system, since international financial arrangements have alternated between fixed– and flexible–exchange-rate systems throughout the 19th and 20th centuries) was that he believed that exchange-rate movements governed purely by private market forces would be large and possibly unstable. Large swings in the values of currencies can be very disruptive for businesses engaged in trade or competing with overseas competition. Based upon what had happened with flexible exchange rates during the Great Depression of the 1930s, President Roosevelt judged that speculation in foreign currencies had exacerbated currency fluctuations.

As World War II ended, the Allies decided to establish a new international economic system that they hoped would avoid both the excessive rigidity of the old international monetary system, under which gold was the international currency, and the instability that was associated with the flexible–exchange-rate system of the 1930s.

The United States and Britain drew up a proposed plan, and delegations from the 44 main industrial countries met in 1948 in Bretton Woods, New Hampshire, to discuss and then ratify this proposed new currency system.

The Bretton Woods plan designated two key currencies: the U.S. dollar and the British pound. Roosevelt had set $35 equal to an ounce of gold, and this value was to be maintained after the war. The British pound was set by making £12.50 equal to an ounce of gold.

The United States and the United Kingdom were to hold gold reserves and maintain their currencies at the fixed values. Other countries were entitled to exchange their dollars or pounds for gold bars at the fixed rates. Other currencies' exchange rates were set in relation to either the dollar or the pound and fixed values were to be maintained as far as possible. Each country's central bank held reserves of dollars or pounds and would buy or sell their own currencies for dollars or pounds to maintain their fixed rates. If there were *chronic* payments deficits or surpluses, these were to be cured by devaluations or revaluations of the currencies. Thus the system was never meant to be one with completely fixed nominal exchange rates. It was intended that the system would provide the best mix of stability and flexibility.

The system worked reasonably well for 20 to 25 years—why? In the period after World War II, U.S. monetary policy did not use expansions and contractions of the money supply in a forceful way in order to maintain full employment. The Fed was trying to maintain stable nominal interest rates. This is a policy that is consistent with a stable exchange rate.

To the extent that the Fed did vary interest rates, this did not create major problems with the exchange rate because the U.S. economy was so large relative

and raises the price of Japanese cars in the United States. In the short run there is little change in the volume of U.S. exports. Also, the U.S. demand for Toyotas, Nissans, and Hondas is quite inelastic, meaning that people keep buying them even at a higher price. Since the price of yen has gone up, it takes more dollars to buy the amount of yen needed to purchase nearly the same number of Japanese cars. In the face of a higher price for foreign exchange, consumers only slightly reduce the quantity of imports they demand; rather, they demand more foreign exchange.

to the rest of the world. The United States determined the world interest rate rather than the other way around.

By the late 1960s the system was in trouble. The Fed policy of maintaining stable nominal interest rates was causing problems as inflation rose. The real rate of interest was diverging from the nominal rate. As the Fed started to play a more active role in controlling the domestic economy, it found it difficult to maintain its pledge to keep the exchange rate constant.

Under the Bretton Woods plan, countries with chronic trade surpluses were supposed to revalue their currencies. So the dollar could have fallen against other currencies and allowed some flexibility. But a failure of the plan was its lack of specificity about how and when currency realignments were to take place. The countries whose currencies became undervalued did not adjust them upward, preferring to run trade surpluses. This created a tendency for the key currencies to become overvalued. In fact, the United Kingdom ran into difficulty first in maintaining the value of its currency, given its desire for an independent monetary policy. The pound lost its status as a key currency and eventually it was devalued against the dollar.

The dollar remained strong for a longer period and took over as the lone key international currency. However, by the late 1960s, the same problem was afflicting the United States. The currencies of Japan, West Germany, and France had been set very low at the end of World War II to compensate for wartime devastation. But these economies recovered, grew rapidly, and began to export very successfully. They piled up surpluses and were not willing to revalue their currencies; instead they demanded that the United States make good on its pledge to maintain the relation of the dollar to gold and they asked to exchange their dollar surpluses for gold bars. U.S. gold reserves held in Fort Knox were falling and, potentially, would run out. Moreover, U.S. manufacturers were complaining about the effects of low-cost foreign competitors.

Under the Bretton Woods system, citizens of the United States, Britain, and other countries were forbidden from holding gold coins or gold bars. Only gold in jewelry or for industrial use was allowed. But some countries permitted gold holdings. As people saw the U.S. gold reserves falling, they began to speculate that gold would rise in price quite sharply. So the worldwide demand for gold increased, as speculators added to the demand by foreign bankers.

In 1971 President Richard Nixon abandoned the commitment to a gold price of $35 an ounce, as part of a package of economic measures that included wage and price controls. Over a two-year period, the Bretton Woods system was effectively abandoned and a flexible–exchange-rate system was adopted. Gold was demonetized—it now has no official relation to the dollar and American citizens can hold gold coins or gold bars. The price of gold shot up to a peak of $850 an ounce, 24 times its old official value, before falling back.

When trade, rather than capital flows, have the dominant influence on the exchange rate and the J-curve is in operation, short-run movements in foreign currencies can be destabilizing. When the exchange rate rises, and foreign currencies become less expensive, the short-run response is not to import more. The demand for foreign currency falls, but at the lower price of foreign currency, there is more foreign currency available for sale than currency traders wish to buy and the price of foreign currency falls even more. If the impact of destabilizing expectations as we described them earlier is added to this scenario, the potential for large swings in the exchange rate, away from equilibrium, could be substantial.

The fact that exchange rates fluctuate so widely creates problems for businesses that have to operate in foreign markets. This has led to two responses. The first is a private-sector response—private businesses buy insurance and mitigate their exchange risk through hedging. The second is that the government intervenes in order to smooth out the fluctuations.

While hedging goes some way toward solving the problems created by exchange-rate fluctuations, private insurers do not have the capacity to provide insurance for large long-term currency swings. This is a task that only governments have tried to take on. When governments have committed themselves to international arrangements for determining currency prices, they have done so in an attempt to eliminate the problems created by fluctuating exchange rates.

A fixed—exchange-rate system

The great advantage of fixed exchange rates is that they encourage trade. The United States has achieved its very high standard of living in part because of the large size and diversity of its economy. Companies in California must compete with companies in New York and bright engineers or managers can learn from working in Boston and take this experience to North Carolina. The fact that the United States has one currency has played a role in this success. There is not a separate dollar for California with a separate fluctuating exchange rate for the dollars of every other state.

One way to get the benefits of reduced uncertainty in the international market is to adopt a government policy of fixed exchange rates. Under this system, the Fed holds reserves of foreign currencies and it buys and sells dollars and foreign currencies in order to maintain equilibrium with supply equal to demand at a fixed exchange rate.[11]

The problem with fixed exchange rates is that maintaining the system is pretty much impossible unless countries are willing to give up their independent control over monetary policy. To see why this is the case, we look at the impact of monetary and fiscal policy in a fixed-rate system.

Monetary policy with a fixed exchange rate.   If exchange rates are really fixed, the expected rate of change of the exchange rate is zero. This means that investors holding U.S. T bills must get the same interest return as they could get from a German short-term asset, because there is no exchange-rate risk. *With fixed exchange rates, there will also be interest-rate equalization.* A world economy in which exchange rates are fixed looks something like the case of a long-run stable equilibrium. But there is a surprise ending. Monetary

---

[11] Policy can go even further toward fixing rates by using gold-backed currencies. See Robert Flood and Peter Garber, "Gold Monetarization and Gold Discipline," *Journal of Political Economy* 92 (February 1984).

FIGURE 12.13   Monetary Policy When the Fed Tries to Fix the Exchange Rate

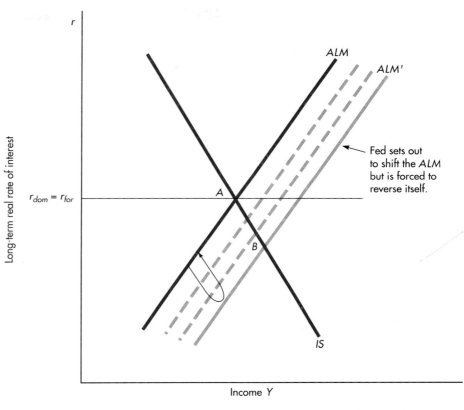

The Fed cannot bring about sustained changes in interest rates and also fix the exchange rate.

policy cannot do anything whereas fiscal policy can! Figure 12.13 illustrates this. The economy is initially shown at point *A,* where the *IS* and *ALM* intersect at the world interest rate. Suppose now that the Fed decides to conduct an expansionary monetary policy and it increases the money supply (moves the *ALM* schedule to *ALM'*). The economy starts to move toward a new equilibrium (intersection of *IS* and *ALM'* at point *B*). But the falling U.S. interest rate generates a capital outflow and this puts downward pressure on the dollar.

The Fed is committed to maintaining the value of the dollar, so it must supply foreign currencies from its own reserves and accept dollars. Foreign-currency trading is carried out through the banking system, so the Fed is selling foreign currencies from its own reserves and is accepting dollars from banks. Banks buy foreign currency from the Fed and pay by reducing their reserve accounts held by the Fed. This reduces the number of dollars available as reserves of U.S. banks. The Fed is automatically reducing the monetary base as it maintains the value of the dollar.

The money supply therefore starts to decline and domestic interest rates rise back up toward equalization with the internationally determined foreign interest rate. (The *ALM* schedule starts to go back from *ALM'* to its initial position. The economy moves from point *B* back toward point *A*.) In fact the process must continue until the old equilibrium is restored, since the economy must return to the world interest rate and goods-market equilibrium has not changed. (The *IS* schedule has not shifted.) *The Fed has found that it cannot maintain a fixed value for the currency and also make independent decisions about domestic monetary policy.*

Fiscal policy with a fixed exchange rate.   Somewhat surprisingly, the reasons that made it impossible to follow an independent monetary policy with fixed exchange rates also make fiscal policy rather effective. Figure 12.14 illustrates how this works. The economy is shown at an initial equilibrium at point *A*, just as before. Now there is an expansionary fiscal policy. (The *IS* schedule shifts out to *IS'*.) The interest rate starts to rise as the economy wants to move to point *B*.

The rising interest rate leads to capital inflows and there is upward pressure on the dollar. The Fed finds that in order to maintain the exchange rate, it must supply dollars to the foreign-exchange market and take in foreign currencies as part of its foreign-currency reserves. As the Fed supplies dollars to the currency market, this automatically increases the U.S. monetary base. With the Fed committed to a fixed exchange rate, a fiscal expansion automatically triggers a monetary expansion (shown in Figure 12.15 as a shift from *ALM* to *ALM'*).

The use of a fiscal-policy expansion in a fixed–exchange-rate system has trapped the Fed. Since the Fed is committed to keeping the exchange fixed, Fed policy cannot help but accommodate the fiscal expansion. Since the U.S. interest rate must be the same as the world interest rate, this monetary expansion must continue until interest rates are equalized as they are in the new equilibrium (point *B* to point *C*). The combination of fiscal expansion and monetary accommodation has also generated a higher level of income.

The inflationary implications of this sort of policy trap for the Fed are serious. In order to maintain a fixed–exchange-rate system, the key-currency country must have a disciplined fiscal policy. If fiscal policy is allowed to be too expansionary (as it was in the U.S. economy in the late 1960s and early 1970s), that expansion will generate an increase in inflation. The Fed will be forced to choose between maintaining a fixed–exchange-rate system (i.e., accommodate the fiscal expansion with a monetary expansion) and fighting inflation. Faced with that choice, any government may well have to abandon its commitment to fixed exchange rates.

FIGURE 12.14   A Fiscal Expansion While the Fed Is Targeting Fixed Exchange Rate

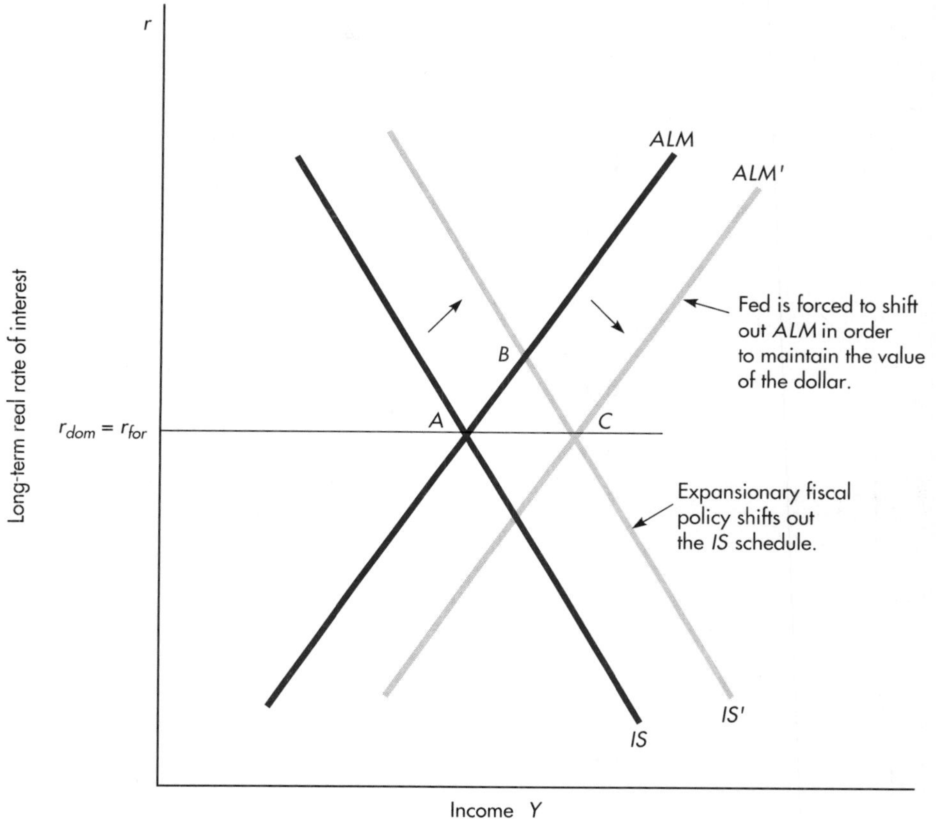

The Fed is forced to respond to the fiscal expansion by increasing the money supply in order to prevent a rise in the dollar.

Policy intervention with flexible exchange rates

For the most part, the current international currency system is one of flexible exchange rates. However, many countries intervene in currency markets. Some developing countries and socialist economies also fix exchange rates and exercise considerable direct control over foreign trade and capital movements. These countries maintain balance-of-payments "equilibrium" with a fixed exchange rate by restricting imports if necessary. Often **black markets** in currency develop to circumvent the restrictions. Sometimes there are special stores where only foreign currency is used, as in the Soviet Union. As these socialist countries move toward greater liberalization of their economies, they

black market
An illegal market that develops in most economies in which the government has placed restrictions on the prices of products, services, and/or assets.

■ Feldstein on the Dollar: Let the Market Decide

Mr. Martin Feldstein, an economic adviser to President George Bush and formerly Chairman of the Council of Economics Advisers under President Reagan, argues that any intervention to alter the value of the dollar will be counter-productive.

The real issue for economic policy is not whether bad policies should be avoided and good policies adopted. The real issue is whether the exchange value of the dollar should be a separate goal of economic policy and, to the extent necessary, the other policy goals should be sacrificed in order to target the dollar's value. My answer is clear. The international value of the dollar should not be a separate target of economic policy. The nation's economic policies should be guided by other considerations, and the dollar's value should be left to the market.

An important reason for this conclusion is the potentially large sacrifice in terms of other economic goals that must be made in order to target the dollar. The cost of managing the dollar would be low if the government could do so simply by buying and selling foreign currencies for dollar securities—i.e., by "sterilised" currency intervention in which America's money supply is left unchanged. But sterilised exchange-market intervention alone is ineffective. Experience continues to confirm that such intervention alters exchange rates for no longer than a few days. Moreover, to the extent that such intervention has any effect at all, it may be only because market participants interpret it as a warning signal that governments may soon shift monetary policy to manage the currency's value.

Although the decline of the dollar after the September 1985 Plaza meeting is frequently pointed to as evidence that intervention works, the dollar's decline actually began in February 1985. Moreover, the pace of decline in the six months before the Plaza meeting was as fast as in the six months after it. The dollar's fall after September 1985 was also spurred by a tightening of monetary policy in Japan

are planning to develop foreign-exchange markets for their currencies and reduce currency restrictions.

Major countries such as Japan, Germany, Britain, and France do not set fixed rates, but they, along with the United States, intervene to influence the values of their currencies. Central bankers have decided that short-term capital movements have driven their currencies away from their underlying equilibrium values, so they intervene to change their values. For example, the German central bank has reserves of dollars and other foreign currencies. Perhaps the mark is falling, but the bank believes it is already too low and wishes to keep the rate from falling further. It will use its reserves to supply dollars and other currencies and to buy marks in exchange.

In order to maintain an independent monetary policy while intervening in the foreign-exchange market, central banks have used a strategy called **sterilized intervention.** When the German central bank buys marks, the German monetary base is decreased, but this is accompanied by an open-market purchase that increases the money base and offsets the domestic monetary consequence of the exchange-rate intervention.

Many economists doubt the ability of such sterilized intervention to support a falling currency even temporarily (see the box, "Feldstein on the Dollar"). The volume of private-sector currency transactions is now very large

sterilized intervention
A central bank buys and sells foreign currencies in order to influence its exchange rate. At the same time it neutralizes the domestic money supply effects of its actions.

and by a decline in the oil price that independently raised the yen and the D-mark relative to the dollar because Japan and West Germany are more dependent on oil imports than the United States. There is no evidence in the Plaza experience to support the efficacy of sterilised intervention. This is true both of the intervention by the United States and of co-ordinated intervention by several countries at once.

The events after the February 1987 Louvre agreement to stabilise the dollar provide further evidence of the ineffectiveness of intervention. Within two months the dollar had fallen 5 percent and the G-7 ministers had to establish new "target ranges" for the dollar. The relative stability of the dollar during the following six months came not from intervention and jawboning, but because America tightened money and raised rates by 2 full percentage points while other central banks kept their interest rates down.

The time has come to abandon the policy of trying to target the dollar. Policymakers should recognise what the market knows: sterilised intervention is ineffective, the use of monetary policy to achieve temporary shifts in the value of the dollar involves a dangerous abandonment of domestic priorities, and the long-run pursuit of sound monetary and fiscal policies is the best way to avoid substantial swings in the dollar's value. Instead of promising more intervention or shifts in monetary policies, it would be far better to echo the reassuring response of Mr. Nicholas Brady, the treasury secretary, to the recent dollar fall: "Markets should go up and down". Monetary and fiscal policies should focus on the performance of the domestic economy, and the value of the dollar should be left to the market.

Adapted from Martin Feldstein, "Feldstein on the Dollar," *The Economist*, December 3, 1988, pp. 21–24.

and makes foreign-currency reserves look small. Monetarists argue that such exchange-rate intervention has an effect only if it also changes the domestic money supply.[12] Exchange-rate intervention will only raise the real exchange rate, they argue, when it is allowed to bring about a domestic–monetary-policy contraction, not when it is a simple exchange of currencies with no change in the equilibrium conditions in the economy.

The monetarists may or may not be correct about this, but it does seem that countries can prevent their currencies from rising by letting their foreign-currency reserves keep piling up. In 1986, Taiwan ran a huge trade surplus, dollars flowed into Taiwan, and, in the absence of any special policy actions, the Taiwan real exchange rate would have risen, making U.S. exports more attractive in Taiwan and Taiwanese exports less attractive in the United States. But the Taiwan government is so committed to generating trade surpluses with the United States that instead of allowing its currency to rise, the Taiwan central bank accumulated huge reserves of dollars. In essence the Taiwan government acted to prevent its residents from reaping the rewards of its export surplus in the form of less expensive U.S. products.

---

[12] Milton Friedman, "The Case for Flexible Exchange Rates."

American policymakers have argued that this strategy of maintaining an undervalued exchange rate is a form of restrictive trade policy. The U.S. Congress has considered proposals to use trade restrictions to penalize countries that follow this strategy.

Conclusions on Exchange-Rate Policies

Flexible exchange rates create uncertainties and difficulties for trading countries, but the post–World War II fixed–exchange-rate system broke down because the key-currency economy (the United States) lost control of domestic inflation and other countries subsequently lost control of their monetary policies. Our current system of flexible exchange rates has probably helped the free economies of the world weather the economic storms of the 1970s. But exchange-rate gyrations have caused problems. We have to make a choice.

The only way to obtain the advantages of fixed exchange rates worldwide is to adopt a system with one currency controlled by one world central bank. Such a system would encourage the growth of trade and eliminate certain kinds of uncertainty. But the single central bank would not be able to use different monetary policies to meet the conflicting needs of all the different countries, some of which might have full employment and some of which might have recession.

In this chapter, we have looked at the effectiveness of monetary and fiscal policies with fixed and with flexible exchange rates and we found rather striking results. With flexible exchange rates, monetary policy becomes more effective and fiscal policy less effective. With fixed exchange rates, the story is reversed. These results may help us understand how the policy environment has changed since World War II. In the 1950s and 1960s, the emphasis was on using fiscal policy, and the automatic stabilizers were seen as an important tool that contributes to economic stability. Starting in the 1970s, monetary policy took over the task of maintaining economic stability. In the light of our discussion in this chapter, this shift in policy strategy does not look like an accident. Once we shifted to a flexible–exchange-rate system, monetary policy was free to act independently and fiscal policy became less effective. In fact, fiscal expansion mostly led to a trade deficit.

In the next two chapters, we will look further at the sources of economic instability and the role of stabilization policy.

SUMMARY

- When net exports are positive, this is a net addition to aggregate demand. When they are negative, this is a subtraction from demand. Net exports fall when income increases with a given exchange rate, so that the multiplier is smaller in an open than in a closed economy. The *IS* schedule will be steeper.

- With flexible exchange rates, the Fed can still control the supply of money in an open economy. If the Fed tries to set the exchange rate it will reduce or eliminate its ability to control the money supply.

- In international financial markets, both domestic and foreign financial investors can shift their portfolios into or out of domestic securities (e.g., U.S. T bills). This means that U.S. interest rates will rise when foreign rates rise. There is an international transmission of interest movements that results from the movements of financial capital across national borders.

- A change in U.S. monetary policy will change the U.S. interest rate and thus the differential between U.S. and foreign interest rates. This will change the exchange rate of the U.S. dollar.

- When foreign interest rates change, this will change U.S. rates and the value of the dollar. This will have an impact on U.S. income and trade.

- Because a sustained increase in export demand sets off a self-correcting rise in the exchange rate, the long-run effect of the increase in export demand will be the tendency to restore the original level of income and restore the original level of net exports.

- In an open economy with flexible exchange rates, *domestic monetary policy is a stronger instrument* for controlling income than in a closed economy. Monetary policy will lower interest rates, lead to a net capital outflow, lower the exchange rate, and increase net exports.

- In an open economy with flexible exchange rates, *fiscal policy has a smaller impact on income* than in a closed economy. A domestic fiscal expansion will raise interest rates, lead to a net capital inflow, raise the exchange rate, and decrease net exports.

- A rise or fall in the exchange rate also decreases or increases the rate of inflation.

- In the long run there is a tendency for complete interest rate equalization. For this to occur in practice would require three conditions: (1) an internationally stable relationship between short-term and long-term interest rates, (2) stability in international inflation expectations, and (3) stable real exchange rates.

- Concerns over the competitive position of the United States have been stimulated by the huge increases in the trade deficit in the 1980s. Improved competitiveness through greater efficiency raises exports and the value of the dollar. Restrictions on trade will reduce the volume of trade and will hurt living standards here, or help them only at the expense of other countries.

- The main cause of the trade deficit is the federal budget deficit. The sustained expansionary fiscal policy experienced during the 1980s generated a government budget deficit. During that period the biggest impact of the large federal deficits was on the foreign sector. (See also Chapter 4 on this issue.)

- An expansionary fiscal policy raises income and interest rates. The increase in the interest rate leads to a capital inflow and the capital inflow then raises the exchange rate. The government deficit is translated into a foreign deficit as the higher exchange rate eventually worsens the trade balance.

- After 1985 the dollar fell as the budget deficit was reduced. The large increase and decrease in the value of the dollar is called *exchange-rate overshooting* and it occurs when there are persistent real interest rate differentials.

■ International trade and financial markets have operated under fixed– or flexible–exchange-rate systems.

■ Flexible exchange rates create uncertainties and difficulties for trade, especially if speculation becomes destabilizing. Some of the problems associated with flexible rates are ameliorated through hedging and speculators can help make the foreign exchange market work well.

■ When fixed–exchange-rate systems were in operation, they reduced uncertainties for awhile; however, they tended to break down whenever the key currency economy lost control of the value of the key currency.

■ With fixed exchange rates, there is interest-rate equalization.

■ Interest-rate equalization that comes from fixed exchange rates *reverses the conclusions about policy that were found under flexible exchange rates:* Monetary policy becomes ineffective whereas fiscal policy becomes effective.

■ In a fixed–exchange-rate system monetary policy is hostage to fixing the exchange rate. A fiscal policy expansion automatically generates an accommodating monetary policy.

■ For the most part, the current international currency system is one of flexible exchange rates, with many countries pursuing exchange-rate policies by intervening in currency markets. Such intervention is thought by many economists to be ineffective.

KEY TERMS

black market

central bank foreign exchange intervention

currency or foreign exchange speculation

exchange-rate overshooting

fixed exchange rates

flexible exchange rates

foreign exchange forward contracts

sterilized intervention

DISCUSSION QUESTIONS AND PROBLEMS

1. Distinguish between domestic macroeconomic policies and international economic policies.

2. If monetary policy works through changing interest rates, how can monetary policy have any effect on an economy where interest rates are determined in worldwide financial markets?

3. Is long-run interest-rate equalization necessary to conclude that fiscal policy is ineffective when exchange rates are flexible?

4. What sort of policy options does the Fed have when it wants to control exchange rates and the domestic money supply?

5. Do you agree or disagree with the following statement? "The source of the U.S. trade deficit in the 1980s is closer to Washington and Detroit than it is to Tokyo." Explain your position.

6. List and compare arguments in favor of a system of fixed or flexible exchange rates.

7. Suppose that domestic investment exceeds private saving by $10 billion and that government expenditure exceeds gross tax revenues by $20 billion. First, write down the relationship between private saving, domestic investment, government's budget balance, and net foreign investment. Then find the numerical value for net foreign investment.

PART VII

Economic Fluctuations and Stabilization Policies

The level of income changes repeatedly. Real GNP could be up by 5 percent, followed by a rise of 1 percent, followed by a gain of 3 percent, and then a fall of 2 percent. Even though there are forces which tend to drive the economy toward equilibrium, that equilibrium itself changes quite frequently. Seemingly small changes in national income (plus or minus 2–3 percent) are keenly felt. The differences among growing, stagnating, or falling economies are amplified in financial markets, employment, business prospects, tax revenues, and public works, and millions of private decisions in the economy. Whether the next quarter is going to be up or down can make or break new business ventures, turn profits to losses, and generate debt repayment or bankruptcy. The economic world is hazardous, subject to wide variation.

Financial asset values are particularly prone to change. Stock markets have a long history of boom and bust. Are the market crashes and recoveries reflecting an underlying economic process or are they simply reacting to the perturbations of speculative fever? There does appear to be a long-term relationship between stock prices and economic performance, but stock markets may overreact to events.

Though we have described a model of how income is determined, we have not focused on what are the causes of fluctuations in income. Do the aggregate demand, supply, financial, policy, inflation, expectations, and international variables simply suffer random change or is there a pattern to the variations and the level of income?

The idea that we explore in the next two chapters is that economic fluctuations follow an irregular pattern of variation called a business cycle. The growth of aggregate demand outraces the growth of aggregate supply. Inflation accelerates and both nominal and real interest rates rise sharply. The reduction in aggregate demand brought on by the rise in rates causes the path of aggregate demand to reverse itself—the economy goes from boom to bust and then recovers toward boom again. The economy is in perpetual motion around a changing target of long-run equilibrium at a growing level of potential output.

CHAPTER 13

Economic Fluctuations
Consumption and Investment Demand

INTRODUCTION

The next two chapters are concerned with the existence and causes of the business cycle—the continuing fluctuations of output around potential output. Output rises and falls, sometimes exceeding potential output and sometimes falling below it. When output is above potential, inflation accelerates and when it is below potential, the economy suffers the costs of excess unemployment and lost output. We have analyzed the way in which a particular equilibrium level of income is determined and the roles played by monetary policy, fiscal policy, and the international economy in changing this equilibrium level of income. But so far, we have not said much about what forces in the economy may either contribute to fluctuations or move the economy toward stability.

An important part of the explanation for the overall pattern of economic fluctuation relates to the expenditure behavior of households and firms. We discover that consumption and investment expenditure, as they were defined in the National Income and Product Accounts, each have components that behave very differently from each other in terms of their variability. Some portion of these expenditures contribute to demand fluctuations which generate instability, while other parts help sustain demand and reduce instability. For example, during recessions, consumers may try to maintain their spending on basic items but they may defer spending on durable goods, like cars and appliances. Under some circumstances, firms may cut back on inventories and postpone new equipment purchases in order to contain cost, but they continue to spend on R&D or other long-run investment plans despite a short-term downturn. Moreover, these patterns of expenditures are subject to further change when the economy experiences shifts in expectations.

We conclude this chapter by tracing out a particular historical episode, the 1958–1962 period, when fluctuations in investment demand and consumer-durable purchases were important contributors to the extended recession of that period. This historical case study helps to illustrate the ideas developed in this chapter. In the next chapter we look at the impact of the international sector and financial markets on the cycle, areas that have been more important in the last few years.

We start our analysis of fluctuations by taking a look at the history of the business cycle in the U.S. economy.

RECESSION AND RECOVERY

The economy is subject to wide swings in the level of GNP, movements that make up the business cycle. Cycles in economic activity are described by a peak, the highest point reached before real GNP begins to turn down; a recession, two or more consecutive quarters of falling real GNP; a trough, the lowest point reached before GNP starts to turn up; and a recovery, where GNP is growing. Over the period between the two World Wars, from 1919 to 1941, there were five cycles of recession and recovery. The Great Depression of the 1930s covered two of these cycles, with the economy declining from 1929 until 1933, recovering (partially) until 1937, and then going into a second decline until 1938.[1]

In the period after World War II, from 1947 until 1982, there were eight peaks and troughs starting with the peak in the fourth quarter of 1948 and ending with the trough that took place in the fourth quarter of 1982. Table 13.1 and Figure 13.1 show the timing of the peaks and troughs of GNP over the period 1919–1982.[2]

The seven recoveries beginning with the 1949–1954 recovery and ending with the 1980–81 recovery have averaged just over 16 quarters in duration. The eight periods of recession from peak to trough have averaged only 2.6 quarters. The increases in real GNP in the recovery phases averaged 21 percent while the recessions showed an average drop of 2.5 percent. Since 1982, the economy has been in a recovery phase, although the rate of growth of real GNP became very slow as of mid-1990; when another recession was imminent.

The recessions prior to World War II were much more severe than the ones since then. *During the five recessions over the period 1919–1938, declines lasted for an average of 6 quarters and GNP fell an average of 14 percent. The*

---

[1] This chapter draws on various material in a paper by Victor Zarnowitz, "Facts and Factors in the Recent Evolution of Business Cycles in the United States," Working Paper no. 2865, (Cambridge, Mass.: NBER, February 1989).

[2] The dating of the peaks and troughs of the business cycle is a subjective evaluation of economic conditions. The U.S. government generally recognizes the dating that is undertaken by the Business Cycle Dating Committee of the National Bureau of Economic Research (NBER), an independent, not-for-profit research institution.

TABLE 13.1   Business-Cycle Peaks and Troughs, 1919–1982

1919–1941:	Peaks, 1920: 1st Qtr., 1923: 2nd Qtr., 1926: 3rd Qtr., 1929: 3rd Qtr., 1937: 2nd Qtr. (five).
	Troughs, 1921:3rd Qtr., 1924: 3rd Qtr., 1927: 4th Qtr, 1933: 1st Qtr., 1938: 2nd Qtr. (five).
1947–1982:	Peaks, 1948: 4th Qtr., 1953: 2nd Qtr., 1957: 3rd Qtr., 1960: 2nd Qtr., 1969: 4th Qtr., 1973: 4th Qtr., 1980: 1st Qtr., 1981: 3rd Qtr. (eight)
	Troughs, 1949: 4th Qtr., 1954: 2nd Qtr., 1958: 2nd Qtr., 1961: 1st Qtr., 1970: 4th Qtr., 1975: 1st Qtr., 1980: 3rd Qtr., 1982: 4th Qtr. (eight)

Source: National Bureau of Economic Research.

greater severity of the cycle prior to World War II is an important fact that we look at in Chapter 14.

In the past, economists studying the business cycle have often assumed that the fluctuations of actual output around potential output describe a repetitive and regular pattern of booms and recessions. But a look at Table 13.1 and Figure 13.1 reveal no clear evidence of a very regular cycle of some set period. Some cycles are very short and others last several years. Also, some have had wide swings away from potential and others have been more mild.

Regardless of the regular or irregular occurrence of fluctuations, they are costly. During recessions people lose their jobs and businesses go broke. Fluctuations in income cause uncertainty which creates anxiety for individuals and risks for businesses planning long-term investments.

Where are these fluctuations coming from? Do businesses increase or decrease investment expenditures in a particular pattern? Do consumers change spending patterns and, if so, why? In order to understand the sources of these economic fluctuations we start by looking at the components of aggregate demand and how and why they change.

CONSUMPTION EXPENDITURES AND ECONOMIC FLUCTUATIONS

In assessing the impact of consumption on economic fluctuations it is important to distinguish between the consumption of nondurable goods and consumer services on the one hand, and the purchases of consumer durables on the other. In this section we will show that households maintain great stability in their consumption of nondurables and services, but that there is considerable variability in household expenditures on durables. So if we ask whether consumers contribute to cyclical fluctuations in the economy, the answer is: Yes, but only through their purchases of cars, houses, and other durable goods.

After showing the relative pattern of durable and nondurable spending,

FIGURE 13.1 Real GNP and Recessions 1919–1941 and 1967–1989

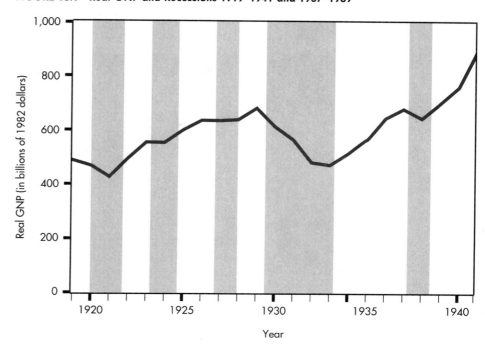

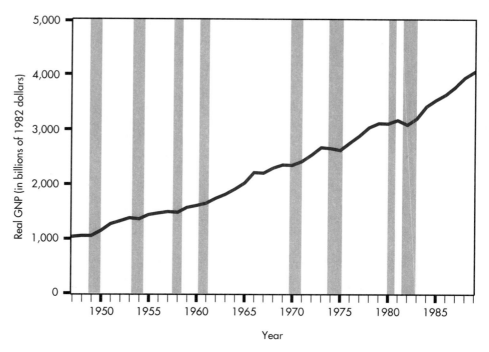

Recessions have been shorter and recoveries longer in the postwar period.

we will concentrate first on the stability of the nondurable part of consumption and discuss alternative theories of consumption and why it is so stable over time. After that we will look at the purchases of consumer durables in combination with investment expenditures and give a general discussion of the demand for durable goods and the accelerator model of investment.

Figure 13.2A shows how the different components of total consumption varied over the course of one recession and recovery that started in the fourth quarter of 1973. Total GNP and total consumption expenditures are also shown, while a pie chart (Figure 13.2B) gives the shares of the components in total consumption at the beginning of the period. In Figure 13.2A all the components of consumption and total GNP are indexed to equal 100 at the start. This allows us to see the extent to which they fluctuate differently from each other over the course of the business cycle.

The figure illustrates that the consumption of nondurable goods and the consumption of services declined very little during this deep recession. This pattern is typical. Purchases of nondurable goods and services (such as food, housing, transportation, medical care, and entertainment) grow rather steadily over time without varying greatly from year to year.

By contrast, consumer expenditures on durable goods have fluctuated substantially. Consumer-durable purchases at the end of 1974 were 11 percent below their initial value. The 1974–75 recession was a particularly severe one for consumer durables because of the energy crisis and the subsequent decline in auto purchases, but it was the case then, as in most recessions, that the purchases of consumer-durable goods (such as autos, TVs, and other electronic and household appliances) varied much more than nondurables. This pattern gives rise to periods of boom and slump in the industries that produce durable goods.

In spite of the large fluctuations in durables, total consumption (shown in Figure 13.2A) remained stable because durable goods were a relatively small portion of total consumption expenditures (13 percent at the start of the cycle, as shown in Figure 13.2B).

Since there are great differences in the variability of components of consumption expenditures, when we analyze fluctuations we need to move away from the expenditure categories that were laid out in the National Income and Product Accounts. In those accounts, we divided aggregate demand into consumption, investment, and government expenditure. We are now going to separate purchases of durable goods from the purchases of nondurable goods and services. We include all consumer purchases of durable goods as part of investment. Since residential housing is already included as part of business investment; we are simply adding consumer purchases of autos and appliances to investment as well.

An important reason for initially following the National Income and Product Accounts in separating aggregate demand into consumption, investment, and government expenditure was that we argued that the decisions to purchase goods and services by consumers, businesses, and the government

FIGURE 13.2A   Components of U.S. Consumption, Fourth Quarter 1973–First Quarter 1977

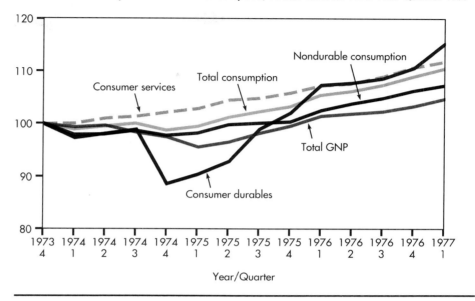

FIGURE 13.2B   Shares of the Components of U.S. Consumption, Fourth Quarter 1973

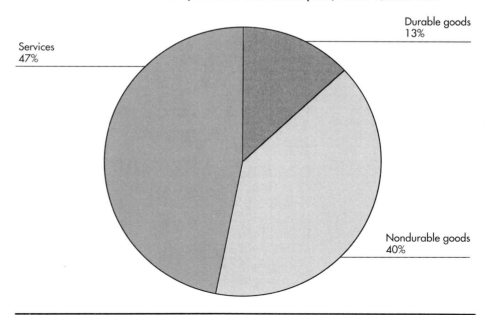

were motivated by different considerations. Expenditure was grouped so that common behavior could be assumed for each of the separate groups.

Changing expenditure categories, by classifying consumer purchases of durable goods as part of investment, still fits with the original reason that we separated consumption and investment decisions. We want to group expenditures that are affected by similar economic forces; this means grouping the components of expenditures so that the decisions to purchase for the items in each group are similarly motivated.

When consumers buy durable goods such as autos and single-family houses, these decisions are similar to business investment decisions. A business decides to purchase machinery or buildings because these assets will yield a flow of productive services to the business over several years. Similarly, households buy consumer durables because they yield a flow of services to the households that own them over a period of several years. Buying a consumer durable, like buying a producer durable, involves an expected commitment over several years and, at a given level of income, the purchase decision is affected by the rate of interest.

The Consumption Standard of Living

The material well-being of the average consumer is an important measure of economic performance. In common usage the *standard of living* has a simple meaning: the quantity and quality of goods and services available to the average consumer. Households consume goods and services through current purchases and through the flow of services that comes from using household "capital" purchased in previous years (that is, homes, autos, appliances, and other consumer durables). We will define now the **consumption standard of living** as equal to *current* household purchases of nondurable goods plus the *flow of services* provided by the existing stock of consumer-durable goods and houses. This concept of consumption (based upon nondurables and the flow of services from durables) is a good measure of consumer living standards.

consumption standard of living The value of goods and services consumed by households through current purchases of nondurables and from the flow of services obtained from consumer capital. Consumer capital includes houses and consumer durable goods owned by households.

Stability in the Consumption Standard of Living

Consumer purchases of nondurable goods and services and the flow of services from durables comprise the consumption standard of living. We have already seen (Figure 13.2) that over time, through a U.S. business cycle, consumer purchases of nondurable goods and services are rather stable. What of the other portion of the standard of living—the flow of services from durables? *The flow of services is likely to be stable from year to year even though the purchases of new consumer durables each year are quite variable.* The flow of services changes as the total stock of consumer durables changes. Changes in the stock of durables (more houses, autos, TVs, and appliances as well as newer and/or higher-priced, higher-quality products) change the

■ **Consumption, Investment, and the Flow of Services in the National Income and Product Accounts**

Even though consumer purchases of durable goods are similar to consumer purchases of houses and to business purchases of durable goods, the conventions of the national income accounts treat them very differently. The accounts assign consumer durables to consumption expenditures, while residential housing is considered to be part of investment, together with business investment. The value of the rental income paid on the existing stock of residential housing is included in GNP as part of consumption, including rent paid to landlords and the implicit rent paid by owner-occupiers to themselves. Implicit rent is an evaluation of the amount homeowners would have paid to rent the house they are living in if they did not own it. By contrast, there is no imputation made for the implicit rent that households pay to themselves for the flow of services provided by the autos or other consumer durables that they own.

The conventions of the National Income and Product Accounts are rather arbitrary. In explaining household behavior, economists often reassign purchases of consumer durables and call them part of total investment and count the flow of services provided by the existing stock of dishwashers and autos as part of the flow of consumption. We are following this procedure as we examine the stability of consumption and the variability of investment. However, the flow of services from autos, appliances, and similar consumer durables does not appear as an observable measure that is included in the National Income and Product Accounts; it has to be imputed or estimated.

flow of services. But the total stock of consumer durables available for use by households is large and each year's purchases of consumer durables and houses adds only a small amount to the household's total accumulation of durables. If a household decided to delay or advance the purchase of a major new appliance, auto, or home, the total flow of services from consumer durables and houses would not change by much, even though there would be a large change in the amount of money spent on consumer durables in that year.

Combining the stability in the purchase of nondurables with the stability in the flow of services from durables means that despite the fact that income varies quite a bit and the purchases of new consumer durables and houses vary quite a bit, *there is considerable stability in the consumption standard of living.* The fact that in a recession families maintain their purchases of nondurable goods and services (such as food and rent) and they do not quickly sell off consumer durables contributes to the overall stability of the aggregate economy. The slow response of households to recessions helps to reduce the size of recessions when they come.

Consumption smoothing

When household incomes fall, people do cut their consumption, but by less than the fall in their income. When consumers increase consumption by

consumption smoothing
The decision to raise or lower consumption less than proportionally to swings in the level of income in order to moderate swings in the consumption standard of living.

less than the rise in income and decrease consumption by less than the fall in income, they are smoothing out the pattern of consumption expenditures over time—this is **consumption smoothing.** This behavior dampens fluctuations in aggregate demand and in order to understand the variability of income, we want to know which economic factors affect the smoothing of consumption.

One explanation of consumption smoothing was put forward by James Duesenberry.[3] He argued that people become accustomed to a particular standard of living and so they choose to cut their saving or even dissave when their incomes fall, rather than cut back much on consumption. Further, it is both costly and difficult for people to adjust many consumption expenditures quickly. People who become unemployed do not want to leave their neighbors and disrupt their families by moving to lower cost apartments. And even if they tried, breaking a lease, finding a new place, and moving are all costly, so the family stays put for awhile. Duesenberry described these ideas in institutional and sociological terms, and pointed out how people who suffer an economic reverse will go to great lengths to prevent that reversal from forcing them to change their life-styles and fall behind their neighbors. Since Duesenberry's analysis, other important analyses of household-expenditure decisions used the more conventional and less sociological tools of economics to explain why households act to maintain their standard of living, even in the face of a fall in income.

Are people being irrational, stubborn, or simply motivated by social habit when they attempt to maintain their consumption living standards in the face of a decline? No. It is not just that in a downturn people do not want to reduce their standard of living. In many cases, they do not have to. They can take concerted action to smooth their consumption standard of living over time.

The permanent-income hypothesis

In a book published in 1957 that still stands as a superb example of economic research, Milton Friedman developed and tested the *permanent-income hypothesis.*[4] His analysis emphasized the relation between the decision to consume and the decision to save.

The decision to save today is also a decision to consume more in some future period. *Saving and dissaving involve reallocating consumption from one period to another.* A major reason why people save in the first place is to allow themselves to smooth out their consumption, so it is natural that saving, as a percentage of income, will go down during recessions and go up in

---

[3] James S. Duesenberry, "Income–Consumption Relations and Their Implications," in *Essays in Honor of Alvin H. Hansen* (New York: W. W. Norton, 1948), pp. 54–81.

[4] Milton Friedman, *A Theory of the Consumption Function* (Princeton, N.J.: Princeton University Press, 1957).

booms. The permanent-income hypothesis argues that consumption is fairly stable because consumers prefer smooth consumption patterns and *they can rationally obtain smooth consumption by varying saving and borrowing in the face of increases or reductions of income that are viewed as temporary.* A worker suffering a period of unemployment probably does not think that the resulting fall in income will last forever. A new job may be obtained or the old one might be restored.

permanent income
The average level of income that households expect to receive over a period of years.

The average income that an individual or household expects to receive over a period of years is **permanent income.** For example, an increase in salary because of an increase in overtime pay is unlikely to change permanent income; however, a promotion coupled with advanced training is likely to change permanently the future course of income.

In Milton Friedman's analysis, the amount of consumption people make depends upon their expectation of permanent income. Thus when a household suffers a drop in income in the current year, the family will not reduce its consumption proportionally because its permanent income has fallen only a small amount. In this case, the household has a *transitory reduction in income—* its current-year income is below its permanent income.

permanent and transitory consumption
Permanent consumption is the average level of consumption that households anticipate undertaking over a period of years, given their permanent income. Transitory consumption is undertaken to meet unexpected needs, such as unexpected medical expenses.

The permanent-income hypothesis also leads to the concepts of **permanent consumption and transitory consumption.** A family that suddenly needs to buy braces for its children may well consume more than usual in that year. It may use up saving it has made in the past. In response to the unusual need for dental expenditures, the family is making transitory consumption in excess of its permanent (meaning usual or average) level of consumption.

There is an important difference between transitory consumption for individual households and for the economy as a whole. The things that lead to individual transitory consumption are generally microeconomic. They depend upon what happens to individuals, families, or small groups. *These shocks to the consumption standard of living will tend to average out over the economy as a whole and they are not directly related to changes in income.* Of course there are changes that lead to transitory increases or decreases in aggregate consumption, but it is unusual for aggregate consumption to be affected significantly by changes in the demand for particular goods or services.

By contrast, it is quite common for there to be aggregate changes in transitory income for the economy as a whole. While there is a substantial amount of individual variability of income, there are also important common fluctuations. A recession is a period when income is low in the aggregate, when many people have unusually low income, not just particular individuals or groups. A change in transitory income is more likely to be experienced economywide than a change in transitory consumption.

This analysis of permanent and transitory income and consumption led Milton Friedman to his version of the consumption function, a relation that helps explain why people maintain consumption levels over the business cycle.

The permanent-income consumption function.   Household consumption is partly related to permanent income and is partly the result of transitory circumstances. This is shown in Equation 13.1 where

$$C = C_{perm} + C_{trans}$$

and

$$C_{perm} = cY_{perm} \tag{13.1}$$

so that

$$C = cY_{perm} + C_{trans}.$$

Consumption (C) over a given time period is the sum of permanent and transitory components. A family's permanent or average level of consumption depends upon its perception of, or expectations about, its permanent or long-run average level of income. In fact, Friedman assumed that the relation was a proportional one—permanent consumption is a fixed proportion, c, of permanent income. The transitory part of consumption varies randomly— in some periods it is positive and in some it is negative.

The actual income received by a family in any period may differ from its permanent level of income because of favorable or unfavorable circumstances that occur. As shown in Equation 13.2, actual income in any period can also be separated into its permanent and temporary components:

$$Y = Y_{perm} + Y_{trans}. \tag{13.2}$$

By combining Equations 13.1 and 13.2, we can obtain the average propensity to consume (Equation 13.3), based upon a family's current consumption (C) and its current actual income (Y).

$$\frac{C}{Y} = \frac{cY_{perm} + C_{trans}}{Y_{perm} + Y_{trans}}. \tag{13.3}$$

Except for transitory consumption behavior, average consumption is determined by the share of permanent income in total income. If a household's income was mostly permanent, it could safely consume a large portion of income. However, if a family's income was mostly transitory, and so subject to variation and risk, then the family would want to save a large portion of income. Farmers and proprietors of small businesses often have quite variable incomes and they save a lot in good years and dissave or borrow in bad years.

Milton Friedman found that this theory fit data on aggregate consumption when he used the average of past income over several years as an estimate of people's perceptions of their permanent incomes. In seeing the implications of his theory for aggregate consumption of all families together, we can use two conclusions from the permanent-income hypothesis:

1. For the whole economy in a given year, the transitory element of consumption should average out to be small, roughly equal to zero.
2. Transitory income will not average out to zero for the whole economy in a given year, because recessions are periods when average transitory income is negative.

This means that in the aggregate we can ignore transitory consumption. The average propensity to consume can then be found from Equation 13.3 by setting C_{trans} equal to zero. This gives Equation 13.4:

$$\frac{C}{Y} = \frac{cY_{perm}}{Y_{perm} + Y_{trans}}. \tag{13.4}$$

This relation indicates that during periods of low income (when Y_{trans} is negative), the average propensity to consume will be high [Y_{perm} is greater than $(Y_{perm} + Y_{trans})$] and saving will be low. During periods of high income (when Y_{trans} is positive), the average propensity to consume will be low [Y_{perm} *is less than* $(Y_{perm} + Y_{trans})$] and households will save a lot.

Here is where Friedman's analysis provides an explanation of why people maintain their consumption standard of living when income changes. *Consumption is stable if average income over several years is more stable than year-to-year income.*

The permanent-income hypothesis emphasized that consumption can be smoothed in the face of the short-run fluctuations or uncertainties of income. But these short-run year-to-year variations in income are not the only important changes that occur in household incomes. Consumers face large but rather predictable changes in income associated with the different stages of life, particularly retirement. Taking these expected longer-term changes in permanent income into account has led to an important variation in the model of consumption smoothing. Changes in permanent income that are anticipated will lead to consumption smoothing that can be planned for through a particular pattern of saving behavior over people's life cycles.

The life-cycle hypothesis

Franco Modigliani added a new element to the theory of consumption.[5] He demonstrated that *the amount households save is affected by the specific ways in which their income is expected to change over the future course of their lifetimes.* He formulated the *life-cycle hypothesis*, pointing out that one of the possible reasons for saving is for retirement.

---

[5] Franco Modigliani and Richard Brumberg, "Utility Analysis and the Consumption Function: An Interpretation of Cross-Section Data," in *Post Keynesian Economics*, ed. K. K. Kurihara (New Brunswick: Rutgers Univ. Press, 1954); and Albert Ando and Franco Modigliani, "The Life-Cycle Hypothesis of Saving: Aggregate Implications and Tests," *American Economic Review* LIII (March 1963).

When people retire they lose their primary source of income, their income from work. In order to maintain their consumption during retirement they draw down their savings accumulated during their working lives. The savings they had available in retirement was not generally the result of simple good fortune, but rather people anticipated their own retirement and provided for that time by saving.

In the early years of adulthood, many people are investing in education and many of them are borrowing to maintain their consumption and pay school fees. They are dissaving by piling up student loans or loans from family members. Then after leaving school most people get married and set up households at a time when their incomes are fairly low. They are usually accumulating a pension and making tax payments to the social security fund, but overall, their net saving is low. As time passes, incomes rise and the peak expenditures of household formation pass, so that net saving is larger. Incomes exceed consumption by a wider margin. At retirement, the situation changes. People's incomes drop and they draw on their pensions, collect social security, and draw on other assets to maintain their consumption during retirement. This pattern of saving over the life cycle is illustrated in Figure 13.3.

At age 18 (point *A*), income is low and many people are taking out student loans. At some point there is a crossover point (point *B*), where consumption levels out and income continues to grow, generating positive saving. Families continue to make positive saving as they age and as their incomes rise toward peak income (point *C*).

At retirement (points *D*) there is a downward drop in income as earned income is replaced by a lower level of retirement income. Families dissave again in the retirement years by drawing down their savings balances. (Pension income and social security income can also be considered as dissaving. See the following box.)

In testing his ideas, Modigliani argued that the consumption of a family will depend upon the total wealth it has accumulated, representing the resources being held for consumption during retirement, and on demographic variables, such as age and the number of people currently in the family who need support. In the determination of aggregate consumption, Modigliani has stressed the importance of variations in aggregate wealth. For example, in Modigliani's model, a decline in the stock market leads to a fall in consumption.[6]

There are important similarities between Modigliani's life-cycle hypothesis and Milton Friedman's permanent-income hypothesis. The permanent-income hypothesis argues that consumption decisions are made with reference

---

[6] Empirical studies of the role of the stock market in consumption are in Barry Bosworth, "The Stock Market and the Economy," *Brookings Papers on Economic Activity, 2:1975;* and Frederic S. Mishkin, "What Depresses the Consumer? The Household Balance Sheet and the 1973–75 Recession," *Brookings Papers on Economic Activity, 1:1977.*

FIGURE 13.3   Income and Consumption over the Life Cycle

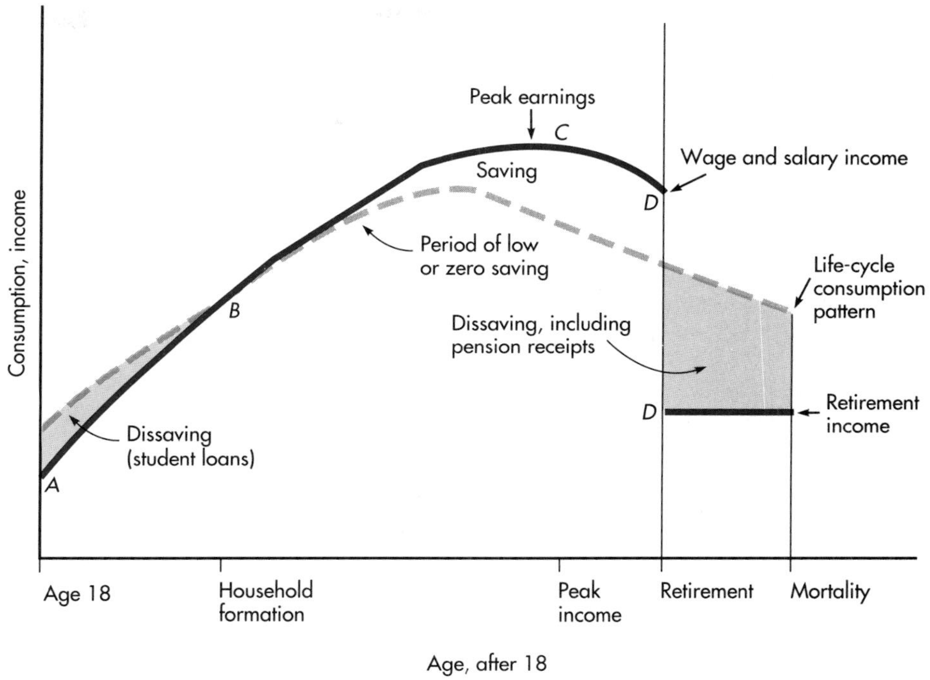

When people are young, earnings are low while consumption exceeds permanent income due to household formation. Earnings and saving peak in late middle age. At retirement, dissaving reappears due to low retirement income.

to permanent income, while the life-cycle hypothesis argues that permanent income, over a lifetime, displays a rising and falling pattern that households anticipate. Both of these models place a strong emphasis on households making decisions on the basis of an expectation of future income and the use of saving and dissaving to smooth consumption over time. Most modern studies of consumption and saving combine elements of both approaches and they indicate that the desire to smooth the consumption standard of living provides an important element of stability in the demand for nondurable consumption.

The constraints on consumption smoothing
The permanent-income hypothesis and the life-cycle hypothesis help explain how consumption smoothing affects consumption patterns in the economy. However, there are limits on most households' ability to smooth consumption. It should come as no surprise that households that suffer a significant reduction

■ Saving for Retirement: Pensions and Social Security

For most people, saving for retirement is done through pension plans and through social security. In private pensions, a certain amount is set aside by employers and invested in stocks or bonds. Either a lump sum or an annuity is then paid out on retirement, and the annuity may be adjusted for changes in the cost of living. Such plans provide protection against risk and allow people to reduce the costs associated with managing their own portfolios. However, there are certain sacrifices in terms of flexibility. Some employers give reduced benefits to employees who leave to change jobs. And if people suddenly need to dip into savings to meet an emergency, they may find it difficult to do this, or may face a penalty for withdrawal of contributions.

In the past, pension plans were not always funded by accumulating stocks and bonds from past contributions. Many plans used a "pay-as-you-go" approach in which benefits for retirees are paid for by the contributions of employees still working. Such an approach was very attractive when pension plans were first being set up, because companies could offer the promise of future pension benefits without actually adding to current labor costs. Some years later these same companies have large hidden liabilities—the amount they owe to their retirees.

Recent changes in federal legislation (the so-called *ERISA provisions*) now require private pensions to set aside amounts for retirees and provide federal insurance if companies or plans go broke.

The social security retirement program has used the same approach as the companies that failed to set aside contributions to retirement funds. The social security payments made to the early participants in the program greatly exceeded the contributions they had made to the plan, with the difference being made up with the social security tax payments made by those still working. At the present time, the program is running a surplus that is offsetting a big chunk of the federal government's budget deficit. But when the baby-boom generation retires, the burden on those who will still be working is likely to be very large.

One problem with pay-as-you-go plans, both private and public, is that they create a genuine asset for individuals. They are part of individual wealth. But they are not actually setting aside much saving themselves. The wealth created for any particular individual is largely a liability for taxpayers, not a net addition to national wealth. Such plans can reduce total national saving.*

---

* This issue has been discussed in Alicia H. Munnell, "The Impact of Social Security on Personal Saving, *National Tax Journal* 27, no. 4 (December 1974), pp. 553–67; and Martin S. Feldstein, "Social Security, Induced Retirement and Aggregate Capital Accumulation," *Journal of Political Economy* 82, no. 5 (September/October 1974), pp. 905–26.

in income will not be able completely to maintain their standard of living. For most families, the largest share of permanent income comes from wages, so that unemployment places constraints on the ability to smooth consumption. The family may be eligible for unemployment insurance and may be able to use credit cards or borrow from friends or family, but only up to a certain point. It is very difficult for some people to maintain their level of consumption through borrowing. An unemployed worker who went to a bank to explain that he wanted to borrow to cover the shortfall in his income resulting from his unemployment would receive a frosty reception. Banks have to lend on the basis of a borrower's future capacity to repay, not on the prospective borrower's need. Of course, prudent individuals who know that they may be laid off can set aside part of their income for saving, but many people fail to do this.

The ability of households to smooth their consumption during recessions will depend on the duration and depth of the decline in their incomes. A household's standard of living can be maintained during a short period of joblessness for one wage earner, but after an extended period without work, or if the entire household is unemployed, consumption is bound to be adversely affected. The long recessions that occurred prior to World War II, when unemployment insurance was much more limited, were hard on people's standard of living. The economic difficulties experienced over this period motivated the establishment of the modern unemployment insurance and social security programs.

We conclude, therefore, that while consumption smoothing contributes to stability in the consumption standard of living, it doesn't guarantee that consumption expenditures remain unchanged in the face of a recession. See the box on pages 536–37.

Furthermore, *aggregate demand is subject to fluctuations in spite of the stabilizing effects of consumption smoothing.* Though consumption expenditures on nondurables are a large part of aggregate demand, the variations in consumer expenditures on durables, together with variations in business investment, lead to substantial variability in overall demand.

CAPITAL INVESTMENT AND ECONOMIC FLUCTUATIONS

A good deal of the instability in aggregate demand comes from the high degree of variation in the level of current expenditures on durable capital goods, particularly given that we are now defining capital investment to include all the investment purchases made by both businesses and households: machinery and equipment, structures, and inventories plus consumer purchases of new residential housing and consumer durables.

Businesses have a stock of capital on hand—the factories, equipment, and office buildings that they have been using to produce output. They assess whether or not the size and composition of their stock of capital will allow them to produce their products at the lowest cost and they then make investment purchases based upon how large a capital stock they have, compared with how much capital they want to hold. They increase or decrease their investment expenditures in order to increase or decrease their current stock of capital. High business investment demand occurs when the current stock of capital is too low. Investment demand is low when the current capital stock is too high, relative to expected needs.

Although there are important differences between a household's decision to buy a new car and a company's decision to buy a new machine, we will group them together and focus on the similarities. Households look at the stock of durable goods that they have and decide whether this stock is large enough. If it is not, then they will purchase more durable goods. The house-

■ Recent Ideas on Consumption

The studies by James Duesenberry, Milton Friedman, and Franco Modigliani are the classic works on consumption behavior, but there have been several more recent studies, some of which have supported the old ideas and some of which have challenged them.*

Robert Hall of Stanford University has come up with an ingenious way of testing the permanent-income hypothesis. He pointed out that if consumption depends upon permanent income, then changes in consumption should depend upon changes in the estimates people make of their permanent income. And Hall then shows that if people are rational in computing their permanent income, changes in permanent income should be random—the only thing that will change the estimate is some new piece of information that was not available before. After taking the trend growth in income, new information will be random in its impact, being equally likely to raise or lower estimated permanent income. According to the permanent income hypothesis, therefore, the pattern of consumption should look like a *random walk*. In this case, consumption in the current period is equal to consumption in the preceding period plus a random error.

$$C_{current} = C_{last\ year} + random\ change.$$

Hall's analysis of U.S. consumption supported the idea that consumption is a random walk and hence he supported the permanent-income hypothesis. But his study sparked an explosion of additional research, extending his idea to other areas of macroeconomics or suggesting that he was wrong.

Criticisms of the permanent-income hypothesis and the life-cycle hypothesis have pointed to two concerns. The first is whether the permanent-income hypothesis can really explain consumption smoothing. When Hall suggested that consumption was a random walk, other people went out and found that income itself is close to being a random walk. And if that is true, *permanent income can be even more variable than current income*. The standard example that is used to illustrate a random walk is the sailor who should be heading back to his ship

---

*Robert E. Hall, "Stochastic Implications of the Life-Cycle-Permanent Income Hypothesis: Theory and Evidence," *Journal of Political Economy* 86, pp. 971–87, 1978; Alan S. Blinder and Angus S. Deaton, "The Time-Series Consumption Function Re-Visited," *Brookings Papers on Economic Activity*, 2:1985; John Y. Campbell and Angus S. Deaton, "Why is Consumption So Smooth?" *Review of Economic Studies*, April 1989; John Y. Campbell and N. Gregory Mankiw, "Consumption, Income, and Interest Rates: Reinterpreting the Time Series Evidence," *NBER Macroeconomics Annual 1989* (Cambridge Mass.: MIT Press, 1989).

---

hold decision on when to buy a durable good is similar to the business decision on when to make a capital expenditure—both are based upon a comparison of a household or firm's actual capital stock and what is called the *desired stock of capital.*

Capital goods do wear out over time and have to be replaced. An important fraction of total gross investment consists of replacement investment. Businesses replace machines as they wear out or when better alternatives become available. Households buy new washing machines when the old ones wear out, or when new models are sufficiently attractive.

but he is so drunk that each step he takes goes in a random direction. As time passes, the sailor will not in general move closer to the ship. The uncertainty about his location rises over time. Similarly, if income is a random walk, changing by a random amount each year, then permanent income is not necessarily smoother or more predictable than current income.

The second concern is based upon evidence from saving and consumption by individual households and whether or not it fits with the life-cycle model. One problem is that elderly people often save quite a bit and the young often save little. Young people do not think much about what will happen when they are old and they spend their current income. Elderly people are worried about becoming sick or needing nursing home care and so they save. A second finding from household surveys is that across different households there tend to be some who save a lot and some who save little, regardless of ages of the people in the households. Much of the variability in saving rates across households seems to come from differences in temperament (preferences), not from the fact that people are at different points in their life cycle. Those households that save a lot end up passing their accumulated wealth on to their children as bequests, not consuming it in retirement.

There has been no consensus as yet on some of these issues, but there are some general conclusions that we draw from the literature.

1. Saving to smooth out the effect of the short-run variability of income and saving for retirement are important reasons why people save. There is a basic validity to the permanent-income and life-cycle hypotheses.

2. It is hard to be sure what fraction of saving is made in order to make bequests to children, but it looks as if this is an important additional motivation for saving.

3. A substantial fraction of the population consists of people who simply spend all of their current income. They do not make rational lifetime saving plans, but rely on social security, unemployment insurance, and company or union pension plans to provide for them in retirement or in the event of unemployment.

4. Those people who make rational, future-oriented plans, have a very strong dislike for variations in their consumption. This is basically what Duesenbery said many years ago, although in the current literature this is described in terms of a low "intertemporal elasticity of substitution in consumption." The size of this elasticity reflects the amount of consumption people are willing to give up in one year in order to get more consumption in another year; and the studies find that the people will not give up much at all. They strongly prefer a smooth pattern of consumption.

The Variability of Total Capital Investment

The components of capital-investment expenditures and their changes over the 1973–1977 business cycles are shown in Figure 13.4.

Figure 13.4A shows changes in GNP and total investment along with the changes in the components of capital investment: business fixed investment in equipment (producer durables), nonresidential-structures investment, residential-housing investment, and consumer-durable purchases, the latter now being considered part of investment. Both the conventional concept

FIGURE 13.4A   Components of U.S. Investment over a Cycle (1973: 4th Qtr = 100)

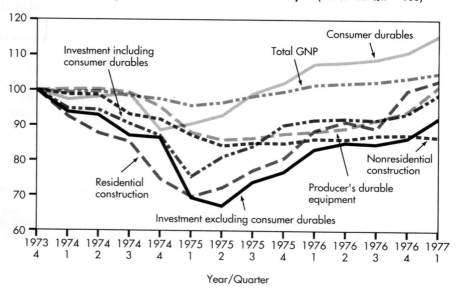

FIGURE 13.4B   Investment Shares at Start of Cycle, 1973: 4th Qtr

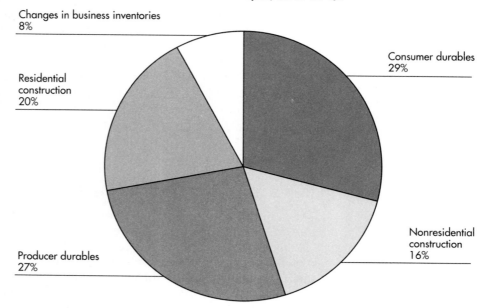

of total investment and total investment including consumer-durable purchases are shown in the figure. There is substantial variability evident in the figure, particularly for total investment, due mostly to changes in investment in producer-durable equipment, residential construction, and inventories.

Changes in business inventories are part of capital investment. Inventory changes are sometimes positive and sometimes negative. Their effect on investment is included in the total but they are not shown separately. The pie chart (Figure 13.4B) shows the component shares of total capital investment at the beginning of the period. At the start of the cycle, all durable products, excluding construction, comprised 56 percent of capital investment and all construction accounted for 36 percent. Changes in business inventories were positive at that time and they accounted for only 8 percent of capital investment. Thus it may appear that because of their small share, fluctuations in inventories are not likely to be an important source of variations in total investment. *However, the variations in inventories are quite large and they do make a strong contribution to the total variability of investments.* Because the economic factors that influence inventories are somewhat different from those affecting overall capital expenditure, we describe and discuss the role of inventories later in this section.

The overall picture from Figures 13.2 and 13.4 is striking. Consumers do not vary their consumption of nondurables much, but total purchases of all durable products by both business and households vary considerably over the course of a business cycle from recession to recovery. This tendency for the variability to be concentrated among durable products and buildings is a feature of business cycles that was studied many years ago, long before Keynes and the monetarists began developing the modern theories of the determination of output. For a long time it has been clear that there is something important about **durability.**

durability
A characteristic of capital goods. They last for more than one year, and they provide a *flow of services* over time.

The fact that capital goods last many years means that the stock of capital goods is large relative to both current investment and current income—business capital stock is approximately three times the level of business output. If businesses and consumers decide to maintain the size of the capital stock in relation to income, then small changes in income or production can lead to big changes in the amount of capital goods that have to be added to or taken away from the stock of capital. When a change in income triggers the desire to increase or decrease the capital stock, that change leads to large fluctuations in investment demand. This idea led to the development of a model called the *accelerator model of investment demand.*

The Accelerator and the Desired Stock of Capital

The idea that investment demand depends upon the way businesses vary the size of the capital stock leads to a simple model of variable investment demand. In this model, an increase in current output and income increases

desired capital stock
The amount of capital businesses would like to have on hand, given current and expected economic conditions.

accelerator
The relationship between an increase in output and the level of investment demand. The accelerator can be *fixed,* reflecting a required relationship between increasing output and the capital necessary to produce more output or *flexible,* reflecting the possibility that other inputs can substitute for capital in production.

desired capital–output ratio
The ratio of the desired capital stock to the level of output.

the **desired capital stock.** Since the actual capital stock was carried over from the past, there is then a discrepancy between the actual capital stock and the desired capital stock. The attempts to close this discrepancy lead to a large rise in investment demand. The model is known as the accelerator model of investment demand because a small increase in output has a larger or accelerated effect on investment demand. Most empirical studies of the demand for consumer and producer durables start with some version of the **accelerator.**[7]

The simple accelerator model of the desired stock of capital assumes that with a given production technology, it takes a fixed collection of capital goods—a particular amount of machinery, plant, and equipment—to produce a particular level of output. The amount of capital that firms want—the desired capital stock—is a fixed multiple of the level of output. The accelerator model can be applied to consumer purchases of durable goods. It says that, based upon the level of their income, households also decide upon a desired size of the stock of cars, houses, and appliances that they want to hold.

Equating income with output and combining the business and household desired capital stocks gives the following expression for the desired stock of capital:

$$K^d = vY. \tag{13.5}$$

The desired capital stock is a fixed multiple of the level of income. The fixed multiple (v) is the ratio of the desired capital stock to output $(v = K^d \div Y)$, called the **desired capital–output ratio.** In the business sector, we are assuming at this point that firms have no choice—they must have capital on hand in an amount equal to (v) times the level of output.

If output is rising in the economy, investment demand is positive because the actual capital stock is below the desired or required stock of capital. Firms and households demand investment goods in an attempt to adjust their actual stock of capital with their desired or required stock of capital. The level of investment then depends upon the amount needed to replace the capital that has worn out in the past year, plus or minus the amount to adjust for any changes in the level of income and output.

We define I_R as the amount of replacement investment, the investment that has to be made simply to keep the stock of capital from declining. Then if there is no change in the amount of output that firms want to produce, they will demand an amount of investment that simply replaces the depreciation. (I will equal I_R.) If there is an increase in the amount that firms want

---

[7] The history and development of the accelerator are surveyed in A. D. Knox, "The Acceleration Principle and the Theory of Investment: A Survey," *Economica*, New Series, 19 (August 1952), pp. 269–97. Peter K. Clark, "Investment in the 1970s: Theory, Performance and Prediction," *Brookings Papers on Economic Activity, 1:1979,* compares the performance of several investment models, including those based upon the accelerator.

■ Net and Gross Investment

Consumer and producer durables wear out over time. Cars last 5 to 10 years, so that 10 to 20 percent of them are retired each year. Some others are lost to accidents. Computers become obsolete after only a few years, but houses and office buildings may last 50 or 100 years. Each year the U.S. Department of Commerce, the agency that constructs the National Income and Product Accounts, makes an estimate of the depreciation of the business capital stock and the stock of residential housing. This figure is called the **capital consumption allowance.** This figure is then subtracted from GNP to measure **net national product** (NNP). The same value is subtracted from *gross* business and residential investment to form the measure of *net* investment. In 1989, gross fixed private investment was $724.5 billion and net investment was $216.2 billion, so the majority of gross investment in the U.S. economy went to replace the capital that has worn out.

The fact that capital wears out means that investment demand can be divided into two parts: the demand for replacement capital and the demand for capital to increase the stock of capital (net investment). Of course, net investment demand can be negative. If companies decide that they have too much capital, they will invest less than the amount necessary to maintain the size of their capital stocks. Individual companies can even sell off assets when they have too much capital—and these transactions happen quite frequently. And for the economy as a whole, used capital goods can be exported. There are substantial costs involved in trading second-hand capital goods, however. When a company buys capital goods, it will not usually plan to resell them except as a last resort.

to produce, then the desired stock of capital will increase (I will be greater than I_R) and investment demand will be equal to depreciation plus the difference between the current desired stock of capital (K^d) and the desired stock in the previous period [$K^d_{prior\ year}$]:

$$I = K^d - K^d_{prior\ year} + I_R. \tag{13.6}$$

Combining 13.5 and 13.6 gives

$$I = vY - [vY_{prior\ year}] + I_R$$
$$I = v[Y - Y_{prior\ year}] + I_R \tag{13.7}$$
$$I = v(\Delta Y) + I_R.$$

In the simple accelerator model, investment demand is equal to replacement investment plus the desired capital–output ratio times the change in income. The desired capital–output ratio (v) is the accelerator coefficient.

Even though it is so simple, the accelerator model can help us understand some important characteristics about the actual economy. In the actual economy, investment demand is much more variable than is income as a whole, and the accelerator predicts this pattern because investment demand depends upon a multiple of the change in income. In addition, we see in the actual economy that investment starts to decline *before* the economy goes into a recession and this too follows from the accelerator. Income is rising in a recovery and this positive change in income keeps a high level of investment. Then as income growth levels off as the top of the boom approaches, the change in income decreases and investment demand actually declines even though income may still be growing. The following worked example helps to show how these results come about.

WORKED EXAMPLE 13.1   The Simple Accelerator Model of Investment

In this example we assume that production requires three units of capital to produce each unit of output. The accelerator coefficient, v, is equal to 3. Replacement investment in each year is equal to 400. The capital stock in year zero is equal to 12,000. The levels of output in the economy over eight years are as follows:

$$Y_1 = 4,000 \qquad Y_2 = 4,040 \qquad Y_3 = 4,120$$
$$Y_4 = 4,140 \qquad Y_5 = 4,120 \qquad Y_6 = 4,080$$
$$Y_7 = 4,000 \qquad Y_8 = 4,000$$

Question: Trace out the path of investment demand over this period.

Answer: The desired capital stock in year one is equal to vY:

$$K^d_1 = 3 \times 4,000 = 12,000.$$

The actual capital stock in year zero is also 12,000, so investment demand in year one will simply equal replacement investment:

$$I_1 = 400.$$

In subsequent years, the level of investment demand is found by substituting into Equation 13.7:

$$I_2 = 3(4,040 - 4,000) + 400 = 520$$
$$I_3 = 3(4,120 - 4,040) + 400 = 640$$
$$I_4 = 3(4,140 - 4,120) + 400 = 460$$
$$I_5 = 3(4,120 - 4,140) + 400 = 340$$
$$I_6 = 3(4,080 - 4,120) + 400 = 280$$
$$I_7 = 3(4,000 - 4,080) + 400 = 160$$
$$I_8 = 3(4,000 - 4,000) + 400 = 400.$$

The example illustrates how volatile investment demand will be as a result of quite moderate changes in income. For example, income rose by only 1 percent from year one to year two (4,000 to 4,040), and yet investment demand grew by 30 percent (from 400 to 520). The following year income grew by about 2 percent (4,040 to 4,120) and investment grew by an additional 23 percent (from 520 to 640).

In years three to four income was still growing, but investment demand actually fell sharply—by 28 percent (640 to 460). Investment demand started to decline even before income started to fall. The subsequent declines in income from year four to year seven then sent investment demand way down until income had stabilized again (between years seven and eight), and investment returned to its original value (equal to replacement investment, 400).

While the accelerator model of investment demand gives us clues as to why there is so much variability in the demand for durables, it is easily criticized as being too abstract. First, the desired capital stock will not remain a fixed proportion of income. The proportion will change with changing economic conditions. Second, following a change in income, firms and households do not attempt to close the gap between actual stocks and the desired stock immediately. Rather, adjustments take place gradually.

The flexible accelerator and capital investment

For considerable periods of time, firms and households can get along with a capital stock that is different from the one that fits exactly with their production needs. Businesses find that adjusting the size of their capital stock is very costly. While they will invest in order to bring the actual and the desired sizes into alignment, they will not close the gap completely in the short run. Companies have alternative strategies they can follow instead of investing in more capital. For example, they can temporarily hire more labor and take some time in adjusting their capital stock while still meeting production requirements. Given that they have this flexibility, firms that want to increase output look at the cost of building up their capital stock quickly. The costs of rapid investment include technical adjustment costs involving premiums paid for quick construction or delivery. So firms facing an increase in demand first use a combination of more labor (new hires, overtime, and/or temporary workers) and some more capital and then later undertake the remainder of the desired capital buildup. Adjustment costs are important in determining how the accelerator works in practice.

The fraction of the gap between the actual and the desired stocks of capital closed by investment in any particular period is the *rate of adjustment* (*d*) and this describes how rapidly firms react to changes in the desired capital stock. Of course in practice, the rate of adjustment is subject to change under varying economic conditions. A high rate of interest or a bout of pessimism about future sales will cause firms to delay their investments and adjust to the desired capital stock more slowly, lowering the rate of adjustment. But we will ignore the changing nature of the rate of adjustment for now by assuming that it is a constant value, and we will concentrate on how incomplete adjustment alone affects the accelerator model.

The lack of complete adjustment by businesses means that the actual capital stock in each period will not always equal the desired stock. *In this case, investment demand depends upon the gap between the desired capital stock this period, the actual capital stock carried forward from the previous period, and the rate of adjustment.* The flexible accelerator is represented in Equation 13.8:

$$I = d[vY - K_{\text{prior year}}] + I_R. \tag{13.8}$$

This equation says that net investment is a fraction (*d*) of the gap between the desired stock and the amount carried forward.

The effect of the partial adjustment is to smooth out over several periods the impact of changes in output on investment demand, thereby sustaining investment demand even when output growth falls. This pattern of investment demand is more realistic than the explosion or contraction of investment demand implied by the simple model. The flexible-accelerator model predicts smoother investment patterns than the simple model, but it still explains the high degree of variability of the demand for durable goods. We illustrate how the flexible accelerator works using another worked example.

WORKED EXAMPLE 13.2   The Flexible Accelerator

We will use the same starting point as we used in Worked Example 13.1. The capital–output ratio, v, is 3. In the initial year (year zero) output is 4,000 and the capital stock is 12,000. Replacement investment is 400.

Question: If the economy follows the same path of output that is given in Worked Example 13.1, show how the level of investment is determined with a flexible accelerator that has an adjustment coefficient of 0.3. Compare the results from the simple-accelerator model and the flexible-accelerator model.

Answer: The desired capital stock in year one is equal to vY with Y equal to 4,000, and the actual capital stock in year zero is 12,000. This allows the computation of investment in the first year, and then in subsequent years, by substituting into Equation 13.8:

$$I_1 = 0.3[(3 \times 4,000) - 12,000] + 400 = 400, \ K_1 = 12,000$$
$$I_2 = 0.3[(3 \times 4,040) - 12,000] + 400 = 436, \ K_2 = 12,036$$
$$I_3 = 0.3[(3 \times 4,120) - 12,036] + 400 = 497, \ K_3 = 12,133$$
$$I_4 = 0.3[(3 \times 4,140) - 12,333] + 400 = 486, \ K_4 = 12,219$$
$$I_5 = 0.3[(3 \times 4,120) - 12,219] + 400 = 442, \ K_5 = 12,261$$
$$I_6 = 0.3[(3 \times 4,080) - 12,261] + 400 = 394, \ K_6 = 12,255$$
$$I_7 = 0.3[(3 \times 4,000) - 12,255] + 400 = 323, \ K_7 = 12,178$$
$$I_8 = 0.3[(3 \times 4,000) - 12,178] + 400 = 347, \ K_8 = 12,125.$$

These figures are calculated using unrounded numbers and then rounded, so that there will be small discrepancies if you check some lines.

The most important difference between the flexible accelerator and the simple accelerator is that the predicted volatility of investment is smaller in the more realistic flexible model than in the highly abstract simple model.

With the simple accelerator, there was a peak of investment of 640 and a trough of 160. With the flexible accelerator, the same path of output led to a peak of 497 and a trough of 323—a much narrower range. The acceleration effect has not disappeared, however. The percent changes in investment are still much greater than the percent changes in output. The reason that the volatility is less is that the impact of a given change in output is spread over several periods. There is not a complete adjustment in the first period.

One important similarity that is carried over to the flexible model is that investment peaks before output peaks. Investment peaked in year three at 497, whereas output did not peak until year four.

The accelerator describes how changes in output lead to larger changes in investment demand. But in our analysis of goods-market equilibrium we have seen that an increase in investment demand will, through the multiplier, raise aggregate demand and output. What happens if we put these two ideas together?

The multiplier–accelerator interaction

In a famous study written in 1939, Paul Samuelson combined a flexible-accelerator model with multiplier analysis into a model in which the increase in income generated by an increase in investment demand (through the multiplier) will lead to a larger increase in the desired capital stock (the accelerator). The higher desired capital stock then leads to a new increase in investment demand, and so on and so on.[8] This interaction of the accelerator and multiplier was used by Samuelson to help explain why the economy is prone to rapid expansions and contractions. The model predicted cycles under some conditions and Samuelson suggested that business cycles in the actual economy might be the result of forces captured by the multiplier–accelerator model. We describe the working of his model and then use an example (Worked Example 13.3) to show how the path of output is traced out in a specific case.

In some versions of Samuelson's model, this process led to explosive growth in income with income pushing investment even higher and then this pushing income even higher, and so on and so on. We know that this does not happen in reality because of rises in interest rates or shortages of workers or other constraints to expansion that prevent the explosive growth. These constraints would have to be incorporated into a more realistic model.

With some values for the multiplier and the accelerator, however, even the very simple model predicts that a boom will run out of gas and the economy will peak and start to turn down. The boost to investment increases income on the next round, but not by enough to increase the growth of income. This means that income is growing still, but *the change in income is smaller*, so that investment starts to fall. Investment expenditures decline even if the economy is growing, as long as the rate of growth is slower this period than last period. At that point, the loss of investment expenditure has a negative impact on aggregate demand. When aggregate demand falls, the actual capital stock exceeds the desired capital stock and investment demand accelerates downward, further driving down aggregate demand. The economy goes from boom to bust as the growth of output changes direction and turns over at a peak and heads for a trough.

The same process then works in the downturn. Provided the model is not unstable, there will be a point where the decline in income is less rapid, and then investment stops falling. Once investment stops falling, income

---

[8] Paul A. Samuelson, "Interaction between the Multiplier Analysis and the Principle of Acceleration," *Review of Economic Statistics* 21 (May 1939).

stops falling and the bottom has been reached. Investment starts to rise again once income has stopped falling. This causes income to start growing and the economy moves into a recovery.

The accelerator–multiplier mechanism is illustrative of an important characteristic of actual economies: *if the growth of income begins to slow down, the economy can move toward recession even while growth is positive.* In order for investment demand to remain strong, the rate of growth of output has to be sustained, and typically that does not happen. The economy approaches full employment and companies find hiring more difficult and anticipate slower growth, so the economy does slow. Then falling investment demand may tip the economy toward recession.

The accelerator–multiplier interaction can also illustrate ways in which recovery takes place. Take an economy that has fallen into a recession. If the economy begins to recover, say as a result of policy action or an upward movement in consumer demand, output will begin to increase and the growth in output will generate a sharp increase in investment demand through the accelerator.[9] As investment demand comes back, this will stimulate further increases in demand through multiplier effects, and the recovery is then well underway.

WORKED EXAMPLE 13.3 The Samuelson Multiplier–Accelerator Model

We give here, with some adaptation, an example that Samuelson used to illustrate how the multiplier and the accelerator can interact. He used a simple consumption function and an investment function that was basically the simple accelerator, except that he used accelerator coefficients that were much smaller than the average ratio of capital to output, because of the kind of partial adjustment of capital that we incorporated here into a flexible accelerator.

His consumption and investment relations differed in one important way from the usual ones that we have used previously. *He allowed for time lags* between income and consumption and between the change of output and the demand for investment. The idea behind this was that consumers decide how much to buy based upon how much income they received in the *previous* period. In the case of investment, it is often true that it takes a while for investment goods to be built and delivered, so that investment this period depends upon the decision to buy that was made in a prior period.

---

[9] If the economy is using capital to capacity, as in a recovery or a boom, then the past year's capital stock will be insufficient to meet this year's need for production, and actual capital will be below the desired level.

If output is rising as the economy is coming out of a recession, there is some question about actual capital being short of desired capital—what of all the capital that was not required or used during the recession, couldn't it be simply brought on line with no need for new capital expenditures? Not really, because if the recession were prolonged, actual capital could still be below desired capital because of past reductions in maintenance and technological obsolescence. New capital expenditures would also be needed if the industrial sectors leading the recovery are distinct from those that suffered the major effects of the recession.

We will use the following consumption and investment equations together with a fixed level for government expenditure. Consumption, investment, and government expenditure in a given year are as follows:

$$C = 100 + 0.7Y_{\text{prior year}}$$
$$= 0.6[Y_{\text{prior year}} - Y_{\text{two years earlier}}] + 400$$
$$I = 0.6[\Delta Y_{\text{prior year}}] + 400$$
$$G = 700.$$

Question: Show that if income was 4,000 in both year zero and year one, then income in year two will be 4,000. Trace out the path of income if government expenditure were to change to 900 in year three and then stay at the new higher level.

Answer: We write down the goods-market–equilibrium condition for this model economy in year two:

$$Y_{\text{two}} = C_{\text{two}} + I_{\text{two}} + G$$
$$= 100 + 0.7Y_{\text{year one}} + 0.6[\Delta Y_{\text{from zero to one}}] + 400 + 700.$$

We can then substitute the value of 4,000 into this expression for the prior values of income and see what the current vlaue of income is. Notice that income was constant at 4,000 during years zero and one, so that there was no change in income from year zero to year one:

$$Y_{\text{two}} = 100 + 0.7(4,000) + 0.6(0) + 400 + 700 = 4,000.$$

This confirms the first part of the answer. We now look at the case where the economy has been at 4,000 for some time, but then it is disturbed by the increase in government expenditure to 900. We trace out what happens to income:

Y_3	=	100	+	$(0.7 \times 4{,}000)$	+	$0.6(\ \ 0)$	+	400	+	900	=	4,200
Y_4	=	100	+	$(0.7 \times 4{,}200)$	+	$0.6(\ 200)$	+	400	+	900	=	4,460
Y_5	=	100	+	$(0.7 \times 4{,}460)$	+	$0.6(\ 260)$	+	400	+	900	=	4,678
Y_6	=	100	+	$(0.7 \times 4{,}678)$	+	$0.6(\ 218)$	+	400	+	900	=	4,805
Y_7	=	100	+	$(0.7 \times 4{,}805)$	+	$0.6(\ 127)$	+	400	+	900	=	4,840
Y_8	=	100	+	$(0.7 \times 4{,}840)$	+	$0.6(\ \ 35)$	+	400	+	900	=	4,809
Y_9	=	100	+	$(0.7 \times 4{,}809)$	+	$0.6(-31)$	+	400	+	900	=	4,748
Y_{10}	=	100	+	$(0.7 \times 4{,}748)$	+	$0.6(-61)$	+	400	+	900	=	4,686
Y_{11}	=	100	+	$(0.7 \times 4{,}686)$	+	$0.6(-61)$	+	400	+	900	=	4,644
Y_{12}	=	100	+	$(0.7 \times 4{,}644)$	+	$0.6(-43)$	+	400	+	900	=	4,625
Y_{13}	=	100	+	$(0.7 \times 4{,}625)$	+	$0.6(-19)$	+	400	+	900	=	4,626
$\cdots$	$\cdot\,\cdot$			$\cdots$		$\cdots$		$\cdot\,\cdot$		$\cdot\,\cdot$		$\cdots$
$Y_{\text{long run}}$	=	100	+	$(0.7 \times 4{,}667)$	+	$0.6(\ \ 0)$	+	400	+	900	=	4,667.

(These figures are calculated using unrounded numbers and then rounded, so that you may note small discrepancies if you check some lines.)

The result of this multiplier–accelerator model, therefore, is that *income will rise and fall following an initial disturbance. The economy is actually tracing out a cycle.* This response of the model economy to the change in government spending is illustrated in Figure 13.5.

In the example we have used here, the up-and-down movements of the economy will die away and the economy will settle down to some long-run level of income.

FIGURE 13.5   The Path of Income over Time following an Increase in Government Expenditure

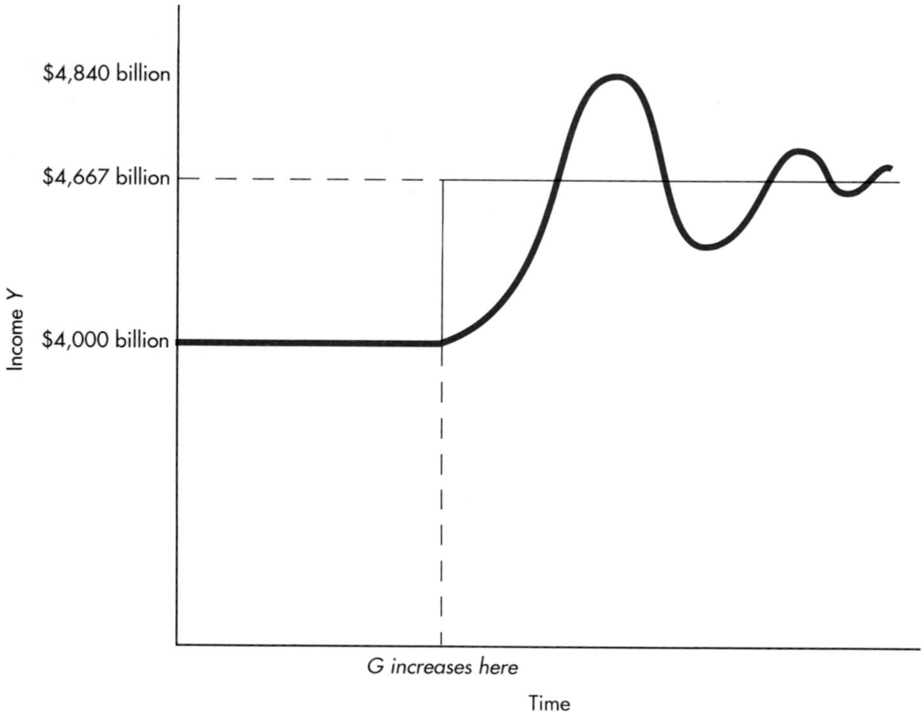

Note: Figure is based on a model adapted from Samuelson's multiplier–accelerator model.

In fact, in this example the economy has come pretty close to its long-run value after 13 years.

The values used in this example insure that the economy will settle down to a stable value. (The system is convergent.) But other values would give different answers. The economy could behave in an unstable way with cycles that get larger and larger, or it could move to its long-run value without cycling.

We have been grouping all kinds of durable goods and construction together in our analysis of the accelerator and the variability of investment. We have argued that there are important common elements in the demand for consumer durables and housing as well as business investment. As we indicated earlier, we put off a discussion of changes in business inventories. Inventory changes are a volatile type of investment that we need to look at separately, and they play a particularly important role in the timing of cyclical fluctuations in economy.

Inventory Investment and the Inventory Cycle

Businesses use inventories in their production processes. Inventories are a capital good, like machinery and equipment, and are a costly necessity for a productive factory. While reducing inventory requirements is a reasonable goal for a firm as it attempts to improve its productive efficiency, at any given state of production technology, there will be a necessary level of inventory associated with a level of output.

To the extent that inventories are simply a part of investment demand, changes in inventories can be analyzed using accelerator models. However, part of the purpose of inventories is to provide product for potential customers more quickly than by producing product on demand. This means that *expectations about future sales play an even more important role in determining inventory investment than other kinds of investment.* Inventory changes are observed to be more volatile than investment in fixed capital.

Inventories played an important role of the discussions of the multiplier and goods-market equilibrium in earlier chapters. We said that in the short run, firms are willing to match supply to demand by allowing inventories to decline when demand exceeds current production or by letting inventories pile up when demand is weak. The change in inventories is partly a residual item—the amount of output that is produced but not sold. When demand is growing strongly, inventories become depleted. Then businesses step up production, both to meet demand and to rebuild the depleted stock of inventories. For a period at the peak of a business-cycle expansion, production exceeds demand. Once demand turns down, inventories pile up. Then businesses cut back production and lay off workers, both because of the fall in demand and in order to get rid of the excess inventories that have piled up. *Over the course of a business cycle, inventories actually add to variability. The variability of production in the U.S. economy is actually greater than the variability of sales.*[10] The effort to rebuild inventories pushes production above sales in cyclical peaks, while the effort to work off excess inventories pushes production below sales at troughs.

In the early chapters, we described a model of equilibrium in the goods market where businesses respond to declining inventories by increasing output following an increase in demand. They respond to rising inventories by decreasing output following a decrease in demand. This meant that in the income–expenditure model the economy was described as moving smoothly from one goods-market equilibrium to another. That was too simple because it ignored the inventory rebuilding that is needed when inventories become depleted or the inventory liquidation needed when they pile up. The adjustment of inventories following a shift in demand can in practice involve some cycling (overshooting and undershooting equilibrium) of the economy around a new equilibrium.

---

[10] Alan S. Blinder, "Can the Production Smoothing Model of Inventory Behavior be Saved?" *Quarterly Journal of Economics* 91 (August 1986), pp. 431–53.

■ Inventories in Production: The Just-in-Time Innovation

While inventories may be necessary for production, actions taken to reduce that necessary level of inventories confer both cost benefits and production-technology benefits on a firm. The use of inventories in production is affected by managerial innovation. Better control systems are designed to make optimal use of inventories. The just-in-time production method, developed in Japan by Toyota and now used worldwide, is a way of reorganizing production that not only uses fewer inventories but more importantly recognizes that the efforts made to reduce inventories reveal inefficiencies in production that were previously masked by the use of inventories as a buffer stock between stages of production or distribution. Correcting those inefficiencies not only reduces the need for inventories, it also increases labor productivity.

As the economy shifts from a period of inventory rebuilding in a business-cycle peak to a period of inventory liquidation in a trough, the shift in inventory investment can be very large. Table 13.2 shows that these swings in inventory investment have been an important part of the decline in GNP in five recessions from 1960 to 1982.[11]

The upper panel of the table shows how the inventories held by different sectors of the economy varied in these recessions. The swings in retail inventories and in manufacturers' inventories of raw materials and partially finished goods are the largest in magnitude. The lower panel of the table shows that, except for the unusual 1980 recession, the swings in inventories were very large indeed relative to the overall swings in GNP, particularly during the 1960s where the inventory cycle was actually larger than the GNP cycle. In these recessions, consumer and government demand actually grew, but the scramble by businesses to work off the excess inventories that had accumulated in the peak pulled GNP down. While improvements in inventory management in the 1980s may have reduced the level of inventory holding, inventories still contribute to economic volatility.

Expectations, Interest Rates, and Investment Demand

The flexible-accelerator model and its interaction with the multiplier along with inventory adjustments provide intriguing insights into the way investment and income might evolve over time. These models are based on the notion that firms and households face adjustment costs that affect the speed with which they match their actual capital stocks to their desired capital stock. Yet they still are lacking an important characteristic of investment demand in that *the desired stock of capital itself changes as economic conditions*

---

[11] Valerie Ramey, "Inventories as Factors of Production and Economic Fluctuations," *American Economic Review*, June 1989.

TABLE 13.2   Swings in Inventory Investment

A. Changes in Inventory by Component
(Billions of 1972 $, Average Annual Rates of Change)

Recessions	Retail	Wholesale	Manufact. Finished Inventories	Manufact. Input Inventories
1960:1st Qtr.–1960:4th Qtr.	−6.3	−1.7	−3.1	−6.3
1969:3rd Qtr.–1970:4th Qtr.	−8.2	+1.2	−0.4	−5.2
1973:4th Qtr.–1975:1st Qtr.	−16.0	−5.8	+2.4	−13.2
1980:1st Qtr.–1980:2nd Qtr.	+3.6	+1.9	−0.3	−4.1
1981:3rd Qtr.–1982:4th Qtr.	−7.6	−2.3	−7.8	−11.1

B. Importance of Inventory Investment in Recessions

Recessions	Total Inventory	GNP	Change in Inventory Investment as a Percentage of Change in Real GNP
1960:1st Qtr.–1960:4th Qtr.	−18.0	−8.6	209
1969:3rd Qtr.–1970:4th Qtr.	−12.3	−7.3	168
1973:4th Qtr.–1975:1st Qtr.	−38.0	−60.7	63
1980:1st Qtr.–1980:2nd Qtr.	−1.6	−35.0	5
1981:3rd Qtr.–1982:4th Qtr.	−38.8	−45.1	86

Note: The rows in Table A do not sum to the inventory numbers in Table B because the latter also include farm inventories.
Source: (A) Valerie Ramey, "Inventories as Factors of Production and Economic Fluctuations," *American Economic Review*, June 1989. In Table A, changes in inventories are calculated from constant-dollar data from the Bureau of Economic Analysis, Department of Commerce.
(B) Alan S. Blinder and Douglas Holtz-Eakin, "Inventory Fluctuations in the United States Since 1929," in *The American Business Cycle, Continuity and Change*, ed. Robert J. Gordon (Chicago: University of Chicago Press, 1986).

change. In practice, the investment decision is affected by factors that these models ignore: expectations and interest rates.

Expectations and variability in investment demand

An important determinant of business investment demand is business expectations. The extent to which businesses adjust their investment demand in response to changes in output will depend upon their expectations about future output. Is an increase in output going to last or not? Is an increase likely to be followed by a decrease? If so, why buy, build, or lease expensive capital this period only to be left with overcapacity next period?

One of the important reasons why firms usually make only a partial adjustment to output changes is connected to their expectations about the duration of the change in demand. They do not necessarily think that increases or decreases in output will persist.[12]

If output is unusually low, then business managers may think it likely that output will rise, so they do not try to match their capital stocks exactly to the current level of output; rather, they invest in excess of their current capital needs. They may continue to replace worn-out capital even though they will not need the replacement machinery right away. If output is unusually high, managers may think that output will fall, so they do not boost their investment by the full amount predicted by the simple accelerator. If families experience an increase or decrease in their income, they may see this as only temporary.

This discussion about expectations assumes that businesses or families will only partially adjust their investment following increases or decreases in output. If there is a recession and people believe that the economy will quickly return to full employment, then this belief actually helps to stabilize the economy. This is the normal case but it is not the only possibility. It presumes that businesses believe that reductions in output will be reversed fairly quickly. If businesses think, instead, that a fall in output will be prolonged or followed by a further fall, then the rate of adjustment can change rapidly and expectations may become destabilizing.

It is quite possible for a household to maintain its standard of living and still make fairly major changes in the timing of the purchase of a house or a car. Suppose the economy is in the early stages of a recession. Households are experiencing reductions in income, but they do not know at this point whether these income changes are transitory or permanent. They can decide either to postpone or go ahead with the purchase of a house or a car. Since they can manage perfectly well in the short run with the house or the car they have now, prudent behavior argues for waiting until they are sure about the nature of the income reduction. They decide to delay the capital expenditure. For example, the worker who thinks that layoffs are coming will not take on installment or lease payments for a new car but rather will continue to use the old car he already has. A middle-aged executive who hears that her company is planning to require early retirement among its staff will not buy a new house with a much larger monthly payment than the one she has now. An economywide postponement in auto, home, and appliance purchases may not initially affect living standards, but it will have quite large effects on aggregate demand.

On the business side, *in a single firm the timing of investment purchases can be changed without necessarily changing production.* For example, the decision to build a new factory could be postponed if a company suddenly decides that a recession is imminent and that demand will fall. A fall in demand would make it unprofitable to operate both the old and the new plants and

---

[12] This issue is discussed in Martin Neil Baily, "Stabilization and Private Economic Behavior," *Brookings Papers on Economic Activity*, 1:1978.

it reduces the payoff to the investment project. If the company foresees a recession, it can continue to make do with the old plant for some period of time, *but an economywide postponement of investment will have a major effect on aggregate demand.*

As summarized next, the speed at which investment adjusts to changes in economic conditions can be quite different depending on expectations.

- If the economy has been stable, where deviations around output are expected to be quickly reversed, a change in output will not lead to a big change in investment demand.
- If the economy is subject to large cycles, where major booms or slumps are expected to follow output changes, a change in output will lead to a larger change in investment demand.
- If businesses' expectations deteriorate such that they completely lose confidence in the economy, then investment can fall precipitously. One reason that the U.S. economy fell into such a deep depression in the 1930s is that business lost confidence in the economy, so gross investment fell almost to zero and net investment was negative.

In general, *the extent to which businesses and households are optimistic or pessimistic about future economic conditions will influence the current level of investment demand.* The fact that business investment and consumer purchases of durables vary with changes in expectations generates variability in investment and makes it hard to predict what investment will be.

The interest rate and the accelerator

We assumed in earlier analysis that the long-term real rate of interest affects investment. How does that fit with the analysis in this chapter, where investment depends upon changes in the desired capital stock? We assume now that the long-term real interest rate affects the size of the desired capital stock.

In the flexible-accelerator model of investment demand, the effect of changes in the real rate of interest on the desired capital stock is captured by allowing the desired capital–output ratio (the accelerator coefficient, v) to depend upon the interest rate. A high interest rate will reduce the amount of capital that firms will choose in order to produce a given level of output.[13] For households, a high rate of interest will encourage them to economize on the amount of durable goods that they will choose at a given level of family income. This idea is expressed by

$$K^d = v(r)Y. \tag{13.9}$$

The desired capital–output ratio depends on the long-term real rate of interest, so the higher is the interest rate, the lower is v.

---

[13] The classic study that brought the interest rate and other elements of the cost of capital into the accelerator framework was undertaken by Dale T. Jorgenson, "Capital Theory and Investment Behavior," *American Economic Review* LIII (May 1963).

When the long-term real rate of interest is high over several years, as it was in the 1980s, this will lower the desired capital–output ratio, reducing the level of investment demand in each period from what it would have been otherwise. Inserting Equation 13.9 into the investment Equation 13.8 gives the following interest-sensitive version of the flexible accelerator:

$$I = d[v(r)Y - K_{\text{prior year}}] + I_R. \tag{13.10}$$

In this version of the flexible-accelerator model of investment demand, the size of investment demand in a given period depends upon the speed of adjustment and the desired capital–output ratio (which depends upon income and the interest rate), the capital stock in the previous period, and the amount of replacement investment.

We use a simplified formulation of this flexible accelerator to see how these various factors affecting investment demand impact overall aggregate demand within the *IS-ALM* framework. We concentrate on three variables in the interest-sensitive flexible-accelerator model—the level of income, the interest rate, and the size of the capital stock in the previous period:

$$I = I[r, Y, K_{\text{prior year}}]. \tag{13.11}$$

This relation is now similar to the investment function that we introduced back in Chapter 2, except for the one additional term. It says that investment demand decreases with increases in the rate of interest and increases with increases in the level of income (just as before) and, in addition, *it decreases with the size of the capital stock carried over from the prior year.* Equation 13.11 summarizes the implication of the accelerator that we will apply to the *IS-ALM* framework. If businesses and households already have a lot of capital, then investment demand will be weak, holding income and the interest rate constant.

THE CAPITAL STOCK, EXPECTATIONS, AND *IS-ALM* EQUILIBRIUM

Introducing the flexible-accelerator model into our analysis provides a previously missing and important element of investment demand. Besides income and the real rate of interest, investment demand also depends upon the amount of capital that is already on hand, carried forward from the previous period.

Since investment demand is affected by how much of the capital stock is carried forward, equilibrium in the goods market is also affected by the size of the capital stock, and we must model the economy so that *the position of the* IS *schedule depends on the capital stock.* Equation 13.12 illustrates:

$$Y = \underset{\text{consumption}}{C(Y,T)} + \underset{\text{investment}}{I[r, Y, K_{\text{prior year}}]} + \underset{\text{government}}{G} \tag{13.12}$$

The condition for goods-market equilibrium given in Equation 13.12 has become a fairly complicated expression, including fiscal-policy variables *(G* and

FIGURE 13.6   Investment Demand and Income Depend upon the Amount of Capital Carried over from the Prior Period

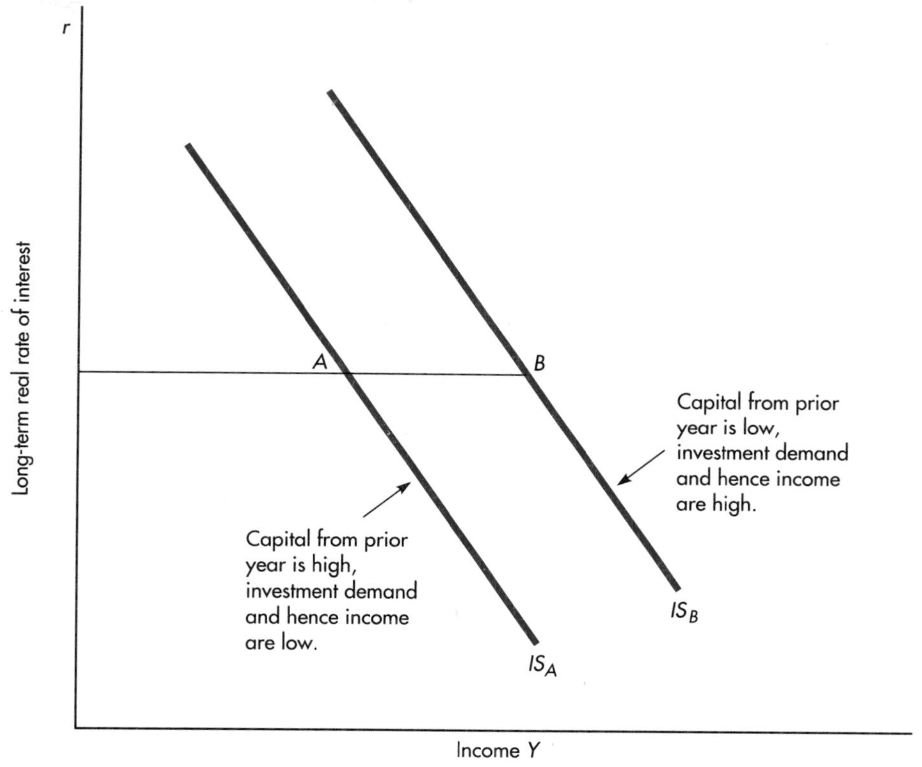

T), the long-term real interest rate *(r)*, and a factor reflecting the capital stock in the prior year ($K_{prior\ year}$). We have omitted net exports from this equation because we are not focusing on international aspects of the economy at this point.

The capital stock last year was determined by economic conditions last year as well as by the capital stock in the year before that, while the capital stock in the year before that was determined by economic conditions in the previous year before and by the capital stock in the year before that, and so on and so on. *Over time, the goods-market equilibrium (the resulting IS schedule) shifts around depending upon the past pattern of output and interest rates.*

Figure 13.6 uses two alternative *IS* schedules to illustrate this dependence on the carryover from past investment. When the capital stock carried forward is large relative to the desired capital stock, investment demand is small and the *IS* schedule *(IS_A)* is shifted inward to the left. The reverse is the case when the capital stock carried forward is small relative to the desired stock *(IS_B)*. When there is a weak economic environment, firms are carrying forward a capital stock that is too large relative to the desired capital stock. They will face excess capacity, resulting in a reduced level of investment even with a low real rate of interest. Conversely, if the economic environment is strong with income rising and/or expected to rise, firms will not have a capital stock equal to their desired capital stock. They will face a shortage of capacity and have trouble meeting demand. In this situation firms will invest in new capital even if the interest rate is high. This makes explicit what was only briefly described when we introduced investment demand in the *IS-ALM* framework in earlier chapters. If economic conditions are such that income is falling, or if firms simply expect a reduction in demand, they will be reluctant to invest, even if the interest rate is low. At the same long-term real rate of interest, the level of investment demand is lower along IS_A (point A) than along IS_B (point B).

Consumer and business expectations are also important. If households think that a decline in the economy is going to get worse, so that their own jobs are threatened, they will be very reluctant to invest in a new car. If people think that a recovery will come soon, they will not fear for their jobs and will be more willing to buy consumer durables.

In general, goods-market equilibrium as reflected in the position of the *IS* schedule will depend on both the past—the size of the existing capital stock—and on future expectations. *The demand for both producer- and consumer-durable goods will be greater (the IS schedule will be further to the right), the lower is the existing stock of these goods and the more optimistic people are about future income and sales. On the other hand, the larger is the existing stock of capital and the more people are pessimistic about the future, the smaller will be investment demand. (The IS schedule will be further to the left.)*

Investment Fluctuations and the Cycle, a Case Study of 1956–1962

We have discussed the way in which investment demand can be both a source of variability and can itself be affected by variability in the economy. We now look at a period of business-cycle history when economic fluctuations were primarily determined by cyclical shifts in investment demand. This is difficult, given the complexity of the issues. Usually economists rely on large computer models to take on that task, and unfortunately those models are not easy to interpret.

Here we use a case-study approach, looking at the two short cycles that the economy went through from 1956–1962. The reason for choosing this period is that inflation was fairly moderate and interest rates did not vary by large amounts. It was a period when both the accelerator and changes in business expectations can be used to explain shifts in investment demand. By looking at this period, we can get a better understanding of the role played by expectations and the capital stock in the fluctuations in the goods market and hence in fluctuations in the aggregate economy.

Over the 1955–1957 period, the U.S. economy was in a boom. Real GNP was 102.8 percent of potential GNP in 1955 and 102.0 percent in 1957. Inflation in consumer prices had been running at only about 1 percent a year, but was starting to increase. Measured in terms of wholesale prices, inflation had increased to over 4 percent a year by the end of 1956. This is not so bad by recent standards, but was considered dangerous by policymakers at the time.

Even though current inflation was rising, people's expectations about long-run future inflation remained optimistic. Chronic inflation had not yet become a problem for the U.S. economy and people did not expect much long-term inflation. We can assume a stable expected rate of inflation of about 1 percent a year over the 1956–62 period.

In order to bring output down below potential output and to ease the pressure on inflation, the Fed decided to allow interest rates to rise, and follow a contractionary policy. The real money supply fell 6 percent from the first quarter of 1956 until the second quarter of 1958, a substantial drop given that potential output kept growing. The monetary contraction did bring about a rise in nominal interest rates. The three-month T-bill rate rose from about 2.4 percent in the first quarter of 1956 to about 3.4 percent in the second half of 1957. There was a reduction in the maturity premium associated with this spike in short-term rates. In the first quarter of 1956, the long-term nominal rate of interest exceeded the short rate by nearly 0.8 percentage points. This difference fell as low as 0.1 by the first quarter of 1957. Nevertheless, there was an increase in long-term real and nominal rates of interest over the period 1956–57.

The rather modest increase in the long-term real interest rate was associated with a rather substantial decline in the real economy. GNP fell absolutely from the second quarter of 1957 until the second quarter of 1958, and relative to potential output the decline was much greater. In 1958, GNP averaged only 96.5 percent of potential—nearly a 6 percent swing compared to 1956. Unemployment rose from 4.1 percent to 6.8 percent.

We cite three reasons why the monetary contraction led to a sharp fall in income even without a large rise in interest rates. The first and most important reason is that growth in the private sector was beginning to slow down on its own. Investment had been strong in 1955 and 1956, but by 1957, the investment boom was already running out of steam because the stock of capital had built up, so that the desired stock of capital was not much bigger than the actual stock. The second reason is that fiscal policy had become contractionary along with monetary policy, and this helped reduce demand also. And the third reason is that even small increases in interest rates had important effects on investment at that time because of credit rationing. The rise in the interest rate was combined with a decrease in the availability of funds.

FIGURE 13.7   The 1958 Recession

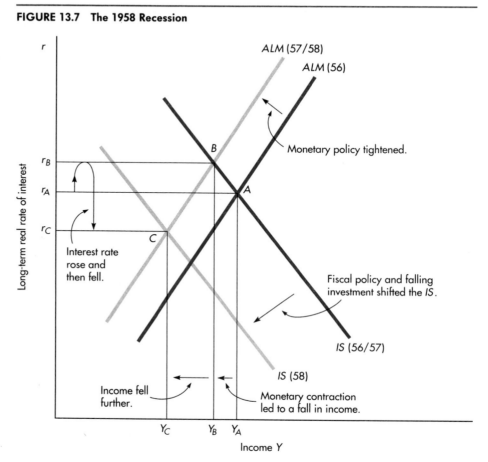

Monetary policy induced a small reduction in income. This triggered a large fall in investment and a further fall in income.

Figure 13.7 uses the *IS-ALM* framework to present a simplified representation of economic events during 1956–1958. The economy started in a boom [at point *A* on *IS*(56/57)] with income Y_A and interest rate r_A. Then the Fed tightened monetary policy, as shown by the shift from *ALM*(56) to *ALM*(57/58). At first, demand remained strong and the real rate of interest rose (from r_A to r_B). Then investment demand started to fall sharply as income growth turned negative. Because of this decline, aggregate demand was falling. [The *IS* schedule was moving to the left to *IS*(58).] Monetary policy remained tight, but interest rates actually fell as the economy went into a recession. This is a common pattern: a tight monetary policy leads to a slowing of

FIGURE 13.8   The Recovery, 1958–1960

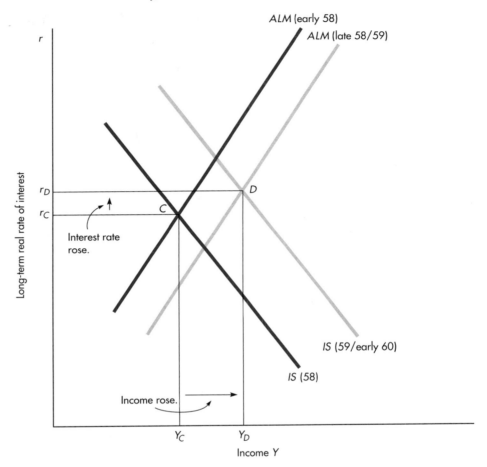

The Fed reversed course and investment and aggregate demand took off again.

income growth, which leads to a sharp fall in investment and a decline in interest rates.

The direction of the economy changed by the second quarter of 1958. GNP had started to grow while the Fed had also turned around and was adopting an expansionary policy. So the end result was a continued decline in the short-term interest rate through June, when it hit a trough below 1 percent. In Figure 13.8, we show the effects of the reversal of Fed policy. Demand for goods and services stopped falling and began to expand. This is reflected in an *IS* schedule that had stabilized and was moving out to the right again. In the second half of 1958 and in 1959 investment demand recovered, and short-term interest rates increased (the *IS* schedule was now moving rapidly to the right).

The movements in the short-term interest rate were tracked to only a limited extent by movements of the long-term nominal rate of interest. (The *ALM* and the *LM* schedules did not always move together.) The sharp dip in the short-term rate in 1958 was seen as only temporary so the maturity premium actually rose to over 2 percent in mid-1958. The rise in the maturity premium in mid-1958 inhibited the recovery, although it did not reverse it.

The Fed had been surprised by the severity of the 1958 recession and as a result had eased monetary policy. Policymakers were then surprised by the strength of the recovery as GNP grew by 8.7 percent from the first quarter of 1958 to the first quarter of 1960. This recovery was certainly due in part to the easing of monetary policy, which lasted through mid-1959, and also by the turnaround in fiscal policy, but was surprisingly strong given the rather mild stimuli these policy shifts provided. The behavior of investment demand helps explain what happened. The changes in income generated large changes in investment demand; business and consumer confidence also played a role. When the economy went into the 1958 recession, confidence in future growth was eroded and investment fell, but then the Fed showed it was able to restore growth and avoid a really deep recession. This triggered a wave of optimism so investment picked up again quickly.

Even though inflation was low and falling, the Fed became concerned about a potential overheating of the economy as the recovery proceeded. A new contraction of the money supply began in mid-1959 and both short- and long-term interest rates went over 4 percent in late 1959 for the first time in the postwar period. The sharp increase in the short-term rate of interest was seen as temporary, however, so that the maturity premium actually went negative in the last quarter of 1959. [The *ALM* schedule stayed shifted out to the right as shown in Figure 13.8 by *ALM* (late 58/59)]. This helped to prolong the economic recovery a little. However, a second recession was on the way as high interest rates were combined with a renewed contractionary fiscal policy—the GNP peaked in the first quarter of 1960 and fell throughout the year. Figure 13.9 represents this period, one that is pretty much a replay of the 1956–1958 recession and recovery. As the Fed tightened monetary policy again, investment fell again. (The *IS* schedule shifted to the left.) This second recession involved large inventory reductions. Businesses had been investing in inventories as the economy expanded in 1958–59. They were caught by surprise when the Fed turned contractionary again so quickly and they suddenly had excess inventories. They cut production sharply in order to work off these excess inventories.

The fact that the economy fell into a second recession in 1960 had important political consequences. John F. Kennedy ran against Richard Nixon by linking him to the economic stagnation, since Nixon was vice president under Eisenhower, the president from 1952–1960. Kennedy pledged to get the country moving again and this theme helped him win the election. The Fed then

FIGURE 13.9   The Second Recession and Recovery, 1960–1962

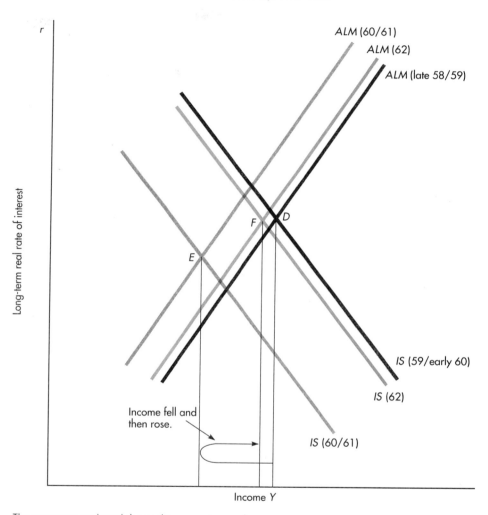

The economy replayed the earlier recession and recovery.

read those election results as a signal to shift toward a more expansionary policy regime. Fiscal policy turned expansionary also, as Kennedy kept another campaign pledge and raised military spending. People foresaw a period of stable short-term rates so there was a flat or even declining maturity premium [*ALM*(60/61) to *ALM*(62)]. The economic recovery that started in 1961 [shown as the shift *IS*(60/61) to *IS*(62)] began the long expansion that lasted until 1969.

The period 1956–62 provides some valuable lessons about the way the goods market and money market interact, in an economy with variable investment spending. Over this period, the combination of moderate monetary-policy changes by the Fed and small fiscal-policy changes were able to trigger fairly large changes in the level of income. These were accomplished with only small changes in interest rates. The *IS-ALM* analysis combined with the accelerator helps us understand how this happened—goods and financial market shifts (*IS* and *ALM* shifts) are taking place together. The tightening of monetary policy raised interest rates, but then aggregate demand contracted because of a cyclical drop in investment demand (the *IS* schedule shifted in), which caused interest rates to fall even though the Fed pursued a contractionary policy.

The variability of investment has fallen somewhat since the 1958–1962 recessions. Back in the 1950s, most business executives and other adults had vivid memories of the Great Depression. There were still substantial fears of a return to depression. When the economy started to turn down, this resulted in sharp declines in investment by businesses and reductions in purchases of durables and houses by families. No one wanted to be caught in a vulnerable economic situation. Another difference at that time is that inflation had not become ingrained in the system. People were not making much adjustment in nominal interest rates for inflation. Today, there are few economic decision makers who expect a return to the Great Depression. When a downturn starts, businesses will cut back, but they will keep some investment projects going, knowing that a recovery will come. Some firms are more concerned about domestic and international competition than they are about a short recession. Because investment demand is less volatile now than it was in the 50s and 60s (the *IS* schedule remains more stable), the Fed can only induce reductions in income with higher interest rates. Moreover, the Fed has to keep interest rates high for some time to establish its credibility.

In the next chapter we will look at additional sources of instability in the economy, starting with international trade and then looking at the dangers of financial crisis. One of the other differences between the economy today and the economy of the 1950s is that companies and families are much more willing to take on debt. When people saw the Great Depression around the corner, they did not want to be caught with a heavy load of fixed debt payments. Today many companies and families must use much of their current flow of income to service their debts.

SUMMARY

- The business cycle is described by a *peak*, the highest point reached before real GNP begins to turn down; a *recession*, when there is falling real GNP; a *trough*, the lowest point reached before GNP starts to turn up; and a *recovery*, where GNP is growing.

- Variability in aggregate demand in both the goods market and the financial market, due to domestic and international forces, contributes to the business cycle.

- The consumption standard of living is composed of household purchases of nondurable goods and services plus the flow of services provided by the existing stock of consumer-durable goods and houses.

- Consumers want to smooth consumption because they dislike large swings in the consumption standard of living. They are able to smooth consumption through borrowing, dissaving, and postponing capital purchases.

- Consumers form an expectation about their average or permanent income over their lifetimes. They set their normal or permanent level of consumption in relation to their permanent income.

- It is generally thought that consumption is smoothed because permanent income is more stable than year-to-year income. This idea has been questioned in recent research.

- Variability in the durable components of consumption and investment expenditure contributes to fluctuations in aggregate demand in the goods market.

- Because of variations in consumer expenditures on durables, together with variations in business investment, aggregate demand is subject to fluctuations in spite of the stabilizing effects of consumption smoothing.

- The stock of consumer-durable goods and houses along with the stock of businesses' equipment, inventories, and plant form the actual stock of capital.

- Businesses and households assess whether or not the size and composition of their actual stock of capital match their desired stock of capital.

- Consumer expenditures on durables and business investment (net additions to the capital stock) take place when the actual stock of capital is below the desired stock of capital.

- The accelerator model of investment demand assumes that investment demand depends upon the gap between actual stock and the desired stock of capital.

- In the accelerator model, an increase in current output and income increases the desired stock of capital. Since the actual capital stock was carried over from the past, there is a discrepancy between the actual capital stock and the desired capital stock. The attempts to close this gap led to a large fluctuation in investment demand.

- When the growth of income slows down, investment starts to decline before the economy goes into a recession.

- Because of the interaction between investment demand and aggregate demand (the accelerator and the multiplier), income will rise and fall following an initial disturbance. The path of income in the economy can trace out a cycle.

- Inventories are a part of investment demand, and they are influenced by expectations about future sales. Expectations can change quickly and inventory changes are observed to be even more volatile than investment in fixed capital.

- The adjustment of inventories following a shift in demand can also contribute to cycling (overshooting and undershooting equilibrium) of the economy around a new equilibrium.

- When economic conditions change, firms and households can respond by changing their desired capital–output ratio.

■ The flexible-accelerator model allows for a partial adjustment of the actual capital stock to a desired capital stock that is itself a moving target.

■ The desired capital–output ratio and thus the desired capital stock are affected by expectations and interest rates. These changes in the desired capital–output ratio and the desired capital stock lead to changes in the level of investment demand.

■ When interest rates are high and/or when expectations deteriorate, firms and households will economize on the amount of capital goods they require and they will postpone their expenditures on durable goods.

■ The amount of investment in one year affects how large a capital stock is carried over into the following year. Investment demand in the current year is affected by how much of the capital stock was carried forward.

■ Equilibrium in the goods market is affected by the size of the capital stock. Since the capital stock that is carried forward each year reflects the economic conditions that existed in previous years, goods-market equilibrium shifts around depending upon the past history of the economy.

KEY TERMS

accelerator

consumption smoothing

consumption standard of living

desired capital–output ratio

desired capital stock

durability

permanent income

permanent and transitory consumption

DISCUSSION QUESTIONS AND PROBLEMS

1. Reconcile the stability of the consumption standard of living with the variability in consumers' purchases of durable goods and housing.

2. How can consumers smooth their income? Why don't they equalize consumption under all circumstances?

3. Does permanent income refer to income which doesn't change?

4. What types of expenditures add to the stock of capital?

5. Can net investment be negative? If so, what is happening to the stock of capital? What are some of the economic conditions which could lead to negative investment?

6. List reasons why actual capital stock can differ from the desired stock of capital?

7. In the simple accelerator model, what is being assumed about the desired capital–output ratio? Describe which behavior of business managers and consumers leads you to believe that those assumptions should be relaxed?

8. How does the discrepancy between actual and desired capital stocks lead to cyclical patterns of income?

9. The capital stock is made up of durable goods which by their nature last from year to year. How does this durability contribute to variability in investment demand?

10. Why are changes in business inventories especially variable?

11. Consider an economy with the following investment equation:

$$I = 0.2[Y_{current\,year} - Y_{prior\,year}] + 500$$

Suppose income has been at 2,000 for several years and then increases to 2,500 and stays at the new level. Trace the pattern of investment over time.

12. Consider an economy with the following consumption function:

$$C = 800 + 0.6Y_{current\,year}$$

Investment is given by the relation shown in question 11. There is no government expenditure or foreign trade. If income is equal to 3,500 in year zero, find the level of income in year one and in subsequent years. Repeat your answer if income is 3,250 in year zero. Discuss your findings in relation to the results of Worked Example 13.3.

CHAPTER 14

Economic Fluctuations
The International Sector,
the Financial Sector,
and Stabilization Policy

INTRODUCTION

The sources of variability in the goods market are not limited to the demands generated by domestic consumption and investment. International trade also provides a potential source of instability or stability. In this chapter we ask how fluctuations in trade flows or the gyrations of currency and asset markets can spread instability across international borders. This discussion of net exports completes the private-sector components of demand in the goods market (C, I, and [X − IM] on the IS side) and so we turn next to a discussion of financial markets and the possible instability coming from the problems of financial intermediaries and the high levels of debt in the economy (the LM or ALM side).

We conclude the chapter by examining stabilization policy. We have, of course, already evaluated the effectiveness of monetary and fiscal policies in changing the level of output and income, but we look here at some of the problems that arise when policymakers try to stabilize an economy that is prone to irregular business-cycle fluctuations. There are important lags involved in both selecting and implementing stabilization policies. These lags may weaken the usefulness of policies that otherwise look effective when analyzed as one-time events. It is hard for policymakers to know whether the economy needs stimulus, restraint, or neither, and to act on that knowledge in a timely fashion. They may make the wrong decisions and make things worse.

Finally we look at a simple test of stabilization policies. Did the economy become more stable after active stabilization policies were introduced and, if so, were the policies responsible?

INTERNATIONAL SOURCES OF FLUCTUATIONS

We look at three ways in which the international economy can affect income and interest rates here at home. Income changes overseas will alter the demand for U.S. exports. When interest rates overseas shift, interest rates here will change too. When a financial crisis occurs domestically or overseas, the transmission of the crisis through international financial markets may exacerbate the crisis, because shifts in international financial markets may affect confidence and have consequences for the interest-rate gap and investment.

Export Demand and Foreign Income

As we saw in Chapters 11 and 12, there can be a direct effect of foreign income on domestic U.S. income. A fall in income, in the rest of the world will reduce domestic exports and hence reduce the level of aggregate demand here in the United States. A recession overseas can lead to a fall in domestic income. This direct effect was important in the Great Depression, especially among European economies. The dramatic falls in income in several countries meant that the demand for imports fell, so that exports fell in the countries that had been selling to them. Income cycled down along with imports, which further drove down income in exporting countries. The reduction in the volume of trade was exacerbated by the fact that countries that suffered a loss of income attempted to improve their trade balances by raising tariffs and quotas.[1]

In the United States in modern times, the possibility of a recession that is induced primarily by a trade war is not very high. There is more cooperation among the major trading countries than was the case in the 1930s, and, in any case, the large size of the U.S. economy makes most countries reluctant to engage in a trade war with the United States.

The international sector has had an important influence on the U.S. business cycle in the 1980s and 1990s, however. The large trade deficit that developed through 1987 helped to reduce aggregate demand, offsetting the fiscal expansion. And the gradual reduction in the trade deficit since 1987 has provided a net stimulus to demand. The economic recovery of the 1980s has been prolonged partly by the expansion of foreign demand.

---

[1] Charles P. Kindleberger, *The World in Depression, 1929–39* (Berkeley: University of California Press, 1973); Philip Friedman, "The Welfare Costs of Bilateralism: German–Hungarian Trade, 1933–1938," *Explorations in Economic History* 13, no. 2 (January 1976), pp. 113–25.

Foreign Interest Rates

As well as the impact of foreign demand on U.S. exports, there is also an international spillover of interest rates. Rising interest rates overseas will pull up U.S. rates as financial investors sell their U.S. assets and purchase foreign assets. This international spillover could conceivably be enough to cause a U.S. recession. If there were contractionary monetary policies in many large foreign countries at once, this would drive up foreign rates and could possibly drive up U.S. rates enough to cause a recession. We do not take that possibility terribly seriously, however, for the following reasons.

1. There is no evidence that we know of that a rise in foreign interest rates has ever brought on a U.S. recession. We may eat those words some time in the future, but until then the experience of the past suggests that the event is unlikely.

2. When foreign central banks are raising interest rates, this is usually in order to restrain a boom that threatens to increase inflation. High overseas interest rates that raise U.S. rates and reduce income here at home will usually coincide with times when foreign income is high and foreign demand for U.S. products is strong.

3. Rising overseas interest rates will lower the exchange rate of the U.S. dollar and increase U.S. exports.

This discussion of the effect of foreign interest rates also has implications for the analysis of export demand and foreign income. When there is a recession in Europe, this will usually mean that European interest rates are low. These low rates will help keep U.S. rates down and thus help to sustain investment demand here. This offsets the fact that the demand for U.S. goods will be weak.

Our conclusion from this discussion of the direct effects of foreign income on the one hand and interest rates on the other on the level of aggregate demand in the United States, therefore, is that they are not large to begin with and they are likely to be offsetting.

Shocks to International Confidence

speculative boom or bust
A situation in which people buy an asset in the expectation that its price will increase. Such a boom can turn into a "bubble" where prices rise rapidly and then collapse. The expectation of further price increases fuels the price rise and then the bubble bursts. This is where the boom becomes a "bust."

Gyrations in stock markets can occur rather easily when irrational **speculative booms or busts** overwhelm more rational investing. And these gyrations may spread from one country to another. Suppose there is a stock-market investor who understands the fundamental determinants of corporate profits and he knows that these fundamentals have not changed in Tokyo or Bonn as result of the fall in the U.S. stock market. Does he quickly rush into these markets to buy when stock prices start to fall? Not necessarily. He knows that there are many investors who have suddenly lost confidence and are selling stocks. As long as bears (investors and traders who expect market prices to decline in the future) are in control of the market, the knowledgeable investor will sell or at least stay out. Speculative movements in stock markets can build their own momentum as prices fall and people come to expect further falls. Bubbles and panics can generate self-fulfilling prophecies in these markets, just as they do in foreign-exchange markets.

Fluctuations in stock markets can spread around the world, but these fluctuations do not generally result in big changes in business investment as a result. The U.S. economy did not suffer any major ill effects from the drop in stock prices in 1987, and gradually prices recovered, while markets in other countries recovered more quickly. The rational investor does not buy immediately in the face of a general wave of selling, but at some point prices will have fallen far enough below their fundamental valuations that bargain hunting takes over and the downward slide is halted and reversed.

Business investment is not very sensitive to short-run changes in the stock market and neither is consumer expenditure. The variations in confidence are enough to give great volatility to stock markets—just as is the case in foreign-exchange markets—but this is because speculative financial investment decisions are made differently. For a speculator, there is great potential profit or loss to be realized by guessing what other people think is going to happen to share prices. The same is not true for business investment, which is based on longer-term considerations. We have not seen the effects of the international transmission of confidence become a major factor in determining the level of income in recent years. However, at one time losses of international confidence did contribute to the business cycle and they may do so once again.

The transmission of international financial crises

During the Great Depression of the 1930s, economic depression spread around the world. Partly this was the result of protectionist trade policies and the direct effects of income on trade. But there was also a role played by financial markets in the international transmission of the crisis. As information about the U.S. stock-market crash, the fall in income and employment, and the bankruptcies of companies and banks spread around the world, it generated a fundamental erosion of confidence that hurt investment demand, foreign stock markets, and then the level of income in other countries. At that time, the international spillovers were more important than they were in recent times. However, there is some fear that an internationally transmitted financial crisis that could cause a recession or worse may reemerge in the 1990s. How would such an internationally based financial crisis affect the U.S. economy?

During the 1980s, the United States had experienced a huge capital inflow that balanced its trade deficits. The capital inflow has taken the form of large stocks of U.S. debt being held by foreign investors, especially investors in Great Britain, Japan, and Germany. A domestic financial crisis that started in any of those major economies could cause foreign holders of U.S. securities to sell off their holdings quickly in the rush to gain liquidity. Since the foreign

BLACK MONDAY: A STOCK MARKET CRASH WITH INTERNATIONAL DIMENSIONS

In October 1987 the Dow-Jones Industrials plummeted 508 points, or more than 22 percent. Some other stock market indexes plunged by even more. By any measure this was the greatest stock market crash in the United States since the October 1929 crash that heralded the Great Depression. However, unlike 1929, the 1987 calamity did not seem to spread to the rest of the economy. The unemployment increase was confined to Wall Street.

Both prior to and after the 1987 crash, there were no fundamental shifts in the economy or in corporate performance. Rather, the crash reflected a change in the psychology of the stock market. It also was influenced by the advent of programmed trading, where computer programs trigger additional sales once the stock market starts to fall.

There are several reasons why the stock market is vulnerable to panics of this kind. Among the elements contributing to the October 1987 crisis are the twin U.S. trade and budget deficits. As the largest debtor nation in the world, the United States has been relying more and more on the influx of foreign capital. Foreigners make loans and investments in the United States in several ways. They buy corporate and government securities, short-term money market instruments, and plain vanilla bank deposits. They also purchase American firms such as Goodyear Tire and Rubber Company, a form of direct investment. The latter kind of investment has accelerated in recent years.

Whether they own real assets, such as factories or firms, or financial assets, such as bonds and stocks, foreign owners will eventually have to be paid dividends and interest. In real economic terms,

Americans will have to sacrifice by consuming fewer foreign goods and selling more of their own. In part, such a process is eased when the international value of the dollar falls, making U.S. goods cheaper to foreigners and foreign goods more expensive to Americans.

Immediately prior to the 1987 U.S. stock market crash, the international value of the dollar was indeed falling. From January 1987 to October 1987 the value of the dollar in relation to the Japanese yen fell from 154.83 yen to 143.32 yen per dollar, on the way to 128.24 yen per dollar by the end of 1987. Unfortunately, a rapidly falling dollar has negative consequences for our foreign creditors. The assets held by foreigners (our liabilities) depreciate in dollar value as the dollar sinks. Upon sale, when Japanese investors convert the value of such assets to their home currency, they end up with fewer yen than they originally expected to gain from their U.S. investments.

Subscribing to this scenario, some people believe that the massive withdrawal of Japanese investors from U.S. equities triggered the October 1987 U.S. stock market crash. A contributing factor might have been the sudden belief that the United States might not be able to make the dividend and interest payments that investors expected in the future. One thing is clear: the world's financial markets have become more and more interdependent during the 1970s and 80s. The day after the American stock market crashed in October 1987, the Japanese stock market followed suit. Financial crisis in one major exchange can spread quickly around the world.

investor who has sold a U.S. T bill still needs to convert dollars to foreign exchange, the sell-off would cause a *run on the dollar*. In the international community, financial markets would experience a loss of confidence in the ability or willingness of the U.S. Treasury to repay its obligations. Explicit failure to repay would be quite unlikely. However, because a financial crisis could lead to unanticipated increases in the inflation rate and/or unanticipated reductions in the real exchange rate, failure to repay in dollars that have maintained their value would be quite likely. The sell-off of U.S. securities by foreign holders could cause a rapid removal of financial capital from the U.S. economy. The resulting increase in U.S. interest rates, along with a possible reduction in the availability of credit, could trigger a serious recession. While we have not returned to the financial fragility of the 1930s, the debt problems of the U.S. economy coupled with the high level of U.S. foreign borrowing have probably heightened the potential for instability. We now examine this issue more closely.

FINANCIAL MARKETS AND ECONOMIC FLUCTUATIONS

financial crisis
A financial crisis occurs when there is a sudden drop in the availability of funds from financial institutions.

Shifts in financial markets have contributed substantially to fluctuations in the U.S. economy. Changes in financial-market conditions can affect wealth and consumption, the cost of capital, investment demand, and expectations. Financial-market contractions have the combined effect of raising interest rates and reducing the supply of credit available to borrowers. Such a contraction can occur endogenously within the economy (i.e., stock-market crashes, banking panics, and credit crunches) or the contraction can stem from policy actions engineered by the Fed. The Fed can bring on a sharp contraction in the economy by contracting the real stock of money—raising interest rates and reducing the supply of loans available from depository institutions. Such a policy was used in 1974–75 and again in the early 1980s. Of course, the Fed induced those recessions in order to deal with inflation. The Fed's bringing on a deep recession as a result of its anti-inflationary policies is one type of **financial crisis** that contributes to economic fluctuations. A financial crisis occurs when there is a sudden drop in the availability of funds from financial institutions. This may occur when the Fed is reducing bank reserves rapidly, so that the banks are in danger of failing to meet their reserve requirements. Banks cut back sharply on new loans. A crisis may also occur when there is a loss of confidence in financial intermediaries so that depositors withdraw funds, once again forcing the institutions to make sharp cuts in lending. Finally, a credit crisis can occur if the financial intermediaries lose confidence in the firms or individuals they are lending to. They fear a rise in the default rate and so they cut back on lending.[2]

The impact of a financial-market crisis upon aggregate demand is heightened when there is an erosion in expectations—a loss of business confidence. As businesses revise downward their evaluations of the flows of revenue from investment projects and revise upward their estimates of the risks and costs of investment projects, the result is a drop in the demand for capital

---

[2] This section draws on Robert J. Gordon, ed., *The American Business Cycle: Continuity and Change* (Chicago: University of Chicago Press for the NBER, 1986); and Victor Zarnowitz, "Fact and Factors in the Recent Evolution of Business Cycles in the United States," NBER Working Paper no. 2865 (February 1989).

goods that reduces aggregate demand. As future business prospects worsen, the expected returns to investment projects deteriorate. Moreover, when stock prices fall, the cost of capital rises directly—firms generate less capital per unit of equity issued on the market. In such a crisis, where falling expectations are coupled with a rise in the cost of capital, the present discounted value of capital investment shrinks as expected future revenues fall and the discount rate rises.

Financial-Market Aspects of a Loss of Business Confidence

In the absence of any Federal Reserve policy changes, a loss of business confidence can contribute to a financial-market crisis even though there was no explicit reduction in the supply of credit made available by financial intermediaries.

Business managers expect to get higher rates of return on investments in real capital assets (new plant or equipment or real estate) than they could have gotten on safe financial investments, such as government bonds. A loss of confidence in the returns expected from real capital investment (a higher probability of loss on investment projects or a greater chance of default on bonds) increases the risk premium associated with those investments. We have seen that there is a gap between the interest rate on short-term nominal assets such as T bills and the rate of return required by businesses in order to invest in real capital assets. This gap depends upon expectations about inflation and about the future path of interest rates. But this gap also depends upon the riskiness of the investment, and the riskiness of investment reflects businesses' expectations about future returns. *When there is a general loss of business confidence, the increased risk of investment raises the long-term real rate of interest relative to the short-term nominal rate of interest in the money market.* We have shown such a change as an upward shift in the *ALM* schedule for any given *LM* schedule, a shift that has an adverse effect on income.

In Figure 14.1 we show how a loss of business confidence results in a change in the interest-rate gap. Pessimistic expectations and the increase in the long-term real rate of interest initiate a downtrend in income, bringing about a recession. The economy is shown initially in equilibrium at points A in both the left and the right panels of the figure. (Income is at Y_A, the long-term real rate of interest is at r_A, and the short-term nominal rate of interest is at i_A.) The *ALM* schedule is shown below the *LM* schedule initially, as the expected rate of inflation more than offsets the maturity premium.

There is then a loss of confidence and an increase in the risk premium. This is shown as an upward shift in the *ALM* schedule to *ALM'*. It moves well above the *LM* schedule as the interest rate on long-term private-sector financial assets rises sharply relative to the interest rate on T bills. The shift in the *ALM* schedule to *ALM'* is also shown in the right-hand panel of Figure 14.1. The economy experiences a decline in income, shown as the shift from

FIGURE 14.1 The Effect of a Loss of Business Confidence

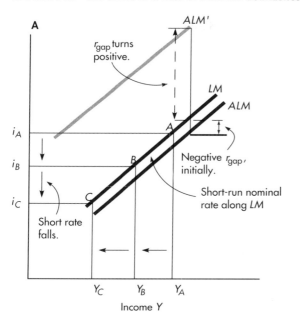

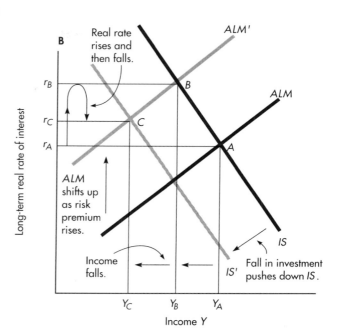

An increase in the risk premium pushes the *ALM* schedule up to the left.

point *A* to point *B*. The long-term real rate of interest is higher (increasing from r_A to r_B) as a result of the loss of confidence.

The fall in income from Y_A to Y_B is also shown in the left-hand panel of Figure 14.1. As income falls, the T-bill rate declines (the decrease from i_A to i_B). The decrease in the T-bill rate has occurred because of the fall in income, which has reduced the transactions demand for money.

Income fell because of the loss of confidence in the economy, but recall that our analysis of the flexible accelerator indicated that investment demand will decline as a result of the initial fall in income, leading to a further fall in income. Though the recession was initiated by a reduction in aggregate demand stemming from the financial market, the cycle is exacerbated by an accelerator reaction in the goods market. The effect of the change in income on investment demand is shown in the figure as a shift from *IS* to *IS'*, leading to a further decline of income to Y_C. The long-term real rate of interest and the short-term nominal interest rate then both decline—to r_C and to i_C, respectively.

The change in the interest-rate gap described in this section was apparent in the Great Depression of the 1930s. The T-bill rate was about one half of

1 percent while the interest rate on Baa bonds was 7.8 percent. This difference of over 7 percentage points between the two nominal interest rates compares with a typical difference of 2 to 4 percentage points.[3] The change in the T-bill rate relative to the long-term *real* rate of interest in the Great Depression was even larger. Prices had been falling from 1929 to 1933, so the expected rate of inflation was low or even negative.

The Great Depression was an extreme case, but it is common in even more moderate recessions for the interest-rate gap to change when there is increased uncertainty in the economy. For example, the difference between the T-bill rate and the Baa rate widened to 5½ percentage points during the 1982 recession.

We have been considering how a financial crisis, through a loss of confidence, increases the long-term real rate of interest. The financial crunch in the case we described did not result either from a Fed policy change or from a crisis in the financial intermediaries themselves. It came from a change in expectations and a rise in the cost of capital. That scenario is quite different from a financial-market crisis where the supply of money and credit is contracted directly.

If the Fed initiates a contraction, it sells T bills to reduce the money supply, thereby contracting bank loans and driving up the short-term rate of interest. Yet, severe financial-market crises can occur even without Fed action, when there is a sizable reduction in the supply of credit made available by financial intermediaries.[4]

Financial Crises and the Supply of Credit

If financial intermediaries either are forced to reduce credit because of large withdrawals of funds or choose to do so because they reassess the risks of lending, then there is a rise in nominal and real interest rates coupled with a reduction in the quantity of credit available to borrowers. With the reduction in bank loans, many firms and consumers search for credit elsewhere; they pay a higher rate of interest if they can secure borrowed funds, or they are forced to reduce expenditures if they cannot. Banking panics and credit crunches that contributed to declines in aggregate demand and income have been part of the story of business-cycle fluctuations in the United States since the 19th century.

Bank failures and panics, 1873–1933

In their monetary history of the United States, Milton Friedman and Anna Schwartz identify the downturns of 1873, 1884, 1890, 1893, and 1907 as banking

---

[3] These figures probably understate the true widening of the gap between rates that took place in the 1930s because many bonds had their ratings downgraded.

[4] Ben Bernanke and Mark Gertler, "Agency Costs, Net Worth, and Business Fluctuations," *American Economic Review* 79 (March 1989), pp. 14–31.

banking panic
Widespread occurrence of **bank runs,** where the rush to withdraw funds from one bank turns into a general withdrawal of funds from all banks, causing large numbers of **bank failures** and a rapid reduction in the supply of money and credit.

panics.[5] There were **banking panics,** when banks refused to convert demand deposits into currency. People lost confidence in the banks and refused to deposit funds in them.

Prior to the creation of the Federal Reserve, bankers voluntarily held reserves. Yet, the profit motives of banks caused them to minimize reserves and maximize loans. Most banks were managed by prudent bankers who held levels of reserves so that the risk of running out of reserves was small. Unfortunately, a small number of "wild cat" banks (banks that attracted deposits and expanded loans without regard to the need for holding reserves or the need for prudent credit creation) contributed to a great deal of financial instability. Further, even if all banks had been well run, the absence of a system to increase reserves quickly in the face of sudden withdrawals meant that the banking system was subject to considerable instability. The economy was subject to repeated banking panics. If depositors feared that withdrawal demands could not be met, they would rush to take out their money, but since banks held only a fraction of their demand-deposit liabilities in the form of reserves, the rush to withdraw funds would create a self-fulfilling prophecy. Thinking that a bank could not meet its obligations caused people to take out funds, which caused a bank not to be able to meet all its obligations. This rush to withdraw further exacerbated the bank's position. The rush to take out funds from an individual bank is called a bank run. A run on an individual bank may be an isolated event. However, if many banks are unable to meet the needs of depositors who want to withdraw funds, then the run on a handful of banks would turn into a *panic*, with large numbers of banks failing. *Bank panics have the effect of rapidly reducing the money supply because the general public shifts from demand deposits to cash—taking reserves out of the banking system.*

The reduction of the money supply brought on by the banking panic reduces the availability of credit, drives up interest rates, drives down investment expenditures, and pushes the economy into recession. Friedman and Schwartz point to the banking panics that occurred during 1930 and 1931 as having exacerbated the Great Depression. During the 1930s, the economy suffered from a two-sided financial crisis—there was a loss of business confidence that reduced the demand for capital investment expenditures and banking panics that reduced the supply of money and credit. The combination of tight money caused by bank failures and increased business risks pushed the economy into the Great Depression, a period of unprecedented reductions in aggregate and income.

The Federal Reserve can prevent bank panics by supplying reserves to banks that are experiencing a run, but historically the Fed has not always

---

[5] Milton Friedman and Anna J. Schwartz, "Money and Business Cycles," *Review of Economics and Statistics: Supplement* 45 (February 1963), pp. 32–64; and *A Monetary History of the United States: Estimates Sources and Methods* (New York: NBER, 1963).

■ Deposit Insurance Prevents Bank Panics

The major reason panics no longer occur is that modern banks have their deposits insured by government-based deposit insurance. *Deposit insurance* convinces the public that their deposits are safe so they should see no reason to rush to a bank and withdraw funds at the slightest hint of a banking problem. In 1933, after the banking crisis, Congress established the Federal Deposit Insurance Corporation, which currently insures deposits of up to $100,000 in commercial banks as well as in S&Ls. Most small depositors are completely covered. Even larger depositors are fairly safe, because the FDIC usually works to find a healthy bank willing to buy a failed bank and honor depositors' claims. Nevertheless, very big depositors will run from a bank in trouble. Because runs and bank closings are rare, the insurance funds do not have to hold enough funds to cover all or even most bank liabilities. Bank failures still occur, and they increased in frequency during the deregulated 1980s, especially among S&Ls. But they did not turn into panics. Banks do not hold large excess reserves because they do not see bank panics as likely within the current system. Bankers do not guard against panics by holding excess reserves because they are convinced that deposit insurance has removed the threat of panic.

As a result of increased bank failures in the last few years, the reserves set aside by the FDIC have been exhausted. Some people are concerned that this will undermine the stability of the banking system. However, it seems clear that the federal government will use general tax revenues to make up for any shortfall in FDIC reserves.

done this. During the Great Depression there were runs on thousands of banks while the Fed waited for the crisis to pass.

Dealing with bank panics that have already started by providing borrowed reserves in a crisis is one way of dealing with the problem. But a better policy would prevent the panics from occurring in the first place. Insuring bank deposits against losses due to bank failures almost eliminates the rationale to withdraw funds from a troubled bank. There were 635 commercial bank failures from 1921 to 1929 and 2,274 between 1930 and 1933. Since the 1930s, there have been no bank crises for many years and the Federal Deposit Insurance Corporation (FDIC) is generally credited with having successfully reduced bank instability.

The Great Depression led to a large reduction in private debt and very conservative financial strategies by banks and other financial institutions. World War II led to a great increase in government-budget deficits and consequently the issuance of large amounts of government bonds. Banks and other institutions decided to hold large fractions of their portfolios in government debt and to avoid stocks and risky bonds. Commercial banks made conservative business loans and S&Ls used real estate to give collateral for conservative mortgage loans. As a result of the salutary lessons from the 1930s, there were no crises in the banks or other financial intermediaries from 1945 until 1966. But crises caused by reductions in the supply of credit did not cease to affect the economy. What changed was that the crises were no longer generated by a withdrawal of bank deposits. From 1966 to 1982 there were mild financial crises because the Fed started to use a more active monetary policy to control inflation. And in the past few years there has been concern that excessive borrowing has raised the possibility of a major financial crisis in the 1990s.

Credit crunches, 1966–1982

credit crunch
A mild financial crisis where there is a sharp reduction in the supply of credit that raises interests rates and reduces access to funds.

A **credit crunch** is a mild financial crisis. It can occur separately from a Fed contraction or as a result of Fed policy. A credit crunch generally involves increases in interest rates, together with a reduction in the availability of credit. Whether or not a credit crunch causes a real economic downturn depends upon the severity of the crunch and the availability of alternative sources of funds. First, we look at how a credit crunch develops and then we look at its impact on the economy.

In 1966 short-term nominal interest rates rose above the levels of previous years. Because the interest rates that banks could offer depositors were restricted by Fed regulation, the rise in market rates sparked a credit crunch. Because they had a competitive disadvantage (being regulated in a high–interest-rate environment), banks were unable to act as intermediaries for those funds. The lower risks and added convenience that banks offered depositors were overwhelmed by the higher returns available elsewhere. Banks suffered from **disintermediation**—depositors' withdrawals of funds in order to purchase higher-yielding financial-market securities. As savers looked for higher returns outside of banks, the flow of funds to banks fell along with the amount of funds that banks could make available for loans. The flow of bank credit to nonfinancial corporations fell by about 40 percent in the second half of 1966. Monetary policy had also become restrictive and the growth rate of the money supply fell sharply.

disintermediation
Withdrawals of funds from financial intermediaries and into direct investments such as financial-market assets. Also used to refer to the withdrawal of funds from banks and S&Ls in the 1960s and 1970s when interest rates on savings accounts were controlled. Funds were withdrawn from controlled accounts and put into other financial intermediaries.

There was not a major downturn in the economy at that time since the funds that were being withdrawn from banks were still available through other financial institutions. However, mortgages and the housing market were affected because at that time most mortgages originated at savings banks.

Following 1966, there were four credit crises or crunches occurring in 1969–1970, 1973–1974, 1978–1980, and 1981–82. In each of these financial crises, the Fed was following a contractionary policy during which a crisis was triggered by a particular shock: The Penn Central railroad went broke in 1970, and the Franklin National bank became insolvent in 1974. In 1980, the First Pennsylvania bank had problems, there was turmoil in the silver market and, for a brief period, the Fed introduced specific restrictions on bank lending. In 1982 there were bank failures, partly associated with energy-related loans, and concerns about the effect of loan defaults by less-developed countries. These financial crises were triggered by a loss of confidence in financial institutions.

The postwar credit crunches have sometimes but not always been associated with downturns in output. One typical pattern of a credit crunch is that a business expansion is associated with increased demands for borrowed funds by business for fixed investment and to finance increases in inventories. Then banks find their default rate rising on loans and they become more cautious in their lending strategies. This is particularly the case when the collateral is risky, as it is for loans to finance inventory. Businesses find it difficult to obtain loans from their usual lenders, while alternative sources of funds demand higher interest rates. They decide to cut production to reduce inventory and increase cash flow. If the Fed engages in restrictive monetary policy, this exacerbates the crunch.

The effect of the credit crunches has usually been to reduce investment and real output. Credit crunches can play an important role in the cycle of inventory investment that we described earlier, but this is not always the case. There were financial crises in the 1980s that did not slow the economy significantly. For example, the problems of the Continental Illinois bank in 1984 and the run on state-insured S&Ls in Ohio in 1985 had little effect. The collapse of the stock market in October 1987 did not bring on a recession either, with many observers crediting the Fed's short-run expansion of the money supply and the bail-out efforts of the federal regulators with preventing a crunch. Just as a temporary spike in short-run interest rates fails to trigger a recession because the impact is not transmitted to long-term real rates, a short-term crisis of confidence does not necessarily lead to a recession because real investment expenditures are not immediately affected and, if the loss of confidence passes quickly, income and output are maintained. Furthermore, if the Fed offsets the impact of a financial crisis with expansionary monetary policies, the crisis will fail to lead to recession. If, on the other hand, it is the Fed that is driving the credit crunch with the aim of reducing output, then a recession is much more likely.

Fears of a Major Financial Crisis in the 1990s

A short-term loss of confidence does not necessarily lead to a recession. But a widespread collapse of confidence could certainly bring on a downturn. There has been increasing concern that the U.S. economy has built up an excessive level of debt that threatens to initiate a financial crisis serious enough to affect output and employment. The savings-and-loan industry is going through an agonizing restructuring in which major bankruptcies are common-place. Major commercial banks and other financial institutions hold loans made to developing countries in Latin America and elsewhere that are now in default. Is the economy threatened by the kind of instability experienced in the Great Depression?

An important difference between the 1930s and the 1990s is that the federal government insures commercial banks and savings and loans through the FDIC. This protects depositors and reduces the chance of sudden mass withdrawal of deposits when there is a threat of bankruptcy. But if the federal government stands behind the banks, who stands behind the federal government? The huge federal-budget deficits of recent years have created some popular concern that even the U.S. federal government might default on its obligations. The threat of default by the federal government is probably not realistic, but the fears of serious financial crisis look much more realistic when we consider the massive increase in corporate debt that has taken place.

Corporate debt, leveraged buyouts, and junk bonds

Concerns about financial instability are not limited to the banks and the federal government. During the 1980s corporate indebtedness increased substantially. Financial restructuring of firms had been underway throughout the period. There was a wave of corporate **leveraged buyouts** (LBOs) where firms repurchased their outstanding equity by issuing large quantities of debt. Even companies that were not directly involved in buyouts or takeovers underwent major restructurings and took on large increases in debt in order to discourage takeovers. Financial innovations such as the marketing of collections of high-interest, high-risk **junk bonds** had facilitated a transformation of corporate capitalization from the use of equity shares to the use of debt. This debt had been successfully sold on two premises. The first is that a portfolio of junk bonds has lower risk than any single junk bond issue because of risk pooling. Failure for one firm will be balanced out by success for another firm. The second premise is that corporate profits in general would continue to rise and that the increased interest payments would be financed out of cash flow. For those investors who accepted these premises, junk bonds offered high returns and reasonable risks. Aggressive banks and wealthy individuals bought many of them.

While the portfolio argument for junk bonds is valid, general business conditions can turn negative for all firms, so that instead of independent risks that are reduced by pooling, a portfolio composed largely of junk bonds is particularly vulnerable to a general economic downturn. A severe recession could strain the ability of corporations to cover their liabilities.

In the 1980s, the rise in corporate debt entailed paying out a larger fraction of cash flow in interest payments. This forces a kind of "backs-to-the-wall" management cycle. One view argues that this will lead to a deterioration in economic performance because it encourages short-term decision making and discourages long-term investments and R&D. A more positive view holds that when corporate managers finance expansion with retained earnings, they are prone to pursue their own interests rather than serving the interests of the shareholders. The increased levels of corporate debt encourage managers to become more efficient and to pursue shareholders' interests.[6] While

leveraged buyouts (LBOs)
Firms repurchase their outstanding equity by issuing large quantities of debt borrowed with the company's own assets as collateral. The companies become private rather than publicly held companies.

junk bonds
High-interest, high-risk corporate debt often used to finance a **leveraged buyout** (LBO).

---

[6] Michael C. Jensen, "Takeovers, Their Causes and Consequences," *Journal of Economic Perspectives* 2 (Winter 1988); and Martin Neil Baily and Margaret Blair, "Productivity and American Management," in *American Living Standards: Threats and Challenges,* ed. Robert E. Litan and Robert Z. Lawrence (Washington, D.C.: Brookings Institution, 1988).

it is still uncertain what the final verdict will be on the wave of corporate restructuring that took place in the 1980s, the rising levels of corporate debts have increased uncertainty about financial stability in the 1990s.

Households in the 1980s and 1990s have also added to the growth of indebtedness and to the perceptions that the financial sector has become less stable. Consumer borrowing has increased along with a rise in the number of personal bankruptcies.

Have government, business, and households all gone on a borrowing spree and banks on a lending spree that could lead to a wholesale collapse of the financial sector? Or are the fears all overblown? So far the financial markets have remained quite stable and the threats to stability are not as severe as feared. The fact that borrowing has gone up may or may not indicate a greater danger of financial crisis. We need to assess how large the increase in borrowing has been and whether or not there has been an increase in the risks associated with borrowing.

Assessing excessive indebtedness

Borrowing becomes excessive when the size of debt is so much larger than income that interest payments claim a significant portion of income. In the United States, has the ratio of debt to income risen to dangerous levels? Data presented by Robert Litan from government sources (Figure 14.2) show the ratio of debt to GNP for business, government, and households and for total debt.[7] It shows that from 1950 to 1980, the ratio of total debt to GNP remained fairly flat at about 1.25. This was the result of a slight up trend in household and business debt and a slight down trend in government debt. After 1980, the trend in total debt shifted abruptly. Household and business debt continued to rise faster than GNP, but government debt reversed its trend and started to rise also. The result was the sharp upward shift that is evident in the ratio of total debt to GNP reaching 1.75 by 1987.

The federal deficits of the 1980s are showing up in the form of an increased debt-to-income ratio, but it is notable that *the ratio of government debt to GNP at the end of the 1980s was still well below the level that existed in 1950.* Even if the federal deficits continue for a number of years, they will not raise the ratio of government debt to income above the range it has had during the post-World War II period. The danger from the federal deficit is not that the government will go broke; rather, it is that the federal deficit is absorbing national saving, thereby reducing domestic investment leading to negative net foreign investment and thereby reducing future living standards.

The most plausible scenario for a serious financial crisis is that a wave of bankruptcies will strike businesses, households, or banks. How likely is this? Figure 14.2 shows the debt-to-GNP ratio, but the increase in private

---

[7] Robert E. Litan, "The Risks of Recession," in *American Living Standards: Threats and Challenges,* ed. Robert E. Litan, Robert Z. Lawrence, and Charles Schultze (Washington, D.C.: Brookings Institution, 1988).

FIGURE 14.2   Ratio of Credit-Market Debt to GNP (nominal) for Households, Businesses, and Government, 1950–1987

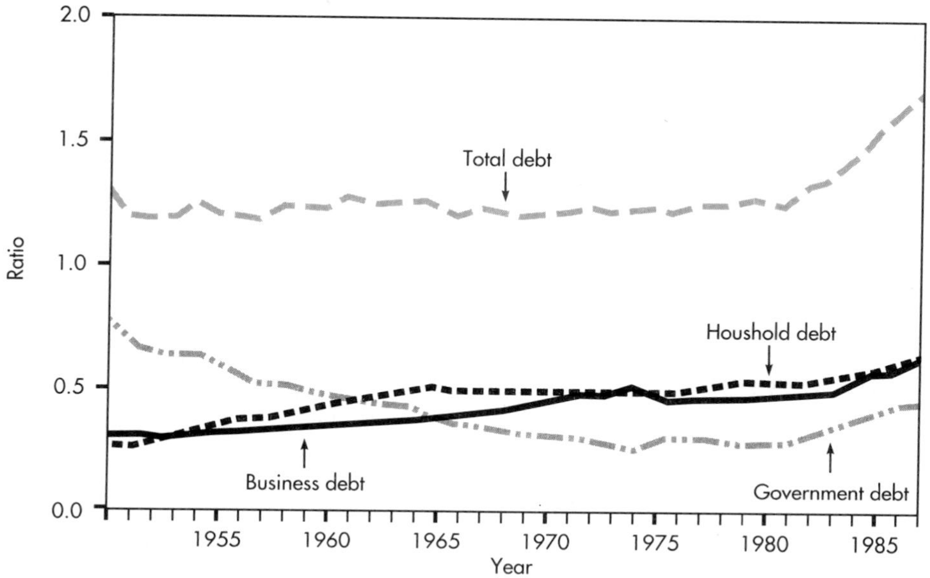

Sources: Board of Governors of the Federal Reserve System, *Balance Sheets for the U.S. Economy, 1948–87* (Washington, D.C., April 1988), pp. 11–15, 16–20, 21–25, and *Flow of Funds Accounts: Financial Assets and Liabilities Year-End, 1963–86,* pp. 3–4; and *Economic Report of the President* (Washington, D.C.: U.S. Government Printing Office, February 1988), p. 260.

borrowing relative to GNP shown in the figure might be appropriate if assets had risen in line with borrowing. Insolvency will occur when there is a fall in asset values that pushes them below the value of liabilities. How close are private borrowers to insolvency? Figure 14.3 shows the ratio of assets to liabilities for nonfinancial corporations and households. It indicates that the ratio of debt to asset values has indeed risen as the debt-to-GNP ratio has risen, particularly for corporations. There is less of a margin of asset values over debt than there used to be.

The asset values used to construct Figure 14.3 reflect the historical cost of purchasing the factories, autos, and houses that provide the collateral for the loans. In the case of corporations, it is possible to use an alternative measure of solvency, the ratio of debt to equity. Figure 14.4 gives the debt–equity ratio for nonfinancial corporations using the market values of both numerator and denominator. The figure shows some upward movement of the debt–equity ratio taking place in the 1970s and then a decline in the 1980s. The ratio is affected primarily by movements in stock prices. The stock market did poorly in the 1970s, particularly in 1974, and has done

FIGURE 14.3.   Nonfinancial-Business and Household Ratios of Total Liabilities to Total Assets, 1948–1987

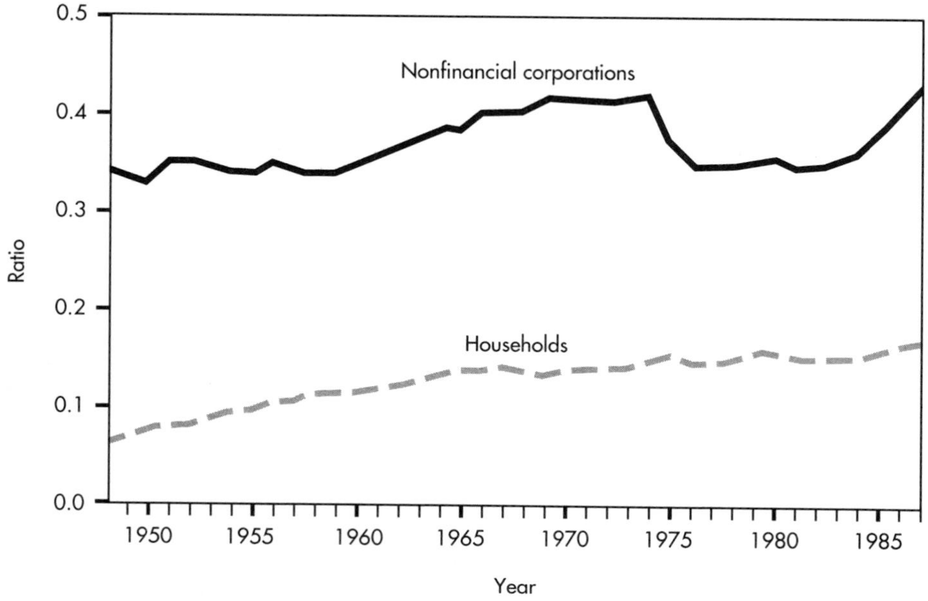

Source: Federal Reserve, Balance Sheets for the U.S. Economy, 1948–87, pp. 11–15, 21–25.

much better in the 1980s, even accounting for the 1987 crash. Using market values, therefore, suggests that the increases in indebtedness in the 1980s were perhaps not an unreasonable response by business to the increased market assessment of the value of their assets.

As a final indicator of the likelihood of financial crisis for households and nonfinancial businesses, we show in Figure 14.5 the ratio of the interest burden to income for households and businesses. This gives a measure of the ability of these groups to service the debt they have acquired. The figure does give some reason for concern. The fact that nominal interest rates have risen over the postwar period means that the debt-service ratio has risen faster than the debt-to-income ratio. The trend for business debt is striking, showing an increase in interest payments from less than 10 percent of cash flow to almost 40 percent. In a 1988 study of corporate indebtedness, Ben Bernanke and John Cambell predicted that if a severe recession, such as the 1981–82 recession, were to strike, it would leave about 10 percent of the large corporations with inadequate cash flows to service their debts.[8]

_____

[8] Ben Bernanke and John Y. Cambell, "Is There a Corporate Debt Crisis?" Brookings Papers on Economic Activity, 1:1988, pp. 83–125.

FIGURE 14.4 Ratio of Nonfinancial-Corporate-Sector Debt to Equity, Market Value, 1961–1987

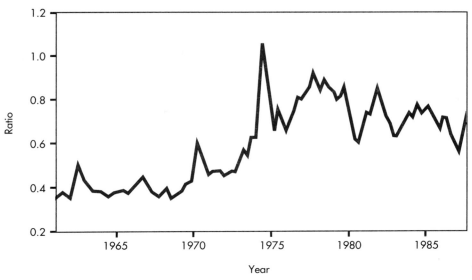

Source: Unpublished data from the Federal Reserve Board.

FIGURE 14.5 Interest Burdens of Nonfinancial Business and Households, 1947–1986

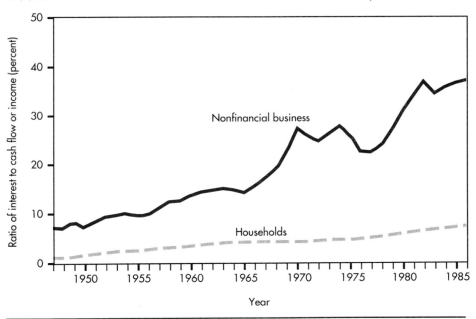

Note: The nonfinancial business measure is the ratio of interest paid to total cash flow. Interest burden of households is the ratio of household interest to disposable income.

Sources: U.S. Department of Commerce, Bureau of Economic Analysis, *National Income and Product Accounts of the United States, 1929–82* (Washington, D.C., 1986), pp. 63–70, 89–98, 392–93; and *Survey of Current Business* 68 (June 1988), pp. 5, 7.

FIGURE 14.6   Number of Business Failures, 1945–1987

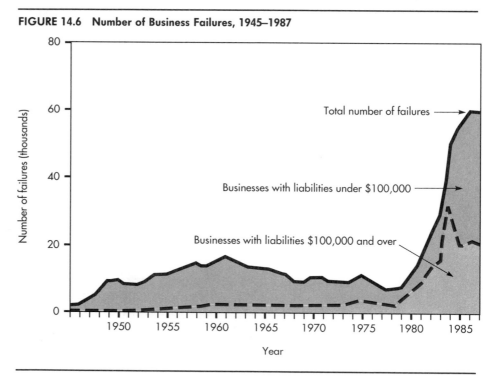

Source: *Economic Report of the President* (Washington, D.C.: U.S. Government Printing Office, February 1988), p. 357.

Not all of these companies would then go bankrupt, but Bernanke and Cambell suggest that corporate bankruptcies would be much more numerous than during the 1981–82 recession. Figures 14.4 and 14.5, therefore, gives somewhat conflicting evidence about the threat of corporate bankrupcies. The market values of assets suggest that the situation during the latter part of the 1980s was fine. The availability of income to service the debt does not look adequate although the improved managerial efficiencies imposed by the debt load mitigate the danger of high interest burdens. The trade-off between debt and efficiency remained unresolved as takeovers and leveraged buyouts pushed up debt-service–to–income ratios at the end of the 1980s. But the fears of a wave of bankruptcies are not purely hypothetical. Figure 14.6 shows the number of corporate bankruptcies over the 1945–87 period. The incidence of bankruptcy rose sharply during the 1980s even though the economy had a long and steady period of economic growth.

The long economic recovery of the 1980s did not reduce the incidence of bankruptcy among industrial corporations, and it did not reduce the bank-

FIGURE 14.7   Bank Failures, 1934–1987

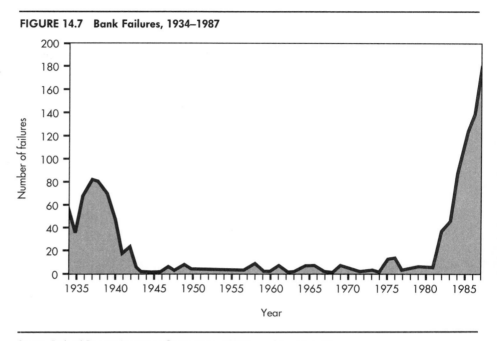

Source: Federal Deposit Insurance Corporation, *1987 Annual Report*, p. 49.

ruptcies among banks and S&Ls either. The FDIC [which in 1989 took over responsibility for its companion organization, the Federal Savings and Loan Insurance Corporation (FSLIC)] is a mixed blessing, because in recent years it has allowed some financial institutions to attract funds at low interest rates by offering security to depositors, and then lending out the money at high interest rates to borrowers undertaking very risky projects. This is a strategy that can yield high profits for the banks if all goes well, but puts the burden on taxpayers if the loans default. In some cases the risky loans have been made to friends or relatives of the managers of the banks.

The high-risk loans that have been made by banks and S&Ls have led to a tremendous increase in the bankruptcy rate for these institutions, as shown in Figure 14.7. The number of bank failures has risen sharply, and more bankruptcies are to be expected.

Despite the weakness in the banking system, there has not been a wholesale banking crisis with a loss of confidence by the public. The reason is that the federal government has stood behind the banks. This has had major benefits for the economy, but there has been a major cost too—the public costs of covering the shortfall and reimbursing depositors. The losses of troubled S&Ls were estimated as $19.2 billion in 1989, a figure that was rising over time. The cost to taxpayers was $29 million a day in the last quarter of that year.[9] Current estimates of the total cost of the crisis exceed $300 billion.

Summarizing the Financial-Market Threat to Stability

Looking at the long-term history of the U.S. economy suggests that financial crises do happen and may have caused recessions. The Great Depression both caused a financial crisis and was itself exacerbated by that crisis. One pattern appears to be policy-driven: rapid increases in inflation, followed by Fed contractionary policies. Another source of financial crisis comes from private-sector financial shocks: losses of business confidence coupled with banking panics and/or credit crunches. These episodes may or may not be connected with Fed policy actions. Regardless, they work to discourage borrowing and spending on interest-sensitive expenditures by businesses and consumers, reducing aggregate demand and income. The lesson of history is that the threat of a major financial crisis is not something to be taken lightly.

For many years after World War II, banks, corporations, and households followed conservative financial strategies. They did not want a repeat of the problems they had experienced in the 1930s. By the 1970s and 1980s, the climate had changed. Banks, S&Ls, corporations, and the federal government itself were all following higher-risk financial strategies. The amount of corporate debt outstanding relative to the value of the corporate business and physical assets is much higher than it used to be. Banks and S&Ls have portfolios of assets that includes many risky loans and many loans that are already in default. Bankruptcy rates have risen sharply for both banks and corporations.

As of 1990, the ratio of federal debt to GNP was not high and consumer confidence in the financial system remained strong in spite of the seemingly large increase in the size of the federal debt. Investor confidence weathered the market collapse of October 1987. The debt–equity ratio for corporations was not unusually high.

In the United States there are three significant differences between the state of financial markets and their relationship to economic fluctuations in the 1990s compared with earlier periods:

1. The combination of increased private-sector debt and a reversal of the down trend in public-sector debt has increased the ratio of total debt to GNP.

2. Real rates of interest are historically high. The amount of money needed to meet interest payments or payments of interest and principle (debt service) is high for any given ratio of debt to income.

---

[9] Values released by federal regulators, reported in *The New York Times*, March 27, 1990, p. A1.

3. In spite of higher debt loads and debt service, the federal government has been able to maintain confidence, particularly by insuring the banks.

The financial sector has probably become less stable than it was during the period from the end of World War II through the 1970s, but not so unstable as to make it a primary cause of economic fluctuations. In the face of a serious recession, there is likely to be a wave of corporate bankruptcies and an increase in the bank failures that are already taking place. The combination could erode confidence and worsen the recession. It is unlikely, although not impossible, for such a crisis to get out of hand and lead to a repeat of the 1930s.

STABILIZATION POLICY

As the world economy emerged from World II, the greatest fear was that there would be a recurrence of the high unemployment of the 1930s or, if not that, then a return to the rather severe and frequent business-cycle fluctuations that occurred throughout the 19th and early 20th centuries. Although there was concern about inflation, the principal goal of stabilization policy in the postwar 1950s was to maintain the level of output close to potential output—to ameliorate the effect of the business cycle. By the 1960s this goal was being compromised by the need to control inflation. And since 1970 there have been several periods during which economic policymakers have tolerated or even induced a recession in order to reduce inflation. Stabilization policy today means trying to form a reasonable compromise between the often conflicting goals of full employment and moderate inflation. A major motivation for delving into the structure of the economy has been to understand how policy could be pursued so as to achieve this reasonable compromise.

In the last section of this chapter, we will analyze the effectiveness of stabilization policy in tackling a recurring business cycle. We focus particularly on the critical issue of the timing of policy actions. Stabilization policy can fail when the direction of the economy changes more quickly than policy can respond and more quickly than policy actions have their effect.

We also review the performance record of stabilization policy by looking at the history of the business cycle. If the stabilization policy that was applied over the past decades is to be judged successful, then it should have reduced the degree of fluctuation and made the economy more stable.

Hitting a Moving Target When Visibility Is Bad

Stabilization policy requires policymakers to steer a very large and sluggish ship with better information about where it has been than where it is currently. The ship has limited controls, with long lags between changes of course and visible reactions. And finally, policymakers are faced with controversy over the appropriate direction in which to steer the ship. At a given point in time, there is reasonably good information available about last year's GNP, inflation, and unemployment. There is only preliminary information about these variables during the nine months prior to the current quarter and there are only very preliminary estimates about the current quarter.

Revisions to preliminary data are often very large. Sometimes preliminary information that indicates that the economy is growing at a rapid rate is later superseded by revised information that indicates that the economy is flat, experiencing no growth at all.

An ideal stabilization policy would have policymakers acting in advance of the onset of the recession and certainly in advance of the time when the experience of a recession is certain. Since policymakers cannot be certain about upcoming change in the direction of the economy and since it takes time for policymakers to react even when they have come to a conclusion about a policy direction, *policy actions are subject to lags between the time policy actions should be initiated and the time that policy actions are in fact initiated.* There is a **recognition lag** between the time an economy starts into a downturn and the time policymakers really know about it, and there is a **decision lag** between the time that the need for policy action is recognized and the time that the levers of policy are actually changed.

Policymaking is not carried out by individuals, but by groups. In a democracy, a majority of decision makers have to be convinced that action is needed and then take the action, and this process takes time. In the case of fiscal policy, that lag can sometimes be very long. Both houses of Congress have to vote on tax and expenditure policies and the president has to sign a bill. During the 1980s the political environment prevented the use of fiscal policy (especially taxes) in the service of stabilization, and this problem is continuing into the 1990s.

In the case of monetary policy, the process is typically much shorter. The Fed's governors (who control the Fed) are not elected officials and there are only a few of them. This can provide an advantage in speedy action. However, even the Fed will take some time to decide its actions, as the open-market committee has to meet and vote to change a policy stance. Further, while the Fed is operationally free to pursue monetary policy, it may well be affected by current political constraints. The recognition lag and the decision lag together make up what is called the **inside lag**—the time it takes the policymaking apparatus to move.

Following the inside lag, there is an **outside lag**—the time before the policy actually takes effect. A tax cut will only boost demand once people know their paychecks will be affected. Monetary policy has to change interest rates and then change investment expenditures. The full effects of monetary and fiscal policy will depend upon the working through of the multiplier and financial-market adjustments.

The outside lag also depends on expectations. We saw in Chapter 8

recognition lag
The time it takes for policymakers to recognize that economic conditions have changed.

decision lag
The time it takes for policymakers to initiate a change in policy following their recognition of the need for a policy action.

inside lag
The time it takes for policymakers to initiate a policy change following a change in economic conditions that requires policy action. This is the sum of the recognition lag and the decision lag.

outside lag
The time it takes for a policy action to take effect after it has been initiated.

that if participants in financial markets do not think that a change in monetary policy is going to last very long, then long-term interest rates may not change by very much when short-term interest rates change. If this is the case, then the effect of a monetary-policy change on investment and output will be small until expectations have changed and long-term rates have moved. Expectations can also affect the fiscal-policy lag. If people know that legislation has been passed to cut taxes, they may even go out and spend more before the policy has actually altered their disposable incomes. If, on the other hand, people believe that a tax cut is only going to be temporary, then they may regard it as a change in transistory income and not change their spending much at all. Since the outside lag depends on expectations, it will be variable and uncertain.

The combination of inside and outside lags makes it difficult to fine-tune the economy. A boom or a slump will certainly have some time to develop before offsetting policy actions can be taken, even assuming that such action is taken. But the problem may be even more severe than that. There is a real risk that by the time a policy change is activated, it hits the economy at exactly the wrong time.

Timing problems

An expansionary policy may just be beginning to kick in when the economy has already turned around and is heading back to full employment on its own. The policy action may then precipitate too strong a boom and an acceleration of inflation. Figure 14.8 illustrates the potential problem caused by lags. The dark line traces out a stylized cyclical fluctuation in output and we assume that the economy would follow this path over time in the absence of any policy intervention. Suppose that at a point in time, the economy is already in a recession with actual output below potential output (point A in the figure). Making the most favorable case for stabilization policy, we assume that an ideal policy would drive actual output toward potential output more quickly and with a less severe recession than if the economy were left to itself.

The alternative paths of adjustment are shown in the figure. If there were no stabilization policies invoked, actual output would reach potential output at a later time (solid line from point A to point C) and with a greater loss of output than it would with an ideal policy (dashed line from point A to point B).

Unfortunately, the inside lag means that the recession has continued and worsened (point A to point D) before an expansionary policy has been enacted. The outside lag means that policy actions taken too late (at point D) do not have a major impact on the economy until well after the business cycle has caused actual income to recover through potential output (point C) and beyond. The effect of the policy is to generate a boom (beyond point C to point E) where output greatly exceeds potential and inflation accelerates.

FIGURE 14.8 Lags in Recognition and Implementation Can Lead to Policies That Worsen Fluctuations

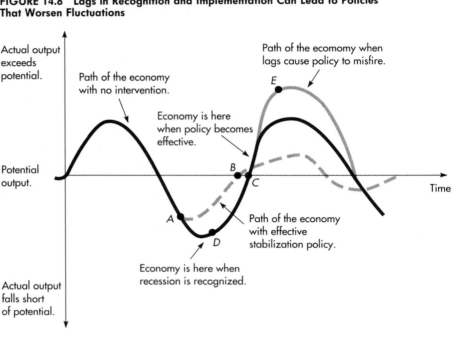

This is a larger and more costly expansion than would have occurred without policy. The effect of policies that misfired is that attempts at stabilization policy have actually increased the amplitude of the business cycle.

How serious is this problem of policy misfiring? In the past, policies have been applied at the wrong time. When John F. Kennedy was elected, he proposed an expansionary fiscal policy to move the economy out of recession. Part of this took effect fairly quickly, but the tax cuts that he proposed did not take effect until 1964, after his death and after the time that they were needed. The 1964 tax cut was one factor pushing the economy into the inflationary boom of the late 1960s. In general, fiscal policy requiring legislative change is difficult to use for countercyclical purposes because of the lags involved and the dangers of making the cycle worse. The lag problem is less severe with monetary policy. The Fed can act quickly, its board members are regularly briefed on the state of the economy, and Fed actions will have immediate effects on interest rates and fairly quick effects on the economy. If recessions turned around quickly on their own, then it would be a mistake to try and offset them with stabilization policy. But since recessions do often lead to persistent excess unemployment, it makes sense to use some combination of monetary and fiscal policies to restore full employment. However, since most of the burden for stabilization policy will fall on monetary policy, the Fed's freedom of action is constrained by the need for inflation to be kept at an acceptable level.

Automatic stabilizers

Policies that require actions by policymakers are called discretionary policies. And the recognition lag and the decision lag that make it difficult to regularly use discretionary fiscal policy can lead to policy misfiring. Moreover, fiscal policy has been caught up in the debate over the deficit and the appropriate size of the federal government, so there is little prospect of using discretionary fiscal policy to stabilize the economy, even if such use were warranted. That does not mean that fiscal policy has no role to play. There are statutory provisions that automatically vary taxes or expenditures in response to changes in the economy. These automatic fiscal stabilizers operate without requiring action by policymakers and they help the economy to avoid booms and slumps. There are two main types:

1. *Automatic changes in tax receipts.* People with very low incomes pay little federal income tax, so as their incomes rise, tax receipts rise. To the degree that the personal income tax is progressive, the fraction of income paid in taxes rises as income rises. This means that a boom will automatically raise federal tax receipts and act as countercyclical fiscal policy. When we studied the multiplier, we saw that its size is reduced by income taxes. This reduction of the multiplier reflects the automatic stabilization of the economy through taxes.

2. *Unemployment compensation and other transfer payments.* In a recession, unemployment rises along with the fall in income. Unemployed workers receive unemployment insurance. This transfer payment, which partially sustains income, is an automatic countercyclical fiscal policy.

In 1978–1979, when unemployment was fairly low, about $9 billion a year was paid out in unemployment benefits. During 1982, when there was a deep recession, nearly $24 billion was paid out.

Aside from workers who are laid off, there is a constant flow of people in and out of the labor force. Mothers with children may decide to look for work. Retirees may find that they need more money and come back into the labor force to look for part-time work. During recessions, it is harder for these labor-force entrants to find jobs. But there are transfer programs that are designed to help them—welfare and social security. During recessions, more people will rely on these transfer programs to sustain their incomes.

In 1979, all transfer payments by government were equal to 10.7 percent of GNP. In the recession year of 1982, this figure rose to 12.8 percent, providing a significant offset to the recession.

Goals and instruments

If stabilization policy is going to be effective, policymakers need to have control over the policy tools or instruments necessary to achieve their goals. Since policymakers are required to deal with a number of different goals for the economy (reduce unemployment, fight inflation, lower interest rates, encourage saving, raise or lower the real exchange rate, etc.) they need to have control over more than one policy instrument (i.e., bank reserves, income taxes, budget expenditures). There has to be a match between goals and instruments because a policymaker cannot cause one instrument (say, the growth of bank reserves) to both increase and decrease at the same time. The classic example is one that is already very familiar. Keeping inflation low may require monetary policymakers to reduce the growth of bank reserves, ultimately driving the level of output below potential output. But the goal of stabilizing output and employment may require an expansionary monetary policy that would cause the Fed to increase the growth of bank reserves.

There have been many suggestions offered over the years for adding an additional instrument in order to solve the trade-off dilemma. The most popular has been wage-and-price guidelines or controls. In the early 1960s, President Kennedy introduced wage-and-price guidelines, hoping to prevent inflation from accelerating. He had a major showdown with the steel industry and persuaded its management to roll back price increases, even though he had no power to force a change. A few months later the industry restored the price increases.

In 1971, President Nixon introduced mandatory wage-and-price controls and kept them in force until 1973, although he loosened them even before this. These mandatory controls were very effective in reducing inflation temporarily, but they failed badly in the longer run as inflation bounced back as soon as the controls were relaxed. Since then there have been proposals to give incentives for wage-and-price restraint—so-called "tax-based incomes policies." But there has not been much recent support for such ideas.

The Fed and President Reagan decided that it was better to pay the prices of high unemployment as the way to reduce inflation. Economists in the Bush administration have accepted the idea that a compromise or trade-off between conflicting goals is the only way to deal with the problem of using stabilization policy when there are more goals than instruments.

Has the Economy Become More Stable?

There are many problems involved in using stabilization policy, including lags, disagreement over direction, and the conflict between inflation and unemployment. Sometimes policymakers find themselves purposely adding to the variability of the economy by trying to push the economy into a recession in order to combat inflation. But despite these considerations, it is important to make a broad-brush comparison of the economy before and after the

■ The Dilemma of Managing with Fewer Instruments than Goals: A Managerial Example

Suppose a corporate manager is told to achieve a rapid increase in market penetration and at the same time to raise profit margins on each item sold. Can this be done? It depends upon how much control the manager has over prices, costs, quality, distribution, marketing, and so on. If the only instrument for achieving these two goals is control over price, she is in trouble. She can raise prices and increase the profit margin on each unit sold, or she can cut prices and go for market share. She is caught in a classic dilemma—armed with only *one* instrument and attempting to achieve *two* goals. She cannot do it, and in general it is impossible to reach more goals than there are instruments unless the goals coincide in some way (i.e., unless the two goals are really one and the same).

The way out for the manager is to garner control over another aspect of her product besides price. If she could reduce costs by raising productivity or cutting the cost of supplies, that additional instrument could allow her to both raise profitability (lower costs) and improve market share (lower prices, though not by as much as costs fall). In fact, in the process of gaining control over additional policy instruments, she may even find that her goals do coincide more than she thought. Raising total sales may allow her to cut unit costs, thereby letting her have her cake and eat it too.

Macroeconomic policymakers face similar problems if they are trying to achieve conflicting goals without enough instruments.

initiation of stabilization policy. The Employment Act of 1946 specified that policy should be used to maintain price stability and full employment. In spite of the apparent contradiction embedded in the act, this date is generally taken to be the starting point of stabilization policies. Is there any evidence that the economy has actually become more stable?

The magnitude of fluctuations in real GNP provides one indicator of the stability or instability of the overall economy. Figure 14.9 shows the rate of growth of GNP over different periods from the 19th century until the 1980s. The reduction in the size of the fluctuations in GNP is dramatic. The period of the Great Depression in the 1930s stand out, but the fluctuations in earlier periods were large also. The period from 1946 to 1983 is much more stable despite the problems in dealing with inflation in the 1970s and 1980s.

The simple conclusion from these figures is that stabilization policies, despite their problems, have worked. This conclusion has been challenged on two grounds.

Christina Romer has argued that problems with the data are distorting the results.[10] There were no National Income and Product Accounts prior

---

[10] Using a highly original approach, she constructs GNP data for the post-1946 period using the methods that were used for the earlier years. She then compares her new post-1946 numbers with the earlier numbers and concludes that the economy was unstable *only* during the Great Depression. Christina Romer, "Spurious Volatility in Historical Unemployment Data," *Journal of Political Economy* 94 (February 1986), pp. 1–37; "Is the Stabilization of the Postwar Economy a Figment of the Data?" *American Economic Review* 76 (June 1986), pp. 314–34.

FIGURE 14.9A   Real Gross National Product, Percentage Changes, Quarterly 1875–1918

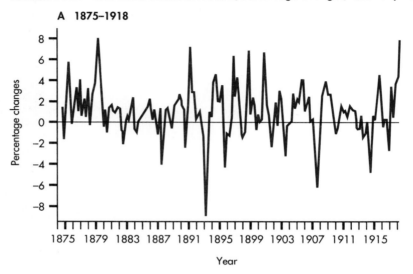

Source: Victor Zarnowitz, "Fact and Factors in the Recent Evolution of Business Cycles in the United States," NBER Working Paper no. 2865 (February 1989). A similar figure was used to illustrate the effects of stabilization policy in Martin Neil Baily, "Stabilization Policy and Private Economic Behavior," *Brookings Papers on Economic Activity,* 1:1978, pp. 11–59.

FIGURE 14.9B   Real Gross National Product, Percentage Changes, Quarterly 1919–1945

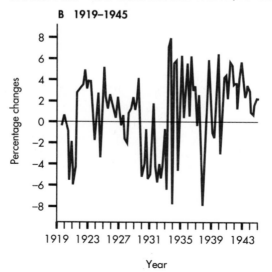

Source: Same as for Figure 14.9A.

FIGURE 14.9C   Real Gross National Product, Percentage Changes, Quarterly 1946–1983

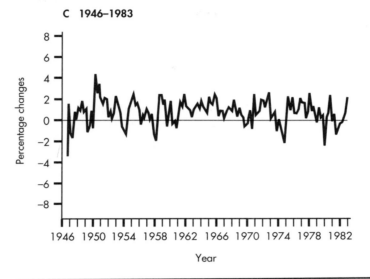

C   1946–1983

Source: Same as for Figure 14.9A.

to World War II and so the figures for real GNP have been pieced together from a variety of different data sources. Romer argues that the way the data were constructed introduced a spurious amount of variability. If variability in the early figures is due to data problems and not to actual variations in GNP, that suggests that instability is the exception rather than the rule for an economy, even one without stabilization policy.

Romer's conclusions have themselves been subject to criticism. For example, Charles Schultze looks at several economic series that have been collected continuously over many years and finds that they all individually show sharp reductions of variability after the war. And Nathan Balke and Robert Gordon construct their own estimates of prewar GNP and find that it varies just as much as the official series.[11] The basic conclusion from Figure 14.9 turns out to be correct: The economy has become much more stable.

A second criticism of the conclusion that stabilization policy has reduced economic variability runs as follows: While variability may have been reduced, it was not stabilization policy and certainly not discretionary policy that caused

---

[11] Charles L. Schultze, *Other Times, Other Places* (Washington D.C.: Brookings Institution, 1986). Nathan S. Balke and Robert J. Gordon, "The Estimation of Prewar Gross National Product: Methodology and New Evidence," *Journal of Political Economy*, February 1989. Another critic of Romer's conclusion is David Weir, "The Reliability of Historical Macroeconomic Data for Comparing Cyclical Stability," *Journal of Economic History*, June 1986.

the greater stability. And there is some force to this argument. A detailed examination of the policy actions that were taken show that policy was often misguided.[12] It is argued that the economy has become more stable as the result of a changed economic structure, in spite of mistaken policy actions. The large service sector of the economy, including the government bureaucracy itself, has increased stability.

Conclusions on increased stability

There is little doubt that the economy is much more stable than it used to be. There are five main reasons for this conclusion. (1) Federal deposit insurance has protected the banking system and the money supply from banking panics. (2) Automatic stabilizers generate fiscal policies that sustain disposable income during recessions and that restrain the growth of disposable income during booms. (3) The structure of the economy has changed so that a smaller fraction of it is in durable-goods manufacturing and agriculture, where fluctuations are most severe. (4) Government policymakers have stepped in on many occasions to offset the cycle, and, even though mistakes have been made, probably they have been smaller or fewer in number in the period since 1946. (5) As a result of all of the preceding reasons, businesses and households have learned that fluctuations are smaller and so their expectations have become more stable and hence so has their behavior.

In this and earlier chapters, we have argued that monetary and fiscal policies can affect real output and inflation, and that on occasions such policies should be used to improve stability. While we do not argue that in practice economic policy has been particularly well executed or well directed—in fact, we believe that on occasion policy has been wrongheaded. However, we do conclude that stabilization policy can be effective and that sometimes it has worked in practice.

In the next two chapters, we will be looking at alternative views of the impact of policy and the desirability of using it. In Chapter 15, we explain the monetarist view that only a strict adherence to rules for monetary policy will work. In Chapter 16 we describe the rational-expectations view that policy cannot work at all. Both of these views come to the opposite conclusion from the one reached in this chapter. They argue that the government is not justified in actively pursuing stabilization policies.

---

[12] George L. Perry, "Stabilization Policy and Inflation," in *Setting National Priorities: The Next Ten Years,* ed. Henry Owen and Charles L. Schultze (Washington, D.C.: Brookings Institution, 1976), pp. 271–321.

SUMMARY

- The international sector can contribute to economic fluctuations.

- The demand for U.S. exports is part of aggregate demand, so that falling exports will reduce aggregate demand. A fall in income overseas will reduce the demand for U.S. exports and reduce income in the U.S. economy.

- Foreign interest rates affect U.S. interest rates. Fluctuations in foreign interest rates will lead to fluctuations in U.S. interest rates.

- The three effects of changes in foreign income and interest rates do not all go in the same direction. (1) High income overseas will help U.S. exports and increase U.S. income. (2) Foreign interest rates will usually be high when foreign income is high, and high foreign rates will pull up U.S. rates. This will reduce U.S. demand through its effect on domestic investment. (3) High foreign interest rates will lower the dollar, increase U.S. exports, and increase U.S. demand.

- When a financial crisis occurs domestically or overseas, the transmission of the crisis through international financial markets may exacerbate the crisis.

- Historically, financial crises have been caused by fluctuations in income and have contributed to those fluctuations.

- A financial crisis can be policy-driven: rapid increases in inflation, followed by monetary contraction, followed by economic downturn.

- A financial crisis can arise without Fed actions as a result of a loss of confidence. If people lose confidence in the banks, this will increase the demand for cash and reduce the money supply. There was a banking crisis in the Great Depression.

- Loss of confidence in the profitability of business investment can lead to an increase in the risk premium, an increase in the long-term real rate of interest, and a decline in income.

- A financial crisis that leads to a fall in income will then be exacerbated by an accelerator reaction in the goods market.

- A credit crunch is a mild financial crisis where there is a rapid reduction in the availability of loans from financial intermediaries. Whether or not a credit crunch reduces aggregate demand and initiates a financial crisis depends upon the reaction of the central bank.

- One form of credit crunch occurred in the past because of disintermediation— depositors' withdrawals of funds in order to purchase higher-yielding financial-market securities.

- The possibility exists that the financial markets of the 1990s have become more prone to instability because of an increased level of indebtedness among all sectors of the U.S. economy. Corporate debt outstanding has risen relative to the value of assets. The loan portfolios of banks and S&Ls have become riskier. Bankruptcy rates have risen sharply for both banks and corporations.

- In the 1970s and 1980s, banks, S&Ls, corporations, and the federal government turned away from the financial policies of the previous several decades by following higher-risk financial strategies. In spite of higher debt loads, the federal government is able to maintain confidence, particularly by insuring the banks.

- The ratio of federal debt to GNP is not high, and consumer confidence in the financial system remains adequate. The debt–equity ratio for corporations is not unusually high, but interest payments have become a very large fraction of corporate cash flow in many companies.

- In the face of a serious recession, there would likely be a wave of corporate and bank bankruptcies that could erode confidence and worsen the recession. But it is unlikely that the crisis would get out of hand and lead to a repeat of the 1930s.

- The goals of stabilization policy are to ameliorate the effect of the business cycle and control inflation. These goals are often in conflict.

- Stabilization-policy actions are subject to lags. There is an inside lag, comprised of a recognition lag (the period from the time of the start of a downturn to the time policymakers recognize the downturn), plus a decision lag (the period from the time of recognition to the time that the policy actions are initiated). There is an outside lag (the period from the time of the initiation of policy actions to the time when policy takes effect).

- The combination of inside and outside lags makes it difficult to fine-tune the economy.

- The timing problem can cause policy to misfire, when it is activated at the wrong time. It can then exacerbate rather than stabilize the business cycle.

- Automatic stabilizers avoid some of the problems of discretionary policies. They come into effect more quickly and are automatically tied to the state of the economy.

- In spite of the mixed record of stabilization policy in practice, the U.S. economy has improved its stability in the period since World War II compared to the prior period.

KEY TERMS

banking panic	junk bond
credit crunch	leveraged buyout
decision lag	outside lag
disintermediation	recognition lag
financial crisis	speculative boom or bust
inside lag	

DISCUSSION QUESTIONS AND PROBLEMS

1. Comment on whether or not debt levels contribute to financial-market instability? How can financial-market instability contribute to fluctuations in the real economy?

2. Compare a banking panic with a credit crunch. Do they have different effects on aggregate demand and instability?

3. (A) In a financial crisis driven by contractionary monetary policy, the short-term nominal rate of interest rises much more than the long-term rate. (B) In a private-sector financial crisis driven by a loss of business confidence, the long-term real rate of interest rises much more than the short-term nominal rate. Compare the way in which these two very different effects both contribute to a decline in aggregate demand?

4. Show how the variability of investment expenditures resulting from accelerator effects can exacerbate a business-cycle downturn that was initiated by a financial crisis.

5. How can a domestic-business-cycle downturn be exacerbated by the international capital flows?

6. "If stabilization policy can only come on line well after a business-cycle downturn has been recognized, the policy action will probably do more harm than good." Comment.

PART VIII

Economic Controversy

It has been said that if you linked all the economists in the world end to end they would never reach a conclusion. There is considerable disagreement among macroeconomists as to the correct way to model economic fluctuations. This text has not emphasized the disagreements; it has brought out the most valuable elements of several alternative approaches. It is time now to present some of the ideas of those macroeconomists whose views of the business cycle are fundamentally different from this one. The disagreement is sharpest on issues of macroeconomic policy and the choice of policies to be used in the face of growing unemployment or inflation. In this chapter and the next we look at the foundations of monetarism, the equilibrium–business-cycle model with rational expectations, and the real–business-cycle model. And we bring out the implications of these models for policymaking.

The alternative approaches to macroeconomics assume that markets are competitive, including labor markets, and that economic agents (institutions, firms, and individuals) act as if they make rational calculations and estimates of their own best interest as well as forecasts of the behavior of the economy. In the view of the economists that have developed these models, market forces work very quickly, prices adjust to differences in supply and demand with great flexibility, rising or falling so as to clear markets. In the monetarist model, the culprit behind income variability is uneven growth in the money supply. In the equilibrium–business-cycle view, the source of instability in income is either a policy action or an exogenous shock that comes as a surprise. Uneven growth in the supply of money is a major cause of cycles in the equilibrium–business-cycle model, just as it is in the monetarist model, but it is only the unexpected fluctuations that will change real output and employment. The real–business-cycle model carries over all the elements of the equilibrium–business-cycle model, but postulates an alternative source of fluctuations, namely real changes in productivity-technology shocks.

These models have their origins in the competitive market models developed by 18th and 19th century economists and they are often referred to as classical or neoclassical models. They are intellectually appealing because they start with clear microeconomic foundations. They start with the assumption that individuals will act rationally to maximize their own self-interest, making the best use of available information.

CHAPTER 15

Monetarism
Classical Roots and
Contemporary Implications

INTRODUCTION

monetarism
A model of the economy in which the economy is self-correcting. Changes in the rate of growth of the money supply are the primary cause of inflation and short-run fluctuations in output.

Monetarism is a view of the aggregate economy that stresses the primacy of changes in the money supply in determining inflation and short-run output fluctuations.[1] A higher growth rate of the money supply means a higher rate of inflation. Monetarists argue that fiscal policy is ineffective as a means of stimulating aggregate demand. Monetarists also argue that expanding the money supply to increase employment and real income is mistaken policy because, fairly quickly, the only result will be more money chasing the same amount of goods and services—more money simply generates higher prices. They believe that the economy is self-correcting and will insure full employment on its own and they conclude that government had best pursue a monetary policy that is predictable and unchanging.

The monetarist model is often seen as an alternative view of the economy from the aggregate supply and demand models or the *IS-ALM* trade-off models that have been presented in this text. However, the models come to similar conclusions about the behavior of the economy in the very long run. We argued in earlier chapters that in the long run, changes in the growth of the money supply will bring about changes in the price level and not changes in output. The economy will operate at potential output when the labor

---

[1] Monetarism is associated most closely with the work of Milton Friedman. See this chapter's box titled "Monetarism and the Monetarists: Milton Friedman and the Monetary Revolution." See also Milton Friedman and Anna J. Schwartz, *A Monetary History of the United States* (Princeton, N.J.: Princeton University Press, 1963); *A Monetary History of the United States: Estimates, Sources and Methods* (New York: NBER, 1963); *The Great Contraction* (Princeton, N.J.: Princeton University Press, 1965); *Monetary Trends in the United States and the United Kingdom* (New York: NBER, 1982). See also Milton Friedman, ed., *Studies in the Quantity Theory of Money* (Chicago: University of Chicago Press, 1956); Friedman, *A Program for Monetary Stability* (New York: Fordham University Press, 1959); and Friedman, *The Optimum Quantity of Money* (Chicago: Aldine, 1969).

market is in long-run equilibrium. These conclusions about the long run are the same as the conclusions of the monetarist model.

The major difference between monetarism and the models we have presented is found in their different assumptions about the short-run behavior of the economy, about the time for the economy to return to full employment following a recession, and specifically about the time it takes for markets to react to changes in the growth of the money supply. The monetarist model assumes that prices and wages are not very sticky, so that markets clear fairly quickly and smoothly. We will return to a discussion and assessment of these differences after we have described the workings of the monetarist model.

Monetarism developed in the 1960s and 1970s as an alternative to the Keynesian analysis that had come to dominate macroeconomics since the publication of Keynes' *General Theory* in 1936. Whereas Keynes had rejected the classical model in which output in the short run is wholly determined by equilibrium in the labor market, monetarists instead built their analysis on classical roots. Whereas some Keynesian writers had emphasized the impact of fiscal policy and played down the importance of monetary policy, monetarists instead stressed the importance of money and minimized the role for fiscal policy. Since monetarism is based on classical roots, we begin our discussion of monetarism by looking at the classical model.

THE CLASSICAL UNDERPINNINGS OF MONETARIST THEORY

classical model
A model of the economy in which all markets clear. Supply and demand in all markets either are in equilibrium or, if disturbed, come quickly back into equilibrium.

The **classical model** is a model of supply and demand where all markets for goods and services are competitive and clear at some set of prices. Similarly, there are competitive markets for the inputs into the production process, and in particular labor is traded like any other commodity at an equilibrium price (the wage rate). The amount of employment is determined in the market-place and this then determines the amount of production in the economy. Goods and services are produced in factories, office buildings, stores, shopping malls, and all the small and large businesses in the economy. The amount of output that firms can produce, as distinct from how much they choose to produce, is determined by (1) the productive resources that the firm has on hand (including capital, labor, purchased materials, and energy); and (2) the way in which those resources are managed and allocated. In those businesses that buy materials and convert those materials to other products, labor and capital costs are in fact a relatively small fraction of the total cost of production. However, the materials that are so processed were produced by labor and capital in the factory that supplied the materials. There is a chain of production where raw-materials suppliers (for example, mining operations supplying iron ore) sell to firms that fabricate semifinished goods (for example, steel mills and metal-stamping companies) which in turn sell to firms that manufacture finished goods (for example, autos, appliances, and metal furniture). Each firm adds value to the materials it buys from supplying firms. In the aggregate, GNP is the sum of the value added by each firm, and purchased materials are intermediate goods that net out of GNP. The economy's productive capacity (potential output) depends upon how much capital and labor are available for production and upon the technology used in production. If more capital and labor are used in production, more output can be produced. The classical model of production starts with this relation between output and the inputs used to produce it, a relation known as the **aggregate production function.**

aggregate production function
The relationship between potential output and the inputs used to produce it (usually capital, labor, and technology).

Equation 15.1a shows the aggregate production function under classical assumptions,

$$Y = F(K,N,T) \tag{15.1a}$$

where output (Y) is produced in firms using capital (K), labor (N) and technology (T). Technology refers to the methods used to organize and manage production as well as the technical aspects of the capital equipment used in production.

In this analysis of how the level of output is determined in the short run, capital and technology are held constant and only the labor inputs varies,

$$Y = F(\overline{K},N,\overline{T}). \tag{15.1b}$$

In this case, the production function relates total output to the total amount of labor employed. Since capital and technology are assumed constant, we can drop them from the function for simplicity:

$$Y = F(N). \tag{15.1c}$$

Output (Y) rises with increases in total employment (N) subject to diminishing returns.[2] As shown in Figure 15.1, this assumes that more workers are required to produce more output—increases in employment lead to increases in output (point A to point B, point B to point C) along the production function. Furthermore, because of diminishing returns, the gain in output that results from more labor $(N_0$ to N_1 to $N_2)$ declines as firms employ more labor. This is shown in the figure by seeing that $(Y_2 - Y_1)$ is smaller than $(Y_1 - Y_0)$.

The Demand for Labor

While the production function describes how much labor is needed in order to produce a certain level of output, it does not describe the decision as to how much labor to hire. That depends on how much labor costs and how

---

[2] In models of long-run growth that we introduce in Chapter 17, the focus will be on the determinant of the growth of potential output, when all inputs are free to vary or grow over time. There we will describe the economy by using a production function that allows for changes in both labor and capital inputs over time. We will look at the effects of capital-intensity on an economy with a labor force that grows at a fixed rate. Also we will look at the role that changes in the quantities and qualities of the labor force, capital, and technology play in the long-run determination of productivity.

FIGURE 15.1   The Aggregate Production Function

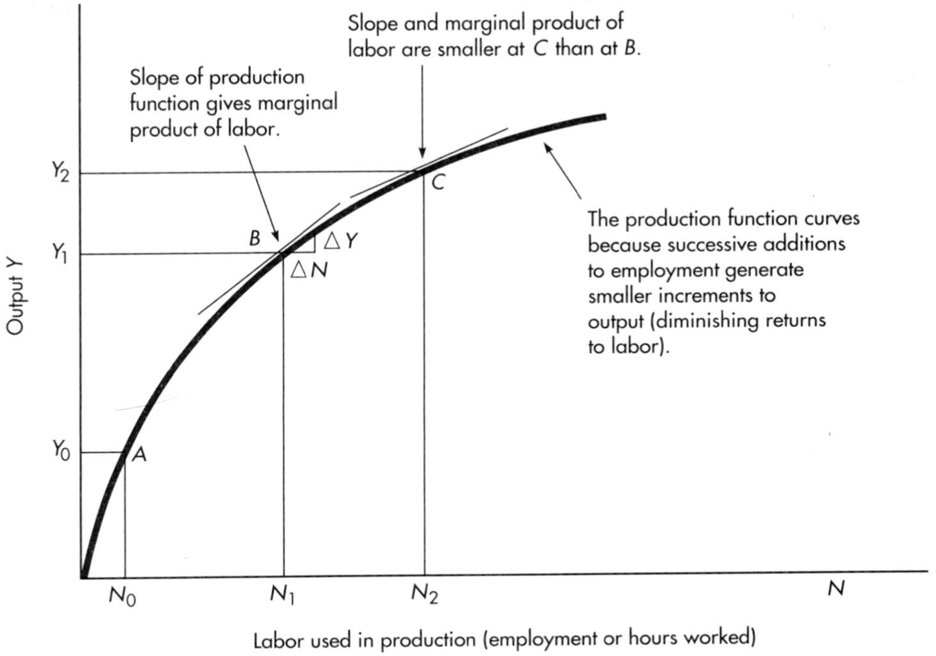

Slope and marginal product of labor are smaller at C than at B.

Slope of production function gives marginal product of labor.

The production function curves because successive additions to employment generate smaller increments to output (diminishing returns to labor).

Output Y

Y_2

Y_1

Y_0

B

$\triangle Y$

$\triangle N$

C

A

N_0 N_1 N_2 N

Labor used in production (employment or hours worked)

much output the firm wants to produce. In the classical model, the amount of labor demanded and the amount of output firms wish to produce are determined together, depending upon the contribution of labor to the profitability of the firm.

Classical economists assumed that firms are competitive profit-maximizers. This means that they decide how much to produce by comparing the extra (marginal) revenue from additional output with the extra (marginal) cost of production. Selling more output increases a firm's revenue and, for firms in competitive markets, marginal revenue is simply equal to the price charged per unit of output times the number of units. If an extra unit of output is sold for $10, then the marginal revenue from one extra unit of output produced is $10. If two extra units are produced, the marginal revenue is $20. (For firms that are not competitive, the price will change with the level of output. Marginal revenue is then no longer equal to price.)

By producing and selling more, firms can increase their revenues. But firms do not attempt to hire more and more workers and produce as much as is possible, because of diminishing returns to labor. Hiring more workers adds to total labor costs, but the increment to employment generates progressively smaller increments to output. This eventually eliminates any additional profit from further hiring. The marginal cost of production is the amount of wages paid out to produce one extra unit of output. Marginal costs rise with successive increases in hiring and output, because each additional hour worked contributes less to output than the previous hours of work. The labor requirement per unit of output rises; that is, there are diminishing returns to labor.

As long as marginal cost is less than the price of the product (which equals marginal revenue with competition), more output is produced and more labor is hired. If marginal cost is above price, then the firm has hired too much labor and will cut its employment and output. When marginal cost equals price, then the firm has hired just the amount of labor and is producing just the amount of output that maximizes its profit.

marginal product of labor
The additional output that results from increasing the amount of labor used in production.

We can illustrate how this condition determines the demand for labor with a figure and equations. In Figure 15.1 we showed the relation between additions to employment and additions to output. If at any level of output (such as point B), employment increases (ΔN), then the increment to output (ΔY) is the difference between the amount of output at two points along the production function. The ratio of the two is the **marginal product of labor** *(MPL)*, which is the additional output that results from hiring additional labor. For small changes in employment, the marginal product of labor is approximated by the slope of the line through point B in the figure. The flattening of the slope as employment rises illustrates the declining marginal productivity of labor due to diminishing returns. Equation 15.2 also shows the marginal product of labor as the ratio of the increments to output and labor:

$$\text{Marginal product of labor} = MPL = \frac{\Delta Y}{\Delta N}. \tag{15.2}$$

For a competitive firm the increase in revenue received from hiring extra labor is equal to the extra output produced by the extra labor times the price per unit ($P \times \Delta Y$). The marginal cost incurred in producing the increment to output is equal to the extra wages paid out ($W \times \Delta N$). Equation 15.3 shows the condition under which a firm will have hired the amount of labor that maximizes its profit:

Increase in revenue from producing ΔY
of extra output $= P \times \Delta Y$

Increase in cost from adding N to   (15.3)
employment to produce ΔY $= W \times \Delta N$

Condition for profit maximization $= P \times \Delta Y = W \times \Delta N.$

Dividing by P and by ΔN gives an equivalent condition for profit maximization:

$$\frac{\Delta Y}{\Delta N} = \frac{W}{P}.$$

(15.3a)

A firm has set the level of employment that maximizes its profit when the marginal product of labor ($\Delta Y/\Delta N$) *equals the real wage* (W/P). Whenever the marginal product exceeds the real wage, the firm hires more workers. Increasing employment drives down the marginal product of labor (diminishing returns) until the firm has hired workers to the point where the marginal revenue from labor equals the wage rate once more. Additional hiring beyond this point would bring on labor whose contribution to revenue was below their wage, thereby reducing profitability.

For example, a bicycle company sells bikes at a price that yields $100 over and above material cost. Hiring another metal worker adds five bikes per week to production. The firm has hired to the profit-maximizing–output level if metal workers earn $500 per week. The real wage is $500/$100 or five bikes per week, which is just equal the marginal product of labor. The bicycle company hires workers until the last worker it hires adds five bikes per week to production and costs the firm wages worth five bikes per week. Having reached this point, the bicycle company then stops hiring.

The condition given in Equation 15.3 describes the hiring decision of a particular firm. In the classical model, this relationship is taken as representative of the economy as a whole and used to determine the aggregate demand for labor in the economy. Total employment increases and the marginal product of labor falls until it equals the real wage prevailing in the economy. The *aggregate demand for labor,* N^d, simply depends upon the real wage:

Labor demand $= N^d \left(\dfrac{W}{P} \right).$

(15.4)

A low real wage is required to induce firms to hire a lot of labor. A high real wage will lead firms to keep their employment low. *In the classical model, the demand for labor in the economy increases when the real wage declines. The demand for labor decreases when the real wage increases.*

In Figure 15.2, the labor-demand relationship in the labor market is illustrated by a downward-sloping demand schedule, N^d. Firms hire workers by paying them the value of their marginal contribution to output. The value of labor's marginal contribution to output (the wage paid) and the amount of labor employed depend on how labor is supplied as well as on the demand for labor services.

The classical model of the demand for labor is oversimplified because, among other things, it assumes firms are perfectly competitive and can sell all the output they want at some given market price. But despite this, the model has direct relevance to a modern economy. If real wages rise with no offsetting improvements in technology and productivity, then employment will in fact suffer.

FIGURE 15.2   The Supply of and Demand for Labor and Labor-Market Equilibrium

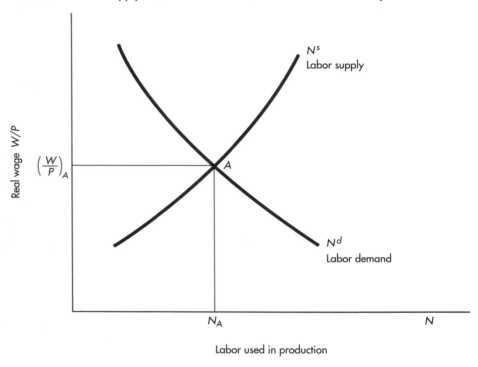

Labor used in production

The Supply of Labor

The classical economists used a labor-supply model based upon the decisions individuals make about whether or not to participate in the labor force—that is, whether or not to look for paid employment. In that model, people decide if they wish to seek work in the market for a wage or do something else—such as looking after their homes without receiving a wage or simply pursuing other activities. The classical model of labor supply argues that higher wages induce more people to decide to seek work in the market-place, or, for hours worked per employee to increase.

When people are making their decisions about work, what wage do they look at? Wages are expressed in dollars per hour (nominal wages). But people are not interested in working for dollars just for the sake of dollars; they want to buy goods and services with those dollars. *Workers who are making rational decisions about work will look at the money or nominal wage* (W) *in relation to the price level* (P). Specifically, if the price level were to double, then the nominal wage would have to double in order to induce the same supply of labor. This construction assumes that potential workers

nominal wage
The average wage paid to labor measured in current dollars.

real wage
The average wage paid to labor measured in constant dollars; that is, after adjustment for inflation.

have an accurate measure of the price level which they use to adjust the **nominal wage** so that they can react to a **real wage.** As is shown in Equation 15.5,

$$\text{Labor supply} = \left(\frac{W}{P}\right). \tag{15.5}$$

In the classical model the supply of labor depends upon the real wage. Labor supply increases when the real wage increases and decreases when the real wage decreases. In Figure 15.2, the labor-supply relationship is shown as the upward-sloping supply schedule, $N^s\left(\frac{W}{P}\right)$.

When this classical model of labor supply is applied to a modern economy in the monetarist or equilibrium–business-cycle models, the decision about *when* to work is stressed. If wages are good in a particular year, some people will decide to work in that year and quit the next year. These intertemporal choices about labor supply are also relevant for seasonal employment changes. Employment and output are much higher in the period up to and including Christmas. Job opportunities are good then, and many people who are not regularly employed take short-term employment.

Equilibrium Output and the Labor Market

The labor market clears (comes into equilibrium) when labor supply equals labor demand at the equilibrium real wage. Even in equilibrium, some workers remain voluntarily unemployed because the market wage is lower than the wage they require to enter employment. In Figure 15.2, an equilibrium real wage $[(W/P)_A]$ and level of employment (N_A) are described by the intersection of labor supply and demand (point A). This model does not say how the wage level and the price level are determined separately; rather, the classical model of the labor market only determines the ratio of the nominal level of wages and the price level (i.e., the real wage). While there may be people who are able to work but who choose not to work at the prevailing wage, there is no involuntary unemployment in this model. It is assumed that wages adjust until all those who want to work at the going wage will work and all those not working are choosing not to work.

The equilibrium level of employment in the labor market implies an equilibrium level of output. Firms demand labor because the output that the workers produce will be sold and generate profits. In terms of the model, the level of output is determined by the amount of labor employed and the production function.

$$Y_A = F(N_A). \tag{15.6}$$

In the classical model, labor supply is determined by people's willingness to work in relation to the real wage. The demand for labor is determined by the marginal productivity of labor in relation to the real wage. *Unless there are changes in the willingness to work or the productivity of labor, then the equilibrium level of output will not change.* In particular, forces that bring about a change in aggregate demand, such as an increase or decrease in the money supply, should not affect either the willingness to work or the productivity of labor and therefore they do not affect employment or output. It is in this sense that the classical model implies that there is a set level of real output determined by a set equilibrium level of employment. This is shown in Equation 15.7.

$$Y_A = Y(\overline{N}_A) = \overline{Y}. \tag{15.7}$$

This view of the labor market is derived from the view that variations in production are solely determined by variations in labor and the assumption of perfectly competitive, quickly clearing product and labor markets. There is no unemployment in this model because excess supply in any market leads to immediate reductions of the work force in that market and the labor released is rehired elsewhere in the economy, even if these people have to be hired at lower wages.

Unemployment in a classical labor market

The classical model of the labor market can generate unemployment, but it has to result from institutional arrangements that prevent workers from reducing their nominal wage in the face of a reduction in the demand for labor. A source of unemployment that stems from such an institutional change is the unemployment created by a minimum wage. Distortions in the labor market such as the introduction of minimum-wage legislation, unemployment insurance, welfare support programs, and unions will produce an equilibrium level of output and employment that is lower than the level achieved with unrestricted labor markets. Minimum-wage legislation has a direct effect in putting a floor under wages. Programs such as unemployment insurance may lead to the same effect by making workers unwilling to accept wages below a certain minimum level. The effect of a minimum level to the real wage is illustrated in Figure 15.3 where the minimum wage creates an excess supply of workers, where the number wishing to work (point B) is greater than the number demanded by firms (point A) given the minimum wage. The excess supply of labor does not lead to a reduction in the real wage in this case, since minimum wage will only lead to unemployment if it exceeds the market-clearing wage.

The classical model of the labor market suggests, therefore, that unemployment is caused only by institutional restraints, such as minimum wages. Many economists blamed the unemployment of the Great Depression on unions or minimum wages that were said to be preventing wage adjustment.

When the classical model of the labor market is used to provide a basis for monetarism, the simple-minded classical model is modified in order to take account of the fact that there is not perfect information available about jobs and wages. Workers are then unemployed because they are searching

FIGURE 15.3 | Unemployment Resulting from a Minimum Wage in the Classical Model

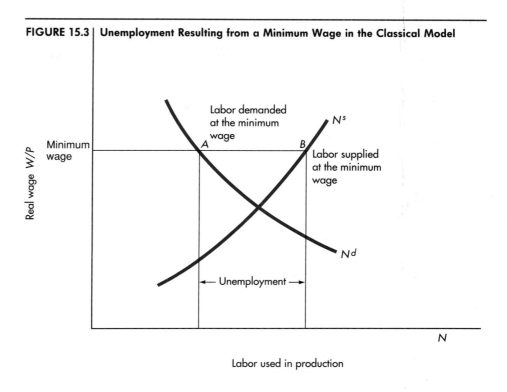

Labor used in production

for the best available job. Variation in overall unemployment can occur if workers' expectations about the likelihood of getting a better wage change over time.

Before turning explicitly to the monetarist framework, however, it is worth looking at how aggregate supply and demand come together in the classical model.

AGGREGATE SUPPLY AND DEMAND IN THE CLASSICAL MODEL

The characteristics of aggregate supply and demand equilibrium in the classical model are different from those in the *IS-ALM* trade-off model in the short run. In the *IS-ALM* trade-off model, increases in demand lead to increases in both output and inflation. Producing more requires hiring more labor at a higher unit cost. The higher unit costs generate an increase in the price level. In terms of the aggregate-supply/aggregate-demand diagram, the aggregate-supply schedule is upward-sloping but not vertical.

In the classical view, output does not change as aggregate demand

FIGURE 15.4   Aggregate Supply and Aggregate Demand in the Classical Model

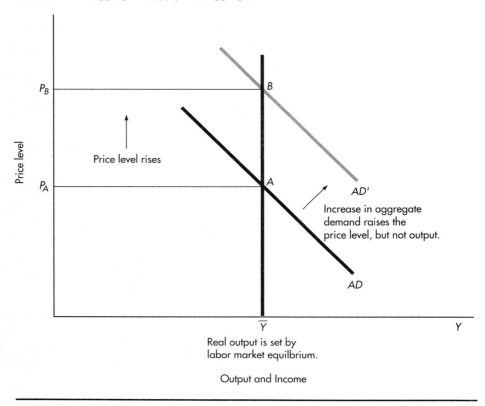

Real output is set by
labor market equilbrium.

Output and Income

changes; rather, the effect of an increase in aggregate demand is solely an
increase in the price level. The aggregate supply schedule is vertical, derived
from the classical model of the supply and demand for labor and not from
the short-run trade-off of output and inflation. This same classical approach
will be carried over to the monetarist framework.

The Role of Aggregate Demand and the Price Level

Since in the classical model the labor market sets the equilibrium amount
of labor supplied which in turn fixes the supply of goods and services, the
aggregate supply schedule is vertical. This is shown in Figure 15.4, where
output $(\overline{Y})$ is set by equilibrium in the labor market. The price level is set
by the level of aggregate demand intersecting the vertical aggregate supply.

Changes in aggregate demand simply lead to changes in the price level at a set level of output $(\overline{Y})$. An increase in aggregate demand (AD to AD'), resulting from, say, an increase in the money supply, raises nominal income, but real income remains unchanged. As shown in the figure, $(P_B \times \overline{Y})$ at point B is greater than $(P_A \times \overline{Y})$ at point A. The increase in aggregate demand simply raises the price level from P_A to P_B.

The classical model seems to have left no room for changes in aggregate demand to affect output. Hence, the classical model implies that there are no changes in output that result from changes in aggregate demand policy, nor are there business cycles or fluctuations in equilibrium output that result from changes in aggregate demand. Consider, for example, whether there would be a rise or fall in output resulting from an increase or decrease in taxes. Since output only changes when there is a change in the amount of labor and there is no mechanism in the classical model by which changes in consumption demand can lead to changes in the real wage, output does not change. Tax-rate changes will only affect output to the extent to which they change the willingness to work or have some other supply-side effect.

If aggregate demand fell (shifted down or inward), equilibrium would be maintained in labor markets without reducing output. In the goods markets, supply would temporarily exceed demand. The excess supply of goods and services would drive down prices and nominal wages. There would be a fall in both the price level and the wage level, but no change in the real wage. With no change in the real wage, there is no change in the level of employment nor in the amount of output produced. This is why, in the classical model, real output, the real wage, and employment are determined independently of fluctuations in aggregate demand.

The classical model does not consider the adequacy of aggregate demand nor whether or not the output level will actually be purchased. The classical model accepts **Say's Law**. This states that the income flowing to suppliers always creates enough demand to match the available supply, so there will always be an adequate level of aggregate demand. Supply creates its own demand; since all revenues flow into someone's income, demand will always be adequate to purchase the level of output generated. The value of production always generates an amount of income equal to the amount of output, with leakages such as saving being offset by injections such as investment.

The classical model implies that even short-run changes in aggregate demand are ineffective in affecting real output. The model implies that only the price level is affected by changes in aggregate demand. This classical link between aggregate demand and the price level provides a foundation of the monetarists' view that changes in the money supply are the primary cause of inflation. With a vertical aggregate supply schedule, an increase in the nominal supply of money will lead to a proportional increase in the price level and no change in the real supply of money—an important monetarist idea.

Say's Law
Supply creates its own demand. The law is part of the classical model. It says that production always generates income such that those who receive the income purchase all that is produced.

The Classical Basis for the Quantity Equation

In the classical model there is a very simple money-demand relation in which money demand is proportional to income. We introduced this classical money demand in Chapter 3, but we need to make clear now that money demand depends upon *nominal* income in the classical framework $(M_d = k \times PY)$. A key feature of classical money demand is that it does not depend upon the rate of interest. When the money market is in equilibrium, money demand equals money supply $(M_d = M_s = M)$, giving the following relation:

$$M = k \times PY.$$

velocity of money
V in the quantity equation. The ratio of *nominal income (PY)* to the money supply.

quantity equation
The money supply times velocity equals nominal income.

Then, since k is assumed to be a constant, the **velocity of money,** V, is also a constant $(V = PY/M = 1/k)$.

Substituting for velocity then gives the famous classical **quantity equation:**

$$M \times V = PY. \tag{15.8}$$

To the classical economists, velocity was a constant with respect to short-run fluctuations in the economy, even though in the long run, velocity might change slowly as a result of such things as increases in the speed with which banks clear checks or the introduction of automatic teller machines.

The quantity equation with the assumption of a constant velocity of money is the classical aggregate demand relation. An increase in the nominal supply of money (an increase in M) must translate into a proportional increase in nominal income, with velocity taken as given. The quantity equation in the classical model takes the place of the *IS-ALM* framework in the model we have used in earlier chapters.

Figure 15.5 illustrates the aggregate demand schedule in the classical model. When the money supply is equal to M, then the schedule is AD. The points A and B on this schedule must then both satisfy the quantity equation:

$$P_A Y_A = P_B Y_B = MV.$$

With fixed velocity and money supply, the aggregate demand schedule is curved in the way shown in the figure. (It is a hyperbola, the figure you get in geometry when xy is constant.)

If the supply of money were to increase to M', there would be a new aggregate demand schedule, AD'. Points along AD' would also have to satisfy the quantity equation:

$$P_C Y_A = P_D Y_B = M'V.$$

A 10 percent increase in money supply will displace the aggregate demand schedule by 10 percent.

When the classical aggregate demand is combined with the vertical aggregate supply, the result is that changes in the supply of money have no effect on real income, but lead to proportional changes in the price level

FIGURE 15.5   The Quantity Equation and the Aggregate Demand Schedule

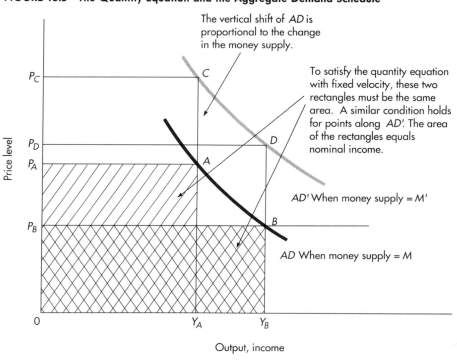

The vertical shift of *AD* is proportional to the change in the money supply.

To satisfy the quantity equation with fixed velocity, these two rectangles must be the same area. A similar condition holds for points along *AD'*. The area of the rectangles equals nominal income.

AD' When money supply = *M'*

AD When money supply = *M*

Output, income

and in nominal income. A 10 percent increase in the money supply raises the price level and nominal income by 10 percent. Figure 15.6 illustrates this.

Monetarists do not take over all the assumptions of the classical model in its most extreme form. They recognize that changes in aggregate demand do have an effect on output as well as on prices. But they have used the classical model as a key starting point to develop their view that the role of money and monetary policy is of primary importance in determining inflation and economic conditions. The monetarist analysis has provided an important alternative to Keynesian analysis and their ideas have been incorporated into modern macroeconomics.

MONETARISM, AGGREGATE DEMAND, AND INFLATION

Just how much does money matter in determining the performance of the macroeconomy? In the early 1960s, when the combination of the Phillips curve and the Keynesian income–expenditure model dominated the general view of macroeconomics, the importance of money and monetary policy

FIGURE 15.6   The Effect of Changes in the Money Supply in the Classical Model

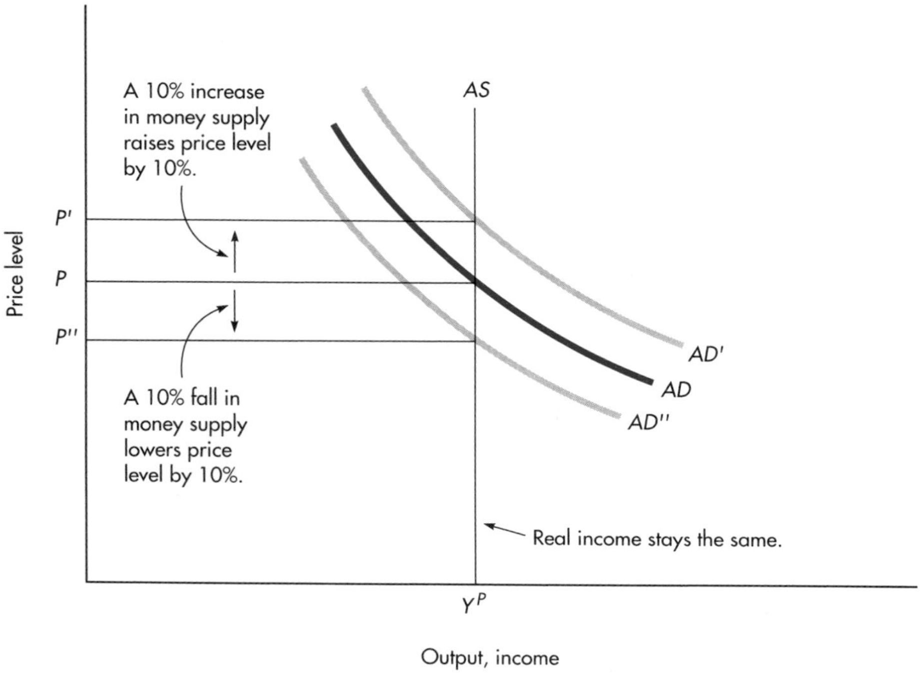

A 10% increase in money supply raises price level by 10%.

A 10% fall in money supply lowers price level by 10%.

AS

AD'

AD

AD''

P'

P

P''

Price level

Real income stays the same.

Y^P

Output, income

were little emphasized. At the time, the view held by some economists and policymakers in the United States and in Britain was that because of the vast range of financial assets that are close substitutes for money, a central bank, such as the Federal Reserve Board or the Bank of England, would be relatively powerless to influence the pace of economic activity in an economy.[3] Trying to control inflation by restricting the money supply, it was argued, is like trying to control alcoholism by restricting the supply of whiskey. People will quickly switch to gin or vodka.

Monetarists used the classical model and the quantity equation to develop arguments to balance the Keynesian focus on fiscal policy as the most important tool of economic policy. In order to counter the view that money does not matter, the monetarists argued that money is all that matters. This went too far, but they made a forceful case for the importance (if not the primacy)

---

[3] J. G. Gurley and E. S. Shaw, *Money in a Theory of Finance* (Washington, D.C.: Brookings Institution, 1960); Committee on the Workings of the Monetary System (generally known as the Radcliffe Committee), *Report* (London, England: Her Majesty's Stationery Office, 1959).

TABLE 15.1   Nominal GNP, the Money Supply, and the Velocity of Money, 1960–1987

	Nominal GNP (billions $)	Money supply		Velocity V1	Velocity V2
		M1	M2		
1960	515.3	140.7	312.4	3.66	1.65
1965	705.1	167.9	459.4	4.20	1.53
1970	1,015.5	214.5	628.1	4.73	1.62
1975	1,598.4	287.6	1,023.2	5.56	1.56
1980	2,732.0	412.2	1,633.3	6.63	1.67
1981	3,052.6	439.1	1,795.9	6.95	1.70
1982	3,166.0	476.4	1,954.5	6.65	1.62
1983	3,405.7	522.1	2,186.0	6.52	1.56
1984	3,772.2	551.9	2,367.2	6.83	1.59
1985	4,014.9	620.5	2,567.4	6.47	1.56
1986	4,231.6	725.9	2,811.2	5.83	1.51
1987	4,524.3	752.3	2,909.9	6.01	1.55
1988	4,880.6	790.3	3,069.6	6.18	1.59
1989	5,233.2	797.6	3,217.0	6.56	1.63

Note: $V1$ = Nominal GNP ÷ $M1$, $V2$ = Nominal GNP ÷ $M2$.
Source: *Economic Report of the President,* 1990

of the money supply in determining equilibrium income in the short run and inflation in the long run. Money does matter, even if it is not the only thing that matters.[4]

This point is illustrated by Table 15.1, which shows actual values for GNP and two versions of the money supply ($M1$ and $M2$), along with their respective velocities. There does appear to be a relationship between the size of the money stock (especially $M2$) and the level of nominal income.

The monetarists are right to say that money does matter. The view that money does not matter has turned out to be fundamentally incorrect. Money matters because there is no ready substitute for it. The Federal Reserve Board's actions in controlling the money base are maintained or strengthened, not diluted, as they work through the extended financial system. Indeed, monetarists have made an important contribution to the mainstream view of the economy.

The Basic Monetarist Framework

Monetarists work with the quantity equation, just as the classical economists did, but they recognize that velocity is not a strict constant. The quantity equation itself is an identity, and so it always holds. But the value of V may change. Moreover, since they apply the monetarist framework to analyze

[4] Franco Modigliani, "The Monetarist Controversy or, Should We Forsake Stabilization Policies?" *American Economic Review* 67 (March 1977), pp. 1–19.

■ Monetarism and the Monetarists: Milton Friedman and the Monetary Revolution

We have only occasionally referred to Keynes and we have avoided use of the term *Keynesianism* to describe the income–expenditure approach to understanding the economy. Today, the *IS-ALM* trade-off model has been changed and developed substantially since Keynes did his original work. By the same token, monetarism is a collection of different ideas and theories developed by different people, each of which can be judged on its merits. Many economists (including Karl Brunner, Allan Meltzer, Bennet McCallum, Phillip Cagan, Anna J. Schwartz, and William Poole as well as the research staffs of

several Federal Reserve Banks, especially the Fed bank of St. Louis) have contributed to the modern development of monetarism. However, of these, Milton Friedman has undoubtedly been the most creative and influential advocate of the monetarists' ideas. Apart from his own contributions to economic literature, Friedman has exercised enormous influence on generations of students and colleagues at the University of Chicago and on public opinion also, through his popular writings and his public-television series. Milton Friedman's name will always be associated with monetarism.

inflation, monetarist ideas can often be understood more easily when the basic quantity equation is transformed into a monetary-growth relation. The quantity equation (15.8) implies that the rate of growth of the money supply plus the rate of change of velocity equals the rate of inflation plus the rate of growth of real income. Equation 15.9 shows what this means:

The Quantity Equation in Growth Rates
$$M \times V \equiv PY$$

$$\frac{\Delta M}{M} + \frac{\Delta V}{V} \equiv \frac{\Delta P}{P} + \frac{\Delta Y}{Y}. \tag{15.9}$$

By subtracting the rate of growth of velocity from both sides of Equation 15.9, the identity is restated so as to allocate the growth of the money supply into its growth components. As shown in Equation 15.10, this describes a **monetary-growth equation:**

monetary-growth equation
The growth version of the quantity equation where the growth of the money supply equals the inflation rate plus the growth of real income less any changes in velocity.

The Monetary-Growth Equation
$$\frac{\Delta M}{M} \equiv \frac{\Delta P}{P} + \frac{\Delta Y}{Y} - \frac{\Delta V}{V}. \tag{15.10}$$

The rate of growth of the money supply is composed of three parts: the rate of growth of prices plus the rate of growth of real income less the rate of growth of velocity. The monetary-growth equation changes from an identity to a substantive tool for analysis when assumptions are made about the relationship of money growth to velocity, prices, and output.

The classical economists assumed that velocity is an institutionally determined constant, so that the change in velocity is zero ($\Delta V/V = 0$). In this case, any given rate of growth of the money supply will determine the rate of growth of nominal income:

$$\frac{\Delta M}{M} = \frac{\Delta P}{P} + \frac{\Delta Y}{Y} \tag{15.10a}$$

$$= \frac{\Delta PY}{PY}.$$

However, the classical model also assumes a vertical supply schedule, which means that real income grows at a rate equal to the rate of growth of potential output ($\Delta Y/Y = \Delta Y^p/Y^p$). This means that changes in the rate of money growth will go one-for-one into changes in the rate of inflation.

The monetarists' version of the monetary-growth equation differs from the classical version in that monetarists realize that velocity and output do fluctuate around their trends, but they argue nevertheless that the classical assumptions of fixed velocity and constant growth of income are good approximations of the actual behavior even over periods of time of a year or two. According to the monetarists, fluctuations in velocity and output are short-lived and they return to their long-term trends rather quickly.

Short-run variations in output

The monetarist version of equilibrium is different from the classical version because of the recognition that wages do not react immediately to changes in the inflation rate. Consequently, in the monetarist framework an increase in the growth of the money supply will, in the short run, lead to temporary changes in the growth rate of real output, as well changes in the inflation rate.

The monetarists recognize that there are many changes going on in the economy as part of its normal operations and that these changes will lead to some frictional unemployment, even when the labor market is in equilibrium. Milton Friedman was the one who first defined the natural rate of unemployment as the rate that occurs as a result of the usual microeconomic changes as workers leave jobs and look for other jobs, even though there is no aggregate disequilibrium.

To see how monetarists analyze the way in which changes in the rate of growth of the money supply affect the real economy, we look again at the classical labor-market model. As shown in Figure 15.7 the economy is initially in equilibrium with output equal to potential output and unemployment at the natural rate (point A). The labor market is in equilibrium; the real wage has adjusted to equate the supply of and demand for labor; and the only unemployment is the result of normal frictions and adjustments. Then, suppose that the rate of growth of the money supply is reduced. In the monetarist framework, this causes an excess demand for money and the price level starts to grow more slowly. This reduction in the rate of increase of prices is unexpected. Firms find that the prices of the products they sell are rising more slowly than expected. There would be no real effect from the deceleration of inflation if the growth of wages slowed down at the same rate, but wage growth does not slow down. Monetarists assume that workers do not realize

FIGURE 15.7   Unexpected Changes in Inflation Leading to Changes in Employment

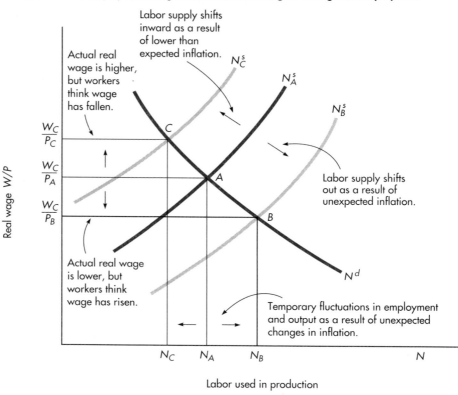

Labor used in production

that the prospective reductions in nominal wage gains are going to be offset by lower-than-expected prices. Workers are making decisions based on nominal wages only. In the short run, as firms cut back on employment, *nominal* wages may fall, but the *real* wages paid to workers are still rising. The unexpected decline in the inflation rate, unmatched by a reduction in nominal wages of the same magnitude, has made labor more expensive (W_A/P_A grows to W_C/P_C even though W_A has fallen). Yet workers do not recognize their good fortune and fewer workers seek employment as employers cut back on nominal wages—labor supply shifts inward (N_A^s to N_C^s). Fewer workers are employed at the higher real wage (point A to point C).

The result of the increase in the real wage is that production is cut back and output and employment fall. (Employment declines from N_A to N_C.) Thus in the monetarist model, the impact of an unexpected reduction in the growth of the money supply is partially transmitted into an unexpected drop in inflation and partly brings about a drop in real output.

In the reverse case, an increase in the growth rate of the money supply will appear to firms as an increase in revenue. The apparent increase in demand generates new hiring and a rise in nominal wages. Workers work more hours at the higher nominal wage $(W_B > W_A)$ even though the real wage falls $(W_B/P_B < W_A/P_A)$. The supply of labor shifts out $(N_A^s$ to $N_B^s)$ and employment rises from N_A to N_B. More workers are employed at a lower wage (shown by the shift from point A to point B).

Changes in employment in the monetarist model depend upon differences in perceptions by workers and firms. Firms immediately recognize that a lower price for their own products means less revenue so that the real cost of any nominal wage has increased, but workers see only their own nominal wages and do not see immediately that there has been a general fall in prices. These differences of perceptions cannot be maintained for long, however. Eventually everybody catches on to reality. This is why the effects on real income only take place in the short run.

Monetarists have modified the classical framework in a way that allows changes in the rate of money growth to change real output, but the effects are strictly temporary. The mechanisms by which the growth of the money supply is connected to real income take place through the less-than-perfect adjustments in labor markets. There is room in this model for different labor markets to adjust to mismatched perceptions and expectations at different speeds, making for an economy that exhibits varying degrees of change in real output over the short run. In some labor markets, the effects on real income are very transitory—workers and firms quickly realize that the wage is out of line and it is adjusted back to equilibrium. The only delay in these cases is to allow expectations to adjust to reality. In other markets, contractual arrangements between workers and firms may delay the adjustment a little longer. Labor contracts act to lengthen the duration of real effects and intensify the impact of monetary changes on real output.

nominal-wage contracts
Agreements between employers and employees that set wages in *nominal terms* (current dollars without inflation adjustments) over a period of time.

Nominal-wage contracts.   Labor contracts that fix nominal wages effectively reduce real wages in the face of inflation. This is also illustrated in Figure 15.7. Because of existing **nominal-wage contracts,** nominal wages are unchanged, leading to a reduction in the real wage and a temporary shift in labor-market equilibrium (point A to point B). But this condition only lasts as long as the contract period. Once this ends, new wage contracts are negotiated that restore the labor market to its previous equilibrium (point B to point A). These wage contracts are seen as a source of rigidity in the economy that prevent the economy from coming into equilibrium as quickly as possible.

Part of the monetarist explanation of the effect of changes in the rate of growth of the supply of money is that these changes lead *directly* to changes in the rate of inflation. Money growth affects inflation and then affects real output because the change in inflation affects the real wage. This is an important difference between monetarism and the model of earlier chapters, where changes in money growth affect interest rates and only then affect real output and inflation. The direct link from money to prices in the monetarist model is an important one to examine.

The monetarist link from money to prices

In the *IS-ALM* framework, an increase in the money supply causes a readjustment of portfolios between bonds and money. Prices are affected when the bidding for bonds drives down the interest rate, and this in turn raises aggregate demand. The increase in aggregate demand increases the purchases of goods and services, which stimulates increases in production. Higher levels of production generate higher costs and markups that increases the price level.

The monetarists argue that an increase in the money supply causes individuals to buy more goods and services, which will directly raise the price level. They infer a relationship between money and prices because almost all goods trade for money and the price level of goods is related to the price of money. The price of goods is how much money is needed to buy a given amount of goods; the **price of money** is how much goods have to be given up in order to obtain a given amount of money. In a very simple economy, with only one good (bread) and money (dollars), the price of bread is the reciprocal of the price of money. If one loaf of bread costs one unit of money ($1), the price of bread is $1 per loaf and the price of money is one loaf per dollar. If one loaf of bread costs two units of money ($2), the price of bread is $2 per loaf and the price of money is one half a loaf per dollar.

Generalize from one good to the many goods and services in the economy, and the price level sets the terms on which money and goods are exchanged. How much money has to be given up to buy a given market basket of goods and services? The answer is proportional to the price level. The higher the price level (P) the greater is the amount of money needed. The reciprocal of the price level $(1/P)$ can be thought of as the price of money.

With this monetarist frame of reference, a simple supply-and-demand analysis leads us expect that an increase in the quantity of money will lead directly to a decrease in the price of money. Since a lower price of money (declining $1/P$) means that the price level rises, increasing the quantity of money leads to inflation. With a given supply of goods and services, an increase in money will create an excess supply of money, and the response of any market to excess supply is to lower the price of the item in excess.

Inflation is popularly characterized as "too much money chasing too few goods." In our judgment, this phrase confuses an effect (inflation) with one of its causes (too much money). To monetarists, that popular statement is exactly on target. Inflation is the direct consequence of an excess supply of money. Whether to view inflation as a wholly monetary process or as a partially monetary process is a central question posed by the monetarist controversy.

---

price of money
A difficult concept because there is no single price of money. Monetarists say that the price of money is the reciprocal of the price level. This price of money is based upon exchanging money for a market basket of goods. Another possible price of money is the short-term nominal interest rate, reflecting the cost of renting money for a short period. One can even think of other prices of money, such as the value of the dollar in foreign exchange. It may be better not to use the concept, the "price of money."

We now go on to discuss that question by taking a more careful look at the quantity equation and the monetarist presumptions about the stability or predictability of velocity.

The stability or predictability of velocity

In the classical model the rate of growth of velocity was zero and the rate of growth of output was constant. The link from money to prices was simple and direct. In the monetarist framework, output growth can fluctuate temporarily and velocity will change.

Table 15.2 shows annual values for the monetary-growth equation. The rate of growth of the money supply ($M1$ or $M2$) equals the rate of growth of the price level (GNP price deflator) plus the rate of growth of real income (GNP/GNP price deflator) minus the rate of growth of the velocity of money (GNP/$M1$ or GNP/$M2$). As shown in the table, the growth of velocity has not been zero. This is true of either the $M1$ or $M2$ version of velocity—it varies from year to year and even changes direction in different periods. The monetary-growth equation reveals variations in velocity that were not readily observable by looking at the levels of the money stock and nominal GNP that were shown in Table 15.1.

Milton Friedman confronted the issue of the stability and predictability of velocity by formulating a more sophisticated version (Equation 15.11) of the quantity equation in which velocity is no longer a constant, but is instead a predictable function of other economic variables:[5]

$$PY = M \times V \, (r, \text{Exp}\Delta P/P). \tag{15.11}$$

In this restatement of the quantity theory, the velocity of money depends upon the real interest rate and the rate of inflation.

Written in this way, Milton Friedman's restatement of the quantity theory is very similar to the money-demand specification used in the *IS-ALM* trade-off model, but in his interpretation, Friedman is able to give an *exclusive* role to monetary policy: The supply of money affects both income and inflation in the short run and affects only inflation in the longer run. He explains his theory by asserting that the real interest rate is constant and that the expected rate of inflation is determined by the expected rate of growth of the money supply. In other words, his response to the criticism that velocity does in fact vary is that *variations in velocity are all caused by changes in monetary policy*—all the sources of variation in the price level are driven by changes

---

[5] Milton Friedman included other variables than those given in Equation 15.11 in his 1956 article, "The Quantity Theory of Money: A Restatement," in *Studies in the Quantity Theory of Money*, ed. Milton Friedman (Chicago: University of Chicago Press, 1956). This issue of predictability as distinct from stability is one of the forecasting accuracy of econometric models of velocity. Though some versions of forecasting models are better than others and some definitions of velocity result in more predictability than others, velocity has in general not proven to be as stable or predictable a macroeconomic variable as is indicated by the monetarists' models of the economy.

TABLE 15.2   The Monetary-Growth Equation: Money Growth Rates (*M1* and *M2*), Inflation, and the Growth of Real Income and Velocity, 1960–1987 (Annual Percent Changes)

	M1 Growth	=	Inflation	+	Real Income Growth	−	Velocity Growth
1960	0.6	=	1.6	+	2.2	−	2.8
1965	4.7	=	2.7	+	5.3	−	3.3
1970	5.3	=	5.5	+	(−0.3)	−	(−0.1)
1971	6.6	=	5.7	+	2.8	−	1.9
1972	9.2	=	4.7	+	5.0	−	0.5
1973	5.5	=	6.5	+	5.2	−	6.2
1974	4.4	=	9.1	+	(−0.5)	−	4.2
1975	4.9	=	9.8	+	(−1.3)	−	3.6
1976	6.6	=	6.4	+	4.9	−	4.7
1977	8.0	=	6.7	+	4.7	−	3.4
1978	8.3	=	7.3	+	5.3	−	4.3
1979	7.7	=	8.9	+	2.5	−	3.7
1980	6.5	=	9.0	+	(−0.2)	−	2.3
1981	6.4	=	9.7	+	1.9	−	5.2
1982	8.6	=	6.4	+	(−2.5)	−	(−4.7)
1983	9.5	=	3.9	+	3.6	−	(−2.0)
1984	5.8	=	3.7	+	6.8	−	4.7
1985	12.5	=	3.2	+	3.0	−	(−6.3)
1986	16.5	=	2.6	+	2.9	−	(−11.0)
1987	3.1	=	3.2	+	3.6	−	3.7

	M2 Growth	=	Inflation	+	Real Income Growth	−	Velocity Growth
1960	4.9	=	1.6	+	2.2	−	(−1.1)
1965	8.2	=	2.7	+	5.3	−	0.8
1970	6.6	=	5.5	+	(−0.3)	−	1.4
1971	13.4	=	5.7	+	2.8	−	4.9
1972	13.0	=	4.7	+	5.0	−	3.3
1973	6.9	=	6.5	+	5.2	−	4.8
1974	5.5	=	9.1	+	(−0.5)	−	3.1
1975	12.6	=	9.8	+	(−1.3)	−	(−4.1)
1976	13.7	=	6.4	+	4.9	−	2.4
1977	10.6	=	6.7	+	4.7	−	0.8
1978	8.0	=	7.3	+	5.3	−	4.6
1979	8.0	=	8.9	+	2.5	−	3.4
1980	8.9	=	9.0	+	(−0.2)	−	(−0.1)
1981	9.9	=	9.7	+	1.9	−	1.7
1982	8.8	=	6.4	+	(−2.5)	−	(−4.9)
1983	11.8	=	3.9	+	3.6	−	4.3
1984	8.5	=	3.7	+	6.8	−	2.0
1985	8.5	=	3.2	+	3.0	−	2.3
1986	9.0	=	2.6	+	2.9	−	2.9
1987	3.3	=	3.2	+	3.6	−	3.5

Note: Inflation = Annual percent change in the GNP price deflator.
Source: *Economic Report of the President,* 1990.

in the money supply. The link between money and prices is maintained and inflation is still always and everywhere a monetary phenomenon.[6]

---

[6] Milton Friedman, "A Theoretical Framework for Monetary Analysis," *Journal of Political Economy,* March/April 1970, p. 217.

According to Friedman, the real rate of interest is a constant because it is tied to stable real factors, such as individuals' attitudes toward consumption now versus consumption in the future (called the rate of time preference) and the rate of profit or marginal productivity of capital. The second assumption is that the expected rate of inflation depends *only* upon monetary policy.

While the monetarist bottom line is that the quantity equation works, modern monetarism differs from the classical framework in its capacity to take account of the observed variability of output and velocity, but it does so in a way that preserves the primacy of money and monetary policy as determinants of inflation.

Monetarist Monetary Policy

Monetarists argue that a monetary policy that changes the rate of growth of the money supply to deal with current economic events should not be used to manage the economy. The monetarist view is that fluctuations in real output are short-lived because the economy is self-correcting and that the growth of the money supply is the primary determinant of nominal income and inflation. This leads them to conclude that an active use of monetary policy will not improve economic performance. Monetarists hold the position that the economy will do better without government action. Attempts to fine-tune the economy through marginal changes in the money supply will only disrupt the economy, resulting in unnecessary fluctuations in inflation and output.

In the face of real shocks to the economy, it may take a while before prices and wages adjust to restore full-employment equilibrium, but not that long. In this view of the world, the private economy is fundamentally self-correcting—it is a stable system that will return to equilibrium quickly unless it is continuously disturbed. Therefore, to monetarists the best monetary policy is a stable and predictable rate of growth in the money supply—one that is matched to the long-run growth of potential output.

Milton Friedman's constant–money-supply-growth rule

In his most famous policy prescription, the **constant–money-supply-growth rule,** Milton Friedman argued that setting a target of a constant percent growth in the money supply would insure price stability, that is to say, roughly a zero rate of inflation.[7] He arrived at that rule by using his assumptions about velocity and the rate of growth of real output and applying them to the monetary-growth equation (Equation 15.10). He assumes that

constant–money-supply-growth rule
The monetarist policy prescription, setting the rate of growth in the money supply equal to the long-term rate of growth of potential output so as to insure price stability and reduce the severity of cyclical fluctuations.

[7] "The precise rate of growth, like the precise monetary total, is less important than the adoption of some stated and known rate. I myself have argued for a rate that would on the average achieve rough stability in the level of prices of final products, which I have estimated would call for something like a 3 to 5 per cent per year rate of growth in currency plus all commercial bank deposits or a slightly lower rate of growth in currency plus demand deposits only." [Milton Friedman, "The Role of Monetary Policy," *American Economic Review* LVIII (March 1968), pp. 1–17.]

the growth of velocity will be close to zero, because the main cause of fluctuations in velocity (namely, fluctuations in the growth rate of money) has been eliminated. In this case (shown in Equations 15.12A and 15.12B), the desired growth rate of money is equal to the desired rate of inflation plus the desired growth rate of real output:

$$\text{Since } \frac{\Delta M}{M} \equiv \frac{\Delta P}{P} + \frac{\Delta Y}{Y} - \frac{\Delta V}{V}. \qquad (15.12)$$

then if the change in velocity is zero, this gives

$$\text{Desired } \frac{\Delta M}{M} = \text{Desired } \frac{\Delta P}{P} + \text{Desired } \frac{\Delta Y}{Y}. \qquad (15.12a)$$

Then if the desired rate of inflation is zero and the desired rate of growth of output is the growth rate of potential output, this gives

$$\text{Desired } \frac{\Delta M}{M} = \text{Constant growth rate of potential output.} \qquad (15.12b)$$

The workings of such a rule-based policy are illustrated in Figure 15.8. The economy is initially pictured at point A, where output is equal to potential output (Y_A is equal to Y^P), aggregate demand is shown by AD_0, and the price level is P_A. Over the course of the next year, potential output grows by a fixed percentage, based upon the trend of potential output (AS to AS'). The increase in the money supply by the same percentage is just enough to increase aggregate demand from AD_0 to AD_1, assuming no change in velocity or no change in the price level.

Friedman recognizes that in practice there may be some change in velocity as a result of all the shocks and changes that go on in a diverse economy. If velocity grows a little, then instead of having aggregate demand of AD_1, there will be aggregate demand of AD'_1. This unexpected increase in velocity will push up the price level (to P_C) and the resulting unexpected inflation will lower the real wage and raise output above potential. (The economy goes to Y_C, moving along the short-run aggregate supply schedule AS.) Similarly, an unexpected decrease in velocity will lead to aggregate demand of AD''_1, an unexpected decrease in the price level (to P_D), and output below potential (at Y_D).

Because the uncertainty of monetary policy has been eliminated, the fluctuations of velocity will be small and so the range of fluctuations of prices and output will be small. The cyclical fluctuations in the economy will have been greatly reduced. Figure 15.8 shows the bands that should cover output and price-level variations, assuming only small changes in velocity.

The analysis could also be extended to cover the possibility of short-run changes in potential output. Small economic fluctuations might take place as a result of changes in technology, consumer preferences, or foreign

FIGURE 15.8   Unexpected Variations in Velocity with Friedman's Money-Growth Rule

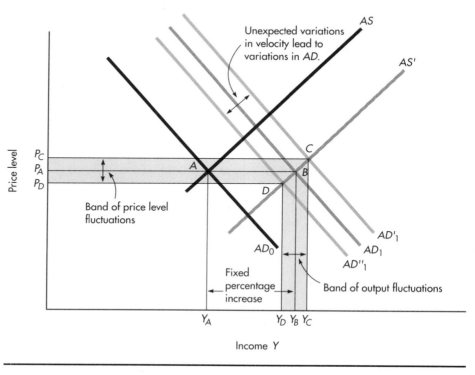

trade and these could lead to a band of variation around the aggregate supply schedule. This would broaden the range of possible output fluctuations that would be experienced in practice, but the business cycle still would be largely attenuated—given Friedman's view that most of the variability in output in the past has been caused by variable monetary policy. Figure 15.9 illustrates the case where there is a band of variability around both the aggregate demand and the aggregate supply schedules. The shaded diamond area indicates the sizes of the price and output variations that would occur with a money-growth rule.

According to the monetarist view, the shaded area between the aggregate supply and demand schedules in Figure 15.9 represents the highest level of performance and the most stability that the economy is capable of obtaining. The unexpected changes in velocity or the unexpected changes in supply conditions cannot be corrected by policy because the policymakers do not know any more about them than the private sector knows. Policy changes that drive the rate of growth of the money supply above or beyond the constant growth rate of potential also drive equilibrium to be temporarily

FIGURE 15.9   The Range of Price and Output Variations with Unexpected Variations in Velocity and Supply Conditions with Friedman's Money-Growth Rule Conditions

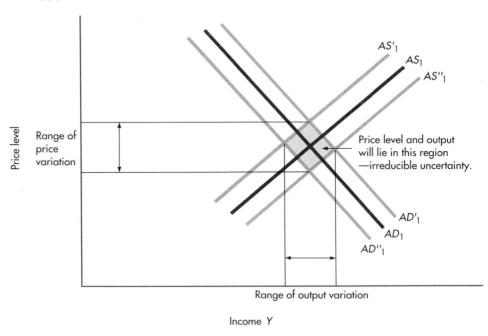

outside of the shaded area. The failure to hold a constant rate of growth in the money supply and the subsequent erratic fluctuations in monetary policy are seen by monetarists as the main sources of the historical business cycle.

There is an important situation where monetarist ideas are clearly applicable. There have been many episodes in the past where governments have been unable or unwilling to raise enough taxes to finance the level of government spending and where they have been unable to borrow enough to pay for the resulting budget deficits. If central banks are then forced to increase the supply of money more and more rapidly in order to buy the government's bonds, the result is a **hyperinflation.**

Hyperinflation

Rates of inflation experienced in the United States in the 20th century have rarely exceeded 10 percent per year. In an economy that experiences any annual growth in real income, inflation rates that remain below 10 percent per year can be attributed to both monetary and nonmonetary causes. But not all inflations are as mild as these. There have been economies that have experienced extraordinarily higher rates of inflation. In those economies,

hyperinflation
A very rapid and escalating inflation. Often defined technically as an inflation where the price level rises at a rate in excess of 50 percent per month for one year.

inflation has been shown to be a purely monetary phenomenon. This is because the extraordinarily large increases in the money supply overpower all other causes of inflation. Monetarists use the examples of extraordinarily rapid inflation to bolster the case for monetarism.

Phillip Cagan, a monetarist who studies rapid inflation, defined hyperinflation as an inflation where the price level rises by more than 50 percent per month or well over 1,000 percent per year.[8] In economies suffering from hyperinflation, the explosive acceleration in the price level is almost completely monetary in nature. The rate of inflation accelerates as the rate of growth of the money supply increases. The growth of the demand for money follows quite closely that which would be predicted by Friedman's version of the quantity equation. There is a rapid growth of velocity as money-supply growth increases and people come to expect rapid inflation. People want to spend money as quickly as possible because its value is falling: the opportunity cost of holding money is rising rapidly. The growth of income and other nonmonetary variables has little impact on inflation compared to the effect of the increase in the money supply. The most well studied hyperinflation took place in Germany from May 1921 to November 1923. Prices and the stock of money in Germany at the end of the hyperinflation had increased by more than one billion times what they were less than two years before. Had such an inflation occurred in the United States in modern times, the price of a loaf of bread would have risen from $1 to $1 billion and the price of a midsized automobile from $12,000 to $12 trillion, all in a very brief 30 months.

The most amazing hyperinflation took place in Hungary in 1945–46, where the price level rose by over one octillion times (5.20×10^{27}) in 13 months. While at the peak of the German hyperinflation, prices were rising at over 300 percent per month or 5 percent per day, in contrast, during the Hungarian hyperinflation prices were rising at almost 20,000 percent per month or almost 40 percent per day! As evidence that there was a rapid increase in velocity that exacerbated the inflationary effects of rapid monetary expansion, German and Hungarian workers demanded to be paid every several hours since the purchasing power of their wages was eroding during the day.

All of the hyperinflations started with a continuing acceleration of the money supply. The hyperinflations typically ended with budgetary reforms to reduce the budget deficits and hence reduce the pressure to expand the money supply. These were also accompanied by the initiation of a currency reform. The growth of the money supply was drastically curtailed and inflationary expectations were rapidly reduced. Following the end of the hyperinflations, people returned to holding money, velocity fell, and the economies stabilized. Yet stopping hyperinflation was not painless; several of the econo-

---

[8] Phillip Cagan, "The Monetary Dynamics of Hyperinflation," in *Studies in the Quantity Theory of Money*, ed. Milton Friedman (Chicago: University of Chicago Press, 1956).

BRAZIL'S HARSH ATTACK ON INFLATION IS RISKING DEEP ECONOMIC SLUMP

SAO PAULO, Brazil—When Fernando Collor de Mello took office in March, he said he had "only one shot" to halt Brazil's hyperinflation. But instead of firing a bullet, the new president dropped a bomb.

"The monetary contraction we imposed on society is fantastic," acknowledges Ibrahim Eris, one of the architects of the harsh anti-inflation plan and now the president of the central bank. "It's probably the first time in the world that a country in time of peace has practically destroyed its monetary standard and replaced it."

Under the plan, Mr. Collor didn't just restrict credit or cut spending, as other governments here have done. He froze about 70% of the money circulating in the economy for 18 months, until the fall of next year, and also replaced the old currency, the cruzado novo, with a new, strictly controlled one, the cruzeiro. If money causes inflation, the thinking goes, then removing money removes inflation.

Fast Medicine

The results have come faster than it takes to say hyperinflation. Inflation, which reached 84.32% in March alone and totaled 4,854% in the 12 months through March, halted completely—in fact, prices fell—in the month following the unveiling of the plan, the government says. (However, some trade unions and economists disagree, charging that the index is based on an incomplete basket of goods.)

But in stopping inflation, the government has also stopped the economy. "To kill the cockroach, they set the apartment on fire," complains former Economic Planning Minister Antonio Delfim Netto.

Deprived of cash, consumers stopped buying, companies stopped producing and exporters stopped exporting. Then, afraid that it had paralyzed the country, the government started reinjecting money into the system to the point that some feared a revival of inflation, and the government closed the tap again. Although the government terms all

mies in central Europe went through severe economic downturns because of the credit crunch that followed the steps taken to end the inflation.

The relationship between the money supply and the price level described by the quantity equation works best in a hyperinflation where the growth of the money supply is so large as to dominate all other economic concerns. But the lessons from hyperinflations do not carry over to the United States. U.S. inflation has had both monetary and nonmonetary causes. The fact that excess money growth is the cause of hyperinflations does not mean that the monetarist model can be applied to the U.S. economy in normal times. In our judgment there are serious difficulties with the monetarist position.

Assessing the Monetarist Model

There is no question that monetarism has contributed to our understanding of the macroeconomy. Indeed, the importance of money to long-run inflation is an idea that has been incorporated in the analysis of earlier chapters. Our emphasis in this book on financial markets and expectations owes a lot to the monetarist revolution. The major differences between the monetarist this as only a short, predictable phase and says economic activity is picking up again, many economists and businessmen think that Brazil has simply traded inflation for recession—and could end up with both if the government errs in its efforts to revive the economy. . . .

"We're walking on a very narrow road," the central bank's Mr. Eris concedes. "On one side is the precipice of recession; on the other is inflation. Today, society thinks we're walking close to recession, but the road is so narrow we could fall the other way. Our problem today is trying to administer this so we don't fall on either side."

Mr. Eris also admits that the plan "has implications that aren't clear. Talk of recession or depression and talk of an explosion of demand prove the economy hasn't found its equilibrium." Inflation, he says, "has been knocked down, and the judge has counted to three. When he says 10, we'll be in another world." But both he and Economics Minister Cardoso are confident of steering the economy through the twin perils of inflation and recession.

If they succeed, economists say, they will have laid the foundations to allow Brazil, at long last, to live up to its huge potential. If they fail, Brazil will have "exhausted the economic encyclopedia" of ways to cure inflation, Mr. Langoni says. The results, all agree, won't be clear for at least another couple of months.

"We're going to have a terrific decade," Abril's Mr. Civita says, "All we have to do is get over the next two months. I'm sure there's a promised land at the end of the desert. The question is: Is there enough water in the canteen to make it across?"

model and the *IS-ALM* trade-off model have to do with the degree to which money is either important or all important, the time it takes for the economy to adjust to equilibrium, and the extent to which wages and prices are flexible in the short run. The trade-off model of inflation has several nonmonetary elements (output, adaptive expectations, supply shocks) that influence inflation, while the monetarist view is that inflation is always and everywhere a monetary phenomenon.

Money and prices

There is a problem with the monetarist analysis of the link between money and the price level. The price level is the aggregate result of thousands of individual price and wage decisions made by firms and workers on the basis of the supply and demand for goods and services. The price of a pair of shoes is not set on the basis of the proportion of the shoe manufacturer's wealth he or she wants to hold in the form of money. When demand increases, each producer sets its own price relative to the prices of other manufacturers and relative to import prices. Inflation increases as a rise in aggregate demand filters down to the individual price and wage decisions. Each decision maker tries to raise his or her relative price, and all prices go up. Similarly, wage rates are set by firms based on wages in other companies, the cost of living, and the state of the labor market. Wages rise more rapidly if companies experience problems in hiring, not directly because cash managers are holding larger checking-account balances. Inflation accelerates as a result of increased aggregate demand for goods and services, and this demand depends upon income and the rate of interest, not particularly on money, which is a tiny fraction of total wealth.

It is misleading to say that the reciprocal of the price level is *the* price of money and hence that changes in the quantity of money will lead directly to changes in the price level. Any durable good has two prices, the purchase price and the rental price; and this is true for money also, in that money can be "rented" by borrowing at the prevailing rate of interest. It is the rental price of money (the interest rate) that adjusts directly when the quantity of money is varied. When the Fed expands the money supply, this leads to an excess supply of money in the money market, where T bills and other short-term assets are traded; and the excess supply of money is then eliminated by a change in the short-term nominal rate of interest. Over time, the change in the interest rate may lead to a change in aggregate demand and hence to a change in the price level.

Real wages over the cycle

The monetarist model argues that changes in real output are the result of changes in the real wage. When the price level increases, the real wage falls and employers hire more workers and produce more output. When the price level falls, this raises the real wage and firms cut back on employment. If this model is correct, it should be possible to look at data on real wages and see their cyclical pattern. Figure 15.10 shows data on the real wage with business-cycle fluctuations marked on the figure. There is no clear tendency in the data for wages to be below their trend during booms and above trend during recessions. Real wages do not seem terribly sensitive to cyclical variations in the economy.

If there is any cyclical pattern to real wages visible in the data, it is a tendency for wages to fall in recessions, suggesting that recessions are periods where product demand is low and employers lay off workers and hold down wages. This does not fit with the monetarist model in which employment losses are driven by high wages.

The behavior of wages over the business cycle is a problem for other models as well as the monetarist model. In the *General Theory*, Keynes also assumed that the real wage would fall in booms; the rational-expectations model that we will discuss in Chapter 16 has the same problem. The reason that all of these models have the same difficulty is that they assume perfectly competitive markets with flexible wages and prices. In a perfectly competitive market, employment and output are determined by the relation between wage cost and product price. Once we recognize the importance of imperfect

FIGURE 15.10   The Real Wage over the Business Cycle

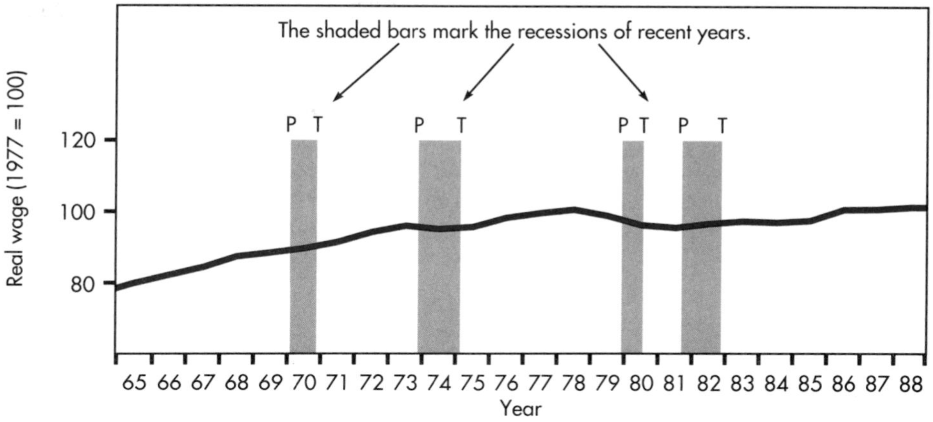

The real wage has increased over time as productivity has increased. It fell with the oil-price increases and other supply shocks. It has not shown much systematic relation to the business cycle.

markets and other market conditions, this is not so. We will return to this issue in Chapter 16.

Monetary aggregates and economic activity

There is general agreement among economists of different schools of thought that monetary policy has played an important role in business-cycle fluctuations. But the monetarist position that money growth dominates all other factors is hard to accept. The surge in inflation in the 1970s is hard to explain without allowing for the OPEC price increase and other supply shocks. Inflation is again being pushed up by the conflict with Iraq in mid-1990 as this is being written. And as another counter-example to monetarism, Table 15.2 documented the rapid growth of the money supply in the 1980s that was not accompanied by any surge in inflation. This period also does not fit well with the monetarist view.

The movements of monetary aggregates are important in explaining the course of economic events, but they are not as all-important as a monetarist model assumes. In the *IS-ALM* model, the power of monetary policy comes from its impact on nominal and real interest rates and on credit conditions, not through a direct link from money to prices. There is room for monetary and nonmonetary influences on the economy.

Even if one disagrees with the monetarist model, however, there is more to monetarism than this. Monetarist economists are not simply developers of an alternative model of the macroeconomy. Much of the literature of monetarism is taken up with reviewing historical economic policy with a very critical eye and with criticizing the Keynesian income–expenditure model for its mechanistic structure, for its excessively constrained role for money and financial markets, and for the imprecision of its forecasts and its policy prescriptions. While many of the monetarist objections to the simple Keynesian models have been answered by extensions of the simple model, it is useful to describe some of that criticism and the responses to it.

Monetarist Criticisms of the Income–Expenditure Model

In the simplest Keynesian models, exogenous shifts in investment or government expenditure lead to large changes in final output because of the induced changes in consumption, investment, imports, and/or government expenditures, net of taxes. The allocation of expenditures using national income accounting led many to believe that the induced change in consumption was the largest contributor to the growth of final output. In those models that described changes in income as a multiplier process, the marginal propensity to consume was a crucial component of the multiplier. The monetarists fiercest criticisms of the simple income–expenditure model were directed toward the multiplier. The criticisms had some validity since the multipliers generated by those models were subject to much more variation than the early Keynesians had realized. The marginal propensity to consume is not a constant; rather, the relationship between short-run changes in income and short-run changes in consumption vary a great deal. The permanent-income hypothesis, which we described in Chapter 13, indicates that families engage in consumption smoothing, so that an increase or decrease in income induces only a small change in consumption.

Monetarists were, and continue to be, very critical of economic-stabilization policy. Such policy is unnecessary, they argue, because the economy is self-correcting. Stabilization policy is unwise because government actions historically have only made things worse. Milton Friedman argues that it was the collapse of the money supply after 1929 that led to the Great Depression. In general he judges that counter-cyclical policies directed against recessions have performed poorly.

At the heart of the monetarist criticism of stabilization policy is the argument that even though the Fed can affect the economy through changes in the growth of the money supply, the Fed is incapable of timing changes so as to match up with the need for intervention. Policy goes wrong so often, not because of bad intentions, but because of bad timing. We never know where the economy is today, only where it was some months ago. Monetarists have argued that even if fiscal policy had an effect on the economy, the problem of timing would almost guarantee that stabilization policy would have the government executing the wrong policy at the wrong time.

Monetarist criticism of fiscal policy

Monetarist criticism of fiscal-stabilization policy extended with the argument that cutting taxes will not induce any increase in consumption. The argument is that households know that a cut in taxes without a corresponding cut in government expenditures will increase their disposable income only temporarily. Suppose the government budget starts in balance, and then there is a stimulative tax cut that generates a budget deficit. Monetarists point out that this deficit must be covered by issuing government bonds. And either these bonds must be repaid in the future, or interest payments must be made indefinitely to service a permanent increase in the national debt. Either way, taxpayers will face higher future tax payments. They will prepare for these payments now by saving the proceeds of the original stimulative tax cut rather than spending it. Thus there is no stimulus to current private expenditure.

While a complete discussion of the proposition that fiscal policy is ineffective awaits in the next chapter, we briefly note that the proposition requires individuals to take account of changes in the federal budget deficit when making private-expenditure decisions. While a sudden rise in the federal deficit may well have a direct impact on financial markets, a similar direct effect of the deficit would be hard to find in consumers' decisions to purchase automobiles and vacations.

Although there are problems with the monetarist model of the economy, the monetarist emphasis on the considerable power of monetary policy to affect real output in the short run and the notion that there is a one-to-one relation between money growth and inflation in the long run are both useful and powerful ideas.

Monetarist criticisms of stabilization policy were the precursors of even more fundamental attacks on the standard models. While monetarism has classical underpinnings, and concludes that stabilization policy is inadvisable, the equilibrium–business-cycle theorists use an approach that is based even more heavily on the classical model and they conclude that systematic stabilization policy has no effect on output and employment.

SUMMARY

- The main core of monetarism holds that: (1) The rate of inflation is strictly determined by the rate of growth of the money supply. (2) The economy is self-correcting so that full employment will be restored fairly quickly in the absence of government intervention. (3) Government policies have contributed to business-cycle fluctuations and were the main cause of the Great Depression. (4) Government should set monetary policy so that the growth of the money supply equals the growth of potential output.

- Most economists agree that in the long run the economy will behave in the way that the monetarist/classsical model describes. The disagreements concern the behavior of the economy over the short and intermediate runs.

- Monetarism has its basis in the classical model of the economy where real output is determined by supply and demand in labor markets that clear fairly quickly and smoothly. The monetarist model rejects the notions of extended price and wage stickiness.

- The classical model is based on the following elements: (1) Output changes come about through changes in the quantity of labor employed. (2) In the short run, capital and technology are held constant and only variations in the amount of labor employed bring about changes in output. (3) Employers determine the demand for labor based upon the condition that the marginal product of labor equals the real wage. (4) Workers decide how much labor to supply based upon the real wage.

- Changes in aggregate demand, such as an increase or decrease in the money supply, should not affect either the willingness to work or the productivity of labor and therefore they do not effect employment or output.

- Changes in aggregate demand simply lead to changes in the price level at a set level of output. With a constant velocity of money, an increase in the money supply will lead to a proportional increase in the price level.

- In the monetarist model, changes in aggregate demand do have an effect on output as well as on prices. A change in the supply of money leads to a change in the price level and hence in the real wage. These changes in the real wage are only temporary and so the deviations of output from potential output are also only temporary.

- Monetarists recognize that velocity changes, but they argue that these changes are the result of changes in the expected rate of growth of the money supply.

- Monetarists say that the role of money and monetary policy is of primary importance in determining inflation and economic conditions.

- Monetarists say that the economy will do better without government action. Attempts to fine-tune the economy through marginal changes in the money supply will only disrupt the economy, resulting in unnecessary fluctuations in inflation and output.

- There are several objections to the monetarist model. Changes in the supply of money may lead to changes in the rate of interest rather than leading directly to changes in the price level. Real wages do not vary over the business cycle in the way that the monetarist model predicts.

KEY TERMS

aggregate production function

classical model

constant–money-supply-growth rule

hyperinflation

marginal product of labor

monetarism

monetary-growth equation   quantity equation

nominal wage   real wage

nominal-wage contracts   Say's Law

price of money   velocity of money

DISCUSSION QUESTIONS AND PROBLEMS

1. Why does output not change in response to aggregate demand changes in the classical model?

2. List reasons why labor markets in an actual economy would or would not resemble the classical labor market. Does the time horizon matter? Why?

3. What is the role of aggregate demand in the classical model?

4. If potential output is determined by aggregate supply, what guarantees that all of potential output will be produced and purchased?

5. Describe the connection between the quantity equation in a classical model and monetarism.

6. Fill in the blanks in the following table.

Growth of nominal money supply	Rate of inflation	Growth of velocity	Growth of real income
5	5	0	—
5	10	0	—
10	—	5	5
0	10	0	—
0	0	5	—
20	—	5	5

7. Discuss the pros and cons of a fixed rule for the growth of the money supply. What do you have to assume about the economy to endorse or reject such a policy?

8. It has been suggested that instead of setting a fixed rate of growth of the money supply, the Fed should vary the rate of growth of money depending upon whether nominal income is growing faster or slower than some target rate of increase. Comment on this proposal.

9. During the period 1980–81, the Keynesian economist James Tobin used the monetary-growth equation to argue that there would be a sharp recession as a result of the Fed's policy of monetary contraction. Try to reconstruct Tobin's argument. Recall that the monetary-growth equation is an identity.

CHAPTER 16

Rational Expectations, Price Flexibility, and Neo-Keynesian Responses

INTRODUCTION

Expectations of future prices, interest rates, exchange rates, and policy actions affect the behavior of the modern economy. Everyone interested in macroeconomic policy agrees that expectations are important, but there is significant disagreement over how they are formed and how they affect income and inflation.

In the 1970s, a group of economists developed a *rational-expectations* model of the economy in which expectations are very important in the determination of income and in which expectations are formed on the basis of a rational forecast of economic conditions. This model accepted many, but not all, of the ideas of monetarism and also relied even more strongly than previous models on classical assumptions about market behavior in the economy. By combining classical assumptions about the quickness with which markets reach equilibrium with the idea that expectations are formed solely on the basis of rational forecasts of economic conditions, the rational-expectations economists developed an alternative view of why there are fluctuations in the economy and what the impact of policy changes will be.

There are two key elements to this new approach to business-cycle analysis. The first is that people form expectations rationally about the future course of the economy. The second is that prices and wages are perfectly flexible and that this flexibility ensures that markets are always in equilibrium or that equilibrium is quickly restored following a shift in supply or demand.

This approach to the analysis of the cycle was developed largely in response to what was seen as a failure of Keynesian analysis. Charles Plosser, a leading advocate of equilibrium–business-cycle models, describes the problem: "The essential flaw in the Keynesian interpretation of macroeconomic

choice-theoretic framework
Models of the economy where the actions of economic agents result from the choices they make, based upon maximizing their self-interest. These choices are often assumed to be made rationally by people with rational expectations.

phenomena was the absence of a consistent foundation based on the **choice-theoretic framework** of microeconomics."[1] And he would certainly make the same criticism of the *IS-ALM* trade-off model that we have used in this book. Equilibrium–business-cycle economists argue that there is no fully rational model of behavior that is consistent with sticky wages and prices. This is what Plosser means by the absence of a "choice-theoretic framework."

As we work through the equilibrium models, their implications will be startling: Government will have no systematic policymaking role in controlling aggregate demand because everyone will know what the effect of an anticipated policy action will be and they will buy or sell goods or assets so as to insulate themselves from its effects. In the view of the rational-expectations economists, output will deviate from potential output only in the short run and only as a result of unexpected shocks. Full employment will quickly be restored without the need to use policy—indeed, systematic policies will have no effect and unexpected policy actions will have adverse effects.

In equilibrium models, systematic stabilization policy is irrelevant with regard to the real economy, but government can affect nominal values in the economy. It can quickly raise the rate of inflation by increasing the rate of growth of the money supply and it can quickly reduce the rate of inflation provided it establishes policy credibility, that is, provided that the government's commitment to reducing the rate of inflation is believed.

If expectations are rational, this means that they are formed using all the available and relevant information about the economy, and further, people do not *consistently* form overestimates or underestimates of future inflation, output, or other economic variables. In this view of the economy, people do not consistently think that inflation is going to be lower or higher than it actually is. Rational expectations result from a knowledge of supply and demand and inferences about the effect of changes in markets upon future equilibrium conditions. If supply and demand conditions are such as to generate economic equilibrium, then participants in the economy will know that that is true and they will act as if they expect supply and demand mechanisms to work accordingly.

In the past few years some of those who advocated the equilibrium–business-cycle approach have concluded that fluctuations in output cannot be explained by unexpected changes in demand. In order to be consistent with the classical assumptions of their model, anticipated fluctuations in the money supply (or in aggregate demand in general) should only lead to changes in the price level and not to fluctuations in real output. These economists began developing models of the business cycle that were strictly classical. In these models, called *real–business-cycle theory*, fluctuations in real output come about because of shifts in aggregate supply as a result of changes in

---

[1] Charles I. Plosser, "Understanding Real Business Cycles," *Journal of Economic Perspectives* 3 (Summer 1989), pp. 51–78.

technology or individual preferences, not because of shifts in aggregate demand.

The complaints voiced by the equilibrium theorists about Keynesian analysis generated a response in a body of theory that is now called *neo-Keynesian analysis*. These models attempt to explain the kind of wage and price stickiness that seem to exist in the actual economy in a way that is consistent with rational behavior. We conclude this chapter with a review of these models.

We begin the discussion of the rational-expectations point of view in the same way that these models were developed, by reconsidering how inflationary expectations are formed.

INFLATIONARY EXPECTATIONS

In the *IS-ALM* trade-off models described in this book, expectations have been important; the expected rate of inflation appeared in the relationship between real and nominal interest rates. Policy expectations were important in the description of the workings of monetary and fiscal policies. And inflationary expectations were a critical part of the output–inflation trade-off. Expectations were also important in the monetarist analysis of the velocity of money, where the expectation of future inflation was a key variable. What distinguishes the rational-expectations view from previous descriptions of the role of expectations are the assumptions made about how expectations are formed.

adaptive expectations
Expectations that are revised based on how closely past expectations conform to reality.

In some of our earlier analyses, we assumed that expectations of the future were formed out of a memory of past inflation in such a way that individuals adapt their expectations to any changes they observe over time in the actual rate of inflation. Under **adaptive expectations** the expected rate of inflation is changed from one period to the next if there is a difference between what was expected last period and what actually happened last period. Adaptive expectations assume that people adapt their beliefs on the basis of how closely they conformed to reality the last time.

In 1961, John F. Muth offered a strong argument that the adaptive-expectations model is wrong.[2] He said that rational economic behavior would lead people to form their expectations by looking at whatever relevant economic information is available. And all of this information is incorporated efficiently into unbiased expectations about the future. Muth found support for his idea in the behavior of agricultural prices.

Applying Muth's approach to the macroeconomy suggests that past inflation is not directly important in forming inflationary expectations. Rather, expectations of future inflation are formed by looking forward, using the economic conditions that generate the future rate of inflation. Past inflation is only important to the extent that it forecasts future inflation. If people

---

[2] John Muth, "Rational Expectations and the Theory of Price Movements," *Econometrica* 29 (July 1961), pp. 315–35.

have reason to think that future inflation will be very different from the rate that has prevailed in the past, then expected future inflation will not simply be an extrapolation of past trends.

The Output–Inflation Trade-Off with Rational Expectations

In Chapter 9, we described a trade-off relation (Equation 9.3 reproduced here as Equation 16.1) in which current inflation is determined by the current level of output relative to potential and the current state of inflationary expectations:

$$\text{Current } \frac{\Delta P}{P} = H\left(\frac{Y}{Y^P}\right) + \text{Exp}\left(\frac{\Delta P}{P}\right). \tag{16.1}$$

While we previously described the two factors that determine how those expectations are formed—by either past history or forward-looking forecasts—we developed the trade-off analysis based on the assumption that the past history of inflation is a major determinant of expected inflation. What characteristics of inflation would be implied by an inflationary process where current inflation is primarily related to forward-looking forecasts rather than to past inflation?

First, inflation should be subject to self-fulfilling prophecies. If everyone thinks that inflation will be high in the current and future periods, then it will be. In terms of Equation 16.1, if the expected inflation rate were to rise, then actual inflation would rise, even if output were to remain equal to potential output. Each individual firm would anticipate larger price increases by all other firms and so would raise its own prices more, even though there was no excess demand in the economy. Second, this purely future-oriented inflationary process should offer the possibility of reducing even a long-entrenched inflation without incurring the cost of prolonged low output. If expected inflation could somehow be reduced, then actual inflation would fall even if output did not fall below potential output. A reduction in the level of inflation in the economy would mean that each individual firm would anticipate smaller price increases by all other firms. In order to remain competitive, each firm would have to reduce its own price increases, bringing about the reduction in inflation even though there was no excess supply in the economy.

If inflation can really be reduced without a prolonged recession, why has past experience with reducing inflation been so painful? Robert Lucas, an economist whose work was instrumental in forming the equilibrium–business-cycle model, has argued that the trade-offs between output and inflation that have been observed in the past were the result of the public's skepticism about the commitment of policymakers to reducing inflation.[3]

---

[3] Robert E. Lucas, Jr., "Some International Evidence on Output–Inflation Tradeoffs," *American Economic Review,* June 1973; and R. E. Lucas, Jr., ed., *Studies in Business Cycle Theory* (Cambridge, Mass.: MIT Press, 1981).

For example, if the Fed restricts credit in the face of a high rate of inflation, this will not reduce inflation by much if few people believe that the Fed will stick with tighter credit over the long term. In terms of Equation 16.1, even at a current level of output different from potential, if there has been no change in inflationary expectations, there will be little change in current inflation.

When expectations of inflation are formed on the basis of future forecasts, then the public's understanding of which policy regime is in force is a more important part of their rational expectations than is the current or past experience with the actual rate of inflation. The credibility of policymakers becomes a primary factor in determining the current rate of inflation.

Credibility issues

In the face of a higher-than-desired rate of inflation, a credible change in policy could reduce inflation without reducing output, according to the rational-expectations view. If somehow policymakers could convince the private sector that the policy change toward a slower rate of growth of the money supply was a clean break between past inflation and future policy actions, then the reduction in the rate of inflation would be fully expected by everyone. Price increases in the private economy, including wage increases, would slow down, reflecting these new expectations. The rate of inflation would in fact decline, with no reduction in employment or output! The key to making such a break, it is argued, is to introduce *credibility* into anti-inflation policy. If policymakers can convince individuals that monetary and fiscal policies will not be adjusted to accommodate inflation, then expectations will change and inflation will end without recession, without output being below potential output.

At the end of Chapter 9, we briefly discussed whether the idea that expectations can be affected directly by policy has been important in practice. We continue that discussion here. Prime Minister Margaret Thatcher of Great Britain came into office in 1979 determined to break an entrenched inflation and vowing not to accommodate inflationary wage and price increases. She believed that an unwavering and credible anti-inflationary policy could bring down an entrenched inflation more quickly than could the gradual reduction of aggregate demand. In effect she was adopting a rational-expectations view of anti-inflationary policy rather than the approach described by anti-inflationary policies moving along a shifting trade-off curve. (See Chapters 9 and 10.) In practice, she succeeded in reducing inflation, but only at the cost of a very long and very severe recession. The credibility approach did not work for Mrs. Thatcher in the way that she hoped. Either she did not establish the necessary credibility required to change expectations, or else the validity of the approach is in doubt. The effects of her anti-inflationary policies were still consistent with the existence of an output–inflation trade-off; they did not supply evidence for the view that inflation expectations are distinct from the past history of inflation.

■ Credibility as a Policy Tool

Neither the United States nor Great Britain was able to reduce inflation in the 1980s without recession, but the idea of using credible policies in order to shift the output–inflation trade-off is one that is still important today. The Council of Economic Advisers is a group of three leading economists that are appointed by the president, and in 1990 President Bush's economic advisers prepared the *Economic Report of the President* that outlined the policy strategy that his administration would be following. There was considerable weight given to the importance of policy credibility and the need to follow credible anti-inflation strategies, as the following excerpt from the *Report* illustrates.

> Credible macroeconomic policies are a key to the Administration's projection of solid growth in the 1990s with gradually declining inflation. The success in containing inflation through seven years of economic expansion has helped to build this credibility. The interest rate projections are influenced by the Administration's commitment to reducing the Federal budget deficit to zero in 1993 and dedicating projected future surpluses thereafter to reducing the national debt. The Federal Government's commitment to reduced borrowing in the future is expected to ease pressure on interest rates. Similarly, the Federal Reserve's continued commitment to move toward price stability is expected to help keep wage increases in line with productivity gains by reducing the expected inflation component of wage decisions.
>
> There is no inconsistency in projecting continued low unemployment and declining rates of inflation. The idea that there is a simple, stable, and permanent trade-off between inflation and unemployment does not accord with modern macroeconomic theory, which emphasizes the importance of expectations, or with historical experience. In the 1970s, inflation and unemployment were high, while in the 1980s, the opposite occurred—inflation and unemployment were relatively low. The United States and other economies are capable of sustaining growth, achieving low unemployment, *and* controlling and reducing inflation simultaneously. The notion that the *only* way to keep inflation in check is to run a slack economy with relatively high unemployment and excess capacity is incorrect.
>
> Economic research and policy experience have led to a growing awareness of the importance of the *credibility* of policymakers to carry out a stated policy. Various definitions of policy credibility have been offered, but the following seems most useful: An announced policy is credible if the public believes that it will be implemented, and acts on those beliefs even in the face of occasional contradictory evidence. Policy credibility is not an all-or-nothing concept, and in many situations credibility can only be achieved gradually.
>
> Policy credibility will often lead to economic performance that is superior to that in which policy is not credible. The more credible a policy, the more likely it is to improve performance. A credible anti-inflation plan initiated by the monetary authorities will bring down inflation more quickly and with less chance of recession than a plan with little credibility. For example, a billion-dollar stabilization fund for Poland, recently established by a group of industrial economies, is designed to lend credibility to the Polish disinflation plan by providing financial backing to help the Polish government stabilize the exchange rate. This will reinforce other policies to reduce inflation and promote external trade.
>
> In addition, credibility can help resolve problems arising from unpredictable shifts in the structural relationships between the policy instruments and the state of the economy. Such changes can make it quite difficult for the public to assess the appropriateness of macroeconomic policies when the policy rules are complicated. If the public is confident that appropriate policies are being followed, households and businesses can plan for the future, which promotes saving, investment, and economic growth.

Source: *Economic Report of the President, 1990, pp. 59, 65–66.*

In the early 1980s, President Reagan and his advisors also wanted to benefit from using a credible anti-inflationary strategy to lower expected inflation. Some economists in his first administration promised that inflation would melt away without recession. Here the prediction of the absence of a trade-off was not borne out. There is some indication that inflation fell a little more quickly in 1983 and 1984 than would have been predicted from past experience. But a major recession was still necessary in order to bring the inflation down.

Credibility in anti-inflationary policy probably does help, but judging by experiences in the United States and the United Kingdom, it cannot be established by simply announcing a firm policy. The Reagan and Thatcher administrations were unrealistic about what could be achieved through the direct effects of policy on inflationary expectations. But despite this, there is wide acceptance of the idea that both past inflation and policy anticipations affect inflationary expectations. Even economists who emphasize the importance of inflation inertia concede that a firm commitment to inflation control can bring down the expected rate of inflation more quickly than would be predicted from past experience with half-hearted inflation control.

The rational-expectations view of credibility was maintained without assuming that markets are neoclassical, that is, competitive and quick to come to equilibrium. It can be argued that expectations are formed rationally but that prices are sticky. If government regulations fix prices, if private institutions set wages or prices with long-term contracts, or if prices or wages are simply adjusted based upon past procedures in some markets, then it is perfectly rational to base expectations of inflation on this behavior. After all, if prices are in fact sticky, it is rational to expect them to be sticky.

However, most rational-expectations economists argued that their view of expectations formation should be combined with the assumption of flexible prices and market equilibrium. The resulting models led to a revolutionary movement in macroeconomics.

COMBINING RATIONAL EXPECTATIONS WITH MARKET CLEARING

Equilibrium–business-cycle economists reject the Keynesian idea that money wages and prices are rigid and the idea that a recession is a period of excess supply for either goods or labor. The reason they give for rejecting these ideas is that if there is price stickiness, so that there is excess supply or demand in a market, then there are opportunities to buy and sell that would be profitable, but these profit opportunities are not being exploited. Markets are always in equilibrium and such opportunities cannot exist, at least not for long, because people will come along to take advantage of any profit that is around.

This group of economists says that the price of a product reflects the terms of a voluntary transaction between two parties. If either party objects to the terms, it can look for a better price. If the transaction goes through, then both parties presumably accept that the price is appropriate. If that price causes no further changes in supply or demand, it is an equilibrium price. The same logic applies to wages. If a company experiences a decline in the demand for its product and lays workers off, then this is the choice of the company and its workers. The parties could always agree to reduce the wage and keep employment higher. Workers who are laid off must prefer this to offering to work at a lower wage. In a sense, they choose to be laid off.

It is acknowledged that declines in wages and prices (outside of agricultural prices) have been relatively rare in the period since 1948, but it is argued that price-flexibility was much greater before World War II. The Wholesale Price Index fell from 158 in 1920 to 102 in 1922. It fell from 100 in 1929 to 74 in 1932. Equilibrium–business-cycle economists claim that the greater apparent stickiness in the postwar period is the result of a change in the policy environment, not because of any change in the structural characteristic of the economy.

Equilibrium Business Cycles

equilibrium–business-cycle model
A model in which fluctuations in output occur as a result of unexpected shocks, especially unexpected money supply changes.

In the **equilibrium–business-cycle model** of the macroeconomy, fluctuations in output occur, but only as a result of unexpected shocks that temporarily drive the economy away from full employment. Individual markets remain in equilibrium over the course of the cyclical fluctuations—hence the name equilibrium business cycles. The unexpected shocks are typically thought to be unexpected changes in the supply of money.

The economy reacts quickly to eliminate any profit opportunities that result from fluctuations in markets, and this has the effect of quickly reversing any deviations from potential output. The result is a pattern in which output oscillates around potential and full employment is quickly restored. In a paper that develops his business-cycle models Robert Lucas describes his main goal in developing his view of the business cycle:

> In all of the models discussed in the paper, real output fluctuations are triggered by unanticipated monetary-fiscal shocks. The first theoretical task—indeed, the central theoretical problem of macroeconomics—is to find an analytical context in which this can occur and which does not at the same time imply the existence of persistent, recurrent, unexploited profit opportunities.[4]

Robert Lucas pictured the economy as made up of separate businesses each of which is on its own island.[5] A business is affected by what happens

---

[4] Robert E. Lucas, Jr., "An Equilibrium Model of the Business Cycle," *Journal of Political Economy* 83 (December 1979), p. 1114.

[5] Robert E. Lucas, Jr., "Understanding Business Cycles," in *Stabilization of the Domestic and International Economy,* ed. Karl Brunner and Allan H. Meltzer, Carnegie-Rochester Series on Public Policy (Amsterdam: North-Holland, 1977), pp. 7–29. The parable of separate islands was first introduced by Edmund S. Phelps in the introduction to the volume he edited, *The Microeconomic Foundations of Employment and Inflation* (New York: W. W. Norton, 1970).

on other islands but no company knows exactly what other companies are doing right away. There is *incomplete information* in the economy.

To make his framework easier to understand, Lucas says that one can think about a representative worker-producer—a firm consisting of one person. And at the outset, suppose that the aggregate price level is constant. Over a given time period, the representative worker-firm finds out what the market price is for her product, a product that requires a fixed number of hours of work for each unit produced. She then determines the amount she wishes to produce, given this price, and thus how many hours she wishes to work that period. In return for the output she makes, she receives money that she then spends on a variety of goods over some period of time.

Suppose that the representative worker-firm starts work one day and finds that the price of her product is now 10 percent higher than it had been the previous day. She does not know why this price increase has occurred, and neither does any other individual worker-firm. Nor does she know how long it will last. Lacking complete information, she makes her best choice, and we can expect that she will choose to work more and produce more output. In fact, if she suspects that the price is only high temporarily, she may respond with even more work and a greater increase in output than if she believes that the increase is permanent. She will want to cash in on a temporary good price while it lasts.

Now suppose that there is not a constant price level, but instead, prices throughout the economy may be changing and the overall price level may change. What happens now when the worker-firm finds that the selling price of her product has risen 10 percent? She does not have complete information about the rest of the economy so she does not know how much of this increase in her own price is paralleled by an increase in the price level. She must form some expectation about what is happening to the price level and what she will be able to buy with the dollars that she earns by working and producing the output. Because she operates in a competitive environment, she cannot control prices; she can only react to price changes by changing output. How much she changes her work hours and output depends upon whether she thinks the rise in price was specific to her product or a general increase in the price level. She will change her work and output depending on how her own actual price compares to her expectation of the overall price level. If she thinks that her own price has risen above the overall price level, she will work and produce more. But if she thinks her own price rise simply reflects the rise in the price level, she will not work or produce more.

The case of a single worker-firm is obviously just a parable, but the equilibrium–business-cycle theorists apply the same idea to the aggregate economy and to the aggregate labor market specifically. Wages are assumed to be flexible and they react quickly to changes in the supply of and demand for labor. Workers expect a particular inflation rate in the future and they

FIGURE 16.1   The Labor Market and Aggregate Supply in the Equilibrium–Business-Cycle Model

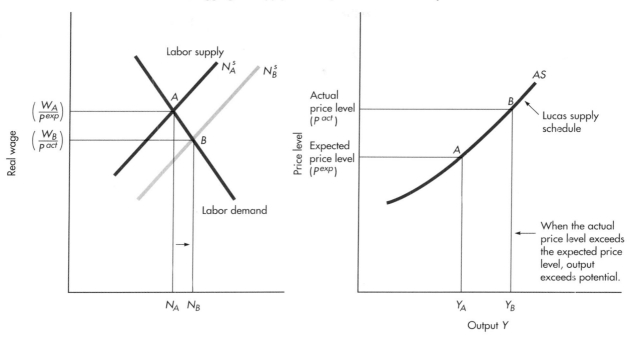

base their decisions about how much to work on the nominal wage they are being paid and their expectations about inflation. Figure 16.1 shows the equilibrium–business-cycle labor market in the left panel. The labor-supply schedule (N_A^s) is based upon workers' expectations about the price level (P^{exp}). This labor supply reflects the amount workers would choose to work based upon different levels of the real wage only if the price level turns out to be what workers expect it to be. In that case, the economy will operate at point A and the level of employment will be N_A.

If the actual price level (P^{act}) turns out to be higher than the expected price level, (P^{exp}), then the actual real wage (W/P^{act}) will be lower than the real wage workers expected (W/P^{exp}). The labor-supply schedule (N_B^s) is based upon the actual price level and not upon the expected price level being realized. It is shifted out compared to the supply when expectations were fulfilled. The economy operates at point B, where the nominal wage is higher than at point A, but the real wage is lower.

The unexpected increase in the price level has raised employment. Workers have worked more because the nominal wage was higher, and they thought that this increase would be reflected in an increase in their real wage. They were faced with the unpleasant surprise of being fooled about how much they would earn in real terms. When they discover the price level is higher than they expected, they find that they have worked more than they wanted. They expected to earn a high real wage and in fact they ended up with a low real wage.

The Lucas supply schedule

Based on the idea of a labor force that offers more labor when workers *mistakenly* believe their real wage is going to rise, Lucas proposed an aggregate-supply schedule—the *Lucas supply schedule*. The Lucas supply schedule is related to the one proposed by Milton Friedman, where output differs from potential output only when the actual price level differs from the expected price level.

When the price level turns out to be higher than expected, this drives down the real wage and firms demand more labor and produce more output. The right-hand panel of Figure 16.1 shows how output will be affected by movements of the actual price level relative to the expected price level. If the actual price level turns out to equal the expected price level, then the economy will produce output equal to potential (Y_B at point B). When the price level is above the expected price level, output exceeds potential output (Y_A at point A). Similarly, when the price level is below the expected price level, then the level of output will be below potential output. For any given level of the expected price level, therefore, increases in the actual price level will lead to higher levels of output. This relation is shown in Figure 16.1 as the Lucas supply schedule.

One important feature of the Lucas aggregate-supply schedule is that its position depends upon the expected price level. When people are expecting a high price level, then the price level must turn out to be high in order to avoid a recession. This idea is illustrated in Figure 16.2. The aggregate-supply schedule shifts up when the expected price level shifts up *(AS')*. The price level shifts down when the expected price level shifts down *(AS")*. When people are expecting a low price level, then the price level must turn out to be low, in order to avoid a boom.

The shifts in the aggregate-supply schedule shown in Figure 16.2 are similar to the shifts in the output–inflation trade-off that we saw in Chapter 9. When the expected rate of inflation is high, there will be large expected increases in the expected price level. An upward or downward shift in the Lucas supply schedule parallels the upward or downward shifts in the trade-off analysis.

While the discussion of the trade-off in Chapter 9 was influenced by the equilibrium–business-cycle model, there is however an important difference. In the equilibrium–business-cycle model, the expected price level is based upon rational, forward-looking forecasts by workers and firms. There is no such thing as an entrenched inflation. The only reason that the price

FIGURE 16.2   The Aggregate-Supply Schedule Shifts Up or Down Depending upon Changes in the Expected Price Level

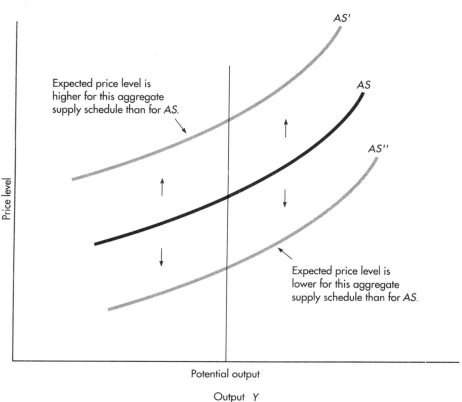

level is expected to rise is the expectation that future economic conditions will generate a higher price level. The case is usually made in reference to expectations about monetary policy. *The price level is expected to increase when the Fed is expected to increase the money supply.* We may observe periods that look as if there is an entrenched inflation. But that is simply because the Fed has followed a pattern of generating inflation through excessive money growth.

Output changes and unrealized expectations of the price level

What could cause the price level to turn out to be different from the expected price level? In equilibrium–business-cycle models, either a supply or a demand shock (for example, an unexpected increase in the money supply) will cause the actual price level to differ from the expected price level. Then the Lucas

■ The Variability of Prices and the Slope of the Lucas Supply Curve

The Lucas supply schedule is based on the assumption that firms and workers do not have complete information. And the slope of the Lucas supply schedule depends upon the difference between the information people have about the prices of the products that they produce and the overall price level. This is why Lucas uses the parable of people being on separate islands. They know much more about what is going on on their own island than what is going on in the whole archipelago.

When a worker-firm finds that the price of its own product has increased, it has to decide to what extent this is an increase in the *relative* price of what it produces, that is, the extent to which its own price has risen relative to the overall price level. For simplicity we will ignore persistent inflation for the present and simply consider increases or decreases in both individual prices and the overall price level.

If the movements of a firm's own price are highly correlated with the movements in the overall price level, then the firm will expect that a given increase in its own price is only a very small increase in its relative price. For example, if, on the average, a 10 percent increase in its own price will be associated with a 9 percent increase in the overall price level, then the firm will expect only a 1 percent increase in its relative price when its own price rises by 10 percent. In this situation the firm will increase its output only very little when it finds its own price has risen.

On the other hand in a firm where changes in the price of its own product are usually unrelated to changes in the overall price level, an increase in its own price will be seen primarily as an increase in its relative price. For example, if, on the average, a 10 percent increase in its own price will be associated with only a 1 percent increase in the overall price level, then the firm will expect a 9 percent increase in its relative price when its own price rises by 10 percent. In this situation the firm will increase its output a lot when it finds its own price has risen.

Differences among firms in a given economy will lead to differences in short-run responses to price changes. And the same idea may lead to overall differences among different economies. In an economy that always maintains stability in its overall price level, firms will come to expect that any changes in the prices of their own products must be changes in the relative prices of those products. In this case, small price changes will lead to large changes in output. If the money supply were to be increased in such an economy and the overall price level were to rise, the result would be a large increase in aggregate output as most firms would assume that their own prices have increased. The Lucas supply curve will be very flat in such an economy. If there has not been much inflation in an economy, then a sudden burst of inflation will fool people into raising output.

The opposite will hold in an economy where there is a great deal of variability in the general price level. Firms will assume that the changes in the prices of their own products are mostly the result of gyrations in the overall price level and they will not respond by changing their production. In such a situation, an increase in the money supply will not result in much increase in aggregate output. The Lucas supply curve will be very steep. A sudden burst of inflation will have very little effect on output.

Lucas has used this analysis to help understand why the relations between output and inflation might be different in different countries. Those with a wide variability of inflation will have steep supply schedules with small increases in output resulting from a given increase in the inflation rate. Those with stable rates of inflation will have flat supply schedules. Lucas found some support for his model in his sample of 18 countries.[*]

To understand his argument, however, it is important to remember that it is the *variability* of inflation that is important, not, directly, the level of inflation. We assumed earlier that there was no persistent inflation, but of course that is not generally the case in practice. In the Lucas model, where people have rational expectations, any stable rate of inflation will simply be factored into people's calculations and should not affect the slope of the supply curve. The slope of the Lucas supply curve will not necessarily be different in economies with different average rates of inflation. This will only be the case if higher average inflation is also associated with greater variability of inflation.

---

[*] Robert E. Lucas, Jr., "Some International Evidence on Output–Inflation Tradeoffs," *American Economic Review*, 63 (June 1973), pp. 326–34.

supply schedule indicates that output will deviate from potential output. For example, an unexpected increase in the money supply leads to an increase in output.

This description of the business cycle may be hard to follow, given that it is being assumed that people have rational expectations. Since expectations are formed rationally, how can expectations fail to be realized? The point is that having rational expectations and using information efficiently do not mean that people know exactly what is going to happen. Rather, it means that they make the best use of the information they have available at the time. The fluctuations of output around potential output reflect the fact that people's expectations are not always realized even though they are formed rationally. A higher-than-expected price level must have resulted from a shock or disturbance to the economy that could not have been foreseen by a rational evaluation of the economy. Only an *unexpected* shock or disturbance to the economy can cause actual prices to exceed expected prices so that actual real wages are lower than the real wages workers expect to receive. Workers therefore work more and output exceeds potential output.

The assumptions of rational expectations and flexible prices and wages play an important role in the analysis. The movement of output above potential output will be only temporary. In the next period, workers make full use of available information to form a new expected price level. And since their expectations are rational, they will not consistently overestimate or underestimate the future price level. In any given period, *there is the same likelihood that the actual price level is above the expected price level as below it, and so output in any period is as likely to be above potential as below it.* Deviations of output from potential output occur randomly.

The monetary basis of aggregate demand and equilibrium

In the rational-expectations model, aggregate demand is a monetary phenomenon determined by a quantity equation—the price level times output is equal to the stock of money times velocity. Provided the actual money supply and velocity turn out to be equal to their expected values, the expected price level will prevail and, by assumption, this price level is the one that will result in output equal to potential output.

Changes in aggregate demand (changes in the money supply or in velocity) come about because of unexpected events. If monetary policy takes an unexpected turn or if velocity changes because asset holders unexpectedly buy or sell securities in financial markets, the money stock and velocity will differ from their expected values. The result will be that the price level will differ from the expected price level and output will be affected.

In Figure 16.3 aggregate equilibrium is shown at potential output (point A) that occurs when expectations about the price level are realized. This occurs when the money stock times velocity (MV) is equal to the expected price level times potential output $(P^{exp} \times Y^P)$. There are no surprises in the growth of the money supply or in the velocity, so the actual price level in

FIGURE 16.3   The Split between Nominal and Real Effects in an Equilibrium Business Cycle

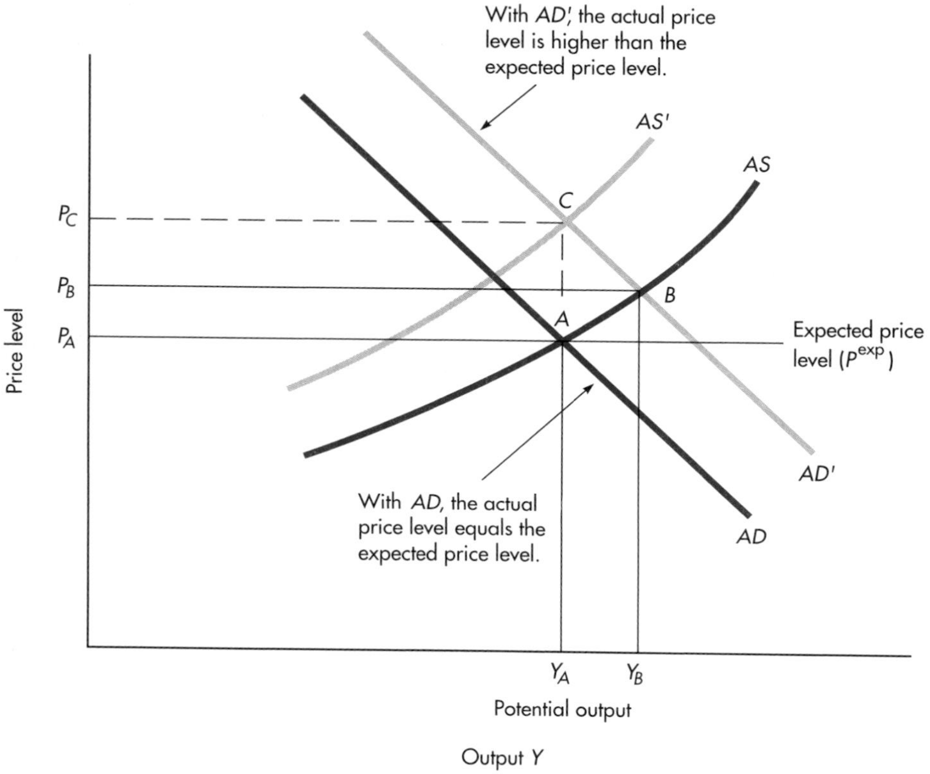

With AD', the actual price level is higher than the expected price level.

With AD, the actual price level equals the expected price level.

Unexpected changes in the money supply and/or velocity lead to short-run changes in output and the price level. In the long run they lead to changes in the price level only.

monetary shock
An unexpected change in the money supply and/or velocity. Also called a **monetary surprise**, a monetary shock is unanticipated and leads to fluctuations in aggregate demand seen as changes in the price level and/or output.

this case (P_A) turns out to be equal to the expected price level. The aggregate-demand schedule, AD, is drawn for this case.

When there is an unanticipated increase in the money supply or velocity, actual aggregate demand is higher than expected and the economy comes into temporary equilibrium (point B) with output exceeding potential. This is shown by the aggregate-demand schedule, AD'. The actual price level in this case (P_B) turns out to be above the expected price level.

The shocks that cause variations in the price level and output occur because of *monetary surprises*—unexpected changes in the money supply and/or velocity. Like the monetarists, equilibrium–business-cycle economists see policy gyrations and **monetary shocks** as the main causes of the business cycle. Monetary shocks are unexpected changes in aggregate demand; changes in the money supply times velocity (changes in $M \times V$). At times monetary shocks can originate in the private sector; for example, if people's preference for holding money changes, then velocity may change. But mostly, monetary shocks come from the inconsistent and highly variable nature of shifts in the money supply brought about by the way in which the Fed uses monetary policy for stabilization. For example, in the face of an increase in the rate of inflation, the Fed will initially take an anti-inflationary position, but it has often switched to an inflation-neutral or inflation-accommodating policy position. The Fed has even moved back and forth from one monetary stance to the other as the goals of Fed policy change. As such, Fed policy actions are often unanticipated—the Fed itself may not know in advance how it will react to economic circumstances.

The effect of monetary shocks on real output and inflation.   In all of the different macroeconomic models, the effect of monetary shocks can be separated into nominal effects (changes in the price level and inflation) and real effects (changes in output and employment). If the effects are all nominal, there is no real impact of a fluctuation on the economy; this is the purely classical result. If the effects are all real, economic fluctuations exact a very large toll in lost output and employment; this is the purely Keynesian result. The *IS-ALM* model uses the output–inflation trade-off to predict how a given change in aggregate demand will be split between changes in output and changes in inflation.

The monetarists used the monetary growth equation to describe aggregate demand, which says that the rate of change of aggregate demand is equal to the rate of change of real income plus the rate of inflation:

$$\frac{\Delta M}{M} + \frac{\Delta V}{V} = \frac{\Delta(MV)}{MV} = \frac{\Delta Y}{Y} + \frac{\Delta P}{P}. \tag{16.2}$$

And in the monetarist model it was assumed that changes in aggregate demand would fall in part on real output in the short run. The changes might be unexpected and it is assumed that there is some short-run stickiness of prices.

In the equilibrium–business-cycle model it is assumed that there is no price stickiness. The *only* reason that changes in aggregate demand will affect real output is if the changes are unexpected. After such an unexpected change, the economy quickly responds to an aggregate-demand shock through readjustments of expected prices. As shown in Figure 16.3, in the long run, as the higher actual price level (P_C) once again is equal to a higher expected price level, equilibrium occurs at potential output (point C). The effect of the shift in aggregate demand only raises the price level.

If aggregate demand (MV) is equal to its expected value, then the rate of growth of real income just equals the rate of growth of potential output and the rate of inflation equals its expected rate. If the rate of change of aggregate demand differs from what is expected, then this will split into real effects (output changes) and nominal effects (inflation). The exact shares of the increase going to real income and to inflation will depend on how much more labor is employed when firms see real wages temporarily drop. The responsiveness of output to the aggregate-demand surprise is illustrated by the shape of the aggregate-supply schedule and the speed with which aggregate supply reacts (*AS* to *AS'*) to the rise in the price level over time.

The equilibrium–business-cycle model is a complete model, therefore, in which aggregate demand and supply interact to determine real output and inflation. It combines the assumption that expectations are formed by making a rational evaluation of future economic conditions with the assumption that the economy is composed of markets that clear quickly in a classical manner. The equilibrium–business-cycle model provides a clear alternative to the other models we have described. Using the *IS-ALM* model, we have argued that the systematic use of economic policies, both monetary and fiscal, affects economic performance. In the equilibrium–business-cycle model, changes in aggregate demand and therefore changes in fiscal- and monetary-policy actions have no effect on the economy unless they are unexpected.[6]

What kind of a business cycle is predicted by this equilibrium model? If this model describes the actual economy, we would expect to see random short-term fluctuations in output. Given that prices and wages are very flexible and move quickly toward equilibrium, the economy can only maintain a level of output that exceeds potential as long as shocks to the economy continue to boost actual prices above expected prices. It would require a series of shocks, all in the same direction, to maintain output either persistently above or persistently below potential output. This is possible but unlikely. Coins do not come up heads many times in a row very often. Therefore, the rational-expectations model predicts that persistent or sustained recessions or booms are unlikely.

THE RATIONALIST CRITIQUE OF STABILIZATION POLICY

The implications of rational-expectations theory for policy are really a strong form of the monetarist position. Monetarists start with the view that the economy is basically stable, but they allow that frictions and even temporary price stickiness can slow the adjustment back to full employment. Monetarists argue that stabilization policy is undesirable, because it is so mistake-prone and subject to lags and inaccuracies. The rational-expectations theorists go further than this. They assume that the private economy is very efficient indeed and that information, including information about economic policy, is incorporated into expectations and acted upon. Economic policies then become a totally ineffective way to stabilize the economy.

---

[6] While the rational-expectations model allows for the possibility that policy could have an effect if it affected aggregate supply, there do not appear to be any supply-side policy instruments (subsidies to education and R&D, immigration policies, changes in tax incentives) that can be made into effective tools for the stabilization of the business cycle.

The Policy-Ineffectiveness Theorem

In an economy with rational expectations, people will form expectations about which policy actions governments will take under different circumstances. And they will adjust their behavior in the light of these expectations. If the government's response to a particular set of economic conditions is predictable, then the government is said to be following a program or regime of **systematic policymaking.** Systematic policymaking will be incorporated into expectations and there will be no unexpected policy shocks. Since, in the rational-expectations view, only an *unexpected* shock can cause output to differ from potential, systematic policy is ineffective as a tool for raising or lowering output.

The notion that policy that is anticipated is policy that is ineffective comes from the work of Thomas Sargent and Neil Wallace.[7] They developed the **policy-ineffectiveness theorem.** This theorem says that any systematic stabilization policy designed to mitigate the business cycle will be ineffective. The theorem is based on the idea that meaningful stabilization policy must be directed at some end or goal and thus it cannot be random or totally unexpected. Then the equilibrium–business-cycle model predicts that a policy that is anticipated is ineffective. Thus the conclusion is that stabilization policy is impotent.

To explain the theorem further, suppose that the Federal Reserve followed a systematic policy rule of setting the growth rate of the money supply at 2½ percent a year in normal times in order to accommodate the trend growth in potential output. Whenever the unemployment rate goes 1 percentage point above or below the natural rate of unemployment, the Fed will expand the money supply at an annual rate higher or lower than 2½ percent. This policy rule could be either explicitly stated or observed over time. Either way, the policy would be anticipated and incorporated into the expected change in the money supply.

Suppose unemployment actually does rise. There will be an expectation that aggregate demand will rise, reflecting the anticipation that the Fed will react to the rise in unemployment by increasing the rate of growth of the money supply. The increase in the expected growth of the money supply leads to an increase in the expected rate of inflation. When the increase in the growth of money supply actually occurs, the subsequent actual rise in the price level will equal the expected rise in the price level. Since output and employment only rise when the actual price level exceeds the expected price level, the result of the application of the policy rule will be that output and unemployment are no different than they would have been in the absence of the policy rule. Inflation will certainly be higher as a result of the attempt at recession fighting. And this is a pure cost, for nothing was gained.

systematic policymaking
A program or regime of policy such that the policy response to a particular set of economic conditions is predictable.

policy-ineffectiveness theorem
If only unexpected changes in policy affect output, systematic or expected changes in policy cannot affect output, and therefore stabilization policy is ineffective.

---

[7] Thomas Sargent and Neil Wallace, "Rational Expectations, the Optimal Monetary Instrument and the Optimal Money Supply Rule," *Journal of Political Economy* 83 (April 1975), pp. 241–54.

In the equilibrium–business-cycle model, the Fed's stabilization policy would only have been effective in increasing output if the Fed had engineered a much larger than anticipated increase in the money supply, but that would mean that the Fed chose not to follow its systematic policy rule, but rather engineered a surprise. Of course that would only work as long as the policy is unexpected. Repeating the same policy in reaction to the same circumstances would surprise no one.

Some critics of the policy-ineffectiveness theorem argue that in practice policy is not made according to a systematic rule that market participants can learn. But this criticism misses the point. If you accept the underlying assumptions of the equilibrium–business-cycle model, the theorem shows that it is only the random or unexpected part of policy that will affect real output. And since stabilization policy by its nature implies that government is expected to take expansionary actions during recessions and contractionary actions during booms, there is no sensible case to be made for a stabilization policy based on always doing the unexpected. A sensible stabilization policy will be contractionary in booms and expansionary in recessions and people will come to expect that pattern. The importance or validity of the policy-ineffectiveness theorem follows directly from the equilibrium–business-cycle model. The validity of the theorem turns on the validity of that model.

In the face of policy ineffectiveness, the equilibrium–business-cycle model does generate a policy prescription, a prescription similar to that offered by the monetarists. If a stable policy regime were followed, such as Friedman's constant–money-supply–growth rule, then cyclical fluctuations would be greatly reduced. There might still be cyclical fluctuations in the economy because there are some shocks to the velocity of money originating in the private sector of the economy. But these fluctuations are unavoidable, because the government has no way of knowing about them any sooner than does the private economy. The private economy will do a better job of offsetting these shocks than will the policymakers.

Taxation and the deficit

In terms of effectiveness, fiscal policy designed to control aggregate demand fares no better than does monetary policy under rational-expectations theory. Consider the following fiscal-policy action. The government attempts to stimulate aggregate demand by cutting taxes, but not expenditures. In order to finance this deficit the government must issue new debt. Since under a rational-expectations view of the world, everyone knows that the debt repayment will raise taxes in the future, saving goes up in anticipation of future tax liabilities. There is no net stimulation to aggregate demand.

This ineffectiveness of fiscal policy is very different from the impact of fiscal policy that we described in the *IS-ALM* trade-off model. In our discussion, an increase in the deficit raises aggregate demand, thereby generating a new equilibrium that had an increased level of output with a higher real interest rate. In the *IS-ALM* trade-off model, the deficit increases aggregate demand through the direct effect of the increased expenditures of households that now receive more after-tax income. According to the rational-expectations view, however, individuals calculate their permanent income and wealth including an expected rate of taxes they believe they (and their children and grandchildren) will be forced to bear in the future. Since a tax cut that generates a budget deficit will have to be financed by the sale of new government bonds, everyone anticipates that the interest on these new bonds will have to be paid for in the future by higher taxes, and this is factored into today's consumption and saving decisions.[8] The bonds do not add to national wealth because the market value of the bonds is just equal to the discounted present value of the principal and interest that will be collected in future taxes and used to pay off the bond. In the context of the *IS-ALM* trade-off model, the *IS* schedule would not move out when the deficit rose because personal saving would increase dollar for dollar with the increase in government expenditure.

These ideas about the ineffectiveness of fiscal policy assume that individuals make rational forecasts of economic conditions. There is general agreement that many (if not all) families make forecasts about their own lifetime income. This is the basis of the permanent-income and life-cycle–consumption models. However, there is doubt about whether individuals make rational forecasts of the future fiscal behavior of government and change their individual behavior on the basis of what they expect to be the course of government action.[9] There is considerable skepticism about the plausibility of a model in which individuals calculate and act upon forecasts of how government policies undertaken now may lead to future changes in taxes. Moreover, the idea that government dissaving (in the form of a deficit) leaves total national saving unchanged does not appear to have been substantiated in practice.

In the early 1980s there were substantial tax cuts unmatched by reductions in government expenditures and the federal budget deficit rose as a percentage of GNP. Not only did the private saving rate fail to rise in the 1980s (it fell a little), but the growth of the deficit appears to have stimulated aggregate demand as predicted by the *IS-ALM* model, and greatly reduced national saving.

Time-inconsistent policies

The rational-expectations analysis of the ineffectiveness of policies designed to control output have suggested a general problem with government policy actions. A policy that works in the short run may not work in the long run. The argument is that if stated policy intentions are carried out, they are anticipated and therefore ineffective. If stated policy intentions are not

---

[8] This idea is developed in Robert Barro, "Are Government Bonds Net Wealth?" *Journal of Political Economy*, December 1974.

[9] Olivier Blanchard, "Debt, Deficits and Finite Horizons," *Journal of Political Economy*, April 1985.

time-inconsistent policies
Policies that, if pursued, realize their intended effects in the short run but have a reversed effect in the long run.

carried out, they suffer from time-inconsistency and are ineffective because they lack credibility.[10]

The problem of **time-inconsistent policies** is familiar to any manager. In the short run it is more efficient for the skilled manager to take on any difficult task that comes along. He can do it better than any of his employees. In the long run, this means that no one else learns how to deal with the problems and the manager is overloaded. Efficiency in the long run requires sacrifices of efficiency in the short run.

Time-inconsistent policies are also familiar in industrial policy. In the 1960s there were many patent-infringement cases brought to court. One company had a patent and another company was producing a product that used the technology. Judges and juries would look at the situation and see a big profitable company that had developed a technology some years before and was now making a ton of money from it by charging consumers a high price for the product. The patent was being infringed by a small company that was cutting its price to sell in the big company's market. The courts very often ruled against the company that held the patent.

Over time, this trend in the courts created problems. Companies that were spending millions on R&D were having trouble getting a return from their ideas. If it is possible to wait and see what another company comes up with and then just imitate that product, why spend millions on R&D? R&D spending fell in the 1970s and there was concern that innovation would suffer. The courts were using a time-inconsistent policy.

Macroeconomic policies to stabilize the economy are time-inconsistent if they rely on surprises. In the equilibrium–business-cycle model policies only affect output if they surprise people, so that stabilization policy is a time-inconsistent policy within this model.

There is a problem of time-inconsistent policies even within the *IS-ALM* trade-off model. We saw how expansionary policies in the 1960s resulted in large output gains in the short run but gradually created inflation problems in the longer run, which could only be cured by recession and high unemployment. The policies of that period were time-inconsistent. Another example we have already seen came up when we talked about the Fed's effort to keep down nominal interest rates. In the short run, the Fed can lower the nominal rate of interest. But when this raises inflation in the longer run, this will push the nominal interest rate higher.

We do not agree, however, that stabilization policies are always time-inconsistent. Indeed, the opposite may be true. If there are fundamental sources of stickiness and instability in the economy, then stabilization policy can work to improve stability in ways that do not rely purely on surprising people. In fact, as the economy became more stable in the postwar period, this actually reinforced stabilization policy because private decisions become

---

[10] Finn Kydland and Edward Prescott, "Rules rather than Discretion: The Inconsistency of Optimal Plans," *Journal of Political Economy*, June 1977.

less volatile as people became more confident that the Great Depression would not return.

The Critique of Econometric-Policy Evaluation

The estimates of the parameters of economic relationships are made using the statistical analysis of economic data, a field called *econometrics*. Econometricians attempt to measure the direction and magnitude of economic relationships as well as assessing the probability that a relationship exists or has a particular value. Econometrics is used to verify or support the implications of economic models and it is often used to evaluate the impact of economic policies. For example, policymakers facing a rise in inflation will not only want to know if raising taxes and/or reducing the growth of the money supply will bring down inflation, they also will want to know how much of a decrease in aggregate demand is required to generate a targeted drop in the inflation rate and how much of a drop in income and unemployment will accompany that policy action. Econometric studies conducted in the 1960s found a correlation between the accelerating inflation and the high level of output. That analysis supported the notion that the trade-off between inflation and output was relevant for policy.

One of the first arguments that Robert Lucas made when introducing rational expectations into the debate over macroeconomics is that much of the econometric work that had been done in the past to test either the effectiveness of policy or the nature of the output–inflation trade-off was invalid.

Lucas critique
Lucas argued that when statistical methods are used on economic data, the results may not provide a reliable guide to policy. When policy changes, this may change the relationship among the economic variables.

The **Lucas critique** focused on the estimates of the parameters of the output–inflation trade-off. Lucas argued that the econometric evidence was misleading and that no such trade-off existed. Rather, the Fed in the 1960s had abandoned its commitment to price stability and allowed the money supply to grow rapidly and inflation to accelerate. This development was not expected by workers and firms, so the price level was consistently higher than anticipated and output was above potential output.

Inevitably, argued Lucas, this situation had to change. Policymakers could not go on indefinitely fooling people in the same direction—by accelerating inflation. Econometric estimates made from data covering primarily the 1960s would not provide a guide to the output–inflation trade-off in other periods.

In a related argument, Lucas also critiqued the policy analysis by both Keynesian and monetarist economists that estimated the impact of monetary- and fiscal-policy changes on output. Relating output changes to monetary-policy changes is again a misspecification, says Lucas, because it does not distinguish between anticipated and unanticipated policy. In historical data there will be a correlation between changes in money and changes in output. But this correlation is being driven by the effect on output of the unanticipated part of the change in the money supply. As was shown in the policy-ineffectiveness theorem, this relation cannot be used as the basis for systematic stabilization policy.

In summary, Lucas argued that if econometric estimates had been made over a period of time when the public correctly anticipated the course of monetary policy, the results would have been different. The estimates of the impact of monetary policy covered a period when much of the movement in the money supply was unanticipated. Estimates made over a period when changes in the money supply were anticipated would not have shown the same policy effects.

REAL–BUSINESS-CYCLE MODELS

technology shock
Any increase or decrease in productivity that is unrelated to changes in the quantity of inputs.

real–business-cycle models
Neoclassical models that argue that all economic fluctuations are the results of technology shocks or labor-supply shocks.

Because of concerns about the ability of the equilibrium–business-cycle model to explain actual economic fluctuations, a new approach has been developed by rational-expectations economists that accepts many of the features of the equilibrium business cycle, but that posits an alternative source of cyclical fluctuations. The new models replace the conclusion of the equilibrium–business-cycle models that fluctuations result from policy surprises, with the hypothesis that fluctuations are the results of shifts in aggregate supply that are the result of **technology shocks** (productivity shifts) or labor-supply shocks (shifts in workers' willingness to work). Shifts in the money market will not change real output; only changes in the real economy can bring about changes in real income—hence these models are called **real–business-cycle models**.[11] The new models (like the equilibrium–business-cycle models) argue that markets are always in equilibrium and they reject the business-cycle analysis of the Keynesian models. The sources of fluctuations in output and employment are traced to shifts in supply and/or demand in the labor market, when the labor market is modeled in much the same way as in the classical model.

Figure 16.4 illustrates the way in which output variations occur in the real–business-cycle model. In the left panel, an increase in output is shown to have occurred because of an increase in the number of people who want to work at a given wage. There has been a shift in people's preference for work. The right panel shows the case of a decline in the demand for labor because of an adverse change in technology. Real–business-cycle theorists regard both shifts in workers' preferences and technology shocks as explanations of cyclical fluctuations in output. But technology shocks have been the focus of most of the attention in these models.

Technology Shocks

In common usage, *technology* generally refers to the technical properties of physical capital (machines, devices, equipment, materials, and structures) and *changes in technology* refer to improvements in productivity associated

---

[11] Finn Kydland and Edward Prescott, "Time to Build and Aggregate Fluctuations," *Econometrica* 50 (November 1982), pp. 1345–70; and Robert G. King and Charles I. Plosser, "Money, Credit and Prices in a Real Business Cycle," *American Economic Review* 74 (June 1984), pp. 363–80.

FIGURE 16.4   Changes in Preferences and Changes in Technology Shift Employment and Hence Output

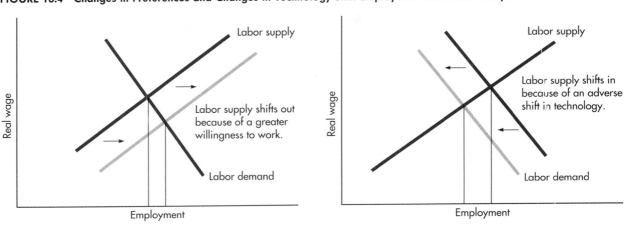

with using physical capital. However, in economic terms, *changes in technology* has a broader meaning. It refers to the manner in which production is undertaken—any increase or decrease in output, unrelated to changes in the quantity of inputs. A positive or negative shift in technology—broadly defined—is a technology shock. Most technology shocks are thought to be positive—innovations in the design and engineering of production technologies and improvements in management practices. But conditions for production can deteriorate as well as improve. The adverse shift in technology shown in the lower panel of Figure 16.4 describes a drop in output due to a reduction of the marginal product of labor and labor productivity has fallen because production conditions have worsened. This adverse shift may have resulted, for example, from changes in the environment or failures of management.

The measure of productivity that fits best with this broad meaning of change in technology is *multifactor productivity*. Multifactor productivity measures productivity net of changes in the amount of labor and capital used in production, thereby providing an indication of how technology is changing.[12]

In support of their model of economic fluctuations, the advocates of real–business-cycle theory point to the close positive relation between changes in multifactor productivity and output. When output is unusually large, then productivity is unusually high; when output is low, productivity is also low. Figure 16.5 shows the year-to-year changes in multifactor productivity and

---

[12] See the discussion in Chapter 18 comparing multifactor productivity with average labor productivity.

FIGURE 16.5   Multifactor-Productivity Growth and Output Growth, 1948–1985

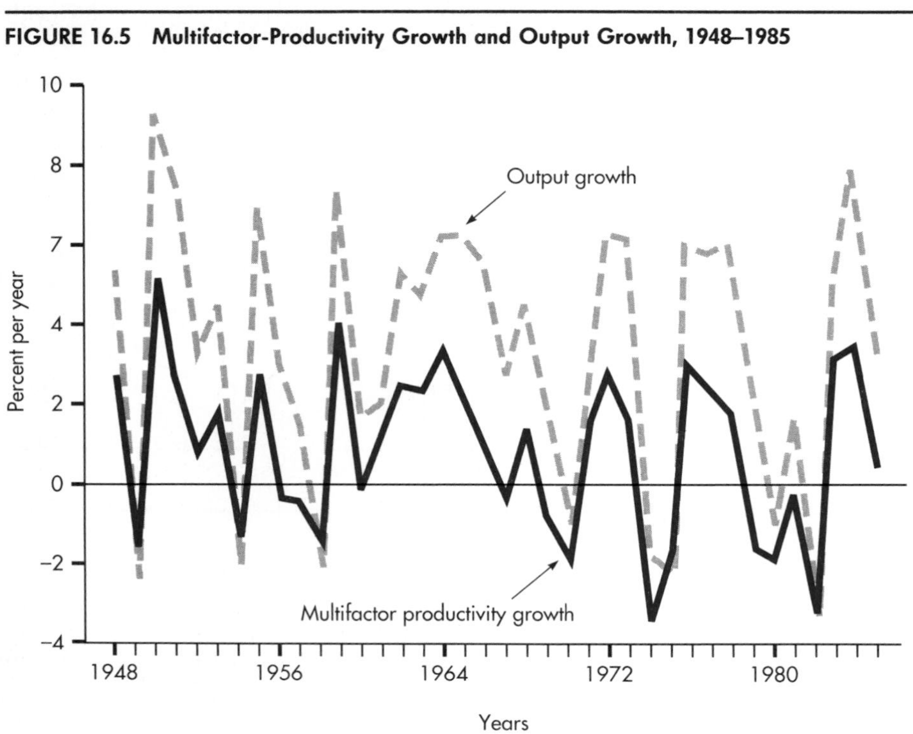

Output growth and multifactor-productivity growth tend to move closely together. Are productivity shocks leading to changes in output? Or are output changes leading to changes in productivity?

in output, with the two series showing a strong positive association.[13] This positive correlation between output and productivity is not what one would expect from a standard analysis of production within the mainstream model. If fluctuations in output are driven by fluctuations in demand, as is assumed in both the mainstream model and in the equilibrium–business-cycle model, and if firms hire more workers and produce more output in booms because of this high demand, then we would expect to see low productivity in booms because of diminishing returns to labor. The advocates of real–business-cycle theory conclude that the year-to-year variations in productivity that are positively correlated with output indicate that there are large technology shocks— shocks to *supply*—that cause changes in output.

It is important to be clear about where the difference of opinion is here.

---

[13] N. Gregory Mankiw, "Real Business Cycles: A New Keynesian Perspective," *Journal of Economic Perspectives* 3 (Summer 1989), p. 84. Mankiw discusses real–business-cycle models in this paper, but he himself is not an advocate of them. His work is neo-Keynesian in approach.

All economists recognize that technology and productivity changes are responsible for most of the long-run changes in output. However, the real–business-cycle models argue that short-run changes in productivity determine changes in output over the business cycle. In some years, the conditions for production are unusually good. Firms go out and bid for workers, driving up the real wage and increasing employment and output. Such periods are then called booms. In some years, the conditions are unusually bad, as the technology of production lowers the marginal productivity of workers and firms lay off workers, drive down the real wage, and reduce output. These periods are recessions.

ASSESSING EQUILIBRIUM–BUSINESS-CYCLE AND REAL–BUSINESS-CYCLE MODELS

There are two key elements in the equilibrium–business-cycle model. (1) People have rational expectations but there is incomplete information so that there are fluctuations in aggregate demand. (2) Wages and prices are not only flexible but they also move toward equilibrium values. The real–business-cycle model essentially carries over these same elements, but argues that incomplete information does not provide an adequate model of the business cycle. Instead, fluctuations in output and employment are driven by aggregate supply shocks, primarily technology shocks.

In assessing these models, we look first at the issue of whether or not people have rational expectations. Proponents of rational expectations point to individual markets for goods and services that appear to work efficiently, with buyers and sellers making good use of information and forming expectations of future market conditions. They argue that the economy, which is the collection of all market activity, should also behave as if driven by rational expectations about the behavior of efficient markets. The case for or against rational expectations depends upon the issues of just how efficient individual markets are and how well rational-expectations models describe the workings of markets and macroeconomic events.

Support from Efficient Markets and Arbitrage

Proponents of the rational-expectations models argue that the assumption that expectations are formed by a rational assessment of future economic conditions does not require that all market participants individually have rational expectations and be wonderfully adept at economic decision making. Many people may not bother to inform themselves about the economy. Many others may be foolish or misunderstand the system. However, because of a phenomenon called **arbitrage,** as long as there are enough buyers and sellers who form rational expectations in any particular market, this may be all that is necessary in order for the market to behave as if all the people held rational expectations. Arbitrage involves people buying assets in order to

arbitrage
Taking advantage of the profit opportunities of either price differences for the same asset in different markets or of price changes over time.

sell them later for a profit. The opportunity to profit from arbitage occurs when market participants hold different expectations about future asset values. Arbitrageurs who expect asset prices to rise will bid for assets from those who do not expect this. If those who hold rational expectations have a demand for assets that is sufficiently large, then arbitrage will drive prices to the same levels that would have prevailed if everyone had rational expectations.

Consider the market in betting on the outcome of NFL football games as an example of how arbitrage can drive a market toward an equilibrium where the price is set by those who hold rational expectations. When a gambler places a bet in Las Vegas, that is the same as having the gambler buy a future contract that pays a stated amount (the size of the bet) conditional upon a team winning by a given amount of points (the point spread). The higher the spread, the more the buyer is willing to "pay" to own a contract that rewards the buyer for betting on the winning team. If there is more money bet on one team than on another, odds makers raise the spread to even out the market because they do not want to be stuck with a net loss regardless of who wins. Plenty of people bet foolishly or with little real knowledge of the game. But the point spread adjusts so that even knowledgeable bettors cannot consistently beat the spread if they rely only on information that is widely available. If this were not the case, then sophisticated bettors would enter the market, betting heavily with or against a particular spread. Then the spread itself would adjust, until it accurately represented an unbiased estimate of the difference between the two teams.

Notice that in this market, the posted point spread rarely turns out to be the actual difference in scores when the game is played. The market has rational expectations, not perfect foresight. There is incomplete information. On any given Sunday a majority of underdogs may beat the spread, or a majority of favorites may do so. Saying that the market is efficient means it is not possible to bet one way or the other and win consistently.

Notice also that someone with inside information may well be able to make money even in an efficient market. For example, if you happen to see a star quarterback injured shortly before a game, you could act on that information by flying to Las Vegas and placing a legal bet against his team. However, once the information becomes widely known, the point spread will change.

Arbitrage also plays an important role in the rationale for the equilibrium–business-cycle model. The advocates of this model argue that the explanation of the business cycle that they propose is the only one consistent with markets that work efficiently. In the *IS-ALM* model, a recession is a time when there are workers who want to work, but who cannot find jobs at the going wage. There are firms who want to make profits, and consumers who want to buy more, but somehow the economy fails to coordinate these activities and exploit this opportunity. Rational-expectations economists argue that this would mean that there are profit opportunities in the economy that are not being exploited, and why should this be? After all, people do not leave $500 bills lying on the sidewalk. Efficient arbitrage should eliminate profit opportunities.

The same point is made in arguing against government policy as a way of improving the efficiency of the economy. How can the government through systematic policy expect to improve on the outcome of a market where arbitrageurs always stand ready to enter? That is like trying to win consistently by betting with or against the point spread.

Doubts about Rational Expectations

When observing the behavior of actual markets to see whether they are consistent with the equilibrium–business-cycle model, we need to separate out the assumption of price flexibility from the assumption of rational expectations. One market where prices are clearly flexible is the stock market, the market in corporate stocks and shares, so by looking at the stock market we can get a good sense of the validity of the rational-expectations assumptions.

Although the final verdict has not yet been given, there have been some tests that have indicated that share prices vary much more than would be predicted from the variability of the dividends and corporate earnings that give value to stocks.[14] The stock market is subject to bouts of speculative fever that drive individual stock prices or even market averages way up and then way down—for example, the run-up of stock prices in 1987 that culminated in the October 1987 crash.

It seems that stock-market traders can be divided roughly into two groups: ordinary investors (noise traders) and smart money. The ordinary investors are influenced by fads and may drive stock prices up and down even when the fundamental determinants of stock values have changed very little. The smart-money investors understand the fundamentals and they should provide the arbitrage that results in a rational-expectations market. But it turns out that being able to read market psychology or being plain lucky is as good a way of making money in the stock market as being an expert in the fundamentals of stock valuation. This means that the smart investors do not necessarily come to dominate the stock market. And if this is the case, arbitrage does not ensure that the stock market behaves with rational expectations.

There is no general agreement concerning the question of whether or not the stock market behaves in a way consistent with rational expectations. Reasonable people can view the evidence and reach different conclusions. Once we look outside markets such as the stock market, however, it is harder to make the case that arbitrage ensures rational expectations.

In markets such as the stock market or the bond market there are many arbitrageurs at work, but the situation is not the same in the markets for the goods and services that make up GNP, nor is it true for the labor market.

---

[14] Robert J. Shiller, *Market Volatility* (Cambridge, Mass.: MIT Press, 1990).

■ Smart Money and Noise Traders

Is modern economics any use in understanding the ups and downs of stock markets?

Market practitioners and academic economists seem further apart than ever in their explanations for the volatility of financial markets, especially stock markets. Most traders find the idea that markets are "optimally forecasting the future flow of real dividends" laughable. Most academic economists regard this notion as so obviously true that they take it as an axiom in their research, not as a claim to be investigated.

If communication is to improve, it will be thanks to those few academics who are both interested in the mechanics of real markets and want a scientific account of the forces that drive them. A leader of this band is Mr. Robert Shiller, a young professor of economics at Yale University. A volume of his papers* has just been published. Here is an economics book about financial markets that thoughtful practitioners will find interesting.

To understand why academics and practitioners cannot agree, it is necessary to understand why the academics cling to their view of financial markets. They say that stock prices reflect the most informed possible view of future streams of dividends (a theory also known as the efficient-market hypothesis or random-walk theory because a price that already reflects all that is known will be knocked either way by the next unknown). That may seem at odds with reality. But once you understand the idea, it is both plausible and resistant to counterargument.

A key point is this: If the idea were not true, it would mean that the market was failing to take account of information that was relevant for predicting future prices. Hence the forecast would not be optimal. In that case, (a) the discovery of such information would yield enormous profits to the discoverer and (b) in collecting those profits by trading in the market the discoverer would incorporate the information in market prices.

So a mechanism exists to make the efficient-market hypothesis true. What about evidence? Well, it is evidence of a sort that share prices are not forecastable. If they were, then the forecasting model would itself be a piece of unexploited information. Over longish periods (a year or more, say) share prices are, in fact, somewhat forecastable. One of Mr. Shiller's papers shows that in years when Wall Street began with a higher-than-average dividend yield (i.e., when prices were low in relation to dividends), prices rose by more than average. The correlation is not strong, but it is there, and it goes against the grain of the optimal-forecast theory.

Over shorter periods, however, many studies have shown that share prices do indeed follow a random walk. Prices are as likely to rise as to fall in the future, regardless of information about prices in earlier periods, or even (in stricter versions of the theory) of all currently available information. Overall, then, the evidence favors the optimal-forecast theory.

But consider another sort of evidence. The sheer volatility of stock markets seems to argue against the optimal-forecast idea. If share prices are a weighted average of discounted future dividends they should iron out any fluctuations in dividends, and thus be less volatile than dividends. Actually,

Many of the people who buy and sell in these markets do not concern themselves with incorporating information about monetary policy or other macroeconomic variables into their decisions. And arbitrage may not be able to introduce rational expectations in this situation.[15]

If money wages are too high, causing unemployment, even a knowledgeable market participant who has rational expectations about future monetary

---

[15] J. Haltiwanger and M. Waldman, "Rational Expectations and the Limits of Rationality," *American Economic Review*, June 1985, pp. 326–40.

they are far more volatile. Mr. Shiller finds that if uncertainty of future dividends can be measured by the past variability of dividends, stock-price volatility is between 5 and 13 times too great (depending on the period examined) to be consistent with optimal-forecast theory.

The theory can be rescued, mind. It might be incorrect to measure uncertainty about future dividends by looking at their past variability. Or you might assume that expected real interest rates vary a lot. This would account for big changes in share prices: it represents a change in the discount rate that the market is applying to the stream of future dividends. But Mr. Shiller works out how far expectations of real interest rates would have needed to move in order to account for the fluctuations in share prices. For 1928–79 the required variation (given certain other assumptions) was from minus-8 percent to plus-17 percent. It is hard to believe that expectations of real interest rates fluctuate within anything like such a wide range.

To reconcile all this conflicting evidence, Mr. Shiller favors a theory that divides stock and other financial markets into two sorts of participants: smart money and "ordinary investors," known unflatteringly in the jargon as noise traders. Broadly, smart money behaves like investors are supposed to behave in the optimal-forecast theory: it searches for all relevant information, incorporating this into prices quickly and smoothly.

Noise traders, who constitute most of the market, are influenced by fads and fashions. They are slow to understand the significance of new information (including advice from smart-money experts). They are not stupid. They might often do better than smart money in the market, by being "wrong" at an auspicious moment. Smart money presumably fled the overvalued stock market in the first half of 1987; some lucky noise traders will have "incorrectly" stayed in, only leaving in the first week of October. Indeed, as Mr. Shiller and others have pointed out, the richest people in the market are unlikely to be smart money; they are more likely to be a tiny fraction of the noise traders who, in their time, have blundered into a fortune through recklessness or plain luck.

Analyzing this two-part market is difficult. Smart money and noise traders will interact in complicated ways—for instance, smart money will monitor not just the "fundamentals" but also the fashions (including the predictions of chartists) that drive noise traders. Working all this out is a matter not just of theory but of lots of close observation. Mr. Shiller is good at both.

This research is still at an early stage. However, it is already clear that the division of the market into smart money and noise traders can solve a big mystery. If smart money finds and exploits the profit opportunities contained in market information, then prices will be pretty unforecastable, as both the optimal-forecast model and the evidence suggest. At the same time, the combination of smart money and noise traders can account for the markets' puzzling volatility.

Source: *The Economist,* June 2, 1990. Reprinted by permission. Review of *Market Volatility* by Robert Shiller (Cambridge, Mass: MIT Press, 1990).

policy cannot immediately profit from that superior knowledge. When the point spread gets out of line with the true probabilities of winning or losing in NFL games, the profit opportunity is clear. Place a bet. If autoworkers are laid off and they are overoptimistic about their chances of getting their old jobs back or they are overoptimistic about the alternative jobs they can obtain elsewhere, then the result will be persistent unemployment. Someone cannot come along and simply bet the unemployed workers that they are wrong. One could prove they are wrong by setting up a competing auto plant that pays lower wages, but it is not easy to start up a new auto plant to compete against an established company. Any such investment decision would have to be based on long-run considerations not on errors in expectations.

The difficulties of making money when people have incorrect expectations also applies to many other situations. When the demand for single-family houses or for commercial real estate declines, we observe that houses stay on the market for many months and that commercial office buildings sit unrented. There is a phenomenon analogous to unemployment in the real-estate market. Prices do not fall quickly to clear the market for single-family houses. Office rentals do not fall to clear the market for commercial space. One explanation for this is that people are overoptimistic about what price they can get for their house or how quickly they can rent their building. If this is indeed the case, there is no arbitrage mechanism by which someone with rational expectations can make a profit by using their superior information. Buying up overpriced houses or office buildings is a way to lose money, not make it.

To conclude on rational expectations: The rational-expectations revolution in economics has had a profound impact. Prior to the work of economists such as Robert Lucas and Thomas Sargent, there were naive macroeconomic models that implied that people repeatedly expected inflation to be lower than it turned out to be. It was a mistake to assume such behavior. The analysis of financial markets, the trade-off, and the foreign-exchange market have all been affected by the idea of rational expectations and these impacts have been reflected in this book. In markets where similar events happen over and over, people will learn rational expectations by experience. In markets where arbitrage is possible, rational expectations will be important and may come to dominate the behavior of the market. These arguments can be taken too far, however. There are many markets where people do not incorporate all available information into their economic decisions. In many cases there are people who do not understand the implications of much of the information that is available to them. And it is unlikely that arbitrage can always lead to markets that act as if everyone had rational expectations.

Doubts about Price and Wage Flexibility

Equilibrium–business-cycle models assume perfect price flexibility as well as rational expectations. And many economists find this assumption to be harder to accept than rational expectations. An important reason for this skepticism is that the equilibrium–business-cycle model does not predict fluctuations in output that fit with the observed pattern of fluctuations in the economy. And the pattern of unemployment in these models does not fit with the kind of unemployment that we observe in recessions.

The persistence problem
An important discrepancy between the rational-expectations models and observation is that these models imply that deviations from potential output

should be short-lived. But the experience of the actual economy is that *output moves slowly and persistently above or below potential for periods of several years at a time*. This was pointed out by Robert Hall, who noted that the assumptions of complete price flexibility and rational expectations left no room for recessions that last a long time.[16] The assumption of rational expectations means that people overestimate the price level as often as they underestimate it. Price flexibility assumes that there are no impediments to adjustment. Rational-expectations models predict that output next period is as likely to be above potential output as below potential output. This will be true regardless of whether the economy is in a boom or a recession in this period. The basic Lucas model, therefore, describes an economy that quickly bounces around full employment. The Great Depression stands out as a particularly difficult period to reconcile with the Lucas model, because output remained greatly depressed below potential for about 10 years.

There have been attempts to incorporate adjustment costs into the analysis so as to develop an equilibrium model with a more realistic business-cycle pattern. Also a reconsideration of the role of inventories can be used to explain persistence.[17] However, to the extent that these modifications succeed, they make the equilibrium model look more like the mainstream models of fluctuations where the basis for fluctuation is due to miscoordination and stickiness, not random shocks (see box). In general, the business cycle is characterized by substantial changes in output and employment and by only a small cyclical response of prices. Equilibrium–business-cycle theorists try to explain this pattern with models where prices are flexible, but where output is costly to adjust. This is bound to be a tough task. The persistence problem remains as a serious objection to the rational-expectations, equilibrium–business-cycle model.

Voluntary or involuntary unemployment

In the equilibrium–business-cycle model, all unemployment is voluntary because the labor market clears at a market wage. A generation of economists that grew up in the Depression years, as well as many contemporary economists, object forcefully to models implying that cyclical unemployment is in any way voluntary. They recall vividly the despair of the unemployed, the soup kitchens, and the overall hardship that accompanied the Depression. Even in later periods, hardship created by severe recessions in 1958, 1975, and 1982 was widespread.

Robert Lucas admits that it is hard to reconcile the 1930s with his model of the cycle. Wages do not appear to have adjusted to restore equilibrium. But advocates of the equilibrium–business-cycle model argue that anecdotes

---

[16] Robert E. Hall, "The Rigidity of Wages and the Persistence of Unemployment," *Brookings Papers on Economic Activity*, 2:1975, pp. 301–50.

[17] Thomas J. Sargent, "Estimation of Dynamic Labor Demand Schedules under Rational Expectations," *Journal of Political Economy*, 86, no. 6 (1978). Alan S. Blinder and Stanley Fischer, "Inventories, Rational Expectations and the Business Cycle," *Journal of Monetary Economics* 6 (November 1981), pp. 277–304.

■ The Persistence of Recessions, Adjustment Costs, and Inventories

Thomas Sargent has argued that recessions are persistent because firms face costs of adjusting output and employment. The cycle, for Sargent, looks as follows. An unexpected decline in aggregate demand *(MV)* induces an unexpected decline in the price level. The real wage rises, and employment and output fall. Then output grows slowly because it is costly for firms to rehire workers and expand production quickly.

Sargent is correct that there are adjustment costs, but it is doubtful whether these costs are large enough to explain the observed persistence of recession. While there are certainly significant managerial costs associated with laying off or firing workers, these are seen to be much less acute for rehiring laid-off workers. Some companies make very large month-to-month adjustments to employment and output because of demand fluctuations specific to their particular industries, and some firms hoard labor rather than letting employees go when faced with a downturn in the business cycle. This suggests that the simple adjustment costs of hiring and firing are a small part of the story. Most firms cite continued inadequate demand as the reason for persistently low output, not an unwillingness to meet the demand because of adjustment costs.

Alan Blinder and Stanley Fischer have offered a different explanation of persistence that is consistent with mainstream models. Inventories accumulated during downturns have to be worked off during booms, thereby dampening the cycle. This creates a carryover effect from recession in one period to the next.

about hardship among the unemployed do not provide a suitable test of alternative macroeconomic models. Workers may indeed be very adversely affected by large, unexpected changes in monetary policy. Such changes mislead workers into believing that they can only remain employed if they accept a lower real wage. Faced with two poor alternatives, workers choose to become unemployed rather than work at lower wages. In the rational-expectations view, it is the bad policy that has created the problem, not a sudden change in the willingness of workers to work.

In the Keynesian view, individual workers are not seen as having a choice between offering to work at a lower wage and taking time at home. Unemployed workers do not have the option of offering to displace an existing employee by taking a wage that is 50 cents an hour less. Labor-market institutions do not allow that kind of competition. This may reflect an implicit social contract or perhaps firms are reluctant to replace workers because of the human capital imbedded in the experience of an in-place work force. Sometimes the threat of violence is used by workers to prevent other workers from undercutting their wages. Regardless, labor markets do not appear to operate in the efficient mode necessary to validate a flexible-wage view of the economy.

Criticisms of the Real–Business-Cycle Model

The problems experienced by the equilibrium model in explaining the observed persistence of output fluctuations were instrumental in motivating the development of the real–business-cycle model. This model suggests that changes in aggregate supply caused by technology shocks have been the reason for cyclical output changes. If there are shifts in technology, it would be hardly surprising that these would lead to persistent output changes.

The new theory has itself been subject to criticisms, however. The first problem with the model is simple but serious. *If changes in output are the result of changes in aggregate supply rather than changes in aggregate demand, then the price level should fall in booms and rise in recessions.* Now we have seen in our earlier discussion of output and inflation that indeed there have been periods when inflation has risen as output has fallen. These episodes of stagflation took place in the 1970s and we identified them as supply-shock inflations. But these episodes are more the exceptions than the rule. *The normal pattern in business cycles is for prices to rise with rising output.* In order to explain the normal pattern of prices over the cycle, real–business-cycle theorists have to suggest that there is some induced change in the money supply when the economy expands or contracts. One cannot explain the normal cyclical pattern by means of supply changes alone.

The second problem with the model is that many economists are skeptical of the idea that declines in output have been caused by technology declines. And the third problem is that the real–business-cycle model does not make realistic predictions about cyclical fluctuations in employment. These two issues need further explanation.

Questions about productivity

The relationship between multifactor productivity and output (Figure 16.5) is the most supportive evidence of real–business-cycle theories. It suggests, at first sight, that output must be fluctuating as a result of shocks to the technology. However, further analysis of this idea reveals some problems with it. In particular, it is hard to know what might be causing these technology shocks and why negative shocks—that reduced productivity—should occur frequently. It is likely that technological change comes about slowly as a result of advances in basic science and engineering, research and development programs, the adoption of improved production methods, and changes in the education and skills of the work force. These changes lead to gradual improvements in productivity, not sudden changes. There may be a sudden breakthrough in technology, but this is likely to affect only a single industry and not bring about a macroeconomic business cycle.

Declines in technology are even harder to explain. There may have been some deterioration in the skills of the work force in the past few years (see Chapter 18), but this is not a plausible reason for short-term fluctuations in productivity. The oil-price increases that took place in 1973 and 1979 are plausible candidates for negative productivity shocks as there were declines in productivity after these episodes. But even if we were to accept the oil-price increases as legitimate technology shocks, however, the other recessions in the postwar period, plus the recessions of previous periods, have no comparable technology-shock explanations. This is particularly true for the Great Depression. Proponents of the real–business-cycle theory have not come up with enough sources of technology shocks, either positive or negative. Technology shocks that are big enough to increase or reduce output in the economy as a whole should be big enough to be directly observable.

Productivity and the business cycle: Cause and effect

The apparent puzzle that productivity is low in recessions and high in booms can be explained by looking at labor markets from the perspective of the business manager. When companies face a reduction in demand, they reduce their output and employment, but employment falls by less than the fall in output. More workers are employed than are immediately needed, reducing productivity. One reason for this is that firms do not want to lay off certain valuable employees who have special skills and knowledge of the production methods in their firms. This phenomen is called **labor hoarding,** and companies report that indeed they do hoard labor during downturns. For many firms, it would not be possible to cut back on employment in proportion to the cut in output, even if there were no workers with special skills. Their plants are designed to operate at a certain level of production and require some level of **overhead labor** in order to operate at all. For example, a steel plant may require almost the same number of workers regardless of how large the flow of production is. And some other industries are the same.

Even though production may generally be subject to constant returns to scale in the long run (so that permanent reductions in output bring about proportional reductions in employment), in the short run, employment variations are less than proportional to output variations. Real–business-cycle theorists see the strong correlation between output and productivity and conclude that technology shocks are causing output changes. The mainstream view is that variations in demand are causing the changes in output and then the changes in productivity. The causality is running from output to productivity and not the other way around.

The economists that have been developing the real–business-cycle models have had great difficulty showing how year-to-year variations in employment could have come about, given their view of the cycle. Figure 16.6 shows the actual growth rate of hours worked in the economy together with the prediction of hours worked from one version of the real–business-cycle model. As is shown, there are noticeable differences between the actual series and the predicted series. The real–business-cycle theorists have not been able to make their models consistent with the ups and downs of employment that we see in actual recessions and booms.

The problems this theory has in explaining employment (or hours worked) are much greater even than this figure suggests. The model that was used to generate the prediction of hours worked shown in the figure assumes that labor supply is very responsive to changes in the real wage. The model

labor hoarding
Retaining employees in the face of a decline in demand.

overhead labor
The minimum level of employment a particular firm needs in order to operate.

FIGURE 16.6   Annual Growth Rate of Hours Worked, 1955–1985

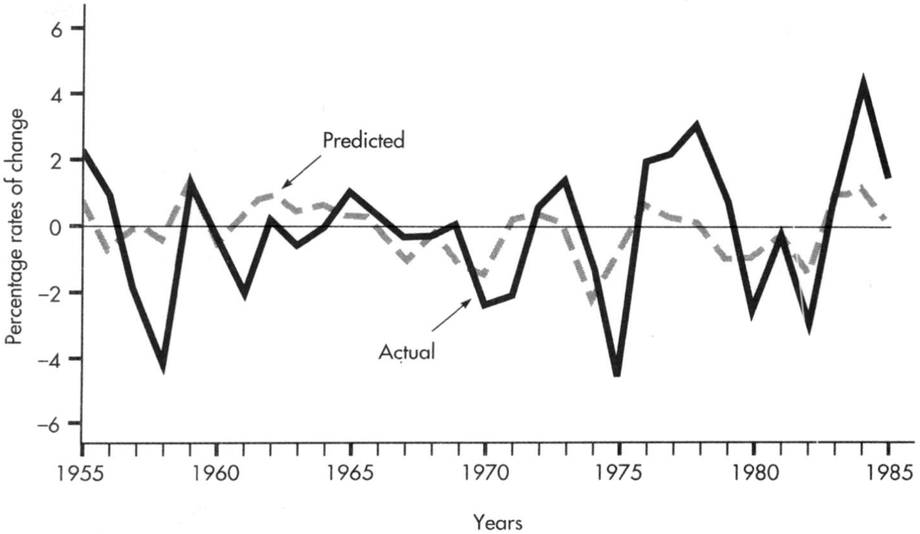

The actual fluctuations in hours worked over time are much greater than those predicted by the real–business-cycle model.

Source: Charles I. Plosser, "Understanding Real Business Cycles," *Journal of Economic Perspectives* 3, no. 3 (Summer 1989), p. 65.

assumes people want to increase their hours of work quite a bit when the wage rises, or lower their work effort when the wage falls. Empirical studies of labor supply do not find such responsiveness.

The real–business-cycle theorists have run into a serious problem in reconciling their model with actual experience because they assume that the labor market is competitive with flexible wages and hence that employment varies only because workers respond to changes in the real wage. This same issue came up in the discussion of the monetarist model where we saw that the real wage does not vary much over the cycle. The only way to explain employment fluctuations in the real–business-cycle model is to assume that people want to increase the amount that they work a lot even though wages have gone up very little, if at all. This does not fit with the studies of how individuals respond to wages.

Conclusions on Equilibrium–Business-Cycle and Real–Business-Cycle Models

There are many ways in which the mainstream model of the macroeconomy has been influenced by the recent developments that have come out of the classical tradition. The assumption of rational expectations has become part of much mainstream analysis and the idea that cycles might be initiated by sudden bursts of technology is potentially an important one.

The advocates of the classical-based theories of the business cycle acknowledge that there are problems with them. But they argue that the alternative mainstream model is fatally flawed because it lacks a microeconomic foundation based on fully rational behavior. The economists that have tried to respond to this criticism are called neo-Keynesians. This is an unfortunate name because Keynes did not believe that such a rationalist framework was necessary or even desirable. But the name itself is not terribly important. What is more important is seeing how well these economists have done in providing explanations for wage and price stickiness.

NEO-KEYNESIAN ANALYSIS OF PRICE STICKINESS

A task that many neo-Keynesians have set themselves is to construct models in which individuals have rational expectations, make rational choices in which they maximize their own utility and companies maximize profit, but nevertheless the resulting decisions made by firms and workers involve slow adjustment of wages and prices. At the macroeconomic level, the sum of the individual decisions should lead to an economy where fluctuations in output result from changes in aggregate demand and there is involuntary unemployment during recessions. This task is an extremely difficult one. Indeed, it may be inherently impossible. But in the process of trying to complete it, much has been learned about price and wage setting and the reasons for price stickiness.

wage contracts
Unions negotiate wage contracts that set wages over periods of one to three years. Union contacts generally allow firms to vary employment but not wages over the business cycle. There are also *implicit wage contracts* based upon an informal understanding between a firm and its workers.

We start by looking at the wage-setting process and the use of **wage contracts.** Then we turn to the price side and the adjustment (or nonadjustment) of markups. We conclude this discussion of **neo-Keynesian analysis** by looking at price flexibility or stickiness in the aggregate as well as the problem of coordinating price adjustments.

neo-Keynesian analysis
Models that accept the framework of rational choice with rational expectations and attempt to show how prices and wages may be sticky and how economy can be described by Keynesian models of aggregate demand.

Wage Contracts

Wages in most companies are adjusted at intervals of six months, a year, or, in the case of many union wage contracts, every three years. Moreover, when the wages are adjusted, they are increased (or occasionally decreased) not primarily on the basis of the short-run conditions in the labor market, but rather on the basis of the long-run trends of the economy. There is frequently some increase in the wage to adjust for the increase in the cost of living and then an additional amount that is linked to individual performance or to general productivity increases. Short-run market conditions do have an impact, particularly if a firm is having trouble recruiting or retaining workers, when it may increase its wages. And if a firm is going broke, it may ask for wage concessions even if a union contract is not up for renegotiation. But the impact of short-run conditions is surprisingly small. Increases or decreases in the queue of unemployed workers have only small impacts on the wages being set for workers who have jobs. Even in recessions when workers are losing their jobs, there is little change in the wages of the workers who keep their jobs. Wages depend upon the overall economic climate, not upon the current weather. Why is this?

The wage in long-term contracts

Young workers change jobs frequently and they may hold short-term jobs while in school. But as people get older, they usually settle down into jobs that last a long time. Looking at data from the 1970s and taking men and women together, it has been found that *half of all work is done in jobs that last 15 years or more.* Among men, half of all work is done in jobs that last 25 years or more.[18] It is possible that job durations have shortened somewhat since then, but it is still the case today that this long-term relationship between workers and the companies they work for is extremely important to both sides. Firms count on having workers who know the ropes and will stay around to help train new hires. It is often necessary to give special training or retraining to employees; in order to make this worthwhile, companies have to know that their employees will remain on the job for some time after the training. From the employee's point of view, changing jobs is very costly. No one enjoys looking for jobs and being evaluated. Losing a job can create a stigma that makes it harder to find a new job.

Given that the employer–employee relationship is often a long-term one, it makes sense for firms to set up a wage policy that is geared, not to short-term conditions, but to the long term. Where there is a union, firms will negotiate a wage contract lasting one or more years that sets out the wages to be paid over the life of the contract. And union contracts usually have provisions governing work rules, hiring and firing, and grievances. When there is not a unionized work force (unions cover only about 15 percent of employment in the U.S. economy), employers will still be concerned about the long term and their reputations as employers. Employers will provide an *implicit contract.* This is an understanding between an employer and its employees as to how wages will be adjusted and it may also cover normal work rules.

Since companies are in long-term relationships with many of their employees and use either implicit or explicit wage contracts, they will view the monthly or even the annual wage as being determined, not by short-run supply and demand in the labor market, but rather as one weekly or monthly payment on a long-term contract. Most people who take out loans to buy houses or cars arrange for stable repayment schedules. The monthly mortgage payment does not usually vary with short-run economic conditions. Similarly,

---

[18] Robert E. Hall, "Employment Fluctuations and Wage Rigidity," *Brookings Papers on Economic Activity 1:1980*, pp. 91–124.

the wage is like a partial payment on a long-term labor contract and it is not varied with short-run conditions.

Wage stability versus employment stability

The analogy between the stable monthly wage and the stable monthly mortgage payment is not an exact one. There is an important difference between the two cases because companies do not guarantee employment. When there is a short-run decline in product demand, workers are laid off. Why is it that implicit and explicit contracts specify that the wage does not respond to short-run market conditions while the level of employment does?

One answer is that firms are trying to reduce the risks faced by workers and *stabilizing wages helps to reduce worker risk, even when employment varies.*[19] Firms find it in their interests to reduce the income risks of workers because it pays off as a long-run strategy. If workers knew that the wage that they would receive would vary with short-run conditions, then they would demand a higher average wage or choose to work at a firm that offered more stability. Providing wage stability is something firms are willing to do as part of their competitive strategy in hiring and retaining workers. Since product demand varies widely over the business cycle, firms do not find that it pays to give employment guarantees, but they can provide some reduction in risk by avoiding variable wages.

A related reason is that workers consider that cutting wages in a downturn is unfair, whereas layoffs are not. Arthur Okun has described an economy with implicit contracts as operating with an invisible handshake, rather than with Adam Smith's invisible hand.[20] Firms have to treat their employees fairly in order to maintain morale, keep up productivity, and encourage workers to stay with the same employer. When the demand for autos or machine tools declines in a recession, workers see the drop in orders and understand that employment must fall. Cutting wages, on the other hand, is divisive. To workers it looks like getting more profit for the company at the expense of workers.

This idea of setting a wage that is higher than the wage that would be required to retain the work force during recessions has recently been described as setting an *efficiency wage*. A firm sets an efficiency wage when it bases its wage decision not only on whether or not it can hire new workers, but also because it believes that there are benefits to productivity and morale from setting wages that are above the minimum required for hiring.

Finally, keeping wages stable while allowing employment to vary is a way of shifting the burden of the recession onto a fraction of the workers,

---

[19] This was shown by Martin Neil Baily, "Wages and Employment under Uncertain Demand," *Review of Economic Studies* 41 (January 1974), pp. 37–50; and Costas Azariadis, "Implicit Contracts and Underemployment Equilibria," *Journal of Political Economy* 83 (December 1975), pp. 1183–1202.

[20] Arthur M. Okun, *Prices and Quantities, A Macroeconomic Analysis* (Washington, D.C.: Brookings Institution, 1981).

typically those that have not been with the company very long. Layoffs are not made randomly. Workers with seniority or skills that the company judges are valuable are retained, while recent hires or workers that the company does not want are let go during recessions.

Wage contracts provide an important reason why wages do not respond much to moderate variations in demand. But wage stickiness is not enough to provide a complete microeconomic foundation for Keynesian models. The neo-Keynesian analysis has also tried to explain price stickiness.

Price Stickiness

The classical model of competitive markets used simple supply and demand schedules. A decline in demand will lead to excess supply and then competition will force the price down. In most actual product markets, however, there is not perfect competition. Firms are choosing the price that they charge in order to maximize the amount of profit they will receive. Firms will usually make strategic decisions about prices. This means that they will take into account the responses of their principal competitors. In particular, a firm deciding to cut its price will know that other firms will probably match the price cut. The gain in profit from reducing price in recessions may be small or nonexistent.

This idea is illustrated in Figure 16.7, where the initial profit schedule for a firm is shown. This schedule indicates how the firm's profit varies with the price that it charges and it implies that the firm will choose initially to be at point A. Its profits are maximized by setting the price P_0 and at this point it has reached the highest level of profit it can, $Profit_A$.

Suppose that there is then a decline in the market demand for the product that is being produced by this firm. Following this decline, the firm's profit will be lower. It can no longer achieve the same level of profit. The figure indicates that the new profit-maximizing price is P_1. This says that it pays the firm to lower its price following the downturn. But the figure also illustrates that if the firm does not lower its price, then the loss of profit will be very small. By lowering its price, it will receive the amount of profit shown at $Profit_B$. But by holding its price constant, it will receive the amount of profit $Profit_C$. The difference between the two is very small.

Menu cost models

Figure 16.8 is only an illustration, of course, but neo-Keynesian economists have worked with models of decision making by firms and concluded that the case shown in the figure is a plausible one. They suggest that the gains to firms from price adjustment may be very small. They then go on to argue that there are costs to adjusting prices so that in fact firms may even be better off to hold price constant because any small gain in operating profit will be less than the cost of adjusting prices. These models, with the unfortunate title **menu cost** models, point out that price lists (such as menus) will

menu cost
The cost of changing price lists or other costs of adjusting prices.

FIGURE 16.7 Effect of a Price Change on Profit

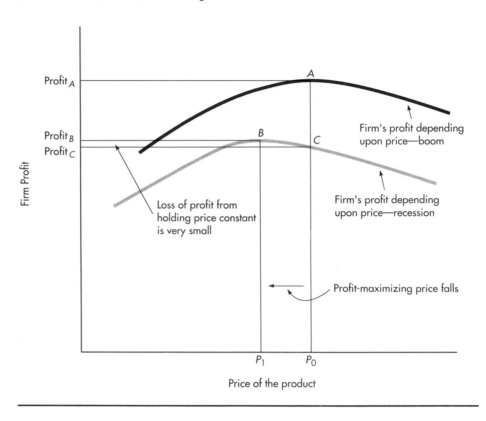

Price of the product

have to be altered when prices are adjusted.[21] More important than the cost of printing price lists are the costs of deciding price changes or the costs of renegotiating prices with suppliers or dealers.

Menu cost models are most applicable to cases where prices are set by contracts between buyers and sellers. Contractual arrangements are common throughout the economy as raw materials and intermediate goods are traded under contractual arrangements and many producers also have long-term contracts with wholesalers and retailers. These contracts may be explicit and are often long, complicated, and costly to renegotiate.

The menu cost model is actually very applicable to the labor market too. An important reason why union contracts are often two or three years

---

[21] Menu cost models have been stressed by N. Gregory Mankiw, "Small Menu Costs and Large Business Cycles: A Macroeconomic Model of Monopoly," *Quarterly Journal of Economics* 100 (May 1985), pp. 529–37.

in duration is that neither side wants to go through the bargaining process more frequently than that. In general, say neo-Keynesians, *firms are willing to give up some short-run profit when demand varies because there are long-term gains from having stable prices and wages.*

The main emphasis of neo-Keynesian analysis has been on developing models of the behavior of individual firms or industries to see if rational behavior can be reconciled with wage and price stickiness. But there has also been another aspect to the theory. What happens when there are many different industries? What is the relation between individual price and wage adjustment and adjustments of the price level?

Coordination Failure and Real and Nominal Stickiness

The equilibrium–business-cycle model assumes complete price and wage flexibility and market efficiency. And the rationale for this is always given in terms of a single market where arbitrage should eliminate any market inefficiency. But even if the assumption of price flexibility were accepted, there is a serious question as to whether the whole economy with thousands of individual markets would converge to a single full-employment equilibrium. Advocates of the equilibrium model assume that there would be aggregate equilibrium, but neo-Keynesians challenge that assumption. There may be a failure of coordination, so that the economy could go to one of several underemployment equilibria. There are no realistic models of adjustment with many different markets that can show a smooth or rapid convergence of all wages and prices to a single full-employment equilibrium. The equilibrium–business-cycle theorists have assumed away a major problem in their analysis.

Real and nominal stickiness

price-coordination problem
A decline in nominal aggregate demand may lead to a decline in real output unless there is a decline in all wages and prices. It may be impossible to obtain a coordinated decline in all prices and wages even if many people in the economy understand that it would be beneficial. The price-coordination problem can cause nominal price stickiness.

The **price-coordination problem** is an important issue for the economists who assume price flexibility. But it becomes even more important in the neo-Keynesian models, where there is price and wage stickiness. There is a specific way in which a coordination failure may occur and make it difficult for the economy to achieve full employment. Coordination problems can mean that small costs of adjusting wages and prices for individual firms can become large costs for the economy as a whole.

The models of wage and price stickiness that we have just described are called models of *real stickiness*. This means that they help us understand why the real wage does not fall during periods when unemployment is high or why firms do not lower the relative prices of their products when their demand curves shift down.[22] But critics of these models have pointed out that if all prices and wages fell together in recessions, there would be

---

[22] The menu cost models that emphasize literally the cost of printing price lists do provide a rationale for nominal stickiness, but such costs alone are not generally considered large enough to be important.

no need for real wages or relative prices to change. For example, if the money supply fell by 10 percent, the chances are that this would lead to a recession. But if all prices and wages fell by 10 percent, then there would be no change in the real money stock and hence no change in real aggregate demand. The fact that this does not happen is called *nominal stickiness.* And some form of nominal wage and price stickiness is essential to any model of the business cycle in which aggregate demand leads to changes in real output. Nominal stickiness means that any decline in the nominal value of output will lead to a decline in real output. How can it be explained?

Neo-Keynesians point out that if all wages and prices were to decline by 10 percent when the money supply (or some other measure of aggregate demand) declined by 10 percent, this would involve an amazing act of coordination by everyone in the economy. How could this occur? Would the natural working of the economy lead to the development of such coordinated behavior? The answer is that it probably would not and the discussion of real stickiness helps to understand why. Suppose the economy were divided into those who followed the Fed's policy changes and understood their implications and those who could care less about such matters. Would the people with rational expectations somehow impose coordination on the others, perhaps by lowering their own prices by more than 10 percent? The analysis of real stickiness suggests that the answer is no. If most firms do not change their wages and prices following a decline in the money supply, then a fall in nominal demand will lead to a decline in real aggregate demand. Moreover, with most prices unchanged, any reduction in wages or prices by the "smart" firms will be a decline in real wages or in relative prices. The models of real stickiness then suggest that profit-maximizing firms will decide that at most only small declines in real or relative wages are indicated. In other words, if some firms have nominal stickiness, then this will tend to spread to all other firms. Unless coordinated adjustments of wages and prices were somehow the norm, it is hard to see how they would ever get started.

This discussion of a coordination failure has been rather abstract, given in terms of a thought experiment following a sudden fall in nominal demand. But the issue itself is far from abstract. If there were some way of encouraging firms to adjust their wages and prices to nominal aggregate demand, it would be possible to reduce the impact of fluctuations in nominal demand on real output and employment. And some small countries have had success in achieving coordination in practice, at least for a while. In Austria most wages are union wages that are all set at the same time in a kind of national wage-bargaining session. The Austrians have been able to cooperate in this bargaining and match wage and price increases to the growth in demand. As a result, they have been able to keep unemployment low. In other countries such attempts have failed, however. Achieving coordination in a large, individualistic economy is hard or impossible, while imposing coordination by government intervention in wage and price setting is likely to create more problems than it solves.

Assessing the Neo-Keynesian Analysis

One criticism of neo-Keynesian analysis is that it is not all that new. The effort to explain why people behave in the way that is assumed in Keynesian or mainstream models has been an ongoing one for 40 years. But this is not a terribly serious criticism. There are important new ideas in this work and there has been a rigorous attempt to build a rational basis for Keynesian analysis.

The serious criticism of neo-Keynesian analysis is that it is trying to do the impossible. The neo-Keynesian models of price and wage stickiness may tell us a lot about why there is stickiness in practice, but these models are not watertight when judged strictly using the axioms of rational choice and rational expectations. Once the extreme rationalist framework has been accepted, it is probably impossible to construct a model of the business cycle that fits with what we observe. In a recession, we observe people being laid off. They are not making rational choices; they are losing their jobs involuntarily. When workers who have been laid off hold out desperately in the hope of getting their old jobs back, they are not using all available information rationally. They are hoping against hope. It is not that the neo-Keynesian analysis is wrong in modeling stickiness, it is that the attempt to reconcile stickiness with a strict rationalist framework may be misguided. This framework may be ignoring much about the way people actually behave.

Good economic science is not based on models that assume that people behave the way economists think they should. It is based upon the way people are actually observed to behave. Long-term experience has demonstrated clearly that wages and prices do not adjust instantly and that markets may take a long time before they adjust to equilibrium. The reasons for this stickiness are not necessarily irrational; they may reflect nonmarket considerations, which make perfectly good sense to managers and employees, but which are not reflected in models of pricing and wage-setting behavior. The fact that economists do not have a fully developed understanding of why there is stickiness is not a reason to assume the behavior away.

Summary

- Equilibrium–business-cycle theorists and real–business-cycle theorists wish to explain fluctuations in output and employment within models that are based on rational individual choice and in which people have rational expectations.

- In the rational-expectations model of the economy, expectations are formed by using all available information efficiently.

- Rational expectations of future inflation are formed by looking forward, using the economic conditions that generate the future rate of inflation. Past inflation is only important to the extent that it forecasts future inflation.

- When expectations of inflation are formed on the basis of future forecasts, the public's understanding of which policy regime is in force is an important part of their rational expectations. The credibility of policymakers becomes a primary factor in determining the current rate of inflation.

- It is possible to assume rational expectations without price and wage flexibility and vice versa. However, equilibrium–business-cycle models assume both price and wage flexibility as well as rational expectations. In the view of the economists that combine rational expectations with price flexibility, markets are always in equilibrium.

- Business cycles occur in the equilibrium models but only because of unexpected shocks to aggregate demand.

- The Lucas supply schedule relates output to the ratio of the actual price level to the expected price level. The actual price level can differ from the expected price level because of a monetary surprise. An unexpected increase in the money supply leads to an increase in output. An unexpected decrease in the money supply leads to a decrease in output.

- Expectations can fail to be realized, because having rational expectations and using information efficiently do not mean people know exactly what is going to happen. Rather they mean that people make the best use of the information available at the time.

- The policy-ineffectiveness theorem argues that stabilization policy is impotent since only an unexpected shock can cause output to differ from potential, and therefore systematic policy is ineffective as a tool for raising or lowering output.

- The real–business-cycle model replaces the conclusion of the equilibrium–business-cycle models that fluctuations result from policy surprises. Instead, it is argued that all fluctuations are the results of technology or labor-supply shocks. Shifts in the money market will not change real output; only changes in the real economy can bring about changes in real income.

- Technology and productivity changes are responsible for most of the long-run changes in output. However, the real–business-cycle models also argue that short-run changes in productivity determine changes in output over the business cycle.

- The case for or against rational expectations depends upon the issues of just how efficient individual markets are and how well rational-expectations models describe the workings of markets and macroeconomic events.

- An important discrepancy between the rational-expectations models and observation is the implication that deviations from potential output should be short-lived. The experience of the actual economy is that output moves slowly and persistently above or below potential for periods of several years at a time.

- Real–business-cycle models assume that output varies as a result of aggregate supply shifts. This should mean that prices fall in booms and rise in recessions. This is not the normal case. The models also are implausible in arguing that technology often declines.

- Neo-Keynesians start with the same framework of rational choice as the equilibrium models and then try to understand how wages and prices could be sticky even under these conditions. Models that look at wage contracts, efficiency wages, and menu costs help us understand how real stickiness occurs. The problem of coordinating price and wage adjustments helps us understand how norminal stickiness can occur.

- The neo-Keynesian models have given insight into stickiness, but it may be a mistake to try and explain actual business cycles using the extreme rational framework.

KEY TERMS

adaptive expectations

arbitrage

choice-theoretic framework

equilibrium–business-cycle model

labor hoarding

Lucas critique

menu cost

monetary shock

neo-Keynesian analysis

nominal price or wage stickiness

overhead labor

policy-ineffectiveness theorem

price-coordination problem

real–business-cycle models

systematic policymaking

technology shock

time-inconsistent policies

wage contracts

DISCUSSION QUESTIONS AND PROBLEMS

1. Do rational expectations require perfect foresight?
2. How can an expectation of future reductions in the rate of inflation lower current inflation?
3. Why does the Lucas supply schedule depend upon surprises to generate an increase in real output? Is such an increase in output a surprise that is likely to be permanent?
4. How does the Fed's establishment of its credibility in pursuing anti-inflationary policies contribute to the ineffectiveness of stabilization policies?
5. In the rationalist view, what might explain an increase in the unemployment rate? Is all unemployment voluntary?
6. In the rationalist view, an unexpected increase in aggregate demand will raise both output and prices. Does the less-than-complete allocation of the increase in demand to prices indicate price stickiness?
7. Contrast the sources of short-term fluctuations around potential output in an equilibrium–business–cycle model and a real–business-cycle model.
8. What is the difference between implicit and explicit contracts? How are implicit contracts enforced? Why do wage contracts typically set wages that do not vary much over the business cycle?
9. What costs will firms face when they change their prices? If menu costs are important, does that mean that the government should subsidize the printing of price lists?

PART IX

Productivity and Long-Term Growth

Improving the standard of living is a fundamental goal of economic development. In the short run, growth in the consumption standard of living can occur if the economy is recovering from a recession, or if the economy is consuming imported goods and borrowing to pay for them. However, in the long run, growth in the consumption standard of living can only be sustained if there is growth in the capacity to produce goods and services—growth in potential output. In fact, if population is growing, then living standards will increase in the long run only if potential output is growing faster than population. And the impact of the growth in potential output compounds in the long run. After several years, large differences in economic performance are the result of small differences in growth rates.

Growth also provides flexibility for an economy where structural changes can have painful effects. There are always some industries that are declining relative to others. There are some regions of the country doing worse than the average and some groups of workers or consumers that are being adversely affected by structural changes. In an economy without growth, every allocation toward one sector, region, or group comes at the expense of another sector, region, or group. The economy becomes what is called a zero sum game, where one person's losses are another person's gains. In such an economy there are often political pressures to protect the incomes of groups that are being hurt. And the result can be policies that adversely effect efficiency. In a growing economy, structural changes will leave fewer people actually worse off, so adjustments are easier.

Up to this point we have focused primarily on the determination of income in the short run, where the status of aggregate demand determined the level of equilibrium income and fluctuations of income around the trend of the growth of potential output. Now we go on to examine how that trend is determined and what may account for long-run changes in the growth of potential output. The characteristics of the growth of potential output are understood by examining the supply side of the economy and the forces that contribute to an expansion of aggregate supply.

CHAPTER 17
Aggregate Supply
Long-Term Growth and Productivity

In 1989 real GNP in the U.S. economy was almost six times the size it had reached in 1929, 60 years before. Over the same period, the U.S. population slightly more than doubled and so GNP per capita rose almost threefold. This represents a dramatic increase in the standard of living, particularly since this period covered the Great Depression and several small recessions, and three wars. The gain in income was not a cyclical phenomenon caused by variations is aggregate demand. Almost all of the growth in per capita income consisted of an increase in our ability to supply goods and services. It was growth in the size of potential output.

In our discussion of income so far we have focused on either determining the level of income or explaining the cyclical relation of actual income to potential income. The primary explanation given for deviations in income was fluctuations in aggregate demand. In these last two chapters the question of whether or not the economy is actually producing its potential is left behind and we turn our attention to the growth of the economy's capacity to produce goods and services—the growth of aggregate supply and the long-run determination of potential output. Over the long run, the shifting out of aggregate supply is a more important determinant of the growth of our living standards than are oscillations of aggregate demand.

Since we are looking at long-run growth trends, even a small difference in growth rates will have large effects. The rate of growth of real income per capita was approximately 1.8 percent per year over the period from 1929 to 1989. If over that same period of time the growth of real income per capita had been either higher (2.3 percent) or lower (1.3 percent) than it actually was by only one half of one percent per year, the level of per capita GNP in 1989 would have turned out to be 35 percent higher or 35 percent lower than was actually obtained. If we look forward 60 years, the effect of rates of growth that differ by only one half of one percent will have just as dramatic an effect on our standard of living and that of our children.

Long-term improvements in the standard of living require growth in income per person (per capita), not just growth in aggregate output. One way income per person can change is because of increases in the number of hours people work or the fraction of the population that is working. Earning more for more hours worked is not an unambiguous gain in living standard— a 70–90-hour workweek, such as was the norm in the 19th century, leaves little time or energy for enjoying the gains in income. Fortunately the modern trend in industrialized economies has been a decline in the number of hours worked per week—below 40 hours in the United States. Alternatively, if family income is increased as a result of an increase in the number of people working, this also represents an increase in the total work hours of the family. The long-term trend in the United States has been a decline in hours worked per employee, but a rise in the fraction of the population that is in the labor force. This has come about through a decline in adult-male labor-force participation and a larger rise in female labor-force participation. In assessing growth in potential output and living standards, the best simple measure is average output per unit of labor input. If output rises faster than employment or hours worked, then living standards will improve— more income is earned by the work force.

In this chapter we look at a model of production, which we use to focus upon the growth of output per worker. We look at the role of saving and capital accumulation in fostering growth as well as the major contribution made by technology. We end this chapter and begin the final chapter by looking at recent trends in growth and productivity in the United States. We go on to examine the recent decline in productivity growth in the United States and in most other economies of the industrialized world.

The first step we take in studying the determination of long-run growth of output per hour is to see how the growth of output per worker is affected by the growth of capital. An increase in the amount of capital per worker will increase output per worker because each worker has more capital on hand to facilitate production. This connection is almost obvious when we reflect on the way in which capital per worker has been increased in industrialized economies—through a greater use of automation in production. With more automation per worker, each worker employed is able to produce a much greater quantity of output. We trace the source of increase in capital per worker to the fraction of income saved. When a larger fraction of income is saved, we also increase the fraction of income that can be allocated to capital for use in production.

PRODUCTION AND A NEOCLASSICAL MODEL OF LONG-RUN GROWTH

We discussed the production function in Chapter 15 when we described the classical model. In that discussion, the production function was used to explain the classical view of short-run fluctuations in the economy. And so we assumed that capital and technology were constant, a reasonable assumption for the short run. Now we use the production function to develop a neoclassical model of long-run growth and we will allow for changes over time in both capital and technology. We use the production function to introduce some ideas that will be important for growth analysis, such as diminishing returns to capital, diminishing returns to labor, and constant returns to scale.

technology
The state of knowledge about methods and techniques used in production.

The amount of output that can be produced depends upon how much capital and labor are employed in production and upon how that capital and labor are used, namely, the state of **technology.** The state of technology includes the cumulative effects of scientific advances and applied research and development that have, over time, led to vast increases in the ability of the economy to produce. Changes in technology also incorporate those important improvements in management methods and ways of organizing production that have raised the productive capacity of the factory and the office.

aggregate-production function
The relationship between potential output and the inputs used to produce it (usually capital, labor, and technology).

We use the concept of an **aggregate-production function** to describe the economywide relationship between potential output (Y^P) and capital (K) and labor (N) inputs, using a particular technology (T). This is shown in Equation 17.1:

$$Y^P = F(K,N,T). \tag{17.1}$$

technological change
Reflects the improvement in technology over time.

Increases in the inputs (capital and/or labor) will raise potential output even if there is no change in technology. Improvements in technology will increase potential output using the same amount of inputs. **Technological change** combined with increases in the amount of capital and/or labor will increase potential output by more than the increase in technology or inputs alone. In the United States, the growth in all three of these factors $(K, N,$ and $T)$ contributed to the economy's history of substantial growth in potential output.

The production function 17.1 is a representation of the way the economy's capacity to produce is affected by technology and the amount of available inputs. Year-to-year changes in actual output (Y) will depend on the extent to which the available capital and labor resources are being utilized. During a downturn, actual employment falls below the available labor force and capital is not fully utilized. But we can study the growth of potential output by computing the growth of actual output between pairs of years where unemployment is equal to its natural rate and capital is fully utilized, so output and potential output are close together. That is one reason we used 1929 and 1989 a little earlier, since these were both years where the economy was close to full employment.

Average Labor Productivity

We argued earlier that output per hour worked is related to living standards. It is an important indicator of economic performance in the economy and is given a specific name: **average labor productivity.** When actual output equals potential output,

average labor productivity
Output per worker or output per hour of work.

$$\text{Average labor productivity} = \text{Output per unit of labor input} = \frac{Y^P}{N}.$$

Average labor productivity is a concept we introduced in Chapter 10 where it played a role in the relation between wage increases and price increases. At that time we were looking at the effect of labor costs on inflation; now we are looking for how labor productivity is determined. Average labor productivity will generally rise when potential output rises, but this is not always the case. It will move in the opposite direction from total output when there is a change in labor input (a change in the denominator N), with no change in capital or technology. If employment increases, with a given technology and given capital, this will raise total output—more labor generates more output—but because of diminishing returns, each additional worker adds less to output than the previously hired workers. The average level of labor productivity will fall. Hiring more workers or using more hours per worker to produce more output will depress average labor productivity unless the amount of capital rises by enough to offset the diminishing returns. An important question for growth theory is: How much capital is needed to prevent running into diminishing returns as the labor force grows?

Constant returns to scale

Labor is not very productive without capital—factories, machinery, offices, computers, and so on. When new workers are hired to produce more output with a given technology, they need the same capital equipment to work with that existing workers have; otherwise, labor productivity will fall.

constant returns to scale
A characteristic of production where a given percentage increase in all inputs leads to an equal percent increase in output.

The need to equip new workers with much the same level of capital as old workers in order to keep productivity from falling is captured in the presumption that production takes place with **constant returns to scale.** For example, if two identical operations (factories or offices) are constructed and set into operation with the same complement of machines, materials, and employees, production under constant returns to scale implies that the two sites will produce twice the output of one operation alone. The idea of constant returns to scale describes production as a process where proportional increases in the scale (amount or size) of capital and labor employed result in output going up proportionally, holding technology constant. A 10 percent increase or decrease in both capital and labor will result in a 10 percent increase or decrease in output.

Returns to scale are assessed by considering the impact of increases in capital and labor with technology taken as given. Of course, in any practical situation, technology will change as the amount of capital and labor change, so statistical methods have to be used to decide whether or not there are constant returns to scale. Studies are done to see how output differs among small and large plants operating with similar technologies. Such studies indicate that constant returns to scale are a reasonable generalization of production in the economy though there may be slight increases in productivity with increases in the scale of operation—output may rise between 10 and 11.5 percent when labor and capital increase by 10 percent.[1] Since the assumption of constant returns to scale greatly simplifies the analysis of productivity with very little loss of realism, we will assume constant returns now and talk about other possibilities later in the chapter.

The relationship between returns to scale and labor productivity is reflected in the production function. Total output per worker (average labor productivity or Y^P/N) is equal to production per worker:

$$\frac{Y^P}{N} = \frac{F(K,N,T)}{N} = \text{average labor productivity.} \tag{17.2}$$

Under constant returns to scale, a proportional increase in capital and labor generates the same level of average labor productivity as before the increase in inputs—average labor productivity does not depend on the size of the economy. This conclusion about constant–returns-to-scale production is shown (Equation 17.3) in an example where capital and labor have doubled (K to $2K$, N to $2N$) and this leads to a doubling of output (Y^P to $2Y^P$). Technology has been held constant.

$$2Y^P = F(2N,2N,T)$$
$$\frac{2Y^P}{2N} = \frac{F(2K,2N,T)}{2N} = \frac{Y^P}{N} \tag{17.3}$$

Notice that constant returns to scale are maintained even though technology stays constant. When a new factory or office is opened or more capacity is added to current operations, the same technology can be replicated. Technology is a form of knowledge and has the property that, when it is applied in one setting, it is not used up so it is available for another. A fixed technology does not mean that technology is spread thinner as production increases, causing diminishing returns. Rather, fixed technology means that the same technology is available at all levels of production. In fact, constant returns to scale would still hold even if a single firm has access to proprietary technology, as long as the increases in the number of operating units occur within the company and the technology is shared.

To summarize, therefore, when production is described by constant returns to scale and there is an increase in the work force, capital has to be

---

[1] Zvi Griliches and V. Ringstad, *Economies of Scale and the Form of the Production Function* (Amsterdam: North-Holland, 1971).

added to the economy so as to prevent a reduction in average labor productivity. Average labor productivity will remain the same if capital is increased in the same proportion as the increase in the labor force.

Capital per Worker and Economic Growth

Proportional increases of capital and labor only keep average labor productivity constant. If there are to be increases in the standard of living, average labor productivity must rise over time. One way to secure higher levels of average labor productivity is to increase capital by more than any increases in labor. In such a case there is an increase in the amount of capital available for each worker and this increases the **capital intensity** of the economy.

capital intensity
The ratio of capital to labor. On average, the amount of capital available for use by each worker.

The intensive production function

The greater is the capital intensity (capital per worker, K/N) of the economy, the greater is output per worker and the greater is the standard of living obtained in the economy. Provided there are constant returns to scale, average labor productivity is determined only by capital intensity—the capital/labor ratio (K/N) with a given technology (T). The **intensive production function** (Equation 17.4) is the production function rewritten so that labor productivity depends upon capital intensity:

intensive production function
A production function in which labor productivity depends upon capital intensity—how much capital is available for use by each worker.

$$\frac{Y^P}{N} = f\left(\frac{K}{N}, T\right). \tag{17.4}$$

With a given technology, the capital intensity of the economy, rather than the separate amounts of capital and labor, determines labor productivity and the standard of living.[2] The intensive production function is illustrated in Figure 17.1. Along a particular production function (f_A), successive increases in capital intensity $[(K/N)_A$ to $(K/N)_B$ to $(K/N)_C]$ bring about increases in average labor productivity. However, raising productivity by raising capital intensity will run into **diminishing returns** to *capital*—average labor productivity rises, but at a declining rate. $(CD$ is less than $BE.)$ Movements along the intensive production function do not represent increases in the scale of operations where all increases are proportional and productivity is unchanged. Rather, they reflect increases in output per worker obtained when capital is increased more than labor— *output increases less than proportionally to the increase in capital.*

diminishing returns
There are *diminishing returns to labor* if the labor input increases but all other inputs remain constant. Output increases by less than the increase in labor. There are *diminishing returns to capital* if the capital input increases but all other inputs remain constant. Output increases by less than the increase in capital.

In the classical model used to describe short-run changes in output (Chapter 15), the production function exhibited diminishing returns to labor as employment varied with capital remaining fixed. Here, where we are describing the growth of output through a strategy of increasing capital over time, the production function illustrates the opposite case—adding capital at a

---

[2] We are ignoring the effect of land or natural resources in this analysis (or grouping them with capital). In addition, for individual industries, labor productivity also depends on intermediate goods and services purchased from other industries.

FIGURE 17.1   The Intensive Production Function: Diminishing Returns

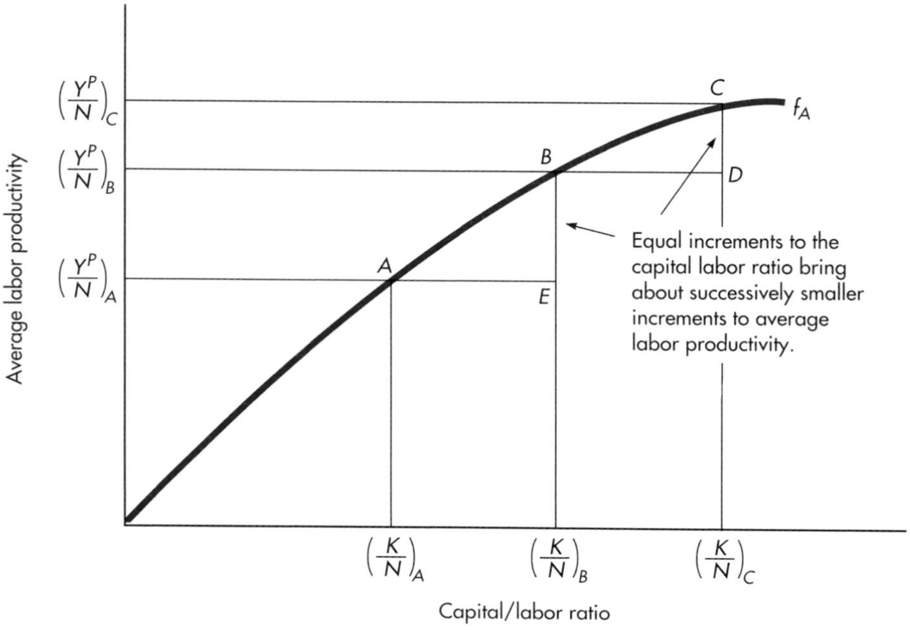

As the capital/labor ratio increases, there are diminishing returns.

faster rate than the growth of the labor force leads to diminishing returns to capital.

The constraints of diminishing returns to capital can be avoided if there is an improvement in technology. In Figure 17.2 we describe several intensive production functions (f_A, f_B, and f_C) where average labor productivity rises because of improvements in technology. Even with no change in capital intensity [points A to B to C line up along the constant capital/labor ratio (K/N)], improvements in the state of technology raise productivity.

Labor-force growth and capital adequacy

In economies with growing populations there will usually be growth in the work force. With a given technology, this growth in the work force requires an equal growth in the stock of capital, just to keep standards of living constant, let alone allow for any improvements. If the work force is growing, and there is not enough new capital added to match the growth of the work force, capital growth will be inadequate and the economy will suffer from a falling standard of living. In this case of inadequate capital growth, there will be a decline in the capital/labor ratio, leading to successively larger

---

FIGURE 17.2 The Intensive Production Function: Shifts in Technology

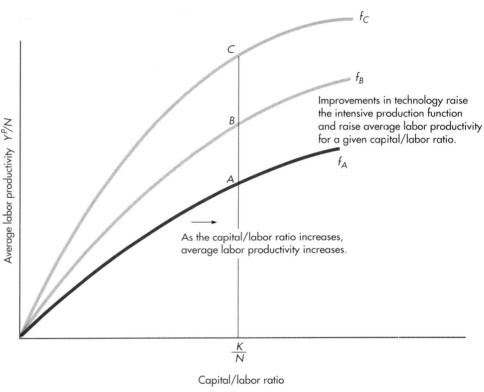

Average labor productivity depends upon the capital/labor ratio and technology.

---

and larger declines in average labor productivity. Increases in capital become essential in order to avoid diminishing returns to labor.

The intensive production function shown in Equation 17.4 describes how average labor productivity depends on the capital/labor ratio (K/N). And the capital/labor ratio depends upon the relative rates of growth of capital and labor. The capital/labor ratio rises when the rate of growth of capital exceeds the rate of growth of the labor input, it falls when the rate of growth of capital is less than that of the labor input, and it stays the same when the two growth rates are equal. This connection between capital intensity and the growth of inputs is set out in Equation 17.5:

K/N is rising when $\Delta K/K > \Delta N/N$
K/N is constant when $\Delta K/K = \Delta N/N$ (17.5)
K/N is falling when $\Delta K/K < \Delta N/N$.

Economies with constant technology that are increasing their stocks of capital at a rate that is just adequate for their rates of labor-input growth will be just maintaining their average labor productivity. In some countries of the world, however, population and labor-force growth have exceeded the ability of the economies to save and increase their capital. These countries have falling standards of living. In Figure 17.1 an economy that starts out (point C) with a high level of average labor productivity $[(Y^P/N)_C]$ will slip back to a lower level of average labor productivity $[(Y^P/N)_B]$ when the labor input grows by more than the capital stock. (K/N falls as labor grows relative to capital.) And if this process continues (point B to point A), the declines of living standards will get even worse. (*BE* exceeds *CD*.)

With a given technology and labor-force growth, the amount of capital growth that is adequate for maintaining living standards is known—it is a growth rate of capital equal to the growth of the work force. But that adequate rate of capital formation may or may not be obtainable. The capacity of an economy to maintain or improve its standard of living is related to the adequacy of its rate of capital formation. *Whether or not an economy is capable of sustaining an adequate level of capital growth depends upon the amount of saving.*

To see just how saving rates affect productivity growth, we now look at the requirements for capital adequacy within a model of economic growth that abstracts from technological change. Changes in technology will be reintroduced later in the chapter. Omitting technology at this point has the advantage that it allows us to focus in a simple fashion on the contribution of capital accumulation to growth and the question of whether economies save too much or too little. When we do reintroduce technological change, we will find that much of the analysis we undertook with a fixed technology is easily transferable to economies experiencing both capital accumulation and technological change.

THE SOLOW LONG-TERM GROWTH MODEL

A major modern contribution to the understanding of long-term growth was the development by Robert M. Solow of a growth model using the production-function framework combined with saving behavior.[3] The Solow model focused on the way in which saving frees up resources that can then be used for capital accumulation. Capital accumulation might then lead to more economic growth and rising living standards.

Saving's contribution to capital accumulation and growth starts with the relationship between saving and income. Since we are analyzing long-term

---

[3] Robert M. Solow, "A Contribution to the Theory of Economic Growth," *Quarterly Journal of Economics*, 70 (February 1956), pp. 65–94; "Investment and Technical Progress," in *Mathematical Methods in the Social Sciences*, ed. K. J. Arrow, S. Karbin, and P. Suppes (Stanford, Calif.: Stanford University Press, 1959), pp. 89–104, and "Technical Change and the Aggregate Production Function," *Review of Economics and Statistics* 39 (1957), pp. 312–20.

Other economists also contributed important work to the early development of growth theory, especially James Tobin and T. W. Swan.

growth, we assume that consumption and hence saving are fixed proportions of income. Using a simple proportional function to describe saving is appropriate in a model of growth since the distinctions between current income and permanent income are issues of concern for explaining fluctuations in income and consumption, not long-term trends during which transitory elements in income will disappear. This assumption corresponds roughly to Milton Friedman's description of consumption as a constant fraction of permanent income. The proportional relationship between saving and potential output is shown in Equation 17.6:[4]

$$S = s \times Y^P. \tag{17.6}$$

Saving is also equal to investment in this model and investment is also equal to the change in the capital stock (ΔK). Again, since this is a long-term model we can safely ignore short-run investment-demand fluctuations. Since saving and investment are proportional to income (Equation 17.7), changes in the capital stock are proportional to income:

$$S = I = \Delta K = s \times Y^P. \tag{17.7}$$

Our analysis is motivated by an interest in living standards and average labor productivity. We want to know how much saving is available per worker because that will translate into how much new capital is available per worker. The amount of new capital per worker will tell us if labor productivity is rising or falling. To see if capital is growing more or less proportionally with labor, in Equation 17.8 we divide output and saving by the size of the labor input, N:

$$\frac{S}{N} = \frac{\Delta K}{N} = \frac{s \times Y^P}{N}. \tag{17.8}$$

Here, we see that the ratio of saving to employment is equal to the amount of new capital per worker $(\Delta K/N)$, and it depends upon output per worker (Y^P/N). Since the propensity to save (s) is set, a fixed proportion of output per worker will be saved.

In Equation 17.9, we replace the term for output per worker $\left(\frac{Y^P}{N}\right)$ with the production function that describes output per worker, the intensive production function. The intensive production function relates output per worker (average labor productivity) to the capital/labor ratio:

Ratio of saving to employment	New capital per worker	Saving rate × Output per worker	Saving rate × Intensive production function	
S/N	$= \Delta K/N$	$= s \times (Y^P/N)$	$= s \times f(K/N).$	(17.9)

---

[4] We are defining both saving and investment *net* of depreciation for simplicity. The growth model can easily be modified to include depreciation explicitly.

Equation 17.9 indicates that the amount of new capital added per worker ($\Delta K/N$) depends upon the existing capital/labor ratio [$f(K/N)$]. The existing capital/labor ratio determines output per worker and a fraction of that output per hour is saved. Total saving divided by employment is the source of investment—new capital per worker. Notice that if there were a rise in the existing capital/labor ratio, current productivity would rise along with future productivity as more output generates more saving, which leads to more new capital.

Having laid out the connection between saving and capital per worker, we are ready to answer the important question about how much capital accumulation is required for growth.

Capital Adequacy in the Growth Model

capital adequacy
The increase in capital required to keep the capital/labor ratio constant. When there is technological change, capital adequacy becomes the increase in capital required to keep the ratio of capital to augmented labor constant.

How do we define **capital adequacy** in a growing economy? Capital adequacy is the increase in capital per worker ($\Delta K/N$) necessary to keep the capital/labor ratio constant, thereby keeping labor productivity constant. It turns out that in the face of a growing labor force, quite a lot of new capital is needed to simply prevent the capital/labor ratio from declining. Even more is needed to raise it. This is because the new entrants to the labor force require a full set of new machines, office space, and so on just to stay even with the existing workers. If the full allocation of new capital is not provided, the growth of the work force will end up diluting the available stock of capital per worker.

We saw in Equation 17.5 that the capital/labor ratio remains constant when the rate of growth of the capital stock is equal to the rate of growth of the labor input ($\Delta K/K = \Delta N/N$). A simple manipulation of this gives us the capital-adequacy condition we need, namely one related to the increase in capital per worker ($\Delta K/N$):

Capital-adequacy condition   (17.10)

The capital/labor ratio remains constant when

$$\Delta K/K = \Delta N/N. \tag{17.10}$$

Multiplying both sides by the capital/labor ratio, K/N, gives

$$\Delta K/N = \Delta N/N \times K/N.$$

This is the capital-adequacy condition.

In general, when the labor force grows, capital growth is adequate if the amount of capital added per existing worker is proportional to the current amount of capital per worker (the capital/labor ratio). The constant of proportionality is the rate of growth of the labor force.

As we showed in Equation 17.9, the amount of new capital added per worker is related to saving and the existing capital/labor ratio. That relationship allows us to describe the connections (Equation 17.1) between saving per worker and capital adequacy:

When Saving per Worker Exceeds Capital Adequacy

$$s \times f\left(\frac{K}{N}\right) = \frac{\Delta K}{N} > \frac{\Delta N}{N} \times \frac{K}{N}$$

Productivity (Y^P/N) and the capital/labor ratio are rising.

When Saving per Worker Equals Capital/Adequacy

$$s \times f\left(\frac{K}{N}\right) = \frac{\Delta K}{N} = \frac{\Delta N}{N} \times \frac{K}{N} \qquad (17.11)$$

Productivity and the capital/labor ratio are constant.

When Saving per Worker Is Less Than Capital/Adequacy

$$s \times f\left(\frac{K}{N}\right) = \frac{\Delta K}{N} < \frac{\Delta N}{N} \times \frac{K}{N}$$

Productivity and the capital/labor ratio are falling.

The amount of saving per worker in the economy $[s \times f(K/N)]$ determines the extent to which new capital can be provided to new entrants to the work force at the same level of capital as it is provided to the ones that are already there $[(\Delta N/N) \times (K/N)]$—the level of capital adequacy. If saving per worker is large, then there is more than enough capital investment being made to equip the new entrants and the rest of the investment can then be used to raise the capital/labor ratio for everyone, a process called **capital deepening.** This is the situation in a successful developing country such as South Korea that is saving enough to spread capital-intensive production methods more widely among its growing work force.

capital deepening
Capital investment taking place at a rate that increases capital intensity and hence raises labor productivity.

If saving per worker is lower than capital adequacy, then the capital/labor ratio in the economy will be falling. The capital stock is growing more slowly than the labor input, so there is not enough extra capital to go around and the capital intensity of the economy is declining and so is output per worker. This is the situation in some struggling developing countries where the labor force, fueled by a population explosion, is growing too fast for its ability to provide new capital. These economies may even have relatively high savings rates, but because their saving per worker cannot maintain their capital/labor ratio in the face of rapid increases in population, their economies are suffering an ongoing decline in productivity and living standards, slipping further and further behind the developed world.

The capital-adequacy conditions under which labor productivity and the capital/labor ratio will rise or fall are illustrated in Figures 17.3 and 17.4. In Figure 17.3, the curve labeled $f(K/N)$ is a particular intensive production function and the curve below it, labeled $s \times f(K/N)$, shows how saving per worker varies with the capital/labor ratio. Total output per worker (at point *A*, measured by *AA''* from the top of the production function to the horizontal

FIGURE 17.3   Capital Adequacy and the Capital/Labor Ratio: Falling Ratio

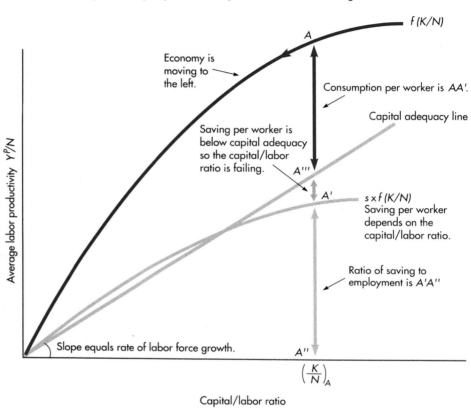

If the capital/labor ratio is $(K/N)_A$, then saving per worker is less than capital adequacy and the capital/labor ratio is falling.

axis) is divided up into consumption per worker (the distance all the way from A, on the intensive production, as far as A', on the saving function). Saving per hour is $(A'A'')$.

The straight line in the figure is the capital-adequacy line $[(\Delta N/N) \times (K/N)]$. The line is straight because the adequate level of capital investment per worker is a constant fraction of the capital/labor ratio. The fraction is equal to an assumed constant rate of growth $(\Delta N/N)$ of the labor force. Even if the rate of growth of the labor input is kept constant, the adequate level of capital rises in proportion with increases in the capital/labor ratio. As the labor force grows, it takes more new capital to stay even if everyone has a higher level of capital to begin with. This is quite reasonable—compare an advanced economy where all employees have a large stock of sophisticated

FIGURE 17.4   Capital Adequacy and the Capital/Labor Ratio: Rising Ratio

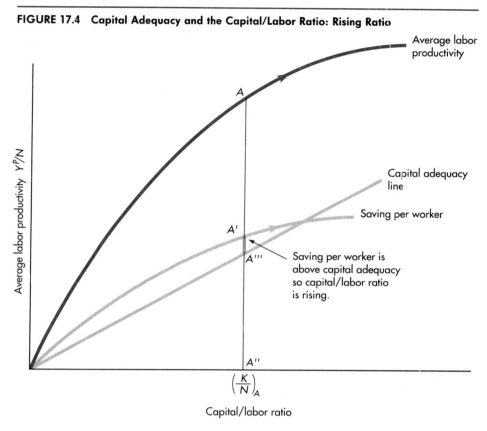

If the capital/labor ratio is $(K/N)_A$, then saving per hour is greater than capital adequacy and the capital/labor ratio is rising.

machinery at their disposal with an economy where workers are forced to produce without very much machinery or equipment at all. While the former is certainly preferable (average productivity and living standards are higher), it is much more expensive to equip new workers in the former economy than in the latter. The problem of capital deepening holds for businesses as well. Giving every employee a personal computer may contribute to productivity, but it will also raise the cost of hiring new employees since each new employee has to be allocated a personal computer to keep even.

Figure 17.3 is drawn so that the economy has an inadequate saving rate. Saving per worker (point A' on the saving function) is below capital adequacy (point A''' on the capital-adequacy line). Saving per worker is insufficient to maintain the capital/labor ratio. Since its capital intensity is falling, productivity in this economy is declining. In order to prevent this decline, there would have to be either more saving, less growth of the labor force, or a combination of the two.

The opposite case, where the capital/labor ratio is rising and average labor productivity is also rising, is shown in Figure 17.4. In this case higher saving and/or a lower rate of labor-input growth has the economy at a point where saving (point A' on the saving function) exceeds capital adequacy (point A''' on the capital-adequacy line). This means that there is more than enough saving to supply the new entrants to the labor force with the same amount of capital per hour as the existing workers. The capital/labor ratio is rising, so there is capital deepening taking place. Increases in the capital/labor ratio will work to increase productivity.

Steady-State Growth

It is apparent from Figures 17.3 and 17.4 that an economy's capital/labor ratio can rise or fall depending upon where saving per worker is in relation to capital adequacy. We take the growth rate of the labor force as given. Just to stay even, an economy that has a very high capital/labor ratio requires much greater increases in capital for new workers than does an economy with the same labor-force growth and a low capital/labor ratio. The economy with a high capital/labor ratio is more likely to experience a declining capital/labor ratio. (As shown in Figure 17.3, $A''' > A'$.) The economy with a low capital/labor ratio is more likely to be experiencing a rising capital/labor ratio. (As shown in Figure 17.4, $A''' < A'$.) *There is a tendency, therefore, for growing economies to move toward the point where the amount of saving and new capital is just equal to the amount of capital adequacy.* Economies move toward a position where capital adequacy is just obtained and growth is constant: At this point, the economy is in **steady-state growth.** The steady state is illustrated in Figure 17.5. Where the economy has a low capital/labor ratio $[(K/N)_A]$, productivity is low (point A) and the saving rate per worker (point A') exceeds capital adequacy. The capital/labor ratio and average labor productivity are both rising. Notice that saving per worker is also rising, but at a declining rate. The economy is heading toward the point where saving per worker is just equal to capital adequacy. This condition is shown at point B', where the saving curve intersects the capital-adequacy line. Since capital adequacy means that just enough new capital is being provided new workers so as to keep the existing capital/labor ratio constant, at points B and B', the capital/labor ratio $[(K/N)_B]$ remains constant.

The situation of an economy with a high capital/labor ratio $[(K/N)_C]$ is depicted at point C' where the saving curve is below the capital-adequacy line. Here, the capital/labor ratio and average labor productivity are both falling. Since capital adequacy is proportional to capital intensity, this situation will also drive the economy to the point where saving per worker is just equal to capital adequacy. Once more, the saving curve intersects the capital-

steady-state growth
The long-run constant rate of growth. Steady state is reached when the amount of saving and new capital is just adequate to maintain capital intensity.

FIGURE 17.5   Capital Adequacy and the Capital/Labor Ratio: Steady State

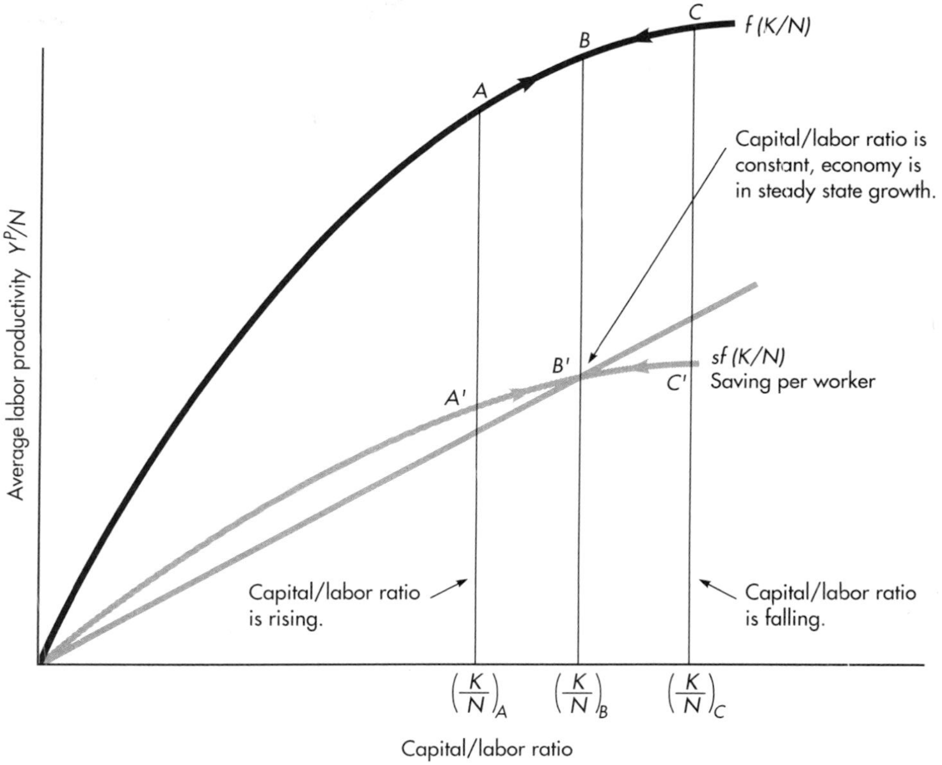

Economies will move toward a point where the capital/labor ratio is constant and there is steady-state growth. There is no technological change.

adequacy line at the same point (point B') this time from above rather than below. Again, the capital/labor ratio will remain constant.

Regardless of its initial capital/labor ratio, therefore, a growing economy will converge to a point where the capital/labor ratio remains constant.[5] At that point (point B on the production function, point B' on the saving curve and the capital-adequacy line) the economy is experiencing steady-state growth. In this discussion, where we have excluded technical change, steady-state growth occurs where the rate of growth of output is equal to the rate

---

[5] This statement has some technical qualifications. It is possible that the saving curve and the capital-adequacy line will not intersect except at the origin or at infinity. These possibilities are not terribly relevant for advanced economies, but it is possible for low-income, high–labor-force–growth economies to get trapped in a downward spiral with no steady state.

of growth of the capital stock and both are equal to the rate of labor-input growth. This means that in steady-state growth, the capital/labor ratio and average labor productivity will both remain constant.

Steady-state growth is important because we have just shown that, regardless of the initial level of productivity and the initial level of the capital/labor ratio, the economy will move over time toward the point of steady-state growth. Steady-state growth is something we would expect to see in mature economies. If we want to see how saving affects growth, we can look first at how it affects steady-state growth, and then we can see how an economy might change from one steady-state growth path to another.

Does thrift lead to more rapid growth?

Prior to the development of the neoclassical theory of growth, many people believed that increasing the fraction of income saved and devoting this increased saving to increased capital accumulation would *indefinitely* generate a higher rate of economic growth. Still today, we hear frequently that the Japanese and the European economies are growing faster than the U.S. economy and they will continue to do so because of their higher rates of saving, compared to spendthrift Americans' rate. *What we will see now is that while more saving does increase the levels of productivity and standard of living, steady-state growth rates are not affected by thrift.* It still pays to save, since an economy with double the standard of living of its neighbor, both having the same growth rate, will continue to have a standard of living double that of its neighbor. The two economies will not grow further apart, but they will not grow closer together either.

Comparing two steady states.   In the steady state, how does the sacrifice of more saving and less consumption in the short term pay off with a higher living standard in the long term? We take a look at this question of the benefits and limitations of saving for economic growth by comparing two economies with the same technologies and different saving rates. Two such economies are described in Figure 17.6. They have the same production technology, shown as a single production function $[f(K/N)]$, and two different saving curves corresponding to an economy that has a low saving rate $[s_A \times f(K/N)]$ and an economy that has a high saving rate $[s_B \times f(K/N)]$. Both economies are assumed to be in steady-state growth.

The level of average labor productivity will be higher in the high-saving economy. *Comparing economies that are in steady-state growth, a higher saving propensity means more capital per worker and a higher level of productivity.* The higher level of productivity will generally mean higher consumption in the high-saving economy. Consumption per worker is probably higher in the high-saving economy (point B to point B') than in the low-saving economy (point A to point A'). But this result is not certain. While output per worker is higher in economy B, saving propensities are higher in economy B. In

FIGURE 17.6   The Effect of Different Propensities to Save

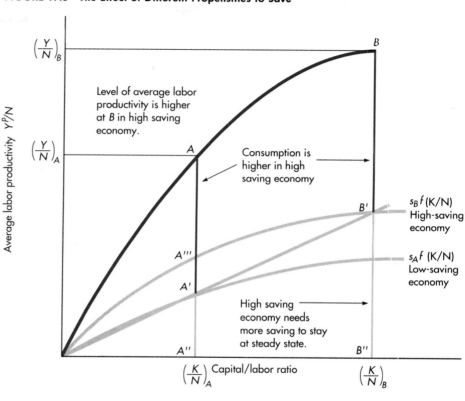

economy B a smaller fraction of output is devoted to consumption, so the consumption standard of living is not higher by the full amount of the difference in productivity between the two economies.[6] *The high-saving economy has to devote a larger share of its higher income to capital accumulation than does the low-saving economy in order to keep its capital/labor ratio constant.* As shown in the figure, at the constant steady-state capital/labor ratio in economy B $[(K/N)_B]$, the segment B' to B'' (saving per worker) is larger than the segment

---

[6] Consumption per worker refers to total consumption divided by the total number of workers. Total consumption includes the consumption made by the owners of capital.

It is possible that consumption per worker in economy B is actually lower than in economy A. In this case, economy B said to be *dynamically inefficient.* The people in economy B could cut their saving, raise their consumption, and be able to consume more in the future as well as in the present. There is no evidence that the U.S. economy is even close to being dynamically inefficient. Japan may find itself moving close to such a situation, although foreign investment, which is not included in this discussion, would solve the inefficiency problem.

A' to A'' at the steady-state capital/labor ratio $[(K/N)_A]$ in economy A. In economies where there is growth in the labor force, like Alice in Wonderland, the economy has to keep running in order to keep its capital/labor ratio still. In the high-saving economy, the steady-state capital/labor ratio is higher so the growing labor force requires more new capital, and the economy has to run even harder to stay still.

We have seen that differences in saving propensities will result in differences in productivity levels and living standards. But the two economies shown operating at points A and B are both in steady-state growth and will, therefore, have the same rates of output growth. *Once an economy has converged to its steady-state growth path, it will keep the same rate of growth regardless of its propensity to save and accumulate capital.* Having a high propensity to save does afford a higher standard of living but not as much higher as the differences in saving among low- and high-saving economies. Moreover, it does not allow an economy to have a higher rate of growth forever.

An important reason why saving and capital accumulation have limited effects is that we have assumed diminishing returns to capital, so that successive increments to capital per worker result in smaller and smaller increments to productivity. The effect of diminishing returns is reflected in the shape of the intensive production function curving over and intersecting the capital-adequacy line.

Changing from one steady state to another.   We have seen how changes in the propensity to save affect steady-state growth. But what about an economy that is growing along a steady-state growth path and then decides to increase its saving propensity? What happens then? We can find the answer by using Figure 17.6, not to compare two economies, but to look at a single economy whose members first have a low saving propensity (s_A at point A') and then change consumption behavior such that there is an increase in the saving rate (s_B at point B'). When the saving rate increases, there will be an immediate sacrifice in the consumption standard of living. Consumption per worker will fall from (AA') to (AA'''). Over time, however, the higher saving rate, now that it is greater than capital adequacy, will raise the capital/labor ratio $[(K/N)_A$ to $(K/N)_B]$. Average productivity and the standard of living will increase as shown by the movement around the intensive production function (point A to point B). During this period of transition, it will have a growth rate of output that exceeds the growth of its labor input, so productivity will be growing. At some point in the transition, it will find that its consumption and living standards have become higher than they were in the previous steady state. And once it has converged to the new steady-state growth path, the economy will have higher living standards forever.

Summarizing the effect of thrift.   Growth theory tells us the following about the role played by saving in economic growth:

1. The long-run (steady-state) growth rate of an economy does not depend on the propensity to save and accumulate capital.

2. For an economy in steady-state growth, the level of output and productivity will be higher, the higher is the level of the propensity to save in the economy.

3. For an economy in steady-state growth, the level of consumption will generally be higher, the higher is the propensity to save. Some part of output has to be used to maintain the ratio of capital to labor. This has the effect of reducing the benefit to consumers of having a higher capital/labor ratio and higher productivity.

4. An economy that decides to raise its saving propensity will make an immediate sacrifice in reduced consumption and living standards. Productivity and living standards will then rise more rapidly for some period, eventually overtaking the former level. They will then be higher for the indefinite future. This process is an important part of economic development. Countries that have stagnated at a low level of income can try to raise their rates of saving and investment and move up toward the developed countries.

5. An economy that decides to lower its saving propensity will gain an immediate benefit in increased consumption and living standards. Productivity and living standards will then fall for some period, eventually falling below the former level. They will then be lower for the indefinite future.

The immediate gains and longer-term losses that result from a reduction in national saving are relevant to the U.S. economy in the 1990s. Americans have been consuming a very high fraction of their income since the 1980s and there is concern that this will erode future living standards. An important difference between the U.S. situation and the model of growth is that foreign saving has provided some alternative to low U.S. saving, allowing capital formation to exceed the supply of domestic saving. We will discuss the U.S. situation more in Chapter 18.

Optimal Growth: Should We Save More?

optimal growth
The rate of growth that balances the sacrifice of current saving and the costs of capital accumulation with the benefits of the consumption standard of living in the future.

It is worth it to raise the rate of saving in an economy? Or, is it better to go on a consumption binge and not worry about the future? The answers to these questions have been sought in models of **optimal growth,** which compare the relative benefits of current and future consumption and the payoff to increased capital accumulation. In a market economy, the natural way to decide whether an economy is saving too much or too little is to look at the choices and preferences of consumers. If individuals can borrow when they want to increase their consumption or buy stocks or bonds when they want to save, they can make their own optimal trade-offs between consumption today and consumption tomorrow by taking into account the long-term real rate of interest that they will pay as borrowers or earn as investors. In terms of the rate of capital accumulation, businesses also look at the real long-term rate of interest in deciding whether the rate of profit they can earn on new capital investments is enough. Their calculations will determine how much investment they will make and the amount of capital they wish to hold.

Thus the long-term real rate of interest can be thought of as the market price that matches the choices of consumers and the choices of businesses. Does this market for saving and investment (capital accumulation) ensure optimal growth? There are several reasons why it does not and hence why there is likely to be too little saving in practice.

1. Some people are shortsighted and do not plan ahead and consider how much they will need for retirement. They may save less than they need for the future.

2. Investing in machinery and other kinds of business capital is risky, and the income that is earned is subject to taxes. The long-term real rate of interest that is used by consumers in making their decisions is much lower than the long-term real rate of interest used by businesses in making their decisions. Thus saving and investment will be equal but at too low a level.[7]

3. The government has taken over part of the task of providing for people in retirement in the form of the social security system. This means that those people who do look ahead in planning for retirement may reduce their saving because they know social security will provide them with support. But the government has not set aside its social security tax receipts and used the revenue to save and accumulate capital. It has paid out the money. This means that the government has been discouraging private saving without saving itself.

In recent decades, the U.S. government has not only been failing to save, it has also been dissaving in the form of a large budget deficit. The downtrend in the national rate of saving has occurred mostly because of government policies that have reduced the total of national saving.

So, should the United States as a nation save more in the long run? We think that the answer is yes and reducing the federal budget deficit is the place to start. The effect of government budget deficits on saving is illustrated in Figure 17.7. Gross saving from all sources as a percentage of national income has had an erratic pattern since 1950. However, the trend

---

[7] This argument assumes that the risk to society from investment is lower than the risk to any individual investor.

[8] Gross saving includes personal and gross business saving and the net effect of the total government (local, state, and federal) budget balance. That measure of saving ranged from about 22 percent to 15 percent of national income over the period. The saving rate that is

FIGURE 17.7   U.S. National Saving (Personal, Business, and Government) as a Share of National Income, Selected Years, 1950–1988)

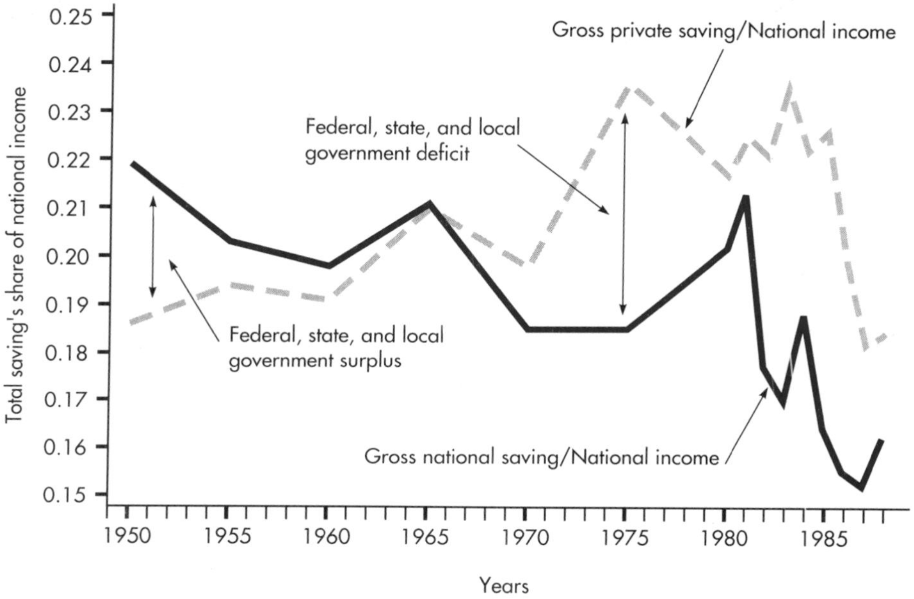

Gross saving has declined as a share of national income. The change from government surpluses to deficits has contributed to the decline.

is unmistakably down—especially in the 1980s.[8] The downtrend in gross saving is matched by a change in government budget balances from surpluses in the 1950s and early 1960s to deficits in the late 1960s through the 1980s.[9]

These reasons why there has been too little saving have been offset, only in part, by one reason why there has been too much saving: People cannot always borrow as much as they would like. This is particularly true of young families who would like to buy a house and other household goods but who are limited by their current borrowing ability.

After balancing this one reason why saving may be too high against the several reasons why it is too low, it seems likely that the U.S. economy has a lower long-run rate of saving and therefore a lower rate of capital accumulation than the optimal rate.

usually reported in the press is personal saving as a percentage of personal disposable income—that saving rate ranged from a high of 8 percent in the late 1960s to a low of 3.2 percent in 1987.

[9] The rate of depreciation has risen subtantially in the past 20 years because investment is more concentrated in short-lived assets. This means that net investment has fallen even more than gross investment.

LONG-TERM GROWTH WITH TECHNOLOGICAL CHANGE

Over the long-term history of the U.S. economy, output has grown more rapidly than has the labor force—productivity has risen very dramatically. How can that growth experience be reconciled with the conclusions of our growth model—that the economy moves toward steady state and in steady state, the capital/labor ratio is constant, and output grows only at the rate of growth of the labor force? In the model, moving from one steady state to another was accomplished through the accumulation of physical capital. Allocating more resources to capital as a way to raise productivity and living standards is limited by diminishing returns. These limits to growth were derived from models in which technology was assumed constant.

Technological change increases the steady-state growth rate, and in practice has been the main source of increases in productivity and living standards.

The Contribution of Technology to Productivity Growth

What portion of the increase that has taken place in average labor productivity in the business sector of the U.S. economy can be attributed to increases in the capital/labor ratio (movements around the intensive production function) and what part to technological change (shifts in the intensive production function)? This question was addressed by Solow when he developed his growth model. Figure 17.8 illustrates his findings. Solow found that, over time, the intensive production function had moved up from f_A to f_B and the economy had moved around the function from point A to point B. Solow estimated that the increase in average labor productivity (the segment BD) had come 87 percent from technological change (the upward shift in the function, point B to point C) and only 13 percent from the increase in capital per worker at the same level of technology (the movement along the function, point D to point C). Other researchers using different methods came up with somewhat different results,[10] but *there was a general and surprising consensus that technological change, rather than the accumulation of capital, was the primary factor in the long-term growth of productivity and hence living standards.* This meant that technological change had to be accounted for in any realistic model of economic growth.

The Solow Long-Term Growth Model Where Technology Augments Labor

The production function and the intensive production function (Equations 17.1 and 17.4) contained the assumption that output and labor productivity

---

[10] Edward F. Denison, *Trends in American Economic Growth, 1929–82* (Washington, D.C.: Brookings Institution, 1985); J. W. Kendrick, *Productivity Trends in the United States* (Princeton, N.J.: Princeton University Press, 1961); and Dale Jorgenson, Frank M. Gollop, and Barbara M. Faumeni, *Productivity and U.S. Economic Growth* (Cambridge, Mass.: Harvard University Press, 1987).

FIGURE 17.8 The Contributions of Capital and Technology to Productivity Growth

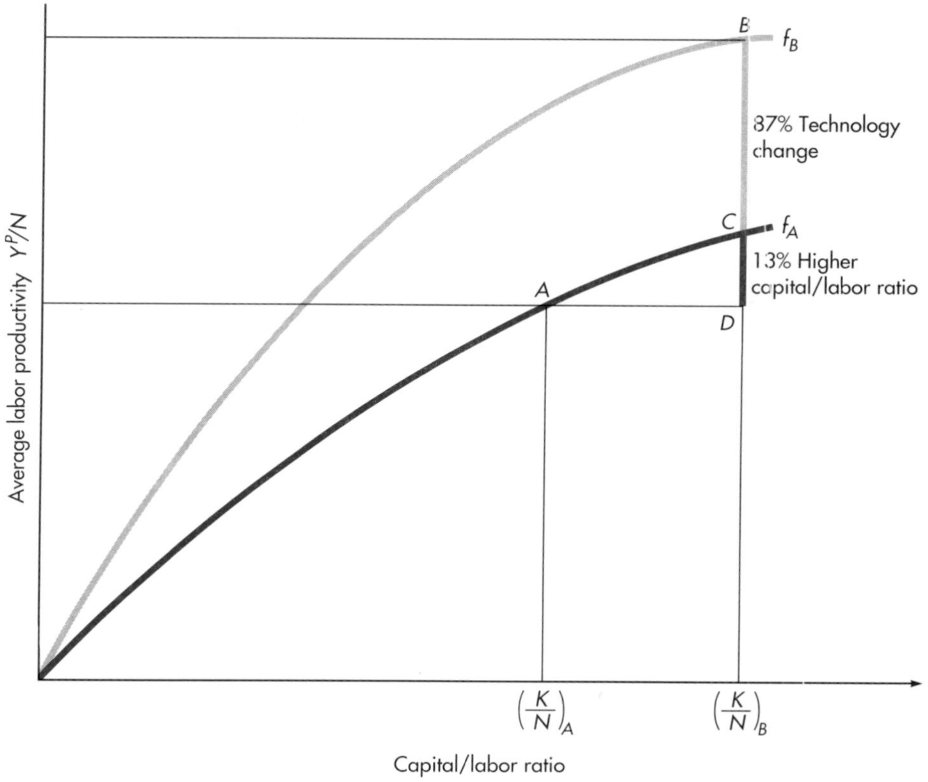

Solow estimated that most of the increase in average labor productivity came from an upward shift in the production function.

depend on the state of technology, *T*. We made no assumption about the way in which technology might affect the contributions of capital and labor to output.

In incorporating the effects of technological change in the Solow model of growth now, we will make an important additional assumption. *We will assume that technological change has the effect of augmenting the labor input to production.* We assume that when technology improves, it augments the productive capacity of labor—it makes each worker or hour of labor more productive. This assumption is a very useful one in that it focuses on the notion that technological change is meant to be a broad technical and managerial term including all sorts of productivity enhancements that, when combined, have the effect of increasing the productivity of workers. This assumption also allows us to make use of the tools we have already developed for analyzing long-term growth.

As the growth of technology augments labor, each hour of work with new technology is equivalent to more than a hour of work with old technology. We now have two ways in which the labor input can grow: more employment or hours worked and more productive workers. We combine these two types of labor growth into a concept called **augmented labor,** N^*. In some initial base year the amount of augmented labor is simply equal to the amount of actual labor, N (set $T = 1$ in the base year). As technology improves over time (T increases), augmented labor grows faster than actual labor. With this assumption, we rewrite the original production function given in Equation 17.1 by combining the labor input, N, and the technology term, T, into the single augmented-labor term, N^*. This is shown in Equation 17.12:

augmented labor
The labor force adjusted by the state of technology. As technology grows, the augmented labor force grows faster than the actual labor force because a unit of augmented labor is equivalent to more than a unit of actual labor.

$$Y^P = F(K,N,T)$$
$$\quad = F(K,N^*) \tag{17.12}$$

The assumption of constant returns to scale is retained, so that a new intensive production function can be used in which output per augmented worker depends upon capital per augmented worker:

$$\frac{Y^P}{N^*} = f\left(\frac{K}{N^*}\right). \tag{17.13}$$

Why would technological change augment labor? One reason is that technical advance can be used to increase the skill and knowledge of each worker. But that is not the only possibility. If technology augments labor, this does not necessarily mean that capital is unaffected. Although it may not be easy to see the intuitive reason for it, technological change that augments labor could come about simply because workers have more efficient machines to work with.

One reason why we assume technology is labor-augmenting is that it fits with an important fact about economic growth observed in several market economies. *Real wages generally increase along with increases in average labor productivity.* Most of the increase in productivity comes from technological change and since labor markets allocate much of those gains to workers, this suggests that technology is augmenting the labor input.

Steady-state growth with labor-augmenting technology

Earlier, we assumed that the labor input grows at a constant rate and we will carry this over and assume that augmented labor grows over time at a constant rate, a rate that is equal to the rate of growth of the labor force plus the rate of technological change:

FIGURE 17.9   The Growth Model with Technical Change

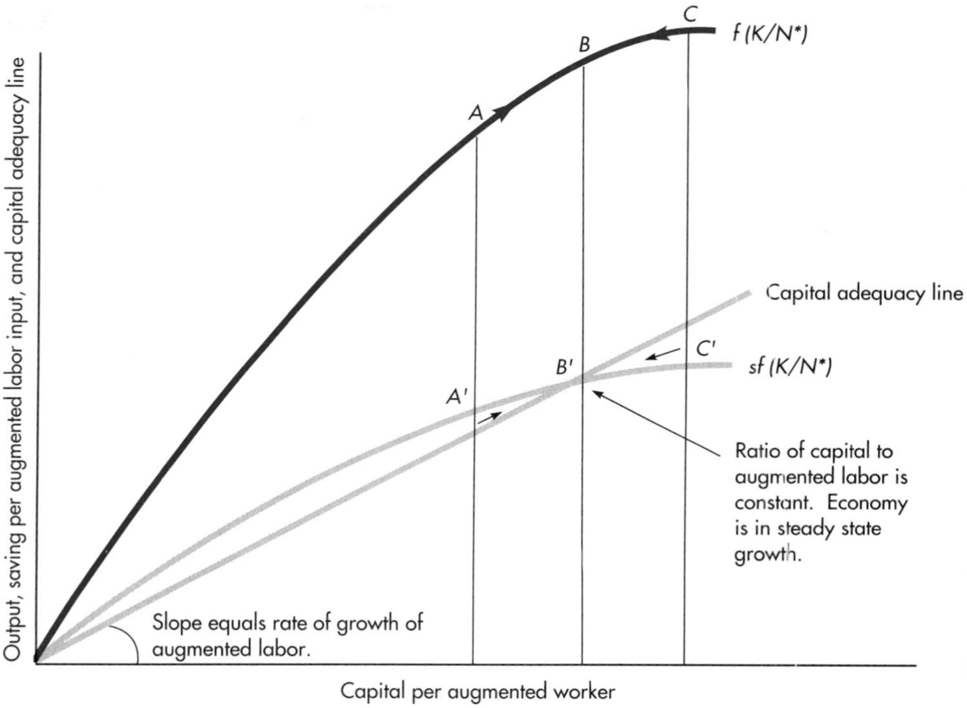

Economies with technological change that augments labor will move toward steady-state growth, with a higher growth rate than in economies with no technological change.

$$\text{Growth rate of augmented labor} = \frac{\Delta N^*}{N^*}$$
$$= \text{Growth rate of labor force}$$
$$+ \text{Rate of labor-augmenting}$$
$$\text{technological change.}$$

Growth in augmented labor is a combination of growth in the actual labor input (the number of workers) and growth in labor-augmenting technology. Looking back at Figure 17.8, there the effect of technological change was to shift the intensive production function upward. By defining the concept of augmented labor, we can now describe a new intensive production function (Figure 17.9) that incorporates changes in technology. The new intensive production function shows how output per augmented worker varies with the amount of capital per augmented worker and the saving curve shows the ratio of saving to the augmented labor input. The capital-adequacy line also involves augmented labor rather than actual labor and this leads to a difference between Figure 17.9 and the earlier figures. The rate of growth of augmented labor is greater than the rate of growth of actual labor, with the difference being the rate of technological change.

In the previous examples, the intersection of the capital-adequacy line and the saving curve (point B') is where the capital/labor ratio is constant at steady-state growth. This is time in Figure 17.9 also, except that it is the ratio of capital to augmented labor that is constant at the steady-state point. If the economy is not in steady-state growth (for example, at points A and A' or at points C and C'), then the ratio of capital to augmented labor will be changing. An economy with technological change that augments labor will move toward the point where steady-state growth occurs. In the steady state, the ratio of capital to augmented labor remains constant at B. And at point B' on the intensive production function, the ratio of output to augmented labor remains constant. The capital-adequacy line is steeper in this case than in previous examples without technological change. It takes more saving per worker to keep the ratio of capital to augmented labor constant than the amount necessary to keep the ratio of capital to actual labor constant. There is a flip side to this, however. With technological change, it is possible to achieve a much higher rate of investment without running into diminishing returns to capital. An economy that experiences labor-augmenting technological change is not free of the need to improve its level of investment in order to maintain its growth rate. However, the steady-state growth rate and standard of living it can obtain are higher because of technological change.

Technological change confers a double productivity benefit for the economy. Improvements in technology generate growth in output and, since saving is a constant proportion of output, this will mean in turn that there will also be a faster rate of growth of the stock of capital. *In an economy with technological change, average labor productivity is growing directly because of the contribution of technology as a factor of production, but it is also growing as an indirect consequence of the technological change because faster output growth leads to faster capital growth.* Success (faster output growth) breeds more success (faster capital accumulation). With technological change, the ratio of capital to actual labor is growing even when there is steady-state growth.

Let's summarize what we have found out from our model of growth in an economy with technological change.

1. The long-run (steady-state) growth rate of output is constant at a rate equal to the rate of labor-augmenting technological change plus the rate of actual labor-input growth (growth of the work force).

2. In steady-state growth, average labor productivity grows at a rate equal to the rate of labor-augmenting technological change.

3. In steady-state growth, the capital stock grows at the same rate as output and the capital/labor ratio grows at a rate equal to the rate of labor-augmenting technological change.

4. For a developing economy that is accumulating capital at a rate that exceeds the rate of growth of augmented labor, the rate of productivity growth will exceed the steady-state rate of growth.

5. For an economy that is "declining," the rate of productivity growth will be below the steady-state rate of growth. Because of technological change, however, the rate of productivity growth will generally still be positive. *Technological change provides an alternative source of productivity growth for an economy where the rate of capital accumulation is low.*

Wages and profits in a growing economy

Before we look at trends in actual growth data for the U.S. economy, we explore the roles of wages and profits in a growing economy. We want to know how growth affects wages and profits because the consumption standard of living in the typical household, though affected by the growth of income, is disproportionally influenced by the growth of wages, since wages account for most of the income of typical households. Also, the shares of income going to wages and profits are used in measuring the relative contributions to productivity improvement from various sources. Information about actual wages and profits allows us to evaluate the U.S. growth experience.

The Solow growth model is neoclassical—it is built on the assumption that in the long run, the markets for capital and labor are perfectly competitive, without price stickiness or wage rigidity, and that businesses are profit maximizers. In perfectly competitive markets, the marginal product of capital determines the rate of profit on capital, while the marginal product of labor determines the wage rate. The marginal product of labor is the increment to output that is achieved if one extra worker is hired, holding the amount of capital and the level of technology constant. In perfectly competitive labor markets, wages are flexible and they adjust until wages equal the marginal product of labor.

The marginal product of capital is the increment to output that is achieved if one more unit of capital is placed into production, holding employment and the level of technology constant. In perfectly competitive capital markets, trading of assets assures that profit (the return on capital) is equal to the marginal product of capital.

We introduced the classical model in Chapter 15 and there we were rather critical of the classical notion of short-run price flexibility. We argued that price stickiness and wage rigidity are important in labor markets in the short run. However, the assumption of price flexibility reacting to competitive market forces is much more appropriate when describing long-run or trend movements of wages and profits.

FIGURE 17.10   Output Divided into Return to Capital and Return to Labor

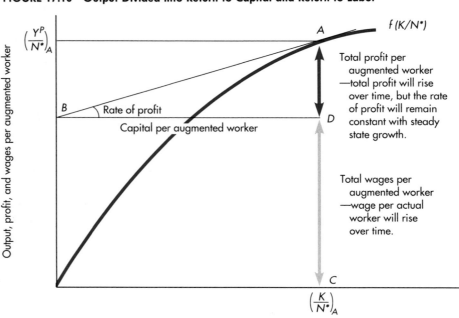

The division of output per worker among profit and wages is shown in Figure 17.10. The economy is operating (at point A) with a particular ratio of capital to augmented labor, $(K/N^*)_A$. Output produced per augmented hour is $(Y^P/N^*)_A$.

The line AB is a tangent to the intensive production function at point A and *the slope of this line represents the marginal productivity of capital.* When the intensive production function is very steep, this means that adding a given amount of capital per augmented worker will add a lot to the amount of output produced. In this case, the marginal productivity of capital is high. When the function is rather flat, then increases in capital per augmented worker add little to output per worker, and the marginal productivity of capital is low.

Since competitive markets drive the marginal productivity of capital to be equal to the rate of profit, the slope of the line AB also gives the rate of profit on capital.

If the economy were to maintain a constant ratio of capital to augmented labor (point A), then the rate of profit would also be constant. It follows, therefore, that *if an economy is in steady-state growth, the rate of profit remains constant over time.* If instead, the capital intensity of the economy were to change (via movement around the intensive production function), the rate of profit on capital would fall if capital grew faster than augmented labor, and it would rise if it grew slower.

Because technological change appears to displace jobs, many people are fearful of the effects of automation and technological change. They believe that workers will suffer losses as company owners retain all of the gains to technology. Analysis using the Solow model of economic growth indicates the opposite. It says that *both technological change and increases in capital per worker will raise wages and hence raise the living standards of workers.*

Wages grow because technology is augmenting the productivity of each worker. At a particular level of capital intensity $[(K/N)_A]$ wages per augmented worker are a portion of total output per augmented worker. The segment AC in Figure 17.10 measures output per worker. The rate of profit, which is the tangent line AB, indicates that the vertical line segment AD represents the portion of income that is received by the owners of capital as profit. The remainder of output per augmented worker, line segment DC, is the wage income that is paid to workers.[11] The point D divides up the line segment AC in a ratio that gives the shares of income going to the two groups.

The segment DC gives the wage income paid per augmented worker, but in the initial or base year the amount of augmented labor is just equal to the amount of actual labor. It follows, therefore, that in the base year, DC simply measures the wage rate paid per worker. Over time, the amount of augmented labor grows at a rate that exceeds the rate of labor-input growth by the rate of technological change. And in the case where the ratio of capital to augmented labor remains constant, the wage will then simply rise at a rate that equals the rate of labor-augmented technological change. *If the economy is in steady-state growth, then wages rise at the same rate as the rate of technological change and hence at the same rate as the rate of growth of average labor productivity.* Wages will rise faster or slower than the rate of growth of average labor productivity if the capital intensity of the economy were to change.

As we noted in discussing the nature of technological change, the wage in the U.S. economy has, in fact, risen at about the same rate as the rate of increase of average labor productivity over the entire postwar period, although real wage increases did exceed productivity increases somewhat in the period after 1973.

In the 19th century, the economist Karl Marx looked at the low wages and poor conditions of workers and concluded that revolutionary change was necessary in order to improve workers' lives. His writings were reflected in the spread of communist revolutions to many countries. Today, we see

---

[11] The slope of the line AB gives the rate of profit, and the segment BD gives the amount of capital per augmented worker. The segment AD is then BD times the slope, which equals the total profit income divided by the quantity of augmented labor. With constant returns to scale, the total wage income will be the amount of total output not paid out as profits, so that DC is the amount of labor income divided by the amount of augmented labor.

that the market economies, by granting personal economic freedom and encouraging efficiency and technological change, have generated much higher wages and better living standards for workers than the communist countries. The desire to emulate the incentives for efficiency and technological change provided in market economies was evident in the dramatic restructuring of Eastern European economies started in the late 1980s, and is continuing into the 1990s.

ECONOMIC GROWTH IN THE U.S. ECONOMY

The long-run implication of the growth model is that economies head for steady state and in the steady state average labor productivity and hence the standard of living only grow to the degree that there is technological improvement. Has the U.S. economy settled into such a steady state? If not, what can the growth model tell us about the prospects for future improvements in productivity and the standard of living?

Whether or not the U.S. economy has entered a steady state can be resolved by analyzing the historical pattern of U.S. growth using the labor-augmenting technical change model of growth.[12] Table 17.1 reports the results of that analysis in rates of growth of output, labor, capital, and average labor productivity over various periods from 1889 to 1987. Output grew very rapidly at the end of the 19th century and into the early part of this century. Since 1929, output has grown at between 2.49 and 3.79 percent a year with the highest rate between 1948 and 1968.

Capital input grew between 3 and 5 percent a year except during the period that included the Great Depression and World War II. Capital grew slower than output before 1968 (the capital/output ratio was rising), but grew faster than output after 1968 (the capital/output ratio was falling).

The growth rate of labor input (hours of work) has been quite variable, reflecting many different factors, such as immigration, changing birth rates, changing participation of women in the work force, early retirement, and reductions in hours per employee. Labor-input growth has always been less than output growth, so that average labor productivity has risen. But the growth of average labor productivity has varied, being around 2 percent a year prior to World War II, somewhat higher than this over the period 1948–68 (2.65 percent a year), and then falling after 1968.

These figures suggest that the U.S. economy has not really converged to a single steady-state rate of growth. In steady-state growth, capital and output grow at the same rate, whereas in practice the capital stock was growing more slowly than output prior to 1968 and more rapidly after that. *The reason that the U.S. economy has not converged to a steady-state growth path*

---

[12] Martin Neil Baily and Charles L. Schultze, "The Productivity of Capital in a Period of Slower Growth," *Brookings Papers on Economic Activity Micro: 1990,* pp. 369–406.

TABLE 17.1 Average Annual Growth Rates of Output, Labor Input (Hours of Work), Capital, Average Labor Productivity, Labor-Augmenting Technical Change, and Augmented Labor Input, Nonfarm Business Sector, 1889–1987

Years	Output $\Delta Y^P/Y^P$	Labor $\Delta N/N$	Capital $\Delta K/K$	Average labor productivity $\left(\dfrac{\Delta Y^P}{Y^P} - \dfrac{\Delta N}{N}\right)$	Labor-augmenting technical change[a]	Augmented labor $\dfrac{\Delta N^*}{N^*}$
1889–1909	5.11	3.01	4.81	2.10	—	—
1909–1929	3.66	1.62	3.02	2.04	2.25	3.87
1929–1948	2.77	0.85	0.72	1.92	2.47	3.32
1948–1968	3.79	1.14	3.27	2.65	2.87	4.01
1968–1973	3.32	1.78	4.25	1.53	1.11	2.89
1973–1979	2.49	2.03	3.72	0.48	−0.04	1.99
1979–1987	2.63	1.43	3.60	1.19	0.77	2.20

[a] The method for computing labor-augmenting technical change and multifactor-productivity growth are described in Chapter 18.

Source: Martin Neil Baily and Charles L. Schultze, "The Productivity of Capital in a Period of Slower Growth," *Brookings Papers on Economic Activity, Micro: 1990*, pp. 369–406.

in practice is that the rate of growth of the labor input and the rate of technological change have not been constant.

Table 17.1 also shows the rate of labor-augmenting technological change.[13] Technological change was rapid and even accelerated slightly through 1968. But then there was a slowdown in technological change after 1968 and a collapse after 1973.

The rate of growth of augmented labor ($\Delta N^*/N^*$) is equal to the sum of the rate of technical change and the rate of growth of labor input; this growth rate is the last column in Table 17.1. The impact of the decline in the rate of technical change is evident in the decline in the growth rate of augmented labor. The slowing of the growth of augmented labor is not as dramatic as the decline in the rate of technical change because the periods when technical change slowed down were periods when the work force grew rapidly.

Looking at the actual experience of growth, therefore, tells that it is not enough to study steady-state growth. The U.S. economy is not typically in steady-state growth. In order to apply the growth model to the actual experi-

[13] In his analysis of growth, Solow showed how to use data on wage and profit income to compute the contribution of technical change to output growth. Assuming a constant-returns–to–scale production function, the wage and profit shares of income are equated to the marginal products of labor and capital. After using the marginal products to account for the actual rates of growth of the capital stock and the labor force, the remaining growth of output, if any, is attributed to the effect of technical change in augmenting the labor force, calculated using his approach.

ence of U.S. growth, we need to look at what happens when there are changes in the rate of labor-input growth and when there is a slowdown in the rate of technological change.

A Fall in the Rate of Technological Change

We can extend the earlier growth analysis to the case where the pace of technical advance slows down. Technological change makes each worker more productive, but the rate of improvement was much slower after 1968. A slowing in the growth rate of technological change will lead to a slowing in the rate of growth of augmented labor. As shown in Table 17.1, the growth rate of augmented labor was over 4 percent a year from 1948 to 1968 and subsequently it dropped to around 2 percent a year. When the economy is not in a steady state, its capital intensity will increase or decrease as will average labor productivity. In terms of the growth model, the economy will move around the intensive production function depending upon whether the saving curve is above or below the capital-adequacy line.

Figure 17.11 uses the Solow model to illustrate the consequences of technological slowdown. As augmented labor grows, the capital-adequacy line shows how much saving is necessary to keep the capital/augmented-labor ratio constant. Remember, when labor is augmented by technological change, capital adequacy requires more capital growth to keep pace with the growth of the labor force since the labor force is growing in augmented terms, not just in size. The slope of the capital-adequacy line is equal to the rate of growth of augmented labor.

The capital-adequacy line, *OA'*, reflects the growth of augmented labor at 4 percent from 1948 to 1968. Capital was growing more slowly than augmented labor as the saving curve was below the capital-adequacy line—capital was growing at about 3¼ percent a year compared to about 4 percent a year for augmented labor. Steady-state growth at that time was equal to the growth of augmented labor, but the actual economy was growing more slowly than that because capital accumulation failed to keep pace with technological change.

When there is a decline in the rate of technological change, the minimum rate of capital accumulation necessary to keep the capital/augmented-labor ratio constant will be smaller than before the decline in technical change. *In the Solow model, a decline in the growth of labor-augmenting technology will be reflected in a decline in the slope of the capital-adequacy line.* The capital-adequacy line *OA'* has rotated and the new capital-adequacy line is *OB'*.

Over the period 1948–68, the U.S. economy had a high rate of labor-augmenting technological change, and capital was growing more slowly than augmented labor as the saving curve was below the capital-adequacy line—capital was growing at 3.27 percent a year compared to 4.01 percent a year for augmented labor. This meant that the economy was not in steady-state growth over this period. The growth rate of output was a little slower than

FIGURE 17.11 A Slowdown in the Rate of Technological Change

Ratio of capital to augmented labor was falling from 1948–68. Economy was moving to the left.

Rate of capital to augmented labor was rising from 1968–87. Economy was moving to the right.

Capital adequacy line rotates as rate of technological change slows.

Saving was less than capital adequacy, 1948–68.

Saving exceeded capital adequacy, 1968–87.

Slope declines when rate of technological change slows.

Output, saving per augmented worker, and capital adequacy

$sf(K/N^*)$

$(K/N^*)_A$ $(K/N^*)_B$

Ratio of capital to augmented labor

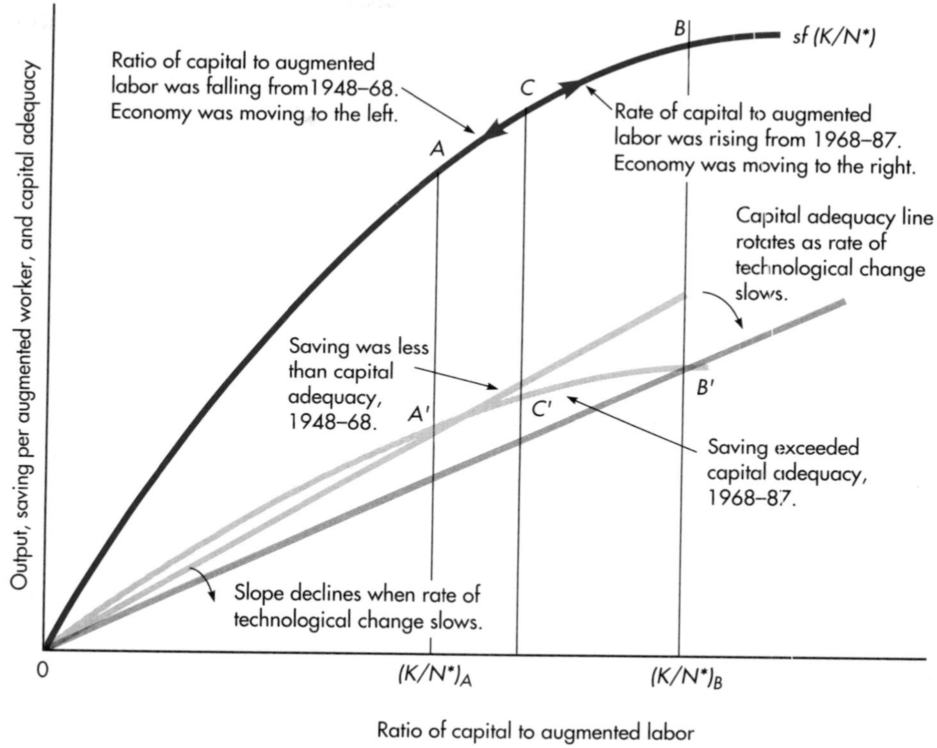

A fall in the rate of technological change will cause the economy to make a transition to a new steady state.

it would have been if capital had grown at the same rate as augmented labor. As seen in Figure 17.11, the economy was at points C and C' in 1948 and then moved gradually toward the steady-state points A and A'. The convergence to the steady state was very slow, but by 1968 the economy was rather close to its steady-state position.

When the rate of technological change fell, the implications for steady-state growth changed. *With a slower rate of technological growth there was an associated reduction in the rate of capital accumulation required to keep the economy from a further slowdown.* In terms of the model, the capital-adequacy line became flatter after the slowdown, while capital accumulation (which was previously inadequate) became more than adequate. Capital intensity started to grow, moving around to the right toward a new steady-state position (points B and B'). The ratio of capital to augmented labor was increasing because of the slower growth of augmented labor, the denominator of the ratio. (Augmented labor was growing at 2–3 percent a year while capital was growing at 3–4 percent a year.) The economy has embarked on a transition. It can be expected to take some years for the new steady-state position to be reached.

As productivity and capital intensity in the economy move around the intensive production function, the ratio of output to augmented labor starts to increase. It looks as if the slowdown in technological change is making the economy more productive! But this is not the case. We commented earlier that technological change brings about a kind of double benefit for average labor productivity. What happens when there is a slowdown is that the decline in the rate of technological change eventually reduces both of its benefits for labor productivity, but only the first of these is affected right away. The rate of growth of labor productivity has certainly slowed down as a result of the slowdown in technological change, but initially the rate of growth of the capital stock does not decline and so the ratio of capital to augmented labor rises. Average labor productivity slows down when the rate of technological change slows, but initially the ratio of capital to actual labor continues to rise at the old rate and this helps to maintain the growth in productivity.

Since saving is a constant proportion of output, however, the slowdown in the rate of growth of output does gradually affect the rate of growth of capital as well, and this leads to the reduction of the second benefit of technological change. *After a time, the economy reaches a new steady state, and then average labor productivity will grow only at the new lower rate of technological change.* The ratio of capital to actual labor is still growing, but it too is now growing at the new lower rate. As the transition to the new steady state proceeds, *the growth rate of average labor productivity in the U.S. economy can be expected to decline further over the next decade, unless there is an increase in the rate of technological change.*

The costs of a technological slowdown

The rate of growth of wages has declined as a result of the decline in technical change. *Workers feel the effect of the slowdown in growth in terms of slower improvements in their living standards.* This has indeed happened in the U.S. economy, where the growth of real wages since 1970 has been very slow indeed.

As the economy makes the transition from the old to the new steady-state growth path, the rate of profit on capital will start to decline. (The slope of the intensive production function becomes flatter.) And the profit rate will remain lower once the new steady-state point is reached. *The owners of capital experience the effect of the slowdown in the form of lower returns to capital.* In the U.S. economy the rate of profit fell from 15.3 percent in 1968 to 12.3 percent in 1987. This is in contrast to the period prior to 1968 when the economy was moving around the intensive production function to the left, and the marginal product of capital/rate of profit was rising—it was 13.6 percent in 1948.[14]

The growth model's description of the response of an economy to periods of rapid technological change after World War II, followed by a sharp slow-down in the 1970s, does seem to fit with what we have seen happening. The decline in the rate of technological change has had a major impact on the rate of growth of wages and the rate of profit on business capital. The slowdown in technological improvement has led to a general deterioration in our economic circumstances.

The figures in Table 17.1 do offer some relief from the conclusions about a slow-growth economy. The rate of technological change was somewhat faster in the 1980s than it was in the 1970s. Technological change may be improving and we can hope this will continue. And perhaps we can do more than this. We can look for explanations of the slowdown and for policies that can increase growth.

In our discussion of growth so far, we have been concerned mostly with putting together a model or framework for growth analysis. Using this framework, we have been able to say something about how changes in the propensity to save will affect the growth rates of output and productivity, and how wages and profits will be affected by a slowdown in the rate of technological change. And we have used the Solow growth model to interpret some aspects of the actual experience of growth in the U.S. economy.

At this point, however, it is time to look beyond the growth model. Models can be a straitjacket as well as a guide and we are going to take a more detailed look at the sources of growth in the U.S. economy. Of course we will not forget the analytical framework, which will continue to inform the discussion.

As we look further at U.S. growth, we want to know more about the concept of technological change. What is it? Where does it come from? Although we have used the word *technological,* in fact it is not just developments related to science and engineering that are driving "technological change." Improvements in management techniques, increases in the amount of training and skill of the work force, and many other possibilities may be causing the upward shifts in the production function. And the apparent decline in the rate of technological change since 1973 may have been caused by a decline in skills or by poor management, as well as by a decline in the pace of technological advance.

Productivity: Accounting for Growth

Many economists have worked to explain the sources of growth. While they ascribed the difference between the growth of inputs and the growth of

---

[14] These figures are taken from Martin Baily and Charles Schultze, "Productivity." The profit rates are gross of depreciation.

output to technological improvement, there was much work to be done on understanding the nature of that improvement. In an early work, Moses Abramovitz referred to technological change as "a measure of our ignorance" since it represents growth that cannot be explained by observing increases in the amount of labor and capital used in production.[15] The task of accounting for the sources of growth is designed to reduce our measure of ignorance— to leave as little of the growth process as possible unexplained by a catchall category of technological change rather than explained by a deeper understanding of how productivity is enhanced, including an understanding of the role of technology and advances in knowledge and practice. A detailed and extensive search of this kind is the **growth-accounting** analysis done by Edward Denison.[16] We summarize Denison's conclusions about the sources of long-term growth in the U.S. economy in Table 17.2, which contains figures drawn from his 1985 study. As his measure of average labor productivity, Y^P/N, Denison uses potential national income per employed person, both for the whole economy and for the nonresidential business sector of the economy. He uses national income, rather than GNP, since the former excludes depreciation and indirect taxes, and he points out that growth in GNP that comes purely from increased depreciation or taxes is not going to help living standards.

He provides figures for the whole economy including the agricultural sector, although he does separate out the residential housing sector because he judges that it is too unlike the other parts of the economy. He starts his analysis back in 1929 because he thinks that data prior to that are not very good; he ends his analysis in 1982, the last year for which he had data at the time of the study.

Denison finds productivity growing at 1.7 percent a year for the nonresidential business sector, somewhat slower than the rates of growth of average labor productivity in Table 17.2. There is a difference in the time periods, but apart from this, much of the difference in productivity growth rates reported comes about because Denison is studying output per worker, or per person employed and the figures in Table 17.1 refer to output per hour. *The number of hours worked per employed person has declined over time in the United States.* Another part of the differences comes about because Denison adjusts his labor input for changes in experience. He finds that the work force has become somewhat less experienced over time. (The labor force became somewhat younger on average over this period and had a higher proportion of women, "whose work histories are often shorter than men's

growth accounting
The identification and measurement of the various factors that contribute to economic growth and the evaluation of their relative importance in bringing about a particular rate of growth.

---

[15] Moses Abramovitz, "Reserves and Output Trends in the United States Since 1870," *American Economic Review* 46 (March 1956), pp. 127–47.

[16] Edward F. Denison, *The Sources of Economic Growth in the United States and the Alternatives Before Us* (Washington, D.C.: Committee for Economic Development, 1962); *Why Growth Rates Differ*, (Washington, D.C.: Brookings Institution, 1967); and *Trends in American Economic Growth, 1929–82* (Washington, D.C.: Brookings Institution, 1985).

TABLE 17.2   Contributions to the Growth of Average Labor Productivity, 1929–1982

	Potential national income per person employed	
	Whole economy	Nonresidential business
Growth rate	1.6	1.7
Percentage of growth rate		
All sources	100	100
Labor input except education	−13	−23
Education per worker	26	30
Capital	15	10
Advances in knowledge	54	64
Improved resource allocation	16	19
Economics of scale	17	20
Changes in legal and human environments	−3	−4
Land	−3	−4
Irregular factors	0	0
Other determinants	−10	−13

Source: Edward F. Denison, *Trends in American Economic Growth, 1929–82* (Washington, D.C.: Brookings Institution, 1985).

due to time spent raising families.") The effect of the reductions in hours and experience are reflected in Denison's value of −23 percent for the contribution of labor (apart from education) to productivity growth in nonresidential business.

An important source of growth that Denison identifies that was not part of the growth model is education per worker. The United States has invested very heavily in **human capital** in the postwar period and this has paid off in additions to productivity. In order to estimate the effect of education, Denison looks at the wages earned by people with different levels of education. Some part of these wage differentials are attributed to differences in innate ability, but the rest is attributed to the human capital embodied in the people. Then data on the number of years of schooling by participants in the work force give the total contribution of education.

Denison assumes that human capital raises the marginal productivity of workers and that the increases in marginal productivity then boost wages. These ideas are familiar from the growth-theory framework. One important omission from Denison's analysis is the contribution of on-the-job training.

The next conclusion from the table is that Denison finds that only 10–15 percent of the growth of average labor productivity comes about through the accumulation of physical capital. Nearly 30 years after Solow's finding of a 13 percent contribution from capital, Denison's work finds a result that

human capital

The capacity to provide value in the labor market through the acquisition of education, training, and work experience.

INCREASING RETURNS AND INTERNATIONAL GROWTH PATTERNS

The neoclassical growth model has been criticised recently by Paul Romer and Robert Lucas of the University of Chicago.* The neoclassical growth model assumes that technology is available to everyone so over time poorer countries should catch up to richer countries. Further, it assumes there will be a gradual convergence of productivity growth rates internationally, and eventually all economies will grow at the same rate. Economies with high saving rates will reach higher levels of productivity but not maintain higher growth rates indefinitely, according to the neoclassical model.

Romer and Lucas point out that this prediction of the neoclassical growth model has not been borne out for the world economy as a whole. The less developed countries, in general, have not grown more rapidly than Europe, the United States, and Japan. The gap between rich and poor countries has not narrowed. The success of such developing countries as South Korea and Hong Kong is an exception, not the rule. Most of the countries of Latin America and Africa, and even many in Asia, remain underdeveloped.

There are many possible explanations for the inconsistency between the neoclassical model and the international pattern of growth. The one suggested by Romer and Lucas is that there are increasing returns to scale. A doubling of the inputs to production will much more than double the output. Countries that become large and rich have advantages that allow them to become larger and richer. Countries that are small and poor have disadvantages that make it difficult for them to develop. Lucas has pointed particularly to the importance of human capital in generating increasing returns. He argues that there are no diminishing returns to human capital. Adding more and more educated people to an economy allows them to interact with each other so that the returns to education are not diminished. Romer has suggested that there are interactions with fixed capital also. When there are several factories or offices together, they generate a more productive business environment and so the effect of diminishing returns to capital is avoided. Romer and Lucas have developed original models to show how individual markets can function well even though there

very closely parallels the original, even though Denison used somewhat different methods and quite different data.

In the growth model it was assumed that there are constant returns to scale. Denison drops this assumption in his analysis and assumes instead that if all of the factors of production were to rise by 10 percent, then the amount of ouput would rise by 11.25 percent. Based on evidence from microeconomic studies, he judges that as the size of the national market expands, firms become larger and can operate more efficiently with longer production runs. Also a larger economy can permit more specialization. Denison finds that increased efficiency resulting from the overall growth of the U.S. economy contributed to a substantial 20 percent of productivity growth from 1929 to 1982.

The extent of increasing returns is a subject of great debate at present. Some economists sugget that there are enormous benefits from increases in scale that help explain why the rich countries keep on growing while many poor countries have remained stagnant (see box, "Increasing Returns and are increasing returns at the aggregate level.

The explanation given by Lucas and Romer for the international pattern of growth is a plausible one. In fact, the idea that poor countries can get stuck at a low level of productivity was introduced many years ago in studies of the problems of economic development. However, other possible reasons why poor countries find it difficult to develop do not involve increasing returns. Some of these countries have economic policies that distort the workings of their economies. Some do not have efficient market systems. Others are politically unstable, which discourages investment.

The most controversial aspect of the Romer and Lucas analysis, however, is whether there are substantial increasing returns to scale in advanced countries. There is some evidence against this idea. First, there is a fairly clear pattern of convergence among the developed countries, as we discuss at greater length in the next chapter. So the neoclassical model fits fairly well with the experience of Europe, North America, and Japan over the period since World War II. And we saw earlier in this chapter that the neoclassical model also fits fairly well with the historical experience of the U.S. economy. In particular, the decline in the rate of profit that has accompanied the decline in productivity growth supports the existence of diminishing returns to fixed capital.

At this time the study of economic growth has become an area of greatly increased interest, and Romer and Lucas get much of the credit. They have stressed the need to integrate the theory of growth with a microeconomic analysis of how new technology is developed and how new knowledge spreads within countries and from country to country. They have not overturned the neoclassical model, but they have shown that it needs to be developed and modified in new ways.

---

* Paul M. Romer, "Increasing Returns and New Developments in the Theory of Growth," NBER Working Paper no. 3098, September 1989, and "Increasing Returns and Long Run Growth," *Journal of Political Economy* 94 (1986), pp. 1002–37; Robert E. Lucas, Jr., "On the Mechanics of Economic Development," *Journal of Monetary Economics* 22 (July 1988), pp 3–42.

International Growth Patterns). Others dispute the idea of increasing returns to scale, noting that countries such as Sweden and Switzerland seem to do well at a small scale, using the benefits of international trade in order to benefit from specialization. Denison's estimate is a reasonable one.

Finally, according to Denison, improved resource allocation has contributed to 19 percent of the productivity growth in nonresidential business, and much of this comes from the movement of workers off the farms. Denison argues that the productivity of workers in small family farms was lower than in the rest of the economy, particularly in the early years of the period. These small farms did not set employment by supply and demand, but instead based it on the number of family members around. The result was that there was surplus labor and inefficiency in the farm sector. As labor migrated off the farms into nonfarm employment, this eliminated the inefficiency and raised overall productivity.

In the original Solow study, 87 percent of the growth in average labor productivity was attributed to technological change. For nonresidential business, Denison finds that his search for alternative sources of growth has trimmed this figure to 64 percent. This is the fraction of the growth in average labor productivity that came about from the source he calls "advances in knowledge." Denison uses this somewhat broader term in order to include improvements in methods as well as new technology, nevertheless, his conclusion is that a substantial fraction of the growth in average labor productivity still remains as a residual item that is attributed to technology and other knowledge improvements.

Denison also looked at the slowdown of productivity growth that took place. And just as we found evidence of a slowing in technological change when we compared actual data with the growth model, Denison also found a sharp drop in growth. He dated this decline in growth at around 1973. In the next chapter we ask why this fall in growth has occurred, we say more about the role of technology in growth, and we look at the challenge long-range policy planners face in response to the slowdown dilemma.

SUMMARY

- In the long run, the growth in potential output is the key determinant of the growth of living standards.

- The economy's productive capacity (potential output) depends upon how much capital and labor are available for production and the technology that is used. If more capital and labor are used in production, more output can be produced.

- With a given technology, increasing labor input to produce more output will depress average labor productivity and living standards for those employed unless the amount of capital rises by enough to prevent the effects of diminishing returns from lowering labor productivity.

- If there are constant returns to scale, then proportional increases or decreases in capital and labor together will result in the same proportional increases or decreases in output with no change in labor productivity at a given level of technology.

- In an economy where production is subject to constant returns to scale, average labor productivity does not depend on the size of the economy. Rather, it depends upon the capital/labor ratio—the capital intensity of the economy.

- An increase in capital intensity is a disproportional increase of capital relative to labor. More capital per worker raises the level of average labor productivity, but there are diminishing returns to capital as capital intensity increases.

- If the labor input is growing and there is not enough new capital added to match the growth of labor, capital growth will be inadequate and the economy will suffer from falling productivity (taking technology as given).

- The simplest growth model assumes no technological change. Saving is the long-run source of the resources that are set aside for investment, and investment is the amount that is added to the capital stock. The amount of saving per worker is assumed to be the same as the amount of new capital per worker in the growth model.

■ The amount of new capital added per worker depends upon output per worker, which is in turn determined by capital intensity—the existing capital/labor ratio.

■ Capital adequacy is the amount of new capital added per worker that is just necessary to maintain the level of capital intensity, thereby keeping labor productivity constant.

■ If saving per worker is larger than necessary to provide for capital adequacy, then there is more than enough capital investment being made to equip new entrants to the labor force, and the rest of the new capital can then be used to raise the level of capital intensity, a process called capital deepening.

■ If saving per worker is lower than capital adequacy, then there is not enough capital investment being made to equip new entrants to the labor force with the same level of capital per worker as present workers have. The average level of capital intensity falls along with a fall in average labor productivity.

■ Regardless of whether an economy is saving at a rate above or below capital adequacy, it tends to move toward steady-state growth, where the amount of saving and new capital is just equal to the amount of capital adequacy.

■ Saving more does increase the level of productivity and consumption but steady-state growth rates are not affected. A high-saving economy has to devote a larger share of its higher income to capital accumulation than does the low-saving economy in order to keep its capital/labor ratio constant.

■ Technological change increases the steady-state growth rate. The simple growth model can be extended to a case where there is labor-augmenting technical change.

■ It has been found that technological change rather than capital accumulation has been the main source of increased productivity and living standards.

■ An economy that experiences labor-augmenting technological change is not free of the need to improve its level of investment in order to maintain its growth rate. However, the steady-state growth rate and standard of living it can obtain are higher because of technological change.

■ In an economy with technological change, average labor productivity is growing directly because of the contribution of technology as a factor of production, but it is also growing as an indirect consequence of the technological change because faster output growth leads to faster capital growth.

■ For an economy in steady-state growth, the wage will rise at the same rate as technical change and hence at the same rate as average labor productivity.

■ Both technological change and increases in capital per worker will raise wages and hence raise the living standards of workers.

■ Average labor productivity slows down when the rate of technological change slows.

■ Somewhere between 1968 and 1973, the rate of technological change seems to have slowed down sharply and thrown the economy away from its postwar path, away from the steady state.

■ Growth accounting has found other sources of growth, not included in the simple growth model, including the effects of education and increasing returns to scale.

KEY TERMS

aggregate-production function	growth accounting
augmented labor	human capital
average labor productivity	intensive production function
capital adequacy	optimal growth
capital deepening	steady-state growth
capital intensity	technological change
constant returns to scale	technology
diminishing returns	

DISCUSSION QUESTIONS AND PROBLEMS

1. How are living standards tied to productivity? Can't wages rise over time even though output levels are constant? What has to happen to the return on capital and the labor force in order to raise wages in this scenario?

2. "Workers are only productive if they have the proper tools. The secret to improving productivity is to make sure employees get more equipment every year." Do you agree with the message offered in this quote? Can productivity continue to grow this way indefinitely?

3. Is capital adequacy a target level of saving that an economy should shoot for, is it a minimum acceptable level, or is it a rate of saving that is inevitable in the steady state?

4. Consider aspects or conditions in the economy that would make labor more productive. Can any of the sources of productivity enhancement be described as an improvement in technology that augments labor? If so, explain.

5. A higher rate of saving frees more resources for capital accumulation than a lower rate of saving. Since a more capital-intensive economy generates a higher level of productivity, saving more should lead to a higher rate of growth. Is this the finding of the growth models? If not, why not? Does saving more buy any improvement in the economy?

6. The U.S. economy has been operating for over 200 years. Aren't we already in the steady state? If so, what would be required to move to another steady state with higher growth? If not, which steady state are we headed for?

7. Consider an economy with the following rates of growth (in percent per year):
Labor input	1.0
Capital input	4.0
Output	3.5
Labor augmenting Technical change	1.5

   Calculate the following: The growth rate of average labor productivity. The growth rate of the capital–output ratio. The growth rate of N^*, the augmented labor input. Is the economy moving around the intensive production function to the left or to the right?

8. Consider an economy in which the saving propensity, s, is equal to 0.10. Average labor productivity is equal to 10, and the capital/labor ratio is equal to 30. There is no technological change. The rate of growth of the labor input is 1.5 percent per year ($\Delta N/N = 0.015$). Is the capital/labor ratio in this economy rising or falling?

9. Consider the economy as described in question 8. Suppose there is labor-augmenting technological change. If the economy is in steady-state growth, what is the rate of technological change?

CHAPTER 18

Productivity, Competitiveness, and Economic Policies for Long-Term Growth

INTRODUCTION

Improvements in the standard of living over the long term come from increases in the availability of goods and services supplied to the economy over and above increases that simply arise because the economy has more people working. How well an economy performs in improving aggregate supply depends upon its own productivity as well as the productivity of economies with which it competes in world markets.

From 1929 until 1948, the United States and the economies of the rest of the industrialized world went through depression, war, and demobilization. The Great Depression, during which income fell and optimistic expectations of recovery were rare, resulted in an understandable unwillingness on the part of companies to commit resources to new risky capital investments or to the lengthy and expensive business of technology development. Since productivity stems from innovation (the industrial application of technological development, not simply the existence of new ideas), the growth of productivity was lower during the Depression than it would have been in an expansionary period. Certainly there was some investment and innovation during the Depression—some opportunities are always too good to pass up. But the slack in the economy and the fear of bankruptcy did not make for a favorable economic climate.[1]

---

[1] The relation between innovation and demand is explored by Jacob Schmookler, *Invention and Economic Growth* (Cambridge, Mass.: Harvard University Press, 1966).

During World War II there was substantial technological development, as the government mobilized industrial and scientific resources for the war effort. But the new technology was being applied to armaments, not to civilian production. As the war ended there were ideas that had not yet been used, new scientific advances, and new products and processes that could generate profits and productivity in the civilian economy.

The United States emerged from World War II as the dominant economy in the world, the leader in technology, and by far the most productive nation. Moreover, the ingredients were available in the postwar period to achieve even more rapid increases in output and productivity than had been achieved in the past. And indeed the postwar period turned out to be one of unusually rapid productivity growth for both the United States and other industrialized nations.

It is not surprising that the rate of productivity growth in the U.S. economy was high in the 1950s and 60s. The expected rate of inflation and the real long-term rate of interest were generally low, and savings rates were high. These favorable business conditions meant that the growth in capital was combined with rapid technological changes to sustain high rate of growth of labor productivity. This period was one of improvement in our social capital as well as business capital investment. There was government investment in roads, schools, bridges, and airports. This growth in what is called the **infrastructure** of the economy also fostered productivity growth. The level of productivity in the U.S. economy was already extremely high in the 1940s and it then grew rapidly in the 1950s and 1960s.

infrastructure
The stock of public capital including roads, bridges, schools, airports, and water and sewer systems.

It took the rest of the industrialized world longer to recover from the depression of the 1930s and the ravages of World War II. But productivity growth was also high in the period after 1950 in Europe and Japan. (The 1960s were the years of most rapid growth for Japan.) Potential output grew fairly steadily and high growth in productivity was assumed to be the dominant characteristic of advanced industrialized economies. Unfortunately this stellar performance did not last. Sometime in the late 1960s and early 1970s there was a significant decline in productivity growth in the United States and most other major industrial economies as well, and this period of slow growth has continued into the 1990s.

The U.S. economy is not the only one to have suffered from a decline in productivity growth, but it is almost alone in the extent of its huge trade deficit. While we are buying far more from overseas than we are selling, our principal economic competitors, Japan and Germany, are running very large trade surpluses. In addition, we are bombarded with reports suggesting that U.S. managers, schools, and technology development are falling behind that of foreigners, especially the Japanese. The management methods introduced by Alfred P. Sloan at General Motors were once considered the model for the industrial world. In the 1990s, General Motors is attempting to use Japanese production methods in order to improve the quality and competitiveness of its products.

competitiveness
A widely used term that lacks a generally accepted definition. U.S. competitiveness is often related to one or more of the following elements: (1) the trade deficit, (2) whether or not U.S. companies can compete internationally without continuous reductions in the value of the dollar, (3) the level of U.S. productivity relative to other countries, (4) the rate of growth of U.S. productivity relative to other countries, (5) whether or not the United States has a lead in technology in key industries.

There is concern today about the long-run **competitiveness** of the U.S. economy, whether it can sell overseas, and whether the U.S. industrial base is being eroded by foreign competition.

In this final chapter we explore two of the most important issues concerning the performance of the U.S. economy: the decline in productivity growth and the loss of competitiveness. We search for the possible causes of the slowdown, the sources of our difficulties with competitiveness, and the consequences of these problems for our future standard of living. The implications for macroeconomic policy of competitiveness and the decline in productivity growth will most probably be central to discussions and debates about economic policy into the next century.

Our discussion of long-run productivity trends follows from Chapter 17, in which the theory of economic growth was developed and the concept of declining growth was introduced. But since Chapter 17 is fairly technical, we have written this chapter so that it can stand alone as a description of the long-run supply issues associated with competitiveness and the growth of productivity. It is not necessary to read Chapter 17 before reading Chapter 18. This does mean, however, that there is some repetition of material. If you have read Chapter 17, you can skim some sections here.

Concepts of Productivity

average labor productivity
Output per worker or output per hour of work.

The concept of productivity we have used so far is **average labor productivity,** defined as real output per unit of labor input:

$$\text{Average labor productivity} = \text{Output per unit of labor input.} \qquad (18.1)$$

Since the largest portion of most people's income is earned by wages and since the growth of wages is closely tied to the growth of labor productivity (see Chapter 10), average labor productivity is closely related to the level of living standards of a country. This concept of productivity is relatively easy to measure. It is an intuitively appealing measure of how well an economy is doing in taking the labor effort of its work force and producing the goods and services that they choose to buy.

multifactor-productivity growth
A measure of the rate of improvement in efficiency or technological change. The rate of growth of output over and above the contributions to growth that stem from the growth of the amount of labor and capital.

Even though it is an attractive measure of productivity, average labor productivity is flawed in that it fails to hold constant changes in the amount of capital available per worker (the capital/labor ratio). A second productivity concept has been developed, **multifactor-productivity growth,** defined as the rate of growth of output net of the contributions to growth of labor and capital. Since output, capital, and labor grow at varying rates, multifactor productivity is defined using the growth rates of outputs and inputs:

$$
\begin{aligned}
\text{Rate of growth of multifactor productivity} \\
= \text{Rate of growth of output} \\
- (\text{Labor's income share} \times \text{Rate of growth of labor input}) \\
- (\text{Capital's income share} \times \text{Rate of growth of capital input}).
\end{aligned} \qquad (18.2)
$$

Multifactor productivity is computed by taking the rate of growth of output and subtracting off a weighted average of the rates of growth of the capital and labor inputs. The weights, or relative contributions to output, of labor and capital are their relative shares in income. Since labor receives about 70 percent of income, the labor input gets a weight of about 0.7 and capital gets a weight of about 0.3. The weights do change over time as the income shares change.

Multifactor-productivity growth measures output growth over and above any increases in the *quantities* of capital and labor inputs. It indicates the amount of output growth attributable to increases in the *efficiency of use* of the factors of production. Improvements in technology, increases in education or skills, and improved management methods will raise multifactor productivity. If the economy becomes less efficient in using the factors of production, then multifactor productivity falls. Because of short-run fluctuations in output, multifactor productivity will fall regularly as capital and labor are not fully utilized during recessions.

There is a direct relation between average labor productivity and multifactor productivity:

Rate of growth of average labor productivity
   = Rate of growth of multifactor productivity
      + [(Capital's income share) ×
      (Rate of growth of the capital/labor ratio)]. $\qquad$ (18.3)

Multifactor-productivity growth measures the growth of output net of increases in labor and capital, while labor productivity measures output growth net of labor inputs only, so multifactor-productivity growth is equated to labor-productivity growth by adding back the contribution to growth of increases in the capital stock relative to the growth of the labor force.[2]

---

[2] The rate of growth of labor productivity is equal to the rate of growth of output minus the rate of growth of labor input:

$$\text{Rate of growth of average labor productivity} = \frac{\Delta Y}{Y} - \frac{\Delta N}{N}.$$

Define the share of income going to capital as the letter a. Then since the capital and labor shares add to unity, the share of income going to labor is $(1 - a)$. The relations between labor productivity growth and multifactor-productivity growth can then be found as follows.

$$\frac{\Delta Y}{Y} - \frac{\Delta N}{N} = \frac{\Delta Y}{Y} - a\frac{\Delta K}{K} - (1 - a)\frac{\Delta N}{N} + a\frac{\Delta K}{K} - a\frac{\Delta N}{N}$$

$$= \text{Rate of multifactor-productivity growth} + a\left[\frac{\Delta K}{K} - \frac{\Delta N}{N}\right]$$

This is then the relation shown in Equation 18.3.

Both average labor productivity and multifactor productivity can be calculated for the economy as a whole or for particular industries or sectors. When industry productivity is computed, it is important to take account not only of the capital and labor inputs used in production, but also of the raw materials and partially finished goods purchased by the industry from other industries. This is done either by using a value-added concept of output (real value added equals the real value of production minus the real value of purchased materials) or, for multifactor productivity, by including purchased materials as an additional factor of production with capital and labor.

■ Multifactor Productivity and the Production Function

This chapter uses the concept of multifactor-productivity growth, a concept that did not appear in the models discussed in Chapter 17. Here we show how this new concept is related to the growth-model framework used in Chapter 17.

In the growth model, we introduced the aggregate-production function and we included in this funciton a term T to represent technology. Later we made an additional assumption, that technological change augments labor. The concept of multifactor-productivity growth defined here is based upon the production function. We start with the basic production function, as in Equation 17.1:

$$Y^P = F(K,N,T).$$

Using calculus, the rate of growth of potential output, Y^P, can be related to the rates of growth of the inputs:

$$\frac{\Delta Y^P}{Y^P} = \left[(\text{Capital's income share}) \times \frac{\Delta K}{K} \right]$$

$$+ \left[(\text{Labor's income share}) \times \frac{\Delta N}{N} \right]$$

$$+ \text{ Proportional shift in the production}$$
$$\text{function due to technological change.}$$

This relationship also assumes that the production function has constant returns to scale and that the income shares are determined in competitive markets. It does not assume, however, that technological change *necessarily* augments labor.

By comparing the preceding expression with the definition of multifactor-productivity growth given in Equation 18.2, we can see that *multifactor-productivity growth is equal to the proportional shift in the production function due to technological change*. Thus when we said in Chapter 17 that Solow estimated

that 87 percent of the increase in average labor productivity had been the result of an upward shift in the production function, this was the same as saying that 87 percent of the increase in average labor productivity had been the result of an increase in multifactor productivity.

Multifactor-productivity growth captures the increase in the efficiency of factor use whether or not technological change augments labor. It is a more general notion of productivity increase and this is why it is used. But suppose that in fact the effect of increases in technology or skills does augment labor, as we assumed in Chapter 17. In this case, how does the rate of labor-augmenting technological change relate to the rate of multifactor-productivity growth? Combining technological change with labor gives a new production function as follows:

$$Y^P = F(K,N^*).$$

Using calculus with this new production function gives

$$\frac{\Delta Y^P}{Y^P} = \left[(\text{Capital's income share}) \times \frac{\Delta K}{K} \right]$$

$$+ \left[(\text{Labor's income share}) \times \frac{\Delta N}{N} \right]$$

$$+ [(\text{Labor's income share}) \times \text{ rate of labor-}$$
$$\text{augmenting technological change}].$$

Comparing this expression with the definition of multifactor productivity shows that *if technological change augments labor, then multifactor-productivity growth is equal to the rate of technological change times the labor share of income* (about 0.7). If the rate of labor-augmenting technological change is about 2.5 percent a year, then the rate of growth of multifactor productivity will be about 1.75 percent a year.

capital deepening
Capital investment taking place at a rate that increases the amount of capital available per worker.

Average labor productivity increases over time for two reasons. First, there is growth in multifactor productivity as the efficiency of factor use increases. And second, average labor productivity increases when **capital deepening** occurs (i.e., when the capital input has increased faster than the labor input). This is the typical case in the U.S. economy and indeed in all of the major economies. The economy is becoming more capital-intensive over time as the amount of capital per worker increases, and this raises productivity.

THE SLOWDOWN IN THE GROWTH OF PRODUCTIVITY IN INDUSTRIAL COUNTRIES

Since the 1970s, a major threat to the standard of living in industrialized economies has been a slowdown in the growth of productivity. The slowdown began in the U.S. economy and was followed by productivity-growth slow-downs in the major economies around the world. We begin our analysis of the slowdown by looking at aspects of the history of productivity in the United States.

Aggregate-Productivity Trends in the United States

Productivity growth in the private business sector of the U.S. economy began to slow in the late 1960s and then collapsed after 1973. Given the high rates of growth immediately following World War II, some slowing of growth was to be expected. However, the collapse of productivity growth represented something deeper than simply a slowdown from an unsustainably high level. There seem to be fundamental problems that initiated a sharp drop in productivity growth and that continue to cause productivity to grow more slowly than has been the typical growth experience in the U.S. economy over the long term.

Table 18.1 gives the growth rates of labor productivity (real output per hour) and multifactor productivity in the business, nonfarm business, manufacturing, and nonfarm nonmanufacturing sectors of the economy over various periods. The two measures of productivity show a similar pattern. There was a decline in growth after 1973 of about 2 percent a year. In fact there was no growth at all in multifactor productivity in the nonfarm business sector in 1973–79, resulting from a combination of a small positive growth in manufacturing and a substantial decline in productivity in the nonmanufacturing sector. The data indicate that efficiency was actually getting worse in nonmanufacturing (a sector that includes the service industries, construction, and mining).

Since 1979, there has been a modest recovery overall, with productivity growing at rates that are well above the dismal rates of the 1973–1979 period, but still well below the rates of the 1950s and 1960s. Multifactor-productivity growth in 1979–87 was equal to about 30 percent, and labor-productivity growth about 45 percent of their pre-1973 rates of increase. The nonfarm, nonmanufacturing sector has made no recovery, however, and still shows a decline in efficiency.

Perhaps it seems that a decline of 1 or 2 percent a year in the rate of growth of productivity is insignificant. Who notices small changes in productivity anyway? The problem with slow growth is that the effects mount

TABLE 18.1   Average Annual Productivity Growth, Percent per Year, 1948–1987

Measure	1948–73	1973–79	1979–87	1973–87	Percentage-point change, 1948–73 to 1973–87
Real output per hour					
Business	2.94	0.62	1.32	1.02	−1.92
Nonfarm business	2.45	0.48	1.11	0.84	−1.61
Manufacturing	2.82	1.38	3.39	2.52	−0.30
Nonmanufacturing	2.32	0.16	0.33	0.25	−2.07
Multifactor productivity					
Business	2.00	0.10	0.61	0.39	−1.61
Nonfarm business	1.68	−0.08	0.45	0.22	−1.46
Manufacturing	2.03	0.52	2.56	1.68	−0.35
Nonmanufacturing	1.55	−0.29	−0.28	−0.30	−1.85

Source: Martin Neil Baily and Robert J. Gordon, "The Productivity Slowdown, Measurement Issues, and the Explosion of Computer Power," *Brookings Papers on Economic Activity 2:1988:* 1948–79 output per hour data taken from U.S. Dept. of Commerce, Bureau of Economic Analysis, *The National Income and Product Accounts of the United States, 1929–82, Statistical Tables* (U.S. Government Printing Office, September. 1986), tables 6.2 and 6.11. Data for 1987 taken from Dept. of Commerce, Bureau of Economic Analysis, *Survey of Current Business* 68 (July 1988), tables 6.2 and 6.11. Multifactor-productivity data taken from U.S. Dept. of Labor, Bureau of Labor Statistics, "Multifactor Productivity Measures, 1987," *News,* September 30, 1988.

up. After 15 or 20 years of slow growth, the economy begins to look very different from the way it would have looked with more rapid growth.

Figure 18.1 shows the shortfall in output associated with slow growth since 1965. We compare the level of output that was actually achieved in the economy after 1965 with the level that would have been achieved if the slowdown had not occurred. The comparison is done twice, using different trends of prior productivity growth to extrapolate past 1965.

The first comparison is shown by the dashed line labeled "Shortfall based on the trend of 1948–65." By using the trend of labor-productivity growth over the period 1948–65 extrapolated forward to 1987, the figure shows that output in 1987 was only about 65 percent of the level it would have achieved with prior trends. This is equivalent to saying that had the U.S. economy been able to sustain the rate of productivity growth that it had achieved following World War II, output could have been almost 50 percent higher in 1987 than actually occurred without requiring any increase in hours worked or number of employed.

Since the U.S. economy was in an unusually strong position for rapid growth at the end of World War II, it would have been surprising if the 1948–1965 productivity-growth trend had in fact been maintained through the 1970s. The comparison of the 1965–87 and 1948–65 periods is possibly misleading. However, the second comparison, shown in the figure by the solid line labeled "Shortfall based on the trend of 1889–65" used the trend of labor-productivity growth over the period 1889–1965 extrapolated forward to 1987. It shows that the period since 1965 has had substantially slower

FIGURE 18.1   The Shortfall in Productivity, 1965–1987

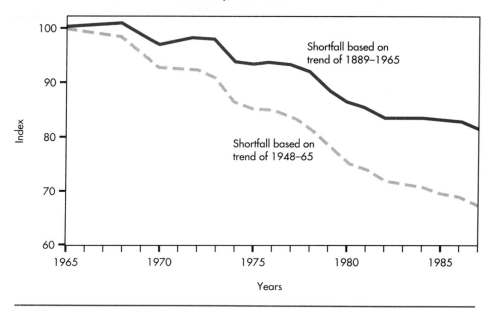

Note: Past trends are based on average annual growth rates of output per hour. For 1889–1948, based on private GDP per hour, from John Kendrick, *Productivity Trends in the United States* (Princeton, N.J.: Princeton University Press for National Bureau of Economic Research, 1961), pp. 298, 301, 311, 313, tables Aiii and Ax. For 1948–87 based on private business output per hour, from U.S. Dept. of Labor, Bureau of Labor Statistics, news release, USDL 87–436 (Oct. 13, 1987) and USDI, 88–98 (March 3, 1988).

Source: Martin Neil Baily and Margaret M. Blair, "Productivity and American Management," in *American Living Standards: Threats and Challenges* (Washington, D.C.: Brookings Institution, 1988).

growth than even the longer period 1889–1965. Output in 1987 was only 80 percent of the level it would have reached had the economy maintained the trend in productivity growth that was achieved over the previous three quarters of a century. If the growth rate since 1889 had continued after 1965, output would have been a third higher in 1987 than was realized. If this extra output had been produced, the additional resources would have been easily sufficient to close the budget and trade deficits and to raise living standards.

Productivity, Consumption, and the Standard of Living

We have suggested here that the growth of productivity is closely related to the growth of living standards. That connection is based on two assumptions: (1) that the growth in actual output is, in the long run, approximately equal to the growth in potential output and (2) that in the long run living standards are determined by per capita income. For periods of several years in the 1970s and 1980s there was a divergence between the growth of productivity and the growth of consumption.

During the 1970s and 1980s the average consumption standard of living of the American family rose faster than per capita income, and income rose faster than productivity. This increase in consumption was achieved at a price. Maintaining the growth of consumption in the face of weak productivity growth has involved more labor, lower saving, and more borrowing.[3] During this period more people worked, private saving declined, private borrowing rose, and government cut taxes and borrowed from overseas to pay for government expenditures. The divergence between productivity growth and consumption is unlikely to be sustained in the long run.

Incomes rose in the 1970s even though productivity hardly grew at all, mostly because of increased labor-force participation. More Americans were working, more families had two or three wage earners, and more people were working at two jobs. The problem with this source of family-income growth is that it is not indefinitely sustainable. In fact the increase in labor-force participation has slowed or stopped since then. Moreover, the gain in the consumption standard of living that was obtained through higher rates of labor-force participation also brought about significant reductions in the time available for nonmarket activities such as family and leisure-time pursuits.

Since 1979 there has been some recovery of productivity growth, and U.S. living standards have continued to grow. But much of the increase in living standards since 1979 has come through foreign borrowing and a lowering of the domestic saving rate. This method for increasing consumption is also problematic. In the longer run, households, firms, and governments in the U.S. economy will have to repay the foreign debts or make interest payments forever. In the long run, the growth of the standard of living depends upon the growth of real income per worker through increases in productivity.

Industry Trends in Productivity Growth

Was the slowdown in productivity growth experienced in a few key industries, pointing to a set of industry-specific causes, or was the slowdown experienced across the board, pointing to economywide sources of the decline in growth?

Table 18.2 shows average labor-productivity growth by major industry group in the United States,[4] together with the magnitude of the slowdown in each industry, based on the difference between the rates of growth before and after 1973. The data indicate that the slowdown in growth after 1973 was experienced across the board. Almost all of the industries had slower growth after 1973 than before. Only in nonelectrical machinery (which includes

---

[3] Frank Levy, *Dollars and Dreams: The Changing American Income Distribution* (New York: Russell Sage Foundation, 1987).

[4] Martin Neil Baily and Robert J. Gordon, "The Productivity Slowdown, Measurement Issues and the Explosion of Computer Power," *Brookings Papers on Economic Activity 2:1988*, pp. 347–431.

TABLE 18.2 Average Annual Growth in GDP per Hour, Major Sectors of the U.S. Economy, Percent per Year, 1948–1987

Sector	1948–73	1973–79	1979–87	1973–87	Percentage-point change, 1948–73 to 1973–87
Business	2.88	0.63	1.36	1.05	−1.83
Goods-producing industries	3.21	0.55	2.39	1.60	−1.61
Farming	4.64	3.09	6.86	5.22	0.58
Mining	4.02	−7.05	2.34	−1.79	−5.81
Construction	0.58	−1.99	−1.67	−1.80	−2.38
Manufacturing	2.87	1.43	3.49	2.61	−0.26
Durable goods excluding nonelectrical machinery	2.56	1.12	2.09	1.67	−0.89
Nonelectrical machinery[a]	2.03	0.70	11.54	6.76	4.73
Nondurable goods	3.40	1.90	2.13	2.03	−1.37
Non–goods-producing industries	2.49	0.73	0.66	0.69	−1.80
Transportation	2.31	1.06	−0.50	0.17	−2.14
Communications	5.22	4.25	5.09	4.73	−0.49
Electricity, gas, and sanitary services	5.87	0.05	1.44	0.84	−5.03
Trade	2.74	0.76	1.68	1.28	−1.46
Wholesale	3.14	0.10	2.39	1.40	−1.74
Retail	2.40	0.87	1.21	1.06	−1.34
Finance, insurance, and real estate	1.44	0.28	−1.15	−0.54	−1.98
Business and personal services	2.17	0.34	0.36	0.35	−1.82
Government enterprises	−0.15	0.94	−0.15	0.32	0.47
General government[a]	0.21	−0.28	0.37	0.09	−0.12
Nonprofit organizations[b]	0.31	0.88	0.32	0.56	−0.87
Employment in private households[c]	−0.35	−0.63	1.98	0.85	1.20

Sources: Hours and GDP from Bureau of Labor Statistics (BLS) data except as noted.

a. GDP and hours for 1948, 1973, and 1979 from National Income and Product Accounts (NIPA); for 1987 from *Survey of Current Business,* 68 (July 1988).

b. GDP from NIPA and *Survey of Current Business.* Hours from *Survey of Current Business* and BLS estimates of military hours.

c. GDP from NIPA and *Survey of Current Business.* Hours from BLS.

the computer industry) and in agriculture was there a reversal of this pattern. (We are ignoring employment in private households, a tiny sector with questionable productivity data.)

The pattern of the slowdowns across industries is also illustrated by Figure 18.2. (The first row of Table 18.2 differs very slightly from the first row of Table 18.1. The aggregate figures in 18.1 were more recently revised.) Each bar indicates the magnitude of the change in growth after 1973 in the given industry. This chart confirms the conclusion that the slowdown was a problem that afflicted all but two of the industry groups. The fact that the slowdown is so widespread strongly suggests that there was some common cause to the slowdown.

Having stressed the similarities across industries, however, we should not slight the differences. If the pre-1973 period is broken down into smaller groups of years, it is very noticeable that construction and mining began to

FIGURE 18.2   Change in Labor-Productivity Growth by Industry, 1948–73 to 1973–1987

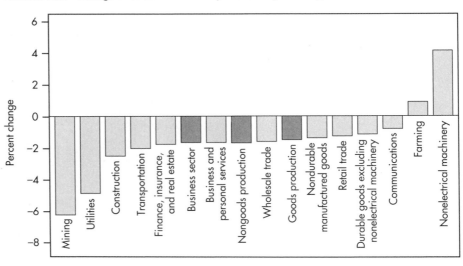

Source: Martin Neil Baily and Robert J. Gordon, "The Productivity Slowdown, Measurement Issues and the Explosion of Computer Power," *Brookings Papers on Economic Activity 2:1988.*

experience falling labor productivity (negative average–labor-productivity growth) in the late 1960s. There was also a slowing of growth in the utility sector at that time.

The collapse of mining productivity is understandable. The United States was running out of the most productive oil and gas reserves, making it harder to find new reserves and most costly to extract what was available. The collapse of mining productivity continued after 1973 as the rise in the price of oil encouraged using even more resources to find reserves and extract the existing stock. This was a rational response to the energy crisis.

The utility industry had achieved very rapid growth by exploiting the benefits of larger and larger generating facilities, but these economies of scale were largely exhausted by the late 1960s; then the energy crisis hit and the demand for electricity fell, leaving the utilities with excess capacity and very inefficient operations.

In both the mining and the utility industries, the scope of health-and-safety regulation also increased in the late 1960s and the 1970s. Both the need to reduce electric–power-plant stack emissions and the Mine Safety Act were costly in productivity terms. This latter observation is made without making a judgment either way about the benefits or desirability of such environmental controls.

The collapse of construction productivity remains something of a mystery. The official data indicate that the level of labor productivity in the industry in 1987 was below the level in the 1940s. This seems absurd. There were real productivity problems in the industry but there were also serious problems in the data. In part, the collapse of productivity in the construction industry is an illusion of the data.

Another important difference among industries is that the manufacturing sector has recovered its rate of productivity increase since 1979, whereas the service industries have not. It is sometimes alleged that the productivity slowdown is due to the expansion in the size of the service sector. This is misleading. It is more accurate to say that *the persistence of the slowdown in the 1980s is associated with a virtual cessation of productivity growth in the service industries in the 1980s.* Productivity growth in the service industries was quite good before 1973, but has become progressively worse since then.

The computer industry is important for understanding the behavior of U.S. productivity. It has played a major role in the recovery of manufacturing growth, so the industry data reveal an interesting puzzle. *The 1980s were a period where the U.S. economy seemed to be doing a terrific job in making computers but did not seem to be able to use these computers to raise productivity in the service industries that were buying them.* So far, this pattern is continuing into the 1990s. The difference between innovative technology and the productivity benefits generated by the innovation is a theme we will return to later.

Aggregate-Productivity Trends in Europe and Japan

There has been much discussion about the apparent decline in U.S. productivity relative to that achieved in other industrialized economies. The belief that U.S. industry has lost its competitive edge is deeply held by many observers of the U.S. economy. Is it a valid belief? Figure 18.3 shows the levels of labor productivity in the aggregate economies of four major industrial countries relative to the United States in various years. Even though actual U.S. productivity changes each year, the data in Figure 18.3 set the level of labor productivity in the United States equal to 100 in every year. This allows the productivity levels in the other countries to be expressed as percentages of the U.S. level on a year-by-year basis.

The data show that the large industrial countries had levels of productivity that were a long way below the U.S. level in 1950 and they have been catching up to the United States since then. But the catch-up has been a long and slow process. As of 1988, *the United States remained the most productive of the major industrial countries.* In fact the U.S. lead is still quite large.

Perhaps the most surprising fact shown in Figure 18.3 is the relatively low level of aggregate productivity in Japan. The Japanese economy has many sectors that are very productive and these sectors are able to compete ferociously in world markets. But there are many inefficient areas of the Japanese economy and, in general, Japan's economy looks weaker outside of the manufacturing industries that compete in international markets. Even within manufacturing, productivity performance is quite uneven. Japan's

FIGURE 18.3   GDP per Employed Person Relative to U.S. Level, 1950–1988

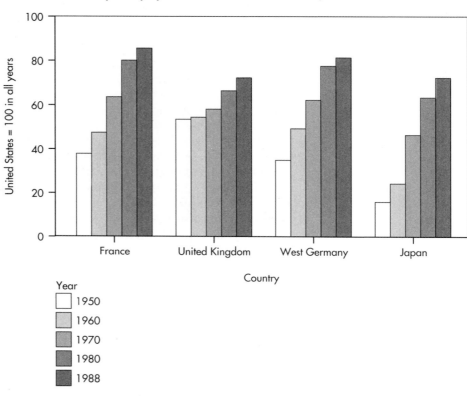

Source: U.S. Dept. of Labor, Bureau of Labor Statistics.

electronics, steel, and chemical industries have overtaken their competitors in the United States in terms of levels of productivity, but other industries remain relatively undeveloped. In 1985, the Japanese food-processing, textile, ceramics, and fabricated-metals industries were all well below U.S. productivity levels.[5] Their productivity was lower even in the transportation-equipment industry, which is surprising given their productivity gains in automobile production. This result comes partly from the fact that transportation equipment includes aerospace where the U.S. lead in productivity has not been lost.

In one important respect, the data we are reporting may understate the level of Japanese productivity. Japanese industry has been able to achieve

_____
[5] Martin Neil Baily and Robert J. Gordon, "Productivity Measurement in Five Large Industrial Countries," paper presented to the conference on technology, OECD, Paris, April 1989.

very high levels of quality in many products (especially in semiconductors, consumer durables, and automobiles), and quality is not well captured by these data.

Comparing the levels of productivity among countries indicates that the U.S. economy remains very strong. But a major part of the concern about the competitiveness of the U.S. economy centers on the slow growth of productivity. Figure 18.3 does show that productivity in the major industrial economies has been catching up to the level generated in the United States.[6] While productivity levels in these countries ranged from approximately 20 to 50 percent of the U.S. level in the 1950s and 1960s, by 1988, they stood at around 70–90 percent of the U.S. level. Europe and Japan's high rates of growth in productivity (rates higher than the U.S. rate) have shrunk the productivity gap, but have not closed it entirely.

The United States has not been alone in finding productivity growth harder to achieve since 1973. In spite of their higher rates of productivity growth, other major industrialized economies have also experienced substantial slowdowns in growth. During the period when the United States was growing rapidly, the other countries were growing even more rapidly and when the U.S. rate of productivity growth slowed down, other countries experienced an even greater reduction in their own high rates.

In summary, *while the United States remained the most productive of the major economies, the other major economies have been catching up to the United States, but the rate of catch-up has slowed down.* While other nations have been able to gain ground on the productivity leadership of the U.S., they have not been able to protect themselves from their own slowdowns in productivity growth.

Just as the inspection of productivity patterns in U.S. industries suggested economywide reasons for a productivity-growth slowdown, so do international comparisons indicate the possibility of either worldwide causes or similarities in the growth history of mature nations that underlie the productivity growth decline.

The international competitiveness of the U.S. economy

The United States has been running a huge foreign-trade deficit. As we showed in Chapters 4 and 12, a major cause of the U.S. trade deficit has been that U.S. interest rates have been well above rates overseas, which kept the dollar above the level needed to eliminate the deficit in the current account. The federal budget deficit was a cause of the interest-rate differential and the attendant capital inflows to U.S. capital markets.

Some have argued that another cause of the U.S. balance-of-trade deficit is that the United States has not been productive enough to compete with

---

[6] The catch-up of other countries to the U.S. level of productivity is analyzed in William J. Baumol, Sue Ann Batey Blackman, and Edward N. Wolff, *Productivity and American Leadership: The Long View* (Cambridge Mass.: MIT Press, 1989).

the other industrialized nations in the world marketplace. But this argument confuses productivity with the competitiveness of products based on relative prices and quality. While the failure to produce competitive products does contribute to trade deficits, low productivity is not necessarily a barrier to a rapid growth of exports. Productivity describes the efficiency with which products are produced; it says nothing about the demand for those products. The emerging Asian countries have much lower levels of productivity than does the United States and yet compete very effectively. And high productivity does not guarantee the ability to sell overseas. After all, we have just seen in Figure 18.3 that through 1988, the United States had a higher level of productivity than the other major industrialized economies.

But even though the attempt to link productivity directly to the trade deficit is mistaken, the concern about U.S. competitiveness is not misplaced. In order to sustain the production of competitive products and services when productivity is growing more slowly than in other economies, we must either continually suffer reductions in real wages in the United States relative to other countries and hence reductions in our relative standard of living, or we must generate improvements in product design and attractiveness that make up for our cost disadvantage.

After World War II the United States had access to unique technologies, used the best methods of management, and produced products that were unavailable elsewhere or unavailable in large quantities. This unique position of the U.S. economy allowed U.S. firms to dominate the markets in many high-tech industries and charge premium prices for their products. Today, U.S. firms have lost this uniqueness in many areas. Producers in other countries now have technology that is as good as or even better than ours, and they have shown that in some cases their business managers have done a better job than ours. The Japanese auto plants in the United States are managed by Japanese managers and they are achieving very high productivity and quality using U.S. production workers.

When the performance of the U.S. economy is compared to the performance of other countries, it no longer looks as if we are doing as well as we can. There are too many cases of U.S. firms or industries not producing the quality of products that match those made overseas. While all firms are not alike, there are successful firms and unsuccessful firms both here and overseas. Case studies of specific industries indicate that management strategies had failed in many firms, particularly in automobiles, consumer electronics, machine tools, steel, semiconductors, and copiers.[7]

In summary, a prolonged trade deficit will be corrected when interest-

---

[7] Michael Dertouzos, Richard K. Lester, and Robert M. Solow, *Made in America: Regaining the Competitive Edge*, Report of the MIT Commission on Industrial Productivity (Cambridge, Mass.: MIT Press, 1989). The commission acknowledged that the macroeconomic problems, such as the budget deficit, that have contributed heavily to the trade deficit also contributed to the productivity decline. Nevertheless, they pointed to several cases of industry-specific failures to retain competitiveness.

rate differentials between the United States and other countries are reduced. For the U.S. economy in the 1990s, that event awaits a reduction in the federal budget deficit. The nature of the long-run equilibrium in trade depends upon whether U.S. industry responds with competitive products and productivity gains or responds with lower export prices from a lowered dollar. In the absence of productivity and quality improvements, U.S. industry will have to compete on world markets by charging lower prices and will end up paying lower wages to its employees than do other countries—hardly a formula for improving the U.S. standard of living. Given the openness of the U.S. economy and the commitment to growth of its standard of living, the nation has to regain its competitive advantage through productivity growth. In order to improve productivity growth, it would help to know what caused its decline. If the factors that led to the decline are responsive to policy changes, then perhaps the slowdown can be reversed. Here we will concentrate on the post-1973 productivity decline.

Some decline in productivity growth started in the United States in the late 1960s. This decline was associated with construction, mining, and utilities and, to some extent, with the ending of the period of very strong aggregate demand after 1968. The decline in growth that began in the late 1960s was specific to a few problem industries. Most economists date the general slowdown from 1973 on. That was when productivity growth collapsed in almost all industries and in many different countries.

Declining Inputs as Candidates for the Slowdown

There is no shortage of possible candidates that may or may not explain the economywide slowdown in productivity growth after 1973. Our search for candidates follows our understanding of the contributors to the rate of growth of average labor productivity (Equation 18.3), both multifactor-productivity growth (which measures the effectiveness of inputs and the role of the economic environment and technology in production) and the rate at which the growth rate of capital exceeds the growth rate of labor.

The first group of candidates that might have caused the slowdown in productivity consists of possible reductions in the effectiveness of the labor force and possible reductions in capital inputs to production. In particular, there is concern about *deteriorating education and labor skills* and *reductions in fixed capital per worker*. Then we turn to the possibility that the *economic environment for productivity enhancement has deteriorated*, including a slowdown in technological advances and problems in taking commercial advantage of technological opportunities.

No single simple culprit emerges as the source of the productivity decline. Rather, a combination of circumstances acting together appear to have been responsible—some are amenable to improvement through policy actions and some are inevitable given the mature nature of industrial economies. Finally, following the search for explanations of the slowdown in productivity in the United States, we examine the case for the U.S.'s productivity slowdown being connected with slowdowns in other industrialized nations.

Limited opportunities and reduced skills in the labor force

During the period after World War II, the work force consisted primarily of mature males. In the 1960s there began an influx of new workers who were predominantly young, female, and/or members of minority groups. Historically, these new workers were denied or otherwise lacked the training and educational opportunities necessary to gain access to the higher-skilled jobs in the labor market. As a result of rarely holding higher-skilled jobs, the new entrants were less able to acquire the level of experience and concomitant productivity skills of the preexisting work force.

While female, youth, or minority workers are certainly not intrinsically less productive (even the evidence of lower wages for these groups can be argued to result from the effects of being channeled into traditional job paths and/or discrimination), there is a reasonable case to be made that the economy's adjustment to the changing composition of the work force has been a costly, although quite necessary, undertaking.

Another labor-quality issue concerns the basic educational capabilities of the labor force. If the quality of education has deteriorated, then this might have contributed to a declining rate of productivity growth. Just as technology was thought to have effectively *increased* the productivity of the labor input, losses in educational quality would have *reduced* the productivity of labor. There is a generally held perception that there has been a long-term decline in educational attainment in the United States during the period of falling productivity growth rates. Much of that perception is connected to trends in test scores—many of which were not designed to measure the productive capacity of the work force, but have been found to be related to it.

Drawing a connection between a deterioration in educational achievement and productivity requires us to resolve (1) whether there were noticeable declines in test scores, (2) whether such declines in educational test scores do in fact indicate a deterioration in actual educational achievement, and (3) if the declines in educational achievement can be related to the productivity decline.

Following improvements in the immediate postwar period, there was a decline in educational test scores, such as the Scholastic Aptitude Test (SAT). The trend in scores bottomed out in the 1980s and started to turn up again, but the test-score declines suggest that there is a cohort of people now in the labor force who have lower educational skills than prior cohorts.

The decline in test scores does appear to reflect an actual decline in educational capabilities.[8] Educational aptitude tests leave significant room

---

[8] John H. Bishop, "Is the Test Score Decline Responsible for the Productivity Growth Decline?" *American Economic Review* 79 (March 1989), pp. 178–97.

for error in measuring the performance of individuals or even groups of individuals, but independent tests of the general levels of intellectual and academic achievement in the population corroborate the conclusions about decline drawn from aptitude tests.

There is a problem, however, in connecting educational decline and the slowdown in productivity growth rates because the timing of the decline in test scores turns out to match the productivity decline only at a superficial level. It was not until the late 1970s that workers with declining scores made up a significant fraction of the work force. So the decline in educational achievement, as indicated by declining SAT scores, could not have been responsible for all or most of the productivity-growth decline. The post-1973 productivity slowdown predated the decline in educationally measured skills.

Overall, however, the decline in educational achievement has been important. Demographic changes lowered growth in the 1970s, and then the weakness in school performance started to have an adverse effect on productivity in the 1980s, just when the flow of young and inexperienced workers slowed down so that demographic change was no longer a problem.

Results from several studies indicate that a decline of approximately 0.3 percent a year in labor-productivity growth after 1973 was due to the combined effects of changes in the demographic composition of the labor force and the decline in educational skills.[9] At most this explains about 15 percent of a slowdown of around 1.5–2.0 percent per year, but it remains an important change for the worse in the quality of the work force. The persistence of the slowdown in the 1980s has been exacerbated by this labor-quality decline.

Lower investment in real capital

The United States has had a low rate of saving and investment for many years, and the rate of capital accumulation was somewhat slower in the 1970s than in the period prior to 1973. Could part of the the slowdown be the result of a lack of investment and capital accumulation?

If the analysis of the sources of growth are based upon the analysis of models of economic growth of the kind we looked at in Chapter 17, the answer is that capital did not play a big role in the slowdown. This can be seen from Table 18.1, because multifactor-productivity growth adjusts labor-productivity growth for the effect of capital accumulation. The fact that the slowdown was as great in terms of multifactor growth as it was in terms of labor-productivity growth provides clear evidence that the slow growth of capital was not a prime cause of the slowdown.

There have been many attempts to dispute this finding and give capital a much bigger role in productivity growth. If capital does have a larger role, then can we point to a slowdown in saving and capital investment as the source of the slowdown in productivity? A key argument that is often

---

[9] The results from these studies are discussed in Baily and Gordon, "Productivity Slowdown."

made in support of a larger role for capital in productivity is that capital is the vehicle by which technology is transmitted to the production process. New pieces of capital equipment embody new technology, so that investment involves applying a combined dose of capital and technology to the factory floor. This suggests that any slowing in the pace of capital investment will slow the rate of technological change. One piece of evidence to support this idea is provided by cross-country comparisons. The countries that have had the most rapid rates of growth in both labor and multifactor productivity since World War II are also the countries that have had the highest rates of investment. This observation contrasts with the analysis underlying the data in Table 18.1 (similar to the growth models described in Chapter 17), which assumes a complete separation between the rate of growth of capital and the rate of technological change.

It turns out that these attempts to give a bigger role to capital as a source of growth and, thus, give a slowdown in capital accumulation a bigger role in the slowdown of productivity growth have had only a limited success. It may well be the case that capital embodies new technology, but this does not imply that the payoff from investment is increased because of faster rates of capital accumulation. The fact that new capital embodies new technology is a plus for investment, but then the capital goods that are put in place become obsolete faster, which is a minus. For a country such as the United States that is already using advanced technology, the growth payoff that comes from faster rates of capital accumulation is only a little higher using models that specify that technology is embodied in capital investment than it is using models where technological change augments labor.[10]

In the case of the European countries and Japan—which grew quickly and invested heavily—their favorable growth experience relative to the United States was achieved in part because they were able to borrow the best of U.S. technology. Capital investment played a vital role in their success; it was a mechanism by which they transferred U.S. technology to their factories. But the United States could not have achieved the same growth rates even if it had had the same rate of capital accumulation.

Another recent attempt to suggest an important role for capital has been to include public capital in the total. Public capital includes the roads, bridges, sewers, and schools that are part of what is called the infrastructure. There is something to this idea, at least as it affected the transportation sector. The transportation industry is one of the service industries that has suffered a fairly substantial decline in productivity growth since 1973. This occurred partly because of the end of the road-building program and other related projects, such as the construction of airports. The development of the interstate highway system in the 1950s and 1960s allowed transportation productivity to rise, but the gains from this source of productivity were exhausted once

---

[10] Edmund S. Phelps, "The New View of Investment: A Neoclassical Analysis," *Quarterly Journal of Economics* 78 (November 1962), pp. 548–67.

the system had been completed. More recently, some of the gains are being eroded because the system has been allowed to deteriorate.[11]

Saving, investment, foreign capital, and growth.   A low rate of saving in the United States jeopardizes future growth, even though capital accumulation has probably not played an important role in explaining the economy's productivity slowdown. If the only source of funds for capital investment were saving, then low saving rates would necessarily generate insufficient resources to match the capital needs of a growing economy. Fortunately for the U.S. economy, saving was not the only source of resources that was used for capital accumulation. During the 1980s the U.S. economy changed from being a net lender to the rest of the world to being in a net-borrowing position. But relying on saving from overseas is not without costs. First, the U.S. economy will have a lower future standard of living because of the need to pay interest and repay principal on the accumulated foreign debt. Second, foreign capital has been attracted to U.S. capital markets because U.S. borrowers (households, corporations, and government) borrowed by selling financial instruments (e.g., mortgages as well as corporate and government bonds) that offered high real rates of interest. As a result, *investment in the U.S. economy is lower than it would have been had there been a higher level of domestic saving and lower interest rates.*

Changes in the Economic Environment as Candidates for the Slowdown

We have found that part, but by no means all, of the productivity slowdown can be traced to an erosion of inputs (capital or labor). This suggests that perhaps there have been changes in the economic environment that have made productivity growth more difficult to obtain, or perhaps the problem is simply that we find it harder to measure the growth that is occurring. We examine the possibility that the slowdown can be linked to a variety of separate changes in the economic environment, all of them candidates for explaining some portion of the decline in growth. The candidates include:

---

[11] The decline in the roads and airports is not the only reason why transportation has had slow growth. This sector is energy-intensive and so was affected by the rise in energy prices. In fact the trucking industry was specifically affected by the reduction of speed limits as a result of the energy crisis. This increased truck transit times—at least for those trucks that observed the limit.

The role of the public capital stock in the slowdown has been investigated by David Aschauer. He greatly exaggerates the impact of public capital, however. Investment of this kind slowed in the late 1960s because of the completion of the highway system and because the end of the baby boom meant that fewer schools were needed. In some ways there was too much public capital at that time as many of the existing schools had to be closed or used unproductively. It is also a mistake to concentrate on public capital in assessing the contribution of government output to private-sector productivity. The government provides services to the private sector, some of which increase and some of which decrease productivity. And the government uses both capital and labor. See David Aschauer, "Is Public Expenditure Productive?" Federal Reserve Bank of Chicago Staff Memorandum SM 88-7, 1988.

1. Changes in the composition of output either toward output that is less susceptible to productivity improvement or toward output where productivity gains are more difficult to observe, especially the move to a service economy and its associated investment in computer technology,

2. Changes in the economic environment that lead to increased errors in the measurement of productivity growth,

3. An increased level of government regulation that may have forced industry to adopt more expensive production technologies,

4. A lowered rate of research and development and innovation that may account for a slowdown in the rate at which technological improvement contributed to growth,

5. A possible erosion of the quality of management, particularly in terms of dealing with the economic disruptions of the past several years, such as the energy crisis.

Computers, services, and errors in measurement

Productivity is measured by comparing output with inputs and this measurement is fraught with the potential for error. The potential for error has led many people to wonder if productivity growth might be much higher than the standard data indicate. And these people may be correct, although it turns out that it is much harder to invoke measurement errors to explain the slowdown in measured productivity growth than it appears at first sight.[12] Some of the ways in which measurement errors could have contributed to making the slowdown appear worse than it actually was include the rise of computer technology (which has accelerated in the service sector, a difficult sector in which to measure productivity gains), the construction industry (where huge declines in productivity occurring after 1968 are implausible), and the growth of resources devoted to convenience in the retail sector (a service unmeasured by conventional methods).

The use of computers has risen enormously and the price of computing has dropped dramatically in recent years, by enough to account for an increase of nearly 12 percent per year in productivity in the nonelectrical-machinery industry (which includes the computer industry) during 1979–87 and an average annual increase of real computing investment over the same period of 24 percent. These gains in an otherwise sluggish economy should have had an impact on overall productivity. Alas, whereas the data show enormous productivity gains in the manufacture of computers, they show apparently little productivity improvement in their use. Why do the official data seem to not show the payoff from investments in computer power? What has all

---

[12] Baily and Gordon, "Productivity Slowdown."

that computer power been doing, and where is the "black hole" into which all those computers are disappearing?

A part of the mystery is resolved by considering how computers are used. Increasing use of computers can lead to more, rather than less, employment because the computers are used to produce a higher quality of output, not more output. And the increased quality is not counted in the usual data. The greatest impact of computers has been in the service sector, in areas such as banking and financial services. These are clearly dynamic areas that have been investing heavily in computerized technology. And yet the official data report no productivity growth in this sector, by assumption. It is assumed that growth in inflation-adjusted output in the banking and financial-services industries is just equal to the growth in the number of people working in the industry. By definition, labor-productivity growth in this industry is zero.

The measurement problems we have described in the banking and financial-services sector apply also to other parts of the service sector, where the quality of the service provided is very difficult to measure. The weak performance of the service sector in the 1980s is explained in part by the fact that official data do not pick up the changing nature of service output.

Even though there are serious measurement errors in the services and construction industries, these errors do not explain much of the slowdown. The reason is twofold. First, many of the errors were occurring before 1973 as well as after 1973. Growth was understated in earlier years as well as in recent years, so the errors do not change the estimates of the change in the growth trend. Second, many of the errors occur in intermediate-goods industries and so do not result in an error in the measurement of final output. For example, there may be errors in the measurement of the output of the banking industry, but since about half of banking output is purchased by other companies as part of their activities, this will give rise to an offsetting error in the output of these other industries. If bank output is understated, then the output of the industries using the banks will be overstated. The error in final output resulting from the error in measuring bank output comes only from the half of bank services that are provided to consumers.

Although it is difficult to be sure of how serious measurement errors really are, it looks as if the magnitude of the slowdown in productivity growth in the business sector of the economy would only be reduced by about 10 percent if output were correctly measured.

Increased government regulation

We have already indicated some areas where the increase in economic regulation has affected productivity—the Mine-Safety Act, and the pollution-control requirements imposed on utilities. But since the 1970s there has been a huge increase in the scope of health-and-safety regulation applied to many industries. There have been two approaches to evaluating the impact of this regulation on productivity growth.[13] One has been to construct measures of regulation and apply them to data on industries. This approach asks: Has there been a relation between the incidence of regulation and the slowdown? The typical answer is that there has been, although the effect that is found is not usually huge. Objections to this approach are that the measures of the incidence of regulation are often rather crude, and that such analysis overstates the effect because other possibilities are often not included in the analysis.

An alternative approach has been used by Edward Denison, who used estimates of the direct costs of regulation, based upon the amount of capital and the number of workers devoted to meeting regulations. Denison found the effect of regulation to have been very small. Overall, these studies indicate that regulation can account for at most 5–10 percent of the slowdown of productivity growth after 1973.

Up to this point we have looked at changes in the quality and quantity of labor inputs, capital inputs, measurement errors, and regulation as sources of the productivity decline, and they have accounted for somewhere around a third to a half of the slowdown. There is still an important part of the story of the slowdown in the growth of productivity left to explain. We suspect that the remainder of the explanation will be found in the post-1973 problems associated with innovation and management.

Reductions in the growth of industrial innovation

Evaluations of the sources of productivity growth involve accounting for input growth and then searching for other sources of improvements in productivity (i.e., measuring multifactor productivity). Since multifactor productivity already accounts for the growth of inputs, increases in multifactor productivity must come about through increases in the effective use of inputs. These increases in efficiency do not simply fall on us like manna from heaven. They are achieved through improvements in the way in which goods and services are produced. A wide variety of activities contribute to these efficiencies including growth in basic knowledge about the material world and about human behavior and organizations, the development of new ideas, inventions and improvements in methods of production, and the delivery of services. The economic payoff from all of these increases in knowledge and methods comes in the form of **innovations,** which are improvements in the commercial applications of inventions and new concepts.

innovation
The introduction into the marketplace of new or improved products, processes, or services.

One way of understanding innovation is to conceive of it as a form of intangible or nonphysical capital that contributes to output. This intangible capital input combines with physical capital and labor hours to generate production. In part this intangible capital is human capital in the form of

---

[13] Edward F. Denison, *Trends in American Economic Growth, 1929–1982* (Washington, D.C.: Brookings Institution, 1985); Wayne B. Gray, "The Impact of OSHA and EPA Regulation on Productivity," Working Paper 1405 (Cambridge, Mass.: NBER, 1984).

increased education embodied in human beings. In part it consists of the stock of knowledge, a stock that is added to when we apply new scientific knowledge and develop innovative products and processes. And of course the increases in the stock of knowledge are often embodied in new equipment and carried throughout the economy.

Studies of productivity growth indicate that advances in knowledge and innovation account for much of the growth in productivity.[14] Since so much of productivity growth in the past has been the result of improvements in technology, it is natural to wonder whether the slowdown indicates lack of growth in the stock of knowledge. *A slowing in the pace of innovation may have caused the slowing of productivity growth.* This possibility has two possible variants. One is that the opportunities for advancement are being depleted. After World War II, there were new technologies waiting to be developed, but perhaps we have exhausted this abundance and the possibilities for further growth will be more limited. Though possible, the exhaustion of opportunities is unlikely—new frontiers for technologies emerge regularly and the opportunities that emerged in the late 1980s appear no less prone to innovation (e.g., superconductivity, genetic engineering, and optical computing) than those that appeared in earlier periods.

A more plausible alternative is that innovation has slowed because we are not putting as much effort into finding innovations, or because we are not getting as much of a payoff from each innovation. Both of these alternatives can be explored by looking at trends in the resources devoted to research and development.

Research and development.   In a modern economy most commercial innovations that are technological in nature trace their initiation to formal research-and-development programs (R&D) conducted by firms, government agencies, public institutions, and universities. R&D combines the activities of acquiring basic knowledge via research with the process of converting research results into new commercial products and processes via development programs. R&D expenditures are a form of investment in intangible capital. Resources allocated to R&D are expected to increase productivity. The capital and labor used in R&D are part of a firm's inputs used in production. These R&D inputs are already included in the calculation of multifactor productivity as if the R&D scientists and engineers were engaged in the direct production of goods and services. But in fact, they are not engaged in direct production, so that the commercial benefits of R&D will increase or decrease multifactor productivity depending upon whether the return to R&D is greater than or less than the return from other investments. Several studies of R&D have shown that the return to R&D substantially exceeds the return to other types

---

[14] Edward F. Denison, *"Trends"*; and Martin Neil Baily and Alok K. Chakrabarti, *Innovation and the Productivity Crisis* (Washington, D.C.: Brookings Institution, 1988).

of investment.[15] This means that the more resources an economy puts into R&D, the higher will be its productivity growth. And of course, the opposite case also applies. A decline in the resources devoted to R&D in the 1970s or 1980s could have caused part or all of the productivity-growth slowdown. Did this happen?

Industry-funded R&D varied between 1.0 and 1.5 percent of private non-farm GNP during the 1960s. And given the excesss return to R&D, this implies that R&D contributed between one fifth and one third of multifactor productivity growth during that period.[16] The rate of growth of both industry R&D and government R&D slowed down in the 1970s, and this slowdown undoubtedly contributed to the slowdown in both labor-productivity growth and multifactor-productivity growth. Thus the conclusion is that part of the productivity slowdown was caused by a reduction in the effort that was being put into R&D. But as with other explanations that we have explored, we find that the fraction of the slowdown that can be explained by this means is fairly small. The ratio of R&D spending to output never fell that much, and indeed R&D spending began to pick up again in the 1980s. At most the decline in the growth rate of R&D led to only about 10 percent of the decline in productivity growth after 1973.

Innovation and commercial applications.   If it is not a decline in the *quantity* of R&D that caused much of the decline in growth, then perhaps it is the productivity payoff per unit of R&D that has declined. Perhaps a given amount of R&D is yielding fewer innovations or the innovations are meeting increasing resistance in the marketplace, thereby yielding less productivity growth.

One way of approaching this possibility is through case studies of particular industries,[17] looking at the relation between the pace of innovation and the rate of productivity growth in each industry. The results of this approach have been mixed. In some cases there seem to be a clear relation between the rate of innovation and the rate of productivity increase. Such a relation indicates that slow productivity growth could well have been caused by a slow pace of innovation. In other cases the relation between innovation and productivity is not so clear.

For example, the chemical industry experienced a major decline in its rate of productivity growth in the 1970s, and it has also undergone a reduction in the flow of innovations it has generated. Thus the chemical industry shows

---

[15] Edwin Mansfield, "Microeconomics of Technological Innovation," in *The Positive Sum Strategy: Harnessing Technology for Economic Growth,* ed. Ralph Landau and Nathan Rosenberg (Washington, D.C.: National Academy Press, 1986). These returns combine private and social returns (i.e., returns to the corporations and spillover returns to society). The differences among private and social returns are discussed later in the section on macroeconomic growth policies and supply-side incentives.

[16] See Baily and Chakrabarti, *Innovation.*

[17] See Dertouzos et al., *Made in Amercia,* and Baily and Chakrabarti, *Innovation.*

support for the innovation–productivity link. For another example, the textile industry also supports the link between innovation and productivity, although in a different way. The textile industry was one of the few industries where productivity had not slowed in the 1970s, and this was also an industry where the pace of innovation had not slowed either.

Other case studies have not shown the same relation between innovation and productivity. In the machine-tool industry, productivity was very weak in the 1970s, but the pace of innovation was not weak. The introduction of numerical and computer-controlled machine tools has made the past 20 years or so a period of high innovation for this industry. In the machine-tool industry, therefore, the relationship between the pace of innovation and productivity appears not to hold. Nevertheless, innovation was a major part of the story of what had happened in this industry. It was innovation in the U.S. machine-tool industry relative to the world industry that was important. The emerging economies of Asia and elsewhere, with very low labor costs, have made it difficult for U.S. companies to compete in the production of basic machine tools. Labor costs are much lower in these developing countries. This has meant that the U.S. industry has had to produce advanced machines in order to remain competitive in world trade. At the same time, Japan was able to develop advanced machines at the top end of the market that were better than the U.S. machines in many cases. To some extent Germany and other European countries did the same. They have innovated more successfully than the U.S. industry was able to do. A heightened level of international competition in commercial innovation became a fact of corporate life in the 1980s. Industry in the United States was squeezed from both the top and the bottom of the market and was unable to remain competitive, and of course the years of an overvalued dollar in the early 1980s did not help either.

In summary, the U.S. machine-tool industry suffered slow productivity growth in the 1970s, not because there were few innovations, but because it was unable to exploit the opportunities for innovation as successfully as its main competitors and ended up contracting its output, its work force, and ultimately its ability to produce efficiently.

Thus there is no simple message from the case studies of specific industries. In some cases, the slowdown in productivity growth can be traced to the exhaustion of opportunities for technological advance, but more likely the decline in the quality and quantity of commercial innovations in the U.S. economy is traceable to the failure of U.S. companies to take full advantage of the opportunities that were there. For example, we have already shown that there have been tremendous innovations in the areas of computers and electronics and tremendous productivity growth in the industries producing them, but there has not been growth in the industries using computers. There has been a failure to take advantage of the potential for productivity growth inherent in the new computer technology.

TRADE POLICY: THE CASE OF THE MACHINE-TOOL INDUSTRY

In the mid-1950s the U.S. machine-tool industry was the world's largest with $1.3 billion in sales. The United States was the biggest exporter of machine tools and had the most advanced technology. Japan's manufacturers produced barely a quarter of the U.S. volume. Moreover, it took two Japanese workers to produce as much as one American worker. The U.S. Air Force funded an effort by the Massachusetts Institute of Technology to improve machining. The resulting development of numerically controlled machine tools meant that computers, rather than humans, could control the movements of machine tools. This revolutionized the industry.

In 1956 the Japanese Ministry of International Trade and Industry (MITI) proposed extraordinary measures for the promotion of the machine-tool industry. In the meantime much of the U.S. technology was offered to the Japanese and to other foreign companies at minimal license fees. MITI called for 50 percent of Japanese production to be accomplished by numerically controlled tools by 1980. Japan actually hit only 49.8 percent! MITI promoted specialization among the Japanese firms so that each manufacturer focused on only one narrow part of the industry. This practice, in effect, created a cartel, which operated until 1983.

By 1986 Japan had become the world's largest producer of machine tools, dominating the most advanced segment of the industry: the numerically controlled machines that had been invented in the United States. By 1982 Japanese firms controlled about 40 percent of the U.S. market. Although MITI had established price floors for exporters in order to avoid charges of "dumping" (selling below actual costs), effective Japanese prices were 20 to 40 percent below U.S. prices. This was done not by reducing the price of the tools but by including in the sale "gift items" such as automobiles.

Throughout policy debates regarding these trade practices, the American government consistently argued that government intervention in efforts to level the playing field would be a form of "industrial policy" and hence undesirable. In the meantime, Japanese manufacturers increased their share of the numerically controlled tool markets to as high as 85 percent, while the U.S. industry contracted.

Was U.S. policy correct, or have we allowed an important and strategic U.S. industry to be destroyed needlessly? Arguments can be made both ways. Allowing Japanese and European machine-tool makers to sell in the U.S. market meant that U.S. companies in other industries had access to the best machine-tools in the world, regardless of where they came from. Access to the best technology worldwide is probably one reason that productivity growth in U.S. manufacturing has remained strong. If we had restricted trade in machine tools we might have shot ourselves in the foot. On the other hand, it is tough for U.S. companies to compete if other countries subsidize their export industries while restricting U.S. firms' access to their markets. The U.S. should pressure Japan and other countries to eliminate both formal and informal trade restrictions.

In order for technological opportunities to be translated into productivity gains, several steps are needed and failure in any one of them can abort the process.

If there is an inadequate level of R&D funding, then the technological opportunity does not result in an innovation.

If a new product cannot be manufactured cost-efficiently, then the market for the product does not develop, or another company or country takes the market away.

If the users of the product do not learn how to use it efficiently, then the potential gains to the economy are reduced.

Some part of the slowdown in productivity may be traced to a failure of one or more of the links in the chain that connect technological opportunities to productivity gains. This may apply to the manufacturing industries that do most of the technological innovating and also to the nonmanufacturing sector, where the new technologies are often used. The people most responsible for translating new ideas into actual productivity gains are the people that manage the companies and their financial, physical, and human resources.

Management failures and economic disruption

In recent years an argument has emerged that slow productivity growth and the inability of U.S. business to compete overseas were the results of serious failures by top management.[18] According to this scenario U.S. managers had abandoned long-term technological superiority as a strategy for success and instead geared their decision making to short-term profits. Studies of the nature of U.S. competitiveness[19] point to the great success that U.S. industry had in turning out standard products in large quantities. This strategy has become outdated, but too many companies stuck to it for too long when the marketplace had changed. In order to meet the needs of customers it has become necessary to develop new products quickly and have the flexibility to produce many different designs at low cost.

The U.S. market was so large and the U.S. lead in technology and efficiency was so great that many companies ignored what foreign companies were doing. They did not realize the extent of the threat from imports and they did not learn about new technologies and management methods developed overseas. This contrasts with foreign companies that were extremely adept at borrowing U.S. methods and then improving on them. This failure is ironic given that the rise of the United States as the leading economic power at the end of the 19th century occurred in part as a result of the "Yankee ingenuity" of borrowing European technology and then improving on it.

The growth of scientific management methods encouraged the use of project analysis by financial executives as the basis for investment decisions. These techniques are fine in principle, but when misapplied they could lead to ineffective decision making by ignoring important but difficult-to-quantify aspects of an investment project. Both the misuse of techniques of financial management and a high real rate of interest contribute to the adoption of short-run strategies. A short-run focus led to investments that paid off quickly and ignored more uncertain investments that in the end would have been more important.

---

[18] Robert H. Hayes and William J. Abernathy, "Managing Our Way to Economic Decline," *Harvard Business Review* 58 (July–August 1980), pp. 67–77.

[19] Dertouzos et al., *Made in America.*

The great success of many companies over the 1950s and 1960s led to corporations with rigid and overstaffed bureaucracies. There were different fiefdoms within a company that often refused to cooperate with people elsewhere in the company. In particular, relations between labor and management were based on fighting over the shares of the profits rather than on seeking ways to improve the efficiency of the overall operation.

These various management problems may well have built up gradually over time and contributed to a gradual slowing of productivity growth over many years.

Management problems may have led to the slowdown that occurred specifically in the late 1960s and early 1970s because it is likely that the economic disruptions that struck at that time interacted negatively with management decisions. For example, energy prices have gyrated since 1973, but since energy is not a major component of total cost in most industries, there is no reason why rational companies should have sacrificed much productivity growth to save energy. Yet the existence of a worldwide slowdown in productivity growth occurring at the time that the energy crisis hit seems more than just a coincidence. Perhaps a key reason why the rise in energy prices was so costly to productivity is that dealing with it, in the crisis atmosphere that prevailed following the energy crisis, took management's attention away from other productivity-enhancing activities.

The energy crisis was only one of the problems that management faced. The argument about energy can also be made for the effects of several other factors: economic regulation; maintaining the skill level of the work force; the problems of recession and inflation; and the difficulties of coping with the tremendous increase in the scope of foreign competition. This last factor required the reassessment of competitive strategies and the shifting of production out of some goods and into others.

Office automation provided the means for reducing white-collar costs, but too often the potential gains were not realized. Capital was less productive in the 1970s than earlier, and management was responsible for the investment decisions and the running of the plants. Innovation slowed in some industries, and while depletion of opportunities was important, superior management might have spurred the search for new areas of opportunity. In other words, there were so many different problems and disruptions to deal with in the 1970s, continuing to the present, that management was understandably overwhelmed and productivity suffered. Management may well have made mistakes in dealing with these problems, but the economic world had changed dramatically and so mistakes were inevitable.

Summing up the causes of the slowdown

We have not identified a smoking gun that points irresistibly to a single suspect in the case of the productivity slowdown. We have, however, identified some likely contributors to the slowdown. These include:

The level of skill and experience of the work force has declined or has grown less rapidly than it did in the 1960s.

There has been some decline in the growth of the quantity and quality of the physical capital stock, both the privately held capital and the publicly held capital.

The severity of the slowdown has been exaggerated because of the way in which productivity is measured. The slowdown is not quite as severe in reality as it looks in official data series.

There has been an increase in the amount of government regulation of the economy and we have paid a productivity price for that.

There was an unusual period after World War II where new technologies were waiting to be exploited, and so part of the slowdown is a return to more normal rates of productivity growth after the unusual 1950s and 1960s.

There has been an exhaustion of technological opportunities in some areas and a failure to open up enough new ones.

Management strategies that led to success in the 1950s and 1960s were no longer appropriate to the changed economic environment of the 1970s and beyond. The misapplication of the principles of scientific management may have actually made things worse. The economic disruptions of the 1970s, including the energy crisis, led to a reduced emphasis on raising average labor productivity.

The United States was not alone in experiencing a slowdown in productivity growth. This suggests a common cause of the different slowdowns and the need to assess any alleged cause of the U.S. slowdown against the experience of the other countries. And if that is done for some of the causes of the U.S. slowdown that we have talked about, there is evidence that similar causes may have affected the other countries. For example, the arguments we have made about economic disruptions and the role of management can be extended to provide an explanation of the slowdowns in other countries. Many of the shifts in the economic environment that disrupted managers in the United States also disrupted managers in other countries—energy prices and regulation are two. But we will argue now that the productivity slowdowns in Europe and Japan are different from the U.S. slowdown, although they are linked to it.

The International Convergence of Productivity Trends

Sometime during the 19th century, the British economy changed from being the leading economy of the industrial world to one that experienced a loss of economic vitality. One of the more intriguing questions facing economic historians has been whether the United States will follow the path of the

United Kingdom as a declining economy. The slowdown in productivity growth has led many people to suggest that this process is indeed happening. An alternative view is that the rest of the industrialized world is following the United States as it experiences declining productivity growth, leaving the United States still as the productivity leader. Which of these alternatives is correct has not yet been resolved, but contrary to much popular opinion, it looks as if the other main industrial countries will eventually catch up to the United States but not exceed the U.S. level of productivity in the near future. This conclusion is suggested by Figure 18.3 and confirmed by estimates made with other countries included.[20]

The slowdowns in the European economies and Japan were different from the U.S. slowdown. These economies grew rapidly in the 1950s and 1960s in large part by rebuilding their economies and then closing the gap with the U.S. level of productivity. They were able to borrow U.S. ideas, buy U.S. machinery, copy U.S. management methods, and in some cases go one better on the U.S. original. *As these countries began approaching the U.S. level of productivity, they were very likely to slow down also.* The opportunities for making large increases in productivity by transforming their industries into modern high-productivity industries have now already been taken. Starting below the U.S. level of productivity gave them certain advantages, but these advantages were bound to diminish and their growth rates were bound to decline.

Figure 18.4 illustrates how the European economies and Japan faced an almost inevitable slowdown in their growth. The figure is a representation of the pattern of convergence between a representative catch-up economy (Europe or Japan) and the U.S. economy. The top line shows the level of productivity in the U.S. economy over time. A ratio or logarithmic scale is used, so that a constant rate of growth of productivity is drawn as a straight line. The figure is drawn to show a constant rate of growth in trend productivity until the slowdown. At that point the line is flatter, representing the slower rate of growth.

The lower curved line shows the path of productivity of a representative catch-up economy. When the catch-up economy is well below the U.S. level of productivity (the distance AA'), then its rate of growth of productivity is rapid—the slope of the line aa is steep. As the catch-up economy moves closer to the level of the United States (the distance BB'), its rate of growth is much smaller—the slope of aa is flatter at B than at A.

The figure also shows the slowdown in the productivity growth rate of the U.S. economy—the line bb becomes flatter. This means that the catch-up economies face a double slowdown. The frontier of productivity and technology that has been located in the U.S. economy in most industries is moving more slowly and the catch-up economies are approaching the frontier

---

[20] See Baumol, Blackman, and Wolff, *Productivity and American Leadership.*

FIGURE 18.4   Productivity Growth in a Catch-up Economy

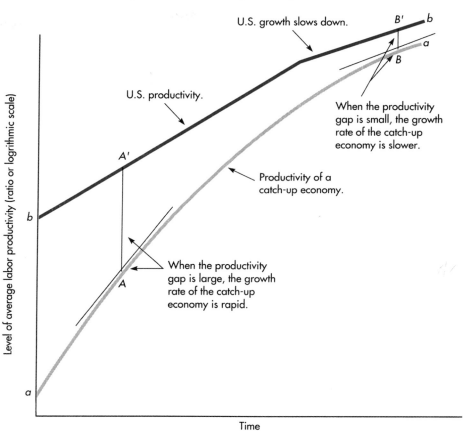

more slowly. The pattern shown in the figure fits with what we saw in Figure 18.3. The large European economies and Japan were catching up to the United States, but the speed of catch-up slowed as they moved closer to the level of productivity of the U.S. economy.

By taking this view and looking at the United States and the other industrialized countries together, one can suggest the following simplified description of the productivity slowdown: *The leading economy lost its capacity to increase its productivity at the pace it achieved in the 1960s, and the catch-up economies have all slowed as they pile up behind it.* Of course, there is an important question as to whether this view of world economic growth will hold in the future. Even though the United States remains the productivity leader on average, other countries are now driving the technology frontier in specific industries.

The United States is becoming one among equals and some of our own industries must learn to play catch-up.

To a great extent, the ability of the U.S. economy to resume a more rapid pace of productivity growth and to retain its position as a productivity leader in the future depends upon the private sector and not on policy. But there are policies that may help growth and stability and there are policies that can hinder growth and contribute to instability.

POLICIES FOR LONG-TERM GROWTH AND STABILITY

Productivity growth is the source of long-term improvements in the standard of living. The prospect of a continuation of slow growth is a cause for concern about the long-run health of the U.S. economy and therefore is of concern to the health of the world economy. If the U.S. economy does not experience improvement in its low rate of saving, does not improve the skills of its work force, and fails to capitalize on new opportunities for innovation and organizational improvement, then the U.S. economy will almost assuredly face a long-term slowdown in the growth of its standard of living.

In this final section we briefly review policies that may stall and reverse the productivity slowdown. We are not presenting a detailed policy analysis. Much of what we say here represents opinion as much as fact. We hope these concluding ideas about long-term growth policies will provoke discussion about the implications for policy brought on by problems of productivity and competitiveness facing the U.S. and world economies.

National Saving and the Federal Budget Deficit

While the growth of the real stock of capital has had only a mild contribution to the productivity decline, the role of capital becomes more important when the effect of replenishing the capital stock with newer, more technologically advanced capital is considered. Investment in new capital is necessary to maintain growth in productivity. Capital (both more of it and with improved technology) has to be added to the economy at a level adequate to meet the needs of the growth of the labor force in order to simply maintain productivity growth. Capital investment at rates that exceed what is required to provide capital for both new and existing workers is necessary for increasing the growth of productivity. Capital investment is spawned in an economy with high income growth and a low long-term real rate of interest. Low real rates require a large supply of national savings and a federal budget deficit nearer to balance than that experienced in the United States in the 1980s. This argues that a long-term supply policy for the U.S. government requires that monetary- and fiscal-policy goals include growth objectives along with short-run stabilization targets.

Investing in Advances in Knowledge

Research and development along with the commercialization of new technologies are necessary activities for productivity growth. We have seen that a major fraction of productivity growth in the past has been the result of advances in knowledge.

A question concerning R&D policy arises when we consider who benefits from the return to R&D. If society benefits by more than any individual company or institution, then there is a case for using government subsidies to support technology development and a related case for arguing that in the absence of such support, there will not be an adequate level of private-sector resources devoted to technology development. An important characteristic of R&D is that the knowledge generated becomes, in part, community property—it is to a degree a *public good*. The company that performs R&D can earn a profit from it, but other companies also find out about the technology. They come up with their own versions of new products and copy new process improvements. The new knowledge generated by R&D spills over and benefits other companies. This means that the social rate of return to R&D is higher than the private rate of return; the payoff to society from developing new technology is greater than the payoff to the company doing the developing.

The U.S. government also provides direct funds for R&D, much of it through the Department of Defense. At times there have been large spillover benefits from this also. For example, the early computers were developed with Department of Defense funding, as were such subsequent developments as hard disks and time sharing. But there are also many examples of direct government support of technology that have turned into pork barrel.

In talking about monetary and fiscal policies, we have said that the government can often make things worse. And the same is true in the area of technology. There are numerous examples where the government has wasted taxpayers' money pursuing expensive programs of technology development that had little chance of paying off. The breeder reactor is one example; experiments in the development of new housing technology are another. To improve U.S. performance in the development and commercialization of technology may require changes in the incentives and behavior of corporations at the microeconomic level that are not amenable to some simple macroeconomic-policy solution.

These high estimates of the social rate of return to R&D imply that there is a substantial basis for treating R&D as a public good. In our judgment, the national support of R&D activities can and should be encouraged, given the public-good nature of much of R&D. Even though it is important to reduce the federal budget deficit, it may be more important to provide public support for basic science and technology and for the development of commercial technologies. Government funds were wasted on the breeder reactor, but government funds were not wasted in developing the jet engine and the computer. The payoff from successful programs has to offset the waste from the unsuccessful ones. The same is true for private-sector projects.

Basic education

It is not enough to make advances in knowledge, as we have already seen in discussing the slowdown. High-tech industries require not only scientists and engineers, but also skilled and capable production workers. Service industries require people who can take advantage of high-tech equipment and adapt to new methods. The problems of our primary and secondary schools have contributed to the slowdown in productivity growth and are hampering the recovery of growth. Companies are reporting that they are having to spend huge sums to provide remedial education and to teach workers how to fill in reports, keep records, and operate sophisticated machinery. The skills that seem most important are "the ability to understand directions (even when the manuals are poorly written), to ask questions, to assimilate and synthesize unfamiliar information, and in short, literacy and problem-solving skills that workers need to function effectively in the labor force."[20]

Any initiative that raises the quality of the schools and hence the quality of the students applying for entry-level jobs would be a major factor in ensuring that the economy avoids the effects of chronic deterioration in productivity, but achieving such initiatives may be difficult. Control of the nation's public schools is spread among 15,000 school districts. And when states try to impose "top-down" programs concerning curricula or organization, these usually misfire because they usurp the authority of the teachers and administrators who will have to make them work. The main initiatives for educational improvement that have shown some promise of success are: (a) Head Start programs for disadvantaged preschoolers, (b) programs to help at-risk youths, (c) summer training for mathematics teachers, (d) incentives for good college graduates to become teachers, and (e) support for curriculum development and test construction.[21]

Macroeconomic Stability

The period from 1948 until the middle or late 1960s was one of greatly increased macroeconomic stability compared to any prior period going back to the 19th century. One reason for this stability was that the economy itself had changed in ways that made it more stable. But a change in the policy environment was also important. On balance, discretionary policies—the deliberate adjustment of monetary and fiscal policies—did increase stability. The auto-

---

[20] Richard J. Murnane, "Education and the Productivity of the Work Force," in *American Living Standards: Threats and Challenges,* ed. Robert E. Litan, Robert Z. Lawrence, and Charles L. Schultze (Washington, D.C.: Brookings Institution, 1988).

[21] Murnane, "Education."

matic stabilizers and the use of the Fed and the FDIC to stabilize the banking system were probably even more important changes in the policy environment. In our judgment, *the improved macroeconomic stability of this period provided an economic environment that encouraged long-term growth and productivity increase,* both here and in many other countries. Such stability is not sufficient to ensure rapid productivity growth, but it is surely necessary. An important ingredient in improving the long-term growth of the economy is maintaining or improving macroeconomic stability.

During the 1970s and 1980s the stability that had been achieved broke down and the resulting instability surely contributed to the slowing of productivity growth both here and overseas. The main reason for the breakdown is that we have never discovered how to deal with bursts of inflation without bringing on recession. The recessions of 1974–1975 and 1982 were engineered by the policymakers in order to fight inflation caused by excessive demand in earlier years and by supply shocks. There is a danger today that we may face a new burst of inflation and hence another round of instability. If so, this will damage the partial recovery of productivity growth that has taken place since 1979. Can this problem be avoided?

Competition may be an important factor in mitigating the inflation problem in the future. The U.S. economy is subject to more competitive pressure today than was the case in the past. In some industries this has come about because of the increase in foreign competition. Three U.S. companies dominated the domestic automobile market for many years, whereas now these companies must compete against Japanese and European manufacturers with significant market shares. And the same is true of many other manufacturing industries. Even in some industries that are not facing much foreign competition, competitive pressure has increased. There was government price regulation in several industries in the past, so that the deregulation that took place in the 1970s and 1980s has opened these industries up to price competition. Examples include transportation (trucks and airlines) and communications (long-distance telephone service). And finally there has been a decline in the fraction of the work force that is unionized, so that there is now more competitive pressure in the labor market. Union plants now have to compete against nonunion plants.

This increase in competitive pressure has had some beneficial effects. Prices and wages are less sticky when there are many competing firms. One of the factors that moderated inflation in the 1980s is that price and wage increases moderated in response to the excess demand for goods and workers that occurred in 1982. If we have to use recession to curb a new supply shock in the future (a very real possibility as of 1990), then greater responsiveness of wages and prices to recession will mean that the recession itself can be shorter or less severe.

The benefits of increased competition come with a cost, however. The decline of unions and the tremendous increase in company restructurings pose new dangers. Unions provided a way for workers to voice grievances and settle conflicts without quitting. When there is very high turnover, when workers have no loyalty to the companies that they work for, and when companies are constantly changing hands and closing down plants, there is no incentive for either a company or its workers to invest in new job skills. There is a dilemma, therefore, because the changes in our economy that have reduced the rigidity of wages and prices and helped the problem of inflation may simultaneously increase the problems of inadequate skills and weak motivation among the work force.

One way in which the twin goals of greater wage flexibility and greater incentives for productivity improvement can be combined is by changing the way in which workers are paid. Martin Weitzman has argued that if workers are paid a share of revenues or are given a stake in the profits of a company, this will automatically increase the flexibility of wages—wage or bonus payments decrease when there is a recession. And Weitzman has also found empirical support for the idea that giving workers a financial stake in their companies improves productivity.[22] Linking wages or bonuses to the performance of companies has the promise of improving both productivity and wage flexibility.

Managers and unions are reluctant to change the traditional ways in which wages are determined, but in facing the need for improved macroeconomic stability and improved productivity growth in the 1990s, it is time for them to try new ideas.

SUMMARY

- Productivity growth is a measure of the growth in output relative to the growth in inputs used to produce it. Average–labor-productivity growth is the growth of output per unit of labor input (output per worker or output per hour of work). Multifactor-productivity growth is the growth of output net of the contribution of both labor and capital.

- When the capital input has increased faster than the labor input, average labor productivity will increase faster than multifactor productivity.

- In 1948 the U.S. economy had by far the highest level of productivity of any country. Productivity growth was rapid in the U.S. economy from 1948 to 1968, but was even more rapid in Europe and Japan. Those countries were catching up to the U.S. level of productivity.

- Since 1968 and especially since 1973 there has been slower growth in all of the major industrial countries. The process of catch-up has continued, but the U.S. remains the most productive of the major economies. Other countries have experienced slower growth too.

---

[22] Martin L. Weitzman and Douglas L. Knuse, ''Profit-Sharing and Productivity,'' in Alan S. Blinder ed., *Paying for Productivity* (Washington, D.C.: Brookings Institution, 1989), pp. 95–141.

- The slowdown in productivity growth meant that there was a slowing in the growth of living standards. Increased numbers of people entering the work force and foreign borrowing allowed consumption to grow faster than productivity during the 1970s and 1980s, but it will be hard to continue this growth in consumption without increased productivity growth.

- In the United States, the slowdown occurred in almost all of the different industries in the economy. The slowdown started earlier and was more severe in mining and construction. The computer industry had no slowdown, nor did farming. Manufacturing has recovered since 1979, but productivity growth in the service sector has been very weak in the 1980s.

- The fact that many industries and countries all slowed down suggests either world-wide causes or similarities in the growth history of mature nations that underlie the productivity decline.

- Productivity and competitiveness in international markets are not the same. Low-productivity economies can be competitive, by adjusting the value of their exchange rates. In the absence of productivity improvements, U.S. industry will have to compete in world markets by letting the dollar decline.

- The technology lead held by the U.S. economy in the 1950s and 1960s allowed U.S. companies to compete even while paying higher wages than other countries. The loss of this lead has contributed to the slow growth of real wages for workers without special skills.

- There is no single cause of the slowdown in productivity. The causes consist of:

    1. Reductions in the effectiveness of inputs; deteriorating education and labor skills; and inadequate growth in the quantity and quality of capital per worker.
    2. A deterioration in the economic environment for productivity enhancement including an increase in regulation, a slowdown in technological advances, and a slowdown in the process of taking commercial advantage of the technological opportunities.

- Productivity is difficult to measure in many industries, particularly in service industries. Productivity is growing somewhat faster than the standard data indicate.

- The prospects for using macroeconomic policies to cure the slowdown are uncertain. However, a few targeted directions for policy exist:

    1. Stimulating national saving and the growth of capital investment.
    2. Treating technology development as a public good.
    3. Increasing the effectiveness and level of support for education.

KEY TERMS

average labor productivity	infrastructure
capital deepening	innovation
competitiveness	multifactor-productivity growth

DISCUSSION QUESTIONS AND PROBLEMS

1. Can the standard of living be improved without productivity growth? If so, how, and is the improvement sustainable?

2. Which measure, the growth of average labor productivity or the growth of multifactor productivity, best reflects improvements in the standard of living? Why? Under what circumstances will these two growth measures be different? What does that difference say about growth in the economy?

3. "The post-1973 productivity slowdown in the United States was inevitable. Our high rate of productivity growth was only a result of being the dominant economy in the world. As soon as Western European and Asian industrialized economies began to catch up, the U.S. lead was bound to evaporate." Comment.

4. "The productivity decline is easily explained—people stopped working hard and they stopped saving." Comment.

5. "The productivity slowdown is a mirage. First of all, most of what we now produce are services, and productivity gains in services can't be measured. Second, the huge investment we've made in computer technology is going to pay off in the 1990s. Economists simply like to worry." Comment.

6. Macroeconomic policies for long-run growth require stimulating aggregate supply. How can government policies contribute to private-sector productivity?

■ GLOSSARY

A

accelerator the relationship between an increase in output and the investment demand. The accelerator can be fixed, reflecting a required relationship between increasing output and the capital necessary to produce more output, or flexible, reflecting the possibility that other inputs can substitute for capital in production, 540

accelerator model the accelerator model of investment says that investor demand depends upon the change in income, 68

adaptive expectations expectations that are revised based on how closely past expectations conform to reality, 640

adverse supply shock a large and rapid increase in the relative prices of key commodities, 391

aggregate demand the amount that households, businesses, and the government decide to purchase, plus net foreign demand, 51

aggregate-production function the relationship between potential output and the inputs used to produce it (usually capital, labor, and technology), 604, 688

aggregate supply the amount of goods and services businesses offer for sale, 51

arbitrage taking advantage of the profit opportunities of either price differences for the same asset in different markets or of price changes over time, 663

augmented labor the labor force adjusted by the state of technology. As technology grows, the augmented labor force grows faster than the actual labor force because a unit of augmented labor is equivalent to more than a unit of actual labor, 710

augmented LM schedule the ALM is an LM schedule that has been augmented by the interest-rate gap. With a particular maturity premium and inflationary expectations, the ALM describes the different levels of income and the long-term real rates of interest that obtain when the money market is in equilibrium, 305

automatic stabilizers transfers and tax reductions that are activated when income falls, without the need for new authorizations or legislation from Congress, 168

autonomous-expenditure multiplier the effect of an increase in autonomous expenditure on equilibrium income when these are taxes, 148

average cash balance the average amount held in all forms of money over a period of time, 223

average labor productivity output per worker or output per hour of work, 689, 732

average propensity to consume (APC) the fraction of income that households spend on consumption, expressed as a ratio C/Y, 62

B

balance of payments the system of accounts describing international financial flows, including the balance of payments on the current account (the value of the trade balance plus the net balances of international items that affect income) and the balance of payments on the capital account (the net exchanges of foreign assets). The current account balance is the negative of the capital-account balance, 440

balance of trade the difference between exports and imports, 81, 440

banking panic widespread occurrence of bank runs, where the rush to withdraw funds from one bank turns into a general withdrawal of funds from all banks, causing large numbers of bank failures and a rapid reduction in the supply of money and credit, 575

barter direct trading for goods and services without using money, 101

black market an illegal market that develops in most economies in which the government has placed restrictions on the prices of products, services, and/or assets, 511

bond a financial claim on an issuer with a specified interest payment and redemption value. The actual return on a bond is a combination of interest payments and any gain or loss in the value of the bond at the time it is sold, 105

budget balance the difference between government receipts and government outlays. When receipts exceed outlays, the budget balance is a budget surplus. When receipts fall short of outlays, the budget balance is a budget deficit, 161

built-in rate of inflation   expectations about inflation based upon the past history of actual inflation, 367

business cycle   a recurring fluctuation of aggregate output in the economy. Each cycle consists of a peak (the highest level of output and employment reached before a sustained decline in output), a recession or contraction (where output is falling for at least two quarters), a trough (the low point for output), and a recovery or expansion (where output is rising), 19

C

capital adequacy   the increase in capital required to keep the capital/labor ratio constant. When there is technological change, capital adequacy becomes the increase in capital required to keep the ratio of capital to augmented labor constant, 696

capital consumption allowance   the allowance reflects depreciation (the extent to which the capital stock wears out in a given period), 43

capital deepening   capital investment taking place at a rate that increases capital intensity and hence raises labor productivity, 697, 734

capital intensity   the ratio of capital to labor. On average, the amount of capital available for use by each worker, 691

capital mobility   the ability of investors to sell assets in one economy purchase foreign exchange, and buy assets in another economy. If there is expected-return equalization, then there is perfect capital mobility, 448

capital stock   the collection of all capital goods (machines, factories, offices, etc.) still in use. Includes those purchased in previous years with adjustment for depreciation, 43

cash management   the movement of funds into and out of money through the purchase and sale of money-market assets. The goal of cash management is to maximize interest earned after deducting financial-transactions costs (FTCs) while providing sufficient cash to cover ongoing expenses, 110, 222

central bank foreign exchange intervention   the buying and selling of foreign exchange by central banks in order to affect the exchange rate, 503

choice-theoretic framework   models of the economy where the actions of economic agents result from the

choices they make based on maximizing their self-interest. These choices are often assumed to be made rationally by people with rational expectations, 639

classical model   a model of the economy in which all markets clear. Supply and demand in all markets either are in equilibrium or, if disturbed, come quickly back into equilibrium, 603

commercial bank   a bank that is authorized to issue checking accounts to individuals and commercial customers, 195

competitiveness   a widely used term that lacks a generally accepted definition. U.S. competitiveness is often related to one or more of the following elements: (1) the trade deficit (2) whether or not U.S. companies can compete internationally without continuous reductions in the value of the dollar (3) the level of U.S. productivity relative to other countries (4) the rate of growth of U.S. productivity relative to other countries (5) whether or not the United States has a lead in technology in key industries, 732

constant-money-supply-growth rule   the monetarist policy prescription, setting the rate of growth in the money supply equal to the long-term rate of growth of potential output so as to insure price stability and reduce the severity of cyclical fluctuations, 625

constant returns to scale   a characteristic of production where a given percentage increase in all inputs leads to an equal percent increase in output, 689

contraction   *see* Business cycle

consumer price index (CPI)   the index tracks the prices of the purchases made by typical households in a given year relative to the prices for the same collection of goods and services in a base year, 28

consumption   the total value of goods and services purchased by households, 38

consumption function   the relationship between consumption and those economic variables that determine the decision to consume, 61

consumption smoothing   the decision to raise or lower consumption less than proportionally to swings in the level of income in order to moderate swings in the consumption standard of living, 528

consumption standard of living   the value of goods and services consumed by households through current purchases of nondurables and from the flow of services obtained from consumer capital. Consumer capital includes houses and consumer durable goods owned by households, 526

contractionary monetary policy when the Fed sets the rate of growth of the money supply to be less than the rate of inflation, 302

credibility the degree to which market participants believe that policymakers will maintain a policy direction (e.g., the believability of the Fed's commitment to an anti-inflationary policy regime), 384, 642

credibility effect the reduction in inflationary expectations that comes from being convinced that the Fed is in fact following a tough anti-inflationary policy, 416

credit crunch a mild financial crisis where there is a sharp reduction in the supply of credit that raises interest rates and reduces access to funds, 577

credit rationing when financial intermediaries reduce the quantity of credit and/or access to credit by rationing rather than only by raising the interest rates they charge on loans, 280

crowding out the reduction in investment resulting from an increase in government spending or a reduction in taxes, 160

currency or foreign exchange speculation buying and selling foreign exchange and/or foreign-exchange futures contracts for the purposes of profiting from changes in exchange rates, 504

currency ratio the ratio of currency held by the public to demand deposits, 205

cyclical deficit the budget deficit minus the structural deficit, 168

cyclically adjusted budget the budget surplus or deficit that would occur with current tax rates and expenditure programs if the level of output and income in the economy were equal to potential output, 168

D

decision lag the time it takes for policymakers to initiate a change in policy following their recognition of the need for a policy action, 588

demand deposits bank deposits that can be withdrawn upon demand, 102

deregulation removal or relaxation of regulations governing the composition of bank assets and the payment of interest on deposit liabilities, 194

desired capital-output ratio the ratio of the level of desired capital stock to the level of output, 540

desired capital stock the amount of capital businesses would like to have on hand, given current and expected economic conditions, 540

diminishing returns there are diminishing returns to labor if the labor input increases but all other inputs remain constant. Output increases by less than the increase in labor. There are diminishing returns to capital if the capital input increases but all other inputs remain constant. Output increases by less than the increase in capital, 691

discounting using an interest rate or discount rate to reduce the value of future cash receipts in order to find out how much those receipts would be worth compared to funds received in the present, 261

discount rate the interest rate that the Fed charges on borrowed reserves, 214

disintermediation withdrawals of funds from financial intermediaries and into direct investments such as financial-market assets. Also used to refer to the withdrawal of funds from banks and S&Ls in the 1980s and 1970s when interest rates on savings accounts were controlled. Funds were withdrawn from controlled accounts and put into other financial intermediaries, 577

disposable income income plus transfers minus gross tax receipts, 144

durability a characteristic of capital goods. They last for more than one year, and they provide a flow of services over time, 539

E

equilibrium-business-cycle model a model in which fluctuations in output occur as a result of unexpected shocks, especially unexpected money supply changes, 645

excess-reserve ratio the ratio of excess reserves to demand deposits, 206

excess reserves the amount of bank reserves held over and above the minimum amount required, 206

exchange rate the number of units of foreign currency that can be purchased for one unit of another currency (for example, the number or fraction of marks, yen, lira, pounds, or other currencies that can be purchased with one U.S. dollar, 428

exchange-rate overshooting   a persistent interest rate differential leads to a large swing in the exchange rate, 500

expansion   *see* Business cycle

expansionary monetary policy   when the Fed sets the rate of growth of the money supply to be faster than the rate of inflation, 302

expectations   a market participant's view of future circumstances (for example, inflationary expectations, interest-rate expectations, and economic-policy expectations), 297

expected-return equalization   the expected returns from holding bonds in two different countries are the same when the foreign interest rate differential is equal to the expected rate of change of the exchange rate, 447

exports   purchases of domestically produced goods and services by foreigners, 29

F

favorable supply shock   a large and rapid reduction in the relative prices of key commodities, 391

federal funds market   the market among banks for short-term borrowing and lending of bank reserves, 206

final sales   GNP minus exports plus imports minus change in business inventory, 41

financial asset   a contract that gives the holder a claim on the user of the asset. The terms of the contract may vary widely from a fixed future payment (as in the case of certain bonds) to a claim that is conditional upon future events (as in the case with certain types of corporate stocks), 104

financial crisis   a situation in which there is a sudden drop in the availability of funds from financial institutions, 571

financial intermediary   any institution that borrows by issuing financial liabilities and that uses the proceeds to purchase assets, both real and financial, 275

financial-transaction costs (FTCs)   the explicit costs (brokerage fees) and implicit costs (cash-management expenses) of exchanging or buying and selling financial assets, 225

fiscal policy   government actions concerning tax revenues, transfers, and the amount of government purchases, 138

fixed exchange rates   prices of foreign currencies set in relationship to each other, either through all currencies having a fixed value in terms of an international monetary standard such as gold or via an arrangement among worldwide central banks such that they intervene in foreign exchange markets to keep exchange rates from changing, 502

flexible exchange rates   exchange rates that can change values in response to changes in supply and demand for currencies in foreign exchange markets, 503

foreign exchange   foreign currency that is purchased or sold in foreign exchange markets, 427

foreign exchange forward contract   a contract to buy or sell a quantity of foreign currency at a set future date, but at a price known today. A forward contract occurs between a bank and an individual or firm, 504

foreign-interest-rate differential   the difference between the nominal rate of interest earned by the holder of a foreign bond and the nominal rate of interest earned by the holder of a domestic bond with the same maturity and risk, 446

fractional reserve system   the system under which banks need only hold a fraction of the funds deposited in the form of reserves, 198

full employment   the level of employment that occurs when the economy is operating at potential output. The benchmark for potential output and for full employment are determined together, 26

G

government expenditures or outlays   the government's purchases of goods and services plus transfer payments and interest on government debts, 136

government purchases of goods and services   the amount that local, state, and federal governments spend on goods and services. Includes such things as school supplies and missiles. Also includes salaries paid to government employees. Transfer payments are excluded, 38, 136

gross domestic product   GNP minus net factor income from overseas. GDP is a measure of the output produced by factors of production residing in the United States, 41

gross national product (GNP) the total amount of goods and services produced in the economy in a given period. Nominal GNP in a given period is measured using the prices that prevail in the same year. Real GNP in a given year values the output in that year in the prices that prevailed in a base year. Base years are changed periodically; the year used now is 1982, 18

gross tax revenue the total of all tax revenue collected by all forms of government, 142

growth accounting the identification and measurement of the various factors that contribute to economic growth and the evaluation of their relative importance in bringing about a particular rate of growth, 722

H–I

human capital the capacity to provide value in the labor market through the acquisition of education, training, and work experience, 723

hyperinflation a very rapid and escalating inflation. Often defined technically as an inflation where the price level rises at a rate in excess of 50 percent per month for one year, 628

identity an equation that is true by definition for all values of the variables in the equation, 57

implicit price deflator for gross national product the price level for all GNP. The deflator is computed as the ratio of nominal GNP to real GNP, 28

imports domestic purchases of foreign goods and services, 29

inflation the rate of increase of the price level. A decrease in the price level—deflation—is measured as the negative of the rate of inflation. Inflation for consumer prices is measured as the rate of increase of the Consumer Price Index, 27

inflation-accommodating monetary policy when the Fed increases the nominal supply of money at the same rate as the rate of inflation. This policy keeps the real money supply constant, 302

infrastructure the stock of public capital including roads, bridges, schools, airports, and water and sewer systems, 731

innovation the introduction into the marketplace of new or improved products, processes, or services, 752

inside lag the time it takes for policymakers to initiate a policy change following a change in economic conditions that requires policy action. This is the sum of the recognition lag and the decision lag, 588

intensive production function a production function in which labor productivity depends upon capital intensity—how much capital is available for use by each worker, 691

interest-rate effect following a shift in conditions in the goods market, the interest-rate effect is the change in income resulting from the change in the rate of interest, 126

interest-rate gap the difference between the long-term real rate of interest and the short-term nominal rate. It is equal to the maturity premium minus the expected rate of inflation, 286

interest-rate risk the risk borne by the owner of a financial asset that the price of the asset will change when the market interest rates change, 247

interest-rate spread the difference between the rate of interest paid to depositors and the rate charged to borrowers, 277

interest-rate targeting a goal for monetary policy that uses changes in the money supply to keep a nominal rate of interest within a target range, 316

intermediate goods and services goods and services sold to other firms to be used up in production or resold, as opposed to those sold for final use, 34

intermediate-run tradeoff the increase in inflation that occurs when the output ratio increases by a given amount for a given period of years, 367

inventory accumulation the change in business inventory in a given period. Goods produced but not yet sold are included in the inventory. It is part of investment and is valued in GNP at the same market prices as comparable items that have been sold, 38

investment gross private domestic investment is the total of new plant and equipment (machines and factories), nonresidential structures (offices, shopping centers), residential structures (houses and apartments), and inventory accumulation purchased in a given period, 38

investment function   the relationship between investment demand and those economic variables that determine the decision by firms to purchase capital goods, 64

J–L

J-curve   the pattern of the trade balance following a reduction in the exchange rate, where the trade balance first worsens and then improves above its initial level, 436

junk bonds   high-interest, high-risk corporate debt often used to finance a leveraged buyout (LBO), 579

labor force   the total number of people in the economy who are either employed or unemployed, 25

labor hoarding   retaining employees in the face of a decline in demand, 672

leveraged buyouts (LBOs)   firms repurchase their outstanding equity by issuing large quantities of debt borrowed with the company's own assets as collateral. The companies become private rather than publicly held companies, 579

liability   any claim that requires future payment, 109

liquidity   the quick-resale characteristic of short-term financial assets. Assets that can be sold quickly for a value close to the value that would be obtained by waiting are called liquid assets, 247

liquidity preference   the preference for liquidity, meaning that investors require a higher rate of return on assets that are less liquid than others. The preference for liquidity can be expressed as a liquidity premium (the difference between long-term and short-term interest rates that holders of long-term assets demand in exchange for the loss of liquidity), 247

long-run tradeoff   the change in the rate of inflation associated with a change in the output ratio that takes place over a period of time long enough for goods-market and labor-market expectations of inflation to completely catch up with the current rate of inflation, 369

Lucas critique   the argument that when statistical methods are used on economic data, the results may

not provide a reliable guide to policy. When policy changes, this may change the relationship among the economic variables, 659

lump-sum taxes   taxes fixed by tax policy in dollar amount and collected from individuals and institutions regardless of their level of income, 152

lump-sum-tax multiplier   the effect of a change in lump-sum taxes on equilibrium income, 152

M

marginal product of labor   the additional output that results from increasing the amount of labor used in production, 606

marginal propensity to consume (MPC)   the amount of increased consumption that results from an amount of increased income, 63

marginal propensity to import (MPM)   the amount of increased imports that results from an amount of increased income, 81

marginal propensity to invest (MPI)   the amount of increased investment that results from an amount of increased income, 66

marginal propensity to tax   the change in net tax revenue resulting from a change in income, 144

maturity premium   the difference in interest rates that investors require in order for them to hold a longer-term, higher-risk asset rather than a shorter-term, lower-risk asset, 283

medium of exchange   an asset that is used for transactions purposes, 102

menu cost   the cost of changing price lists or other costs of adjusting prices, 677

merchandise exports   the sale of goods abroad, 440

merchandise imports   expenditures on goods purchased from other countries, 440

misery index   the sum of the unemployment rate and the rate of inflation. The misery index rises particularly during stagflation, 361

monetarism   a model of the economy in which the economy is self-correcting. Changes in the rate of growth of the money supply are the primary cause of inflation and short-run fluctuations in output, 602

monetary base the sum of bank reserves and cash held by the public, 204

monetary-growth equation the growth version of the quantity equation where the growth of the money supply equals the inflation rate plus the growth of real income less any changes in velocity, 618

monetary shock an unexpected change in money supply and/or velocity. Also called a monetary surprise, a monetary shock is unanticipated and leads to fluctuations in aggregate demand seen as changes in the price level and/or output, 652

money an asset that can be used to make transactions; that is, money is used to buy things and is accepted by people selling things, 101

money market where people increase or decrease the amount of money they hold by selling or buying short-term bonds that carry very little risk of default, such as Treasury bills, 100, 222

money multiplier the money supply divided by the monetary base. The money-multiplier equation shows how the multiplier depends upon the currency ratio and the reserve ratio, 204

multifactor-productivity growth a measure of the rate of improvement in efficiency or technological change. The rate of growth of output over and above the contributions to growth that stem from the growth of the amount of labor and capital, 732

multiplier in the simple income determination model the level of equilibrium income is proportional to autonomous expenditure. The factor of proportionality is called the multiplier, so that, for example, if the multiplier were three, then equilibrium income would be three times autonomous expenditure, 70

multiplier effect the change in income that would occur following a shift in the IS schedule if there were no change in the rate of interest, 126

N

national income the sum total of all income received by those who contributed to production. This includes the compensation of employees, proprietors' income, rental income, profit, and net interest, 42

National Income and Product Accounts the accounting system used to organize and define aggregate economic measures. These accounts form the basis for macroeconomic analysis of output, income, and expenditure, 38

national saving the total of private saving plus the government's budget surplus (or minus the government's budget deficit). It can be given gross or net of depreciation, 164

national wealth all tangible assets plus net foreign-asset holdings, 44

natural rate of unemployment the level of unemployment that occurs when output equals potential output, 26, 356

Neo-Keynesian analysis models that accept the framework of rational choice with rational expectations and attempt to show how prices and wages may be sticky and how the economy can be described by Keynesian models of aggregate demand, 674

net exports exports minus imports. Exports of goods and services minus imports of goods and services, 38

net foreign investment purchases of foreign assets by U.S. residents minus purchases of U.S. assets by foreign residents. It equals net exports, 161

net national product (NNP) the value of total production after the capital consumption allowance (depreciation) is deducted from GNP, 43

net tax revenue the total gross tax revenue collected by the government minus transfer payments (including interest on the debt), 143

nominal exchange rate index an index of the values of the dollar where the contribution of any particular nominal exchange rate for any one foreign currency contributes to the value of the index based upon the share of total trade conducted with that country. The index is denoted by the symbol ex, 431

nominal gross national product *see* Gross national product

nominal values values of such things as the money supply and income expressed in current-dollar terms. Interest rates and rates of return unadjusted for inflation, 227

nominal wage the average wage paid to labor measured in current dollars, 609

nominal-wage contracts agreements between employers and employees that set wages in nominal terms (current dollars without inflation adjustments) over a period of time, 621

nonbank intermediaries   intermediaries that are prevented by regulations from issuing checking accounts and making loans, 276

O

Okun's law   the relationship between output and unemployment. If output exceeds potential output, then the unemployment rate will be below the natural rate of unemployment, 358

open-market operations   the buying and selling of government securities, that is, Treasury bills and bonds. They are used to vary the size of bank reserves, 209

opportunity cost of funds   the rate of interest on financial assets that could have been earned had the funds that are used for other purposes been used instead to purchase a financial asset. That rate represents the opportunity cost of investment, 260

optimal growth   the rate of growth that balances the sacrifice of current saving and the costs of capital accumulation with the benefits of the consumption standard of living in the future, 705

output gap   the difference between actual output and potential output. Can also be expressed as the percent difference between the two, 23

output-inflation tradeoff   the change in the rate of inflation associated with a change in the output ratio, 351

output ratio   the ratio of actual output to potential output, usually given in percent terms, 23, 357

outside lag   the time it takes for a policy action to take effect after it has been initiated, 588

overhead labor   the minimum level of employment a particular firm needs in order to operate, 672

P

peak   *see* Business cycle

perfect capital mobility   *see* Capital mobility

permanent and transitory consumption   permanent consumption is the average level of consumption that households anticipate undertaking over a period of years, given their permanent income. Transitory consumption is undertaken to meet unexpected needs, such as unexpected medical expenses, 529

permanent income   the average level of income that households expect to receive over a period of years, 529

planned investment   the amount businesses want to spend on capital goods including the amount they want to add to their inventories. Planned investment differs from actual investment by the amount of unplanned changes in inventory accumulation, 65

policy-ineffectiveness theorem   if only unexpected changes in policy affect output, systematic or expected changes in policy cannot affect output, and therefore stabilization policy is ineffective, 655

policy regime   the policymakers' actions over time indicate how the Fed is likely to react to economic events. People then form their expectations about future policy on the basis of this regime, 326

portfolio   a listing of the set of assets and liabilities held by a household or organization, 109

portfolio choice   the decision about the proportions of different assets and liabilities held in a portfolio, 109

potential output or potential gross national product   the level of output (usually real GNP) that is produced when the capital and labor resources of the economy are fully utilized but not overutilized. Benchmark levels of unemployment and capital utilization have to be set to determine potential output, 21

present discounted value   the total discounted value of a stream of future returns, 261

price-coordination problem   a decline in nominal aggregate demand may lead to a decline in real output unless there is a decline in all wages and prices. It may be impossible to obtain a coordinated decline in all prices and wages even if many people in the economy understand that it would be beneficial. The price-coordination problem can cause nominal price stickiness, 679

price level   a price index set equal to unity (or 100) in the base year. Changes in the price level over time reflect the average change of all prices. The implicit price deflator for GNP is one measure of the price level, equal to the ratio of nominal GNP to real GNP, 22

price of money   a difficult concept because there is no single price of money. Monetarists say that the price of money is the reciprocal of the price level. The price of money is based upon exchanging money for a market basket of goods. Another possible price of money is the short-term nominal interest rate, reflecting the cost of renting money for a short period. One can even think of other prices of money, such as the value of the dollar in foreign exchange. It may be better not to use the concept "price of money," 622

price stickiness a characteristic of the economy wherein prices do not immediately and completely adjust to changes in supply and/or demand, 355

price-wage spiral the ongoing process whereby increases in wages raise unit labor costs, contributing to a higher rate of inflation and still higher wages, 404

private saving the part of income not consumed. It is computed as total income minus net taxes minus consumption. Private saving can be split into personal saving and business saving (retained earnings), 164

productivity the amount of output produced per unit of input. Often measured by average labor productivity—output per hour of work. Output per worker is often used as an alternative measure, 26, 360

public goods goods and services that to some extent have the properties of nonrivalry and nonexcludability, 139

Q–R

quantity equation the money supply times velocity equals nominal income, 614

real and nominal rates of interest the nominal rate of interest is the one reported by a bank or financial institution. The real rate of interest is adjusted for inflation, 229

real-business-cycle model neoclassical models that argue that all economic fluctuations are the results of technology shocks or labor-supply shocks, 660

real exchange rate index the nominal exchange rate index adjusted for changes in the relative price levels in the United States and its trading partners. Relative to the nominal index, it changes over time depending on whether inflation is more or less rapid in the United States than in other countries. The index is denoted by the symbol rex, 432

real gross national product *see* Gross national product

real gross national product per person real GNP divided by the population, 19

real values values of such things as the money supply, income, and interest rates adjusted for inflation, 227

real wage the average wage paid to labor measured in constant dollars; that is, after adjustment for inflation, 609

recession *see* Business cycle

recognition lag the time it takes for policymakers to recognize that economic conditions have changed, 588

recovery *see* Business cycle

required reserves the minimum level of reserves that must be held. The required reserve ratio is the ratio of required reserves to demand deposits, 206

reserve account banks and other depository institutions hold funds in accounts with the Federal Reserve. These reserve accounts are included in total bank reserves, 198

reserves a depository institution's reserve-account balances plus cash held in the bank (vault cash). Reserves held by depository institutions are available to meet withdrawal demands that exceed deposits, 198

S

sacrifice ratio the loss in GNP, measured as a percentage, associated with a one percent reduction in the rate of inflation, 382

saving the part of income that is not used for consumption, 93

savings-and-loan banks (S&Ls) banks where customers hold savings accounts. Prior to deregulation, they could not issue checking accounts. They were directed to specialize in residential mortgage loans as their primary asset. Now they are similar to commercial banks, 196

Say's Law supply creates its own demand. The law is part of the classical model. It says that production always generates income such that those who receive the income purchase all that is produced, 613

short-run output-inflation tradeoff the change in the rate of inflation associated with a change in the output ratio that takes place over a short period of time, before goods-market and labor-market expectations of infla tion are revised in the face of changes in the current rate of inflation, 356

speculative boom or bust   a situation in which people buy an asset in the expectation that its price will increase. Such a boom can turn into a "bubble" where prices rise rapidly and then collapse. The expectation of further price increases fuels the price rise and then the bubble bursts. This is where the boom becomes a "bust," 568

stagflation   a worsening of the output-inflation trade-off where the rate of inflation rises while there is a constant or reduced level of output, 361

steady-state growth   the long-run constant rate of growth. Steady state is reached when the amount of saving and new capital is just adequate to maintain capital intensity, 700

sterilized intervention   a central bank buys and sells foreign currencies in order to influence its exchange rate. At the same time it neutralizes the domestic money supply effects of its actions, 512

stocks   a term having two definitions to be used in context: (1) the plural of stock—a fixed quantity, as in the stock of money, meaning the fixed amount of money. (2) corporate equities, a particular type of asset. These are the common or preferred stocks, which are the ownership shares of corporations, 104

structural deficit   if the cyclically-adjusted budget is in deficit, then the economy has a structural deficit, 168

supply shock   a change in supply conditions, often associated with a large and rapid rise in the relative prices of commodities or raw materials, 391

systematic policymaking   a program or regime of policy such that the policy response to a particular set of economic conditions is predictable, 655

T

tax leakages   the increased net tax revenue associated with an increase in income. Because tax leakages reduce the increase in spending that follows an increase in income, they reduce the multiplier, 149

Technological change   reflects the improvement in technology over time, 688

technology   the state of knowledge about methods and techniques used in production, 688

technology shock   any increase or decrease in productivity that is unrelated to changes in the quantity of outputs, 660

terms of trade   the value of imports received in exchange for exports, measured by comparing the prices of exports to the prices of imports, 438

term structure of interest rates   the relationship among interest rates depending upon the maturity of the assets, 245

term to maturity   the length of time between the current period and an obligation's date of required payment of principal, 247

time-inconsistent policies   policies that, if pursued, realize their intended effects in the short run but have a reversed effect in the long run, 658

trade adjustment lag   in international trade, the time delay between a change in the exchange rate and changes in the volumes of imports and exports, 436

trade balance   the difference between exports and imports of goods, 29

transaction   a single act of exchange of goods or services between a buyer and a seller, 102

transfer payments   income payments made by the government to households and institutions. Interest payments on the debt are included in transfers, 142

trough   *see* Business cycle

U–Y

unemployment rate   the percentage of the labor force that is unemployed. The unemployed are those looking for work or on layoff, 25

value added   the net contribution to the final value of a product made at each stage of production. Calculated by subtracting the cost of intermediate goods and services purchased from the value of sales plus additions to inventory, 34

velocity of money   the ratio of income to money, usually described by the term V. Velocity measures the number of times a dollar turns over in a year, 107, 614

wage contracts unions negotiate wage contracts that set wages over periods of one to three years. Union contracts generally allow firms to vary employment but not wages over the business cycle. There are also *implicit wage contracts* based on an informal understanding between a firm and its workers, 674

wealth the total value of all assets, 104

weighted average used for calculating an overall measure when not all items are equally important. Instead of calculating an average by adding all the elements and dividing by the number of items, in a weighted average each item is counted (weighted) for relatively more or less in arriving at the average. The weight of an item reflects the relative importance or impact of that item in the aggregate measure, 29

yield curve the array of interest rates on bonds by term to maturity. A normal yield curve has short-term rates lower than long-term rates. An inverted yield curve has short-term rates higher than long-term rates, 250

INDEXES

■ NAME INDEX

■ SUBJECT INDEX